CRIMINAL LAW

CRIMINAL LAW

A Comparative Approach

Markus D. Dubber
and Tatjana Hörnle

OXFORD

UNIVERSITY PRESS

UNIVERSITY PRESS

Great Clarendon Street, Oxford, OX2 6DP,
United Kingdom

Oxford University Press is a department of the University of Oxford.
It furthers the University's objective of excellence in research, scholarship,
and education by publishing worldwide. Oxford is a registered trade mark of
Oxford University Press in the UK and in certain other countries

Published in the United States of America by Oxford University Press
198 Madison Avenue, New York, NY 10016, United States of America

British Library Cataloguing in Publication Data
Data available

Library of Congress Control Number: 2013952449

ISBN 978-0-19-958960-9

PREFACE

Criminal Law: A Comparative Approach is a criminal law text written from a comparative perspective, featuring cases and materials on the central issues in criminal law from two representative common law and civil law jurisdictions, the United States and Germany.

The idea for this book emerged from several years of searching for a format that allows teachers and scholars to unlock the potential of comparative analysis. *Criminal Law: A Comparative Approach* does not attempt to present an encyclopedic overview of the world's criminal law systems.[1] It is both narrower and deeper in conception; it presents a systematic and comprehensive comparative analysis of the substantive criminal law of two jurisdictions, covering both the fundamental principles of the so-called general part and a selection of offenses drawn from the so-called special part of criminal law.[2]

The present book, then, is about criminal law first, and about comparative law second. Its primary audience is criminal law scholars and teachers interested in a deeper understanding of their own field, not card carrying comparativists. It presupposes no familiarity with either U.S. or German criminal law—or with any other criminal law system, for that matter.[3] All foreign-language sources have been translated into English.[4] Cases and materials are accompanied by heavily cross-referenced introductions and notes that place them within the framework of each country's criminal law system and highlight issues ripe for comparative analysis. Throughout, readers are exposed to alternative approaches to familiar problems in criminal law, and as a result will have a chance to see "their" country's criminal law doctrine, on specific issues and in general, from the critical distance of comparative analysis.

The bulk of the materials is drawn from U.S. and German criminal law; materials from other jurisdictions, common and civil, have been included where appropriate— notably from Canadian criminal law, which has come to occupy an intermediate position between common law and civil law approaches in general, and between U.S. and German criminal law in particular. Of course each reader is free—and, in fact, encouraged—to adapt the text to her needs, by highlighting and exploring contrasts and comparisons with her domestic criminal law system.

---

[1] For a fuller picture of approaches to substantive criminal law around the world, based on the same conceptual structure that shapes the present book, see Kevin J. Heller and Markus D. Dubber (eds.), *Handbook of Comparative Criminal Law* (2010); see also Markus D. Dubber and Tatjana Hörnle (eds.), *Oxford Handbook of Criminal Law* (forthcoming 2014).

[2] The book is yet narrower, in another sense: Rather than trying to capture "American criminal law" in its entirety (consisting of over fifty jurisdictions), we focus on the Model Penal Code. The Model Penal Code was drafted by the American Law Institute, an influential law reform organization, between 1952 and 1962, under the direction of Professor Herbert Wechsler, with the assistance of a cast of collaborators, which included law professors, lawyers, and judges, as well as psychiatrists, a criminologist, and a professor of English. The Model Penal Code triggered widespread reform in American criminal law, remains the most systematic statement of American criminal law, has been called "the principal text in criminal law teaching," and—as a code—is particularly well suited for comparative analysis with civil law systems. See generally Markus D. Dubber, *Criminal Law: Model Penal Code* (2002).

[3] Those seeking more detailed, independent, accounts of American criminal law or German criminal law (in English), may wish to consult the following texts. Wayne R. LaFave, *Criminal Law* (5th edn. 2010); Joshua Dressler, *Understanding Criminal Law* (6th edn. 2012); Volker Krey, *Deutsches Strafrecht: Allgemeiner Teil / German Criminal Law: General Part pts. I & II* (2002/2003) (bilingual textbook); Michael Bohlander, *Principles of German Criminal Law* (2008).

[4] In fact, the primary texts by themselves add up to the most comprehensive English-language collection of criminal law materials from a non-Anglophone legal system. For a collection of essays reflecting on formative texts in criminal law scholarship, see Markus D. Dubber (ed.), *Foundational Texts in Modern Criminal Law* (forthcoming 2014).

The comparative study of criminal law thus can lay the foundations for critical analysis not only of another system or systems, but also of one's own. Taking a comparative perspective facilitates a more nuanced analysis of the criminal law system familiar to a given reader, both at the specific level of individual criminal law doctrines and at the general level of the two representative systems as a whole. This enhanced understanding of one's "home" system may lead to a more critical engagement with, and appreciation of, specific features of that system along with its conceptual and historical foundations.

Beyond the realm of domestic criminal law systems, a comparative view of criminal law is conducive to the study of international criminal law. This rapidly emerging field, still in the early stages of its development, has relied heavily on a comparative analysis of domestic systems of criminal law, both in the scholarly literature and in the growing jurisprudence of international criminal courts.

To unlock its considerable potential, domestic and international, comparative criminal law must take a comprehensive and contextual approach that enables rich comparative analysis, rather than collect point-by-point contrasts or make grand but vague statements about essential systemic distinctions and similarities. Ideally, in criminal law scholarship, doctrinal comparison will be placed within a broad historical and extra-legal context, and will reflect the necessary sensitivity to the difference between "law in the books" and "law in action." In criminal law teaching, we ordinarily do not have the luxury to fill in quite as much of the conceptual and empirical framework as we might in scholarship, except perhaps in upper-level seminars of sufficiently narrow topical focus. The present book nonetheless draws on what we hope is a suitably rich body of primary and secondary materials on two major criminal law systems that makes meaningful and rewarding comparative analysis possible, adjusting the resolution of our comparative lens as appropriate to find a happy medium between generality and specificity, the forest and the trees. Similarities at the level of general doctrine will go hand in hand with differences in detail, while differences in general approach may, upon closer inspection, make less of a difference on the ground than might first appear.

It is tempting, in this preface, to attempt to trace grand themes that run through this book, and to try in broad strokes to set out a general comparative analysis of common law and civil law systems of criminal law, or at any rate of U.S. and German criminal law, but it is a temptation we will resist. Developing and discarding, then reviving and constantly revising hypotheses on the subject of systemic comparison will be among the chief pleasures of reading and working through the book, or so we hope.

Markus D. Dubber
Tatjana Hörnle

ACKNOWLEDGMENTS

We are happy to acknowledge the assistance of colleagues, friends, and institutions in the completion of this project. First and foremost, our thanks go to Raymond Youngs who did a wonderful job translating dozens of German judgments. Others who helped in various ways and at different times include Alan Brudner, Andreas Dürr, Lindsay Farmer, Simon Stern, and Leo Zaibert. Among our students and assistants we would like to thank John Koziar, James Marton, Sarah Rankin, Brittany Shamess, and Cate Simpson (in Toronto) and Beatrice Brunhöber (in Berlin), along with the participants in our Toronto seminar on *Comparative Criminal Law*, where we test drove an early draft of these materials. Work on this project was supported by generous grants from the Social Sciences and Humanities Research Council of Canada (SSHRC) and the Deutsche Forschungsgemeinschaft (DFG).

Finally, we are grateful for permission to reprint excerpts from the following publications:

Binder, Guyora, "The Rhetoric of Motive and Intent," 6 *Buffalo Criminal Law Review* (2002), 1.

Chin, Gabriel J., "Unjustified: The Practical Irrelevance of the Justification/Excuse Distinction," 43 *University of Michigan Journal of Law Reform* (2009), 79.

Davis, Kenneth Culp, *Administrative Law* (2nd edn. 1979).

Dubber, Markus D., "American Plea Bargains, German Lay Judges, and the Crisis of Criminal Procedure," 49 *Stanford Law Review* (1997), 547.

——, "Criminalizing Complicity: A Comparative Analysis," 5 *Journal of International Criminal Justice* (2007), 977.

——, "Policing Possession: The War on Crime and the End of Criminal Law," 91 *Journal of Criminal Law and Criminology* (2002), 829.

——, "The Promise of German Criminal Law: A Science of Crime and Punishment," 6 *German Law Journal* (2005), 1049.

——, "The Victim in American Penal Law: A Systematic Overview," 3 *Buffalo Criminal Law Review* (1999), 3.

——, "Theories of Crime and Punishment in German Criminal Law," 53 *American Journal of Comparative Law* (2006), 679.

——, "Toward a Constitutional Law of Crime and Punishment," 55 *Hastings Law Journal* (2004), 509.

Hörnle, Tatjana, "Distribution of Punishment: The Role of a Victim's Perspective," 3 *Buffalo Criminal Law Review* (1999), 175.

——, "Hijacked Airplanes: May They Be Shot Down?," 10 *New Criminal Law Review* (2007), 582.

——, "Offensive Behavior and German Penal Law," 5 *Buffalo Criminal Law Review* (2001), 255.

——, "Penal Law and Sexuality: Recent Reforms in German Criminal Law," 3 *Buffalo Criminal Law Review* (2000), 639.

——, "Social Expectations in the Criminal Law: The 'Reasonable Person' in a Comparative Perspective," 11 *New Criminal Law Review* (2008), 1.

Kay, Julie, "Heat is on Attorneys in Drug Trafficking Cases: Florida Lawyer Is Accused of Taking 'Dirty Money'," *Miami Daily Business Review*, May 25, 2001.

Lynch, David, "The Impropriety of Plea Agreements: A Tale of Two Counties," 19 *Law & Social Inquiry* (1994), 115.

Naucke, Wolfgang, "An Insider's Perspective on the Significance of the German Criminal Law Theory's General System for Analyzing Criminal Acts," *Brigham Young University Law Review* [1984], 305.

Nestler, Cornelius, "Sentencing in Germany," 7 *Buffalo Criminal Law Review* (2003), 109.

Sayre, Francis Bowes, "Public Welfare Offenses," 33 *Columbia Law Review* (1933), 55.

Streng, Franz, "Sentencing in Germany: Basic Questions and New Developments," 8 *German Law Journal* (2007), 153.

Weigend, Thomas, "*Societas delinquere non potest*? A German Perspective," 6 *Journal of International Criminal Justice* (2008), 927.

SUMMARY CONTENTS

PART III THE SPECIAL PART

CONTENTS

PART II THE GENERAL PART

PART III THE SPECIAL PART

TABLE OF CASES

TABLE OF LEGISLATION

LIST OF ABBREVIATIONS

German Language Abbreviations

AG	Amtsgericht (local court)
ALR	Allgemeines Landrecht für die Preußischen Staaten (General Land Law for Prussian States)
AnwBl	*Anwaltsblatt* (journal)
BayObLG	Bayerisches Oberstes Landesgericht (Bavarian higher regional court)
BayObLGSt	Sammlung des BayObLG in Strafsachen (Decisions of the BayObLG in Criminal Matters)
BGB	Bürgerliches Gesetzbuch (Civil Code)
BGBl	Bundesgesetzblatt (Federal Gazette)
BGH	Bundesgerichtshof (Federal Court of Justice)
BGHSt	Entscheidungen des BGH in Strafsachen (Decisions of the BGH in Criminal Matters)
BMJ	Bundesministerium für Justiz (Federal Justice Ministry)
BT-Dr	Bundestag-Drucksachen (*Bundestag* Documents)
BtMG	Betäubungsmittelgesetz (Narcotics Act)
BVerfG	Bundesverfassungsgericht (Federal Constitutional Court)
BVerfGE	Sammlung der Entscheidungen des BVerfG (Decisions of the BVerfG)
DM	Deutsche Mark (Germany's pre-1999, pre-Euro currency, DM 2 = €1)
EuGRZ	*Europäische Grundrechte-Zeitschrift* (journal)
FS	Festschrift
GA	*Goltdammers Archiv für Strafrecht* (journal)
GDR	German Democratic Republic
GG	Grundgesetz (Basic Law)
GmbH	Gesellschaft mit beschränkter Haftung (limited liability corporation)
GrS	Großer Senat (en banc court)
GSSt	Großer Senat des BGH für Strafsachen (en banc BGH in Criminal Law Matters)
GVG	Gerichtsverfassungsgesetz (Judiciary Act)
h.L.	herrschende Lehre (prevailing doctrine)
h.M.	herrschende Meinung (prevailing opinion)
i.d.F.	in der Fassung (in the version of)
JR	*Juristische Rundschau* (journal)
Jura	*Juristische Ausbildung* (journal)
JuS	*Juristische Schulung* (journal)
JZ	*JuristenZeitung* (journal)
KG	Kammergericht (higher regional court, Berlin)
KritV	*Kritische Vierteljahresschrift für Gesetzgebung und Rechtswissenschaft* (journal)
LG	Landgericht (district court)
NJW	*Neue Juristische Wochenschrift* (journal)
NS	National Socialist
NStZ	*Neue Zeitschrift für Strafrecht* (journal)
NStZ-RR	*NStZ-Rechtsprechungs-Report Strafrecht* (journal)

OGHSt	Entscheidungen des Obersten Gerichtshofs für die Britische Zone in Strafsachen (Decisions of the Supreme Court of Justice for the British Zone in Criminal Matters)
OLG	Oberlandesgericht (higher regional court, court of appeal)
OWiG	Gesetz über Ordnungswidrigkeiten (Administrative Offenses Act)
PolG NRW	Polizeigesetz des Landes Nordrhein-Westfalen (Police Law of the Land North Rhine-Westfalia)
PStGB	Preußisches Strafgesetzbuch (Prussian Criminal Code)
RG	Reichsgericht (Imperial Court)
RGBl	Reichsgesetzblatt (Imperial Gazette)
RGSt	Entscheidungen des RG in Strafsachen (Decisions of the RG in Criminal Matters)
RStGB	Reichsstrafgesetzbuch (Imperial Criminal Code)
StGB	Strafgesetzbuch (Criminal Code)
StPO	Strafprozeßordnung (Code of Criminal Procedure)
StrafR	Strafrecht (criminal law)
StV	*Strafverteidiger* (journal)
StVollzG	Strafvollzugsgesetz (Prison Act)
TierSchG	Tierschutzgesetz (Animal Protection Act)
VO	Verordnung (regulation)
VVDStRL	*Veröffentlichungen der Vereinigung der Deutschen Staatsrechtslehrer* (journal)
WStG	Wehrstrafgesetz (Military Criminal Law Act)
WiStG	Wirtschaftsstrafgesetz (Economic Crimes Act)
ZIS	*Zeitschrift für Internationale Strafrechtsdogmatik* (journal)
ZStW	*Zeitschrift für die gesamte Strafrechtswissenschaft* (journal)

English Language Abbreviations

A.2d	Atlantic Reporter (Second Series)
A.C.	Appeal Cases
Ak.	Alaska
Ala.	Alabama
Ala. Crim. App.	Alabama Court of Criminal Appeals
ALI	American Law Institute
Allen	Allen Reports (Massachusetts)
Am.	Amendment
Ark.	Arkansas Reports
art., Art.	Article
BAC	Blood alcohol content
Buff. Crim. L. Rev.	*Buffalo Criminal Law Review*
BYU L. Rev.	*Brigham Young University Law Review*
C. & K.	Carrington & Kirwan Reports (England)
Cal. App. 3d	California Appellate Reports (Third Series)
Cal. Rptr.2d	California Reporter (Second Series)
Calif. L. Rev.	*California Law Review*
C.C.C.	Canadian Criminal Cases
C.C.R.I.	Circuit Court for Rhode Island
C.F.R.	Code of Federal Regulations
ch.	Chapter
Cir.	Circuit
Colum. L. Rev.	*Columbia Law Review*
cmt.	Comment

Conn.	Connecticut Reports
Const.	Constitution
Cox Crim. Cas.	Cox Criminal Cases (England)
Ct. Crim. App. Okla.	Oklahoma Court of Criminal Appeals
D.C. Cir.	United States Court of Appeals for the District of Columbia
D.D.C.	District Court for the District of Columbia
D.L.R.	Dominion Law Reports
Duke L.J.	*Duke Law Journal*
EED	Extreme emotional disturbance defense
El. & Bl.	Ellis & Blackburn Reports (England)
Eng. Rep.	English Reports
F.2d	Federal Reports (Second Series)
F.3d	Federal Reports (Third Series)
F. Cas.	Federal Cases
F. Supp.	Federal Supplement
Fed. Sentencing Rep.	*Federal Sentencing Reporter* (journal)
Harv. L. Rev.	*Harvard Law Review*
Hastings L.J.	*Hastings Law Journal*
J. Crim. L. & Criminology	*Journal of Criminal Law and Criminology*
L.A.	Los Angeles
Law & Contemp. Probs.	*Law and Contemporary Problems* (journal)
Leach	Leach Reports (England)
L.Q.R.	*Law Quarterly Review*
LWOP	Life imprisonment without parole
Mass.	Massachusetts Reports
Mass. App.	Appeals Court of Massachusetts
Me.	Maine Reports
Misc.2d	New York Miscellaneous Reports (Second Series)
Mo.	Missouri Supreme Court
Mo. App.	Missouri Appeals Reports
Mont.	Montana Supreme Court
MPC	American Law Institute, Model Penal Code
N.C.	North Carolina Reports
N.D.	North Dakota
Nev.	Nevada Reports
N.J.	New Jersey Reports
N.J. Super.	New Jersey Superior Court Reports
N.Y.	New York
N.Y.2d	New York Reports (Second Series)
N.Y.S.2d	New York Supplement (Second Series)
N.Y. Sup. Ct.	New York Supreme Court
N.W.2d	Northwestern Reporter (Second Series)
Nw. U. L. Rev	*Northwestern University Law Review*
Ohio St.3d	Ohio State Reports (Third Series)
Ohio St. L.J.	*Ohio State Law Journal*
P.2d	Pacific Reporter (Second Series)
Pa.	Pennsylvania State Reports
Pa. D. & C.2d	Pennsylvania District and County Reports (Second Series)
Pa. Super.	Pennsylvania Superior Court Reports
Prop. New Fed. Crim. Code	Proposed New Federal Criminal Code

Restatement (Second) of Torts	American Law Institute, Restatement of Torts, Second
Rutgers L.J.	*Rutgers Law Journal*
Q.B.	Queen's Bench
Q.B.D.	Queen's Bench Division
S.C.R.	Supreme Court Reports
S.D.	South Dakota
S.D.N.Y.	Southern District of New York
S.E.2d	Southeastern Reporter (Second Series)
So.	Southern Reports
So.2d	Southern Reports (Second Series)
Stan. L. Rev.	*Stanford Law Review*
S.W.2d	Southwestern Reporter (Second Series)
tit.	Title
U. Chi. L. Rev.	*University of Chicago Law Review*
U.S.	United States Reports
U.S.C.	United States Code
U.S.C.M.A.	Decisions of the United States Court of Military Appeals
U.S.S.G.	United States Sentencing Guidelines
Va.	Virginia Supreme Court
Veh. & Traf.	Vehicle and Traffic

PART I
FOUNDATIONS

In this, the first part of the book, we deal with an eclectic mix of preliminary issues, ranging from the foundational to the taxonomical, and everywhere in between. We start with a discussion of the various rationales for punishment. Here we encounter the traditional, and now well established, quartet of justifications: specific and general deterrence, rehabilitation, and incapacitation, on the one ("consequentialist") side, and retribution, on the other ("deontological") side. We will observe these rationales in action, rather than merely in the abstract, by taking a close look at a fascinating, and helpfully foundational, opinion in a U.S. federal criminal law case involving two interior decorators who found themselves convicted of money laundering. For comparative effect, we will also turn our attention to the currently leading rationale for punishment in Germany, positive general prevention (*positive Generalprävention*), which sets out to combine all the positive elements of the familiar justifications while avoiding the negative ones. Along the way, we will encounter the distinctly American phenomenon of an elaborate set of sentencing guidelines: in this case the influential, ambitious, and highly controversial Federal Sentencing Guidelines.

The victim's role in the contemporary system of criminal law in general, and in the law of sentencing in particular, has received considerable attention in recent decades and we too will take a comparative glance at this issue. We will see that while both criminal law systems under investigation have professed a commitment to victims' rights, this commitment has manifested itself differently, doctrinally and institutionally.

A look at the types of sanction in American and German criminal law reveals much in common, but also significant differences. There is of course the obvious, and important, difference that capital punishment remains alive—if perhaps not quite as well as in the past—in the U.S., but was abandoned in Germany, with the support of a remarkable left–right coalition, during the drafting of the German Basic Law (*Grundgesetz*, GG) after World War II. But there is also the less symbolic, but more practically significant, difference in the default sanction: imprisonment in the U.S., and the fine in Germany. This raises the related issue of the radical severity gap separating the U.S. from Germany, which puts the U.S. atop the list of country incarceration rates, and Germany somewhere near the bottom, between Canada and Japan.

After having thus set the stage, we proceed to consider what, if any, constitutional limits both countries recognize as constraining, or at least guiding, the legislative choice of prescribed punishment and its judicial imposition in a particular case. Capital punishment passed constitutional muster in the United States, after some prolonged hesitation on the part of the U.S. Supreme Court, which instead launched a decades-long, and ongoing, effort to micromanage death penalty schemes through the blunt tool of the Eighth Amendment's cruel and unusual punishments clause. The German Constitutional Court (*Bundesverfassungsgericht*, BVerfG) likewise managed to affirm the constitutionality of life imprisonment despite concerns about its consistency with the commitment to human dignity and autonomy associated with German constitutional law. In the U.S., life imprisonment—even without the possibility of parole (LWOP for short)—has been portrayed by death penalty opponents as a far preferable, and unquestionably constitutional, alternative to capital punishment. Limits on the quantity, rather than the quality, of punishment meted out in the abstract, or in a particular case, have been (even) harder to come by. Until recently, the

U.S. Supreme Court was unclear about whether the Eighth Amendment imposed any proportionality requirement on non-capital sentences (consistent with a general tendency to treat capital punishment as a *sui generis* punishment subject to unique constitutional constraints).

A particularly fruitful topic for comparative analysis is the distinction between "punishment" and "measure," which is a central feature of the German penal process, whose two-track sanction system differentiates categorically—and constitutionally—between guilt-based punishment and risk-based preventive detention. Although a similar distinction also appears in pockets of American criminal law, notably in the treatment of so-called "sexual predators," where it has similar constitutional implications, it plays a much less systematic, and more controversial, role, at least so far. (Other common law jurisdictions, such as Canada, more closely resemble the German dualistic approach.)

The next Chapter in Part I is devoted to the legality principle, also known by its Lawyer Latin moniker—ordinarily attributed to the early nineteenth-century German criminal law scholar (and codifier/judge/author) Paul Johann Anselm Feuerbach—*nulla poena sine lege* (among others: e.g., *nullum crimen sine lege*).* We will pay particular attention to two aspects of the principle, the requirements of prospectivity and specificity (the affirmative flipsides of the prohibitions of retroactivity, or *ex post facto*, and vagueness, for which no Latin version has been coined, so far[†]). It will turn out, perhaps not surprisingly, that both systems recognize these requirements, and assign them constitutional status, even if significant differences in formulation, interpretation, and application remain. The German case on retroactivity (Chapter 2), dealing with the criminal liability of former East German border guards under the Communist regime prior to 1989, is interesting in its own right. It is one of several cases in this book that explore the interplay between criminal law doctrine (and institutions) and behavior, by officials and others, under an oppressive political regime, of which there have been several in recent German history.

The interplay between constitutional law and criminal law presents another opportunity for comparative reflection. In the U.S., it has become an old saw that procedural criminal law is almost completely constitutionalized, thanks to the Warren Court (i.e., the U.S. Supreme Court under Chief Justice Earl Warren) in the 1950s and 60s, whereas substantive criminal law has remained almost entirely untouched by constitutional scrutiny. While it is certainly true that the general principles of criminal liability, which make up the general part of substantive criminal law, cannot as a rule claim constitutional status, the U.S. Supreme Court has been more willing—at least recently—to take a closer constitutional look at the special part of criminal law, i.e., the legislature's authority to criminalize particular conduct in the first place. In both the general part and the special part, the firstness of the First Amendment—protecting free speech—has made its mark, triggering greater scrutiny of doctrines and offenses that may chill the exercise of free speech rights. In Germany— unlike, say, in Canada—there is also little constitutional criminal law, as criminal law principles so far have claimed pre- if not super-constitutional status. This makes recourse to constitutional principles unnecessary, except perhaps to suggest that already-established criminal law doctrines have constitutional foundations (such as the ubiquitous culpability— or guilt—principle). Constitutional or not, two principles that are often invoked as possible limits on the scope of criminal law—the harm principle in Anglo-American criminal law, and the *Rechtsgut* principle in German law—are primed for comparative analysis, with similarly mixed results.

The question of criminal jurisdiction, i.e., the applicability of the criminal norms of a particular state (or other political community, such as a tribe, for instance), tends to get little attention in criminal law teaching, and scholarship, with the noteworthy exception of international criminal law, where it is recognized for its foundational significance. We will

---

* See Tatjana Hörnle, "Paul Johann Anselm von Feuerbach and His Impact on Contemporary Criminal Law Theory," in Markus D. Dubber (ed.), *Foundational Texts in Modern Criminal Law* (forthcoming 2014).
[†] Unless one counts the not particularly common *nulla poena sine lege certa* (see Chapter 2). We will also touch on the legislativity principle in that Chapter.

take a comparative look at Anglo-American and German conceptions of criminal jurisdiction, both of which revolve around the notion of territoriality, but with noteworthy differences in historical and doctrinal context.

A basic understanding of the procedural and institutional aspects of the penal process is essential, or at least useful, for a comparative study—and in fact, for any study—of substantive criminal law. The next to last Chapter in Part I gives readers a quick sense of how a criminal case makes its way through the procedural maze and what officials and institutions it may encounter en route to what form of disposition. One feature of the German law of criminal procedure is particularly worth highlighting here: the principle of compulsory prosecution, or *Legalitätsprinzip*. This principle seeks to bring prosecutorial (and police) discretion within the rule of law by eliminating it, except in cases covered by a countervailing principle, the opportunity principle (*Opportunitätsprinzip*), with interesting implications for the practice of plea bargaining, the existence of which has only recently been acknowledged in Germany.

Part I ends with a comparative overview of the schemes for the analysis of criminal liability in Anglo-American, and the American Law Institute's Model Penal Code in particular, and German criminal law. This Chapter is important for the rest of the book as it sets the general framework for the comparative analysis to follow, in Parts II and III, which are devoted to the general part and special part of criminal law, respectively.

PUNISHMENT: CONCEPTS, FORMS, LIMITS

A. Concepts and Forms of Punishment

Criminal Law is the law of punishment, as the German terms *Strafrecht* (literally, punishment law) and *Strafgesetzbuch* (literally, punishment code) make clear. Even those who prefer the moniker *Kriminalrecht*, or criminal law, to reflect the existence of (ostensibly) non-punitive "sanctions"—most notably the "measures" of rehabilitation and protection (*Maßregeln der Besserung und Sicherung*, originally, until 1975, dubbed measures of protection and rehabilitation) that supplement the expressly punitive sanctions labeled "punishments" in German criminal law—must acknowledge that punishment remains a central aspect of criminal law. Previous attempts to replace the punishment paradigm with a treatment paradigm altogether, as reflected, for instance, in the American Law Institute's Model Penal Code project, have not managed to turn punishment into a taboo. At any rate, criminal law is about a particularly—even uniquely—intrusive exercise of state power by any name, punishment or "hard" or "peno-correctional" treatment. No relabeling exercise can, or should, obviate the need for the justification of punishment.

And so we begin with a discussion of the so-called rationales for punishment. One would think, given that punishment is an exercise of state power, that these rationales would be framed in political terms. Instead, however, they have tended to be treated as an exercise in applied moral philosophy, illustrating the distinction between consequentialist—and particularly utilitarian—and deontological, or desert-based, moral theories (*ne peccetur* vs. *quia peccatum*, if you prefer Latin). This is particularly true of the Anglo-American literature, where the debate about "punishment theory" has continued for some two hundred years, swaying back and forth between consequentialism and retributivism. In Germany, the discussion has produced a wide consensus around a theory of punishment, "positive general prevention," which one might consider not so much an alternative to, as a combination of, the traditional accounts. Unlike the bulk of Anglo-American rationales, however, the German consensus view at least acknowledges the legal-political dimension of the problem, by addressing itself to citizens whose loyalty to the state's legal order is bolstered by the state's punishing those who violate its legal norms. (We will return to the question of the justification of punishment in our discussion of the constitutional limits on the state's penal power, in Chapter 3.)

While rationales for punishment also figure in the doctrine of the law of *crime* (i.e., substantive criminal law, narrowly speaking), if perhaps not as much as one might think (or perhaps as they should, given how much time is devoted to them in teaching and scholarship), they most directly influence the law of *punishment* (i.e., the law of sentencing). A court may turn to the rationales for punishment when deciding, say, a question in the law of attempt: an incapacitative approach might yield a more expansive view of the scope of attempt, moving the *locus poenitentiae* farther away from the consummation of the offense and thereby permitting state interference at an earlier point in the timeline from preparation to attempt to consummation, than would a retributive approach, which may struggle to justify attempt liability except for conduct that comes perilously close to the consummation of the offense. But it is when determining the appropriate sentence, as opposed to considering the preceding question of criminal liability, that a court will find the rationales for punishment directly relevant: should this person be punished and, if so, how (quality) and how much (quantity)? Of course, one would hope that the rationales for punishment would also shape the *legislature*'s decision (or that of some state official to whom the legislature has delegated the power to generate norms, within some area of administrative expertise, backed by the threat of punishment for noncompliance), whether, and if so in what way, to threaten certain behavior with criminal punishment in the first place.

i. Rationales

United States v. Blarek
U.S. District Court, Eastern District of New York
7 F. Supp. 2d 192 (E.D.N.Y. 1998)

Weinstein, Senior District Court Judge.

Facts

Defendants Blarek and Pellecchia . . . were charged with Racketeering, 18 U.S.C. § 1962(c), Racketeering Conspiracy, 18 U.S.C. § 1962(d), and Conspiring to Launder Monetary Instruments, 18 U.S.C. §§ 371 and 1956(h) . . . Blarek was additionally charged with one count of Interstate Travel in Aid of Racketeering, 18 U.S.C. § 1952(a)(1). By way of indictment, the government sought the forfeiture of defendants' property traceable to their alleged criminality. Both defendants pleaded not guilty.

Blarek, while operating his own interior design firm in Coconut Grove, Florida, met Pellecchia in 1980. They worked together, and became intimate, cohabitating as homosexual partners. Quickly they established a new decorating company. Blarek was President and Pellecchia Vice-President. The venture was successful. Defendants designed, remodeled, and renovated homes and offices for a broad range of private persons and businesses.

Beginning in the early-1980's, the nature of defendants' operation changed. From that time forward they worked almost exclusively for a single, ill-famed and powerful criminal client—José Santacruz Londoño. Blarek met Santacruz by chance in 1979 during a visit to friends in Colombia. He agreed to work for Santacruz, designing the interior of the drug lord's new ostentatious home. . . .

Other dealings with Santacruz followed. Over a twelve year period, the defendants designed and decorated a number of offices and living spaces for Santacruz, his wife, his mistresses, and his children. . . .

Defendants knowingly laundered tainted cash for Santacruz in the United States in order to continue exercising their own craft and to enhance their own lives. . . . Both Blarek and Pellecchia knew who José Santacruz was, what he did, and from where his money was derived. Yet, each voluntarily agreed to, and in fact did, "wash" his drug proceeds . . .

Nearly all transactions between Santacruz and defendants were in cash. Defendants traveled to Miami, New York City, and other pre-determined locations to receive large sums of money from Santacruz's couriers. Payments as high as one million dollars at a time were hand-delivered to defendants in piles of fifty and one-hundred dollar bills. Defendants moved the cash between cities, traveling by car or train to avoid airport searches.

Portions of the funds were deposited in defendants' safe deposit boxes, or in bank accounts in amounts of less than $10,000 at a time to avoid federal bank transaction reporting requirements. See 31 C.F.R. § 103.22; see also 31 U.S.C. § 5324. In addition, defendants' own accountant, who pleaded guilty to money laundering and testified as a government witness, converted some one million dollars of the drug cash into checks for the defendants, thus "cleaning" the money for routine use in defendants' business operations . . .

After a two week trial, in February 1997, defendants were each found guilty of the Racketeering Conspiracy and Money Laundering Conspiracy counts. The jury also returned a verdict of Blarek's guilt of Interstate Travel in Aid of Racketeering.

Following trial, defendants entered into a stipulation with the government, forfeiting nearly all of their property, including their home in San Francisco worth over two millions dollars, three Harley

Davidson motorcycles, a Mercedes Benz automobile, approximately $75,000 worth of jewelry, and hundreds of thousands of dollars in bank accounts and safe deposit boxes.

According to the Presentence Reports prepared by the United States Probation Office, defendants' offense conduct after 1986 involved at least $5.5 million dollars. In the process of "grouping" the counts, Guideline level 20 was used as an appropriate base offense level reflecting a determination that violation of section 1956(a)(1)(b)(i) of Title 18 of the United States Code was one of the underlying objectives of the conspiracies. See U.S.S.G. § 2S1.1(a)(2). Additionally, enhancements were made to the initial offense levels based upon defendants' knowledge that the monies received were drug proceeds and for their supervisory role in the crimes. Further upward adjustment to Blarek's offense level was predicated upon obstruction of justice for his alleged false testimony at the trial.

Taking these factors into account, the Presentence Report indicates Blarek has a combined adjusted offense level of 33 based upon the three counts for which he was convicted. His criminal history category is I, since he has no prior record. His Guidelines imprisonment range would then be 135 to 168 months. A fine range for Blarek's crimes of $20,000 to $14,473,063, as well as a required period of supervised release of at least two but not more than three years is also indicated.

Pellecchia's combined adjusted offense level, according to the Presentence Report, is 33. He, too, was assigned a criminal history category of I by the Probation Office since he has no prior convictions. This assessment results in an imprisonment range of 135 to 168 months. The Presentence Report also indicates a fine range of $17,500 to $14,473,063 and a required period of supervised release of at least two but not more than three years ...

Law

A. Sentencing Statute: 18 U.S.C. § 3553

1. Sufficient But Not Greater Than Necessary

Congress restructured the federal sentencing law in the 1980's to create the current Guidelines-based system. See Sentencing Reform Act of 1984, Pub. L. No. 98-473, § 211, 98 Stat. 1987, 1989–90 (1984). It expressly stated that courts "shall impose a sentence sufficient, but not greater that necessary," to comply with the purposes of criminal sanctions.18 U.S.C. § 3553(a). Harshness greater than that required is statutorily prohibited by this portion of the Sentencing Reform Act. Excessive leniency is also forbidden.

2. Seriousness of the Offense, Adequate Deterrence, Protection of the Public, and Correctional Treatment

The Sentencing Reform Act went on to explicitly delineate the purposes of criminal sanctions. Section 3551(a) provides that every defendant "shall be sentenced ... so as to achieve the purposes set forth in subparagraphs (A) through (D) of section 3553(a)(2) to the extent that they are applicable in light of all the circumstances of the case."

Subparagraphs (A) through (D) of section 3553(a)(2) instruct courts to consider the necessity of the sentence imposed:

(A) to reflect the seriousness of the offense, to promote respect for the law, and to provide just punishment for the offense;
(B) to afford adequate deterrence to criminal conduct;
(C) to protect the public from further crimes of the defendant; and
(D) to provide the defendant with needed educational or vocational training, medical care, or other, correctional treatment in the most effective manner.

... (A) above largely constitutes a summary of the just deserts theory and (B), (C), and (D) encompass utilitarian concerns. In creating the sentencing statutes, "Congress spelled out the four traditional justifications of the criminal sentence—deterrence, incapacitation, retribution and rehabilitation—and expressly instructed the sentencing court to keep these purposes in mind ..." Kenneth R. Feinberg, The Federal Guidelines as the Underlying Purposes of Sentencing, 3 Fed. Sent. Rep. 326, 326 (May/June 1991).

When enforcing the complex federal sentencing scheme, courts are required to consider six factors, subsidiary to the traditional sentencing rationales set out above. These are:

(a) "the nature and circumstances of the offense and the history and characteristics of the defendant";
(b) "the kinds of sentences available";
(c) "the kinds of sentence and the sentencing range established" by the Sentencing Guidelines;
(d) "the need to avoid unwarranted sentence disparities among defendants with similar records who have been found guilty of similar conduct";

(e) "any pertinent policy statement issued by the Sentencing Commission"; and
(f) "the need to provide restitution to any victims of the offense."

18 U.S.C. § 3553(a)(1), (3)–(7).

To understand how these statutory provisions should be applied, a brief review of the theory and background of the purposes of criminal sentences is required.

B. Traditional Sentencing Rationales

Sentencing is a critical stage of a criminal prosecution. See Gardner v. Florida, 430 U.S. 349, 358, 51 L. Ed. 2d 393, 97 S. Ct. 1197 (1977). It represents an important moment in the law, a "fundamental judgment determining how, where, and why the offender should be dealt with for what may be much or all of his remaining life." Marvin E. Frankel, Criminal Sentences vii (1973). It is significant not only for the individual before the court, but for his family and friends, the victims of his crime, potential future victims, and society as a whole.

Four core considerations, in varying degrees and permutations, have traditionally shaped American sentencing determinations: incapacitation of the criminal, rehabilitation of the offender, deterrence of the defendant and of others, and just desert for the crime committed . . .

Ascertaining priorities among these potentially conflicting notions has long been a point of contention amongst legislators, scholars, jurists, and practitioners. Somewhat oversimplifying, there are two basic camps. Retributivists contend that "just deserts" are to be imposed for a crime committed. Utilitarians, in their various manifestations, suggest that penalties need to be viewed more globally by measuring their benefits against their costs . . .

Implied in this debate are questions about our basic values and beliefs:

Why do we impose punishment? Or is it properly to be named "punishment"? Is our purpose retributive? It is to deter the defendant himself or others in the community from committing crimes? Is it for reform? rehabilitation? incapacitation of dangerous people? Questions like these have engaged philosophers and students of the criminal law for centuries.

Frankel, supra, at 7.

In the nineteenth and most of the twentieth century American prison and punishment system reforms were designed primarily to rehabilitate the prisoner as a protection against further crime. In more recent years there has been a perception by many that attempts at rehabilitation have failed; a movement towards theoretically based, more severe, fixed punishments, based upon the nature of the crime gained momentum. Two eighteenth and nineteenth century philosophers set the terms of the current . . . debate.

1. Kant's Retributive Just Desert Theory

Immanuel Kant, born in East Prussia in 1724, [famously held that] "the moral worth of an action does not depend on the result expected from it, and so too does not depend on any principle of action that needs to borrow its motive from this expected result . . ." Immanuel Kant, Groundwork of the Metaphysics of Morals 68–69 (H.J. Paton ed. & trans., Hutchinson Univ. Library 3d ed. 1965) (1785) (italics omitted).

. . . . Kant's anti-utilitarian thesis on criminal penalties is reflected in an oft-cited passage from his work, The Metaphysical Elements of Justice:

Juridical punishment can never be used merely as a means to promote some other good for the criminal himself or for civil society, but instead it must in all cases be imposed on him only on the ground that he has committed a crime; for a human being can never be manipulated merely as a means to the purposes of someone else and can never be confused with the objects of the Law of things . . .

Immanuel Kant, The Metaphysical Elements of Justice (Part I of The Metaphysics of Morals) 100 (John Ladd ed. & trans. 1965) (1797).

It follows from this position that the sole justification for criminal punishment is retribution or "jus talionis." See Leon Pearl, A Case Against the Kantian Retributivist Theory of Punishment: A Response to Professor Pugsley, 11 Hofstra L. Rev. 273, 274 (1982) ("Immanuel Kant . . . held that only a retributivist theory is properly responsive to the criminal's dignity as a rational agent capable of moral conduct, a dignity which he retains despite his commission of a legal offense.") . . . For Kant and his adherents, "punishment that gives an offender what he or she deserves for a past crime is a valuable end in itself and needs no further justification." Paul H. Robinson & John M. Darley, The Utility of Desert, 91 Nw. U. L. Rev. 453, 454 (1997). "It is not inflicted because it will give an opportunity for reform, but because it is merited." Edmund L. Pincoffs, The Rationale of Legal Punishment 7 (1966). Kantian "just deserts" theory, therefore, focuses almost exclusively on the past to determine the level of punishment that should be meted out to right the wrong that has already occurred as a result of the defendant's delict . . .

2. Bentham's Utilitarian Theory

Jeremy Bentham, an English philosopher born in 1748, advocated a far different, more prospective approach through his "Principle of Utility." For him, law in general, and criminal jurisprudence in particular, was intended to produce the "greatest happiness for the greatest number," a concept sometimes referred to as the "felicity calculus."

This is not to say that Bentham did not believe in sanctions. It was his view that punishment was sometimes essential to ensure compliance with public laws. See Jeremy Bentham, Bentham's Political Thought 167–68 (Bhikhu Parekh ed. 1973) ("For the most part it is to some pleasure or some pain drawn from the political sanction itself, but more particularly . . . to pain that the legislator trusts for the effectuation of his will.").

Unlike his contemporary, Kant, Bentham was not interested in criminal punishment as a way of avenging or canceling the theoretical wrong suffered by society through a deviation from its norms. Rather, a criminal sanction was to be utilized only when it could help ensure the greater good of society and provide a benefit to the community. Bentham's writings in An Introduction to the Principles of Morals and Legislation explain this theory:

> . . . all punishment is mischief: all punishment in itself evil. Upon the principle of utility, if it ought at all to be admitted, it ought only to be admitted in as far as it promises to exclude some greater evil . . . in the following cases punishment ought not to be inflicted.
> I. Where it is groundless: where there is no mischief for it to prevent: the act not being mischievous upon the whole.
> II. Where it must be inefficacious: where it cannot act so as to prevent the mischief.
> III. Where it is unprofitable, or too expensive: where the mischief it would produce would be greater than what it prevented.
> IV. Where it is needless: where the mischief may be prevented, or cease of itself, without it: that is, at a cheaper rate . . .
>
> Jeremy Bentham, An Introduction to the Principles of Morals and
> Legislation, in The Great Legal Philosophers: Select Readings
> in Jurisprudence 262, 270 (Clarence Morris ed., 1959).

Under the Benthamite approach, deterring crime, as well as correction and reformation of the criminal, are primary aspirations of criminal law. While "the theory of retribution would impose punishment for its own sake, the utilitarian theories of deterrence and reformation would use punishment as a means to [a practical] end—the end being community protection by the prevention of crime." Charles E. Torcia, 1 Wharton's Criminal Law § 1, at 3 (15th ed. 1993).

3. Sanctions in Strict Retributive and Utilitarian Models

Given the divergence in underlying assumptions and theory, the competing retributivist and utilitarian theories suggest opposing methods for ascertaining proper penalties. Under a Kantian model, the extent of punishment is required to neatly fit the crime. "Whoever commits a crime must be punished in accordance with his desert." Pincoffs, supra, at 4.

In the case of murder, some believe that just desert is clear. A taker of life must have his own life taken. Even in the case of killings, however, there are degrees of mens rea, and over large portions of the world capital punishment is outlawed on a variety of just desert and utilitarian grounds. Cf. Alan I. Bigel, "Justices William J. Brennan, Jr. and Thurgood Marshall on Capital Punishment: Its Constitutionality, Morality, Deterrent Effect, and Interpretation by the Court," 8 Notre Dame J.L. Ethics & Pub. Pol'y 11, 44 (1994) (statistics show that utilization of death penalty does not significantly lower murder rate).

For lesser offenses, reaching a consensus on the proper "price" for the criminal act under the Kantian approach is even more difficult. As one scholar has written:

> The retributivist can perhaps avoid the question of how we decide that one crime is morally more heinous than another by hewing to his position that no such decision is necessary so long as we make the punishment "equal" to the crime. To accomplish this, he might argue, it is not necessary to argue to the relative wickedness of crimes. But at best this leaves us with the problem of how we do make punishments equal to crimes, a problem which will not stop plaguing retributivists.
>
> Pincoffs, supra at 16.

Two main theoretical problems are presented by this just deserts approach. The degree of the earned desert—that is to say the extent or length of the appropriate punishment—is subjective. The upper and lower limits of the punishment can be very high or very low, justified on personal views and taste. The "earned" punishment may be quite cruel and do more harm to society, the criminal, and his family, than can be justified on utilitarian grounds.

Determining the appropriateness of sanction differs under Bentham's utilitarian approach, although it too poses challenging theoretical and practical tasks for the sentencer. Under this model, among:

the factors ... [to be considered] are the need to set penalties in such a way that where a person is tempted to commit one of two crimes he will commit the lesser, that the evil consequences ... of the crime will be minimized even if the crime is committed, that the least amount possible of punishment be used for the prevention of a given crime.

See id. at 23.

Obviously, one problem with utilizing a system based only upon this approach is that "it is difficult ... to determine when more good than harm has been achieved. ... " United States v. Concepcion, 795 F. Supp. 1262, 1272 (E.D.N.Y. 1992).

As in the case of Kantian just deserts, the felicity calculation is subject to considerable difficulty and dispute. Another major problem with the utilitarian approach is that the individual criminal can be treated very cruelly, to gain some societal advantage even though the crime is minor—or very leniently, despite the shocking nature of the crime—if that will on balance benefit society.

Given these problems, it may make sense to continue to equivocate, oscillating between these poles, tempering justice with mercy, just deserts with utility calculations, in varying pragmatic ways. "Pragmatism," one of the hallmarks of the American political and legal system, itself suggests a leaning toward utilitarianism. See Webster's New Twentieth Century Dictionary (William Collins ed., 2d ed. 1979) ("in philosophy [pragmatism] ... tests the validity of all concepts by their practical results").

C. Utility and Retribution Under Sentencing Guidelines

The Sentencing Guidelines, written by the United States Sentencing Commission pursuant to the Sentencing Reform Act, see Pub. L. 98-473, § 217, 98 Stat. 1987, 2019 (1984), purport to comport with the competing theoretical ways of thinking about punishment. The Guidelines state that they [seek to] "further the basic purposes of criminal punishment: deterrence, incapacitation, just punishment, and rehabilitation." See U.S.S.G. Chap. 1, Pt. A(2). A systematic, theoretical approach to these four purposes was not, however, employed by the Commission:

A philosophical problem arose when the Commission attempted to reconcile the differing perceptions of the purposes of criminal punishment. Most observers of the criminal law agree that the ultimate aim of the law itself, and of punishment in particular, is the control of crime. Beyond this point, however, the consensus seems to break down. Some argue that appropriate punishment should be defined primarily on the basis of the principle of "just deserts." Under this principle, punishment should be scaled to the offender's culpability and the resulting harms. Others argue that punishment should be imposed primarily on the basis of practical "crime control" considerations. This theory calls for sentences that most effectively lessen the likelihood of future crime, either by deterring others or incapacitating the defendant.

Id. at A(3).

The Commission decided not to create a solely retributivist or utilitarian paradigm, or "accord one primacy over the other." Id.

It is claimed that, "as a practical matter this choice [between the competing purposes of criminal punishment] was unnecessary because in most sentencing decisions the application of either philosophy will produce the same or similar results." Id. This premise is flawed. In practice, results may vary widely depending upon theory. A penalty imposed based upon pure utilitarian considerations would hardly ever be identical to one that was imposed in a pristine retributive system. While it cannot be said that one is always harsher than the other, seldom would their unrestrained application produce the same sentence.

D. Deference to Sentencing Judge on Guidelines' Critical Sentencing Issues

Since the Sentencing Commission did not say how competing rationales should shape individual sentencing decisions, courts are left to make that judgment. ...

In writing the initial Guidelines, the Commission "sought to solve both the practical and philosophical problems of developing a coherent sentencing system by taking an empirical approach that used as its starting point data estimating pre-guidelines sentencing practice." U.S.S.G. Ch. 1, Pt. A(3). It contended that this:

empirical approach ... helped resolve its philosophical dilemma. Those who adhere to a just deserts philosophy may concede that the lack of consensus might make it difficult to say exactly what punishment is deserved for a particular crime. Likewise, those who subscribe to a philosophy of crime control may acknowledge that the lack of sufficient data might make it difficult to determine exactly the punishment that will best prevent that crime. Both groups might therefore recognize the wisdom of looking to those distinctions that judges and legislators have, in fact, made over the course of time. These established distinctions are ones that the community believes, or has found over time, to be important from either a just deserts or crime control perspective.

Id.

This statistically based foundation has proven inadequate to administer individual criminal litigations except in "routine" cases upon which there may be a "consensus." . . .

E. Application of the Guidelines

Until broad-based transformation of the current complex federal system takes place, individual judges have a duty under the statutes to consider all traditional purposes of sentencing when determining an appropriate penalty. Such "purpose-based analysis by judges may be the best hope for bringing justification to sentences imposed in the federal guideline system." Marc Miller, Purposes at Sentencing, 66 S. Cal. L. Rev. 413, 478 (1992).

1. Heartland

The Guidelines established base offense levels for criminal acts, representing an assessment of the quantity of punishment required for the "average" crime of that sort. As a result, "sentencing courts [are] to treat each guideline as carving out a 'heartland,' a set of typical cases embodying the conduct that each guideline describes." U.S.S.G. Ch.1, Pt.A(4)(b). What this means, the Supreme Court has recently explained, is that "[a] district judge now must impose on a defendant a sentence falling within the range of the applicable Guideline, if the case is an ordinary one." Koon v. United States, 518 U.S. 81, 92 (1996).

The Guidelines, while intended to ensure "a more honest, uniform, equitable, proportional, and therefore effective sentencing system," U.S.S.G. Ch.1, Pt.A(3), must not be interpreted as eliminating judicial sentencing discretion. See Koon, 518 U.S. at 92. The traditional task of imposing a just and fair sentence based upon an independent view integrating all philosophical, statutory, Guidelines and individual particulars of the case at hand remains the job of the . . . judge.

2. Departures

Congress provided for judicial departure from the Sentencing Guidelines whenever a "court finds that there exists an aggravating or mitigating circumstance of a kind, or to a degree, not adequately taken into consideration by the Sentencing Commission in formulating the guidelines that should result in a sentence different from that described." 18 U.S.C. § 3553(b).

In the same way that the Commission could not have foreseen every type of criminal case, it could not have foretold every potential ground justifying departing from the Guidelines. Except perhaps for a limited few grounds that the Commission has expressly stated should not be considered as reasons for departing, it "does not intend to limit the kind of factors, whether or not mentioned anywhere else in the guidelines, that could constitute grounds for departure in an unusual case." U.S.S.G. Ch.1, Pt. A(4)(b). . . .

Law Applied to Facts

A. Guidelines Computations

. . . Probation's Presentence Report recommends that defendant Blarek should incur an upward adjustment for obstruction of justice based upon perjury in his trial testimony. See U.S.S.G. § 3C1.1. The government's argument supporting this view is rejected. Blarek appeared to be forthright in his presentation. Inconsistencies in his testimony might be attributed to the tricks memory often plays when a person wishes the past were different from what it was. See U.S.S.G. § 3C1.1 cmt.1 ("inaccurate testimony or statements sometimes may result from confusion, mistake, or faulty memory and, thus, not all . . . reflect a willful attempt to obstruct justice"). An allegation of perjury is not supported. See U.S.S.G. § 3C1.1 cmt.3(b) ("committing, suborning, or attempting to suborn perjury" warrant obstruction of justice enhancement).

Based upon these findings, defendant Blarek's total offense level should be reduced to 32, while defendant Pellecchia's is reduced to 30. Blarek faces a period of imprisonment of 121 to 151 months. Pellecchia faces 97 to 121 months' incarceration. . . .

B. Traditional and Statutory Sentencing Rationales

1. Incapacitation

Incapacitation seeks to ensure that "offenders . . . are rendered physically incapable of committing crime." Arthur W. Campbell, Law of Sentencing § 2:3, at 27–28 (1991). In colonial America, incapacitation was sometimes imposed in a literal sense. Id. at 28 (loss of organs). With the development of the penitentiary system, incarceration was seen as "a more reliable means of incapacitation." Adam J. Hirsch, The Rise of the Penitentiary: Prisons and Punishment in Early America 44 (1992).

In the instant case, incapacitation is not an important factor. First, these defendants have no prior criminal record indicating any propensity towards crime. Second, their connection to the criminal world, Santacruz, is now deceased. Third, it does not appear that long term restriction is necessary to ensure that defendants do not reenter a life of crime.

Consistent with utilitarian-driven analysis, little would be gained if the sentences emphasized incapacitation.

2. Rehabilitation

Rehabilitation is designed to instill "in the offender proper values and attitudes, by bolstering his respect for self and institutions, and by providing him with the means of leading a productive life. . . . " Wharton's Criminal Law, supra, at 18. Neither of these men is wayward or in need of special instruction on the mores of civilized society. They have in place strong communal support systems, as evidenced by the many letters submitted to the court by family and friends. They know how to live a law abiding life. It is not required that a penalty be fashioned that teaches them how to be moral in the future. This criterion, rehabilitation, therefore, is not one that is useful in assessing a penalty.

3. Deterrence

Of the two forms of deterrence that motivate criminal penalties—general and specific—only one is of substantial concern here.

Specific deterrence is meant to "disincline individual offenders from repeating the same or other criminal acts." Campbell, supra, at 25. Such dissuasion has likely already occurred. Defendants regret their actions. The ordeal of being criminally prosecuted and publicly shamed by being denominated felons and the imposition of other penalties has taught them a sobering lesson.

General deterrence attempts to discourage the public at large from engaging in similar conduct. It is of primary concern in this case. Defendants' activities have gained a great deal of attention. Notorious cases are ideal vehicles for capturing the attention of, and conveying a message to, the public at large. While it is not appropriate under just desert views for defendants in famous cases to be treated more harshly than defendants in less significant ones simply for the sake of making an example of them, under a utilitarian view, the notoriety of a particular defendant may be taken into account by sentencing courts provided the punishment is not disproportionate to the crime.

4. Retribution

Retribution is considered by some to be a barbaric concept, appealing to a primal sense of vengeance. See Wharton's Criminal Law, supra, at 24. It cannot, however, be overlooked as an appropriate consideration. When there is a perception on the part of the community that the courts have failed to sensibly sanction wrongdoers, respect for the law may be reduced. This is a notion applicable under both just deserts and utilitarian balancing concepts that has had some resurgence with the current growth of the rights of victims to be heard at sentencing. See, e.g., 18 U.S.C. § 3555 (order of notice to victims). But see Susan Bandes, "Empathy, Narrative, and Victim Impact Statements," 63 U. Chi. L. Rev. 361, 365 (1996) ("victim impact statements are narratives that should be suppressed because they evoke emotions inappropriate in the context of criminal sentencing").

Should punishment fail to fit the crime, the citizenry might be tempted to vigilantism. This may be why, according to one group of scholars, "a criminal law based on the community's perceptions of just desert is, from a utilitarian perspective, the more effective strategy for reducing crime." Robinson & Darley, supra, at 454. "White collar" "victimless" offenses, such as the ones committed by these defendants, are harmful to all society, particularly since drugs are involved. It is important, therefore, that the imposition of a penalty in this case captures, to some rational degree, the "worth" of defendants' volitional criminal acts.

5. Sufficient But Not Greater Than Necessary

Mercy is seldom included on the list of "traditional" rationales for sentencing. It is, however, evinced by the federal sentencing statute, 18 U.S.C. § 3553(a), which provides, as noted above, that the lowest possible penalty consistent with the goals of sentencing be imposed. See also United States v. Johnson, 964 F.2d 124, 125 (2d Cir. 1992) ("the United States Sentencing Guidelines do not require a judge to leave compassion and common sense at the door to the courtroom").

The notion that undue harshness should be avoided by those sitting in judgment has long been a part of the human fabric and spirit. Lenity is often the desirable route.

C. Departures

To impose the harsh sentence suggested by Probation and the government under the Guidelines without appropriate downward departures would amount to an act of needless cruelty given the nature of the crimes committed and the personal circumstances of these defendants. Reasoned application of both sets of philosophical considerations—just desert and utilitarian—lead to amelioration.

1. Not a Heartland Case

This case is outside of the heartland of racketeering and money laundering conspiracy cases contemplated by the Guidelines. Under such circumstances the law requires the exercise of a large degree of discretion as bridled and channeled by the sentencing statutes and Guidelines.

Unlike those in most prosecutions in drug money laundering cases, the acts of these defendants were not ones of pure personal greed or avarice. While their manner of living did greatly improve with the receipt of their drug-tainted income, their state of mind was one that was much more complicated—driven largely by excessive artistic pride. So obsessed were defendants with creating art that they lost sight of reality. Abandoned was their previously unblemished law abiding life. In exchange for professional glory and economic freedom to create, they chose to live by the credo of the Cali drug cartel. Cf. Irving Stone, The Agony and the Ecstasy (New American Library, 1996) (Medici family's support [of] Michelangelo). Unfortunately for these defendants, in our world Mephistophelean deals are circumscribed by the law.

The unique motivations behind their crimes do make defendants' acts somewhat different from those in the mainstream of criminality. While still morally culpable, the state of mind of these defendants must be taken into account when considering the various rationales behind criminal penalties. Because this and other factors "distinguishes the case from the 'heartland' cases covered by the guidelines in a way that is important to the statutory purposes of sentencing," departure is encouraged. U.S.S.G. § 5K2.0.

2. Vulnerability of Blarek and Pellecchia

The defendants are homosexual lovers in a case that has been broadly publicized. The sexual proclivity of these men will likely be well known to fellow inmates and others in the correctional facilities. Their status will, no doubt, increase their vulnerability in prison.

The Guidelines purport to prohibit sex from being taken into account in the determination of a sentence. See U.S.S.G. § 5H1.10. No mention is made of sexual orientation. See id. Sexual orientation as a basis for departure has been questioned on constitutional grounds. See United States v. Lara, 905 F.2d 599, 603 (2d Cir. 1990) ("That the district court did not base its sentence upon the defendant's bisexual orientation is of some significance because to have done so might have raised serious constitutional concerns."); see also United States v. Wilke, 995 F. Supp. 828 (N.D. Ill. 1998) (collecting cases indicating "one's status as a member of a particular group ... cannot alone provide sufficient reason for departure from the otherwise applicable guideline range").

While sexual orientation may not be an appropriate ground for departure, related ancillary issues presented in some such cases support a reduction in sentence. The reality is that homosexual defendants may need to be removed from the general prison population for their own safety. This would amount to a sentence of almost solitary confinement, a penalty more difficult to endure than any ordinary incarceration. See, e.g., United States v. Lara, 905 F.2d at 603 ("severity of [defendant's] prison term is exacerbated by his placement in solitary confinement as the only means of segregating him from other inmates").

There is ample authority for the proposition that the likelihood of a defendant being abused while in prison supports a downward departure. See Koon v. United States, 518 U.S. at 111–12 (departure based upon "susceptibility to abuse in prison"); United States v. Gonzalez, 945 F.2d 525, 527 (2d Cir. 1991) (departure based upon defendant's small frame and feminine looks resulting in extreme vulnerability in prison). Because these defendants will be especially vulnerable to abuse in prison given their sexual orientation as well as their demeanor and build, downward departure is warranted.

3. Pellecchia's Medical Condition

Defendant Pellecchia is HIV positive and has been for fifteen years. While he currently appears to be in stable condition and has not developed discernable AIDS related symptoms, there is no question that this defendant suffers from a serious medical condition. See Reid J. Schar, Comment, Downward Sentencing Departures for HIV-Infected Defendants: An Analysis of Current Law and a Framework for the Future, 91 Nw. U. L. Rev. 1147, 1154 (1997) ("although the [HIV-positive] individual may feel fine, the infected patient is capable of spreading the disease and the patient's immune system is deteriorating"). This defendant has an extraordinary and unpredictable impairment. See, U.S.S.G. § 5H1.4 ("extraordinary physical impairment may be a reason to impose a sentence below the applicable guidelines range").

Defendant represents that much of his relative well-being is attributable to a special regimen to which he has adhered. He has maintained a strict diet, exercised regularly, received acupuncture frequently, and taken a combination of vitamins and other natural supplements under the close supervision of a medical professional. Following a similar holistic plan within a correctional facility will likely be impossible. Federal prisons do provide appropriate medical care to those who are infected by HIV. Nevertheless, there will be no substitute for his present living arrangements.

While the government may be correct that it cannot be proven that defendant's unique treatment has contributed to his stable condition, defendant believes that it has. Since cruelty and its perception is as much a state of mind as a physical reality, he will suffer at least emotionally from the deprivation of his choice of treatment.

The extent to which inmates are exposed to diseases such as tuberculosis in prison is well documented. See Schar, supra, at 1156–57 ("The incidence of TB in prisons has recently been on the rise, and not surprisingly, those who tend to suffer most are HIV-infected prisoners."). Despite federal authorities' concern for prisoners' welfare, incarceration is likely to be detrimental to this defendant's health, resulting in a lessening of his present life expectancy. On this ground a reduction in defendant Pellecchia's sentence is required. . . .

D. Individual Sentences

The final task is weighing the sentencing considerations already delineated, with particular emphasis on general deterrence and imposition of a punishment that can be viewed as deserved in light of the seriousness and danger to society of the crimes. While defendants have [surrendered] most of their property to the government via forfeiture, and do deserve a downward departure from the Guidelines, a stiff fine to eliminate all assets as well as a substantial period of incarceration is required.

1. Blarek

Blarek, whose actions indicate a somewhat greater culpability than do Pellecchia's, begins with a computed offense level of 32. For reasons already indicated, the sentence imposed should reflect a downward departure of six levels to offense level 26. Blarek is sentenced towards the lower end of the Guidelines' range for level 26 to a concurrent term of 68 months' incarceration for his conviction on the three counts. A lesser or greater departure would not be appropriate in view of the facts and law.

In addition, Blarek is fined a total of $305,186, which represents his approximate total net worth after his forfeiture of over $2,000,000 in cash and property to the government, and his payment of attorney's fees. See 18 U.S.C. §§ 1956(a)(1), 1963(a), and U.S.S.G. 5E1.2(c)(4).

The maximum period of supervised release, three years, is imposed. U.S.S.G. §§ 5D1.1(a), 5D1.2 (a)(2). During the time that defendant is under supervision, he may not work for any clients or employers outside of the United States to ensure that he is not tempted again into money laundering. A mandatory special assessment of $150 is also imposed. 18 U.S.C. 3013(a)(2)(A) and U.S.S. G. § 5E1.3.

2. Pellecchia

Pellecchia's total offense level is computed at 30. The sentence should reflect a downward departure of seven levels to offense level 23. This represents the same six-level departure granted for defendant Blarek with an addition level of downward departure based upon defendant's health as well as his lesser culpability. A concurrent term of incarceration of 48 months, at the lower end of offense level 23, is imposed for his conviction on two counts. A lesser or greater departure would not be sufficient on the facts or the law.

No fine has been imposed for Pellecchia since he will have a negative net worth of over $100,000 after payment of attorney's fees.

Three years of supervised release is ordered. U.S.S.G. §§ 5D1.1(a), 5D1.2(a)(2). Like his co-defendant, Pellecchia may not be employed by anyone outside of this country during his period of supervision to minimize chances of his being tempted again into money laundering. A special assessment of $100 is also imposed. 18 U.S.C. § 3013(a)(2)(A) and U.S.S.G. § 5E1.3.

German Federal Constitutional Court (*Bundesverfassungsgericht*)
BVerfGE 45, 187 (June 21, 1977)
Life Imprisonment Case

[The defendant, a police officer, had been convicted of murder and received a mandatory sentence of life imprisonment. In addressing a constitutional challenge to his mandatory sentence of life imprisonment, the court also commented on various justifications for criminal punishment.*]

The Federal Constitutional Court has repeatedly concerned itself with the meaning and purpose of state punishment without taking a position in principle on the theories of punishment, which have been propounded in the literature. Even in the present case there is no ground for giving consideration to the various punishment theories, because it cannot be the task of the Federal Constitutional Court to decide for constitutional reasons the theoretical dispute in criminal law jurisprudence. Nor has the legislature wanted to take a conclusive position in the criminal law reform statutes since 1969 on the purposes of punishment, and has contented itself with an open regime within limits which would not obstruct the further development of any of the jurisprudentially recognized theories (see BTDrucks. V/4094, p. 4 f.; Dreher, Criminal Code, 36th edit 1976, notes 3 and 4 on § 46 Criminal Code; Lackner, § 13 Criminal Code—eine Fehlleistung des Gesetzgebers?, in: Festschrift for Wilhelm Gallas, Berlin-New York 1973, pp. 117, 121, 136). The current criminal law and the case law of the German courts follows to a large extent the so-called unification theory, which—admittedly with various set main focuses—attempts to bring all the purposes of punishment into a balanced relationship to each other. This is in keeping with the framework of freedom of formulation under the constitutional separation of powers: it falls within the purview of the legislature, not the judiciary, to recognize individual purposes of punishment, to balance them against each other, and to coordinate them with each other. Consequently the Federal Constitutional Court has in its case law not only emphasized the culpability principle [*Schuldgrundsatz*], but also recognized the other purposes of punishment. It has described the general task of criminal law as being the protection the fundamental values of communal life. Attribution of guilt, prevention, resocialization of the perpetrator, expiation and retribution for wrong committed are described as aspects of an appropriate criminal sanction (see BVerfGE 32, 98 [109]; 28, 264 [278]).

Franz Streng, "Sentencing in Germany: Basic Questions and New Developments," 8 *German Law Journal* (2007), 153

German law is codified law. This means that not only the individual crimes are laid down in the German Criminal Code, but also the general principles concerning sentencing are contained therein. The constitutional basis of the sentencing structure can be drawn from the notion of the Rechtsstaat, which can be translated with the term "rule of law." This principle, which is laid down in Article 20 § 1 Grundgesetz (German Constitution—Basic Law), encompasses the culpability principle, under which the punishment must be proportionate to the individual guilt of the offender. Thus, section 46 § l of the Criminal Code (Strafgesetzbuch—Criminal Code) reads: "the guilt of the perpetrator is the foundation for determining punishment." The culpability principle is a specific expression of the proportionality principle, which is also a constitutional requirement of the "rule of law."

In sec. 46 § l S. 2 of the Criminal Code the law clarifies that the likely effect of the punishment on the perpetrator's future social life shall be considered. One of the principal aims of sentencing is therefore the rehabilitation of the offender. Apart from these two notions, the culpability principle and rehabilitation, the law stresses the importance of other, positive aims of sentencing, such as the preservation of the legal order or the confirmation of the norm (Verteidigung der Rechtsordnung).

However, the courts and legal scholars also draw upon other sentencing aims and objectives found in German criminal law theory: these include individual deterrence and incapacitation, and the deterrent effect a sentence might have on the general public.

In evaluating the role of the judge in sentencing one must take into account that German criminal law is in a specific sense democratic in principle. What I mean here is that German criminal law is a law for citizens. These citizens are not only addressees of the criminal law but also its carriers. And this is not to be understood in a purely formal democratic sense. Rather, the judge himself acts as a citizen when determining the punishment, who reflects society's values when assessing the

---

* [For a more detailed statement of the facts, see Chapter 1.B.i.]

appropriate punishment, whilst keeping within the statutory boundaries. In contrast to a technocratic or an authoritarian criminal law system the judge in our law system relies on values which are coined by his social and professional personality. Under this perception of his role the German judge thus demands for a wide sentencing range, from which he is free to choose a just and fair sanction in accordance to his persuasion. Mandatory sentencing guidelines would contradict this self-conception of the judges. The restrictive and problematic use of the only mandatory life sentence for murder under sec. 211 of the Criminal Code and for genocide under sec. 6 of the International Criminal Law Code also points to the necessity to open up a leeway for the judges in determining the punishment.

The seemingly harmless discourse of adapting the sanction to fit the individual case carries with it some substantial questions. Two important factors must be addressed. Firstly, it is difficult to find adequate parameters for comparing the individual case and the punishment. Without such a measure one cannot properly talk about a sanction which is proportionate to the crime committed. Second, it is questionable whether the general aims and objectives of criminal law besides retribution are relevant to the admeasuring of the sanction at all. I shall discuss these questions with regard to the so-called Spielraum-theory, Spielraum meaning "margin" or "leeway," which is the prevailing theory of sentencing in German jurisprudence and criminal law theory.

The Spielraum-theory, which is sometimes called Schuldrahmen-theory, that means framework of guilt-theory, is based on the proposition that the judge establishes a specific framework for the individual guilt derived from the general statutory provisions. Within this margin the judge then takes account of utilitarian, or as Germans prefer to say preventive aims, avoiding both overstepping and undershooting the guilt of the accused. One can call this method: "prevention within the limits of repression," i.e. the individual guilt of the accused sets the limits to the objective of prevention. The term "guilt" in this context signifies a certain Strafzumessungsschuld, a specific "sentencing-guilt," quantifying the guilt of the offender and at the same time encompassing to a certain extent characteristics both preceding and following the criminal act.

Cornelius Nestler, "Sentencing in Germany," 7 *Buffalo Criminal Law Review* (2003), 109

Statutory penalty ranges tend to be fairly broad, thus allowing significant room for judicial sentencing discretion. This can be demonstrated with a few examples from the German Criminal Code:

223. Bodily Injury

(1) Whoever physically maltreats or harms the health of another person, shall be punished with imprisonment for not more than five years or a fine.

Section 223 is exemplary for many provisions that give a range of punishment up to a maximum penalty of (most often) three or five years while also allowing for a fine. Whether the sanction will be imprisonment or a fine is then structured by general provisions on sentencing: According to section thirty-eight, the minimum fixed term of imprisonment is one month, and according to section forty-seven an imprisonment of less than six months shall only be imposed in extraordinary cases. Fines are imposed in daily rates with the maximum of 360 days, the amount of each daily rate depending on the income of the convicted person.

224. Dangerous Bodily Injury

(1) Whoever commits bodily harm:
    1. through the administration of poison or other substances dangerous to health;
    2. by means of a weapon or other dangerous tool;
    3. by means of a sneak attack;
    4. jointly with another participant; or
    5. by means of a treatment dangerous to life,
    shall be punished with imprisonment from six months to ten years, in less serious cases with imprisonment from three months to five years.

Section 224 is an example for a provision regarding a more serious offense, setting a range between a minimum and a maximum punishment.

212. Intentional Manslaughter

(1) Whoever kills a human being without being a murderer, shall be punished for manslaughter with imprisonment for not less than five years.

Intentional Manslaughter is an example of a provision with a high minimum fixed term of imprisonment, and according to section thirty-eight the maximum fixed term of imprisonment is generally fifteen years. The more serious offenses of the Criminal Code usually have a minimum term of imprisonment of one year (which does not allow for sentencing with a fine) or two years (which does not allow for suspended execution of the punishment) or even five years as in the case of Intentional Manslaughter . . .

German sentencing over the past thirty years can be summarized by describing two dominant tendencies: First, the number of long-term prison sentences has increased, primarily because of an increased number of drug convictions. Second, the total number of prison sentences has decreased due to more case dismissals by the prosecution, a shift from prison sentences to fines, and an increase in the numbers of suspensions of prison sentences. As a result, the numbers of adults in prison were the same for 1968 and 1996, although the numbers of registered and investigated crime nearly doubled between those years.

All these trends probably have very little to do with the theory of sentencing. Not only based on academic work but also from my practical experience as a defense counselor, I fully agree with Thomas Weigend's statement that the theory of sentencing is complicated, conceptually murky, and of very little practical relevance.[33]

Although rehabilitation does and should somewhat influence the sentence according to section 46 subsection 1, the basic guideline for sentencing, it is uncontested that the seriousness of the offense and the offender's blameworthiness are the most important considerations in sentencing. The predominant theory conceives that, starting with the range given by the offense's sentencing provision (in a serious drug case that would be for instance two to fifteen years), the offender's desert should define the sanction by setting a fairly broad range within the statutory range (using the same example, this could be a range between six and nine years); any sentence within this new narrowed range would then be in accordance with the principle of proportionality between guilt and punishment. The specific length of the sentence is then determined with the help of preventive considerations.

All this is rhetoric and has little to do with the practice of sentencing for a variety of reasons:

First, in its verdict the court must not indicate which narrowed range it has chosen for the determination of the sentence. Therefore the theoretically proscribed method of finding the right punishment is a virtual one; the court's translation of sentencing considerations into concrete levels of punishment are not subject to any procedural control (although the reasoning of the sentencing in the court's verdict will indicate which factors the court regards as mitigating or aggravating, it is entirely in the discretion of the court whether, for instance, an attempted homicide or the import of one kilogram of cocaine will be punished with six or with nine years of imprisonment). A second procedural reason for the disparity between the practice and the theory of sentencing is that issues of guilt and issues of sentencing are decided in a comprehensive case—there is no separate sentencing stage comparable to the one in the U.S. procedure. Therefore, in their sentencing, courts often have very little information outside of the facts of the case.

Empirical research has shown that the sentence is usually based on four factors: The circumstances of the offense, the damage caused, the defendant's prior convictions, and the defendant's behavior in court. In recent years, the bargaining position of the defendant has become probably the most important factor in the determination of the sentence in more serious cases.

The motives by which sentencing is driven in Germany are primarily retribution, deterrence, a little bit of rehabilitation, and a lot of pragmatism. Even though retribution and deterrence are dominant factors in sentencing, they do not necessarily translate into prison sentences. The concept that offenders deserve punishment but nevertheless should not go to prison appears to be of high importance in German sentencing. Only once imprisonment has been deemed to be necessary are the concepts of retribution, deterrence, and incapacitation used to support relatively harsh sentences.

Markus D. Dubber, "Theories of Crime and Punishment in German Criminal Law," 53 *American Journal of Comparative Law* (2006), 679

In the Anglo-American literature, the debate about the rationale, or rationales, of punishment largely remains within the familiar framework of consequentialist and deontological theories of punishment. Ordinarily, lists of the rationales of punishment include the following four: deterrence (general and special), incapacitation, rehabilitation (or reformation), and retribution (or just deserts), with the first three classified as consequentialist and the fourth as deontological. The "consequences" that the first seek to achieve might differ from account to account, but the prevention of crime, or reduction of the crime rate, is certain to be among them.

---

[33] Thomas Weigend, Sentencing and Punishment in Germany, in Sentencing and Sanctions in Western Countries 188, 203 (Michael Tonry & Richard S. Frase eds., 2001).

After roughly two centuries of hostilities between the consequentialist and deontological camps, general exhaustion has set in. By and large, punishment theorists—and legislatures as well as sentencing commissions—have settled on some "mixed theory" or other, generously combining elements of what once were thought to be deeply irreconcilable views.

The analytic work of the English legal philosopher H. L. A. Hart proved to be particularly helpful in this regard. By differentiating between the different questions that a theory of punishment should answer, Hart made different answers to these questions possible. So one might be a consequentialist with respect to the justification of the institution of punishment in general, while choosing retributivism when it comes to justifying the infliction of punishment in a particular case. More specifically, we might think that we need punishment to deter people from committing crimes, but at the same time that we should not punish people unless they in fact deserve it.

Given the widely acknowledged staleness of debates about the rationales for punishment in Anglo-American law, one might be tempted to turn to the German literature on the subject. And indeed, it turns out that German criminal law theory has made a conscious effort to break out of the consequentialist-deontological rut. Whether the effort succeeds in the end remains to be seen.

German criminal law, too, once witnessed intense battles pitting consequentialists against deontologists, those who proposed punishment ne peccetur against those who preferred punishing quia peccatum est. The fiercest, and most prolonged, period of this dispute even had its own name, the "Clash of the Schools" (Schulenstreit), whose main protagonists were Franz v. Liszt, the founder of German criminology, for the "progressive school," and Karl Binding, the originator of "norm theory" in German criminal law, for the "classical school."

To characterize the dispute between Liszt and Binding (and their associates and successors) as one between consequentialism and retributivism, however, could be misleading. It is important to keep in mind that both Liszt and Binding were thoroughgoing legal positivists. Binding argued that punishment was justified, and only justified, as the state's response to a violation of a state norm. The essence of crime thus was the violation of a norm of positive law, rather than the commission of a wrongful act. The criminal law was not so much a demand of justice, or as Kant would have it, a "categorical imperative," as a state tool for the enforcement of state authority that the state may or may not choose to employ.

The "right to punishment," to Binding, was "nothing but the right to obedience of the law, which has been transformed by the offender's disobedience." The purpose of punishment thus was "the inmate's subjugation under the power of law for the sake of maintaining the authority of the laws violated." As such, punishment was to "represent the holiness and inviolability of the duties to which it is attached."

Liszt, by contrast, accused Binding and his fellow classicists of advocating pointless punishment. (That's not quite fair, as we just saw, since Binding thought punishment served the purpose of maintaining state authority.) Liszt insisted that punishment, to be legitimate in a modern enlightened state, had to serve some purpose. Punishment could never be an end in itself. More specifically, Liszt argued that punishment must (and does) seek to protect legal goods (Rechtsgüter) against criminal violation. These legal goods, in Liszt's view, included, broadly speaking, "the life conditions" of a given community so that crimes were all "those acts that this people at this time perceives as disturbances of its life conditions." Punishment served its purpose through rehabilitation (education), deterrence, or incapacitation, depending on the type of offender. The recidivist, for instance, would, upon his third conviction of an offense motivated by "the strongest and most basic human drives" (including theft, robbery, arson, and rape, but also damaging property), be sentenced to an indeterminate prison term, to be served in a state of "penal servitude," with the use of corporal punishment to enforce prison discipline. Truly incorrigible offenders were to be imprisoned for life, because "we do not wish to behead or hang and cannot deport" them—why that would be so Liszt did not explain.

In keeping with their broadly treatmentist approach, Liszt and his fellow progressives called for more or less radical legislative reforms. The cumbersome, and legalistic, construct of criminal law doctrine was to be replaced by a more flexible, modern, scientific ("progressive") system for the proper diagnosis, and classification, of offenders, which was crucial for the prescription of the correction quality and quantity of peno-correctional treatment. Ironically, these reform proposals did not come to fruition until after the National Socialists took power in 1933. One of the Nazis' first criminal law reforms was the Law Against Dangerous Recidivists and Regarding Measures of Protection and Rehabilitation of November 1933, which established the "two-track" sanctioning system that remains in place today. Since then, two general types of sanction have been available: punishments and measures. Only punishments "properly speaking" are subject to constraints of proportionality between culpability and sanction. "Measures" instead are unrelated to culpability and are determined exclusively by the offender's peno-correctional diagnosis. So if she requires rehabilitative treatment, she might be sent to a drug rehabilitation clinic; if she requires incapacitative treatment, she might be incarcerated indefinitely. Freed of the constraints of proportionality between offense and sanction, "measures" are served independently—and where appropriate consecutively—to whatever "punishments" are imposed.

At the same time, the retention of the distinction between punishments and measures indicates that the victory of the progressive treatmentists was not complete. While "progressive" considerations governed the realm of "measures," that of "punishments" remained subject to "classical" quia peccatum considerations. In the end, then, a statutory compromise was reached. Strafrecht (literally, the law of punishment) remained, but was now only one component of the comprehensive vision of Kriminalrecht (literally, criminal law), which encompassed both punishment and treatment.

The German theory of punishment thus combined once incommensurable deontological and consequentialist elements, much like Anglo-American punishment theory. Unlike Anglo-American punishment theory, however, which has been content to resolve the tension between deontology and consequentialism, and between utilitarianism and retributivism, by combining these ingredients in "mixed" theories, German punishment theory eventually produced an altogether new theory of punishment that aims to reconcile the differences between what the Germans call "relative" and "absolute" theories of punishment.

This is the theory of "positive general prevention" (positive Generalprävention, or PGP for short), which today is the dominant theory of punishment in German criminal law. There are many varieties of positive general prevention, so many in fact that discussions of the theory as a matter of course caution that it may well be misleading to speak of the theory, rather than theories, of positive general prevention. Still, the basic features of positive general prevention can be discerned easily enough. It is "general" to distinguish itself from special prevention, which uses punishment to prevent crime by the particular offender subject to punishment, rather than by others. It is also "positive" because it seeks to prevent crime not by scaring potential lawbreakers into compliance, but by bolstering the law-abidingness of the rest of the population. Finally, and relatedly, it is about "prevention" generally speaking, rather than "deterrence" as a particular means of prevention. There could be no such thing as positive deterrence, after all.

It is pretty clear, therefore, what positive general prevention is not. One might think of it, in fact, as being constructed specifically to take advantage of the consensus that special deterrence is an entirely inappropriate attempt to legitimate punishment. Positive general prevention clearly is not negative special prevention (or special deterrence for short). That theory, after all, is generally thought to have been thoroughly, and permanently, laid to rest by the father of modern German criminal law, P. J. A. Feuerbach, at the turn of the 19th century.

But positive general prevention is also not positive special prevention, or rehabilitation. It is no accident that positive general prevention arose out of another, much later and somewhat narrower, consensus in German criminal legal science, namely that—to quote the familiar American phrase— "nothing works." While American criminal law, in particular, responded to the perceived failure of rehabilitative measures by (re)turning to retributivism, or "just deserts" as it was now called, the German response shifted emphasis among the objects of prevention, rather than leaving the realm of consequentialist punishment altogether. If positive special prevention did not work, then perhaps positive general prevention might. If punishment cannot rehabilitate offenders, perhaps it could stiffen the resolve of non-offenders not to become (unrehabilitatable) offenders.

More generally, it was hoped that positive general prevention would steer clear of the normative and empirical problems that had plagued consequentialist theories of punishment, without endorsing a retributive theory of punishment for its own sake, which was dismissed as literally pointless, and hence barbaric.

The normative problems with deterrence theory have been familiar at least since Kant. The categorical imperative, after all, instructs us never to treat a person merely as a means to an end. And what is punishing one person to deter another from committing a crime, if not treating him as a means to the end of crime control? Invoking Kant in support of positive general prevention, however, is not without irony. Kant, after all, was an arch retributivist, and therefore was very much passé. Moreover, Kant's objection was not limited to deterrence, special or general, but applied to any consequentialist theory of punishment. For what is punishing one person to prevent another from committing a crime—no matter how—if not treating him as a means to the end of crime prevention?

But there was another normative problem with deterrence theories in particular, which a preventive theory, and more specifically a positive one, might avoid. This objection was formulated by another famous German retributivist, Hegel, who argued that prevention through deterrence was illegitimate because it disrespected the dignity of the deterred. For what, Hegel asked, is punishing for deterrence's sake if not treating the intended audience of this spectacle as animals, dogs to be precise, which (not who) are to be scared, and (in the case of special deterrence) beaten, into submission?

Positive general prevention did not threaten dogs with raised sticks, but instead addressed human beings capable of making choices, including the choice to follow or to break the law. It sought to deter no one, neither the person punished nor anyone else. It merely aimed to reinforce the "general legal consciousness" of the community at large, perhaps including, but certainly not limited to, the specific offender.

But positive general prevention was to be more than the kinder, gentler version of general deterrence, thus solving, or at least circumventing, the normative problems that had dogged general deterrence for centuries. It was to solve consequentialist theory's empirical problems as well. For not only special prevention, or rehabilitation, had run into empirical difficulties, captured dramatically in the "nothing works" slogan. General deterrence, too, had never quite managed to bolster its scientific claims with hard empirical evidence. There certainly was a strong common sense notion that punishment would have a deterrent effect, but not much else. But common sense hardly seemed enough for a theory of punishment whose central claim was that punishment without a point (or for its own sake) was patently illegitimate. Unlike retributivism, consequentialism was not to rest a state institution as intrusive and violent as punishment on some metaphysics of crime and punishment, or on some abstract principle of justice (such as the categorical imperative). Instead, what was needed was hard evidence of results. Without that evidence, consequentialism was no better than retributivism. To persist in punishing in the absence of evidence of punishment's beneficial effects would be barbaric indeed.

Deterrence theory's most embarrassing empirical problem is that the mere fact of crime appears to disprove it. After all, if the point of punishment is deterrence then it becomes difficult, at least after a while, to ignore the fact that crime persists, and even increases, despite continued punishment. Positive general prevention, however, is thought to blunt the force of this empirical objection, largely by virtue of its very positiveness, so to speak. Who knows, after all, what positive effects the threat and infliction of punishment might have on the law-abidingness of the law-abiding? The mere existence of considerable numbers of undeterrable offenders does not imply the absence of scores of people who never even consider a life of crime because they see their trust in the authority of law reaffirmed, all contrary appearances in the form of continued lawbreaking notwithstanding. Clearly, not everyone is committing crimes all the time. Why should that not be the result of positive general prevention through punishment? Surely, punishment can claim to have made some contribution here.

This speculation, however, if it can be said to prove anything, proves not only the empirical soundness of positive general prevention, but of any method of preventive punishment, including through deterrence. And so one can find arguments that positive general prevention is attractive precisely because of the very absence of empirical evidence for its effectiveness—or more precisely, the impossibility of ever producing empirical evidence. For all intents and purposes, it is said, positive general prevention is empirically immune; it is "hardly falsifiable."

Nonfalsifiability might appear as an odd benefit of a punishment theory that is designed to combat the nonfalsifiable nature of retributivist metaphysics. In fact, at some point it becomes difficult to tell the difference between positive general prevention and retributivism. For many retributivists too were concerned with using punishment to manifest the authority of the state, or at least the force of criminal (or social, or moral, or legal) norms (see Binding above). Unlike most supporters of positive general prevention today, they did not claim that asserting the authority of law required any end beyond itself, but if achieving that end becomes so irrelevant as to not require verification (or even verifiability), then one might suspect that positive general prevention adds little to retributivism.

The line between retributivism and consequentialism becomes particularly blurry in a recent, and quite influential, variety of positive general prevention. Echoing Hegel's theory of punishment as the negation of the negation (of crime), Günther Jakobs regards the function of criminal law as "contradicting the contradiction of norms defining the identity of society." "Punishment," in Jakobs's conception, "is not only a means for the maintenance of societal identity, but already is this maintenance itself." As such, the efficacy of punishment is beyond empirical falsifiability; maintaining societal identity is what punishment means. That's not to say, of course, that retributivism, or any other theory of punishment that does not turn on empirical falsifiability, should for that reason be dismissed, only that nonfalsifiable varieties of positive general prevention cannot dismiss it for that reason.

The less emphasis is placed on the effects, the more weight is shifted onto the meaning of punishment. And the more positive general prevention insists that punishment is about meaning something, as opposed to accomplishing something (like prevention, say), the less it appears as a justification of punishment, as opposed to an analysis of it. At some point, positive general prevention becomes not a theory of punishment, but a function of punishment. Perhaps it is true that punishment "demonstrates to the community of law the inviolability of the legal order and thereby strengthens the population's loyalty to the law." But does this demonstration and strengthening justify punishment?

Here positive general prevention faces the same difficulties as the so-called expressive theory of punishment. The expressive theory of punishment, in fact, never claimed to justify punishment at all. The expression of the communal condemnation was not a purpose, or rationale, of punishment, but, as the title of the article popularizing it makes plain, a (not even the) "function of punishment." As an expressive analysis of the function of punishment, positive general prevention fits into a long tradition of sociological accounts, reaching at least as far back as Durkheim, who regarded state punishment as a medium for the satisfaction of society's collective feelings of revenge and, for that reason, as playing a crucial role in the maintenance of communal identity in modern societies devoid of substantive commonalities.

NOTES

1. Both the U.S. District Court and the German Federal Constitutional Court are reluctant to express a clear preference for one justification of punishment over another. Are they too reluctant or is a mix-and-match approach convincing? Does the notion of "oscillating" between the poles of just deserts and preventive thinking as expressed by the U.S. District Court make sense? Are the alternative approaches compatible?

2. Kant's and Hegel's objections to consequentialist uses of punishment are cited frequently, at least in the German literature. Are they well-founded? Or are they dogmatic remnants of a time before crime and punishment came to be seen in the context of a general project of social ordering through law and other means? Can they be accommodated simply by assigning "retributivism" a limiting function (to prevent punishing the innocent, however great the deterrent effect, for instance), rather than a (or even *the*) justificatory function?

3. The U.S. District Court speaks of retribution with a fairly critical undertone, as "considered by some to be a barbaric concept, appealing to a primal sense of vengeance." Could one describe the criminal justice system's function in relation to a "primal sense of vengeance" in a positive light? For instance, might humankind consider it an achievement to have moderated, mediated and formalized the need for revenge that victims and their communities may feel after a crime? Nevertheless, within the moderation and barriers erected by state criminal law, the primary driving force behind all criminal justice systems still might be victims' need to have the wrong done to them condemned. Was James Fitzjames Stephen right that "criminal law is in the nature of a persecution of the grosser forms of vice, and an emphatic assertion of the principle that the feeling of hatred and the desire of vengeance . . . are important elements of human nature which ought in such cases to be satisfied in a regular public and legal manner"?*

4. From a European perspective, but not only from that perspective, the severity of the approach taken by the U.S. Sentencing Guidelines to the offenses in *United States v. Blarek* is startling. The German legislature took a different stance: for ordinary cases of money laundering, the penalty range in § 261 para. 1 Criminal Code (*Strafgesetzbuch*, StGB) is three months to five years. In severe cases, where the offender drew a continuous income from money laundering (§ 261 para. 4 StGB), the prescribed range is six months to ten years. German courts tend to choose from the lower ends of sentence ranges.[†] It is very rare that defendants are sentenced to more than two years' (twenty-four months') imprisonment, especially if they have no prior record. Compare this to the U.S. Guidelines range applicable in *Blarek*: 135–168 months.[‡]

The U.S. District Court relied on the defendants' lives and personal circumstances (their motive of "creating art," their homosexuality, Pellecchia's HIV infection) to mitigate their sentences, which the judge obviously considered too high. For the Court, there was no alternative to this line of argument because the Guidelines were mandatory.[§] But consider

---

* James Fitzjames Stephen, *Liberty, Equality, Fraternity* (1873), 149.
† For more on money laundering, see Chapter 17.C.
‡ On the severity discrepancy between U.S. and German criminal sentences, see Chapter 1.A.iii and B.
§ This is no longer the case, see Note 5.

the Guidelines from a broader perspective. While the Guidelines explicitly demand that the sentence reflect the seriousness of the offense, are the relevant sentence ranges themselves based on this principle? Blarek and Pellecchia did not kill, mutilate or rape fellow human beings. Nor were they involved in drug sales, for instance, or inducing minors to become addicted to drugs. Of course, saying that their personal contribution to a dangerous market is remote does not mean that it is not blameworthy. Those who transfer funds and launder money share responsibility for the continuing existence of drug markets and, therefore, also for the harm done as a result of drug addiction. But in grading the seriousness of the offense, one cannot simply equate money laundering with the sale of drugs. The agent's responsibility is more diluted in the former case. Does a sentence range that starts with more than eleven years' imprisonment still seem proportionate, even in so-called "heartland cases" (in standard cases of money laundering)? In other words, do you agree that "the imposition of a penalty in [Blarek] captures, to some rational degree, the 'worth' of defendants' volitional criminal acts"? Or is it, in the end, about general deterrence only? About sending a message? What message? And to whom? Is the judge signaling that "'white collar' 'victimless' offenses'" are serious, too, "particularly since drugs are involved"?

5. Since *Blarek*, the U.S. Supreme Court has downgraded the Sentencing Guidelines from mandatory to advisory, not because they resulted in disproportionate sentences, but because they violated the right to a jury trial under the Seventh Amendment to the U.S. Constitution. In *United States v. Booker*, 543 U.S. 220, 125 S. Ct. 738 (2005), the Court held that the Guidelines permitted—indeed required—courts to make an end-run around the constitutional jury trial guarantee by calculating sentences on the basis of facts established at the (judicial) sentencing hearing under a standard of "preponderance of the evidence," rather than the "beyond a reasonable doubt" standard required at the guilt phase of the (jury) trial. In *Booker* itself, for instance, the sentence authorized by the jury verdict was 210 to 262 months in prison; that sentencing range increased to 360 months to life on the basis of facts established at the sentencing hearing following the guilty verdict, resulting in a thirty-year sentence, rather than the maximum sentence of twenty-one years, ten months that the judge could have imposed based on the facts found by the jury beyond a reasonable doubt at trial.[*]

6. Judges (and commentators) complained about the U.S. Sentencing Guidelines early and often.[†] Judge Weinstein, the district court judge in *Blarek* (and former Columbia Law School professor), was one of the Guidelines' earliest and most vociferous critics. His opinions in sentencing cases include extended scholarly and systematic assaults on the entire guidelines scheme as well as more subtle internal critiques, as illustrated by *Blarek*, a masterpiece of judicial guidelines avoidance.[‡] How does Judge Weinstein try to produce a sentence that he considers just and appropriate without jettisoning the guidelines framework itself? Does he succeed? What about cases involving less sympathetic defendants, as, for instance, the beating of Rodney King by Los Angeles police officers, where the district judge also opted for a significant downward departure—again after a lengthy opinion—partly on a similar basis (vulnerability in prison)?[§]

---

[*] Note that this issue would not have arisen in German criminal law; there is no constitutional right to a jury trial, and lay participation in the criminal process has been limited to the participation of lay judges on panels alongside professional judges; there is no procedural separation between the guilt phase and the sentencing phase of a trial, with the court—whether a professional judge sitting alone, or a panel of professional and lay judges—deliberating on both guilt and, if appropriate, sentence, at the same time; and there is no distinction between the standard of proof on matters of liability and of sentence. On lay participation in German criminal cases in comparative perspective, see Markus D. Dubber, "American Plea Bargains, German Lay Judges, and the Crisis of Criminal Procedure," 49 *Stanford Law Review* (1997), 547; for a general overview of the German and U.S. criminal process, see Chapter 5.

[†] For an exhaustive overview, see Daniel J. Freed, "Federal Sentencing in the Wake of Guidelines: Unacceptable Limits on the Discretion of Sentencers," 101 *Yale Law Journal* (1992), 1681.

[‡] See generally Kate Stith, "Weinstein on Sentencing," 24 *Federal Sentencing Reporter* (2012), 217; Jeffrey B. Morris, *Leadership on the Federal Bench: The Craft and Activism of Jack Weinstein* (2011), ch. 8.

[§] See *United States v. Koon*, 833 F. Supp. 769 (C.D. Cal. 1993), aff'd in part & rev'd in part, 518 U.S. 81 (1996).

7. The establishment of the U.S. federal sentencing guidelines was motivated in large part by an effort to limit judicial discretion. Ironically, federal district judges—notably Marvin E. Frankel, the author of the influential *Criminal Sentences: Law Without Order* (1972) (like Weinstein, a former Columbia Law School professor)—were among the loudest critics of what they regarded as arbitrary, even lawless and discriminatory, sentencing practices that were either unpredictable, or predictable by irrelevant factors (namely what judge happened to be assigned to the case or, more generally, "luck"). Since guidelines, and especially mandatory guidelines, limit judicial discretion, should one take judicial outrage about sentencing guidelines with a grain of salt? Are guideline-driven sentences any more lawful, or less lawless, than judge-driven ones? Are they more, or less, just? Or does the push-and-pull between guidelines and discretion merely reflect the tension between different conceptions, or perhaps aspects, of justice—one concerned with individual justice, the other with equality?

8. A common criticism of the U.S. federal sentencing guidelines was that, rather than guiding (never mind eliminating) judicial sentencing discretion, they simply shifted discretion—and therefore power—to federal prosecutors, who now controlled the sentence, within a narrow range, by deciding which offenses to charge. Prosecutorial discretion in the U.S. system, however, is essentially unconstrained, leaving prosecutors a largely free hand to engage in plea bargaining, or in this case *charge* bargaining (and in some cases even *fact* bargaining, insofar as findings of fact at the sentencing hearing—in particular about the quantity of drugs possessed, or distributed—could have a dramatic impact on the sentencing guidelines range). The guidelines, by this account, had not only retained sentencing discretion, but removed it from the open courtroom into the prosecutor's office, or the courtroom hallway, and took it out of the hands of the judicial branch and placed it into those of the executive branch, from an objective arbiter to a partisan party occupying the dominant position in an essentially unregulated process.*

The German literature, and jurisprudence, on sentencing does not reflect a similarly wide and deep concern about the exercise of judicial discretion by state officials in the criminal process.† Judicial discretion is not regarded as troubling. Prosecutors are seen as having no influence on sentencing, even indirectly through charging decisions; at any rate, the problem of prosecutorial discretion is thought to have been addressed by the introduction of the so-called *Legalitätsprinzip*, or principle of compulsory prosecution (literally, but confusingly, "principle of legality"), which requires prosecutors to charge every offense supported by credible evidence. This principle was more recently joined by a counter principle, the opportunity principle (*Opportunitätsprinzip*), which permits prosecutors to drop a charge in cases of minor culpability in the public interest. (This counter principle does not apply to police, who are subject only to the principle of compulsory prosecution.)‡

What is the connection between discretion (by whom?) and the various justifications for punishment? And conceptions of the role of judges and prosecutors in the criminal process? And trust in state officials (or in some officials rather than in others)?

9. What, exactly, is wrong with the federal sentencing guidelines? Too harsh? Too rigid? Too mandatory? Too detailed? Too retributive? Too consequentialist? Too administrative (after all, they're drafted by a "commission")? What else? Is the very project of sentencing guidelines doomed? Or can one imagine crafting guidelines that avoid some, all, or any of the problems associated with the U.S. Sentencing Guidelines in particular? The Minnesota

---

* Note that federal judges and prosecutors, unlike many of their state colleagues, are appointed, not elected: federal judges are appointed by the U.S. President for life, upon Senate confirmation, as members of the federal judicial branch, 28 U.S.C. § 134(a) ("during good behavior"); U.S. Attorneys are appointed to four-year terms but, as members of the executive branch, "are subject to removal by the President," 28 U.S.C. § 541(c).

† See Tatjana Hörnle, "Moderate and Non-Arbitrary Sentencing Without Guidelines: The German Experience," 76 *Law and Contemporary Problems* (2013), 189.

‡ See German Code of Criminal Procedure (*Strafprozeßordnung*, StPO) § 153ff.

Sentencing Guidelines are often held up as an example of an acceptable—kinder, gentler—alternative to the federal guidelines.*

10. *A note on the Model Penal Code and treatmentism.* It is worth taking a closer look at the rationale of punishment that underlies the Model Penal Code, both because the Model Penal Code plays such a central role in the present book and because its rationale of punishment plays such a central role in the Code itself. The MPC was a child of its time, which means that it reflects a treatmentist approach to criminal law. The treatmentist influence on the Code is strong, and can help one make sense of the Code in many respects (both large and small), but it was also tempered somewhat by two facts: it was drafted by Herbert Wechsler, who at bottom always remained a lawyer (rather than a social scientist, or penologist), and it was designed as a model code, which meant that it had to appeal to legislators (many of whom were lawyers), lawyers, and judges (law professors were less important in this regard). Treatmentism, according to Wechsler's 1930s manifesto "A Rationale of the Law of Homicide,"[†] reconceptualized criminal punishment as peno-correctional treatment for abnormal dangerousness. Crime was a symptom of that dangerousness, rather than some evil act that required retribution. Punishment was taboo, and retributivism was atavistic and barbaric. (Do you see traces of this view in Judge Weinstein's opinion in *Blarek*?) The criminal code, to put it pointedly, amounted to a rough manual for the pre-diagnosis of dangerousness, to be confirmed and refined by penological experts during the course of the implementation of sanctions of indeterminate duration.[‡]

11. *Culpability principle, take one.* The German Federal Constitutional Court opinion and Streng's overview of German sentencing law both refer to a norm that will make frequent appearances throughout this book: the culpability principle (also sometimes referred to as the guilt principle), or *Schuldprinzip* (or *Schuldgrundsatz*). This is a fascinating and central concept in contemporary German criminal law, with enormous range and power: range because it covers much doctrinal ground, from the proportionality—if not the justification—of punishment (as in the present context), to the law of *mens rea* (i.e., subjective offense elements), and eventually to the law of excuse.

It is the culpability principle that requires that punishment be proportionate to the offense, and to the offender, in the sense that the punishment reflect the offender's culpability, or desert. In other words, the culpability principle represents the idea of so-called limiting retributivism, which insists that punishment, apart from any consequentialist functions it might serve, not exceed the offender's desert. Some even ascribe to the culpability principle a more ambitious function, of justifying—rather than merely limiting—punishment as the consequence ("just deserts") of an ascription of culpability.[§]

As we will see later on, it is also the culpability principle that requires proof of *mens rea*, accounting for the categorical rejection of strict (or absolute) liability in German criminal law.[¶] (Along the way, the culpability principle also has been invoked to support the similarly categorical rejection of corporate criminal liability,** on the ground that corporations are incapable of culpability.)

Finally, the culpability principle has been interpreted to require the recognition, and even the particular interpretation, of excuses. For instance, the culpability principle is taken to require a broad interpretation of the insanity defense to cover cases of extreme

---

* See Richard S. Frase, "Sentencing Guidelines in Minnesota, 1978–2003," 32 *Crime and Justice: A Review of Research* (2004), 139.

† Jerome Michael and Herbert Wechsler, "A Rationale of the Law of Homicide I," 37 *Columbia Law Review* (1937), 701; Jerome Michael and Herbert Wechsler, "A Rationale of the Law of Homicide II," 37 *Columbia Law Review* (1937), 1261.

‡ See generally Markus D. Dubber, *Criminal Law: Model Penal Code* (2002).

§ Contrast Claus Roxin, *Strafrecht: Allgemeiner Teil* (3rd edn. 1997), vol. 1, 59–60, with Hans-Heinrich Jescheck and Thomas Weigend, *Lehrbuch des Strafrechts: Allgemeiner Teil* (5th edn. 1996), 23–4.

¶ See Chapter 8.B.

** See Chapter 11.

intoxication as well as a broad reading of the mistake of law defense to cover (unavoidable) ignorance of law.*

The power of the culpability principle, however, is at least as impressive as its range. Already considered a fundamental principle of German criminal law science, it has not only been constitutionalized, but constitutionalized in the most dramatic form, by grounding it in the first and highest norm in German constitutional law: the inviolability of human dignity guaranteed in Article 1, section 1 of the Basic Law. For good measure, it has also been associated with the fundamental constitutional *Rechtsstaatsprinzip*, or rule-of-law principle.

The range and power of the culpability principle, however, is more easily identified than its substance, which—not surprisingly—depends on one's preferred notion of culpability (or guilt).† It is clear that the culpability principle is a *principle*, but what *culpability* does it protect? Consider this question any time you encounter a reference to the culpability principle in this book.

For now, here is a standard statement of the principle (cited in its Latinate version: *nulla poena sine culpa*), from elsewhere in the Federal Constitutional Court opinion excerpted below:‡

> The free human personality and its dignity represent the highest legal value within the constitutional order. The duty is imposed on state power in all forms of its manifestation to have regard to and to protect the dignity of the human being.
>
> This is based on the idea of the human being as a spiritual and moral being, intended for self-determination and self-development in freedom. . . . The maxim "a human being must always remain a goal in himself" applies without restriction for all areas of law, because the dignity of the human being as a person, which cannot be lost, consists in the fact that he continues to be recognized as a self-responsible personality.
>
> In the area of criminal justice in which the highest requirements are placed upon justice, art. 1 para. 1 Basic Law determines the conception of the nature of punishment and the relationship of guilt and expiation. The principle *nulla poena sine culpa* has the status of a constitutional principle. Every punishment must have a just relationship to the seriousness of the crime and to the guilt of the perpetrator.

ii. The victim's role

The victim's role in criminal law has received considerable attention in the United States and Germany, particularly during the last decades of the twentieth century. The victims' rights movement in the United States has proved very influential, particularly as an important plank in eventually ubiquitous tough-on-crime platforms. During the heyday of the so-called war on crime, the pursuit of victims' rights became largely indistinguishable from the attack on defendants' rights, in a backlash against the U.S. Supreme Court's concerted effort starting in the 1950s to revamp the criminal process, particularly, but not exclusively, in Southern states, through the enforcement of federal constitutional protections, which until then had been limited to federal criminal cases, which accounted for only a small fraction of criminal cases in the United States. Despite a wave of largely symbolic "victims' bills of rights" that swept the nation, however, the precise impact on legal doctrine and practice can be difficult to detect. Interestingly, the victims' rights movement showed little interest in, and had little effect on, crime victim compensation in the United States; yet, by the early 1990s the U.S. Supreme Court cited the victims' rights movement in support of a decision to reverse its previous rejection of victim impact statements in capital sentencing hearings.

---

* See Chapter 8.C.ii and 8.D.
† For a discussion of some of the various conceptions of culpability circulating in German criminal law scholarship, see Chapter 8.A.
‡ Other parts of the opinion are reproduced in Chapter 1.B.i.

Although the victims' rights discussion in Germany was less politicized, or at least less heated, and less focused on expanding victims' rights by limiting defendants' rights, it also produced fairly modest reforms. Still, considering the victim's role in criminal law remains a promising point of entry into a critical analysis of the enterprise of criminal law as a whole. Shifting one's perspective from the offender to the victim opens up a view of an alternative approach to the state's response to the phenomenon of crime, one focused on the determination of victimhood, rather than offenderhood, and of compensation, rather than of punishment, and of a road (so far) not taken.

Compensation and restitution

Uniform Victims of Crime Act (1992)*

Summary of Contents

The fundamental objective underlying this Act is the protection of the best interests of victims of crime. This Act seeks to ensure that crime victims are treated with the dignity and respect they deserve while functioning in a system in which they find themselves through no fault of their own. The Act seeks to accommodate that objective and crime victims' needs and rights with defendants' constitutional rights. . . .

§ 101. Definitions

In this [Act]:

(1) "Crime" means an act or omission committed by a person, whether or not competent or an adult, which, if committed by a competent adult, is punishable by [incarceration].

. . .

(6) "Victim" means a person against whom a crime has been committed, but does not include a person who is accountable for the crime or a crime arising from the same conduct, criminal episode, or plan and does not include a government or a governmental subdivision, agency, or instrumentality.

§ 304. Eligibility for Compensation

The following are eligible to receive compensation under this [Article]:

(1) a victim who has suffered physical, emotional, or psychological injury or impairment as a result of a crime [of violence, including driving while impaired and domestic abuse];
(2) an individual who, as a result of a crime [of violence, including driving while impaired and domestic abuse], has lost care or support from a victim;
(3) an individual who has suffered physical, emotional, or psychological injury or impairment as a result of preventing or attempting to prevent the commission of a crime, apprehending or attempting to apprehend a suspected criminal, aiding or attempting to aid a [law enforcement officer] to apprehend or arrest a suspected criminal, or aiding or attempting to aid a victim of a crime. . . .

§ 305. Award of Compensation

(a) The [agency] may award compensation for any economic loss directly caused by death or physical, emotional, or psychological injury or impairment, including:
   (1) reasonable expenses related to medical care, including prosthetic or auditory devices; ophthalmic care, including eye glasses; dental care, including orthodontic or other therapeutic devices; mental health care; and rehabilitation;
   (2) loss of income;
   (3) expenses reasonably incurred in obtaining ordinary and necessary services instead of those the victim, if not injured, would have performed, not for income but for the benefit of the victim or a member of the victim's family;

---

* [A model statute prepared by the National Conference of Commissions on Uniform State Laws, a non-profit association comprised of state commissions on uniform laws from each state. The Act has been approved by the American Bar Association.—Eds.]

(4) loss of care and support; and

(5) reasonable expenses related to funeral and burial or crematory services.

(b) An award may be made whether or not a person is charged, indicted, prosecuted, or convicted of a crime giving rise to the claim.

German Victim Compensation Act
(*Opferentschädigungsgesetz*, OEG)

§ 1

(1) Who has suffered harm to his health through an intentional, unlawful physical assault against himself or another person or in defense against such an assault in the area where German law applies or on a German ship or aircraft, shall on demand receive financial assistance by the state for health or economic damages, according to the regulations in the Federal Assistance Act [*Bundesversorgungsgesetz*, traditionally applied to war victims—Eds.] . . .

(2) Equal to physical assaults are intentional poisoning and endangering others' life or health through the commission of a crime that endangered a great number of persons if this was done at least negligently. . . .

Sentencing

Payne v. Tennessee
United States Supreme Court
501 U.S. 808 (1991)

[Our decision in Booth v. Maryland, 482 U.S. 496 (1987), was] based on two premises: that evidence relating to a particular victim or to the harm that a capital defendant causes a victim's family do not in general reflect on the defendant's "blameworthiness," and that only evidence relating to "blameworthiness" is relevant to the capital sentencing decision. However, the assessment of harm caused by the defendant as a result of the crime charged has understandably been an important concern of the criminal law, both in determining the elements of the offense and in determining the appropriate punishment. Thus, two equally blameworthy criminal defendants may be guilty of different offenses solely because their acts cause differing amounts of harm. "If a bank robber aims his gun at a guard, pulls the trigger, and kills his target, he may be put to death. If the gun unexpectedly misfires, he may not. His moral guilt in both cases is identical, but his responsibility in the former is greater." *Booth*, 482 U. S., at 519 (Scalia, J., dissenting).

. . .

"The first significance of harm in Anglo-American jurisprudence is, then, as a prerequisite to the criminal sanction. The second significance of harm—one no less important to judges—is as a measure of the seriousness of the offense and therefore as a standard for determining the severity of the sentence that will be meted out." S. Wheeler, K. Mann, & A. Sarat, Sitting in Judgment: The Sentencing of White-Collar Criminals 56 (1988).

. . .

"We have held that a State cannot preclude the sentencer from considering 'any relevant mitigating evidence' that the defendant proffers in support of a sentence less than death." Eddings v. Oklahoma, 455 U.S. 104, 114 (1982). Thus we have . . . required that the capital defendant be treated as a "uniquely individual human being." *Booth*, 482 U.S., at 504 (quoting Woodson v. North Carolina, 428 U.S. 280, 304 (1976)). . . . *Booth* has, we think, unfairly weighted the scales in a capital trial; while virtually no limits are placed on the relevant mitigating evidence a capital defendant may introduce concerning his own circumstances, the State is barred from either offering "a quick glimpse of the life" which a defendant "chose to extinguish," Mills v. Maryland, 486 U.S. 367, 397 (1988) (Rehnquist, C.J., dissenting). or demonstrating the loss to the victim's family and to society which has resulted from the defendant's homicide.

The *Booth* Court reasoned that victim impact evidence must be excluded because it would be difficult, if not impossible, for the defendant to rebut such evidence without shifting the focus of the sentencing hearing away from the defendant, thus creating a " 'mini-trial' on the victim's character." *Booth*, 482 U.S., at 506–507.

Payne echoes the concern voiced in Booth's case that the admission of victim impact evidence permits a jury to find that defendants whose victims were assets to their community are more deserving of punishment than those whose victims are perceived to be less worthy. As a general matter, however, victim impact evidence is not offered to encourage comparative judgments of this kind—for instance, that the killer of a hardworking, devoted parent deserves the death penalty, but that the murderer of a reprobate does not. It is designed to show instead each victim's "uniqueness as an individual human being," whatever the jury might think the loss to the community resulting from his death might be. . . .

"Within the constitutional limitations defined by our cases, the States enjoy their traditional latitude to prescribe the method by which those who commit murder shall be punished." Blystone v. Pennsylvania, 494 U.S. 299, 309 (1990). The States remain free, in capital cases, as well as others, to devise new procedures and new remedies to meet felt needs. Victim impact evidence is simply another form or method of informing the sentencing authority about the specific harm caused by the crime in question, evidence of a general type long considered by sentencing authorities. We think the *Booth* Court was wrong in stating that this kind of evidence leads to the arbitrary imposition of the death penalty. . . . Courts have always taken into consideration the harm done by the defendant in imposing sentence. . . .

We thus hold that if the State chooses to permit the admission of victim impact evidence and prosecutorial argument on that subject, the Eighth Amendment erects no per se bar. A State may legitimately conclude that evidence about the victim and about the impact of the murder on the victim's family is relevant to the jury's decision as to whether or not the death penalty should be imposed. . . .

Tatjana Hörnle, "Distribution of Punishment: The Role of a Victim's Perspective," 3 *Buffalo Criminal Law Review* (1999), 175

Relying on a victim's perspective clarifies issues that have been treated rather superficially in traditional sentencing doctrine. For this reason, it is useful to mention a few distinctions in German criminal doctrine. The first is the distinction between wrongdoing (*Unrecht*) and culpability of the offender (*Schuld*). "Wrongdoing" refers to the criminal act; its wrongfulness and its consequences are judged from an outside perspective. Establishing culpability, on the other hand, means evaluating the offender's personal deficiencies from an internal perspective. Thus, the crucial determination is whether wrongdoing can be fully attributed to the offender.

A victim's perspective is relevant in assessing the degree of wrongdoing. The judgment of wrongdoing is a social one. It indicates borders between differing interests, the interest of the victim in having her rights preserved and the interest of the offender in exercising her liberty. The formal distinction between wrongful and legitimate conduct matters, but the qualitative judgment of "how much wrongdoing" has occurred confirms the extent to which the victim's sphere has been violated.

"Wrongdoing" is occasionally equated with "harm." . . . But reference to harm, that is, to the result of an intrusion, does not fully cover the range of objective circumstances that influence the degree of wrongdoing. Certain modes of acting do not affect the victim but nevertheless can affect the judgment about the offender's conduct, for example, if an armed burglar was lucky enough not to encounter anybody. A second distinction in the German literature, between *Erfolgsunrecht* and *Handlungsunrecht*, classifies the circumstances of an offense and clarifies their relevance. The second concept, *Handlungsunrecht*, cannot be translated literally, but I will explain the difference. *Erfolgsunrecht* refers to the negative consequences of the criminal act; thus, the concept is analogous to harm. It is the *Handlungsunrecht* that widens the perspective; it denotes the wrongdoing of the act but not the act's result.

[A] victim's perspective is most useful with respect to the *Handlungsunrecht*. Like any other event, each offense can be described with an infinite number of details; for example, the temperature at the location, the time of the day, a description of the clothes the actors wore, or the contents of the offender's jacket pockets. This listing might look odd at first, but courts and commentators frequently cite aggravating circumstances that raise additional questions about an offender's culpability. Should it matter that the offender was a foreigner or, most important in practice, that he had numerous prior convictions? Does the definition of crime change when an act is committed by members of a very sophisticated criminal organization like a gang, rather than an unorganized group of offenders? Is it a greater wrong to plan an offense carefully in advance? Is it relevant that the offender carried tools (like a screwdriver) that could be used to hurt people? In order to separate relevant from irrelevant details, one must consider a victim's perspective. This process distinguishes which circumstances characterize the wrongdoing and which will be significant merely for preventive reasons. . . .

Take, for instance, mitigating circumstances that can be determined empirically. In German law, abnormal mental conditions not only can excuse the offender, but also are important for sentencing. The sentence can be mitigated considerably when the offender's ability to recognize the wrongfulness of his conduct or his ability to act according to this insight are substantially reduced. The victim does not, and, logically, cannot play a role in determining whether the offender was mentally ill or psychologically disturbed.

Some mitigating circumstances under German law are based not on empirically measurable internal conditions but on normative considerations. For example, an offense committed to ward off present danger to life, health, or liberty is excused. This excuse occasionally is said to derive from an abnormal mental condition that leads to an inaccurate assessment of danger. A straightforward normative justification, however, which bases the excuse on the general principle that one cannot be expected to avoid illegal behavior in the face of immediate danger clearly is preferable (*Theorie der Zumutbarkeit*). This principle can be extended to other situations in which attendant circumstances can mitigate a sentence.

The criteria for excuses and mitigations are not influenced by a victim's perspective. The normative perspective requires the judge to place herself in the position of the offender, that is, in the situation of an endangered person. What matters is the internal conflict the actor had to struggle with—the conflict between his interest in self-preservation and his general interest in obeying the law. The social conflict between the demands of the victim and the offender has already been examined on the level of wrongdoing. With respect to the narrower question of culpability, the interests of the victim have no specific relevance.

Markus D. Dubber, "The Victim in American Penal Law: A Systematic Overview," 3 *Buffalo Criminal Law Review* (1999), 3

In the theoretical underpinnings of the substantive criminal law, the so-called theory of punishment, the role of victims differs from theory to theory. Rehabilitation, the reigning ideology in American penal law until the late 1960s, had little use for victims. Punishment or, as the rehabilitationist would have it, peno-correctional treatment, turns on the offender's criminal pathology, as diagnosed by penological experts. Victims are no more relevant to this view of punishment than they are to the medical treatment of any other patient. This is not to say that victims are irrelevant, only that their characteristics or conduct matters merely insofar as they affect the diagnosis and treatment of a particular offender's deviance. So the victim's age might indicate a diagnosis of pedophilia. Similarly, her conduct might help the penologist identify the specific behavioral trigger of the offender's criminal episode, such as in provocation cases, or even constitute strong evidence against a diagnosis of criminal pathology, such as in cases of victim consent. More recently, victim participation has been said also to contribute to the offender's rehabilitative treatment. Victim offender meetings, for example, may assist the offender's rehabilitation by forcing her to confront the devastating and long term impact her deviant behavior has on the immediate victim and her community. . . .

By the 1970s, rehabilitationism began to give way to retributivism as the dominant ideology of punishment in the United States. . . .

Retributivism made room for victims insofar as its assessment of desert turned in part on the harm inflicted by the defendant's conduct not only in the abstract, i.e., in the definition of the offense, but also in the particular case, provided the offender displayed an attitude toward the harm that would permit the assignment of blame. The victim's role in retributivism, however, was not uncontested. Many retributivists, after all, rebelled against what they perceived as the rehabilitationists' ill-advised attention to the particular characteristics and circumstances of the offender, rather than to the nature of the offense, for two reasons. First, such efforts at particularization placed excessive discretion in the hands of those charged with applying penal norms, a discretion that in turn led to non-uniform punishment practices in general, and to discriminatory punishment practices in particular. Second, any offender-based punishment practice risked the degrading stigmatization of its object, who was marked as deviant, rather than judged as having wronged. In its most abstract form, retributivism thus viewed punishment as the vindication of a general penal norm (e.g., against homicide), rather than retribution for the particular harm suffered by a particular victim. The victim's experience was significant only insofar as it established the norm violation. Once the norm violation had been established, the particular sentence imposed on the offender could reflect the particular harm inflicted only insofar as the offender was aware of it (or possessed some other mental state).

This deontological interlude, however, proved short-lived. Certainly in practice, if not in theory, retributivism quickly gave way to its consequentialist analogue, vengeance, and the crudest form of consequentialist penology, incapacitation. The rise of the so-called victims' rights movement in the United States formed an important part of this consequentialist (re)turn. . . .

In the absence of a coherent theory underlying the victims' rights movement . . . , one is forced instead merely to identify the symptoms of this sociological phenomenon. . . . [T]he victims' rights movement can be thought of as the manifestation of a communal self-protective reflex or impulse. The victim would play a central role in such a phenomenology of reflex punishment. It is the injury to a fellow community member by an outsider that triggers the penal impulse. Through identification with the victim, other community members re-experience her suffering. Moreover, they may experience the injury inflicted upon the individual victim as an injury to the community as a whole, and perhaps even as a threat to its continued existence. The victim, in the end, becomes an icon to a community of potential victims. The victim is entitled to an unrestrained manifestation of her pain and confusion, with her fellow community members as empathic onlookers.

In this model, everything would turn on the onlooker's identification with the iconic victim. Without identification, she cannot experience the victim's pain as her own, nor does she consider an injury to the victim as a threat to her own community . . .

[T]hough based on the perception of fellow community membership with respect to victims, the victims' rights movement, at the same time, has worked to block that identification when it comes to certain offenders. One might even go so far as to say that the victims' rights movement set out to replace offender identification with victim identification.

The inclusionary exclusionary nature of the victims' rights movement becomes most obvious in capital cases. Here identification with the victim is said not only to permit but to require differentiation from the offender. By declaring the offender an outsider so alien to the community that identification is simply impossible for lack of even the most basic similarity, the community purges itself of deviant elements and thereby heals itself as it salves the victim's pain. . . .

Once the offender is excluded from the realm of identification, the question "how could someone like us (or, stronger, like me) have done something like this" no longer arises. To the extent curiosity survives, it does not concern the offender's behavior, but the victim's suffering. Making room for victims thus often amounts to facilitating the search for an answer to the altogether different, passive, question "how could something like this have happened to someone like us (or me)." The offender and her behavior remains significant only insofar as it can help answer this elusive question, most obviously in the case of victim offender meetings after conviction. . . .

Jörg-Martin Jehle, Criminal Justice in Germany: Facts and Figures
(Federal Ministry of Justice, 2009)

Offender–Victim Mediation (*Täter-Opfer-Ausgleich*; abbreviated: TOA), which was given a legislative basis for the first time in 1990, refers to an offender's efforts to achieve a settlement with the injured party and in doing so to make good his or her offense, or to go a long way towards doing so. A settlement of this kind can take place at any stage during criminal proceedings and can cause the authorities to refrain from prosecution (§ 45 section 3 of the Act on Juvenile Courts), to drop the prosecution (§ 153a section 1 line 2 Nr. 5 Code of Criminal Procedure, § 47 section 1 no. 3 Act on Juvenile Courts) or to refrain from imposing a or mitigating the sanction (§ 46a StGB). According to juvenile criminal law, the judge can issue the instruction that the judged offender is to make efforts towards Offender–Victim Mediation (§ 10 section 1 line 3, no. 7 Juvenile Criminal Code). In order to enable TOA to be used more frequently and easily the criminal code provisions were augmented procedurally in 1999 with the new paragraphs 155a and 155b in the Code of Criminal Procedure. These oblige the prosecution service and the court to consider the possibilities for reaching a settlement between the accused and the victim at all procedural stages.

Offender–Victim Mediation is usually achieved upon prosecution service initiative, although a TOA institution, usually the juvenile court service, the court service or a specialist independent organization will be involved. This organization will consider whether a case is generally suited for TOA, whether the victim and perpetrator are prepared to enter settlement discussions, lead these discussions, record the result of these, supervise the actual compensatory efforts and inform the prosecution service and court of success or failure.

German Criminal Code
(*Strafgesetzbuch*, StGB)

§ 46a Offender–Victim Mediation, Compensation for Damages

If the offender has:
1. in an effort to achieve mediation with the injured person (offender–victim mediation), completely or substantially made restitution for his act or earnestly tried to do so; or
2. in a case in which the restitution of damages required substantial personal accomplishments or personal sacrifice, completely or substantially compensated the victim,
the court may mitigate the sentence according to § 49 para. 1 or, if the maximum punishment would be imprisonment for up to one year or a fine, dispense with punishment.

NOTES

1. Considering the role of victims in the criminal law raises important questions. First, should or must the state offer financial compensation to the victims of crime? Second, may victims take an active role in the criminal trial, specifically by delivering victim impact statements at the sentencing stage? Third, should the law support and encourage victim-offender mediation or compensation? Fourth, as a matter of substantive criminal law, how should the victim's conduct or characteristics affect the offender's criminal liability?

2. The first issue, financial compensation by the state for victims of crime, tends to be thought of, in Germany, as the provision of a social service to citizens in need (analogous to other services such as medical insurance, workers' compensation, emergency aid, and so on), rather than as a matter of criminal law in general, or of criminal trials in particular. The German "federal support law" (*Bundesversorgungsgesetz*, BVG) was introduced in 1950 for victims of the Second World War. While it is easy to see why harm caused by the decisions of state organs (like the decision to declare war) ought to be compensated by the state, it is less evident in cases where the harm is caused by other citizens (which in general is the subject of civil lawsuits). But the German state now also compensates the victims of crime; the Victim Compensation Law (*Opferentschädigungsgesetz*, OEG) for violent crimes was introduced in 1985. It is not only a symbol of an extended welfare state; more importantly, it signifies a growing trend in German society to sympathize and identify with victims.[*]

In the U.S., crime victim compensation tends to attract little attention, and in general is under-theorized. The "victims' rights" agenda of the so-called "war on crime" instead regarded the protection of victims' and defendants' rights as a zero sum game; much of the pursuit of victims' rights, then, amounted to a restriction of defendants' rights and general calls for greater punitiveness (three-strikes laws for repeat offenders; increased and mandatory minimum sentences; expansion of capital punishment; restrictions on federal habeas corpus; primarily as an avenue to challenge state capital sentences; and so on).[†]

Crime victim compensation schemes in the U.S. appear less as a service provided by the general welfare state (which, in comparison to Germany, is much less developed, and far more controversial) than as a specific and more limited attempt to provide crime victims with financial assistance, as reflected in the crime-focused financing models adopted by various jurisdictions, for example, drawing on a portion of salaries earned by offenders from prison work or while on work release or parole, collecting forfeited assets from criminal activity, or allowing taxpayers to designate a part of their income tax refund to be used for crime victim services.

Victim compensation schemes in other common law countries pursue aims similar to the German scheme. For instance, the provision of financial assistance to victims of violent crime in the Canadian province of Ontario is said to further the following policy rationales:

(a) Criminal injuries financial assistance reflects society's compassion for innocent victims and a collective desire to help those who have been harmed as a result of violent crime.

(b) Governments fund a number of programs that are designed to promote the welfare of its citizenry and financial assistance for victims of violent crime is a reasonable extension of these kinds of state funded programs.

(c) Similarly, governments provide several insurance-like programs such as health care insurance, unemployment insurance and workplace injury insurance that spread certain inevitable risks in society. Victim financial assistance is seen, again, as a reasonable extension of these kinds of programs.[‡]

---

[*] See generally "Symposium: Victims and the Criminal Law: American and German Perspectives," 3 *Buffalo Criminal Law Review* (1999), 1.

[†] See generally Markus D. Dubber, *Victims in the War on Crime: The Use and Abuse of Victims' Rights* (2002).

[‡] Report on Financial Assistance for Victims of Violent Crime in Ontario (2008), 17–18.

3. Consider the relationship between crime victim compensation law and criminal law. They can be seen as parallel mirror-image state responses to the phenomenon of crime, each focused on one of the persons constituting the legal event "crime": "offender" and "victim." Criminal law investigates the offender's punishability; compensation law the victim's compensability. The offender's punishability turns on her guilt; the victim's compensability on his innocence. Note that the Uniform Victims of Crime Act, in § 101(6), excludes from the definition of "victim" anyone "accountable for the crime": victims cannot be offenders, and innocence cannot be guilt. Similarly, under New York law, a "victim" for purposes of crime victim compensability is "an innocent person who suffers personal physical injury as a direct result of a crime."* The prerequisite of innocence can raise the specter of a second victimization, in the very process of victim compensation, by inquiring into the victim's "contribution" to the criminal offense against him or her.†

Can the requirement of innocence be squared with the view of victim compensation schemes as providing a state social service to the needy? To what extent are crime victim compensation schemes *crime* victim compensation schemes? Should they be?

4. Should victims be able to express their suffering and needs in criminal trials through victim impact statements? The answer to this question is not obvious. If the evolution of state punishment is seen as a crucial step in civilizing and restricting vindictive reactions, we might be reluctant to provide extensive victims' rights and specifically victim impact statements.

Under German law, victims in general are not entitled to participate actively in criminal trials and there are no victim impact statements. However, there are important exceptions to this rule of the "passive victim." The German Code of Criminal Procedure allows certain types of victims to appear as "accessory prosecutor" (*Nebenkläger*): §§ 395–402. This right is mainly available to victims of sexual offenses, assault and attempted murder, as well as to relatives of murder and homicide victims. The position of an "accessory prosecutor" includes a right to make statements. It does not, however, oblige the judge to put particular emphasis on the victim's suffering in his or her sentencing decision. Independent of the procedural aspect, even if victims do not themselves make statements about the crime's impact on their lives, judges will take evidence about harm (from medical reports, for instance) into account in sentencing.‡

5. Another question is whether the criminal justice system should consider attempts to improve the relationship between offender and victim as a mitigating factor or even promote and instigate mediation and compensation. In contemporary German criminal law theory, the issue of "restorative justice" plays a prominent role, and multiple forms of victim-offender mediation and compensation schemes are applied in practice. German criminal law does not include mediation as a feature of the criminal trial as such, but it encourages such procedures outside of the courtroom. Mediation may lead to termination of the criminal proceedings before trial, or, if a trial takes place, § 46a StGB allows a judge to reduce the sentence or, in less serious cases, to abstain from imposing punishment.

With respect to sentencing theory, this raises the question of whether mitigation of punishment (for actual, or even for attempted, mediation) can fit into a coherent approach. Could one argue that offenders' conduct after the crime should influence the assessment of their crimes insofar as it affected—and perhaps reduced—the harm done? What if efforts at victim–offender mediation, however genuine, have the opposite, even if unintended, effect and aggravate the victim's suffering? How would one measure this effect? Should a good faith effort by the offender be enough? Should victims be forced, or at least induced, to participate

---

* See Markus D. Dubber, *Victims in the War on Crime: The Use and Abuse of Victims' Rights* (2002), 9–10, 233–5.

† See, e.g., *Re Jane Doe and Criminal Injuries Compensation Board*, (1995) 22 O.R. (3d) 129, [1995] O.J. No. 278 (reversing victim compensation board's 40 percent reduction of award for failure to take reasonable precautions against exposure to H.I.V.); *Sheehan and Criminal Injuries Compensation Board*, (1975) 5 O.R. (2d) 781 (upholding board's dismissal of prison inmates' claim on the ground that "but for their own prior criminal activity these applicants would not have found themselves in Kingston Penitentiary where they were injured").

‡ See generally William T. Pizzi and Walter Perron, "Crime Victims in German Courtrooms: A Comparative Perspective on American Problems," 32 *Stanford Journal of International Law* (1996), 37.

in mediation sessions? What about unsympathetic victims (e.g., someone who harbors racial prejudices against the offender)? Paranoid, traumatized, indifferent victims?*

6. What role does—should—the victim play in substantive criminal law? For instance, does it make the offender any less guilty if the victim consented to the offender's conduct, or does it make the conduct less criminal, or less wrongful, or harmful? We will take up the issue of consent later on, but for now think about what it means for the ostensible victim of a crime if the criminal law—i.e., the state in defining, applying, and enforcing criminal norms—declares that his or her consent is immaterial. (Think of adult partners in a consensual sado-maso-chistic sexual relationship, or terminally ill patients seeking the assistance of others in ending their lives, and thereby their suffering.[†]) Does the irrelevance of victim consent to the offender's criminal liability amount to a violation of "victims' rights"?[‡]

iii. Types of sanction

The *Blarek* opinion features a wide palette of sanctions: imprisonment (which gets all the attention, not just in this case, but in general, at least in Anglo-American criminal law), along with fine, forfeiture, supervised release, and a "special assessment" to boot. This list is fairly representative, even if it does not include the death penalty and so-called "alternative punishments," which is often taken as a synonym for (more or less) tailored shaming sanctions of some sort. We will pay particular attention to the fine, which is of considerable comparative interest because it is as irrelevant in Anglo-American criminal law as it is central to German criminal law (and to the criminal law of many other European countries, notably in Scandinavia).[§]

Apart from the retention of capital punishment in many American jurisdictions, the most obvious difference between criminal sentences in the United States and Germany (and, in fact, between the United States and any other Western country, and many non-Western countries besides) is the frequent use of imprisonment, which—combined with harsh sentences—has placed the United States at, or near, the top of incarceration rates worldwide. Even with recent developments in the direction of reducing the prison population, or at least of slowing its exponential growth (from 166 per 100,000 population in 1970 to 760 in 2009)—which tend to be driven by budgetary concerns about the high cost of imprisonment, rather than by a rejection of imprisonment as the sanction of choice—this radical distinction will remain in place for some time to come.

In the context of the American penal regime, every other sanction is measured against the paradigm of imprisonment. Against this backdrop, every other type of punishment appears as an alternative, as a deviation from the standard of imprisonment, in both directions of severity. The death penalty is an upward deviation from the norm, everything else a downward deviation, and both must be justified in these terms. The death penalty, as a *type* of sanction, is thought to be reserved for cases in which imprisonment, even life imprisonment without the possibility of parole, is considered insufficient for one reason or another (e.g., it does not reflect the seriousness of the crime, the offender's blameworthiness or dangerous-ness). Non-incarcerative types of sanction other than the death penalty are, by definition, considered less severe than a prison sentence, and thus regarded as an exceptional downward departure from the norm. In fact, so close is the association between punishment and

---

* See, e.g., *People v. Mooney*, 133 Misc. 2d 313, 506 N.Y.S.2d 991 (Co. Ct. 1986) (imposing community-based sentence in a case of violent crime "in a small cohesive community" despite victim's "continu[ing] in a state of reproachment, with strong feelings of anger and revenge," where "victim's mother expressed a less hostile attitude and was more receptive to a conciliatory process to eliminate the destructive nature of such feelings to his own future welfare").

† See Chapters 13.C (on consent) and 15.A.v (on assisted suicide).

‡ See generally Vera Bergelson, *Victims' Rights and Victims' Wrongs: A Theory of Comparative Criminal Liability* (2009).

§ For a detailed discussion of ostensibly non-punitive "measures," see Chapter 1.B.iii.

imprisonment that a common criticism of non-incarcerative sanctions—most notably fines—is that they are not "really" punishments. This political-conceptual context accounts, at least in part, for the interest in so-called "alternative" shaming sanctions, which are portrayed as alternatives to imprisonment that, to put it mildly, are less likely to be taken as insufficiently punitive than other alternatives, such as fines. At the same time, fines face the general objection that they discriminate against poor defendants, which is a serious concern in a country of greater income inequality than, say, Germany or Sweden, which rely heavily on criminal fines, even with a so-called day fine system aimed at addressing this problem. Nonetheless, it is a concern that pales in comparison to the reality of mass incarceration of predominately poor and, what is more, minority status persons. In 2005, 8.1 percent of all black males age 25 to 29 were in prison, compared to 1.1 percent of white males.[*]

Incarceration Rates (prisoners per 100,000 population, 2009)

U.S.A.	760
Russian Federation	624
South Africa	329
Israel	325
England	140
Australia	129
Canada	116
France	96
Germany	90
Sweden	74
Japan	63

Source: Organization for Economic Co-Operation and Development, Factbook 2010, Economic, Environmental and Social Statistics

---

Verdict, disposition, and sentence received in cases terminated in U.S. district court, 2009

	Number	*Percent*
Total Cases Terminated	95,891	100
Convicted	86,975	90.7
Plea	84,326	87.9
Bench/jury trial	2,649	2.8
Not convicted	8,916	9.3
Dismissed	8,425	8.8
Bench/jury trial	491	0.5
Sentence imposed		
Total convicted defendants	86,975	100
Prison	67,499	78.2
Probation only	9,401	10.9
Fine only	2,747	3.2
Suspended sentence	6,626	7.7

Source: Bureau of Justice Statistics, Federal Justice Statistics, 2009 (December 2011, NCJ 234184), <http://bjs.ojp. usdoj.gov/content/pub/pdf/fjs09.pdf>.

---

[*] U.S. Dep't of Justice, Prisoners in 2005 (2006).

Sentence received in cases terminated in German courts, 2009

	Number	Percent
Total convicted adults	727,641	100
Prison	37,911	5.2
Suspended prison	96,585	13.3
Fine only	593,128	81.5

Source: German Federal Office of Statistics (Statistisches Bundesamt, Fachserie 10, Reihe 3, Strafverfolgung)

United States Sentencing Guidelines

§ 5E1.2 (Fines for Individual Defendants)

(a) The court shall impose a fine in all cases, except where the defendant establishes that he is unable to pay and is not likely to become able to pay any fine. . . .

. . .

(d) In determining the amount of the fine, the court shall consider:
  (1) the need for the combined sentence to reflect the seriousness of the offense (including the harm or loss to the victim and the gain to the defendant), to promote respect for the law, to provide just punishment and to afford adequate deterrence;
  (2) any evidence presented as to the defendant's ability to pay the fine (including the ability to pay over a period of time) in light of his earning capacity and financial resources;
  (3) the burden that the fine places on the defendant and his dependents relative to alternative punishments;
  (4) any restitution or reparation that the defendant has made or is obligated to make;
  (5) any collateral consequences of conviction, including civil obligations arising from the defendant's conduct;
  (6) whether the defendant previously has been fined for a similar offense;
  (7) the expected costs to the government of any term of probation, or term of imprisonment and term of supervised release imposed; and
  (8) any other pertinent equitable considerations.
  The amount of the fine should always be sufficient to ensure that the fine, taken together with other sanctions imposed, is punitive.
(e) If the defendant establishes that (1) he is not able and, even with the use of a reasonable installment schedule, is not likely to become able to pay all or part of the fine required by the preceding provisions, or (2) imposition of a fine would unduly burden the defendant's dependents, the court may impose a lesser fine or waive the fine. In these circumstances, the court shall consider alternative sanctions in lieu of all or a portion of the fine, and must still impose a total combined sanction that is punitive. Although any additional sanction not proscribed by the guidelines is permissible, community service is the generally preferable alternative in such instances.
(f) If the defendant establishes that payment of the fine in a lump sum would have an unduly severe impact on him or his dependents, the court should establish an installment schedule for payment of the fine. The length of the installment schedule generally should not exceed twelve months, and shall not exceed the maximum term of probation authorized for the offense. The defendant should be required to pay a substantial installment at the time of sentencing. If the court authorizes a defendant sentenced to probation or supervised release to pay a fine on an installment schedule, the court shall require as a condition of probation or supervised release that the defendant pay the fine according to the schedule. The court also may impose a condition prohibiting the defendant from incurring new credit charges or opening additional lines of credit unless he is in compliance with the payment schedule.
(g) If the defendant knowingly fails to pay a delinquent fine, the court shall resentence him in accordance with 18 U.S.C. § 3614.

Commentary

Application Notes:

1. A fine may be the sole sanction if the guidelines do not require a term of imprisonment. If, however, the fine is not paid in full at the time of sentencing, it is recommended that the court sentence the defendant to a term of probation, with payment of the fine as a condition of probation. If

a fine is imposed in addition to a term of imprisonment, it is recommended that the court impose a term of supervised release following imprisonment as a means of enforcing payment of the fine.

2. In general, the maximum fine permitted by law as to each count of conviction is $250,000 for a felony or for any misdemeanor resulting in death; $100,000 for a Class A misdemeanor; and $5,000 for any other offense. 18 U.S.C. § 3571(b)(3)–(7). However, higher or lower limits may apply when specified by statute. 18 U.S.C. § 3571(b)(1), (e). As an alternative maximum, the court may fine the defendant up to the greater of twice the gross gain or twice the gross loss. 18 U.S.C. § 3571(b)(2), (d).

3. The determination of the fine guideline range may be dispensed with entirely upon a court determination of present and future inability to pay any fine. The inability of a defendant to post bail bond (having otherwise been determined eligible for release) and the fact that a defendant is represented by (or was determined eligible for) assigned counsel are significant indicators of present inability to pay any fine. In conjunction with other factors, they may also indicate that the defendant is not likely to become able to pay any fine.

4. The Commission envisions that for most defendants, the maximum of the guideline fine range . . . will be at least twice the amount of gain or loss resulting from the offense. Where, however, two times either the amount of gain to the defendant or the amount of loss caused by the offense exceeds the maximum of the fine guideline, an upward departure from the fine guideline may be warranted.

Moreover, where a sentence within the applicable fine guideline range would not be sufficient to ensure both the disgorgement of any gain from the offense that otherwise would not be disgorged (e.g., by restitution or forfeiture) and an adequate punitive fine, an upward departure from the fine guideline range may be warranted. . . .

. . .

6. The existence of income or assets that the defendant failed to disclose may justify a larger fine than that which otherwise would be warranted under this section. The court may base its conclusion as to this factor on information revealing significant unexplained expenditures by the defendant or unexplained possession of assets that do not comport with the defendant's reported income. If the court concludes that the defendant willfully misrepresented all or part of his income or assets, it may increase the offense level and resulting sentence in accordance with Chapter Three, Part C (Obstruction). . . .

Judith A. Greene, "Structuring Criminal Fines: Making an 'Intermediate' Penalty More Useful and Equitable," 13 *Justice System Journal* (1988), 37

First developed in Scandinavia in the 1920s and 1930s, and introduced into West Germany during the late 1960s and early 1970s, the day fine system of setting variable rather than fixed fine amounts rests upon a simple two step [process that embraces both proportionality and equity]. First, the court sentences the offender to a certain number of fine units according to the gravity of the offense, but without regard to his or her means. The value of each unit is then established as a share of the offender's daily income (hence the name "day fine"), and the total fine amount is determined by simple multiplication.

German Criminal Code

§ 40 (Day Fine Units)

(1) Fines are imposed in daily units. The minimum fine consists of five daily units and, unless the law provides otherwise, the maximum fine of three hundred and sixty full daily units.

(2) The court determines the amount of the daily unit taking into consideration the personal and financial circumstances of the offender. As a rule, it shall typically base its calculation on the average net income the offender achieves for one day or could achieve. A daily unit shall not be set at less than one euro and shall not exceed thirty thousand euros.

(3) The offender's income, his assets and other relevant factors may be estimated when setting the amount of a daily unit.

(4) The number and amount of the daily units must be indicated in the decision.

NOTES

1. The sentencing tables of U.S. district courts and German courts demonstrate remarkable differences in sentence severity. Of course, one has to be cautious with this comparison. The German data includes *all* sentencing decisions in criminal cases (including 176,091 criminal traffic offenses). The courts are administered by the sixteen states' Departments of Justice, but the German Federal Office of Statistics aggregates data the states supply and thus gives a comprehensive picture of German courts. The data about U.S. district courts above only portray one segment of the American criminal justice system—sentences handed out in federal trial courts, applying federal criminal law. Nonetheless, some general comparisons are permissible: German courts hand out lower sentences overall and more fines in particular. In U.S. federal courts (as well as state courts), very few cases end in a "fine only" sentence; in German criminal courts, only very few cases do not. Imprisonment is the penalty of choice in U.S. federal courts, while the fine is the default punishment in German criminal courts.*

2. The U.S. Sentencing Guidelines emphasize the "combined sentence" approach, that is, fines complementing prison sentences. Under German law, combinations of imprisonment and fines are possible,† but they are rarely applied in practice. "Fine only" sentences are the far more popular choice. Fining the offender is seen as sufficient punishment for the offenses that make up the daily business of local courts (minor property crimes like theft, fraud, and drunk driving).

That the day fine system is the standard form of punishment is not to say that offenders engaged in economic crimes, drug crimes or other forms of criminal enrichment may keep the proceeds. The German Criminal Code allows for forfeiture of both the means for committing crimes (weapons, computers, etc.) and the financial proceeds (confiscation and deprivation orders, §§ 73–76a). For most offenses, proof is required that assets found in the offender's possession are in fact the profits of the crimes charged; but for certain crimes (for instance, organized money laundering), a reasonable assumption is sufficient.‡ Confiscation and deprivation orders are not considered criminal punishment and the law distinguishes between such orders, on one hand, and fines as punishment, on the other.§

Anglo-American law distinguishes between civil and criminal forfeiture: Civil forfeiture is an *in rem* proceeding against the tainted asset itself;¶ criminal forfeiture is a type of punishment. In a civil forfeiture case, the government must establish the asset's connection to criminal activity, with no need to obtain, or even to seek, a criminal conviction. The Eighth Amendment's prohibition of "excessive fines" (U.S. Const. Amendment VIII: "Excessive bail shall not be required, nor excessive fines imposed, nor cruel and unusual punishments inflicted.") is not limited to forfeitures labeled "criminal"; it also applies to "civil" forfeitures used for a "punitive" purpose, i.e., to civil *in rem* forfeitures that amount to punishment in fact, if not by label.** Not surprisingly, civil forfeiture is far more common than criminal forfeiture. It is also considerably more controversial, not only because it is said to pursue punitive aims without the procedural safeguards available in a criminal proceedings, but also because the ease and scale of civil forfeiture, particularly in the so-called War on Drugs, may be seen as creating perverse incentives for police departments.†† Between 1989 and 2010, the

---

* On the severity of punishment in U.S. and German criminal law, see Chapter 1.B.ii.
† See Criminal Code § 41.
‡ See Criminal Code § 73d.
§ See Note 5.
¶ E.g., *Various Items of Personal Property v. United States*, 282 U.S. 577 (1931).
** See *Austin v. United States*, 509 U.S. 602 (1993) (applying Eighth Amendment to "civil" forfeiture of mobile home and auto body shop under 21 U.S.C. § 881(a)(4), applying to "conveyances...used, or... intended for use, to transport, or in any manner to facilitate the transportation, sale, receipt, possession, or concealment" of controlled substances and § 881(a)(7), covering "real property,...which is used, or intended to be used, in any manner or part, to commit, or to facilitate the commission of, a [federal drug offense] punishable by more than one year's imprisonment").
†† Donald J. Boudreaux and A.C. Pritchard, "Civil Forfeiture and the War on Drugs: Lessons from Economics and History," 33 *San Diego Law Review* (1996), 79.

value of asset forfeitures recovered by U.S. federal prosecutors—not counting property seized by state law enforcement agencies—exceeded US$12 billion.*

3. Any system that includes fines among the range of criminal punishments has to deal with at least two questions: how to determine the amount of the fine in a given case, and how to deal with those who fail to pay the fine. Obviously, these questions are related: the higher fines are, the more offenders will be unable to pay. In the German system, the fine depends on the offender's income. Two defendants who have committed the same crime (for instance as co-perpetrators) can receive rather different sentences. The number of daily units would be the same (for instance, both may be sentenced to ninety daily units), but one could be fined ninety daily units of €200 each, that is, €18,000, and the other ninety daily units of €10, that is €900. Although the total amount can be quite small for low-income offenders, there are no signs of public discontent with the German day fine system. Does this differential treatment of equally culpable offenders raise justice concerns? Do these particularized sentences violate the right to equal treatment? Or are they perhaps less, rather than, more objectionable on equality grounds, insofar as they equalize the effect of a sentence on two differently situated defendants? But then should all punishments be tailored to the particular situation, mental and physical capacities and characteristics, vulnerabilities, pain threshold, job prospects, family situation, etc. of each defendant?[†]

4. A day fine system might initially address the problem of unpaid fines by setting a very low minimum day unit (like the €1 in the German Criminal Code), which an offender might be expected to afford to contribute, particularly if he or she applies for any social benefits that might be available. What happens if no social benefits are available, either because the offender is not entitled to them or because he lives in a jurisdiction that does not provide social benefits?

In Germany, failure to pay traditionally resulted in imprisonment. Section 43 StGB stipulates that one day-fine results in one day of imprisonment. The prosecution office (which supervises the execution of sentences) will try to work with the offender to create an installment plan before ordering imprisonment as a substitute for payment. But, if this fails, offenders will be incarcerated for trifling offenses. Does this raise concerns about proportionality? About equality, more generally, by distinguishing among offenders based on their economic resources? Or based on their willingness, rather than their ability, to pay the fine?

Prosecution offices in Germany are beginning to develop models that allow offenders to do community service if they fail to pay their fines. Does this place too much power in the hands of prosecutors?[‡]

5. So far we have dealt with fines as criminal punishment. German law distinguishes between criminal punishment and administrative penalties (addressed in more detail in Chapter 1.B. iii), and a large portion of fines for contraventions of the law belong to the area of administrative penalties. This is captured in a linguistic differentiation between *Geldstrafe* (monetary punishment) and *Geldbuße* (something like "monetary penalty"), which disappears once one uses the common English translation "fine." Does this linguistic distinction make a legal difference? German law places great weight on this distinction. For instance, corporations in German criminal law are said to be incapable of committing crimes (for various reasons, including that they cannot commit a criminal act, cannot form criminal intent, and cannot be criminally culpable). Even though corporations as a result cannot be punished criminally, they can be penalized administratively—they cannot receive something

---

* Kathleen Maguire (ed.), *Sourcebook of Criminal Justice Statistics, U.S. Department of Justice, Bureau of Justice Statistics* (2009), table 4.45.2010, <http://www.albany.edu/sourcebook/pdf/t4452010.pdf>.
† Compare here Judge Weinstein's consideration of the defendants' sexual orientation in reducing their prison sentence in *Blarek*, Chapter 1.A.i.
‡ See the discussion of the principle of compulsory prosecution, *Legalitätsprinzip*, in Chapter 5.C.

called a *Geldstrafe*, but they can receive something called a *Geldbuße*, even if the amount of the fine is the same in both cases or, in fact, even if the *Geldbuße* exceeds the *Geldstrafe*.*

6. Take another look at the fine line between fine as criminal punishment and fine as administrative penality. Are fines really punishments? Or are they mere slaps on the wrist that cannot reflect the seriousness of crime—of most crime, of some crime, or of crime in general? Does the significance of the fine as a sanction depend on the context of the criminal (and in fact the administrative) sanctioning system as a whole? More specifically, does a fine mean the same thing in U.S. and German criminal law, as they exist today?

The common perception of fines as non-punitive played a significant role in the search for so-called "alternative" sanctions in the United States. These sanctions, notoriously including shaming, were proposed as a viable alternative to the paradigmatic sanction in U.S. criminal law: imprisonment. Fines, the argument went, are thought to carry no condemnatory meaning, so that their imposition in fact may signal impunity; this leaves shaming sanctions, which are condemnatory by their very nature, as a viable alternative to imprisonment. Examples of shaming sanctions include publishing offenders' personal information in the newspaper, on local television, on billboards, or on the internet and requiring offenders to wear shirts or carry signs indicating their crime of conviction, or to perform public labor (commonly street cleaning).[†] Many advocates of shaming penalties cite their supposed superior efficiency relative to imprisonment. This claim may be difficult to verify. It may also be neither here nor there. Are shaming penalties, or could they be, more *just*?

Consider this dissent from a federal appellate court opinion affirming "the legality of a supervised release condition that requires a convicted mail thief to spend a day standing outside a post office in San Francisco wearing a signboard stating, 'I stole mail. This is my punishment.'":

> There is precious little federal authority on sentences that include shaming components, perhaps indicative of a recognition that whatever legal justification may be marshaled in support of sentences involving public humiliation, they simply have no place in the majesty of a [federal] courtroom. Some state courts have reviewed such sentences and the results have been mixed.
>
> *People v. Hackler*, 13 Cal. App. 4th 1049, 16 Cal.Rptr.2d 681, 686–87 (Cal. Ct. App. 1993), involved a condition that required a shoplifting offender to wear a court provided t shirt whenever he left the house that read: "My record plus two six packs equals four years" on the front and "I am on felony probation for theft" on the back. Applying a state sentencing regime similar to the federal guidelines—authorizing the imposition of reasonable conditions of probation to foster rehabilitation and to protect public safety—the court struck down the condition. The court held that the relationship between the required conduct (wearing the t shirt) and the defendant's crime (stealing beer) was so incidental that it was not reasonable and that the true intent behind the condition was to expose Hackler to "public ridicule and humiliation" and not "to foster rehabilitation."
>
> As in Hackler's case, the purpose behind the sandwich board condition was not to rehabilitate Gementera, but rather to turn him into a modern day Hester Prynne.[4] This sort of condition is simply improper under the Sentencing Reform Act.
>
> *Ballenger v. State*, 210 Ga. App. 627, 436 S.E.2d 793 (Ga. Ct. App. 1993), approved a condition that a convicted drunk driver wear a fluorescent pink identification bracelet identifying him as such. . . .
>
> Just as in *Hackler* and *Ballenger*, the true intention in this case was to humiliate Gementera, not to rehabilitate him or to deter him from future wrongdoing. When the district court initially imposed the sandwich board condition, . . . Gementera filed a motion to correct the sentence by having the sandwich board condition removed. He urged that humiliation was not a legitimate objective of punishment or release conditions. Only at the hearing on Gementera's motion did the district court change its characterization of the shaming punishment, remarking that the punishment was one of deterrence and rehabilitation and not merely humiliation.

---

* See also the discussion of corporate criminal liability, in Chapter 11.
† See Dan M. Kahan, "What Do Alternative Sanctions Mean?," 63 *University of Chicago Law Review* (1996), 591.

---

4 *See* Hawthorne, *The Scarlet Letter*...

...To affirm the imposition of such punishments recalls a time in our history when pillories and stocks were the order of the day. To sanction such use of power runs the very great risk that by doing so we instill "a sense of disrespect for the criminal justice system" itself. *Ballenger*, 436 S.E. 2d at 796 (Blackburn, J. dissenting).

I would vacate the sentence and remand for re sentencing, instructing the district court that public humiliation or shaming has no proper place in our system of justice.

United States v. Gementera, 379 F.3d 596 (9th Cir. 2004)
(Hawkins, J., dissenting).

Note that the dissenting judge frames his objection in terms of "the majesty of a federal courtroom" and "disrespect for the criminal justice system"? Note also that the billboard was a condition of supervised release from federal prison, so (literally) an alternative to imprisonment, rather than as an independent punishment. Should this make a difference? Can treatment that is illegitimate on its own become legitimate if it is offered as an alternative to another, legitimate, sanction? Is (chemical, or even physical) castration of sexual offenders legitimate if it is offered as an alternative to imprisonment?

"Dignity" does not appear in the dissent, nor anywhere in the majority opinion (except as part of the standard reference to "the dignity of man" as "[t]he basic concept underlying the Eighth Amendment."). Unlike in German constitutional law, which assigns pride of place (as does the German Basic Law) to the protection of dignity, the concept of dignity does not figure prominently in U.S. constitutional law in general, and the U.S. Supreme Court's Eighth Amendment jurisprudence in particular, despite the reflexive reference to dignity as the "basic concept underlying" the prohibition of "cruel and unusual punishments" in the Eighth Amendment to the U.S. Constitution.* Eighth Amendment analysis, if it has any bite in noncapital cases at all, instead focuses on a comparison between the challenged sentence and sentences imposed in other—relevantly similar—cases (to determine whether the sentence is not only cruel but also "unusual").[†]

7. In Germany, community service is not a common type of punishment. Prosecutors may allow offenders to substitute community service for payment of fines, and in the case of a suspended prison sentence the court can also require the offender to do community service, § 56b StGB. But there is no independent sanction that consists of community service alone. Proposals for such sanctions have been made, but a crucial constitutional question arises. Article 12, para. 2 Basic Law prohibits forced labor with the exception of duties imposed on everyone; Article 12 para. 3 Basic Law makes an exception for work during imprisonment.[‡]

B. Limits on Punishment

U.S. constitutional law draws an important distinction between constitutional limits on capital punishment and on non-capital punishment. The relevant constitutional provision here is the Eighth Amendment to the U.S. Constitution, which prohibits "cruel and unusual punishments." Much of modern Eighth Amendment jurisprudence has been concerned with the question whether capital punishment is unconstitutional *per se*, and if not, under what circumstances it could meet Eighth Amendment criteria. After a five-year moratorium on

---

* See generally James Q. Whitman, "The Two Western Cultures of Privacy: Dignity Versus Liberty," 113 *Yale Law Journal* (2004), 1151.

† For further discussion of constitutional limitations on criminal law, see Chapters 1.B and 3.

‡ Compare this to the Thirteenth Amendment to the U.S. Constitution (1865), which is famous for abolishing slavery, but also contains a lesser known exception: "Neither slavery nor involuntary servitude, *except as a punishment for crime whereof the party shall have been duly convicted*, shall exist within the United States, or any place subject to their jurisdiction." (Emphasis added.) The association of imprisonment and slavery, and between prisoners and slaves, has a long history. See, e.g., *Ruffin v. Commonwealth*, 62 Va. 790 (1871) (imprisonment as civil death: "[The prisoner] is for the time being the slave of the State. He is *civiliter mortuus*; and his estate, if he has any, is administered like that of a dead man."); see also Cesare Beccaria, *Of Crimes and Punishments* (1764), 16, 30.

capital punishment, the U.S. Supreme Court, in *Furman v. Georgia*,* struck down all existing state and federal death penalty statutes. *Furman* did not produce a majority opinion setting out the Court's rationale; instead each Justice wrote a separate opinion. Three of the Justices in the 5-4 majority raised concerns about arbitrariness; only two (Brennan and Marshall) found the death penalty unconstitutional *per se*. In the years after *Furman*, dozens of states set out to craft capital punishment schemes that would address the arbitrariness concerns raised in *Furman*, setting the stage for *Gregg v. Georgia* and its companion cases in 1976 (*Proffitt v. Florida*, *Jurek v. Texas*, *Woodson v. North Carolina*, and *Roberts v. Louisiana*).

While the U.S. Supreme Court, after *Gregg*, got into the business of subjecting the procedure for the imposition of capital punishment and even, though to a lesser extent, the substantive law of capital murder,† to constitutional scrutiny, it lavished considerably less attention on noncapital sentences. Only recently did the Court show a willingness to scrutinize sentences of imprisonment under the Eighth Amendment, which as a general matter were previously thought to fall within the states' sovereign authority to develop their criminal law as they saw fit. Currently, the Supreme Court appears to have settled on a narrow proportionality requirement for noncapital sentences, illustrated in *United States v. Angelos*, excerpted in Chapter 1.B.ii.

The German case addressing the constitutionality of life imprisonment *per se* parallels *Gregg v. Georgia* insofar as it concerns a qualitatively different, and more serious, punishment: mandatory life imprisonment. Yet, at the same time, it also differs significantly from *Gregg* in that it deals with a noncapital sentence, which under U.S. law would be subject at best to a narrow proportionality analysis. There is no doubt, then, that the mandatory life imprisonment at issue in the German case would pass constitutional muster in the U.S. Note simply that the case, which is usually cited as the origin of the narrow proportionality analysis in noncapital cases, *Harmelin v. Michigan*, 501 U.S. 957 (1991) (in a concurring opinion by Justice Kennedy), considered—and, by a 5-4 vote, affirmed—the constitutionality of a mandatory sentence of life imprisonment without the possibility of parole for simple possession of "650 grams or more" of cocaine. Compare this sentence to that in the German case: mandatory life imprisonment with the possibility of parole for murder with base motives. In the U.S., given the existence of capital punishment, this sentence for murder would be held up, also and especially by death penalty opponents, as an example of constitutional punishment.

We shift gears at the end of this Section to throw light on a central distinction in the German law of punishment, between punitive and non-punitive sanctions, between punishments and "measures." This distinction lies at the heart of the German two-track sanction system of backward-looking, guilt-based punishment and forward-looking, dangerousness-based preventive detention. The two-track system is interesting in its own right, from a theoretical and historical perspective, as it tests the boundaries of the concept of punishment. More particularly, it also tests the boundaries of constitutional scrutiny, insofar as constitutional constraints that apply to punishment, narrowly speaking, may not apply to non-punitive sanctions. From a comparative perspective, the German two-track system is worth a closer look because there is nothing quite like it in American criminal law.

i. Ultimate sanctions: death and life imprisonment (quality)

Gregg v. Georgia
United States Supreme Court
428 U.S. 153 (1976)

[U]ntil Furman v. Georgia, 408 U.S. 238, 92 S.Ct. 2726, 33 L.Ed.2d 346 (1972), the Court never confronted squarely the fundamental claim that the punishment of death always, regardless of the enormity of the offense or the procedure followed in imposing the sentence, is cruel and unusual

---

* *Furman v. Georgia*, 408 U.S. 238 (1972).
† See Chapter 15.

punishment in violation of the Constitution. Although this issue was presented and addressed in Furman, it was not resolved by the Court. Four Justices would have held that capital punishment is not unconstitutional per se; two Justices would have reached the opposite conclusion; and three Justices, while agreeing that the statutes then before the Court were invalid as applied, left open the question whether such punishment may ever be imposed. We now hold that the punishment of death does not invariably violate the Constitution.

The history of the prohibition of "cruel and unusual" punishment already has been reviewed at length. The phrase first appeared in the English Bill of Rights of 1689, which was drafted by Parliament at the accession of William and Mary. See Granucci, "Nor Cruel and Unusual Punishments Inflicted: The Original Meaning," 57 Calif. L. Rev. 839, 852–853 (1969). The English version appears to have been directed against punishments unauthorized by statute and beyond the jurisdiction of the sentencing court, as well as those disproportionate to the offense involved. The American draftsmen, who adopted the English phrasing in drafting the Eighth Amendment, were primarily concerned, however, with proscribing " 'tortures' and other 'barbarous' methods of punishment."

In the earliest cases raising Eighth Amendment claims, the Court focused on particular methods of execution to determine whether they were too cruel to pass constitutional muster. The constitutionality of the sentence of death itself was not at issue, and the criterion used to evaluate the mode of execution was its similarity to "torture" and other "barbarous" methods. See Louisiana ex rel. Francis v. Resweber, 329 U.S. 459, 464, 67 S.Ct. 374, 376, 91 L.Ed. 422 (1947) (second attempt at electrocution found not to violate Eighth Amendment, since failure of initial execution attempt was "an unforeseeable accident" and "(t)here was no purpose to inflict unnecessary pain nor any unnecessary pain involved in the proposed execution").

But the Court has not confined the prohibition embodied in the Eighth Amendment to "barbarous" methods that were generally outlawed in the 18th century. Instead, the Amendment has been interpreted in a flexible and dynamic manner. . . . As Mr. Chief Justice Warren said, in an oft-quoted phrase, "(t)he Amendment must draw its meaning from the evolving standards of decency that mark the progress of a maturing society." Trop v. Dulles, 356 U.S. 86, 101, 78 S.Ct. 590, 598, 2 L.Ed.2d 630 (1958). Thus, an assessment of contemporary values concerning the infliction of a challenged sanction is relevant to the application of the Eighth Amendment. . . . [T]his assessment does not call for a subjective judgment. It requires, rather, that we look to objective indicia that reflect the public attitude toward a given sanction.

But our cases also make clear that public perceptions of standards of decency with respect to criminal sanctions are not conclusive. A penalty also must accord with "the dignity of man," which is the "basic concept underlying the Eighth Amendment." Trop v. Dulles, 356 U.S., at 100, 78 S.Ct., at 597 (plurality opinion). This means, at least, that the punishment not be "excessive." When a form of punishment in the abstract (in this case, whether capital punishment may ever be imposed as a sanction for murder) rather than in the particular (the propriety of death as a penalty to be applied to a specific defendant for a specific crime) is under consideration, the inquiry into "excessiveness" has two aspects. First, the punishment must not involve the unnecessary and wanton infliction of pain. Second, the punishment must not be grossly out of proportion to the severity of the crime. . . .

[I]n assessing a punishment selected by a democratically elected legislature against the constitutional measure, we presume its validity. We may not require the legislature to select the least severe penalty possible so long as the penalty selected is not cruelly inhumane or disproportionate to the crime involved. And a heavy burden rests on those who would attack the judgment of the representatives of the people.

This is true in part because the constitutional test is intertwined with an assessment of contemporary standards and the legislative judgment weighs heavily in ascertaining such standards. "[I]n a democratic society legislatures, not courts, are constituted to respond to the will and consequently the moral values of the people." Furman v. Georgia, 408 U.S., at 383 (Burger, C.J., dissenting). The deference we owe to the decisions of the state legislatures under our federal system is enhanced where the specification of punishments is concerned, for "these are peculiarly questions of legislative policy." Gore v. United States, 357 U.S. 386, 393 (1958). . . .

In the discussion to this point we have sought to identify the principles and considerations that guide a court in addressing an Eighth Amendment claim. We now consider specifically whether the sentence of death for the crime of murder is a per se violation of the Eighth and Fourteenth Amendments to the Constitution. We note first that history and precedent strongly support a negative answer to this question.

The imposition of the death penalty for the crime of murder has a long history of acceptance both in the United States and in England. The common-law rule imposed a mandatory death sentence on all convicted murderers. And the penalty continued to be used into the 20th century by most American States, although the breadth of the common-law rule was diminished, initially by narrowing the class of murders to be punished by death and subsequently by widespread adoption of laws expressly granting juries the discretion to recommend mercy.

It is apparent from the text of the Constitution itself that the existence of capital punishment was accepted by the Framers. At the time the Eighth Amendment was ratified, capital punishment was a common sanction in every State. Indeed, the First Congress of the United States enacted legislation providing death as the penalty for specified crimes. C. 9, 1 Stat. 112 (1790). The Fifth Amendment, adopted at the same time as the Eighth, contemplated the continued existence of the capital sanction by imposing certain limits on the prosecution of capital cases:

> No person shall be held to answer for a capital, or otherwise infamous crime, unless on a presentment or indictment of a Grand Jury . . . ; nor shall any person be subject for the same offense to be twice put in jeopardy of life or limb; . . . nor be deprived of life, liberty, or property, without due process of law. . . .

And the Fourteenth Amendment, adopted over three-quarters of a century later, similarly contemplates the existence of the capital sanction in providing that no State shall deprive any person of "life, liberty, or property" without due process of law . . .

Four years ago, the petitioners in Furman and its companion cases predicated their argument primarily upon the asserted proposition that standards of decency had evolved to the point where capital punishment no longer could be tolerated. The petitioners in those cases said, in effect, that the evolutionary process had come to an end, and that standards of decency required that the Eighth Amendment be construed finally as prohibiting capital punishment for any crime regardless of its depravity and impact on society. This view was accepted by two Justices. Three other Justices were unwilling to go so far; focusing on the procedures by which convicted defendants were selected for the death penalty rather than on the actual punishment inflicted, they joined in the conclusion that the statutes before the Court were constitutionally invalid.

The petitioners in the capital cases before the Court today renew the "standards of decency" argument, but developments during the four years since Furman have undercut substantially the assumptions upon which their argument rested. Despite the continuing debate, dating back to the 19th century, over the morality and utility of capital punishment, it is now evident that a large proportion of American society continues to regard it as an appropriate and necessary criminal sanction.

The most marked indication of society's endorsement of the death penalty for murder is the legislative response to Furman. The legislatures of at least 35 States have enacted new statutes that provide for the death penalty for at least some crimes that result in the death of another person. . . . [A]ll of the post-Furman Statutes make clear that capital punishment itself has not been rejected by the elected representatives of the people.

The jury also is a significant and reliable objective index of contemporary values because it is so directly involved. The Court has said that "one of the most important functions any jury can perform in making . . . a selection (between life imprisonment and death for a defendant convicted in a capital case) is to maintain a link between contemporary community values and the penal system." Witherspoon v. Illinois, 391 U.S. 510, 519 n.15 (1968). It may be true that evolving standards have influenced juries in recent decades to be more discriminating in imposing the sentence of death. But the relative infrequency of jury verdicts imposing the death sentence does not indicate rejection of capital punishment per se. Rather, the reluctance of juries in many cases to impose the sentence may well reflect the humane feeling that this most irrevocable of sanctions should be reserved for a small number of extreme cases. Indeed, the actions of juries in many States since Furman are fully compatible with the legislative judgments, reflected in the new statutes, as to the continued utility and necessity of capital punishment in appropriate cases. At the close of 1974 at least 254 persons had been sentenced to death since Furman, and by the end of March 1976, more than 460 persons were subject to death sentences.

As we have seen, however, the Eighth Amendment demands more than that a challenged punishment be acceptable to contemporary society. The Court also must ask whether it comports with the basic concept of human dignity at the core of the Amendment. Trop v. Dulles, 356 U.S., at 100, 78 S.Ct., at 597 (plurality opinion). Although we cannot "invalidate a category of penalties because we deem less severe penalties adequate to serve the ends of penology," Furman v. Georgia, 408 U.S., at 451 (Powell, J., dissenting) the sanction imposed cannot be so totally without penological justification that it results in the gratuitous infliction of suffering.

The death penalty is said to serve two principal social purposes: retribution and deterrence of capital crimes by prospective offenders.[28] In part, capital punishment is an expression of society's moral outrage at particularly offensive conduct. This function may be unappealing to many, but it is essential in an ordered society that asks its citizens to rely on legal processes rather than self-help to vindicate their wrongs.

---

[28] Another purpose that has been discussed is the incapacitation of dangerous criminals and the consequent prevention of crimes that they may otherwise commit in the future.

[Retribution is not] a forbidden objective nor one inconsistent with our respect for the dignity of men. Indeed, the decision that capital punishment may be the appropriate sanction in extreme cases is an expression of the community's belief that certain crimes are themselves so grievous an affront to humanity that the only adequate response may be the penalty of death.

Statistical attempts to evaluate the worth of the death penalty as a deterrent to crimes by potential offenders have occasioned a great deal of debate. The results simply have been inconclusive. As one opponent of capital punishment has said:

(A)fter all possible inquiry, including the probing of all possible methods of inquiry, we do not know, and for systematic and easily visible reasons cannot know, what the truth about this "deterrent" effect may be....

The inescapable flaw is . . . that social conditions in any state are not constant through time, and that social conditions are not the same in any two states. If an effect were observed (and the observed effects, one way or another, are not large) then one could not at all tell whether any of this effect is attributable to the presence or absence of capital punishment. A "scientific" that is to say, a soundly based conclusion is simply impossible, and no methodological path out of this tangle suggests itself.

C. Black, Capital Punishment: The Inevitability of Caprice and Mistake 25–26 (1974).

Although some of the studies suggest that the death penalty may not function as a significantly greater deterrent than lesser penalties, there is no convincing empirical evidence either supporting or refuting this view. We may nevertheless assume safely that there are murderers, such as those who act in passion, for whom the threat of death has little or no deterrent effect. But for many others, the death penalty undoubtedly is a significant deterrent. There are carefully contemplated murders, such as murder for hire, where the possible penalty of death may well enter into the cold calculus that precedes the decision to act. And there are some categories of murder, such as murder by a life prisoner, where other sanctions may not be adequate.

The value of capital punishment as a deterrent of crime is a complex factual issue the resolution of which properly rests with the legislatures, which can evaluate the results of statistical studies in terms of their own local conditions and with a flexibility of approach that is not available to the courts. Indeed, many of the post-Furman statutes reflect just such a responsible effort to define those crimes and those criminals for which capital punishment is most probably an effective deterrent.

In sum, we cannot say that the judgment of the Georgia Legislature that capital punishment may be necessary in some cases is clearly wrong. Considerations of federalism, as well as respect for the ability of a legislature to evaluate, in terms of its particular State, the moral consensus concerning the death penalty and its social utility as a sanction, require us to conclude, in the absence of more convincing evidence, that the infliction of death as a punishment for murder is not without justification and thus is not unconstitutionally severe.

Finally, we must consider whether the punishment of death is disproportionate in relation to the crime for which it is imposed. There is no question that death as a punishment is unique in its severity and irrevocability. When a defendant's life is at stake, the Court has been particularly sensitive to insure that every safeguard is observed. But we are concerned here only with the imposition of capital punishment for the crime of murder, and when a life has been taken deliberately by the offender,[35] we cannot say that the punishment is invariably disproportionate to the crime. It is an extreme sanction, suitable to the most extreme of crimes. We hold that the death penalty is not a form of punishment that may never be imposed, regardless of the circumstances of the offense, regardless of the character of the offender, and regardless of the procedure followed in reaching the decision to impose it.

German Federal Constitutional Court
BVerfGE 45, 187 (June 21, 1977)
Life Imprisonment Case

A.

The subject matter of the proceedings is the question of whether life imprisonment for a murderer who commits his crime insidiously or in order to conceal another crime is compatible with the Basic Law.

---

[35] We do not address here the question whether the taking of the criminal's life is a proportionate sanction where no victim has been deprived of life for example, when capital punishment is imposed for rape, kidnaping, or armed robbery that does not result in the death of any human being.

Facts

The regional court of Verden has suspended criminal proceedings and in accordance with art. 100 para. 1 Basic Law referred to the Federal Constitutional Court for decision the question of whether § 211 para. 1 Criminal Code is unconstitutional in so far as it determines that murder is punishable by life imprisonment.

1. The charge and the initial decision in the original proceedings accuse the defendant Detlev R., who is a 31-year-old Berlin police officer that on the night of May 13, 1973 in Nienburg / Weser* he murdered the 22-year-old drug addict Günter L. The outcome of the main proceedings so far is that the lay assessor's court found the defendant guilty of murder. It has in essence established the following facts:

The defendant had dealt in drugs for a long time. He was sentenced to five years and six months imprisonment for drug dealing concomitantly with tax offenses by a legally effective judgment of the regional court of Verden on March 5, 1976. At the end of April 1973 the defendant became acquainted with the drug addict Günter L. through a Turkish intermediary in Nienburg. He sold him morphine base in return for cash. As the defendant wanted to transfer his drug dealing to West Germany, he travelled to Nienburg again a few days later, and gave L. morphine base to sell on commission. L. was to pay 1000 DM to the defendant for this. However, on a police search of L's home the majority of the drugs were seized, so he was short of drugs. In order to force the defendant to supply him with drugs again, in spite of the morphine base not having been paid for, he telephoned the defendant in Berlin, and threatened to report him to the police if he did not provide more drugs. As a result of this the defendant decided to travel to Nienburg and shoot L.; in this way he intended to prevent the threatened accusation and continuing blackmail by L. At the same time he lulled him into a sense of false security by promising him over the telephone to supply morphine base. The defendant drove to Nienburg in the night of May 13, 1973 together with the Turk, and gave L. the promised morphine base at his home. L. wanted immediately to prepare some "Berliner Tinke" from this for an injection. Whilst the Turk went into the kitchen with him, the defendant waited in the living room. When L. was sitting with his back to the door in the kitchen and was in the course of preparing the injection, the defendant approached L., who was distracted by the injection, from behind and fired three shots at his head from a distance of half a meter. All the shots met their mark and Günter L. died instantly.

2. The regional court of Verden states that if § 211 para. 1 Criminal Code was compatible with the Constitution, the defendant should be sentenced to life imprisonment. However, if the norm was unconstitutional, a fixed term imprisonment of fifteen years at the most (§ 38 para. 2 Criminal Code) would fall to be considered.

3. The regional court holds the norm referred for examination to be incompatible with art. 1, art. 2 para. 2 sentence 2 in combination art. 19 para. 2 and further with art. 3 para 1 Basic Law. It explains its reasoning as follows: Scientific investigations about personality changes in imprisonment had confirmed that lengthy deprivation of freedom caused harm to the personality. After a period of detention of ten, fifteen, twenty or in any case twenty-five years, the stage would be reached in practice with every prisoner in which the abatement of good feelings, resignation, apathy and indifference would cause a change in personality that would end in unsuitability for life, sophistry about innocence, and pre-senile delusions about pardon, and frequently stupefaction. After about twenty years' stay in prison the prisoner would become physically and mentally no more than a wreck. In agreement with the Prison Commission, the legislator had therefore refused to prescribe a maximum term of more than fifteen years for a fixed term of imprisonment, as a longer period was not defensible either for protection of legal goods or from the aspect of resocialization. The criminal's final exclusion from society by life imprisonment, and his psychological destruction associated with it, violated the duty set for the legislature in art. 1 Basic Law to have regard to human dignity to which every human being, even the common criminal, is entitled . . .

Reasons

B.

The reference is permissible. . . .

C.

§ 211 Criminal Code is compatible with the Basic Law in the scope to be examined here according to the following observations and in the restrictive interpretation that arises from these.

[* A medium-sized county seat halfway between Hannover and Bremen.—Eds.]

I.

1. Life imprisonment represents an extraordinarily severe invasion of the basic rights of the person affected. Freedom of the person, which art. 2 para. 2 sentence 2 Basic Law guarantees as inviolable, is taken away on a permanent basis by this punishment, which stands at the summit of the catalogue of punishments in current criminal law. The verdict "lifelong" in the strict sense means the final exclusion of the criminal from the society of free citizens. Not only is the basic right under art. 2 para. 2 sentence 2 Basic Law restricted by the implementation of life imprisonment, but there are— depending on the situation in the individual case—also numerous other basic rights guaranteed in the Constitution that are affected. This makes the weight and significance of the constitutional law problem clear.

It is true that the right to personal freedom in accordance with art. 2 para. 2 sentence 3 Basic Law can be curtailed on the basis of a statute. The legislative freedom of formulation is, however, limited in several ways by the Constitution. The legislature must in exercising the power given to it have regard to the inviolability of human dignity (art. 1 para. 1 Basic Law), the highest principle of the constitutional order, and further constitutional norms, in particular the requirement of equality (art. 3 para. 1 Basic Law) and the requirement of the constitutional and social state (art. 20 para. 1 Basic Law). If the freedom of the person is such an elevated legal good that it may only be limited on especially important grounds (BVerfGE 22, 180 [219]), the lifelong deprivation of this freedom needs an especially strict examination against the standard of the proportionality principle.

Within these boundaries there remains room for legislative decision-making. Life imprisonment, from the point of view of the role of criminal law in modern society, raises a string of questions about legal and criminal policy. The resolution of these falls on the legislature. It has so far decided in favor of the retention of life imprisonment for the most serious crimes. The Federal Constitutional Court only can, within the framework of this reference, examine whether this decision is compatible with the Constitution.

2. Since time immemorial life imprisonment has belonged to the core stock of criminal law sanctions. Its significance was, however, smaller, in comparison to the present time, because the death penalty headed the list of punishments. The dispute over the death penalty made "life" the alternative, and the permissibility of "life" in constitutional law was not generally called into question. There is nevertheless a not insignificant older literature that concerned itself rather thoroughly with the effect of lifelong deprivation of freedom on the human personality and its consequences (see M. Liepmann, Die Todesstrafe (The Death Penalty), Berlin 1912, Gutachten für den 31. Deutschen Juristentag). It was a popular argument with supporters of the death penalty that life imprisonment was crueler and less humane ("agony without end") than the death penalty ("end by agony"). Only after the arguments about the death penalty had subsided did the academic community begin towards the end of the 1960s to concern itself with the problem of lifelong deprivation of freedom again. Since then the discussion about this maximum penalty is no longer fragmentary. In this connection a prominent feature is that the argument in the academic literature in recent years has become continually more vigorous, but the case law on the other hand has as good as not concerned itself with the problems raised thereby at all, until the reference from the regional court of Verden. The criminal courts have assumed the permissibility in constitutional law of life imprisonment without further discussion until recent times. . . .

II.

1. Regard for and protection of human dignity are constitutional principles of the Basic Law. The free human personality and its dignity represent the highest legal value within the constitutional order (see BVerfGE 6, 32 [41]; 27, 1 [6]; 30, 173 [193]; 32, 98 [108]). The duty is imposed on state power in all forms of its manifestation to have regard to and to protect the dignity of the human being.

This is based on the idea of the human being as a spiritual and moral being, intended for self-determination and self-development in freedom. The Basic Law understands this freedom not as that of an isolated and autocratic individual but as of one who is related to and tied to society (see BVerfGE 33, 303 [334] with further references). In view of this commitment to society the freedom cannot be "unlimited in principle." The individual must accept those limits of his freedom of action which the legislature draws for the cultivation and furtherance of social communal life within the limits of what is generally reasonable in relation to the given facts; the independence of the person must however be preserved (BVerfGE 30, 1 [20]—eavesdropping case). This means that even within society each individual must in principle be recognized as a member with equal rights and an intrinsic value. It therefore contradicts human dignity to make a human being a mere object within the State (see BVerfGE 27, 1 [6] with further references). The maxim "a human being must always remain a goal in himself" applies without restriction for all areas of law, because the dignity of the human being as a person, which cannot be lost, consists in the fact that he continues to be recognized as a self-responsible personality.

In the area of criminal justice in which the highest requirements are placed upon justice, art. 1 para. 1 Basic Law determines the conception of the nature of punishment and the relationship of guilt and expiation. The principle *nulla poena sine culpa* has the status of a constitutional principle (BVerfGE 20, 323 [331]). Every punishment must have a just relationship to the seriousness of the crime and to the guilt of the perpetrator (BVerfGE 6, 389 [439]; 9, 167 [169]; 20, 323 [331]; 25, 269 [285 f.]). The requirement to have regard to human dignity means in particular that cruel, inhuman and demeaning punishments are forbidden (BVerfGE 1, 332 [348]; 6, 389 [439]). The perpetrator ought not to be made a mere object of the battle against crime in such a way as to violate his claim to social value and regard that is protected in constitutional law (BVerfGE 28, 389 [391]). The fundamental prerequisites of individual and social existence of human beings must be maintained. The duty of the state to provide the minimum requirements for livelihood that contribute to an existence worthy of a human being is therefore derived from art. 1 para. 1 Basic Law in combination with the social state principle—and that applies in particular for the implementation of punishment. It would be incompatible with human dignity understood in this way if the State were to claim for itself the right to strip human beings of their freedom by force without them at least having the chance of being able to obtain freedom again.

For all that, it must not be forgotten that human dignity is something inalienable. The knowledge of what the requirement to have regard to it demands cannot however be separated from historical developments. The history of the administration of criminal justice shows clearly that the cruelest punishments have continually been replaced by milder punishments. Progress from the more brutal to the more humane, from the more simple to the more differentiated forms of punishment has continued and in this connection the path that is still to be covered can be recognized. A judgment on what corresponds to human dignity can therefore only be based on the current state of knowledge and no claim can be made to timeless validity.

2. If the content and effects of life imprisonment are tested according to these standards, it follows that there is no violation of art. 1 para. 1 Basic Law.

a) The regional court bases violation of human dignity chiefly on the reference to scientific investigations of personality changes during imprisonment and prison experience that on a lengthy deprivation of freedom consequences damaging to the personality arise, which, "after a period of detention, assessed variously at 10, 15, 20 or in any case 25 years, reach a stage with practically every prisoner in which the abatement of good feelings, resignation, apathy and indifference cause a change in personality that ends in unsuitability for life, sophistry about innocence, and presenile delusions about pardon; and frequently stupefaction."

The regional court did not carry out its own surveys on this question. If the literature that is described by the court or otherwise pertinent is examined, substantial doubts arise as to whether the evidence quoted for the harmful effects asserted in respect of life imprisonment is underpinned methodically and objectively in such a way that conclusions in constitutional law can be derived from it in order to assess the legislature's decision. It is noticeable in particular that few authors can rely on their own investigations. Many assertions are ultimately based on the opinion of M. Liepmann for the 31st German Jurists Conference in 1912. . . . The results of Liepmann's investigation are based on extensive findings and the analysis of information about more than 2000 life prisoners from various European countries as well as on preliminary work of other academics. The opinion accordingly doubtless represents a well-founded investigation of the effects of life imprisonment. It must however be borne in mind that the implementation of prison sentences at the beginning of this century cannot be compared to the present-day circumstances in prisons in the Federal Republic. Even if the buildings of numerous prisons may originate from this period, the decisive factor is the treatment of prisoners in them in day-to-day life. It is precisely in this respect that fundamental alterations have occurred through the change from mere "detention" to "treatment," even though much may still need to be improved. . . .

Views in the more recent literature about the consequences of detention in cases of life imprisonment show a very broad spectrum. They stretch from assertion of severe personality changes to description of successful resocialization of the vast majority of prisoners after their discretionary release. . . . Even where occurrence of harm in the case of long-term prisoners is confirmed in principle, opinions differ strongly about the point in time from which permanent personality damage to the prisoners has to be reckoned with. . . .

b) Even the hearing of evidence that occurred in these proceedings did not lead to an unambiguous conclusion. The experts who gave evidence at the oral hearing on the question of harm caused by life imprisonment came to similarly varied conclusions, like those already to be gleaned from the literature. Professors Dr. Dr. Bressner and Dr. Rasch—both psychiatrists—were in the end result united in their testimony, in spite of substantially differing investigation methods, that their investigations did not reveal that life imprisonment as a rule caused irreparable damage to the personality or to the health of the prisoners....On the other hand the experts Dr. (Mrs.) Einsele and Dr. Stark—both prison practitioners—agreed on substantial points in explaining that according to their experiences substantial damage of a physical as well as of a psychological and mental kind arose after a certain period of detention and that this could scarcely be remedied.

It is not a matter for the Federal Constitutional Court to decide on how such differing assessments can be reached....It must further be borne in mind that the experiences on which the experts' statements are based are proportionately small according to their own admissions. Sufficient experience about the effects of life imprisonment cannot be available because as a rule early release ensues, and the hope of this release could have influenced the development of the prisoner. The differing conditions of detention in the individual prisons can also have played a role. Important points of view can be asserted for both standpoints. But the difficulty consists in the fact that at present neither is verifiable by sufficiently reliable investigations....

c) In a situation of this kind, restraint is required in the examination by the Constitutional Court (see BVerfGE 37, 104 [118]; 43, 291 [347], with further references). It is true that the protection of the basic rights as against the legislature is transferred to the Federal Constitutional Court. The Court is not therefore bound to the legislature's view about the law in its examination. However, in so far as evaluations and factual assessments of the legislature are of importance here, the Court can in principle only disregard them if they are refutable. It might seem questionable that obscurities in the assessment of facts should operate to the disadvantage of the holder of a basic right. If the Federal Constitutional Court nevertheless denies an infringement of human dignity through possible harm resulting from detention, the following grounds are decisive for this:

aa) The threat of life imprisonment finds the complement it needs in constitutional law in meaningful treatment of prisoners. Prisons are obligated to work for the resocialization of prisoners, including those sentenced to life imprisonment, to maintain their ability to cope with life, and to combat harmful effects of the deprivation of freedom, and therefore also (and primarily) distorting changes to the personality...these tasks are fulfilled by prisons to the required extent, they make a fundamental contribution to combating threatened personality changes with prisoners.

Punishment in the Federal Republic is already no longer simple "detention"; the goal is now "treatment" directed at resocialization of prisoners. This also corresponds with the case law so far of the Federal Constitutional Court on questions of punishment. The Court has emphasized on a number of occasions that the requirement for resocialization corresponded in constitutional law to the self-image of a society that placed human dignity at the center, and was committed to the social state principle. This resocialization interest for the perpetrator arose from art. 2 para. 1 in combination with art. 1 Basic Law. The convicted perpetrator had to be given a chance to fit into the community again after serving his sentence (BVerfGE 35, 202 [235 f.]—Lebach; 36, 174 [188])...If it is assumed that even a person sentenced to life imprisonment must in principle be allowed a chance of being able to obtain his freedom again, then logically he must also have a claim to resocialization, even if he only has the prospect of preparing himself for life in freedom after serving a lengthy sentence (see on this the decision BVerfGE 40, 276 [284], which concerned a murderer sentenced to life imprisonment).

The Prison Act (StVollzG) of 16 March 1976 (BGBl I p. 581) takes account of these requirements for punishment in conformance with the Constitution. The goal is described in § 2 sentence 1 StVollzG Act as being that the prisoner should be capable of leading a life of social responsibility without crime in the future. According to § 2 sentence 2 StVollzG, implementation of punishment also serves to protect the general public from further crimes. At the same time life in detention should as far as possible be brought into line with the general circumstances of life. Harmful consequences of the deprivation of freedom must be counteracted—....The Act incorporates life imprisonment in this, and assumes that the carrying out of this sentence ought not to isolate the prisoner more severely than is necessary for the implementation of imprisonment and treatment of the prisoner. The prisoner should remain able to cope with life to such an extent that he can come to terms with normal life again if he is released from detention....

bb) According to the findings made, serving the full sentence of life imprisonment is a rare exception. People who are sentenced to life imprisonment—except in a few cases in which the social prognosis is unfavorable, and further implementation of the sentence is required on grounds of public security—are released early by way of reprieve. This creates a further fundamental restriction to the risk of serious personality alterations. The established practice of reprieve in the federal states over a period of thirty years shows that out of the 702 released prisoners only a few (48) were reprieved before ten years and also only a few (27) after an extreme length of detention of up to thirty years. The majority of reprieves takes place between the fifteenth and the twenty-fifth year of detention. On average the length of detention is approximately twenty years....

III.

We agree with the referring court that the present state of the law according to which life imprisonment can only be suspended or remitted by way of reprieve gives rise to doubts based on the principle of the constitutional state. The constitutional state principle requires legal regulation of the practice of reprieve.

The right of reprieve belongs to the President of the Federal Republic, to the First Ministers in the states, to the Council of Ministers in Saarland, and to the Senates in the city states. This amounts to a diverse treatment of the right of reprieve. In particular, it leads to convicted persons in the individual federal states needing to have served terms of differing length before they can expect release from life imprisonment by way of reprieve. Thus according to communications from the states the average length of sentence in the period from May 8, 1945 to December 31, 1975 was about sixteen years in Hamburg, seventeen and a half years in Berlin, around eighteen years in Baden-Württemberg, between twenty and twenty-one years in Bayern, Bremen, Hessen, Niedersachsen, Saarland und Schleswig-Holstein, between twenty-one and twenty-two years in Nordrhein-Westfalen and something over twenty-two years in Rheinland-Pfalz....

On examination of the constitutionality of life imprisonment, it has appeared, in particular from the viewpoint of art. 1 para. 1 Basic Law and the constitutional state principle, that implementation of such imprisonment in accordance with human dignity is only ensured if the convicted person has a concrete chance, which can also in principle be realized, of being able to obtain his freedom again at a later point in time. This is because the core of human dignity is affected when the convicted person has to give up any hope of winning his freedom once more, regardless of the development of his personality. The institution of reprieve on its own is not enough to ensure this prospect (which is the only thing that makes implementation of life imprisonment in accordance with the understanding of the personal dignity endurable) in a manner that corresponds with constitutional law requirements.... The practice of the States in relation to reprieve admittedly reveals considerable care in the preparation of the reprieve decisions. However, substantial differences exist in the procedure and the determination of the time of release, without the grounds for this being available for examination....

On the facts present here, which concern a decision about a serious question of existential significance for the person affected, the principle of legal certainty as well as the requirement for substantive justice demand that the prerequisites under which life imprisonment can be suspended and the procedure to be applicable are regulated by statute....

Whether early release should be orientated exclusively towards a favorable social prognosis and a certain minimum term served is another question.... Consideration could, for instance, be given to taking also into account the degree of wrong and guilt in the murder in question when establishing the point in time for release. A possibility of differentiation in this manner could do justice to the special character of the individual case in question. It is the task of the legislature to find a meaningful regime here.... From the above considerations, it follows that the legislature has a duty in constitutional law to introduce an appropriate statutory regime....

IV.

If the legislature regards life imprisonment as a necessary and reasonable sanction for the worst kind of crimes against life, this does not violate the constitutional law requirement of sensible and moderate punishment.

1....*

2. The referring court states that life imprisonment was not justified according to the purposes of punishment recognized by the Federal Constitutional Court. It did not have the deterrent effect assumed by the legislature, it was superfluous in most cases as a safeguard against possible recidivists, and it contradicted the claim to resocialization based on constitutional law. It was also not appropriate for expiation and retribution.

This view cannot be acceded to. An examination according to the standard of the purposes of punishment recognized by the Federal Constitutional Court, and corresponding in essence to the prevailing unification theory, reveals instead that life imprisonment, as a sanction for the most serious crimes against life, fulfills an important function for the protection of human life as an outstanding legal good. It corresponds with the concepts of values existing in the population today, and at the same time proclaims a negative value judgment that inculcates deeper awareness. This sanction is not in any way inconsistent with a later resocialization of murderers who are not in danger of relapse,

[* This section, concerning the purposes of punishment in general, is excerpted in Chapter 1.A.i.—Eds.]

and corresponds to the punishment functions of settlement for culpability and expiation. When seen as a whole, life imprisonment for murder is not therefore a senseless punishment.

a) If the chief goal of punishment is to preserve society from socially harmful behavior and to protect the fundamental values of communal life ("common general prevention"), it is necessary first to proceed on the basis of the value of the violated legal good and the extent of social harmfulness of the violating act—in comparison also with other acts subjected to punishment—when carrying out the overall survey that is required here. The life of every individual human being is included in the highest legal goods. The duty of the state to protect it arises directly from art. 2 para. 2 sentence 1 Basic Law. Besides this it follows from the provisions of art. 1 para. 1 sentence 2 Basic Law. If the legislature imposes the most severe sanction at its command for especially reprehensible violations of this highest legal good (described with the traditional concept of "murder"), this cannot be objected to—at any rate as a starting point—on constitutional law grounds.

Admittedly the general preventive effect of life imprisonment for murder is evaluated in very varied ways. See Röhl, Über die lebenslange Freiheitsstrafe, Berlin 1969, p. 201 ff. A distinction must be made between the negative and positive aspects of general prevention here, as the experts, in agreement with the relevant criminological and criminal law literature, have explained.

aa) The negative viewpoints are traditionally described with the concept of deterrence of others who are in danger of committing similar crimes ("special general prevention" See BGHSt 24, 40 [44]). On this issue the experts have unanimously stated that a deterrent effect of life imprisonment for murder could not be established for the potential circle of perpetrators. Admittedly, special studies are to a large extent lacking here. The general empirical investigations on the problem of deterrence are also, as was explained in the oral hearing, to be regarded with reservations as to their methodological reliability, capacity for generalization, and therefore meaningfulness.

Certainly a large proportion of murderers act in a conflict situation. However, it cannot be deduced from this alone that the threat of punishment in these cases is ineffectual. This is because even the perpetrator in a conflict case does not necessarily decide rashly, thoughtlessly or carelessly to remove the difficulties that exist by a murder. Even this perpetrator will rather consider various possibilities for resolution of the conflict situation, and only plan murder when he sees no other way out. It is precisely in this phase in which the potential murderer seeks a way out of his situation that the assessment of human life that exists in the general consciousness, and therefore the assessment of murder, can prevent him from carrying out the deed. Life imprisonment can even have a direct effect upon him so that he seeks for other solutions in order to avoid this punishment. The case is admittedly otherwise with compulsive or passionate perpetrators who as a rule do not carry out this kind of assessment and search for a way out. But even in this respect, as the criminal law practitioners who gave evidence have indicated, complete ineffectiveness of the threat of punishment cannot be assumed from the outset.

bb) The positive aspect of general prevention is generally seen in the maintenance and strengthening of confidence in the power of the legal order to survive and assert itself (see BGHSt 24, 40 [46]; 24, 64 ([66]; BGH GA 1976, p. 113 [114]). One of the purposes of punishment is to enforce the law against the wrong committed by the perpetrator, in order to demonstrate before the legal community the inviolability of the legal order and thus to strengthen the population's fidelity to the law. Admittedly there are so far no well-founded investigations of the effectiveness of this. Probably, in relation to the most serious crimes against life, effects that reduce crime cannot be measurably proved at all from a certain threat of punishment or punishment practice. On the other hand there are sufficiently certain grounds for saying that the threat and imposition of life imprisonment are of importance for the status attached to human life by the general public's sense of right and wrong. . . .

For this reason the objection that life imprisonment is not necessary for the purposes of general prevention is wrong. Admittedly, reference can be made to the fact that even at the time when the death penalty was still permissible, murders were committed, and that in the countries that do not recognize life imprisonment any more, no clear increase in capital crime has taken place. It is, however, an open question according to the present state of criminological research whether a thirty or twenty-five or even twenty year term of imprisonment could also achieve a sufficient general preventive effect. In this situation the legislature is keeping within the framework of its freedom of formulation if it not only limits itself to the negative aspects of general prevention but also attaches importance to the effects explained above of life imprisonment for the general public's sense of right and wrong, which would not follow from the threat of fixed term imprisonment.

b) The purpose of negative special prevention by the securing the individual perpetrator can be perfectly attained by his detention for the period of his life. But whether lifelong imprisonment is necessary on security grounds depends on the danger of relapse. It is, as appears from the survey of the states, small with murderers (about 5%), whilst the usual frequency of relapse is 50 to 80%. This circumstance makes the argument employed by the regional court appear well founded, that the purpose of securing the perpetrator does not on its own justify the imposition of life imprisonment for murder without exception. But regular sentencing of all murderers to life imprisonment at any rate ensures that the level of the punishment, and therefore the length of the detention, of murderers does not depend from the outset on the result of a long term criminal prognosis that is extraordinarily difficult and often also very uncertain. Otherwise there would be a greater risk that dangerous and violent criminals would attain freedom again after serving a fixed term of imprisonment on the basis of an incorrect prognosis. It must certainly not be overlooked that under the current regime even those murderers who could be released into freedom without risk to the general public after serving a certain term are sentenced to life imprisonment. This can, however, be corrected by the practice of release referred to above.

c) Taking into account the practice of reprieve so far and the required legal regulation of penal suspension proceedings, the imposition of life imprisonment does not contradict the resocialization concept, which is based on constitutional law (positive special prevention). The murderer sentenced to life imprisonment has the chance in principle to obtain his freedom again after serving a certain term. For him as well the resocialization goal secured by the Prison Act has a positive effect. It guarantees that on a later release he will still be able to cope with life and reintegrate. It is only with criminals who continue to be dangerous to the general public that the resocialization goal of criminal enforcement cannot be realized. That is however not based on the sentence of life imprisonment but on special personal circumstances of the convicted person concerned, which exclude successful resocialization on a permanent basis.

d) Finally, so far as the goals of settlement of culpability and expiation are concerned, it corresponds with the existing system of criminal sanctions that murder is punished with an especially high penalty because of the extreme wrongfulness and culpability of the act. This penalty is also in harmony with the general expectation of justice. It was logical for the legislature to threaten the highest penalty available to it for the destruction of human life in the especially reprehensible form of murder.

The expiation function of the penalty is admittedly vigorously disputed at a time when the concept of "*défense sociale*" is given a continually more prominent place. If the legislature still regards expiation as a legitimate purpose, then it can be guided by the fact that the criminal, in destroying a human life by murder, incurred a heavy burden of guilt, and his reintegration into the legal community presupposes that he will come to terms with guilt, and this also is facilitated by a very long sentence of imprisonment with the chance of early release.

The references to an alleged development in a different direction in other countries do not take matters any further. In most countries that have abolished the death penalty, a life sentence is still threatened as a sanction for the most serious crimes. The Italian Constitutional Court has expressly confirmed its compatibility with art. 27 para. 3 of the Italian Constitution in its decision of November 7/22 1974 (no. 264—Racc. Uff. Vol. XLII [1974], p. 353). The purpose and goal of the penalty was not only to reintegrate the criminal. Deterrence, prevention and social protection were permissible reasons for a penalty, to no lesser an extent than improvement.

German Basic Law*
(*Grundgesetz*, GG)

Art. 1

(1) Human dignity shall be inviolable. To respect and protect it shall be the duty of all state authority.
(2) The German people therefore acknowledge inviolable and inalienable human rights as the basis of every community, of peace and of justice in the world.
(3) The following basic rights shall bind the legislature, the executive, and the judiciary as directly applicable law.

Art. 2

(1) Every person shall have the right to free development of his personality insofar as he does not violate the rights of others or offend against the constitutional order or the moral law.

[* The German Constitution of May 23, 1949, BGBI 1.—Eds.]

(2) Every person shall have the right to life and physical integrity. Freedom of the person shall be inviolable. These rights may be interfered with only pursuant to a law.

Art. 102

Capital punishment is abolished.

German Prison Act
(*Strafvollzugsgesetz*, StVollzG)*

§ 2

During the execution of a prison sentence, the imprisoned person should learn to lead her future life in a socially responsible way, without committing further offenses (goal of imprisonment). The execution of a prison sentence also serves to protect the public against future offenses.

NOTES

1. Unlike the U.S. Constitution (and the European Convention on Human Rights (ECHR)), the text of the German Basic Law does not explicitly prohibit "cruel and unusual punishments" (or "inhuman or degrading treatment or punishment," in the ECHR's case). However, such a prohibition has been developed by the Federal Constitutional Court, following its standard practice of deducing unwritten principles from cornerstone provisions of the Basic Law, notably the guarantee that "human dignity shall be inviolable," in art. 1 para. 1. The U.S. Supreme Court has been considerably more reluctant to adopt a similarly flexible approach, instead generally insisting on hewing more closely to the constitutional text. Does this difference in general approach, and in textual foundation, affect the analysis of the constitutionality under German and U.S. law?

2. That art. 102 is part of the Basic Law does not necessarily mean that the death penalty could never be reintroduced in Germany. Changes of the Basic Law are in general possible; they require a two-thirds majority in the *Bundestag*, the Federal Parliament, and also in the *Bundesrat*, the Federal Council (representing the German states, or *Länder*).[†] However, art. 79 para. 3 prohibits changes that affect the principles in art. 1. Thus, the crucial constitutional question would be whether the death penalty is incompatible with human dignity. In the literature on this question, some come to the same result as the U.S. Supreme Court, arguing that the death penalty does not *per se* (that is, independent of the procedures involved and the mode of execution) violate the convicted person's human dignity. But the majority of German constitutional lawyers take the position that art. 1 para. 1 Basic Law would stand in the way of abolishing art. 102, even with two-thirds majorities in both houses. Under this view, art. 102 Basic Law may never be abolished. Who has the better of this argument? Is capital punishment compatible with human dignity, or is it not? Is it more, or less, compatible than, for instance, life imprisonment without the possibility of parole? How would one go about deciding this question, or about resolving differences of opinion? Does the answer depend on cultural, historical, political context? Is it possible that something violates "human dignity" in one legal system—say, the United States—but not in another—say, Germany? Or, within a given system, at one point in time, but not at another?

   On the history of the abolition of the death penalty in art. 102, see Richard J. Evans, *Rituals of Retribution: Capital Punishment in Germany, 1600–1987* (1996). Evans, in this exhaustive historical study of the German death penalty, found that at the deliberations over the Basic Law in 1948 the proposal to abolish capital punishment was raised by the leader of the far-right German Party (*Deutsche Partei*), at a time when opinion polls indicated that 77 percent

---

[* The federal Prison Act will be partly replaced by state statutes, due to a reform of the federalist system initiated in 2006.—Eds.]

[†] See Basic Law art. 79, para. 2.

of the West German population favored it. According to Evans, "only the hope of being able to save Nazi criminals from the gallows . . . persuaded conservative deputies from the German Party and the Christian Democrats to cast their votes in favor of abolition in sufficient numbers to secure its anchorage in the Basic Law."

3. Note that the German case concerning life imprisonment did not reach the Federal Constitutional Court because the offender, Detlef R., filed an appeal. Rather, the judges at the regional court made use of a provision in the Basic Law, art. 100 para. 1: if a court doubts whether the law to be applied is compatible with the Basic Law, it can refer this question to the Federal Constitutional Court. Note that, in the United States, constitutional questions also are not reserved for the U.S. Supreme Court (or, in the case of state constitutional law, for the highest state court), but may be—and, if properly raised, must be—addressed by any court.*

4. After the German Federal Constitutional Court's decision about life imprisonment, the German parliament responded to the Court's demand to regulate discharge from lifelong imprisonment by federal statute, rather than leaving this as a matter of mercy. Section 57a German Criminal Code now provides that those sentenced to life imprisonment be released on parole if the following three conditions are fulfilled: the offender has served 15 years, the offense was not particularly serious, and no strong countervailing security interests exist.

What, precisely, is wrong with leaving the decision about parole as a matter of mercy (or reprieve, or pardon)? The Court praises the care with which the responsible authorities in the various states discharged their obligation in these cases. What is added by passing a provision like § 57a? Does it make it more likely that inmates will be paroled? That officials denying parole will think more deeply about their decision, take into account other (better, more relevant) considerations or weigh these considerations more carefully, or appropriately, or sensitively? Is the underlying concern one about equality of treatment? But why is this a concern in these cases, in this particular question, at the back end of the penal process, and not in the much more common *ex ante* sentencing decision, where the exercise of unbridled judicial discretion does not attract similar attention in German criminal law? What is the difference, if any, between the reasons for constraining the discretion of officials who make decisions on parole in cases of life imprisonment, on the one hand, and the reasons for guiding the discretion of those who impose a criminal sentence, on the other? Or is this the German system's attempt to deal with the extraordinary case of a mandatory sentence, which contrasts so starkly with the wide sentencing discretion available in other cases? If so, would it not make more sense to address the issue directly, by eliminating the initial requirement of a life sentence? For a sustained critique of life imprisonment in a European context, see Dirk van Zyl Smit, *Taking Life Imprisonment Seriously in National and International Law* (2002).

5. The U.S. Sentencing Guidelines, discussed in Chapter 1.A.i, abolished parole altogether, to make sentencing determinate not only at the front end (by "guiding" judicial discretion) but also at the back end (by eliminating early release), all in the name of predictability. This goal was endorsed even by prisoners' rights advocates, who regarded indeterminate sentences that were subject to adjustment by prison officials as oppressive attempts to force inmates into compliance with prison regulations at best, and to wield power arbitrarily, and discriminatorily, at worst. Liberal reformers, presumably, did not envision the sentencing guidelines system that emerged in the end, which combined determinacy with severity. Why would a system that—like the U.S. one—gives prosecutors virtually unlimited discretion drastically constrain the discretion of other officials at later stages in the penal system? Conversely, why would a system that—like the German one—virtually eliminates prosecutorial discretion grant wide discretion to other officials at later stages in the penal system?

6. Do you find the courts' rejection of constitutional attacks on capital punishment and life imprisonment persuasive? What about moral or political objections? Do these considerations

---

* See the constitutional analysis of the application of a statute to a particular case by the federal district judge in *U.S. v. Angelos*, in Chapter 1.B.ii.

affect the constitutional legal analysis in these cases? Should they? Should murder (or some other crime, or crimes) receive a punishment that is qualitatively different than other crimes? Why? If so, will not this punishment be subject to the same objections that were raised to the punishments at issue in the two cases above? If so, is it possible to argue that murder *requires* capital punishment? Or that murder requires (legally, morally, politically?) some qualitatively more serious punishment than other crimes? Or would the quantitatively most serious punishment be enough?*

ii. Proportionality (quantity)

We now descend from the heights of constitutional scrutiny of the most serious, and qualitatively unique, punishment in American and German criminal law, to the constitutional constraints, if any, governing the imposition of a sentence along a quantitative spectrum, and along the spectrum of imprisonment in particular.

United States v. Angelos
U.S. District Court for the District of Utah
345 F. Supp. 2d 1227 (D. Utah 2004)

Paul G. Cassell, United States District Judge:

Defendant Weldon Angelos . . . is a twenty-four-year-old first offender who is a successful music executive with two young children. Because he was convicted of dealing marijuana and related offenses, both the government and the defense agree that Mr. Angelos should serve about six to eight years in prison. But there are three additional firearms offenses for which the court must also impose sentence. Two of those offenses occurred when Mr. Angelos carried a handgun to two $350 marijuana deals; the third when police found several additional handguns at his home when they executed a search warrant. For these three acts of possessing (not using or even displaying) these guns, the government insists that Mr. Angelos should essentially spend the rest of his life in prison. Specifically, the government urges the court to sentence Mr. Angelos to a prison term of no less than 61½ years—six years and a half (or more) for drug dealing followed by 55 years for three counts of possessing a firearm in connection with a drug offense. In support of its position, the government relies on a statute (18 U.S.C. § 924 (c) which requires the court to impose a sentence of five years in prison the first time a drug dealer carries a gun and twenty five years for each subsequent time. Under § 924(c), the three counts produce 55 years of additional punishment for carrying a firearm.

Mr. Angelos . . . argues that his 55-year sentence under § 924(c) violates the Eighth Amendment's prohibition of cruel and unusual punishment. . . .

[T]he court must engage in a proportionality analysis guided by factors outlined in Justice Kennedy's concurrence in Harmelin v. Michigan, 501 U.S. 957 (1991). In particular, the court must examine (1) the nature of the crime and its relation to the punishment imposed, (2) the punishment for other offenses in this jurisdiction, and (3) the punishment for similar offenses in other jurisdictions.

Before turning to these Harmelin factors, it is important to emphasize that the criminal conduct at issue is solely that covered by the three § 924(c) counts. Mr. Angelos will be fully and appropriately punished for all other criminal conduct from the sentence on these other counts. Thus, the proportionality question in this case boils down to whether the 55-year sentence is disproportionate to the offense of carrying or possessing firearms three times in connection with dealing marijuana.

The first Harmelin factor requires the court to compare the seriousness of the three § 924(c) offenses to the harshness of the contemplated penalty to determine if the penalty would be grossly disproportionate to such offenses. In weighing the gravity of the offenses, the court should consider the offenses of conviction and the defendant's criminal history, as well as "the harm caused or threatened to the victim or society, and the culpability of the offender."[82] . . .

The criminal history in this case is easy to describe. Mr. Angelos has no prior adult criminal convictions and is treated as a first time offender under the Sentencing Guidelines.

The sentence triggering criminal conduct in this case is also modest. Here, on two occasions while selling small amounts of marijuana, Mr. Angelos possessed a handgun under his clothing, but he

---

* For a detailed discussion of the law of murder, see Chapter 15.

---

[82] Solem v. Helm, 463 U.S. 277, 292 (1983).

never brandished or used the handgun. The third relevant crime occurred when the police searched his home and found handguns in his residence. These handguns had multiple purposes—including recreational activities—but because Mr. Angelos also used the gun to protect himself while dealing drugs, the possession of these handguns is also covered by § 924(c).

Mr. Angelos did not engage in force or violence, or threats of force or violence, in furtherance of or in connection with the offenses for which he has been convicted. No offense involved injury to any person or the threat of injury to any person. . . .

It is relevant on this point that the Sentencing Commission has reviewed crimes like Mr. Angelos' and concluded that an appropriate penalty for all of Mr. Angelos' crimes is no more than about ten years (121 months). With respect to the firearms conduct specifically, the Commission has concluded that about 24 months (a two level enhancement) is the appropriate penalty. The views of the Commission are entitled to special weight, because it is a congressionally established expert agency which can draw on significant data and other resources in determining appropriate sentences. Comparing a recommended sentence of two years to the 55-year enhancement the court must impose strongly suggests not merely disproportionality, but gross disproportionality.

The next Harmelin factor requires comparing Mr. Angelos' sentence with the sentences imposed on other criminals in the federal system. Generally, "if more serious crimes are subject to the same penalty, or to less serious penalties, that is some indication that the punishment at issue may be excessive."[155] This factor points strongly in favor of finding that the sentence in this case is excessive. . . . Mr. Angelos will receive a far longer sentence than those imposed in the federal system for such major crimes as aircraft hijacking, second degree murder, racial beating inflicting life threatening injuries, kidnapping, and rape. Indeed, Mr. Angelos will receive a far longer sentence than those imposed for three aircraft hijackings, three second degree murders, three racial beatings inflicting life threatening injuries, three kidnappings, and three rapes. Because Mr. Angelos is "treated in the same manner as, or more severely than, criminals who have committed far more serious crimes,"[156] it appears that the second factor is satisfied.

The final Harmelin factor requires the court to examine "sentences imposed for the same crime in other jurisdictions."[157] Evaluating this factor is also straightforward. Mr. Angelos' sentence is longer than he would receive in any of the fifty states. The government commendably concedes this point in its brief, pointing out that in Washington State Mr. Angelos would serve about nine years and in Utah would serve about five to seven years. Accordingly, the court finds that the third factor is satisfied.

Having analyzed the three Harmelin factors, the court believes that they lead to the conclusion that Mr. Angelos' sentence violates the Eighth Amendment. But before the court declares the sentence unconstitutional, there is one last obstacle to overcome. The court is keenly aware of its obligation to follow precedent from superior courts—specifically the Tenth Circuit and, of course, the Supreme Court. The Supreme Court has considered one case that might be regarded as quite similar to this one. In Hutto v. Davis, the Supreme Court held that two consecutive twenty year sentences—totaling forty years—for possession of nine ounces of marijuana said to be worth $200 did not violate the Eighth Amendment. If Davis remains good law, it is hard see how the sentence in this case violates the Eighth Amendment. Here, Mr. Angelos was involved in at least two marijuana deals involving $700 and approximately sixteen ounces (one pound) of marijuana. Perhaps currency inflation could equate $700 today with $200 in the 1980's. But as a simple matter of arithmetic, if 40 years in prison for possessing nine ounces marijuana does not violate the Eighth Amendment, it is hard to see how 61 years for distributing sixteen ounces (or more) would do so.

The court is aware of an argument that the 1982 Davis decision has been implicitly overruled or narrowed by [more recent decisions of the Supreme Court.] [Nonetheless,] in light of . . . continued references to Davis [by the Supreme Court], the court believes it is obligated to follow its holding here. Indeed, in Davis the Supreme Court pointedly reminded district court judges that "unless we wish anarchy to prevail within the federal judicial system, a precedent of this Court must be followed by the lower federal courts. . . ."[164] Under Davis, Mr. Angelos' sentence is not cruel and unusual punishment. Therefore, his Eighth Amendment challenge must be rejected. . . .

The 55-year sentence mandated by § 924(c) in this case appears to be unjust, cruel, and irrational. But our constitutional system of government requires the court to follow the law, not its own personal views about what the law ought to be. Perhaps the court has overlooked some legal point, and that the appellate courts will find Mr. Angelos' sentence invalid. But applying the law as the court understands it, the court sentences Mr. Angelos to serve a term of imprisonment of 55 years and one day. The court recommends that the President commute this unjust sentence and that the Congress modify the laws that produced it. The Clerk's Office is directed to forward a copy of this

---

[155] Solem, 463 U.S. at 291.
[156] Solem, 463 U.S. at 299.
[157] Harmelin, 501 U.S. at 1005 (Kennedy, J., concurring).
[164] Hutto v. Davis, 454 U.S. 370, 375 (1982).

opinion with its commutation recommendation to the Office of Pardon Attorney and to the Chair and Ranking Member of the House and Senate Judiciary Committees.

Higher Regional Court (*Oberlandesgericht*, OLG) Braunschweig
1 Ss 52/0176, NStZ-RR 2002, 75 (October 25, 2001)

Facts

The accused stole a packet of cigarettes to the value of five DM from a supermarket. The local court sentenced him to two months imprisonment for this. Following his appeal in law the sentence was reduced to one month.

Reasons

II.

The appeal in law has been lodged in a permissible manner and is well founded; it is partially successful. This is because a sentence of imprisonment of two months cannot be regarded as a just settlement of culpability if the defendant is merely accused of having stolen a packet of cigarettes to the value of five DM from a shop.

It is true that both courts below correctly proceeded on the basis that in the light of the accused's extraordinary number of previous convictions for theft and considerable number of sentences of imprisonment served, there are special circumstances in his personality in the sense of § 47 para. 1 Criminal Code that make the imposition of a sentence of imprisonment indispensable both for its effect on the accused and for defense of the legal order. This applies particularly in view of the fact that the accused committed the current theft after less than a month from his release from custody. It applies—even in taking the aspect of proportionality into account—to trivial offenses as well (Oberlandesgericht Düsseldorf, NStZ 1986, 512, for theft of tobacco to a value of 8.80 DM; Bayerisches Oberstes Landesgericht, NStZ 1989, 75, for theft of coffee to a value of 13.99 DM).

To this extent the appeal in law must be rejected on the application of the public prosecutor's office and after hearing the defense in accordance with § 349 para. 2 Code of Criminal Procedure.

In view of the length of the two month sentence of imprisonment imposed, though, the appeal in law cannot be unsuccessful. It is true that in principle determination of sentence is a matter for the judge of fact. The court hearing the appeal in the law can only intervene if the judge of fact leaves legally recognized purposes of criminalization out of consideration or if the punishment abandons, either upwards or downwards, its purpose of being a just settlement of culpability (BGHSt 24, 132 [134] = NJW 1971, 61; Tröndle/Fischer, Criminal Code, 50th edit, § 46 marginal no. 108). The latter is the case here. The basis for punishment of the perpetrator is the culpability that is expressed in the crime. This relates to taking an item valued at five DM from a department store. The wrongness of the act here must be regarded as extremely small in a double sense: for one thing because of the trivial value of the packet of cigarettes and for another thing having regard to the merely abstract removal of an object of value in a department store without any actual personal sphere being affected. If the state reacts to this with a sentence of imprisonment of two months, it exceeds the scope of what is reasonable with regard to the guilt; the punishment is out of proportion to the crime, which is located in the most trivial category. It is not possible to speak of a just settlement of culpability here even if the numerous previous convictions and the considerable number of prison sentences served are considered.

The Senate* is also of the view that the sentence of two months' imprisonment here violates the constitutional principle of proportionality. According to the consistent case law of the Federal Constitutional Court, punishment must be in a just relationship to the seriousness of the crime and to the culpability of the perpetrator; it ought above all to be "not simply inappropriate" to the action that is being punished (BVerfGE 50, 205 [215] = NJW 1979, 1039). The Senate regards it as being "simply inappropriate" to punish the theft of a packet of cigarettes from a department store with a sentence of imprisonment of two months.

This outcome is indirectly confirmed by the fact that according to the statutory position applying between 1912 and 1974, a maximum penalty of six weeks "detention" (and therefore not prison) was provided for this contravention on the basis of the privileged definition of petty theft (§ 370 para. 1 no. 5 Criminal Code, old version). Certainly it was not the intention of the legislature when abolishing this definition of the contravention of petty theft, to increase the threatened penalty in

---

* [A "senate" is a panel of a German appellate court, of varying size: e.g., three (at a Higher Regional Court, OLG), as in this case, or nine (at the Federal Court of Justice, *Bundesgerichtshof*, BGH).—Eds.].

relation to this trivial crime. Even the Second Senate of the Federal Constitutional Court in its decision of January 17, 1979 (BVerfGE 50, 205 = NJW 1979, 1039), in which it confirms the constitutionality of the definition of theft of an item of trivial value in accordance with §§ 248a, 242 Criminal Code, certainly did not proceed on the basis that the criminal courts, after the abolition of contraventions and therefore also the definition of petty theft, would use the new statutory situation as an opportunity for punishing trivial crimes more severely, in the case of "incorrigible" perpetrators, than was possible under the previous statutory situation applying since 1912. This ought in any case to be accepted for theft crimes like the present one, which would come within the earlier privileged definition of petty theft.

III.

On the application of the chief public prosecutor the Senate has not referred the matter back, but has stipulated the sentence here of one month as what would reasonably be regarded as the lowest statutory punishment (§§ 38 para. 2, 47 para. 1 Criminal Code).

NOTES

1. What does the reasoning in *U.S. v. Angelos* tell us about the relationship between the courts and the legislature? Which constitutional principles could be cited either to defend a strong role for the legislature or to demand greater power for the courts when confronted with harsh laws such as the one at issue in *Angelos*? Does it make a difference that in this case—in contrast to Blarek*—the sentence resulted from an application of a (legislative) statute, rather than a set of (administrative) guidelines drafted by an unelected sentencing commission? Even if the commissioners are appointed by the (elected) chief executive (here, the U.S. President) and include several (life-term federal) judges, and the commission's guidelines are subject to approval by the legislature (here, the U.S. Congress)?†

How about the relationship between courts and the executive, or law and mercy? The district judge in *Angelos* takes the highly unusual step of urging the President to exercise his constitutional pardon power: "The court recommends that the President commute this unjust sentence and that the Congress modify the laws that produced it." Compare the famous nineteenth-century case of *Dudley & Stephens*,‡ where the court affirmed the defendants' death sentences for murder, only to have the Queen commute the sentences to time served (six months' imprisonment). Does this division of labor reflect poorly on a legal system—including the substantive norms, and the institutions and people who apply them? What sort of conception of law, and the relationship between law and justice—and between courts and law and justice—underlies it? What does it mean to reach a result that complies with the law but not with justice? Does it indicate a failure of law, or of those who apply it?§

Angelos's sentence was affirmed on appeal. *United States v. Angelos*, 433 F.3d 738 (10th Cir. 2006) (Angelos's sentence not "disproportionate to his crimes"). As of November 2013, Angelos's sentence had not been commuted.¶

2. What sort of guidance might a trial court derive from the opinion of the appellate court in the German shoplifting case? What does it mean to say that a punishment is "simply inappropriate"? Does it add anything to calling it "out of proportion to the crime"? Wouldn't the trial court be in a better position to determine the "appropriateness" of a sentence, or for that matter its proportionality? What sort of comparative analysis does the appellate court undertake, if any? Is the remedy (the reduction of a sentence by one month) proportionate to the supposed constitutional nature of the question? Or does this case illustrate German courts' general reluctance to impose prison terms? Compare this case to *Angelos*.

---

* See Chapter 1.A.i.
† See generally *Mistretta v. United States*, 488 U.S. 361 (1989) (rejecting nondelegation challenge to federal sentencing scheme).
‡ See Chapter 6.C.
§ See the discussion of *Rechtsbeugung* ("bending the law") in Chapter 17.B.
¶ See Editorial, *Salt Lake Tribune*, November 15, 2013, <http://www.sltrib.com/sltrib/opinion/57134523-82/angelos-former-letter-president.html.csp>.

3. To what extent does proportionality of the punishment depend on prior convictions? Are repeat offenders punished for their most recent offense only, or also for their previous ones? Or are they punished for their likely future offenses as well? Does it help to think of the punishment for a first offense as reflecting a first-timer discount, rather than of the punishment for a second offense as a second-timer "recidivist premium"?* Do prior convictions increase culpability, or decrease it, or do they make no difference? Do they reveal the offender's dangerousness, recalcitrance, evil character, lack of impulse control, antisocial personality? If so, should these factors affect punishment?

4. The sentence in *U.S. v. Angelos*, once again, illustrates the comparative severity of U.S. criminal sentences. While it may be justifiable in principle to aggravate sentences if an offender carried a weapon, because this means risks for others involved in the interactions and for innocent bystanders, the amount of additional punishment in the U.S. Code appears excessive. Under German law, the basic sentence range proscribed by the Narcotics Act (*Betäubungsmittelgesetz*, BtMG) for drug dealing is 2–15 years and, if the offender carried a handgun, the range is 5–15 years. But independent of the increased mandatory penalty, if an offender is sentenced for multiple counts of drug dealing (even of large quantities) while carrying a gun, he could not be sentenced to more than 15 years under German law. One might debate whether the German legislature's decision to set 15 years as the upper limit in all cases except murder[†] is compelling. But the crucial point (which the U.S. Court in the *Angelos* decision clearly points out) is that relative, and not only absolute, proportionality matters: even if a 55-year sentence for simple gun possession is not disproportionate on its terms, punishing the mere possession of a gun more severely than aircraft hijacking, kidnapping or rape surely is.

The district judge in *Angelos* agrees with all this, and finds the sentence grossly disproportionate even under the narrow *Harmelin* standard. At least as noteworthy as this conclusion (which is rare enough) is the ultimate decision, which nonetheless upholds the sentence, not because it is not grossly disproportionate, but because invalidating it would conflict with (another) Supreme Court precedent: *Hutto v. Davis* (which, however, itself is difficult to square with subsequent decisions by the Supreme Court).

Of course, one might attack *Davis* on the merits, but that would be beside the point. The district judge may very well share the view that *Davis* was wrongly decided, but the point is that having decided that it is on all fours with the case before him and remains good law (both conclusions that are not inescapable), he has no choice but to follow it. This situation would not arise in Germany, or other civil law countries, that do not follow the rule of *stare decisis*. The U.S. federal trial judge is free to undertake a constitutional analysis, but that analysis is bound by precedential decisions of higher courts (in particular the superior federal appellate court, here the U.S. Court of Appeals for the Tenth Circuit—which, as we noted, in fact affirmed Angelos's sentence, though on other grounds than did the district court—and the supreme federal appellate court, the U.S. Supreme Court).

5. Is U.S. criminal punishment so harsh, and the severity discrepancy between U.S. and German criminal punishment so stark, that comparing one with the other amounts to comparing apples with oranges?

Accounting for the difference between criminal punishment in the U.S. and Europe is tricky. Whitman,[‡] recently has proposed a sociological explanation (contrasting American "leveling-down" with European "leveling-up," so that American offenders were all treated equally poorly, and European ones equally princely); the prevalence and persistence of slavery, and its lingering after effects, will have to feature prominently in any account (not

---

* See Andrew von Hirsch, *Past or Future Crimes: Deservedness and Dangerousness in the Sentencing of Criminals* (1985).

† See German Criminal Code § 38 para. 2.

‡ James Q. Whitman, *Harsh Justice: Criminal Punishments and the Widening Divide Between America and Europe* (2003).

only because inmates were classified at one point as rightless "slaves of the state";* perhaps a political-legal account can make a contribution as well (building on the recognition that U.S. penality never underwent a radical reform in light of constitutional principles, instead adapting the patriarchal mode of penal governance from its erstwhile colonial master in the guise of the essentially unlimited and discretionary "police power."[†] There are signs, however faint, that Whitman's "divide between America and Europe" at least may no longer be "widening," even if it is not narrowing just yet. The police power in the U.S. being a state power, and emphatically not a federal power, criminal law has always been, and will always remain, primarily a state matter, which means—among other things—that change, if it comes, comes slowly and sporadically. Even the U.S. Supreme Court can do little more than patrol the constitutional margins of state action, unless it were to commit itself to an all-out national reform effort as did the Warren Court some fifty years ago, but only in the area of criminal procedure, not substantive criminal law.[‡]

That said, the Supreme Court at least has begun to show a greater willingness to place constitutional constraints, if not on norms of the general or special part of criminal law, then at least on the law of punishment, narrowly speaking, particularly in the area of juvenile criminal law.[§] We have already noted the Court's greater scrutiny of cases involving the death penalty, which it regards as a *sui generis* sanction; while the vast bulk of this attention has fallen on procedural criminal law, the Court occasionally has recognized constitutional limits on substantive criminal law in capital cases.[¶]

iii. Punishment vs. measure

The law of punishment is one thing. The law of criminal sanction is another. Both legal systems under analysis in this book differentiate between punitive and non-punitive criminal sanctions, with the latter being exempt from the legal (and perhaps constitutional) constraints governing the state's exercise of its power to "punish" (which is not to say that they may not be subject to other legal and constitutional limits). A prohibition of "cruel and unusual punishments" obviously does not apply, on its face, to a state action that does not qualify as "punishment," and so on. Not surprisingly, this differentiation between punitive and non-punitive sanctions has been controversial.

The 1997 U.S. Supreme Court decision in *Kansas v. Hendricks*, the "sexually violent predator" case excerpted below, attracted considerable attention, and widespread criticism. It was attacked as an attempt by the Court to exempt preventive detention schemes from significant constitutional scrutiny, by allowing legislatures to sidestep constitutional constraints on "punishment" (however weak), including not only the Eighth Amendment's "cruel and unusual punishments" prohibition, but also the Fifth Amendment's double jeopardy clause and the *ex post facto* prohibitions in §§ 9 and 10 of Article 1 of the U.S. Constitution. On the other side of the Atlantic, the far more ambitious, and long-standing, German two-track system of criminal sanctions labeled "punishments" and

---

* See Chapter 1.A.iii, Note 7.
† See Markus D. Dubber, *The Police Power: Patriarchy and the Foundations of American Government* (2005).
‡ The discrepancy between U.S. constitutional protections in procedural and substantive criminal law is explored in Chapter 3.
§ See, e.g., *Roper v. Simmons*, 543 U.S. 551 (2005) (Eighth Amendment's "cruel and unusual punishments" clause prohibits capital punishment for juveniles); *Graham v. Florida*, 560 U. S. ___ (2010) (Eighth Amendment prohibits life without parole for juveniles convicted of a non-homicide offense); *Miller v. Alabama*, 567 U.S. ___ (2012) (Eighth Amendment prohibits mandatory life without parole for juveniles); see also *Kennedy v. Louisiana*, 554 U.S. 407 (2008) (Eighth Amendment prohibits death as punishment for child rape).
¶ See, e.g., *Enmund v. Florida*, 458 U.S. 782 (1982) (*mens rea*; felony murder); *Tison v. Arizona*, 481 U.S. 137 (1987) (same); *Atkins v. Virginia*, 536 U.S. 304 (2002) (mental retardation).

"measures" has faced similar criticism, if not by German courts, then by the European Court of Human Rights.

Kansas v. Hendricks
United States Supreme Court
521 U.S. 346 (1997)

Justice Thomas delivered the opinion of the Court.

The Kansas Legislature enacted the Sexually Violent Predator Act (Act) in 1994 to grapple with the problem of managing repeat sexual offenders. . . . In the Act's preamble, the legislature explained:

> [A] small but extremely dangerous group of sexually violent predators exist who do not have a mental disease or defect that renders them appropriate for involuntary treatment pursuant to the [general involuntary civil commitment statute]. . . In contrast to persons appropriate for civil commitment under the [general involuntary civil commitment statute], sexually violent predators generally have anti-social personality features which are unamenable to existing mental illness treatment modalities and those features render them likely to engage in sexually violent behavior. The legislature further finds that sexually violent predators' likelihood of engaging in repeat acts of predatory sexual violence is high. The existing involuntary commitment procedure . . . is inadequate to address the risk these sexually violent predators pose to society. The legislature further finds that the prognosis for rehabilitating sexually violent predators in a prison setting is poor, the treatment needs of this population are very long term and the treatment modalities for this population are very different than the traditional treatment modalities for people appropriate for commitment under the [general involuntary civil commitment statute].

Kan. Stat. Ann. § 59-29a01 (1994).

As a result, the Legislature found it necessary to establish "a civil commitment procedure for the long term care and treatment of the sexually violent predator."

The Act defined a "sexually violent predator" as:

> any person who has been convicted of or charged with a sexually violent offense and who suffers from a mental abnormality or personality disorder which make the person likely to engage in the predatory acts of sexual violence.

Kan. Stat. Ann. § 59-29a02(a).

A "mental abnormality" was defined, in turn, as a "congenital or acquired condition affecting the emotional or volitional capacity which predisposes the person to commit sexually violent offenses in a degree constituting such person a menace to the health and safety of others." § 59-29a02(b).

As originally structured, the Act's civil commitment procedures pertained to: (1) a presently confined person who, like Hendricks, "has been convicted of a sexually violent offense" and is scheduled for release; (2) a person who has been "charged with a sexually violent offense" but has been found incompetent to stand trial; (3) a person who has been found "not guilty by reason of insanity of a sexually violent offense"; and (4) a person found "not guilty" of a sexually violent offense because of a mental disease or defect.

The initial version of the Act, as applied to a currently confined person such as Hendricks, was designed to initiate a specific series of procedures. The custodial agency was required to notify the local prosecutor 60 days before the anticipated release of a person who might have met the Act's criteria. The prosecutor was then obligated, within 45 days, to decide whether to file a petition in state court seeking the person's involuntary commitment. If such a petition were filed, the court was to determine whether "probable cause" existed to support a finding that the person was a "sexually violent predator" and thus eligible for civil commitment. Upon such a determination, transfer of the individual to a secure facility for professional evaluation would occur. After that evaluation, a trial would be held to determine beyond a reasonable doubt whether the individual was a sexually violent predator. If that determination were made, the person would then be transferred to the custody of the Secretary of Social and Rehabilitation Services (Secretary) for "control, care and treatment until such time as the person's mental abnormality or personality disorder has so changed that the person is safe to be at large."

In addition to placing the burden of proof upon the State, the Act afforded the individual a number of other procedural safeguards. In the case of an indigent person, the State was required to provide, at public expense, the assistance of counsel and an examination by mental health care professionals. The individual also received the right to present and cross examine witnesses, and the opportunity to review documentary evidence presented by the State.

Once an individual was confined, the Act required that "[t]he involuntary detention or commitment...shall conform to constitutional requirements for care and treatment." Confined persons were afforded three different avenues of review: First, the committing court was obligated to conduct an annual review to determine whether continued detention was warranted. Second, the Secretary was permitted, at any time, to decide that the confined individual's condition had so changed that release was appropriate, and could then authorize the person to petition for release. Finally, even without the Secretary's permission, the confined person could at any time file a release petition. If the court found that the State could no longer satisfy its burden under the initial commitment standard, the individual would be freed from confinement....

[Hendricks] contends that where, as here, newly enacted "punishment" is predicated upon past conduct for which he has already been convicted and forced to serve a prison sentence, the Constitution's Double Jeopardy and Ex Post Facto Clauses are violated....

The categorization of a particular proceeding as civil or criminal "is first of all a question of statutory construction." We must initially ascertain whether the legislature meant the statute to establish "civil" proceedings. If so, we ordinarily defer to the legislature's stated intent. Here, Kansas' objective to create a civil proceeding is evidenced by its placement of the Sexually Violent Predator Act within the Kansas probate code, instead of the criminal code, as well as its description of the Act as creating a "civil commitment procedure." Kan. Stat. Ann., Article 29 (1994) ("Care and Treatment for Mentally Ill Persons"), § 59-29a01 (emphasis added). Nothing on the face of the statute suggests that the legislature sought to create anything other than a civil commitment scheme designed to protect the public from harm.

Although we recognize that a "civil label is not always dispositive," we will reject the legislature's manifest intent only where a party challenging the statute provides "the clearest proof" that "the statutory scheme [is] so punitive either in purpose or effect as to negate [the State's] intention" to deem it "civil." United States v. Ward, 448 U.S. 242, 248–249 (1980). In those limited circumstances, we will consider the statute to have established criminal proceedings for constitutional purposes. Hendricks, however, has failed to satisfy this heavy burden.

As a threshold matter, commitment under the Act does not implicate either of the two primary objectives of criminal punishment: retribution or deterrence. The Act's purpose is not retributive because it does not affix culpability for prior criminal conduct. Instead, such conduct is used solely for evidentiary purposes, either to demonstrate that a "mental abnormality" exists or to support a finding of future dangerousness. We have previously concluded that an Illinois statute was nonpunitive even though it was triggered by the commission of a sexual assault, explaining that evidence of the prior criminal conduct was "received not to punish past misdeeds, but primarily to show the accused's mental condition and to predict future behavior." In addition, the Kansas Act does not make a criminal conviction a prerequisite for commitment—persons absolved of criminal responsibility may nonetheless be subject to confinement under the Act. An absence of the necessary criminal responsibility suggests that the State is not seeking retribution for a past misdeed. Thus, the fact that the Act may be "tied to criminal activity" is "insufficient to render the statute punitive." United States v. Ursery, 518 U.S. 267, 292 (1996).

Moreover, unlike a criminal statute, no finding of scienter is required to commit an individual who is found to be a sexually violent predator; instead, the commitment determination is made based on a "mental abnormality" or "personality disorder" rather than on one's criminal intent. The existence of a scienter requirement is customarily an important element in distinguishing criminal from civil statutes. See Kennedy v. Mendoza Martinez, 372 U.S. 144, 168 (1963). The absence of such a requirement here is evidence that confinement under the statute is not intended to be retributive.

Nor can it be said that the legislature intended the Act to function as a deterrent. Those persons committed under the Act are, by definition, suffering from a "mental abnormality" or a "personality disorder" that prevents them from exercising adequate control over their behavior. Such persons are therefore unlikely to be deterred by the threat of confinement. And the conditions surrounding that confinement do not suggest a punitive purpose on the State's part. The State has represented that an individual confined under the Act is not subject to the more restrictive conditions placed on state prisoners, but instead experiences essentially the same conditions as any involuntarily committed patient in the state mental institution. Because none of the parties argues that people institutionalized under the Kansas general civil commitment statute are subject to punitive conditions, even though they may be involuntarily confined, it is difficult to conclude that persons confined under this Act are being "punished."

Although the civil commitment scheme at issue here does involve an affirmative restraint, "the mere fact that a person is detained does not inexorably lead to the conclusion that the government has imposed punishment." United States v. Salerno, 481 U.S. 739, 746 (1987). The State may take measures to restrict the freedom of the dangerously mentally ill. This is a legitimate non punitive governmental objective and has been historically so regarded. The Court has, in fact, cited the confinement of "mentally unstable individuals who present a danger to the public" as one classic example of nonpunitive detention. Id., at 748–749. If detention for the purpose of protecting the community from harm necessarily constituted punishment, then all involuntary civil commitments would have to be considered punishment. But we have never so held.

Hendricks focuses on his confinement's potentially indefinite duration as evidence of the State's punitive intent. That focus, however, is misplaced. Far from any punitive objective, the confinement's duration is instead linked to the stated purposes of the commitment, namely, to hold the person until his mental abnormality no longer causes him to be a threat to others. If, at any time, the confined person is adjudged "safe to be at large," he is statutorily entitled to immediate release. Kan. Stat. Ann. § 59-29a07 (1994).

Furthermore, commitment under the Act is only potentially indefinite. The maximum amount of time an individual can be incapacitated pursuant to a single judicial proceeding is one year. If Kansas seeks to continue the detention beyond that year, a court must once again determine beyond a reasonable doubt that the detainee satisfies the same standards as required for the initial confinement. This requirement again demonstrates that Kansas does not intend an individual committed pursuant to the Act to remain confined any longer than he suffers from a mental abnormality rendering him unable to control his dangerousness.

Hendricks next contends that the State's use of procedural safeguards traditionally found in criminal trials makes the proceedings here criminal rather than civil.... The numerous procedural and evidentiary protections afforded here demonstrate that the Kansas Legislature has taken great care to confine only a narrow class of particularly dangerous individuals, and then only after meeting the strictest procedural standards. That Kansas chose to afford such procedural protections does not transform a civil commitment proceeding into a criminal prosecution....

Where the State has "disavowed any punitive intent"; limited confinement to a small segment of particularly dangerous individuals; provided strict procedural safeguards; directed that confined persons be segregated from the general prison population and afforded the same status as others who have been civilly committed; recommended treatment if such is possible; and permitted immediate release upon a showing that the individual is no longer dangerous or mentally impaired, we cannot say that it acted with punitive intent. We therefore hold that the Act does not establish criminal proceedings and that involuntary confinement pursuant to the Act is not punitive. Our conclusion that the Act is nonpunitive thus removes an essential prerequisite for both Hendricks' double jeopardy and *ex post facto* claims.

German Federal Constitutional Court
BVerfGE 109, 133 (February 5, 2004)

Facts

The complainant, who was born in 1957, has only spent a few weeks in freedom since he was 15 years old. He would have been released on August 18, 2001, because of the expiry of the ten year maximum period for detention had it not been for the new regime, which he [is] challenging.

1. After he had had to be judicially cautioned in 1971 for shoplifting, he served five days in youth detention about a year later for theft and stealing food. Almost a month later, amongst other things he broke into a number of vehicles and caravans with other young people. In September 1972 he was given a youth custody sentence of undetermined duration, because of continued aggravated joint theft in three cases, amongst other things. He completed the maximum period of detention of three years on July 5, 1975. During the sentence he escaped on a total of three occasions. Less than three weeks after his release from the youth detention center he again committed offenses of, amongst other things, breaking into several cars, and was finally sentenced in November 1975 to a youth custody sentence of ten months. During this detention period, he was at large for a week. The sentence ended in July 1976.

2. A week after his release from detention he committed a joint robbery concomitantly with joint infliction of grievous bodily harm and extortion by force; an attempted murder on the following day; and on a subsequent day, a joint theft in a particularly serious case.

The regional court of Kassel sentenced the complainant to youth detention of six years because of these crimes in October 1977. He first completed two thirds of this sentence in July 1980, before the sentence was interrupted in favor of the two following sentences, and he finally completed it in October 1984.

3. In November 1977, the complainant committed another criminal offense during his detention. For some trivial reason, he threw a heavy metal box at a supervisor, and then stabbed him with a

screwdriver. The regional court of Wiesbaden therefore sentenced him to a term of imprisonment of one year and nine months in March 1979 for infliction of grievous bodily harm.

4. Before the imposition of this sentence, a dispute with a fellow prisoner about an open cell window had led to the infuriated complainant kicking the head of a fellow prisoner, who was severely disabled and physically weaker, with all his might, pouncing on him, and striking and throttling him. The regional court of Marburg sentenced the complainant, inclusive of the punishment mentioned under 3 above, to a total sentence of imprisonment of two years and six months for infliction of bodily harm.

5. The complainant at first behaved in an unobtrusive and compliant manner, but then decided to escape in July 1985. On the basis of the relaxation of his prison arrangements he went on parole for several hours with a voluntary prison assistant who had kept in touch with him since 1980. The prison assistant first invited the complainant to lunch. They then went for a walk, and the complainant suddenly knocked his companion down and throttled her, intending to kill her. He only desisted when three young people approached the spot. He fled, taking her handbag with him. A few days later—after a planned robbery of a user of a multi-story car park failed just before its execution—he was captured. The regional court of Marburg sentenced him to a term of imprisonment of five years in November 1986 for attempted murder, concomitantly with robbery, and ordered him to be committed to preventive detention. The court assumed on the basis of expert evidence that the complainant had been fully responsible for his crimes. He had, however, a deep-rooted and intensive inclination to violations of the law by which his victims were severely harmed psychologically, and above all physically. He was inclined to rash aggressive reactions, and these were also to be expected in future. It had to be assumed that the complainant when free would regard any lack of money as a reason for committing acts of violence against people, and would not even shrink from killing his victims. Preventive detention was imposed from August 18, 1991.

6. During the detention the complainant took advantage of a day's parole in October 1995 to escape. But in November he gave himself up to the police. In July 1996, he broke a fellow prisoner's nose, in order to give emphasis to an alleged claim for 100 DM. In 1998, the prison reported that the complainant was increasingly showing impulsive aggressive behavior. Inconsiderateness had become a principle in his life. For some time he had identified with the skinhead scene. SS signs, swastikas and pictures of Hitler and Goebbels had been taken from his cell. He refused to co-operate with foreign prisoners. His hatred for the prison governor had become deeper; he had described him as a "worthless life" who "in the Third Reich would have ended up in a concentration camp," because of a back problem.

7. After seeking an expert's opinion from a psychiatrist, the criminal sentencing chamber again declined, by the decision that is being challenged here, to suspend the preventive detention on probation. There was no question of the complainant having a psychiatric illness. But he showed histrionic personality traits, which were embedded in a distinctive narcissistic problematic nature. In addition, he had a very pronounced lack of empathy. It was true that he had learnt to assess social situations cognitively, but he had no emotional barriers that prevented him from asserting himself in a way that harmed others. He had isolated himself, and, with his highly narcissistic need to be noticed and receive attention, was in danger of falling "by the wayside." It was to be expected that he would take new ways to resolve things, and in this context would commit new crimes that would seriously harm the victims psychologically or physically.

There were no objections in constitutional law to the new statutory regime, which permitted a continuation of the preventive detention originally ordered beyond ten years.*

Reasons

C.

The constitutional complaint is unfounded.

I.

Confinement in preventive detention, without an upper time limit regulated by statute, does not violate the guarantee of human dignity contained in art. 1 para. 1 Basic Law.

1.

a) Respect for and protection of human dignity are constitutional principles of the Basic Law (see BVerfGE 45, 187 [227]; BVerfGE 87, 209 [228]; BVerfGE 96, 375 [398]; BVerfGE 102, 370 [389]). The social claim of human beings to value and respect is protected by human dignity. This claim

---

* [The retroactivity of this change is considered in the two following judgments.—Eds.]

forbids human beings being made a mere object of the state or being exposed to treatment that in principle puts their subject quality in question (see BVerfGE 27, 1 [6]; BVerfGE 45, 187 [228]). Human dignity in this sense is also the entitlement of somebody who cannot act sensibly because of his physical or mental condition. It is not lost even by "unworthy" behavior. It cannot be taken away from any human being. The claim to respect that arises from it can however be violated (see BVerfGE 87, 209 [228]).

b) For the administration of criminal justice, the requirement to respect human dignity means, in particular, that cruel, inhuman and demeaning punishments are forbidden. The perpetrator may not be made a mere object of the fight against crime by violation of his social claim to value and respect, which is protected in constitutional law (BVerfGE 45, 187 [228]). The fundamental prerequisites for individual and social existence of human beings must be maintained, even when the person entitled to the basic right does not do justice to his free responsibility and the community takes away his freedom because of crimes that he has committed. The duty of the state to formulate even the deprivation of freedom in a manner consistent with human dignity follows from art. 1 para. 1 Basic Law. It would be incompatible with the guarantee of human dignity if the State were to claim for itself the right to strip human beings of their freedom compulsorily without their having at least the chance of ever enjoying freedom again (see BVerfGE 45, 187 [229]).

The court has decided that, for the threat and implementation of a life prison sentence, . . . constitutional law requires meaningful treatment. Prisons are obliged, having regard to the basic rights of a prisoner serving a life sentence, to combat, as far as possible, the harmful effects of deprivation of freedom, above all distorting personality changes that seriously put the prisoner's ability to cope with life in question and prevent him from being able to cope in normal life in the case of a release from captivity (see BVerfGE 64, 261 [272f.]). Harmful effects for the physical and mental constitution of the prisoner must so far as is possible be counteracted.

c) These standards also apply when accommodating criminals in preventive detention. Human dignity is not violated by lengthy detention if this is necessary because of continuing danger posed by the detainee. The state community is not prevented from protecting itself against dangerous criminals by taking their freedom away (see BVerfGE 45, 187 [242]). The individual's relationship and commitment to the community that are prescribed in the Basic Law justify the taking of indispensable measures to preserve essential community interests from harm. It is, however, also necessary in these cases to preserve the independence of the detainee, and to respect and to protect his dignity. Therefore preventive detention must, in the same way as punishment for crime, be orientated towards creating the prerequisites for a responsible life in freedom. It is necessary to work towards resocialization of the detainee within the framework of preventive detention also. If hardened criminal tendencies are present, this may be more difficult than with those imprisoned as punishment. However, the protection of human dignity requires statutory guidelines as well as implementation programs that give detainees a real chance of recovering their freedom.

2. Preventive detention in its present formulation satisfies this standard.

a) Preventive detention for continuing danger does not violate the basic right under art. 1 para. 1 Basic Law when regard is had to the individual's commitment to the community.

The Basic Law has resolved the tension between the individual and the community in favor of the individual's relationship with and commitment to the community, but without thereby encroaching on his intrinsic value (see BVerfGE 4, 7 [15f.]). Because of this picture of the human being, preventive detention is compatible with the Basic Law even as a preventive measure for the protection of the general public. The person affected is not in this way turned into a mere object of state action; he is not reduced to a mere means to an end or a commodity.

b) There is no requirement in constitutional law arising from art 1 para. 1 Basic Law in relation to preventive detention that a maximum time limit should be set when the detention is ordered or at a later point when it is reviewed. This is because the prognosis of a danger is always only possible in the present for the future. How long this danger will continue depends on future developments that cannot be reliably predicted. There is therefore no objection to the legislature providing that a binding decision about the detainee's expected time of release will not be made in advance.

aa) The statute guarantees reviews at each stage of the measure, which can lead to the release of the person affected: . . . the court must before the end of the sentence examine whether the convicted person will still after the end of it represent a danger that requires implementation of preventive detention, taking into consideration his development during the sentence (see BVerfGE 42, 1 [6ff.]). After commencement of the detention, investigations will be made on the state's initiative at intervals of two years as to whether the measure can be suspended for a probationary period . . . This system of recurring reviews of readiness for suspension and completion guarantees to the person affected the appropriate procedural legal security.

bb) The information from the state governments in the present proceedings confirms the effect-iveness of the normative guidelines. Even if this information is only based on partial surveys over a limited period of time, and there is so far no representative collection of data based on uniform standards, they allow the conclusion that detainees have a concrete and realizable chance of being released from preventive detention. It is true that preventive detention is only rarely suspended on probation before the execution of detention. On the other hand the regular review of preventive detention after the commencement of its implementation frequently leads, even though with regional variations, to decisions about suspension of detention.

c) The statutory framework conditions of preventive detention are interpreted in such a way as to counteract as far as possible harmful effects for the physical and mental constitution of the detainee.

aa) Preventive detention does not violate art. 1 para. 1 Basic Law on account of possible harm caused by custody (see, for life imprisonment, BVerfGE 45, 187 [237ff.]). New research on the effects of lengthy deprivation of freedom does not support the idea that the standard period of preventive detention inevitably leads to irreparable harm of a psychological or physical kind. Impairment of health on the basis of lengthy imprisonment cannot be excluded; however, the statute and implementation practice curb such harm.

bb) Preventive detention that is not limited in time finds the supplementation required by consti-tutional law in meaningful treatment (see BVerfGE 45, 187 [237ff.]; BVerfGE 98, 169 [200f.]). Preventive detention is both normatively and factually orientated towards the concept of resocialization. The goal of resocialization (§ 2 sentence 1 Prison Act) applies also for prisoners against whom subsequent preventive detention is ordered....

II.

There is likewise no violation of the basic right to freedom under art. 2 para. 2 Basic Law. The preventive detention regime that the complainant challenges is, bearing in mind the following considerations, a limitation of a basic right that conforms to the Constitution (art. 2 para. 2 sentence 3 Basic Law).

1....

2. Freedom of the person—as the foundation and prerequisite of the citizen's opportunities for -development—occupies high rank among the basic rights. This is expressed by the fact that art. 2 para. 2 sentence 2 Basic Law describes it as "inviolable." ... Invasions of this legal good are in general only permissible if they are required by the protection of others or the general public, having regard to the principle of proportionality (see BVerfGE 90, 145 [172]). The need for the security of the general public from expected substantial violations of their legal goods is countered by the detainee's claim to freedom as a corrective; they are to be weighed against each other in the individual case....

a) In assessing the suitability and necessity of the chosen means of attaining the goals sought, as well as the evaluation and prognosis of the dangers threatening the individual or the general public that has to be undertaken in this connection, the legislature has a margin of discretion that can only be examined by the Federal Constitutional Court to a limited extent, according to the particular nature of the subject area in question, the opportunities of forming a sufficiently safe judgment and the legal interests at stake (BVerfGE 90, 145 [173]). Against this background there is no objection to the legislature having regarded it as appropriate and necessary to delete the maximum limit for first time preventive detention, in order to improve the protection of the general public from dangerous criminals. Whether this increase in the severity of the law of preventive detention was caused by an objective increase in violent criminality or—as many critics think—whether it merely took account of an increased feeling on the part of the general public that they were under threat does not have to be assessed by the Federal Constitution Court. This is because it is primarily a matter for the legislature to decide on the basis of its concepts and goals in relation to criminal policy within the scope of its prerogative of assessment, which measures it will take in the interest of the common good. It is only obviously defective decisions of the legislature that are subject in this respect to correction by the Constitutional Court (see BVerfGE 30, 292 [317]; BVerfGE 77, 84 [106]); there can be no question of that here.

The uncertainties of the prognosis that is the foundation of the detention (see Dünkel/Kunkat, Neue Kriminalpolitik 2001, 16 [17f.]; Adams, StV 2003, 51 [53]; Kinzig, NJW 2001, 1455 [1458]; Ullenbruch, NStZ 2001, 292 [295]; Nedopil, NStZ 2002, 344 [349]; Streng, in: Festschr.f. Lampe, p. 611 [621f.]) have effects on the minimum requirements for a prognosis opinion and its assessment in connection with the prohibition on excess.... They remove however neither the suitability of nor the necessity for the invasion of freedom. Prognosis decisions always carry the risk of being defective, but in law they are unavoidable. The prognosis as a basis for avoiding any danger is and remains indispensable, even if it is inadequate in individual cases. Moreover, in the practice of forensic psychiatry, understanding of risk factors has significantly improved in recent years so that in relation to some delinquents relatively good and reliable prognostic statements can be made (see Nedopil, NStZ 2002, 344 [346]). Both experts heard in the oral hearing have submitted that a determined and determinable proportion of the subjects acquire an accumulation of risk factors of such a kind that a prognosis of danger can be given with certainty . . .

<hr>

M. v. Germany
European Court of Human Rights
Application no. 19359/04 (December 17, 2009)

The facts

Circumstances of the case

The applicant was born in 1957 and is currently in Schwalmstadt Prison. . . . * Since 18 August 1991 the applicant, having served his full prison sentence, has been in preventive detention in Schwalmstadt Prison . . . On 10 April 2001 the Marburg Regional Court dismissed the applicant's requests to suspend on probation his preventive detention . . . On 26 November 2001 the applicant lodged a complaint with the Federal Constitutional Court against the decisions ordering his continued preventive detention even on completion of the ten-year period . . . On 5 February 2004 a panel of eight judges of the Federal Constitutional Court dismissed the applicant's constitutional complaint as ill-founded. [BVerfGE 109, 133 (February 5, 2004)—Eds.] . . .

Relevant domestic, comparative and international law and practice

At the time of the applicant's offense and his conviction, Article 67d of the Criminal Code, in so far as relevant, was worded as follows:

Article 67d Duration of detention

(1) Detention in a detoxification facility may not exceed two years and the first period of preventive detention may not exceed ten years. . . .

Article 67d of the Criminal Code was amended while the applicant was in preventive detention for the first time, by the Combating of Sexual Offenses and Other Dangerous Offenses Act (*Gesetz zur Bekämpfung von Sexualdelikten und anderen gefährlichen Straftaten*) of 26 January 1998. The amended provision, in so far as relevant, provided:

Article 67d Duration of detention

(1) Detention in a detoxification facility may not exceed two years . . .

According to the information and material before the Court, the member States of the Council of Europe have chosen different ways of shielding the public from convicted offenders who acted with full criminal responsibility at the time of the offense (as did the applicant at the relevant time) and who risk committing further serious offenses on release from detention and therefore present a danger to the public. Apart from Germany, at least seven other Convention States have adopted systems of preventive detention in respect of convicted offenders who are not considered to be of unsound mind, in other words, who acted with full criminal responsibility when committing their offense(s), and who are considered dangerous to the public as they are liable to re-offend. These include Austria (see Articles 23 et seq. and 47 et seq. of the Austrian Criminal Code, and Articles 435 et seq. of the Austrian Code of Criminal Procedure), Denmark (see Articles 70 et seq. of the Danish Criminal Code), Italy (see Articles 199 et seq. of the Italian Criminal Code), Liechtenstein (see Articles 23 et seq. and 47 of the Liechtenstein Criminal Code and Articles 345 et seq. of the Liechtenstein Code of Criminal Procedure), San Marino (see Articles 121 et seq. of the San Marinese Criminal Code), Slovakia (see Articles 81 and 82 of the Slovakian Criminal Code) and Switzerland (see Articles 56 et seq. of the Swiss Criminal Code). Preventive detention in these States is ordered, as a rule, by the sentencing courts and is generally executed after the persons concerned have served their prison sentences (with the exception of Denmark, where preventive detention is ordered instead of a prison sentence). The detainees' dangerousness is reviewed on a periodic basis and they are released on probation if they are no longer dangerous to the public. . . . In many other Convention States, there is no system of

---

* [The applicant is the same as in the decision of the German Federal Constitutional Court of February 5, 2004, above.—Eds.]

preventive detention and offenders' dangerousness is taken into account both in the determination and in the execution of their sentence. On the one hand, prison sentences are increased in the light of offenders' dangerousness, notably in cases of recidivism. In this respect, it is to be noted that, unlike the courts in the majority of the Convention States, the sentencing courts in the United Kingdom expressly distinguish between the punitive and the preventive part of a life sentence. The retributive or tariff period is fixed to reflect the punishment of the offender. Once the retributive part of the sentence has been served, a prisoner is considered as being in custody serving the preventive part of his sentence and may be released on probation if he poses no threat to society (see, *inter alia*, sections 269 and 277 of the Criminal Justice Act 2003 and section 28 of the Crime (Sentences) Act 1997).

As regards the distinction between penalties and preventive measures in the Convention States and the consequences drawn from the qualification of the sanction in question, it must be noted that the same type of measure may be qualified as an additional penalty in one State and as a preventive measure in another. Thus, the supervision of a person's conduct after release, for example, is an additional penalty under Articles 131-36-1 et seq. of the French Criminal Code and a preventive measure under Articles 215 and 228 of the Italian Criminal Code... The French Constitutional Council, in its decision of 21 February 2008 (no. 2008-562 DC, Official Gazette (*Journal officiel*) of 26 February 2008, p. 3272), found that such preventive detention, which was not based on the culpability of the person convicted but was designed to prevent persons from re-offending, could not be qualified as a penalty (§ 9 of the decision). Nevertheless, in view of its custodial nature, the time it may last, the fact that it is indefinitely renewable and the fact that it is ordered after conviction by a court, the French Constitutional Council considered that post-sentence preventive detention could not be ordered retrospectively against persons convicted of offenses committed prior to the publication of the Act (§ 10 of the decision). In this respect, it came to a different conclusion than the German Federal Constitutional Court.

The Law

. . .

Alleged Violation of Art. 7 of the Convention

The applicant... complained that the retrospective extension of his preventive detention from a maximum period of ten years to an unlimited period of time violated his right not to have a heavier penalty imposed on him than the one applicable at the time of his offense. He relied on Article 7 § 1 of the Convention, which reads:

> 1. No one shall be held guilty of any criminal offense on account of any act or omission which did not constitute a criminal offense under national or international law at the time when it was committed. Nor shall a heavier penalty be imposed than the one that was applicable at the time the criminal offense was committed.

. . .

The concept of "penalty" in Article 7 is autonomous in scope. To render the protection afforded by Article 7 effective the Court must remain free to go behind appearances and assess for itself whether a particular measure amounts in substance to a "penalty" within the meaning of this provision (see *Welch v. the United Kingdom*, 9 February 1995, § 27, Series A no. 307-A; *Jamil v. France*, 8 June 1995, § 30, Series A no. 317-B). The wording of Article 7 paragraph 1, second sentence, indicates that the starting-point in any assessment of the existence of a penalty is whether the measure in question is imposed following conviction for a "criminal offense." Other relevant factors are the characterisation of the measure under domestic law, its nature and purpose, the procedures involved in its making and implementation, and its severity (see *Welch*, 9 February 1995, cited above, § 28; *Jamil*, cited above, § 31; *Adamson v. the United Kingdom* (dec.), no. 42293/98, 26 January 1999; *Van der Velden v. the Netherlands* (dec.), no. 29514/05, ECHR 2006-XV; and *Kafkaris*, cited above, § 142). The severity of the measure is not, however, in itself decisive, since, for instance, many non-penal measures of a preventive nature may have a substantial impact on the person concerned (see *Welch*, cited above, § 32; compare also *Van der Velden*, cited above).

The Court shall thus examine, in the light of the foregoing principles, whether the extension of the applicant's preventive detention from a maximum of ten years to an unlimited period of time violated the prohibition of retrospective penalties under Article 7 § 1, second sentence. The Court observes that at the time the applicant committed the attempted murder in 1985, a preventive detention order made by a sentencing court for the first time, read in conjunction with Article 67d § 1 of the Criminal Code in the version then in force, meant that the applicant could be kept in preventive detention for ten years at the most. Based on the subsequent amendment in 1998 of Article 67d of the Criminal

Code . . . , which abolished that maximum duration with immediate effect, the courts responsible for the execution of sentences then ordered, in 2001, the applicant's continued preventive detention beyond the ten-year point. Thus, the applicant's preventive detention was prolonged with retrospective effect, under a law enacted after the applicant had committed his offense—and at a time when he had already served more than six years in preventive detention.

The Court, having regard to the criteria established in its case-law, therefore needs to determine whether the applicant's preventive detention constitutes a "penalty" within the meaning of the second sentence of Article 7 § 1 . . .

As to the characterization of preventive detention under domestic law, the Court observes that in Germany, such a measure is not considered as a penalty to which the absolute ban on retrospective punishment applies. Under the provisions of the German Criminal Code, preventive detention is qualified as a measure of rehabilitation and protection. Such measures have always been understood as differing from penalties under the long-established twin-track system of sanctions in German criminal law. Unlike penalties, they are considered not to be aimed at punishing criminal guilt, but to be of a purely preventive nature aimed at protecting the public from a dangerous offender. This clear finding is, in the Court's view, not called into question by the fact that preventive detention was first introduced into German criminal law, as the applicant pointed out, by the Habitual Offenders Act of 24 November 1933, that is, during the Nazi regime.

However, as reiterated above, the concept of "penalty" in Article 7 is autonomous in scope and it is thus for the Court to determine whether a particular measure should be qualified as a penalty, without being bound by the qualification of the measure under domestic law. . . .

The Court shall therefore further examine the nature of the measure of preventive detention. It notes at the outset that, just like a prison sentence, preventive detention entails a deprivation of liberty. Moreover, having regard to the manner in which preventive detention orders are executed in practice in Germany, it is striking that persons subject to preventive detention are detained in ordinary prisons, albeit in separate wings. Minor alterations to the detention regime compared to that of an ordinary prisoner serving his sentence, including privileges such as detainees' right to wear their own clothes and to further equip their more comfortable prison cells, cannot mask the fact that there is no substantial difference between the execution of a prison sentence and that of a preventive detention order. . . .

Furthermore, having regard to the realities of the situation of persons in preventive detention, the Court cannot subscribe to the Government's argument that preventive detention served a purely preventive, and no punitive purpose. It notes that, pursuant to Article 66 of the Criminal Code, preventive detention orders may be made only against persons who have repeatedly been found guilty of criminal offenses of a certain gravity. It observes, in particular, that there appear to be no special measures, instruments or institutions in place, other than those available to ordinary long-term prisoners, directed at persons subject to preventive detention and aimed at reducing the danger they present and thus at limiting the duration of their detention to what is strictly necessary in order to prevent them from committing further offenses . . .

Furthermore, given its unlimited duration, preventive detention may well be understood as an additional punishment for an offense by the persons concerned and entails a clear deterrent element. In any event, as the Court has previously found, the aim of prevention can also be consistent with a punitive purpose and may be seen as a constituent element of the very notion of punishment (see *Welch*, 9 February 1995, cited above, § 30).

As regards the procedures involved in the making and implementation of orders for preventive detention, the Court observes that preventive detention is ordered by the (criminal) sentencing courts. Its execution is determined by the courts responsible for the execution of sentences, that is, courts also belonging to the criminal justice system, in a separate procedure. . . .

In view of the foregoing the Court, looking behind appearances and making its own assessment, concludes that preventive detention under the German Criminal Code is to be qualified as a "penalty" for the purposes of Article 7 § 1 of the Convention.

. . . In view of the foregoing, the Court concludes that there has been a violation of Article 7 § 1 of the Convention.

[The Court awarded the applicant €50,000 in respect of non-pecuniary damage.]

German Federal Constitutional Court
BVerfGE 128, 326 (May 4, 2011)

The complainants object to the continuation or retrospective ordering of their confinement in preventive detention . . . [T]he constitutional complaints are well-founded.

The provisions [in the German Criminal Code] on which the disputed decisions are based are incompatible with art. 2 para. 2 sentence 2,* art. 104 para. 1 sentence 1† and art. 2 para. 2 sentence 2 in combination with art. 20 para. 3 Basic Law.‡

The provisions [in the German Criminal Code] do not infringe this basic right in its core content (see BVerfGE 109, 133, 156 [excerpted in Chapter 1.B.iii]. However, they do not satisfy the principle of proportionality. The serious invasion of the basic right to freedom inherent in preventive detention can only be justified by strict examination in the light of proportionality. The rules about preventive detention are not compatible with the (minimum) requirements in constitutional law concerning the execution of these measures.

... [T]he value judgements of art. 7 para. 1 ECHR lead to the refinement of the requirements, which apply anyway in constitutional law, for the execution of a preventive deprivation of freedom that is independent of guilt and differs qualitatively from criminal punishment (the so-called distinction requirement, *Abstandsgebot*). . . .

The distinction requirement is based on the differing grounds of legitimation in constitutional law and differing purposes of imprisonment and preventive detention:

Imprisonment and preventive detention differ fundamentally with regard to their legitimation in constitutional law. The state's entitlement to impose criminal punishment in form of imprisonment and to execute such sentences is based in essence on the culpable commission of a crime. A perpetrator should only be sentenced and subjected to imprisonment if he has done wrong in a reprehensible manner. This is based on the conception of man in the Basic Law as a human being capable of free self-determination, which is to be taken into account with the culpability principle, which is rooted in human dignity (see BVerfGE 123, 267, 413) . . . On the other hand, the entitlement to order and implement measures that take away freedom like preventive detention follows from the principle of the prevailing interest (see Radtke, in: Münchener Kommentar zum StGB, vol 1, 1st edit. 2003, intro. to §§ 38 ff. marginal no. 68). Such ordering and execution are only legitimate if the general public's interest in protection outweighs the right to freedom of the person affected in the individual case (see BVerfGE 109, 133, 159). . . .

As the execution of the measure is only justified on the principle of the prevailing interest, it must immediately be terminated if the protected interests of the general public no longer outweigh the detainee's right to freedom. The state has the duty at the same time to provide appropriate concepts from the start when executing the measure in order if possible to eliminate the danger posed by the detainee. . . .

A freedom-oriented observation of the distinction requirement will take account of the value judgments underlying the case law of the European Court of Human Rights on art. 7 para. 1 ECHR. The Court has in this connection referred to the fact that in the light of the undetermined length of preventive detention special efforts were necessary for the support of detainees who as a rule were not in a position to achieve progress in the direction of release by their own endeavors. A high degree of care by a multi-disciplinary team was necessary as well as intensive and individual work with the detainees on the basis of individual plans that should be drawn up without delay (see ECtHR, Judgment of December 17, 2009, complaint no. 19359/04, M. v. Germany, marginal no. 129).

The concept for the regime of preventive detention, for formulation by the legislature, must . . . include at least the following aspects:

Preventive detention can only be ordered as a last resort if other less radical measures do not suffice to take the general public's safety interest into account. This *ultima ratio* principle in the ordering of preventive detention is followed by the idea that execution must also correspond with this principle. Where preventive detention comes into consideration all possibilities must be exhausted during the execution of the sentence in order to reduce the danger posed by the convicted person.

A comprehensive investigation, corresponding to modern scientific requirements, with respect to treatment must take place without delay, and at the latest at the start of the execution of preventive detention. The individual factors that are decisive for the danger posed by the detainee are at the same time to be analyzed in detail. An execution plan must be drawn up on this basis that will indicate in detail whether and, if necessary, with which measures the risk factors present can be minimized or compensated for by strengthening protective factors . . .

---

* ["Freedom of the person shall be inviolable."—Eds.]
† ["Liberty of the person may be restricted only pursuant to a formal law and only in compliance with the procedures prescribed therein."—Eds.]
‡ ["The legislature shall be bound by the constitutional order, the executive and the judiciary by law and justice."—Eds.]

The undetermined length of preventive detention can have serious psychological effects, demotivating the detainee and leading him into lethargy and passivity. This is to be dealt with first by an offer of therapy and care, which if possible opens up a realistic prospect of release (thus also ECtHR loc. cit. marginal nos. 77 and 129). Besides this, the preparedness of the detainee to co-operate in his treatment by well-directed motivational work must be aroused and promoted.

The existing regulations about preventive detention do not satisfy these demands.

Since 1998 the legislature has . . . continually expanded preventive detention, but without—contrary to the Senate's guidelines in its judgment of February 5, 2004 (BVerfGE 109, 133, 166 f.)—developing an overall concept for the detention that is orientated in favor of freedom and directed towards therapy and that would do justice to the distinction requirement . . .

The psychological or psychiatric care of those in preventive detention is in practice insufficient. According to studies, an average of only about 30% of those in preventive detention are receiving any therapy, although the proportion of detainees with a distinctive characteristic requiring therapy is clearly higher at 79.3% (see Bartsch, Sicherungsverwahrung [Preventive detention], 2010, p. 228; Habermeyer, Die Maßregel der Sicherungsverwahrung [The measure of preventive detention], 2008, p. 54). . . .

According to the judgment of the chamber of the 5th Section of the European Court of Human Rights of December 17, 2009 (complaint no. 19359/04, M. v. Germany) retrospective lengthening of the earlier maximum period of ten years . . . violates art. 7 para. 1 ECHR, because preventive detention is a punishment in the sense of art. 7 ECHR. This classification of preventive detention in Convention law is based amongst other things on the fact that it, like a sentence of imprisonment, results in a deprivation of freedom and is executed in prisons. Also, according to the chamber of the 5th Section of the European Court, having regard to the factual situation of detainees in preventive detention it was not comprehensible that preventive detention only had a preventive function and did not serve any purpose of punishment.

This interpretation of art. 7 para. 1 ECHR argues in favor of delineating the distinction requirement more clearly but it does not require the interpretation of art. 103 para. 2 Basic Law to be brought completely into line with that of art. 7 para. 1 ECHR . . .

There is accordingly no reason to adapt the Basic Law concept of punishment in the art. 103 II GG to the concept of punishment in art. 7 para. 1 ECHR. The European Court of Human Rights itself explains in this respect that the concept of "penalty" in the sense of art. 7 ECHR should be interpreted "autonomously"; it—the Court—was not bound by the classification of a measure under national law (ECtHR, Judgment of December 17, 2009, complaint no. 19359/04, M. v. Germany, marginal no. 126). . . . The concept of punishment in art. 103 Basic Law will continue to be interpreted as expressed in the decision of February 5, 2004 (BVerfGE 109, 133, 167ff.) under the constitutional order of the Basic Law as it has evolved . . .

Having regard to the value judgments [of art. 5 ECHR] and in view of the substantial invasion of the trust of persons in preventive detention affected in their basic right under art. 2 para. sentence 2 and art. 104 para. 1 sentence 1 Basic Law, the purpose of protecting the general public from dangerous criminals to a large extent takes second place to the trust protected by the basic rights in termination of preventive detention after the expiry of ten years . . . A deprivation of freedom by preventive detention that is retrospectively ordered or extended can therefore only be regarded as proportionate if the required distinction from punishment is maintained, extreme danger of the most serious violent or sexual crimes can be deduced from actual circumstances in the personality or behavior of the detainee (see also BGH, Judgment of November 9, 2010, 5 StR 394/10, 440/10, 474/10, NJW 2011, 240, 243) and the prerequisites of art. 5 para. 1 sentence 2 letter e ECHR* are fulfilled. Only in such exceptional cases can predominance of the public interests in safety still be assumed . . .

NOTES

1. Note that the four judgments excerpted above all address the distinction between punishment and some other form of carceral sanction: civil commitment, preventive detention, or more generally, a "measure." But only one of the excerpts—the first decision by the German Federal Constitutional Court, from 2004—addresses the constitutionality of the supposedly non-punitive measure itself. The other three consider indirect constitutional challenges that apply only once the distinction between punishment and "measure" has been rejected: double jeopardy, or more precisely double punishment for the same

---

* [ECHR Art. 5 para. 1 sentence 2: No one shall be deprived of his liberty save in the following cases and in accordance with a procedure prescribed by law: . . . (e) the lawful detention of persons for the prevention of the spreading of infectious diseases, of persons of unsound mind, alcoholics or drug addicts or vagrants. . . . —Eds.]

offense (*ne bis in idem*) (in *Hendricks*) and retroactivity (*ex post facto*) (in *Hendricks, M. v. Germany*, and the 2011 decision by the German Constitutional Court.*

On the first question, the constitutionality of preventive detention *per se*, what work, if any, does the concept of dignity do in the court's reasoning? Note that the German Constitutional Court's 2011 judgment in the same case makes much less of dignity, and instead relies heavily on the right to freedom.

On the second question, do you find the rationales in *Hendricks*, on one hand, and in the German Constitutional Court's 2004 and 2011 judgments, on the other, convincing? (How do they differ?) Or are they a series of taxonomical sleights of hand that, in the end, amount to little more than the repetitive insistence on the reality, and constitutional significance, of the distinction between punishment and measure?

Should it make a difference whether the legislature deliberately labeled a sanction a "measure" or something, anything, other than a "punishment" partly, or even entirely, in order to escape the constitutional limits (e.g., double jeopardy, retroactivity) that apply only to something called a "punishment"? What do you think of the ECHR's professed effort to "go behind appearances"? How willing are the domestic courts (both the U.S. and the German court) to question "their" legislatures' labeling efforts? How comfortable are they with engaging in labeling exercises themselves?

2. There are different ways and techniques to organize preventive detention. In the U.S., over the last two decades, state legislatures have introduced Sexually Violent Predator Acts, which allow civil commitment of persons with mental abnormality or personality disorder and the tendency to commit, acts of sexual violence.

In Germany, preventive detention has a longer history. The Criminal Code distinguishes between criminal punishment and measures of rehabilitation and protection (*Maßregeln der Besserung und Sicherung*), which aim to rehabilitate dangerous offenders and to protect the public. This two-track system of sanctions was created in November 1933 by the so-called Habitual Offenders Act: Law Against Dangerous Habitual Offenders and Regarding Measures of Incapacitation and Rehabilitation (*Gewohnheitsverbrechergesetz*) of November 24, 1933, RGBl. I 995, art. 3, § 17.[†] Preventive detention (§§ 66–66b StGB) is not limited to sexual offenders. Until recently, preventive detention required (besides a criminal sentence of at least two years imprisonment plus previous convictions) a general propensity "to commit serious offenses, notably those which seriously harm their victims physically or mentally or which cause serious economic damage." In 2010, the legislature eliminated the "serious economic damage" clause from § 66 StGB. But the Act still applies to a larger group of offenders than does the Kansas Sexually Violent Predator Law.

In 1965, 1,430 persons were being held in preventive detention in Germany, and this included chronic property offenders. As preventive detention increasingly became the subject of criticism, the numbers dropped to 183 persons in 1995. Since then, the numbers have risen again, to 536 in 2010 (out of 60,693 prison inmates).

Does it make sense to extend preventive detention to some dangerous offenders, but not to others? Put another way, if preventive detention of some dangerous offenders is constitutionally unobjectionable, then why would it be objectionable to preventively detain all dangerous offenders? Does the selective preventive detention of some dangerous offenders, but not others, raise constitutional (equal treatment) concerns? Other common law countries have preventive detention schemes that rival the breadth of Germany's.[‡]

---

* For a detailed discussion of retroactivity, see Chapter 2.A.

† The original title of the relevant section of the German Criminal Code was revised, in 1975, from "Measures of Protection and Rehabilitation" to "Measures of Rehabilitation and Protection." Compare StGB § 42a (old version) with StGB § 61 (current version), respectively.

‡ See, e.g., Can. Crim. Code pt. xxiv ("dangerous offenders"); *R. v. Lyons*, [1987] 2 S.C.R. 309 (reviewing history of preventive detention in English law, and rejecting constitutional challenge—under prohibition of "cruel and unusual treatment or punishment" in § 12 Canadian Charter of Rights and Freedoms—to revised Canadian dangerous offender scheme, "now carefully tailored so as to be confined in its application to those habitual criminals who are dangerous to others"); see generally Christopher Slobogin, "Preventive Detention in Europe and the United States," Vanderbilt Public Law Research Paper Working Paper No. 12-27 (June 27, 2012).

3. Decisions of the European Court of Human Rights (ECtHR) are strictly binding for Germany only with regard to the individual case (the obligation to pay compensation to individual claimants). The legal document that is the source for the ECtHR's jurisprudence, the European Convention on Human Rights (ECHR), has the status of a simple statute in German law. The ECHR does not have the constitutional status of the German Basic Law. It is therefore not evident that general rules and principles developed by the ECtHR are mandatory for the application of German law. How far the German courts will go in adapting their case law to conform to principles appearing in the European Court's jurisprudence is mainly a political matter. In recent years, the political will has, however, grown so that a victory before the European Court will have wider consequences beyond merely affirming the claimant's view and granting him or her financial compensation.

In the United Kingdom, the ECHR has had a noticeable impact on English criminal law in the wake of the Human Rights Act 1998, which requires that, "[s]o far as it is possible to do so, primary legislation and subordinate legislation ... be read and given effect in a way which is compatible with the Convention rights."*

Compare the relationship between the U.S. Supreme Court and the legislatures of U.S. states (Kansas in this case), on one hand, and that between the ECtHR and the member states (Germany in this case), on the other. Might the ECtHR's relative lack of power help to account for its relative lack of deference? Note that a negative decision by the U.S. Supreme Court—as the final arbiter of matters of federal constitutional law—is not merely advisory, but renders a state (and federal) statute null and void.

How does the German Federal Constitutional Court's 2011 decision deal with the ECtHR's critical review (if not the literal overturning) of its 2004 decision? Does it accept the ECtHR's central conclusion that preventive detention is "punishment," all "appearances"—including its own previous decision—to the contrary notwithstanding? Or does it treat what appears as dismissal by the ECtHR instead as confirmation of the central holding in its 2004 decision, namely that the distinction between punishment and measure must make a difference, i.e., it must result in palpable differences in the conditions of incarceration?

4. After the European Court of Human Rights decided *M. v. Germany*, a number of other claimants who were detained in Germany demanded to be released immediately. In the time period after the European Court decision, there was a state of confusion among German courts that supervise the execution of preventive detention. Some courts released detainees who fell under the retroactive extension of preventive detention through the 1998 legislation. Other courts did not. The German Federal Constitutional Court had to take up the matter again because new complaints were filed. Those were decided in the second ruling from May 4, 2011, excerpted above.

The German Federal Constitutional Court was in a somewhat awkward position. On the one hand, it would have meant complete capitulation before the European Court to accede now that preventive detention was criminal punishment—exactly what the German Federal Constitutional Court had denied in 2004. On the other hand, simply restating what they had said in 2004 would have been interpreted as a blatant sign of disrespect for the European Court of Human Rights. Therefore, the judges at the German Federal Constitutional Court had to find a compromise.[†]

The crucial point in the 2011 decision is to stress what the Court calls *Abstandsgebot*, a distinction requirement; the execution of preventive detention must be made (yet) more distinct from imprisonment than it had previously been. In December 2012 (Law for the Implementation of the Distinction Requirement in Federal Law), the German legislature introduced § 66c German Criminal Code which stipulates some general principles

---

* UK Human Rights Act (1998) § 3(1).
† See generally, Kirstin Drenkhahn, Christine Morgenstern, and Dirk van Zyl Smit, "What Is in a Name? Preventive Detention in Germany in the Shadow of European Human Rights Law," *Criminal Law Review* [2012], 167.

for the administration of preventive detention according to the 2011 decision by the Federal Constitutional Court. With respect to the narrower problem of "old cases" (persons in preventive detention who would have been released under the "ten-years-only-for-first-time-preventive-detention" rule abolished in 1998), the Court tightened the requirements without totally giving in to the European Court. According to the ECtHR, applying art. 7 para. 1 ECHR, a retroactive extension of the period in preventive detention is prohibited without exceptions. The German Federal Constitutional Court does allow for limited exceptions under the following conditions: the required distinction from punishment is maintained, extreme danger of the most serious violent or sexual crimes can be deduced from actual circumstances in the personality or behavior of the detainee, and the detained person suffers from an "unsound mind" in the sense of art. 5 para. 1 sentence 2 number (e) ECHR.

Assuming this account captures the Constitutional Court's reasoning well enough, what do you think of making constitutional law through compromise? Should decisions about fundamental constitutional principles—dignity, freedom, *Rechtsstaat*—be subject to considerations of inter-curial (or more broadly political, international, or intranational, i.e., federal) deference, or lack thereof?

5. In the German Criminal Code, there is a range of other measures of rehabilitation and protection. They include placement in a psychiatric hospital (§ 63, not as civil commitment but ordered through a criminal court) or in a detoxification facility (§ 64), but also somewhat less intrusive measures like the revocation of drivers licenses after traffic offenses (§ 69) or employment restrictions (§ 70). In the U.S., some of these sanctions, along with a long list of others (including disenfranchisement, deportation, and loss of welfare and housing benefits), are classified as "collateral consequences" and have been subjected to vigorous debate, largely focused on obligations (by defense attorneys, prosecutors, judges) to inform defendants of their potential, if not mandatory, application as a result of certain convictions, the vast majority of which in the U.S. result from guilty pleas.*

---

* See, e.g., Uniform Law Commission, Uniform Collateral Consequences of Conviction Act (2009); see generally Meda Chesney-Lind and Marc Mauer (eds.), *Invisible Punishment: The Collateral Consequences of Mass Imprisonment* (2003).

THE LEGALITY PRINCIPLE
(*NULLA POENA SINE LEGE*)

The principle of legality is generally presented as a key commitment of Anglo-American and German criminal law alike. Upon closer inspection, however, whether this is in fact the case is a little less obvious than it might first appear. U.S. constitutional law certainly is familiar with a prohibition of *retroactivity* (an *ex post facto* prohibition appears not once, but twice, and not in the Bill of Rights, but in the original text of the U.S. Constitution, though neither version—as we will see—turns out to cover judicial decisions) and a *vagueness* prohibition has been traced to the general due process protection in the Fifth and Fourteenth Amendments. But there is no constitutional principle of *legislativity* (which would require the legislative definition of offenses, despite the centuries-long tradition of judicially created crimes, a practice that has fallen into disuse without having aroused constitutional scrutiny); the rule of *lenity*, also known as the rule of strict construction, is of dubious constitutional status (there is no "prohibition of analogy") and, even as a maxim of statutory interpretation, is honored in its breach; and the requirement of *publicity*, which is also often mentioned in connection with the principle of legality, has no practical significance, even if it were recognized as a constitutional principle. What is more important, however, regardless of the status or critical bite these principles, rules, and maxims might have, they are rarely, if ever, considered as manifestations of some more general principle like, say, the "principle of legality."

A note on terminology and translations: German treatises on criminal procedure refer to a principle by the name *Legalitätsprinzip*. But keep in mind that the meaning of the term *Legalitätsprinzip* in this context is not identical with the meaning of the English expression "principle of legality," that is, the principle examined in this chapter. Rather, the German procedural principle demands compulsory prosecution: it aims to eliminate prosecutorial discretion.*

In Germany, the principle of legality instead is known as the principle of *nulla poena sine lege*, which is attributed not to Roman law, or canon law, as the use of Latin might suggest, but to the German criminal law scholar P.J.A. Feuerbach, who, in § 20 of his influential criminal law textbook,† postulated not one, but three versions of the principle—*nulla poena sine lege* (no punishment without law), *nulla poena sine crimine* (no punishment without a crime), *nullum crimen sine poena legali* (no crime without a legal punishment)—each deduced from "the highest principle of penal law":

---

* See Chapter 5.C.

† P.J.A. Feuerbach, *Lehrbuch des gemeinen in Deutschland geltenden peinlichen Rechts* (1st edn. 1801). For a translation of excerpts from Feuerbach's textbook, see Markus D. Dubber (ed.), *Foundational Texts in Modern Criminal Law* (forthcoming 2014). On Feuerbach, see generally Tatjana Hörnle, "Paul Johann Anselm von Feuerbach and His Impact on Contemporary Criminal Law Theory," in ibid; see also Markus D. Dubber, "The Legality Principle in American and German Criminal Law: An Essay in Comparative Legal History," in Georges Martyn et al. (eds.), *From the Judge's Arbitrium to the Legality Principle: Legislation as a Source of Law in Criminal Trials* (2013), 365.

§ 19

From the above deduction the following highest principle of penal law arises: *Every legal punishment in the state is the legal consequence of a statute that is based on the necessity of maintaining the rights of others and that threatens the violation of a right with a sensual evil.*

Today, the *nulla poena* principle is part of the German Constitution. Article 103 para. 2 Basic Law provides:

An act can be punished only if its punishability was specified by a law before the act was committed.

Since Feuerbach, the original *nulla poena* principle has spawned several variations each of which is said to capture one of its aspects:

nulla poena sine lege scripta (no punishment without *written* law): legislativity
nulla poena sine lege praevia (. . . without *prior* law): prospectivity
nulla poena sine lege certa (. . . without *specific* law): specificity
nulla poena sine lege stricta (. . . without *strict* law): strict construction/no analogy.*

A. Retroactivity

Rogers v. Tennessee
United States Supreme Court
532 U.S. 451 (2001)

Justice O'Connor delivered the opinion of the Court.

[Wilbert Rogers stabbed a man, who died some 15 months later. After his conviction of second degree murder, he appealed on the basis of the common law "year and a day rule," which provides that no defendant can be convicted of murder, or any other form of homicide, unless his victim died by the defendant's act within a year and a day of the act. The Tennessee Supreme Court abolished the rule and applied its decision to petitioner to uphold his conviction.]

This case concerns the constitutionality of the retroactive application of a judicial decision abolishing the common law "year and a day rule." . . .

Although petitioner's claim is one of due process, the Constitution's Ex Post Facto Clause figures prominently in his argument. The Clause provides simply that "no State shall . . . pass any . . . ex post facto Law." Art. I, § 10, cl. 1. The most well known and oft repeated explanation of the scope of the Clause's protection was given by Justice Chase, who long ago identified, in dictum, four types of laws to which the Clause extends:

1st. Every law that makes an action done before the passing of the law, and which was innocent when done, criminal; and punishes such action. 2d. Every law that aggravates a crime, or makes it greater than it was, when committed. 3d. Every law that changes the punishment, and inflicts a greater punishment, than the law annexed to the crime, when committed. 4th. Every law that alters the legal rules of evidence, and receives less, or different, testimony, than the law required at the time of the commission of the offense, in order to convict the offender.

Calder v. Bull, 3 Dallas 386, 390 (1798).

[L]imitations on ex post facto judicial decisionmaking are inherent in the notion of due process. . . . [T]his Court has often recognized the "basic principle that a criminal statute must give fair warning of the conduct that it makes a crime." Deprivation of the right to fair warning, we continued, can result both from vague statutory language and from an unforeseeable and retroactive judicial expansion of statutory language that appears narrow and precise on its face. For that reason, "if a judicial construction of a criminal statute is 'unexpected and indefensible

---

* For another variation, *nulla poena sine culpa*, see the discussion of the so-called "culpability principle" in, for example, Chapter 1.A.i. There was even a variant in (pre-1989) socialist criminal law: *nulla poena sine periculo sociali* (. . . without social dangerousness). See, e.g., Andrzej Zoll, "Die Gesellschaftsgefährlichkeit der Tat als Element des Verbrechensaufbaus," in Klaus Lüderssen et al. (eds.), *Modernes Strafrecht und ultima-ratio-Prinzip* (1990), 149.

by reference to the law which had been expressed prior to the conduct in issue,' [the construction] must not be given retroactive effect." Bouie v. City of Columbia, 378 U.S. 347, 354 (1964) (quoting J. Hall, General Principles of Criminal Law 61 (2d ed. 1960))....

Petitioner observes that the Due Process and Ex Post Facto Clauses safeguard common interests—in particular, the interests in fundamental fairness (through notice and fair warning) and the prevention of the arbitrary and vindictive use of the laws. While this is undoubtedly correct, petitioner is mistaken to suggest that these considerations compel extending the strictures of the Ex Post Facto Clause to the context of common law judging. The Ex Post Facto Clause, by its own terms, does not apply to courts. Extending the Clause to courts through the rubric of due process thus would circumvent the clear constitutional text. It also would evince too little regard for the important institutional and contextual differences between legislating, on the one hand, and common law decisionmaking, on the other.

Petitioner contends that state courts acting in their common law capacity act much like legislatures in the exercise of their lawmaking function, and indeed may in some cases even be subject to the same kinds of political influences and pressures that justify ex post facto limitations upon legislatures. A court's "opportunity for discrimination," however, "is more limited than [a] legislature's, in that [it] can only act in construing existing law in actual litigation." James v. United States, 366 U.S. 213, 247, n. 3, 6 L. Ed. 2d 246, 81 S. Ct. 1052 (1961) (Harlan, J., concurring in part and dissenting in part). Moreover, "given the divergent pulls of flexibility and precedent in our case law system," incorporation of the Calder categories into due process limitations on judicial decisionmaking would place an unworkable and unacceptable restraint on normal judicial processes and would be incompatible with the resolution of uncertainty that marks any evolving legal system....

[A]t the time of petitioner's crime the year and a day rule had only the most tenuous foothold as part of the criminal law of the State of Tennessee. The rule did not exist as part of Tennessee's statutory criminal code. And while the Supreme Court of Tennessee concluded that the rule persisted at common law, it also pointedly observed that the rule had never once served as a ground of decision in any prosecution for murder in the State. Indeed, in all the reported Tennessee cases, the rule has been mentioned only three times, and each time in dicta....

The judgment of the Supreme Court of Tennessee is accordingly affirmed.

Justice Scalia, dissenting.

The Court today approves the conviction of a man for a murder that was not murder (but only manslaughter) when the offense was committed. It thus violates a principle—encapsulated in the maxim nulla poena sine lege which "dates from the ancient Greeks" and has been described as one of the most "widely held value judgments in the entire history of human thought." J. Hall, General Principles of Criminal Law 59 (2d ed. 1960). Today's opinion produces, moreover, a curious constitution that only a judge could love. One in which (by virtue of the Ex Post Facto Clause) the elected representatives of all the people cannot retroactively make murder what was not murder when the act was committed; but in which unelected judges can do precisely that. One in which the predictability of parliamentary lawmaking cannot validate the retroactive creation of crimes, but the predictability of judicial lawmaking can do so. I do not believe this is the system that the Framers envisioned—or, for that matter, that any reasonable person would imagine....

Madison wrote that "ex post facto laws ... are contrary to the first principles of the social compact, and to every principle of social legislation." The Federalist No. 44, p. 282 (C. Rossiter ed. 1961). I find it impossible to believe, as the Court does, that this strong sentiment attached only to retroactive laws passed by the legislature, and would not apply equally (or indeed with even greater force) to a court's production of the same result through disregard of the traditional limits upon judicial power. Insofar as the "first principles of the social compact" are concerned, what possible difference does it make that "[a] court's opportunity for discrimination" by retroactively changing a law "is more limited than a legislature's, in that it can only act in construing existing law in actual litigation"? The injustice to the individuals affected is no less.

Even if I agreed with the Court that the Due Process Clause is violated only when there is lack of "fair warning" of the impending retroactive change, I would not find such fair warning here. It is not clear to me, in fact, what the Court believes the fair warning consisted of. Was it the mere fact that "the year and a day rule is widely viewed as an outdated relic of the common law"? So are many of the elements of common law crimes, such as "breaking the close" as an element of burglary, or "asportation" as an element of larceny. See W. LaFave & A. Scott, Criminal Law 631–633, 708–710 (1972). Are all of these "outdated relics" subject to retroactive judicial rescission? Or perhaps the fair warning consisted of the fact that "the year and a day rule has been legislatively or judicially abolished in the vast majority of jurisdictions recently to have addressed the issue." But why not count in petitioner's favor (as giving him no reason to expect a change in law) those even more numerous jurisdictions that have chosen not "recently to have addressed the issue"?...

In any event, as the Court itself acknowledges, "due process . . . does not require a person to apprise himself of the common law of all 50 States in order to guarantee that his actions will not subject him to punishment in light of a developing trend in the law that has not yet made its way to his State." . . .

German Federal Court of Justice
(*Bundesgerichtshof*, BGH)
BGHSt 39, 1 (November 3, 1992)
Border Guard Case*

Facts[†]

A.

. . .

The defendants, as members of the border troops of the GDR[‡]—W. as non-commissioned officer and as leader of a post consisting of two persons, and H. as a soldier—were stationed at the Berlin Wall. There, on Dec. 1, 1984, at 3:15 a.m. they fired at S. who was 20 years old and came from the GDR. He was preparing to climb over the wall, from the city district of Pankow in the direction of the district of Wedding. S., while he was climbing up a ladder leaning against the wall, was hit by bullets from the automatic infantry rifles of the defendants. A bullet from the weapon of the defendant W. penetrated his back, when he had already laid one hand on the top of the wall; this injury was fatal. S. was also hit in the knee by a bullet from the weapon of the defendant H.; this injury had no connection with his death. The time sequence of the two gunshot wounds has not been established. S. was not brought into the People's Police Hospital until shortly before 5:30 a.m., where he died at 6:20 a.m. He would have been saved by immediate assistance from a doctor. The delay was the consequence of rules as to secrecy and competence, which were not known to the defendants. The defendants were not employed in the recovery and removal of victim.

For the shots which hit S., the rifles of both defendants were adjusted to "continuous firing." The defendant H. fired twenty-five rounds altogether in the five seconds during which S. climbed up the ladder; from the rifle of the defendant W. twenty-seven rounds were fired. The defendant W. who had previously shouted to S. to stop, and had given warning shots, fired at S. from a distance of 150 m, from the watch tower. The defendant H., who on the appearance of the fugitive, had left the tower at the direction of the defendant W., fired, leaning against the wall, from a distance of about 110 m. Neither of the defendants intended to kill S. whom they did not consider to be a spy, saboteur or "criminal." But they recognized the possibility of a fatal hit. "Even at this price, however, they intended to prevent the success of the flight, in accordance with the command which they considered to be binding. In order to secure in any event the carrying out of the command, which even included the conscious killing of the fugitive so as to frustrate the flight, they fired—omitting as a first stage the prescribed aimed individual shots—in short bursts of continuous fire. They knew that this increased the probability of a hit, even if not in the area aimed at, and with that also the risk of a fatal shot."

The defendants were asked before the start of their service at the border whether they were prepared to use weapons against "border violators"; they answered the question in the affirmative without inward reservations. §§ 26, 27 East German Border Act of March 25, 1982 (DDR-GBI I, 197) had been discussed during their training. According to § 27 para. 1 sentence 1 of this Act, the use of the gun was "justified in order to prevent the immediately impending execution or continuation of a punishable act, which in the circumstances presents itself as a felony." The regional court accepted as true that contraventions of § 213 Criminal Code GDR ("unlawful crossing of the border") in direct contact with the Berlin Wall at the time of the Act were in most cases assessed to be a felony in accordance with § 213 para. 3 Criminal Code GDR and were punished with more than two years imprisonment . . .

As to the general command situation, the regional court explains: "The general command situation which was authoritative for the defendants as well and was so understood and accepted by them,

---

* [This is based on a translation which appears in Raymond Youngs (ed.), *Sourcebook on German Law* (2nd edn. 2002) and is reproduced with the permission of Routledge Cavendish.—Eds.]

† [For further information about the political background, see the judgment of July 26, 1994, against the members of the National Defense Council of the German Democratic Republic. See BGH, July 26, 1994, 5 StR 98/94, BGHSt 40, 218.—Eds.]

‡ [The former German Democratic Republic ("East Germany"), under socialist rule, reunified with the Western parts of Germany, the Federal Republic of Germany, in 1990.—Eds.]

was to the effect that the reaching of 'enemy territory' (here: West Berlin) by the fugitive was to be prevented in every case and, in the end, by all methods. Accordingly one of the formulations used, to the defendants as well, at the 'gatherings' [meaning a "pep-talk," or indoctrination session] stated in its key sentence: 'Border escapes are not to be permitted in any case. Border violators are to be arrested or destroyed' . . . Before every move out to border service, the "gathering" took place; by it, once again, the specific action and, in general form, the duty imposed were made known to the border guards." The general command situation, as dealt with in training, provided for the following scheme of action, under which at any time the next action stage was to be proceeded to if the previous one showed no result or showed itself from the outset not to promise results: calling to the fugitive—attempt by the guard to reach the fugitive on foot—warning shot—aimed single shots, several times if necessary, at the legs—"further shooting, no matter how, if necessary also shooting to kill, until the flight has been prevented." The rule of thumb was: "Better that the fugitive should be dead than that the flight should succeed."

The regional court Berlin assumes that the defendants committed joint homicide: It applied §§ 212, 213 Criminal Code GDR as the more lenient law (art. 315 para. 1 Introductory Law to the Criminal Code in association with § 2 para. 3 Criminal Code). . . . The regional court further states: Even if a justification under the law of the GDR is considered, it would nevertheless not be applicable to the shots of the defendants because of the special circumstances of the act. §§ 26 and 27 of the GDR Border Law are orientated by the principle of proportionality; § 27 para. 1 sentence 1 describes the use of firearms as "the most extreme measure of the application of force." An interpretation which has regard to the viewpoint of proportionality would result here in the continuous fire given by the defendants not being covered by § 27 of the GDR Border Law and only single shots having been permitted. The requirement of § 27 para. 5 of the GDR-Border Law that human life is to be spared if possible also argues in favor of this. Admittedly the defendants aimed at the legs. They were however aware that with continuous fire in short bursts, the weapon "breaks out" after the first shot. . . .

The regional court convicted the accused W. (born on April 11, 1964) and H. (born on July 16, 1961) of homicide, and sentenced the accused W. to juvenile detention of one year and six months and the accused H. to a prison sentence of one year and nine months; it suspended the execution of both sentences.

The appeals in law were rejected.

Reasons

. . .

C.

The factual and legal examination shows that the appeals in law of the defendants are, in their outcome, unfounded.

I.

The lives of the defendants and the victim were based in the GDR at the time of the deed; there the victim was hit by the defendants' shots and died . . .

II.

The law of the former GDR would, in the sense of § 2 para. 3 Criminal Code . . . be, in comparison with the law of the Federal Republic of Germany, the more lenient law if the fatal of use of firearms had been justified in accordance with the law of the GDR (§ 27 para. 2 GDR Border Law in combination with § 213 para. 3 GDR Criminal Code), and this ground of justification had to be taken into consideration even today in favor of the defendants. The examination shows that the defendants—according to the interpretation employed in the GDR at the time of the act—complied with the requirements described in § 27 para. 2 GDR Border Law but that no effective justification follows from this. . . .

2. Contrary to the view of the regional court, it is possible to interpret these provisions as meaning that the conduct of the defendants was covered by them.

a) The literal meaning of § 27 GDR Border Law permits such an interpretation: the crossing of the border which, by application of § 213 para. 3 Criminal Code GDR was regarded as a crime, should, so far as it was directly imminent, be "prevented" by the use of firearms (§ 27 para. 1 GDR Border Law). The act described the use of firearms as the "ultimate measure" (§ 27 para. 1 sentence 1 GD Border Law); however, other means of preventing the crossing of the border were not available for the defendants. According to § 27 para. 5 GDR Border Law, lives were to be spared "as far as possible," and therefore not in every case. . . .

The prerequisite for this interpretation of § 27 GDR Border Law is, of course, that the objective of preventing border violations had priority over the sparing of human life. How the balancing of the life of the fugitive with the "inviolability of the state border" was to turn out could not be gathered from the Act. Case law of courts of the GDR on this question has not been published. . . . Under these circumstances, the general command situation . . . surrounding the occurrence of the act is crucial to ascertain how the provisions of § 27 GDR Border Law were understood by those responsible for its application and interpretation at the time of the act.

aa) The general command situation included "even the deliberate killing of the fugitive in order to frustrate the flight" if less severe means did not suffice for the prevention of the flight. The reaching by the fugitive of the western sector of Berlin was "to be prevented in every case and in the end by all means." . . . The interest in prevention of the flight accordingly had priority over the life of the fugitive. A successful flight was "the worst thing that could happen for the company as it would not be consistent with the duty placed upon it." On the other hand, the fatal shooting of a fugitive at the wall had "no negative consequences"; it never led to proceedings against the marksman. Instead, the guard who had, in whatever way, prevented a flight would be treated with distinction and rewarded. The judge of fact states that courts, public prosecutors' offices or other state authorities of the GDR had never objected that the use of firearms described in the general command exceeded the boundaries laid down in § 27 GDR Border Law.

bb) The fact that the protection of the life of "border violators" receded behind other objectives, even the objective of keeping serious injuries secret, is also shown by the following findings of the judge of fact:

. . . None of the members of the border troops and other units arriving after the shots helped S. although he asked for this several times. He was "dragged" to a tower and "put down" there in a place which was not visible from the West. S. was not taken away by the usual ambulance of the "Rapid Medical Aid," but by a regimental ambulance which took forty-five minutes to arrive, and not to the nearest hospital but to the more distant hospital of the Peoples Police, where he was delivered more than two hours after the injuries. There was no doctor in the ambulance, because on the requesting of the ambulance no communication was permitted to the effect that someone had been seriously injured. With rapid medical assistance, S. could have been saved. The measures mentioned, which produced a substantial delay, corresponded to the general command situation which was primarily orientated not towards the saving of life, but towards the interest in ensuring that the incident remained unknown on both sides of the border . . .

cc) The Senate therefore concludes that, according to state practice in the GDR at the time of the act, the use of continuous fire without preliminary single shots directed at the legs had not been regarded as unlawful. The defendants, by continuous fire, increased the chance of preventing the flight (although admittedly also the risk of a fatal shot) and thereby complied with what was, in harmony with the prevailing interpretation of the GDR Border Law, conveyed to them as the most important objective, namely the prevention of crossings of the border. They would . . . possibly have laid themselves open to criticism . . . if there was a high probability that single shots at the legs would have reliably prevented flight. That is certainly not the position here in view of the timing: S. was, when the defendants fired, rapidly climbing the ladder. He needed five seconds to reach a height from which he could grasp the top of the wall. It must be accepted that he was at this point in time in a position to climb over the top of the wall within a few seconds and thereby to bring himself into safety. On the firing of single shots, according to the findings, the least interval between two shots amounted to 1.5 seconds; in view of the shortness of the time remaining for prevention of flight, the chance of attaining this objective was accordingly substantially higher with continuous fire (with a frequency of ten shots per second). Incidentally, it must also be borne in mind that the distance of the marksmen from S. was not inconsiderable and that the events took place at night.

dd) Accordingly, the conduct of the defendants complied with the justification provisions of § 27 para. 2 GDR Border Law as they were applied in state practice . .

b) However, one must distinguish from the question of whether the conduct of the defendants was justified by the law of the GDR as it was applied in state practice another question: whether a justification understood in this way (§ 27 para. 2 GDR Border Law) must be left out of consideration because it infringes preordained general legal principles which should have been observed in the GDR as well, and because of an extreme violation of the principle of proportionality. . . . The Senate answers this question in the affirmative . . .

aa) Cases in which a justification accepted at the time of the act is regarded as not appropriate for consideration must certainly remain limited to extreme exceptions.

The fact that a justification offends against the public order of the Federal Republic of Germany . . . is—contrary to the view of Küpper-Wilms, ZRP 1992, 91 (93)—not on its own a sufficient ground . . .

bb) A justification accepted at the time of the act can only remain out of consideration because of a violation of law with a higher priority if an obviously gross violation of basic concepts of justice and humanity is expressed in it; the violation must be so serious that it offends against convictions about law, which are common to all people, referring to the worth and dignity of the human being (BGHSt 2, 234 (239)). The conflict of positive law with justice must be so intolerable that the statutory provision has, as false law, to give way to justice (Radbruch, SJZ 1946, 105, 107). An attempt was made (see also BVerfGE 3, 225 (232) = NJW 1954, 65; BVerfGE 6, 132 (198 f.) = NJW 1957, 579) after the end of the National Socialist despotism to characterize the most serious violations of law in this way. The transfer of these points of view to the present case is not simple, because the killing of human beings at the internal German frontier cannot be equated with Nationalist Socialist mass murder. Nevertheless, the insight obtained at that time remains valid, that in assessing acts which have been committed at the order of the state, regard has to be had to whether the state has overstepped the utmost limit which is set for it according to the general conviction in every country.

cc) Today, more concrete standards for investigation have been added: international human rights treaties offer criteria for saying when the state violates human rights according to the belief of the worldwide legal community. In this connection, the International Covenant on Civil and Political Rights of December 19, 1966 (ICCPR) is of special importance. The GDR acceded to it in 1974 (GDR GBl II, 57). . . . The GDR, however, neglected to use the treaty in accordance with art. 51 GDR Constitution as an opportunity for internal statutory amendments and to have it "confirmed" on this occasion by the Peoples Chamber in accordance with the said constitutional provision. These circumstances do not change anything so far as the international law obligation of the GDR is concerned. A state can "not evade the fulfillment of obligations entered into by it by an appeal to its internal legal order" (Völkerrecht, Lehrb., Berlin-Ost 1981, I, p. 59) . . .

(1) Art. 12 para. 2 ICCPR states: "Every person is free to leave any country including his own" (translation in the GDR Law Gazette: "Everyone is free to leave any country and also his own") . . . it follows from the binding English wording of art. 12 para. 3 ICCPR ("The . . . rights shall not be subject to any restrictions except . . . ") and the history of origin as well as the international interpretation of the provision that a comprehensive statutory reservation was not intended; the limitations should much rather remain limited to exceptional cases and not in any way destroy the substance of the freedom to move around and the right to travel abroad . . . Economic or social welfare points of view, as the materials show, should not be a permissible motive for the limitation of the freedom to move around. . . .

(2) The human right of freedom to travel abroad described in art. 12 of the ICCPR was violated by the border regime of the GDR because the right to freely travel abroad was withheld from inhabitants of the GDR not only in exceptional cases but as a rule . . .

(3) In particular, the restrictive provisions as to passport and travel abroad cannot be appreciated from the point of view of human rights without having regard to the actual circumstances at the border, which were characterized by "wall, barbed wire, no man's land and command to shoot" (BVerfGE 36, 1 (35) = NJW 1973, 1539) and therefore violated art. 6 of the ICCPR. According to this provision "every human being has an inherent right to life"; "no one may be deprived of his life arbitrarily" (art. 6 para. 1 sentence 1 and 3). Even if the interpretation of the term "arbitrarily" has up until now, on the whole, not been very productive (see Nowak, art. 5 marginal nos. 12 ff.; Polakiewicz, EuGRZ 1992, 177 (182); Ramcharan, Netherlands Internat. Law Review 30, (1983), 297 (316 ff.); . . .), the tendency becomes apparent in the case law of other States as well (see in particular US Supreme Court 471 US 1 in the case of Tennessee v. Garner, 1985) to limit state organs' use of firearms which have possible fatal effect, by strong emphasis on the principle of proportionality, to cases in which an endangering of life and limb of others is to be feared . . .

The limit of arbitrary action is, according to the view of the Senate, in particular overstepped if the use of firearms at the border serves the purpose of frightening third persons away from the unauthorized crossing of the border . . .

dd) The violation of the human rights guarantees in arts. 6 and 12 ICCPR in their specific context, characterized by the situation at the inner German border, makes it impossible for the Senate to base a justification on the provisions of § 27 GDR Border Law as well as those of § 213 para. 3 GDR Criminal Code to the extent to which they were understood in the State practice of the GDR. The circumstances at the border were, even considering the economic and social disadvantages which would be connected with a substantial emigration of persons, an expression of an attitude which valued the right of human beings to life at a lower level than its interest in preventing them from leaving the State. The justification provided for in GDR law and described in § 27 GDR Border Law was for this reason ineffective from the start . . .

3. The Senate then had to investigate whether § 27 GDR Border Law could, by interpretation methods which were peculiar to the law of the GDR, have been interpreted in such a way as to avoid the violations of human rights mentioned; a justification limited in this manner should then be considered. . . .

In contrast to the National Socialist dictator state there was no doctrine in the GDR according to which the mere will of the possessor of factual power was able to make law. Statutes were binding (see art. 49 I GDR Constitution). The administration of justice, which had to protect freedom, peaceful life and the rights and dignity of human was called to "realize Socialist legality" (art. 90 I GDR Constitution) . . . Accordingly statutes laid claim to a validity which was not determined by directions or actual state practice. A person who seeks today to ascertain the content of the statutes of the GDR by having regard to the Constitution of the GDR and the fact that the GDR was bound by international human rights agreements does not thereby impute to the law of the GDR contents which would be irreconcilable with this law's own pretensions. The First Deputy for the President of the Council of Ministers of the GDR . . . explained on the introduction of the GDR Border Law that the regime regarding the use of firearms § 27 GDR Border Law) contained "no more and no less than other states have laid down for their protective organs"; the use of firearms was "the most extreme measure" against persons who "have committed crimes against the legal order of the GDR or seek to evade responsibility for the violation of the law they have committed" (Peoples Chamber, 8. Wahlper., 4. Tagung, p. 88 f. of the shorthand copy). . . . The wording of § 27 para. 2 GDR Border Law permitted an interpretation which took into account the principle of proportionality . . . § 27 para. 2 sentence 1 GDR Border Law is then to be understood in this way: border soldiers might use firearms for prevention of flight . . . but the justification reached its limit when shots were fired at a fugitive, who, according to the circumstances, was unarmed and not otherwise a danger to the life and limb of others with the—conditional or unconditional—intention to kill him. Accordingly, the conditionally intentional killing, as expressed in the use of continuous fire, was not covered by § 27 para. 2 GDR Border Law as interpreted in a manner sympathetic to human rights . . .

. . .

c) On this interpretation, the conduct of the defendants was not covered by justification in § 27 para. 2 GDR Border Law; and accordingly they have committed unlawful homicide according to the law of the GDR.

4. According to art. 103 para. 2 Basic Law, an act can only be punished if criminal liability was determined by statute at the time of the act (prohibition on retroactivity). This constitutional provision does not forbid the punishment of the complainants.

a) In the circumstances explained above, there are grounds for the view that art. 103 para. 2 Basic Law does not prevent, from the outset, punishment of the defendants because the act was punishable according to the law of the GDR at the time of the act as correctly interpreted. Whether the defendants knew this is a question which merely concerns grounds of excuse.

b) The Senate has not however overlooked the fact that with regard to art. 103 para. 2 Basic Law the question can be raised as to which understanding of the law at the time of act is to be taken as a basis. If the law at the time of the act is interpreted in a way which causes the action, although it was commanded by the state, to appear as contrary to law [see C.II.2 and C.II.3 of this judgment], it follows that the prohibition on retroactivity does not oppose punishment. If on the other hand the actual conditions of power in the state are taken chiefly into consideration, the application of art. 103 para. 2 Basic Law could lead to another result. That applies primarily if the defendant has been commanded by a state department to violate a generally recognized law, especially the right to life . . .

aa) The question of what meaning art. 103 para. 2 Basic Law has for the assessment of actions which have been undertaken by order of the State under a former regime, and which violate human rights like the right to life, has not yet been clearly answered (see Schünemann, in: Festschr. f. Hans-Jürgen Bruns, 1978, pp. 223 ff.; Dencker, KritVSchr 1990, 299 (304) and Polakiewicz, EuGRZ 1992, 177 (188)). . . . The problem of the prohibition on retroactivity in relation to justifications has been raised in German case law by the Supreme Court for the British Zone (OGHSt. 2, 231 ff.).

The points of view developed under substantial influence of Anglo-Saxon legal opinions in the case law of the International Military Tribunal of Nuremberg as well as in particular in the decision in the so-called lawyer's proceedings (III. US Military Court, Judgment of Dec. 4, 1947, pp. 29 ff. of the official text) were not taken over by later German case law. The prohibition against conviction in respect of acts which were not punishable at the time they were committed also appears in art. 15 of the ICCPR as well as in art. 7 of the European Human Rights Convention. But a second paragraph is added to both provisions in which it says that the prohibition in principle on retroactivity does not exclude the conviction of persons whose act was punishable at the time it was committed according to the general principles of law recognized by the international community. The Federal Republic of Germany has however made the reservation (art. 64 ECHR) in respect of art. 7 para. 2 ECHR that the provisions would only be applied within the limits of art. 103 para. 2 Basic Law ...

Justifications in criminal law are not generally excluded from the area of protection of art. 103 para. 2 Basic Law. ... The Senate does not follow the proposition (see recently Schroeder, JZ 1992, 990 (991)) that the prohibition on retroactivity applies only to the constituent elements of the crime and not to justifications ... The decision of the legislature to limit the constituent elements or to provide instead for a justification is in certain circumstances only of a technical nature ... If an action was justified at the time of the act, it cannot be punished if the justificatory norm is subsequently abolished (Eser, in: Schönke-Schröder, 24th edit., § 2 marginal no. 3) ...

From this consideration, some authors conclude in the recent discussion with regard to cases of the present kind that a justification employed in state practice at the time of the act, even if it contradicts superior norms, may not be left out of consideration to the disadvantage of the accused. Otherwise, a criminal liability, which did not exist at the time of the act, would be established in a manner which violates art. 103 para. 2 Basic Law (Jakobs, in: Isensee, Vergangenheitsbewältigung durch Recht (Overcoming the past by law), 1992, pp. 36 ff.; also, in the same volume, Isensee, p. 91 (105 ff.); Grünwald, StrVerf 1991, 31 (33); Rittstieg, DuR 1991, 404; Pieroth, VVDStRL 51 (1992), 92 ff. (102 ff., 144 ff., 168 ff.); also, in the same volume Isensee, pp. 134 ff.; Dencker KritVschr 73 (1990), 299, 306; differentiating, Polakiewicz, EuGRZ 1992, 117 (188 ff.); see also Dreier, VVDStRL 51 (1992), 137).

bb) The Senate does not follow this opinion.

(1) ...

(2) The Senate is, for the following reason, of the view that art. 103 para. 2 Basic Law is not opposed to the proposition that the act is unlawful; the decisive issue is, as stated, whether criminal liability "was determined by statute" before the act was committed. In examining whether this was the case, the judge is not bound in the sense of pure factuality to that interpretation which found expression in state practice at the time of the act. If the law at the time of the act could, taking into account the limits provided by the literal meaning of the statute and in the light of the Constitution of the GDR be so interpreted that the international law obligations of the GDR with regard to human rights were complied with, the law at the time of the act is to be understood according to this interpretation sympathetic to human rights as the law which "statutorily determined" criminal liability in the sense of art. 103 para. 2 Basic Law (similarly Alexy, VVDStRL 51 (1992), 132 ff.; Schünemann, loc. cit; Lüderssen, ZStW 104 (1992), 735 (779 ff.); see further Starck-Maurer VVDStRL 51 (1992), 141 ff. (147 f.)). A justification applicable to the defendants' conduct was in fact accepted in state practice as expressed in the general command situation. But it ought not to be inferred at that time from the statute as correctly interpreted. The prohibition on retroactivity should protect the accused from arbitrary action and limit penal authority to the enforcement of general laws (Schreiber, Gesetz und Richter (Law and judges), 1976, p. 217). It protects the trust which the defendant has put, at the time of the act, in the continuing existence of the law applicable at that time (Rüping, in: BK, art. 103 para. 2 Basic Law marginal no. 16 with further references). These protective principles of constitutional law are not being ignored here: the expectation that the law would also be applied in the future as it was in state practice at the time of the act, in such a way that a justification which was contrary to human rights was acknowledged, is not worthy of protection. It is not arbitrary treatment if the accused, so far as the unlawfulness of his action is concerned, is judged in the way in which he ought to have been treated on the correct interpretation of GDR law at the time of the act ...

III.

1. On this basis the relevant factual and legal examination shows that the regional court correctly assessed the conduct of the defendants as manslaughter ...

[For the part of the decision that concerns culpability, i.e., the absence of excuse, see Chapter 8.C.ii.]

NOTES

1. Both in the U.S. and in Germany, there is a constitutional rule against "*ex post facto* laws" in the criminal law (in Germany, the common term is: prohibition of retroactivity, part of *nulla poena sine lege*, no punishment without law, art. 103 para. 2 Basic Law). At its core, this rule is clear and beyond dispute: legislatures may pass new criminal law norms, but they may not demand that these new norms be applied to crimes already committed. This applies to the creation of norms prohibiting conduct which was legal before, to the aggravation of existing prohibitions, and to the infliction of greater punishment than the law provided for at the time when the crime was committed. This core is captured by the first three of the four rules the U.S. Supreme Court lists in *Rogers v. Tennessee*, quoting *Calder v. Bull* (1798).

Calder v. Bull, as the title of the case suggests, was not a criminal case, but a civil case. The Supreme Court's discussion of the application of the federal constitutional *ex post facto* prohibition to *criminal* cases is therefore, strictly speaking, dictum—even if one that has been quoted for over two centuries as the still definitive discussion of constitutional limits on the retroactivity of changes in criminal law. The constitutional prohibition itself makes no mention of the distinction between criminal and civil norms (nor of any of the further distinctions *Calder v. Bull* draws among criminal norms). But why should it matter whether a norm is classified as criminal or civil for purposes of its retroactivity? Do persons (citizens?) have less of a right to be apprised of changes in civil norms than in criminal ones? Is it merely a matter of the quantity (or quality) of the sanction attached to the violation of a criminal or a civil norm? What about administrative (and therefore "civil") fines (or even taxes) that exceed criminal ones? Civil confinement that exceeds criminal incarceration, in quantity (i.e., length) or in quality (i.e., in the conditions of confinement—solitary confinement, access to privileges, opportunities for early release, etc.)? For purposes of the retroactivity prohibition, does it matter in the end whether a state action is classified as civil or criminal, or whether its quantity and quality, i.e., the degree and nature of its interference with personal rights?

2. Although the *ex post facto* rule is firmly established, questions about its scope remain. One was covered in the section about preventive detention: it can be disputed whether legal consequences count as "criminal punishment" or not, see the opinions about the nature of preventive detention in Chapter 1.B.3. Another topic of discussion concerns retroactive changes to rules of evidence to the defendant's disadvantage. From a German perspective, the fourth rule which the U.S. Supreme Court cites in *Rogers v. Tennessee* does not belong to the reach of the constitutional prohibition against retroactive laws. German constitutional doctrine does not apply art. 103 para. 2 Basic Law to procedural law. Rules of evidence are part of procedural law rather than of substantive criminal law. The idea is that prohibitions address citizens and inform them of whether the law condones the conduct in question, by listing the appropriate punishment. Rules of procedure are, however, not this kind of rule of conduct.

Do you think that this distinction between substance and procedure is convincing? What is the difference between substance and procedure? When does a procedural rule become so fundamental that its retroactive change would seem unfair (e.g., eliminating the right to a jury trial for an offense, lowering the burden of proof at the sentencing hearing)?

What about other substantive norms that are not rules of conduct in the sense of prohibitions (don't do this, or else): what about "defenses," i.e., norms about when it is permissible to do something that is prohibited ("justifications," such as self-defense), or norms about when you will not be punished even though you did something that was not justified but excusable ("excuses," such as duress)? Can such "defenses" be eliminated with retroactive effects? Note that in the German *Border Guard Case*, the central legal problems concerned the justificatory defense that § 27 GDR Border Law might have provided—there was no debate about the existence of a prohibition against homicide (to kill another person was a crime in the GDR as well as in other countries).*

---

* For more on defenses, see Chapters 13 & 14.

3. Analyze the *ex post facto* prohibition from the perspective of the various rationales of punishment (see Chapter 1.A.1) and expand this analysis to the principle of legality as a whole. To what extent is Feuerbach's formulation of the *nulla poena* principle (or rather principles) tied to a consequentialist, deterrence-based, approach to punishment?

4. The question in *Rogers v. Tennessee* was whether the *ex post facto* prohibition (in the U.S. Constitution) applies to changes in case law. A case before the German Federal Court (Judgment of June 28, 1990, 4 StR 297/90, BGHSt 37, 89) concerned the amount of alcohol which renders driving a motor vehicle absolutely unsafe, even if the individual driver does not show visible signs of incompetence, § 316 StGB. In that case, the Court decided to lower the threshold for absolute incompetence from 0.13 percent to 0.11 percent blood alcohol content (BAC). Addressing the question whether this new regime could be applied retro-actively to the defendant in the case before it, the Court reached the same result as did the U.S. Supreme Court in *Rogers*: it distinguished between the legislature passing new laws and the judiciary's mere interpretation of legal terms. It also emphasized the need to take new scientific evidence into account when interpreting the law.

Do you find the courts' reasoning in *Rogers v. Tennessee* and the German BAC case convincing? Do judges in complicated cases create new law, or is the task of interpretation of legal texts different from creating new law? How do the majority and dissenting opinions in *Rogers* relate to different principles like democracy, rule of law, separation of powers, and the protection of citizens' trust in the law?

What difference does it make whether retroactivity is measured against an "explicit *ex post facto*" prohibition or against a more general right to "due process"? Note that the issue in *Rogers* was not *whether* there are constitutional constraints on judicial retroactivity, but *which ones*. Only the (federal and state) legislature—so the Supreme Court argues on the basis of the constitutional text—is subject to the *ex post facto* prohibition. Both the legislature and the courts are subject to due process constraints. The difference appears to be that a due process violation is harder to make out than an *ex post facto* violation, as illustrated in *Rogers* itself. But what does the due process analysis add other than to make explicit the notice (reliance? fairness?) concerns that underlie the *ex post facto* prohibition? If so, is the difference between the due process analysis and the *ex post facto* analysis then simply a difference in the strictness of review (less strict for due process, more for *ex post facto*)? Does that make any sense? (Note that this distinction is not uncommon in U.S. constitutional law, and constitutional criminal procedure in particular, where the general and weaker due process guarantee operates, at least in theory, as a broad safety net in the event other, more specific and stronger, protections do not catch.) Or are there other considerations that drive the (double!) *ex post facto* prohibition in the federal constitution?)

5. Difficult issues of retroactivity can arise after the collapse of a political regime under which state officials disregarded fundamental human rights. May criminal courts of the new regime punish those who gave orders and those who executed orders? The situation is less difficult if the conduct in question was illegal not only under the new legal order, but also under the old legal order. In the *Border Guard Case*, the regional court of Berlin tried this approach. It started with the (undisputed) rule that if conduct could be judged either according to the law of the German Democratic Republic (GDR) valid in 1984 or according to the Law of the Federal Republic of Germany, the milder provision governed.* The judges at the regional court Berlin rejected the argument that the milder law was GDR law, holding that the acts fell outside the scope of the justification under § 27 GDR Border Law.

The Federal Court of Justice took a different approach. Their more complicated arguments take the following route: if one looks at the wording of § 27 GDR Border Law and applies it in this case, a certain degree of ambiguity remains. One could solve this problem by considering the state practice as it was. From this angle, one would arrive at the conclusion that under East German law in 1984, the defendants acted in a legally permissible way when they shot at

---

* See EGStGB (Introductory Law StGB) art. 315 para. 1; StGB § 2 para. 3.

S. But the Senate argues that § 27 GDR Border Law must be read not with view to *actual* state practice but as it *should* have been interpreted. At this point in their arguments, the Court considers a proposal by the famous criminal law theorist and legal philosopher (and also Social Democratic politician and minister of justice in the 1920s) Gustav Radbruch. In a short article published in 1946, after the breakdown of the National Socialist regime, Radbruch argued for priority of "natural law" over positive law under extreme circumstances: if a conflict between positive law and justice is intolerable, the positive law ought to give way to justice (the so-called "Radbruch formula"). Although the Federal Court of Justice appears to have been sympathetic to Radbruch's approach—after all, it cites the Radbruch formula—the judges did not go so far as to dispose of the case by merely treating it as a problem of legal philosophy. Instead, the Federal Court of Justice attempted to relate its decision to the East German legal system at the time of the act. The Senate developed an interpretation of § 27 GDR Border Law that would have been appropriate in the GDR in the year 1984—with a view to the fact that the GDR had signed the International Convention on Civil and Political Rights and thus acceded to the duty to obey human rights in general and in particular the right of freedom to travel abroad. Accordingly, they concluded that, while border guards could in general use firearms, this did not cover the intentional killing of a fugitive who was unarmed and posed no danger to the life and limb of others.

The relevant constitutional provision, art. 103 para. 2 Basic Law, appears rather late in the written reasons. The Federal Court of Justice had to decide whether its creative interpretation of § 27 GDR Border Law with a view to the GDR's commitments concerning human rights was compatible with the constitutional prohibition of retroactive extensions of the criminal law. After all, the defendants in 1984 had no idea that the law could be interpreted in the way the West German Federal Court of Justice did twelve years later—for them, the only plausible and accessible way of interpretation was the one practiced in their own legal system. For this reason, some authors still claim that the judgment of the Federal Court of Justice shows disregard for art. 103 para. 2 Basic Law because it neglects the fact that the change of the law was surprising and unforeseeable for the defendants. However, the Court rejects this argument, stating that the defendants' trust in the law as it was interpreted was not worthy of protection. (What does that mean? Does the Court's long and winding doctrinal analysis come down to an obscure and, ultimately, unsupported value judgment about another legal life world or value system? Is the Court's decision more moral, or political, than legal? Does it uphold, or ignore, the rule of law?)

On the question of retroactivity, does the Court's reasoning fit the rationale for the prohibition of retroactive criminal law? If the issue is citizens' "trust in the law," should this mean their actual state of mind at the time of the act or (as the German courts argued) merely what they *should* have believed?

After this decision, more former East German border guards were convicted,[*] as were state officials who were higher up in the military and political hierarchy,[†] the latter typically receiving longer sentences. The Federal Constitutional Court confirmed the view that art. 103 para. 2 Basic Law does not require protection of defendants' trust in the ways the law in their country was in fact interpreted at the time of their actions.[‡]

6. It may be helpful to compare criminal prosecution of crimes committed in the GDR with those of Nazi crimes in West Germany after 1945, if only because the comparison was frequently drawn, even in post-1989 judicial opinions.[§] Prosecutions of Nazi crimes in (West and East) Germany were sporadic and tended to focus on those who were the lowest in the chain of command.[¶] The *Border Guard Case*, and in particular the Federal Court of Justice's

---

[*] See, e.g., Federal Court of Justice, March 20, 1995, 5 StR 111/94, BGHSt 41, 101.

[†] See, e.g., Federal Court of Justice, July 26, 1994, 5 StR 98/94, BGHSt 40, 218.

[‡] See Judgment of October 24, 1996, 2 BvR 1851, 1853, 1875 u. 1852/94, BVerfGE 95, 96.

[§] See also the discussion of bending the law (*Rechtsbeugung*) in Chapter 17.B.

[¶] See, e.g., Joachim Perels, "Perceptions and Suppression of Nazi Crimes by the Postwar German Judiciary," in Nathan Stolzfus and Henry Friedlander (eds.), *Nazi Crimes and the Law* (2008), 87.

opinion, illustrates the difficulties of condemning egregious pre-1989 wrongdoing in the wake of the widely perceived failure to bring Nazi offenders to justice after 1945, without violating the prohibition of retroactivity (a charge often leveled against the Nuremberg Tribunals) or denying the incommensurable enormity of Nazi atrocities. The comparison with Nuremberg may also be instructive. Nuremberg, of course, was not a domestic proceeding, but is now considered, and celebrated, as the origin of international criminal law. At the time, it was perceived—also by German criminal lawyers—as an unfair instance of victor's justice, and more particularly (incidentally) retroactive imposition of foreign norms on domestic defendants. This other-judgment, however, was not followed by a concerted effort at self-judgment, of Germans, by Germans, under German law, in German courts. The post-GDR cases were supposed to be different, not instances of victor's other-judgment, but of self-judgment (hence the significance of applying East German law, if "properly interpreted"). Does the *Border Guard Case* succeed in this respect?

7. The German Federal Court of Justice repeatedly talks about the "judge of fact" (singular)—this refers to the division of labor between the court of first instance (the "judge of fact") and the appellate court. In an important case like the *Border Guard Case*, the trial court in fact includes five judges (three professional judges and two lay judges*).[†]

Readers of the *Border Guard Case* might wonder why the defendant W. received a sentence of juvenile detention although he was twenty years old at the time of the shooting and twenty-eight years at trial. The reason for this is that the rules of juvenile criminal law can be applied to persons who are younger than twenty-one at the day of the offense, depending on individual maturity at that point in time. Only at the stage of sentence execution—rather than of sentence imposition—does the actual age matter, and the convicted person will serve her (juvenile) sentence in a correctional facility for adults if she is older than twenty-four years.[‡]

The general trend toward punitiveness in U.S. criminal law has also affected the treatment of young offenders.[§] In the country that established the first separate juvenile courts, in Chicago, some one hundred years ago, it is today a sign of progress that the U.S. Supreme Court has begun to place constitutional limits, under the Eighth Amendment's cruel and unusual punishments clause, on legislatures who subject youths to sentences of life imprisonment without the possibility of parole and even capital punishment.[¶]

B. Vagueness

Besides the prohibition of retroactivity, the prohibition of vagueness also enjoys constitutional status in American law, though indirectly, through the general due process guarantee (in the Fifth and Fourteenth Amendment), rather than directly, through an explicit constitutional provision (as in the case of the *ex post facto* clauses in Article 1 of the U.S. Constitution. German law also recognizes a vagueness prohibition, as part of the general principle of *nulla poena sine lege*, found in art. 103 para. 2 Basic Law.

---

* See JGG (Juvenile Courts Act) § 33b and GVG (Judiciary Act) § 76 para. 1.
† On the (limited) significance of lay judges in German criminal trials, see Markus D. Dubber, "American Plea Bargains, German Lay Judges, and the Crisis of Criminal Procedure," 49 *Stanford Law Review* (1997), 547.
‡ See Juvenile Courts Act §§ 89b para. 1, 105 para. 1.
§ See Chapter 1.A.3.
¶ See *Roper v. Simmons*, 543 U.S. 551 (2005) (capital punishment for juveniles); *Graham v. Florida*, 560 U. S. ___ (2010) (life without parole for juveniles convicted of a non-homicide offense); *Miller v. Alabama*, 567 U.S. ___ (2012) (mandatory life without parole for juveniles). On the early juvenile courts in Chicago, see Julian Mack, "The Juvenile Court," 23 *Harvard Law Review* (1909), 104.

Chicago v. Morales
United States Supreme Court
527 U.S. 41 (1999)

Justice Stevens announced the judgment of the Court.

In 1992, the Chicago City Council enacted the Gang Congregation Ordinance, which prohibits "criminal street gang members" from "loitering" with one another or with other persons in any public place ...

Before the ordinance was adopted, the city council's Committee on Police and Fire conducted hearings to explore the problems created by the city's street gangs, and more particularly, the consequences of public loitering by gang members. Witnesses included residents of the neighborhoods where gang members are most active, as well as some of the aldermen who represent those areas. Based on that evidence, the council made a series of findings that are included in the text of the ordinance and explain the reasons for its enactment.

The council found that a continuing increase in criminal street gang activity was largely responsible for the city's rising murder rate, as well as an escalation of violent and drug related crimes. It noted that in many neighborhoods throughout the city, "the burgeoning presence of street gang members in public places has intimidated many law abiding citizens." 177 Ill. 2d 440, 445, 687 N.E.2d 53, 58, 227 Ill. Dec. 130 (1997). Furthermore, the council stated that gang members "establish control over identifiable areas ... by loitering in those areas and intimidating others from entering those areas; and ... members of criminal street gangs avoid arrest by committing no offense punishable under existing laws when they know the police are present...." Ibid. It further found that "loitering in public places by criminal street gang members creates a justifiable fear for the safety of persons and property in the area" and that "aggressive action is necessary to preserve the city's streets and other public places so that the public may use such places without fear." Moreover, the council concluded that the city "has an interest in discouraging all persons from loitering in public places with criminal gang members." Ibid.

The ordinance creates a criminal offense punishable by a fine of up to $500, imprisonment for not more than six months, and a requirement to perform up to 120 hours of community service. Commission of the offense involves four predicates. First, the police officer must reasonably believe that at least one of the two or more persons present in a "public place" is a "criminal street gang member." Second, the persons must be "loitering," which the ordinance defines as "remaining in any one place with no apparent purpose." Third, the officer must then order "all" of the persons to disperse and remove themselves "from the area." Fourth, a person must disobey the officer's order. If any person, whether a gang member or not, disobeys the officer's order, that person is guilty of violating the ordinance.

Two months after the ordinance was adopted, the Chicago Police Department promulgated General Order 92-4 to provide guidelines to govern its enforcement. That order purported to establish limitations on the enforcement discretion of police officers "to ensure that the anti-gang loitering ordinance is not enforced in an arbitrary or discriminatory way." Chicago Police Department, General Order 92-4. The limitations confine the authority to arrest gang members who violate the ordinance to sworn "members of the Gang Crime Section" and certain other designated officers, and establish detailed criteria for defining street gangs and membership in such gangs. In addition, the order directs district commanders to "designate areas in which the presence of gang members has a demonstrable effect on the activities of law abiding persons in the surrounding community," and provides that the ordinance "will be enforced only within the designated areas." Id. at 68a-69a. The city, however, does not release the locations of these "designated areas" to the public.

[The Supreme Court struck down the Chicago ordinance because it "fails to give the ordinary citizen adequate notice of what is forbidden and what is permitted" and "provides absolute discretion to police officers to determine what activities constitute loitering."]

Skilling v. United States
United States Supreme Court
561 U.S. ___, 130 S. Ct. 2896 (2010)

Justice Ginsburg delivered the opinion of the Court.

In 2001, Enron Corporation, then the seventh highest-revenue-grossing company in America, crashed into bankruptcy. We consider in this opinion two questions arising from the prosecution of Jeffrey Skilling, a longtime Enron executive, for crimes committed before the corporation's collapse. First, did pretrial publicity and community prejudice prevent Skilling from obtaining a fair trial?

Second, did the jury improperly convict Skilling of conspiracy to commit "honest-services" wire fraud, 18 U.S.C. §§ 371, 1343, 1346?

Answering no to both questions, the Fifth Circuit affirmed Skilling's convictions. We conclude, in common with the Court of Appeals, that Skilling's fair-trial argument fails; Skilling, we hold, did not establish that a presumption of juror prejudice arose or that actual bias infected the jury that tried him. But we disagree with the Fifth Circuit's honest-services ruling. In proscribing fraudulent deprivations of "the intangible right of honest services," § 1346, Congress intended at least to reach schemes to defraud involving bribes and kickbacks. Construing the honest-services statute to extend beyond that core meaning, we conclude, would encounter a vagueness shoal. We therefore hold that § 1346 covers only bribery and kickback schemes. Because Skilling's alleged misconduct entailed no bribe or kickback, it does not fall within § 1346's proscription. We therefore affirm in part and vacate in part.

I.

Founded in 1985, Enron Corporation grew from its headquarters in Houston, Texas, into one of the world's leading energy companies. Skilling launched his career there in 1990 when Kenneth Lay, the company's founder, hired him to head an Enron subsidiary. Skilling steadily rose through the corporation's ranks, serving as president and chief operating officer, and then, beginning in February 2001, as chief executive officer. Six months later, on August 14, 2001, Skilling resigned from Enron.

Less than four months after Skilling's departure, Enron spiraled into bankruptcy. The company's stock, which had traded at $90 per share in August 2000, plummeted to pennies per share in late 2001. Attempting to comprehend what caused the corporation's collapse, the U.S. Department of Justice formed an Enron Task Force, comprising prosecutors and FBI agents from around the Nation. The Government's investigation uncovered an elaborate conspiracy to prop up Enron's short-run stock prices by overstating the company's financial well-being. In the years following Enron's bankruptcy, the Government prosecuted dozens of Enron employees who participated in the scheme. In time, the Government worked its way up the corporation's chain of command: On July 7, 2004, a grand jury indicted Skilling, Lay, and Richard Causey, Enron's former chief accounting officer.

These three defendants, the indictment alleged,

engaged in a wide-ranging scheme to deceive the investing public, including Enron's shareholders, ... about the true performance of Enron's businesses by: (a) manipulating Enron's publicly reported financial results; and (b) making public statements and representations about Enron's financial performance and results that were false and misleading.

App. P5, p. 277a.

Skilling and his co-conspirators, the indictment continued, "enriched themselves as a result of the scheme through salary, bonuses, grants of stock and stock options, other profits, and prestige." App. P14, at 280a.

Count 1 of the indictment charged Skilling with conspiracy to commit securities and wire fraud; in particular, it alleged that Skilling had sought to "depriv[e] Enron and its shareholders of the intangible right of [his] honest services." The indictment further charged Skilling with more than 25 substantive counts of securities fraud, wire fraud, making false representations to Enron's auditors, and insider trading.

The mail- and wire-fraud statutes criminalize the use of the mails or wires in furtherance of "any scheme or artifice to defraud, or for obtaining money or property by means of false or fraudulent pretenses, representations, or promises." 18 U.S.C. § 1341 (mail fraud); § 1343 (wire fraud). The honest-services statute, § 1346, defines "the term 'scheme or artifice to defraud'" in these provisions to include "a scheme or artifice to deprive another of the intangible right of honest services." ...

Following a 4-month trial and nearly five days of deliberation, the jury found Skilling guilty of 19 counts, including the honest-services-fraud conspiracy charge, and not guilty of 9 insider-trading counts. The District Court sentenced Skilling to 292 months' imprisonment, 3 years' supervised release, and $45 million in restitution.

On appeal, Skilling raised a host of challenges to his convictions, including the ... honest-services argument[] he presses here. ... Arguing that the Fifth Circuit erred in its consideration of these claims, Skilling sought relief from this Court. We granted certiorari, 558 U.S. ___, 130 S. Ct. 393, 175 L. Ed. 2d 267 (2009), and now affirm in part, vacate in part, and remand for further proceedings. ...

We also granted certiorari and heard arguments this Term in two other cases raising questions concerning the honest-services statute's scope. See Black v. United States, No. 08-876, 561 U.S. ___ (2010); Weyhrauch v. United States, No. 08-1196, 561 U.S. ___ (2010). Today we vacate and remand those decisions in light of this opinion.

. . .

III.

[Skilling argues that his] conspiracy conviction was premised on an improper theory of honest-services wire fraud. The honest-services statute, § 1346, Skilling maintains, is unconstitutionally vague. Alternatively, he contends that his conduct does not fall within the statute's compass.

A.

To place Skilling's constitutional challenge in context, we first review the origin and subsequent application of the honest-services doctrine.

1.

Enacted in 1872, the original mail-fraud provision, the predecessor of the modern-day mail- and wire-fraud laws, proscribed, without further elaboration, use of the mails to advance "any scheme or artifice to defraud." See McNally v. United States, 483 U.S. 350, 356, 107 S. Ct. 2875, 97 L. Ed. 2d 292 (1987). In 1909, Congress amended the statute to prohibit, as it does today, "any scheme or artifice to defraud, or for obtaining money or property by means of false or fraudulent pretenses, representations, or promises." § 1341 (emphasis added); see id., at 357–358, 107 S. Ct. 2875, 97 L. Ed. 2d 292. Emphasizing Congress' disjunctive phrasing, the Courts of Appeals, one after the other, interpreted the term "scheme or artifice to defraud" to include deprivations not only of money or property, but also of intangible rights.

In an opinion credited with first presenting the intangible-rights theory, Shushan v. United States, 117 F.2d 110 (1941), the Fifth Circuit reviewed the mail-fraud prosecution of a public official who allegedly accepted bribes from entrepreneurs in exchange for urging city action beneficial to the bribe payers. "It is not true that because the [city] was to make and did make a saving by the operations there could not have been an intent to defraud," the Court of Appeals maintained. Id., at 119. "A scheme to get a public contract on more favorable terms than would likely be got otherwise by bribing a public official," the court observed, "would not only be a plan to commit the crime of bribery, but would also be a scheme to defraud the public." Id., at 115.

The Fifth Circuit's opinion in Shushan stimulated the development of an "honest-services" doctrine. Unlike fraud in which the victim's loss of money or property supplied the defendant's gain, with one the mirror image of the other, see, e.g., United States v. Starr, 816 F.2d 94, 101 (CA2 1987), the honest-services theory targeted corruption that lacked similar symmetry. While the offender profited, the betrayed party suffered no deprivation of money or property; instead, a third party, who had not been deceived, provided the enrichment. For example, if a city mayor (the offender) accepted a bribe from a third party in exchange for awarding that party a city contract, yet the contract terms were the same as any that could have been negotiated at arm's length, the city (the betrayed party) would suffer no tangible loss. Cf. McNally, 483 U.S., at 360, 107 S. Ct. 2875, 97 L. Ed. 2d 292. Even if the scheme occasioned a money or property gain for the betrayed party, courts reasoned, actionable harm lay in the denial of that party's right to the offender's "honest services." See, e.g., United States v. Dixon, 536 F.2d 1388, 1400 (CA2 1976).

"Most often these cases . . . involved bribery of public officials," United States v. Bohonus, 628 F.2d 1167, 1171 (CA9 1980) but courts also recognized private-sector honest-services fraud. In perhaps the earliest application of the theory to private actors, a District Court, reviewing a bribery scheme, explained:

> When one tampers with [the employer-employee] relationship for the purpose of causing the employee to breach his duty [to his employer,] he in effect is defrauding the employer of a lawful right. The actual deception that is practised is in the continued representation of the employee to the employer that he is honest and loyal to the employer's interests.

> United States v. Procter & Gamble Co., 47 F. Supp. 676, 678 (Mass. 1942).

Over time, "[a]n increasing number of courts" recognized that "a recreant employee"—public or private—"c[ould] be prosecuted under [the mail-fraud statute] if he breache[d] his allegiance to his employer by accepting bribes or kick-backs in the course of his employment," United States v. McNeive, 536 F.2d 1245, 1249 (CA8 1976); by 1982, all Courts of Appeals had embraced the honest-services theory of fraud, Hurson, Limiting the Federal Mail Fraud Statute—A Legislative Approach, 20 Am. Crim. L. Rev. 423, 456 (1983).

2.

In 1987, this Court, in McNally v. United States, stopped the development of the intangible-rights doctrine in its tracks. McNally involved a state officer who, in selecting Kentucky's insurance agent, arranged to procure a share of the agent's commissions via kickbacks paid to companies the official partially controlled. 483 U.S., at 360, 107 S. Ct. 2875, 97 L. Ed. 2d 292. The prosecutor did not charge that, "in the absence of the alleged scheme[,] the Commonwealth would have paid a lower premium or secured better insurance." Ibid. Instead, the prosecutor maintained that the kick-back scheme "defraud[ed] the citizens and government of Kentucky of their right to have the Commonwealth's affairs conducted honestly." Id., at 353, 107 S. Ct. 2875, 97 L. Ed. 2d 292.

We held that the scheme did not qualify as mail fraud. "Rather than constru[ing] the statute in a manner that leaves its outer boundaries ambiguous and involves the Federal Government in setting standards of disclosure and good government for local and state officials," we read the statute "as limited in scope to the protection of property rights." Id., at 360, 107 S. Ct. 2875, 97 L. Ed. 2d 292. "If Congress desires to go further," we stated, "it must speak more clearly." Ibid.

3.

Congress responded swiftly. The following year, it enacted a new statute "specifically to cover one of the 'intangible rights' that lower courts had protected . . . prior to McNally: 'the intangible right of honest services.' " Cleveland v. United States, 531 U.S. 12, 19–20, 121 S. Ct. 365, 148 L. Ed. 2d 221 (2000). In full, the honest-services statute stated:

> For the purposes of th[e] chapter [of the United States Code that prohibits, inter alia, mail fraud, § 1341, and wire fraud, § 1343], the term 'scheme or artifice to defraud' includes a scheme or artifice to deprive another of the intangible right of honest services.
>
> § 1346.

B.

Congress, Skilling charges, reacted quickly but not clearly: He asserts that § 1346 is unconstitutionally vague. To satisfy due process, "a penal statute [must] define the criminal offense [1] with sufficient definiteness that ordinary people can understand what conduct is prohibited and [2] in a manner that does not encourage arbitrary and discriminatory enforcement." Kolender v. Lawson, 461 U.S. 352, 357, 103 S. Ct. 1855, 75 L. Ed. 2d 903 (1983). The void-for-vagueness doctrine embraces these requirements.

According to Skilling, § 1346 meets neither of the two due process essentials. First, the phrase "the intangible right of honest services," he contends, does not adequately define what behavior it bars. Brief for Petitioner 38–39. Second, he alleges, § 1346's "standardless sweep allows policemen, prosecutors, and juries to pursue their personal predilections," thereby "facilitat[ing] opportunistic and arbitrary prosecutions." Id., at 44 (quoting Kolender, 461 U.S., at 358, 103 S. Ct. 1855, 75 L. Ed. 2d 903).

In urging invalidation of § 1346, Skilling swims against our case law's current, which requires us, if we can, to construe, not condemn, Congress' enactments. . . . Alert to § 1346's potential breadth, the Courts of Appeals have divided on how best to interpret the statute. Uniformly, however, they have declined to throw out the statute as irremediably vague.

We agree that § 1346 should be construed rather than invalidated. First, we look to the doctrine developed in pre-McNally cases in an endeavor to ascertain the meaning of the phrase "the intangible right of honest services." Second, to preserve what Congress certainly intended the statute to cover, we pare that body of precedent down to its core: In the main, the pre-McNally cases involved fraudulent schemes to deprive another of honest services through bribes or kick-backs supplied by a third party who had not been deceived. Confined to these paramount applications, § 1346 presents no vagueness problem.

1.

There is no doubt that Congress intended § 1346 to refer to and incorporate the honest-services doctrine recognized in Court of Appeals' decisions before McNally derailed the intangible-rights theory of fraud. Congress enacted § 1346 on the heels of McNally and drafted the statute using that decision's terminology. As the Second Circuit observed in its leading analysis of § 1346:

> The definite article "the" suggests that "intangible right of honest services" had a specific meaning to Congress when it enacted the statute—Congress was recriminalizing mail- and wire-fraud schemes to deprive others of that "intangible right of honest services," which had been protected before McNally, not all intangible rights of honest services whatever they might be thought to be.
>
> United States v. Rybicki, 354 F.3d 124, 137–138 (2003) (en banc).

2.

Satisfied that Congress, by enacting § 1346, "meant to reinstate the body of pre-McNally honest-services law," we have surveyed that case law. In parsing the Courts of Appeals decisions, we acknowledge that Skilling's vagueness challenge has force, for honest-services decisions preceding

McNally were not models of clarity or consistency. While the honest-services cases preceding McNally dominantly and consistently applied the fraud statute to bribery and kickback schemes—schemes that were the basis of most honest-services prosecutions—there was considerable disarray over the statute's application to conduct outside that core category. In light of this disarray, Skilling urges us . . . to invalidate the statute in toto.

It has long been our practice, however, before striking a federal statute as impermissibly vague, to consider whether the prescription is amenable to a limiting construction.

Arguing against any limiting construction, Skilling contends that it is impossible to identify a salvageable honest-services core; "the pre-McNally caselaw," he asserts, "is a hodgepodge of oft-conflicting holdings" that are "hopelessly unclear." . . . Although some applications of the pre-McNally honest-services doctrine occasioned disagreement among the Courts of Appeals, these cases do not cloud the doctrine's solid core: The "vast majority" of the honest-services cases involved offenders who, in violation of a fiduciary duty, participated in bribery or kickback schemes. Indeed, the McNally case itself, which spurred Congress to enact § 1346, presented a paradigmatic kickback fact pattern. Congress' reversal of McNally and reinstatement of the honest-services doctrine, we conclude, can and should be salvaged by confining its scope to the core pre-McNally applications.

As already noted, the honest-services doctrine had its genesis in prosecutions involving bribery allegations.

In view of this history, there is no doubt that Congress intended § 1346 to reach at least bribes and kickbacks. Reading the statute to proscribe a wider range of offensive conduct, we acknowledge, would raise the due process concerns underlying the vagueness doctrine. To preserve the statute without transgressing constitutional limitations, we now hold that § 1346 criminalizes only the bribe-and-kickback core of the pre-McNally case law.

3.

The Government urges us to go further by locating within § 1346's compass another category of proscribed conduct: "undisclosed self-dealing by a public official or private employee—i.e., the taking of official action by the employee that furthers his own undisclosed financial interests while purporting to act in the interests of those to whom he owes a fiduciary duty." . . . In light of the relative infrequency of conflict-of-interest prosecutions in comparison to bribery and kickback charges, and the intercircuit inconsistencies they produced, we conclude that a reasonable limiting construction of § 1346 must exclude this amorphous category of cases.

Further dispelling doubt on this point is the familiar principle that "ambiguity concerning the ambit of criminal statutes should be resolved in favor of lenity." Cleveland, 531 U.S., at 25, 121 S. Ct. 365, 148 L. Ed. 2d 221 (quoting Rewis v. United States, 401 U.S. 808, 812, 91 S. Ct. 1056, 28 L. Ed. 2d 493 (1971)). . . . Holding that honest-services fraud does not encompass conduct more wide-ranging than the paradigmatic cases of bribes and kickbacks, we resist the Government's less constrained construction absent Congress' clear instruction otherwise.

4.

Interpreted to encompass only bribery and kickback schemes, § 1346 is not unconstitutionally vague. Recall that the void-for-vagueness doctrine addresses concerns about (1) fair notice and (2) arbitrary and discriminatory prosecutions. A prohibition on fraudulently depriving another of one's honest services by accepting bribes or kickbacks does not present a problem on either score.

As to fair notice, "whatever the school of thought concerning the scope and meaning of" § 1346, it has always been "as plain as a pikestaff that" bribes and kickbacks constitute honest-services fraud, and the statute's mens rea requirement further blunts any notice concern. See also Broadrick v. Oklahoma, 413 U.S. 601, 608, 93 S. Ct. 2908, 37 L. Ed. 2d 830 (1973) ("[E]ven if the outermost boundaries of [a statute are] imprecise, any such uncertainty has little relevance . . . where appellants' conduct falls squarely within the 'hard core' of the statute's proscriptions."). Today's decision clarifies that no other misconduct falls within § 1346's province. See United States v. Lanier, 520 U.S. 259, 266, 117 S. Ct. 1219, 137 L. Ed. 2d 432 (1997) ("[C]larity at the requisite level may be supplied by judicial gloss on an otherwise uncertain statute.").

As to arbitrary prosecutions, we perceive no significant risk that the honest-services statute, as we interpret it today, will be stretched out of shape. Its prohibition on bribes and kickbacks draws content not only from the pre-McNally case law, but also from federal statutes proscribing—and defining—similar crimes. See, e.g., 18 U.S.C. §§ 201(b), 666(a)(2); 41 U.S.C. § 52(2) ("The term 'kickback' means any money, fee, commission, credit, gift, gratuity, thing of value, or compensation of any kind which is provided, directly or indirectly, to [enumerated persons] for the purpose of improperly obtaining or rewarding favorable treatment in connection with [enumerated circumstances]."). . . . A criminal defendant who participated in a bribery or kickback scheme, in short, cannot tenably complain about prosecution under § 1346 on vagueness grounds.

C.

It remains to determine whether Skilling's conduct violated § 1346.... The Government charged Skilling with conspiring to defraud Enron's shareholders by misrepresenting the company's fiscal health, thereby artificially inflating its stock price....

The Government did not, at any time, allege that Skilling solicited or accepted side payments from a third party in exchange for making these misrepresentations. It is therefore clear that, as we read § 1346, Skilling did not commit honest-services fraud.

Because the indictment alleged three objects of the conspiracy—honest-services wire fraud, money-or-property wire fraud, and securities fraud—Skilling's conviction is flawed. See Yates v. United States, 354 U. S. 298 (1957) (constitutional error occurs when a jury is instructed on alternative theories of guilt and returns a general verdict that may rest on a legally invalid theory). This determination, however, does not necessarily require reversal of the conspiracy conviction; we recently confirmed that errors of the Yates variety are subject to harmless-error analysis. The parties vigorously dispute whether the error was harmless.... We leave this dispute for resolution on remand.

Whether potential reversal on the conspiracy count touches any of Skilling's other convictions is also an open question. All of his convictions, Skilling contends, hinged on the conspiracy count and, like dominoes, must fall if it falls. The District Court, deciding Skilling's motion for bail pending appeal, found this argument dubious, but the Fifth Circuit had no occasion to rule on it. That court may do so on remand.

For the foregoing reasons, we [vacate] the Fifth Circuit's ruling on Skilling's ... conspiracy conviction, and remand the case for proceedings consistent with this opinion.

It is so ordered.

Justice Scalia, with whom Justice Thomas joins, and with whom Justice Kennedy joins except as to Part III, concurring in part and concurring in the judgment.

The Court strikes a pose of judicial humility in proclaiming that our task is "not to destroy the Act...but to construe it." But in transforming the prohibition of "honest-services fraud" into a prohibition of "bribery and kick-backs" it is wielding a power we long ago abjured: the power to define new federal crimes. See United States v. Hudson, 11 U.S. 32, 7 Cranch 32, 34, 3 L. Ed. 259 (1812).

I.

A criminal statute must clearly define the conduct it proscribes, see Grayned v. City of Rockford, 408 U.S. 104, 108, 92 S. Ct. 2294, 33 L. Ed. 2d 222 (1972). A statute that is unconstitutionally vague cannot be saved by a more precise indictment, see Lanzetta v. New Jersey, 306 U.S. 451, 453, 59 S. Ct. 618, 83 L. Ed. 888 (1939), nor by judicial construction that writes in specific criteria that its text does not contain, see United States v. Reese, 92 U.S. 214, 219-221, 23 L. Ed. 563 (1876). Our cases have described vague statutes as failing "to provide a person of ordinary intelligence fair notice of what is prohibited, or [as being] so standardless that [they] authoriz[e] or encourag[e] seriously discriminatory enforcement." United States v. Williams, 553 U.S. 285, 304, 128 S. Ct. 1830, 170 L. Ed. 2d 650 (2008). Here, Skilling argues that § 1346 fails to provide fair notice and encourages arbitrary enforcement because it provides no definition of the right of honest services whose deprivation it prohibits.... The Court...knows that adopting by reference "the pre-McNally honest-services doctrine," is adopting by reference nothing more precise than the referring term itself ("the intangible right of honest services"). Hence the deus ex machina: "[W]e pare that body of precedent down to its core." Since the honest-services doctrine "had its genesis" in bribery prosecutions, and since several cases and counsel for Skilling referred to bribery and kickback schemes as "core" or "paradigm" or "typical" examples, or "[t]he most obvious form," of honest-services fraud, and since two cases and counsel for the Government say that they formed the "vast majority," or "most" or at least "[t]he bulk" of honest-services cases, THEREFORE it must be the case that they are all Congress meant by its reference to the honest-services doctrine.

Even if that conclusion followed from its premises, it would not suffice to eliminate the vagueness of the statute. It would solve (perhaps) the indeterminacy of what acts constitute a breach of the "honest services" obligation under the pre-McNally law. But it would not solve the most fundamental indeterminacy: the character of the "fiduciary capacity" to which the bribery and kickback restriction applies. Does it apply only to public officials? Or in addition to private individuals who contract with the public? Or to everyone, including the corporate officer here? The pre-McNally case law does not provide an answer. Thus, even with the bribery and kickback limitation the statute does not answer the question "What is the criterion of guilt?"

But that is perhaps beside the point, because it is obvious that mere prohibition of bribery and kickbacks was not the intent of the statute. To say that bribery and kickbacks represented "the core" of the doctrine, or that most cases applying the doctrine involved those offenses, is not to say that they are the doctrine. All it proves is that the multifarious versions of the doctrine overlap with regard to those offenses. But the doctrine itself is much more. Among all the pre-McNally smorgasbord-offerings of varieties of honest-services fraud, not one is limited to bribery and kickbacks. That is a dish the Court has cooked up all on its own.

Thus, the Court's claim to "respec[t] the legislature" is false. It is entirely clear (as the Court and I agree) that Congress meant to reinstate the body of pre-McNally honest-services law; and entirely clear that that prohibited much more (though precisely what more is uncertain) than bribery and kickbacks. Perhaps it is true that "Congress intended § 1346 to reach at least bribes and kickbacks." That simply does not mean, as the Court now holds, that "§ 1346 criminalizes only" bribery and kickbacks.

Arriving at that conclusion requires not interpretation but invention. The Court replaces a vague criminal standard that Congress adopted with a more narrow one (included within the vague one) that can pass constitutional muster. I know of no precedent for such "paring down," and it seems to me clearly beyond judicial power. This is not, as the Court claims, simply a matter of adopting a "limiting construction" in the face of potential unconstitutionality. To do that, our cases have been careful to note, the narrowing construction must be "fairly possible," Boos v. Barry, 485 U.S. 312, 331, 108 S. Ct. 1157, 99 L. Ed. 2d 333 (1988), "reasonable," Hooper v. California, 155 U.S. 648, 657, 15 S. Ct. 207, 39 L. Ed. 297 (1895), or not "plainly contrary to the intent of Congress," Edward J. DeBartolo Corp. v. Florida Gulf Coast Building & Constr. Trades Council, 485 U.S. 568, 575, 108 S. Ct. 1392, 99 L. Ed. 2d 645 (1988). As we have seen (and the Court does not contest), no court before McNally concluded that the "deprivation of honest services" meant only the acceptance of bribes or kick-backs. If it were a "fairly possible" or "reasonable" construction, not "contrary to the intent of Congress," one would think that some court would have adopted it. The Court does not even point to a post-McNally case that reads § 1346 to cover only bribery and kickbacks, and I am aware of none.

The canon of constitutional avoidance, on which the Court so heavily relies, states that "when the constitutionality of a statute is assailed, if the statute be reasonably susceptible of two interpretations, by one of which it would be unconstitutional and by the other valid, it is our plain duty to adopt that construction which will save the statute from constitutional infirmity." Until today, no one has thought (and there is no basis for thinking) that the honest-services statute prohibited only bribery and kickbacks.

I certainly agree with the Court that we must, "if we can," uphold, rather than "condemn," Congress's enactments. But I do not believe we have the power, in order to uphold an enactment, to rewrite it. Congress enacted the entirety of the pre-McNally honest-services law, the content of which is (to put it mildly) unclear. In prior vagueness cases, we have resisted the temptation to make all things right with the stroke of our pen. I would show the same restraint today, and reverse Skilling's conviction on the basis that § 1346 provides no "ascertainable standard" for the conduct it condemns. Instead, the Court today adds to our functions the prescription of criminal law.

German Federal Constitutional Court
BVerfGE 87, 209 (October 29, 1992)
"Dance of the Devils"

Facts

The complainant, a film distributor, had acquired the rights for the cinema version of the film "The Evil Dead"—German title: "Dance of the Devils." The film describes the visit of three women and two men to a weekend house situated in a forest. There they are disturbed by inexplicable apparitions. After playing a magic formula spoken on a tape, all save one of them metamorphose one after the other. They take on features of inhuman beings and pursue each other with the intention of annihilation. The ones who are not possessed in this way fend off the attacks and those possessed are finally killed or annihilated. This is all presented in a graphic manner. The film version and the video version sold by a different organization were confiscated by the regional court of Munich, judgment of October 7, 1985. The film violated § 131 Criminal Code because it trivialized acts of violence and represented them in a way which violated human dignity. The complainant edited a video cassette of the film and submitted the edited version to the Voluntary Self-Regulation of the Film Industry (*Freiwillige Selbstkontrolle der Filmwirtschaft, FSK*) applying for it to be categorized for public viewing as "not suitable for under 18s." In the course of these proceedings the cassette was submitted to the public prosecutor's office in order to resolve the question of whether this office had any criminal law reservations about it. The office applied for the confiscation of the cassette.

The local court granted this application in accordance with §§ 74d, 76a Criminal Code, because any intentional dissemination of the film in the knowledge of its contents would satisfy the definition of § 131 para. 1 no. 4 Criminal Code. It contained sequences which described cruel or otherwise inhuman acts of violence against human beings in a way that presented the cruelty or inhumanity of the events so as to violate human dignity:

"There is a close-up of the head of a possessed woman catching fire, and the facial skin burning. A further scene shows how one of the men is strangled. Then there is a close-up of the men chopping up the body of one of the possessed with an axe, and the limbs of the body are twitching. In a further scene, a possessed woman stabs a man with a stiletto and wounds him. She then licks the blood-smeared weapon with relish. In the following fight the possessed woman falls on the stiletto. The close-up shows how the weapon penetrates her body and great quantities of blood gush from the wounds and from her mouth. When one man has buried a possessed woman, she reaches out towards him from the grave and a fight begins. He beats her with a wooden beam, and a white liquid gushes from her mouth. The possessed woman prepares for an unnaturally high leap on to the man who is lying on the ground. He grabs a spade and holds it in front of himself for protection. When the woman lands on the spade, her head is severed from her body and it strikes the ground next to the man. The close-up shows him holding in his hands the woman's body without its head, with blood gushing from the stump of its neck. A further scene shows a shot fired at the head of a possessed woman which tears it partially apart. Another close-up shows how one of the men strikes a hand with the butt of a gun and crushes it.

The film consisted overwhelmingly of brutal, cruel and tasteless scenes. Severe pain and agony were inflicted on human beings. The participants were acting in a feelingless and merciless cast of mind. A ruthless and indifferent tendency showing contempt for human beings found concrete expression in the portrayal of violent events. The offending scenes were scarcely linked due to poor treatment. Crude acts of violence were shown in an intrusive and lurid way without any socially meaningful motivation, for their own sake and for mere entertainment and stimulation of emotions. The portrayal of excessive violence and cruelty was therefore promoted to an end in itself."

The regional court rejected the immediate complaint raised against the confiscation as unfounded and in this connection referred to two further scenes in the film: "At 1.20 on the counter the video cassette shows for example how a man fighting a possessed woman who is strangling him presses his thumb into her eye sockets and a bloody liquid gushes over her face. At 1.22 on the counter there is a close-up of a possessed woman beating a man lying on the ground with a hook."
The constitutional complaint was successful.

Reasons

C.

The constitutional complaint is well founded. The decisions under challenge violate the complainant's basic right under Art. 5 para. 1 sentence 2 Basic Law* and its right under Art. 103 para. 2 Basic Law.

§ 131 para. 1 no. 4 Criminal Code on which the decisions are based is, in relation to the feature of the definition "in a manner violating human dignity," only compatible with the Basic Law in accordance with the reasons. . . .

II.

1. In so far as the complainant objects to a violation of Art. 103 para. 2 Basic Law, the subject matter for examination is the provisions of § 131 para. 1 no. 4 Criminal Code to the extent that they formed the basis of the decisions by the local court and the regional court. These courts based the confiscation on the fact that the film submitted by the complainant to the FSK was intended for dissemination and described inhuman acts of violence against human beings so as to present the cruelty or inhumanity of the occurrence in a manner violating human dignity.

2. Art. 103 para. 2 Basic Law obliges the legislature to describe the prerequisites of criminal liability so concretely that the consequences and area of application of the definitions of crimes can be recognized and can be ascertained by interpretation. This duty serves a double purpose. On the one hand it is a question of constitutional protection of the addressee of the norm: everyone should be able to foresee what behavior is forbidden and threatened with punishment. On the other hand it

---

* [Freedom of the press, freedom of publication.—Eds.]

is necessary to ensure that only the legislature decides on criminal liability (see BVerfGE 71, 108 (114)). Art. 103 para. 2 Basic Law contains a strict commitment to statutory regulation which prevents the executive and judicial powers from deciding about the prerequisites for punishment (BVerfGE 71, 108 (114)).

That does not exclude the use of concepts which need interpretation by the judge to a special extent. Even in criminal law the legislature has to take account of the varied nature of life. Because of the generality and abstractness of criminal norms it is also unavoidable that in borderline cases it can be doubtful whether behavior already or still falls within the statutory definition or not. In any case the addressee of the norm must as a rule be able to foresee on the basis of the statutory regime whether the behavior is criminal. In borderline cases he can in this way at least recognize the risk of punishment. From this point of view, what is decisive for the certainty of a criminal provision is primarily the wording of the statutory definition which is recognizable and comprehensible for the addressee and which represents the outer boundary of permissible judicial interpretation (see BVerfGE 75, 329 (341); BVerfGE 85, 69 (73)).

3. Measured by these principles the crime definition, which has to be examined in relation to the feature "in a manner violating human dignity," is still sufficiently certain if interpreted so as to conform to the Constitution. The remaining features of the definition in question here give no cause for assuming a lack of certainty. However, the interpretation and application of § 131 I no. 4 Criminal Code by the local court and the regional court on confiscation of the film in the edited version violates Art. 103 para. 2 Basic Law because they extend the wording of the norm in a manner which is impermissible in constitutional law.

a) § 131 Criminal Code is not too uncertain simply because of an excessive number of offense elements which need interpretation—although this has been assumed in the literature (see for instance Lenckner, in: Schönke-Schröder, Criminal Code, 24th edit. (1991), § 131 marginal no. 2; v. Bubnoff, in: LK, 10th edit. (1988), § 131 marginal no. 4 on previous version; . . .).

In determining the question of the certainty of the criminal norm with regard to Art. 103 para. 2 Basic Law the concepts "human being," "cruel," "inhuman," "acts of violence," "describe" and "in a manner which violates human dignity" need to be interpreted here. This is a manageable number of normative concepts which—apart from the last mentioned concept—can be determined by means of traditional statutory application.

aa) The offense element "human being" is sufficiently certain simply because it is unmistakably linked to the biological concept of a human being. On the other hand creatures of fantasy similar to humans cannot be understood as included within it, as has been propounded in the discussions on the Act for the New Regime for Protection of Young People in Public (see Recommended Decision and Report of the Committee for Youth, Family and Health, BT-Dr 10/2546, p. 22). The sense of the word alone excludes such an interpretation. If the concept "human being" were intended to be otherwise understood, it would violate the prohibition of analogy under art. 103 para. 2 Basic Law. If the legislature wanted to penalize the portrayal of violence against creatures resembling humans (primarily so-called zombies), it would have had to express this in the wording of the provision.

The required differentiation between human beings and creatures resembling humans does not exclude the possibility that in an individual case there could be doubt as to whether the victims of acts of violence shown in a film were humans or creatures resembling them. That does not however lead to uncertainty of the provision. Subsumption under the statutory definition is the task of the criminal courts. If they reached the view here that the creatures shown in the film, who are at first unambiguously humans and in the course of the plot change into possessed persons, nevertheless remain human beings in the eyes of the viewer as well as in the sense of the film, that is an assessment of ordinary law which is in principle removed from constitutional law examination (see BVerfGE 18, 85 (92)).

bb) Admittedly the offense element "cruel" in § 131 Criminal Code is not from its wording so unambiguously determinable as the concept "human being." That does not however prevent its certainty being sufficient to satisfy art. 103 para. 2 Basic Law. "Cruel" also in an offense element in the description of murder in § 211 Criminal Code and, according to the prevailing opinion, it is to be interpreted in the same way as in this criminal law norm (see Lackner, Criminal Code, 19th edit. (1991), § 131 marginal no. 4; Maurach-Schroeder-Maiwald, marginal no. 6; Dreher-Tröndle, § 131 marginal no. 5 . . .). An action is accordingly cruel if it is carried out with the infliction of severe pain or agony of a physical or emotional kind, and besides this reveals a brutal and merciless attitude by the person who commits it (see Lenckner, in: Schönke-Schröder, § 131 marginal no. 10).

cc) The offense element "inhuman" is supposed to express the idea that action is taken with a cast of mind which shows contempt for humanity, or is inconsiderate, callous or merciless (see BT-Dr VI/3521, p. 7), perhaps because it is gives the perpetrator satisfaction to mistreat or kill human beings completely unscrupulously and in cold blood. There is also extensive unanimity in the legal literature about this (see Lenckner, in: Schönke-Schröder, § 131 marginal no. 10; Rudolphi, in: SK, § 131 marginal no. 7 . . .).

dd) It is true that the concept of "acts of violence" in § 131 para. 1 Criminal Code is described as ambivalent (Geilen, in: LdR/StrafR, 1989, p. 355). However, from the viewpoint of sufficient certainty of the norm there are no doubts about understanding it as including aggressive active conduct by which, through the direct or indirect use or initiation of physical force, a human body is affected in a way which impairs or concretely endangers its physical or emotional integrity (see Lenckner, in: Schönke-Schroeder, § 131 marginal no. 9; Lackner, § 131 note 4a . . .). . . .

b) However, the "human dignity" provision which was introduced by the Act for the New Regime for Protection of Young People in Public of February 25, 1985 (BGBl I, 425) requires constitutional scrutiny. This element is described as problematic not only because of its uncertainty, but also because the violation of human dignity by portrayals of violence is hardly suited to demarcation (see Maurach-Schroeder-Maiwald, marginal no. 9). With view to the constitutional requirement of certainty of a definition (art. 103 para. 2 Basic Law), it is regarded as a questionable borderline case of legislative reform which is legitimate in itself, but in its "nebulousness" is very unwieldy (see Geilen, in: LdR/StrafR, p. 356). The provision is however in this respect also sufficiently certain when it is interpreted in conformity with Constitution.

aa) With the concept of human dignity the statute is obviously making a link to the content of art. 1 para. 1 sentence 1 Basic Law. The Federal Constitutional Court understands it as a basic constitutional principle in the system of basic rights (see BVerfGE 6, 32 (36, 41); BVerfGE 45, 187 (227)). It is associated with the claim of human beings to social value and regard which prevents them being made mere objects of the state or being exposed to treatment which in principle calls in question their subject quality. Human dignity in this sense is not only the individual dignity of the person in question but the dignity of humans as generic beings. Everyone possesses it without regard to his characteristics, his achievements and his social status. It also belongs to the person who cannot act meaningfully because of his physical or mental condition. It is not lost even by "unworthy" conduct. It cannot be taken away from any human being. However the claim to regard which arises from it can be violated.

bb) The certainty of the offense element in § 131 para. 1 Criminal Code related to human dignity does not pose problems in so far as it encompasses cases in which the dignity of actual persons is violated in the way they are portrayed in the film.

That does not however cover the whole sense of the provision. It follows from the wording and systematic context of it that it is primarily to include those cases in which the description of the cruel and inhumane aspects of an event is calculated to produce or strengthen an attitude in the viewer which denies the fundamental claim to value and regard which belongs to every human being. That occurs in particular when cruel or otherwise inhuman events are shown in order to give the viewer sadistic pleasure or cause people or groups to appear unworthy of humanity. Such a tendency includes the idea of human beings being available as mere objects, to be dealt with as one wishes. For this reason even purely fictional events which demonstrate contempt for humanity can violate the requirement to have regard to human dignity. This can encourage a general brutalization, diminish respect for the dignity of fellow human beings in the eyes of an observer, and thus also increase the danger of actual violations of this legal good. The statutory materials confirm that such portrayals should also fall within the definition. The report of the Principal Committee for Youth, Family and Health quotes "gleeful" preoccupation with an inhuman event as an example for application of the norm (BT-Dr 10/2546, p. 21 f.).

c) The local court and the regional court have however based their decision on an interpretation of § 131 para. 1 Criminal Code which does not satisfy the certainty requirement of art. 103 para. 2 Basic Law. They base their opinion that a portrayal violating human dignity was present essentially on the fact that crude acts of violence were shown for their own sake in an intrusive and lurid manner, and without any socially meaningful motivation. This interprets the offense element of a portrayal violating human dignity in a manner which does not sufficiently acknowledge certain contours. Acts of violence in films do not on their own violate human dignity. That follows from the simple fact that portrayal in a manner violating human dignity is named as a special offense element. It must be fulfilled in addition to the description of acts of violence. Neither the large number nor the intrusive and lurid portrayal of acts of violence can fulfill the definition on their own. If it was a question of these criteria, the acts forbidden by § 131 para. 1 Criminal Code could not be sufficiently clearly distinguished from, for instance, adventure and crime films, which should be regarded as permissible.

For this reason alone, the reasoning of the decisions under challenge does not withstand a constitutional law examination by the standard of art. 103 para. 2 Basic Law. Besides this, application to the actual case shows that the courts assumed an impermissibly wide understanding of the criminal provision. There were no findings that the viewer would be stimulated to affirmative interest in the horror scenes. Instead it seems likely that he would not identify with the violent possessed, but with the untransformed human beings who are fighting against them. The overall impression given by the film may cause him to see the events as quite ridiculous and grotesque because of its bizarre exaggeration. There are such forms of entertainment—even though toned down—in other fantasy productions like horror stories and ghost stories. If they were simply to be included in the human dignity alternative, this offense description would not be apt for the demarcation of criminal conduct.

NOTES

1. The legal technique applied by the Chicago City Council to prevent "gang loitering" is not entirely unfamiliar to German jurists. German towns and cities have passed ordinances that prohibit specific kind of conduct on public streets (for instance aggressive begging or feeding pigeons), and typically they threaten fines. However, such contraventions belong to the class of administrative (non-criminal) offenses (*Ordnungswidrigkeiten*, "order contraventions"). The German system distinguishes between criminal offenses in a strict sense and administrative penalties for minor wrongdoing that does not deserve the blame connected with a criminal conviction. The threat of a fine often appears in the last section of administrative laws passed by the federal or state legislature, or, as mentioned, in municipal ordinances. These administrative norms cover a wide range of subjects, for instance, traffic rules (to prevent, among others, speeding or illegal parking), safety regulations concerning consumer goods, regulations to protect minors etc. There is a general federal law (Administrative Offenses Act, *Gesetz über Ordnungswidrigkeiten*, OWiG) which sets out, in a streamlined general part, the procedure and general rules for administrative offenses but also contains a short special part describing some forms of conduct subject to administrative penalties, for example, causing undue noise that seriously offends neighbors or the public (§ 117 Administrative Offenses Act).

There is one difference, however, between German law and the Chicago ordinance: The former does not provide for imprisonment or community service, only fines which, unless otherwise specified in the law, may not exceed €1000 (§ 17 para. 1 Administrative Offenses Act).

Administrative offenses used to be called police offenses (*Polizeivergehen*), and municipal ordinances were known as police ordinances (*Polizeiverordnungen*), in the sense of offenses against "the police," a term originally used synonymously with welfare, order, or peace, familiar to Anglo-American ears from terms such as offenses against the king's (or queen's) peace, peace (police) officers, justices of the peace, and peace bonds, and—particularly in the U.S.—the *police power*, one of the central, and broadest, state power in American constitutional history, akin to the king's power to maintain the (royal) peace.* Police offenses hovered at the outskirts of German criminal law (and criminal codes) for over a century, until they were removed from the criminal code and placed in a separate code of "order contraventions" in the second half of the twentieth century.

It is tempting to distinguish order contraventions from "real" crimes by associating one with order maintenance and the other with wrongdoing. Is it the case, however, that order contraventions do not carry condemnation no matter how high the fine (which may reach €1,000,000, in the case of corporate offenses, § 30 OWiG)? That "real" criminal law is always, and only, concerned with the condemnation of wrongdoing (rather than, say, order maintenance through positive and negative incentives)? Also, is a monetary sanction for prohibited conduct labeled a *Geldstrafe* relevantly distinguishable from a monetary sanction for

---

* See Markus D. Dubber, *The Police Power: Patriarchy and the Foundations of American Government* (2005).

prohibited conduct labeled a *Geldbuße* (especially in a legal system whose paradigmatic punishment is a monetary sanction)? Is prohibited conduct defined in something called a *Strafgesetzbuch* relevantly distinguishable from prohibited conduct defined in something called a *Gesetz über Ordnungswidrigkeiten* (especially if many of the offenses in the latter piece of legislation originally were defined in the former)?*

2. If lawmakers attempt to curb socially disruptive or offensive behavior, it can be difficult to define with great precision the relevant kind of conduct. Thus, the temptation to use general, unspecific descriptions is especially great in this area. The German Federal Constitutional Court and the Federal Court of Justice point out that the prohibition of vagueness (art. 103 para. 2 Basic Law) applies to town and city ordinances and to administrative penalties.[†] However, the Federal Constitutional Court also argues in a rather pragmatic way that the sanction's seriousness matters. The more severe the sanction, the more precise the legislature must be in describing both the prohibited conduct and its possible legal consequences (Judgment of May 6, 1987, 2 BvL 11/85, BVerfGE 75, 329). (What is the connection between the seriousness of the threatened sanction and the constitutional requirement of specificity? Is this connection limited to the particular constitutional protection at issue, or does it reflect a general view that the scrutiny of the fit between ends and means depends on the seriousness of the state interference at stake?)

Accordingly, in 2002, the Court declared unconstitutional a newly introduced criminal sanction (meant to combat organized crime) that could have deprived offenders of all or substantial parts of their assets (*Vermögensstrafe*, § 43a StGB, now revoked). The argument was that the law did not spell out under what circumstances judges may opt for this severe sanction in addition to imprisonment.[‡] On the other hand, when administrative penalties are to be evaluated, the Court tends to be more generous towards the legislature. The German Administrative Offenses Act contains, for example, a requirement that one is not "to act in a grossly inappropriate way that offends or endangers the public and disturbs public order" (§ 118). Without the Federal Constitutional Court's pragmatic approach towards minor penalties, it would be hard to explain how such a vague offense description could survive. From a German perspective, the U.S. Supreme Court in *Chicago v. Morales* took a surprisingly firm stance despite the comparatively minor sanctions at stake.

Were you similarly surprised? What might have motivated the U.S. Supreme Court in *Morales*, given the nature of the offense and its intended effect? Does it make a difference to you that the law was not only a local ordinance, but an ordinance backed by community groups, including churches, in the affected Chicago neighborhoods? Would it have made a difference if the police had published its internal regulations that (could have?) put meat on the bare bones of the ordinance? Could the ordinance have been saved by transferring discretion onto higher level officials in the police department (perhaps relying on statistical patterns of criminal activity)?

3. *Skilling v. United States* leads into another area of criminal law haunted by vagueness concerns: economic crimes. Most legal systems include provisions against fraud in the classical sense, which require symmetry between financial losses to a third party, on the one hand, and financial profit for the offender, on the other. Legislatures, however, have been eager to capture forms of economic crime that cannot be captured by the traditional notion of fraud, often testing the limits of the constitutional vagueness prohibition in the process. The German Federal Constitutional Court decided three relevant cases in 2011.[§] In the first

---

[*] On distinctions within the realm of criminal sanctions, between "civil" and "criminal" forfeiture, and between "measures" and "punishments" see Chapters 1.A.iii and 1.B.iii, respectively.

[†] See, e.g., Federal Constitutional Court, Judgment of February 23, 1972, 2 BvL 36/71, BVerfGE 32, 346; Federal Court of Justice, Judgment of March 15, 1996, 3 StR 506/95, BGHSt 42, 79.

[‡] Judgment of March 20, 2002, 2 BvL 794/95, BVerfGE 105, 135.

[§] Judgment of June 23, 2010, 2 BvR 2559/08, 105/09, 491/09, BVerfGE.

case, the CEO of a health insurance company rewarded employees with excessive bonuses; in the second, a bank manager approved a €20 million loan for a construction firm without proper examination of their credit rating (no proof of kickback schemes or offenders' personal gain). In the third high-profile case, employees of the Siemens corporation were convicted for creating hidden funds to secure contracts for Siemens in foreign countries where business partners and state officials expected "gifts." Again, there was no proof of personal profit, nor, one could argue, was harm done to Siemens, because the hidden funds were used to promote the corporation's business interests (Siemens had adopted an anti-corruption-policy, which meant losing some contracts and thus was ignored by some employees).

The German Federal Constitutional Court had to deal with these cases for the same reason *Skilling* reached the U.S. Supreme Court: the defense challenged the statute as being too vague. In German law, this was § 266 Criminal Code (*Untreue*: "disloyalty" or "abuse of trust"), a prohibition whose current wording was introduced on May 26, 1933. (The significance of the introduction of this section during the Nazi regime is contested; notions of duty and loyalty played a central role in Nazi criminal law ideology.*)

Section 266 para. 1 German Criminal Code provides:

> Who abuses the power (accorded to him by statute, public authority or legal contract) to dispose of assets of another or to make binding agreements for another, or who violates a duty (imposed by statute, public authority, legal contract or a fiduciary relationship) to safeguard property interests of another, and thereby causes damage to the other whose property interests he had to safeguard, will be punished with imprisonment of not more than five years or a fine.

The Federal Constitutional Court acknowledged that the wording is not exactly precise. (Compared to the "honest services" provision at stake in *Skilling*, however, this appears like a model of precision, doesn't it?) But, in the end, the Court did not declare the norm to be unconstitutional, and it upheld the criminal convictions (with one exception: in the case of the bank manager, the Court demanded that the criminal court compute the actual financial harm caused). The Court also commented on the rationale behind the constitutional prohibition of vagueness in art. 103 para. 2 Basic Law. Similar to the U.S. Supreme Court's reference to "fair warning," it stressed that citizens must be able to recognize from the wording of the law what is prohibited. It also emphasized that in a democratic state, the legislature (not the judiciary, or for that matter, the executive) must decide about the scope of criminal liability. (Why is that?) But it acknowledged at the same time that lawmakers often have no alternative but to rely on general terms to ensure that different situations in real life are covered. Therefore, the Court accepted offense elements such as "duty," "abuse," and "fiduciary relationship." (What is the argument here? That vagueness is prohibited, except when it isn't, or except when it would make the legislature's life harder?)

4. Are the two decisions by the U.S. Supreme Court (*Morales* and *Skilling*) consistent in light of the relationship between legislature and judiciary they reflect? What role, if any, should the judicial interpretation of a statute that is concededly vague on its face play in the constitutional vagueness analysis *of the statute*? The Court in *Skilling* acknowledges that federal courts have given the honest-services statute different interpretations, agreeing only in their rejection of vagueness attacks on the statute. Ironically, the Court also acknowledges that the statute, on its face, is indeed vague, and that it can survive vagueness scrutiny only in light of judicial interpretations. Just what can a person fairly be expected to do in order to determine the scope of a vague statutory prohibition? In Skilling's case, this would have required carefully studying the winding legislative and judicial history of federal mail fraud, then poring over years of diverging judicial readings of the honest-services statute, boiling all of it down to what the Supreme Court in *Skilling* discovers to be the common core. This seems fanciful even in the case of a highly sophisticated, extremely wealthy business executive who

---

* See, e.g., Georg Dahm, "Verrat und Verbrechen," 95 *Zeitschrift für die gesamte Strafrechtswissenschaft* (1935), 283.

has the best legal advice money can buy at his fingertips; what about others less fortunate, or at least less well heeled?

5. The *"Dance of the Devils" Case* belongs to yet another area of criminal law legislation perpetually raising vagueness concerns: attempts to keep some media content away from minors, but also the general public. The German legislature added § 131 to the Criminal Code in 1973. Section 131 allows punishment in form of a fine or imprisonment up to one year for the distribution, production, delivery, etc. of media content that shows "cruel or otherwise inhuman acts of violence against human beings in a way which either glorifies or plays down such violent acts or which portrays the cruelty or inhumaneness of the event in a manner which violates human dignity."

From the beginning, there was a debate whether the lawmakers had succeeded in drawing the line between permissible and prohibited portrayals of violence or whether the offense description ran afoul of the vagueness prohibition under art. 103 para. 2 Basic Law. Citing the need for interpretation of legal terms, the Federal Constitutional Court found no vagueness problems with several offense elements: "human being," "cruel," and "acts of violence." When examining the element "human being," the Court pointed out that art. 103 para. 2 Basic Law bars its application to creatures that are clearly non-human. (In response, the German parliament quickly amended § 131 StGB to cover "beings resembling humans" as might appear in "zombie films" and the like.) But the main focus of the Court's ruling concerned the elements in § 131 that the legislature had introduced to limit the scope of application. The Court voiced no general objections against relying on a "violation of human dignity," even though the depiction of merely fictional events can be said to violate human dignity as long as the producers aim to create or strengthen among viewers an attitude "that denies the fundamental claim to value and regard which belongs to every human being."

Are the contours of the concept of "dignity" any clearer in this context than they are in the application of the constitutional right to dignity in the German Basic Law, which plays a key role in German constitutional criminal law?* Apart from obvious substantive concerns about infringing freedom of speech, how can an offense that criminalizes the "violation of human dignity" pass constitutional muster under a vagueness test, particularly if it is interpreted so broadly as to include the depiction of fictional events, of fictional characters' actions (attitudes?) toward other fictional characters in fictional places and fictional times?

In an attempt to flesh out its clarifying reading of "violation of human dignity," the Court stressed that a lurid and detailed portrayal of violence does not necessarily imply the work's tendency to foster in viewers an attitude of contempt for human dignity. According to the Federal Constitutional Court's reasoning, even the most graphic portrayals of violence might have an entertainment purpose only. (Due to the difficulties of applying these standards, there are not many successful prosecutions under § 131: in 2009, twenty offenders were convicted. Does this strike you as a small number? Does the number of successful prosecutions under a statute affect the analysis of its constitutionality?) Does this attempt at clarification succeed? Or is this rather an attempt to preserve the constitutionality of the statute in the face of other challenges, notably one based on the right to free speech?

6. So far we have focused on judicial attempts to preserve the constitutionality of a legislative norm through interpretation. What constrains judicial interpretation? Our decisions mention two different principles: the prohibition of analogy on the one hand, and the so-called rule of lenity on the other. The U.S. Supreme Court in *Skilling* cites the so-called rule of lenity (also known as the rule of strict construction) on its way to discussing the vagueness challenge: "the familiar principle that 'ambiguity concerning the ambit of criminal statutes should be resolved in favor of lenity.'" Familiar the rule may be, but it is also widely ignored. The Court's reference to it in *Skilling*, as a supplementary consideration confirming a result reached on other grounds, is no exception. If the Court had taken

---

* See, e.g., Chapter 1.B.i.

the rule seriously, could it have resolved the case without having to delve into the issue of vagueness?*

In German constitutional law, there is no rule that obliges judges to choose the less strict of two (or more) reasonable interpretations of a legal term in criminal prohibitions. German constitutional law instead recognizes the "prohibition of analogy" (*Analogieverbot*). This prohibition is, like the retroactivity and vagueness prohibitions, derived from art. 103 para. 2 Basic Law ("An act may only be punished if it was defined by a law as a criminal offense before the act was committed.").†

While the prohibition of vagueness is addressed to the legislature (laws must be phrased in a clear and understandable way), the prohibition to draw analogies addresses the courts. It instructs courts to respect the meaning of a legal term that it has in ordinary language; a court's interpretation of a legal term must not exceed the scope of meaning drawn by ordinary language. In the *"Dance of the Devils" Case*, the German Federal Constitutional Court points to the sense of the word "human being" (which is one of the relevant legal terms in § 131 Criminal Code) and concludes that the criminal norm must not be applied if a film etc. features non-human beings such as fictional creatures like "zombies." An even more clear-cut example would be the following: a film shows horrible cruelty against animals, and a court contemplates that this deserves punishment and thus considers applying § 131 German Criminal Code. This would be considered a flagrant disregard for the constitutional prohibition against analogy (in ordinary language, animals cannot be called "human beings").

Consider the relationship between interpretation and analogy.‡ Where does one stop, and the other start? Put another way, where does permissible "interpretation" cross the line into impermissible "analogy"? How does one—a court, say—determine what a statutory term means in ordinary language, or what qualifies as a possible—or, for that matter, a "reasonable"—interpretation of that term? What role, if any, would consideration of legislative intent play? More generally, how does the prohibition of analogy interact with the principle of separation of powers?

7. Note that in 1935, during the National Socialist period, the German Criminal Code was amended with a new § 2 (abolished again after 1945): "That person will be punished who commits an act which the law declares to be punishable or which deserves punishment according to the fundamental principle of a penal statute and the healthy sentiment of the people." This amendment meant to give true flexibility to judges: "the healthy sentiment of the people" could be cited and supported criminal punishment even if the wording of the criminal norm evidently did *not* describe the conduct in question. This was a tool to implement National Socialist policies immediately, without "formal obstacles" such as a requirement of changing the wording in criminal laws.§

Under this view, the amendment to § 2 is treated as an exceptional deviation from the analogy prohibition, which was corrected after 1945. For a differentiated historical analysis of the status of the analogy prohibition in particular, and the legality principle in general, in German criminal law, see Hans-Ludwig Schreiber, *Gesetz und Richter: Zur geschichtlichen Entwicklung des Satzes* nullum crimen, nulla poena sine lege (1976).¶

---

* On the questionable (constitutional) status of the rule of lenity, see Dan M. Kahan, "Lenity and Federal Common Law Crimes," *Supreme Court Review* [1994], 345; see also *R. v. Paré*, [1987] 2 S.C.R. 618 (Can.) (insisting on "continued vitality of the doctrine" in Canadian law).

† See also StGB § 1 ("An act may only be punished if its punishability was determined by law before the act was committed.").

‡ See generally Wolfgang Naucke, "Interpretation and Analogy in Criminal Law," *Brigham Young University Law Review* [1986], 353.

§ See generally Markus D. Dubber, "Judicial Positivism and Hitler's Injustice," 93 *Columbia Law Review* (1993), 1807.

¶ See also Wolfgang Naucke, "Der Zustand des Legalitätsprinzips," in Klaus Lüderssen et al. (eds.), *Modernes Strafrecht und ultima-ratio-Prinzip* (1990), 149; Markus D. Dubber, "The Legality Principle in American and German Criminal Law: An Essay in Comparative Legal History," in Georges Martyn et al. (eds.), *From the Judge's Arbitrium to the Legality Principle: Legislation as a Source of Law in Criminal Trials* (2013), 365.

8. How would the "representation of violence" statute in the *"Dance of the Devils" Case* (§ 131 StGB) and the "disloyalty" statute at issue in the economic crime cases discussed in Note 3 (§ 266 StGB) fare under the two-part vagueness test enunciated by the U.S. Supreme Court, and cited in *Morales* and *Skilling*: (1) fair notice, (2) arbitrary enforcement? (A version of this test is also used in other jurisdictions. (See, e.g., *R. v. Nova Scotia Pharmaceutical Society*, [1992] 2 S.C.R. 606 (Can.).)

9. Does the (first) fair notice prong of the vagueness analysis mean what it says? Is the fair notice requirement realistic, given the enormous and evergrowing multitude of criminal norms? Would the modern state not come to screeching halt if we took a fair notice requirement seriously? How does the fair notice requirement sit with the categorical rejection of an ignorance of law defense in common law countries?* With the very lax publicity requirements characteristic of modern criminal law, which—if they persist at all—are satisfied through publication in obscure government gazettes, if not the (nominally) public consideration of proposed legislation (a far cry from the original rule that norms did not come into force until their publication through oral or written announcement in a public place, such as a the town square)?†

At any rate, even if notice still makes sense in modern criminal law (with its mass of statutory and regulatory norms, each subject to judicial and executive interpretation), why do we need a separate vagueness doctrine if due process requires fair notice in all cases?‡

10. What does the (second) arbitrary discretion prong have to do with vagueness? This prong tends to do most of the work, given the thinness of the fair notice requirement (*Skilling* notwithstanding). But is this not a rule of criminal procedure, rather than of substantive criminal law, one that attaches a presumption of arbitrariness to certain provisions that are so likely to produce arbitrary police behavior as to be not only constitutionally suspect, but infirm? Is this an irrebuttable presumption, or could it be rebutted through the introduction of evidence demonstrating the non-arbitrary application of the provision in general, or even in the particular case?

11. Consider how a vagueness challenge in a particular case might be used to raise different concerns about a legislative act. In the most famous U.S. vagueness case, *Papachristou v. City of Jacksonville*, 405 U.S. 156 (1972), the U.S. Supreme Court struck down a city vagrancy ordinance (closely modeled after a fourteenth-century English statute) that provided, among other things, that "[r]ogues and vagabonds, common gamblers, common drunkards, common night walkers, thieves, pilferers or pickpockets, lewd, wanton and lascivious persons, common railers and brawlers, habitual loafers, disorderly persons, shall be deemed vagrants." The Court spent much time celebrating aimless wandering and loafing around as quintessentially American pursuits (citing, among others, Walt Whitman); the case also had strong racial undertones, featuring interracial couples who had been arrested in a Southern city (Jacksonville, Florida). In other words, the vagueness analysis was less about vagueness than about other concerns—overbreadth and racial discrimination, which might have been more difficult to address head-on, for different reasons (the weakness of overbreadth doctrine in cases not implicating the First Amendment, i.e., free speech rights, and the need to establish racial discriminatory intent). Recall that vagueness is not overbreadth, or that a broad statute is not necessarily a vague one. Overbreadth goes to the substantive limits on state power; vagueness concerns the form of a state norm, not its substance. On the distinction (in Canadian constitutional law), see *R. v. Heywood*, [1994] 3 S.C.R. 761.

---

* See Chapter 8.C.ii.
† See, e.g., *United States v. Casson*, 434 F.2d 415 (D.C. Cir. 1970).
‡ See the discussion of the retroactivity of judicial changes in criminal law, in Chapter 2.A.

CONSTITUTIONAL LIMITS ON SUBSTANTIVE CRIMINAL LAW

This Section deals with constitutional limits, if any, on the law of crime, rather than the law of punishment (addressed in Chapter 1.B). The question here is whether, and if so how, the general part and special part of Anglo-American and German criminal law can be said to be constrained by, or grounded in, principles of constitutional law. In the United States, constitutional law, in the hands of the U.S. Supreme Court, has had very little to say about the general principles of criminal liability. Among the more charitable assessments of the Supreme Court's constitutional jurisprudence on *mens rea*, for instance, is the remark—made twice, several decades apart—that "*Mens Rea* is an important requirement, but it is not a constitutional requirement, except sometimes."* Less charitable, and more common, is the view that the Supreme Court has expended all its constitutional ambitions on procedural criminal law, showing virtually no interest its substantive cousin. And there are those who think this is a good thing, too.[†]

Efforts to place limits on the special part are easier to come by in American constitutional jurisprudence, though they tend to reflect a general interest in protecting free speech rights under the First Amendment rather than in constraining the state's criminal lawmaking power in general. The one possible exception: the U.S. Supreme Court's decision in *Lawrence v. Texas*, 539 U.S. 558 (2003), which—in striking down a Texas homosexual sodomy law—made reference to the "autonomy of the self."

Given the dearth of American constitutional criminal law, especially when it comes to the general part, we lead off with a Canadian case. The Canadian Supreme Court, since the adoption of the Charter of Rights and Freedoms in 1982 (and the failure of a comprehensive criminal code reform effort), embarked on an ambitious attempt to explore the constitutional foundations of the general principles of criminal liability. Along the way, it has struck a balance between American and German approaches. The case excerpted here, the *Motor Vehicle Reference* of 1985, is an example: unlike the U.S. Supreme Court, it recognizes a constitutional *mens rea* requirement, but then, unlike German law, limits it to certain (imprisonable) offenses.

Constitutional principles play an interesting, and contested, role in German criminal law. Constitutional law (still) tends to be treated as a recent arrival on the criminal law scene, one dominated by a system of norms, principles, standards, and rules developed by German criminal law scientists, i.e., German professors of criminal law, over the past century or two. The question is less what criminal law principles constitutional law might generate than to which constitutional provisions long-established principles of criminal law science might be attached. As constitutional law, and the German Constitutional Court, have become more

---

* Compare Herbert L. Packer, "*Mens Rea* and the Supreme Court," *Supreme Court Review* [1962], 107, with Richard Singer and Douglas Husak, "Of Innocence and Innocents: The Supreme Court and *Mens Rea* Since Herbert Packer," 2 *Buffalo Criminal Law Review* (1999), 861.

[†] Louis Bilionis, "Process, the Constitution, and Substantive Criminal Law," 96 *Michigan Law Review* (1998), 1269.

established, this relationship between constitutional law and criminal law as a source of general principles has become more controversial, as illustrated by the Constitutional Court's decision in the *Incest Case* of 2008 (which drew a strong dissent from a Judge who, not coincidentally, had been a distinguished criminal law professor before his appointment).

A. General Part

Reference Re: Section 94(2) of the Motor Vehicle Act
Supreme Court of Canada
[1985] 2 S.C.R. 486
"Motor Vehicle Reference"

Lamer J.:—

Introduction

A law that has the potential to convict a person who has not really done anything wrong offends the principles of fundamental justice and, if imprisonment is available as a penalty, such a law then violates a person's right to liberty under s. 7 of the *Canadian Charter of Rights and Freedoms (Part* I of the *Constitution Act, 1982*, as enacted by the *Canada Act, 1982* (U.K.), c. 11).

In other words, absolute liability and imprisonment cannot be combined.

The facts

On August 16, 1982, the Lieutenant-Governor in Council of British Columbia referred the following question to the Court of Appeal of that province, by virtue of s. 1 of the *Constitutional Question Act*, R.S.B.C. 1979, c. 63:

Is s. 94(2) of the Motor Vehicle Act, R.S.B.C.1979, as amended by the Motor Vehicle Amendment Act, 1982, consistent with the *Canadian Charter of Rights and Freedoms*?

On February 3, 1983, the Court of Appeal handed down reasons in answer to the question in which it stated that s. 94(2) of the Act is inconsistent with the *Canadian Charter of Rights and Freedoms*: 4 C.C.C. (3d) 243, 147 D.L.R. (3d) 539, 33 C.R. (3d) 22, [1983] 3 W.W.R. 756, 42 B.C.L.R. 364, 5 C.R.R. 148, 19 M.V.R. 63. The Attorney-General for British Columbia launched an appeal to this Court.

The legislation

Motor Vehicle Act, R.S.B.C. 1979, c. 288, s. 94, as amended by the *Motor Vehicle Amendment Act*, 1982, c. 36, s. 19:

94 (I) A person who drives a motor vehicle on a highway or industrial road while

    (a) he is prohibited from driving a motor vehicle under section 90, 91, 92 or 92.1, or

    (b) his driver's licence or his right to apply for or obtain a driver's licence is suspended under section 82 or 92 as it was before its repeal and replacement came into force pursuant to the *Motor Vehicle Amendment Act, 1982*,

commits an offense and is liable

    (c) on a first conviction, to a fine of not less than $300 and not more than $2000 and to imprisonment for not less than 7 days and not more than 6 months, and

    (d) on a subsequent conviction, regardless of when the contravention occurred, to a fine of not less than $100 and not more than $2000 and to imprisonment for not less than 14 days and not more than one year.

  (2) Subsection (1) creates an absolute liability offense in which guilt is established by proof of driving, whether or not the defendant knew of the prohibition or suspension.

Canadian Charter of Rights and Freedoms; Constitution Act, 1982:

1. The Canadian Charter of Rights and Freedoms guarantees the rights and freedoms set out in it subject only to such reasonable limits prescribed by law as can be demonstrably justified in a free and democratic society.

7. Everyone has the right to life, liberty and security of the person and the right not to be deprived thereof except in accordance with the principles of fundamental justice.

11. Any person charged with an offence has the right . . .

(d) to be presumed innocent until proven guilty according to law in a fair and public hearing by an independent and impartial tribunal;

52. (1) The Constitution of Canada is the supreme law of Canada, and any law that is inconsistent with the provisions of the Constitution is, to the extent of the inconsistency, of no force or effect.

. . .

Section 7

1. Introduction

The issue in this case raises fundamental questions of constitutional theory, including the nature and the very legitimacy of constitutional adjudication under the Charter as well as the appropriateness of various techniques of constitutional interpretation. I shall deal first with these questions of a more general and theoretical nature as they underlie and have shaped much of the discussion surrounding s. 7.

2. The nature and legitimacy of constitutional adjudication under the Charter

The British Columbia Court of Appeal has written in the present case that the *Constitution Act, 1982* has added a new dimension to the role of the courts in that the courts have now been empowered by s. 52 to consider not only the *vires* of legislation but also to measure the content of legislation against the constitutional requirements of the Charter.

The concerns with the bounds of constitutional adjudication explain the characterization of the issue in a narrow and restrictive fashion, *i.e.*, whether the terms "principles of fundamental justice" have a substantive or merely procedural content. In my view, the characterization of the issue in such fashion pre-empts an open-minded approach to determining the meaning of "principles of fundamental justice" . . .

The task of the court is not to choose between substantive or procedural content *per se* but to secure for persons "the full benefit of the Charter's protection" (Dickson C.J.C. in *R. v. Big M Drug Mart Ltd.* (1985), 18 C.C.C. (3d) 385 at p. 424, 18 D.L.R. (4th) 321 at p. 360, [1985] 1 S.C.R. 295 at p. 344), under s. 7, while avoiding adjudication of the merits of public policy. This can only be accomplished by a purposive analysis and the articulation (to use the words in *Curr v. The Queen* (1972), 7 C.C.C. (2d) 181 at p. 192, 26 D.L.R. (3d) 603 at p. 614, [1972] S.C.R. 889 at p. 899) of "objective and manageable standards" for the operation of the section within such a framework . . .

The main sources of support for the argument that "fundamental justice" is simply synonymous with natural justice have been the Minutes of the Proceedings and Evidence of the Special Joint Committee on the Constitution and the *Bill of Rights* jurisprudence. In my view, neither the minutes nor the *Bill of Rights* jurisprudence are persuasive or of any great force. The historical usage of the term "fundamental justice" is, on the other hand, shrouded in ambiguity. Moreover, not any one of these arguments, taken singly or as a whole, manages to overcome in my respectful view the textual and contextual analyses . . .

Consequently, my conclusion may be summarized as follows:

The term "principles of fundamental justice" is not a right, but a qualifier of the right not to be deprived of life, liberty and security of the person; its function is to set the parameters of that right.

Sections 8 to 14 address specific deprivations of the "right" to life, liberty and security of the person in breach of the principles of fundamental justice, and as such, violations of s. 7. They are therefore illustrative of the meaning, in criminal or penal law, of "principles of fundamental justice"; they represent principles which have been recognized by the common law, the international conventions and by the very fact of entrenchment in the Charter, as essential elements of a system for the administration of justice which is founded upon a belief in the dignity and worth of the human person and the rule of law.

Consequently, the principles of fundamental justice are to be found in the basic tenets and principles, not only of our judicial process, but also of the other components of our legal system.

We should not be surprised to find that many of the principles of fundamental justice are procedural in nature. Our common law has largely been a law of remedies and procedures and, as Frankfurter J. wrote in *McNabb v. U.S.* (1942), 318 U.S. 332 at p. 347, "the history of liberty has largely been the history of observance of procedural safeguards." This is not to say, however, that the principles of fundamental justice are limited solely to procedural guarantees. Rather, the proper approach to the determination of the principles of fundamental justice is quite simply one in which, as Professor Tremblay has written, "future growth will be based on our historical roots": 18 U.B.C. L. Rev. 201 at p. 254 (1980).

Whether any given principle may be said to be a principle of fundamental justice within the meaning of s. 7 will rest upon an analysis of the nature, sources, *rationale* and essential role of that principle within the judicial process and in our legal system, as it evolves.

Consequently, those words cannot be given any exhaustive content or simple enumerative definition, but will take on concrete meaning as the courts address alleged violations of s. 7...

Absolute liability and fundamental justice in penal law

It has from time immemorial been part of our system of laws that the innocent not be punished. This principle has long been recognized as an essential element of a system for the administration of justice which is founded upon a belief in the dignity and worth of the human person and on the rule of law. It is so old that its first enunciation was in Latin *actus non facit reum nisi mens sit rea.*

As Glanville Williams said:

> There is no need here to go into the remote history of *mens rea*, suffice it to say that the requirement of a guilty state of mind (at least for the more serious crimes) had been developed by the time of Coke, which is as far back as the modern lawyer needs to go. "If one shoot at any wild fowl upon a tree, and the arrow killeth any reasonable creature afar off, without any evil intent in him, this is *per infortunium.*"

> (Glanville Williams, *Criminal Law, The General Part*, 2nd ed. (1961), p. 30, London, Stevens & Sons Limited.)

One of the many judicial statements on the subject worth mentioning is of the highest authority, *per* Lord Goddard C.J. in *Harding v. Price*, [1948] 1 K.B. 695 at p. 700, where he said:

> The general rule applicable to criminal cases is actus non facit reum nisi mens sit rea, and I venture to repeat what I said in *Bread v. Wood* ((1946), 62 T.L.R. 462, 463): "It is of the utmost importance for the protection of the liberty of the subject that a court should always bear in mind that, unless a statute either clearly or by necessary implication rules out mens rea as a constituent part of a crime, the court should not find a man guilty of an offense against the criminal law unless he has a guilty mind."

This view has been adopted by this Court in unmistakable terms in many cases, amongst which the better known are *Beaver v. The Queen* (1957), 118 C.C.C. 129, [1957] S.C.R. 531, 26 C.R. 193, and the most recent and often-quoted judgment of Dickson J. (as he then was), writing for the court in *R. v. City of Sault Ste. Marie* (1978), 40 C.C.C. (2d) 353, 85 D.L.R. (3d) 161, [1978] 2 S.C.R. 1299.

This Court's decision in the latter case is predicated upon a certain number of postulates one of which, given the nature of the rules it elaborates, has to be to the effect that absolute liability in penal law offends the principles of fundamental justice. Those principles are, to use the words of Dickson J., to the effect that "there is a generally held revulsion against punishment of the morally innocent" [at p. 363 C.C.C., p. 170 D.L.R., p. 1310 S.C.R.]. He also stated [at p. 363 C.C.C., p. 171 D.L.R., p. 1311 S.C.R.] that the argument that absolute liability "violates fundamental principles of penal liability" was the most telling argument against absolute liability and one of greater force than those advanced in support thereof.

In my view, it is because absolute liability offends the principles of fundamental justice that this Court created presumptions against Legislatures having intended to enact offenses of a regulatory nature falling within that category. This is not to say, however, and to that extent I am in agreement with the Court of Appeal, that, as a result, absolute liability *per se* offends s. 7 of the Charter.

A law enacting an absolute liability offense will violate s. 7 of the Charter only if and to the extent that it has the potential of depriving of life, liberty or security of the person.

Obviously, imprisonment (including probation orders) deprives persons of their liberty. An offense has that potential as of the moment it is open to the judge to impose imprisonment. There is no need that imprisonment, as in s. 94(2), be made mandatory.

I am therefore of the view that the combination of imprisonment and of absolute liability violates s. 7 of the Charter and can only be salvaged if the authorities demonstrate under s. 1 that such a deprivation of liberty in breach of those principles of fundamental justice is, in a free and democratic society, under the circumstances, a justified reasonable limit to one's rights under s. 7....

Before considering s. 94(2) in the light of these findings, I feel we are however compelled to go somewhat further for the following reason. I would not want us to be taken by this conclusion as having inferentially decided that absolute liability may not offend s. 7 as long as imprisonment or probation orders are not available as a sentence. The answer to that question is dependent upon the content given to the words "security of the person." That issue was and is a live one. Indeed, though the question as framed focuses on absolute liability (s. 94(2)) in relation to the whole Charter, including the right to security of the person in s. 7, because of the presence of mandatory imprisonment in s. 94(1) only deprivation of liberty was considered. As the effect of imprisonment on the right to liberty is a foregone conclusion, *a fortiori* minimum imprisonment, everyone directed their arguments, when discussing s. 7 to considering whether absolute liability violated the principles of fundamental justice, and then subsidiarily argued *pro* or *contra* the effect of s. 1 of the Charter.

Counsel for those opposing the validity of s. 94(2) took the position in this Court that absolute liability and severe punishment, always referring to imprisonment, violated s. 7 of the Charter. From the following passage of the judgment in the Court of Appeal it would appear that counsel for those opposing the validity of the section took the wider position in that court that all absolute liability offenses violated s. 7 because of "punishment of the morally innocent" at p. 250 C.C.C., p. 546 D.L.R.:

> In seeking to persuade the court to that conclusion counsel opposing the validity of s. 94(2) contended all absolute offenses are now of no force and effect because of s. 7 of the Charter and that the provisions of s. 1 of the Charter should not be invoked to sustain them. In support of this submission counsel relied upon the view expressed by Mr. Justice Dickson in *Sault Ste. Marie* that there was "a generally held revulsion against punishment of the morally innocent." They contended that had the Charter been in effect when *Sault Ste. Mane* was decided all absolute liability offenses would have been struck down.

We accept without hesitation the statement expressed by the learned justice but do not think it necessarily follows that because of s. 7 of the Charter this category of offense can no longer be legislated. To the contrary, there are, and will remain, certain public welfare offenses, *e.g.*, air and water pollution offenses, where the public interest requires that the offenses be absolute liability offenses.

While I agree with the Court of Appeal, as I have already mentioned, that absolute liability does not *per se* violate s. 7 of the Charter, I am somewhat concerned with leaving without comment the unqualified reference by the Court of Appeal to the requirements of the "public interest."

If, by reference to public interest, it was meant that the requirements of public interest for certain types of offenses is a factor to be considered in determining whether absolute liability offends the principles of fundamental justice, then I would respectfully disagree; if the public interest is there referred to by the court as a possible justification under s. 1 of a limitation to the rights protected at s. 7, then I do agree.

Indeed, as I said, in penal law, absolute liability always offends the principles of fundamental justice irrespective of the nature of the offense; it offends s. 7 of the Charter if, as a result, anyone is deprived of his life, liberty or security of the person, irrespective of the requirement of public interest. In such cases it might only be salvaged for reasons of public interest under s. 1.

In this latter regard, something might be added.

Administrative expediency, absolute liability's main supportive argument, will undoubtedly under s. 1 be invoked and occasionally succeed. Indeed, administrative expediency certainly has its place in administrative law. But when administrative law chooses to call in aid imprisonment through penal law, indeed sometimes criminal law and the added stigma attached to a conviction, exceptional, in my view, will be the case where the liberty or even the security of the person guaranteed under s. 7 should be sacrificed to administrative expediency. Section 1 may, for reasons of administrative expediency, successfully come to the rescue of an otherwise violation of s. 7, but only in cases arising out of exceptional conditions, such as natural disasters, the outbreak of war, epidemics and the like. . . .

Section 94(2)

No doubt s. 94(2) enacts in the clearest of terms an absolute liability offense, the conviction for which a person will be deprived of his or her liberty, and little more, if anything, need be added. . . .

In the final analysis, it seems that both the appellant and the respondent agree that s. 94 will impact upon the right to liberty of a limited number of morally innocent persons. It creates an absolute liability offense which effects a deprivation of liberty for a limited number of persons. To me, that is sufficient for it to be in violation of s. 7.

Section 11

Having found that s. 94(2) offends s. 7 of the Charter there remains the question as to whether the appellants have demonstrated that the section is salvaged by the operation of s. 1 of the Charter. No evidence was adduced in the Court of Appeal or in this Court. The position in that regard and the argument in support of the operability of s. 94(2) is as follows in appellant's factum:

If this Court rules that s. 94(2) of the Motor Vehicle Act is inconsistent with S. 7 (or S. 11(d)) of the Charter, then it is submitted that S. 1 of the Charter is applicable. It is submitted that Laskin J. (as he then was) made it clear in *Curr v. The Queen*, supra, that it is within the scope of judicial notice for this Court to recognize that a statutory provision was enacted as part of a legislative scheme aimed at reducing the human and economic cost of bad driving. S. 94 is but part of the overall scheme laid out in the Motor Vehicle Act by which the Legislature is attempting to get bad drivers off the road. S. 94 imposes severe penalties on those who drive while prohibited from driving and those who drive while their driver's licence is suspended.

It is submitted that if S. 94(2) is inconsistent with one of the above-noted provisions of the Charter, then S. 94(2) contains a "reasonable limit, etc." within the meaning of S. 1 of the Charter.

I do not take issue with the fact that it is highly desirable that "bad drivers" be kept off the road. I do not take issue either with the desirability of punishing severely bad drivers who are in contempt of prohibitions against driving. The bottom line of the question to be addressed here is: whether the Government of British Columbia has demonstrated as justifiable that the risk of imprisonment of a few innocent is, given the desirability of ridding the roads of British Columbia of bad drivers, a reasonable limit in a free and democratic society. That result is to be measured against the offense being one of strict liability open to a defence of due diligence, the success of which does nothing more than let those few who did nothing wrong remain free.

As did the Court of Appeal, I find that this demonstration has not been satisfied, indeed, not in the least.

Appeal dismissed

Markus D. Dubber, "Toward a Constitutional Law of Crime and Punishment," 55 *Hastings Law Journal* 509 (2004), 509

It has become a commonplace that there are no meaningful constitutional constraints on [U.S.] substantive criminal law. While procedural criminal law is thoroughly constitutionalized, so much so that criminal procedure has become synonymous with constitutional criminal procedure, the law of crime and punishment has remained virtually untouched by constitutional scrutiny.

The failure to place constitutional limits upon substantive criminal law reflects two common features of the constitutional jurisprudence of the United States Supreme Court: the prioritization of process over substance and, relatedly, the prioritization of states' rights over individual rights, where criminal lawmaking is taken to be one, perhaps the, manifestation of the power of governance most closely associated with the states, the police power, which is also widely recognized as the power of governance least susceptible to definition, never mind limitation. . . .

[T]here is great need for constitutional principles of criminal law. The war on crime of the past thirty-odd years has wrought havoc on the traditional principles of American criminal law, exposing their fundamental weakness. The foundation of "*mens rea*" and "*actus reus*" in common law precedent did not stand in the way of the transformation of criminal law into a system of risk administration, which began over a century ago with the medicalization and bureaucratization of criminal law and culminated in the war on crime, an increasingly ambitious social control program launched by President Richard Nixon and continued, and continually expanded, by succeeding administrations that eventually encompassed all levels of American government.

The venerable principles of common criminal law—imported from foreign soil and associated with an undemocratic, unrepublican system of governance that regarded criminal law as an order main-tenance system, where they long ago had been eviscerated through the gradual displacement of common law crimes by statutory crimes—crumbled under the pressure of crime waves and crime scares, political opportunism and populist one-up-manship. After a gradual, but accelerating, process of evisceration . . . the once vaunted principles of the English common law eventually came, at best, to retain a largely antiquarian significance, as relics from a mythical time when *mens rea* meant *mens rea* and *actus reus, actus reus*. At worst, they helped to legitimize the transmogrification of modern criminal law, as they stood for the reassuring notion that in the realm of "real" criminal law—of "true" or "traditional" crimes—the world was still in order, while outside, on the "periphery," strict liability crimes spread in open defiance of the *mens rea* requirement, possession offenses flouted the purportedly non-negotiable act requirement, and defenses, like insanity and intoxication, were either crippled or eliminated altogether.

NOTES

1. The question of whether lawmakers have unlimited discretion when deciding about criminal prohibitions or whether there are restrictions binding even legislatures has been discussed intensively since the Enlightenment. Today, the idea of protecting persons' liberty

is no longer left exclusively to political theory in general and criminal law theory in particular. The crucial question now is also a legal question: What limits does constitutional law place on legislative decision-making? One important constitutional principle of this kind is the principle of legality, or *nulla poena sine lege* (prohibiting, for instance, retroactive and vague criminal prohibitions) discussed in Chapter 2. While something like a formal principle of legality—or at least more specific constitutional norms that might be bundled into a general principle—is widely recognized as an ideal, the constitutionalization of substantive principles, either in the general part or in the special part of criminal law, differs considerably among legal systems, both in conception and in degree.

In the United States, for instance, the very notion of constitutionalizing substantive criminal law is contested (by contrast, procedural criminal law has been thoroughly constitutionalized since the Warren Court of the 1960s, though also hardly without controversy). In Canada, the Supreme Court began to constitutionalize the substantive criminal law, and the general part of the criminal law in particular, following the enactment in 1982 of the Canadian Charter of Rights and Freedoms. In Germany, the constitutionalization of criminal law has been largely a question of locating existing criminal law principles within a constitutional framework.

This overview of different approaches raises the basic question: who needs constitutional law? The constitutionalization of criminal law principles in Germany has been not only slow, but also controversial, because German criminal law scholars insist that criminal law does not need constitutional law to generate fundamental principles. Take *nulla poena*: the German Criminal Code has since 1871 included a *nulla poena* provision (now in § 1). What does a constitutional *nulla poena* prohibition add? Alternatively, one might ask: who needs criminal law? What exactly is the contribution that criminal law can make to constitutional analysis? A rights-based constitutional law analysis asks which right, if any, has been infringed, and (perhaps), if so, whether that infringement can be justified (as reasonable, proportional, and so on). Where do criminal law "principles"—like the requirement of *mens rea* or *actus reus*, or the harm principle, the *Schuldgrundsatz* (or culpability principle), or the *Rechtsgutsprinzip**—enter this inquiry?

2. Unlike in the United States, in Germany *nulla poena sine culpa* (no punishment without culpability) is recognized as a constitutional principle. Unlike the U.S. Constitution, the text of the German Constitution does not contain a "cruel and unusual punishments" clause. The culpability principle is also not written explicitly in the Basic Law. But the Federal Constitutional Court specifies unwritten constitutional requirements by drawing together general maxims and principles.

A frequently cited description of what culpability means appeared in a decision by the Federal Court of Justice from March 18, 1952 (GSSt 2/51, BGHSt 2, 194, 200):

> The internal ground for the accusation of culpability lies in the fact that the human being is destined for free, responsible and moral self-determination, and is therefore enabled to decide for the right and against the wrong, to order his conduct according to the norms of the legally required and to avoid what is legally prohibited as soon as he has attained moral maturity and as long as his aptitude for free moral self-determination has not been temporarily paralyzed or permanently destroyed by the pathological events mentioned in § 51 [old version, now § 20] German Criminal Code.

The Federal Constitutional Court links the culpability principle to one of the keystones of German constitutional theory, the *Rechtsstaatsprinzip*, which can be roughly translated as "rule of law principle." This includes the principle of substantive justice, and to punish an offender for past wrongdoing would be unjust if he acted without fault.[†] (Compare the fault principle in Canadian constitutional law, framed as a prohibition of "punishment of the morally innocent."[‡]) In addition, the German Federal Constitutional Court relies on human

---

* See Chapter 3.B.
[†] See Federal Constitutional Court, Judgment of October 25, 1966, 2 BvR 506/63, BVerfGE 20, 323, 331.
[‡] See, e.g., *R. v. Wholesale Travel Group Inc.*, [1991] 3 S.C.R. 154.

rights clauses: human dignity and autonomy as guaranteed in art. 1 para. 1 and art. 2 para. 1 Basic Law. These human rights provisions conceptualize human beings as autonomous agents and moral beings capable of self-determination and development who should not be treated as mere objects of state intervention.*

Emphasizing the culpability principle as a constitutional principle has one important consequence: criminal punishment for strict liability offenses would be unconstitutional under the German Basic Law. In fact, the legislature has abstained from passing criminal laws based on strict liability.

Given the central importance of the culpability principle in German criminal law, it is worth considering its content and its constitutional status in greater detail. To recognize a culpability principle is one thing: to clarify what it is, another; and to justify it yet a third. The 1952 German case cited above, which is often cited as an authoritative statement of the culpability principle, dealt with a mistake of law (a *Verbotsirrtum*), not with a mistake of fact (a *Tatbestandsirrtum*). It did not address the question of strict (or absolute) liability in the sense of an absence of a requirement of *mens rea* attached to a particular offense element. (This question only would have arisen in the case of a mistake of *fact*, i.e., a mistake that could have negated a *mens rea* requirement.) The Federal Court of Justice in this case held that mistake of law must be a defense. Why? Because of the culpability principle, as defined in the quote above. "Culpability," again, is here understood not in the sense of "mode of culpability" (or type of *mens rea*), as a subjective offense element, but in the sense of "accountability" or "blameworthiness" (or absence of excuse). It may well be that the broad "culpability principle" set out by the Federal Court of Justice in the 1952 case implies the recognition not only of an excuse of mistake of law (along with, perhaps, any other type of excuse) but also of a *mens rea* requirement (attaching to each offense, or to each offense element?), which could then be negated by a mistake of fact. But this application would exceed the holding of the case, and therefore require further elaboration. For a detailed discussion of *mens rea*, mistake of law, and excuse, see Chapter 8.

This ambiguity inherent in the *Schuldprinzip* between culpability as *mens rea* and (absence of) excuse (leaving aside the further complication that it also encompasses proportionality in sentencing, see Chapter 1.B.) merely reflects the ambiguity between *mens rea* and excuse in criminal law doctrine generally speaking. The line between *mens rea* and excuse is not always obvious (within a given legal system, at any given time, never mind across legal systems, or within a given legal system over time), and the development of the modern law of culpability is also the development of a separate category of excuse, and the gradual recognition that not all matters of culpability can (or should) be addressed as a matter of *mens rea*, or modes of culpability.

As a matter of translation, it is important, however, to recognize that, at least today (if not always), the "culpability" in the "culpability" principle (or *Schuldprinzip*) refers *both* to subjective offense elements (i.e., types of *mens rea*) and to the absence of excuse. The translation "guilt principle" would minimize the risk of misinterpreting the principle as speaking *only* to *mens rea*, but at the cost of increasing the risk of misinterpreting it as speaking only to the issue of excuse.

It is worth noting in this context that the quoted passage from the 1952 decision appears in the middle of a review of the criminal law literature and jurisprudence on mistake of law over the preceding century, with some commentators and courts taking one position on mistake of law, and others another. The moment of constitutionalization occurred only later, in judgments of the German Federal Constitutional Court, which relate the culpability principle, thus defined, to various notions of constitutional law—rule of law, dignity, autonomy. But how does one get from such general abstract concepts: (1) to any culpability principle; (2) to the culpability principle as formulated by the Federal Court of Justice in 1952; (3) to the requirement that the criminal law recognize mistake of law as a defense, (4) to the requirement that the criminal law recognize other excuses; and, finally, (5) to a general *mens rea*

---

* See Federal Constitutional Court, Judgment of February 26, 1969, 2 BvL 15, 23/68, BVerfGE 25, 269, 285.

requirement (attached to every offense, or to every offense element)? Given the potential significance of constitutionalizing criminal law principles, and of the often invoked culpability principle in particular, it is perhaps surprising that traditionally little effort has been made to enunciate the precise constitutional foundation of the culpability principle. Until recently, the constitutional status of a criminal law norm tended to be announced, rather than justified.*

But note that in contemporary German constitutional law the culpability principle is firmly entrenched. In its important Lisbon Decision of June 30, 2009 (dealing with the Lisbon Treaty, which changed the European Union's foundations), the German Federal Constitutional Court reiterated its opinion concerning the importance of the culpability principle in criminal law. The Court emphasizes: "Criminal law is based on the culpability principle. This principle presupposes the principle of responsibility of human beings who decide autonomously about their acts and are capable to decide between right and wrong on the basis of their freedom of will."†

3. The decision of the Canadian Supreme Court shows some similarities to the principles enunciated by the German Federal Constitutional Court. It also takes as its starting point a very general constitutional notion, in this case, s. 7 of the Canadian Charter of Rights and Freedoms, and the phrase "principles of fundamental justice" in particular. The line from "principles of fundamental justice" to a prohibition of strict liability requires is no more direct than that from the various principles cited by the German Federal Constitutional Court (rule of law, dignity, autonomy). However, due to the wording of s. 7 ("right to life, liberty and security"), strict liability offenses only are deemed unconstitutional if they infringe liberty by including imprisonment as a sanction. On this point, the German Federal Constitutional Court comes to a different conclusion. From the beginning, the German Court held that the culpability principle applies to penalties of any kind, including fines and other "punishment-like penalties."‡

4. The Canadian Supreme Court has fleshed out the conception of criminal law, and of crime, invoked in *Motor Vehicle Reference* in later cases, for instance in *R. v. Wholesale Travel Group Inc.*, [1991] 3 S.C.R. 154:

> Criminal law is rooted in the concepts of individual autonomy and free will and the corollary that each individual is responsible for his or her conduct. It assumes that all persons are free actors, at liberty to choose how to regulate their own actions in relation to others. The criminal law fixes the outer limits of acceptable conduct, constraining individual freedom to a limited degree in order to preserve the freedom of others. Thus, the basis of criminal responsibility is that the accused person has made a deliberate and conscious choice to engage in activity prohibited by the Criminal Code. The accused person who is convicted of an offence will be held responsible for his or her actions, with the result that the opprobrium of society will attach to those acts and any punishment imposed will be considered to be deserved.

Compare this passage to the above-quoted passage in the German Federal Constitutional Court's Lisbon Decision. Do they set out a common core of commitments that could generate basic principles of criminal law (in a modern? liberal? Western? democratic? society). What might those principles look like? If one starts with some basic commitment to "dignity" or "autonomy," which is supposed to give rise to a "culpability principle," what is added by the latter principle? (Similarly, in the law of sentencing, if "[t]he culpability principle is a specific expression of the proportionality principle, which is also a constitutional requirement of the 'rule of law,'"§ what does the "culpability principle" add to the analysis?) Is a (specifically criminal) culpability principle more specific than, say, a (general constitutional) principle of dignity, or autonomy, or proportionality, and therefore more suitable as the basis for specific doctrinal rules?

---

* See generally Tatjana Hörnle, "Die verfassungsrechtliche Begründung des Schuldprinzips," in Ulrich Sieber et al. (eds.), *Strafrecht und Wirtschaftsstrafrecht: Dogmatik, Rechtsvergleich, Rechtstatsachen* (2008), 325.
† BVerfGE 123, 267, 413.
‡ See Judgment of October 25, 1966, 2 BvR 506/63, BVerfGE 20, 323, 331.
§ See Chapter 1.B.

Now consider the opening paragraph from the U.S. Supreme Court's opinion in *Lawrence v. Texas*, 539 U.S. 558 (2003) (excerpted in Chapter 3.B), striking down a Texas anti-sodomy statute:

> Liberty protects the person from unwarranted government intrusions into a dwelling or other private places. In our tradition the State is not omnipresent in the home. And there are other spheres of our lives and existence, outside the home, where the State should not be a dominant presence. Freedom extends beyond spatial bounds. Liberty presumes an autonomy of self that includes freedom of thought, belief, expression, and certain intimate conduct. The instant case involves liberty of the person both in its spatial and more transcendent dimensions.

Does this passage suggest that U.S. constitutional law shares these commitments, and that they could give rise to a set of constitutionally grounded principles of substantive criminal law? Or is the "autonomy of self" in *Lawrence* fundamentally different than the self-determination and autonomy in the German and Canadian cases?*

5. Let us leave constitutional law aside for the moment, and focus on the content of the culpability principle, constitutionalized or not, as a principle of (criminal) law. The question then becomes whether there is something like a culpability principle in Anglo-American criminal law. In fact, given the deep historical roots that tend to be claimed for the culpability principle, it would be odd if the culpability principle would be limited to a body of law as modern as "German criminal law," or the criminal law in other civil law countries for that matter, without having left at least some trace in English law, or the law of any other common law jurisdictions. (In this context, it is worth pointing out that the Latinate version of the culpability principle—*nulla poena sine culpa*—is of recent vintage. It does not even go as far back as P.J.A. Feuerbach's formulation of the *nulla poena sine lege* maxim in the early nineteenth century, despite occasional assertions to the contrary.[†])

It is not surprising, then, that Anglo-American criminal law might lay claim to a culpability principle of its own: *actus non facit reum nisi mens sit rea*, the vaunted common law "*mens rea* requirement," usually traced to Sir Edward Coke in the seventeenth century and from there to medieval canon law (which tends to be enlisted as the source of the German culpability principle as well). (Or as Blackstone put it a century later: "An involuntary act, as it has no claim to merit, so neither can it induce any guilt: the concurrence of the will, when it has its choice either to do or to avoid the fact in question, being the only thing that renders human actions either praiseworthy or culpable.") To identify a "culpability principle" in Anglo-American criminal law, however, is not the end of the inquiry, but barely the beginning. For the question that has exercised Anglo-American lawyers for centuries is: Just what does this requirement mean, if anything? Is it so vague as to be toothless? How does it affect doctrinal analysis? Consider, for instance, this characteristic passage from James Fitzjames Stephen in the famous case of *R. v. Tolson*, 23 Q.B.D. 168 (1889):

> Like most legal Latin maxims, the maxim on *mens rea* appears to me to be too short and antithetical to be of much practical value. It is, indeed, more like the title of a treatise than a practical rule. . . .
> The principle involved appears to me, when fully considered, to amount to no more than this. The full definition of every crime contains expressly or by implication a proposition as to a state of mind. Therefore, if the mental element of any conduct alleged to be a crime is proved to have been absent in any given case, the crime so defined is not committed; or, again, if a crime is fully defined, nothing amounts to that crime which does not satisfy that definition. Crimes are in the present day much more accurately defined by statute or otherwise than they formerly were. The mental element of most crimes is marked by one of the words "maliciously," "fraudulently," "negligently," or "knowingly" but it is the general—I might, I think, say the invariable—practice of the legislature to leave unexpressed some of the mental elements of crime. In all cases whatever, competent age, sanity, and some degree of freedom from some kinds of coercion are assumed to be essential to criminality, but I do not believe they are ever introduced into any statute by which any particular crime is defined.

---

* See generally James Q. Whitman, "The Two Western Cultures of Privacy: Dignity Versus Liberty," 113 *Yale Law Journal* (2004), 1151.
† See Chapter 2.

In other words, in Stephen's view, the culpability principle has no significance other than as a maxim of statutory interpretation, according to which the legislature is presumed to have intended to require proof of *mens rea* with respect to all crimes and that infancy, insanity, and duress preclude criminal liability. Does this amount to a culpability principle? Or is a principle a norm without exception, an irrebuttable presumption? Does Anglo-American criminal law lack a culpability principle? Or, still leaving aside the question of constitutional status, does it have a culpability principle that differs from that found in German criminal law in definition, in scope, or in rigidity, or all three?

6. *A note on judicial style.* Chief Justice Lamer, like other common law judges, refers to himself in the first personal singular. German judges would not do this, nor would they give any other hint of opinions being held by them personally in contrast to their colleagues. Rather, with the exception of dissenting opinions in constitutional cases,* all judicial statements are made by "the Senate," "the Court," and so on. What does this practice reveal about underlying conceptions of the judicial role and the functions of a judicial opinion (and the relationship between its author and its audience)? About the judicial role in German *constitutional* cases and in other non-constitutional ones?

Even in the Constitutional Court, dissenting opinions (or rather minority votes, including separate concurring opinions) were not permitted (by statute!) until 1970. In the common law, including U.S. criminal law, dissenting opinions have long been an important feature of judicial decision-making. They allow for a public dialogue among judges on a given court and help dispel the notion that the majority position is the only possible, viable, just, or correct resolution of a given issue. They also allow judges to set out arguments that, though unsuccessful in a given court at a given time, may garner the requisite votes on that court in the future or may influence other courts (or anyone else, for that matter, including legislators, other officials, or public discourse). Many dissenting views, in that way, have been transformed into majority positions, even during the term of the once dissenting judge (who may end up writing the majority opinion in the later case . . .).†

Note also that German criminal cases identify defendants, victims, and witnesses only by the first initial of their last name. Likewise, and as a result, German criminal cases are not identified by the name of the defendant, or in any way other than by referring to the court, date of decision, case number, etc. Other than protect the privacy of the persons involved, does this contribute to an image of objective, expert, scientific, or correct decision-making, driven by the syllogistic application of general norms to particular cases, unaffected by personal bias?

The history of the common law, in criminal law as elsewhere, is very much a history of judges and their judgments. The development of the law is measured in opinions strung together through the rule of precedent, *stare decisis*, according to which prior judgments exert greater or lesser influence over later ones, depending on the relationship between the courts rendering the two decisions (between higher and lower courts within a given jurisdiction, or on particular issues) or, more flexibly, the status or reputation of the first court or even the judge who signed a given opinion. Some courts, in particular the U.S. Supreme Court, which functions not only as the final arbiter of (federal) constitutional questions but also as the highest federal court in the land (combining the role played in the German system by the Federal Constitutional Court and the Federal Court of Justice), have become so influential within a given legal system, that the judges who sit on them are subjected to intense scrutiny from the moment of their nomination to the day of their retirement (or their death, which in the U.S. may coincide since Supreme Court Justice serve for life) and legal strategies are designed to sway particular judges, notably those who are thought to hold the "swing vote" that could tip the balance in favor of one perceived faction of the court over another. Judges, through their decisions, are seen—and see themselves—as developing a

---

* See, e.g., Judge Hassemer's dissent in the *Incest Case*, reproduced in Chapter 3.B.
† See, e.g., *People v. Sanchez*, 98 N.Y.2d 373, 777 N.E.2d 204 (N.Y. 2002) (Rosenblatt, J., dissenting); *People v. Payne*, 3 N.Y.3d 266, 819 N.E.2d 634 (2004) (opinion by Rosenblatt, J.) (excerpted in Chapter 15.A.ii).

judicial philosophy or approach, both in form (regarding their perception of the judicial role) and in substance (regarding their views on particular subjects).*

In civil law systems, and in German criminal law in particular, which operate without this system of precedent, prior judgments are less significant and so are their authors. Even referring to prior decisions is cumbersome, given the absence of case names, except in some cases, like the *"Dance of the Devils" Case* or the *Border Guard Case*, that come to be identified through a moniker of some sort. Referring to the judicial author of a prior decision is, as a rule, impossible (again with the exception of dissenting votes in the German Constitutional Court, which occupies a distinct position in the German judicial landscape).

B. Special Part: *Rechtsgut* and Harm Principle

As an exercise of state power, the decision to criminalize is subject to general principles of constitutional law. For instance, the U.S. Supreme Court has struck down on First Amendment (free speech) grounds a number of statutes that threaten the protected conduct with criminal punishment. The criminal nature of the norm in these cases, however, was incidental to the analysis of its constitutionality. By contrast, this Section instead is concerned primarily with constitutional norms that govern the exercise of the criminal law power in particular. Two leading candidates suggest themselves: the harm principle in Anglo-American law and the *Rechtsgut* principle in German law. The most detailed analysis of the constitutional status of the harm principle appears in a Canadian case, *R. v. Malmo-Levine*, denying the harm principle the status of a "principle of fundamental justice," alongside a Pennsylvania case, *Commonwealth v. Bonadio*, which heavily relies on the harm principle, to the point of quoting extensively from John Stuart Mill's *On Liberty*. The *Rechtsgut* principle fared little better in the *Incest Case* before the German Constitutional Court than the harm principle had in *Malmo-Levine*. *Lawrence v. Texas* and the German *Abortion Case* illustrate more general constitutional analyses of criminal prohibitions, beyond the question of the *constitutionalization* of principles set out elsewhere, be it in a foundational nineteenth-century text of Anglo-American liberalism (as in the case of the harm principle) or in the writings of German criminal law science (as in the case of the *Rechtsgut* principle).

Lawrence v. Texas
United States Supreme Court
539 U.S. 558 (2003)

Justice Kennedy delivered the opinion of the Court.

In Houston, Texas, officers of the Harris County Police Department were dispatched to a private residence in response to a reported weapons disturbance. They entered an apartment where one of the petitioners, John Geddes Lawrence, resided. The right of the police to enter does not seem to have been questioned. The officers observed Lawrence and another man, Tyron Garner, engaging in a sexual act. The two petitioners were arrested, held in custody over night, and charged and convicted before a Justice of the Peace.

The complaints described their crime as "deviate sexual intercourse, namely anal sex, with a member of the same sex (man)." App. to Pet. for Cert. 127a, 139a. The applicable state law is Tex. Criminal Code Ann. § 21.06(a) (2003). It provides: "A person commits an offense if he engages in deviate sexual intercourse with another individual of the same sex." The statute defines "deviate sexual intercourse" as follows:

"(A) any contact between any part of the genitals of one person and the mouth or anus of another person; or

---

* For an interesting study of judicial style (on appellate courts), see Karl Llewellyn, *The Common Law Tradition: Deciding Appeals* (1960).

"(B) the penetration of the genitals or the anus of another person with an object."

§ 21.01(1)

. . .

The petitioners were adults at the time of the alleged offense. Their conduct was in private and consensual . . .

At the outset it should be noted that there is no longstanding history in this country of laws directed at homosexual conduct as a distinct matter. . . . Laws prohibiting sodomy do not seem to have been enforced against consenting adults acting in private. A substantial number of sodomy prosecutions and convictions for which there are surviving records were for predatory acts against those who could not or did not consent, as in the case of a minor or the victim of an assault. . . . Instead of targeting relations between consenting adults in private, 19th-century sodomy prosecutions typically involved relations between men and minor girls or minor boys, relations between adults involving force, relations between adults implicating disparity in status, or relations between men and animals . . .

[F]or centuries there have been powerful voices to condemn homosexual conduct as immoral. The condemnation has been shaped by religious beliefs, conceptions of right and acceptable behavior, and respect for the traditional family. For many persons these are not trivial concerns but profound and deep convictions accepted as ethical and moral principles to which they aspire and which thus determine the course of their lives. These considerations do not answer the question before us, however. The issue is whether the majority may use the power of the State to enforce these views on the whole society through operation of the criminal law. "Our obligation is to define the liberty of all, not to mandate our own moral code." Planned Parenthood of Southeastern Pa. v. Casey, 505 U.S. 833, 850 (1992).

. . . . In Casey, the Court . . . confirmed that our laws and tradition afford constitutional protection to personal decisions relating to marriage, procreation, contraception, family relationships, child rearing, and education. In explaining the respect the Constitution demands for the autonomy of the person in making these choices, we stated as follows:

> These matters, involving the most intimate and personal choices a person may make in a lifetime, choices central to personal dignity and autonomy, are central to the liberty protected by the Fourteenth Amendment.* At the heart of liberty is the right to define one's own concept of existence, of meaning, of the universe, and of the mystery of human life. Beliefs about these matters could not define the attributes of personhood were they formed under compulsion of the State.

Persons in a homosexual relationship may seek autonomy for these purposes, just as heterosexual persons do. . . .

As an alternative argument in this case, counsel for the petitioners . . . contend that . . . the Texas statute [is] invalid under the Equal Protection Clause. That is a tenable argument, but . . . [w]ere we to hold the statute invalid under the Equal Protection Clause some might question whether a prohibition would be valid if drawn differently, say, to prohibit the conduct both between same-sex and different-sex participants. . . .

The present case does not involve minors. It does not involve persons who might be injured or coerced or who are situated in relationships where consent might not easily be refused. It does not involve public conduct or prostitution. . . . The case does involve two adults who, with full and mutual consent from each other, engaged in sexual practices common to a homosexual lifestyle. The petitioners are entitled to respect for their private lives. The State cannot demean their existence or control their destiny by making their private sexual conduct a crime. Their right to liberty under the Due Process Clause gives them the full right to engage in their conduct without intervention of the government. "It is a promise of the Constitution that there is a realm of personal liberty which the government may not enter." Casey, supra, at 847. The Texas statute furthers no legitimate state interest which can justify its intrusion into the personal and private life of the individual.

Had those who drew and ratified the Due Process Clauses of the Fifth Amendment or the Fourteenth Amendment known the components of liberty in its manifold possibilities, they might have been more specific. They did not presume to have this insight. They knew times can blind us to certain truths and later generations can see that laws once thought necessary and proper in fact serve only to oppress. As the Constitution endures, persons in every generation can invoke its principles in their own search for greater freedom . . .

---

* ["No State shall make or enforce any law which shall abridge the privileges or immunities of citizens of the United States; nor shall any State deprive any person of life, liberty, or property, without due process of law; nor deny to any person within its jurisdiction the equal protection of the laws."—Eds.]

Justice O'Connor, concurring in the judgment.

.... I agree with the Court that Texas' statute banning same-sex sodomy is unconstitutional. See Tex. Criminal Code Ann. § 21.06 (2003). Rather than relying on the substantive component of the Fourteenth Amendment's Due Process Clause, as the Court does, I base my conclusion on the Fourteenth Amendment's Equal Protection Clause.

The Equal Protection Clause of the Fourteenth Amendment "is essentially a direction that all persons similarly situated should be treated alike." *Cleburne* v. *Cleburne Living Center, Inc.*, 473 U.S. 432, 439 (1985). Under our rational basis standard of review, "legislation is presumed to be valid and will be sustained if the classification drawn by the statute is rationally related to a legitimate state interest." *Cleburne* v. *Cleburne Living Center, supra,* at 440. . . .

The statute at issue here makes sodomy a crime only if a person "engages in deviate sexual intercourse with another individual of the same sex." Tex. Criminal Code Ann. § 21.06(a) (2003). Sodomy between opposite-sex partners, however, is not a crime in Texas. That is, Texas treats the same conduct differently based solely on the participants. Those harmed by this law are people who have a same-sex sexual orientation and thus are more likely to engage in behavior prohibited by § 21.06.

The Texas statute makes homosexuals unequal in the eyes of the law by making particular conduct—and only that conduct—subject to criminal sanction. It appears that prosecutions under Texas' sodomy law are rare. . . . [W]hile the penalty imposed on petitioners in this case was relatively minor, the consequences of conviction are not. [P]etitioners' convictions, if upheld, would disqualify them from or restrict their ability to engage in a variety of professions, including medicine, athletic training, and interior design. See, *e.g.,* Tex. Occ. Code Ann. § 164.051(a)(2)(B) (2003 Pamphlet) (physician); § 451.251 (a)(1) (athletic trainer); § 1053.252(2) (interior designer). Indeed, were petitioners to move to one of four States, their convictions would require them to register as sex offenders to local law enforcement. See, *e.g.,* Idaho Code § 18-8304 (Cum. Supp. 2002); La. Stat. Ann. § 15:542 (West Cum. Supp. 2003); Miss. Code Ann. § 45-33-25 (West 2003); S. C. Code Ann. § 23-3-430 (West Cum. Supp. 2002). . . .

Texas attempts to justify its law, and the effects of the law, by arguing that the statute satisfies rational basis review because it furthers the legitimate governmental interest of the promotion of morality. . . . Moral disapproval of a group cannot be a legitimate governmental interest under the Equal Protection Clause because legal classifications must not be "drawn for the purpose of disadvantaging the group burdened by the law." *Romer* v. *Evans*, 517 U.S. 620, 633 (1996). Texas' invocation of moral disapproval as a legitimate state interest proves nothing more than Texas' desire to criminalize homosexual sodomy. But the Equal Protection Clause prevents a State from creating "a classification of persons undertaken for its own sake." *Id.,* at 635. And because Texas so rarely enforces its sodomy law as applied to private, consensual acts, the law serves more as a statement of dislike and disapproval against homosexuals than as a tool to stop criminal behavior. The Texas sodomy law "raises the inevitable inference that the disadvantage imposed is born of animosity toward the class of persons affected." *Id.,* at 634. . . .

Commonwealth v. Bonadio
Supreme Court of Pennsylvania
490 Pa. 91, 415 A.2d 47 (1980)

This is an appeal from an Order of the Court of Common Pleas of Allegheny County granting appellees' Motion to Quash an Information on the ground that the Voluntary Deviate Sexual Intercourse Statute* is unconstitutional. Appellees were arrested at an "adult" pornographic theater on charges of voluntary deviate sexual intercourse and/or conspiracy to perform the same.

The Commonwealth's position is that the statute in question is a valid exercise of the police power pursuant the authority of states to regulate public health, safety, welfare, and morals. Yet, the police power is not unlimited, as was stated by the United States Supreme Court in *Lawton v. Steele*, 152 U.S. 133, 137, 14 S.Ct. 499, 501, 38 L.Ed. 385 (1894).

---

* The relevant portions of the statute are the following:

"A person who engages in deviate sexual intercourse under circumstances not covered by section 3123 of this title (related to involuntary deviate sexual intercourse) is guilty of a misdemeanor of the second degree." Act of December 6, 1972, P.L. 1482, No. 334 § 1, 18 Pa.C.S.A. § 3124 (1973).

" 'Deviate sexual intercourse.' Sexual intercourse *per os* or *per anus* between human beings who are not husband and wife, and any form of sexual intercourse with an animal." Act of December 6, 1972, P.L. 1482, No. 334, § 1, 18 Pa.C.S.A. § 3101 (1973).

To justify the State in thus interposing its authority in behalf of the public, it must appear, first, that the *interests of the public generally*, as distinguished from those of a particular class, require such interference; and, second, that the means are reasonably necessary for the accomplishment of the purpose, and *not unduly oppressive upon individuals.* (Emphasis added.)

The threshold question in determining whether the statute in question is a valid exercise of the police power is to decide whether it benefits the public generally. The state clearly has a proper role to perform in protecting the public from inadvertent offensive displays of sexual behavior, in preventing people from being forced against their will to submit to sexual contact, in protecting minors from being sexually used by adults, and in eliminating cruelty to animals. To assure these protections, a broad range of criminal statutes constitute valid police power exercises, including proscriptions of indecent exposure, open lewdness, rape, involuntary deviate sexual intercourse, indecent assault, statutory rape, corruption of minors, and cruelty to animals. The statute in question serves none of the foregoing purposes . . . The Voluntary Deviate Sexual Intercourse Statute has only one possible purpose: to regulate the private conduct of consenting adults. Such a purpose, we believe, exceeds the valid bounds of the police power while infringing the right to equal protection of the laws guaranteed by the Constitution of the United States and of this Commonwealth.

With respect to regulation of morals, the police power should properly be exercised to protect each individual's right to be free from interference in defining and pursuing his own morality but not to enforce a majority morality on persons whose conduct does not harm others.

No harm to the secular interests of the community is involved in atypical sex practice in private between consenting adult partners.

MODEL PENAL CODE § 207.5—Sodomy & Related Offenses. Comment
(Tent. Draft No. 4, 1955).

Many issues that are considered to be matters of morals are subject to debate, and no sufficient state interest justifies legislation of norms simply because a particular belief is followed by a number of people, or even a majority. Indeed, what is considered to be "moral" changes with the times and is dependent upon societal background. Spiritual leadership, not the government, has the responsibility for striving to improve the morality of individuals. Enactment of the Voluntary Deviate Sexual Intercourse Statute, despite the fact that it provides punishment for what many believe to be abhorrent crimes against nature and perceived sins against God, is not properly in the realm of the temporal police power.

The concepts underlying our view of the police power in the case before us were once summarized as follows by the great philosopher, John Stuart Mill, in his eminent and apposite work, ON LIBERTY (1859):

[T]he sole end for which mankind are warranted, individually or collectively, in interfering with the liberty of action of any of their number, is self-protection . . . [T]he only purpose for which power can be rightfully exercised over any member of a civilised community, against his will, is to prevent harm to others. His own good, either physical or moral is not a sufficient warrant. He cannot rightfully be compelled to do or forbear because it will be better for him to do so, because it will make him happier, because, in the opinions of others, to do so would be wise, or even right. These are good reasons for remonstrating with him, or reasoning with him, or persuading him, or entreating him, but not for compelling him, or visiting him with any evil in case he do otherwise. To justify that, the conduct from which it is desired to deter him must be calculated to produce evil to some one else. *The only part of the conduct of any one, for which he is amenable to society, is that which concerns others. In the part which merely concerns himself, his independence is, of right, absolute. Over himself, over his own body and mind, the individual is sovereign.*

It is, perhaps, hardly necessary to say that this doctrine is meant to apply to human beings in the maturity of their faculties . . .

But there is a sphere of action in which society as distinguished from the individual, has, if any, only an indirect interest; comprehending all that portion of a person's life and conduct which affects only himself, or if it also affects others, only with their free, voluntary, and undeceived consent and participation . . .

This, then, is the appropriate region of human liberty. It comprises, first, the inward domain of consciousness; demanding liberty of conscience, in the most comprehensive sense; liberty of thought and feeling; absolute freedom of opinion and sentiment on all subjects, practical or speculative, scientific, *moral, or theological* . . . Secondly, the principle requires liberty of tastes and pursuits; of framing the plan of our life to suit our own character; of doing as we like, subject to such consequences as may follow: without impediment from our fellow-creatures, *so long as what we do does not harm them, even though they should think our conduct foolish, perverse, or wrong.* Thirdly, from this liberty of each individual, follows the liberty, within the same limits of combination among individuals; freedom to unite, for any purpose not involving harm to others: the persons combining being supposed to be of full age, and not forced or deceived.

No society in which these liberties are not, on the whole, respected, is free, whatever may be its form of government; . . .

The only freedom which deserves the name, is that of pursuing our own good in our own way, so long as we do not attempt to deprive others of theirs, or impede their efforts to obtain it. Each is the proper guardian of his own health, whether bodily, or mental or spiritual. Mankind are greater gainers by suffering each other to live as seems good to themselves, than by compelling each to live as seems good to the rest. (Emphasis Supplied)

This philosophy, as applied to the issue of regulation of sexual morality presently before the Court, or employed to delimit the police power generally, properly circumscribes state power over the individual . . .

Order affirmed.

R. v. Malmo-Levine
Supreme Court of Canada
[2003] 3 S.C.R. 571

The judgment of McLachlin C.J. and Gonthier, Iacobucci, Major, Bastarache and Binnie JJ. was delivered by

Gonthier and Binnie JJ.:

In these appeals, the Court is required to consider whether Parliament has the legislative authority to criminalize simple possession of marihuana and, if so, whether that power has been exercised in a manner that is contrary to the *Canadian Charter of Rights and Freedoms*. The appellant Caine argues in particular that it is a violation of the principles of fundamental justice for Parliament to provide for a term of imprisonment as a sentence for conduct which he says results in little or no harm to other people. The appellant Malmo-Levine puts in issue the constitutional validity of the prohibition against possession for the purpose of trafficking in marihuana.

The British Columbia Court of Appeal rejected the appellants' challenges to the relevant provisions of the *Narcotic Control Act*, R.S.C. 1985, c. N-1 ("NCA"), and, in our view, it was right to do so. Upholding as we do the constitutional validity of the simple possession offense, it follows, for the same reasons, that Malmo-Levine's challenge to the prohibition against possession for the purpose of trafficking must also be rejected.

All sides agree that marihuana is a psychoactive drug which "causes alteration of mental function." That, indeed, is the purpose for which the appellants use it. Certain groups in society share a particular vulnerability to its effects. While members of these groups, whose identity cannot in general be distinguished from other users in advance, are relatively small as a percentage of all marihuana users, their numbers are significant in absolute terms. The trial judge estimated "chronic users" to number about 50,000. A recent Senate Special Committee report estimated users under 16 (which may overlap to some extent with the chronic user group) also at 50,000 individuals (*Cannabis: Our Position for a Canadian Public Policy* (2002) (the "Senate Committee Report"), vol. I, at pp. 165–66). Pregnant women and schizophrenics are also said to be at particular risk. Advancing the protection of these vulnerable individuals, in our opinion, is a policy choice that falls within the broad legislative scope conferred on Parliament.

A conviction for the possession of marihuana for personal use carries no mandatory minimum sentence. In practice, most first offenders are given a conditional discharge. Imprisonment is generally reserved for situations that also involve trafficking or hard drugs. . . . The appellants have assembled much evidence and argument attacking the wisdom of the criminalization of simple possession of marihuana. They say that the line between criminal and non-criminal conduct has been drawn inappropriately and that the evil effects of the law against marihuana outweigh the benefits, if any, associated with its prohibition. These are matters of legitimate controversy, but the outcome of that debate is not for the courts to determine. The Constitution provides no more than a framework. Challenges to the wisdom of a legislative measure within that framework should be addressed to Parliament. Our concern is solely with the issue of constitutionality. We conclude that it is within Parliament's legislative jurisdiction to criminalize the possession of marihuana should it choose to do so. Equally, it is open to Parliament to decriminalize or otherwise modify any aspect of the marihuana laws that it no longer considers to be good public policy.

. . .

Relevant Statutory and Constitutional Provisions

Canadian Charter of Rights and Freedoms

7. Everyone has the right to life, liberty and security of the person and the right not to be deprived thereof except in accordance with the principles of fundamental justice.

Constitution Act, 1867

91. It shall be lawful for the Queen, by and with the Advice and Consent of the Senate and House of Commons, to make Laws for the Peace, Order, and good Government of Canada, in relation to all Matters not coming within the Classes of Subjects by this Act assigned exclusively to the Legislatures of the Provinces; and for greater Certainty, but not so as to restrict the Generality of the foregoing Terms of this Section, it is hereby declared that (notwithstanding anything in this Act) the exclusive Legislative Authority of the Parliament of Canada extends to all Matters coming within the Classes of Subjects next herein-after enumerated; that is to say, . . .

(27) The Criminal Law, except the Constitution of Courts of Criminal Jurisdiction, but including the Procedure in Criminal Matters.

. . .

(d) The "Harm Principle"

The appellants contend that unless the state can establish that the use of marihuana is harmful *to others*, the prohibition against simple possession cannot comply with s. 7. Our colleague Arbour J. accepts this proposition as correct to the extent that "the state resorts to imprisonment". . . . Accordingly, a closer look at the alleged "harm principle" is called for. . . .

(i) History and Definition of the Harm Principle

What is the "harm principle"? The appellants rely, in particular, on the writings of the liberal theorist, J. S. Mill, who attempted to establish clear boundaries for the permissible intrusion of the state into private life . . .

Mill's principle has two essential features. First, it rejects paternalism—that is, the prohibition of conduct that harms only the actor. Second, it excludes what could be called "moral harm." Mill was of the view that such moral claims are insufficient to justify use of the criminal law. Rather, he required clear and tangible harm to the rights and interests of others.

At the same time, Mill acknowledged an exception to his requirement of harm "to others" for vulnerable groups. He wrote that "this doctrine is meant to apply to human beings in the maturity of their faculties. . . . Those who are still in a state to require being taken care of by others, must be protected against their own actions as well as against external injury."

Mill's statement has the virtues of insight and clarity but he was advocating certain general philosophic principles, not interpreting a constitutional document. Moreover, even his philosophical supporters have tended to agree that justification for state intervention cannot be reduced to a single factor—harm—but is a much more complex matter. One of Mill's most distinguished supporters, Professor H. L. A. Hart, wrote:

> Mill's formulation of the liberal point of view may well be too simple. The grounds for interfering with human liberty are more various than the single criterion of 'harm to others' suggests: cruelty to animals or organizing prostitution for gain do not, as Mill himself saw, fall easily under the description of harm to others. Conversely, even where there is harm to others in the most literal sense, there may well be other principles limiting the extent to which harmful activities should be repressed by law. So there are multiple criteria, not a single criterion, determining when human liberty may be restricted. [Emphasis added.]
>
> H. L. A. Hart, "Immorality and Treason," originally appearing in *The Listener* (July 30, 1959), at pp. 162–63, reprinted in *Morality and the Law* (1971), 49, at p. 51)

To the same effect, see Professor J. Feinberg, *The Moral Limits of the Criminal Law* (1984), vol. 1: *Harm to Others*, at p. 12; vol. 4: *Harmless Wrongdoing*, at p. 323.

(ii) Is the Harm Principle a Principle of Fundamental Justice?

The appellants submit that the harm principle is a principle of fundamental justice for the purposes of s. 7 that operates to place limits on the type of conduct the state may criminalize. This limitation exists independently of the division of powers under the *Constitution Act, 1867*. In other words, the appellants contend that there is a double threshold. Even if the Crown is able to establish that the creation of a particular criminal offense is a valid exercise of the criminal law power, there is a second level of constraint on the type of conduct that can be made criminal by virtue of s. 7 of the *Charter*.

We agree that there is a form of "double threshold," in that the *Charter* imposes requirements that are separate from those imposed by the *Constitution Act, 1867*. However, we do not agree with the attempted elevation of the harm principle to a principle of fundamental justice. That is, in our view the harm principle is not the constitutional standard for what conduct may or may not be the subject of the criminal law for the purposes of s. 7.

In *Re B.C. Motor Vehicle Act*, [1985] 2 S.C.R. 486, Lamer J. (as he then was) explained that the principles of fundamental justice lie in "the basic tenets of our legal system. They do not lie in the realm of general public policy but in the inherent domain of the judiciary as guardian of the justice system" (p. 503). This Court provided further guidance as to what constitutes a principle of fundamental justice for the purposes of s. 7, in *Rodriguez v. British Columbia (Attorney General)*, [1993] 3 S.C.R. 519, *per* Sopinka J. (at pp. 590–91 and 607):

> A mere common law rule does not suffice to constitute a principle of fundamental justice, rather, as the term implies, principles upon which there is *some consensus* that they are vital or fundamental to our societal notion of justice are required. Principles of fundamental justice must not, however, be so broad as to be no more than vague generalizations about what our society considers to be ethical or moral. They must be capable of being *identified with some precision* and *applied* to situations in a manner which yields an understandable result. They must also, in my view, be *legal principles*. . . .
>
> While the principles of fundamental justice are concerned with more than process, reference must be made to principles which are "fundamental" in the sense that they would have *general acceptance among reasonable people*. [Emphasis added.]

. . . In short, for a rule or principle to constitute a principle of fundamental justice for the purposes of s. 7, it must be a legal principle about which there is significant societal consensus that it is fundamental to the way in which the legal system ought fairly to operate, and it must be identified with sufficient precision to yield a manageable standard against which to measure deprivations of life, liberty or security of the person.

a. Is the Harm Principle a Legal Principle?

In our view, the "harm principle" is better characterized as a description of an important state interest rather than a normative "legal" principle. Be that as it may, even if the harm principle could be characterized as a legal principle, we do not think that it meets the other requirements, as explained below.

b. There Is No Sufficient Consensus that the Harm Principle Is Vital or Fundamental to Our Societal Notion of Criminal Justice

Contrary to the appellants' assertion, we do not think there is a consensus that the harm principle is the sole justification for criminal prohibition. There is no doubt that our case law and academic commentary are full of statements about the criminal law being aimed at conduct that "affects the public," or that constitutes "a wrong against the public welfare," or is "injurious to the public," or that "affects the community." No doubt, as stated, the *presence* of harm to others may justify legislative action under the criminal law power. However, we do not think that the *absence* of proven harm creates the unqualified barrier to legislative action that the appellants suggest. On the contrary, the state may sometimes be justified in criminalizing conduct that is either not harmful (in the sense contemplated by the harm principle), or that causes harm only to the accused . . .

Several instances of crimes that do not cause harm to others are found in the *Criminal Code*, R.S.C. 1985, c. C-46. Cannibalism is an offense (s. 182) that does not harm another sentient being, but that is nevertheless prohibited on the basis of fundamental social and ethical considerations. Bestiality (s. 160) and cruelty to animals (s. 446) are examples of crimes that rest on their offensiveness to deeply held social values rather than on Mill's "harm principle." . . .

c. Nor Is There Any Consensus that the Distinction Between Harm to Others and Harm to Self Is of Controlling Importance

Our colleague Arbour J. takes the view that when the state wishes to make imprisonment available as a sanction for criminal conduct, it must be able to show the potential of such conduct to cause harm to others (para. 244). With respect, we do not think there is any such principle anchored in our law. As this Court noted in *Rodriguez, supra*, attempted suicide was an offense under Canadian criminal law (found in the original *Code* at s. 238) until its repeal by S.C. 1972, c. 13, s. 16. Sopinka J. emphasized, at p. 597, that the decriminalization of attempted suicide cannot be said to represent a consensus by Parliament or by Canadians in general that the autonomy interest of those wishing to kill themselves is paramount to the state interest in protecting the life of its citizens.

The offense of attempted suicide was removed from the *Criminal Code* because Parliament came to prefer other ways of addressing the problem of suicide. In that case, as here, there was an important distinction between constitutional competence, which is for the courts to decide, and the wisdom of a particular measure, which, within its constitutional sphere, is up to Parliament.

We do not accept the proposition that there is a general prohibition against the criminalization of harm to self. Canada continues to have paternalistic laws. Requirements that people wear seatbelts and motorcycle helmets are designed to "save people from themselves." There is no consensus that this sort of legislation offends our societal notions of justice. Whether a jail sentence is an appropriate penalty for such an offense is another question . . .

In short, there is no consensus that tangible harm to others is a necessary precondition to the creation of a criminal law offense.

d. The Harm Principle Is Not a Manageable Standard Against Which to Measure Deprivation of Life, Liberty or Security of the Person

Even those who agree with the "harm principle" as a regulator of the criminal law frequently disagree about what it means and what offenses will meet or offend the harm principle. In the absence of any agreed definition of "harm" for this purpose, allegations and counter-allegations of non-trivial harm can be marshalled on every side of virtually every criminal law issue, as one author explains:

> The harm principle is effectively collapsing under the weight of its own success. Claims of harm have become so pervasive that the harm principle has become meaningless: the harm principle no longer serves the function of a *critical principle* because non-trivial harm arguments permeate the debate. Today, the issue is no longer *whether* a moral offense causes harm, but rather what type and what amount of harms the challenged conduct causes, and how the harms compare. On those issues, the harm principle is silent. [Emphasis in original.]

B. E. Harcourt, "The Collapse of the Harm Principle" (1999), 90 *J. Crim. L. & Criminology* 109, at p. 113 . . .

Harm, as interpreted in the jurisprudence, can take a multitude of forms, including economic, physical and social (e.g., injury and/or offense to fundamental societal values). In the present appeal, for example, the respondents put forward a list of "harms" which they attribute to marihuana use. The appellants put forward a list of "harms" which they attribute to marihuana prohibition. Neither side gives much credence to the "harms" listed by the other. Each claims the "net" result to be in its favour.

In the result, we do not believe that the content of the "harm" principle as described by Mill and advocated by the appellants provides a manageable standard under which to review criminal or other laws under s. 7 of the *Charter* . . .

German Federal Constitutional Court
BVerfGE 39, 1 (February 25, 1975)
Abortion Case

A.

The subject matter of the proceedings is the question of whether the so-called abortion limit according to which termination of pregnancy remains free from punishment in the first twelve weeks from conception under certain prerequisites is compatible with the Basic Law.

The Fifth Criminal Law Reform Act of June 18, 1974, (BGBl I, 1297) has regulated the criminality of termination of pregnancy in a new way. §§ 218 to 220 Criminal Code have been replaced by provisions which, as compared to the previous state of the law, contain the following amendments:

In principle, anyone who terminates a pregnancy later than on the thirteenth day after conception will be punished (§ 218 para. 1). However, a termination of pregnancy undertaken by a doctor with the consent of the pregnant woman is not punishable under § 218 if no more than twelve weeks have passed since conception (§ 218a—abortion limit). Further, a termination of pregnancy undertaken by a doctor with the consent of the pregnant woman after the expiry of the period of twelve weeks is not punishable under § 218 if it is indicated by findings of medical science either to avert a risk to the life of the pregnant woman or the risk of a serious impairment of her state of health in so far as this cannot be averted in some other reasonable manner (§ 218 b no. 1—medical indication), or because there are compelling grounds for assuming that the child, because of an hereditary disposition or harmful influences before the birth, would suffer from irremediable damage to its state of health which would be so serious that the pregnant woman cannot be expected to continue the pregnancy, provided that no more than 22 weeks have elapsed since conception (§ 218 b no. 2—eugenic indication) . . .

C.

The statutory regime can only be examined by the Federal Constitutional Court from the point of view of whether it is reconcilable with the Basic Law as the highest form of law applying in the Federal Republic. The importance and seriousness of the constitutional law question are clear when it is considered that this is a question of the protection of human life, a central value of every legal order.

I.

1. Art. 2 para. 2 sentence 1 Basic Law* also protects the life developing in the mother's womb as an independent legal good.

a) The express inclusion of the right to life, which is in itself taken for granted, in the Basic Law—in contrast to the position for example in the Weimar Constitution—is explained principally as a reaction to the "destruction of life which does not deserve to live," to the "final solution" and "liquidations" which were implemented by the national socialist regime as state measures. Art. 2 para. 2 sentence 1 Basic Law contains, as well as the abolition of the death penalty by art. 102 Basic Law, "a declaration of the basic value of human life and of an opinion of the state which positions itself in deliberate contrast to the views of a political regime to which individual life meant little and which therefore abused in an unbridled manner the right which it asserted over the life and death of the citizen" (BVerfGE 18, 112, 117).

b) In interpreting art. 2 para. 2 sentence 1 Basic Law it is necessary to proceed from its wording: "Everyone has the right to life. . . ." Life in the sense of the historical existence of a human individual exists, according to verified biological and physiological findings at any rate from the 14th day after conception (implantation, individuation) (see on this the statement of Hinrichsen before the Special Committee for Criminal Law Reform, 6th parliamentary term, 74th session, stenographer's report p. 2142 ff.). The development process thereby begun is a continuous event, which shows no sharp turning points and does not allow for a precise demarcation of the different stages of development of human life . . . The protection of art. 2 para. 2 sentence 1 Basic Law cannot therefore be limited to the "complete" human being after birth nor to the independently viable unborn child. . . . "Everyone" in the sense of art. 2 para. 2 sentence 1 Basic Law is "every living person," or, to express it otherwise, every human individual possessing life. "Every" therefore also includes the human being yet unborn.

2. The duty of the state to protect every human life can simply be derived directly from art. 2 para. 2 sentence 1 Basic Law. Over and above this it arises also from the provisions of art. 1 para. 1 sentence 2 Basic Law.† This is because the developing life also shares in the protection which art. 1 para. 1 Basic Law grants to human dignity. Where human life exists it is entitled to human dignity; it is not decisive whether the person entitled is aware of this dignity and knows how to preserve it. The potential faculties inherent in human existence from the very beginning suffice to found human dignity.

II.

1. The protective duty by the state is comprehensive. It does not—self-evidently—only prohibit direct invasions by the state into the developing life, but also requires the state to put itself in a position to protect and support this life; this means above all to protect it from illegal invasions by others as well . . . The higher the rank the legal good in question should have within the order of values under the Basic Law, the more seriously must the state's duty of protection be taken. Human life represents—and it is not necessary to give more detailed reasoning for this—a value of the highest rank within the Basic Law order; it is the vital basis for human dignity and the prerequisite for all other basic rights . . .

---

* [Basic Law, art. 2 para. 2 sentence 1: "Every person shall have the right to life and physical integrity."—Eds.]
† [Basic Law, art. 1 para. 1: "Human dignity shall be inviolable. To respect and protect it shall be the duty of all state authority."—Eds.]

III.

How the state fulfills its duty to protect the developing life effectively is primarily to be decided by the legislature. It decides on what protective measures it regards as appropriate and necessary to guarantee an effective protection of life.

...

The question of how far the state is obliged by the Constitution to deploy the tool of criminal law, as the sharpest weapon available to it, to protect the unborn life cannot be answered by simply asking whether the state must punish certain actions. An overall view is necessary which on the one hand has regard to the value of the legal good infringed and the extent of social harm arising from the infringing action – in comparison also with other actions subjected to punishment and to be assessed similarly from a socio-ethical point of view – and on the other hand considers the traditional legal regimes for this area of life as well as the development of ideas about the role of criminal law in modern society, and finally does not leave out of account the practical effectiveness of threats of punishment and the possibility of their replacement by other legal sanctions.

...

a) The task of criminal law has always been to protect the fundamental values of communal life. It has been explained above that the life of each individual human being belongs to the most important of legal goods. The termination of a pregnancy irrevocably destroys a human life which has come into existence ... No legal regime can ignore the fact that by this action the fundamental inviolability and inalienability of human life guaranteed in art. 2 para. 2 sentence 1 Basic Law is violated. Seen from this angle, the use of criminal law to punish abortions is undoubtedly legitimate; it is current law in most civilized states—under differently formulated prerequisites—and also corresponds in particular to the German legal tradition. It likewise follows from this that it is not possible to dispense with a clear legal characterization of this occurrence as "wrong."

b) However, punishment can never be an end in itself. Its use is subject in principle to the legislature's decision. The legislature is not prevented, if it observes the viewpoints given above, from also expressing legal disapproval of termination of pregnancy required by the Basic Law in another way than by the method of threatening punishment. The decisive question is whether the totality of measures serving the protection of the unborn life, whether they are of a civil law, public law, or in particular social law or criminal law nature, guarantee a factual protection corresponding to the importance of the legal good to be protected. In the worst case, that is when the protection required by the Constitution cannot be attained in any other way, the legislature can be obliged to employ the method of criminal law to protect the developing life. The criminal law represents so to speak the "last resort" in the legislature's apparatus. According to the constitutional state principle of proportionality, which controls the whole of public law, including constitutional law, it may only make use of this method cautiously and sparingly. Yet this final method also must be employed if an effective protection of life is not otherwise to be attained ...

The objection that a state duty to punish could never be derived from a basic right norm guaranteeing freedom cannot succeed. If the state is obliged to protect an especially important legal good against attacks by third parties as well, measures will often be unavoidable through which the areas of freedom of other holders of basic rights are affected. In this respect the legal situation on the deployment of social law or civil law methods is not in principle different to the enactment of a criminal norm. Differences exist at the most in relation to the strength of the necessary intervention. The legislature must resolve the conflict arising here by a balancing of the two basic values or areas of freedom set against each other in accordance with the order of values in the Basic Law and having regard to the constitutional state principle of proportionality. If the duty to employ the means of criminal law as well were to be in general denied, the protection of life which is to be guaranteed would be substantially limited ...

D.

[T]he time periods regime which is under challenge [has] not done justice to the duty under art. 2 para. 2 sentence 1 in combination with art. 1 para. 2 Basic Law effectively to protect the developing life to the required extent ...

The legal disapproval of the termination of pregnancy which is required by the Constitution must also become clearly evident in the legal order beneath the Constitution.... The negative value judgment is not expressed in the provisions about termination of pregnancy in the first twelve weeks. This is because the Statute leaves it unclear as to whether, when the termination of pregnancy is not indicated, it is still right or wrong after the repeal of the threat of punishment under § 218 a StGB.

...

Dissenting opinion of Judge Wiltraut Rupp-v. Brünneck and Judge Dr. Helmut Simon*

The life of every individual human being is self-evidently a central value of the legal order. The constitutional law duty to protect this life indisputably covers even its preliminary stage before birth. The debate in Parliament and before the Federal Constitutional Court did not concern the *whether* but only the *how* of this protection. The decision about this is the responsibility of the legislature. Under no circumstances can a state duty be derived from the Constitution to make termination of pregnancy punishable at every stage of the pregnancy ...

Our strongest reservation is directed against the fact that for the first time in the Constitutional Court case law an objective value decision is to be used as a *duty* for the legislature *to enact criminal norms* and thus to demand the strongest conceivable intrusion into the area of the citizen's freedom. This distorts the function of the basic rights into their opposite. If the objective value decision contained in a basic right norm for the protection of a particular legal good is to suffice for the derivation of a duty to punish, the basic rights could turn covertly from being a bulwark for safeguarding freedom to being the basis for a wealth of regulations limiting freedom ... The Constitution naturally assumes that the state can deploy its power to punish for the protection of orderly communal life. The purpose of the basic rights is not however to demand such deployment, but to create boundaries to it. Thus the Supreme Court of the United States has regarded punishment for terminations of pregnancies which are undertaken by a doctor in the first trimester of the pregnancy with the consent of the pregnant woman as even being a violation of a basic right [*Roe v. Wade*, 411 U.S. 113 (1973)]. This, according to German constitutional law, would admittedly go too far. However, under the liberal character of our Constitution the legislature needs constitutional law justification for punishing, but not for refraining from punishment ...

The opposing view leads inevitably to a questionable extension of constitutional court control: it no longer has merely to be examined whether a criminal provision intrudes too far into the citizen's legal sphere, but also conversely whether the state is punishing *too little*. The Federal Constitutional Court, contrary to the view of the majority, will not be able to stop here at the question of whether the enactment of any criminal norm, no matter what the content, is required, but must resolve which criminal sanction suffices for the protection of the legal good in question. Ultimately the court could even be compelled to examine whether the application of a criminal norm satisfies the protective concept in the individual case.

Establishing criminal norms in constitutional law—as the majority requires—is finally also to be rejected because the central themes of criminal law according to the experiences of the last decades and the development to be expected in the realm of social sciences are subject to rapid and deep changes. This is not only demonstrated by looking at the fundamental changes for example in the assessment of moral crimes—e.g., homosexuality, procuration of spouses, exhibitionism—but can also be especially substantiated for the criminal provisions against abortion ...

German Federal Constitutional Court
BVerfGE 120, 224 (February 26, 2008)
Incest Case

Facts

The complainant by his constitutional complaint challenges his conviction for sexual intercourse between siblings, and seeks a finding of invalidity in respect of § 173 para. 2 sentence 2 Criminal Code, on which the conviction was based. The local court sentenced the complainant for a misdemeanor under § 173 para. 2 sentence 2 Criminal Code to a term of imprisonment of a year and two months ...

As to the personal circumstances of the complainant who was born in 1976 and his natural sister who was born in 1984, the co-defendant K., the local court made, amongst others, the following findings: The parents of both defendants were divorced shortly before K's birth. In the ensuing period the mother had exercised the right to care for K. and a younger brother alone, without any contact with the father. The upbringing had been extremely strained. The family had been looked after by social services. Since the age of five, K. had been in youth care institutions. After the death of the mother in 2000, K. had been under the guardianship of the youth office and with her younger brother had lived with the younger brother's natural father. The complainant had lived in children' homes and

---

* [Dissenting opinions were first permitted in the Constitutional Court in 1970. To this day, they are permitted in no other German court. See, e.g., Peter E. Quint, "Leading a Constitutional Court: Perspectives from the Federal Republic of Germany," 154 *University of Pennsylvania Law Review* (2006), 1853.—Eds.]

with several foster families from the age of three, after his alcoholic father had repeatedly abused him. At the age of seven the complainant had been adopted by his foster parents at that time, and had taken their name. Since then he had had no contact with his original family. In 2000 he had recommenced contact via the youth office with his natural mother, and had come to know K., whose existence had been unknown to him until then. He had remained with K. after the mother's death. A close relationship developed between the complainant and K. In 2001, 2003, 2004 and 2005 K. had given birth to four children whose natural father was the complainant. K. had an anxious, withdrawn and dependent personality which in combination with the existing unsatisfactory family situation had led to significant dependence on the complainant. The local court saw this as severe personality disturbance which in combination with a slight mental handicap had led to diminished responsibility on K.'s part.

The complainant had already been sentenced in 2002 and 2004 for sexual intercourse between relations . . . to a term of imprisonment of one year, the execution of which had been suspended on probation, and to a term of 10 months. Incorporating the last prison sentence of 10 months, he had further been sentenced for intentional infliction of bodily harm to an overall prison term of 11 months (the complainant had struck his sister K. in the face with his fist, which had caused her to suffer a swollen lip and nosebleed).

. . . The complainant contests the judgment of the local court and the decision of the court of appeal. He indirectly contests the constitutionality of § 173 para. 2 sentence 2 Criminal Code.

The constitutional complaint was rejected.

Reasons

B.

The constitutional complaint is admissible but not well founded.

I.

The criminal provision in § 173 para. 2 sentence 2 Criminal Code, which penalizes sexual intercourse between siblings, is compatible with the Basic Law.

1. The decision of the legislature to criminalize incest between siblings is not open to objection in constitutional law according to the primary standard to be applied under art. 2 para. 1 in combination with art. 1 para. 1 Basic Law.

a)

   aa) The Basic Law has placed the intimate and sexual sphere of human beings, as a part of their private sphere, under the constitutional law protection of art. 2 para. 1 in combination with art. 1 para. 1 Basic Law. This means that individuals have the right to decide about their sexuality and their sexual relations with a partner; and they are in principle left free to decide for themselves on whether, within what boundaries and with what objectives to accept the influences of third persons (see BVerfGE 47, 46 [73f.]; BVerfGE 60, 123 [134]; BVerfGE 88, 87 [97]; BVerfGE 96, 56 [61]).

   The general personality right, in its manifestation as a right to sexual self-determination, is admittedly not guaranteed without reservation. The individual must, so long as there is no invasion of the inviolable sphere of his private life, accept state measures which are taken in the overwhelming interest of the general public, or with regard to interests of third parties protected by basic rights, provided that the requirement of proportionality is strictly observed (see BVerfGE 27, 344 [351]; BVerfGE 65, 1 [44]; BVerfGE 96, 56 [61]). A core area of private life is absolutely protected and therefore excluded from the effect of public authority (see BVerfGE 80, 367 [373]; BVerfGE 90, 145 [171]; BVerfGE 109, 279 [313]). Whether facts belong to the inviolable core area depends on whether their content is such that they are of a highly personal nature, and also on the way in which and the intensity with which they affect the sphere of others or the interests of community; the special features of each case are decisive (see BVerfGE 34, 238 [248]; BVerfGE 80, 367 [374]; BVerfGE 109, 279 [314f.]).

   bb) Limitations of the general personality right need, according to art. 2 para. 1 in combination with art. 1 para. 1 Basic Law, a statutory basis which conforms to the Constitution, and from which the prerequisites and the scope of the limitations appear clearly and in a way which is recognizable for the individual (see BVerfGE 65, 1 [44]. The legislature is under a duty to preserve the principle of proportionality.

   The principle of proportionality requires . . . that a criminal norm serves the protection of others or the general public (see BVerfGE 90, 145 [172, 184] . . .). Criminal law is used as the "ultima ratio" to protect legal goods if . . . certain behavior is particularly socially harmful and intolerable for ordered communal life of human beings, and its prevention is therefore especially urgent. To avoid excess is especially important for the examination of criminal norms because of the negative socio-ethical value judgment expressed by the threat, imposition and implementation of punishment (see BVerfGE 90, 145 [172]; BVerfGE 92, 277 [326]; BVerfGE 96, 10 [25]). But it is in principle a matter for the legislature to determine the scope of the criminal law. The legislature is in principle free to decide whether a certain legal good, the protection of which is deemed fundamental, should be protected by means of criminal law and, if appropriate, how to do this (see BVerfGE 50, 142 [162]...).

A criminal norm must be appropriate and necessary in order to attain the goal sought for.

A means is appropriate if the desired result can be promoted with its assistance...A statute is necessary if the legislature could not have chosen another equally effective means which would not limit the basic right or would limit it less severely. In assessing the appropriateness and necessity of the chosen means to attain the objectives sought for, as well as the evaluation and prognosis of the dangers threatening the individual or the general public, the legislature has a margin of appreciation. The Federal Constitutional Court can only examine this to a limited extent....

Finally in the overall balancing of the severity of the invasion with the weight as well as the urgency of the reasons which justify it, it is necessary to maintain a limit based on what can reasonably be expected of the addressee of the prohibition (proportionality in the narrow sense). The measure ought not to burden the addressee excessively. In the realm of state punishment, it follows from the culpability principle and the principle of proportionality that the seriousness of a crime and the culpability of the perpetrator must be in a just relationship to the punishment. The threat of punishment ought not to be unreasonable according to the nature and extent of the conduct which is penalized...

It is in principle a matter for the legislature to establish the area of criminal activity.... The Federal Constitutional Court merely has to assess that criminal provisions are in harmony with the provisions of the Constitution and correspond with the unwritten constitutional principles as well as the basic decisions of the Basic Law...

cc) Criminal norms are not, for constitutional reasons, subject to stricter requirements concerning the goals pursued by them. In particular, no such requirements can be derived from the doctrine about "legal good" in criminal law.

There is no unanimity even about the concept of the legal good (see the contributions in Hefendehl/v. Hirsch/Wohlers [eds.], Die Rechtsgutstheorie (The Legal Good Theory), 2003...). If legal good was what the legislature regards as worth of protection, expressed in current law, the concept is reduced to explaining the ratio legis of the particular criminal norm, and it cannot then take on a guiding role for the legislature (see Weigend, in: LK-StGB, Vol. 1, 12th edit. [2007], Intro. marginal no. 7). If on the other hand on the basis of a "naturalistic" legal good theory only certain "conditions of social life" are recognized as legitimate legal goods, or in some other way a concept of legal goods beyond positive law is assumed, this comes into conflict with the idea that under the Basic Law the democratically legitimated legislature has to establish the interests to be protected by means of criminal law (in the same way as the purposes of punishment) (see BVerfGE 45, 187 [253]) and to adjust criminal norms to social developments. The legislature cannot be restricted by appealing to supposedly pre-existing legal goods or to those "recognized" by courts beyond the legislature. Legislative authority finds its limit—in the area of criminal law as elsewhere—only in the Constitution itself if and in so far as this excludes the pursuit of a certain purpose from the outset. No judgment is necessary here as to the contribution which the concept of legal goods may be able to make for legal policy and criminal law doctrine (see on the historical genesis of the legal good theory Amelung, Rechtsgüterschutz und Schutz der Gesellschaft (Legal good protection and protection of society), 1972, pp. 15ff.). In any case it provides no standards within constitutional law which sets the legislature ultimate limits to its power of regulation (see Lagodny, Strafrecht vor den Schranken der Grundrechte (Criminal law in the light of the limits of the basic rights), 1996, pp. 143ff., 536; Appel, Verfassung und Strafe (Constitution and punishment), 1998, p. 390...Hörnle, Grob anstößiges Verhalten (Grossly offensive behavior), 2005, p. 11ff.; for a different view Roxin, StrafR AT, 4th edit. [2006], § 2 marginal nos. 27, 86ff.

b) The legislature limits physical siblings' right to sexual self-determination by the criminal law norm of § 173 para. 2 sentence 2 Criminal Code which threatens a fine or sentence of imprisonment of up to two years for sexual intercourse. It is true that boundaries are thereby set to private formulation of life, in particular by the fact that certain forms of expression of sexuality between persons close to one another (see BVerfGE 109, 279 [314, 321f.]) are penalized. This is however no intrusion into that core area of private life which is denied to the legislature. Sexual intercourse between siblings does not affect them exclusively; it can also have effects on the family and society, and besides it has consequences for the children produced by the liaison. As the criminal law prohibition of incest only has as its object narrowly circumscribed conduct, and the possibilities of intimate communication are reduced only in a particular respect, the persons affected are not placed in a hopeless situation which would be irreconcilable with respect for human dignity.

c) The legislature pursues purposes by the norm under challenge which are not open to objection in constitutional law, and in any case in their totality legitimate the limitation of the general personality right. The legislature has not exceeded its margin of appreciation by regarding the preservation of the family order from the damaging effects of incest, the protection of the "inferior" partner in an incestuous relationship and in addition the avoidance of serious genetically-based diseases in the offspring of incestuous relationships as sufficient to impose criminal law sanctions parallel to the incest taboo which is anchored in society.

aa) The protection of marriage and the family required by art. 6 Basic Law takes first place in the considerations of the legislature (see BT-Dr VI/1552, p. 14; BT-Dr VI/3521, p. 17) and the case law (see RGSt 57, 140; BGHSt 3, 342 [343f.]; BGHSt 39, 326 [329]). Even in the more recent literature the purpose of § 173 Criminal Code is primarily seen to be an objective protection of marriage and the family, although this legitimization is at the same time partly regarded as insufficient (see Dippel, in: LK-Criminal Code, 11th edit., § 173 marginal no. 10 with further references; Schönke/Schröder/Lenckner, Criminal Code, 27th edit. [2006], § 173 marginal no. 1; . . . .) . . .

The negative effects of sibling incest on families and society may be difficult to isolate by social science methods from the effects of other influences, and may therefore not be easily identified (on the absence of empirical foundations, see Dippel, in: LK-Criminal Code, § 173 marginal nos. 7, 13, 15; Hörnle, p. 454). This does not however affect the plausibility of assumption of this kind which are also presented in the opinion of the Max Planck Institute commissioned by the Senate. According to this, the following negative consequences may arise: diminished self-confidence, functional sexual disturbances in adulthood, retarded individuation, deficiency in discovering psycho-sexual identity and the capacity to form relationships, difficulties in forming and maintaining an intimate relationship, failure in the work environment, general dissatisfaction with life, strong feelings of guilt, distressing recollections of the incest experience, depression, drug and alcohol misuse, self-harm, eating disorders, suicidal thoughts, sexual promiscuity and post-traumatic experiences as well as indirect harm for other members of the family, for instance through exclusion or social isolation. The empirical studies which were evaluated as a basis for these findings had, as the opinion of the Max Planck Institute concedes, shortcomings. But they show that the legislature is not moving outside its margin of appreciation, when it assumes that harmful effects can arise from incestuous liaisons between siblings . . .

bb) In so far as the protection of sexual self-determination is invoked to justify the criminal norm (see Frommel, in: NK-Criminal Code, § 173 marginal nos. 1, 6), this normative purpose is relevant not only in the relationship between children and adults, but also in the relationship between siblings.

In the literature of medical anthropology, cases of sibling incest are reported in which the brother was "successor" to the father. So-called "despot incest" accompanied by violence also occurs in the relationship between siblings. . . . In the legal literature, in cases in which, as here, there is a significant difference in age between the siblings, a certain plausibility of harmful effects is assumed (see Hörnle, p. 453). The facts in the present case point in the same direction.

The objection that sexual self-determination is comprehensively and sufficiently protected by other norms (§§ 174ff.) in the Criminal Code and therefore does not justify § 173 para. 2 sentence 2, especially having regard to its limited area of application (see Tröndle, in: Tröndle/Fischer, Criminal Code, 54th edit. [2007], § 173 marginal no. 2; Al-Zand/Siebenhüner, KritV 2006, 68 [74] . . .), ignores the fact that § 173 Criminal Code has in view specific dependencies associated with closeness in the family. . . . The case law shows that sexual intercourse between relations often occurs in combination with sexual abuse such as penalized in §§ 174ff. Criminal Code. But sexual intercourse between relations anyway acquires even in these cases an independent significance if the abuse of a child extends beyond the age of 18—for example in a situation in which, after the a victim of longstanding abuse or rape attains majority, further sexual acts occur, and the victim, because of a dependence which has its roots in the existing family relationship does not refuse the still undesired sexual intercourse sufficiently clearly. . . . The thesis which suggests . . . that young victims of sexual abuse do not always succeed in breaking out of the family structures which facilitated the abuse before attaining majority, can also apply in cases of sibling incest, especially where there is a distinct difference in age between the siblings or in cases in which the older sibling adopts the role of a parent.

cc) The legislature additionally relied on eugenic arguments, and assumed that the risk of inherited defects could not be excluded for children produced from an incestuous relationship because of the increased possibility of combinations of recessive hereditary dispositions (see BT-Dr VI/1552, p. 14; BT-Dr VI/3521, pp. 17f.). The objections made against this in the criminal law literature because of the lack of empirical proof (see Roxin, p. 27; Dippel, in: LK-Criminal Code, § 173 marginal no. 12; Ritscher, in: MünchKomm-Criminal Code, 2005, § 173 marginal no. 3; . . . art.) are not convincing. In the medical and anthropological literature reference is made to the special risk of inherited defects (see Szibor, Rechtsmedizin, 2004, p. 387ff. with further references; Staudacher, pp. 152f.) and it is partly accepted that these are more serious in liaisons between brother and sister than in those between father and daughter (see Staudacher, p. 153). These findings are supported by empirical studies which are reported in the opinion of the Max Planck Institute commissioned by the Senate. Against this background the prohibition of incest cannot be regarded as irrational from the viewpoint of avoiding hereditary defects (see Schubarth, in: Festschr. f. Grünwald, 1999, p. 641, with reference to the investigations of Eibl-Eibesfeld, Wickler and Bischof). The supplementary reference to this argument is not excluded just because it has been historically misused to deprive people with hereditary diseases and handicaps of their rights.

dd) In the legislative proceedings it was emphasized on several occasions that a break with the tradition of a prohibition on incest was not desired. Reference was also made, in relation to the social taboo on incest, to the risk of children of an incestuous relationship being exposed to discrimination because of their descent (see BT-Dr VI/1552, p. 14; VI/3521, pp. 17f.). The purposes already explained are therefore supported by the conviction of the legislative bodies that a consciousness of wrong anchored in society ought to be taken up and further supported by means of criminal law . . . It can be left undecided whether the distinction between criminal norms which are only based on moral concepts, and those which serve the protection of legal goods is workable (see for § 173 Criminal Code Dippel, in: LK-Criminal Code, § 173 marginal no. 14; Tröndle/Fischer, § 173 marginal no. 1 . . .), and whether, if this is the case, criminal norms of the first kind would be open to objection in constitutional law. Such a case is not present here. Instead the criminal norm under challenge is justified by the bringing together of comprehensible goals against the background of a social conviction based on cultural history and still effective, that incest deserves to be punished, as can also be established by international comparison. The criminal norm, as an instrument for the protection of sexual self-determination, the health of the population, and in particular the family, fulfills an appellative function of strengthening norms which has a general preventive character. It manifests the setting of values by the legislature and therefore contributes to their maintenance.

d) The norm under challenge satisfies the constitutional law requirements of appropriateness, necessity and proportionality. . . .

aa) . . . The objection that § 173 para. 2 sentence 2 Criminal Code fails to achieve its intended purposes due to its incomplete formulation (see Dippel, in: LK-Criminal Code, § 173 marginal no. 24; Hörnle, pp. 454f. . . . .) does not recognize that by prohibiting sexual intercourse a central aspect of sexual liaison between siblings is made punishable. . . . The fact that the legislature has selected the core area of the punishable conduct and has not also penalized other sexual activities is therefore acceptable in constitutional law . . .

Not extending the crime definition to include sexual intercourse between step, adoptive or foster siblings can for one thing be based on such acts contradicting the traditional image of the family to a lesser extent . . . For another thing there are in this respect no comparable genetic reservations, and it is not unlikely that dependency could exist to a greater extent between physical siblings than between step, adoptive or foster siblings . . .

bb) The norm under attack is not subject to any reservations in constitutional law with regard to its necessity either. Guardianship court measures and youth social welfare measures need to be considered in cases of sibling incest (see Deutscher Bundestag, Protokolle der Beratungen des Sonderausschusses für die Strafrechtsreform (German Parliament, Minutes of the deliberations of the Special Committee for Criminal Law Reform), vol 1, 28th session, pp. 919, 922). But in comparison to the protection of the criminal law they do not represent a more lenient means which has equal effectiveness. Criminal law cannot be denied—either generally or in connection with the present issue—to have an independent effect which goes beyond public welfare measures. . . .

cc) Finally, the threat of punishment is not disproportionate. It only affects a narrow area of personal lifestyle. Probably, due to a inhibition about incest, only few pairs of siblings are affected by the prohibition. The threatened punishment—imprisonment of up to two years or a fine—is moderate and a minimum penalty is not provided for . . .

The law permits courts to take account of special types of cases in which the limited degree of the accused's culpability makes punishment appear unreasonable. They may terminate proceedings, refrain from punishment or apply special considerations in sentencing decisions.... Against this background, which was taken into consideration in the legislative proceedings, the criminal law prohibition on sexual intercourse between siblings does not violate the constitutional prohibition against excessive state reactions....

...

Dissenting opinion of Judge Hassemer

I cannot support the decision that § 173 para. 2 sentence 2 Criminal Code satisfies the prerequisites which the Basic Law places on the definition of a crime. The norm is not in harmony with the principle of proportionality which creates boundaries for the legislature in criminal matters; to let such a disastrous criminal norm pass constitutional scrutiny endorses serious defects and omissions by the legislature and overextends the legislative margin of appreciation in criminal law at the cost of the Federal Constitutional Court's competence to exercise control.

The norm does not pursue any regulatory goal which would in itself be free from contradiction and reconcilable with the offense definition (I). § 173 para. 2 sentence 2 Criminal Code is not suited for the goals which are read into the definition today (II). There are more lenient instruments than the threat of punishment which are also more appropriate (III) and the provision prescribes excessively burdensome legal consequences (IV).

I.

1. Criminal law interventions weigh especially heavily. They wield the sharpest weapon which is available to the legislature (see BVerfGE 39, 1 [45]) ... The case law of the Federal Constitutional Court has always taken account of this, in harmony with criminal law doctrine:

a) The legislature is not free in its choice of the causes and objectives of its action; it is limited to the protection of the fundamental values of communal life (see BVerfGE 27, 18 [29]; BVerfGE 39, 1 [46]; BVerfGE 45, 187 [253]), to the safeguarding of the foundations of an ordered society (see BVerfGE 88, 203 [257]) and the preservation of important communal interests (BVerfGE 90, 145 [184]). A criminal norm must accordingly not only pursue a legitimate objective ... It must additionally relate to an important interest, a fundamental value, a foundation of our communal life.

b) The limits of constitutional law for criminal legislation also affect the choice and deployment of criminal law instruments. Criminal law is ultimo ratio, the last available means of protecting an interest of the general public, and therefore only falls to be considered when the behavior to be criminalized is socially harmful in a special way and intolerable for human communal life, and its prevention is especially urgent (see BVerfGE 88, 203 [257f.]).

c) The legislature has to determine in each case the causes, objectives and instruments of criminal law requirements and prohibitions. This limits the controlling competence of the Federal Constitutional Court. The Court does not examine whether the legislature has found the solution which is most appropriate to its purpose, wisest or most just; it does however watch over whether the legislature's decision is substantively in harmony with the order of values in constitutional law and corresponds with the unwritten principles and the fundamental decisions of the Basic Law (see BVerfGE 27, 18 [30]; BVerfGE 37, 201 [212]).

d) An indispensable component of the legislative decision is in any case clarity about the objectives which it is pursuing by regulation. The legislature is not permitted to leave it to legal practice or jurisprudence subsequently to read a purpose into its criminal norm. This is based amongst other things on the fact that the examination of the proportionality of a norm cannot succeed without clarity about its objective.... What is appropriate, necessary and reasonable is indissolubly related to what should be attained and by which means....

So, for example, the legislature's decision to limit the criminality of sibling incest to sexual intercourse and to leave other sexual activities unpunished is possibly appropriate to meet the danger of reproduction, but not appropriate to safeguard sexual self-determination and certainly inappropriate for the protection of marriage and the family. That has been developed over a long period in the legal goods doctrine, which the Senate holds at arm's length. The subsequent attribution of a purpose to a norm, a purpose which the legislature was not pursuing, changes the coordinates, contours and contents of proportionality.

2. It is not consistent with these basic requirements of limitation and clarity when the majority of the Senate sees § 173 para. 2 sentence 2 Criminal Code as justified by the "bringing together of comprehensible goals against the background of a social conviction based on cultural history, and still effective that incest deserves to be punished, as can also be established by international

comparison." Neither a nebulous effective social conviction based on cultural history (if it really relates to incest deserving to be punished and not merely social disapproval) nor international comparisons (incidentally, incomplete and in many ways divergent) can justify a criminal norm in constitutional law. The legal goods cited as such by the Senate either pursue no legitimate goal in the protection of our society (a), or are not found in the actual form of § 173 para. 2 sentence 2 Criminal Code which in any case in this formulation does not pursue the purposes read into it by the Senate (b)....

a) Eugenic aspects are from the outset not a legitimate purpose for a criminal norm in constitutional law. The protection of the population's health, which has "special importance" according to the intention of the legislature (BT-Dr VI/3521, p. 18), because eugenic considerations which make it comprehensible why the law limits criminal liability to vaginal intercourse (BT-Dr VI/1552, p. 14), cannot be the protected interest.

It is not necessary to consider whether there is in fact a special danger of hereditary defects with children produced from incestuous liaisons. For constitutional reasons alone it is in any case forbidden to make the protection of health of potential offspring the basis for criminal law interventions. No holder of a legal good whose presumed interests could be invoked exists at the point in time of the act besides the pair of siblings affected. The notion of criminal law protection of potential offspring from genetic defects furthermore assumes the absurd balancing of a presumed interest in a life with genetic defects on the one hand with a presumed interest in its own non-existence on the other. Therefore for good reasons we do not criminalize sexual intercourse even in other cases where the probability of handicapped offspring is higher and the expected handicaps are more substantial than in the case of incest....

Consideration of eugenic aspects can also not be justified by the possible argument of disadvantage to third parties, for instance the family into which a handicapped child is born, or the general public who are required to bear the welfare expenses. This would be to deny the right to life of handicapped children merely on the grounds of interests contrary to life and financial concerns of others.

Nor would it be convincing to point to the health of the population as an—abstract—protected object. In contrast to, for instance, the criminal law about drugs, because of the recognized rarity of possible hereditary defects resulting from sibling incest, no impairment worthy of mention can be predicted, either for the health of the population or that of individual distinguishable population groups ...

b) § 173 para. 2 sentence 2 Criminal Code is also not a means for protection of sexual self-determination. The legislature has not yet referred to this on any occasion (cf. BT-Dr VI/3521, p. 17f.) and the majority of the Senate had to read this purpose into the statutory regime subsequently. Neither the wording nor the statutory system give any indications that the, or one, purpose of the provision could lie in the protection of the right to sexual self-determination. In fact they tend to disprove this assumption.

The wording of § 173 para. 2 sentence 2 Criminal Code demands, in contrast to provisions for the protection of children and young people (§§ 174, 176 and 182 Criminal Code) only sexual intercourse between siblings. Other particulars of the contact play no role: neither the age of the younger sibling who is worthy of protection nor for instance dependency of the victim (see § 174 para. 1 no. 2 Criminal Code), nor a predicament (§ 182 para. 1 Criminal Code), nor the absence of capacity for sexual self-determination (see § 182 para. 2 Criminal Code). § 173 para. 2 sentence 2 Criminal Code contains no sort of indication that it is intended to cover precisely those circumstances which demonstrate an impairment of sexual self-determination....

The limitation of criminality to adult siblings makes it completely clear that the criminal law protection of sexual self-determination cannot be a purpose which shapes the norm.... It is only in well-founded and clearly formulated exceptional cases where a person is not capable of self-determined action—on the application of compulsion or where there is an absence of capacity to resist—that the Criminal Code guarantees the protection of sexual self-determination for victims who are not minors.

The Senate majority are leaving out of consideration this unambiguous and plausible basic decision of the legislature on the boundaries of criminal liability... It cannot be deduced from the assumption that sexual autonomy is possibly not yet fully developed in the transition to majority that the criminal norm was intended to include such cases ...

c) Neither can the prohibition of sibling incest find its possible legal good and justification in constitutional law in the protection of marriage and the family. It is true that the legislature took the prohibition on incest into consideration primarily from the aspect of an effect which destroys marriage and the family; and the Federal Court of Justice has also seen the protection of marriage and the family as an outstanding legal good of § 173 Criminal Code (see BGHSt 39, 326 [329]).

Nevertheless it is not evident that it is really tailor-made for the protection of marriage or the family.

The Federal Constitutional Court has established in an earlier decision in 1973 that the prevention of sexual relationships within a family, apart from such relationships within marriage, amounts to good sense because the vital function of the family for human society would be crucially disturbed (see BVerfGE 36, 146 [167]). Whether this notion of ordered families could still be maintained today, for example in view of the abolition of a crime called adultery, which means to accept sexual behavior harming the family, can be left undecided. In any case the criminal norm in its concrete form does not in fact aim to protect the family from sexual activities of siblings.

It is only vaginal intercourse between natural siblings which is criminalized. All other sexual activities between brothers and sisters are excepted. Sexual relationships between siblings of the same sex are also not covered, as well as those between siblings who are not natural siblings i.e. step, adoptive and foster siblings. This means that this definition is not concerned with protection of the family from sexual activities of siblings, and the possible negative consequences for the family associated with this, but only with penalizing sexual intercourse between natural siblings. If the criminal provision was really intended for protection of the family from sexual activities, it would extend to these activities which disturb the family...

A further factor to be taken into account is that the legislature has only imposed criminal liability under § 173 para. 3 Criminal Code for siblings from the age of 18 years upwards. This limitation is not consistent with protection of the family, as generally understood, either. The fact that sibling incest is limited by a minimum age, but that no other restrictive features are prescribed, means that the age of the siblings (and their capacity for action and decision which changes with this) plays no role; the same holds for the fact that there might be no functioning family community based on close social relationships or that a "community of house and life" originally formed with the parents has possibly become a "mere meeting community" without a real "family life" (on these lines of development in a family community see BVerfGE 10, 59 [66]).

According to the clear wording of the criminal norm none of these aspects matter even though the possible harmful effects for the family accompanying the incestuous relationship, which the Senate explains in detail, depend upon the relationship which actually exists and therefore in such types of case could be smaller or even not detectable at all. This also proves that the offense description is not compatible with a statutory purpose of "protection of the family."

Nor can any different conclusion be derived from possible overlapping of roles which could occur with children from incestuous relationships... there is no longer any concrete probability, in times where reliable contraception is possible and in which sexual intercourse can simply have no consequences, of the procreation of children actually following sexual intercourse...

d) None of the legal goods attributed by the Senate to the provision import into it a legitimate purpose in constitutional law...

Much is to be said for the view that the provision in the existing form—and a broad section of the criminal law literature also indicates this (see for instance the references in Dippel, in: LK-Criminal Code, 11th edit, marginal nos. 4, 14)—merely has in view existing or even only presumed moral judgments, but not a concrete legal good. The legislature did not in the end want to decide in favor of abolition because the general public regarded sibling incest as wrong and the removal of the norm could weaken consciousness of the abnormality of the behavior.

But the synthesis or maintenance of a social consensus about values cannot be the direct goal of a criminal norm. There are other and better suited methods for this in the sense of the ultimate ratio principle and the principle of proportionality as constitutional restrictions of criminal law intervention. The strengthening of moral concepts may at best be expected—indirectly—as a long-term result of a just, clear, rational and constant administration of criminal justice.

... [The Senate] considers that this is not a type of case in which criminal law is only protecting moral concepts. But the regulatory purposes explained by the majority of the Senate cannot in fact convey a protection of legal goods. The Senate seeks to shelter behind the "totality of regulatory purposes pursued by the norm" or the "combination of comprehensible purposes." This makes clear that each individual purpose, taken by itself, obviously also in the view of the majority of the Senate, cannot serve as a legitimate goal for the legislature. But it remains open why the sum of purposes which are unsuitable, not wholly sufficient, and not founded on the offense description should provide compelling legitimation. Finally, the Senate makes no secret of the fact that it has in the end no objection to criminal law protecting the "social conviction founded in cultural history" that incest deserves to be punished. I consider this to be protection of a societal moral judgment...

Markus D. Dubber, "Theories of Crime and Punishment in German Criminal Law," 53 *American Journal of Comparative Law* (2006), 679

The significance, and meaning, of the distinctive nature of crime—and therefore, by implication, the proper scope of criminal law—has long befuddled Anglo-American criminal jurisprudence.... [T]he Anglo-American criminal lawyer might do well to consult German criminal law [on this point,] for German law offers a well-developed account of the nature of criminal harm and the point of criminal law: the theory of *Rechtsgut*, or legal good. Let us then take a closer look at the *Rechtsgut* theory to see whether it can inform the development of a more sophisticated account of the nature of criminal harm in Anglo-American criminal law.

Rechtsgut, or legal good, is one of the foundational concepts underpinning the German criminal law system. The concept is so basic and essential, in fact, that German criminal lawyers find it difficult to imagine a system of criminal law without it. The concept of legal good serves several crucial functions, at various levels of generality within the German criminal law system. Most fundamentally, the concept of legal good defines the very scope of criminal law. By common consensus, the function of criminal law is the "protection of legal goods," and nothing else. Anything that does not qualify as a legal good falls outside the scope of criminal law, and may not be criminalized. A criminal statute, in other words, that does not even seek to protect a legal good is prima facie illegitimate. This principle has been invoked in favor of decriminalizing various morals offenses, such as homosexual sex and the distribution of pornography.

To perform this basic critical function, the concept of legal good must be defined with reasonable clarity, and it must be given normative bite. There is much less of a consensus in the German literature on these two points, however, than there is on the general commitment to the concept of *Rechtsgut* in the abstract.

A. Positivism and Normativism

To appreciate the scope of the concept of *Rechtsgut* in the literature, as well as the variety of its manifestations, let us consider the treatment of the topic in two leading, and fairly representative, treatises. Hans-Heinrich Jescheck and Thomas Weigend, in their popular Textbook of Criminal Law: General Part, declare categorically that "criminal law has the objective of protecting legal goods," and then go on to explain that legal goods, or "life goods" (*Lebensgüter*), come in two varieties. Among "elementary life goods" that "are indispensable for the coexistence of humans in the community (*Gemeinschaft*) and therefore must be protected by the coercive power of the state through public punishment" one finds, for example, human life, bodily integrity, personal freedom of action and movement, property, wealth, traffic safety, the incorruptibility of public officials, the constitutional order, the public peace, the external security of the state, the impunity of foreign state organs and indicia, the security of national, ethnic or cultural minorities against extermination or undignified treatment, international peace.

Besides these elementary goods there are also those that "consist exclusively of deeply rooted ethical convictions of society (*Gesellschaft*) such as the protection good of the criminal prohibition of cruelty against animals," which "become legal goods through their adoption into the legal order."

By contrast, Claus Roxin, in his influential Criminal Law: General Part, does not assemble a list of legal goods, not even an exemplary one. In passing, however, he does mention a number of things that have been considered legal goods at some point in time, including, in order of appearance in the text, life, bodily integrity, honor, the administration of law, ethical order, sexual autonomy, property, the state, the currency, dominant moral opinions, heterosexual structure of sexual relations, undisturbed operation of administration, purity of German blood, public peace, traffic congestion, the life and well-being of animals, the environment, morality, "purity of soil, air, water, etc.," the variety of species in flora and fauna, maintenance of intact nature, the people's health, life contexts as such, purity of the system of proof. Also unlike Jescheck and Weigend, Roxin hazards a definition of *Rechtsgut*:

> Legal goods are conditions or chosen ends, which are useful either to the individual and his free development within the context of an overall social system based on this objective, or to the functioning of this system itself.

Roxin's definitional venture is motivated by an attempt to put some teeth into the concept of legal good. While Jescheck and Weigend appear content to follow up their declaration that criminal law protects legal goods with a list of legal goods the criminal law in fact does protect, Roxin strives to give the concept of legal good normative bite. The concept of legal good by itself is supposed to tell the legislature "what it may punish and what it shall leave without punishment."

The tension between positivism (here represented by Jescheck and Weigend) and normativism (Roxin) is inherent in the concept of legal good itself. On the face of it, the concept appears to be in conflict with itself, for it conjoins two very different concepts: *Recht* and *Gut*. The translation of *Gut*, as "good," is fairly straightforward. What is not so clear is what sort of "good" one has in mind here. While the term is familiar enough, it is familiar from moral, or perhaps political, philosophy, but not from legal theory, never mind from blackletter law. What's more, those disciplines that do concern themselves with the concept of "good" (or "goods") have had considerable difficulty defining it. Even if moral theory had produced a neat and widely shared notion of good, it is not immediately obvious why that notion should have any application to the field of law, particularly since German criminal law since P. J. A. Feuerbach (or Kant, whoever came first) has maintained a strict distinction between morality and legality, and criminal law especially.

But it is the other of the concepts welded together in the word "*Rechtsgut*" that presents the real difficulty. *Recht* is well known for its ambiguity. With no equivalent in the English language, it straddles the distinctions between justice and law, rightness and legality, natural and positive law, and even rights and right. This inherent ambiguity means, for one, that the question about the relevance of an apparently moral concept like "good" to a system of law cannot simply be answered—as it sometimes is—by pointing out that we are, after all, talking about a legal good, rather than a moral one. The mere invocation of the label "*Rechtsgut*"—with an appropriate emphasis on the first syllable—cannot stem any unwanted incursion of moral notions into law in general, and criminal law in particular.

B. From Feuerbach to Birnbaum

The impression of a concept at odds with itself is only strengthened when one considers the origins and subsequent development of *Rechtsgut*. In a very real sense, the tension between a positivist and a normative approach to the concept of legal good is as old as the concept itself. According to the standard account, the concept of legal good was discovered by an otherwise rather undistinguished criminal law scholar by the name of Birnbaum, who first reported his discovery in an often cited article published in 1834. In that article, Birnbaum attacked Feuerbach's view of crime as a violation of "subjective right." According to Feuerbach, in committing a crime the offender did not just violate "the law," or "a statute," but the rights of her individual victim. Birnbaum pointed out that this view of crime was much too narrow, as it could not account for a great many criminal statutes which did not concern themselves with violations of individual rights at all, and yet were not considered to be any less criminal as a result.

Feuerbach's cramped view of crime might work for traditional crimes like murder and theft, but it did not have room for such familiar crimes as "unethical and irreligious acts." Birnbaum had a point. In fact, Feuerbach himself had never denied that crimes against morality and religion were crimes, even though everyone agreed they did not violate anyone's individual rights and therefore did not fit Feuerbach's definition of crimes as violations of individual rights. Instead he had, with some embarrassment, simply categorized them as "crimes in the broad sense" and labelled them "police offenses."

Birnbaum clearly did a much better job capturing the nature of crime as a matter of positive law. Instead of a violation of individual rights (*Rechte*), a crime was now to be regarded as a violation of or a threat to goods (*Güter*) protected by the state. But whatever Birnbaum's definition of crime gained in accuracy, it lost in critical purchase.

Eventually the notion of legal good, rather than limiting the power of the state to criminalize, turned into a convenient trope for its expansion. By the late 19th century, when Birnbaum's discovery of the legal good was rediscovered by the committed positivist architects of the new national German criminal law, Karl Binding chief among them, the point of the legal good was to justify the expansion of criminal law beyond the protection of individual rights to the protection of communal goods, societal interests, and eventually the state itself. Legal goods became "interests of the law," transforming law from a means to an end in itself. If crime was thought to violate any right, it was not the rights of individuals but the state's right to obedience.

Accordingly, Binding defined legal good as "anything that the legislature considers valuable and the undisturbed retention of which it therefore must ensure through norms." In Binding's influential norm theory of criminal law, legal goods (e.g., life) were protected by norms (e.g., do not kill) that the legislature, in its discretion, translated into legal prescriptions and prohibitions, including, but not limited to, criminal statutes (e.g., whoever causes the death of another person is guilty of murder and punishable by death).

At the same time as the move from the protection of individual rights to that of legal goods broadened the scope of criminal law, the move from violations to threats widened its grasp. Where criminal law was once—at least in theory, however awkwardly—limited to the punishment of violations of individual rights, it now reached the prevention of threats to any good, individual or not, that the state declared worthy of its penal protection.

Since Binding's rediscovery of Birnbaum, the basic framework of the occasionally heated debate about the definition and the function of the concept of legal good has remained fairly constant. Contributors to the debate took their place along the spectrum marked by Feuerbach's notion of crime as a violation of individual right and Binding's as a threat to state interests. Even Nazi criminal law, after some initial attempts to discard the notion of legal good altogether as an outdated liberal constraint upon state power, was content to develop new legal goods worthy of penal protection, rather than doing away with the concept altogether (e.g., "race and the substance of the people," "Germanness").

C. Constitutional Foundations?

Today, the formal-positivist and the material-normative approach to the concept of legal good are represented by Jescheck and Weigend, and Roxin, respectively, and among many others. What's "new" about Roxin is the attempt to derive the content of legal good not from some more or less explicit notion of "law" or "good," but from constitutional principles, for only they limit legislative discretion in a modern democratic state: "A concept of legal good that constrains penal policy . . . can only derive from those objectives of our law state (*Rechtsstaat*) grounded in the freedom of the individual which are articulated in the Basic Law," i.e., the German constitution. Just what these constitutional principles are, however, Roxin does not say. From the quoted declaration, he proceeds immediately to the above-quoted definition of legal goods as "conditions or chosen ends, which are useful either to the individual and his free development within the context of an overall social system based on this objective, or to the functioning of this system itself."

Roxin's failure to derive his definition of legal good from the constitution is of course problematic, given that he simultaneously asserts that any such definition must be constitutionally derived. Upon closer inspection one begins to suspect that the definition derives not from its source, constitutional or not, but from its effect. So Roxin explains that the inclusion of "chosen ends," in addition to preexisting "conditions" (presumably including individual rights), was meant to "express" a prior, unexplored, judgment that his view of legal good does not exclude by definition any crimes that Anglo-American lawyers might call *mala prohibita*, and that he calls "duties to obey norms generated by law itself." In other words, he insists on critical bite, but not on too much.

It is no surprise, therefore, that Roxin spends considerably more time illustrating various applications of his definition than he does justifying it. The definition is correct, the implication appears to be, because it leads to correct results, legitimizing just the right sorts of crimes, while delegitimizing only those that are beyond the pale of the state's penal power. In fact, Roxin identifies not a single case of a German criminal statute that is illegitimate because it does not protect a legal good.

The statutes, and policies, that fail Roxin's legal good test are either fanciful or obsolete. "Arbitrary threats of punishment" are illegitimate because they do not protect legal goods. No one may be forced, by fear of punishment, to pay homage to some "symbol" or other, for this "serves neither the freedom of the individual in a state committed to freedom nor the ability of a social system based on such principles to function." The purity of German blood likewise does not count as a legal good because "protecting ideological objectives through penal norms is prohibited." Criminalizing homosexual sex is also improper. Morally offensive behavior, Roxin points out, does not violate legal goods because it does not interfere with "the social system's ability to function." In fact, it is the criminalization of morally offensive behavior, rather than the behavior itself, which causes such interference "because it creates unnecessary societal conflict by stigmatizing socially integrated humans."

All existing criminal statutes pass the test, even if not always with flying colors. So Roxin struggles to justify the continued punishability of assisted suicide, which arguably interferes with no legal good, on the ground that it is difficult to prove the decedent's "autonomous decision" to end her life and that, at any rate, "the norm of protection of life demands the tabooization of others' life." Drug criminal law is legitimate—despite strong criticism that it protects no legal good, individual or communal—because it abates the dangers of drugs "for consumers incapable of responsibility"; the crime of abortion protects the fetus' "emerging life," which is a legal good because the German Constitutional Court has held that it is constitutionally protected; cruelty to animals is properly criminalized not because it offends deeply held and widely shared moral convictions (which do not qualify as legal goods in Roxin's definition), but because "it is to be assumed that the legislature, in a kind of solidarity among creatures, also regards the higher animals as fellow creatures, or 'foreign brothers,' and protects them as such"; and environmental crimes too pass muster because "the variety of the species in flora and fauna and the preservation of intact nature belong to a life with human dignity." Not even "symbolic legislation," including obviously ineffective policies designed merely to placate voters or to signal the legislature's commitment to certain values, fails the legal good test, at least not without "a comprehensive study from the perspective of criminal and constitutional law," which, however, is yet to be undertaken.

Considering the toothless nature of Roxin's normative theory of legal good, its bark turns out to be worse than its bite. In fact, one might even wonder just what critical point the concept of legal good retains, when all is said and done. Even Roxin himself acknowledges that, by his own account, it is not clear just what the notion of legal good adds to constitutional constraints upon criminal law-making. (He concludes that the concept can still serve to "bundle" the various constitutional limitations.) After all, the definition of legal good is supposed to be derived exclusively from constitutional principles, as it must be as no other constraints upon the legislature are said to be permissible.

D. Internal Constraints

At this point, it is worth noting that even a merely—and explicitly—positivist notion of legal good, such as the one favored by Jescheck and Weigend, is not without critical potential, though from within an existing system of criminal law, rather than from without. Even if the ends of criminal law are beyond reproach, the means need not be. In German criminal law, a criminal statute that sets out to protect a legal good—however defined—and therefore has the proper end, may nonetheless be open to criticism if it is insufficiently connected to that good, and thus constitutes an improper means. This means–ends test has been used to criticize so-called "abstract dangerousness offenses," which criminalize conduct that in the abstract poses a threat to some legal good, without any need to prove that the specific conduct posed such a threat in fact. The classic example here is driving while intoxicated.

Recall that Birnbaum expanded the scope of criminal law not only in breadth, but also in depth, by recognizing the punishability of mere threats to legal goods, as opposed to actual violations. Modern German criminal law, and in fact modern criminal law in general, has been much concerned with reaching, and neutralizing, ever more remote, and ever more abstract, threats to legal goods. German criminal law distinguishes between concrete and abstract dangerousness offenses. In the former case, the definition of the offense includes actual endangerment, as in the offense of "endangering rail, ship, and air traffic" which criminalizes "endangering another's life, limb, or property of significant value" in certain circumstances. Abstract endangerment offenses, by contrast, do not include actual endangerment in their definition. They instead cover conduct that "typically creates a concrete danger," whether or not that danger was in fact created by the particular conduct in question. Examples include slander, which requires only an act "capable of" stigmatizing another and drunk driving, which requires no showing that the drunk driver posed a threat to anyone or anything.

Finally, a criminal statute that does set out to protect a legal good still may be illegitimate if it is not necessary to achieve its end. The criminal law, in other words, is said to be the state's *ultima ratio* in its effort to protect legal goods; it must employ less intrusive, civil, means if they can provide sufficient protection for the legal good in question. The status, and origin, of this so-called subsidiarity principle of German criminal law is not entirely clear. Roxin claims, once again, that the *ultima ratio* principle derives from the constitution, in this case the principle of proportionality which, he continues, "can be deduced from the constitutional principle of the rule of law: Since criminal law enables the harshest of all state interferences with the liberty of the citizen, it may only be applied if milder means do not promise sufficient success." Later on, however, Roxin acknowledges that the legislature enjoys wide discretion in choosing among available means, criminal and noncriminal, concluding somewhat anticlimactically "the subsidiarity principle is more of a guideline for penal policymaking than a compelling requirement."

E. Doctrinal Significance

Apart from its various critical functions, external or internal, toothless or not, the notion of legal good performs several more mundane, doctrinal tasks. The justification of necessity, for instance, requires a balancing of the affected legal goods (the protection of one legal good making the violation of the other necessary). The American Model Criminal Code captures very much the same idea when it allows for a justification of "choice of evils" in the case of "conduct which the actor believes to be necessary to avoid a harm or evil to himself or to another is justifiable, provided that . . . the harm or evil sought to be avoided by such conduct is greater than that sought to be prevented by the law defining the offense charged."

The balancing act required takes into account both the relative significance of the legal good, and the degree of its interference. So "personality values" (*Persönlichkeitswerte*)—like "human freedom"—rank higher than "thing goods" (*Sachgüter*)—like "property"—and "life and limb" trump not only other "personality values" but also "supraindividual legal goods." Yet trivial interferences with "personality values" may be justified for the sake of preventing serious interferences with "thing goods," such as a minor assault necessary to avert a major fire. The origin, as well as the precise order, of the ranking remains, once more, somewhat doubtful. As might be suspected, the ranking of legal goods on occasion is said to derive from constitutional principles.

Certain *de minimis* conduct that fits the definition of an offense is nonetheless declared noncriminal (or not "subsumed" under the offense definition) because it does not "really" violate the legal good protected by the statute in question. So tipping the mailman is not bribery, playing penny poker not gambling, and calling your brother a bad name not a criminal insult. The Model Criminal Code likewise provides for judicial dismissal of a prosecution for prima facie criminal conduct that "did not actually cause or threaten the harm or evil sought to be prevented by the law defining the offense or did so only to an extent too trivial to warrant the condemnation of conviction."

German criminal law also distinguishes between different types of legal good that a criminal statute might protect, individual legal goods, such as life and liberty, and communal ones, such as peace and security. And it may make a doctrinal difference which type of legal good is implicated. For instance, self-defense is not available against attacks on communal—as opposed to individual— goods. "Otherwise every citizen could set himself as auxiliary policeman and annul the state's monopoly on violence." That's not to say, however, that no justification would be available, just that the justification of self-defense would not. A citizen who wishes to defend communal goods against attack instead would have to rely on the justification of necessity.

Consent is also only available as a justification in cases involving an offense protecting an individual legal good. Here the reason is that the individual cannot be justified in waiving the criminal law's protection of a communal legal good, i.e., of an interest that is not merely his own and therefore not his to give away.

Though of no immediate doctrinal significance, the role of the concept of legal good as a method of categorization also deserves mention. The special part of the German criminal code is divided up into sections that contain offense definitions designed to protect a common legal good or set of legal goods, including "crimes against peace" and "crimes endangering the democratic rule of law" (sec. 1), "crimes against sexual autonomy" (sec. 13), "crimes against personal freedom" (sec. 18), and "crimes against environment" (sec. 29). The Model Criminal Code similarly arranges the crimes defined in its special part according to the "individual or public interests" they protect.

By figuring in both the general part and the special part of criminal law, the concept of legal good highlights the connection between the two parts. Issues in the general part, like necessity, involve consideration of the same interests—or goods—that are protected by the offenses in the special part. This common conceptual foundation is obscured by the nomenclature in the Model Criminal Code, for instance, which frames questions relating to legal goods in terms of "harms or evils" or "individual or public interests," depending on whether they arise in the general or special part.

F. *Rechtsgut* as Analytical Tool

In the end, the most important function of the concept of legal good may well be the facilitation of critical analysis, rather than critique itself. The very existence of the concept stands for the proposition that there are limits within which modern criminal law must operate if it is to claim legitimacy, and ultimately obedience, and therefore effectiveness. The notion of legal goods provides critical analysis of German criminal law with a language for expressing itself, no less, but also not much more.

There is clearly a danger in overestimating the significance of the mere existence of a concept called *Rechtsgut*. Yet, one should also resist the opposite impulse to dismiss the concept as meaningless, or even hypocritical, simply because it has never been invoked to invalidate a single piece of criminal legislation. In American criminal law, a constant reminder—even a purely formal one—of the intimate connection between criminal law and the rule of law might prove useful as state programs such as the "war on crime," the "war on drugs" or, most recently, the "war on terror" draw into question the identity of criminal law as a species of law, rather than a system for the policing of human threats. Still, there is nothing magical about the concept of *Rechtsgut* itself. In American criminal law, at least, another concept—such as a concept of criminal harm based on rights of personal dignity and autonomy recently reaffirmed in *Lawrence v. Texas*—may be able to perform the same function, with more substantive bite and a more solid grounding in American constitutional principles.

Even if the concept of a legal good turns out not to be constitutionally based, and therefore to have no destructive potential, it still can play a constructive role in a general account of the criminal law, perhaps even as a guideline for policy makers, and certainly as an interpretative tool for the courts. At the very least, it would be preferable to have courts ponder the question what legal good, or interest, a particular statute was designed to protect, rather than unsystematically divining the "gist" or "crux" or "gravamen" or "focus" or "scope" or "object" or "hard core" of a particular criminal statute, the "harm or evil," just plain "evil," or "injury" it seeks to prevent, or the "individual or public interests" or "rights" it is meant to protect, or worse yet, to wonder which "class of persons" or "bad men" it might have been intended to reach.

NOTES

1. The cases show that it is not easy to delineate constitutional boundaries for criminalization (or, in other words, limits on the special part of the criminal law, as opposed to its general part, which deals not with specific offenses but with general principles of liability, such as *mens rea*, culpability, and so on). None of the constitutions contains a specific provision that addresses this issue with a general, abstract description of what can be legitimately prohibited by criminal law means, perhaps as part of a broader provision setting out the foundation and nature of the state's criminal law power. It is theoretically conceivable to formulate such a constitutional clause but it is not part of the constitutions in the legal systems compared here. (What might such a clause look like?)

In the United States, courts and commentators tend to cite an implied power, the power to police, as the source of the *states'* power to criminalize.[*] The police power, however, as an essential attribute of sovereignty, was explicitly retained by the states; the federal government in the United States does not have a general power to police. This means that the federal government has had to ground its criminal lawmaking—which has expanded dramatically since the American Revolution, and even since the early twentieth century—in other powers, which the states granted to it explicitly in the federal constitution. Chief among these is the commerce clause, i.e., the power to regulate interstate (and international) commerce.[†] Along the way, the federal government has stretched these alternative constitutional powers to such an extent that it is widely conceded that it now possesses a police power *de facto*, if not *de jure*.[‡] The Supreme Court by and large has turned a blind eye to this development, with occasional, highly controversial, exceptions.[§]

Here it is worth noting that the police power, which has quietly and implicitly underlain the legislature's exercise of the power to criminalize, also has been invoked, explicitly, by *courts*. The doctrine of "common law misdemeanors," under which courts took it upon themselves to recognize behavior as criminal that had escaped the legislature's attention as late as the second half of the twentieth century. Consider this passage from *Commonwealth v. Keller*, 35 Pa. D. & C.2d 615 (1964), a Pennsylvania trial court opinion that crafted the novel offense of "indecent disposition of a dead body":

> The landmark case in this Commonwealth which enounces the principle of preserving common law offenses is Commonwealth v. McHale, 97 Pa. 397 [1881]. After analyzing and determining that common law crimes are preserved, Mr. Justice Paxton, at page 408, asks the question, "What is a common-law offense?"
>
> The highest authority upon this point is Blackstone. In chap. 13, of vol. 4, of Sharswood's edition, it is thus defined: "The last species of offenses which especially affect the Commonwealth are those against the public police or economy. By the public police and economy I mean the due regulation and domestic order of the kingdom, whereby the individuals of the state, like members of a well-governed family, are bound to conform their general behavior to the rules of propriety, good neighborhood and good manners, and to be decent, industrious and inoffensive in their respective stations. This head of offenses must therefore be very miscellaneous, as it comprises all such crimes as especially affect public society, and are not comprehended under any of the four preceding series. These amount some of them to felony, and other to misdemeanors only."

---

[*] See generally Markus D. Dubber, *The Police Power: Patriarchy and the Foundations of American Government* (2005).

[†] See, e.g., 21 U.S.C. § 801 (federal drug criminal law based on commerce clause because of drug traffic's "substantial and direct effect upon interstate commerce").

[‡] See already Ernst Freund, *The Police Power: Public Policy and Constitutional Rights* (1904), 63.

[§] See *United States v. Lopez*, 514 U.S. 549 (1995) (striking down a federal gun possession statute ostensibly based on the commerce clause).

Just two years earlier, across the Atlantic, the House of Lords had reaffirmed its role as "the *custos morum* of the people" and its "superintendency of offences *contra bonos mores*," giving rise to the "residual power, where no statute has yet intervened to supersede the common law, to superintend those offences which are prejudicial to the public welfare."* Common law misdemeanor doctrine has since fallen into disuse in common law countries, including the U.S., England, and Canada, as a result of judicial self-limitation or legislative reform (rather than a finding of unconstitutionality, say, on the ground that it violated the principle of legality in general, and the principle of legislativity in particular).[†] For present purposes, however, the point is that the police power's foundational function was not limited to legislative ("statutory") crimes, but extended to judicial ("common law") ones, even at a time when the primary locus of criminal lawmaking had shifted from the judiciary to the legislature.[‡]

Grounding the criminal law power in the police power makes generating constitutional limits on criminal law difficult, if not impossible. The police power is, after all, generally thought to be—by both proponents and critics—beyond principled constraint, constitutional or otherwise, which is precisely why the states were so careful *not* to cede it to the federal government and why progressive reformers at the turn of the twentieth century vigorously opposed the U.S. Supreme Court's attempts to place it within constitutional limits (culminating in the decades-long battle over *Lochner v. New York*, 198 U.S. 45 (1905)). As an "idiom of apologetics," the police power shields the exercise of state power, including criminal law, from constitutional control.[§]

The majority in the German *Abortion Case* of 1975 tried another approach: it derived from the right to life in art. 2 para. 2 sentence 1 Basic Law (along with art. 1 para. 1 Basic Law, the human dignity clause) the state's *duty* to protect human life. The duty of protection includes, according to this view, unborn human life. Note that even the majority did not derive a straightforward duty to utilize the criminal law (rather than other legal means) to achieve protection. But with respect to the norms in question, they regarded the relatively liberal abortion law that the German legislature had passed in 1974 as unconstitutional. In contrast, the two dissenting judges—one of them, Wiltraut Rupp-von Brünneck, was one of the few female judges in the history of the German Federal Constitutional Court—expressed concern about turning human rights that traditionally serve to protect liberty into reasons for criminalization that curtail it.

Is it possible to derive limits on the state's exercise of its criminal law power (the culpability principle, for instance, discussed in Chapter 1) from the constitutional requirement to protect a fundamental right, such as the inviolable right to human dignity in art. 1 of the German Basic Law, without at the same time deriving from it the duty to exercise that power in the protection of that same right? In other words: Does it make sense to acknowledge defensive rights, that is constitutional rights of a defensive nature (defending the individual against the state) while at the same time being more skeptical about protective rights (rights of individuals to be protected by means of the criminal law)? What conceptions of crime, of the state, and of the separation of powers, might come into play here?

2. The dispute about abortion laws did not end in Germany with the judgment excerpted above. The legislature later tried again to pass a more liberal abortion law; once more, the German Federal Constitutional Court objected,[¶] again by pointing to the unborn's right to life and human dignity, and the state's duty to protect those rights even against the mother of

---

* *Shaw v. DPP*, [1962] A.C. 220.

[†] See Chapter 2; see also Pa. Crimes Code § 107(b) ("Common law crimes abolished") (Pennsylvania); *Knuller v. DPP*, [1973] A.C. 435 (England); *Frey v. Fedoruk*, [1950] S.C.R. 517, § 9 Canadian Criminal Code (Canada).

[‡] See generally Markus D. Dubber, "The Story of *Keller*: The Irrelevance of the Legality Principle in American Criminal Law," in Robert Weisberg and Donna Coker (eds.), *Criminal Law Stories* (2012), 23.

[§] See Walton H. Hamilton and Carlton C. Rodee, "Police Power," in *Encyclopedia of the Social Sciences* (1933), vol. 12, 190.

[¶] See Judgment of May 28, 1993, BVerfGE 88, 203.

the unborn child. Note that the Court's articulation of a state duty to protect unborn life does *not* mean that in fact abortions are categorically prohibited, or even significantly restricted, under German criminal law as it is today. The compromise after the second abortion decision in 1993 was to somewhat vaguely label abortion by a doctor within twelve weeks of conception and after abortion counseling as "not being a criminal offense," rather than declaring abortion under such circumstances justified, or not unlawful. (Why would this make a difference, from the perspective of the rightsholder? Is my right any less violated because the act in question is labeled one way, rather than another? If labels matter, does it reflect lesser or greater respect for a right to label its violation not a criminal offense, as opposed to labeling it as a criminal offense that may be justified in certain, limited, circumstances?*)

3. If one moves beyond the abortion debate, which might (or might not) be anchored in a constitutional "right to life" provision, it becomes even more difficult to draw inferences from human rights clauses to specific prohibitions within the criminal law. Therefore, it is necessary to expand one's focus from potential victims' human rights to offenders' rights. Obviously, every criminal prohibition curtails liberty. How far the state may go in doing so could potentially be derived from general constitutional provisions concerning liberty and the curtailment of liberty. However, those provisions tend to be formulated in a very abstract way. What restrictions on criminalization can be derived from "due process of law" (U.S. Constitution, 14th amendment), "principles of fundamental justice" (Canadian Charter of Rights and Freedoms), or "dignity" (German Basic Law)? Is it any harder to derive constitutional norms governing criminalization (i.e., the special part of criminal law) from these abstract provisions than constitutional norms governing the ascription of criminal liability for any given offense (i.e., the general part of criminal law), such as the German culpability principle (*Schuldprinzip*),[†] or the fault principle in Canadian constitutional law? See *R. v. Wholesale Travel Group Inc.*, [1991] 3 S.C.R. 154.

One could try to narrow this gap by turning to criminal law theory and, more generally, moral and political theory. The Pennsylvania Supreme Court, in *Bonadio*, for instance, strikes down a criminal statute after quoting extensively from John Stuart Mill's discussion of the so-called "harm principle" in his classic text *On Liberty*. The Supreme Court of Canada also turns to Mill and his harm principle, but reaches the opposite conclusion: while the principle is well and good, it does not have constitutional standing (at least in Canada, in 2003) and, by itself, cannot decide the constitutional fate of a criminal statute, though a legislature may do well to take it into account when making decisions about criminalization.

The German tradition that the Federal Constitutional Court considers is also a product of the nineteenth century. Mill and the harm principle, until very recently, were hardly mentioned in the German literature, as the focus was on the legal good (*Rechtsgut*) doctrine. Note that the German Constitutional Court, in the *Incest Case*, was no more impressed with the attempt to claim constitutional status for the legal good doctrine than the Canadian Supreme Court, in *Malmo-Levine*, had been with the same attempt regarding the harm principle. Compare the harm principle and the *Rechtsgut* doctrine. Do they differ in substance? In significance? Do (*should*) they have bite, leaving aside the question of their constitutional status?

4. The more general question is whether constitutional limits for the legislature can be derived straightforwardly from criminal law theory. The judges at the Federal Constitutional Court were, similar to their Canadian colleagues, not willing to ground constitutional interpretation in pre-existing concepts developed in political theory and criminal law theory. The German judges emphasize that a democratically legitimated legislature is not obliged to adhere to "pre-discovered legal goods."

---

* Compare N.Y. Penal Law § 125.05(3) ("justifiable abortional act").
† See Chapter 1.

Despite its reluctance to accept the legal good doctrine, the German Federal Constitutional Court does not argue that parliament has unlimited discretion when deciding to criminalize conduct. Rather, the German Court applies the same test that it would for any other limitation of liberty: the constitutional test of proportionality. According to this test, the legal prohibition has to pursue a specific goal, i.e., the protection of others or the general public, and this intrusive measure must be appropriate, necessary and proportional in a narrower sense. As rational as this test might sound, one can also read the *Incest Case* as a demonstration that the general constitutional proportionality test is a rather blunt instrument when applied to criminalization.

Is this a problem with the proportionality test, or perhaps with the Court's interpretation and application of the test? Did the Court, for instance, consider illegitimate rationales for the provision, including reliance on a supposed social taboo and communal consciousness (see below)? Did it engage in a slipshod analysis of existing criminal prohibitions? Did it rely on insufficient empirical evidence? What's the connection between these concerns and the choice of constitutional test? Could one sharpen the proportionality test to address the question of criminalization in particular, rather than the question of state interference in general?

The Court argues that the prohibition of siblings' incest serves to protect others (the weaker sibling, the family, the public against handicapped offspring). Criminal law theorists who share the dissenting judge's opinion (Judge Hassemer, who was a professor of criminal law at the University of Frankfurt joining the Federal Constitutional Court) are more skeptical about these purported goals.

The majority opinion in the German *Incest Case* relies on eugenic reasons as one argument to justify why prohibition of sibling incest serves a constitutionally acceptable goal. But are eugenic arguments really appropriate in contemporary societies, and what does this mean for persons with hereditary diseases who wish to have children?

The Court also mentions the "social conviction based on cultural history and still effective, that incest deserves to be punished" and uses the word "social taboo" (while claiming that this only gives additional reasons). How would one go about measuring this conviction? Assuming one could measure it, what relevance would it have? Should the state use law (any law, a criminal law, a criminal offense punishable—as in the case of the incest provision in the German Criminal Code—with up to three years' imprisonment) to protect a "social taboo"?

5. Both the majority opinion in the German *Incest Case* and Judge Hassemer insist that the criminal law must be *ultima ratio*, the last resort, a phrase that can be found repeatedly in the Court's rulings and in the German literature. Does this principle do any work in the opinion? What does the *ultima ratio* requirement mean in the context of a general inquiry into constitutionality on the basis of the principle of proportionality? If the legislation is proportional, what difference does it make to say it is, or is not, also *ultima ratio*? Does not the retention of the *ultima ratio* requirement amount to precisely the sort of importation of external concepts (developed in the criminal law literature) into constitutional analysis that the Court rejected in the case of another concept, *Rechtsgut*?

The *ultima ratio* principle also appears occasionally in the Anglo-American literature (less so in judicial opinions). It is unclear, however, what it requires and what motivates it, other than a general preference for less over more criminal law. Like the harm principle, it may amount to little more than a general recommendation to lawmakers, a reminder that there are ways of dealing with a problem other than through the often knee-jerk response of criminalization. In that case, its constitutionalization would add little bite to constitutional review of exercises of the state's criminal law power.*

---

* See generally Panu Minkkinen, "The 'Last Resort': A Moral and/or Legal Principle?," 3 *Oñati Socio-legal Series* 21 (2013); Douglas Husak, "Applying Ultima Ratio: A Skeptical Assessment," 2 *Ohio State Journal of Criminal Law* (2005), 535.

6. Compare *Lawrence* and the *Incest Case*. In both cases, it is clear that there is a core of intimate (sexual) life which the state may not regulate. However, while the U.S. Supreme Court proceeds to strike down the Texas anti-sodomy statute, the German Federal Constitutional Court upholds the incest statute. Does this difference in outcome reflect different conceptions of privacy rights (their nature, their scope, their significance)?

In its early years, the German Federal Constitutional Court also had to decide about a norm that prohibited sexual contacts between adult men (§ 175 StGB, reduced to contacts with minors in 1973, abolished 1994). In the ruling from May 10, 1957 (1 BvR 550/52, BVerfGE 6, 389), the German Court declared that the fact that homosexual acts between female partners were not punishable while males had to expect penal consequences did not violate the equality principle (art. 3 para. 2 sentence 2 Basic Law). The argument was that male homosexuality is different from female homosexuality (the "expert opinions" cited in this judgment about women's tenderness and male aggressiveness will strike contemporary readers as odd). In discussing the right to liberty in art. 2 para. 1 Basic Law, the Court pointed to the fact that art. 2 explicitly lists (to this day) "the moral law" as a possible restriction of liberty. This "moral law" clause hardly plays a role in modern constitutional jurisprudence—in fact, it is mostly ignored today—but in the 1950s, it made it easy to uphold the criminal prohibition against male homosexual acts. (Is it appropriate for courts to ignore constitutional provisions, as opposed to interpreting them differently? If so, when? How would a court differentiate between provisions that deserve attention, and those that do not?)

Note that *Lawrence* overturned *Bowers v. Hardwick*, a 1986 case in which the Supreme Court, in an opinion by Justice White, had upheld the Georgia anti-sodomy statute, rejecting precisely the privacy arguments that carried the day seventeen years later in *Lawrence*, 478 U.S. 186 (1986). Leaving aside the details, the *Lawrence* majority declared that "[t]he rationale of *Bowers* does not withstand careful analysis," that it "was not correct when it was decided, . . . is not correct today," and that Justice Stevens's dissent in *Bowers* had the better of the argument (and for that reason "should have been controlling in *Bowers* and should control here"). On a comparative note, *Lawrence* is one of the few cases in which the U.S. Supreme Court, over vigorous dissent, invoked non-U.S. jurisprudence, and the jurisprudence of the ECtHR in particular:

> To the extent *Bowers* relied on values we share with a wider civilization, it should be noted that the reasoning and holding in *Bowers* have been rejected elsewhere. The European Court of Human Rights has followed not *Bowers* but its own decision in *Dudgeon v. United Kingdom*. See *P. G. & J. H. v. United Kingdom*, App. No. 00044787/98, ¶ 56 (Eur. Ct. H. R., Sept. 25, 2001); *Modinos v. Cyprus*, 259 Eur. Ct. H. R. (1993); *Norris v. Ireland*, 142 Eur. Ct. H. R. (1988). Other nations, too, have taken action consistent with an affirmation of the protected right of homosexual adults to engage in intimate, consensual conduct. The right the petitioners seek in this case has been accepted as an integral part of human freedom in many other countries. There has been no showing that in this country the governmental interest in circumscribing personal choice is somehow more legitimate or urgent.

What, if any, is the relevance of foreign judgments in determining the constitutionality of a given piece of domestic legislation? What if it turned out that the presumed German "social taboo" against consensual adult sibling incest was (not) shared by other countries? How would this attitude be measured? What does it mean to suggest that a particular conduct is consistent, or inconsistent, with a "wider civilization"? How would one draw the borders of this civilization?

7. With respect to the question of whether the mere possession of marihuana can be a criminal offense, a ruling by the German Federal Constitutional Court from March 9, 1994 (2 BvL 43, 51, 63, 64, 70, 80/92, 2 BvR 2031/92, BVerfGE 90, 145) matches the result of the Canadian Supreme Court. With respect to the infringement of liberty, the same proportionality test as in the *Incest Case* was applied. The Constitutional Court accepted the purposes pursued by the legislature (protection of public health, protection of minors). It did express some concern about proportionality in the narrower sense, with view to possession of small amounts. However, this concern was addressed by pointing to the availability of conditional and unconditional discharge in cases of minor harm and culpability (§§ 153, 153a German Code of Criminal Procedure). (The opportunity principle, as an exception from the general principle of compulsory prosecution.*) This allowed the Court to reject the constitutional challenge. Is it appropriate to preserve the constitutionality of a provision of substantive criminal law by procedural means? Is it appropriate for the judiciary to discharge its obligation to review the constitutionality of legislative acts by delegating the matter to the discretion of prosecutors, or for that matter of other participants in the criminal process? A similar move appears in common law judgments, where concerns about the constitutionality, or general propriety, of a substantive norm are assuaged by referring to the "good sense" of prosecutors, jurors, and trial judges. Does it matter here whether prosecutors regard themselves as partisan participants in an adversarial process or as objective state officials seeking truth and justice, or whether there is meaningful lay participation in the criminal process (through independent juries, rather than through lay judges sitting on panels with professional judges), or whether trial judges are elected or appointed? Does it matter whether the exercise of discretion by prosecutors is subject to meaningful review?

---

* See Chapter 5.C.

JURISDICTION

It is commonly said that the Anglo-American law of criminal jurisdiction rests on the principle of territoriality. Among the comparatively curious, this may also be considered a unique feature of the common law, in contrast to civil law systems, which also emphasize personal relations (mainly offenders' and victims' nationality) in addition to the principle of territoriality. As with other aspects of the distinction between common law and civil law systems, however, the treatment of jurisdiction in both systems turns out to bear a remarkable resemblance, even if each may have arrived at its current position from different starting points.

Today, territoriality is generally cited as the central principle of criminal jurisdiction in both common law and civil law systems. Just what this means, however, is another question, since—as we will see—territoriality tends to be given such a broad—and expansive—interpretation that it may be difficult to distinguish it, in the end, from other traditional bases of criminal jurisdiction: active and passive personality (turning on the citizenship of the alleged offender or victim, respectively), the protective principle (focusing on the act's impact on interests of the state seeking to extends its jurisdiction to it), and the universality principle (attaching to the nature of the act as an offense against the worldwide community, and therefore to be punished even if it was not committed on the punishing state's territory, nor committed by one of its citizens, nor against one of its citizens or one of its domestic interests).

United States v. Rodriguez
U.S. District Court for the Southern District of California
182 F. Supp. 479 (S.D. Cal. 1960)

The present case raises this question: May aliens, found within the United States, be prosecuted here for the commission of crimes allegedly committed outside the territorial limits of the United States, when the crimes charged concern the use of false statements to secure the documents necessary for admission into the United States?

[The defendants are charged with making false statements in an immigration application, in violation of 18 U.S.C. § 1546 ("fraud and misuse of visas, permits, and other documents"), for trying to obtain immigrant visas at American consulates and embassies abroad on the basis of sham marriages with American citizens.]

A Harvard research project, Research in International Law, considered various problems of international criminal jurisdiction, reporting its conclusions in 1935 (see Research on International law, Part II, Jurisdiction with Respect to Crime, 29 Am. J. Int'l L. Supp. 435 (1935)). The reporter for that portion of the project, Professor E. D. Dickinson, summarized their findings concerning five general principles of international jurisdiction:

> These five general principles are: first, the territorial principle, determining jurisdiction by reference to the place where the offence is committed; second, the nationality principle, determining jurisdiction by reference to the nationality or national character of the person committing the offence; third, the protective principle, determining jurisdiction by reference to the national interest injured by the offence; fourth, the universality principle, determining jurisdiction by reference to the custody of the person committing the offence; and fifth, the passive personality principle, determining jurisdiction by reference to the nationality or national character of the

person injured by the offence. Of these five principles, the first is everywhere regarded as of primary importance and of fundamental character ... The third is claimed by most states, regarded with misgivings in a few, and generally ranked as the basis of an auxiliary competence.

Id. at 445.

...

The protective principle was codified by the Harvard group in Article 7 of their report:

A state has jurisdiction with respect to any crime committed outside its territory by an alien against the security, territorial integrity or political independence of that state, provided that the act or omission which constitutes the crime was not committed in exercise of a liberty guaranteed the alien by the law of the place where it was committed.

Id. at 543.

It is clear that international law recognizes not only the territorial theory of jurisdiction, but also the protective principle and several others as well. Having these principles in mind, it is now necessary for us to consider their effect upon the potential exercise of jurisdiction by our constitutionally created government.

A state might seek to exercise its jurisdiction in two general localities: First, it can attempt to impose its laws upon those found within its boundaries, holding these persons, whoever they may be, liable for acts committed within or without the territorial limits of the State. Second, the state might seek to control the actions of those physically in some other sovereign nation. . . .

. . . Entry by an alien into the United States secured by means of false statements or documents is an attack directly on the sovereignty of the United States. The effect of such an entry in connection with espionage or subversive activities clearly pinpoints the great impact such an entry could have on sovereignty.

To put it in more general terms, the concept of essential sovereignty of a free nation clearly requires the existence and recognition of an inherent power in the state to protect itself from destruction. This power exists in the United States government absent express provision in the Constitution, and arises from the very nature of the government which was created by the Constitution. . . .

Possessing this power of protection, Congress is entitled to utilize it to the full extent. From the body of international law, the Congress may pick and choose whatever recognized principle of international jurisdiction is necessary to accomplish the purpose sought by the legislation. The mere fact that, in the past, Congress may not have seen fit to embody in legislation the full scope of its authorized powers is not a basis for now finding that those powers are lacking. Disuse, or even misuse of power inherent in the federal government, or given to it by the Constitution, is not a valid basis for us to hold that this power may not later be employed in a proper fashion.

United States v. King
U.S. Court of Appeals for the Ninth Circuit
552 F.2d 833 (9th Cir. 1976)

Appellants King . . . and Powell . . . were both convicted of unlawful distribution in Japan of heroin intended for importation into the United States in violation of 21 U.S.C. § 959 [Manufacture or distribution for purposes of unlawful importation]. Adopted in 1970, the statute is expressly aimed at having extraterritorial effect, but King and Powell protest that its attempted reach exceeds the legislative power vested in Congress by the Constitution.

There is no constitutional bar to the extraterritorial application of penal laws. . . . In upholding statutes with extraterritorial impact, courts have recognized that the territorial concept of jurisdiction is neither exclusive nor a full and accurate characterization of the powers of states to exercise jurisdiction beyond the confines of their geographical boundaries. . . .

Thus, [appellants] have not established that authority under one of the other three principles would not be acceptable. Since both appellants are United States citizens, the nationality principle would apply: American authority over them could be based upon the allegiance they owe this country and its laws if the statute concerned as does § 959, evinces a legislative intent to control actions within and without the United States.

R. v. Stucky
Ontario Court of Appeal
(2009) 303 D.L.R. (4th) 1

The following judgment was delivered by

K.M. Weiler and E.E. Gillese JJ.A.:—

1. Mr. Stucky, a resident of Ontario, operated a direct mail business in Ontario that sold lottery tickets and merchandise only to persons outside of Canada. He was charged with sixteen counts of making false or misleading representations "to the public" between 1995 and 2002 in order to promote his business interests, contrary to s. 52(1) of the *Competition Act*, R.S.C. 1985, c. C-34 (the "Act"). The charges pertained to four direct mail promotions sent primarily to people in the United States, Great Britain, Australia, and New Zealand. The promotions were not mailed to anyone in Canada.

2. Section 52(1) of the Act currently reads as follows:

> No person shall, for the purpose of promoting, directly or indirectly, the supply or use of a product or for the purpose of promoting, directly or indirectly, any business interest, by any means whatever, knowingly or recklessly make a representation *to the public* that is false or misleading in a material respect. [Emphasis added.]

3. The trial judge found Mr. Stucky not guilty of the charges because he held that the phrase "to the public" means "to the *Canadian* public" and none of the mailings were made to persons in Canada.

. . .

24 Based on *Criminal Code* jurisprudence, it is our view that the meaning of "the public" is not restricted to the Canadian public where there is a real and substantial link or connection between the offence and Canada.

. . .

26 [I]n *Libman v. The Queen*, [1985] 2 S.C.R. 178, the accused was charged with seven counts of fraud and one count of conspiracy to commit fraud arising from a telephone solicitation sales scheme operated from Canada, whereby residents in the United States were induced to purchase shares in Central American companies. Purchasers sent money to the Central American countries and, eventually, some of the proceeds returned to Canada. La Forest J., on behalf of the court, began by noting that the presumption against extraterritoriality in criminal law was codified in s. 5(2) (now s. 6(2)) of the *Criminal Code*, R.S.C. 1970, c. C.34, which states that no person "shall be convicted in Canada for an offence committed outside of Canada." However, he concluded that the offences in question had taken place in Canada. The commission of the offences had a real and substantial connection to Canada, in that the scheme was devised in Canada, and the operation and directing minds were situated in Canada. . . .

27 The reasoning La Forest J. followed is equally applicable to this case and may be summarized along these lines: Canada has a legitimate interest in prosecuting persons for unlawful activities that take place abroad when the activities have a "real and substantial link" or connection to Canada. The fact that the only victims are outside of Canada does not make the activity any the less unlawful or mean that no crime has been committed in Canada when there exists "a real and substantial link" or connection to this country. The court must take into consideration all the facts that give Canada an interest in prosecuting the offence and then consider whether international comity would be offended in the circumstances. The principle of extraterritoriality has not prevented courts from taking jurisdiction over transnational offences whose impact is felt within the country. The purpose of criminal law is to protect the public from harm. That purpose is not achieved only by direct means, but also by underlining the fundamental values of our society and, in so doing, reinforcing the law-abiding sentiments of our society. La Forest J. reflected at p. 212 that utilizing a "real and substantial link" approach is necessary in order to reinforce the fundamental values of society:

> It would be a sad commentary on our law if it was limited to underlining society's values by the prosecution of minor offenders while permitting more seasoned practitioners to operate on a world-wide scale from a Canadian base by the simple manipulation of a technicality of the law's own making. What would be underlined in the public's mind by allowing criminals to go free simply because their operations have grown to international proportions, I shall not attempt to expound.

. . .

Canadian Criminal Code

§ 6

. . .

(2) Subject to this Act or any other Act of Parliament, no person shall be convicted . . . of an offence committed outside Canada.

§ 7

. . .

Space Station — Canadian crew members

(2.3) Despite anything in this Act or any other Act, a Canadian crew member who, during a space flight, commits an act or omission outside Canada that if committed in Canada would constitute an indictable offence is deemed to have committed that act or omission in Canada, if that act or omission is committed

(a) on, or in relation to, a flight element of the Space Station; or

(b) on any means of transportation to or from the Space Station.

Space Station — crew members of Partner States

(2.31) Despite anything in this Act or any other Act, a crew member of a Partner State who commits an act or omission outside Canada during a space flight on, or in relation to, a flight element of the Space Station or on any means of transportation to and from the Space Station that if committed in Canada would constitute an indictable offence is deemed to have committed that act or omission in Canada, if that act or omission

(a) threatens the life or security of a Canadian crew member; or

(b) is committed on or in relation to, or damages, a flight element provided by Canada.

. . .

(2.33) No proceedings in relation to an offence referred to in subsection (2.3) or (2.31) may be instituted without the consent of the Attorney General of Canada.

Extraterritorial Criminal Jurisdiction (Canada)*

1. Overview

Every state assumes jurisdiction over the prosecution and punishment of crimes committed within its borders (the territorial principle of jurisdiction).

In addition, states generally assert some criminal jurisdiction over at least certain of their nationals when they commit crimes abroad (the active personality principle of jurisdiction). States' global criminal jurisdiction over their military personnel is a common example of this. Some states—particularly, many continental European states—exercise general extraterritorial criminal jurisdiction over all their citizens.

States sometimes assert extraterritorial jurisdiction in cases where one of its nationals is the victim of a crime (the passive personality principle of jurisdiction). However, this basis of jurisdiction is less common than either the territorial principle or the active personality principle.

For states such as Canada, whose criminal law is based on English law, the territorial principle of jurisdiction is the rule and extraterritorial jurisdiction is the exception. Section 6(2) of the Canadian *Criminal Code* provides that, subject to the Code or other federal legislation to the contrary, no person may be convicted of an offence committed outside Canada. However, even for states such as Canada, which favour the territorial principle, there has been a progressive increase in assertions of extraterritorial criminal jurisdiction to deal with international and trans-national crime, often pursuant to international treaty commitments.

2. Canadian Extraterritorial Jurisdiction

Canadian law currently provides for general extraterritorial jurisdiction in the following contexts:

Context	Legislative Provision
Offences committed by Canadian military personnel and other persons subject to the Code of Service Discipline.	*National Defence Act*, ss. 67, 130, 132
Any indictable offence committed by a Canadian federal public servant.	*Criminal Code*, s. 7(4)
Any indictable offence committed on or in respect of Canadian aircraft.	*Criminal Code*, s. 7(1)(a)
Any indictable offence committed on an aircraft in flight where the aircraft lands in Canada.	*Criminal Code*, s. 7(1)(b)
Various offences pertaining to Canada's exclusive economic zone or continental shelf.	*Criminal Code*, s. 477.1(a) and (b)

---

* [*Source*: David Goetz, "International Criminal Law," Law & Gov. Div., PRB 01-17E (2001), Government of Canada—Eds.]

Offences committed in the course of "hot pursuit" from Canada.	*Criminal Code*, s. 477.1(d)
Any offence committed by a Canadian citizen which is outside the territory of any state.	*Criminal Code*, s. 477.1(e)
Any indictable offence committed during a space flight in connection with the Civil International Space Station by a Canadian crew member.	*Criminal Code*, s. 7(2.3)
Any indictable offence committed during a space flight in connection with the Civil International Space Station by a non-Canadian crew member: against a Canadian crew member; or on, or in relation to, a Canadian flight element of the Space Station.	*Criminal Code*, s. 7(2.31)

Canada also asserts specific extraterritorial jurisdiction over the following offences where there is some specified nexus between Canada and the offender, the victim or intended victim, or the circumstances of the offence:

Offence	*Legislative Provision*
High treason or treason against Canada	*Criminal Code*, s. 46(3)
Piracy	*Criminal Code*, s. 74 & 75
Forgery or fraud in relation to Canadian passports	*Criminal Code*, s. 57
Fraudulent use of Canadian citizenship certificate	*Criminal Code*, s. 58
Bigamy	*Criminal Code*, s. 290
Hijacking or endangering the safety of an aircraft or airport	*Criminal Code*, s. 7(2)
Seizing control, or endangering the safety of, a ship or fixed platform at sea	*Criminal Code*, ss. 7(2.1) & (2.2)
Various offences directed against "internationally protected persons" (i.e., various national and international officials and their families)	*Criminal Code*, s. 7(3)
Hostage taking	*Criminal Code*, s. 7(3.1)
Various offences involving nuclear material	*Criminal Code*, s. 7(3.2), (3.3), 3.4)
Torture	*Criminal Code*, s. 7(3.7)
Genocide	*Crimes Against Humanity and War Crimes Act*, ss. 6 & 8
Crimes against humanity	*Crimes Against Humanity and War Crimes Act*, ss. 6 & 8
War crimes	*Crimes Against Humanity and War Crimes Act*, ss. 6 & 8
Breach of command responsibility in relation to genocide, a crime against humanity or a war crime	*Crimes Against Humanity and War Crimes Act*, ss. 7 & 8
Various sexual offences against children	*Criminal Code*, s. 7(4.1)
Conspiracy to commit an offence	*Criminal Code*, s. 465(3) & (4)

German Criminal Code

§ 3 (Applicability for Domestic Offenses)

German criminal law applies to acts committed on German territory.

§ 4 (Applicability for offenses committed on German Ships and Aircrafts)

German criminal law applies, regardless of the law applicable in the place where the act was committed, to acts committed on a ship or an aircraft entitled to carry the federal flag or the national insignia of the Federal Republic of Germany.

§ 5 (Offenses Committed Abroad against Domestic Legal Goods)

German criminal law applies, regardless of the law applicable in the place where the act was committed, to the following acts committed abroad:

1. preparation of a war of aggression (§ 80);
2. high treason against the Federation (§§ 81 to 83);
3. endangering the democratic state under the rule of law
   (a) in cases under § 89 and § 90a para. 1, and § 90b, if the offender is German and has his center of existence in the territory of the Federal Republic of Germany; and
   (b) in cases under § 90 and § 90a para. 2;
4. treason and endangering external national security (§§ 94 to 100a);
5. offenses against the national defense:
   (a) in cases under § 109 and §§ 109e to 109g; and
   (b) in cases under § 109a, § 109d and § 109h, if the offender is German and has his center of existence in the territory of the Federal Republic of Germany
6. causing the danger of political persecution (§ 234a, § 241a) if the act is directed against a German who has his domicile or usual residence in Germany;
6a abduction of minors in cases under § 235 para. 2 no. 2, if the act is directed against a person who has his domicile or usual residence in Germany;
7. violation of business or trade secrets of a business physically located within the territory of the Federal Republic of Germany, or of an enterprise, which has its seat there, or of an enterprise with its seat abroad and which is dependent on an enterprise with its seat within the territory of the Federal Republic of Germany and which forms a group with the latter;
8. offenses against sexual self-determination:
   (a) in cases under § 174 para. 1 and 3, if the offender and the victim are German at the time of the offense and have their center of existence in the territory of the Federal Republic of Germany; and
   (b) in cases under §§ 176 to 176b and § 182, if the offender is German;
9. abortion (§ 218), if the offender at the time of the offense is German and has his center of existence in the territory of the Federal Republic of Germany;
10. false testimony, perjury and false sworn affidavits (§§ 153 to 156) in proceedings before a court or another German authority within the territory of the Federal Republic of Germany that has the authority to administer oaths or affirmations instead of oath;
11. offenses against the environment under § 324, § 326, § 330 and § 330a committed within Germany's exclusive economic zone, to the extent that international conventions on the protection of the sea allow for their prosecution as criminal offenses;
11a offenses under § 328 para. 2 no. 3 and 4, para. 4 and 5, also in conjunction with § 330, if the offender is German at the time of the offense;
12. offenses committed by a German public official or a person entrusted with special public service functions during their official stay or in connection with their official duties;
13. acts committed by a foreigner as a public official or as a person entrusted with special public service functions;
14. acts committed against public officials, persons entrusted with special public service functions, or soldiers in the Armed Forces during the execution of their duties or in connection with their duties;
14a bribing delegates (§ 108e) if the offender is German at the time of the offense or the offense was committed vis-à-vis a German;
15. trafficking in human organs (§ 18 of the Transplantation Act), if the offender is German at the time of the offense.

§ 6 (Offenses committed abroad against Internationally Protected Legal Goods)

German criminal law applies further, regardless of the law of the place where they are committed, to the following offenses committed abroad:

1. (repealed); [This concerned offenses like crimes against humanity, war crimes etc.; in 2002, these were shifted to the new German International Criminal Law Code which in § 1 claims universal jurisdiction.–Eds.]
2. offenses involving nuclear energy, explosives and radiation under § 307 and § 308 para. 1 to 4, § 309 para. 2 and § 310;

3. attacks on air and maritime traffic (§ 316c);
4. human trafficking for the purpose of sexual exploitation, for the purpose of work exploitation and assisting human trafficking (§§232 to 233a);
5. unlawful drug dealing;
6. distribution of pornography under §§ 184a, 184b para. 1 to 3, and § 184c para. 1 to 3, also in conjunction with § 184d sentence 1;
7. counterfeiting money and securities (§ 146, § 151 and § 152), credit cards and blank eurocheques (§ 152b para. 1 to 4,) as well as the relevant preparatory acts (§§ 149, 151, 152 and 152b para. 5);
8. subsidy fraud (§ 264);
9. offenses which on the basis of an international agreement binding on the Federal Republic of Germany must be prosecuted even though committed abroad.

§ 7 (Offenses committed Abroad in Other Cases)

(1) German criminal law applies to offenses committed abroad against a German, if the act is a criminal offense at the place of its commission or if that place is not subject to any criminal jurisdiction.

(2) German criminal law applies to other offenses committed abroad if the act is a criminal offense at the place of its commission or if that place is not subject to any criminal law jurisdiction, and if the offender:
1. was German at the time of the offense or became German after the commission; or
2. was a foreigner at the time of the offense, is discovered in Germany and, although extradition law would permit extradition for such an offense, is not extradited because a request for extradition within a reasonable period of time is not made, is rejected, or the extradition is not feasible.

§ 8 (Time of the Offense)

An offense is committed at the time when the principal or the participants acted, or, in the case of an omission, should have acted. The time when the result occurs is irrelevant.

§ 9 (Place of the Offense)

(1) An offense is committed in every place where the offender acted or, in the case of an omission, should have acted, or in which the result which is an element of the offense occurs or should have occurred according to the intention of the offender.

(2) Acts of participation are committed not only in the place where the offense was committed, but also in every place where the participant acted or, in the case of an omission, should have acted or where, according to his intention, the offense should have been committed. If the participant to an offense committed abroad acted within the territory of the Federal Republic of Germany, German criminal law applies to the participation even though the act is not a criminal offense according to the law of the locality of its commission.

NOTES

1. The backbone of national laws concerning criminal jurisdiction is the territoriality principle: states claim the right not only to enact, but also to enforce, criminal norms with respect to any act that occurs on their territory. The territoriality principle is firmly entrenched in common law systems, as well as in the German Criminal Code, § 3 StGB.

The application of the territoriality principle to particular cases has occupied courts for some time. Beyond the core cases where it is obvious that the crucial act (for instance, stabbing another person with a knife) was committed within the state's territory, there are more difficult legal questions such as what counts as an act in the first place, or how to decide if an act and its effects occurred within the same territory (for instance, if the offender sends a bomb to another country where it explodes). For the latter case, the German law contains a rule in § 9 para. 1 StGB: an offense is committed either where the agent acted or where the effects took place. Also, this norm declares that an omission is committed wherever the agent should have acted.

English criminal courts in particular have developed a rich, even interesting, jurisprudence over the centuries, in an effort to determine whether or not a given act fell under the territoriality principle and was therefore subject to English criminal jurisdiction, an inquiry often further complicated by the existence of international treaties governing conduct beyond the territorial jurisdiction of any sovereign, on the high seas.*

2. The internet age poses new questions, as an agent can physically act (add content to the internet) from a foreign country and use a server for data storage that does not fall within a given state's territory—but can make content accessible to any internet user in that country, and elsewhere.† Is it sufficient that readers or viewers sitting in front of a screen in Germany, say, can access content created and stored anywhere in the world for German courts to claim jurisdiction, and to apply German criminal law? The German Federal Court of Justice had to decide about this in the *Töben Case* (Chapter 17.A.).

The German Court in *Töben* held that the territoriality principle (by itself) covered the defendant's conduct, on the ground that the conduct's results occurred (also) in Germany. For a similar argument, see the following "Statement on Internet Jurisdiction" by the Minnesota Attorney General:

STATEMENT OF MINNESOTA ATTORNEY GENERAL ON INTERNET JURISDICTION

WARNING TO ALL INTERNET USERS AND PROVIDERS

THIS MEMORANDUM SETS FORTH THE ENFORCEMENT POSITION OF THE MINNESOTA ATTORNEY GENERAL'S OFFICE WITH RESPECT TO CERTAIN ILLEGAL ACTIVITIES ON THE INTERNET.

PERSONS OUTSIDE OF MINNESOTA WHO TRANSMIT INFORMATION VIA THE INTERNET KNOWING THAT INFORMATION WILL BE DISSEMINATED IN MINNESOTA ARE SUBJECT TO JURISDICTION IN MINNESOTA COURTS FOR VIOLATIONS OF STATE CRIMINAL AND CIVIL LAWS.

The following discussion sets out the legal basis for this conclusion. Minnesota's general criminal jurisdiction statute provides as follows:

A person may be convicted and sentenced under the law of this State if the person:
(1) Commits an offense in whole or in part within this state; or
(2) Being without the state, causes, aids or abets another to commit a crime within the state; or
(3) Being without the state, intentionally causes a result within the state prohibited by the criminal laws of this state.
It is not a defense that the defendant's conduct is also a criminal offense under the laws of another state or of the United States or of another country.

Minnesota Statute § 609.025.

This statute has been interpreted by the Minnesota Supreme Court. In *State v. Rossbach*, 288 N.W.2d 714 (Minn. 1980), the defendant appealed his conviction for aggravated assault. The defendant, standing inside the border of an Indian Reservation, had fired a rifle across the boundary line at a person outside the border. The defendant claimed that Minnesota courts did not have jurisdiction because his act took place off of Minnesota lands. Applying Minnesota Statute § 609.025 and the common law, the Minnesota Supreme Court affirmed the conviction, holding that the intentional impact within Minnesota land created jurisdiction....

The above principles of Minnesota law apply equally to activities on the Internet. Individuals and organizations outside of Minnesota who disseminate information in Minnesota via the Internet and thereby cause a result to occur in Minnesota are subject to state criminal ... laws.

---

* For a discussion of this jurisprudence in historical and theoretical context, see Lindsay Farmer, "Jurisdiction and Criminalization," 63 *University of Toronto Law Journal* (2013), 225; for a contemporary account of the doctrine in action, see Michael Hirst, *Jurisdiction and the Ambit of the Criminal Law* (2003).

† See generally Mireille Hildebrandt, "Extraterritorial Jurisdiction to Enforce in Cyberspace: Bodin, Schmitt, Grotius in Cyberspace," 63 *University of Toronto Law Journal* (2013), 196.

An Example of Illegal Activity on the Internet: Gambling

Gambling appears to be an especially prominent aspect of criminal activity on the Internet. There are a number of services outside of Minnesota that offer Minnesota residents the opportunity to place bets on sporting events, purchase lottery tickets, and participate in simulated casino games. These services are illegal in Minnesota. . . .

Gambling is just one example of illegal activity on the Internet. However, the same jurisdictional principles apply with equal force to any illegal activity.*

Does this interpretation of territoriality strain the principle "to the breaking point"?†

3. The extension of the territoriality principle is particularly tempting in criminal law systems that, unlike Germany, recognize no other basis of criminal law jurisdiction. Canada is an example. Note how the Canadian Criminal Code, rather than citing alternative theories of criminal jurisdiction, retains the exclusive commitment to territoriality (in Can. Crim. Code § 6(2)), but then uses "deeming" provisions to reach conduct considerably beyond Canadian territory, including acts committed on an international space station, either by Canadians, or by others against Canadians or "a flight element provided by Canada" (§ 7(2.3) and (2.31)).

The Canadian Supreme Court took another step in *R. v. Libman*, when it recognized criminal jurisdiction on the basis of a "real and substantial link or connection" between the act and Canada, applied by the Ontario Court of Appeal in *R. v. Stucky*. Is this still consistent with an exclusive commitment to territoriality?

4. The more complex the organization of the nation states involved, the more complex questions of jurisdiction can become. If states with a federal system enact or enforce criminal laws, several questions arise: first, how to decide if several states within the same system could claim jurisdiction; second, how to decide on the relationship between a system as a whole and foreign countries. For the states that constitute the United States, it makes sense to delineate jurisdiction carefully because each state enforces its own criminal law, presumably relying on the territoriality principle. In Germany, the questions of which prosecution office and which local or regional court takes control are considered less important. The goal is uniform enforcement of the federal criminal law (both the German Criminal Code and the Code of Criminal Procedure are federal laws‡). German states do not in general strive to assert cultural or political identity in this area. Therefore, for practical reasons, there are rules about this matter (which can be found in §§ 7–21 Code of Criminal Procedure). But they reflect the need to find a feasible modus operandi, not an ambition to resolve claims made by several states.

In the United States, the applicability of a particularly state's criminal law is not a matter of prosecutorial coordination, but of the enforcement of sovereignty. It is, in other words, a matter of jurisdiction, as opposed to a matter of venue—where jurisdiction here concerns the applicability of a body of law and venue the application of that body of law by a particular court (though these terms are not always used consistently).§ In contrast, the question whether one federal district court or another adjudicates a federal offense is a matter of venue, not jurisdiction, as is the question of whether one county or another adjudicates a state offense.

But, since each state is a sovereign with a separate, independent, right to enforce its criminal law, state jurisdiction is not an exclusive affair: several states can have and exercise

---

* [<http://cyber.law.harvard.edu/ilaw/Jurisdiction/Minnesota_Full.html>—Eds.]

† Compare *People v. Werblow*, 241 N.Y. 55 (1925) (Cardozo, J.) (rejecting invitation to extend New York state law under a "territorial" jurisdiction theory to an alleged conspiracy "if only some overt act can be found to have been here committed in furtherance of the conspiracy, even though the act is not a constituent" of the consummated object offense, in this case a bank theft committed in London, England).

‡ See Chapter 5.A.

§ Compare N.Y. Crim. Proc. L. § 20.20 with § 20.40; see generally Glanville Williams, "Venue and the Ambit of Criminal Law," 81 *Law Quarterly Review* (1965), 276–88, 395–421, 518–38 (1965).

jurisdiction over a given act. So, theoretically at least, a person can be punished twice (or more often) for the same act, without running afoul of the federal constitutional double jeopardy prohibition (*ne bis in idem*), which—in the Fifth Amendment—provides that no one shall "be subject for the same offense to be twice put in jeopardy of life or limb." (Under German law, this would be impossible. Even if a crime had effects both in, say, Lower Saxony and Bavaria, a criminal judgment in one state would preclude prosecution for the same acts in the other, due to the double jeopardy prohibition (art. 103 para. 3 Basic Law). Note that in Germany the states are not just administrative units, but they do have powers of sovereignty—but not in the area of passing criminal laws (this right is reserved for the Federal Republic*).) According to the dual sovereignty doctrine set out in *Heath v. Alabama*, 474 U.S. 82, 88–90 (1985), one act can amount to more than one "offense" insofar as it offends more than one sovereign:

> The dual sovereignty doctrine is founded on the common law conception of crime as an offense against the sovereignty of the government. When a defendant in a single act violates the "peace and dignity" of two sovereigns by breaking the laws of each, he has committed two distinct "offences." As the Court explained in *Moore v. Illinois*, 14 How. 13, 19 (1852), "[a]n offence, in its legal signification, means the transgression of a law." Consequently, when the same act transgresses the laws of two sovereigns, "it cannot be truly averred that the offender has been twice punished for the same offence; but only that by one act he has committed two offences, for each of which he is justly punishable."
>
> In applying the dual sovereignty doctrine, then, the crucial determination is whether the two entities that seek successively to prosecute a defendant for the same course of conduct can be termed separate sovereigns. This determination turns on whether the two entities draw their authority to punish the offender from distinct sources of power. Thus, the Court has uniformly held that the States are separate sovereigns with respect to the Federal Government because each State's power to prosecute is derived from its own "inherent sovereignty," not from the Federal Government....
>
> The States are no less sovereign with respect to each other than they are with respect to the Federal Government. Their powers to undertake criminal prosecutions derive from separate and independent sources of power and authority originally belonging to them before admission to the Union....

Under the dual sovereignty doctrine, of course, it is also theoretically—and constitutionally— possible for one act to give rise to criminal prosecutions under state and federal law, since the federal government can also claim sovereign status, not just externally vis-à-vis other countries, but also internally, vis-à-vis the states. The exercise of federal criminal jurisdiction, however, is a matter of discretion and subject to flexible guidelines. For instance, the U.S. Department of Justice's so-called *Petite* Policy (named after the U.S. Supreme Court case of *Petite v. United States*, 361 U.S. 529 (1960)), "precludes" a successive federal prosecution for "substantially the same act(s) or transactions" unless the following require-ments are met:

> first, the matter must involve a substantial federal interest; second, the prior prosecution must have left that interest demonstrably unvindicated; and third, applying the same test that is applicable to all federal prosecutions, the government must believe that the defendant's conduct constitutes a federal offense, and that the admissible evidence probably will be sufficient to obtain and sustain a conviction by an unbiased trier of fact. In addition, there is a procedural prerequisite to be satisfied, that is, the prosecution must be approved by the appropriate Assistant Attorney General.
>
> United States Attorneys' Manual § 9-2.031

More generally, the same U.S. Attorneys' Manual sets out general "Grounds for Commen-cing or Declining Prosecution":

> The attorney for the government should commence or recommend Federal prosecution if he/ she believes that the person's conduct constitutes a Federal offense and that the admissible

---

* See Basic Law art. 74 para. 1 no. 1.

evidence will probably be sufficient to obtain and sustain a conviction, unless, in his/her judgment, prosecution should be declined because:
1. No substantial Federal interest would be served by prosecution;
2. The person is subject to effective prosecution in another jurisdiction; or
3. There exists an adequate non-criminal alternative to prosecution.

§ 9-27.220(A)

Interesting questions of internal criminal jurisdiction tend to come up not in the context of the relationship between the federal government and the states, but of that between the federal government and Indian tribes. While there is no doubt that the federal government and the states are independent sovereigns, and therefore that questions of jurisdiction must be resolved as between sovereigns, the sovereignty of Indian tribes is contested, and evolving.*

5. If one turns to the relationship among national states again, the territoriality principle often is regarded as too narrow. It applies to ships and aircraft (see § 4 StGB) but also is extended in other more important ways. A state's claim to jurisdiction can be broadened by declaring its criminal law applicable to acts committed abroad by evoking one of the following principles: the principle of nationality or active personality principle; the passive personality principle; protection of a state's public interests; or the principle of universal jurisdiction. German law recognizes the active personality principle, which emphasizes offenders' German nationality, and the passive personality principle (German citizens as victims) in § 7 StGB, with the restriction that the act in question must be a criminal act at the location of its commission. Also, some crimes are classified as touching upon national public interests even if the act in question occurred abroad. That is the rationale behind § 5 StGB, see for instance "preparation of war" (§ 5 nr. 1) or the false testimony of witnesses that were questioned in their home country to give evidence for a German trial (§ 5 Nr. 10).

Which reasons might be cited in favor of extending a state's criminal jurisdiction beyond the territoriality principle? What does a strong emphasis on the active or passive personality principle imply about the relationship between a state and its citizens, about duties of the state to protect and duties of citizens as representatives of their country when abroad?[†]

In thinking about the foundations of criminal jurisdictions, consider an(other) alternative conception of jurisdiction, one not based on territory, but on group membership: military criminal law.

United States Uniform Code of Military Justice

Art. 2. Persons subject to this chapter

(a) The following persons are subject to this chapter:
   (1) Members of a regular component of the armed forces . . . ; volunteers . . . ; inductees . . . ; and other persons lawfully called or ordered into, or to duty in or for training in, the armed forces. . . .

Art. 5. Territorial applicability of this chapter

This chapter applies in all places.

Can. National Defence Act
Code of Service Discipline

Persons subject to Code of Service Discipline:

60. (1) The following persons are subject to the Code of Service Discipline:
   (a) an officer or non-commissioned member of the regular force; . . .

---

* See, e.g., *United States v. Lara*, 541 U.S. 193 (2004).
† See generally Markus D. Dubber, "Criminal Jurisdiction and Conceptions of Penality in Comparative Perspective," 63 *University of Toronto Law Journal* (2013), 247; Michael Pawlik, "Strafe oder Gefahrenbekämpfung?: Die Prinzipien des deutschen Internationalen Strafrechts vor dem Forum der Straftheorie," 7 *Zeitschrift für Internationale Strafrechtsdogmatik* (2006), 274.

Place of Commission of Offence

Service offence, wherever committed, is triable

67. [E]very person alleged to have committed a service offence may be charged, dealt with and tried under the Code of Service Discipline, whether the alleged offence was committed in Canada or outside Canada.

German Military Criminal Law Act
(Wehrstrafgesetz, WStG)

§ 1 Jurisdiction

(1) This statute applies to criminal acts committed by soldiers of the German armed forces (*Bundeswehr*). . . .

§ 1a Acts Abroad

(1) German criminal law applies, regardless of the law of the place of the act, for acts that this statute threatens with punishment and are committed abroad, if the perpetrator
1. Is a soldier . . .

Does greater reliance on the personality principle (active or passive? both? based on nationality or based on a person's close relationship to the state such as being member of the military?) reflect a more communitarian conception of law in general, and of criminal law in particular? Consider in this context also the recent history of the law of criminal jurisdiction in Germany, which fluctuated between territoriality and personality throughout the nineteenth and twentieth centuries, most recently returning to the territoriality principle, in 1975, after thirty-five years under the personality principle.*

6. The most controversial extension beyond the territoriality principle is the principle of universal jurisdiction. It is based on the claim that certain types of crime affect all states because they often are committed across borders or indiscriminately against any state, or because of their particular seriousness. Paradigm cases include piracy (this is covered by § 6 no. 2 StGB), as pirates in international waters tend to attack regardless of the vessel's nationality, and crimes against humanity (previously § 6 no. 1 StGB, now § 7 German Code on International Criminal Law (VStGB)).

Although Germany is by no means alone in asserting universal jurisdiction, German law is rather broad here: it claims, for instance, universal jurisdiction for any act of unlawful drug dealing anywhere in the world. What do you think about such broad claims, and what could be an appropriate notion of "universal jurisdiction"? Is there a relevant distinction here between offenses such as drug dealing or subsidy fraud (§ 6 no. 8 StGB), on the one hand, and the offenses now covered in the German Code on International Criminal Law (genocide, § 6 VStGB; crimes against humanity, § 7; war crimes, §§ 8–12), and those listed in the 2001 Princeton Principles on Universal Jurisdiction (piracy; slavery; war crimes; crimes against peace; crimes against humanity; genocide; torture)? If there is such a distinction, is one type of offense more appropriately subjected to universal jurisdiction than the other?

If we leave aside offenses like drug dealing and subsidy fraud, is there something troubling about turning the power of criminal punishment on the *hostis humani generis*, the enemy of mankind, the universal outlaw, expressions historically associated with the pirate? For a common passage denouncing piracy, see William Blackstone, Commentaries on the Laws of England, vol. 4, at 71 (1769):

[T]he crime of *piracy,* or robbery and depredation upon the high seas, is an offence against the universal law of society; a pirate being, according to Sir Edward Coke, *hostis humani generis.* As therefore he has renounced all the benefits of society and government, and has reduced himself afresh to the savage state of nature by declaring war against all mankind, all mankind

---

* See German Criminal Code (1940) § 3 ("German criminal law applies to the act of a German national whether or not he commits it in Germany or a foreign country."); see generally Markus D. Dubber, "Criminal Jurisdiction and Conceptions of Penality in Comparative Perspective," 63 *University of Toronto Law Journal* (2013), 247.

must declare war against him: so that every community hath a right, by the rule of self-defence, to inflict that punishment upon him which every individual would in a state of nature have been otherwise entitled to do, for any invasion of his person or personal property.

Is the identification and prosecution of acts of "such a heinous nature as to warrant the application of universal jurisdiction," in the language of the Princeton Principles, a step toward the global triumph of legality over impunity or a move in the opposite direction, away from the realm of law and toward the creation of a realm of global outlawry?

Might it be useful here to draw another distinction, between the issue of universal jurisdiction in general and of universal jurisdiction in particular? Or, more specifically, between the universal jurisdiction of an international tribunal, on the one hand, and of a domestic tribunal, on the other? Might one conclude, say, that the idea of a universal crime made sense—theoretically—without also thinking that the courts of a(ny) particular state, applying that state's substantive and procedural law, should be in the business of adjudicating cases based on the accusation that a universal crime has been committed?

The first question—about the possibility of universal crime—goes to the heart of the notion of international criminal law, which is not concerned with conduct that is a crime in the traditional sense of giving "offense" to a sovereign through disobedience of its commands backed by the threat of criminal sanction. For this reason—at least for those who insist on a sovereignty-based conception of law in general, and of criminal law in particular—an international "crime" appears at best as the violation of a universal *moral* norm, and therefore not properly subject to any form of *juris*diction. But even if one accepts the notion of a universal crime as a legal concept, should its adjudication be entrusted to a universal court, one presumably beyond the institutional, political, and generally parochial limitations inherent in any domestic legal system?

PROCEDURAL CONTEXTS

Some sense of the procedural and institutional framework is helpful in making sense of the norms of substantive criminal law that operate within this framework and that are the subject of the present book. This is true for the study of a given domestic criminal law system and doubly true of a comparative study; it is perhaps triply true of the present comparative study of systems that reflect differing conceptions of the relationship between substantive and procedural norms, and of the priority among them. (In the United States, procedural criminal law has attracted the bulk of scholarly, and judicial, attention; in Germany, it is the other way around.) Of course, the comparative analysis of procedural criminal law is also interesting in its own right. Even a moderately close comparative look at criminal procedure draws into question the usefulness, never mind the accuracy, of the traditional distinction between adversarial and inquisitorial systems as reflected in the Anglo-American and the German criminal process, respectively.* As in the case of substantive criminal law, this is not to say that significant differences do not remain after one moves beneath a general level of analysis. The principle of compulsory prosecution, for instance, has no analog in Anglo-American criminal procedure, even after one takes account of the countervailing opportunity principle in the German Code of Criminal Procedure. Likewise, even after one acknowledges the existence of bargained outcomes in the German criminal process, important differences between bargaining in the context of the American and the German criminal process remain.

A. Criminal Justice in a Federal System

The Federal Republic of Germany consists of sixteen states (*Länder*). Each state has its parliament, as does the Federal Republic (the *Bundestag*). Federal legislation dominates in the area of criminal law. Both the Criminal Code and the Code of Criminal Procedure are federal laws. This was different until the late nineteenth century, but the creation of a German nation state (*Deutsches Reich*) in 1871 also meant that major statutes, among them the Criminal Code and the Code of Criminal Procedure, were introduced as federal legislation to promote unity. The German Criminal Code was enacted in 1871, and the German Code of Criminal Procedure in 1877. (The German Civil Code, the *Bürgerliches Gesetzbuch*, did not come into force until 1900.) The German Criminal Code was based closely on the criminal code of the North German Federation of 1870, which in turn was derived from the criminal code of the most powerful German state, the Prussian Criminal Code of 1851. The Bavarian Criminal Code of 1813 (drafted by P.J.A. Feuerbach)[†] is generally considered the first modern German criminal code.

---

* See, for instance, the debate about the treatment of defense attorneys' fees under money laundering statutes, Chapter 17.C.

[†] On Feuerbach, see Chapter 2; see generally Tatjana Hörnle, "Paul Johann Anselm von Feuerbach and His Impact on Contemporary Criminal Law Theory," in Markus D. Dubber (ed.), *Foundational Texts in Modern Criminal Law* (forthcoming 2014).

The criminal courts in Germany apply the same (federal) Criminal Code and Code of Criminal Procedure, but they are (with the exception of the Federal Court of Justice) organized by the sixteen states, and only by the states. Unlike in the U.S., there is no side-by-side of state court systems and a federal court system. Only the Federal Court of Justice (*Bundesgerichtshof*), which only decides about appeals in law in serious cases, is a federal court. Occasionally, but not very often, the German Federal Constitutional Court (*Bundes-verfassungsgericht*) will hear a case that originated in a criminal court. But the Constitutional Court emphasizes that it is not an additional appellate court. Its task is not to determine the correct interpretation of the Criminal Code or the Code of Criminal Procedure but only to decide if constitutional norms and principles have been misinterpreted or violated.

Until recently, a federal statute (the Prison Act, *Strafvollzugsgesetz*) laid down the fundamental principles for corrections. However, in 2006, the federal system was reorganized. Since then, it is up to the sixteen states to pass prison law codes.

In the United States, the vast bulk of criminal cases are state cases, dealing with state crimes investigated by state police officers, prosecuted by state prosecutors (often called district attorneys, who run the prosecutor's office in a district, and assistant district attorneys, who litigate cases), adjudicated by state judges (who, like district attorneys, often are elected), and juries (drawn from the district, who are selected for each trial, with input from both parties), resulting (upon conviction) in criminal sentences to be served in state prisons (staffed by state prison wardens and guards) or under the supervision of state probation or parole officers.

Each state is an independent sovereign, which has ceded some rights to the federal government, enumerated in the federal constitution; as such, each state has the power to criminalize, based on its broad power to police.* There are state trial courts, appellate courts from intermediate to the highest court in the state (often called Supreme Court, as in California Supreme Court†). The highest court in the state is the final instance on all matters of state law, including state criminal law and state *constitutional* law (every state will also have a separate state constitution).

The federal government does not have a police power, and must rely on the powers enumerated in the federal constitution in all matters, including matters of criminal law; much of federal criminal law is said to be an exercise of the federal power to regulate interstate commerce. This explains why federal criminal statutes often read like jurisdictional provisions first, and criminal offense definitions second. So, for instance, the infamous Unabomber, Ted Kaczynski, whose mail bombs killed three people and injured over twenty others across the United States between 1978 and 1995, was charged with "transport[ing] and attempt[ing] to transport . . . *in interstate commerce* an explosive with the knowledge and intent that it would be used to kill, injure and intimidate an individual" (emphasis added).

Federal crimes are handled by federal officials: federal law enforcement (*not* police!) officers (e.g., FBI), federal prosecutors (called U.S. Attorneys, appointed by the President), federal judges (also appointed by the President), federal probation officers (federal parole was abolished with the introduction of the federal sentencing guidelines‡), prison wardens and guards.

The federal court system parallels the state court systems: there are trial courts (district courts, run by district judges—sometimes with the assistance of magistrate courts, run by magistrate judges), intermediate appellate courts (called Courts of Appeals, which generally sit in panels of three judges), and the U.S. Supreme Court. The U.S. Supreme Court is both the highest federal appellate court (it sits atop the federal court hierarchy) and the final arbiter on questions of federal constitutional law.

---

* On the police power, see Chapter 3; see generally Markus D. Dubber, *The Police Power: Patriarchy and the Foundations of American Government* (2005).

† As always in American criminal law, there are exceptions. For instance, the highest court in New York State is the seven-judge New York Court of Appeals; the New York Supreme Court is the ordinary trial court in New York State, with a branch in each of the state's sixty-plus counties.

‡ See Chapter 1.A.iii.

B. Overview of the Criminal Process

Overview of the American Criminal Justice Process*

Law enforcement agencies learn about crime from the reports of victims or other citizens, from discovery by a police officer in the field, from informants, or from investigative and intelligence work.

Once a law enforcement agency has established that a crime has been committed, a suspect must be identified and apprehended for the case to proceed through the system. Sometimes, a suspect is apprehended at the scene; however, identification of a suspect sometimes requires an extensive investigation. Often, no one is identified or apprehended. In some instances, a suspect is arrested and later the police determine that no crime was committed and the suspect is released.

After an arrest, law enforcement agencies present information about the case and about the accused to the prosecutor, who will decide if formal charges will be filed with the court. If no charges are filed, the accused must be released. The prosecutor can also drop charges after making efforts to prosecute (*nolle prosequi*).

A suspect charged with a crime must be taken before a judge or magistrate without unnecessary delay. At the initial appearance, the judge or magistrate informs the accused of the charges and decides whether there is probable cause to detain the accused person. If the offense is not very serious, the determination of guilt and assessment of a penalty may also occur at this stage.

Often, the defense counsel is also assigned at the initial appearance. All suspects prosecuted for serious crimes have a right to be represented by an attorney. If the court determines the suspect is indigent and cannot afford such representation, the court will assign counsel at the public's expense.

A pretrial-release decision may be made at the initial appearance, but may occur at other hearings or may be changed at another time during the process. Pretrial release and bail were traditionally intended to ensure appearance at trial. However, many jurisdictions permit pretrial detention of defendants accused of serious offenses and deemed to be dangerous to prevent them from committing crimes prior to trial.

The court often bases its pretrial decision on information about the defendant's drug use, as well as residence, employment, and family ties. The court may decide to release the accused on his/her own recognizance or into the custody of a third party after the posting of a financial bond or on the promise of satisfying certain conditions such as taking periodic drug tests to ensure drug abstinence.

In many jurisdictions, the initial appearance may be followed by a preliminary hearing. The main function of this hearing is to discover if there is probable cause to believe that the accused committed a known crime within the jurisdiction of the court. If the judge does not find probable cause, the case is dismissed; however, if the judge or magistrate finds probable cause for such a belief, or the accused waives his or her right to a preliminary hearing, the case may be bound over to a grand jury.

A grand jury hears evidence against the accused presented by the prosecutor and decides if there is sufficient evidence to cause the accused to be brought to trial. If the grand jury finds sufficient evidence, it submits to the court an indictment, a written statement of the essential facts of the offense charged against the accused.

Where the grand jury system is used, the grand jury may also investigate criminal activity generally and issue indictments called grand jury originals that initiate criminal cases. These investigations and indictments are often used in drug and conspiracy cases that involve complex organizations. After such an indictment, law enforcement tries to apprehend and arrest the suspects named in the indictment.

Misdemeanor cases and some felony cases proceed by the issuance of an information, a formal, written accusation submitted to the court by a prosecutor. In some jurisdictions, indictments may be required in felony cases. However, the accused may choose to waive a grand jury indictment and, instead, accept service of an information for the crime.

In some jurisdictions, defendants, often those without prior criminal records, may be eligible for diversion from prosecution subject to the completion of specific conditions such as drug treatment. Successful completion of the conditions may result in the dropping of charges or the expunging of the criminal record where the defendant is required to plead guilty prior to the diversion.

---

* [Excerpted from U.S. Bureau of Justice Statistics, Office of Justice Programs, "The Justice System," <http://bjs.ojp.usdoj.gov/content/justsys.cfm#>—Eds.]

Once an indictment or information has been filed with the trial court, the accused is scheduled for arraignment. At the arraignment, the accused is informed of the charges, advised of the rights of criminal defendants, and asked to enter a plea to the charges. Sometimes, a plea of guilty is the result of negotiations between the prosecutor and the defendant.

If the accused pleads guilty or pleads nolo contendere (accepts penalty without admitting guilt), the judge may accept or reject the plea. If the plea is accepted, no trial is held and the offender is sentenced at this proceeding or at a later date. The plea may be rejected and proceed to trial if, for example, the judge believes that the accused may have been coerced.

If the accused pleads not guilty or not guilty by reason of insanity, a date is set for the trial. A person accused of a serious crime is guaranteed a trial by jury. However, the accused may ask for a bench trial where the judge, rather than a jury, serves as the finder of fact. In both instances the prosecution and defense present evidence by questioning witnesses while the judge decides on issues of law. The trial results in acquittal or conviction on the original charges or on lesser included offenses.

After the trial a defendant may request appellate review of the conviction or sentence. In some cases, appeals of convictions are a matter of right; all States with the death penalty provide for automatic appeal of cases involving a death sentence. Appeals may be subject to the discretion of the appellate court and may be granted only on acceptance of a defendant's petition for a writ of certiorari. Prisoners may also appeal their sentences through civil rights petitions and writs of habeas corpus where they claim unlawful detention.

After a conviction, sentence is imposed. In most cases the judge decides on the sentence, but in some jurisdictions the sentence is decided by the jury, particularly for capital offenses.

In arriving at an appropriate sentence, a sentencing hearing may be held at which evidence of aggravating or mitigating circumstances is considered. In assessing the circumstances surrounding a convicted person's criminal behavior, courts often rely on presentence investigations by probation agencies or other designated authorities. Courts may also consider victim impact statements.

The sentencing choices that may be available to judges and juries include one or more of the following:

- the death penalty
- incarceration in a prison, jail, or other confinement facility
- probation—allowing the convicted person to remain at liberty but subject to certain conditions and restrictions such as drug testing or drug treatment
- fines—primarily applied as penalties in minor offenses
- restitution—requiring the offender to pay compensation to the victim.

In some jurisdictions, offenders may be sentenced to alternatives to incarceration that are considered more severe than straight probation but less severe than a prison term. Examples of such sanctions include boot camps, intense supervision often with drug treatment and testing, house arrest and electronic monitoring, denial of Federal benefits, and community service.

In many jurisdictions, the law mandates that persons convicted of certain types of offenses serve a prison term. Most jurisdictions permit the judge to set the sentence length within certain limits, but some have determinate sentencing laws that stipulate a specific sentence length that must be served and cannot be altered by a parole board.

Offenders sentenced to incarceration usually serve time in a local jail or a State prison. Offenders sentenced to less than 1 year generally go to jail; those sentenced to more than 1 year go to prison. Persons admitted to the Federal system or a State prison system may be held in prisons with varying levels of custody or in a community correctional facility.

A prisoner may become eligible for parole after serving a specific part of his or her sentence. Parole is the conditional release of a prisoner before the prisoner's full sentence has been served. The decision to grant parole is made by an authority such as a parole board, which has power to grant or revoke parole or to discharge a parolee altogether. The way parole decisions are made varies widely among jurisdictions.

Offenders may also be required to serve out their full sentences prior to release (expiration of term). Those sentenced under determinate sentencing laws can be released only after they have served their full sentence (mandatory release) less any "goodtime" received while in prison. Inmates get goodtime credits against their sentences automatically or by earning them through participation in programs.

If released by a parole board decision or by mandatory release, the releasee will be under the supervision of a parole officer in the community for the balance of his or her unexpired sentence. This supervision is governed by specific conditions of release, and the releasee may be returned to prison for violations of such conditions.

Criminal Procedure in Germany: A Brief Overview*

The police register criminal offenses that they have discovered through their own investigations or that have otherwise been made known to them. After the police have processed the case, they pass it on to the Public Prosecution Office. The Public Prosecution Offices are state agencies (with one exception: at the Federal Court of Justice, there is a Federal Prosecution Office). Public prosecution is organized in a hierarchical way within the states: the state's attorney general can issue orders to the state's public prosecutors (in this way, there can be some political pressure in cases of specific public and political interest). As it is "in charge" of the investigation, the Public Prosecution Office may take further steps to clear up the case. The Public Prosecution Office can order coercive measures or apply for their imposition by a judge (seizure of evidence, searches etc.). Pre-trial detention can only be ordered by a judge if the accused is strongly suspected of having committed the crime (i.e. it is very likely that he will be punished), if the detention is not disproportionate to the significance of the case and to the likely punishment, and if there are risks if the accused is not detained, such as the risk of flight or the risk of evidence being tampered with (§ 112 Code of Criminal Procedure [StPO]) or the risk of re-offending (§ 112a German Code of Criminal Procedure). The vast majority of accused are not detained, but this depends on the severity of the crime and the personal circumstances of the accused—in cases of intentional killing, pre-trial detention will be the rule, see § 112 para. 3 German Code of Criminal Procedure. The possibility of bail is recognized in the law (§ 116 para. 1 no. 4 German Code of Criminal Procedure), however, it does not play much of a role in German practice.

The Public Prosecution Office will drop the case if no suspect is found, if the evidence is not sufficient or if it is likely that the suspect is not criminally liable (§ 170 German Code of Criminal Procedure), or if the weight of the offense is of a minor nature (§ 153 German Code of Criminal Procedure). Furthermore, the Public Prosecution Office can terminate the case with the requirement that the accused fulfills certain conditions (§ 153a German Code of Criminal Procedure). These can be financial compensation paid to the victim, payments to the state or a charity, community service or offender–victim mediation. This option for terminating cases is only available for misdemeanors (*Vergehen*) when the minimum statutory penalty is a fine or less than one year imprisonment, not in felony cases (*Verbrechen*) for which the law proscribes a minimum of one year imprisonment. But as a large proportion of the cases to be processed are *Vergehen*, § 153a German Code of Criminal Procedure plays an important role in contemporary case management by the Public Prosecution Office. Another possibility exists for dealing with rather trivial misdemeanors (trespass, minor bodily injury, criminal damage etc.): the Public Prosecution Office can advise that a private prosecution be pursued if there is no public interest (§§ 374–394 German Code of Criminal Procedure). Such private charges are not much used in practice.

In the remaining cases, the Public Prosecution Office applies either for a penal order, which can be issued by a single professional judge at the local court, or it prepares an indictment to commence a criminal trial. In fact, the majority of cases are processed without trial, if not with conditional discharge as just described, then with a penal order (*Strafbefehl*, §§ 407–412 German Code of Criminal Procedure). A penal order will be the option for uncomplicated "run-of-the-mill" cases of lower severity. Beside the fact that is must be a *Vergehen*, there are limits to the sanctions that can be imposed by way of a penal order: either a fine or a suspended term of imprisonment up to one year.

If the Public Prosecution Office hands in an indictment, in the next step the court examines the charge(s) and (usually) commences the main proceedings. The Judiciary Act (*Gerichtsverfassungsgesetz* [GVG]) determines which type of court will hear the case. German law does not know jury trials any more. Until 1924, a jury of twelve jurors (*Geschworene*) had to decide about the conviction in serious cases at the regional courts. These courts were called *Schwurgericht*. Today, the expression *Schwurgericht* still is used for the criminal chamber at the regional court which decides about murder, homicide etc. (see § 74 para. 2 GVG). However, this is merely a historical reminiscence without actual legal significance. Courts consist of professional judges and, in more serious cases, two lay persons will also sit on the judges' bench (they are called *Schöffen*). In courts that include *Schöffen*, they decide together with the professional judges about both conviction and sentencing. The professional judges are not elected but enter the judiciary after their legal training at a rather young age for a life-long career in the judiciary. Selection depends on the grades obtained in two state exams, which follow law school and two years of practical training. Entry into the Public Prosecutor Office is organized in a similar way: not as elected office but according to the grades in the state exams.

---

* [Some of the text is taken, with permission of the author, from Jörg-Martin Jehle, *Criminal Justice in Germany: Facts and Figures* (2009).—Eds.]

If the crime is one where the punishment is not likely to be more than two years' imprisonment, the case will be heard by a single professional judge at the local court (*Amtsrichter*). If imprisonment of between two and four years is likely or the case concerns a felony (*Verbrechen*, with a minimum punishment of a one year prison sentence), one professional judge and two *Schöffen* at the local court will deal with it (*Schöffengericht*). The regional court (*Landgericht*, two or three professional judges and two lay persons as *Schöffen*) is responsible for serious cases: if imprisonment of more than four years or commitment to a psychiatric hospital or to preventive detention is to be expected. There are special juvenile courts for cases against juveniles and young adult offenders.

Some trials end with discharge, without conditions (e.g., because the accused's culpability is of a minor nature and there is no public interest in prosecution) or with a condition being imposed (§§ 153, 153a German Code of Criminal Procedure). Otherwise the trial will end with conviction or (very rarely) acquittal after the evidence has been heard.

Both defendants and the public prosecutor can appeal against judgments. If the local court has decided, the regional court will review the facts of the case. Instead of such an appeal on the facts, it is also possible to lodge an appeal with the Higher Regional Court (*Oberlandesgericht*) on points of law. If the court of first instance was a criminal chamber at the regional court, an appeal can be made only on points of law to the Federal Court of Justice (*Bundesgerichtshof*).

C. Compulsory Prosecution (*Legalitätsprinzip*)

Kenneth Culp Davis,
Administrative Law (2nd edn. 1979), 216–35

The American legal system—federal, state, and local—is shot through with excessive and unnecessary discretionary power in the hands of miscellaneous and diverse administrators of many kinds, but one kind of discretionary power, representing more than half of all unnecessary such power, is the seemingly ever present discretionary power not to enforce . . .

All the regulatory agencies have important power not to enforce—to push a little more or a little less, to be more aggressive or more empathetic, to hold out against pressures for nonenforcement or weak enforcement or to yield to such pressures, to carry out the intent behind the legislation or to allow regulated parties to get the upper hand. Discretion not to enforce is most damaging when it is unevenly exercised from case to case . . .

Whenever an officer properly applies the law to a private party, he is enforcing the law. And, strangely, any officer having such power to enforce almost always (legally or illegally) has discretionary power not to enforce. Even if a statute provides with clarity and force that the officer "shall" or "must" enforce, or that he has a "duty" to enforce, still the vital practical fact usually is that the officer may exercise a discretion not to enforce.

Furthermore, whether the failure to enforce is legal or illegal may often be of no consequence because of lack of authority elsewhere in the system to compel the officer to perform his mandatory duty to enforce . . .

But why should we be concerned with the negative power, the power not to enforce? . . . Discretionary power not to enforce is the power to discriminate.

On the question whether the police have a mandatory duty to enforce the law, the formality of the law (what the statutes say) is at one extreme and the reality of the law (what the officers do) is at the opposite extreme. Furthermore, neither of the two extremes has any effect upon the other . . .

Statutes are quite clear in requiring policemen to arrest for crimes committed in their presence . . . The law is not what the statutes provide, because (a) police nullify the statutes by not arresting, and their superiors do not require them to arrest, (b) legislators who are informed take no action against police nullification of the full enforcement statutes, and (c) legislators participate in the nullification by appropriating only enough for partial enforcement. No one would assert that police nullification of clear statutes is a good system, but anyone who examines the reality is forced to conclude that the effective law is the opposite of what the full enforcement statutes clearly provide.

Whether prosecutors, including those in regulatory agencies, have a mandatory enforcement duty is much more complex. A fact of considerable importance is the pervasive assumption that mandatory prosecution would be impossible. Even though the assumption is strongly dominant, it can be conclusively rebutted. Some discretion is inherent in finding facts and in interpreting law, but other discretion can be eliminated from most enforcement functions (though probably not all). A statute could provide that whenever a prosecutor finds that the evidence is enough to convict for a serious crime he has an enforceable legal obligation to bring the prosecution unless one of a dozen specified reasons for not prosecuting is also found . . .

Even though compulsory prosecution is exceptional in the United States, we have a substantial amount of it, and American experience shows that it is a viable system. . . . [Some] statutes governing transportation agencies, including the Federal Aviation Act, allow compulsory prosecution: "If . . . there shall appear to be any reasonable ground for investigating the complaint, it shall be the duty of the administrator or the Board to investigate the matters complained of." . . . Under that provision, when a bus company complained of airline family fares, the Civil Aeronautics Board dismissed the complaint without a hearing, but the reviewing court emphasized the "duty" of the Board, held the dismissal reviewable, held that the statute did not vest "anything near absolute discretion in the Board," held that the APA . . . required the Board to state grounds for dismissal, and held that "standards for the Board's exercise of discretion must exist." *Trailways of New England, Inc. v. CAB*, 412 F.2d 926, 931–32 (1st Cir. 1969) . . .

German Code of Criminal Procedure
(*Strafprozeßordnung*, StPO)

§ 152

(1) The public prosecution office has to decide about public charges.

(2) Unless otherwise provided by law, the public prosecution office is obliged to take action in the case of all criminal offenses which may be prosecuted, provided there are sufficient factual indications.

§ 153

(1) If a less serious criminal offense is the subject of the proceedings, the public prosecution office may dispense with prosecution with the approval of the court competent to open the main proceedings if the offender's culpability is considered to be minor and if there is no public interest in the prosecution. . . .

§ 153a

(1) In a case involving a less serious criminal offense, the public prosecution office may, with the consent of the court competent to open the main proceedings and with the consent of the accused, dispense with preferment of public charges and concurrently impose conditions and instructions upon the accused if these are suitable to eliminate the public interest in criminal prosecution, and if the degree of culpability does not present an obstacle. In particular, the following conditions and instructions may be chosen:

1. to make a contribution towards reparation for damage caused by the offense,
2. to pay a sum of money to a non-profit making institution or to the Treasury,
3. to perform some other public service,
4. to comply with duties to pay maintenance, or
5. to make a serious attempt to reach a mediated agreement with the victim (offender-victim mediation) . . . ; or
6. to participate in a seminar pursuant to . . . Road Traffic Act.

. . .

German Criminal Code

§ 258 Obstruction of Punishment

(1) Who intentionally or knowingly obstructs in whole or in part the punishment of another in accordance with the Criminal Code or becomes subject to a measure (§ 11 para. 1 no. 8) will be punished with imprisonment of not more than five years or a fine.

§ 258a Obstruction of Punishment in a Public Office

(1) If the perpetrator in cases under § 258 para. 1 is a public official who has to participate in the criminal proceedings or the proceedings which lead to a measure, or if he as a public official

is involved in the execution of criminal punishment or measure, then the punishment is imprisonment from six months to five years, in less serious cases, imprisonment of not more than three years or a fine.

Markus D. Dubber, "Comparative Criminal Law," in Mathias Reimann and Reinhard Zimmermann (eds.), *Oxford Handbook of Comparative Law* (2006), 1287

Continental criminal law...has developed a more systematic approach to the question of the constraints of legality on criminal law [than has Anglo-American criminal law]. Driven by the Enlightenment critique of state power in all forms, and in the guise of criminal law in particular, the principle of *nulla poena sine lege* attempted to place principled constraints on official discretion—notably in its judicial and executive manifestations (with legislative constraints lagging behind). In the executive realm, the principle of legality (*Legalitätsprinzip*) was thought to require eliminating official discretion altogether. Prosecutors (who now performed functions traditionally performed by judges, in an attempt to limit judicial discretion) and police were obligated—under threat of criminal punishment—to pursue all reasonably suspected violations of a criminal statute...

The legality principle in the U.S., then, is considerably narrower than in other countries. Violations of those (few) aspects of the legality principle that are recognized in the U.S., however, face a stiffer sanction than mere judicial disapproval: they result in the invalidation of the offending statute. Also note that the (nonconstitutional) norms that add up to a broad legality principle in non-U.S. countries are not always as categorical as they might at first appear. The well-known (nonconstitutional) principle of compulsory prosecution (*Legalitätsprinzip*) in the German Code of Criminal Procedure, for instance, has for some time been subject to an exception that has begun to threaten the rule—the (nonconstitutional) *Opportunitätsprinzip*, or principle of appropriateness. The latter principle releases prosecutors (but, at least in theory, not police officers, who are thought not to deserve the same level of trust) from the former in cases where the public interest does not require prosecution. As one might suspect, the principle of appropriateness played a central role in the spread of plea bargaining in Germany over the past few decades, after—and even while—this practice was universally disavowed and, in fact, derided as a typical example of the pervasive lawlessness of the U.S. criminal process and the principled superiority of German criminal procedure law.

D. Plea Bargaining

David Lynch, "The Impropriety of Plea Agreements: A Tale of Two Counties," 19 *Law and Social Inquiry* (1994), 115

The academic defense of plea-bargaining has generally taken one or more of three forms. First, many have concluded that plea bargaining is indispensable to the system of criminal justice—that without it, the courts would be overwhelmed by a mass of trials they would be unable to handle. A second defense is that plea bargaining is both constitutionally permissible and morally legitimate, since both sides voluntarily engage in and benefit from the practice. Finally, some commentators suggest that the abolition of plea bargaining would be impossible because the parties would continue the practice even if higher authorities tried to curb it.

Although there is a substantial literature on plea bargaining, little of it originates from the vantage point of someone who knows the system from the inside. Plea bargaining, by its very nature, is a closed-door affair that is not readily amenable to observation by outsiders. I bring to this discussion a perspective based on experience with the system: I worked for nearly five and one-half years as a "professional plea bargainer," both as a public defender and as a prosecutor, in the criminal courts of two very different midsized jurisdictions...

In my view, plea bargaining is not an administrative necessity for two reasons. First, most criminal defendants do not want trials and would not choose to go to trial even if they faced no penalty for doing so. Moreover, my experience suggests that with appropriate administrative reforms and changes in attitudes, courts are actually capable of handling substantially more trials than they currently do...

Whether or not plea bargaining is constitutional in the narrow legal sense, I think it is wrong to think of it as a voluntary practice—a deal that makes both sides better off. For the small number of defendants who actually want to go to trial . . . plea bargains must be enforced by substantial coercion from judges, prosecutors, and even public defenders. It is these groups who most strongly support plea bargaining and who work the system to their advantage (and to the disadvantage of defendants).

Finally, even though many actors in the judicial system have substantial discretion, I do not believe that this discretion must inevitably be used to sneak plea bargaining back in through the back door when higher authorities try to curb it. My experience suggests that when a legal culture develops that allows or encourages trials, all the parties involved find a way to adapt to that legal culture . . .

It has been my experience that judges, lawyers, and even police officers often love plea bargaining. They love it not because it prevents the breakdown of the criminal justice system but because it helps them avoid work and stress. Defense attorneys universally collected their fees up front, public defenders were paid a set salary, and salaried prosecutors and judges all got paid no differently whether a case was settled in a 60-second negotiation or disposed of by a trial. So, unlike the medical specialist, who is paid handsomely for the stress and work of an intense surgical procedure, and who is rewarded and admired by a professional peer group as well, the attorney pushing for trials received no financial or professional rewards of any kind. Indeed, the opposite was true. Defense attorneys all knew that if they brought too many cases to trial, they would be seen as either unreasonable and worthy of professional ostracism or as a fool who was too weak to achieve "client control."

Many attorneys I knew became masters of the fine art of controlling their clients. Some liked to engage in "chair therapy," in which a client who insists on a trial is made to sit in the hall of the courthouse (or in the courthouse lockup) for days on end during courthouse trial terms, waiting for his day in court, until he accepts a deal. Some (usually unintentionally) resorted to "good cop/bad cop" routines, in which a resistant defendant is subjected to the screams of his or her attorney, followed by the lawyer's associate, who tries to calmly help the accused to see the light. Usually, however, defense attorneys, aware that incredible trial penalties were attached to the "right" to a jury trial, only needed to tell a defendant of the unconscionable sentences that had been meted out to others who dared to create work for a judge.

The Prosecutor as Judge, Jury, and Sentencer

I quickly learned that prosecutors . . . were the real judges when it came to sentencing decisions. By allowing plea bargaining judges successfully dumped the burdens of sentencing most criminal defendants onto prosecutors. How did prosecutors handle this sentencing burden? The answer, I soon learned, was "any way they wanted to." There were no official rules that bound me or my fellow prosecutors in the making of plea-bargaining offers. (The only unwritten rule was to avoid creating bad public relations, either with the press or with the judiciary). Prosecutors, then, had nearly complete discretion in deciding what offers to make to defense counsel. There were many instances in which prosecutors would decide the appropriate sentence; offer it to defense counsel who then accepted; then search the crimes code for some offense that would produce the "correct" sentence.

This is not to say that prosecutors spent long periods of time agonizing over appropriate sentences. A prosecutor would often work through a pile of cases in machine-gun fashion, making snap decisions as to appropriate punishments in just a few minutes per case. These few minutes (perhaps 3 or so for misdemeanors and 10 for serious felonies) included all the time devoted to (1) examining police reports and all the evidence; (2) reviewing the defendant's prior criminal history; (3) deciding the defendant's fate as to sentencing; and (4) putting the plea offer into a form letter to be sent to defense counsel.

The speed at which assistant district attorneys decide sentences, often involving substantial periods of incarceration, was amazing. But what was also noteworthy was the surprising lack of training we prosecutors received for our sentencing roles. Given no official training, new prosecutors (and almost all prosecutors I encountered were relatively "new" in the sense that most saw the district attorney's office as merely a career steppingstone) were forced to go by their instincts or by the instincts of benighted others around them.

Other Negative Aspects of Plea Bargaining

Although quality of defense counsel, in my opinion, never seemed to make much difference during trials (the witnesses, after all, do most of the talking), defense counsel quality seemed to make an enormous difference in plea bargaining. Some attorneys were skillful at power-coercive brinkmanship. Others were completely incompetent at negotiations . . .

. . . Although civility and intelligence are usually assets in most professions, plea bargaining tends to exalt the negative traits of human character. Some of the most effective negotiators were arrogant, aggressive, unreasonable, and even ill informed as to the law. These attorney traits formed part of the calculus that prosecutors used in deciding what to offer. Fortunately . . . most attorneys chose to be reasonably pleasant, but the more crude, hot tempered, and unreasonable an attorney was, the more many felt obliged to appease him or her with a better deal. Plea bargaining thus made the practice of criminal law one in which legal knowledge and civility took a back seat . . .

That plea bargaining has little to do with practicing a learned profession can be illustrated in a different way through the story of someone I shall refer to as Bill White, who was the office manager of the . . . District Attorney's Office. Although he never attended a day of law school, White was offering plea bargains to defense attorneys just three months into his job. In court, judges would sometimes ask, "Who made that deal?" If a defense attorney answered, "Bill White," it was accepted by all parties as completely legitimate. Ironically, Bill White was one of the most competent people I have ever known and an excellent plea bargainer. The fact that he lacked any legal education or a license to practice law was of little practical consequence. I am convinced that the average car salesman or real estate agent with a few days of instruction could become an adequate plea bargainer . . .

The danger of convicting an innocent person pursuant to a plea bargain . . . is real. For reasons I have never fully understood, many prosecutors are loath to risk losing a case at trial. They will therefore resort to offering incredibly lenient punishments to assure the entry of guilty pleas in those weak cases that probably would and should be lost at trials (in which the reasonable doubt standard would necessarily come into play). For instance, I have witnessed cases in which the charge of rape was ultimately reduced to harassment; armed robbery that should have called for a five-year sentence reduced to a sentence of a few months; and countless cases calling for some jail time reduced to probationary cases. In such situations, no good is done. The guilty get off so easily that they can only lose respect for the system. And the few innocent here and there (those the system was originally designed to protect but probably no longer does) are stigmatized by a criminal conviction and must feel constitutionally abandoned. One might say that the innocent could insist on their day in court. But with their own lawyer forcefully urging them to accept an offer, and given the typically outrageous generosity of the offer coupled with the typically outrageous penalty if they go to trial and lose, only the most courageous among them would refuse this safe but dehumanizing way out. As Albert Alschuler wrote, "to turn a substantial portion of a defendant's punishment on a single tactical decision is . . . to assign to the defendant a responsibility that he cannot fairly be required to bear."

Markus D. Dubber, "American Plea Bargains, German Lay Judges, and the Crisis of Criminal Procedure," 49 *Stanford Law Review* (1997), 547

One must exercise caution when applying the term "plea bargaining" to German bargaining practices because there is no such thing as a plea in German criminal procedure. The German defendant who seeks to obtain a lighter sentence may not enter a plea of guilty; instead, she must confess to the crime. Although a confession in German criminal court, like a guilty plea in the United States, may be withdrawn, the court may include the withdrawn confession in its consideration of the case in its entirety.

Bargaining in German criminal cases can take many different forms. Section 153a of the German Code of Criminal Procedure has given rise to what might be called "diversion bargains." Section 153a permits the prosecution to divert (i.e., conditionally suspend) proceedings in exchange for paying a sum of money to a charitable organization or the state or performing charitable work. Prosecutors make particularly frequent use of section 153a in cases of serious white collar crime.

The limitation of section 153a to *Vergehen* should not lead an American reader to underestimate its scope. German *Vergehen* include several quite serious crimes that are considered felonies in the United States. These include lesser crimes against the person (such as battery), most drug offenses, environmental crimes, and property crimes (such as larceny and virtually all business crimes, regardless of the financial harm caused).

Plea bargaining in Germany also occurs by means of the penal order (*Strafbefehl*). Issued without a hearing, the penal order informs the defendant that she will receive a specified sentence for a specified crime unless she objects within two weeks, in which case the matter will proceed to trial before the appropriate court, generally the single professional judge. The prosecutor may submit an application for a penal order at any time, even after the beginning of trial. The judge must issue the penal order as requested "if no concerns suggest otherwise." This means judges grant virtually all applications for a penal order as a matter of course. Until recently, the prosecutor could seek only fines by penal order. Now, she can request a suspended prison sentence of up to one year, provided the defendant has legal representation.

In penal order bargains, the prosecutor may offer to initiate a penal order proceeding instead of filing the case in the single judge court, thereby limiting the defendant's maximum exposure to a suspended one year prison sentence, instead of the four years' imprisonment in the single judge court. Alternatively, she may offer to specify a particular sentence in her application for a penal order. In exchange, the defendant would agree not to object to the penal order, thus saving the prosecutor the trouble of a trial.

The penal order's limited punishment range should not obscure its significance as a bargaining mechanism. In Germany, fines—which may reach millions of dollars—are imposed in over 80 percent of criminal cases. By contrast, prison sentences of over one year are imposed in only 3 percent of cases. Fines are routinely imposed for any Vergehen, which include, as noted earlier, many crimes that would be felonies under U.S. law.

In addition to diversion and penal order bargaining, bargaining also occurs in non-Vergehen cases and in Vergehen cases in which the defendant refuses a deal under section 153a or objects to the penal order and requests a trial. In these "judgment bargains," the judge normally offers the defendant more lenient treatment in exchange for a confession in open court.

As German judges routinely initiate plea bargaining, defendants regularly face substantial pressure to plead guilty in exchange for leniency. Not only may the defendant hesitate to rebuff an offer from the very judge who will decide her fate at trial, the judge herself may find her impartiality sorely challenged by a recalcitrant defendant.

In contrast to their professional colleagues, lay judges do not participate in plea bargaining. The German [Federal Court of Justice] recently reminded professional judges that their lay colleagues must be consulted about plea agreements. Nonetheless, bargaining continues to be limited to the professional court elite. Lay judges tend to be informed of the terms of the bargain only after it has been struck...

Based on an account of the traditional German criminal process as an inquisitorial proceeding dominated by a powerful judge whose sole aim is to obtain a confession from the defendant, some German commentators have welcomed plea bargaining. According to this account, the German defendant's role in the proceedings is entirely passive, and is limited to responding to the interrogation by the presiding judge who knows the case file prepared by the prosecution that contains all facts relevant to the resolution of the case. The defendant develops no evidence on her own; she merely motions the court to do the investigating for her. She may request that the court call certain witnesses and appoint certain experts, but she never takes the active role of developing a case and presenting it to the court.

Against the background of this image of the German criminal process, some German commentators regard plea bargaining as an opportunity for the defendant to take a more active role in the process. In this view, plea bargaining strengthens the defendant's position by permitting her to shape the proceedings that will settle her fate. Plea bargaining appears as a process that permits the resolution of disputes in the course of a rational discourse among equals. With an occasional nod in the direction of modern discourse and process theories, it is said that the participation of the defendant in the dialogic process both improves the quality of its resolution and legitimizes it. In this light, plea bargaining appears as the paradigm of a new rational approach to criminal procedure that seeks to replicate the rational "seminar atmosphere" of certain German white collar trials.

Professor Klaus Luderssen has gone one step further: he sees the rise of plea bargaining as an important indication of an actual paradigm shift. He calls for the abandonment of traditional substantive and procedural criminal law and advocates the resolution of what are now criminal cases in private tort actions. According to Lüderssen, plea bargaining serves as a model for the rational, dialogic resolution of disputes between victim and offender. Lüderssen views this dialogic resolution as the only way to legitimize the imposition and infliction of sanctions in our modern society of autonomous persons.

German Code of Criminal Procedure

§ 257b

At trial, the court may discuss the status of the proceedings with the participants if this appears suitable to expedite the proceedings.

§ 257c

(1) In suitable cases, the court may, in accordance with the following subsections, reach an agreement with the participants on the further course and outcome of the proceedings....

(2) Subject of this agreement may only be the legal consequences which could be the content of the final judgment and of associated rulings, other procedural measures relating to the proceedings, and the participants' course of conduct during the trial. A confession should be part of any negotiated

agreement. The verdict of guilt as well as measures of rehabilitation and prevention may not be the subject of a negotiated agreement.

(3) The court announces what content a negotiated agreement could have. It may also indicate an upper and lower limit for the sentence, based on free assessment of all the facts and general principles of sentencing. The participants have the opportunity to make submissions. A negotiated agreement requires that the defendant and the public prosecution office agree to the court's proposal.

(4) The court is no longer bound by a negotiated agreement if legal or factually significant circumstances have been overlooked or have arisen and the court therefore becomes convinced that the prospective sentencing range does not correspond to the seriousness of the offense or the degree of culpability. The same applies if the defendant's legal actions at trial do not correspond to that upon which the court's prediction was based. The defendant's confession may not be used under such circumstances. . . .

NOTES

1. The German Code of Criminal Procedure (*Strafprozeßordnung*, StPO) was introduced in 1877. It covers the whole area of criminal procedure and addresses police officers, public prosecutors, and judges. The code contains rules for investigations, trials (including the law of evidence), special proceedings, appeals, and finally for the supervision of sentence execution. The conduct of police officers in their *proactive* role (to avert dangers for public security) is regulated by "police law," with its own police codes (*Polizeigesetze*), which—unlike substantive and procedural criminal law—is state law, not federal. When police officers act in their *reactive* role, i.e., when they investigate crimes already committed, however, they have to adhere to the rules in the federal Code of Criminal Procedure.

The Code of Criminal Procedure from 1877 was never replaced through enactment of a new code; however, there has been a continuous stream of legislative changes and amendments to adapt legal provisions to changing realities. Technical and social developments (phones, computers, DNA-testing, etc.), legal progress (the introduction of the Basic Law in 1949 with its emphasis on human rights) and new police strategies (undercover investigations, extensive search strategies, etc.) required new regulations regarding the conduct of investigations and trials.

By contrast, criminal procedure law in the United States is driven largely not by codes, but by constitutional law, and by federal constitutional law in particular. (State constitutional law can also be significant, within the state in question, but only if it grants greater protections than does federal constitutional law.) The U.S. Supreme Court, in a series of decisions during the Warren Court era (named after Earl Warren, a former Republican Governor of California who served as Chief Justice from 1953–1969), applied the federal bill of rights (including the Fourth, Fifth, and Sixth Amendments, reproduced below) to the states and, for all intents and purposes, transformed the federal constitution into a federal code of criminal procedure, with constitutional force. This program was highly controversial at the time, particularly among Southern states, which bore the brunt of the Supreme Court's actions; the Supreme Court, in fact, since has scaled back several of the constitutional protections as the Court shifted to the right under Chief Justices Burger, Rehnquist, and Roberts, all appointed by Republican Presidents (as was Warren, incidentally, whose appointment President Eisenhower called "the biggest damned-fool mistake I ever made").

Fourth Amendment

The right of the people to be secure in their persons, houses, papers, and effects, against unreasonable searches and seizures, shall not be violated, and no warrants shall issue, but upon probable cause, supported by oath or affirmation, and particularly describing the place to be searched, and the persons or things to be seized.

Fifth Amendment

No person shall be held to answer for a capital, or otherwise infamous crime, unless on a presentment or indictment of a grand jury, except in cases arising in the land or naval forces, or in the militia, when in actual service in time of war or public danger; nor shall any person be subject for the same offense to be twice put in jeopardy of life or limb; nor shall be compelled in any criminal case to be a witness against himself, nor be deprived of life, liberty, or property, without due process of law; nor shall private property be taken for public use, without just compensation.

Sixth Amendment
In all criminal prosecutions, the accused shall enjoy the right to a speedy and public trial, by an impartial jury of the state and district wherein the crime shall have been committed, which district shall have been previously ascertained by law, and to be informed of the nature and cause of the accusation; to be confronted with the witnesses against him; to have compulsory process for obtaining witnesses in his favor, and to have the assistance of counsel for his defense.

Is codification of norms of criminal procedure required? What if the norms governing the behavior of state officials are derived from the constitution, and developed and enforced by the courts? Who is the audience of a code of criminal procedure, as opposed to a code of criminal law? What about a code of punishment execution (or prison law)? The German Federal Constitutional Court held in 1972 that the legislature was constitutionally required to codify prison law, rather than leaving it to executive regulations (BVerfGE 33, 1). To whom is a code of punishment execution, or prison law, addressed? Does it matter whether a norm only applies to someone who already has been convicted of an offense, as opposed to someone who is presumed innocent prior to judgment?

2. One of the leading ideas behind the German Code of Criminal Procedure (StPO) is the idea that the criminal law should be applied equally and uniformly everywhere and to every case. Therefore, § 152 para. 2 indicates that the public prosecution office must indict if there is sufficient evidence. The purpose of this norm is to eliminate discretion. This notion of compulsory prosecution, which is in German called *Legalitätsprinzip,* should not be confused with *nulla poena sine lege* (*Gesetzlichkeitsprinzip* in German, but "legality principle" in English).* *Nulla poena sine lege,* "no punishment without law," serves (not exclusively but importantly) to protect individuals against unforeseeable restrictions of their liberty. The legislative choice to remove prosecutorial discretion is not directly connected to individuals' liberty rights. The rationale, besides guaranteeing equality before the law, is instead to support the separation of powers as a constitutional principle, and also to promote a law-oriented, duty-oriented attitude among public prosecutors and police officers, instead of trusting state officials to exercise their discretion appropriately.

How does the elimination of discretion by officials in the executive branch reflect a separation of powers among branches, as opposed to a limitation of power of a particular branch (the executive) vis-à-vis another (the legislature)? Is the idea that granting members of the executive discretion as to how to enforce legislative commands means granting them quasi-legislative power? What conception of the relationship between legislature and executive underlies this concern?

In theoretical reflections about German criminal law and criminal procedure, there is not much fundamental dispute about the principle of compulsory prosecution—which does not preclude acknowledging certain situations where permitting discretion might actually be the better choice.

In what circumstances would exercising discretion *not* to prosecute be preferable? (How would we measure this preference? Justice, efficiency, equality, fairness?) Does a system of compulsory prosecution discourage legislatures from passing unenforceable criminal statutes, and thereby limit proliferation of offenses and, ultimately, the scope of criminal law?

The real question is whether it is correct to describe the German system today as a system with compulsory prosecution. First, often it is unavoidable that police officers exercise discretion—they have to cope with limits on resources and cannot devote the same degree of rigorous investigation to all offenses coming to their attention. They may also see it as a matter of justified leniency to ignore petty offenses. Such examples of police discretion tend to fly "under the radar." Second, the law itself contains numerous exceptions that allow public prosecutors† to exercise discretion, see §§ 153–154f German Code of

---

* See Chapter 2.
† Note that the opportunity principle does not apply to police officers; they are bound by the *Legalitäts-prinzip*, without exceptions.

Criminal Procedure. Besides §§ 153, 153a there is, for instance, § 153c German Code of Criminal Procedure, which concerns offenses committed abroad—a necessary legislative measure: even if they knew about them, it would be impossible for German prosecutors to work, for example, on cases of drug dealing committed elsewhere on the planet. (Recall that drug dealing is among the offenses subject to universal jurisdiction of German courts.* There is an extensive reading of even the territoriality principle of jurisdiction, extending to acts committed in Australia in the *Töben Case*.[†]) It has been argued that there are so many holes in the principle of compulsory prosecution that it can no longer be regarded as a main pillar of the German criminal justice system. However, there remain important areas of criminal offenses that must be investigated and prosecuted without discretion: robberies, intentional killings, rape and other serious crimes (these are felonies which do not fall under §§ 153, 153a German Code of Criminal Procedure). If a prosecutor failed to deal with an unpleasant case (and hide the file in the closet), he or she would face criminal charges according to § 258a StGB (obstruction of punishment, punishable by up to five years' imprisonment).

U.S. law takes a diametrically opposed view of prosecutorial discretion. It pays almost no attention to the decision *not* to prosecute (absent some victims' rights provisions designed to give victims a voice in charging decisions, in theory, if not in practice[‡]); what applies to the lack of interest in prosecutors' decision not to pursue a charge applies doubly to police officers' choice not to investigate (absent evidence of accessorial or conspiratorial intent). The decision to prosecute is left entirely to prosecutorial discretion; police officers' decisions to investigate (search and arrest) are subject to constitutional analysis under the Fourth Amendment prohibition of unreasonable searches and seizures: unconstitutionally obtained evidence may be inadmissible at trial. More important, this grant of discretion is thought to be desirable, as it allows prosecutors (and police officers) to exercise their judgment in determining whether facially criminal conduct should in fact be subject to criminal punishment, both on grounds of fairness, but also in light of limited public resources and the perceived needs of law enforcement (for instance, the recruitment of prosecution witnesses who agree to cooperate, and perhaps to testify, in exchange for leniency).

3. Reconsider the relationship between the procedural *Legalitätsprinzip* and the principle of *nulla poena sine lege*, the *Gesetzlichkeitsprinzip*, which confusingly in English is called principle of legality. German commentators point out that the former is concerned with separation of powers and control of prosecutorial discretion, and the latter with giving citizens' fair notice. It would be odd, however, if the two concepts were entirely unrelated. Note the following overlap: first, the constitutional principle of legality (*nulla poena sine lege*) is concerned not only with fair notice, but also with the control of discretion—though not the discretion of law enforcement officials (prosecutors, police officers), but the discretion of legislatures (through the vagueness prohibition, for instance) and of judges (through the analogy prohibition). Second, the constitutional legality principle is also concerned with separation of powers; as we have seen previously[§] both the prohibition of vagueness and that of analogy serve to police the distinction between the generation of norms (which is to be limited to the legislature) and their application (the province of the judiciary).

Would it not make sense to see both the German principle of compulsory prosecution and the legality principle (*nulla poena sine lege*) as manifestations of the rule of law (or legality), as opposed to rule of persons, extended to all aspects of the system of criminal law (including substance and procedure, generation, application, as well as execution)? If this makes sense, does this mean that the absence—in fact the rejection—of the principle of compulsory prosecution in the U.S. implies a rule of law deficit? Or is a different, less categorical, approach to the challenge of discretion possible, one that acknowledges the necessity and desirability of discretion, rather than attempts to eliminate it, or deny its existence, altogether?

---

* See Chapter 4.
[†] See the *Töben Case*, Chapter 17.A.
[‡] See Chapter 1.A.ii.
[§] See Chapter 2.B.

In the American context, is it any more naïve to think that the discretion of law enforcement officials (prosecutors and police officers) could be subjected to enforceable guidelines than to think that guiding judicial sentencing discretion is possible (assuming it is desirable)?

4. During the last decades, a shift can be observed, first and foremost in German criminal practice, but also seeping into the text of the Code. It is a move from the formal, time-consuming criminal trial towards more flexible handling of cases. Prosecutors and judges have a strong interest in avoiding traditional trials. As in the U.S., it is debated whether this is a matter of sheer necessity because of increasing caseloads and complicated cases of economic crime in particular, or, as David Lynch argues in his article, of the personal interests of the professional agents (prosecutors, defense counsels, judges). It seems likely that the latter does play a role. Most, or at least many, people who are able to get around procedures perceived as tedious will do so. In the case of German judges, avoiding a formal trial has the advantage of not only limiting time spent in the courtroom but also of saving time after a trial. It takes time to formulate written reasons for conviction (evaluating evidence, explaining the legal outcome, justifying the sentence; see for the requirement of written reasons § 267 German Code of Criminal Procedure). Thus, it is advantageous to rely not only on unconditional discharge for the more trivial offenses (§ 153 German Code of Criminal Procedure), but also on discharge in more serious cases—the legislature accommodated this by introducing § 153a German Code of Criminal Procedure in 1975. In many cases, especially when § 153a is applied in cases of complicated economic crimes, this is preceded by negotiations with defense counsel.

If there is no way around conviction, the question arises whether the duration of the criminal trial can be shortened. German law does not know guilty pleas; conviction requires full evidence. However, even with this requirement there are shortcuts if the defendant confesses and foregoes the right to appeal (then the written judgment can be considerably shorter).* The practice of inducing defendants' cooperation has become an important feature in German courtrooms over the last decades. As there are no statistics available, it is hard to assess the ratio of negotiated-sentences-after-confessions to the "ordinary procedure." The practice, the motives behind it and its dangers for defendants have evoked strong criticism. Within the framework of German criminal procedure, agreements are alien and problematic. The Federal Court of Justice has decided several times about the evolving court practice (Judgment of August 28, 1997, 4 StR 240/97, BGHSt 43, 195; Judgment of March 3, 2005, GSSt 1/04, BGHSt 50, 40). The Court tried to develop restrictions on plea bargaining, struggling to keep this practice within the boundaries of criminal procedure principles, and it also demanded that the legislature regulate such procedures. In the year 2009, § 257b and § 257c were introduced into the German Code of Criminal Procedure. Note that § 257c para. 2 German Code of Criminal Procedure limits negotiations and agreements to the sentencing decision and prohibits so-called "charge bargaining"—agreements concerning the applicable offense description. It is still debatable whether sentence bargaining is compatible with important principles including, foremost, the constitutional culpability principle.[†] Either incentives or threats are necessary to induce confessions. Defendants must either be offered considerable mitigation or the information they receive on the otherwise applicable "normal" sentence range must be exaggerated.

After the judgments by the Federal Court of Justice and the amendment of the German Code of Criminal Procedure, it soon became evident that attorneys, prosecutors and judges did not comply with these attempts to regulate the growing practice of plea bargaining in Germany. In 2013, the German Federal Constitutional Court had to address constitutional complaints against criminal convictions based on an agreement between the defendant and the court and against § 257c German Code of Criminal Procedure (Judgment of March 19, 2013, BVerfGE ___). In preparation, the Constitutional Court commissioned an empirical study based on interviews with a large number of judges. According to this study, judges

---

* See German Code of Criminal Procedure § 267 para. 4.
† See, e.g., Chapter 1.

admitted disregarding the rules for agreements established by the Federal Court of Justice and the Code of Criminal Procedure in about half of the cases. It is common practice to keep agreements "informal," that is, to not include them in the court records as required. Also, practitioners do not limit themselves to agreements about sentence length but practice charge bargaining. The Federal Constitutional Court criticized these deficiencies and emphasized, among other points, that agreements must be noted in the court records and that sentencing must be compatible with the culpability principle. Note also that the Court condemned "slim" confessions (that is, a practice similar to the American guilty plea). It emphasizes that proof of guilt is required in all cases, that is, a confession must be comprehensive and credible. The Court, however, did not in principle criticize the practice of exchanging confessions for reduced sentences. Nor did it declare § 257c German Code of Criminal Procedure unconstitutional. Given the apparently widespread disregard of previous attempts to formalize the informal process of plea bargaining, what do you think will be the effect of declaring that agreements (really) must be recorded, that they must comply with the culpability principle, and that confessions must be comprehensive and credible (rather than "slim")?

5. Read against the background of plea bargaining in the U.S., § 257c StPO demonstrates another feature of criminal trials which is characteristic of the German system: the strong position of the trial judge. Judges are the dominant figures and both prosecution and defense play a much more passive role than their U.S. counterparts. Often judges will propose negotiations with the aim of shortening proceedings through a confession. In other cases, defense counsel makes the first move and talks to the prosecutor, but any agreement the two parties might achieve is meaningless unless they can convince the trial judge. Judges are not bound by what the prosecutor suggests nor will they accept a confession as conclusive evidence if they have doubts. The dominant position of the trial judge can also be observed in trials without negotiations. Judges not only question witnesses, but also work through the extensive dossier developed in the pre-trial stage, mainly by the public prosecution office, in order to determine which evidence ought to be heard in court. Prosecution and defense counsels may make motions for additional evidence, but the collection and introduction of evidence is a matter of judicial discretion. Behind this stands an assumption of fundamental importance: according to the German understanding, the goal of the trial is to discover the truth, to establish the facts as accurately as possible. The emphasis is not on procedural justice but on substantive justice.

Would it fair to say that in the U.S. procedural justice is privileged over substantive justice, and in Germany it is the other way around? Is one approach preferable to the other?

6. *Felonies and misdemeanors.* The distinction between serious and less serious offenses, between felonies (*Verbrechen*) and misdemeanors (*Vergehen*), plays an important role in procedural criminal law, and in U.S. constitutional criminal procedure in particular (even if many of the formal "procedural niceties" between felony and misdemeanor trials at common law have disappeared, *Callanan v. United States*, 364 U.S. 587 (1961)).

For our purposes more important, the distinction between felony and misdemeanor, and between *Verbrechen* and *Vergehen* appears in substantive criminal law, since—particularly in German criminal law—substantive norms are defined in terms of their application to one type of crime or another (for instance, attempts are punishable only in cases of *Verbrechen*, unless otherwise specified in the Code). It is therefore important to get at least a comparative sense of these terms, and to keep in mind significant differences when considering the materials in this book.

The distinction between *Vergehen* and *Vergehen* is defined in the German Criminal Code:

German Criminal Code § 12

(1) Felonies are unlawful acts punishable by a minimum sentence of one year's imprisonment.
(2) Misdemeanors are unlawful acts punishable by a lesser minimum term of imprisonment or by fine.

Contrast this distinction with that drawn in the New York Penal Law:

N.Y. Penal Law § 10.00 Definitions of terms of general use in this chapter

4. "Misdemeanor" means an offense, other than a "traffic infraction," for which a sentence to a term of imprisonment in excess of fifteen days may be imposed, but for which a sentence to a term of imprisonment in excess of one year cannot be imposed.

5. "Felony" means an offense for which a sentence to a term of imprisonment in excess of one year may be imposed.

Note that, while both legal systems draw the line between the two types of offense at one year's imprisonment, the German definition of *Verbrechen* includes all crimes punishable by a *minimum* one year sentence (minimum exposure), while the U.S. definition of felony includes all crimes punishable by a *maximum* sentence of more than one year's imprisonment (maximum exposure). As long as a sentence of less than one year's imprisonment, including a fine, is possible for a given offense, that offense is a *Vergehen* under German law, even if the maximum possible sentence far exceeds one year in prison. So, a crime punishable by, say, "imprisonment of not more than five years," for example, § 242 German Criminal Code (theft), or by "imprisonment from six months to ten years," § 244 German Criminal Code (theft while carrying a weapon, burglary into a residential building), would be a *Vergehen* in Germany, but a felony in New York.

ANALYSIS OF CRIMINAL LIABILITY

Much, if not all, of this book could be consumed with a comparative discussion of various approaches to the analysis of criminal liability found throughout the history of common law scholarship and jurisprudence, on the one hand, and the array of approaches to the same issue developed over the course of German criminal law history, on the other. Then the rest of the book, should there be any space left, could be devoted to a discussion of whether there should be any generalized scheme for the analysis of criminal liability in the first place, thus questioning the need of the exercise, and of the book, in the first place.

Alternatively, one might highlight the commonalities between the general conceptions of the task at hand—i.e., the search for an answer to the question of who is criminally liable for what—on both sides of the systemic divide, and then use the resulting conceptual framework as the basis for a comparative analysis of particular legal norms.

In the present book, we have chosen the second path. The proof will be in the pudding: if the resulting conceptual backbone makes possible, and perhaps even facilitates, a comparative analysis of Anglo-American and German criminal law, then it will have done its job.

A. The German Scheme

Wolfgang Naucke, "An Insider's Perspective on the Significance of the German Criminal Law Theory's General System for Analyzing Criminal Acts," *Brigham Young University Law Review* [1984], 305

German courts are time and again confronted by the following set of facts: A group of young people has difficulty gaining public attention for their political views, and to remedy this problem they decide to "advertise." They have some posters printed and paste them up as firmly as possible in as many locations as they see fit. The modern glues are quite permanent, and the material is often bonded to the surface to which it is attached. It is usually a tremendous inconvenience to remove the posters or fliers, and is sometimes impossible.

Under German criminal law, the question is whether the foregoing conduct is sufficient to constitute the crime of damaging property under section 303 of the German Criminal Code. There are conflicting opinions, and the courts and scholars defend their views with numerous arguments. It is unsettled whether firmly pasting a flier or poster on an object damages that object.* Those who believe that it does must turn to further questions. Conceivably, such property damage is justified by the right to freedom of speech. Even someone who does not accept the argument that free speech rights legitimize property damage might still argue that the young people should not be punished because they (mistakenly) thought that their right to freedom of speech justified their actions. . . .

. . . . In [the general system for analyzing criminal acts] are collected those features of crime that are common to all crimes, whether it be damaging property, theft, murder, or anything else. If, therefore, unauthorized advertising is to be punishable under German law, it must be found to exhibit the general paradigmatic features of crime as determined by German criminal theory, as well as the particular elements of section 303 established by statute.

---

* [The legislature has since made it an offense to alter the "appearance" of an object belonging to another substantially and permanently without actually damaging its substance. German Criminal Code § 303 para. 2.—Eds.]

The general analytical system describes the main features of criminal action with the German terms *Tatbestandsmässigkeit* (definition of the offense), *Rechtswidrigkeit* (wrongfulness), and *Schuld* (culpability). Whatever the governing code provision may be, every criminal act must be wrongful and culpable conduct that conforms to (i.e., is violative of) the definition of the offense. Unauthorized advertising can only be punished if it violates the definition, is wrongful, and is culpable. These central elements are discussed with much effort and pomp in Germany. The discussion . . . has not achieved a conclusive result. A few main points, however, are undisputed.

a. The definition of an offense. The word *Tatbestandsmässigkeit* embraces all of the elements of a particular crime that are found in the applicable code section. A rough American equivalent would be the phrase "elements of the offense." There is a *Tatbestand* or definition of theft, homicide, fraud, and so on. The problems . . . with applying section 303 to "wild postering" are questions about whether such conduct fits within the scope of the definition of damaging property. A German law student writing an exam on the issue, or for that matter, a German judge deciding a "wild postering" case, would be regarded as engaging in improper analysis if he or she tried to treat these question at a different stage of the analysis—i.e., as an issue of wrongfulness or culpability.

Demanding that the problem of determining which legal good is protected by section 303 be treated as a problem of the definition of damaging property affects more that the mere formal ordering of legal analysis. This demand also aids the decision of substantive issues. The content of the definition of a crime cannot be extended beyond that formulated by the legislature. In the context of section 303, for example, the authority of the property owner to determine what may happen to his property is protected only to the extent this authority is asserted to prevent damage to, or destruction of, the property. From this perspective it would take a strained interpretation to hold unauthorized advertising to be a violation of section 303, since such conduct leaves the property intact and intrudes solely upon the owner's authority. . . . If however, the definition of the crime of damaging property were tied to the authority of the owner to control his property, the determination of whether a particular act satisfied the element of the definition would be dependent upon whether the property owner viewed the act as an incursion upon his authority. . . .

b. Wrongfulness. *Rechtswidrigkeit*, or wrongfulness, embraces all the statutory and extra statutory general grounds for holding that conduct which is violative of the definition may still be found to be justified, thereby escaping punishment. Self-defense is a classic justification that negates the wrongfulness of an act. The right to free speech, which some "wild posterers" cite as the source of the legitimacy of their activity, is a doubtful justification in their case. But it is in any event an argument that must be legally analyzed under the heading of wrongfulness. The category of wrongfulness in the general analytical system not only proves the proper place for the discussion of such justifications but also provokes the discussion of doubtful justification.

c. Culpability. The first task of the element of *Schuld* or culpability in the general analytical system is to secure the status of culpability as an indispensable prerequisite to punishment. A result of the culpability requirement is that the lawyer must carefully consider possible grounds for excusing the actor, even though his conduct is violative of the definition of the crime and is wrongful. Insanity and duress are illuminating examples of the doctrines that serve to negate culpability in this manner. A party availing himself of either of these defenses typically claims that while he has engaged in conduct specified in the definition of some crime, and though he has done so without justification, he cannot fairly be held responsible for what he did.

Legal discussions of unauthorized advertising commonly encounter the view that this conduct conforms to the definition of damaging property and is wrongful. Those who defend this position are not, however, finished with their analysis. They must take up the further problem presented by the possibility that the actor thought he had a right to paste up posters. In the terms of the theory of the general analytical system, this is a problem of culpability. A perhaps overly simplistic formulation is that the category of culpability marshals all of the arguments favoring a finding of not guilty that are based on the subjective state of the accused and insures that they are considered in every case.

**Markus D. Dubber, "The Promise of German Criminal Law:
A Science of Crime and Punishment,"
6 *German Law Journal* (2005), 1049**

A natural science to which German criminal legal science might be fruitfully compared is botany, or zoology. Much of German criminal law theory is devoted to classification. Once the basic impetus for classification has been provided, often by the kind of insight into the order of things just mentioned, the German criminal legal scientist seeks to assign each element of the doctrine its proper place in the classificatory system of the criminal law.

[T]he taxonomical mode of German criminal law lends itself to a certain formalism. Arguments are not infrequently resolved by definition, or rather by classification. Once an issue has been properly classified, it has been properly resolved. Given the care with which it has been assembled, and continues to be maintained, it is perhaps not surprising that the classificatory system of German criminal law is asked to do considerable rhetorical work. if the categories are correct, and an issue has been correctly categorized, then the issue has been correctly resolved, or so the syllogism goes. In other words, the time that common criminal lawyers spend on fretting over the proper resolution of a particular case, German criminal lawyers instead dedicate to the correct construction of a system for the resolution of all cases. The more effort goes into the building and quality control of the juridical apparatus, the less effort need go into output control. And so indefinite preventive detention, for instance, is legitimate because it is classified not as a "punishment," but as a "measure," and large fines against corporations are legitimate because they are classified as "monetary fines" (or, once again, as a "measure") for "order violations" rather than as "punishments" for "crimes," and so on.

To pursue the analogy to botany for a moment, consider the recent dispute over the proper classification of a tomato in the state of New Jersey. After the tomato was beaten out by the blueberry in the competition for designation as the state's official "state fruit," a campaign was launched to have it recognized as the official "state vegetable" instead. Botanists insisted that the tomato is a fruit. Supporters of the tomato's bid for state vegetabledom, however, cited the U.S. Supreme Court decision in *Nix v. Hedden*, declaring the tomato a vegetable under the Tariff Act of Mar. 3, 1883, which imposed a duty on vegetables, but not on fruits. The Court reasoned that

> [b]otanically speaking, tomatoes are the fruit of a vine, just as are cucumbers, squashes, beans, and peas. But in the common language of the people, whether sellers or consumers of provisions, all these are vegetables which are grown in kitchen gardens, and which, whether eaten cooked or raw, are, like potatoes, carrots, parsnips, turnips, beets, cauliflower, cabbage, celery, and lettuce, usually served at dinner in, with, or after the soup, fish, or meats which constitute the principal part of the repast, and not, like fruits generally, as dessert.

Why indeed should the botanists' classification carry the day? Why should the vice chairman of the New Jersey Assembly's agriculture and natural resources committee adopt the scientists' preferred classification, when in his thirty-year career as a grocer, he didn't "ever recall putting tomatoes in the fruit section"? As another (pro-tomato) participant in the New Jersey debate put it, "Everybody knows, botanically, it's a fruit, but legally it's a vegetable."

The danger of this taxonomical formalism is, of course, that it may deflect attention from the search for justification, and ultimately legitimation. If the task of the criminal law scientist consists exclusively of identifying—and then filling—gaps within the entirely autonomous system of criminal law, the scientific achievements of German criminal law will be appreciated only by fellow practitioners. Outside observers . . . may find themselves mystified and, ultimately, unconvinced.

B. The American (Model Penal Code) Scheme

Setting out a common scheme for the analysis of criminal liability that captures American criminal law in the full variety of its fifty-plus manifestations is a hopeless, and ultimately pointless, endeavor, though possibly slightly less hopeless and pointless than the attempt to distill a common position on any given point of substantive criminal law doctrine. Luckily, the Model Penal Code drafters, after extensive (internal) comparative research (there is no evidence of the systematic consideration of other legal systems, with the exception of England's, which hardly qualifies as "other"), already came up with a structure that would be familiar enough to policymakers and lawyers in the fifty-odd American jurisdictions that made up the Code's audience to at least not stand in the way of seriously considering the adoption of the Code in full or in part. The Model Penal Code, as a systematic and comprehensive code (at least with respect to the general part, including the general approach to the analysis of criminal liability), also recommends itself as a promising point of contrast for a comparative analysis of American and German criminal law, which has long been codified—although it will turn out that interesting differences in the conception of a criminal code, and of codification in general, remain. It is also helpful that the Model Penal Code's basic analytic scheme bears a quite close resemblance to that developed in German criminal law—perhaps surprisingly, given the absence of external comparative research (in contrast, incidentally, to German criminal codification efforts, one of which produced a preparatory sixteen-volume treatise on comparative criminal law*).

It is easy to overstate the difference between "the German scheme" and "the Anglo-American scheme." While German criminal law certainly has worked harder to precisely differentiate the various levels of analysis and, not unrelatedly, to assign substantive significance to the resulting taxonomy, the general distinction between elements of an offense, on the one hand, and defenses, and more specifically justifications and excuses, on the other, was not foreign to Anglo-American criminal law. So, in the eighteenth century, Blackstone distinguished between "justifiable" and "excusable" homicide in still familiar terms:

> In . . . instances of justifiable homicide, . . . the slayer is in no kind of fault whatsoever, not even in the minutest degree. . . . But that is not quite the case in excusable homicide, the very name whereof imports some fault, some error, some omission; so trivial however, that the law excuses it from the guilt of felony. . . . [†]

A century later James Fitzjames Stephen's draft of an English criminal code (unsuccessful in England, but adopted in Canada) drew a general distinction between justification and excuse:

> There is a difference in the language used in [this draft] which probably requires explanation. Sometimes it is said that the person doing an act is "justified" in so doing under particular circumstances. The effect of an enactment using that word would be not only to relieve him from punishment, but also to afford him a statutable defence against a civil action for what he had done. Sometimes it is said that the person doing an act "is protected from criminal responsibility" under particular circumstances. The effect of an enactment using this language is to relieve him from punishment, but to leave his liability to an action for damages to be determined on other grounds, the enactment neither giving a defence to such an action where it does not exist, nor taking it away where it does. [‡]

Another century later, the Model Penal Code drafters themselves made "a rough analytical distinction" between justification and excuse, while at the same time refusing "to draw a fine line" between the two: "To say that someone's conduct is 'justified' ordinarily connotes that the conduct is thought to be right, or at least not undesirable," while "to say that someone's conduct is 'excused' ordinarily connotes that the conduct is thought to be undesirable but that for some reason the actor is not to be blamed for it." [§]

Model Penal Code

§ 1.02. Purposes; Principles of Construction

(1) The general purposes of the provisions governing the definition of offenses are:
    (a) to forbid and prevent conduct that unjustifiably and inexcusably inflicts or threatens substantial harm to individual or public interests; . . .

Analysis of Criminal Liability (citations to Model Penal Code)

1. *Criminality (arts. 1–2, 5)*: Does the behavior constitute criminal conduct?
    A. What are the elements of the offense as defined? (§ 1.13 (9))
        1. Conduct (§ 1.13 (5))
        2. Circumstances
        3. Result

---

* Karl Birkmeyer (ed.), *Vergleichende Darstellung des deutschen und ausländischen Strafrechts: Vorarbeiten zur deutschen Strafrechtsreform*, 16 vols. (1905–1909).
† William Blackstone, *Commentaries on the Laws of England* (1769), vol. 4, 182.
‡ Criminal Code Bill Commission, Report 11 (1879).
§ Model Penal Code Commentaries art. 3, introduction, at 2–3.

4. Mode of Culpability (as to each element)
  - purpose, knowledge, recklessness, negligence (§ 2.02)
  - none (strict liability, § 2.05)
  - rules of interpretation (§§ 2.02 (3), (4), 2.05)

B. Does the behavior satisfy each element of the offense?
1. Conduct
  - act (§ 2.01)
  - voluntariness (§ 2.01)
  - omission (§ 2.01)
  - complicity (§ 2.06)
2. Circumstances
  - consent (§ 2.11)
3. Result
  - causation (§ 2.03)
    – but for (§ 2.03 (1)(a))
    – proximate (§ 2.03 (1)(b)–(4))
4. Mode of Culpability (as to each element)
  - mistake (§ 2.04 (1))
  - intoxication (§ 2.08)
  - diminished capacity (§ 4.02 (1))
5. Inchoate Crimes (art. 5)
  - attempt (§ 5.01)
  - solicitation (§ 5.02)
  - conspiracy (§ 5.03)

2. *Illegality (Justification) (art. 3)*: Is the criminal conduct unlawful generally speaking?

A. Necessity (choice of evils) (§ 3.02)
B. Self-defense (§ 3.04); defense of another (§ 3.05); defense of property (§ 3.06)
C. Law enforcement (§ 3.07)
D. Public duty (§ 3.03)
E. Special responsibility (§ 3.08)
F. Consent (§ 2.11)

3. *Culpability (Excuse) (arts. 2, 4)*: Is the accused blameworthy for her criminal and unlawful conduct?

A. Duress (§ 2.09)
B. Military orders (§ 2.10)
C. Entrapment (§ 2.13)
D. Ignorance of Law (§ 2.04 (3))
E. Provocation and Diminished Capacity (§ 210.3 (1)(b))
F. Insanity and Infancy (§§ 4.01, 4.10)
  - involuntary intoxication (§ 2.08 (4))

Gabriel J. Chin, "Unjustified: The Practical Irrelevance of the Justification/Excuse Distinction," 43 *University of Michigan Journal of Law Reform* (2009), 79

The distinction [between justification and excuse] is important as a matter of legal philosophy, because it describes reasons for withholding criminal liability. However, as Professor Westen writes, "[t]he measure of any internally-consistent distinction between justification and excuse is its usefulness."[8] Its utility to the criminal justice system—to judges, juries, legislatures, law students and lawyers—has not yet been demonstrated.

. . . The justification/excuse distinction plays no significant role in contemporary criminal doctrine. For example, the legal consequence of a successful defense in an individual case does not turn on whether it is a justification or excuse; any complete defense ends a prosecution. There are no general rules applicable to justifications that do not apply to excuses (or vice versa), say, with regard to allocation or nature of the burden of proof, or the mitigating effect of a failed defense at sentencing.

Nevertheless, . . . major contributors to this debate assert that categorizing defenses correctly is important because whether a defense is classified as a justification or an excuse should affect the

---

[8] Peter Westen, An Attitudinal Theory of Excuse, 25 Law & Phil. 289, 328 (2006).

outcome in particular cases or shape other aspects of the criminal justice system. This claim is initially plausible. Some defense classifications are clearly important to the outcomes of criminal cases. For example, it matters whether a defense is complete or partial, affirmative or ordinary, constitutionally mandated or potentially subject to abolition by a court or legislature. It is also true that moral philosophy and jurisprudence are often relevant to criminal law doctrine, because persuasive arguments may affect decision makers' criminalization of particular conduct or lead to other rule changes to conform the law to principles of justice. But when attempting to identify precisely how the justification/excuse distinction, in itself, suggests anything about how cases should be disposed of in actual court systems, the question becomes more problematic.

A general warning sign suggesting that the concepts might be difficult to apply in a legal system is the broad scholarly dissensus about what they mean. If experts disagree about definitions and concepts, those definitions and concepts may also be difficult for lay jurors and non-academic lawyers. Scholars disagree about the concepts of justification and excuse in multiple dimensions. They disagree at the conceptual level whether justification is defined objectively or subjectively (and therefore whether reasonably mistaken justification is justification or excuse), and, if objectively, whether "unknowing justification" is either the superior defense of justification or, instead, no defense at all.

Scholars also disagree about categorization as justification or excuse of many individual defenses, including duress, provocation, and others. Yet, scholars recognize that defenses they categorize as excuses can be satisfied by conduct fitting the definition of justification—and vice versa.... Some versions differentiate between actual threats of harm and mere reasonable appearances of threat that did not actually exist. To apply these distinctions, juries must determine the actual intentions and future plans of, say, a perceived arsonist shot dead while reaching for the match.

Notwithstanding the impressive intellectual efforts devoted to the task, no single scholar or viewpoint appears to be on the verge of generating practical consensus about the concepts of justification and excuse, categorization of the defenses, or categorization of difficult individual cases. Justification and excuse, then, will likely remain contested and controversial in broad concept, in individual cases, and at the intermediate level of particular defenses.... Any legal system must pause before making its most important decisions rest on precise application of concepts that lack accepted definitions and appear difficult, perhaps impossible, to administer.

Advocates of the distinction make three main claims for the importance of developing and elaborating the justification/excuse distinction: that it 1) could with feasible changes in the law send clear moral messages about the disposition of criminal charges, particularly "not guilty" verdicts; 2) now shapes third party and accomplice liability; and 3) should be used to generate procedural rules, such as with respect to the burden of proof, for categories of defenses. [As Mitchell Berman[17] and Kent Greenawalt[18] have suggested,] none of these goals can be usefully advanced through the justification/excuse distinction....

[First,] defenses need not be categorized and labeled as precisely as crimes, either for jurisprudential or for practical purposes. Because the various crimes have different punishments and moral implications, they must be precisely defined in general and carefully ascribed in particular cases. By contrast, all non-convictions have identical punishment and the same criminal implications, and rest on the same general ground—given the procedural structure, there is insufficient evidence of guilt....

[Second,] the major claim for the practical utility of the justification/excuse distinction [is unconvincing]: sending clear moral messages in cases of acquittal. Professors Robinson, Dressler and others argue that acquittal based on justification implies that the conduct was good or tolerable, while acquittal based on an excuse defense appropriately suggests that the conduct was undesirable. This argument is not correct.

An acquittal on any ground, including, for example, a reasonable doubt that any crime was committed, carries no legal implication of good behavior. One reason for the moral neutrality of acquittals is the burden of proof, necessitated by the inability of trials to determine absolute truth. Strong evidence of guilt of murder falling just short of the "beyond a reasonable doubt" standard results in an acquittal, but does not imply that the defendant did not in fact murder.... Similarly, strong disproof of a self-defense defense to murder falling just short of the prosecution's required burden results in acquittal based on justification, but does not mean that the defendant in fact acted in self-defense. Under our system, a conviction assigns moral and legal guilt, but an acquittal does not necessarily indicate moral or legal innocence.

---

[17] Mitchell N. Berman, Justification and Excuse, Law and Morality, 53 Duke L.J. 1 (2003)....
[18] Kent Greenawalt, Distinguishing Justifications from Excuses, 49 Law & Contemp. Probs. 89 (1986)....

Criminal trials could be restructured to provide moral messages, but this would be no small project. Presumably, there is no point in generating more specific, but inaccurate moral messages. Accurate messages would require changing defenses and procedures so that in addition to determining legal guilt, they generated morally meaningful findings. . . . The constitutional, financial, practical and technical problems with this project are daunting, and are probably sufficient to explain why it has apparently never been attempted.

[Third,] the claim that the justification/excuse distinction helps allocate aider and abettor liability under existing law [also falls short]. The argument is that one helping a merely excused principal, say, an insane killer, should not have a defense, but helping a justified principal, one acting in self-defense, for example, should not be punished. However, modern codes, appropriately, impose liability based on the defendant's conduct and mental state. Thus, the real question is what the defendant thought they were doing. If a defendant intended to aid a felonious killer but in fact aided a lawful actor, they should at least be liable for attempt; by the same token, a defendant who reasonably believed she aided lawful conduct should not be condemned because the principal unexpectedly turned out to be a criminal. On the modern view, whether the principal was justified, excused or engaged in no criminal activity is less important than is the evaluation of the defendant's personal culpability.

C. An Illustration: *Dudley and Stephens,* (1884) 14 Q.B.D. 273

To close this chapter of the book, we use the famous case of *Dudley and Stephens* (known in Germany as the *Mignonette Case,* after the defendants' shipwrecked yacht) to illustrate briefly the basic scheme for the analysis of criminal liability that structures the comparative analysis in the remainder of this book. This quick snapshot of the analytic scheme in action also serves as a convenient point of departure for references to other parts of the book, where topics lightly touched upon here are handled at greater length and, hopefully, depth.

The Queen v. Dudley and Stephens
Queen's Bench Division
(1884) 14 Q.B.D. 273

INDICTMENT for the murder of Richard Parker on the high seas. . . .

At the trial before Huddleston, B., at the Devon and Cornwall Winter Assizes, November 7, 1884, the jury, at the suggestion of the learned judge, found the facts of the case in a special verdict which stated "that on July 5, 1884, the prisoners, Thomas Dudley and Edward Stephens, with one Brooks, all able-bodied English seamen, and the deceased also an English boy, between seventeen and eighteen years of age, the crew of an English yacht [the Mignonette], a registered English vessel, were cast away in a storm on the high seas 1600 miles from the Cape of Good Hope, and were compelled to put into an open boat belonging to the said yacht. That in this boat they had no supply of water and no supply of food, except two 1 lb. tins of turnips, and for three days they had nothing else to subsist upon. That on the fourth day they caught a small turtle, upon which they subsisted for a few days, and this was the only food they had up to the twentieth day when the act now in question was committed. That on the twelfth day the turtle were entirely consumed, and for the next eight days they had nothing to eat. That they had no fresh water, except such rain as they from time to time caught in their oilskin capes. That the boat was drifting on the ocean, and was probably more than 1000 miles away from land. That on the eighteenth day, when they had been seven days without food and five without water, the prisoners spoke to Brooks as to what should be done if no succour came, and suggested that someone should be sacrificed to save the rest, but Brooks dissented, and the boy, to whom they were understood to refer, was not consulted. That on the 24th of July, the day before the act now in question, the prisoner Dudley proposed to Stephens and Brooks that lots should be cast who should be put to death to save the rest, but Brooks refused consent, and it was not put to the boy, and in point of fact there was no drawing of lots. That on that day the prisoners spoke of their having families, and suggested it would be better to kill the boy that their lives should be saved, and Dudley proposed that if there was no vessel in sight by the morrow morning the boy should be killed. That next day, the 25th of July, no vessel appearing, Dudley told Brooks that he had better go and have a sleep, and made signs to Stephens and Brooks that the boy had better be killed. The prisoner Stephens agreed to the act, but Brooks dissented from it. That the boy was then lying at the bottom of the boat quite helpless, and extremely weakened by famine and by drinking sea water, and unable to make any resistance, nor did he ever assent to his being killed. The prisoner Dudley offered a prayer asking forgiveness for them all if either of them should be tempted to commit a rash act, and that their souls might be saved. That Dudley, with the assent of Stephens, went to the boy, and telling him that his time was come, put a knife into his throat and killed him then and there; that the three men fed upon the body and blood of the boy for four days; that on the fourth day after the act had been committed the boat was picked up by a passing vessel, and the prisoners were rescued, still alive, but in the lowest state of prostration . . . That if the men had not fed upon the body of the boy they would probably not have survived to be so picked up and rescued, but would within the four days have died of famine. That the boy, being in a much weaker condition, was likely to have died before them. That at the time of the act in question there was no sail in sight, nor any reasonable prospect of relief. That under these circumstances there appeared to the prisoners every probability that unless they then fed or very soon fed upon the boy or one of themselves they would die of starvation. That there was no appreciable chance of saving life except by killing some one for the others to eat. . . . "

The learned judge then adjourned the assizes until the 25th of November at the Royal Courts of Justice. On the application of the Crown they were again adjourned to the 4th of December, and the case ordered to be argued before a Court consisting of five judges . . .

Dec. 9.

The judgment of the Court (Lord Coleridge, C.J., Grove and Denman, JJ., Pollock and Huddleston, B-B.) was delivered by LORD COLERIDGE, C.J.

The two prisoners, Thomas Dudley and Edwin Stephens, were indicted for the murder of Richard Parker on the high seas on the 25th of July in the present year. They were tried before my Brother Huddleston at Exeter on the 6th of November, and under the direction of my learned Brother, the jury returned a special verdict, the legal effect of which has been argued before us, and on which we are now to pronounce judgment.*

. . . From the[] facts, stated with the cold precision of a special verdict, it appears sufficiently that the prisoners were subject to terrible temptation, to sufferings which might break down the bodily power of the strongest man and try the conscience of the best. . . . But nevertheless this is clear, that the prisoners put to death a weak and unoffending boy upon the chance of preserving their own lives by feeding upon his flesh and blood after he was killed, and with the certainty of depriving him of any possible chance of survival. The verdict finds in terms that "if the men had not fed upon the body of the boy they would probably not have survived," and that, "the boy being in a much weaker condition was likely to have died before them." They might possibly have been picked up next day by a passing ship; they might possibly not have been picked up at all; in either case it is obvious that the killing of the boy would have been an unnecessary and profitless act. It is found by the verdict that the boy was incapable of resistance, and, in fact, made none; and it is not even suggested that his death was due to any violence on his part attempted against, or even so much as feared by, those who killed him. . . .

. . . [T]he real question in the case [is] whether killing under the circumstances set forth in the verdict be or be not murder . . . First it is said that it follows from various definitions of murder in books of authority, which definitions imply, if they do not state, the doctrine, that in order to save your own life you may lawfully take away the life of another, when that other is neither attempting nor threatening yours, nor is guilty of any illegal act whatever towards you or any one else. But if these definitions be looked at they will not be found to sustain this contention . . .

Now it is admitted that the deliberate killing of this unoffending and unresisting boy was clearly murder, unless the killing can be justified by some well-recognised excuse admitted by the law. It is further admitted that there was in this case no such excuse, unless the killing was justified by what has been called "necessity." But the temptation to the act which existed here was not what the law has ever called necessity. Nor is this to be regretted. Though law and morality are not the same, and many things may be immoral which are not necessarily illegal, yet the absolute divorce of law from morality would be of fatal consequence; and such divorce would follow if the temptation to murder in this case were to be held by law an absolute defence of it. It is not so. To preserve one's life is generally speaking a duty, but it may be the plainest and the highest duty to sacrifice it. War is full of instances in which it is a man's duty not to live, but to die. The duty, in case of shipwreck, of a captain to his crew, of the crew to the passengers, of soldiers to women and children, . . . these duties impose on men the moral necessity, not of the preservation but of the sacrifice of their lives for others, from which in no country, least of all, it is to be hoped, in England, will men ever shrink as indeed, they have not shrunk . . .

---

* [For centuries, common law judges have referred to each other as brothers, or brethren.—Eds.]

It is not needful to point out the awful danger of admitting the principle which has been contended for. Who is to be the judge of this sort of necessity? By what measure is the comparative value of lives to be measured? Is it to be strength, or intellect, or what? It is plain that the principle leaves to him who is to profit by it to determine the necessity which will justify him in deliberately taking another's life to save his own. In this case the weakest, the youngest, the most unresisting, was chosen. Was it more necessary to kill him than one of the grown men? The answer must be "No"—

> So spake the Fiend, and with necessity,
> The tyrant's plea, excused his devilish deeds."[a]

It is not suggested that in this particular case the deeds were devilish, but it is quite plain that such a principle once admitted might be made the legal cloak for unbridled passion and atrocious crime. There is no safe path for judges to tread but to ascertain the law to the best of their ability and to declare it according to their judgment; and if in any case the law appears to be too severe on individuals, to leave it to the Sovereign to exercise that prerogative of mercy which the Constitution has intrusted to the hands fittest to dispense it.

. . . . It is therefore our duty to declare that the prisoners' act in this case was wilful murder, that the facts as stated in the verdict are no legal justification of the homicide; and to say that in our unanimous opinion the prisoners are upon this special verdict guilty, of murder.

THE COURT then proceeded to pass sentence of death upon the prisoners. [This sentence was afterwards commuted by the Crown to six months' imprisonment.]

NOTES

1. The scheme sketched by Wolfgang Naucke is familiar to anyone who underwent legal training at a German university. Criminal law students are taught to structure the legal opinions they write in the order of: 1. Elements of the Offense; 2. Wrongfulness; 3. Culpability—and they are taught never to deviate from this sequence of examination. The "elements of the offense" category becomes more varied if the offense is not a standard "one offender—intentional act"—type but involves variations such as omissions, forms of complicity, negligence etc., but the basic three-part-structure is not challenged in contemporary German doctrine. This scheme is not explicitly mentioned in the Criminal Code. It has evolved in the literature under the heading *Verbrechenslehre* (the doctrine of the analysis of crime), and it also forms the unwritten background for both the legislature and the courts.

The evolution of what today is taken for granted involved, of course, some debate. Until a few decades ago, it was disputed whether intent belongs to "elements of the offense" or to "culpability," i.e., to the first or to the third level of the analysis of criminal liability. Today, the former view is generally accepted.[*]

2. Is this way of framing criminal law problems a self-referential and ultimately pointless, if not distracting or even obscurantist, exercise in pressing the world into neat schemes? Or is there more to it? The (limited) significance might be illuminated if one looks at a still existing dispute about categorization. (This will require the consideration of details about the prerequisites of criminal liability that we will not discuss until later on, in particular the distinction between justification and excuse, and the doctrine of accomplice liability.) It concerns situations where the offender erroneously believed facts that would, if they were present, constitute a justification (for instance, if he or she wrongly believed that there was an imminent attack). Do such circumstances negate wrongdoing (i.e., do they amount to a "justification") or only culpability (i.e., do they amount to an "excuse")? A pragmatic response might be: it does not matter, it is a defense either way (another question is whether the mistake must have been reasonable). But the more systematic approach sharpens awareness that classification might be unavoidable with view to further consequences (for

---

[a] Milton, Paradise Lost iv. 393 (1667).

---

[*] See, on this issue, the 1952 opinion by the Federal Court of Justice on the "culpability principle," which was handed down at a time when this dispute about the scope of "culpability" had not been resolved definitively. See Chapter 3.

example, if an error about justifying circumstances negates culpability, the offender still acts wrongfully, and thus the person who was mistaken for an attacker responds to an unlawful act and may exercise the right to self-defense). Still, if there is a choice to be made between different legal interpretations, the answer "solution X fits the overall system better than solution Y" will have weight inside a given legal system but hardly for the observer from outside.

More generally, there is a difference between justifying a particular analytic scheme in terms of its usefulness (as the above example does) and justifying it in terms of its truth, or correctness. One might argue, for instance, that the distinction between justification and excuse reflects something about the nature of crime, or at least criminal liability; to adopt a different analytic scheme therefore would be simply wrong, or inaccurate, ontologically, or perhaps phenomenologically, speaking.

Note also possible interactions between criminal law theory in general and the analytic scheme in particular, and features of criminal procedure. German criminal law does not draw the common law's categorical distinction between offenses and defenses; it focuses on pre-requisites for criminal liability—unlawfulness (wrongfulness) and culpability (accountability, responsibility, blameworthiness)—rather than referring to their absence, i.e., justification (absence of unlawfulness) and excuse (lack of culpability). This way of framing the problems can be related to differences in criminal procedure. The German criminal trial is not only shaped by the strong position of the presiding judge who is responsible for presenting *all* facts, including those concerning justifications and excuses (neither defense counsel nor prosecutor carry a responsibility of their own for presenting facts). It is also characterized by the fact that the burden of proof for all facts lies with the state (the defense does not carry any burden of proof). This might explain why the German *Verbrechenslehre* presents the levels 2 und 3— "wrongfulness" and "culpability"—as positive elements along with "definition of offence" while in Anglo-American law defenses are features that negate. Another feature (mentioned by Chin) that will obviously impact the complexity of an analytical framework concerns the question: who has to decide (non-lawyers such as jurors or persons with legal education).

3. From the perspective of contemporary German criminal law, *Dudley and Stephens* would be a fairly straightforward case turning on the distinction between justifying necessity (§ 34 German Criminal Code) and excusing necessity (§ 35 German Criminal Code). Cutting the unfortunate cabin boy's throat constituted murder (because it satisfied the elements of murder), a murder that was not justified by necessity (because the balance of evils did not come out in the defendants' favor—why? because life is incommensurable*). The question would be whether, under the extreme and unusual circumstances of the case, the defendants' personal culpability nonetheless was low enough to foreclose punishment, in other words whether they qualified for an excuse, namely excusing necessity (§ 35). To this the answer would be: probably yes (assuming the circumstances were sufficiently dire).

From the perspective of contemporary U.S. criminal law, the analysis would proceed along similar lines. Using the Model Penal Code's (MPC) approach, Dudley and Stephens would have committed murder (because their act satisfied the elements of murder: homicide committed purposely or knowingly, in this case purposely, one as principal, the other as accomplice). Was that murder justified by necessity? That depends again on whether the circumstances were sufficiently dire to create a situation of necessity that would justify the criminal act in question, here the murder of the cabin boy. (The MPC would not object to throwing the value of the cabin boy's life into the balance; and the balance would come out in the defendants' favor, since the taking of one life saves three others.) Assuming the conduct was not justified, the question then would be whether the defendants would qualify for an excuse. To this the answer would be: no (because the defense of "duress" is only personal, not circumstantial; in other words, the MPC does not recognize general necessity as an excuse, only necessity that is caused by another person).[†]

---

   * See Chapter 13.B.
   † See Chapters 13.B and 14.A.

4. If the discussion turns to "*should* there be an excuse?" as a matter of criminal policy, or as a reason perhaps to change the positive law, the system as such can no longer serve as a heuristic device. Lawyers who are only trained in understanding the interconnections in their own system reach their limits at this point. In *Dudley and Stephens*, the ultimate question is whether the community who passes criminal judgment may demand that an individual sacrifice his or her life. The nineteenth-century court clearly answers this in the affirmative. From this point of view, a rule about excusing necessity such as in § 35 German Criminal Code would deserve criticism. In the twenty-first century, however, and definitely in Germany, visions of heroic sacrifice have lost glamor and desperate acts of self-preservation are met with some tolerance.

To take a more contemporary example, the Model Penal Code drafters do not explain their decision to reject excusing necessity (also known as circumstantial, "situational," duress) but to accept personal duress in terms of heroic norms of behavior—which would eliminate any sort of duress defense. Instead, they remark that situational duress has more drastic consequences than personal duress; the latter type of duress shifts liability from one person (the duressee) to another (the duresser), while the former eliminates criminal liability altogether. Whether this argument is persuasive is another question.*

Of course, Dudley and Stephens's conduct also met with tolerance, quite literally: they were pardoned by the Queen. Arguably, then, the question in the case is not whether their conduct was thought to be excusable, but whether courts had the doctrinal means, or the institutional competence—as adjudicators of legal liability (lawfulness, in other words), not dispensers of mercy—to recognize an excuse. It should also be mentioned that, at the time *Dudley and Stephens* was decided, German doctrine on culpability and excuse was not as clear-cut and uniform as it appears today (recall once more the often-quoted 1952 Federal Court of Justice decision setting out the culpability principle). In fact, the defense of necessity—either as justification, or as excuse—was not recognized in the German Criminal Code at the time *Dudley and Stephens* was decided (1884). Necessity did not appear in the German Criminal Code until 1975 (some thirteen years after it appeared in the Model Penal Code), although German *courts* had begun to develop the defense some decades earlier.†

Again, whether the division of labor in *Dudley and Stephens* between judicial law and executive mercy is defensible, is another question. But even at the time, there was widespread consensus that the defendants deserved mercy.‡

Note, finally, that the court in *Dudley and Stephens* dealt with a case of murder, and therefore with defenses to murder, not with defenses in general. It is one thing to recognize an excuse defense (as either personal or circumstantial duress) in general, and quite another to recognize it even in cases of intentional homicide. In fact, many common law jurisdictions today—not including the Model Penal Code—exclude murder from the scope of whatever version of the duress defense they make available. The reason is not so much that people should be held to heroic standards of behavior, but that the value of human life is such that even non-heroes can fairly be expected to refrain from intentionally taking another's life even under circumstances that would amount to an excuse for any other offense. The recognition of the (immeasurably high, incommensurable) value of human life, as we have seen, underlies the unavailability in German criminal law of necessity as a justification in intentional homicide cases. *Dudley and Stephens* extends this recognition to all forms of necessity, as justification or as excuse.

5. Few would question the desirability of a consistent, clear, accessible, and internally and externally consistent framework for the analysis of legal liability. The choice of framework, however, would seem to be of secondary importance. It is not immediately obvious why, say,

---

* See, e.g., Peter Westen and James Mangiafico, "The Criminal Defense of Duress: A Justification, Not an Excuse—And Why It Matters," 6 *Buffalo Criminal Law Review* (2003), 833, 937–9.

† See Chapter 13.B.

‡ See generally A.W.B. Simpson, *Cannibalism and the Common Law: The Story of the Tragic Last Voyage of the* Mignonette *and the Strange Legal Proceedings to Which It Gave Rise* (1984).

the German analytic scheme of today is preferable to (a) the German analytic scheme, or rather schemes, endorsed (b) thirty years ago, (c) one hundred years ago, or (d) the Model Penal Code scheme, or, for that matter, (e) the sort of scheme that critics of the justification/ excuse defense (like Chin) might prefer. At the same time, ontological or phenomenological commitments aside, few would deny the risk of coming to regard an analytic tool as having a life of its own, apart from its function, and detached from its origins and broader questions of legitimacy, resulting in an internal debate among experts in the operation and maintenance of a taxonomical device that spits out the correct solution to questions of considerable significance to those whose lives it affects. The challenge, it seems, would be to find the right balance of a sensible system critically administered.

6. The fact that in Germany there is strong emphasis on an elaborate and coherent system of analyzing the elements of crimes also influences legal teaching and the way courts work with precedents (even apart from the absence of *stare decisis*). Unlike in the Anglo-American system, German courts only rarely cite older cases, for instance cases from the nineteenth century, and those cases do not appear in the materials used in legal education. As the doctrinal approach to crime has been refined so much since then, older court rulings are mostly considered outdated and not useful.[*]

Of course, it is also the case that court opinions in general, no matter their date, play a less central role in legal education and scholarship in German criminal law than they do in U.S. criminal law; textbooks—not casebooks—remain the primary teaching materials, the lecture method—not the case method—the primary mode of instruction, and the task of doctrinal refinement primarily the business of legal scholars—not the courts.

7. More prosaically, *Dudley and Stephens*—on the basis of engaging, if fairly ghastly, facts— touches on so many issues that it may serve to illustrate the operation of the contemporary analysis of criminal liability. Not surprisingly, given that it is a late-nineteenth-century English decision, *Dudley and Stephens* does not address these issues in what today might be considered the "proper" order in contemporary German (or, for that matter, U.S.) criminal law. (The following can also serve as a preview of what is to come; in fact, it may be worthwhile to return to *Dudley and Stephens* later on, at various points throughout the book.)

(a) *Level One: Offense Elements.* Beginning with the first level of inquiry, the court spends a good deal of time addressing the question whether the defendants have committed a crime. Contemporary German or U.S. law would have little difficulty with this issue. Starting with the *actus reus*, or the objective offense elements: Dudley stabbed Parker. But did he kill him, or doctrinally speaking, did he *cause* his death (as required by the offense definition of homicide)? The Model Penal Code makes this requirement explicit: § 210.1(1) ("A person is guilty of criminal homicide if he purposely, knowingly, reck- lessly or negligently causes the death of another human being."). The German Criminal Code's definition of homicide speaks only of "killing" (*töten*) which is interpreted as requiring causation. (It is not unusual for the Model Penal Code to be more detailed, both in the general part and the special part, than the German Criminal Code, which by design leaves many issues—including, for instance, the definition of mental states, one of the centerpieces of the Model Penal Code—to criminal law scholars, and the courts.) Homicide is discussed in Chapter 15.A.

Assuming that Parker was about to die anyway, does hastening his inevitable and imminent death amount to causing it? Yes (after all, every homicide does no more than hasten the inevitable).[†]

---

[*] For a rare exception, see German Federal Court of Justice, Judgment of October 25, 1990, 4 StR 371/90, BGHSt 37, 214, excerpted in Chapter 8.C.i (citing, without discussion, the *Rose-Rosahl Case* of 1859, but only because there had been no high court decision on the issue since then).

[†] For more on causation, see Chapter 9.

Does stabbing Parker count as an act? Yes, regardless of what definition of act is in play: broadly, as *any* bodily movement (as in the Model Penal Code), or narrowly, as only *voluntary* bodily movements. The Model Penal Code would ask the additional question whether the act was voluntary, to which the answer would also be "yes" (given criminal law's generally undemanding view of voluntariness). Although Dudley might have been parched, starving, and weak, he was neither suffering an epileptic seizure, nor was he sleepwalking, two typical examples of involuntary acts.*

To sum up, using the Model Penal Code's detailed definition of homicide as the backdrop: Dudley's behavior satisfies every *objective* element of the offense of murder: he "caused" the death of another human being, as we just saw. (If he hadn't managed to cause Parker's death, but tried to, he would be liable for attempted murder.) He caused the "death" of another human being, as opposed to merely causing some other, less serious, physical harm. (In that case, he would have committed assault, not homicide.) Now, if Parker had already been dead when Dudley stabbed him, Dudley could still be liable for some other—less serious—offense, such as abuse of a corpse.† (Actually, he may also be liable for attempted murder, provided he thought Parker was still alive at the time. Attempt is covered in Chapter 12.A.) Dudley caused the death of "another" human being, rather than his own death. (Suicide is no longer a crime in the U.S. or in Germany, though assisting suicide still is.) And he caused the death of another "human being," rather than that, say of an animal. (Killing an animal, of course, may be a separate offense.)

So much for Dudley. What about Stephens? Although only Dudley commits the act of killing, Stephens nonetheless is held liable for the murder as well, but not as a principal, but as an accomplice. As a result of his (rather minimal) involvement in the events culminating in the act of killing, the principal's (Dudley's) conduct is imputed to Stephens; "the law," it is said, treats him as though he had wielded the knife himself. (Accessorial liability is covered in Chapter 10.)

And Brooks (who tends to get lost in the shuffle)? Since he did nothing to encourage or help Dudley in committing the act of stabbing, he cannot be held liable for homicide as an accomplice—even though he too "fed upon the body and blood of the boy." (Even in jurisdictions that retain the traditional concept of "accessory after the fact," Brooks wouldn't qualify because his "after-the-fact" behavior was not intended to aid Dudley.) His failure to act, specifically to come to Parker's aid, could generate criminal liability for homicide only if he owed Parker a duty to aid, which he did not. (The criminal law, in the U.S. and Germany, is fairly stingy about extending criminal liability to omissions beyond a narrow class of relatives and dependents, though Germany recognizes a general, less serious, offense of failure to aid without substantial risk to oneself: § 323c German Criminal Code. If Dudley and Stephens were a contemporary case to be judged under German law, one of the interesting questions would be: Could the law expect Brooks to intervene under these very special circumstances?) Interestingly, Dudley—as the captain of the shipwrecked vessel—might have had a duty to all three of his boatmates.‡

Next: *mens rea*, or subjective offense elements. On the basis of English law at the time, the defendants argued that they lacked the requisite *mens rea*, in that they did not act "willfully" (or with "malice") because they harbored no ill will against the cabin boy, but acted purely out of necessity. This argument fails, however, because—and here the court sounds quite modern—*mens rea* does not require an "evil mind" (or some other character deficiency) but merely intent: specifically, in the case of murder, it requires

---

* On voluntariness, see Chapter 7.A.

† This notion is not as far-fetched as it may seem in this case. Although Dudley and Stephens were indicted only for murder, all three men (including the reluctant Brooks), cannibalized Parker's body. For a contemporaneous discussion of their potential liability for a "common law misdemeanor," i.e., a judge-created offense, see Herbert Stephen, "Homicide by Necessity," 1 *Law Quarterly Review* (1885), 51. See also Chapter 2 (discussing common law misdemeanors).

‡ For more on omissions, see Chapter 7.D.

the intent to cause the death of another person. If Dudley intended to kill Parker (where much judicial and scholarly ink has been, and continues to be, spilled, in the U.S. and in Germany, on the question of just what "intent" encompasses—purpose, knowledge, recklessness, *dolus eventualis*, etc.), he is guilty of murder, regardless of his (benevolent or malevolent) motives (with almost as much ink spilled on the question of what, exactly, differentiates motive from intent).*

(b) *Level Two: Justification.* Assuming that the defendants have committed the offense on its face, i.e., that—as the court puts it—"the deliberate killing of this unoffending and unresisting boy was clearly murder," the analysis of criminal liability can move on to the next step: the availability of defenses.†

The court begins by looking at self-defense. (And so do we, in Chapter 13.A.) The status of this defense is unclear in the opinion, though today we would most likely say that the court treats it as a justification. (A hundred years earlier, self-defense in homicide (*se defendendo*) in English law was (still) considered an excuse, requiring royal pardon.) At any rate, self-defense is not available to Dudley and Stephens because, as the court puts it, Parker was "unoffending and unresisting." Putting a modern gloss on this point, we might say that Dudley was not justified in defending himself, presumably against Parker, simply because Parker did not threaten him with unlawful force: even if one could say that Parker posed a threat to Dudley through his very existence (as a competitor for food and water), he did not attack Dudley unlawfully—nor did Dudley (mistakenly) believe that he did. Without an unlawful attack, however, Dudley's act of self-defense was itself unlawful, and therefore not justified.

The court also considers necessity as a justification, i.e., whether "the killing was justified by what has been called 'necessity'"? Necessity, however, turns out not to be available in this case because taking the life of another (innocent) person is always wrong, i.e., unlawful, and therefore unjustifiable. (Today's German criminal law would agree, on account of the incommensurability of human life, even against other lives. The Model Penal Code, by contrast, would permit necessity as a justification even for homicide, provided the "harm or evil" avoided outweighs the "harm or evil" committed, as, for instance, in the present case, which saved more lives than it cost.)‡

Another possible justification hovers in the background of *Dudley and Stephens*, without being made explicit: consent. In the end, Dudley and Stephens may have been done in by their failure to draw lots, apparently the established practice in shipwreck scenarios at the time. Leaving aside offenses that are defined in terms of non-consent, e.g., rape or assault, in which case the presence of consent would negate an offense element already at the first level of the analysis of criminal liability, the status of consent as a general (justification) defense is contested. And even if consent were available as a justification in some cases, it would not reach homicide.§

(c) *Level Three: Excuse.* Assuming, then, that Dudley acted both criminally (engaging in conduct that matches the definition of an offense, murder) and unlawfully (without justification), the next—and last—question is whether he also acted culpably, i.e., without excuse. The court in *Dudley and Stephens* has no difficulty dismissing this possibility: there is no defense of necessity to murder, as justification or excuse. Or put less anachronistically, there is no necessity defense to murder, no matter how dire the circumstances. These circumstances may call for executive mercy (which the defendants received), but it cannot influence the analysis of *legal* liability.¶

---

* For a discussion of *mens rea*, see Chapter 8.
† For an overview of defenses, see Chapter 13.
‡ On necessity as a justification, see Chapter 13.B.
§ Consent is discussed in Chapter 13.C; consent in homicide, and the distinction between consented-to homicide and assisted suicide, is explored in Chapter 15.A.v.
¶ For a more detailed discussion of this aspect of the rationale in *Dudley and Stephens*, which tends to attract the most attention, see Note 4.

There is another excuse that one might think could apply in a case like *Dudley and Stephens*: insanity (discussed in Chapter 14.C). This defense was not considered by the court; it would have been clearly unavailable since the English insanity test at the time (established in *M'Naghten's Case*, (1843) 8 ER 718, and still in force in many U.S. and other common law jurisdictions) limited the defense to those who were incapable of telling right from wrong because of a mental defect (so-called cognitive insanity). Dudley did not suffer from a mental defect and, even if he did, no one argued that he at the time, and *for that reason*, did not realize that stabbing Parker was wrong. (Today, the Model Penal Code and German criminal law both recognize another type of insanity, volitional insanity, which would excuse someone who was incapable, again because of a mental defect, of *not* doing what he or she recognizes as wrong. Volitional insanity also would not apply to Dudley, however, once more because it would not have been caused by a mental defect, but by the dire circumstances.)

PART II
THE GENERAL PART

The general part—or what not too long ago was called the philosophical part—of criminal law is concerned with the general principles of criminal liability. It has long been the focus of comparative criminal law, which since its early days around the turn of the nineteenth century has been driven in large part by an interest in theoretical, and foundational, questions. As criminal law theory has lavished most of its attention on the general part, so has comparative criminal law.

As a result, many issues in the general part have received sustained comparative attention, including, for instance, *mens rea* (or subjective offense elements), particularly the distinction between recklessness and conditional intent, intoxication, corporate criminal liability, justifications (particularly self-defense, but also necessity), and the law of mistake (particularly mistakes regarding the elements of self-defense and ignorance of law). These issues, though already well plowed, will receive our attention in Part II, but so will many others that so far have largely escaped comparative analysis.

The discussion in Part II will generally follow the analytic framework laid out at the end of Part I: beginning with offense elements, then moving onto defenses, first justifications, then excuses. From a distance, the general parts of American criminal law (once again taking the Model Penal Code as the closest thing to a systematic representative statement of that conglomerate of fifty-plus sovereign criminal law systems) and German criminal law appear quite similar, or at any rate similar enough to make comparison possible, and possibly useful (and hopefully interesting!). Nonetheless, a closer look will often reveal noteworthy differences, or similarities. For instance, while both American and German criminal law require the commission of a voluntary act, German criminal law does without a general "act requirement," constitutional or otherwise. While both American and German criminal law feature negligence as a mode of culpability, German law does not distinguish between the definitions of criminal and civil negligence. On the flipside, while German law continues to reject criminal liability for corporations in principle, it now provides for significant administrative corporate fines. While German criminal law does not recognize a separate inchoate offense of conspiracy, it punishes the agreement to commit a felony as attempted participation. And so on.

Whether the differences and similarities, in matters large and small, add up to a pattern is another question, the answer to which will only emerge, if at all, from a careful comparative analysis of specific doctrines. The present book hopes to facilitate this sort of detailed study, at the cost of impeding facile, or at least premature, comparisons at a higher level of generality.

ACTUS REUS (OBJECTIVE ELEMENTS)

The next six chapters deal with the various prerequisites for a finding of criminality, formally speaking. In other words, they address the question whether behavior has occurred that satisfies the definition of an offense, including all of its objective and subjective elements. If *prima facie* criminal behavior is present, i.e., if an offense has been committed, then the inquiry proceeds to the question whether a defense is available, either a justification, or an excuse. This question is addressed in Chapters 13 and 14, respectively.

We begin with the term *actus reus*, which in Anglo-American criminal law can mean any number of things. Here we use it to refer to the totality of objective elements in the definition of a criminal offense, as distinguished from the subjective elements (or *mens rea*). We will pay particular attention to the so-called act requirement in Anglo-American criminal law, at least some aspects of which are thought to be constitutionalized in U.S. law, while at the same time being dismissed as pointless by some commentators. Both Anglo-American and German criminal law make use of possession offenses, though arguably with differing levels of enthusiasm and critical attention to the difficulty of fitting possession into an act requirement; both also have generated—roughly similar—doctrinal tools to extend criminal liability to literal non-acts, i.e., omissions.

A. Voluntary Acts

The Model Penal Code (MPC) drafters, through their narrow definition of act as a bodily movement, combined with their refusal to provide an affirmative definition of voluntariness, differentiated between an act and its voluntariness. This distinction not only has met with criticism, if not confusion, on the part of those who find that the very notion of an act already implies voluntariness, but also has raised the question whether the so-called act requirement is about voluntariness, or actness, or both. There appears to be more of a consensus on requiring voluntariness than on requiring an act. But even if one recognizes an act requirement of some sort, questions about its scope remain.

State v. Tippetts
Court of Appeals of Oregon
180 Or. App. 350, 43 P.3d 455 (2002)

Kistler, J.

Defendant appeals from a judgment of conviction for supplying contraband. He argues that the trial court should have granted his motion for a judgment of acquittal because he did not voluntarily introduce marijuana into the Washington County Jail...

In October 1998, police officers obtained a warrant to search defendant's house. The officers located the house and, after knocking on the door and announcing their presence, forced the door open. Once inside, the officers saw defendant running towards the back of the house. They followed and subdued him. They placed him in handcuffs, read him his Miranda rights, and searched him. The officers found no drugs or other contraband on defendant. The officers then searched defendant's home, where they found methamphetamine and a weapon.

The officers formally placed defendant under arrest and took him to the Washington County Jail, where they turned him over to Officer Morey. Before searching him, Morey asked defendant whether he had any knives, needles, or drugs on him that he was bringing into the jail. Morey then searched defendant and found a small bag of marijuana in his pants pocket. Based on the marijuana Morey found, the state charged defendant with supplying contraband. A person commits the crime of supplying contraband if "the person knowingly introduces any contraband into a correctional facility, youth correction facility or state hospital[.]" Ore. Rev. Stat. § 162.185(1)(a).

At trial, defendant moved for a judgment of acquittal on the charge of supplying contraband. . . . [H]e argued that he could be found guilty of that crime only if he voluntarily introduced the contraband into the jail. Defendant contended that no reasonable juror could find that he acted voluntarily. He argued that, once he was arrested, he could not avoid taking the marijuana with him into the jail. The trial court denied defendant's motion, reasoning that defendant could have avoided the charge by admitting to possession of the marijuana before the officer discovered it.

On appeal, defendant renews his argument [based] on Ore. Rev. Stat. § 161.095(1), which provides:

> The minimal requirement for criminal liability is the performance by a person of conduct which includes a voluntary act or the omission to perform an act which the person is capable of performing.

The state, for its part, does not defend the trial court's ruling on the ground that the court articulated,[2] nor does the state argue that there is evidence in this case from which a reasonable juror could find that defendant chose to take the marijuana into the jail with him.[3] . . .

. . . By its terms, [Ore. Rev. Stat. § 161.095(1)] requires (1) that the act that gives rise to criminal liability be performed or initiated by the defendant and (2) that the act be voluntary. Ore. Rev. Stat. § 161.085(2), in turn, defines the phrase "voluntary act." It means "a bodily movement performed consciously[.]" Ore. Rev. Stat. § 161.085(2).

The texts of Ore. Rev. Stat. §§ 161.095(1) and 161.085(2) support defendant's position. Applied to the charge of supplying contraband, they require (1) that defendant either initiate the introduction of contraband into the jail or cause it to be introduced and (2) that he do so consciously. Defendant, however, did not initiate the introduction of the contraband into the jail or cause it to be introduced in the jail. Rather, the contraband was introduced into the jail only because the police took defendant (and the contraband) there against his will.

The state argues, however, that the use of the word "consciously" in the definition of the phrase "voluntary act" somehow changes that conclusion. The state reasons that the word consciously means "aware" and that an act will be voluntary as long as the defendant is aware that it is occurring. In explaining its position at oral argument, the state reasoned that, under its interpretation, if the police forcibly took a minor who was intoxicated out of his or her house and brought the minor into a public area, he or she could be convicted of public intoxication. In the state's view, the police's movement of the person into a public area would be a "voluntary act" that would satisfy Ore. Rev. Stat. § 161.095(1), as long as the person was aware that he or she was being moved . . .

[A] voluntary act requires something more than awareness. It requires an ability to choose which course to take—i.e., an ability to choose whether to commit the act that gives rise to criminal liability. Conversely, a person may be aware that a particular act is being committed during a seizure or during a reflexive act, but that fact alone does not make the act voluntary.

. . . The state does not argue that there is any evidence from which a reasonable juror could find that defendant had such a choice, and we turn to the alternative basis that the state advances for upholding the trial court's ruling.

[In the alternative], the state argues that, even if the introduction of the drugs into the jail was not itself a "voluntary act," Ore. Rev. Stat. § 161.095(1) requires only "the performance by a person of conduct which includes a voluntary act[.]" The state reasons that, even if defendant did not voluntarily introduce the marijuana into the jail after the police arrested him, he voluntarily possessed

---

[2] The state does not dispute that, without a sufficient promise of immunity, Article I, section 12, of the Oregon Constitution and the Fifth Amendment to the United States Constitution prevent the state from forcing defendant to choose between admitting to possession of a controlled substance and being charged with introducing that substance into a correctional facility. There is no evidence in this record that defendant was promised immunity from criminal liability if he admitted to possessing controlled substances.

[3] The state does not argue that, even if defendant's interpretation of the statute were correct, we may affirm the trial court's ruling because there is circumstantial evidence that would permit a reasonable juror to infer that defendant made a conscious choice to take the contraband with him into the jail. For example, the state does not argue that there is any evidence that would permit a reasonable juror to find that defendant could have disposed of the contraband after he was arrested but chose not to do so.

it before he was arrested. The earlier voluntary act of possession, the state concludes, is sufficient to hold defendant criminally liable for the later involuntary act of introducing the marijuana into the jail. Defendant responds that Ore. Rev. Stat. § 162.185(1)(a) punishes the act of introducing the contraband into a correctional facility; it does not punish the act of possessing drugs. Defendant reasons that turning the voluntary act of possession into the predicate for holding him liable for involuntarily introducing marijuana into the jail stretches the word "includes" too far...

Ore. Rev. Stat. § 161.095(1) derives from the Model Penal Code. The commentary to the analogous section of the Model Penal Code explains:

> It will be noted that the formulation does not state that liability must be based on the voluntary act or the omission simpliciter, but rather upon conduct which includes such action or omission. The distinction has some analytical importance. If the driver of an automobile loses consciousness with the result that he runs over a pedestrian, none of the movements or omissions that accompany or follow this loss of consciousness may in themselves give rise to liability. But a prior voluntary act, such as the act of driving, or a prior omission, such as failing to stop as he felt illness approaching, may, under given circumstances, be regarded as sufficiently negligent for liability to be imposed. In that event, however, liability is based on the entire course of conduct, including the specific conduct that resulted in the injury.
> American Law Institute, Model Penal Code § 2.01, 120 (Tentative Draft No. 4 1955).

The commentary to the Model Penal Code makes clear that the mere fact that defendant voluntarily possessed the drugs before he was arrested is insufficient to hold him criminally liable for the later act of introducing the drugs into the jail. Rather, to satisfy Ore. Rev. Stat. § 161.095(1), the involuntary act must, at a minimum, be a reasonably foreseeable or likely consequence of the voluntary act on which the state seeks to base criminal liability. On these facts, no reasonable juror could find that the introduction of contraband into the jail was a reasonably foreseeable consequence of possessing it. Moreover, the state does not dispute that, in this case, the police's act of arresting defendant and transporting him to the jail was an intervening cause that resulted in the marijuana's being introduced into the jail....

Conviction for supplying contraband reversed.

Martin v. State
Court of Appeals of Alabama
31 Ala. App. 334, 17 So. 2d 427 (1944)

Appellant was convicted of being drunk on a public highway, and appeals. Officers of the law arrested him at his home and took him onto the highway, where he allegedly committed the proscribed acts, viz., manifested a drunken condition by using loud and profane language.

The pertinent provisions of our statute are: "Any person who, while intoxicated or drunk, appears in any public place where one or more persons are present, . . . and manifests a drunken condition by boisterous or indecent conduct, or loud and profane discourse, shall, on conviction, be fined," etc. Code 1940, Title 14, Section 120.

Under the plain terms of this statute, a voluntary appearance is presupposed. The rule has been declared, and we think it sound, that an accusation of drunkenness in a designated public place cannot be established by proof that the accused, while in an intoxicated condition, was involuntarily and forcibly carried to that place by the arresting officer.

Conviction of appellant was contrary to this announced principle and, in our view, erroneous. It appears that no legal conviction can be sustained under the evidence, so, consonant with the prevailing rule, the judgment of the trial court is reversed and one here rendered discharging appellant.

Of consequence, our original opinion of affirmance was likewise laid in error. It is therefore withdrawn.

Reversed and rendered.

People v. Decina
New York Court of Appeals
2 N.Y.2d 133, 138 N.E.2d 799 (1956)

[The defendant experienced an epileptic seizure while driving his car down Delaware Avenue in Buffalo on "a bright, sunny day" in March of 1955. His car jumped the curb and ran into a group of six schoolgirls, killing four of them. He had suffered several seizures in the previous years, including one in September of 1954, and took daily medication to help prevent seizures.]

Defendant was indicted and charged with violating section 1053-a of the Penal Law.[a] ...

[Defendant argues] that his demurrer should have been sustained, since the indictment here does not charge a crime. The indictment states essentially that defendant, knowing "that he was subject to epileptic attacks or other disorder rendering him likely to lose consciousness for a considerable period of time," was culpably negligent "in that he consciously undertook to and did operate his Buick sedan on a public highway" and "while so doing' suffered such an attack which caused said automobile "to travel at a fast and reckless rate of speed, jumping the curb and driving over the sidewalk" causing the death of 4 persons. In our opinion, this clearly states a violation of section 1053-a of the Penal Law. The statute does not require that a defendant must deliberately intend to kill a human being, for that would be murder. Nor does the statute require that he knowingly and consciously follow the precise path that leads to death and destruction. It is sufficient, we have said, when his conduct manifests a "disregard of the consequences which may ensue from the act, and indifference to the rights of others." ...

Assuming the truth of the indictment, as we must on a demurrer, this defendant knew he was subject to epileptic attacks and seizures that might strike at any time. He also knew that a moving motor vehicle uncontrolled on public highway is a highly dangerous instrumentality capable of unrestrained destruction. With this knowledge, and without anyone accompanying him, he deliberately took a chance by making a conscious choice of a course of action, in disregard of the consequences which he knew might follow from his conscious act, and which in this case did ensue ...

To hold otherwise would be to say that a man may freely indulge himself in liquor in the same hope that it will not affect his driving, and if it later develops that ensuing intoxication causes dangerous and reckless driving resulting in death, his unconsciousness or involuntariness at that time would relieve him from prosecution under the statute ... To have a sudden sleeping spell, an unexpected heart or other disabling attack, without any prior knowledge or warning thereof, is an altogether different situation, and there is simply no basis for comparing such cases with the flagrant disregard manifested here.

Higher Regional Court (OLG) Hamm
4 Ss 942/78, NJW 1979, 438 (September 20, 1978)

Facts

The accused was driving a stolen car on a federal road at around 22.30 hours. As a result of his unfitness to drive due to alcohol and because of his excess speed he went into a skid with the car on a left-hand bend, and collided with the witness K.'s approaching truck. Although K. was able to stop, his vehicle was scraped by the skidding car on the right hand front side; property damage of about 1200 DM occurred. The car driven by the accused left the road, turned over and remained lying on its roof in a ditch beside the road. The witness K. first notified the police from a public house, before he, together with a driver who had stopped, shone a light over the overturned Volkswagen. He could not find anyone inside the vehicle. When the police arrived at the site of the accident soon after this, the accused was present amongst the onlookers. When the witness police sergeant F. spoke to him about the accident, he explained that he had had nothing to do with it and had come to the site of the accident on foot. As the accused gave unclear information about himself, and the Volkswagen involved in the accident was reported as stolen, he was brought to the police station to establish his personal details and taken into custody.

The local court sentenced the accused to a term of imprisonment of one year and six months and confiscation of his driving license for three years. His appeal in law was successful.

Reasons

... 1. Contrary to the assumption of the judgment under challenge, the defendant has not fulfilled the definition of leaving the scene of an accident.*

---

[a] § 1053-a (Criminal negligence in the operation of a vehicle resulting in death) applies to any "person who operates or drives any vehicle of any kind in a reckless or culpably negligent manner, whereby a human being is killed."

* [§ 142 German Criminal Code (Leaving the Scene of an Accident without Cause).

(1) A party to a road traffic accident who leaves the scene of the accident before:

a) This applies first for the behavior of the accused until the arrival of the police. The judgment under challenge expressly explains that it could not be established whether the accused had left the scene of the accident before the return of the witness K. It cannot therefore be ruled out that the accused remained at the scene of the accident and was merely not noticed by the witness K. Such behavior does not fulfill the definition in the sense of § 142 para. 1 Criminal Code. The concept of leaving the scene by which the 13th Criminal Law Amendment Act has replaced the word "flight" requires a change of place (Oberlandesgericht Hamm, DAR 1978, 139 [140]; Berz, DAR 1975, 310; Cramer, in: Schönke-Schröder, StGB, § 142 marginal no. 37 with further references), as was also mainly assumed for § 142 Criminal Code, old version. The new wording was merely to make it terminologically clear that a removal from the scene of the accident will fulfill the definition, even if there were no persons there who were available for making determinations (see BT-Dr 7/2434, p.7). The text of the statute confirms this by the fact that it imposes on the participant in the accident the duty to facilitate determinations, amongst other things, "by his presence." A participant in an accident does not therefore commit the crime of leaving the scene of the accident if and so long as he remains at the scene of the accident. Whether the accused had decided, at the point in time when the witness K. returned, to move away from the scene of the accident in the near future does not need to be discussed as an attempt to leave the scene of an accident is not a crime . . .

c) The judgment under challenge is obviously based on the view that the definition of leaving the scene of the accident would also be fulfilled if participation in the accident was untruthfully denied. This view is incorrect. It is true that the participant in the accident would not in this way fulfill his interview duty. However, the violation of this duty is not made punishable as such, but only subject to the prerequisite that the participant in the accident moved away from the scene of the accident. This follows from the clear wording of the statute which restricts the space for interpretation according to § 1 Criminal Code, art. 103 para. 2 Basic Law.

d) Nor is the definition in § 142 para. 1 no. 1 Criminal Code fulfilled by bringing the accused to the police station . . . The accused was provisionally arrested by the police officers and taken away from the scene of the accident against his will. The definition however requires leaving, that is self-removal which is produced by the will of the participant in the accident. The accused has obviously not undertaken any such action. Whether a different decision would have to be made if a participant in an accident consciously brought about his removal in order to evade the necessary determinations can be left open as the reasoning in the judgment contained no grounds for this. Nor has the accused fulfilled the definition of § 142 para. 1 no. 1 Criminal Code by omission (see BGH, VRS 5 [1953], 44; Cramer, in: Schönke-Schröder, StGB, § 142 marginal no. 39), as he had no influence on his removal which took place in the form of an arrest, and consequently he could not prevent this . . . .

The conviction of the accused under § 142 Criminal Code can therefore not stand.

Higher Regional Court (OLG) Hamm
5 Ss 331/74, NJW 1975, 657 (July 16, 1974)

Reasons

The local court sentenced the defendant to a fine of 150 DM for negligent infliction of bodily harm under § 230 Criminal Code.* The local court proceeded on the basis that a fly flew into the defendant's eye as she drove her car around a gentle right-hand bend with a window open. She fended off this fly with one hand while holding the steering wheel with the other. The local court

---

1. he has made it possible, in the interest of the other parties to the accident and any persons suffering injury or damage, to establish his identity, his vehicle and the nature of his involvement through his presence and a statement that he was involved in the accident; or
2. has waited for a period of time which was appropriate under the circumstances, during which no one was willing to establish these facts,

will be punished with imprisonment of not more than three years or a fine.—Eds.]

* [German Criminal Code § 229 (Causing Bodily Harm through Negligence), formerly § 230
Who causes bodily harm to another person through negligence will be punished with imprisonment of not more than three years or with a fine.—Eds.]

further established that the defendant's "jerky defensive movement" transmitted itself to her body and from there to the steering wheel. The result was that the car veered off the carriageway to the right, on to an unmetalled verge, causing the defendant to lose control over the vehicle so that it skidded and crossed on to the opposite carriageway where it struck a car coming in the opposite direction. This caused injury to the defendant's two children travelling with her in her car as well as to a passenger in the colliding vehicle. The local court considers that the defendant's violent defensive movement causing the vehicle she was driving to skid and her culpable failure to take into account that such a jerky movement could transfer itself to the steering of the vehicle amounted to conduct in breach of duty on the defendant's part.

The defendant's appeal in law against this is permissible, but in its outcome is not well founded. ... 2. The Senate cannot agree with the appeal in law in so far as it, by its substantive challenge, disputes the presence of an action in the criminal law sense. If the appeal in law considers that the defensive movement was a shock reaction in the sense of a mere reflex movement, it fails to appreciate the concept of the reflex or reflex movement. It is generally only possible to speak of a mere reflex with those physical movements as to which the stimulation of the motor nerves is not under mental control, but is triggered directly by a physical physiological stimulus, i.e. as to which a stimulus is transferred without the involvement of consciousness from a sensory center to a motor center and hence into movement, and consequently the voluntary element of a reaction, directing action, is absent (see Oberlandesgericht Hamburg, JR 1950, 408, 409; Jescheck, AT, 2nd edit. 1973, p. 169 f., Maurach, AT, 4th edit. 1971, p. 188 ...). Fending off a fly is however not in any way an involuntary defensive reaction in the sense of a purely physiological stimulus being translated directly into a motor reaction. Examples of such direct motor reactions are to be assumed for instance in the case of convulsions, vomiting or medical reflex testing. Even the reaction of the eye closing itself momentarily when a foreign body, like for instance a fly, flies into it may be included in the category of reflex movements. On the other hand, the defensive movement with the hand to ward off such a foreign body involves the circuit of voluntary control, and defensive movements of this kind can in principle be avoided because of other necessities, for instance on the basis of a contrary motivation caused by the threatened risk of an accident. Whether such contrary motivation is present in the actual case, or indeed could have been present, is not a question of the reflex movement, but is a problem of the so-called "semi-automatic" reactions.

Yet there are no sufficient grounds present here for accepting even a "semi-automatic" reaction (Oberlandesgericht Frankfurt, VRS 28, 364) or an "automatized readiness to act" (Welzel, Fahrläs-sigkeit und Verkehrsdelikte (Negligence and Traffic Offences), 1961, p. 33 f.). It is typical of such reactions that the behavior triggered by the stimulus occurs more or less automatically on the basis of a practiced readiness to act arising from a long-established pattern of behavior (see Oberlandes-gericht Frankfurt, loc. cit.). The intention-forming process is thereby transferred to the subliminal by long practice; nevertheless the reaction remains "governable" although it no longer needs to be controlled by actual deliberateness (Maurach, AT, p. 188). So, for example if, when driving a car, individual or partial acts of driving, like for instance the making of traffic signals or changing gear are automatized on the basis of constant practice, the necessary behavior in question remains never-theless controllable because of the diversity of the situations, like e.g. the need to change gear or stop at a traffic light. So far as the issue here, fending off a fly, is concerned, it seems questionable whether this is to be seen as a part of driving at all or not rather as a separate act which is to be looked at individually. It is also scarcely possible to speak here of a learnt or practiced form of behavior. It could seem more appropriate to describe such reactions as impulsive. Yet this would not in any case be meant as an instinctive movement, which could possibly be equated with a reflex movement (Mezger, LK, 8th edit 1957/58). This is because whilst an instinctive movement can be involuntary behavior, an impulsive action represents a voluntary occurrence even if it frequently takes the form of a so-called sudden irrational act, for which a psychological impulse is present, and which is translated into action by merely excluding contrary motives (Schönke-Schröder, preliminary note 27 a before § 1).

Even the appeal in law does not exclude the possibility that the defendant's defensive movement is to be assumed to be a sudden irrational act of this kind. The defensive movement cannot therefore in any case be denied the quality of an action. It is true that in actions of this kind, the intent, as for instance here to fend off the foreign body, is activated or formed so quickly through the sensory nerves and is so quickly translated into a motor reaction that no time remains for the formation of a contrary motivation, however compelling the facts on which it is based. In this respect the sudden irrational act, because of the course it takes, resembles the so-called shock reaction in which the primitive reactions which emerge from the depths of the personality (senseless substitute actions or incapability of action) arise so quickly and directly that the so-called I function (the "person level") as a controlling power cannot move into action at all (Spiegel, DAR 1968, 290). In spite of the speed of this event, such processes do not however lack any voluntary impulse, so the defensive movement at issue here is an act in the sense of the criminal law ...

NOTES

1. Unlike the Oregon Statute, the text of the German Criminal Code does not explicitly demand a voluntary act as a "minimal requirement for criminal liability." But there is a general consensus within German criminal law doctrine and judicial practice about the requirement of an act as an (unwritten) pre-condition of offense definitions. The majority opinion advocates a very broad conception of act as "socially relevant conduct," while others emphasize the offender's will to achieve something. Despite some uncertainty about how to define "act" positively, all agree about a negative core definition: acts do not include uncontrollable incidents such as sudden seizures or unforeseeable heart attacks and reflexes.

The Oregon criminal code is based on the Model Penal Code, and the provision at issue in *Tippetts* is no exception.* Unlike the Oregon code, however, the MPC does not attempt to define "voluntariness." Instead, paralleling the German consensus, the drafters were content to list *involuntary* acts:

(2) The following are not voluntary acts within the meaning of this Section:
   (a) a reflex or convulsion;
   (b) a bodily movement during unconsciousness or sleep;
   (c) conduct during hypnosis or resulting from hypnotic suggestion;
   (d) a bodily movement that otherwise is not a product of the effort or determination of the actor, either conscious or habitual.

The MPC drafters shied away from defining voluntariness for fear of "inject[ing] into the criminal law questions about determinism or free will."† (Is this a valid concern? How could one *not* inject questions of free will into the criminal law? If one is a treatmentist, perhaps?‡) Note that the Restatement of Torts (Second), which the American Law Institute drafted roughly contemporaneously with the Model Penal Code, did manage to produce just such a definition: "The word 'act' is used throughout the Restatement of this Subject to denote an external manifestation of the actor's will and does not include any of its results...."§ (Does it make more sense to think of *criminal* liability without reference to "will" than to think of *tort* liability in this way? Wouldn't you expect it to be the other way around?)

This attempt to evade intractable philosophical difficulties presumably also accounts for the Model Penal Code's distinction, followed in the Oregon code, between acts and voluntary acts. This made possible an apparently unproblematic definition of act as "a bodily movement whether voluntary or involuntary" (§ 1.13(2)). But doesn't that just pass the buck from one intractable problem (philosophy) to another (neurology)? What is a bodily movement anyway?

Then again, is *Tippetts* an illustration of just what can happen if a legislature does try to define voluntariness? Consider the trouble the word "consciously" causes the court in *Tippetts*. Or is the trouble with "consciously" not that it raises questions of free will, but that it confounds the distinction between *actus reus* and *mens rea*, and purpose in particular, which the Code defines as, among other things, "conscious object" (and knowledge, perhaps even recklessness, insofar as they require awareness).¶

2. In German criminal law, outside the general agreement about an act requirement of some kind, there are borderline cases, sometimes because we tend to apply the term "reflex" in ordinary language in a broader sense than a doctor of neurology would. The second German case decided by the Higher Regional Court of Hamm (it is a coincidence that we have here two cases by the same appellate court) analyzes phenomena like semi-automatic reactions and sudden irrational acts. The judges conclude that only reflexes in the narrow, medical

---

* See Model Penal Code § 2.01(1) ("A person is not guilty of an offense unless his liability is based on conduct which includes a voluntary act or the omission to perform an act of which he is physically capable.")
   † Model Penal Code Commentaries § 2.01, at 215.
   ‡ On the MPC and treatmentism as a rationale for punishment, or rather for "peno-correctional treatment," see Chapter 1.A.i.
   § Restatement (Second) of Torts § 2.
   ¶ MPC § 2.02; see also the discussion of *mens rea* in Chapter 8.

sense do not count as acts, whereas semi-automatic reactions and sudden irrational acts are acts in a legal sense.

What is the significance of the "medical" or "scientific" definition of a term in this opinion? As opposed to the commonsensical, or everyday, sense of the term? If science changes (hopefully improves!) over time, should legal analysis follow suit? If there is a conflict between scientific and everyday senses, which one should win the day? How about conflicts *among* scientific senses (or everyday ones, for that matter)? This issue will reappear in the discussion of intoxication and insanity, in Chapters 8.D and 14.C. Is a juror worse (or better?) suited to assess the relevance of scientific evidence, or to determine the everyday sense of a term, than a judge? Are you convinced by the Hamm court's attempt to differentiate automatic from "semi-automatic" from sudden irrational acts? Is it trying to get at something important, something the MPC approach to acts and voluntariness is missing?*

3. In German criminal law, there is also general consensus about the circumstances in *State v. Tippetts* and in *People v. Decina*, that is, a driver's sudden loss of consciousness. The legally relevant conduct under such conditions might be a prior act or omission, like starting to drive or failing to stop despite awareness of illness or despite knowledge about the danger of seizures.

The doctrine of "concurrence" in Anglo-American criminal law generally requires that *actus reus* and *mens rea* coincide: to have the requisite *mens rea* at time A, and commit the requisite act at time B would not amount to a criminal offense. Courts have a way of getting around this requirement (1) by stretching the "relevant act" to cover time A or (2) by finding concurrence between the requisite *mens rea* and some *failure to act* (i.e., an omission) at time A.[†] This move is controversial in the concurrence context, so why shouldn't it be controversial here? Why do we get to broadly define the "legally relevant" conduct to start when someone gets behind the wheel of a car, even if the offense does not criminalize getting behind the wheel of car, but driving (or at least "operating") it? If we are not stretching the legally relevant act, but concede that the first act (getting behind the wheel of the car) and the second act (driving) are separate, how can the first act generate criminal liability for the second act, even if at the time of the first act the defendant had the requisite *mens rea* (in the driving cases: recklessness? negligence?)?[‡] Are we prepared to say that defendant engaged in the proscribed conduct (let's say, reckless driving) the moment he gets into the car, walks to the car, picks up the keys, puts on his coat, gets up from the breakfast table, eats his cereal, etc.? Where do we draw the line between "legally relevant" conduct and other conduct, once we leave behind the definition of the offense (which requires "driving")? In other words, is what's missing in these cases the *actus reus*, or the *mens rea*? A similar problem arises in cases of intoxication.[§]

4. The act requirement has very limited meaning in German criminal law. Only in very rare and unusual cases can one conclude that there was no legally relevant act at all. This is also the case in Anglo-American law, to the point where most scholarly discussions about the act requirement wonder aloud whether it is (still?) necessary, or whether it still exists (assuming it ever did).[¶] Does it matter that one of the paradigmatic offenses of contemporary criminal law, possession, appears to fly in the face of the act requirement—or would, if such a requirement existed.[**] Do you think the requirement of an act, or of a voluntary act, makes

---

* See MPC § 2.01(2)(a): "reflex or convulsion" not voluntary act.
† See *R. v. Miller*, [1983] 1 All E.R. 978 (discussing *Fagan v. Metropolitan Police Commissioner*, [1968] 3 All E.R. 442).
‡ For more—*much* more—on *mens rea*, see Chapter 8.
§ See Chapter 8.D. For a general discussion of "time framing" devices in criminal law, see Mark Kelman, "Interpretive Construction in the Substantive Criminal Law," 33 *Stanford Law Review* (1981), 591.
¶ See, e.g., Douglas Husak, "Rethinking the Act Requirement," 28 *Cardozo Law Review* (2007), 2437; Paul H. Robinson, "Should the Criminal Law Abandon the Actus Reus/Mens Rea Distinction?," in Stephen Shute et al. (eds.), *Action and Value in Criminal Law* (1996), 187.
** See Chapter 7.A.

sense? Consider this question in light of the various rationales of punishment. Is it the actness of the requirement that does the work, or the voluntariness?

Consider the rationale for the (voluntary) act requirement offered in the Model Penal Code Commentaries:

> It is fundamental that a civilized society does not punish for thoughts alone. Beyond this, the law cannot hope to deter involuntary movement or to stimulate action that cannot physically be performed; the sense of personal security would be undermined in a society where such movement or inactivity could lead to formal social condemnation of the sort that a conviction necessarily entails. People whose involuntary movements threaten harm to others may present a public health or safety problem, calling for therapy or even for custodial commitment; they do not present a problem of correction.
>
> Commentaries § 2.01, at 214–15.

Can these arguments be squared with the Model Penal Code's treatmentist approach?

5. With regard to cases like *State v. Tippetts*, *Martin v. State*, and the first German case (leaving the scene of an accident), it is questionable whether the decisive legal question really concerns the act requirement. The act requirement obviously would be relevant if police officers had not only handcuffed Tippetts, but also bound his feet and carried him into the building. But if he walked into the jail building, why should this not count as an act?

In the German case, we can assume that a police car took the defendant away from the scene of the accident to the police station. Thus, it is easier to argue that he did not act because the movement of the police car was beyond his control (getting into the car through bodily movements of his own would not be crucial as long as the car was still parked at the scene of the accident). But should criminal punishment really depend on whether a defendant was transported by car or was made to walk (for instance, if a police car had broken down)? Arguably, such coincidences should not determine the legal outcome—but one has to keep in mind that there are other ways to negate criminal liability if someone moves his body in a controlled way but is forced by others to do so. Therefore, a judgment that "the offender did move his muscles consciously, according to his own will" does not imply that he or she will be punished.

First, the specific offense definition is more important rather than the general act requirement. Offense elements ("introducing contraband into a correctional facility," "leaving the scene of an accident," and "appearing in public") could be interpreted in a restrictive way. Even if the defendant did act by moving his body, this act might not fall under the scope of the prohibition as it was intended by the legislature. Such a restrictive interpretation would exclude situations when the "offender" was forced by others to move his body. (Admittedly, the German ruling does not make it clear whether the judges referred to the general act requirement or a restrictive interpretation of § 142 para. 1 Criminal Code when coming to the conclusion that there was no criminal liability.) Second, one could think about a justification or excuse under the heading of "duress" if the offender was forced by others to move his body.*

Martin v. State is a classic American case on the act requirement, and is usually taken to illustrate a clear-cut violation of the act requirement. The (very short) opinion in this case is reproduced here in its entirety. Note that the Alabama appellate court changed its mind: in this opinion overturning the conviction, the court takes the highly unusual step of withdrawing its own previous opinion in the same case, which had affirmed the conviction. The obvious violation of the act requirement, in other words, only became obvious after further reflection (and, at any rate, was not obvious to the trial court). But does *Martin* in fact turn on the act requirement? Or can it be handled as an exercise in statutory interpretation? Just how many acts does the statute in *Martin* require? If it's more than one, does the act requirement require that at least one act be voluntary, or must all be voluntary? Can you square *Martin* with *Decina*? Why doesn't the *Martin* court extent the "legally relevant

---

* For more on duress, see Chapter 14.A.

conduct" to an earlier point at which Martin did engage in voluntary conduct? Drinking? In private? In public?

6. Actus reus *and offense element types.* More generally, it is worth exploring the connection between the act requirement and statutory interpretation. It may well be that the act requirement is less significant today because offense definitions have become more detailed than they once were. In an age of vague (or nonexistent) offense definitions, where courts have little more to go on than a general threat of punishment attached to an otherwise undefined term (say, "murder is punishable by death through hanging" or "thieves are punished by having their ears cut off"), they may well turn to a general requirement such as *actus reus* to guide their analysis of the situation before them. As offense definitions— developed in the common law by courts, and then increasingly by legislatures—become more specific, and actually define the conduct subject to punishment, the act requirement adds little to the analysis of the question of whether the behavior in the case matches the elements of the offense definition. (Note that the *actus reus* requirement, as the *mens rea* requirement, applied only to common law crimes, i.e., judicially created offenses, not to statutory offenses, i.e., those defined by parliament.) In fact, today "*actus reus*" is often used in precisely this sense: the objective elements of the offense. Alternatively, it might refer to (only) the conduct element of an offense, so that the *actus reus* requirement would amount to a requirement that every offense definition must include a conduct element. Consider the following excerpt from the Model Penal Commentaries, discussing the three different *offense element types* (conduct, attendant circumstance, result):

> The "circumstances" of the offense refer to the objective situation that the law requires to exist, in addition to the defendant's act or any results that the act may cause. The elements of "nighttime" in burglar, "property of another" in theft, . . . and "dwelling" in arson are illustrations. "Conduct" refers to "breaking and entering" in burglary, "taking" in theft, "sexual intercourse" in rape and "burning" in arson. Results, of course, include "death" in homicide.

Model Penal Code Commentaries § 5.01, at 301 n.9.

B. Constitutional Constraints?

The act requirement is often mentioned as one of the few exceptions (if not the only one) to the rule that U.S. constitutional law does not concern itself with substantive criminal law. To what extent the act requirement is in fact constitutionalized—based on the Eighth Amendment prohibition of "cruel and unusual punishments"—is unclear, however. Also unclear is whether the constitutional act requirement, however it might be defined, in fact has any teeth.

People v. Davis
Court of Appeals of New York
33 N.Y.2d 221, 306 N.E.2d 787 (1973)

Jasen, Judge:

Wilbert Davis, a heroin addict, has been convicted of criminal possession of a dangerous drug in the sixth degree and criminal possession of a hypodermic instrument . . .

The facts are undisputed. On February 4, 1971, the landlord of the premises at 34 Fort Green Place, Brooklyn, approached a uniformed patrolman on duty in the area. He led the officer to that address, a three story "walk up," and permitted him to enter. The officer ascended one flight of stairs and observed the defendant standing in a bathroom, about to inject himself with a syringe later determined to contain heroin. When approached by the officer, the defendant pleaded with him to be allowed to take the injection. In effecting the arrest, the officer observed fresh needle marks on defendant's right arm. Defendant admitted that he had been using heroin for about a year and one half.

At trial, the defendant offered evidence designed to show the nature of narcotic addiction and that he was, in fact, a narcotic addict. The defendant conceded his addiction to heroin and this concession was amply supported by medical testimony not disputed by the People.

The argument for reversal is predicated on *Robinson v. California*, 370 U.S. 660, 82 S.Ct. 1417, 8 L. Ed.2d 758 and *Powell v. Texas*, 392 U.S. 514, 88 S.Ct. 2145, 20 L.Ed.2d 1254. In *Robinson*, the petitioner was convicted under a California statute making it a criminal offense for a person to be addicted to narcotics. The Trial Judge instructed the jury that it was a misdemeanor under the statute "either to use narcotics, or to be addicted to the use of narcotics," that the "portion of the statute referring to 'addicted to the use' of narcotics is based upon a condition or status," and that "(i)t is a continuing offense" which "subjects the offender to arrest at any time before he reforms."

The Supreme Court reversed. Implicitly recognizing that narcotic addiction is a disease, the court held that a State law making the "status" of narcotic addiction a criminal offense inflicted cruel and unusual punishment in violation of the Eighth and Fourteenth Amendments. By way of rationale, the court emphasized the absence of an *actus reus*, that under the statute the criminal sanction was imposed even though a person has "never touched any narcotic drug within the State or been guilty of any irregular behavior there." The court was careful to point out, however, that the States retained broad power to regulate narcotic drugs traffic within their borders. Such regulation, it said, could take a variety of valid forms, citing, by way of example, the power to impose criminal sanctions against the unauthorized sale, manufacture, purchase or possession of narcotics.

In dissent, Justice White voted to affirm the conviction, being of the view that the appellant was not being punished on the basis of status, illness or condition, but for the regular and habitual use of narcotics in violation of California law. In dicta, particularly pertinent here, he observed: "If it is 'cruel and unusual punishment' to convict appellant for addiction, it is difficult to understand why it would be any less offensive to the Fourteenth Amendment to convict him for use on the same evidence of use which proved he was an addict. It is significant that in purporting to reaffirm the power of the States to deal with the narcotics traffic, the Court does not include among the obvious powers of the State the power to punish for the use of narcotics. I cannot think that the omission was inadvertent."

In *Powell v. Texas*, supra, the Supreme Court . . . was asked to extend *Robinson* by prohibiting a State from punishing a chronic alcoholic for public drunkenness. Leroy Powell was convicted of violating a Texas statute declaring it unlawful to "get drunk or be found in a state of intoxication in any public place." The Trial Judge, sitting without a jury, made certain "findings of fact": that "chronic alcoholism is a disease which destroys the afflicted person's will power to resist the constant, excessive consumption of alcohol"; that "a chronic alcoholic does not appear in public of his own volition but under a compulsion symptomatic" of his disease; and that Powell was afflicted with disease as described.

The Supreme Court affirmed. The plurality opinion per Justice Marshall, rejecting the trial court's findings of fact, observed that one could not "conclude, on the state of this record or on the current state of medical knowledge, that chronic alcoholics in general, and Leroy Powell in particular, suffer from such an irresistible compulsion to drink and to get drunk in public that they are utterly unable to control their performance of either or both these acts and thus cannot be deterred at all from public intoxication." Robinson was distinguished on the ground that Powell was not convicted for being a chronic alcoholic, but for being in public while drunk. Unlike *Robinson*, the sanctions of the Texas statute were not directed at "mere status," but at socially offensive behavior: appearing in public drunk.

In a dissent joined by three Justices, Justice Fortas adopted the trial court's findings and viewed the Texas statute as imposing punishment for the "mere condition of being intoxicated in public" and read *Robinson* as barring the imposition of criminal sanctions "upon a person for being in a condition he is powerless to change." As a corollary, Justice Fortas declared that "a person may not (consistent with the Eighth Amendment) be punished if the condition essential to constitute the defined crime is part of the pattern of his disease and is occasioned by a compulsion symptomatic of the disease." Justice White . . . observed: "If it cannot be a crime to have an irresistible compulsion to use narcotics, *Robinson v. California*, 370 U.S. 660, 82 S.Ct. 1417, 8 L.Ed.2d 758 (1962), I do not see how it can constitutionally be a crime to yield to such a compulsion. Punishing an addict for using drugs convicts for addiction under a different name. Distinguishing between the two crimes is like forbidding criminal conviction for being sick with flu or epilepsy but permitting punishment for running a fever or having a convulsion. Unless Robinson is to be abandoned, the use of narcotics by an addict must be beyond the reach of the criminal law. Similarly, the chronic alcoholic with an irresistible urge to consume alcohol should not be punishable for drinking or for being drunk." . . .

Implicit in the defendant's argument that it constitutes cruel and unusual punishment to impose a criminal penalty upon an addict who possesses narcotics and associated paraphernalia for his own use, is an appeal for judicial recognition of a drug dependence defense to criminal responsibility, an argument better addressed, at this juncture, to the Legislature.* Doubtless, the argument is logically appealing that if an addict cannot, consistent with the Federal and State Constitutions, be punished for being in the status or condition of addiction, he cannot be punished for the acts of possessing for his personal use narcotics and associated instruments, the necessary incidents of his condition, which acts are realistically inseparable from the status or condition itself.

There is, however, no square holding for defendant's position that acts incident to addiction may not be punished. Robinson did not so hold. Indeed it is authority for the proposition that actual behavior may be punished but not the condition or status of addiction itself...[Moreover,] it is unmistakably clear that the majority in Powell recoiled from the asserted Eighth Amendment claim and the recognition of new lines of defense to criminal accountability by reason of the compulsions attributable to alcoholism, and presumably narcotic addiction, conditions from which it is still widely assumed, rightly or wrongly, that the victim retains some capacity to extricate himself....

...The ramifications of recognizing the asserted cruel and unusual punishment defense, and impliedly the defense of drug dependence, are startling. The difficulty lies in knowing where to stop. The obvious danger is that the defense will be extended to other crimes— robberies, burglaries and the like—which can be shown to arise from the compulsive craving for drugs. And if "mere purchase or possession" by the addict for his own use is protected, what of the "mere sale" to the same addict by an obliging trafficker in illicit drugs? Could not the sale to the addict who is driven to acquire drugs by his compulsive craving be defended as a humane act inflicting no harm on other members of society?

Moreover, any attempted limitation on the availability of the drug dependence defense to those acts such as purchase, possession or receipt of narcotics for the addict's personal use, finds little justification in the cruel and unusual punishment clause with which it intertwines. For example, assuming the drug dependence defense be recognized, is it somehow less offensive to contemporary concepts of human decency, as embodied in the constitutional proscription of cruel and unusual punishment (*Trop v. Dulles*, 356 U.S. 86, 101) to punish an addict who, out of a compulsive craving for drugs, steals to fund his habit than it is to punish an addict who, out of the same craving, merely purchases or possesses illicit drugs for his own use? If the compulsion is the same, why is the one act blameworthy and not the other? Such a distinction smacks of limitation by fiat and invites accusations of arbitrariness...

[W]hile it may be that the policy of rehabilitation would be well served by affording addicts a cruel and unusual punishment and drug dependence defense to possession for their own use, we should not lose sight of the utility of such penalties to law enforcement. For example, these possible penalties may, through the exercise of prosecutorial discretion, enable law enforcement to enlist addict informers in ferreting out the wholesalers of illicit drugs, thereby facilitating the policy of elimination of the drug traffic. Then, too, punishment may persuade some addicts to undertake rehabilitation through various State or private programs. On the other hand, recognition of the defense might conceivably make the addict the witting or unwitting tool of the drug trafficker.

In sum, recognition of defendant's constitutional claim and implicitly, at least, the drug dependence defense, does not follow inexorably from the Robinson and Powell decisions and, indeed, strong reasons of public policy militate against any such recognition by this court.

The order of the Appellate Term should be affirmed.

NOTES

1. The German Federal Constitutional Court would analyze cases like *Robinson v. California* and *Powell v. Texas* (which are mentioned in *People v. Davis*) by pointing to the constitutional culpability principle. The text of the German Basic Law does not contain an explicit "cruel and unusual punishment" clause, but the culpability principle, which the Court derives from basic human rights and constitutional maxims,** serves similar functions. If the German legislature introduced an offense description that would base criminal punishment on status or events like "being addicted to the use of narcotics" or "being found in public," the Federal Constitutional Court could be expected to declare this a violation of the culpability

---

* The drug dependence defense would appear to be premised on the theory that addiction involves a compelling propensity to use narcotics, amounting to a loss of self-control, depriving the addict's acts of possession and use, etc., of volition, a theory about which debate rages.

** See, e.g., Chapter 1.

principle. The crucial point would be that the status of "being addicted" or "being found" can be entirely beyond the individual's control. For instance, addiction can be the product of drugs administered by others against one's will, and one can be found somewhere after being transported there against one's will by others.

2. If one turns to circumstances like those in *People v. Davis*, that is, possession offenses, the German Federal Constitutional Court also dismisses constitutional challenges. Under German law, illegal possession of drugs is a criminal offense (§ 29 para. 1 no. 3 Narcotics Act). There was a constitutional case arguing that the act requirement is a constitutional requirement and that therefore possession offenses must be regarded as unconstitutional. But the Court rejected this view.* In this decision, the Court cites the culpability principle and demands that the conduct in question must be under the offender's control—which is compatible with the existence of possession offenses. The offender can choose between continuing to possess and giving up his or her possession. With respect to drug dependence, the German Federal Constitutional Court has not demanded that drug dependence count as an excuse in the criminal law. It seems that the Court's underlying concept of "offender's control" as part of the culpability principle is not a very ambitious vision of control.

3. Somewhat surprising for a German reader is the recourse in *People v. Davis* to a "utility to law enforcement" argument—the German Federal Constitutional Court tends to avoid such openly pragmatic views. Is that because pragmatic views of this sort do not influence legal analysis in German courts? Or because they *may* not influence it? Or because they cannot be accommodated, given the norms of German legal reasoning? Either way, what is objectionable about (openly) considering the utility of a given norm to law enforcement? Recall[†] the problems with acknowledging the practice of plea bargaining in German criminal law and the difficulty in accommodating exceptions to the principle of compulsory prosecution (*Legalitätsprinzip*), eventually through the establishment of a counter-principle, the opportunity principle (*Opportunitätsprinzip*), which as a matter of principle authorizes prosecutors (but not police officers) to deviate from the principle of compulsory prosecution on the basis of general "pragmatic" considerations such as the "public interest." Is it possible to weigh "policy" against "principle," or should one not stray from the path of principle, as a matter of principle, perhaps for fear of attracting Kant's famous curse, in the *Metaphysics of Morals*, directed at those who deviate from the criminal law's categorical imperative and engage in consequentialist penal thinking: "woe to him who slithers through the serpent-windings of utilitarianism"? (Recall, in this context, the discussion of rationales, mixed or not, of punishment, in Chapter 1.A.i.)

C. Possession

The notion of criminal liability for possession is worth closer attention than it has received, at least until recently, for several reasons. As a matter of the general part, it raises interesting questions about the criminal law's commitment to an act requirement, since possession as a status, or perhaps as a relationship between a person and an object, is not obviously compatible with even the narrow definition of an act as a bodily movement (voluntary or not) favored by the drafters of the Model Penal Code.

At the same time, through the use of the concepts of "constructive" and "joint" possession, the law of possession circumvents ordinary requirements of accessorial liability, instead deriving nonexclusive possession liability from a person's indirect relationship to an object in the form of actual, or potential, dominion or control over an area containing it or over

---

* German Federal Constitutional Court, Judgment of June 16, 1994, 2 BvR 1157/94, NJW 1994, 2412.
† See Chapter 5.D.

another person in physical possession of it. In other words, possession is both a mode of criminal liability—in the general part—and an offense with as many variations as there are objects to possess—in the special part.

More generally, possession liability fits into, and highlights, a complex doctrinal system of multiply inchoate liability, in conjunction with implicit as well as explicit, irrebuttable as well as rebuttable, backward- and forward-looking, presumptions. As such, the range of possession offenses, a fairly recent addition to the state's penal toolkit, perform an important function in a modern regime of crime control aimed at the efficient identification and elimination of human threats, characteristic of the often cited preventive turn in contemporary criminal law and manifested most comprehensively in the so-called war on crime.

People v. E.C.
Supreme Court of New York
195 Misc. 2d 680, 761 N.Y.S.2d 443 (2003)

The issue presented in this case is whether . . . the temporary and lawful possession of one-eighth of an ounce of cocaine is a defense to criminal possession of a controlled substance in the fourth degree (Penal Law § 220.09 [1]) . . .

. . . [T]he defendant . . . was employed by Primo Security to work as a bouncer at a bar, was told to confiscate illegal contraband before anyone was allowed inside, and that their policy was that if anything was confiscated, he should contact Primo who would turn in the contraband to the police. On the night in question, the defendant confiscated 14 packets of cocaine from a patron on his way into the bar. Prior to his having an opportunity to contact Primo, the police responded to noise outside the bar at which time the defendant gave the police the 14 packets of cocaine . . .

The foundation for the common law defense [of temporary and lawful possession] originates with the possession of a weapon. In *People v. Persce*, 204 NY 397, 97 N.E. 877, 27 N.Y. Cr. 41 (1912), the defendant possessed a "slungshot." The court, in dicta, recognized that the possession of a weapon as part of a criminal act did not mean mere possession. In *Persce*, the court mentioned two exceptions: (1) "legal ownership of a weapon in a collection of curious and interesting objects" and (2) possession "which might result temporarily and incidentally from the performance of some lawful act, as disarming a wrongful possessor."

. . . The People do not dispute the existence of this common law defense with respect to weapons, rather they argue against applying it to other possessory crimes such as criminal possession of a controlled substance . . .

The People seem to be taking an absolutist position to the temporary and innocent possession of a controlled substance. This position makes little sense in real life and runs contrary to public policy considerations. It also allows for certain factual situations to be criminalized where it is clear that the state would not want to punish people doing the right thing. While many real life situations come to mind, three intriguing ones came up in oral argument.

First, if a parent discovers illegal drugs in their child's bedroom and decided to confront the child with these drugs—just like we see on the public service announcements on television—the parent would be guilty of a degree of criminal possession of a controlled substance under the People's absolutist position.

Second, if a teacher, dean, guidance counselor or principal in a school came into possession of a controlled substance by either taking it from a student or finding it in a desk, open locker, the hall or any other part of the school, the teacher, dean, guidance counselor or principal would be guilty of a degree of criminal possession of a controlled substance under the People's absolutist position.

The third example might be the most intriguing especially in drug cases. During the trial, like other drugs cases, after the People entered into evidence the 14 packets of cocaine, they published them to the jury. The jurors, one-by-one, took the cocaine into their hands and looked at it and then passed them to the next juror. The last juror returned the 14 packets to the court. Under this situation, each juror would be guilty of a degree of criminal possession of a controlled substance under the People's absolutist position.

The same policy considerations for weapons are equally valid for controlled substances. We want people, not just law enforcement, to confiscate illegal drugs from their children and students and turn them in to the proper authorities. We want people who find drugs on the street to pick them up and turn them in to the proper authorities. We want jurors to be able to examine evidence without fear of prosecution. It makes no sense whatsoever to criminalize this type of behavior. It runs contrary to public policy . . .

Accordingly, the jury will be instructed [on the temporary and lawful possession defense.] [I]t will be up to the jury to decide whether the defendant was telling the truth and whether the defense applies.

Model Penal Code

§ 2.01. Possession as an Act

(4) Possession is an act... if the possessor knowingly procured or received the thing possessed or was aware of his control thereof for a sufficient period to have been able to terminate his possession.

Higher Regional Court (OLG) Zweibrücken
1 Ss. 171/81, AnwBl. 1983, 126 (July 7, 1982)

Reasons

The defendant is charged with obstruction of punishment (§ 258 Criminal Code)* and a misdemeanor against the Narcotics Act (unauthorized possession of hashish).

The local court acquitted the defendant. On appeal by the public prosecutor's office, the criminal chamber of the regional court sentenced the defendant for obstruction of punishment to a fine of 80 daily amounts of 100 DM each.

The regional court has made the following findings:

On Oct. 22 or 24, 1977, the court employee A. entrusted the defendant, who runs a lawyer's office, to represent her interests and those of her son. She was afraid that her son, who repeatedly stayed at a certain residence which, according to police information, was used as a place of resort for consumers, dealers and couriers of hashish, could be involved in a drugs affair. An incident on Oct. 21, 1977, gave concrete ground for her fear. On this day, Wolfgang A. asked his mother, as is described in the judgment, "to lend him her car, a V W, which Mrs. A. did, as she had frequently done in the past. He told his mother that he wanted to travel to Ludwigshafen. In fact he drove there that evening and stayed in front of or in the public house S. in Ludwigshafen-Friesenheim, frequented by known drug dealers and consumers. On the return journey to Neustadt a d. Weinstr., he took a person with him, whose identity remained unknown. On Saturday, October 22, 1977, Mrs. A. discovered in the course of the morning that the passenger door of her car was unlocked. She found a plastic bag with a T-shirt and other pieces of clothing on the back seat. The witness (Mrs. A) noticed on the floor behind the driver's seat, or on the passenger seat, a dark green-brown slab almost turning black 5 x 10 cm in area and 3–5 mm thick which was wrapped or sealed in firm transparent foil. It was a slab of hashish of unknown weight. This hashish had either been acquired on the previous evening by Wolfgang A. who had left it lying in the car or it had been left behind in the car by the unknown third person.

Mrs. A. was very shocked about the discovery of the packet. Because of knowledge acquired by her from work, she immediately assumed that it was hashish... She contacted the defendant on Oct. 24, 1977, at the latest. At the discussion with him when she gave instructions, so far as the criminal chamber could obtain information about this, what essentially happened was that Mrs. A. pleaded for the defendant's assistance in a state of the greatest agitation, as she feared that her son was slipping away. She asked the defendant to exercise influence over him. In the following days the defendant had a discussion with Wolfgang A. at his office. The content of this conversation could not be established, apart from the fact that the defendant talked generally with Wolfgang A. about drug problems, established his knowledge of the subject and obtained information about drugs, their origin and effect. In the context of the information from his client, the defendant discovered all the circumstances relating to the find, and in particular that Wolfgang A. had taken an unknown person with him in his mother's car.

At a point in time which can no longer be established, but at the latest on Nov. 5, 1977, Mrs. A. handed over to the defendant the packet with hashish. The defendant thought it was highly probable that it was hashish. He said to Mrs. A. that the packet would be destroyed in the proper way. The defendant kept the packet with him for several days at least and considered what to do. It is not disputed that he contacted the head of a drug department of a public prosecutor's office outside Rheinland-Pfalz who was known to him and asked for advice. This public prosecutor, who remains unknown, explained to the defendant that in practice cases of this kind are entered under an "AR" number, and the drug is then later handed over to the competent state police office for destruction. It would be possible to proceed in this way in the present case.

On Nov. 17, 1977, the defendant brought the packet with the hashish to the private residence of the unknown public prosecutor and departmental head. It is not disputed that during the ensuing period he weighed the hashish and sent the drug for destruction to the state police office. He communicated the fact of destruction to the defendant before Nov. 29, 1977. According to the

* [§ 258 StGB is reprinted above, in Chapter 5.C.—Eds.]

findings in the judgment, the defendant knew when the drug was handed over for destruction "that it was an important form of evidence. He also knew that there had been possession relevant in criminal law on the part of his client Wolfgang A. or another possessor. By getting rid of this form of evidence he intended to secure primarily his client Wolfgang A., but in any case the last possessor of the drug, against criminal prosecution . . .

The defendant explained his conduct in a letter of Nov. 18, 1977, to the chief public prosecutor amongst other things by saying that he had had doubts giving the drug to the local police office because one of his clients would have been disadvantaged by this.

In the intervening period criminal proceedings were commenced against Wolfgang A. for prohibited possession of a drug. The local court acquitted the defendant's client because it could not be established whether the package in question had contained hashish. The public prosecutor's appeal was rejected by the regional court by a judgment of January 26, 1979, which had become legally effective. The chamber assumed that the substance in question was hashish, but that possession relevant in criminal law by Wolfgang A. could not be proved.

The defendant is of the opinion that he has not made himself criminally liable. He considered himself to be justified in acting as he had, especially as he had not expected that investigatory proceedings would be taken against Wolfgang A. His own transitory power over the packet, during which he had not known for certain but had merely suspected that it contained a drug, had not been illegal because in the circumstances of the case he had acted under a justifying or excusing necessity.

The criminal chamber considers the defendant to be guilty of a misdemeanor of obstructing punishment (§ 258 Criminal Code) because he as a defense attorney had removed a form of evidence. In this context the judgment explains: The defendant intended "to preserve his client Wolfgang A. from punishment for unauthorized possession of narcotics under §§ 3, 11 para. 1 no. 6b Narcotics Act by removal of a form of evidence. The defendant was at the same time aware on the basis of his conversation with Wolfgang A. and Mrs. A. that by destroying the form of evidence he would prevent the punishment of a possible other possessor of the drug. The defendant intended this and acted deliberately in this respect. . . .

The chamber did not regard the defendant's possession of the drug as criminal.

The defendant is appealing against this judgment by his appeal in law by which he objects to the violation of procedural and substantive law. The appeal in law, which is admissible, is successful in relation to the substantive objection.

The defendant must be acquitted. According to the findings of the appeal judgment, the objective definition of obstructing punishment (§ 258 Criminal Code) is not fulfilled. Nor do the findings support a conviction for an attempt to commit this crime.

According to this provision, a person is to be punished if he obstructs another being punished or made subject to a measure in accordance with criminal statute because of an unlawful act. Obstruction here means an improvement, even if only partial, of the position of the person benefited by the perpetrator's action as against the State claim to prosecution or punishment (see e.g.: Dreher-Tröndle, StGB 40th edit., § 258 marginal no. 5 with further references). The defendant has not objectively brought about any such hindrance to the State claim to prosecution either in favor of his client or an unknown third party.

So far as his behavior is to be assessed with regard to his clients Wolfgang A. and Wolfgang A.'s mother, criminal conduct by them is lacking. According to the findings of the appeal court and their legal assessment within the framework of the definition of the crime, the defendant's client, Wolfgang A, did not have possession. It is true that the packet of hashish which was found inside the car used by Wolfgang A was within the area of his power and this formed the basis of suspicion of a crime. The circumstances of the present case and the conclusions arising from them do not however support this suspicion when looked at sensibly. . . .

The concept of possession in the sense of this provision has not been unambiguously elucidated either in the literature (see Joachimsky, Betäubungsmittelrecht, 3rd edit. § 11 note 15 and 27a, c; . . .) or in the case law (see OLG Hamburg MDR 74, 954; BGHSt 26, 117). Nor has there been a conclusive determination in the most recent decision of the Federal Court of Justice (BGHSt 27, 380). There is however unanimity in so far as possession according to the meaning and purpose of the rule—as was expressed in the reasoning to the draft of an Opium Act of Dec. 18, 1970,—represents not for instance a condition but causal conduct, and that the bringing about or maintenance of this condition should be made punishable (BT-Drucks. 665/70 p.16); a deliberate factual holding, a factual power relationship is to suffice for the assumption of this possession according to these observations (see also the reasoning to the draft of a Statute to amend the Opium Act of February 25, 1971, BT-Drucks. VI 1877 p. 9). The deliberate factual power relationship over the drug is accordingly decisive (see BGHSt 27, 380; 26, 117; OLG Karlsruhe GoldtArch 75, 183 and KG GoldtArch 79, 427).

Proceeding from these principles, criminal possession of drugs by Wolfgang A. cannot be based on the findings made by the regional court and the factual circumstances and relationships to be derived from them. Instead the circumstances even argue in favor of his innocence. If Wolfgang A., who, according to the findings, had had experience in dealing with drugs (hashish) and had already emerged as a consumer and dealer, had known of the existence of the packet in his mother's car, it would have been the "sensible thing to do" to secure and hide the drug and not to leave it in a parked car with an unlocked door available to possible access by third parties. The lack of concern displayed by omitting to check whether the car, which anyway did not belong to him but to his mother, was locked, argues decisively in favor of the assumption that parking the car raised no anxiety on his part about securing or hiding something. This behavior cannot be reconciled with a conscious power relationship over the drug packet; it is more consistent with the third party, who remains unknown and whom Wolfgang A. took with him as a favor, leaving behind a packet over which he had the power of disposal without the driver having any knowledge of this . . .

There is also no crime and therefore no obstruction of a criminal prosecution in regard to Wolfgang A.'s mother. Her power over the hashish is also not possession which is significant in criminal law in the sense of narcotics law.

According to its purpose in criminal policy, penalization of the possession of drugs was intended to create a device to facilitate the battle against drug crime. It enables the criminal prosecution of all persons who are found in possession of drugs whose acquisition, import or manufacture of drugs or trading in them, or other activities criminalized under earlier law is not provable (see BGHSt26, 118 with reference to the official reasoning). According to this intention on the part of the legislature, a restrictive interpretation of the concept of possession, according to subjective criteria and the type and purpose of the intention to control of the person who exercises power over the item from an objective point of view, appears to be both possible and required. The possessor who has the drug in his power for his own sake, for the realization of his purpose in the modalities described in the statute, acts criminally. In this connection it is enough if he at the same time intends to secure or to facilitate this determined goal of another person. A person who on the other hand is guided by other ideas which are directed towards detaining the drug, withholding it from addicted or endangered persons, withdrawing it from circulation to a certain extent, as for instance teachers, parents and supervisory persons, who, for the protection of the persons entrusted to their upbringing, take away drugs from such persons, do not fall under the criminal definition of possession of drugs. Instead they help to realize the protective purpose which the Narcotics Act pursues, similarly to the persons entrusted with criminal prosecution on the acquisition of drugs which is taken away from drug offenders.

Accordingly, the defendant's client, who according to the findings in the judgment took possession of the packet in question and kept it with her only out of concern that her son could come into contact with the hashish or that it could otherwise come into the hands of an unauthorized person, did not fulfill the definition of possession.

Therefore the defendant has not committed obstruction of punishment in relation to his client.

Markus D. Dubber, "Policing Possession: The War on Crime and the End of Criminal Law," 91 *Journal of Criminal Law and Criminology* (2002), 829

Possession is not a conduct offense. As commentators have pointed out for centuries, possession is not an act, it is a state of being, a status.[287] To possess something is to *be* in possession of it.

To dismiss possession simply on the ground that it violates the so-called act requirement of Anglo-American criminal law, however, would be premature. The act requirement, from the outset, applied to common law offenses only, i.e., to offenses that traced their origins back through a grand chain of common law precedents, rather than to a specific statute that created a new offense. . . . English judges from very early on threw out possession indictments as violative of the act requirement only if they alleged a common law offense of possession, rather than invoked a statutory possession provision. Once it was settled that the possession indictment was brought under one of the increasing number of possession statutes, the common law's act requirement was no longer an issue.[288] The act requirement was as irrelevant to statutory possession as the mens rea requirement was to "statutory" rape.[289]

---

[287] *E.g.,* Regina v. Dugdale, 1 El. & Bl. 435, 439 (1853) (Coleridge, J.).
[288] *See, e.g.,* Rex v. Lennard, 1 Leach 90 (1772) (applying 8 & 9 Will. 3, c. 26 (Eng.)).
[289] *See* Regina v. Prince, 2 L.R. Cr. Cas. Res. 154 (1875).

The common law's act requirement, therefore, does not stand in the way of modern possession statutes. And the thin slice of the act requirement constitutionalized by the U.S. Supreme Court in . . . *Robinson v. California*[290] also can do little, by itself, to challenge possession offenses. The constitutional act requirement merely prohibits the criminalization of addiction in particular, and of sickness in general (or at least "having a common cold"). Possession doesn't criminalize an illness, at least not directly. The Supreme Court in Robinson went out of its way to reassure legislatures that they remained free to "impose criminal sanctions . . . against the unauthorized manufacture, prescription, sale, purchase, or possession of narcotics."

Then there is the general uneasiness regarding omission offenses characteristic of American criminal law. Absent a clear duty to act, the failure to act is not criminal. If possession isn't an act, perhaps one should think of it as an omission, the omission to get rid of the item one possesses. But what is the duty that compels me to drop the shiny new pistol that my friend has just bought himself at the local gun store, or to toss out the baggie of cocaine I noticed in the glove compartment of my rental car? If one looked hard enough, perhaps one could find such a duty nestled in the criminalization of a possession that is defined as the failure to end it. But the point of requiring a specific duty for omission liability, the significance of the general unwillingness to criminalize omission, is precisely to reject omission liability absent specific and unambiguous provisions to the contrary . . .

Possession offenses . . . are everywhere in modern American criminal law, on the books and in action. They fill our statute books, our arrest statistics, and, eventually, our prisons. By last count, New York law recognized no fewer than 153 possession offenses; one in every five prison or jail sentences handed out by New York courts in 1998 was imposed for a possession offense. That same year, possession offenses accounted for over 100,000 arrests in New York State, while drug possession offenses alone resulted in over 1.2 million arrests nationwide . . . .

So broad is the reach of possession offenses, and so easy are they to detect and then to prove, that possession has replaced vagrancy as the sweep offense of choice. Unlike vagrancy, however, possession offenses promise more than a slap on the wrist. Backed by a wide range of penalties, they can remove undesirables for extended periods of time, even for life . . .

New York boasts no fewer than 115 felony possession offenses, all of which require a minimum of one year in prison; eleven of them provide for a maximum sentence of life imprisonment . . .

One way of thinking of possession offenses is to view them as criminalized presumptions of some other offense. In criminalizing possession, the legislature really criminalizes import, manufacture, purchase. Or forward-looking, the legislature really criminalizes use, sale, or export. In the latter variety, the prospective presumption resembles an implicit inchoate offense. So possession really is an attempt to use, sell, or export, or more precisely, possession is an attempt to attempt to use, sell, or export, that is, an inchoate inchoate offense . . .

[T]he implicit presumption inherent in the concept of a possession offense reveals the modus operandi of possession, the secret of its success as a policing tool beyond legal scrutiny. Possession succeeds because it removes all potentially troublesome features to the level of legislative or executive discretion, an area that is notoriously difficult to scrutinize. In its design and its application, possession is, in doctrinal terms, a doubly inchoate offense, one step farther from the actual infliction of personal harm than ordinary inchoate offenses like attempt. In practical terms, it is an offense designed and applied to remove dangerous individuals even before they have had an opportunity to manifest their dangerousness in an ordinary inchoate offense. On its face, however, it does not look like an inchoate offense, nor does it look like a threat reduction measure targeting particular types of individuals.

NOTES

1. As a general trend, one could also say for German criminal law that possession offenses gained importance in the last decades—but to a lesser degree than in U.S. law. The most important example is possession of child pornography, which was introduced into the German Criminal Code in 1993. However, there is a crucial difference: possession offenses in German law, be it possession of drugs, weapons, or child pornography, are typically not felonies and are punished leniently. Although consumers of illicit goods are thought to share responsibility for the harm done through those illegal markets, their individual responsibility is thought to be somewhat diluted, making high felony penalties appear disproportionate.

That said, lesser punishments may lessen the challenge of legitimating possession in the face of purportedly fundamental principles of criminal liability—the act requirement in

---

[290] Robinson v. California, 370 U.S. 660 (1962).

Anglo-American criminal law or the culpability principle in German criminal law—but they cannot dispose of it. Otherwise it would be difficult to object to the less than categorical rejection of strict (or rather, absolute) liability in Canadian criminal constitutional law on the ground that punishing strict liability is illegitimate, period, even for offenses not subject to imprisonment.*

Possession, of course, sweeps more broadly than consumption, nor does it require consumption; consumption is an act, possession is a state of affairs. Nor does it require other acts, such as acquisition, never mind purchase, or participation in any market, either as supplier or as consumer. Possession includes consumption by implication, as a non-technical presumption; but it bears the same constructive relationship to distribution, or sale, i.e., it reaches the high-rolling callous drug dealer as easily as it does the hapless addict. Insofar as suppliers bear greater responsibility for the harm caused (?) by a market in addictive substances than do consumers (do they? why?), then presumably greater punishments would be appropriate. Could the higher punishments for, say, drug possession in U.S. reflect a different standard presumption—i.e., from possession to distribution, rather than to consumption? What if—as tends to be the case—the punishment of possession offenses is proportioned to the quality and quantity of drugs possessed, so that the greater the quantity and the more potent or addictive the drug, the higher the punishment? Would this address the proportionality concern about the punishment of possession offenses?

2. The crucial question of what rationale could support possession offenses therefore remains. Neither the U.S. Supreme Court (or the New York Court of Appeals) nor the German Federal Constitutional Court so far has registered a concern with criminalizing possession on constitutional grounds. It is worth noting, however, that a recent comprehensive study of German constitutional criminal law concluded that, while the vast bulk of German criminal law passes constitutional muster, the criminalization of simple possession offenses does not.[†]

Leaving the constitutional question aside, one still can ask whether there are good reasons for criminalization. The passive status of merely possessing an object (not using it and not participating in an illegal market through acquisition or sale) is as such harmless and does not violate or endanger legal goods, rights of others etc. It is therefore understandable that the Higher Regional Court of Zweibrücken insists that there must be some kind of conduct beyond the status as such. It seems that similar concerns underlie the decision in *People v. E.C.*: the exceptions spelled out there only make sense if one relates them to a lack of danger under these specific circumstances. (Again, what precisely is the danger ordinarily associated with possession? Is not possession a classic *malum prohibitum* offense that threatens disobedience of a state prohibition with punishment? So that possession is not an offense if, and only if, it does not in fact, as determined by a state official, challenge the authority of the state, e.g., by state officials or by those licensed—explicitly or implicitly—by the state.) Or is the significant distinction not between possession and some other status or conduct offense, but between different types of possession offenses (say, possession of drugs vs. possession of guns or explosives)?

This leaves two possible explanations: either possession is punished in lieu of prior or future acts by the offender which are closer to harm but harder to prove, or the crucial point is really the omission: failing to get rid of a potentially dangerous object. With respect to the latter explanation, Dubber questions the existence of a duty to act. However, from the perspective of German legal doctrine, this does not pose a serious problem: dominion over dangerous objects establishes responsibility (for instance, criminal liability occurs when the owner of a factory, a house, a car etc. omits measures necessary to avert dangers stemming from these objects).

---

* See Chapter 3.
[†] Otto Lagodny, *Strafrecht vor den Schranken der Grundrechte* (1996), 534 ("Possession offenses are unconstitutional insofar as they attach to simple possession and therefore do not presuppose behavior.").

Anglo-American criminal law appears to be less comfortable with recognizing general duties to act (also illustrated by the absence of a general duty to rescue of the sort found in German law (§ 323c Criminal Code)); see the discussion of omission liability in Chapter 7.D. A duty-based conception of criminal liability may have less difficulty with possession offenses for the simple reason that it would not see the point of an act (i.e., a commission) requirement in the first place. For a recent discussion of the difficulty (in Anglo-American law) of justifying possession offenses on an omission theory, see Andrew Ashworth, "The Unfairness of Risk-Based Possession Offences," 5 *Criminal Law and Philosophy* (2011), 237, 242–3. Ashworth concludes:

> Offences of simple possession are to be found in many modern legal systems. They have the great rule-of-law merits that usually they are clearly defined and give fair warning of the reach of the criminal law. But they fail to meet many of the standard requirements of the criminal law: they do not require a voluntary action, they do not always require awareness and/or intention, they often depart from the presumption of innocence, by penalising people on the basis of what they might subsequently decide to do they do not measure up to the requirements for inchoate offences, and they also criminalise people on the basis of what other individuals might decide to do.
>
> . . .
>
> If the pressure for political compromise is irresistible, then . . . this may be an appropriate point for the criminal law to borrow from the principles applicable to incapacitative measures such as civil detention, and to demand that possession offences be enacted only if and insofar as they require proof of the probable danger of the article being used to cause serious harm. If as criminal lawyers we are not seriously committed to limits of this kind, then we must reflect on our commitment to principle more generally. In view of their practical on-the-street effects and the substantial sentences to which they can now lead, many risk-based possession offences are unfair in their present form. In particular, simple possession is an insufficient foundation for anything more than regulatory liability, and a substantial sentence for that is unjustifiable.
>
> Andrew Ashworth, "The Unfairness of Risk-Based Possession Offences,"
> 5 *Criminal Law and Philosophy* (2011), 254, 256.

What, then, is the appropriate response to the claim that possession offenses, a central tool in the arsenal of modern criminal law, cannot be reconciled with one (or more) of the fundamental principles of (at least Anglo-American) criminal law? (1) There is no problem: they do not violate the act requirement (never mind the others); (2) There is no problem: the act requirement is empty or, at best, superfluous; (3) There is a problem: but it's easily fixed by (a) imposing only light criminal sanctions for possession, (b) imposing only non-criminal sanctions, (c) requiring proof of probable danger; (4) Something else altogether?

D. Omissions

Omission liability, like possession liability, is difficult to square with an act requirement, taken seriously. Unlike in the case of possession liability, however, an elaborate body of doctrine has developed to extend criminal liability to omissions. Omission is not simply declared an act by codificatory fiat (as possession is in the Model Penal Code, § 2.01(4)), perhaps because omission liability does not merely extend liability to a non-act (as in the case of possession), but to the *absence* of an act. As with possession, omission, in Anglo-American and German criminal law, is both a mode of liability in the general part (in the form of "constructive" [*unecht*], or indirect, omission liability for commission offenses) and a type of offense in the special part (in the form of "real" [*echt*], or direct, omission offenses). In both systems, indirect omission liability requires the existence of a duty to act, external to the definition of the offense. Unlike in Anglo-American criminal law, however, German criminal law recognizes a general duty to aid.

State v. Miranda
Supreme Court of Connecticut
245 Conn. 209, 715 A.2d 680 (1998)

Katz, J.

...The defendant commenced living with his girlfriend and her two children in an apartment in September, 1992. On January 27, 1993, the defendant was twenty-one years old, his girlfriend was sixteen, her son was two, and her daughter, the victim in this case, born on September 21, 1992, was four months old. Although he was not the biological father of either child, the defendant took care of them and considered himself to be their stepfather. He represented himself as such to the people at Meriden Veteran's Memorial Hospital where, on January 27, 1993, the victim was taken for treatment of her injuries following a 911 call by the defendant that the child was choking on milk. Upon examination at the hospital, it was determined that the victim [suffered from multiple injuries] . . . [T]he trial court found that the injuries, many of which created a risk of death, had been caused by great and deliberate force [and] that the defendant had been aware of [the injuries] . . .

The trial court . . . found the defendant guilty of one count of § 53-21* and six counts of § 53a-59(a)(3).[†] The trial court found the defendant not guilty of nineteen counts of assault in the first degree. Those counts had charged him with either personally inflicting the injuries or not preventing the child's mother from inflicting the injuries.[4] The court imposed a total effective sentence of forty years imprisonment.

The defendant appealed to the Appellate Court, which . . . reversed the assault convictions concluding that the defendant had no legal duty to act under the circumstances of this case . . .

I

Before addressing the . . . issue of whether the facts and circumstances of this case were sufficient to create a legal duty to protect the victim from parental abuse pursuant to § 53a-59 (a) (3), we turn our attention to the question of whether, even if we assume such a duty exists, the failure to act can create liability under that statute. In other words, by failing to act in accordance with a duty, does a defendant commit a crime, such as assault in the first degree in violation of § 53a-59 (a) (3), that is not specifically defined by statute in terms of an omission to act but only in terms of cause and result? . . .

The trend of Anglo-American law has been toward enlarging the scope of criminal liability for failure to act in those situations in which the common law or statutes have imposed an affirmative responsibility for the safety and well-being of others. Criminal liability of parents based on a failure to act in accordance with common-law affirmative duties to protect and care for their children is well recognized in many jurisdictions. See, e.g., People v. Stanciel, 153 Ill. 2d 218, 606 N.E.2d 1201, 180 Ill. Dec. 124 (1992) (mother guilty of homicide by allowing known abuser to assume role of disciplinarian over child); State v. Williquette, 129 Wis. 2d 239, 385 N.W.2d 145 (1986) (mother guilty of child abuse for allowing child to be with person known previously to have been abusive and who subsequently abused child again) . . .

[C]riminal conduct can arise not only through overt acts, but also by an omission to act when there is a legal duty to do so. "Omissions are as capable of producing consequences as overt acts. Thus, the common law rule that there is no general duty to protect limits criminal liability where it would otherwise exist. The special relationship exception to the 'no duty to act' rule represents a choice to retain liability for some omissions, which are considered morally unacceptable." State v. Williquette, supra, 129 Wis. 2d 253. Therefore, had the defendant been the victim's parent—someone with an undisputed affirmative legal obligation to protect and provide for his minor child—we would conclude that his failure to protect the child from abuse could constitute a violation of § 53a-59 (a) (3).

---

* [General Statutes § 53-21. Injury or risk of injury to, or impairing morals of, children.
Any person who (1) wilfully or unlawfully causes or permits any child under the age of sixteen years to be placed in such a situation that the life or limb of such child is endangered, the health of such child is likely to be injured or the morals of such child are likely to be impaired, or does any act likely to impair the health or morals of any such child, . . . shall be guilty of a class C felony.—Eds.]

† [General Statutes § 53a-59. Assault in the first degree: Class B felony.
(a) A person is guilty of assault in the first degree when . . . (3) under circumstances evincing an extreme indifference to human life he recklessly engages in conduct which creates a risk of death to another person, and thereby causes serious physical injury to another person . . . .—Eds.]

[4] Although the trial court never stated who actually had caused the injuries, we take judicial notice that the child's mother entered a plea of nolo contendere to the crimes of intentional assault in the first degree and risk of injury to a minor. She received a sentence of twelve years' incarceration suspended after seven years.

II

We next turn to the issue of whether the duty to protect can be imposed on the defendant, an adult member of the household unrelated to the child . . .

The defendant argues that there is no statutory or common-law precept "authorizing the expansion of assault under § 53a-59 (a) (3)." The state argues that there is both. We conclude that, based on the trial court's findings that the defendant had established a family-like relationship with the mother and her two children, that he had voluntarily assumed responsibility for the care and welfare of both children, and that he had considered himself the victim's stepfather, there existed a common-law duty to protect the victim from her mother's abuse, the breach of which can be the basis of a conviction under § 53a-59 (a) (3).

There are many statutes that expressly impose a legal duty to act and attach liability for the failure to comply with that duty. With other statutes, however, the duty to act can be found outside the statutory definition of the crime itself, either in another statute; or in the common law.

We note initially that the question of whether a duty, and thus, liability for the breach of that duty, should be recognized in this state is not foreclosed by our penal code . . . Section 53a-4 of the code provides: "The provisions of this chapter shall not be construed as precluding any court from recognizing other principles of criminal liability or other defenses not inconsistent with such provisions." The official commentary to that provision states: "The purpose of this savings clause is to make clear that the provisions of §§ 53a-5 to 53a-23, which define the principles of criminal liability and defenses, are not necessarily exclusive. A court is not precluded by sections 53a-5 to 53a-23 from recognizing other such principles and defenses not inconsistent therewith." Commission to Revise the Criminal Statutes, Penal Code Comments, Conn. Gen. Stat. Ann. (West 1985) § 53a-4, p. 196.

We do not believe that the principle of imposing a common-law duty in and of itself is inconsistent with any other principle of criminal liability provided in the code. "Failure to act when there is a special relationship does not, by itself, constitute a crime. The failure must expose the dependent person to some proscribed result. The definition of proscribed results constitutes the substantive crime, and it is defined in the criminal code . . . ." *State v. Williquette*, supra, 129 Wis. 2d 254 . . . .

. . . Although one generally has no legal duty to aid another in peril, even when the aid can be provided without danger or inconvenience to the provider, there are four widely recognized situations in which the failure to act may constitute breach of a legal duty: (1) where one stands in a certain relationship to another; (2) where a statute imposes a duty to help another; (3) where one has assumed a contractual duty; and (4) where one voluntarily has assumed the care of another. 1 W. LaFave & A. Scott, supra, § 3.3 (a) (1)–(4), pp. 284–87.[14] The state argues that this case falls within both the first and fourth situations, or some combination thereof.

We begin with the duty based upon the relationship between the parties. One standing in a certain personal relationship to another person has some affirmative duties of care with regard to that person. "Legal rights and duties . . . may arise out of those complex relations of human society which create correlative rights and duties the performance of which is so necessary to the good order and well-being of society that the state makes their observance obligatory." Annot., supra, 100 A.L.R.2d 488.

It is undisputed that parents have a duty to provide food, shelter and medical aid for their children and to protect them from harm. "The inherent dependency of a child upon his parent to obtain medical aid, i.e., the incapacity of a child to evaluate his condition and summon aid by himself, supports imposition of such a duty upon the parent." Commonwealth v. Konz, 498 Pa. 639, 644, 450 A.2d 638 (1982). Additionally, "the commonly understood general obligations of parenthood entail these minimum attributes: (1) express love and affection for the child; (2) express personal concern over the health, education and general well-being of the child; (3) the duty to supply the necessary food, clothing, and medical care; (4) the duty to provide an adequate domicile; and (5) the duty to furnish social and religious guidance." In re Adoption of Webb, 14 Wash. App. 651, 653, 544 P.2d 130 (1975) . . .

In addition to biological and adoptive parents and legal guardians, there may be other adults who establish familial relationships with and assume responsibility for the care of a child, thereby creating a legal duty to protect that child from harm. "Recognizing the primary responsibility of a natural parent does not mean that an unrelated person may not also have some responsibilities incident to the care

---

[14] A leading case first outlining these four situations added a requirement to the fourth that appears to have been omitted in recent years. See *Jones* v. *United States*, 113 U.S. App. D.C. 352, 308 F.2d 307, 310 (D.C. App. 1962) ("where one has voluntarily assumed the care of another and *so secluded the helpless person as to prevent others from rendering aid*" [emphasis added]). This refinement would not seem applicable to an infant, or for that matter a child of tender years, because a child is *always* dependent on others for care and intervention when sick or in danger.

and custody of a child. Such duties may be regarded as derived from the primary custodian, i.e., the natural parent, or arise from the nature of the circumstances." People v. Berg, 171 Ill. App. 3d 316, 320, 525 N.E.2d 573, 121 Ill. Dec. 515 (1988).

Most courts deciding whether, under a particular set of facts, liability for an omission to act may be imposed under a statute that does not itself impose a duty to act, have looked to whether a duty to act exists in another statute, in the common law or in a contract. Of those courts acting outside the context of a statutory or contractual duty that have held a defendant criminally liable for failing to protect a child from injury, most have relied on a combination of both the first and fourth situations described by Professors LaFave and Scott to establish a duty as the predicate for the defendant's conviction. More specifically, these courts have examined the nature of the relationship of the defendant to the victim and whether the defendant, as part of that relationship, had assumed a responsibility for the victim.[15] ...

In State v. Orosco, 113 N.M. 789, 833 P.2d 1155 (1991), the court examined whether the defendant, who lived with the victim and his mother and who failed to intervene when one of his friends sexually abused the victim, could be held criminally liable for the abuse. [T]he court held that, by assuming the care and welfare of the child, the defendant stood in the position of a parent.

In Leet v. State, 595 So. 2d 959 (Fla. App. 1991), the court examined whether the defendant could be held criminally responsible for abuse of a child by his mother although he was not the child's father ... Although the defendant had argued that he was not financially responsible for the child and could not have authorized his medical treatment, the court, nevertheless, concluded that he had the authority, and indeed, the duty to prevent the mother's conduct.

In People v. Wong, 182 A.D.2d 98, 588 N.Y.S.2d 119 (1993), the court examined whether the defendants, who had been babysitters for the child victim's parents, could be convicted of manslaughter for harming the child and for failing to provide him with necessary medical care. To support a conviction based upon their failure to provide medical attention, the prosecution relied on two theories: (1) that the defendants had contracted with the child's parents to care for the child while the parents worked; and (2) that the defendants voluntarily had assumed care for the child ...

As these cases demonstrate, the traditional approach in this country is to restrict the duty to save others from harm to certain very narrow categories of cases. We are not prepared now to adopt a broad general rule covering other circumstances. We conclude only that, in accordance with the trial court findings, when the defendant, who considered himself the victim's parent, established a familial relationship with the victim's mother and her children and assumed the role of a father, he assumed, under the common law, the same legal duty to protect the victim from the abuse as if he were, in fact, the victim's guardian ... That duty does not depend on an ability to regulate the mother's discipline of the victim or on the defendant having exclusive control of the victim when the injuries occurred. Nor is the duty contingent upon an ability by the state or the mother to look to the defendant for child support. Moreover, whether the defendant had created a total in loco parentis relationship with the victim by January, 1993, is not dispositive of whether the defendant had assumed a responsibility for the victim. "If immediate or emergency medical attention is required from a child's custodian it should not matter that such custodian is not the primary care provider or for that matter a legally designated surrogate." People v. Berg, supra, 171 Ill. App. 3d 320.

Nor should we reject the concept of a duty in this case because the defendant might not have been able to authorize medical treatment for the victim had he taken her to the hospital. The status required to impose the legal duty to safeguard the victim is not coextensive with the status that permits one to authorize treatment ...

Finally, we recognize the continuing demographic trend reflecting a significant increase in non-traditional alternative family arrangements. Consequently, more and more children will be living with or may depend upon adults who do not qualify as a natural or adoptive parent ... To distinguish among children in deciding which ones are entitled to protection based upon whether their adult caregivers have chosen to have their relationships officially recognized hardly advances the public policy of protecting children from abuse ...

The judgment of the Appellate Court is reversed and the case is remanded to that court for consideration of the defendant's remaining claims.

Palmer, J., with whom McDonald, J., joins, concurring.

I join the opinion of the majority. A serious question remains, however, as to whether the defendant, Santos Miranda, had fair warning that his failure to act, in the particular circumstances of this case, could give rise to the crime of assault in the first degree in violation of General Statutes § 53a-59 (a) (3).

---

[15] As we have stated, some courts in other jurisdictions have held that liability can flow from the breach of a duty created by contract. The state is not relying on that theory as a basis for conviction and, therefore, we express no opinion as to whether that relationship can serve as a theory of liability.

The legal duty that we recognize today has never before been expressly recognized in this state; indeed, the Appellate Court, upon consideration of the defendant's appeal, unanimously concluded that no such duty existed. In such circumstances, it is by no means clear that the due process clauses of the federal and state constitutions permit such a duty to be imposed on this defendant for purposes of criminal liability under the assault statute.[1] Since the defendant will have the opportunity to raise a due process claim on remand, however;[2] and because I agree with the analysis and conclusions of the majority, I join the opinion of the majority.

Berdon, J., dissenting.

...

The majority's determination that the facts in this case were sufficient to create a legal duty on the part of the defendant to protect the child from parental abuse pursuant to § 53a-59 (a) (3) is premised on its unsupported conclusion that had the defendant been the victim's parent, he would have had an undisputed affirmative legal obligation to protect the child from assault pursuant to § 53a-59 (a) (3). There is an affirmative obligation on the defendant and the parent, under the circumstances of this case, to protect the child, but that duty does not arise under § 53a-59 (a) (3). Rather, in this state, the obligation to act arises under § 53-21, entitled "injury or risk of injury to, or impairing the morals of, children," which was enacted by the legislature many years ago to address the failure to act with respect to the welfare of a child .... Here, the trial court found the defendant guilty of risk of injury with respect to the child, for which he was sentenced to the maximum term of ten years. The defendant's conviction under § 53-21, however, is not before us ...

II

The majority addresses [the] issue ... whether the "conduct" referred to in § 53a-59 (a) (3) includes the failure to act ... Section 53a-59 (a) provides in part that "[a] person is guilty of assault in the first degree when ... (3) under circumstances evincing an extreme indifference to human life he recklessly engages in conduct which creates a risk of death to another person, and thereby causes serious physical injury to another person ... " Although "conduct" can include the failure to act under circumstances when there is a duty to act; 1 W. LaFave & A. Scott, Substantive Criminal Law (1986) § 3.3, p. 282; the majority points to nothing in the text of § 53a-59 (a) (3), or its legislative history, to support its conclusion that conduct under § 53a-59 (a) (3) includes the failure to act. In fact, both the common definition of assault—"a violent attack with physical means"; Webster's Third New International Dictionary; and the legal definition of assault—"any wilful attempt or threat to inflict injury upon the person of another"; Black's Law Dictionary (6th Ed. 1990); belie the majority's claim.

Moreover, by construing § 53a-59 (a) (3) to include the duty to act, the majority stands a longstanding and fundamental principle of statutory construction on its head: Penal statutes "are to be expounded strictly against an offender, and liberally in his favor. This can only be accomplished, by giving to them a literal construction, so far as they operate penally ... " Daggett v. State, 4 Conn. 60, 63 (1821). While a criminal statute is not to be defeated by an unreasonably strict construction of its language, it must be rather strictly construed so that the conduct made criminal will be ascertainable with reasonable certainty from a careful reading of the statute ... A careful reading of § 53a-59 (a) (3) would never lead a rational reader to believe that a person was subject to criminal liability under the statute for the failure to act—whether the person is a stranger, a live-in boyfriend, or a parent ...

III

Nevertheless, even if the majority were correct that one person can assault another person under § 53a-59 (a) (3) by failing to act, the defendant's conviction in this case cannot stand. By superimposing on § 53a-59 (a) (3) a common-law duty on the part of a person to act in order to protect a child from harm when that third person voluntarily assumes responsibility for the care and the welfare of the child and considers himself to have a stepfather–stepchild relationship with the child, the majority has created a new crime. In crafting this new crime, the majority ignores the fact that it is the legislature that defines substantive crimes. This division between the legislature and the court was established

---

[1] There is, of course, a difference between the recognition of an existing duty, on the one hand, and the creation of an altogether new duty, on the other. Whether that distinction is significant for due process purposes under the specific facts of this case remains to be seen.

[2] The importance of this issue to the defendant cannot be overstated in view of the fact that he received a cumulative sentence of thirty years imprisonment on the six counts of assault in the first degree. Because the defendant also received a consecutive ten year prison term on the one count of risk of injury to a child, his total effective sentence is forty years imprisonment. By contrast, the child's mother, who, it appears, actually caused the child's injuries, received a total effective sentence of only seven years imprisonment.

in 1971 when the legislature adopted the penal code and repealed General Statutes (Rev. to 1968) § 54-117, which recognized common-law crimes . . .

The majority argues that it may recognize a duty to protect a child from abuse under § 53a-59 (a) (3) because it is merely applying a long-standing principle of liability consistent with the principles of liability permitted by § 53a-4. Even if we assume that it is merely applying a principle of liability rather than creating a substantive crime, the majority, however, . . . fails to cite any cases in which this court has applied this principle of liability for acts of omission.

Moreover, the majority makes no attempt to explain why the "principle of imposing a common-law duty" to protect a child from abuse is not inconsistent with the [general] principles of liability set forth in . . . the penal code. Indeed, the majority ignores the fact that the recognition of this new duty under § 53a-59 (a) (3) is inconsistent with the notion of accessory liability . . . For example, this court consistently has held that one cannot be held liable under a theory of aiding and abetting, for merely being present at the time of the crime and acquiescing to the commission of the crime . . .

IV

The legislature will be very much surprised to discover that we have in place, under § 53a-59 (a) (3), a law that provides that the failure to act is punishable criminal conduct. Although the legislature recently has grappled with the issue of imposing an affirmative obligation on the part of a parent and an unrelated adult to protect children from abuse see Substitute House Bill No. 5283 (1988) (H.B. No. 5283), entitled "An Act Concerning Facilitation of Abuse of a Child"; it did not enact the proposed legislation. Nevertheless, the majority of this court, without any understanding of the implications of its decision today and without the aid of expert advice that is available to the legislature through the public hearing process, impetuously and presumptuously crafts a crime of assault that was never intended by the legislature. Clearly, if the legislature agreed with the majority that, pursuant to § 53a-59 (a) (3), parents as well as unrelated adults had an affirmative legal obligation to protect children from abuse, it never would have had a need to consider H.B. No. 5283, a bill that explicitly criminalizes the conduct with which the defendant was charged in the present case.

The representatives of several state agencies and several non-profit groups created to support victims of abuse spoke out against H.B. No. 5283 at the public hearing before the legislature's select committee on children . . .

First, those who testified before the committee expressed unanimous concern that holding persons liable for not protecting children from abuse actually would cause more harm than it would prevent . . . Second, nearly every speaker at the public hearing before the select committee on children testified that the legislature did not need to enact H.B. No. 5283 because "the situation that [it] is intended to address is already covered by" § 53-21, the risk of injury to a child statute . . . Third, the speakers at the public hearing before the select committee on children agreed that, even if the committee approved H.B. No. 5283, the bill would have to be made more specific in order to set forth the effort that must be extended to satisfy the duty to protect children from abuse . . .

Clearly, all of these delineated issues are best left for the legislature's consideration, not ours.

V

Finally, in crafting this new common-law crime, the majority acknowledges constitutional problems in attempting to apply it in this case. For example, the majority has created an ex post facto law in its classic sense. Furthermore, there is at least a question as to whether the defendant's convictions for assault and risk of injury violate the constitutional prohibition against double jeopardy . . . I would affirm the judgment of the Appellate Court.

Accordingly, I dissent.

Model Penal Code

§ 2.01 Omission as Basis of Liability

(3) Liability for the commission of an offense may not be based on an omission unaccompanied by action unless:
    (a) the omission is expressly made sufficient by the law defining the offense; or
    (b) a duty to perform the omitted act is otherwise imposed by law.

German Criminal Code

§ 13 (Commission by Omission)

(1) Whoever fails to avert a result, which is an element of an offense definition will only be punished for this offense if he is legally responsible for the fact that the result does not occur, and if the omission is equivalent to the realization of the statutory elements of the crime through action.
(2) The punishment can be mitigated according to § 49 para. 1.

Vermont Statutes, Title 12

§ 519. Emergency medical care

(a) A person who knows that another is exposed to grave physical harm shall, to the extent that the same can be rendered without danger or peril to himself or without interference with important duties owed to others, give reasonable assistance to the exposed person unless that assistance or care is being provided by others.
(b) A person who provides reasonable assistance in compliance with subsection (a) of this section shall not be liable in civil damages unless his acts constitute gross negligence or unless he will receive or expects to receive remuneration. Nothing contained in this subsection shall alter existing law with respect to tort liability of a practitioner of the healing arts for acts committed in the ordinary course of his practice.
(c) A person who willfully violates subsection (a) of this section shall be fined not more than $ 100.00.

Wisconsin Statutes

§ 940.34. Duty to aid victim or report crime [; misdemeanor]

(2) (a) Any person who knows that a crime is being committed and that a victim is exposed to bodily harm shall summon law enforcement officers or other assistance or shall provide assistance to the victim.
. . .
(d) A person need not comply with this subsection if any of the following apply:
   1. Compliance would place him or her in danger.
   2. Compliance would interfere with duties the person owes to others.
   3. In the circumstances described under par. (a), assistance is being summoned or provided by others.
. . .
(3) . . . Any person who provides . . . reasonable assistance under this section is immune from civil liability for his or her acts or omissions in providing the assistance. This immunity does not apply if the person receives or expects to receive compensation for providing the assistance.

German Criminal Code

§ 323c (Failure to Render Assistance)

Who does not render assistance in the case of a misadventure, common danger or disaster, although it is required and can be expected of him under the circumstances, especially, if assistance is possible without substantial danger to himself and without violation of other important duties, will be punished with imprisonment of not more than one year or a fine.

German Federal Court of Justice
3 StR 153/03, BGHSt 48, 301 (July 24, 2003)

Facts

The regional court established the following facts:

On the evening of June 1, 1996, both defendants forced their way into a house in O., which was occupied by the divorced first husband of the defendant S. (J.). In the absence of the divorced first husband, the defendant M. started a fire in the bedroom and the defendant S. in the attic...On January 25, 2001, the defendant M. strangled the husband of the accused, W., until he lost consciousness, and struck him in the stomach with his fist. He was angry with his victim for having reported him to the police for theft. The defendant S. had obtained knowledge of M.'s plan shortly before the crime, but refrained from warning her husband, from whom she had separated about four weeks previously, of the attack. She also made no efforts to prevent the defendant M. from committing his crime.

The regional court sentenced the defendant M. to juvenile detention of four years for aggravated arson and to a total sentence of one year and four months for inflicting dangerous bodily harm taking into account earlier sentences; it sentenced the defendant S. to a total sentence of three years and one month for aggravated arson and assisting infliction of bodily harm by omission.

The defendants' appeal was only partially successful.

Reasons

The defendant S.'s conviction for assisting infliction of bodily harm by omission does not withstand legal examination.

a) Contrary to the challenges of the appeal in law, it can be deduced from the judgment that the defendant M.'s crime would at least have been made more difficult if the defendant S. had tried to prevent him from committing it or if she had warned her husband by telephone. This is sufficient. It is not necessary in order to find assisting by omission that the omitted action would have prevented the success of the crime (see BGH, NJW 1953, 1838 with further references).

b) The findings of the regional court do not however indicate that the defendant was under a duty to act for the benefit of the victim as would be necessary for her conviction for assisting infliction of bodily harm by omission. According to these findings it is instead possible that the guarantor duty arising from the marriage no longer applied here because the defendant separated from her husband about four weeks before the crime and took another man.

    aa) In relation to the guarantor duty between spouses it is undisputed that spouses in a life relationship are obliged to protect each other as guarantors and therefore in each case have to assume responsibility in the sense of § 13 Criminal Code that no harm is inflicted on the other party which appears as the "result" of a crime. Accordingly it cannot be doubted that the defendant—if she had not separated from her husband—would have been obliged to warn him about the threatened bodily harm by the co-defendant M. or to attempt to prevent M. from committing his intended crime.

    bb) There are different views as to the basis for this guarantor duty and what significance separation of the spouses has for it.

       In this respect on the one hand it is argued that the guarantor duty of spouses arises from § 1353 para. 1 sentence 2 Civil Code* without regard in principle to the factual existence of a life relationship (Jakobs, StrafR AT, 2nd edit., p. 823 . . .). Proponents of this approach do concede that the factual existence of a relationship is not without any meaning; without it, one would deny a guarantor duty for other legal interests than body, life and freedom (Jescheck, in: LK-StGB, 11th edit., § 13 marginal no. 23a.E.). The duty to assume responsibility for the protection of the named legal interests (body, life, freedom) was however simply linked to the continued existence of the marriage and would not be terminated simply by the spouses giving up living together and going separate ways—with the consequence that the conviction here met with no doubts.

       According to another view the guarantor duty between spouses does not find its basis in § 1353 Civil Code. The decisive factor for assuming a guarantor position should instead only be the factual existence of a mutual relationship of trust and dependence between the spouses (Rudolphi, in: SK-StGB, § 13 marginal no. 50 with further references). If this was absent and it would be as a rule if the spouses were leading factually separate lives, omissions would not

---

* [Civil Code, § 1353 para. 1: Marriage is entered into for life. The spouses have a mutual duty of conjugal community; they are responsible for each other.—Eds.]

be equal to the active causing of the wrongful consequence in the crime definition. The legal duty arising from § 1353 Civil Code to re-enter conjugal community could not change anything as long as the spouse does not fulfill this legal duty and a mutual relationship of trust and dependence is lacking....

The Federal Court of Justice has not yet decided this question...A compromise view seems to be indicated in the end:

The answer to the question about criminal law protective duties between spouses must take its starting point with § 1353 Civil Code. It is not evident why, if spouses bear responsibility for each other according to this norm (§ 1353 para. 1 sentence 2), this should not in principle also apply for the criminal law. Accordingly the mutual duty of assistance cannot be regarded as terminated with for instance the mere departure of a spouse from the marital home as such, i.e. with the mere spatial separation. The absence of a domestic relationship does not—according to the actual circumstances—necessarily mean that the marital life relationship has been given up (Palandt/Brudermüller, BGB, 62nd edit., § 1565 marginal no. 2). Marriage is distinguished in this way from a mere communal relationship intended for mutual assistance, as may for instance be present with a group sharing a house. With the latter, the criminal law guarantor duty will in general end with the factual end of the relationship.

On the other hand it would amount to an unjustifiable overextension of the criminal law duty of assistance between spouses if it were to be accepted that this only terminates with the end of the marriage, and thus only when the divorce decree becomes effective. There are numerous conceivable arrangements in life in which—regardless of the formal continuing marriage bond—neither of the two spouses actually trusted, or even had cause to trust, that the other party would assist him for the protection of his legal interests. That applies in an especially striking way, for instance, when the spouses had already been separated for years, and possibly even linked to other partners in a life relationship, as well as when they—perhaps for purely economic reasons—live in the same house or in the same residence separately from one another after severe unilateral or bilateral marital transgressions or quarrels...

Accordingly the criminal law guarantor duty between spouses ends when one spouse has separated from the other with the serious intention of not restoring this relationship...

This compromise view...coincides to a large extent with the opinion that the criminal law guarantor duty between spouses in its basis and in its scope can only be derived from the factual existence of a mutual relationship of trust. If the supporters of this opinion explain for instance that the guarantor duty will not apply "as a rule in the case of factually separate lives of the spouses" (see for example Rudolphi, in: SK-StGB, § 13 marginal no. 50), then they presumably allow for an exception if spouses have separated in order to test whether their relationship has a chance, whilst in cases in which separation is the final cancellation of the relationship, a guarantor duty no longer exists.

On the basis of this opinion the conviction of the defendant S. for assisting infliction of bodily harm by omission cannot subsist. According to the findings so far it is possible that the departure of the defendant S. was based on a serious decision not to continue the marriage life relationship and the guarantor duty was thereby terminated. The fact that the defendant had taken another man could argue in favor of this.

On the other hand, the departure from the marital home only took place a short time before the moment of the crime. It may have been the case that the defendant still wished to consider continuation of the marriage. Therefore, it is conceivable that further examination of facts might lead to the assumption of a continuing guarantor duty. The Senate cannot therefore acquit the defendant.

German Federal Court of Justice
StR 34/82, BGHSt 30, 391 (February 24, 1982)

Facts

The chief perpetrator B., a Turkish citizen, together with four other men—all of them masked—attacked and, with blows and other violence, abducted the 18-year-old witness S., also Turkish, early in the morning January 29, 1981, in the street and took her in a vehicle to the residence of his brother M. He had intended to have sexual intercourse with her there—if necessary by violence—in order to make her comply with his expressed desire for marriage, which until now had been fruitless. His plan however failed at first because of the witness's violent resistance. He had then decided to take the witness to another safer place, i.e., the residence of the two defendants, also Turks in S., because he considered the attic of the small house which was partially occupied by them as tenants to be a suitable hideout in order to complete his intentions. B. and one of his assistants carried the witness, who was tied up, blindfolded and continually shouting for help, up the stairway. At this point at the latest, the defendant Ü., a 41-year-old partially sighted man who had taken early retirement, noticed what was happening. He asked who the girl was and was told he could not know this. In the attic B. tried again to have sexual intercourse with the witness by means of violence; he struck her and kicked her. When the defendant Ü. then appeared in the attic, the witness told him what had happened and asked for his help. B then threatened to kill the defendant. The defendant left the attic rooms saying that he wanted to call his wife, the defendant E. She worked nearby and appeared in the residence at 9 a.m., during the coffee break. The witness told her what had happened so far and asked for her help as well. The defendant promised help, but stated that she could not provide it at the moment. She would however later inform the victim's parents. She merely cleaned traces of blood off the witness's face with a damp cloth. She also vacuumed up the fragments of a table lamp destroyed in the struggles. After B. had threatened to kill her as well, and had also thrown an ashtray at her, she returned at around 9.20 a.m. to her workplace. Like her husband, under the influence of the threats uttered by B. she did nothing to free the witness. Both defendants realized that B. had violently abducted the witness, that he intended to have sexual intercourse with her by the use of force, and that he would ill-treat her further physically on the premises of the communal residence. B. now bound the witness's hands again (she had temporarily freed herself), beat her once more, and finally attained his goal of having sexual intercourse with her by force. About half an hour later—more than five hours having passed since the departure of the defendant Ms. Ü—the witness was freed by the police who had been anonymously informed.

The regional court sentenced B. to seven years imprisonment for rape concomitantly with abduction against the victim's will and infliction of dangerous bodily harm (§§ 177, 237, 223a, 52 Criminal Code). In this respect the judgment is final. The complainant married couple were sentenced by the regional court to 10 months imprisonment each for assisting B.'s crime by omission. It suspended the execution of this sentence on probation. Their appeals in law were successful.

Reasons

II.

1. The regional court assesses the behavior of the complainants only from the legal viewpoint of assisting by omission. It deduces a guarantor relationship as the basis of a legal duty to act from the fact that "both possessed the power of disposition over the premises used by the defendant for his crime." It bases this primarily on the Senate decision BGHSt 27, 10. In that case, the defendant had however taken the victim into his residence and had made its protection available to him. His guarantor status arose from the foundation of trust that this created. Whether the proprietor of a residence must also protect persons who have arrived in his residence without his involvement could be left open by the Senate in the prior judgment.

2. According to § 13 para. 1 Criminal Code a person who fails to avert the result contained in a definition in a criminal statute is only punishable if he is legally responsible for that result not arising; further the omission must be equivalent to the statutory definition by an act. The first of these two criteria—a guarantor status of the possessor [*Inhaber*] of a residence for a legal interest threatened on his premises—cannot be assumed here.

The legal concept of guarantor status is not described in greater detail in statute law. Before the introduction of § 13 Criminal Code it has been traced through case law and legal doctrine to a number of origins. Common to these is a special protective function of the guarantor, whether arising from his statutory duty, from factual acceptance or from a previous act creating danger. The mere factual possibility of preventing a result or a moral duty to do this have never been regarded as a sufficient ground for a guarantor duty. A duty on the part of the possessor of a residence to protect any person on his premises against criminal acts by other persons is derived by part of the literature from the basic right of inviolability of his residence (art. 13 para. 1 Basic Law) granted to him by the legal order which restricts interference by third parties or the police (art. 13 para. 2 Basic Law, §§ 103, 104 Code of Criminal Procedure). Corresponding protective duties are inferred for the person thus privileged— as reflexively increased rights (Blei, StrafR AT, 17th edit, p. 295)—from these special defensive powers. However this conclusion is not convincing. It must first be pointed out that the protection of the owner's right to undisturbed possession does not exist in the case of serious crimes which are directly impending . . . It must further be considered that the view mentioned forces every possessor of a residence into the role of protector of people in his residence, and into that of a supervisory person as against those of them who inflict bodily harm on others, without any evident legal foundation for imposing such a legal duty on everyone, and without the possessor of the residence having contributed anything to it except renting or possessing his residence. When he fails in this role, which is allocated to him without regard to guilt or even to the cause of the danger which has arisen to others, criminal liability is imposed upon him for the legal interest violation which took place on his premises. This extensive approximation of the possessor of the residence who merely remains inactive with the real violator of the law, by which the possessor becomes the violator's accomplice, is not reconcilable with the meaning of guarantor liability which assumes a "taking of responsibility" for the inviolability of the legal interest to be protected. It extends the scope of duties to act reinforced with the consequences of criminal liability into the realm of merely moral duties in an impermissible manner . . .

A guarantor status which is only derived from a person's capacity as possessor of a residence is mainly denied in the legal literature (Jescheck, in: LK, 10th edit, § 13 marginal no. 44; Stree, in: Schönke-Schröder, StGB, 20th edit., § 13 marginal no. 54; Rudolphi, in: SKStGB, § 13 marginal no. 37; Herzberg, Die Unterlassung im StrafR und das Garantenprinzip (The omission in criminal law and the guarantor principle), p. 332 ff.; . . .). Case law has also only made the possessor of a residence or other premises liable in criminal law for legal interest violations committed on these premises if special circumstances appear which form the basis of a legal duty to act. Such circumstances have been seen in the position of the head of a household as against a woman who killed a child (RGSt 72, 373; OGHSt 1, 87), in the position of a husband of a woman who has an abortion (BGH, NJW 1953, 591; BGH, GA 1967, 115), in the running of a public house (RGSt 58, 299; BGH, NJW 1966, 1763; deviating BGH, GA 1971, 336 where in a similar case only the legal aspect of failure to provide assistance is stressed) and in the case BGHSt 27, 10 mentioned above in the taking of the victim into the protective area of the residence.

A guarantor duty on the part of a possessor of a residence can admittedly arise if the residence, because of its special nature or position, represents a source of danger which he must secure and watch over in such a way that it cannot be made the means for easy commission of crimes (Jescheck, in: LK, § 13 Rdnr. 44; Rudolphi, in: SKStGB, § 13 marginal no. 37; Herzberg, pp. 331, 334; . . .). That the defendant's dwelling—beyond its character as a dwelling and therefore as an area shielded from the outside world and concealing events occurring there—represents a special source of danger in this sense cannot however be deduced from the findings of the regional court.

3. The finding of a guarantor duty by the regional court is incorrect and leads to quashing of the judgment.

In the new main proceedings the judge of fact will also have the opportunity to look into the question of whether the defendants possibly encouraged B.'s crimes by positive action . . . If the new proceedings should lead again to findings which do not permit a conviction for participation in B's crime, the regional court will have to examine whether the defendants are guilty of omission to provide assistance. The rape of a woman is recognized in the case law as a misadventure in the sense of § 323c Criminal Code (BGHSt 3, 65 (66); BGH, GA 1971, 336).

German Federal Court of Justice
2 StR 221/70, BGHSt 23, 327 (July 29, 1970)

The defendant was charged with homicide because he killed a drinking companion in a fight on the way home by stabbing him in the heart. The regional court (juvenile chamber) acquitted him of the charge of completed homicide because of self-defense. It further assumes that the injured man could not have been saved after the stabbing. The defendant however left him behind helpless without knowledge of this and thereby accepted and condoned the occurrence of death as a result of failure to provide assistance. The young persons' chamber therefore sentenced him to two years youth detention for attempted homicide.

. . . The view of the regional court that the defendant had committed attempted homicide by omission to provide assistance meets with legal doubts which prevail.

The regional court assesses the defendant's conduct as a crime by omission. The pre-requisite for this is that the perpetrator was obliged to prevent the result. He must be a guarantor for the protection of the threatened legal interest. That is the case when he has—with or without culpability—brought about the dangerous situation. The question of whether the prior conduct causing the danger must be wrongful does not need to be answered generally here (see on this BGHSt 19, 152). In any case injuring an attacker in self-defense does not as a rule suffice to establish a guarantor status of the person attacked.

As far as is evident, the question has not yet been decided. The opinions in the literature are divided. Guarantor status of the person attacked is denied by, amongst others, Welzel, Deutsches Strafrecht § 28 A I 4; Dreher, StGB, 31st edit., before § 1 note D I 4; Schönke-Schröder, StGB, 15th edit., preliminary note, marginal no. 120 d; Mezger, Strafrecht 13th edit., § 29 III 2 c; . . . A contrary view is expressed by, amongst others, Maurach, Deutsches Strafrecht, Allg. Teil, § 46 III C 4; Baumann, Strafrecht, Allg. Teil, § 18 II 3 c; . . .

It must be assumed that the person who acts in self-defense finds himself in a substantially different situation than the initiator of a situation of danger normally does. The action of the person attacked which causes danger, i.e. the defense against the attacker, is not based on his free decision, but is provoked and triggered by the attacker's illegal behavior. This special circumstance must have an effect on the legal status of the attacker endangered by the defensive action. The person who causes self-endangerment by an illegal attack cannot thereby force the person attacked to become his protector as a guarantor. The attacker is not thereby in any way left unprotected. The general claim to help under § 330c Criminal Code* enforced by the criminal law remains for him anyway, because a misadventure in the sense of this provision is also present when the person affected has provoked the plight himself (BGHSt 6, 147, 152). To burden the person attacked over and above this with guarantor status contradicts the purpose of the law of self-defense. This is because the attacker would thereby be more effectively protected than an accident victim for whom neither he nor anyone else is to blame. What decision should be made when, in a case of true self-defense, the attacker is not responsible for his actions or can otherwise not act in a culpable way, can be left open here.

A homicide crime committed by omission is therefore ruled out here. On the other hand, the defendant is guilty of failure to render assistance . . . [now § 323c]

NOTES

1. Can punishing persons who have done nothing, who could only be blamed for remaining passive, be legitimate? In addressing this question, it is helpful to distinguish between omission offenses that are explicitly defined as omissions and offenses that are defined as active behavior (such as, for instance, "to kill a person"). German law contains few offenses of the first kind ("real omissions" in German criminal law). Besides § 323c Criminal Code (failure to render assistance), it is also a criminal offense not to report one's knowledge of an impending serious crime such as homicide, murder, robbery, arson, etc. to state authorities or the potential victim (§ 138 Criminal Code). Such crimes do not punish the occurrence of harmful results as such, but the omission of assistance. If, in this mode, a statute describes the relevant conduct explicitly as omitting to act, there is no problem in terms of "fair warning" of citizens.

But why is this not a violation of the act requirement? How can a non-act be an act? Can this sort of question be answered by definition, so that as long as the state (in a statute? a court opinion?) defines X as Y (even if Y=non-X), no legitimacy concerns remain? Recall the Model Penal Code's "definition" of possession as an act in § 2.01(4), quoted in Chapter 7.C. Note that the Code, in § 2.01(1), formulates the act requirement as a "conduct" requirement, and then defines conduct as "includ[ing] a voluntary act or *the omission* to perform an act" (emphasis added). Is this a sleight of hand that achieves at best drafting consistency, without addressing the underlying challenge of justifying the punishment of non-acts in the face of an act requirement (or, alternatively, punishing *some* non-acts, namely those backed by a duty, but not others, such as statuses, or thoughts)? Or does it suggest an altogether different—duty-based—conception of criminal law (revolving around the *failure* to comply with a duty)?

One can debate whether (and to what degree) duties of compassion and solidarity exist between citizens, and whether the state should punish their violation. Note that the punishment ranges for "real omission" offenses tend to be moderate—which might influence the evaluation of their legitimacy. Do these statutes blur the line between moral and legal duties? Do they violate the *ultima ratio* principle (the "last resort"[†])? The German duty-to-aid statute (§ 323c) in particular has a checkered history; it was introduced in 1935, in the following form (since amended):

German Criminal Code § 330c (Failure to Render Assistance)

Who does not render assistance in the case of a misadventure or common danger, or necessity, even though this is his duty according to sound popular sentiment and, in particular, does not comply with the request for assistance of a police agent, even though he could comply with the

---

* [Note: old version, now § 323c.–Eds.]

---

† See Chapter 3.B.

request without serious danger and without the infringement of other important duties, is punishable with prison for up to two years or with a fine.

Leaving aside the ideological reference to "sound popular sentiment" in the original version of the German provision, is the criminal enforcement of general duties to aid more consistent with communitarian conceptions of legality than with traditionally liberal ones? General criminal duty-to-aid statutes are rare in the United States (and throughout the common law world); the Vermont and Wisconsin statutes reproduced above are often cited as exceptions. Note the reference to tort liability arising out of Good Samaritan acts in both the Vermont and the Wisconsin provision, along with the narrow scope of the duty (including the requirement of willfulness) and the minimal punishment (particularly within the context of the severity of U.S. criminal punishment in general).

Germany is not alone among civil law countries to criminalize the failure to comply with a general duty to aid. Consider also the following French provisions:

French Penal Code

Art. 223–6

Anyone who, being able to prevent by immediate action a felony or a misdemeanor against the bodily integrity of a person, without risk to himself or to third parties, wilfully abstains from doing so, is punished by five years' imprisonment and a fine of €75,000.

The same penalties apply to anyone who wilfully fails to offer assistance to a person in danger which he could himself provide without risk to himself or to third parties, or by initiating rescue operations.

Art. 223–7

Anyone who voluntarily abstains from taking or initiating measures, which involve no risk to himself or to third parties, to combat a natural disaster likely to endanger the safety of others is punished by two years' imprisonment and affine of €30,000.

Like German criminal law, U.S. criminal law also distinguishes between "direct" omission and "indirect" omission liability. The former arises, directly, out of offenses defined explicitly in terms of a failure to act, a typical example being tax evasion, which criminalizes—in one of its permutations—the failure to file a tax return, 26 U.S.C. § 7203 ("willful failure to file return, supply information, or pay tax").

2. Things are more complicated if one turns to the second type of omission offenses, which focus on certain harmful results. The relevant provisions in criminal codes typically describe affirmative acts (for example, killing or injuring another person). What to do about a defendant who remained passive but who could have averted the crucial result (death or injury)? There is a widely shared intuition that, under certain circumstances, results may legitimately be attributed to the passive person. The paradigm example, which also figures in *State v. Miranda*, is the situation of traditional parenthood (biologically and socially within a family). A mother who does not feed her starving child has to expect punishment for causing death through omission in all legal systems. Under such circumstances, if the conviction is for murder or manslaughter through omission, the punishment typically is considerably more severe than for the "failure-to-render-assistance"-type of offenses.

"Indirect" omission liability attaches to offenses that are defined in terms of an act, rather than a failure to act. This includes the vast bulk of offenses (except, interestingly, in corporate criminal law, which in many ways is an upside-down version of the criminal law of natural persons; the paradigmatic corporate crime is a strict liability direct omission offense*). Indirect omission liability thus has the effect of dramatically expanding the scope of criminal liability, by extending every offense to those who did not engage in proscribed conduct, but are treated *as if* they had because of their *failure* to engage in *required* conduct. A person who does nothing can thus "commit" homicide "by omission," assuming a duty required him or her to come to the aid of the eventual homicide victim (and, of course, assuming as well that

---

* See Chapter 11.

he or she satisfies all the other elements of the offense, including *mens rea*, and no defenses apply). Indirect omission is simply another, indirect, way of satisfying the conduct element of the crime in question. Most offenders satisfy the conduct element of a crime by commission; others satisfy it, indirectly, by commission through omission. Indirect omission is a form of liability (general part); direct omission is a form of offense (special part).

3. In cases of "indirect" omission liability, legal problems emerge, which are mentioned in the other opinions in *State v. Miranda*. Offense descriptions might be formulated to emphasize activity rather than harmful outcome (see Judge Berdon's reading of what the phrase "assault" means). If the legislature opts for such formulations, it is debatable whether this may be circumvented through judicial decisions to include passive conduct. Also, if one turns to the question of "fair warning," obviously it is preferable if a criminal code (any statute? a court opinion?) describes under which circumstances passive conduct will be treated as equivalent to actively causing certain outcomes.

In German law, § 13 Criminal Code contains a provision of this kind, albeit a rather vague one. The passage in § 13 para. 1 Criminal Code requires that the offender must be "legally responsible for the fact that the result does not occur." The Code does not, however, specify which circumstances make one "legally responsible." Therefore, case law and German criminal doctrine had to delineate the duties that are important enough to justify punishment for omission. Consider this as an example of how the differences between a "common law system" and a "civil law system" might be smaller than are sometimes assumed. The German Criminal Code contains many expressions that are in need of interpretation and specification through case law. (For instance, the German Criminal Code does not contain definitions of mental states (*Vorsatz* and *Fahrlässigkeit*); by contrast, the Model Penal Code's definition of modes of culpability (purpose, knowledge, recklessness, negligence) is considered one of its central achievements.*)

Does the failure to include in the criminal code a definition of duties that can give rise to criminal indirect omission liability constitute a violation of the principle of legality?[†]

4. Which duties create "legal responsibility" for a harmful outcome even if one remains passive? In German case law, the expression "guarantor duty" (*Garantenpflicht*) is the central term when § 13 Criminal Code is under consideration. There is some dispute about which circumstances create such a guarantor duty. One approach puts strong emphasis on legal regulations such as contracts, legal provisions within family law, etc. An alternative way to found duties pays more attention to social realities and perhaps also to moral obligations (although the German Federal Court of Justice in the case of the abducted young woman explicitly rejected moral notions as foundations for criminal liability!). The German case concerning the hostile wife who did not warn her husband of the attack illustrates these viewpoints. Note that the German Court of Justice points in a similar direction as the Supreme Court of Connecticut in *State v. Miranda*: towards factual social arrangements rather than legal categories such as not-being-divorced or not-being-an-adoptive-parent. What is troubling about basing legal liability, and criminal legal liability, on moral notions of appropriate (ethical, prudent?) behavior? About basing criminal liability on factual arrangements? Who finds these facts, who interprets them? What about the principle of legality?

Another distinction that emerges from the German case law is the following: the distinction between guarantor duties of care toward a specific individual and guarantor duties to protect unspecified others against a danger for which one is responsible. The first category is probably the less disputed one. Duties of care towards a child (one's own biological or

---

* See the discussion of *mens rea* in Chapter 8.

† See Chapter 2. See further Don Stuart, "Supporting General Principles for Criminal Responsibility in the Model Penal Code with Suggestions for Reconsideration: A Canadian Perspective," 4 *Buffalo Criminal Law Review* (2000), 13, 42 ("Allowing criminal responsibility to rest not only on breach of statutory duty outside the Criminal Code but on any common law duty such as those found in torts is a fundamental breach of the principle of legality. Duties imposed in the context of civil compensation where the issue is often which party can better bear the risk of harm may well be inappropriate to the issue of just punishment.").

adoptive child or step child) and towards one's spouse belong to this group, for example *State v. Miranda* and the German case concerning spousal omission liability. The two other German judgments concern the "responsible for danger" category. The accused in these cases had no special relationship of care with the victim; the victims were strangers. But German case law does acknowledge guarantor duties (with the potential of much harsher punishment than § 323c Criminal Code) if the victim was endangered by a prior act of the offender or if the offender is in other ways responsible for the danger. For instance, if a driver in a state of drunkenness causes an accident and injures another person, and then leaves without helping the injured, he will be punished for homicide or murder through omission if the victim of the accident dies (see Federal Court of Justice, decision from May 6, 1986, 4 StR 150/86, BGHSt 34, 82). For another German case exploring a guarantor duty based on prior dangerous conduct, see the *Leather Spray Case*, Chapter 9 (not to be confused with the *Leather* Strap *Case*, in Chapter 8.A). A well-known English case on the issue is *R. v. Miller*, [1983] 1 All E.R. 978 (affirming arson conviction of a squatter who, having inadvertently set fire to a mattress with his cigarette, did nothing about it and went back to sleep in another room).

The Federal Court of Justice emphasized that the prior conduct that creates guarantor duties must be wrongful, that is, not covered by a justification. Therefore, one who acts in self-defense and then leaves a seriously injured attacker without calling for medical assistance will not be punished for homicide through omission should the attacker die (though he or she would still be liable under § 323c Criminal Code!).* Assuming the defendant, Bonnie Kuntz, had stabbed the victim, Warren Becker, in self-defense, the court explored the interaction between duties arising out of "creation of the peril" and justification:

> Undoubtedly, when a person places another in a position of danger, and then fails to safeguard or rescue that person, and the person subsequently dies as a result of this omission, such an omission may be sufficient to support criminal liability. . . .
> Although the use of force may be justified, to not hold such a person criminally accountable for the subsequent omission would, according to the State, "encourage revenge and retaliation."
> Whether inflicted in self-defense or accidentally, a wound that causes a loss of blood undoubtedly places a person in some degree of peril, and therefore gives rise to a legal duty to either 1) personally provide assistance; or 2) summon medical assistance. Even so, the performance of this legal duty does not require that a person place herself at risk of serious bodily injury or death. . . .
> [T]he duty to summon aid may in fact be "revived" as the State contends, but only after the victim of the aggressor has fully exercised her right to seek and secure safety from personal harm. Then, and only then, may a legal duty be imposed to summon aid for the person placed in peril by an act of self-defense.
> [A] person, who is found to have used justifiable force, but who nevertheless fails to summon aid in dereliction of the legal duty as defined here, may be found criminally negligent only where the failure to summon aid is the cause-in-fact of death, rather than the use of force itself.

The dissenting judge disagreed:

> [T]he majority opinion predicates criminal liability on a finding that the failure to summon aid is the cause in fact of death. However, where a person is placed in peril by another's justified use of force it can never be said that the failure to summon aid, rather than the original act of force, is the cause in fact of death, because presumably death would never have occurred but for the original act of self-defense. . . .
> A person driven to the point of having to violently defend herself from a violent attack should not, at the risk of criminal punishment, be required to know that at some undefined point in time she has a duty to save that same person. A normal person under those circumstances is incapable of undertaking such an intellectual process. To require her to do so is inconsistent with the traditional notion that when criminal liability is based on the failure to perform a duty, it must be a plain duty which leaves no doubt as to its obligatory force.

---

* For a similar U.S. case on this point, consider *State ex rel. Kuntz v. Montana*, 298 Mont. 146, 995 P.2d 951 (2000).

Who has the better of this argument?

In the German case of the abducted young woman, the court had to deal with the question of whether possession (occupancy, as opposed to ownership) of a residence generates a duty of care toward any person on the premises. There is a hint in the ruling that this is conceivable, although not in a situation like the one before the court. If the possessor had created unusual sources of dangers in a dwelling (for instance, by drilling big holes into stairs, having unsafe lines of electricity, etc.), he or she would have a guarantor duty if others injured themselves; but the mere possession of the residence could not generate such a duty.

5. The last sentences of the German decision concerning duties among spouses might require some explanation with respect to procedures after appeals in law. The Federal Court of Justice reverses the judgment by the district court but refuses to acquit the defendant S. because there remain uncertainties of a factual kind. This means that the case goes back to another chamber of the district court, which has to collect additional evidence on the background of the separation between S. and her husband (see § 354 German Code of Criminal Procedure).

MENS REA (SUBJECTIVE ELEMENTS)

In Anglo-American criminal law, as in German criminal law, there are two sides to a crime: *actus reus* and *mens rea*, in one system, objective and subjective elements, in the other. So far we have dealt with one side; now it is time to have a look at the other. In fact, it is the other side, that of *mens rea* or subjective offense elements, that tends to attract far more attention than the first. It is the *mens rea* that turns the *actus reus* into a crime, that puts the *reus* into the *actus*, so to speak: *actus non facit reum nisi mens sit rea*, as the old common law saw puts it, not the other way around. When the Model Penal Code drafters went to work, they focused much of their attention on the question of *mens rea*, not only because they thought that the law on this subject was particularly rife with inconsistencies and irrationalities, but also because—not unrelatedly—the problem of *mens rea* lay at the heart of the inquiry into criminal liability. The resulting Code section on *mens rea* is the most carefully drafted, most significant, and most influential part of the Code, featuring not only (arguably overly detailed) definitions of four modes of culpability (purpose, knowledge, recklessness, negligence), but also a set of supplementary provisions, including maxims of statutory interpretation to guide courts in determining which mental state requirement attached to each element of the offense.

The German Criminal Code may not contain a similarly detailed and comprehensive set of provisions on the subject of *mens rea* (although definitions of the various mental states— *Vorsatz, Wissentlichkeit, Fahrlässigkeit, Leichtfertigkeit*—were proposed in the preliminary official and alternative drafts), but ironically this *absence* reflects a similar sense of the importance and the complexity of the issue: so important and complex is the doctrine of subjective offense elements that it should be left to the continuous consideration and refinement of criminal law science, rather than attempting to capture it, once and for all, in a legislative definition. (Interestingly, similar arguments were advanced in nineteenth century England, except that there and then consideration of the issue tellingly was assigned not to criminal law scholars but to common law judges.*)

The Anglo-American and German approaches to the issue of subjective offense elements are sufficiently similar to support meaningful comparison, which then reveals interesting distinctions at a higher resolution. For instance, a question that continues to attract attention is that of the distinction (or lack thereof) between (Anglo-American) recklessness and (German) conditional intention (*bedingter Vorsatz, dolus eventualis*). But there are other issues that may be worth a longer comparative look, including the relationship between (Anglo-American) negligence and (German) *Fahrlässigkeit*, the (legitimate) role of motive in the assessment of criminal liability, and the meaning and significance of reasonableness in the law of *mens rea*, as well as generally in Anglo-American and German criminal law.

---

* See Martin L. Friedland, "R.S. Wright's Model Criminal Code: A Forgotten Chapter in the History of the Criminal Law," 1 *Oxford Journal of Legal Studies* (1991), 307.

A. Modes of Culpability

People v. Baker
Supreme Court of New York, Appellate Division
4 A.D.3d 606, 771 N.Y.S.2d 607 (2004)

Rose, J.

Appeal from a judgment of the County Court of Tioga County (Sgueglia, J.), rendered April 7, 2000, upon a verdict convicting defendant of the crime of murder in the second degree.

After a three-year-old child died while defendant was babysitting in the child's home, she was charged with both intentional and depraved indifference murder. At trial, the evidence established that, on a warm summer night, the victim died of hyperthermia as a result of her prolonged exposure to excessive heat in a bedroom of her foster parents' apartment. The excessive heat was caused by the furnace having run constantly for many hours as the result of a short circuit in its wiring. The victim was unable to leave her bedroom because defendant engaged the hook and eye latch on its door after putting her to bed for the night. Defendant then remained in the apartment watching television while the furnace ran uncontrollably. The victim's foster parents and another tenant testified that when they returned in the early morning hours and found the victim lifeless in her bed, the living room of the apartment where defendant sat waiting for them felt extremely hot, like an oven or a sauna, and the victim's bedroom was even hotter. Temperature readings taken later that morning during a police investigation while the furnace was still running indicated that the apartment's living room was 102 degrees Fahrenheit, the victim's bedroom was 110 degrees Fahrenheit and the air coming from the vent in the bedroom was more than 130 degrees Fahrenheit.

In characterizing defendant's role in these events, the prosecutor argued that the key issue for the jury was whether or not defendant had intended to kill the victim. The prosecution's proof on this issue consisted primarily of the second of two written statements given by defendant to police during a four-hour interview conducted a few hours after the victim was found. In the first statement, defendant related that she had been aware of the oppressive heat in the victim's bedroom, kept the victim latched in because the foster parents had instructed her to do so, had not looked at or adjusted the thermostat even though the furnace was running on a hot day, heard the victim kicking and screaming to be let out and felt the adverse effects of the heat on herself. The second statement, which defendant disavowed at trial, described her intent to cause the victim's death by turning up the thermostat to its maximum setting, closing all heating vents except the one in the victim's bedroom and placing additional clothing on the victim which she then removed after the victim died . . .

After trial, the jury acquitted defendant of intentional murder (see Penal Law § 125.25 [1]), thereby rejecting the second statement, and instead convicted her of depraved indifference murder of a child (see Penal Law § 125.25 [4]). County Court sentenced her to a prison term of 15 years to life, and she now appeals . . .

We agree with defendant . . . that the evidence in the record is legally insufficient to prove the gross recklessness and additional aggravating circumstances necessary for a conviction of depraved indifference murder. In our view, the jury could not reasonably infer from the evidence a culpable mental state greater than criminal negligence due to the unique combination of events that led to the victim's death, as well as the lack of proof that defendant actually perceived and ignored an obvious and severe risk of serious injury or death.

A verdict is supported by legally sufficient evidence when the proof, viewed in the light most favorable to the prosecution, establishes the elements of the crime beyond a reasonable doubt. Here, County Court instructed the jury as to the elements of intentional murder in the second degree, depraved indifference murder in the second degree, as well as the lesser included offenses of manslaughter in the first degree with intent to cause physical injury (see Penal Law § 125.20 [1], [4]), reckless manslaughter in the second degree (see Penal Law § 125.15 [1]) and criminally negligent homicide (see Penal Law § 125.10). The jury's finding that defendant was not guilty of intentional murder clearly indicates that it rejected defendant's second statement. That statement contains an explicit admission of an intent to kill the victim and a description of a series of acts reflecting such an intent. Inasmuch as there is no other evidence, and no argument, that these acts were done for any other purpose, we must assume that the jury rejected the acts when it rejected the charge of intentional murder. Thus, we look elsewhere in the record to ascertain whether there is other evidence establishing first, that the circumstances surrounding defendant's conduct evince a depraved indifference to human life, and second, that defendant perceived and disregarded a substantial risk of serious injury or death.

To support defendant's conviction of depraved indifference murder of a child, there must be proof that, "based on an objective assessment of the risk defendant recklessly created and disregarded, the likelihood of causing [serious physical injury or] death from defendant's conduct was so obviously severe that it evinced a depraved indifference to human life" (People v. Sanchez, 98 N.Y.2d 373, 384 [2002]). Although the excessive heat in the victim's bedroom ultimately proved fatal and defendant failed to provide relief from the heat by removing the victim from her bedroom or attempting to reduce the heat, the evidence does not establish that her acts and omissions were "committed under circumstances which evidenced a wanton indifference to human life or a depravity of mind" (People v. Register, 60 N.Y.2d 270, 274 [1983]). "Illustrative of such conduct is driving an automobile on a city sidewalk at an excessive speed and striking a pedestrian without applying the brakes, firing several bullets into a house, beating an infant over a five day period, and placing a bomb in a public place. In each illustration the basic crime was aggravated by additional egregious conduct" (People v. Murphy, 235 A.D.2d 933, 936 [1997]). In cases where the victim is a child, there typically are one or more instances of direct harmful contact with the child, as well as other egregious conduct (People v. Dexheimer, 214 A.D.2d 898, 901 [1993] [adult repeatedly struck young child and failed to summon emergency aid]; cf. People v. Sika, 138 A.D.2d 935, 935–936 [1988] [mother's failure to provide adequate nourishment and seek medical assistance for infant son was held not to be "so brutal, callous or wanton that it evinced a depraved indifference to human life"]). Here, by contrast, there was neither obviously dangerous conduct by defendant nor harmful physical contact between defendant and the victim.

In addition to the lack of physical contact, there is no evidence that defendant knew the actual temperature in any portion of the apartment or subjectively perceived a degree of heat that would have made her aware that serious injury or death from hyperthermia would almost certainly result. Put another way, the risk of serious physical injury or death was not so obvious under the circumstances that it demonstrated defendant's actual awareness. There was only circumstantial evidence on this point consisting of the subjective perceptions of other persons who later came into the apartment from cooler outside temperatures. Defendant, who had been in the apartment as the heat gradually intensified over many hours, and who was described by others as appearing flushed and acting dazed, could not reasonably be presumed to have had the same perception of oppressive and dangerous heat. Rather, defendant testified that she knew only that the heat made her feel dizzy and uncomfortable, and denied any awareness of a risk of death. Most significantly, there is no dispute that defendant remained in a room that was nearly as hot as the victim's bedroom for approximately nine hours and checked on the victim several times before the foster parents returned. This evidence of defendant's failure to perceive the risk of serious injury stands unrefuted by the prosecution.

Defendant's ability to appreciate such a risk was further brought into doubt by the prosecution's own expert witness, who described her as having borderline intellectual function, learning disabilities and a full scale IQ of only 73. We also note that here, unlike where an unclothed child is shut outside in freezing temperatures, the circumstances are not of a type from which it can be inferred without a doubt that a person of even ordinary intelligence and experience would have perceived a severe risk of serious injury or death.

For these reasons, we find that defendant's conduct was not proven to have been "so wanton, so deficient in a moral sense of concern, so devoid of regard of the life or lives of others, and so blameworthy as to warrant the same criminal liability as that which the law imposes upon a person who intentionally causes the death of another" (People v. Fenner, 61 N.Y.2d 971, 973 [1984]). Accordingly, no valid line of reasoning and permissible inferences could have led the jury to the conclusion that it reached.

We turn next to the issue of whether the record evidence establishes, beyond a reasonable doubt, one or more lesser-included offenses. As to manslaughter in the first degree, there is no proof, other than defendant's discredited second statement, that she intentionally caused "serious physical injury" (Penal Law § 125.20 [1]) or "physical injury" (Penal Law § 125.20 [4]). As to the lesser included offenses of manslaughter in the second degree and criminally negligent homicide, we must compare the requisite culpable mental states. A person is guilty of manslaughter in the second degree when he or she recklessly causes the death of another person (see Penal Law § 125.15 [1]) and of criminally negligent homicide when, with criminal negligence, he or she causes the death of another person (see Penal Law § 125.10). Reckless criminal conduct occurs when the actor is aware of and consciously disregards a substantial and unjustifiable risk, and criminal negligence is the failure to perceive such a risk (see Penal Law § 15.05 [3], [4]).

As we have noted, there is no support for a finding that defendant perceived and consciously disregarded the risk of death which was created by the combination of the "runaway" furnace and her failure to release the victim from her bedroom (see Penal Law § 15.05 [3]; § 125.15 [1]). None of defendant's proven conduct reflects such an awareness and the fact that she subjected herself to the excessive heat is plainly inconsistent with a finding that she perceived a risk of death.

However, the evidence was sufficient to establish defendant's guilt beyond a reasonable doubt of criminally negligent homicide. A jury could reasonably conclude from the evidence that defendant should have perceived a substantial and unjustifiable risk that the excessive heat, in combination with her inaction, would be likely to lead to the victim's death. Since defendant was the victim's caretaker, this risk was of such a nature that her failure to perceive it constituted a gross deviation from the standard of care that a reasonable person in the same circumstances would observe in such a situation (see Penal Law § 15.05 [4]; § 125.10). Thus, defendant's conduct was shown to constitute criminal negligence and such a finding would not be against the weight of the evidence. Accordingly, we reduce the conviction from depraved indifference murder to criminally negligent homicide and remit the matter to County Court for sentencing on the reduced charge.

Model Penal Code

§ 2.02 General Requirements of Culpability

(1) *Minimum Requirements of Culpability.* Except as provided in Section 2.05, a person is not guilty of an offense unless he acted purposely, knowingly, recklessly or negligently, as the law may require, with respect to each material element of the offense.

(2) *Kinds of Culpability Defined.*

    (a) Purposely. A person acts purposely with respect to a material element of an offense when:

        (i) if the element involves the nature of his conduct or a result thereof, it is his conscious object to engage in conduct of that nature or to cause such a result; and

        (ii) if the element involves the attendant circumstances, he is aware of the existence of such circumstances or he believes or hopes that they exist.

    (b) Knowingly. A person acts knowingly with respect to a material element of an offense when:

        (i) if the element involves the nature of his conduct or the attendant circumstances, he is aware that his conduct is of that nature or that such circumstances exist; and

        (ii) if the element involves a result of his conduct, he is aware that it is practically certain that his conduct will cause such a result.

    (c) Recklessly. A person acts recklessly with respect to a material element of an offense when he consciously disregards a substantial and unjustifiable risk that the material element exists or will result from his conduct. The risk must be of such a nature and degree that, considering the nature and purpose of the actor's conduct and the circumstances known to him, its disregard involves a gross deviation from the standard of conduct that a law-abiding person would observe in the actor's situation.

    (d) Negligently. A person acts negligently with respect to a material element of an offense when he should be aware of a substantial and unjustifiable risk that the material element exists or will result from his conduct. The risk must be of such a nature and degree that the actor's failure to perceive it, considering the nature and purpose of his conduct and the circumstances known to him, involves a gross deviation from the standard of care that a reasonable person would observe in the actor's situation.

(3) *Culpability Required Unless Otherwise Provided.* When the culpability sufficient to establish a material element of an offense is not prescribed by law, such element is established if a person acts purposely, knowingly or recklessly with respect thereto.

(4) *Prescribed Culpability Requirement Applies to All Material Elements.* When the law defining an offense prescribes the kind of culpability that is sufficient for the commission of an offense, without distinguishing among the material elements thereof, such provision shall apply to all the material elements of the offense, unless a contrary purpose plainly appears.

(5) *Substitutes for Negligence, Recklessness and Knowledge.* When the law provides that negligence suffices to establish an element of an offense, such element also is established if a person acts purposely, knowingly or recklessly. When recklessness suffices to establish an element, such element also is established if a person acts purposely or knowingly. When acting knowingly suffices to establish an element, such element also is established if a person acts purposely.

(6) *Requirement of Purpose Satisfied if Purpose Is Conditional.* When a particular purpose is an element of an offense, the element is established although such purpose is conditional, unless the condition negatives the harm or evil sought to be prevented by the law defining the offense.

(7) *Requirement of Knowledge Satisfied by Knowledge of High Probability.* When knowledge of the existence of a particular fact is an element of an offense, such knowledge is established if a person is aware of a high probability of its existence, unless he actually believes that it does not exist.

(8) *Requirement of Wilfulness Satisfied by Acting Knowingly.* A requirement that an offense be committed wilfully is satisfied if a person acts knowingly with respect to the material elements of the offense, unless a purpose to impose further requirements appears.

(9) *Culpability as to Illegality of Conduct.* Neither knowledge nor recklessness or negligence as to whether conduct constitutes an offense or as to the existence, meaning or application of the law determining the elements of an offense is an element of such offense, unless the definition of the offense or the Code so provides.

(10) *Culpability as Determinant of Grade of Offense.* When the grade or degree of an offense depends on whether the offense is committed purposely, knowingly, recklessly or negligently, its grade or degree shall be the lowest for which the determinative kind of culpability is established with respect to any material element of the offense.

R. v. G. and another
House of Lords
[2003] UKHL 50

Lord Bingham of Cornhill:—
My Lords,

The point of law of general public importance certified by the Court of Appeal to be involved in its decision in the present case is expressed in this way:

> Can a defendant properly be convicted under s 1 of the Criminal Damage Act 1971 on the basis that he was reckless as to whether property was destroyed or damaged when he gave no thought to the risk but, by reason of his age and/or personal characteristics, the risk would not have been obvious to him, even if he had thought about it?

The appeal turns on the meaning of "reckless" in that section. This is a question on which the House ruled in R. v. Caldwell [1981] 1 All ER 961, [1982] AC 341, a ruling affirmed by the House in later decisions. The House is again asked to reconsider that ruling.

The agreed facts of the case are very simple. On the night of 21–22 August 2000 the appellants, then aged 11 and 12 respectively, [set fire to some garbage cans, which spread to an adjacent shop, causing extensive damage.]

An indictment was preferred against the appellants charging them with arson contrary to s 1(1) and (3) of the 1971 Act.... Section 4(1) of the Act provides that a person guilty of arson under s 1 shall on conviction on indictment be liable to imprisonment for life...

The appellants stood trial before Judge Maher in March 2001. At the outset of the trial, submissions were made on the meaning of "reckless" in s 1(1) of the 1971 Act since the appellants were charged with being reckless whether the premises would be destroyed or damaged and not with intending to destroy or damage them. The judge ruled (in effect) that he was bound to direct the jury in accordance with R. v. Caldwell, [1982] A.C. 341....

[After the jury returned a guilty verdict,] the judge made a one-year supervision order in the case of each appellant. It was not suggested in argument before the House that the judge's directions to the jury were other than correct on the law as then understood and applied....

In a leading opinion [in R v Caldwell] with which Lord Keith of Kinkel and Lord Roskill agreed, but from which Lord Wilberforce and Lord Edmund-Davies dissented, Lord Diplock... held [that it was] no less blameworthy for a man whose mind was affected by rage or excitement or drink to fail to give his mind to the risk of damaging property than for a man whose mind was so affected to appreciate that there was a risk of damage to property but not to appreciate the seriousness of the risk or to trust that good luck would prevent the risk occurring. He observed ([1981] 1 All ER 961 at 965, [1982] AC 341 at 352):

> My Lords, I can see no reason why Parliament when it decided to revise the law as to offences of damage to property should go out of its way to perpetuate fine and impracticable distinctions such as these, between one mental state and another. One would think that the sooner they were got rid of the better....

Lord Diplock... preferred the ordinary meaning of "reckless" which—

> surely includes not only deciding to ignore a risk of harmful consequences resulting from one's acts that one has recognised as existing, but also failing to give any thought to whether or not there is any such risk in circumstances where, if any thought were given to the matter, it would be obvious that there was.
>
> If one is attaching labels, the latter state of mind is neither more nor less "subjective" than the first. But the label solves nothing. It is a statement of the obvious; mens rea is, by definition, a state of mind of the accused himself at the time he did the physical act that constitutes the actus reus of the offence; it cannot be the mental state of some non-existent hypothetical person.

To decide whether a person had been reckless whether harmful consequences of a particular kind would result from his act it was necessary to consider the mind of "the ordinary prudent individual" ([1981] 1 All ER 961 at 966, [1982] AC 341 at 354).

In a passage which has since been taken to encapsulate the law on this point, and which has founded many jury directions (including that in the present case) Lord Diplock then said ([1981] 1 All ER 961 at 967, [1982] AC 341 at 354):

In my opinion, a person charged with an offence under s 1(1) of the 1971 Act is "reckless as to whether or not any property would be destroyed or damaged" if (1) he does an act which in fact creates an obvious risk that property will be destroyed or damaged and (2) when he does the act he either has not given any thought to the possibility of there being any such risk or has recognised that there was some risk involved and has none the less gone on to do it. That would be a proper direction to the jury; cases in the Court of Appeal which held otherwise should be regarded as overruled.

. . . .

In his dissenting opinion Lord Edmund-Davies . . . observed ([1981] 1 All ER 961 at 970, [1982] AC 341 at 358):

In the absence of exculpatory factors, the defendant's state of mind is therefore all-important where recklessness is an element in the offence charged, and s 8 of the Criminal Justice Act 1967 has laid down that:

"A court or jury, in determining whether a person has committed an offence, (a) shall not be bound in law to infer that he intended or foresaw a result of his actions by reason only of its being a natural and probable consequence of those actions; but (b) shall decide whether he did intend or foresee that result by reference to all the evidence, drawing such inferences from the evidence as appear proper in the circumstances." . . .

The task confronting the House in this appeal is, first of all, one of statutory construction: what did Parliament mean when it used the word "reckless" in s 1(1) and (2) of the 1971 Act? In so expressing the question I mean to make it as plain as I can that I am not addressing the meaning of "reckless" in any other statutory or common law context. . . .

Since a statute is always speaking, the context or application of a statutory expression may change over time, but the meaning of the expression itself cannot change. So the starting point is to ascertain what Parliament meant by "reckless" in 1971. . . . It cannot be supposed that by "reckless" Parliament meant anything different from the Law Commission. The Law Commission's meaning was made plain both in its report (Law Com no 29) and in Working Paper No 23 which preceded it. These materials (not, it would seem, placed before the House in R. v. Caldwell) reveal a very plain intention to replace the old-fashioned and misleading expression "maliciously" by the more familiar expression "reckless". . . . In treating this authority as irrelevant to the construction of "reckless" the majority fell into understandable but clearly demonstrable error. No relevant change in the mens rea necessary for proof of the offence was intended, and in holding otherwise the majority misconstrued s 1 of the Act. . . .

First, it is a salutary principle that conviction of serious crime should depend on proof not simply that the defendant caused (by act or omission) an injurious result to another but that his state of mind when so acting was culpable. This, after all, is the meaning of the familiar rule *actus non facit reum nisi mens sit rea*. The most obviously culpable state of mind is no doubt an intention to cause the injurious result, but knowing disregard of an appreciated and unacceptable risk of causing an injurious result or a deliberate closing of the mind to such risk would be readily accepted as culpable also. It is clearly blameworthy to take an obvious and significant risk of causing injury to another. But it is not clearly blameworthy to do something involving a risk of injury to another if (for reasons other than self-induced intoxication (see D.P.P. v. Majewski [1976] 2 All ER 142, [1977] AC 443)) one genuinely does not perceive the risk. Such a person may fairly be accused of stupidity or lack of imagination, but neither of those failings should expose him to conviction of serious crime or the risk of punishment.

Secondly, the present case shows, more clearly than any other reported case since R. v. Caldwell [1981] 1 All ER 961, [1982] AC 341, that the model direction formulated by Lord Diplock is capable of leading to obvious unfairness. [T]he trial judge regretted the direction he (quite rightly) felt compelled to give, and it is evident that this direction offended the jury's sense of fairness. The sense of fairness of 12 representative citizens sitting as a jury (or of a smaller group of lay justices sitting as a bench of magistrates) is the bedrock on which the administration of criminal justice in this country is built. A law which runs counter to that sense must cause concern. . . . I share their sense of unease. It is neither moral nor just to convict a defendant (least of all a child) on the strength of what someone else would have apprehended if the defendant himself had no such apprehension. Nor, the defendant having been convicted, is the problem cured by imposition of a nominal penalty.

Thirdly, I do not think the criticism of R. v. Caldwell expressed by academics, judges and practitioners should be ignored. A decision is not, of course, to be overruled or departed from simply because it meets with disfavour in the learned journals. But a decision which attracts reasoned and outspoken criticism by the leading scholars of the day, respected as authorities in the field, must command attention. One need only cite (among many other examples) the observations of Professor John Smith [1981] Crim LR 392 at 393–396 and Professor Glanville Williams "Recklessness Redefined" (1981) 40 CLJ 252. This criticism carries greater weight when voiced also by judges as authoritative as Lord Edmund-Davies and Lord Wilberforce in R. v. Caldwell itself, Robert Goff LJ in Elliott v. C. (a minor) [1983] 2 All ER 1005, [1983] 1 WLR 939 and Ackner LJ in R. v. Stephen Malcolm R (1984) 79 Cr App R 334. The reservations expressed by the trial judge in the present case are widely shared. The shop floor response to R. v. Caldwell may be gauged from the editors' commentary, to be found in Archbold's Pleading, Evidence and Practice in Criminal Cases (41st edn, 1982) pp 1009–1010 (para 17–25). The editors suggested that remedial legislation was urgently required.

Fourthly, the majority's interpretation of "reckless" in s 1 of the 1971 Act was, as already shown, a misinterpretation. If it were a misinterpretation that offended no principle and gave rise to no injustice there would be strong grounds for adhering to the misinterpretation and leaving Parliament to correct it if it chose. But this misinterpretation is offensive to principle and is apt to cause injustice. That being so, the need to correct the misinterpretation is compelling. . . .

In the course of argument before the House it was suggested that the rule in R. v. Caldwell might be modified, in cases involving children, by requiring comparison not with normal, reasonable adults but with normal, reasonable children of the same age. This is a suggestion with some attractions but it is open to four compelling objections. First, even this modification would offend the principle that conviction should depend on proving the state of mind of the individual defendant to be culpable. Second, if the rule were modified in relation to children on grounds of their immaturity it would be anomalous if it were not also modified in relation to the mentally handicapped on grounds of their limited understanding. Third, any modification along these lines would open the door to difficult and contentious argument concerning the qualities and characteristics to be taken into account for purposes of the comparison. Fourth, to adopt this modification would be to substitute one misinterpretation of s 1 for another. There is no warrant in the Act or in the travaux préparatoires which preceded it for such an interpretation.

A further refinement, advanced by Professor Glanville Williams (1981) 40 CLJ 252 at 270–271, adopted by the justices in Elliott's case and commented upon by Robert Goff LJ in that case is that a defendant should only be regarded as having acted recklessly by virtue of his failure to give any thought to an obvious risk that property would be destroyed or damaged, where such risk would have been obvious to him if he had given any thought to the matter. This refinement also has attractions, although it does not meet the objection of principle and does not represent a correct interpretation of the section. It is, in my opinion, open to the further objection of over-complicating the task of the jury (or bench of justices). It is one thing to decide whether a defendant can be believed when he says that the thought of a given risk never crossed his mind. It is another, and much more speculative, task to decide whether the risk would have been obvious to him if the thought had crossed his mind. The simpler the jury's task, the more likely is its verdict to be reliable. . . .

I cannot accept that restoration of the law as understood before R. v. Caldwell would lead to the acquittal of those whom public policy would require to be convicted. There is nothing to suggest that this was seen as a problem before R. v. Caldwell, or . . . before the 1971 Act. There is no reason to doubt the common sense which tribunals of fact bring to their task. In a contested case based on intention, the defendant rarely admits intending the injurious result in question, but the tribunal of fact will readily infer such an intention, in a proper case, from all the circumstances and probabilities and evidence of what the defendant did and said at the time. Similarly with recklessness: it is not to be supposed that the tribunal of fact will accept a defendant's assertion that he never thought of a certain risk when all the circumstances and probabilities and evidence of what he did and said at the time show that he did or must have done. . . .

German Federal Court of Justice
5 StR 35/55, BGHSt 7, 363 (April 22, 1955)
Leather Strap Case

Facts

The defendant K. had come to know the insurance salesman M., who was homosexually inclined, in December 1953. A friendly relationship arose between M. and K. with occasional minor indecent activities. M. had given K. money on many occasions. In the course of December 1953, the defendant K. became friends with the defendant J. They both had the idea of obtaining from M. at least a suit each and the money necessary to rent a room. For this purpose they intended to take violent action against M., render him incapable of resistance, and then without disturbance take from his home the things they wanted, to use them for their own purposes. When considering how they could make M. incapable of resistance, they at first had the idea of secretly administering sleeping tablets to him, and thereby sending him to sleep. After they had attempted this unsuccessfully, K. proposed throttling M. with a leather trouser belt, and then tying him up and gagging him. J. was in agreement with this. Both defendants recognized that such throttling could lead not only to unconsciousness, but also to serious harm and could even cause M.'s death. K., when making a visit on February 8, 1954, intended to carry out the crime in J.'s presence; however his courage deserted him. He passed the belt on to J. who likewise did nothing. But the defendants did not in principle give up their plan. J. however now advised against throttling M. with a leather belt, because the defendants saw the danger that M. could not only become unconscious as a result, but could die. Therefore J. made the proposal of stunning M. with a sandbag, to which K. finally declared his agreement. They both considered that the sandbag would adapt itself to the shape of the skull on impact to the head, and therefore no serious injuries could occur.

On February 15, 1954, in the evening the defendants visited M. J. had the sandbag in his trouser pocket. K. had taken the leather belt with him on his own decision without J.'s knowledge, to cover any eventuality. The defendants asked M. to let them stay the night with him. M. complied with this request. K. slept in M's room, and J. in another room. At about four o'clock in the morning J. struck M.'s head twice powerfully with the sandbag in K.'s presence. The blows did not however have the desired effect, but they awoke M. On a further blow the sandbag burst. M. climbed out of bed, and became involved in a fight with J. K. had in the meantime rushed to the hall, and fetched the belt. He approached M., who until then had not noticed that K. was also one of his attackers, from behind, and threw the belt over his head from this position, but the belt stayed hanging round his chin. J. pressed M.'s hands and arms downwards to lend support to the action with the belt which he now recognized. As a result of this M. was thrown on the bed again. Here K. again threw the belt over his head while J. secured M.'s arms. The belt was now lying round M.'s neck; both ends were slung crosswise on his neck. Each of the defendants now pulled on an end of the belt with all their force until M. let his arms fall and sank into the bed. Then the defendants began to tie M up. When he sat up, J. threw himself on his back, and pressed him down again. K. began once more to throttle M. with the belt. In doing so he had put the belt around M.'s neck in such a way that the end of the belt went through the buckle which was lying close to the left side of M.'s neck. K. pulled on the belt again until M. no longer moved, nor made any sound. When J. noticed this he called to K.: "Stop it!" K. then gave up the throttling. Both defendants now tied M. up. They then took a number of things from his linen and clothing. After this they looked round at M. They now had doubts about whether he was still alive. They tried in vain to resuscitate him. Then they left the residence.

Reasons

The regional court comes to the conclusion that the defendants had killed M. with conditional intention; they had also acted insidiously and with base motives. In the end result there are no doubts about this.

1. The regional court observes as follows on the subject of conditional intention:
K. took the leather belt with him on February 15, 1954, because he reckoned on the possibility that the attack with the sandbag would fail and because for him it was "a matter of putting himself in possession of the desired pieces of clothing and objects of value belonging to M. under all circumstances, cost what it might." Both defendants had then carried out the attack with the sandbag, at first without intention to kill. During the attack with the leather belt however they had both acted with conditional intention. Both defendants had been aware earlier, when they had taken the decision for the first time to throttle M. with a leather belt, of the danger of their action. They had been aware that this throttling could have fatal consequences for M. For this reason they had at first given up their plan to throttle after the failure of February 8, 1954. When they had now decided to throttle M. with the leather belt, they had thereby resumed their old plan formed earlier, with all the consequences already foreseen by them as possible and approved at that time. Just as then, they had been aware of the danger of their action and the possibly fatal consequences for the victim arising from it, and all the more when M. defended himself, and they applied considerable force when they both pulled the leather belt tight, in order to break his resistance. It then says: "The throttling of the victim was undertaken by them not only once but twice, and on the second occasion in an especially dangerous manner. While at the first throttling the leather belt had merely been put on the victim crosswise round the neck, and could work itself loose after the termination of the throttling, the defendant K. had on the second throttling formed a noose from his leather belt with the help of the metal buckle.

He pulled this noose so tight that the victim's neck was still tied up when the defendant let go. In these circumstances, the court is persuaded that it is established that both defendants during the whole course of implementation of the crime realized the extraordinary danger of their plan and reckoned with the possibility of the occurrence of serious consequences for M., and even imagined the occurrence of death as a possible result of their actions. This result of their actions imagined by both defendants as possible, the victim's death, was, in case it occurred, also approved and intended by both of them. On February 15, the last opportunity, which would not occur again, of carrying out the crime and putting themselves in possession of stolen goods had offered itself to both defendants. The defendants had already begun the attack against M. They could not carry it out in the way they had first intended, as the sandbag used by them for the crime had burst. When they now decided to fall back on their original plan and went over to throttling the victim, in spite of the serious and very grave consequences which they had imagined as possible from their course of action, they proceeded with the intention of carrying out the crime under all circumstances and at all costs, regardless of what happened to the victim, and even at the risk they had clearly recognized and imagined as possible that M. could die as a result." At a later point it then says: "Even if this result had not in any way been attractive for them, they had nevertheless wanted it in the case of its occurrence."

2. Both appeals in law criticize the regional court for having failed to appreciate the concept of conditional intention . . . The Chief Federal Prosecutor endorsed this argument, elaborating as follows: The observations in the judgment reproduced above verbatim give rise to the suspicion that the regional court had believed that a finding that the defendants had imagined the victim's death necessarily implies that the approved of the death as well. Such a view would be erroneous in law. It could not be excluded that the regional court held this view, in particular because, apart from the established imagination of the defendants that death was possible, all the other circumstances of the case argued against approval and even revealed a clear feeling of reluctance, of not wanting it. The following circumstances cause this to become especially apparent:

a) The original plan had related unambiguously to merely rendering the victim unconscious.
b) The first attempts were undertaken with sleeping tablets. J. had not (at the second attempt) been afraid himself to drink the coffee into which the tablets had been put.
c) Even in relation to the strangling, the plan had only logically been to strangle M. until he became unconscious.
d) Both defendants had even after the third attempt (February 8) consciously refrained from strangulation, as a throttling could "go wrong," in order not to incur the "risk" of killing M. It had been "too dangerous" for them. Thus the opposite of an approval was present here, i.e., an expressed feeling of reluctance, a clear contrary intention.
e) The suddenness of the decision (during the "implementation" of the crime) now to strangle again makes it appear questionable whether at such a moment of the highest excitement a new factor, i.e., an inward approval, deviating from the situation so far, could arise.
f) The first strangulation on February 16 had obviously only been strong enough to make M. unconscious, because he had awoken again from unconsciousness after a few moments.
g) When on the second strangulation on February 16 (the third part of the crime) M. had no longer moved, J. had immediately shouted: "Stop it," and K. had immediately let go of the belt.
h) After that both defendants had carried out attempts to resuscitate.

Even if these circumstances would not awaken the suspicion that the regional court had incorrectly assumed that a person who reckons on a result with a certain probability also approves of it in the legal sense, there was at least a misuse of discretion in the fact that the court had not concerned itself in detail with the extent to which the points mentioned contradicted its opinion.

3. The Senate cannot endorse these observations by the Chief Federal Prosecutor. It is correct that knowledge of the possible consequences of a course of action and approval of these consequences are two independent prerequisites of conditional intention. The regional court did not however fail to appreciate this. It did not assume that the perpetrator intended a result in the legal sense if he only foresaw it as possible. . . . The parts of the judgment mentioned verbatim deal with foresight and approval of the result expressly as special characteristics of conditional intention. If the Chief Federal Prosecutor argues that the remaining established circumstances argued so strongly against an approval of the result by the perpetrators, and that on this ground the suspicion existed that the findings on the subject of intention were only formulaic, and in truth were derived exclusively from the knowledge of the danger, then he cannot be followed in this respect. The circumstances mentioned admittedly suggest the occurrence of M.'s death was highly undesired by the defendants. The regional court did not fail to appreciate this; it expressly mentioned it. Approval of the result, which according to the case law of the Imperial Court (RGSt 72, 36,43; 76, 115) and of the BGH (BGH

1 StR 436/51 of October 2, 1951) forms the decisive feature of conditional intention, distinguishing it from conscious negligence, does not however mean that the result has to correspond with the wishes of the perpetrator. Conditional intention can also be present if the occurrence of the result is undesired by the perpetrator. In the legal sense he approves of this result nevertheless if he, for the sake of the goal which he seeks, if necessary, i.e., provided that he cannot attain his goal otherwise, comes to terms with the fact that his action will bring about the result, though undesired in itself, and therefore wants it in the case of its occurrence (see for a similar case RGSt 67, 424). Even in the case of unconditional intention the occurrence of the result can be unattractive to the perpetrator. That is so in all cases in which someone in order to attain a definite goal, unwillingly applies a method to do so, because he knows that he can only attain the result which he seeks through this method. Conditional intention is distinguished from unconditional intention by the fact that the undesired result is not foreseen as necessary but only as possible. It differs from conscious negligence by the fact that the perpetrator who acts with conscious negligence trusts that the result foreseen as possible will not occur, and therefore accepts the risk, whilst the perpetrator acting with conditional intention accepts it because, if he cannot attain his goal otherwise, he nonetheless wants to attain it by the undesired method.

The context of the judgment shows clearly that the regional court proceeded on the basis of the following ideas: The defendants intended to appropriate the objects in M.'s possession in all circumstances. They wanted to do it in a way which harmed M. as little as possible. Therefore they began with the least dangerous method. They tried first to administer sleeping tablets to M. When that did not succeed, they turned to the more dangerous—although in their view not life endangering—attack with the sandbag. Only when this also failed did they decide in favor of throttling; they had previously recognized and discussed the danger which this posed to life. They did not do this because they now—in contrast to earlier—trusted that the result foreseen as possible would not occur, but because they now intended not to give up the theft of the items on any account, and intended to carry it out even if throttling would lead to M.'s death. Even now they only wanted his death if there was no other way. They therefore stopped when they believed that M. was unconscious.

German Criminal Code

§ 15 (Intentional and Negligent Conduct)

Criminal liability presupposes intentional conduct, unless the law expressly prescribes criminal punishment for negligent conduct.

German Federal Court of Justice
2 StR 239/02, NStZ 2003, 657 (March 14, 2003)

Facts

According to the findings of the regional court the defendant worked from 1975 until 2001 (when he became an emeritus professor) as professor of the medical faculty of a University and directed the clinic there for chest, heart and vascular surgery. The defendant, who was also extensively active in the academic field, enjoyed an excellent reputation as a heart surgeon and operated personally on several hundred patients per year. The conviction was based on the infection of 12 patients with hepatitis B by the defendant.

The defendant was not medically examined either on the commencement of his duties or in the following years. After discovery of the hepatitis B virus in 1970 and the later development of vaccines, regular precautionary and monitoring examinations were undertaken in the clinic from the 1980s onwards for the doctors and medical personnel, a compulsory part of which was also the establishment of the hepatitis B status. This practice went back to dissemination of the discovery at that point in time in Germany and other western lands that medical personnel were susceptible in a special way to the risk of infection with contagious diseases, and in particular hepatitis B, and that conversely the danger also existed of patients being infected by infected employees. The examinations to which almost all personnel at the University clinic were called in, took place until the beginning of 1999 at regular intervals of three years; persons who were in areas especially at risk were monitored at shorter intervals. The only people who were not covered by the duty to be examined were the employees who had already been appointed as officials, in particular the heads of specialist departments and their deputies. The overwhelming part of the medical personnel availed themselves of the offer to be vaccinated voluntarily against hepatitis B.

The defendant also knew about the problem, discussed in detail in medical circles and the specialist literature, of the risk of mutual HBV infections between doctors and patients—including the special risk from surgical activity. Since the beginning of the 1990s the general state of medical knowledge also included the fact that in certain circumstances minute amounts of blood or traces of serum which were not visible with the naked eye (e.g. drops of sweat) were sufficient for transmission of the virus. The defendant likewise knew that all the personnel in the clinic which he led—with the exception of himself and his deputy—were summoned for monitoring at regular intervals. His deputy however arranged for himself to be voluntarily examined elsewhere for infectious diseases every one or two years. But the defendant did not submit himself either to an investigation by the University doctor or outside the clinic; he also did not have himself vaccinated.

At the latest in 1992 the defendant became infected with hepatitis B, without ever establishing symptoms of the disease in himself. The disease took a chronic course, and the defendant became highly infectious. In the period from May 27, 1994, to Nov. 6, 1998, he infected 12 of his patients in heart operations. Substantial health problems arose for some of them; in three cases the infection became chronic.

The regional court sentenced the defendant for negligent infliction of bodily harm in twelve cases (acquitting him of the remainder) to a total fine of 300 day fines of 1500 DM each. His appeal in law was unsuccessful.

Reasons

The defendant's conduct had to be classified here, according to all the circumstances of the commission of the act, as active behavior . . . In the present case the main focus of the conduct relevant in criminal law is to be seen in carrying out heart operations, which led directly to the infection of the patients without any further intermediate steps . . . Failing to undergo the required monitoring examinations—taken by itself—cannot lead on its own to criminal liability, as the infection only occurs with the carrying out of the operation, which leads directly to the realization of the harm to health required by the definition . . .

The fact that the defendant refrained from undergoing monitoring examinations in breach of his duty is the basis for the violation of the duty of care which is fundamental for a negligent crime. This "omission component"—which for negligence crimes frequently consists of omitting care precautions—is in its nature necessarily associated here with negligent action, and does not change the active character of the behavior, but is inherent in it (see SK-StGB-Rudolphi preceding § 13 marginal no. 27; Kühl StrafR AT, 4th edit., § 18 marginal no. 24; AK-StGB-Seelmann § 13 marginal no. 27; . . . see BGH, Judgment of Nov. 27, 1951, —1 StR 439/51).

The criminal chamber has affirmed an objective and subjective violation of the defendant's duty of care in a manner not open to objection. In particular it considered that the type and extent of the care to be applied arise from the requirements which should be made of a prudent and conscientious person in the actual situation and social role of the person acting, on a consideration of the risk situation "ex ante." The decisive factor is thus how a circumspect and experienced doctor from the same field would have behaved in the same situation, so subsequent scientific discoveries have to be left out of account (see BGH NStZ 2000, 2754, 2758).

The regional court explains in detail in this respect that at the point in time in question the risk of a transmission of viruses from the doctor to the patients as well had moved into the general consciousness not only of virologists but doctors in general, and why this had happened. According to the court's findings, which are free from legal error, a high risk of transmission of hepatitis B to patients existed according to the state of knowledge at that time, and in particular from surgeons even when using surgical gloves. The criminal chamber has therefore drawn the conclusion without legal error that the defendant was under a duty at least to undergo regular monitoring examinations if he did not have himself vaccinated.

The criminal chamber was able to base its assumption of an annual duty of examination on the defendant's part on the idea that in the light of the large number of operations conducted by him and the particularly high risk of infection associated with his activity, responsible fulfillment of his duty of care in any case required monitoring at yearly intervals for attaining even only approximately the goal pursued of a minimization of the risk. The practice in the defendant's clinic at that time in formulating the intervals for examinations as well as the practice—mentioned in another place in the judgment— in other hospitals and the implementation of voluntary monitoring by the defendant's deputy had a certain significance here as circumstantial evidence. Besides this, the regional court has correctly considered the defendant's elevated status in determining the standards of care required specially of him.

Accordingly the defendant should have had himself examined in any case before the first operation (May 27, 1994) condemned here as negligent infliction of bodily harm, and then in the knowledge of his own infection ought not to have carried out further operations.

Alternative Draft, German Criminal Code (1969)*

§ 16 Intentional and negligent conduct [*vorsätzliches und fahrlässiges Handeln*]

(1) If the statute does not expressly threaten negligent conduct with punishment, punishability requires intentional conduct.
(2) In the case of minimally negligent conduct the actor remains unpunished.
(3) If the statute attaches a more severe punishment to a particular result of the act, it applies to the actor or participant only if he brought about the result negligently.

§ 17 Intention and Knowledge [*Vorsatz und Wissentlichkeit*]

(1) He acts intentionally who satisfies the statutory offense elements with knowledge and volition.
(2) He also acts intentionally who seriously thinks it possible, and accepts, that the offense elements have been satisfied.
(3) He acts knowingly who knows that the elements for which the statute requires knowing conduct are satisfied, or anticipates with certainty that they will be satisfied.

§ 18 Negligence

He acts negligently who disregards that diligence which he is duty bound to exercise, and which he is capable of exercising, and thereby satisfies a statutory offense definition.

NOTES

1. Section 2.02, is, arguably, the single most important provision in the Model Penal Code (well, perhaps excepting the definition of crime in § 1.02(1)(a) ("conduct that unjustifiably and inexcusably inflicts or threatens substantial harm to individual or public interests")). The Code drafters considered the widespread confusion about the meaning of *mens rea* as perhaps the single most important problem their model code was meant to fix. They were not the first—nor the last—to record dissatisfaction with the state of the law of *mens rea*. Here is what James Fitzjames Stephen had to say, in *Queen v. Tolson*, 23 Q.B.D. 168 (1889) (Stephen, J.), to those who thought there was such a thing as a single notion of *mens rea*, or "*mens rea* requirement," rather than a potpourri of meanings:

> Though this phrase (non est reus, nisi mens sit rea) is in common use, I think it most unfortunate, and not only likely to mislead, but actually misleading, on the following grounds. It naturally suggests that apart from all particular definitions of crimes, such a thing exists as a "mens rea," or "guilty mind," which is always expressly or by implication involved in every definition. This is obviously not the case, for the mental elements of different crimes differ widely. "Mens rea" means, in the case of murder, malice aforethought; in the case of theft, an intention to steal; in the case of rape, an intention to have forcible connection with a woman without her consent; and in the case of receiving stolen goods, knowledge that the goods were stolen. In some cases it denotes mere inattention. For instance, in the case of manslaughter by negligence it may mean forgetting to notice a signal. It appears confusing to call so many dissimilar states of mind by one name. It seems contradictory indeed to describe a mere absence of mind as a "mens rea," or guilty mind. The expression again is likely to and often does mislead. To an unlegal mind it suggests that by the law of England no act is a crime which is done from laudable motives, in other words, that immorality is essential to crime.

---

* [This so-called Alternative Draft (*Alternativ-Entwurf*) was part of the lively discussion in Germany in the 1960s and 1970s concerning the reform of the Criminal Code. The group of people who produced it did not belong to an officially appointed reform commission—they were criminal law professors who wished to voice a (in general) more liberal conception of the criminal law. The sections reprinted above, however, correspond with standard definitions of intention, conditional intention and negligence that are applied today by the courts and in textbooks about German criminal law. See *Alternative Draft of a Penal Code for the Federal Republic of Germany (American Series of Foreign Penal Codes: Vol 21)* (Joseph J. Darby, trans. 1977) (also available at <heinonline.org>).–Eds.]

Herbert Packer contributes a more recent example, from *The Limits of the Criminal Sanction* (1968), 104–5:

> When we speak of Arthur's having the mens rea of murder, we may mean any one or more of the following things: that he intended to kill Victor; or that he was aware of the risk of his killing Victor but went ahead and shot him anyhow; or (more dubiously) that he ought to have known but didn't that there was a substantial risk of his killing Victor or that he knew it was wrong to kill a fellow human being, or that he ought to have known it; or that he didn't really think that Victor was trying to kill him; or that he did think that, but only a fool would have thought it; or that he was not drunk to the point of unconsciousness when he killed Victor; or that even though he was emotionally disturbed he wasn't grossly psychotic, etc., etc.

Before his appointment to the bench, Stephen just a few years before *Tolson* had punted on the issue of the definition of *mens rea* in his draft of a criminal code (which failed in England, but was enacted, with few changes, in Canada, and elsewhere in the Commonwealth). His draft contained no definition of *mens rea*, instead leaving by default the matter to judges (who, of course, were precisely the people who had made such a hash of the law of *mens rea* to begin with). Incidentally, his fellow—and even less successful, if generally better suited—criminal codifier, R.S. Wright, did set out definitions of *mens rea*.[*]

The Model Code drafters, however, decided to tackle the issue head-on: § 2.02 is the result. Whether they succeeded in clarifying the concept of *mens rea*, or rather replacing one type of obscurity with another, and insufficient specificity with excessive detail, is another question (and one worth pondering). At any rate, their scheme proved extremely influential, not only in American criminal law, but in other common law systems as well; even if drafters, judges, and commentators may not have swallowed the Model Penal Code's taxonomy of culpability hook, line, and sinker, the MPC scheme became the place to start serious thought about *mens rea*.

When contemplating the Code it is important to keep in mind that the drafters saw it not only as a piece of model legislation, but also as a manual, or a textbook: to reform American criminal law meant not only inducing legislatures to rethink existing criminal statutes, but also educating judges (and lawyers, and even law professors!), and guiding their interpretation of a necessarily incomplete statutory system of criminal law. The Code, then, is as detailed and explicit as it is not only to conform to the principle of legality, but also to train the judiciary. (What significance does the principle of legality have for a treatmentist code, anyway? In fact, what is the point of a code from a treatmentist perspective? If deterrence failed, after all, is it more than a (very rough) manual for the diagnosis of criminal dangerousness with various attendant treatment options?[†]) The chief drafter of the Code, Herbert Wechsler, was an important contributor to the Legal Process school in American law, which devoted itself to determining which official is best suited to perform the panoply of functions, and to occupy the myriads of pockets of discretion, found throughout a given legal system, including a system of criminal law, or rather peno-correctional treatment.[‡]

2. Note that the Model Penal Code scheme differentiates between definitions of mental states for each type of offense element (conduct, attendant circumstance, result). Not to lose the forest for the trees, let's take a moment to get the gist of the various mental state definitions.

Purpose. The core concept here is "conscious object"; the definition of purpose most likely to matter is that with respect to a result element. The roughly contemporaneous ALI Restatement of Torts (Second) makes this explicit (in § 8A cmt. a.):

---

[*] See generally Martin L. Friedland, "R.S. Wright's Model Criminal Code," 1 *Oxford Journal of Legal Studies* (1981), 307.

[†] See generally Markus D. Dubber, "Penal Panopticon: The Idea of a Modern Model Penal Code," 4 *Buffalo Criminal Law Review* (2000), 53.

[‡] On the Code's treatmentism, see Chapter 1.A.i. On Legal Process, see Henry M. Hart, Jr. and Albert M. Sacks, *The Legal Process: Basic Problems in the Making and Application of Law* (William N. Eskridge and Philip P. Frickey eds., 1994) [1958]; see also Henry M. Hart, Jr., "The Aims of the Criminal Law," 23 *Law and Contemporary Problems* (1958), 401.

"Intent," as it is used throughout the Restatement of Torts, has reference to the consequences of an act rather than the act itself. When an actor fires a gun in the midst of the Mojave Desert, he intends to pull the trigger; but when the bullet hits a person who is present in the desert without the actor's knowledge, he does not intend that result.

The Model Penal Code does its best to avoid use of the term "intent" (or "intention") because courts have struggled to differentiate among varieties of intent, including intent-as-purpose and intent-as-knowledge.* Many legislatures decided to keep "intent" (or "intention") in their criminal law vocabulary, even combining the old with the new, and complicating things further, by replacing "purpose" with "intent."[†]

For completeness's sake, the Code drafters also defined purpose with respect to conduct and attendant circumstances. Purpose regarding an attendant circumstance does not require awareness; a subjective belief, or even hope, that the attendant circumstance is present would suffice, even if it turns out to be mistaken.

Knowledge. The key concept is "awareness." Knowledge means awareness, no matter what the offense element type; knowledge with respect to result, however, requires not awareness of a fact, but of a "practical certainty," so a likelihood close, but not equal, to 100 percent. (Why?) One interesting question is whether it is possible to act purposely with respect to a result without also acting knowingly. The answer is yes, under the Model Penal Code, because purpose requires that it be your "conscious object" to bring about the result, while knowledge requires awareness of a practical certainty that the result will come about: you can desire to cause a result without being practically certain of your success.[‡]

Recklessness and negligence. Quantitatively, recklessness and negligence differ from knowledge in the magnitude of the risk, the degree of certainty: knowledge requires "practical certainty," recklessness and negligence only "substantial risk." Knowledge requires awareness; recklessness requires "conscious disregard." (Does conscious disregard require more than cognitive awareness? Perhaps acceptance of the risk, making your peace with the occurrence of the manifestation of the risk? The choice to go ahead in the face of the recognition of the risk?) Note that this "disregard" is also supposed to be measured against some control group ("law abiding" persons) and must amount to a "gross deviation" from that group's "standard of conduct." This aspect of the definition of recklessness tends to attract little attention; courts generally are content to treat recklessness as awareness of a substantial risk.

Unlike purpose and knowledge, recklessness and negligence have a one-size-fits-all definition that applies to any objective offense element type they may accompany; they are the conscious disregard and culpable ignorance of a substantial risk, respectively.

At any rate, the MPC's distinction between recklessness and negligence, and in particular its definition of recklessness as requiring actual awareness of a risk, rather than constructive awareness (via a reasonable person standard of some sort), has not found universal acceptance. For the struggle in English criminal law on this issue, compare *R. v. Caldwell*, [1981] 1 All ER 961, and *R. v. G and another*, [2003] UKHL 50 (excerpted above).

3. It may be helpful to consider the Model Penal Code's taxonomy of mental states from the perspective of its underlying treatmentist ideology, which regarded the function of criminal law (assuming it failed in its effort to prevent criminal conduct) as diagnosing types and levels of criminal dangerousness. The Code in general, and the *mens rea* provisions in

---

* Many still do. See, e.g., *R. v. Buzzanga*, [1979] O.R. (2d) 705 (Can.) (intention, regarding result, can mean purpose or knowledge).

[†] E.g., N.Y. Penal Law § 15.05(1)) ("A person acts intentionally with respect to a result or to conduct described by a statute defining an offense when his conscious objective is to cause such result or to engage in such conduct.").

[‡] See *People v. Steinberg*, 79 N.Y.2d 673 (1992) (purposely [intentionally] vs. knowingly causing serious physical injury).

particular, served to "describe the character deficiencies of those subjected to [the criminal law] in accord with the propensities that they manifest."[*] In this account, the definitions of different forms of *mens rea* attempt to capture differences in criminal dangerousness. The person who acts purposely is more dangerous than the one who acts knowingly, and so on.

One question is whether (any of) these distinctions are differences in quality, or in quantity, in type or in degree. Can it be argued that there is a qualitative distinction between, say, purpose and knowledge, and only a quantitative one between knowledge, recklessness, and negligence? Is a subjective mental state always an indicator of greater dangerousness than an objective one (i.e., one defined in terms of some standard, of a "law-abiding," or more normally a "reasonable" person)?

4. *The Model Penal Code scheme meets reality.* The MPC's carefully constructed taxonomy of mental states may have reoriented the jurisprudence of *mens rea* in the U.S., and—to a lesser extent—elsewhere in the common law world, but it did not manage to erase centuries of nomenclature. Despite the drafters' best efforts, the common law of crime continues to be populated by such concepts of intent, intention, malice, depravity, and wilfulness (or willfulness). Even the New York Penal Law, a code that otherwise followed the Model Penal Code quite closely (though not as closely as the Pennsylvania or New Jersey codes), adopted the Model Code's definition of "purpose," but stuck with its traditional concept of "intent," by simply replacing all references to "purpose" in the Model Code with references to "intent," presumably to the displeasure of Herbert Wechsler, the Model Code's chief architect, who also served on New York's criminal code revision commission. As a result, the Model Code's scheme requires some adaptation when applied to real-life cases and statutes. The Code itself acknowledges this need in one case, the once (and still) popular mental state requirement of "wilfulness"; or, as Wechsler put it, "because it is such a dreadful word and so common in the regulatory statutes," the drafters decided "to superimpose some norm of meaning on it,"[†] by declaring that a "requirement that an offense be committed wilfully is satisfied if a person acts knowingly with respect to the material elements of the offense, unless a purpose to impose further requirements appears" (§ 2.02(8)).

The drafters, unfortunately, did not provide a similarly handy guide to the interpretation of "depraved indifference," which along with "depraved heart," "abandoned heart," and "malice aforethought" has long been a staple of the law of murder in particular (but not exclusively), including in Wechsler's home state of New York. Perhaps not surprisingly, in a criminal code that otherwise followed the Model Penal Code's approach, "depraved indifference" has wreaked havoc ever since, and no more than since 2004, when the New York Court of Appeals decided, in *People v. Payne*, 3 N.Y.3d 266 (2004), that depraved indifference toward a result was inconsistent with intent toward it. This subject is taken up at greater length in the discussion of homicide in Chapter 15.A. For present purposes, it is enough to see why the notion of depraved indifference, which makes an appearance in *Baker* (above), sits so uneasily with the other New York mental states considered in the opinion: because it is a pre-Model Penal Code remnant that survived the Model Penal Code-based revision of the New York Penal Law. The very notion of depravity is foreign to the Model Penal Code approach.

Then again, is it that difficult to fit depravity into a treatmentist scheme of modes of culpability? Perhaps it could be a term for a diagnosis of heightened dangerousness, even beyond the level marked by "purpose." Or could it qualitatively different than purpose? Not a greater dangerousness, but a dangerousness of a different kind, a generic sort of dangerousness, rather than one focused on a particular object, a total lack of empathy for the suffering of others, no matter who they might be ("indifference")?

---

[*] Model Penal Code Commentaries §§ 220.1–230.5, at 157 n.99.
[†] ALI Proceedings (1955), 160.

Or is "depravity" so vague, even (or especially?) in combination with "indifference," as to be useless for diagnostic purposes? Is it one of those concepts that are simply beyond hope of clarification (unlike, presumably, purpose, knowledge, recklessness, and negligence) and best relegated to the junkyard of discarded doctrinal tools?

5. *Motive.* In Anglo-American criminal law, motive is generally said to be irrelevant to criminal liability. Here is a typical statement of the rule, taken from an opinion of the Ohio Supreme Court, *State v. Wyant*, 64 Ohio St.3d 566 (1992) (discussed in detail in Chapter 17.A):

> Motive, in criminal law, is not an element of the crime. In their textbook, 1 Substantive Criminal Law (1986) 318, Section 3.6, LaFave and Scott argue that if defined narrowly enough, motive is not relevant to substantive criminal law, although procedurally it may be evidence of guilt, or, in the case of good motive, may result in leniency. Other thought-related concepts such as intent and purpose are used in the criminal law as elements of crimes or penalty-enhancing criteria, but motive itself is not punished.
>
> There is a significant difference between why a person commits a crime and whether a person has intentionally done the acts which are made criminal. Motive is the reasons and beliefs that lead a person to act or refrain from acting. The same crime can be committed for any of a number of different motives. Enhancing a penalty because of motive therefore punishes the person's thought, rather than the person's act or criminal intent. . . .
>
> Culpable mental state, or intent, is usually required to find one guilty of a crime. "Intent" refers to the actor's state of mind or volition at the time he acts. Did A intend to kill B when A's car hit B's, or was it an accident? This is not the same as A's motive, which is why A intentionally killed B. When A murders B in order to obtain B's money, A's intent is to kill and the motive is to get money. One can have motive without intent, or intent without motive. For instance, the wife of a wealthy but disabled man might have a motive to kill him, and yet never intend to do so. A psychopath, on the other hand, may intend to kill and yet have no motive.
>
> Purpose to commit an additional criminal act is frequently seen in criminal statutes as a basis for enhanced penalty or as creating a separate, more serious crime. For example, burglary is a trespass "with purpose" to commit a theft offense or felony. Purpose in this context is not the same as motive. What is being punished is the act of trespass, plus the additional act of theft, or the intent to commit theft. Upon trespassing, A's intent is to commit theft, but the motive may be to pay debts, to buy drugs, or to annoy the owner of the property. The object of the purpose is itself a crime. Thus the penalty is not enhanced solely to punish the thought or motive.
>
> Criminal penalties are often enhanced using the concept of an aggravating circumstance. These also are distinguishable from motive. For example, under Rev. Code § 2929.04, any of a number of aggravating circumstances can increase the penalty for aggravated murder to death. Among these is murder committed "for the purpose of" escaping another offense. The basis for enhancing the penalty in this case is once again an additional act or intent. Escaping another offense is in itself a crime. The enhanced penalty for murder does not stem from motive (i.e., preference of life on the street to life in prison), but from the additional act of escape, or the intent to escape.
>
> Rev. Code § 2929.04(A)(2) declares murder for hire to be an aggravating circumstance. This is not properly seen as enhancing the penalty for a mercenary motive. Hiring is a transaction. The greater punishment is for the additional act of hiring or being hired to kill. The motive for the crime (such as jealousy, greed or vengeance) is not punished.
>
> Some aggravating circumstances involve the identity of the victim, such as a peace officer or governmental official. Rev. Code § 2929.04(A)(1), (6). The legislature has decided, in these instances, that acts against certain individuals are more serious criminal acts. Imposing a higher penalty for killing the Governor than for killing an ordinary citizen is similar to imposing a higher penalty for stealing a painting worth $1,000 than for stealing one worth only $5.

Does it make sense to distinguish between (impermissible) motive and (permissible) mental states? In particular, does the distinction between motive and purpose as "conscious object" make sense? Does the above excerpt, meant to illustrate the operation of the rule that motive is irrelevant, in fact manage to illustrate the opposite, by listing so many apparent exceptions that they swallow the rule?*

---

* See generally Carissa Byrne Hessick, "Motive's Role in Criminal Punishment," 80 *Southern California Law Review* (2006), 89.

Other courts such as the Canadian Supreme Court have been more willing to acknowledge the difficulty of distinguishing motive from *mens rea*, without, however, abandoning the effort: *R. v. Lewis*, [1979] 2 S.C.R. 821:

> In ordinary parlance, the words "intent" and "motive" are frequently used interchangeably, but in the criminal law they are distinct. In most criminal trials, the mental element, the mens rea with which the court is concerned, relates to "intent," i.e. the exercise of a free will to use particular means to produce a particular result, rather than with "motive," i.e. that which precedes and induces the exercise of the will. The mental element of a crime ordinarily involves no reference to motive: 11 Hals. (4th ed., 1976), para. 11.
>
> Difficulty arises, however, from the vagueness in law of the notion of "motive." There would appear to be substantial agreement amongst textwriters that there are two possible meanings to be ascribed to the term. Glanville Williams in his Criminal Law, The General Part (2nd ed., 1961) distinguishes between these meanings:
>
> "(1) It sometimes refers to the emotion prompting an act, e.g., 'D killed P, his wife's lover, from a motive of jealousy.' (2) It sometimes means a kind of intention, e.g., D killed P with the motive (intention, desire) of stopping him from paying attentions to D's wife." (p.48)

It is this second sense, according to Williams, which is employed in criminal law:

> "Motive is ulterior intention–the intention with which an international act is done (or, more clearly, the intention with which an intentional consequence is brought about). Intention, when distinguished from motive, relates to the means, motive to the end. (p. 48)"

Smith and Hogan in their Criminal Law (4th ed., 1978) put the matter in slightly sharper perspective. Dealing with the first of the above meanings:

> "If D causes an actus reus with mens rea, he is guilty of the crime and it is entirely irrelevant to his guilt that he had a good motive. The mother who kills her imbecile and suffering child out of motives of compassion is just as guilty of murder as is the man who kills for gain." (p. 63)

The authors discuss also the species of intention implicit in the second meaning above:

> "For example, D intends to (a) put poison in his uncle's tea, (b) to cause his uncle's death and (c) to inherit his money. We would normally say that (c) is his motive. Applying our test of 'desired consequence' (c) is certainly also intended. The reason why it is considered merely a motive is that it is a consequence ulterior to the mens rea and the actus reus; it is no part of the crime. If this criterion as to the nature of motive be adopted then it follows that motive, by definition, is irrelevant to criminal responsibility—that is, a man may be lawfully convicted of a crime whatever his motive may be, or even if he had no motive." (pp. 63–4)

Both of these texts were drawn upon in a brief discussion of motive by Lord Hailsham in Hyam v. D.P.P. [[1975] A.C. 55 (H.L.)], at pp. 73–4. The appellant in that case had had a relationship with a man who became engaged to another woman B. The appellant had gone to B's house at night and set fire to the house. While B escaped, her two daughters did not and the two died of suffocation. The appellant's defence was that she had only intended to frighten B. If one were to use the first sense of motive as emotion, the appellant's admitted motive was jealousy of B; if the second sense of motive as ulterior intention, her motive was to frighten B so that she would leave the neighbourhood. In the former sense, states Lord Hailsham, "it is the emotion which gives rise to the intention and it is the latter, and not the former, which converts an actus reus into a criminal act."

> It is, however, important to realise that in the second sense too motive, which in that sense is to be equated with the ultimate "end" of a course of action, often described as its "purpose" or "object" although "a kind of intention," is not co-extensive with intention, which embraces, in addition to the end, all the necessary consequences of an action including the means to the end and any consequences intended along with the end. (p. 73)

In *Lewis*, the Canadian Supreme Court went on to list a set of guidelines to help judges decide about the admissibility of motive evidence:

(1) As evidence, motive is always relevant and hence evidence of motive is admissible.
(2) Motive is no part of the crime and is legally irrelevant to criminal responsibility. It is not an essential element of the prosecution's case as a matter of law.

(3) Proved absence of motive is always an important fact in favour of the accused and ordinarily worthy of note in a charge to the jury.

(4) Conversely, proved presence of motive may be an important factual ingredient in the Crown's case, notably on the issues of identity and intention, when the evidence is purely circumstantial. . . .

(6) Each case will turn on its own unique set of circumstances. The issue of motive is always a matter of degree.

Even if motive is irrelevant for purposes of *mens rea*, i.e., for purposes of determining whether the defendant has satisfied the elements of the offense, does this mean it's also irrelevant for purposes of determining whether the defendant may have a defense (in particular, a justification, like self-defense)? (Its relevance at sentencing is widely acknowledged.) Is a claim of self-defense not simply a claim that I intentionally used physical force against my attacker with the "ulterior intention" of protecting myself from physical harm?

Is the motive/intent not only unsustainable, but also anachronistic? Consider the following excerpt:

It has often been said that the criminal law is concerned only with intent, not motive. . . . [U]nderstanding the motive/intent distinction and the irrelevance of motive maxim requires understanding the changing context in which these rhetorical constructions have been invoked. . . . [T]he original point of the irrelevance of motive maxim was to urge courts to apply formal offense definitions and to encourage legislatures to supply them. Legal reformers associated "intentions" with behavior, which could be compared to rules of conduct. By contrast, they associated "motives" with character, which could only be evaluated by discretionary moral judgment. Thus, the irrelevance of motive maxim implied that courts should assess behavior by applying conduct rules rather than by engaging in discretionary moral judgment. An intention was supposed to be somehow more legal than a motive and the irrelevance of motive connoted fidelity to the principle of legality. The motive/intent distinction was part of the rhetoric of the rule of law in criminal law, and stood for a particular allocation of discretion among courts and legislatures. . . .

[W]hen twentieth century lawyers encountered the irrelevance of motive maxim in older cases and treatises, . . . they interpreted the distinction between motive and intent as a psychological distinction, among the kinds of mental states that should inculpate offenders. But here they faced the difficulty that the terms "intent" and "motive" are used interchangeably in ordinary language. These terms could only be distinguished as technical terms of art.

Twentieth century legal scholars came up with three different candidates for such a technical distinction between intent and motive. According to one version, intentions were cognitive states of mind, like expectations or perceptions of risk. Motives, by contrast, were desiderative states—desires, purposes, or ends. The difficulty with this version of the distinction was that it seemed to render the motive is irrelevant maxim descriptively false, since criminal law often conditioned liability on these desiderative states.

A second version of the distinction divided desiderative states into immediate and remote goals, identifying intention with the former and motive with the latter. The difficulty with this version of the distinction was that any act might be explained by not just two, but perhaps a very great number of goals. Any goal might be denominated an intention when compared to a more remote goal, and a motivation when compared to a more immediate goal.

In an effort to sort goals into just two categories, some commentators suggested that intentions were only those goals that were offense elements, while motives were any more remote goals. This version of the motive/intent distinction certainly accorded with the motive is irrelevant maxim, but at the price of reducing it to an empty tautology, true by definition.

If the motive is irrelevant maxim is true by definition, it has no normative bite. If the only identifying characteristic of motives is that they are not offense elements, the irrelevance of motive maxim can tell us nothing about how to define offenses. It can have no implications regarding hate crimes, mercy killing, transferred intent, necessity, provocation, or criminal negligence. On the other hand, the irrelevance of motive maxim will have law reform implications if we take it to mean that criminal liability should never be predicated on desiderative states. But this version of the irrelevance of motive maxim has law reform implications only because it is (and has long been) at odds with so much criminal law doctrine. . . .

Guyora Binder, "The Rhetoric of Motive and Intent,"
6 *Buffalo Criminal Law Review* (2002), 1, 1–5.

6. In the German Criminal Code, § 15 requires intention (*Vorsatz*, or *dolus*) as a prerequisite for criminal liability, unless the Code explicitly mentions negligence as sufficient. There are few examples of negligent crimes in the German Criminal Code. For most crimes in most cases, an important question to be examined at trial typically is: Did the offender act with intention concerning all the elements of this crime? The German Criminal Code does not define what counts as "intentional," but there is well-established case law on this point (one of the most important questions in criminal law doctrine). There are a few similarities with the American approach expressed in the Model Penal Code, but also meaningful differences. In German law, the expression "intention" is used as a generic term that encompasses subgroups, that is, direct intention (*dolus directus*) and conditional intention (*dolus eventualis*).*

Direct intention can take the form of purpose (*Absicht*): the offender wants the result to occur, the act to take place etc.; this corresponds to the Model Penal Code's approach ("purposely"). Alternatively, direct intention can be present in the form of knowledge (*sicheres Wissen*): the offender knows or is practically certain of what is going to happen; again, this parallels the Model Penal Code's approach ("knowingly"). Conditional intention, however, does not have a direct analogue in the Model Penal Code scheme. It requires both that the offender is aware that the outcome described in the offense description is possible and not entirely unlikely *and* that he or she condones or accepts this outcome.

7. The concept of conditional intention in German criminal law must be differentiated carefully from that of recklessness in U.S. criminal law. The case law and the majority opinion in the German literature, as illustrated in the leading case on conditional intent (the often-cited *Leather Strap Case*, above), emphasize the need of a *volitional* element beyond the *cognitive* requirement of risk awareness. (Other views supported in the literature place the emphasis on one or another of these aspects, with some abandoning the volitional element altogether and resting conditional intention solely on awareness of the probability ("probability theory"), or even the possibility ("possibility theory"), of the proscribed result.)

This volitional element must be distinguished from straightforwardly wanting something to occur (the latter would be purpose, direct intention). In the *Leather Strap Case*, the German Federal Court of Justice emphasized that a volitional element can be present even if the offender honestly claims that he had preferred the victim's survival to the victim's death. It is sufficient that, in order to achieve his goal (for example, immobilizing the victim), the offender condones or accepts the harmful outcome or at least comes to terms with it because it is the necessary means to his end. An often mentioned test question asks whether an offender honestly (albeit irrationally) trusted that death (or other harm) would not happen, and so acted only negligently, or if he thought, "if things go the worst possible way, so be it."†

According to the German concept of conditional intention, the volitional element needs to be proven in addition to the cognitive element (i.e., awareness of risk). In practice, this may create considerable evidentiary problems. Only few defendants will freely admit to having inwardly accepted the harmful result. Typically, they will deny this either to themselves or at least to the investigating authorities, and claim to have hoped for a different outcome. Therefore, on the level of evidence, German courts are often forced to infer volition from cognition, by determining whether the defendant's acceptance of the possible occurrence of harm may be inferred based on (his or her awareness of) the gravity of the risk. In many cases, the actual outcome with respect to a finding of conditional intent is not different than it would be in legal systems that rely on a (purely cognitive) standard of recklessness, because

---

* Not to be confused with "conditional purpose," a term occasionally found in common law jurisprudence, and used to refer to the controversial, and arguably oxymoronic, notion of the "conscious object" (or intent, in the sense of purpose) of engaging in some conduct or of bringing about some result, that is nonetheless predicated on the occurrence of some other event—such as the purpose of causing physical harm in the event a theft victim offers resistance. See, e.g., *Holloway v. United States*, 526 U.S. 1 (1999) (carjacking: intent to use violence in the event driver resists).

† See also the *AIDS Case* in the discussion of homicide, Chapter 15.A.iii.

awareness of a substantial risk will be taken as proof of the volitional element. Under this approach, the volitional aspect of the inquiry into intention is in danger of being collapsed into the cognitive aspect.

In order to give some substance to an independent assessment of the volitional aspect, courts often apply the "overall view" mentioned by the Federal Court of Justice, and examine the defendant's attitudes, his or her personality and so on. Consider the problems connected with this: it makes the finding of *mens rea* dependent on defendants' ability to present themselves as "essentially good guys," and invites stricter evaluations if a judge is not sympathetic toward the defendant and thus ascribes a "bad attitude" to him, demonstrating the volitional element.

8. Just how different is conditional intent in German criminal law from recklessness in the Model Penal Code? To begin with, note that the Model Penal Code test—unlike the *Caldwell* rule rejected by the English House of Lords in *R. v. G*—also has a subjective aspect: the defendant must "consciously disregard" the relevant risk. Conscious disregard (for that matter, any other kind of disregard) implies prior awareness. Awareness is a subjective mental state (referring to the subject's perception of a state of affairs—which in the case of "awareness" is objectively correct, and in the case of "belief" may or may not be correct). This means, among other things, that MPC recklessness and the cognitive prong of German *dolus eventualis* are both subject to the same evidentiary problems facing any subjective test (and therefore, absent a credible confession, present the fact finder, judge or jury, with the same challenge of either inferring a subjective state of mind from objective facts or basing his or her conclusion on other factors, including possibly the defendant's character).

But there is the additional question of whether the requirement of "conscious disregard" adds an additional subjective requirement beyond mere awareness to the Model Penal Code's recklessness definition. After all, what would be the point of framing recklessness in terms of "conscious disregard" if all the drafters had in mind was a purely cognitive (if subjective) requirement of "awareness"? Does disregard imply more than "dis-regarding," that is, literally "not-seeing"? Or does it suggest an attitudinal component, beyond a merely cognitive one? Some independently normatively significant decision to proceed despite having seen the risk? What does the word "conscious" add to "disregard"? If it adds nothing, then why is it there? If it does add something significant, does it confirm the sense that (dis-) regard is more than (dis-)awareness, and that recklessness requires a conscious (perhaps even deliberate?) decision to go ahead and take the chance? Is it too far a stretch to see this as a requirement of acceptance, of acquiescence? If so, is this still significantly different than the volitional aspect of the German inquiry into "conditional intention," though one that perhaps ties the inquiry into the volitional aspect more closely to that into the cognitive one—perhaps thereby expressing a preference for the cognitive aspect as the decisive, or primary, one, and perhaps also safeguarding against the "personality"-based analysis of the volitional prong mentioned above?*

9. *Default.* The default mental state requirement in the German Criminal Code is intention (*Vorsatz*). The Model Penal Code has a default mental state requirement as well: recklessness (§ 2.02(3)). (Not all legislatures followed the Model Code on this point; some instead adopted negligence as the default mental state requirement.†) The significance of the difference between the former and the latter default requirement obviously depends on what significance one attaches to the distinction between conditional intention in German criminal law and recklessness under the Model Code.‡ The Model Penal Code's choice of recklessness as a default mental state requirement was meant as a manifestation of the common law's so-called *mens rea* requirement, which was interpreted as, among other

---

* See generally Alan C. Michaels, "Acceptance: The Missing Mental State," 71 *Southern California Law Review* (1998), 953.

† See, e.g., N.Y. Penal Law § 15.15(1).

‡ See Note 7.

things, a requirement of "general intent," which in turn came to be interpreted as awareness (of a risk or practical certainty), in contrast to "specific intent," which the Model Code attempts to capture with its concept of "purpose." Note that the Code recognizes another guide for statutory interpretation with respect to *mens rea* requirements: § 2.02(4) sets out the one-for-all rule, which establishes a rebuttable presumption that the legislature intended the mental state requirement attached to one offense element to apply to the other offense elements as well.

The one-for-all (or "travel") rule makes sense only against the background of the Model Penal Code's so-called "element analysis." In contrast to "offense analysis," the Model Code calls for an inquiry into the mental state attaching to each element, rather than to the offense as a whole. Under the Code's differentiated analysis, different objective elements of an offense can be accompanied by different subjective offense elements, i.e., mental states (or modes of culpability, or types of *mens rea*). A court interpreting a statutory offense definition, then, must determine not which *mens rea* the offense requires, but which *mens rea* each and every element requires.* German criminal law takes the same approach: the subjective element needs to be established for each element in the objective offense description.

10. So far, we have focused on the question of whether conditional intention in German criminal law is *narrower* than recklessness under the Model Penal Code. Could it be *broader* as well, so that some cases that qualify as conditional intention would not qualify as recklessness, rather than vice versa? If we leave aside the volitional aspect, it appears that MPC recklessness requires a greater risk, on the cognitive axis, than does German criminal law. While there is disagreement in the German literature on this point, the majority position appears to be that it is enough, for conditional intention, that the defendant considered the result as possible and not entirely unlikely. (Others argue for a requirement of awareness of probability, not merely of possibility.) By contrast, the Model Penal Code requires a "substantial risk." Whether this actually makes a difference is unclear, as unclear as the difference between "possibility" and "substantial risk." It is difficult to say what makes a risk substantial, other than that a substantial risk captures a lower probability than the "practical certainty" required for MPC knowledge (since otherwise the distinction between recklessness and knowledge would collapse). Presumably, under the Model Penal Code, "substantial risk" would also fall short of "high probability," referred to elsewhere in the Code.[†]

At any rate, the cognitive test in MPC recklessness may be more demanding than the cognitive test in conditional intention, at least under some versions of the definition of conditional intention, including the majority view of German courts and commentators reflected in the *Leather Spray Case*. (In fact, it can be argued that some instances of conditional intention would fall outside the criminal realm altogether, insofar as the requirements of "substantial" risk, along with that of a "gross deviation" from the relevant standard of care, which apply to both recklessness and negligence, are seen in U.S. law as minimum requirements for criminal, as opposed to civil, liability.[‡] German criminal law, however, does not recognize a distinction between criminal and civil negligence in the first place.[§])

In general, it appears that the German debate has focused on the volitional, rather than on the cognitive, prong, with disagreements arising both about the appropriateness of engaging in a volitional analysis in the first place and, assuming a volitional inquiry should occur, what shape it should take. Common law jurisdictions also have shown little appetite for policing the degree of known risk required for recklessness, particularly in cases of serious crime, notably reckless homicide.[¶]

---

* For the various rules in action, see, e.g., *State v. Lozier*, 101 Ohio St.3d 161 (2004).

[†] See generally Kenneth W. Simons, "Should the Model Penal Code's *Mens Rea* Provisions Be Amended?," 1 *Ohio State Journal Criminal Law* (2003), 179.

[‡] See, e.g., *People v. Haney*, 30 N.Y.2d 328 (1972).

[§] See Chapter 15.A.iv.

[¶] See, e.g., *R. v. Moo*, [2009] O.J. No. 3706 (Ont. Ct. App.) ("use of 'danger' instead of 'likelihood' in the definition of recklessness recedes to background noise"); see also Kenneth W. Simons, "Should the Model Penal Code's *Mens Rea* Provisions Be Amended?," 1 *Ohio State Journal Criminal Law* (2003), 179, 190

What is the point of requiring a volitional inquiry? What is lost in abandoning it? What is lost in including it? Given the problems of its definition, and its application, does it make sense to eliminate the volitional inquiry altogether? Is it any easier—more predictable, consistent, raising fewer evidentiary difficulties—to undertake a cognitive analysis? Could one compensate for eliminating the volitional prong by strengthening the cognitive one (by, say, requiring awareness of a higher risk)? Consider these questions from the various rationales of punishment, including the Model Penal Code's treatmentist approach.

11. The second German case, concerning the surgeon infected with Hepatitis B, illuminates the notion of negligence (*Fahrlässigkeit*) under German law. There are not many offenses that can be committed in the absence of direct or conditional intent, but causing bodily harm and causing the death of a person (§§ 229, 222 German Criminal Code) are criminal offenses if done negligently. Note that the punishment range is much lower than for intentional acts: fines or punishment up to 3 years' imprisonment (bodily harm) and 5 years' imprisonment (negligent homicide) as the maximum penalty. (The Model Penal Code, with its default mental state requirement, recognizes few negligence crimes: homicide (§ 210.4) and assault (with a deadly weapon), § 211.1(1)(b); criminal mischief by fire, explosives, or other dangerous means is a "non-criminal" violation (§ 220.3(1)(a)).)

There are some differences between the German concept of negligence and the definition in MPC § 2.02. However, before turning to these, the common feature is worth mentioning. The core task in assessing cases of possible negligence is the same in both legal systems: the court needs to establish what standard of care "a reasonable person would observe in the actor's situation." The German Federal Court of Justice could solve this task without much difficulty because there are widely acknowledged professional standards for surgeons, which the defendant had ignored. It can be more of a challenge to identify the required behavior if persons behave carelessly outside of clearly defined professional or social roles—especially if the principle of "fair warning" is taken seriously.

Under German law, in contrast to the Model Penal Code's approach, negligence includes both cases when the offender is aware of the risk, but lacks the volitional element[*] (conscious *Fahrlässigkeit*) and cases when he only should have been aware of it (unconscious *Fahrlässigkeit*). In other words, if one reads the Model Penal Code's definition of recklessness as adopting a purely cognitive standard, then German negligence straddles the line between recklessness and negligence under the Model Code.

Also, German courts do not emphasize that it must be a *gross* deviation of the standards of care. In U.S. law, this distinction, between "deviation" and "gross deviation" from the relevant standard of care, marks the line between civil and criminal liability: only "gross" deviations generate criminal liability (both in the case of negligence and of recklessness).[†] Just where that line is to be drawn, and just when a deviation turns into a gross deviation, is unclear, of course. Nonetheless, this distinction is thought to be of critical importance, as a bulwark—however illusory—against the transformation of civil liability into criminal liability. Again and again, courts emphasize that, no matter how difficult it may be to determine what constitutes criminal negligence, one thing remains clear: it requires more than civil negligence.[‡]

Finally, the Federal Court of Justice mentions the requirement of an "objective and subjective" violation of the defendant's duty of care. It is not sufficient to establish that the conduct was not in accordance with standards of care, but it must also be shown that the defendant could adhere to these standards. In the particular case, like in many others,

(suggesting that the substantiality requirement in recklessness "might vary according to the seriousness of the harm": from 1 percent in case of death, to 10 percent in case of physical injury).

[*] See Note 7.

[†] See generally Tatjana Hörnle, "Social Expectations in the Criminal Law: The "Reasonable Person' in a Comparative Perspective," 11 *New Criminal Law Review* (2008), 1.

[‡] See, e.g., *People v. Haney*, 30 N.Y.2d 328 (1972); *R. v. Beatty*, [2008] 1 S.C.R. 49 (Can.) ("marked departure").

however, there was not much to be said about subjective negligence on the surgeon's part. Usually, there is no reason why the individual defendant should have been unable to do what was objectively required, especially if professional standards are at issue. However, it is conceivable in other areas that measures of care which are evident to most persons are beyond the grasp of a particular defendant, for instance, if a very young person is not capable to see what is obvious for the more mature observer.* Under such circumstances, there would be a lack of "subjective negligence" and thus no criminal liability.

From the U.S. perspective, this talk of "subjective negligence" may appear as an attempt in German criminal law to differentiate criminal from civil negligence, a difficult task U.S. law attempts to perform elsewhere in the doctrinal construction of criminal negligence—notably the requirements of a "gross" deviation and of the putative failure to recognize a "substantial" risk, as well as in the adaption of the "reasonable person" standard to the defendant's "situation," including his or her relevant characteristics and background.†

Nonetheless, the general point that (German) *Fahrlässigkeit* and (Anglo-American) negligence should not be treated as synonyms any more than *bedingter Vorsatz* and recklessness, is well taken.‡

12. *A note on reasonableness and comparative criminal law.*

While the "reasonable person" appears frequently in the criminal laws of America and England, this is not the case in Germany. To readers with an American or English legal background, references to the "reasonable person" are familiar. The American Model Penal Code, for instance, uses this expression in the definitions of negligence, to define the defense of duress, or to describe when a mistake of law can exceptionally be a defense (when acting in reasonable reliance upon an official statement of the law). Legal rules about self-defense require that the defendant reasonably believe he or she is being attacked and also that self-defense is necessary. If one searches the German Criminal Code or the indices of German criminal law text books, however, for a literal translation of the "reasonable person," one finds nothing. It is not a legal term German criminal law theorists discuss. For a German lawyer, it is therefore initially puzzling that it appears in such different contexts in the English speaking legal world.

George Fletcher argued in his comparative analysis of "The Right and the Reasonable" that the pervasive reliance upon the "reasonable" in English and American criminal law can be traced back to a different style of reasoning.[§] Thinking along these lines, the conclusion might be that comparative enterprises could not add much new insights beyond the diagnosis of fundamental differences. . . .

However, it would be premature to stop at this point. A closer look at the German system reveals that it also has to deal with some of the issues which stand behind references to the "reasonable person." It is possible to extract a rough idea from the legal provisions where this figure appears: the central feature of the "reasonable person" is that she meets social expectations. The expression serves as a metaphor which stands for social expectations about how one should evaluate situations and how one should respond to them. If one formulates the matter this way, it becomes obvious that all legal systems somewhere have mechanisms built into their doctrines which serve to integrate social expectations into the evaluation of a criminal offense. That German law does not use the phrase "reasonable person" does not mean that there are no related questions to be discussed.

In certain contexts, the offender's conduct must be measured against standardized models of behavior. This is evident with respect to negligent crimes: it is impossible to define all offenses in a succinct and understandable way and at the same time to state what is prohibited in detail. Even if one looks at the core of "mala per se," the imperative "do not kill," this is only a

---

* See, e.g., *R. v. G.*, Chapter 8.A.

† See, e.g., *State v. Leidholm*, 334 N.W.2d 811 (N.D. 1983) (in a battered woman's syndrome case, explaining that "an accused's actions are to be viewed from the standpoint of a person whose mental and physical characteristics are like the accused's and who sees what the accused sees and knows what the accused knows").

‡ See Thomas Weigend, "Zwischen Vorsatz und Fahrlässigkeit," 93 *Zeitschrift für die gesamte Strafrechtswissenschaft* (1981), 657; L.A. Zaibert, "Philosophical Analysis and the Criminal Law," 4 *Buffalo Criminal Law Review* (2001), 100. On the mental state of *Leichtfertigkeit*, which appears to sit somewhere between *Vorsatz* and (ordinary) *Fahrlässigkeit*, see Note 14 and Chapter 15.A.ii (felony murder).

§ [George Fletcher, "The Right and the Reasonable," 98 *Harvard Law Review* (1985), 949.—Eds.]

clear command as long as it is combined with intention. Otherwise, it needs to be detailed what kind of risks which might result in the death of a person are prohibited, and this can only be achieved if criminal law doctrine and the courts specify objective standards.

Tatjana Hörnle, "Social Expectations in the Criminal Law:
The 'Reasonable Person' in a Comparative Perspective,"
11 *New Criminal Law Review* (2008), 1.

13. So far, we have focused on distinctions among mental states, including the distinction between intention, and recklessness, on one hand, and negligence, on the other. The difficulty of distinguishing criminal from civil negligence, however, raises the question whether it is legitimate to punish negligent behavior at all. Negligence has long been accepted as a basis for civil liability in the law of tort. But does it warrant punishment? (How) can punishing negligent conduct be justified under the traditional rationales for punishment? What about the culpability principle? Recall the much quoted 1952 definition by the German Federal Court of Justice:*

> The internal ground for the accusation of culpability lies in the fact that the human being is destined for free, responsible and moral self-determination, and is therefore enabled to decide for the right and against the wrong, to order his conduct according to the norms of the legally required and to avoid what is legally prohibited as soon as he has attained moral maturity and as long as his aptitude for free moral self-determination has not been temporarily paralyzed or permanently destroyed. . . .

In the case of negligent behavior, in what sense has the actor "decide[d] for the right and against the wrong," or exercised "his aptitude for free moral self-determination"? Is there a justification for threatening negligent behavior with punishment other than as deterrence? (Even from a deterrent perspective, how does the threat of punishment deter someone from *not* recognizing a risk? Or is it perhaps an encouraging threat, one that encourages people to be more vigilant in their daily lives, so that they may recognize risks they otherwise might have missed?) Is there a justification for punishing negligent behavior, the effort at deterrence having failed, other than on grounds of incapacitation or rehabilitation? From the Model Penal Code's perspective, does negligence—i.e., unreasonable inadvertence, or the failure to recognize a risk a reasonable person would have recognized—indicate sufficient dangerousness to warrant peno-correctional treatment? Why does the nature of the harm matter? Why, in other words, should we (the German Criminal Code, the Model Penal Code) limit negligence liability to murder and assault? Is the failure to recognize the risk of hitting a person more culpable, more self-determined than the failure to recognize the risk of hitting a car? More criminally dangerous?

The inclusion of negligence liability in the Model Penal Code (even if only in a few cases) was heavily criticized by a leading American criminal law scholar at the time, Jerome Hall, who considered criminal liability for negligence at best an anachronistic remnant of "the rigorous mediaevalism that some time in the past, the actor 'willed not to will,'"† noting "the progressive restriction of the range of negligence in penal law in many, perhaps all, modern legal systems during the past millennium."‡ Hall argued that the proper response to negligent behavior was not punishment, but education, to bring the person up to the level of the reasonable person; of course, there is also the law of torts.

Despite the apparent absence of a decision "for the right and against the wrong," it is sometimes suggested that negligent behavior could be *more* culpable than intentional behavior, on the ground that the person who ignores the risk of harm his conduct poses to others at least recognized that there was a risk in the first place. The negligent person, by contrast, is so indifferent to the existence of others (and their interests?) as to not even see the risk the reckless (or conditionally intentional) actor ignores. Does that make sense? What

---

* See Chapter 3.A.

† Jerome Hall, "Interrelations of Crime and Torts: II," 43 *Columbia Law Review* (1943), 967, 981.

‡ Jerome Hall, "Negligent Behavior Should Be Excluded from Criminal Behavior," 63 *Columbia Law Review* (1963), 632.

conception of culpability, and wrong, does this suggestion reflect? How would this suggestion affect the relationship between civil and criminal wrong, and between inadvertent (unconscious) and advertent (conscious) negligence?*

14. *Leichtfertigkeit, Rücksichtslosigkeit,* and *Böswilligkeit. Vorsatz* and *Fahrlässigkeit* tend to get all the attention in accounts of German criminal law. There is one mental state, *Leichtfertigkeit,* that fits—somewhat uneasily—between the classic alternatives of *dolus* and ordinary *Fahrlässigkeit* and, for that reason alone, is of comparative interest. After all, the comparative sweet spot lies closer to the middle of the *mens rea* spectrum than to its ends, purpose and unconscious *Fahrlässigkeit.*†

(a) *Leichtfertigkeit* is regarded as a variation on the theme of negligence, and is often described as aggravated negligence. The most common definition, or rather label, for *Leichtfertigkeit* is *grobe Fahrlässigkeit,* or gross negligence; this is the definition of *Leichtfertigkeit* in the 1962 proposed draft of the German Criminal Code, E 1962 § 18(3), which follows the definition of negligence in the section on "Negligence and *Leichtfertigkeit.*" The Alternative Draft, prepared by a group of law professors, however, omitted this definition of *Leichtfertigkeit* as "superfluous."‡

The distinction between "gross" and "ordinary" remains somewhat unclear (no less than, say, that between "gross" and ordinary deviations from the standard of care in the U.S. definition of criminal negligence§), with a wide range of suggestions on offer, some emphasizing the attitudinal aspect (so that grossness would reflect a greater, or otherwise more objectionable indifference), others the probabilistic aspect (so that grossness would reflect a greater risk of harm).¶ Note that the distinction between "conscious" and "unconscious" is irrelevant: *Leichtfertigkeit* does not require awareness of risk. To draw a simple parallel to "recklessness," at least in the Model Penal Code sense—as a(nother) mental state between negligence and intention—would therefore be misleading. *Leichtfertigkeit* does not require, as MPC-recklessness would, an awareness of the risk. A subjective deficit (i.e., lack of awareness) can be compensated for by an objective surplus (i.e., level of risk and importance of the threatened legal good).

The concept of *grobe Fahrlässigkeit* stems from German civil law, which also draws a distinction between ordinary negligence and gross negligence. As we have already noted, German criminal law—unlike Anglo-American criminal law—does not draw a categorical distinction between civil and criminal negligence, so that a straight transfer of the distinction between types of negligence from civil to criminal law would not be objectionable in principle. Even so, it is widely acknowledged that the civil law also has not managed to work out the distinction with particular precision.

(b) *Rücksichtslosigkeit* appears in one offense definition in the German Criminal Code, § 315c (Endangering Road Traffic):

(1) Who in road traffic:

. . .

---

* See also Chapter 15.A (homicide).
† *Leichtfertigkeit* appears frequently throughout the German Criminal Code, both in offense definitions and as an aggravating element or factor. See §§ 97 (Revelation of State Secrets), 109g (Security Endangering Images), 138 (Failure to Report Planned Crimes), 176b (Serious Sexual Abuse of Children), 178 (Sexual Coercion and Rape Resulting in Death), 218 (Termination of Pregnancy), 239a (Extortionate Kidnapping), 251 (Robbery Resulting in Death), 261, (Money Laundering), 264 (Subsidy Fraud), 283 (Bankruptcy), 306c (Arson Resulting in Death), 307 (Causing an Explosion by Nuclear Power), 308 (Causing an Explosion by Use of Explosives), 309 (Misuse of Ionizing Radiation), 312 (Defective Construction of a Nuclear Facility), 316a (Car Robbery), 316b (Interference with Public Operations), 316c (Assaults on Air and Sea Traffic), 325 (Air Pollution), 329 (Endangering Areas Requiring Protection), 330a (Serious Endangerment by Release of Poison), 345 (Punishment Execution against the Innocent); see also §§ 74a (forfeiture), 74f (compensation).
‡ *Alternativ-Entwurf eines Strafgesetzbuches: Allgemeiner Teil* (2d edn. 1969), 57.
§ See Note 11.
¶ See generally Claus Roxin, *Strafrecht: Allgemeiner Teil* (4th edn. 2006), vol. 1, 1092–6.

2. in gross violation of traffic regulations and recklessly [*grob verkehrswidrig und rücksichtslos*]:
   a) does not observe the right of way;
   b) improperly passes or drives improperly in the process of passing;
   c) improperly drives over pedestrian crosswalks;
   d) drives too fast in places with poor visibility, at road crossings or junctions or railroad crossings;
   e) fails to keep to the right hand side of the road at places with poor visibility;
   f) turns, drives backward or contrary to the direction of traffic, or attempts to do so, on a highway or motorway; or
   g) fails to make vehicles that are stopped or have broken down recognizable from a sufficient distance, although it is required for traffic safety, and thereby endangers the life or limb of another human being or others' property of significant value,
   shall be punished with imprisonment of not more than five years or a fine.

Compare this to a standard definition of "reckless driving," from the N.Y. Vehicle and Traffic Law:

N.Y. Veh. & Traf. Law § 1212. Reckless Driving

Reckless driving shall mean driving or using any motor vehicle, motorcycle or any other vehicle propelled by any power other than muscular power or any appliance or accessory thereof in a manner which unreasonably interferes with the free and proper use of the public highway, or unreasonably endangers users of the public highway. Reckless driving is prohibited. Every person violating this provision shall be guilty of a misdemeanor.

(c) If one might be tempted to translate *Leichtfertigkeit* (or for that matter, *Rücksichtslosigkeit*) *as* recklessness, another mental state in the German Criminal Code, *Böswilligkeit*, might be taken for a German analogue to the long familiar common law mental state of *malice*, with an emphasis on the dispositional aspect of the term. *Böswilligkeit*, literally "evilwillness" (or, less awkwardly, "illwill") appears in only three offense definitions in the German Criminal Code §§ 90a(1), 130(1) and (2), 225(1), and is often assigned a place in the traditional German *mens rea* taxonomy not between negligence and intention (as in the case of *Leichtfertigkeit*) at the low end of the culpability spectrum, but at the top, beyond purpose (*Absicht, dolus directus of the first degree*). It fits with the base motives required for liability as a murderer in § 211 StGB, as a dispositional requirement (*Gesinnungsmerkmal*).* A person has been said to mistreat others by disregarding his or her duty of care with *Böswilligkeit*, under § 225(1) StGB, if he or she "repudiates the duty because of a bad disposition, a base motive, e.g., hatred, avarice, egotism, sadistic tendencies."[†]

15. Apart from the details in the definitions of various mental states in German criminal law and the Model Penal Code, one general, structural, distinction deserves mention. The German system turns on a dichotomy, by drawing a sharp, and categorical, distinction between *dolus* or *Vorsatz* and *Fahrlässigkeit*. Everyone would agree that this distinction—unlike that between justification and excuse, say—is critical because it makes a difference: *Vorsatz* is the default mental state requirement, so that a finding of *Vorsatz* rather than *Fahrlässigkeit* will make the difference between criminal liability and no criminal liability (except in the few offenses that require only negligence for conviction, where it would make the difference between more and less serious threatened punishment).

In contrast, the MPC scheme is designed as a spectrum, occasionally described as a hierarchy, of mental states, from negligence on one end to purpose on the other. There is no radical distinction among groups of mental states in the MPC scheme; rather, each mode of culpability falls on various points on different axes. On the objective, or probabilistic, axis, knowledge differs from both recklessness and negligence by requiring 100 percent (or as close to 100 percent as humanly possible, in the case of result), while recklessness and negligence make do with a lower likelihood ("substantial risk"). Purpose finds no place on

---

* See Chapter 15.A.
† See generally Brigitte Kelker, *Zur Legitimität von Gesinnungsmerkmalen im Strafrecht* (2007), 547.

the objective axis because it is defined exclusively in subjective terms, except when it comes to attendant circumstances (in which case it requires awareness, or 100 percent). On the subjective, or attitudinal, axis, purpose requires conscious object, awareness, belief, or hope, depending on the offense element type to which it is attached in the offense definition; knowledge requires awareness (of a fact, or a practical certainty); recklessness requires "conscious disregard." Negligence requires nothing (except putative awareness), being defined exclusively in objective terms.

Recklessness being the default mental state requirement, the line between (default) criminality and non-criminality in the MPC scheme falls between recklessness and negligence. In the German scheme, it falls between *Vorsatz* and *Fahrlässigkeit* or, since conditional intention is considered the least demanding form of *Vorsatz*, between conditional intentional and negligence.

Traditionally, the common law—like German law—drew a categorical distinction between intent (or intention) and negligence (which is not to say that this distinction was clearly or consistently drawn). The Model Penal Code drafters, however, abandoned the concept of intent because it did not provide courts with a sufficiently fine grid for the analysis of the subjective element of crimes, and instead obfuscated the *mens rea* analysis. Presumably it might have been possible to clarify matters by clarifying the definition of intent, and differentiating carefully between purpose, knowledge, and recklessness within that definition. The drafters, instead, chose to make a fresh start and abandon the concept of intent altogether. Assuming that clarity was gained, was something lost in the process? Does the distinction between intent and negligence—still maintained by German criminal law (and many common law jurisdictions)—capture something significant about the nature of criminality? From the treatmentist perspective? From the perspective of other approaches to criminal law?

If we were to draw a line between (default) criminality and non-criminality, where should it be drawn? At the point of volition (as in the German system, at least under the majority view illustrated in the *Leather Strap Case*)? Or at the point of (subjective) awareness (as in the Model Penal Code)?

16. The German Criminal Code does not include an analogue to the taxonomy of mental states set up in Model Penal Code § 2.02. Many criminal law codes in common law countries are criticized for their failure to define mental states; the absence of such definitions is often taken as a prime illustration of the absence of a general part. Correspondingly, the need for statutory definitions of mental states tends to be at, or near, the top of the list of reasons for criminal code reform in the first place. The 1962 draft of a revised German Criminal Code included mental state definitions; so did the 1969 Alternative Draft of a German Criminal Code assembled by a group of law professors (excerpted above). As the Commentary to the Alternative Draft put it: "Like the 1962 draft, but in contrast to the current Criminal Code, the Alternative Draft presents legal definitions of intention and negligence, because the code should not, without need, remain silent on such central issues."*

In the end, no definitions of mental state were introduced into the revised German Criminal Code, on the ground that this matter was too important, and too disputed, *not* to be left to criminal law scientists (i.e., German criminal law professors) and courts. A similar argument was made against criminal codification in general in nineteenth-century England, as judges insisted that they, not the legislature, were best equipped to deal with the intricacies of criminal law doctrine, which therefore should be left to the time-tested continued development, and refinement, of (judge-made) common law.

Does the failure to define the types of *mens rea* raise concerns in light of the principle of legality?† Or would the definitions, to accommodate the variety of approaches found in the German literature, have to remain so abstract that they would provide neither meaningful

---

* *Alternativ-Entwurf eines Strafgesetzbuches: Allgemeiner Teil* (2d edn. 1969), 57.
† See Chapter 2.

notice to the public nor guidance to the courts? Compare the mental state definitions in the Model Penal Code (in § 2.02) and the Alternative Draft (§§ 16–18), in form and substance.

B. Strict (or Absolute) Liability

Much of the comparative analysis of *mens rea*, or subjective offense elements, in Anglo-American and German criminal law has been devoted not to differences and similarities of the various types of mental state requirement, discussed in Chapter 8.A, but instead to the absence of such a requirement in some criminal offenses under Anglo-American criminal law. In other words, while the absence of a general act requirement in German criminal law might perhaps surprise those steeped in the Anglo-American criminal law tradition (assuming they are not among those who think that there is—or should, or need—be no such requirement), the lack of a *mens rea* requirement in Anglo-American criminal law may have a similar effect on a German observer, except that the absence of a *mens rea* requirement is likely to appear more significant, reflecting the greater importance accorded that requirement in criminal law generally speaking. Insofar as *mens rea* is essential to, and distinctive of, criminal behavior, as opposed to behavior unlawful generally speaking, the notion of a crime without *mens rea* is either nonsensical or, at least, deeply objectionable as indicative of a fundamental misunderstanding of the distinction between conduct that does or does not deserve criminal punishment.

While this objection is often based on a general requirement of culpability, or guilt (notably in the form of the German "culpability principle"), it might also be put in terms of some other distinctive feature of the offender, such as abnormal dangerousness, that is said to justify the exercise of the state's penal power in a particular case, or class of cases. The latter objection would draw on an interpretation of the various requisite mental states as indicators not of levels, or types, of culpability in a normative sense, but instead of degrees, and types, of dangerousness. From this, treatmentist perspective, an act committed with, say, purpose (or *Absicht*), for instance, would not render the actor more culpable and therefore deserving of greater punishment, but instead indicate a diagnosis of greater criminal dangerousness, than an act committed, with, say, negligence. And the line between criminal liability and no criminal liability would be the line between the presence and absence of criminal dangerousness, rather than the presence or absence of "guilt."*

Morissette v. United States
Supreme Court of the United States
342 U.S. 246 (1952)

Mr. Justice Jackson delivered the opinion of the Court.

On a large tract of uninhabited and untilled land in a wooded and sparsely populated area of Michigan, the Government established a practice bombing range over which the Air Force dropped simulated bombs at ground targets. These bombs consisted of a metal cylinder about forty inches long and eight inches across, filled with sand and enough black powder to cause a smoke puff by which the strike could be located. At various places about the range signs read "Danger—Keep Out—Bombing Range." Nevertheless, the range was known as good deer country and was extensively hunted.

Spent bomb casings were cleared from the targets and thrown into piles "so that they will be out of the way." They were not sacked or piled in any order but were dumped in heaps, some of which had been accumulating for four years or upwards, were exposed to the weather and rusting away.

Morissette, in December of 1948, went hunting in this area but did not get a deer. He thought to meet expenses of the trip by salvaging some of these casings. He loaded three tons of them on his truck and took them to a nearby farm, where they were flattened by driving a tractor over them. After expending this labor and trucking them to market in Flint, he realized $84.

---

* On treatmentism and the Model Penal Code, see Chapter 1.A.i.

Morissette, by occupation, is a fruit stand operator in summer and a trucker and scrap iron collector in winter. An honorably discharged veteran of World War II, he enjoys a good name among his neighbors and has had no blemish on his record more disreputable than a conviction for reckless driving.

The loading, crushing and transporting of these casings were all in broad daylight, in full view of passers-by, without the slightest effort at concealment. When an investigation was started, Morissette voluntarily, promptly and candidly told the whole story to the authorities, saying that he had no intention of stealing but thought the property was abandoned, unwanted and considered of no value to the Government. He was indicted, however, on the charge that he "did unlawfully, wilfully and knowingly steal and convert" property of the United States of the value of $84, in violation of 18 U.S.C. § 641, which provides that "whoever embezzles, steals, purloins, or knowingly converts" government property is punishable by fine and imprisonment. Morissette was convicted and sentenced to imprisonment for two months or to pay a fine of $200. The Court of Appeals affirmed, one judge dissenting.

On his trial, Morissette, as he had at all times told investigating officers, testified that from appearances he believed the casings were cast-off and abandoned, that he did not intend to steal the property, and took it with no wrongful or criminal intent. The trial court, however, was unimpressed, and ruled: "(H)e took it because he thought it was abandoned and he knew he was on government property.... That is no defense."....

The contention that an injury can amount to a crime only when inflicted by intention is no provincial or transient notion. It is as universal and persistent in mature systems of law as belief in freedom of the human will and a consequent ability and duty of the normal individual to choose between good and evil.[4] A relation between some mental element and punishment for a harmful act is almost as instinctive as the child's familiar exculpatory "But I didn't mean to," and has afforded the rational basis for a tardy and unfinished substitution of deterrence and reformation in place of retaliation and vengeance as the motivation for public prosecution. Unqualified acceptance of this doctrine by English common law in the Eighteenth Century was indicated by Blackstone's sweeping statement that to constitute any crime there must first be a "vicious will." Common-law commentators of the Nineteenth Century early pronounced the same principle, although a few exceptions not relevant to our present problem came to be recognized.[8]

Crime, as a compound concept, generally constituted only from concurrence of an evil-meaning mind with an evil-doing hand, was congenial to an intense individualism and took deep and early root in American soil.[9] As the state codified the common law of crimes, even if their enactments were silent on the subject, their courts assumed that the omission did not signify disapproval of the principle but merely recognized that intent was so inherent in the idea of the offense that it required no statutory affirmation. Courts, with little hesitation or division, found an implication of the requirement as to offenses that were taken over from the common law. The unanimity with which they have adhered to the central thought that wrongdoing must be conscious to be criminal is emphasized by the variety, disparity and confusion of their definitions of the requisite but elusive mental element. However, courts of various jurisdictions, and for the purposes of different offenses, have devised working formulae, if not scientific ones, for the instruction of juries around such terms as "felonious intent," "criminal intent," "malice aforethought," "guilty knowledge," "fraudulent intent," "wilfulness," "scienter," to denote guilty knowledge, or "mens rea," to signify an evil purpose or mental culpability. By use or combination of these various tokens, they have sought to protect those who were not blameworthy in mind from conviction of infamous common-law crimes.

However, [there exist] offenses [that] belong to a category of another character, with very different antecedents and origins. The[se] crimes... depend on no mental element but consist only of forbidden acts or omissions. This, while not expressed by the Court, is made clear from examination of a century-old but accelerating tendency, discernible both here and in England, to call into existence new duties and crimes which disregard any ingredient of intent. The industrial revolution multiplied the number of workmen exposed to injury from increasingly powerful and complex mechanisms, driven by freshly discovered sources of energy, requiring higher precautions by employers. Traffic of

---

[4] ... "Historically, our substantive criminal law is based upon a theory of punishing the vicious will. It postulates a free agent confronted with a choice between doing right and doing wrong and choosing freely to do wrong." Pound, Introduction to Sayre, Cases on Criminal Law (1927).

[8] Exceptions came to include sex offenses, such as rape, in which the victim's actual age was determinative despite defendant's reasonable belief that the girl had reached age of consent.... Most extensive inroads upon the requirement of intention, however, are offenses of negligence, such as involuntary manslaughter or criminal negligence and the whole range of crimes arising from omission of duty.

[9] Holmes, The Common Law, considers intent in the chapter on The Criminal Law, and earlier makes the pithy observation: "Even a dog distinguishes between being stumbled over and being kicked." ...

velocities, volumes and varieties unheard of came to subject the wayfarer to intolerable casualty risks if owners and drivers were not to observe new cares and uniformities of conduct. Congestion of cities and crowding of quarters called for health and welfare regulations undreamed of in simpler times. Wide distribution of goods became an instrument of wide distribution of harm when those who dispersed food, drink, drugs, and even securities, did not comply with reasonable standards of quality, integrity, disclosure and care. Such dangers have engendered increasingly numerous and detailed regulations which heighten the duties of those in control of particular industries, trades, properties or activities that affect public health, safety or welfare.

While many of these duties are sanctioned by a more strict civil liability, lawmakers, whether wisely or not, have sought to make such regulations more effective by invoking criminal sanctions to be applied by the familiar technique of criminal prosecutions and convictions. This has confronted the courts with a multitude of prosecutions, based on statutes or administrative regulations, for what have been aptly called "public welfare offenses." These cases do not fit neatly into any of such accepted classifications of common-law offenses, such as those against the state, the person, property, or public morals. Many of these offenses are not in the nature of positive aggressions or invasions, with which the common law so often dealt, but are in the nature of neglect where the law requires care, or inaction where it imposes a duty. Many violations of such regulations result in no direct or immediate injury to person or property but merely create the danger or probability of it which the law seeks to minimize. While such offenses do not threaten the security of the state in the manner of treason, they may be regarded as offenses against its authority, for their occurrence impairs the efficiency of controls deemed essential to the social order as presently constituted. In this respect, whatever the intent of the violator, the injury is the same, and the consequences are injurious or not according to fortuity. Hence, legislation applicable to such offenses, as a matter of policy, does not specify intent as a necessary element. The accused, if he does not will the violation, usually is in a position to prevent it with no more care than society might reasonably expect and no more exertion than it might reasonably exact from one who assumed his responsibilities. Also, penalties commonly are relatively small, and conviction does not grave damage to an offender's reputation. Under such considerations, courts have turned to construing statutes and regulations which make no mention of intent as dispensing with it and holding that the guilty act alone makes out the crime....

Neither this Court nor, so far as we are aware, any other has undertaken to delineate a precise line or set forth comprehensive criteria for distinguishing between crimes that require a mental element and crimes that do not. We attempt no closed definition, for the law on the subject is neither settled nor static....

Stealing, larceny, and its variants and equivalents, were among the earliest offenses known to the law that existed before legislation; they are invasions of rights of property which stir a sense of insecurity in the whole community and arouse public demand for retribution, the penalty is high and, when a sufficient amount is involved, the infamy is that of a felony, which, says Maitland, is "...as bad a word as you can give to man or thing."...

Congress, therefore, omitted any express prescription of criminal intent from the enactment before us in the light of an unbroken course of judicial decision in all constituent states of the Union holding intent inherent in this class of offense, even when not expressed in a statute. Congressional silence as to mental elements in an Act merely adopting into federal statutory law a concept of crime already so well defined in common law and statutory interpretation by the states may warrant quite contrary inferences than the same silence in creating an offense new to general law, for whose definition the courts have no guidance except the Act....

We find no grounds for inferring any affirmative instruction from Congress to eliminate intent from any offense with which this defendant was charged.

Francis Bowes Sayre, "Public Welfare Offenses," 33 *Columbia Law Review* (1933), 55.

Blackstone, ... summarizing the classical conception of a crime, declared that "to constitute a crime against human laws, there must be first a vicious will, and secondly an unlawful act consequent upon such vicious will." "There can be no crime large or small without an evil mind," says Bishop. "It is therefore a principle of our legal system, as probably it is of every other, that the essence of an offense is the wrongful intent, without which it cannot exist."

In the face of an almost unbroken line of authorities to similar effect we are witnessing today a steadily growing stream of offenses punishable without any criminal intent whatsoever. Convictions may be had for the sales of adulterated or impure food, violations of the liquor laws, infractions of anti-narcotic acts, and many other offenses based upon conduct alone without regard to the mind or intent of the actor...

What does this... movement portend?... Are we to look forward to a day when criminality will be based upon external behavior alone irrespective of intent?

No such conclusion is warranted. Criminality is and always will be based upon a requisite state of mind as one of its prime factors... "Public welfare offenses," if one may coin the phrase, constitute, however, a noteworthy exception...

All criminal law is a compromise between two fundamentally conflicting interests, that of the public which demands restraint of all who injure or menace the social well-being and that of the individual which demands maximum liberty and freedom from interference... During the nineteenth century it was the individual interest which held the stage; the criminal law machinery was overburdened with innumerable checks to prevent possible injustice to individual defendants. The scales were weighted heavily in his favor, and, as we have found to our sorrow, the public welfare often suffered. In the twentieth century came reaction. We are thinking today more of the protection of social and public interests; and coincident with the swinging of the pendulum in the field of legal administration in this direction modern criminologists are teaching the objective underlying correctional treatment should change from the barren aim of punishing human beings to the fruitful one of protecting social interests....

[S]wamped with... inundations of cases of petty violations, the lower criminal courts would be physically unable to examine the subjective intent of each defendant, even were such determination desirable. As a matter of fact it is not; for the penalty in such cases is so slight that the courts can afford to disregard the individual in protecting the social interest.

The ready enforcement which is vital for effective petty regulation on an extended scale can be gained only by a total disregard of the state of mind...

How then can one determine practically which offenses do and which do not require mens rea, where the statute creating the offense is entirely silent as to requisite knowledge? Although no hard and fast lines can be drawn, two cardinal principles stand out upon which the determination must turn.

The first relates to the character of the offense. All criminal enactments in a sense serve the double purpose of singling out wrongdoers for the purpose of punishment or correction and of regulating the social order. But often the importance of the one far outweighs the other. Crimes created primarily for the purpose of singling out individual wrongdoers for punishment or correction are the ones commonly requiring mens rea; police offenses of a merely regulatory nature are frequently enforceable irrespective of a guilty intent.

The second criterion depends upon the possible penalty. If this be serious, particularly if the offense be punishable by imprisonment, the individual interest of the defendant weighs too heavily to allow conviction without proof of a guilty mind. To subject defendants entirely free from moral blameworthiness to the possibility of prison sentences is revolting to the community sense of justice; and no law which violates this fundamental instinct can long endure.

R. v. City of Sault Ste. Marie
Supreme Court of Canada
[1978] 2 S.C.R. 1299

The judgment of the court was delivered by Dickson, J.:

In the present appeal the Court is concerned with offences variously referred to as "statutory," "public welfare," "regulatory," "absolute liability," or "strict responsibility," which are not criminal in any real sense, but are prohibited in the public interest: *Sherras v. De Rutzen*, [1895] 1 Q.B. 918. Although enforced as penal laws through the utilization of the machinery of the criminal law, the offences are in substance of a civil nature and might well be regarded as a branch of administrative law to which traditional principles of criminal law have but limited application. They relate to such everyday matters as traffic infractions, sales of impure food, violations of liquor laws, and the like. In this appeal we are concerned with pollution.

The doctrine of the guilty mind expressed in terms of intention or recklessness, but not negligence, is at the foundation of the law of crimes. In the case of true crimes there is a presumption that a person should not be held liable for the wrongfulness of his act if that act is without *mens rea*: *R. v. Prince* (1875), L.R. 2 C.C.R. 154; *R. v. Tolson* (1889), 23 Q.B.D. 168; *R. v. Rees* (1955), 115 C.C.C. 1, 4 D.L.R. (2d) 406, [1956] S.C.R. 640; *Beaver v. The Queen* (1957), 118 C.C.C. 129, [1957] S.C.R. 531, 26 C.R. 193; *R. v. King* (1962), 133 C.C.C. 1, 35 D.L.R. (2d) 386, [1962] S.C.R. 746. Blackstone made the point over two hundred years ago in words still apt: " ... to constitute a crime against human laws, there must be, first, a vicious will; and secondly, an unlawful act consequent upon such vicious will . . . ": see *Commentaries on the Laws of England* (1809), Book IV, 15th ed., c. 15, p. 21. I would emphasize at the outset that nothing in the discussion which follows is intended to dilute or erode that basic principle . . .

The City of Sault Ste. Marie was charged that it did discharge, or cause to be discharged, or permitted to be discharged, or deposited materials into Cannon Creek and Root River, or on the shore or bank thereof, or in such place along the side that might impair the quality of the water in Cannon Creek and Root River, between March 13, 1972 and September 11, 1972. The charge was laid under s. 32(1) of the *Ontario Water Resources Act*, R.S.O. 1970, c. 332, [formerly *Ontario Water Resources Commissary Act*, renamed by 1972, c. 1, s. 70(1)] which provides, so far as relevant, that every municipality or person that discharges, or deposits, or causes, or permits the discharge or deposit of any material of any kind into any water course, or on any shore or bank thereof, or in any place that may impair the quality of water, is guilty of an offence and, on summary conviction, is liable on first conviction to a fine of not more than $5,000 and on each subsequent conviction to a fine of not more than $10,000, or to imprisonment for a term of not more than one year, or to both fine and imprisonment . . .

To relate briefly the facts, the City on November 18, 1970, entered into an agreement with Cherokee Disposal and Construction Co. Ltd., for the disposal of all refuse originating in the City. Under the terms of the agreement, Cherokee became obligated to furnish a site and adequate labour, material and equipment. The site selected bordered Cannon Creek which, it would appear, runs into the Root River. The method of disposal adopted is known as the "area," or "continuous slope" method of sanitary land fill, whereby garbage is compacted in layers which are covered each day by natural sand or gravel. . . .

Prior to 1970, the site had been covered with a number of freshwater springs that flowed into Cannon Creek. Cherokee dumped material to cover and submerge these springs and then placed garbage and wastes over such material. The garbage and wastes in due course formed a high mound sloping steeply toward, and within 20 ft. of, the creek. Pollution resulted. Cherokee was convicted of a breach of s. 32(1) of the *Ontario Water Resources Act*, the section under which the City has been charged. The question now before the Court is whether the City is also guilty of an offence under that section . . .

The *mens rea* point

The distinction between the true criminal offence and the public welfare offence is one of prime importance. Where the offence is criminal, the Crown must establish a mental element, namely, that the accused who committed the prohibited act did so intentionally or recklessly, with knowledge of the facts constituting the offence, or with wilful blindness toward them. Mere negligence is excluded from the concept of the mental element required for conviction. Within the context of a criminal prosecution a person who fails to make such inquiries as a reasonable and prudent person would make, or who fails to know facts he should have known, is innocent in the eyes of the law.

In sharp contrast, "absolute liability" entails conviction on proof merely that the defendant committed the prohibited act constituting the *actus reus* of the offence. There is no relevant mental element. It is no defence that the accused was entirely without fault. He may be morally innocent in every sense, yet be branded as a malefactor and punished as such.

Public welfare offences obviously lie in a field of conflicting values. It is essential for society to maintain, through effective enforcement, high standards of public health and safety. Potential victims of those who carry on latently pernicious activities have a strong claim to consideration. On the other hand, there is a generally held revulsion against punishment of the morally innocent . . . Various arguments are advanced in justification of absolute liability in public welfare offences. Two predominate. Firstly, it is argued that the protection of social interests requires a high standard of care and attention on the part of those who follow certain pursuits and such persons are more likely to be stimulated to maintain those standards if they know that ignorance or mistake will not excuse them. The removal of any possible loophole acts, it is said, as an incentive to take precautionary measures beyond what would otherwise be taken, in order that mistakes and mishaps be avoided. The second main argument is one based on administrative efficiency. Having regard to both the difficulty of proving mental culpability and the number of petty cases which daily come before the Courts, proof of fault is just too great a burden in time and money to place upon the prosecution. To require proof of each person's individual intent would allow almost every violator to escape. This, together with the glut of work entailed in proving *mens rea* in every case would clutter the docket and impede adequate enforcement as virtually to nullify the regulatory statutes. In short, absolute liability, it is contended, is the most efficient and effective way of ensuring compliance with minor regulatory legislation and the social ends to be achieved are of such importance as to override the unfortunate by-product of punishing those who may be free of moral turpitude. In further justification, it is urged that slight penalties are usually imposed and that conviction for breach of a public welfare offence does not carry the stigma associated with conviction for a criminal offence.

Arguments of greater force are advanced against absolute liability. The most telling is that it violates fundamental principles of penal liability. It also rests upon assumptions which have not been, and cannot be, empirically established. There is no evidence that a higher standard of care results from absolute liability. If a person is already taking every reasonable precautionary measure, is he likely to take additional measures, knowing that however much care he takes, it will not serve as a defence in the event of breach? If he has exercised care and skill, will conviction have a deterrent effect upon him or others? Will the injustice of conviction lead to cynicism and disrespect for the law, on his part and on the part of others? These are among the questions asked. The argument that no stigma attaches does not withstand analysis, for the accused will have suffered loss of time, legal costs, exposure to the processes of the criminal law at trial and, however one may downplay it, the opprobrium of conviction. It is not sufficient to say that the public interest is engaged and, therefore, liability may be imposed without fault. In serious crimes, the public interest is involved and *mens rea* must be proven. The administrative argument has little force. In sentencing, evidence of due diligence is admissible and therefore the evidence might just as well be heard when considering guilt . . .

Public welfare offences involve a shift of emphasis from the protection of individual interests to the protection of public and social interests: see F. B. Sayre, "Public Welfare Offences," 33 *Columbia Law Rev.* 55 (1933); Hall, *General Principles of Criminal Law* (1947), c. 13, p. 427; R. M. Perkins, "Civil Offence," 100 *U. of Pa. L. Rev.* 832 (1952); Jobson, "Far From Clear," 18 *Crim. L. Q.* 294 (1976). The unfortunate tendency in many past cases has been to see the choice as between two stark alternatives: (i) full *mens rea*; or (ii) absolute liability. In respect of public welfare offences (within which category pollution offences fall) where full *mens rea* is not required, absolute liability has often been imposed. English jurisprudence has consistently maintained this dichotomy: see "Criminal Law, Evidence and Procedure," 11 Hals., 4th ed., pp. 202, para. 18. There has, however, been an attempt in Australia, in many Canadian Courts, and indeed in England, to seek a middle position, fulfilling the goals of public welfare offences while still not punishing the entirely blameless. There is an increasing and impressive stream of authority which holds that where an offence does not require full *mens rea*, it is nevertheless a good defence for the defendant to prove that he was not negligent.

Dr. Glanville Williams has written: "There is a half-way house between *mens rea* and strict responsibility which has not yet been properly utilized, and that is responsibility for negligence" (*Criminal Law: General Part*, 2nd ed. (1961), p. 262). Morris and Howard, in *Studies in Criminal Law* (1964), p. 200, suggest that strict responsibility might with advantage be replaced by a doctrine of responsibility for negligence strengthened by a shift in the burden of proof. The defendant would be allowed to exculpate himself by proving affirmatively that he was not negligent . . . The correct approach, in my opinion, is to relieve the Crown of the burden of proving *mens rea* . . . In a normal case, the accused alone will have knowledge of what he has done to avoid the breach and it is not improper to expect him to come forward with the evidence of due diligence. This is particularly so when it is alleged, for example, that pollution was caused by the activities of a large and complex corporation. Equally, there is nothing wrong with rejecting absolute liability and admitting the defence of reasonable care.

In this doctrine it is not up to the prosecution to prove negligence. Instead, it is open to the defendant to prove that all due care has been taken. This burden falls upon the defendant as he is the only one who will generally have the means of proof. This would not seem unfair as the alternative is absolute liability which denies an accused any defence whatsoever. While the prosecution must prove beyond a reasonable doubt that the defendant committed the prohibited act, the defendant must only establish on the balance of probabilities that he has a defence of reasonable care.

I conclude, for the reasons which I have sought to express, that there are compelling grounds for the recognition of three categories of offences rather than the traditional two:

1. Offences in which *mens rea*, consisting of some positive state of mind such as intent, knowledge, or recklessness, must be proved by the prosecution either as an inference from the nature of the act committed, or by additional evidence.
2. Offences in which there is no necessity for the prosecution to prove the existence of *mens rea*; the doing of the prohibited act *prima facie* imports the offence, leaving it open to the accused to avoid liability by proving that he took all reasonable care. This involves consideration of what a reasonable man would have done in the circumstances. The defence will be available if the accused reasonably believed in a mistaken set of facts which, if true, would render the act or omission innocent, or if he took all reasonable steps to avoid the particular event. These offences may properly be called offences of strict liability . . .

3. Offences of absolute liability where it is not open to the accused to exculpate himself by showing that he was free of fault.

Offences which are criminal in the true sense fall in the first category. Public welfare offences would, *prima facie*, be in the second category. They are not subject to the presumption of full *mens rea*. An offence of this type would fall in the first category only if such words as "wilfully," "with intent," "knowingly," or "intentionally" are contained in the statutory provision creating the offence. On the other hand, the principle that punishment should in general not be inflicted on those without fault applies. Offences of absolute liability would be those in respect of which the Legislature had made it clear that guilt would follow proof merely of the proscribed act. The over-all regulatory pattern adopted by the Legislature, the subject-matter of the legislation, the importance of the penalty, and the precision of the language used will be primary considerations in determining whether the offence falls into the third category.

Ontario Water Resources Act, s. 32(1)

Turning to the subject-matter of s. 32(1)—the prevention of pollution of lakes, rivers and streams—it is patent that this is of great public concern. Pollution has always been unlawful and, in itself, a nuisance: *Groat v. City of Edmonton*, [1928] 3 D.L.R. 725, [1928] S.C.R. 522. A riparian owner has an inherent right to have a stream of water "come to him in its natural state, in flow, quantity and quality": *Chasemore v. Richards* (1859), 7 H.L. Cas. 349 at p. 382. Natural streams which formerly afforded "pure and healthy" water for drinking or swimming purposes become little more than cesspools when riparian factory owners and municipal corporations discharge into them filth of all descriptions. Pollution offences are undoubtedly public welfare offences enacted in the interests of public health. There is thus no presumption of a full *mens rea*...

The present case concerns the interpretation of two troublesome words frequently found in public welfare statutes: "cause" and "permit." These two words are troublesome because neither denotes clearly either full *mens rea* nor absolute liability. It is said that a person could not be said to be permitting something unless he knew what he was permitting. This is an over-simplification. There is authority both ways, indicating that the Courts are uneasy with the traditional dichotomy...

Since s. 32(1) creates a public welfare offence, without a clear indication that liability is absolute, and without any words such as "knowingly" or "wilfully" expressly to import *mens rea*, application of the criteria which I have outlined above undoubtedly places the offence in the category of strict liability.

Proof of the prohibited act *prima facie* imports the offence, but the accused may avoid liability by proving that he took reasonable care.

The present case

As I am of the view that a new trial is necessary, it would be inappropriate to discuss at this time the facts of the present case...

Appeal dismissed.

NOTES

1. U.S. law has long struggled with the distinction between so-called "public welfare" (*malum prohibitum*) offenses and traditional (*malum in se*) crimes. *Morissette* draws a stark all-or-nothing contrast between a full-blown *mens rea* requirement, variously described (by the Court) as "'felonious intent,' 'criminal intent,' 'malice aforethought,' 'guilty knowledge,' 'fraudulent intent,' 'wilfulness,' 'scienter,' to denote guilty knowledge, or 'mens rea,' to signify an evil purpose or mental culpability."

Morissette does not consider the possibility of a halfway house between "felonious intent," etc.—which, in Model Penal Code hindsight, we might interpret as a reference to recklessness as a default mental state requirement—and strict liability. *Sault Ste. Marie* does just that, by setting up a third, intermediate option of an affirmative "defense" of due diligence (i.e., the absence of negligence), along the way somewhat confusingly relabeling *Morissette's* "strict liability" as "absolute liability" and assigning the label "strict liability" to the new, compromise, position.

The potpourri of mental states cited in *Morissette*—and in fact the opinion itself—illustrate the confused, and confusing, state of the law of *mens rea* when the Model Penal Code drafters began their work. *Morissette* was decided the same year the Code project began in earnest

(1952), and immediately drew heavy criticism, most famously in an article by Henry Hart, who went so far as to draft a bitingly ironic, and highly entertaining, concurring opinion, by a fictional Justice Tenthjudge:

Mr. Justice Tenthjudge, concurring in result.

While I have an emotional sympathy with most of what is said in my brother Jackson's engaging opinion in this case, I should not wish to be understood as expressing judicial agreement with any part of it, except the very limited part which is necessary for decision of the narrow issue before us.

We ought to refrain from writing discursive essays on the law, if only to spare law students the burden of reading them and law professors the pain of deciding whether to reproduce them in their casebooks. But there is a still more compelling reason for restraint. We cannot possibly apply our minds to all the considerations which are relevant to all the propositions which the Court's opinion advances. We cannot possibly be sure, therefore, that each proposition will stand up when it is tested in the crucible of a litigation squarely involving it. Thus, to the peccadillo of announcing too much law in this case, we add the cardinal sin of announcing law of dubious reliability.

We have to deal here with a typical modern statute consolidating—with typical looseness of draftsmanship—the various forms of theft, so far as these crimes are of concern to the United States as a governmental entity. With respect to all these forms of theft—not only those which are of judicial origin, like trespassory larceny and larceny by trick, but those which have their origin in statutes, like obtaining property by false pretenses and embezzlement—a "claim of right" has traditionally been a defense. Morissette's claim falls comfortably with the types of claims which have traditionally been recognized as affording this defense.

Hence the simple question before us is whether the vague and general language of the "knowingly converts" clause of 62 Stat. 725 (1948), 18 U.S.C. § 641 (1952) should be read as incorporating this established element of the crime of theft or as eliminating it.

There are a plethora of good reasons for the narrower reading.

Statutes, generally, should be read in the light of the common law, save where they make plain a purpose to depart from it.

This is doubly true of statutes defining crimes, which ancient learning tells us should be strictly construed, if a strict construction is sensible.

It is trebly true of statues defining federal crimes, which are not readily to be given an expansive interpretation overlapping the criminal prohibitions of the states.

It is quadruply true of a section which the statutory revisers tell us simply "consolidates" previous provisions of the code, which provisions, as we know, had never been held to dispense with the common law defense.

It is quintuply true when the section in question is contained in a recodification which, as the Court's opinion tells us, was generally "not intended to create new crimes, but to recodify those then in existence."

It is sextuply true when the recodification in question—why not come right out and say it?—is one for which the spadework was done by the hired hands of three commercial law-book publishers, on delegation from a congressional committee desirous of escaping the responsibility of hiring and supervising its own staff.

In these circumstances, the case against finding a major change of public policy in the interstices of this slovenly enactment is overwhelming.

If the Court's opinion had chosen merely to add as a seventh reason that it is a general principle of our law that criminal condemnation imports moral blameworthiness and that the legislature ought not lightly to be taken as wishing to weaken this principle, I should have had no objection; indeed, I should have applauded.

But I see no occasion for examination and labored distinction of the notorious instances in which Congress and this Court have sanctioned blatant defiance of this principle. . . .

[I]t may not be inappropriate to call attention to the paradox in which my brother Jackson's ratiocinations have involved him.

In relation to offenses of a traditional type, the Court's opinion seems to be saying, we must be much slower to dispense with a basis for genuine blameworthiness in criminal intent than in relation to modern regulatory offenses. But it is precisely in the area of traditional crimes that the nature of the act itself commonly gives some warning that there may be a problem about is propriety and so affords, without more, at least some slight basis of condemnation for doing it. Thus, Morissette knew perfectly well that he was taking property which, at least up to the moment of caption, did not belong to him.

In the area of regulatory crimes, on the other hand, the moral quality of the act is often neutral; and on occasion, the offense may consist not of any act at all, but simply of an intrinsically innocent omission, so that there is no basis for moral condemnation whatever....

Henry M. Hart, Jr., "The Aims of the Criminal Law,"
23 *Law and Contemporary Problems* (1958), 401, 431–2 n.70.

2. Still it is important to recognize that both *Morissette* and *Sault Ste. Marie* are presented as exercises in statutory interpretation, exercises that turn on an inquiry into legislative intent. They are not, at least not explicitly, general explorations of the merits and demerits of a piece of legislation, or of a general approach to criminal lawmaking (which is not to say, of course, that they do not reflect an opinion on these matters—more on this below).

Nor are they exercises in constitutional scrutiny. This bears emphasis: neither *Morissette* nor *Sault Ste. Marie* address questions of constitutionality. *Sault Ste. Marie* was decided before the enactment of the Canadian Charter in 1982; for a Canadian decision considering the constitutionality of absolute liability.*

There is no U.S. analogue to the *Motor Vehicle Reference Case*, although scholars have long argued in favor of a general constitutional *mens rea* requirement, often tracing the U.S. Supreme Court's jurisprudence to see whether such a requirement could be found, if only implicitly.[†] That said, the Court has been more willing to recognize a constitutional dimension to the *mens rea* inquiry in cases involving statutes that, without a *mens rea* requirement, might affect the exercise of free speech rights under the First Amendment.[‡]

As exercises in statutory interpretation, the two opinions—*Morissette* and *Sault Ste. Marie*—follow similar, and familiar, paths. They begin with an absence: the absence of a requirement of intent of any kind. Does the legislature's failure to include a *mens rea* requirement attached to the relevant offense element indicate that it meant (1) to require proof of *mens rea*, after all, but did not bother spell this out or (2) to dispense with the requirement of proof of *mens rea*? This way of framing the question is, of course, already tendentious, to the extent that it puts it in terms of "failing" to do something, of "dispensing" with a requirement, implying that there was a requirement to be dispensed with. But that is exactly how both courts approach the question: in light of a general common law (*not* constitutional) requirement of *mens rea*, is there sufficient evidence of the legislature's intent to carve out an exception from this requirement by "dispensing" with it in the present case? Again, there is no suggestion that the legislature would not have been free to do just that; the long-standing common law *mens rea* requirement only establishes a rebuttable presumption that the legislature intended to require *mens rea*, a presumption, however, that can be rebutted by a clear (enough) indication of contrary legislative intent.

The two-part and three-part schemes in *Morissette* and *Sault Ste. Marie* are, in the end, guidelines for the interpretation of criminal statutes with missing (or ambiguous) mental state requirements, one more elaborate than the other. (The Model Penal Code, as you may recall, developed similar interpretive devices on this issue: the (recklessness) default rule and the one-for-all rule.[§])

3. The—or one—trouble with *Morissette* and *Sault Ste. Marie* is that the distinctions underlying their interpretive guidelines can be difficult to trace. Does it make sense to classify some offenses as "public welfare" offenses, but not others? Isn't the protection of public welfare one of the—if not the—function of criminal law as a whole? Similarly, isn't every offense also a *malum prohibitum* in the sense that it is punishable at least part because it disobeys a state norm, apart from its content? Looking at the distinctions from the other

---

* See the *Motor Vehicle Reference Case*, excerpted in Chapter 3.A (finding that absolute liability is constitutionally incompatible with imprisonment).

[†] See, e.g., Richard Singer and Douglas Husak, "Of Innocence and Innocents: The Supreme Court and Mens Rea Since Herbert Packer," 2 *Buffalo Criminal Law Review* (1999), 859.

[‡] See, e.g., *United States v. X-Citement Video, Inc.*, 513 U.S. 64 (1994); *Virginia v. Black*, 538 U.S. 343 (2003).

[§] See Chapter 8.A.

direction (in a liberal state?) is the protection of public welfare by itself, and independent of its connection to the rights—or perhaps the welfare—of individuals ever a sufficient justification for the invocation of criminal sanctions?

Now, *Morissette* and *Sault Ste. Marie*, along with the article by Sayre, which first set out an account of "public welfare offenses," can be read as limited endorsements of strict liability, and as endorsements of limits on strict liability. In the face of legislative developments—in particular, the multiplication of strict liability offenses—Sayre can be seen as trying to preserve a *mens rea* requirement, while also leaving room for strict liability, if restricted to minor offenses. Is the problem that, once the genie of "public welfare offenses" had been let out of the bottle, it became impossible to place meaningful limits on strict liability? (Of course, German criminal law avoids this problem of framing an exception that does not swallow the rule by categorically rejecting strict liability.)

4. Even the Canadian Supreme Court, though otherwise clearly critical of absolute liability, does not dismiss pragmatic considerations altogether. Rather than implement its vision of *mens rea* at the expense of efficiency considerations, it sees its task as balancing considerations of justice and efficiency. This approach is foreign to a German observer; German courts, as noted previously, would shy away from explicitly engaging in this sort of balancing exercise, even if there were more reliable evidence in support of the claimed efficiencies of various alternatives, ranging from proof of intent, to proof of negligence, to a reverse burden of proof on the issue of negligence, to absolute liability. Although Justice Dickson summarily dismisses the "administrative argument," one might have expected a more careful investigation of such questions as why a requirement of negligence should seriously hamper criminal prosecution (compared to an affirmative "defense" of non-negligence)? In the area of public and professional duties, after all, it is generally not difficult to describe why the defendant had not acted according to the required standards. Absent constitutional principles, and the institution of judicial review of legislation in light of these principles (neither of which was available in Canada at the time of *Sault Ste. Marie*, which was decided before the enactment of the Canadian Charter of Rights and Freedoms in 1982) what would authorize a court to implement its view on a legal issue if that view conflicted with that of the legislature? What theory of statutory interpretation, and of the relationship between the judicial and the legislative branches, and the separation of powers, would such a decision imply?

5. Absolute liability offenses are, from the German viewpoint, in violation of an important constitutional principle, that is, the culpability principle, which the Federal Constitutional Court derives from human rights and basic constitutional maxims.* The fact, pointed to in *Morissette,* that penalties tend to be small ameliorates the size of the problem but does not solve it. It is understandable that the Canadian court searched for a way out by allowing defendants to escape liability by proving that they took reasonable care (strict liability rather than absolute liability). However, seen against the German constitutional culpability principle, such a way of distributing the burden of proof would hardly survive constitutional scrutiny. Under German law, defendants in criminal trials have no burden of proof at all; the state must prove even the non-existence of possible justifying or excusing circumstances. In the recent decision on "sentence bargaining" (or, more correctly, agreements between defendants and courts, rather than prosecutors) from March 19, 2013, BVerfGE ___, the German Federal Constitutional Court held that the constitutional framework for criminal trials demands that the state prove all matters concerning the offense and the offender's culpability. (Incidentally, to the extent that this reverse burden would amount to a requirement that the defendant disprove an element of the offense, in this case the element of "negligence," it would violate the due process guarantee of the U.S. Constitution as well.†)

6. Both *Morissette* and *Sault Ste. Marie* spend a great deal more time on the supposed exception to the rule than the rule itself; neither opinion gets around to setting out in any

---

* See Chapter 1.A.
† *In re Winship*, 397 U.S. 358 (1970); see also *Patterson v. New York*, 432 U.S. 197 (1977).

detail the basis of the *mens rea* requirement, or what Justice Dickson calls the "fundamental principles of penal liability" that the exception of absolute liability violates. Both opinions are remarkably content to rely on Blackstone and other previous statements of the *mens rea* rule, without giving a contemporary justification for it. As a result, the discussion is framed, even in the Canadian case and in Sayre's article, by a stark, and inapposite, contrast, between an eighteenth-century invocation of a "vicious will" as the benchmark of crime, on one hand, and a (similarly rudimentary) pragmatic efficiency calculus on the other.

Do not references to "vicious will" reflect a problematic and outdated conception of the essence of crime? (Is this the conception that underlies the Model Penal Code?) Why focus on "vicious will" and, for that matter, on intention as the core of wrongdoing? A strong emphasis on the subjective aspect of crime, including the offender's subjective state of mind makes sense in canon law or other religious notions of, for instance, divine judgment after death. For a secular criminal law in a liberal democracy, shouldn't the emphasis instead lie on the conduct's impact, for instance on other persons or the community? Sayre—and, following him, *Morissette* and *Sault Ste. Marie*—recognize the significance of protecting public welfare against offense. But why is the protection of public welfare necessarily incompatible with a commitment to principles of criminal liability? Is perhaps the source of the perceived incompatibility a conception of crime that revolves around a distinctly pre-liberal and radically subjective notion of crime as the manifestation of a "vicious will"?

The Canadian Supreme Court, in the context of considering the constitutional status of *Sault Ste. Marie*'s approach to absolute liability in the *Motor Vehicle Reference Case*, and subsequent cases on constitutional criminal law, has sought to develop a more contemporary account of crime, which attempts to go beyond Coke and Blackstone. Whether such an account, based on the recognition that "criminal law is rooted in the concepts of individual autonomy and free will,"* necessarily implies the rejection of absolute liability in all cases, is another question, which the Canadian Supreme Court answers one way (in the *Motor Vehicle Reference Case* in Chapter 3.A), and German criminal law answers in another.

C. Mistake

In general, mistake, like consent, comes in two forms: as an element-negating "defense" (*Tatbestandsirrtum*) and as a separate excuse (*Verbotsirrtum*), or—as the common law would have it, somewhat misleadingly—as a mistake of fact and a mistake of law. The latter type of mistake is by far the more interesting, and controversial, of the two. Here, it turns out, German criminal law is considerably more generous than Anglo-American criminal law. Common law courts still delight in invoking the maxim of "*ignorantia juris non excusat*," and even the Model Penal Code only carved out a narrow ignorance of law defense that might more properly be called a reliance on official mistake defense.

i. As element-negating

People v. Gudz
Supreme Court of New York, Appellate Division
18 A.D.3d 11, 793 N.Y.S.2d 556 (2005)

Cardona, P.J.

In July 2002 in the Town of Livingston, Columbia County, a witness observed defendant slowly drive his car across the center line of a road and strike a female bicyclist stopped alongside the road. The witness further observed defendant pull the struggling victim toward his vehicle. As the witness and other bystanders moved to intervene, the victim wriggled free and, after exchanging words with

---

* *R. v. Wholesale Travel Group Inc.*, [1991] 3 S.C.R. 154.

those seeking to intervene, defendant fled the scene. Defendant was subsequently arrested and charged with attempted kidnapping in the second degree.*

At his trial, defendant testified that the aforementioned events were the result of mistaken identity. In sum, defendant claimed that, after meeting an individual named "Judith" on the Internet, the two arranged to have defendant simulate an "abduction" of Judith and thereafter engage in sexual role-playing activities together. According to defendant, he and Judith planned this mock abduction for a number of months and the preparation included defendant scouting the location of the event in Livingston, observing Judith while she rode her bicycle in the neighboring countryside, and Judith executing a "consent form" in which she agreed to her own capture. Numerous electronic communications between defendant and Judith were introduced into evidence at trial in support of defendant's case. Finally, although the mock abduction was originally scheduled for March 2002, defendant claimed at trial that he and Judith had rescheduled for July 2002 and that, on the day he encountered the victim, he believed that she was Judith due to her physical appearance and the model of her bicycle.

Defendant was subsequently convicted as charged and sentenced, as a second felony offender, to 15 years in prison. Defendant now appeals, . . . challenging . . . the manner in which County Court instructed the trial jury on the legal precepts applicable to defendant's "mistake of fact" defense.

Penal Law § 15.20 provides, as is relevant here, that "[a] person is not relieved of criminal liability for conduct because he [or she] engages in such conduct under a mistaken belief of fact, unless . . . such factual mistake negatives the culpable mental state required for the commission of an offense" (Penal Law § 15.20 [1] [a]). In the instant matter, County Court began its jury instruction concerning defendant's mistake of fact defense with an appropriate recitation of this principle. However, the court continued its instruction [and] imposed a two-step analytical framework for the jury to follow. In order to find the defense applicable, the jury was first required to conclude that defendant's mistake was, in fact, subjectively and honestly believed in the mind of defendant. The jury was then instructed to make a second, objective determination as to whether such belief was reasonable under the circumstances. Because imposition of this second requirement does not comport with the plain wording of the defense as codified, we find it to be error and, accordingly, reverse defendant's conviction and remit for a new trial.

We first note that, as a matter of pure statutory construction, Penal Law § 15.20 (1) (a) is silent in terms of a reasonableness requirement, a factor which, in and of itself, should lead us to conclude that no such requirement was intended by the Legislature.[2] . . . Moreover, it has been recognized that, at the time that the mistake of fact defense was first codified in New York during the wholesale revision of the Penal Law in 1965, the Legislature was influenced by the promulgation of the Model Penal Code (hereinafter MPC) and intended that analogous provisions of the new Penal Law would be construed consistent therewith. Reasonableness is not set forth as an element of the mistake of fact defense in the MPC (see Model Penal Code § 2.04[1][a] [1985]; see also Model Penal Code § 2.04, Comment 1 [1985]). . . .

Turning to whether County Court's error can be deemed harmless, we note that defendant's mens rea was the predominant issue at trial and was the subject of considerable proof on both sides. . . . [T]here is simply no way of telling whether . . . the jury accepted defendant's version of events but did not find his beliefs to be objectively reasonable in compliance with the court's two-tier instruction. Under these circumstances, we cannot conclude that County Court's erroneous jury instruction was harmless beyond a reasonable doubt.

German Criminal Code

§ 16. Mistake of fact

(1) Who at the time of the commission of the offense is unaware of a fact which is a statutory element of the offense does not act with intention. Liability for negligent behavior remains unaffected.

---

* [N.Y. Penal Law §§ 135.20 ("A person is guilty of kidnapping in the second degree when he abducts another person."), 135.00(2) (" 'Abduct' means to restrain a person with intent to prevent his liberation by either (a) secreting or holding him in a place where he is not likely to be found, or (b) using or threatening to use deadly physical force.").—Eds.]

[2] It should also be noted that the legislatures of some other jurisdictions have affirmatively made the objective reasonableness of an accused's purported mistake a prerequisite to invocation of the mistake of fact defense (see e.g. Ind Stat Ann, § 35-41-3-7; Tex Stat Ann, Penal Code § 8.02 [a]).

(2) Who at the time of commission of the offence mistakenly assumes the existence of facts which would satisfy the elements of a more lenient provision, may only be punished for an intentional offense under the more lenient provision.

German Federal Court of Justice
3 StR 358/02, StV 2003, 393 (October 29, 2002)

Reasons

The regional court sentenced the defendant to a total sentence of imprisonment of three years for rape and sexual abuse of children in nine cases, and in one of these concomitantly with sexual coercion. The appeal was successful on the substantive issue.

The findings of the regional court do not support the conviction for rape or sexual coercion . . . Nor does the conviction for sexual abuse of children in nine cases (§ 176 para. 1 Criminal Code)* withstand legal examination. The finding of the regional court that the defendant had considered it at least to be possible that the children abused by him were not yet 14 years old is based on an assessment of the evidence which is defective in law. The defendant had admittedly confessed but did not admit knowledge about the children's ages. Neither the fact that the defendant had known the children "over a long period" nor the actual ages of the children at the time in question (13, 12 and 10 years old) justify the conclusion, without further findings for instance on physical development and appearance of the victims at the time in question, that the defendant had considered it at least to be possible that the boys were each not yet 14 years old.

German Federal Court of Justice
4 StR 371/90, BGHSt 37, 214 (October 25, 1990)

Facts

The defendant had decided in 1984 to kill M. who was his son from his first marriage and the heir to the defendant's farm. He had handed over the farm to his son in return for a grant of a usufruct [the legal right to derive profits from the farm—Eds.]; M. however disputed his right to the usufruct. M. was also responsible—mostly under the influence of alcohol—for a number of physical attacks. The defendant therefore feared, in addition to his destruction, the loss of his home, and experienced persistent disturbance of household peace. Although he himself profited financially from his son's land sales, and the handing over of the farm had freed him from his debts, he believed that the killing of his son was necessary to save himself and his family. He succeeded in persuading the co-defendant S. to carry out the killing in return for the promise of a sum of money; he felt himself as a father unable to commit the act. S. was to kill M. in the stable, which M. regularly crossed on his return home; the details were left to S. To ensure that other people came to no harm, the defendant informed the co-defendant S. about his son's habits and appearance, and also showed him a photograph. He called on S. on Nov. 24, 1985, and as there had been several failed attempts—in one of which S. had also seen the son—he set S. a deadline for carrying out the deed, which was now to be carried out with a small caliber firearm which had been found by the defendant. S. went to the defendant's farm on Nov. 25, 1985 and entered the stable. By coincidence he met the defendant there, who understood his plan and questioned him to make sure that he would be able to identify M. S. then waited in the stable for the victim to appear. It was dark, a certain amount of brightness only being generating by the snow on the ground. At about 7 p.m. B., a neighbor, visited the farm and opened the stable door. He resembled M. in stature and carried a bag in his hand, as M. was in the habit of doing. S. therefore assumed that this was M. and shot the unsuspecting victim from a short distance.

The regional court did not regard the defendant's behavior leading to the crime of Nov. 25, 1985 as a completed but only as an attempted incitement, because the killing of B. had not been included in his intention. The appeal in law by the public prosecutor's office is directed against this decision.

The appeal was successful and led to the quashing of the sentence.

---

* [§ 176 German Criminal Code (Sexual Abuse of Children)
(1) Who performs sexual acts with a person under fourteen years of age (child) or lets the child perform sexual acts with himself shall be punished with imprisonment from six months to ten years.—Eds.]

Reasons

1. The defendant intended to induce S. to kill his son. The regional court was correct not to regard him as the perpetrator but to examine his participation in the trial from the legal viewpoint of incitement.

2. The co-defendant S. killed B. thinking that he was M. Such a mistake by the perpetrator about the identity of the victim (*error in persona*) is of no legal significance so far as he is concerned (BGHSt 11, 268 (270)). The question of whether the perpetrator's mistake affects the criminal liability of the inciter is however disputed in the legal academic literature (references in Bemmann, MDR 1958, 817) since a decision of the Prussian Supreme Court [*Obertribunal*] in 1859 [*Rose-Rosahl Case*]—which answered the question in the negative (GA vol. 7, 332). There has so far been no recent decision by the highest courts.

a) In the literature one opinion stresses that the inciter has persuaded the perpetrator to kill a human being. This was a result which conformed sufficiently to the definition of the crime. In the same way as the perpetrator bore the risk of confusion as to the person concerned, so the inciter had to bear it also; he could not evade it by inducing another person directly to carry out the crime (see Cramer, in: Schönke-Schröder, StGB, 23rd edit., preliminary note to §§ 25 ff. marginal no. 47 with further references).

The contrary opinion emphasizes in essence that the inciter had to have had the actual crime in his mind. If the perpetrator killed a person other than the victim chosen by the inciter, the crime committed deviated in an essential respect from the inciter's purpose, and the incitement had therefore not succeeded. It is also claimed here that the mistaken killing appeared in relation to the inciter as a case of so-called miscarriage of an attack (*aberratio ictus*) leading to punishment for attempted incitement or for incitement to the attempt. This is confirmed by the consideration that otherwise the inciter would have to be held responsible for two (or more) killings if the perpetrator, after realization of his error, now killed the correct victim; this could not be correct because the inciter was only after one person (Roxin, in: LK, 10th edit., § 26 marginal no. 26 with further references).

Compromise opinions might accordingly differentiate between whether the inciter had left it to the perpetrator to individualize the victim, or whether the attack was directed against a highly personal legal interest or not . . .

b) According to the view of the Senate, the starting point must be the relationship of principal perpetration and participation which is regulated by statute. According to § 26 Criminal Code, the inciter is punished in the same way as the perpetrator. According to this the inciter in principle realizes the same wrong as the perpetrator and should be liable in the same way as he. No different considerations arise from the rationale of punishing incitement i.e. that the inciter causes the crime as a distant author of it and therefore causes the legal interest violation of the main act. The inciter attacks the protected legal interest by his influence on the perpetrator (Roxin, in: LK, 10th edit., preliminary note § 26 marginal nos. 1, 7; Jescheck, StrafR A T, 4th edit, p. 621; Otto, JuS 1982, 557 (558)). The protected legal interest in the crime of homicide is life; it is also violated—and not for instance merely endangered in the sense of an attempt—if the perpetrator is mistaken about the identity of the victim.

Accordingly special justification would be needed if a fact which is of no significance in relation to the perpetrator is in contrast to this, to be treated as legally significant in relation to the inciter. The Senate cannot see such a justification in the differing direction of purpose of the two defendants.

aa) Admittedly the legal association of principal perpetration and participation is not absolute. The inciter must, according to statute, act intentionally.* He is not liable in criminal law if the main crime deviates from his concept of it. The Senate is not able to acknowledge that the mistake of S. has made the crime into an event which is materially different for the defendant and which is not covered by his intention. The mistake of the co-defendant admittedly appears to the defendant to be a deviation from his own plans. But the deviation is legally insignificant because it remains within the boundaries of what is foreseeable according to general experience of life, so that a different assessment of the crime is not justified (BGHSt 7, 325 (329)). That also arises from the parallels which exist between the provisions about perpetration and participation; it must lead as a rule to the perpetrator's mistake about the person of the victim being also insignificant for the inciter. Admittedly the defendant did not intend here that B. should be killed. But he intended the killing of his son and he must allow the deviation of the course of the crime from this plan to be attributed to himself, as a confusion by the perpetrator about the victim was not outside any experience of life.

---

* [§ 26 StGB: Who intentionally induces another to intentionally commit an unlawful act, shall, as an inciter, be punished the same as a perpetrator.—Eds.].

The defendant, when he left the stable, actually deliberately left the matter out of his hands. In view of the lack of light, there was clearly a danger that the perpetrator would confuse other persons who coincidentally came to the stable with the intended victim. The defendant was in fact aware of this possibility because before going away he made sure by asking a question that S. could identify his son.

The fact that the course of events was not desired by the defendant does not prevent it being attributed to his intention. The Federal Court of Justice decided this in a case in which a participant in a crime mistakenly shot at a co-participant whom he thought to be a pursuer and wanted to eliminate; that pursuers should be shot had been agreed before the crime (BGHSt 11, 268). In that case the person injured by the shot had also to be punished as a co-perpetrator of the attempted homicide because the mistake of his accomplice about the identity of the supposed pursuer was insignificant for all the participants. The same applies for attribution in the relationship between perpetrator and inciter.

bb) The rules for miscarriage of an attack (*aberratio ictus*) are not applicable in cases like the present one. They have been developed—as a special case of causal deviation—for courses of events in which the perpetrator sees the object of attack in front of him, but injures another object in its place (see Puppe, GA 1984, 101 (121)). The transfer of these rules to other sets of facts causes difficulties (see BGHSt 9, 240 (242); Streng, JR 1987, 431 (433)) and is also not necessary.

The category of attribution of deviations from the imagined course of events where those deviations are within the boundaries of what is foreseeable according to general experience of life (BGHSt 9, 240 (242)) allows to prevent unreasonable results which are cited as an objection to the Senate's solution. If the perpetrator, after the recognition of his mistake, kills the victim described by the inciter as well, both homicides are as a rule to be attributed to the inciter even though he should only be convicted of one act of incitement to both killings. If however the perpetrator's mistake is based on circumstances which are not attributable to the inciter, i.e. are outside the experience of life, criminal liability is in this respect ruled out.

3. The defendant is therefore guilty not of attempted but of completed incitement to murder (§§ 211, 26 Criminal Code). The Senate has altered the conviction accordingly.

NOTES

1. The question discussed in *People v. Gudz* (are any mistakes of fact relevant when assessing intention, or only reasonable mistakes?) has not been the subject of a prominent appellate decision in Germany. There was never a serious dispute about the interpretation of the relevant provision in the statute, § 16 Criminal Code. Section 16 para. 1 sentence 1 does not refer to reasonableness. It is irrelevant why a defendant was unaware of a fact constituting an element of the offense description—*any* error of fact, be it stupid and careless, or not, means lack of intention. (But not lack of negligence. Why?)

Beyond the interpretation of the existing law, if one turns to criminal policy, there is some debate in the German literature about the appropriateness of the legislature's decision. If the crime in question was a crime against life or against physical integrity, § 16 para. 1 sentence 2 Criminal Code (mistake has no impact on criminal liability for negligence) provides a fallback position: the careless offender will be punished for negligent homicide or negligent causation of bodily harm. But there are offenses that can only be committed with intention, without a corresponding negligence offense in the code. (Recall that there are only very few negligence offenses in the German Criminal Code.) Important examples for this are sexual offenses. If a perpetrator in a sexual abuse case did not recognize the victim's age (see the first German case above, the judgment by the German Federal Court of Justice from 2002), although a reasonable person would have seen that this is a child, or if he carelessly assumed consent in the case of rape, German law demands acquittal. In contrast to other legal systems, German law does not define sexual abuse as a strict liability offense with view to a child's age (which is a consequence of the constitutional culpability principle*). But it would not pose constitutional problems if the legislature would add an offense of negligence to cover unreasonable mistakes of fact.

---

* See Chapter 1.B.

How should a legislature go about deciding in which offenses negligence should suffice for criminal liability, as a fallback for cases of unreasonable—in the sense of negligent—mistake? Are there any limits, constitutional or otherwise, on how negligence liability might be extended? At this point, negligence liability, in the German Criminal Code and the Model Penal Code, is limited to offenses against the person—homicide and (certain types of) assault. Could it be extended to offenses against property, against public safety, the environment, and so on?

2. As *Gudz* notes, the Model Penal Code does not limit mistake of fact to reasonable mistakes. It does, however, specify elsewhere that a "reasonable belief" includes "a belief which the actor is not reckless or negligent in holding," § 1.13(16), so that an unreasonable mistake would include both reckless and negligent beliefs. The question under the Model Penal Code would not be whether the mistake was reasonable or unreasonable, but whether it was reckless or negligent, in which case it would expose the defendant to liability for a recklessness or negligence offense, provided such an offense exists, of course.*

3. In general, the Model Penal Code drafters sought to simplify the analysis of questions of mistake, and to avoid classificatory difficulties of distinguishing between various types of mistake, notably mistakes of fact and mistakes of law. Mistakes of fact instead were reconceptualized as mistakes regarding elements of the offense, i.e., as mistakes that "negative[] the purpose, knowledge, belief, recklessness or negligence required to establish a material element of the offense" (§ 2.04(1)(a)), or element-negating mistakes for short. They were labeled "defenses," but not "affirmative defenses," clarifying substantively that they related to elements of the offense, rather than some defense, and procedurally that the defendant would not bear the burden of proof on the issue.† The Code also makes clear that element-negating mistakes could come either in the form of mistakes of fact or of law; if a matter of law appears as an element in the definition of an offense ("unlawfully," property of "another"), then a mistake regarding that element would count as an element-negating mistake. Again, what mattered was not the label, but the mistake's negation of an element of the offense. (The same analysis applies in German criminal law.)

An element-negating mistake was distinguished from the "belief that conduct does not legally constitute an offense" (§ 2.04(3)), formerly known as mistake or ignorance of law. This defense (to be proved by a preponderance of the evidence, § 2.04(4)) was available even if no element-negating mistake had occurred, and is better thought of as an excuse. For more on this type of mistake defense, see the next subsection.

Strictly speaking, the Model Code could have done without a provision on element-negating mistake. After all, this provision only spells out one implication of the general rule that criminal liability requires behavior that satisfies every offense element, including subjective offense elements, i.e., mental states. That the defendant could not be assigned the burden of proving this "defense" in turn follows from the rule that the state bears the burden of proving each element of the offense (§ 1.12(1)).

4. German criminal law doctrine has developed several categories to deal with "deviations from the imagined course of events." Often, events will not develop exactly as the offender had anticipated. For instance, if the offender planned to drown the victim in a river by throwing him from a bridge, the victim might die by falling on the concrete base of the bridge before getting in contact with water. The Federal Court of Justice's reference (in the case about the ex-farmer and his son) to "what is foreseeable according to the general experience of life" is meant to deal with such deviations. If, like in the bridge example, the deviation is within limits and foreseeable, the perpetrator will be punished for intentional homicide or murder despite the slight difference between his plan and the actual course of events.

---

* For a discussion of this issue in the context of defense elements, rather than offense elements, see Chapter 13.
† For the MPC's treatment of "affirmative defenses," see MPC § 1.12(1)–(3).

But German case law and the majority opinion in the literature draw the line where the act goes astray in a more pronounced way, amounting to a deviation labeled with the Latin phrase *aberratio ictus* ("deviation of the stroke"). This refers to missing the person one has aimed at and accidentally hitting another person. Under such circumstances, the error concerning the course of events will be a relevant one and the injury to the accidental victim will not count as intentional (but will be punished as negligent homicide or assault). This is the majority opinion; others treat *aberratio ictus* as irrelevant, under an "equivalence" theory: (1) equivalence: if the affected legal good is equivalent to the targeted one (e.g., the offender kills one person rather than another) or (2) if the actual harm can be causally attributed to the offender's act as foreseeable.*

From such *aberratio ictus*-cases, another category is distinguished, labeled *error in persona* ("error about the person"). The difference is the following: the perpetrator sees a person, aims at her and hits her—afterwards, it turns out to be a case of misidentification. This was the situation for the defendant S. in the German case, who wanted to kill the man he saw but erred about his identity. The Federal Court of Justice reiterates the general opinion: such an error is irrelevant. The defendant knows the relevant facts (he saw a human being and killed it), and the error concerning identity is not covered by § 16 para. 1 Criminal Code. There was agreement on this before the judgment, but it got more complicated because the Court needed to decide what S.'s error meant for M., who had incited S. to the killing. The Court here emphasized that the wording of § 26 Criminal Code provides that inciters will be punished as if they were principals.†

5. The Model Penal Code would handle these scenarios not under the rubric of mistake (and *mens rea*), but under that of causation (discussed in Chapter 9).

(1) The bridge scenario would be analyzed as a matter of (proximate, or legal) causation, on the assumption that the *mens rea* requirement had been satisfied: the question would be whether "the actual result . . . is not *too remote or accidental* in its occurrence to have a [just] bearing on the actor's liability or on the gravity of his offense."‡ Whether the same result would be reached under German and American law would depend on the difference—or lack thereof—between the relevant standards: foreseeability and "not too remote or accidental." (Foreseeability would be among the considerations to be taken into account in applying the deliberately flexible MPC standard. In New York criminal law, it is the decisive consideration.§)

(2) An "error in persona" (more generally an "*error in persona vel in obiecto*") would be considered a "divergence between result designed or contemplated and actual result."¶ The test would be whether "the actual result differs from that designed or contemplated, as the case may be, only in the respect that a *different person or different property* is injured or affected" (emphasis added).

(3) The same test would be applied to "*aberratio ictus*" cases. Here too the defendant would be held to have had the requisite *mens rea* with respect to the general result element of the offense: in the case of homicide, the death of "another human being." Since the definition of homicide does not specify a particular human being, the *mens rea* requirement is satisfied as long as the defendant has the requisite *mens rea* with respect to the death of anyone who qualifies as "another human being."**

Does it make sense to treat the third "deviation from the imagined course of events" differently from the first two? From an *error in persona* in particular? Leaving aside the technical question of the choice of the proper doctrinal tool of analysis (*mens rea* vs.

---

* See Note 5 on the Model Penal Code position.
† For more on accomplice liability, see Chapter 10.
‡ MPC § 2.03(2)(b) (emphasis added)).
§ See *People v. Kibbe*, 35 N.Y.2d 407 (1974).
¶ MPC § 2.03(2)(a).
** Compare the German "equivalence" theory, discussed in Note 4.

causation), what may account for the difference in outcome (in the case of *aberratio ictus*, if not in the other two)? Consider these cases from the Model Penal Code's treatmentist perspective (focusing on a diagnosis of the offender's criminal dangerousness)? What conception of *mens rea*, and of culpability, might be seen to underlie the German approach to these questions? Does the German culpability principle come into play here?

6. Note that the German Federal Court of Justice in the case against M. cites a nineteenth-century ruling by the Prussian Obertribunal. This rarely happens—after all, the text of the Criminal Code and foremost the state of criminal doctrine has evolved much since the nineteenth century so that there is not much to be gained by referring to older court decisions. Here, the unusual features of the case might have prompted the Federal Court of Justice to mention the one precedent available in German legal history (but only in passing, without seriously analyzing the older ruling).

The *Rose-Rosahl Case* was decided in 1858 (and published a year later); the German Criminal Code was not enacted until 1871, though the Prussian Criminal Code, upon which it is based, stems from 1851. (The date of the codes is of limited significance since neither code settles the issue.) Given the relative, and deliberate, sparseness of the German Criminal Code then and now, the decision instead turns on a consideration of arguments developed in the criminal law literature, i.e., in criminal law science.

The facts in the case are suitably Romantic, possibly contributing to its continuing attraction. The "wood merchant Rosahl" hired the "laborer Rose" to kill the "carpenter Schliebe," with whom he had a business dispute. Rose waylaid Schliebe on a country road in the woods between the towns of Lieskau and Schiepzig. When he saw a man approach him in the dusk, he fired, only to find out later that the man he had killed was not Schliebe, but the seventeen-year-old "cantor's son Harnisch," who happened to be walking by. To this day, a small memorial stone marks the spot (the "bloodstone of Lieskau"), bearing the inscription "Here fell by murderer's hand on 11 September 1858 Ernst Heinrich Harnisch." There is a famous, and still very entertaining and illuminating, collection of early nineteenth century criminal cases by P.J.A. Feuerbach, available in English translation.*

ii. As excuse (ignorance of law)

People v. Marrero
Court of Appeals of New York
69 N.Y.2d 382, 507 N.E.2d 1068 (1987)

Bellacosa, Judge.

The defense of mistake of law (Penal Law § 15.20[a], [d]) is not available to a Federal corrections officer arrested in a Manhattan social club for possession of a loaded .38 caliber automatic pistol who claimed he mistakenly believed he was entitled, pursuant to the interplay of CPL 2.10, 1.20 and Penal Law § 265.20, to carry a handgun without a permit as a peace officer . . .

Defendant was a Federal corrections officer in Danbury, Connecticut, and asserted that status at the time of his arrest in 1977. He claimed at trial that there were various interpretations of fellow officers and teachers, as well as the peace officer statute itself, upon which he relied for his mistaken belief that he could carry a weapon with legal impunity.

The starting point for our analysis is the New York mistake statute as an outgrowth of the dogmatic common-law maxim that ignorance of the law is no excuse. The central issue is whether defendant's personal misreading or misunderstanding of a statute may excuse criminal conduct in the circumstances of this case.

The common-law rule on mistake of law was clearly articulated in *Gardner v. People*, 62 N.Y. 299. In Gardner, the defendants misread a statute and mistakenly believed that their conduct was legal. The court insisted, however, that the "mistake of law" did not relieve the defendants of criminal liability . . .

---

* See P.J.A. Feuerbach, *Narratives of Remarkable Criminal Trials* (trans. Lady Duff Gordon, 1846).

The desirability of the Gardner-type outcome, which was to encourage the societal benefit of individuals' knowledge of and respect for the law, is underscored by Justice Holmes' statement: "It is no doubt true that there are many cases in which the criminal could not have known that he was breaking the law, but to admit the excuse at all would be to encourage ignorance where the lawmaker has determined to make men know and obey, and justice to the individual is rightly outweighed by the larger interests on the other side of the scales." (Holmes, The Common Law, at 48 [1881]).

The revisers of New York's Penal Law intended no fundamental departure from this common-law rule in Penal Law § 15.20, which provides in pertinent part:

§ 15.20. Effect of ignorance or mistake upon liability.

2. A person is not relieved of criminal liability for conduct because he engages in such conduct under a mistaken belief that it does not, as a matter of law, constitute an offense, unless such mistaken belief is founded upon an official statement of the law contained in (a) a statute or other enactment ... (d) an interpretation of the statute or law relating to the offense, officially made or issued by a public servant, agency, or body legally charged or empowered with the responsibility or privilege of administering, enforcing or interpreting such statute or law.

This section was added to the Penal Law as part of the wholesale revision of the Penal Law in 1965. When this provision was first proposed, commentators viewed the new language as codifying "the established common law maxim on mistake of law, while at the same time recognizing a defense when the erroneous belief is founded upon an "official statement of the law' " (Note, Proposed Penal Law of New York, 64 Colum L. Rev. 1469, 1486 [1964]).

The defendant claims as a first prong of his defense that he is entitled to raise the defense of mistake of law under section 15.20(2)(a) because his mistaken belief that his conduct was legal was founded upon an official statement of the law contained in the statute itself. Defendant argues that his mistaken interpretation of the statute was reasonable in view of the alleged ambiguous wording of the peace officer exemption statute, and that his "reasonable" interpretation of an "official statement" is enough to satisfy the requirements of subdivision (2)(a). However, the whole thrust of this exceptional exculpatory concept, in derogation of the traditional and common-law principle, was intended to be a very narrow escape valve. Application in this case would invert that thrust and make mistake of law a generally applied or available defense instead of an unusual exception which the very opening words of the mistake statute make so clear, i.e., "A person is not relieved of criminal liability for conduct ... unless" (Penal Law § 15.20). The momentarily enticing argument by defendant that his view of the statute would only allow a defendant to get the issue generally before a jury further supports the contrary view because that consequence is precisely what would give the defense the unintended broad practical application.

The prosecution further counters defendant's argument by asserting that one cannot claim the protection of mistake of law under section 15.20(2)(a) simply by misconstruing the meaning of a statute but must instead establish that the statute relied on actually permitted the conduct in question and was only later found to be erroneous. To buttress that argument, the People analogize New York's official statement defense to the approach taken by the Model Penal Code (MPC). Section 2.04 of the MPC provides:

Section 2.04. Ignorance or Mistake.

(3) A belief that conduct does not legally constitute an offense is a defense to a prosecution for that offense based upon such conduct when ... (b) he acts in reasonable reliance upon an official statement of the law, *afterward determined to be invalid or erroneous*, contained in (i) a statute or other enactment" (emphasis added).

Although the drafters of the New York statute did not adopt the precise language of the Model Penal Code provision with the emphasized clause, it is evident and has long been believed that the Legislature intended the New York statute to be similarly construed. ...

It was early recognized that the "official statement" mistake of law defense was a statutory protection against prosecution based on reliance of a statute that did in fact authorize certain conduct. "It seems obvious that society must rely on some statement of the law, and that conduct which is in fact 'authorized' ... should not be subsequently condemned. The threat of punishment under these circumstances can have no deterrent effect unless the actor doubts the validity of the official pronouncement—*a questioning of authority that is itself undesirable*" (Note, Proposed Penal Law of New York, 64 Colum.L.Rev. 1469, 1486 [emphasis added]). While providing a narrow escape hatch, the idea was simultaneously to encourage the public to read and rely on official statements of the law, not to have individuals conveniently and personally question the validity and interpretation of the law and act on that basis. If later the statute was invalidated, one who mistakenly acted in reliance on the authorizing statute would be relieved of criminal liability. That makes sense and is fair. To go further does not make sense and would create a legal chaos based on individual selectivity.

In the case before us, the underlying statute never in fact authorized the defendant's conduct; the defendant only thought that the statutory exemptions permitted his conduct when, in fact, the primary statute clearly forbade his conduct. Moreover, by adjudication of the final court to speak on the subject in this very case, it turned out that even the exemption statute did not permit this defendant to possess the weapon. It would be ironic at best and an odd perversion at worst for this court now to declare that the same defendant is nevertheless free of criminal responsibility.

The "official statement" component in the mistake of law defense in both paragraphs (a) and (d) adds yet another element of support for our interpretation and holding. Defendant tried to establish a defense under Penal Law § 15.20(2)(d) as a second prong. But the interpretation of the statute relied upon must be "officially made or issued by a public servant, agency or body legally charged or empowered with the responsibility or privilege of administering, enforcing or interpreting such statute or law." We agree with the People that the trial court also properly rejected the defense under Penal Law § 15.20(2)(d) since none of the interpretations which defendant proffered meets the requirements of the statute. The fact that there are various complementing exceptions to section 15.20, none of which defendant could bring himself under, further emphasizes the correctness of our view which decides this case under particular statutes with appropriate precedential awareness.

[M]istake of law is a viable exemption in those instances where an individual demonstrates an effort to learn what the law is, relies on the validity of that law and, later, it is determined that there was a mistake in the law itself.

The modern availability of this defense is based on the theory that where the government has affirmatively, albeit unintentionally, misled an individual as to what may or may not be legally permissible conduct, the individual should not be punished as a result. This is salutary and enlightened and should be firmly supported in appropriate cases. However, it also follows that where, as here, the government is not responsible for the error (for there is none except in the defendant's own mind), mistake of law should not be available as an excuse.

We recognize that some legal scholars urge that the mistake of law defense should be available more broadly where a defendant misinterprets a potentially ambiguous statute not previously clarified by judicial decision and reasonably believes in good faith that the acts were legal. Professor Perkins, a leading supporter of this view, has said: "[i]f the meaning of a statute is not clear, and has not been judicially determined, one who has acted 'in good faith' should not be held guilty of crime if his conduct would have been proper had the statute meant what he 'reasonably believed' it to mean, even if the court should decide later that the proper construction is otherwise." (Perkins, Ignorance and Mistake in Criminal Law, 88 U.Pa.L.Rev. 35, 45.) In support of this conclusion Professor Perkins cites two cases: State v. Cutter, 36 N.J.Law. 125 and Burns v. State, 123 Tex.Cr.R. 611, 61 S.W.2d 512. In both these cases mistake of law was viewed as a valid defense to offenses where a specific intent (i.e., willfully, knowingly, etc.) was an element of the crime charged. In Burns, the court recognized mistake of law as a defense to extortion. The statute defining "extortion" made the "willful" doing of the prohibited act an essential ingredient of the offense. The court, holding that mistake of law is a defense only where the mistake negates the specific intent required for conviction, borrowed language from the Cutter case: "In State v. Cutter . . . the court said: "The argument goes upon the legal maxim ignorantia legis neminem excusat. But this rule, in its application to the law of crimes, is subject . . . to certain important exceptions. Where the act done is malum in se, or where the law which has been infringed was settled and plain, the maxim, in its rigor, will be applied; but where the law is not settled, or is obscure, *and where the guilty intention, being a necessary constituent of the particular offence, is dependent on a knowledge of the law, this rule, if enforced, would be misapplied*' " (Burns v. State, 123 Tex.Cr.R. at 613, 61 S.W.2d at 513, supra [emphasis added]). Thus, while Professor Perkins states that the defense should be available in cases where the defendant claims mistaken reliance on an ambiguous statute, the cases he cites recognize the defense only where the law was ambiguous and the ignorance or mistake of law negated the requisite intent. In this case, the forbidden act of possessing a weapon is clear and unambiguous, and only by the interplay of a double exemption does defendant seek to escape criminal responsibility, i.e., the peace officer statute and the mistake statute.

We conclude that the better and correctly construed view is that the defense should not be recognized, except where specific intent is an element of the offense or where the misrelied-upon law has later been properly adjudicated as wrong. Any broader view fosters lawlessness . . . Strong public policy reasons underlie the legislative mandate and intent which we perceive in rejecting defendant's construction of New York's mistake of law defense statute. If defendant's argument were accepted, the exception would swallow the rule. Mistakes about the law would be encouraged, rather than respect for and adherence to law. There would be an infinite number of mistake of law defenses which could be devised from a good-faith, perhaps reasonable but mistaken, interpretation of criminal statutes, many of which are concededly complex. Even more troublesome are the opportunities for wrongminded individuals to contrive in bad faith solely to get an exculpatory notion before the jury. These are not in terrorem arguments disrespectful of appropriate adjudicative procedures; rather, they are the realistic and practical consequences were the dissenters' views to prevail. Our holding comports with a statutory scheme which was not designed to allow false and diversionary stratagems to be provided for many more cases than the statutes contemplated. This would not serve the ends of justice but rather would serve game playing and evasion from properly imposed criminal responsibility.

Accordingly, the order of the Appellate Division should be affirmed.

Hancock, Judge (dissenting).

The rule adopted by the majority prohibiting the defense of mistake of law under Penal Law § 15.20 (2)(a) in the circumstances here is directly contrary to the plain dictates of the statute and a rejection of the jurisprudential reforms and legislative policies underlying its enactment. For these reasons, as more fully explained herein, we cannot agree with this decision.

I

The basic difference which divides the court may be simply put. Suppose the case of a man who has committed an act which is criminal not because it is inherently wrong or immoral but solely because it violates a criminal statute. He has committed the act in complete good faith under the mistaken but entirely reasonable assumption that the act does not constitute an offense because it is permitted by the wording of the statute. Does the law require that this man be punished? The majority says that it does and holds that (1) Penal Law § 15.20(2)(a) must be construed so that the man is precluded from offering a defense based on his mistake of law and (2) such construction is compelled by prevailing considerations of public policy and criminal jurisprudence. We take issue with the majority on both propositions.

There can be no question that under the view that the purpose of the criminal justice system is to punish blameworthiness or "choosing freely to do wrong,"[1] our supposed man who has acted innocently and without any intent to do wrong should not be punished. Indeed, under some standards of morality he has done no wrong at all.[2] Since he has not knowingly committed a wrong there can be no reason for society to exact retribution. Because the man is law-abiding and would not have acted but for his mistaken assumption as to the law, there is no need for punishment to deter him from further unlawful conduct. Traditionally, however, under the ancient rule of Anglo-American common law that ignorance or mistake of law is no excuse, our supposed man would be punished.

The maxim "ignorantia legis neminem excusat"[3] finds its roots in Medieval law when the "actor's intent was irrelevant since the law punished the *act itself*" (United States v. Barker, D.C.Cir., 514 F.2d 208, 228 [Bazelon, Ch. J., concurring]; emphasis in original) and when, for example, the law recognized no difference between an intentional killing and one that was accidental. Although the common law has gradually evolved from its origins in Anglo-Germanic tribal law (adding the element of intent [*mens rea*] and recognizing defenses based on the actor's mental state . . .) the dogmatic rule that ignorance or mistake of law is no excuse has remained unaltered. Various justifications have been offered for the rule, but all are frankly pragmatic and utilitarian—preferring the interests of society (e.g., in deterring criminal conduct, fostering orderly judicial administration, and preserving the primacy of the rule of law) to the interest of the individual in being free from punishment except for intentionally engaging in conduct which he knows is criminal.

Today there is widespread criticism of the common-law rule mandating categorical preclusion of the mistake of law defense (see, e.g., Model Penal Code § 2.04, comment 3, at 274–276 [Official Draft and Revised Comments 1985]). The utilitarian arguments for retaining the rule have been drawn into serious question but the fundamental objection is that it is simply wrong to punish someone who, in good-faith reliance on the wording of a statute, believed that what he was doing was lawful. It

---

[1] "Historically, our substantive criminal law is based upon a theory of punishing the vicious will. It postulates a free agent confronted with a choice between doing right and doing wrong and choosing freely to do wrong" (Pound, Introduction to Sayre, Cases on Criminal Law [1927], quoted in Morissette v. United States, 342 U.S. 246, 250, n. 4, 72 S.Ct. 240, 243, n. 4, 96 L.Ed. 288).

[2] Kant, Philosophy of Law, at 13, 14, 28, 37 (Hastie trans. 1887); cf., Bentham, Theory of Legislation, at 1–4 (Ogden ed. 1931).

[3] Although "ignorantia legis" does not literally refer to mistake of law, the maxim is ordinarily understood, as we use it here, to include both ignorance and mistake of law.

is contrary to "the notion that punishment should be conditioned on a showing of subjective moral blameworthiness." This basic objection to the maxim "ignorantia legis neminem excusat" may have had less force in ancient times when most crimes consisted of acts which by their very nature were recognized as evil (malum in se). In modern times, however, with the profusion of legislation making otherwise lawful conduct criminal (malum prohibitum), the "common law fiction that every man is presumed to know the law has become indefensible in fact or logic" ...

II

.... It is fundamental that in interpreting a statute, a court should look first to the particular words of the statute in question, being guided by the accepted rule that statutory language is generally given its natural and most obvious meaning. Here, there is but one natural and obvious meaning of the statute: that if a defendant can establish that his mistaken belief was "founded upon" his interpretation of "an official statement of the law contained in ... statute" (Penal Law § 15.20[a]), he should have a defense. No other natural and obvious meaning has been suggested.

It is difficult to imagine a case more squarely within the wording of Penal Law § 15.20(2)(a) or one more fitted to what appears clearly to be the intended purpose of the statute than the one before us ...

Defendant stands convicted after a jury trial of criminal possession of a weapon in the third degree for carrying a loaded firearm without a license (Penal Law § 265.02).... On defendant's motion before trial the court dismissed the indictment, holding that he was a peace officer as defined by CPL 2.10(26) and, therefore, exempted by Penal Law § 265.20 from prosecution under Penal Law § 265.02.[7] The People appealed and the Appellate Division reversed and reinstated the indictment by a 3–2 vote.[8] Defendant's appeal to this court was dismissed for failure to prosecute and the case proceeded to trial. The trial court rejected defendant's efforts to establish a defense of mistake of law under Penal Law § 15.20(2)(a). He was convicted and the Appellate Division has affirmed [without an opinion].

Defendant's mistaken belief that, as a Federal corrections officer, he could legally carry a loaded weapon without a license was based on the express exemption from criminal liability under Penal Law § 265.02 accorded in Penal Law § 265.20(a)(1)(a) to "peace officers" as defined in the Criminal Procedure Law and on his reading of the statutory definition for "peace officer" in CPL 2.10(26) as meaning a correction officer "of *any* penal correctional institution" (emphasis added), including an institution not operated by New York State. Thus, he concluded erroneously that, as a corrections officer in a Federal prison, he was a "peace officer" and, as such, exempt by the express terms of Penal Law § 265.20(a)(1)(a). This mistaken belief, based in good faith on the statute defining "peace officer" (CPL 2.10), is, defendant contends, the precise sort of "mistaken belief ... founded upon an official statement of the law contained in ... a statute or other enactment" which gives rise to a mistake of law defense under Penal Law § 15.20(2)(a). He points out, of course, that when he acted in reliance on his belief he had no way of foreseeing that a court would eventually resolve the question of the statute's meaning against him and rule that his belief had been mistaken, as three of the five-member panel at the Appellate Division ultimately did in the first appeal.

The majority, however, has accepted the People's argument that to have a defense under Penal Law § 15.20(2)(a) "a defendant must show that the statute *permitted his conduct*, not merely that he believed it did." Here, of course, defendant cannot show that the statute permitted his conduct. To the contrary, the question has now been decided by the Appellate Division and it is settled that defendant was not exempt under Penal Law § 265.20(a)(1)(a). Therefore, the argument goes, defendant can have no mistake of law defense. While conceding that reliance on a statutory provision which is later found to be invalid would constitute a mistake of law defense (see Model Penal Code § 2.04 [b][i]), the People's flat position is that "one's mistaken reading of a statute, no matter how reasonable or well intentioned, is not a defense."

[This] construction leads to an anomaly: only a defendant who is not mistaken about the law when he acts has a mistake of law defense. In other words, a defendant can assert a defense under Penal Law § 15.20(2)(a) only when his reading of the statute is correct—not mistaken. Such construction is

---

[7] By virtue of Penal Law § 265.20(a)(1)(a) "peace officers," as defined in the CPL 1.20, are expressly exempt from criminal liability under Penal Law § 265.02. CPL 1.20 incorporates the definition of "peace officer" in CPL 2.10, which includes "correction officers of any state correction facility or of any penal correctional institution." Penal Law § 265.20 (a) was amended in 1980 to remove "peace officer" from (a)(1)(a) and to include "peace officer" in (a)(1)(c) (L.1980, ch. 843, §§ 44, 45).

[8] The majority held that Penal Law § 265.20(a)(1)(a) included only State correction officers. The dissenters agreed with Supreme Court that under the unambiguous language of CPL 2.10 defendant was a "peace officer" within the meaning of Penal Law § 265.20(a)(1)(a) and exempt from prosecution under Penal Law § 265.02.

obviously illogical; it strips the statute of the very effect intended by the Legislature in adopting the mistake of law defense. The statute is of no benefit to a defendant who has proceeded in good faith on an erroneous but concededly reasonable interpretation of a statute, as defendant presumably has. An interpretation of a statute which produces an unreasonable or incongruous result and one which defeats the obvious purpose of the legislation and renders it ineffective should be rejected.

Finally, the majority's disregard of the natural and obvious meaning of Penal Law § 15.20(2)(a) so that a defendant mistaken about the law is deprived of a defense under the statute amounts, we submit, to a rejection of the obvious legislative purposes and policies favoring jurisprudential reform underlying the statute's enactment. It is self-evident that in enacting Penal Law § 15.20(2) as part of the revision and modernization of the Penal Law the Legislature intended to effect a needed reform by abolishing what had long been considered the unjust archaic common-law rule totally prohibiting mistake of law as a defense. Had it not so intended it would simply have left the common-law rule intact. In place of the abandoned "ignorantia legis" common-law maxim the Legislature enacted a rule which permits no defense for ignorance of law but allows a mistake of law defense in specific instances, including the one presented here: when the defendant's erroneous belief is founded on an "official statement of the law."

This reform, like the changes adopted in Model Penal Code § 2.04(3) and those proposed by various legal commentators, was prompted by the prevailing dissatisfaction with the common-law rule. Both the Model Penal Code and Penal Law § 15.20(2) accept the general concept that the outright prohibition of the mistake of law defense under the common law should be replaced with a rule permitting "a limited defense based on a reasonable belief on the part of the defendant that the law is such that his conduct does not constitute an offense" (Model Penal Code § 2.04, comment 3, at 274 [Official Draft and Revised Comments 1985]).

The majority construes the statute, however, so as to rule out any defense based on mistake of law. In so doing, it defeats the only possible purpose for the statute's enactment and resurrects the very rule which the Legislature rejected in enacting Penal Law § 15.20(2)(a) as part of its modernization and reform of the Penal Law. It is fundamental that a construction of a statute which does not further the statute's object, spirit and purpose must be rejected . . .

III

Any fair reading of the majority opinion, we submit, demonstrates that the decision to reject a mistake of law defense is based on considerations of public policy and on the conviction that such a defense would be bad, rather than on an analysis of CPL 15.20(2)(a) under the usual principles of statutory construction. The majority warns, for example, that if the defense were permitted "the exception would swallow the rule"; that "[m]istakes about the law would be encouraged"; that an "infinite number of mistake of law defenses . . . could be devised"; and that "wrongminded individuals [could] contrive in bad faith solely to get an exculpatory notion before the jury."

These considerations, like the People's argument that the mistake of law defense "would encourage ignorance where knowledge is socially desired," are the very considerations which have been consistently offered as justifications for the maxim "ignorantia legis." That these justifications are unabashedly utilitarian cannot be questioned. It could not be put more candidly than by Justice Holmes in defending the common-law maxim more than 100 years ago: "*Public policy sacrifices the individual to the general good* . . . It is no doubt true that there are many cases in which the criminal could not have known that he was breaking the law, but to admit the excuse at all would be to encourage ignorance where the law-maker has determined to make men know and obey, and *justice to the individual is rightly outweighed by the larger interests on the other side of the scales*" (Holmes, The Common Law, at 48 [1881]; emphasis added). Regardless of one's attitude toward the acceptability of these views in the 1980's, the fact remains that the Legislature in abandoning the strict "ignorantia legis" maxim must be deemed to have rejected them . . .

It is no answer to protest that the defense may become a "false and diversionary stratagem[ ], or that "wrongminded individuals [could] contrive" an "infinite number of mistake of law defenses"; for it is the very business of the courts to separate the true claims from the false. Such in terrorem arguments should have no more force here than similar objections which doubtless were voiced with equal intensity to the long-accepted defenses of justification, accident, mistake of fact, insanity, entrapment, duress and intoxication. As Justice Holmes wrote in commenting on John Austin's argument that permitting the mistake of law defense would present courts with problems they were not prepared to solve: "If justice requires the fact to be ascertained, the difficulty of doing so is no ground for refusing to try" (Holmes, The Common Law, at 48 [1881]) . . .

German Federal Court of Justice
5 StR 370/92, BGHSt 39, 1 (November 3, 1992)
Border Guard Case*

[For the facts of the case, see Chapter 2.A above]

2. The defendants committed the—in default of any ground of justification which could be taken into account, unlawful—killing on command. The findings showed that they did not recognize as they committed their act that the carrying out of the command violated criminal statutory provisions. This does not, however, negate their culpability.

(a) ...

(b) According to § 5 para. 1 Military Criminal Law Act (WStG)† the subordinate is only guilty if he recognizes that it is a question of an unlawful act or this is obvious according to the circumstances known to him. The first of the stated prerequisites is ... not present. Whether the defendants are excused in accordance with § 5 para. 1 Military Criminal Law Act is consequently dependent on whether it was obvious according to the circumstances known to them that a command had been given to them to commit an unlawful act in the sense of the Criminal Code....

The regional court accepts that it was obvious for the defendants according to the circumstances known to them that they were committing a crime of homicide in the sense of the Criminal Code by the shooting which was the subject of the command to them. This assessment cannot be refuted. The regional court did not overlook the fact that the defendants as border soldiers of the GDR were exposed to an especially intensive political indoctrination and that they had previously "grown up in the spirit of socialism with corresponding hostile images of the Federal Republic of Germany and of persons who wanted to leave the GDR by surmounting the barrier installations." Even in these circumstances the chamber did not ignore the high requirements which are to be placed on obviousness in the sense of § 5 para. 1 Military Criminal Law Act. The soldier has no duty of examination (Scherer-Alff, SoldatenG, 6th edit. (1988), § 11 marginal no. 29). If he harbors doubts which he cannot get rid of, he may follow the command; the violation of the criminal law is only obvious when it is beyond all doubt...

There can be no objection on legal grounds to the district court nevertheless finding that it was obvious in the circumstances that the shooting here violated criminal law. The district court emphasizes pertinently the "requirement of humanity" which includes, amongst other things, the principle that the criminal also has a right to life. By this it meant that it was plainly self-evident that the State does not have the right, in order to prevent this impermissible crossing of the border, to cause the killing of a person who, without threatening others, intended to go from one part of Berlin into another by surmounting the wall. It is conceded in favor of the appeals in law that the application of the element "obvious" is very difficult here. After all, during the long years in which there were shootings at the wall and at the other inner German borders, the people in the GDR who bore responsibility in politics, the military, justice and scholarship were not known to have expressed a view publicly about killing on the border. Proceedings against marksmen had not been taken. In the light of the life history and environment of the defendants it also does not seem appropriate to reproach them with "complacency," "blindness to the law" and not thinking for themselves. Finally, it should not be held against the accused H. that "according to his own admission he recognized immediately after the act that his action against S. was inhuman"; this circumstance can also have as its explanation that confrontation with the consequences of the shots awoke the conscience of the accused for the first time.

Nevertheless, the view of the regional court chamber that the killing of an unarmed fugitive by continuous fire in the given circumstances was an act so dreadful and so beyond any rational justification that the violation of the elementary prohibition of killing was easily comprehensible, and therefore obvious, even for an indoctrinated person, should, in the end, be accepted. The fact that the great majority of the population of the GDR disapproved of the use of firearms at the border corresponds with this. It is generally known that this was the case. Even the circumstance that the general command situation gave secrecy priority over taking rapid steps to save the life of the victim shows to what degree those responsible assumed disapproval by the population. The victim S., a carpenter, had strictly refused to join the border troops.

---

* [This is based on a translation which appears in Sourcebook on German Law, Raymond Youngs, 2nd edition, Cavendish (London) 2002 and is reproduced with the permission of Routledge Cavendish.—Eds.]

† [Military Criminal Law Act § 5(1) (Acts on Command) ("A subordinate who commits a wrongful act which fulfils the elements of a criminal offense on command only acts culpably if he recognises that this is a wrongful act or if this is obvious according to the circumstances know to him.")—Eds.]

3. The judge of fact did not exclude the possibility that the defendants believed, in accordance with the command, they had to kill a violator of the border in order to prevent his flight even if the command was unlawful. There can be no objection on legal grounds to the fact that the judge of fact accepted that this mistake represented, as an assumption of a ground of justification which was not recognized, a mistake of law which, in the sense of § 17 sentence 2 Criminal Code, could have been avoided by the defendants. The judge of fact again referred to the fact that life was the highest of all legal interests. That cannot be opposed on legal grounds. The judge of fact would also have been able to refer in this connection to the fact that the defendants were told in their training that commands which offended against humanity did not need to be followed...

4. The assessment of the sentencing decision withstands the factual and legal examination. The judge of fact did not overlook the fact that the defendants had only grown up after the building of the Berlin Wall and according to their origin and life history had no opportunity to subject their indoctrination to a critical assessment. Their vocational training as manual workers and likewise their school education obviously could not have contributed to this. The defendants were quite far down in the military hierarchy. They are in a certain way also victims of the circumstances connected with this border. As the defence pertinently explained, circumstances which the defendants do not have to defend have led to being called to account under the criminal law prior to trials against GDR officials who had a larger overview and a more discriminating education. All this urged towards lenient punishments. The regional court took account of this.*

German Criminal Code

§ 17. Mistake about the Prohibition

If at the time of the commission of the offense the offender does not understand the wrongfulness of his act, he acts without culpability if the mistake was unavoidable. If the mistake was avoidable, the sentence can be mitigated according to § 49 para. 1.

NOTES

1. Should mistakes about the law excuse an offender? In criminal law theory, a starting point for answering this question could be to distinguish between three kinds of mistakes: first, any mistake about the law, including sheer ignorance; second, a mistake by an offender who knows the relevant legal provisions but misinterprets them (mistake of interpretation); third, beliefs about the scope of a legal provision which actually were correct at the time of the offense but are no longer correct as a result of subsequent events. The narrowest approach to mistake about the law only accepts this third version. A mistake of law would accordingly only be legally relevant under unusual, unexpected circumstances, for instance, if the offender could at the time of his act point to a favorable statement of the law subsequently reversed, such as a court decision later overturned by the same, or a higher, court (on the inapplicability of the *ex post facto* prohibition to judicial changes in the law[†]) or an opinion by an official later revised by the same official, overridden by a superior, or invalidated in court. The most liberal approach would accept *any* mistake of law as excuse, even if the offender was ignorant in a blameworthy way.

People v. Marrero concerns the interpretation of the mistake-of-law-clause in the New York Penal Law. The debate revolves around the question of whether the relevant New York statute must be read as opting for the third, most restrictive approach or whether it also covers the middle approach, that is, mistakes of interpretation. Judge Hancock refers to notions that go beyond mere statutory interpretation. He takes up again the point of "vicious will" as the core of crime which is lacking if the offender was not aware of doing wrong,[‡] and he rejects the pragmatic and utilitarian reasons given in the majority opinion for the narrowest approach.

---

* [The defendants were sentenced to one year six months' and one year nine months' imprisonment, respectively; execution of this sentence was suspended.—Eds.]

---

† See Chapter 2.
‡ For a critique of this view, see Chapter 8.B., Note 6.

Note also Judge Hancock's point that it is misleading to put the most restrictive alternative chosen in the ruling under the heading "mistake" (because it is not really a mistake at all). What is the significance of this miscategorization? Does it matter whether the defense in this form is characterized as "mistake of law" or, perhaps, as "reliance on official statement of the law"? Is this not the core of the defense in its New York Penal Law formulation: that it is unfair for the state to tell me one day that the conduct I am about to engage in is not criminal (how about not illegal, even in a civil sense?) and then to turn around the next day, after I have gone ahead and done it, to tell me that it was criminal after all? In other words, is this version of the "mistake of law" defense not really a due process defense akin to the *nulla poena* principle?

2. Under German law, the crucial question is not what kind of mistake of law the offender has committed—even sheer ignorance, not knowing the law at all, could count as a mistake of law. But the relevant provision, § 17 Criminal Code, demands another crucial condition that narrows the scope of the excuse considerably. The test question is: was this error avoidable? If the answer is no, if the mistake was unavoidable, it negates culpability—i.e., it operates as an excuse (rather than negating a subjective offense element). But if the mistake was avoidable, the offender will be convicted (with the option for the judge of fact to mitigate the sentence). In applying this test, German case law demands a lot from offenders and therefore most mistakes will be labeled "avoidable." For instance, courts require offenders to think carefully (even if they in fact were completely unaware they were about to commit an offense), and not only under *malum in se*-conditions, but also for *mala prohibita*. The simple argument "I did not know the law" will almost never count as an excuse, except in extremely rare circumstances (perhaps if a new statute in a remote area of law was enacted days before the offense and even a lawyer would have been unaware of its existence).

A dominant feature in rulings concerning § 17 Criminal Code is the assumption of a duty to seek expert opinions rather than to trust one's own interpretation of the law. In a case like *People v. Marrero*, German courts would not find an unavoidable mistake. Rather, they would demand that the defendant check his own interpretation of the law with a lawyer or the public prosecutor's office. Therefore, under German law, the defendant would have been convicted of unlawful possession of a weapon as well.

Is there not a significant distinction between seeking—and then relying on—the (paid?) advice of a private attorney and that of a state official? Of a state official whose area of competence includes the issue under consideration? Does this depend on one's perception of defense lawyers' role (officers of the court vs. private counsel)?

3. *Wilfulness and taxes.* The rigid adherence to the time-honored maxim *ignorantia legis non excusat* is subject to at least one exception, or perhaps two, depending on who's counting. The mental state requirement of "wilfulness" has long been interpreted as requiring proof of the awareness of illegality in a more or less specific sense. At the same time, or as a particular example, federal courts have been generous in permitting ignorance of law arguments in criminal tax cases, i.e., cases involving federal criminal tax provisions that require "wilful" violation. This is a significant exception to the *ignorantia legis* maxim because legislatures are fond of transforming wide swaths of regulatory provisions into criminal offenses through the insertion, often at the end of a long list of regulations, of a general clause criminalizing all "willful" violations of the above. Consider the following case, *People v. Coe*, 71 N.Y.2d 852 (1988), also from the New York Court of Appeals:

> Defendant, a registered nurse employed at the Isabella Geriatric Center in Manhattan, was convicted under Public Health Law § 12-b(2), after a bench trial, of wilfully violating a provision of the Public Health Law and regulations adopted thereunder (see, Public Health Law § 12-b[2]) in connection with the alleged abuse or mistreatment of an elderly resident (see, Public Health Law § 2803Bd[7]; 10 N.Y. Comp. Codes R. & Regs. § 81.1[a], [b]) ... Public Health Law § 2803Bd(7) proscribes acts of physical abuse, neglect or mistreatment of residents or patients in facilities such as the Isabella Geriatric Center. Under 10 N.Y. Comp. Codes R. & Regs. § 81.1 (a) the term "abuse" is defined as "inappropriate physical contact with a patient or resident of a residential health care facility ... Inappropriate physical contact includes, but is not limited to, striking ... shoving." Under 10 N.Y. Comp. Codes R. & Regs. § 81.1(b) "mistreatment" is

defined as, among other things, "inappropriate use of physical . . . restraints on . . . a patient or resident of a residential health care facility."

According to the evidence adduced at trial defendant—attempting to locate two missing $5 bills—forcibly searched an 86-year old resident who had a history of heart disease. Despite the resident's repeated objections, defendant went through his pockets while an attendant pinned his arms behind him. Shortly after the incident, the resident died. . . . On appeal, after a unanimous affirmance by the Appellate Division, defendant contends that the People did not make the required showing that she wilfully violated a provision of the Public Health Law or a Public Health Law regulation.

We decline to adopt the People's contention that for criminal liability under Public Health Law § 12-b(2) it need only be shown that the defendant acted deliberately and voluntarily, as opposed to accidentally. This construction requires reading the word "wilfully"—not as modifying "violates," the word which immediately follows it in the statute—but rather as describing the manner in which the underlying act was committed. In short, the People would have us read the statute as stating that any person who consciously performs an act, when such act happens to contravene some provision or regulation of the public health laws, is guilty of a misdemeanor. . . .

We also reject defendant's contention, however, that for liability under Public Health Law § 12-b it must be shown that defendant acted with an "evil motive, bad purpose or corrupt design." We hold that the Legislature, in using the term "wilfully" in Public Health Law § 12-b, intended a culpable mental state generally equivalent to that required by the term "knowingly" (see, Model Penal Code § 2.02[8]). To require proof of an evil motive or intent to injure—higher culpable mental states appropriate for intentional crimes classified as felonies—for conduct in violation of a statute or regulation which the Legislature has seen fit to classify under Public Health Law § 12-b(2) as a misdemeanor would be impermissible judicial legislation. It would also be inconsistent with the legislative purpose of protecting the public against Public Health Law violations by criminalizing a broad range of conduct under Public Health Law § 12-b but, at the same time, treating such regulatory or statutory violations as crimes of less serious degree.

Nor were the People required, as defendant impliedly argues, to demonstrate that she knew she was violating a specific statute or regulation. Rather, the People were required to show only that defendant was aware that her conduct was illegal. Here, defendant admitted receiving a copy of the patient's bill of rights (codified in Public Health Law § 2803-c) and attending lectures regarding its contents. The bill of rights mandates, among other things, that residents must be free from having their personal privacy invaded; being physically or mentally abused; and being forced to do anything against their will. Moreover, defendant admitted that she knew that it would be inappropriate to search a patient who physically resisted. There is ample support in the record for the Trial Judge's undisturbed finding that the People established "a knowing violation . . . of the statute."

What might explain courts' willingness to interpret willfulness as requiring awareness of illegality? In federal tax criminal law, willfulness is interpreted as requiring a "voluntary, intentional violation of a known legal duty." This means, for instance, that an airline pilot—in a well-known case—was permitted to argue, in his defense, that he did not know that the U.S. federal tax code (Internal Revenue Code) treated wages as income, *Cheek v. United States*, 498 U.S. 192 (1991), and that reliance on one's lawyer's advice can bolster a mistake of law defense, *Bursten v. United States*, 395 F.2d 976 (5th Cir. 1968). In tax cases, courts often stress the complexity of the relevant norms. How about the norms in *Coe*?

4. The *Border Guard Case* illustrates how strict German courts are with respect to mistakes of law. One part of the arguments concerned a special provision of military law, § 5 Military Criminal Law Act. The crucial term for conviction was "obvious": even if the offender was not himself aware of committing a wrongful act, the defense of mistake of law would not be available if the act's wrongfulness was obvious according to the circumstances known to him. Consider whether you find the arguments of the court convincing in this respect: Would it have been obvious to the young men who had grown up in the GDR and who underwent strong indoctrination to see the regular activities of the border guard troops as wrong (in other words, not only criminal on its face, but also unlawful, i.e., not justified)?* After all, the larger part of the reasons point in the opposite direction. Take into account the "command

---

* For further discussion of the concept of wrongfulness, see Chapter 13.

situation" described in the facts of the case. Unfortunately, the case is rather brief on the matter of § 17 Criminal Code. Again, there would be strong reasons in favor of arguing that this was one of the (rare) cases when a defendant actually could not have avoided being mistaken about the wrongfulness of what he was doing. Labeling the fatal shots at the inner German border as "wrong" while recognizing an excuse for the young men concerned might have been a fair compromise—one, however, the court eschewed.

Compare this case to *Dudley and Stephens*, where the English court also failed to recognize an excuse (of necessity) after having rejected a claim of justification, instead insisting that the defendants' conduct was both wrongful and blameworthy. Could similar considerations account for the decision to insist on rejecting the excuse compromise in both cases? Recall that in *Dudley and Stephens*, the Queen pardoned the defendants and that in the *Border Guard Case*, only "lenient punishments" were imposed. Do these cases, then, reflect a similar compromise position—insisting on criminal liability, but then exercising mercy in punishment?

D. Intoxication

Anglo-American and German criminal law approach the significance of intoxication for the assessment of criminal liability in significantly different ways. Anglo-American criminal law reflects a general reluctance to recognize intoxication as a defense, or as a reason for mitigating liability or punishability in general. At best, and in extreme cases, intoxication may negate some, but not all, mental state requirements: traditionally, intoxication could negate "specific intent," but not "general intent," an instrumental, and even concededly "illogical," distinction that did little more than allow courts to permit intoxication as a defense in some cases, but not in others, on the basis of some "policy consideration" or other. Here, too, as in the case of ignorance of law (and, arguably, in the case of felony murder*), the Model Penal Code drafters rejected common law orthodoxy in form, while retaining some version of it in substance: the Code dismisses the distinction between specific and general intent, but declares intoxication incapable of negating recklessness, with the same effect of eliminating it for the bulk of offenses, since recklessness is the default mental state requirement in the Code (see MPC §§ 2.02(3), 2.08(2)).

By contrast, German criminal law treats intoxication only as a separate excuse defense, under the same general provision regarding mental disorders that also covers cases of insanity. Having recognized extreme intoxication as a complete defense, German criminal law, however, then imposes liability either under a separate extreme intoxication offense in the German Criminal Code or, using a construction called *actio libera in causa*, under the offense committed in the state of intoxication, provided the offender intoxicated him- or herself with the intent to commit that offense or with negligence regarding its commission.

State v. Cameron
Supreme Court of New Jersey
104 N.J. 42, 514 A.2d 1302 (1986)

Clifford, J.

This appeal presents a narrow, but important, issue concerning the role that a defendant's voluntary intoxication plays in a criminal prosecution. The specific question is whether the evidence was sufficient to require the trial court to charge the jury on defendant's intoxication, as defendant requested. The Appellate Division reversed defendant's convictions, holding that it was error not to have given an intoxication charge. We granted the State's petition for certification and now reverse.

---

* See Chapter 15.A.ii.

Defendant, Michele Cameron, age 22 at the time of trial, was indicted for second degree aggravated assault, in violation of N.J. Stat. Ann. § 2C:12-1(b)(1);* possession of a weapon, a broken bottle, with a purpose to use it unlawfully, contrary to N.J. Stat. Ann. § 2C:39-4(d);† and fourth degree resisting arrest, a violation of N.J. Stat. Ann. § 2C:29-2.‡ A jury convicted defendant of all charges. After merging the possession count into the assault charge, the trial court imposed sentences aggregating seven years in the custody of the Commissioner of the Department of Corrections, with a three year period of parole ineligibility and certain monetary penalties.

The charges arose out of an incident of June 6, 1981, on a vacant lot in Trenton. The unreported opinion of the Appellate Division depicts the following tableau of significant events:

The victim, Joseph McKinney, was playing cards with four other men. Defendant approached and disrupted the game with her conduct. The participants moved their card table to a new location within the lot. Defendant followed them, however, and overturned the table. The table was righted and the game resumed. Shortly thereafter, defendant attacked McKinney with a broken bottle. As a result of that attack he sustained an injury to his hand, which necessitated 36 stitches and caused permanent injury.

Defendant reacted with violence to the arrival of the police. She threw a bottle at their vehicle, shouted obscenities, and tried to fight them off. She had to be restrained and handcuffed in the police wagon.

The heart of the Appellate Division's reversal of defendant's conviction is found in its determination that voluntary intoxication is a defense when it negates an essential element of the offense—here, purposeful conduct. We agree with that proposition. Likewise are we in accord with the determinations of the court below that all three of the charges of which this defendant was convicted—aggravated assault, the possession offense, and resisting arrest—have purposeful conduct as an element of the offense; and that a person acts purposely "with respect to the nature of his conduct or a result thereof if it is his conscious object to engage in conduct of that nature or to cause such a result"...

Under the common law intoxication was not a defense to a criminal charge... [T]he early cases nevertheless held that in some circumstances intoxication could be resorted to for defensive purposes—specifically, to show the absence of a specific intent. The exceptional immunity extended to the drunkard is limited to those instances where the crime involves a specific, actual intent. When the degree of intoxication is such as to render the person incapable of entertaining such intent, it is an effective defence. If it falls short of this it is worthless.

The principle... developed from the foregoing approach, that intoxication formed the basis for a defense to a "specific intent" crime but not to one involving only "general" intent...

N.J. Stat. Ann. § 2C:2-8 provide[s]:

a. Except as provided in subsection d. of this section, intoxication of the actor is not a defense unless it negatives an element of the offense.
b. When recklessness establishes an element of the offense, if the actor, due to self-induced intoxication, is unaware of a risk of which he would have been aware had he been sober, such unawareness is immaterial.
c. Intoxication does not, in itself, constitute mental disease....
d. Intoxication which (1) is not self-induced or (2) is pathological is an affirmative defense if by reason of such intoxication the actor at the time of his conduct lacks substantial and adequate capacity either to appreciate its wrongfulness or to conform his conduct to the requirement of law.
e. Definitions. In this section unless a different meaning plainly is required:
  (1) "Intoxication" means a disturbance of mental or physical capacities resulting from the introduction of substances into the body;
  (2) "Self-induced intoxication" means intoxication caused by substances which the actor knowingly introduces into his body, the tendency of which to cause intoxication he knows

---

* [2C:12-1(b) Aggravated assault.
A person is guilty of aggravated assault if he (1)[a]ttempts to cause serious bodily injury to another, or causes such injury purposely or knowingly or under circumstances manifesting extreme indifference to the value of human life recklessly causes such injury.—Eds.]
† [2C:39-4(d). Possession of weapons for unlawful purposes.
Any person who has in his possession any weapon, except a firearm, with a purpose to use it unlawfully against the person or property of another is guilty of a crime of the third degree.—Eds.]
‡ [2C:29-2. Resisting Arrest; Eluding Officer.
[A] person is guilty of a crime of the fourth degree if he, by flight, purposely prevents or attempts to prevent a law enforcement officer from effecting an arrest.—Eds.]

or ought to know, unless he introduces them pursuant to medical advice or under such circumstances as would afford a defense to a charge of crime;

(3) "Pathological intoxication" means intoxication grossly excessive in degree, given the amount of the intoxicant, to which the actor does not know he is susceptible.

As is readily apparent, self-induced intoxication is not a defense unless it negatives an element of the offense. Under the common-law intoxication defense . . . intoxication could either exculpate or mitigate guilt "if the defendant's intoxication, in fact, prevents his having formed a mental state which is an element of the offense and if the law will recognize the proof of the lack of that mental state. "[U]nder pre-Code law, intoxication was admissible as a defense to a "specific" intent, but not a "general" intent, crime.

The original proposed Code rejected the specific/general intent distinction, choosing to rely instead on the reference to the four states of culpability for offenses under the Code: negligent, reckless, knowing, and purposeful conduct . . . In essence, "[t]hat which the cases now describe as a "specific intent' can be equated, for this purpose, with that which the Code defines as 'purpose' and 'knowledge.' See § 2C:2-2b. A 'general intent' can be equated with that which the Code defines as 'recklessness,' or criminal 'negligence.'" Code Commentary at 68 . . .

N.J. Stat. Ann. § 2C:2-8 was modeled after the Model Penal Code (MPC) § 2.08. The drafters of the MPC, as did the New Jersey Commission, criticized the specific-general intent distinction, and adopted instead the same four states of culpability eventually enacted in the Code. In the commentary, the drafters of the MPC expressly stated their intention that intoxication be admissible to disprove the culpability factors of purpose or knowledge, but that for crimes requiring only recklessness or negligence, exculpation based on intoxication should be excluded as a matter of law.

The drafters explicitly determined that intoxication ought to be accorded a significance that is entirely co-extensive with its relevance to disprove purpose or knowledge, when they are the requisite mental elements of a specific crime . . . [W]hen the definition of a crime or a degree thereof requires proof of such a state of mind, the legal policy involved will almost certainly obtain whether or not the absence of purpose or knowledge is due to the actor's . . . intoxication or to some other cause.

The policy reasons for requiring purpose or knowledge as a requisite element of some crimes are that in the absence of those states of mind, the criminal conduct would not present a comparable danger, or the actor would not pose as significant a threat. Moreover, the ends of legal policy are better served by subjecting to graver sanctions those who consciously defy legal norms. It was those policy reasons that dictated the result that the intoxication defense should be available when it negatives purpose or knowledge. The drafters concluded: "If the mental state which is the basis of the law's concern does not exist, the reason for its non-existence is quite plainly immaterial."

Thus, when the requisite culpability for a crime is that the person act "purposely" or "knowingly," evidence of voluntary intoxication is admissible to disprove that requisite mental state. . . .

The foregoing discussion establishes that proof of voluntary intoxication would negate the culpability elements in the offenses of which this defendant was convicted.

The charges—aggravated assault, possession of a weapon with a purpose to use it unlawfully, and resisting arrest—all require purposeful conduct (aggravated assault uses "purposely" or "knowingly" in the alternative). The question is what level of intoxication must be demonstrated before a trial court is required to submit the issue to a jury . . .

The guiding principle is simple enough of articulation. We need not here repeat the citations to authorities already referred to in this opinion that use the language of "prostration of faculties such that defendant was rendered incapable of forming an intent." . . .

So firmly fixed in our case law is the requirement of "prostration of faculties" as the minimum requirement for an intoxication defense that we feel secure in our assumption that the legislature intended nothing different in its statutory definition of intoxication: "a disturbance of mental or physical capacities resulting from the introduction of substances into the body." N.J. Stat. Ann. § 2C:2-8(e)(1). In order to satisfy the statutory condition that to qualify as a defense intoxication must negative an element of the offense, the intoxication must be of an extremely high level . . .

Measured by the foregoing standard and evidence relevant thereto, it is apparent that the record in this case is insufficient to have required the trial court to grant defendant's request to charge intoxication . . . True, the victim testified that defendant was drunk, and defendant herself said she felt "pretty intoxicated," "pretty bad," and "very intoxicated." But these are no more than conclusory labels, of little assistance in determining whether any drinking produced a prostration of faculties . . .

Ordinarily, of course, the question of whether a defendant's asserted intoxication satisfies the standards enunciated in this opinion should be resolved by the jury. But here, viewing the evidence and the legitimate inferences to be drawn therefrom in the light most favorable to defendant, the best that can be made of the proof of intoxication is that defendant may have been extremely agitated and distraught. It may even be that a fact-finder could conclude that her powers of rational thought and deductive reasoning had been affected. But there is no suggestion in the evidence that defendant's faculties were so prostrated by her consumption of something less than a pint of wine as to render her incapable of purposeful or knowing conduct. The trial court correctly refused defendant's request.

German Federal Court of Justice,
4 StR 117/90, BGHSt 37, 231 (November 22, 1990)

Facts

The regional court sentenced the defendant, who at the time of the crime had a blood alcohol concentration of about .232%, to life imprisonment for robbery and murder.

The defendant by his appeal in law, which is limited to the sentence, objected to the violation of substantive law. The appeal was well founded. The finding of full culpability on the defendant's part was not free from legal error.

Reasons

The regional court calculated from the defendant's indications of quantity of drink for the seven hours from drinking until the crime, according to the principles in the case law, a blood alcohol concentration of .232% at the time of the crime....However it then endorsed the observations of the psychiatric expert according to which, in spite of this alcoholic influence, there was no substantial impairment. This view is based on the following considerations: the overall conduct of the defendant, who had been accustomed and tolerant to alcohol as a result of substantial regular alcohol consumption over a period of years, showed no deficiency symptoms associated with alcohol. Witnesses had not been able to recognize in him any impairment caused by alcohol before the crime. His capability of action had also been maintained at the time of crime, which was demonstrated by the fact that the defendant had "proceeded logically, purposefully and consistently" and had acted methodically and in accordance with the situation. His behavior after the crime, when he had looked for possible items of evidence incriminating him at the scene of crime, could be described as "decidedly thought-out and appropriate to the situation." His capacity for recollection of the events had also remained intact. Finally the defendant had not felt himself hampered, according to the information which he gave, and still "could think...clearly"...The "maximum blood alcohol level as obtained exclusively by calculation which" was based "always on an uncertain foundation" was displaced by the "priority of assessment of the psycho-pathological picture." Following all this, the regional court did find full culpability on the part of the defendant. This does not stand up legal examination in the appeal in law.

1. Medical alcohol research has established on the basis of experience over many years that certain ("stochastic") dependencies can be established between increasing blood alcohol concentration and the psychological state of a person at the time of a crime (Gerchow, BA 1985, 152 (156); the same, Forensia 1986, 155 (163); Witter, Der psychiatrische Sachverständige im Strafrecht (The psychiatric expert in criminal law), 1987, p. 1 (21)). Accordingly between blood alcohol concentration on the one hand and impairment of culpability on the other hand, there is admittedly no linear relationship governed by natural laws but there are statistically verifiable regularities which are more or less distinctive and which in any case permit statements of probability about the reduction or disappearance of capacity for control...In the medical literature, there is some discussion how far this applies to § 21 Criminal Code. According to Rasch (Forensische Psychiatrie, 1986, p. 199) it is scarcely tenable to exclude a substantial reduction in criminal capacity on a blood alcohol concentration of .2%...Others formulate the position in a more restricted way. Thus with a blood alcohol concentration at the time of the crime of .2% the application of § 21 Criminal Code should at least be considered or may only be rejected by special reasoning (Langelüddeke-Bresser, Gerichtliche Psychiatrie, 4th edit. (1976), p. 291)...

From these statements, a generally recognized medical empirical principle can be deduced: a blood alcohol level from .2% upwards indicates a substantial reduction in the capacity for control. For the judge who always has to consider reliable scientific findings (BGHSt 21, 157 (159); BGHSt 30, 251 (252 f.); BGHSt 34, 133 (134);...) this means that a blood alcohol concentration of .2 % and more represents a fact which on the basis of a reliable—statistical—empirical principle facilitates the conclusion that there is substantial reduction of the capability to control...

2 . . . .

3. The established blood alcohol concentration at the time of the crime—whether it is established directly or calculated for a period of up to 10 hours—is the decisive factor in relation to drunkenness in

the sense of an intoxication psychosis as a pathological psychological disorder or a profound consciousness disorder in accordance with § 20 Criminal Code, with the further possible consequence of impairment of the capacity for insight or the ability for inhibition. For the latter the empirical principle of a substantial impairment of the capacity for control based on a level of blood alcohol content of .2% and more is directly meaningful (Judgment of the Senate of Sept. 13, 1990, 4 StR 376/90). If such a blood alcohol concentration is the only assessment criterion, the judge must find the presence of the prerequisites of § 21 Criminal Code according to the unanimous case law of the Federal Court of Justice.

4. Admittedly a conclusion which is only based on a—statistical—empirical principle is no longer justified if it is shaken in the individual case by the presence of generally recognized conflicting assessment criteria (see Herdegen, in: KK, 2nd edit., § 244 marginal no. 5; Gollwitzer, in: Löwe-Rosenberg, § 261 marginal no. 47). In this case the judge must, within the framework of an overall assessment, undertake an evaluation of the opposing criteria . . .

5. . . . In the ideal case of a subtle psycho-diagnosis undertaken in direct connection with the occurrence of the crime by an expert doctor, it is possible from the appearance, the (active) conduct of the perpetrator or other circumstances to draw reliable conclusions about whether the capability for inhibition remained preserved or was impaired. Also in cases in which the perpetrator shows in connection with the crime, in spite of substantial inebriation, extraordinary (fine) motor control of the body (see for instance BGH, Judgment of Oct. 21, 1981, 2 StR 264/81—Cat Burglar Case; also the facts underlying the decision in BGHSt 35, 308 might be included: lame man who in spite of substantial inebriation escapes his pursuers and during his flight discharges his revolver and loads it again) it is possible to conclude from the established active conduct that he has retained ability for control. Apart from exceptional cases of this kind, no assessment criteria on the reconstruction of the perpetrator's physical state at the time of the crime are evident which are of such a convincing nature as to be apt to refute the above empirical principle in relation to a blood alcohol content of two parts and more per thousand (see Renzikowski, NJW 1990, 2905 ff.). It is true that a psychiatric expert will as a rule have the opportunity to investigate the defendant before the main proceedings. But the circumstances which are crucial here at the time of the crime—in particular the defendant's physical and emotional state—cannot be reconstructed by an expert even one day after the crime . . .

6. . . . As a rule therefore a blood alcohol concentration of two parts and more per thousand remains the only circumstance capable of consideration which leads, according to reliable scientific experience and having regard to the principle of doubt, to the finding of substantially diminished culpability in the sense of § 21 Criminal Code.

7. The judgment under challenge cannot therefore stand so far the sentence is concerned. The new criminal chamber to which the case will be referred will have to discuss the complainant's culpability again having regard to the above considerations, including in its assessment the occurrence of the crime, spontaneous as to cause and course, senseless and indicating alcoholic influence. A murder based on fear of discovery is not as such a criterion which excludes substantial limitation of culpability. The behavior after the crime described as "thought through" and "appropriate to the situation" could also be based on a possible "sobering-up effect" which is mentioned in medical science. The complainant's own assessment of his state (tipsy, drunk) has hardly any evidential value . . .

German Federal Court of Justice
5 StR 93/04, BGHSt 49, 239 (August 17, 2004)

Facts

The regional court sentenced each of the defendants to imprisonment for three years and six months for inflicting dangerous bodily harm concomitantly with wrongful detention and coercion—allowing the reduction of the statutory punishment range according to §§ 21, 49 para. 1 Criminal Code on the basis of substantial inebriation.

According to the findings of the regional court the defendant G. drank alcohol from adolescence onwards and is clearly accustomed to alcohol. He has a number of previous convictions for property and traffic crimes, including drunkenness in traffic. On the day of the crime he had from the early morning and throughout the day drunk several bottles of beer before going with the defendant M. (likewise already slightly drunk but with no prior convictions) to see the victim P. in order to maltreat him. The defendants had heard a rumor about P., which they had not further checked, that he had raped a small girl. Together they wanted "to pursue their delight in violence." At P.'s residence the defendants immediately struck and kicked him, and demanded that he admit to having raped the girl. The victim was compelled to come with them in a car, driven by the defendant G., to K. G. and M. maltreated and abused their victim there so that P. in the end was bleeding from the face and could hardly stand on his legs. Then they all drove together in G.'s car to a fast food place and then across the countryside; the victim now had to climb into the car boot. He was partly stripped of his clothing by the defendants at a weir and pushed into the cold water which was between 15° and 18° Celsius. After some time the defendants finally pulled the victim to land again, kicked him until he lost consciousness, and left him half naked and unconscious. P. suffered multiple bruises from the defendants' maltreatment, a fracture of the ribs and a traumatic brain hemorrhage which would have been life-threatening if untreated, and in addition hypothermia and disturbances of cardiac rhythm. During the events, which dragged on for several hours, both defendants had consumed not insubstantial quantities of beer and other alcoholic drinks.

The regional court mitigated the punishment range of § 224 para. 1 no. 4 Criminal Code (dangerous bodily harm)* in accordance with §§ 21, 49 para. 1 Criminal Code on the basis of the defendants' inebriation and the substantial reduction of the "capacity for control and insight" caused thereby (correctly: capacity for control, see Tröndle/Fischer, StGB, 52nd edit., § 21 marginal no. 5 with further references). It gave as its reasoning that the defendant G.'s drunkenness had not been culpable on the day of the crime because he had so far been controlled to a large extent by alcohol; in the absence of testimony by the defendant M. it was also to be assumed in his favor that his drunkenness had not been culpable.

The appeals in law of the public prosecutor's office, limited to the legal consequences, are successful.

Reasons

1 ....

2. The regional court has without any legal error and on expert advice reached the conclusion that the defendant's capacity for control was substantially reduced, on the ground of G.'s plausible statements about quantity of drink, of witness descriptions about the condition of the defendants and the depiction of the events which points to substantial loss of inhibition.

3. The public prosecutor's office nevertheless correctly objects to the mitigation of the punishment ...

a) The Third Criminal Senate [of the Federal Court of Justice—the Eds.] has expressed the view that the case law of the Federal Court of Justice so far—which tends to lack uniformity and is partly even contradictory—on mitigation of punishment in the case of reprehensible inebriation in principle requires further reflection (BGH, NJW 2003, 2394, with note by Foth, NStZ 2003, 597; Frister, JZ 2003, 1019; ... agreeing, the Second Criminal Senate, BGHR StGB § 2 Strafrahmenverschiebung 32). The Senate shares this concern but reaches the following result which differentiates and does not basically contradict the previous case law:

The judge of fact decides about the mitigation of the punishment range under §§ 21, 49 para. 1 Criminal Code in accordance with his duty to exercise his discretion on the basis of an overall consideration of all the circumstances relevant to guilt. If the substantial reduction in culpability is based upon drunkenness for which the defendant is responsible, this argues as a rule against alteration of the punishment framework, if inebriation had increased in a foreseeable and significant way the risk of crimes with view to the personal or situational background. The judge of fact has to determine whether this is the case. His decision is only subject to limited scrutiny by the court hearing the appeal in law and must as a rule be accepted in so far as the essential factual foundations for it have been sufficiently ascertained and have been sufficiently weighed in the evaluation.

b) The solution found by the Senate is based in particular on the following considerations:

In the case law of the Federal Court of Justice it is recognized that a substantial limitation of the capacity for understanding wrongfulness or control in principle reduces culpability (see BGHSt 7, 28 [30]; ... also RGSt 69, 314 [317]). But this alone does not compel mitigation of the punishment range. The judge of fact is in principle allowed discretion in cases of substantially reduced culpability ... According to the statutory wording of § 21 Criminal Code the punishment merely

---

* [§ 224 StGB (Dangerous Bodily Harm)
(1) Who causes bodily harm
...
4. together with another perpetrator,
...
will be punished with imprisonment from six months to ten years, in less serious cases with imprisonment from three months to five years.—Eds.]

"can" be reduced; the punishment range neither "must" nor "ought to" be altered. The legislature has thereby ordered that even a substantial reduction of culpability in the sense of § 21 Criminal Code does not on its own lead either necessarily or as a rule to a considerable reduction of punishment (see also Foth, in: Festschr. f. Salger, 1995, pp. 31, 37).

The reduction of culpability due to the limitation of capacity can in fact be compensated by circumstances increasing culpability (consistent case law, see Tröndle/Fischer, § 21 marginal nos. 20ff. with further references; BVerfGE 50, 5 [11f.]). The Third Criminal Senate sees such a circumstance generally in every inebriation with reprehensible causes (BGH, NJW 2003, 2394). It is not however sufficiently recognized that this presupposes at least (simple) negligence. Foreseeability and avoidability of the unlawful result are necessary elements of negligence generally (objective) and specifically for the perpetrator (subjective). Additionally, the point of reference for any factor increasing culpability must be a wrong actually committed...

In spite of widespread and frequent use and misuse of alcohol, an unlawful act arises in only a fraction of cases of substantial inebriation...On the other hand it cannot be ignored that alcohol generally increases the risk of commission of criminal acts; a large part of the crimes against body and life as well as against sexual self-determination is committed under the influence of alcohol. These results do not however justify the assumption that it is always objectively and subjectively foreseeable that in cases of substantial inebriation crimes by the drunken person are to be expected. This depends on the person of the perpetrator in question and on the situation in which the drinking is taking place or into which the perpetrator goes when he is drunk.

(1) According to the case law of the Federal Court of Justice so far, reduction of punishment should be denied if the perpetrator knew consumption of alcohol to have an especially unfavorable effect on him, and knew or should have known that he then had a tendency to acts of violence or other crimes. It is thus a question of whether special circumstances in the person of the perpetrator in the actual individual case have foreseeably increased the risk of commission of unlawful acts to a significant extent. It has been additionally required that the perpetrator must have previously committed crimes which are comparable in extent and intensity with the present crime (see BGHR StGB § 21 Strafrahmenverschiebung 6, 14, 16; further reference in Lenckner/Perron, in: Schönke/Schröder, StGB, 26th edit., § 21 marginal no. 20), but the Senate does not adhere to this view...Previous experiences need not have led to previous convictions or criminal proceedings. The perpetrator's knowledge of the danger he poses matters, and not necessarily the possible additional aspect of warning created by an earlier conviction.

(2) The danger of committing crimes in a substantially inebriated condition can be significantly and foreseeably increased not only by the perpetrator's personality, but also by the circumstances of the situation. The person who, in a situation fraught with danger, drinks alcohol in substantial quantities can be accused of having brought himself into a crime situation by a certain carelessness which increases his guilt (BGH, NStZ 1990, 537 [538]). The reprehensible feature here is continuing to drink in such a situation in spite of actual foreseeability of breaches of the law threatened by further inebriation (see also Jähnke, in: LK, § 21 marginal no. 22). The danger of violence is as a rule foreseeably increased by the disinhibiting effect of substantial inebriation particularly in strongly emotionally charged crisis situations (see BGH, NStZ 1990, 537 [538]). The same applies with drinking in groups from which—simply on the basis of group dynamics—crimes are easily committed against others. A person who gets drunk for instance in a group of marauding hooligans or radicals ready to use violence must actually expect the commission of crimes in a drunken state. Furthermore, inebriation cannot—if the principles of actio libera in causa do not already exclude reduction in punishment—benefit the person who gets drunk when he is ready to drive and therefore knows or must expect he will participate as a driver in public road traffic (see Tröndle/Fischer, § 316 marginal no. 54; König, in: LK, § 316 marginal no. 243).

It makes no relevant difference whether the perpetrator drinks alcohol so as to reduce inhibition in a situation which is recognizably potentially violent, or consciously goes into such a situation, already disinhibited by drunkenness. A person who is already slightly drunk and joins a group which is ready for violence can be accused of having sought a potentially violent situation in spite of the known disinhibiting effect of his inebriation...Within the overall assessment of all circumstances relevant to culpability it is possible to accuse an alcohol-dependent perpetrator not of the inebriation as such but of having—with in this respect a still existing capacity for inhibition—consciously gone into a potentially violent situation even though he knew or ought to have known that he would only be able to control himself there to a limited extent as a result of being under the influence of alcohol...

(3) ...According to the principles of actio libera in causa—which apply within the framework of § 21 Criminal Code (see Lenckner/Perron, in: Schönke/Schröder, § 21 marginal no. 11 with

further references)—as a rule there should be no reduction in punishment if the perpetrator had already intended to commit a specific crime while being in an unintoxicated state (see BGH, BGHR StGB § 20 actio libera in causa 3; . . .). If the decision for the offense was made at a time at which substantial impairment of the capability for inhibition was not yet present, there will be no room for a mitigation of the punishment range under §§ 21, 49 para. 1 Criminal Code (see BGHSt 34, 29 (33); BGH, quoted in Detter, NStZ 1999, 495; . . .). This applies to an increased extent if the perpetrator has become intoxicated purposely in order to breakdown his inhibitions against execution of a crime.

(4)   . . . In applying the above principles to violent crimes, a mitigation of the punishment range under §§ 21, 49 para. 1 Criminal Code after a reprehensible inebriation will in many cases be ruled out. For the most part circumstances will be present, either in the personality of the perpetrator or at least in the situation, which in connection with the inebriation have significantly and foreseeably increased the risk of commission of crimes. Excessively high requirements ought not to be placed here on the formation of belief of the judge of fact; the devastating effects in many different ways of excessive alcohol consumption are generally known. . . .

(5)   . . .

(6)   The Senate points out as a precaution that what applies to alcohol cannot simply be transferred equally to other substances (see Senate, Judgment of August 17, 2004, 5 StR 591/03). The disinhibitory effect of alcohol and its tendency to promote aggression are generally known. On the other hand, the effects of narcotics are more diverse and possibly less concretely foreseeable, especially as the dosage and the individual toleration are mostly subject to substantial variations from case to case.

The mitigation of the punishment range under §§ 21, 49 para. 1 Criminal Code by the court of fact meets in the end with prevailing doubts.

In applying the above mentioned principles, the regional court should not have contented itself in connection with the reasoning for alteration of the punishment framework under §§ 21, 49 para. 1 Criminal Code with the consideration that G.'s inebriation was not blameworthy because he was addicted to alcohol to a large extent. It ought also to have considered whether it should for instance be set against this that this defendant went to see the future victim with the firm intention of giving full rein to the defendant's delight in violence, obviously accepting the special loss of inhibition resulting from his inebriation, and the increasing loss of it which further inebriation would cause. Even the person who is extensively dependent on alcohol can in certain circumstances be accused (in such a way as to increase his culpability) of having deliberately gone into a potentially violent situation in spite of the foreseeability of loss—and especially the further loss—of inhibition through alcohol . . . It is also possible that the above-mentioned principles of actio libera in causa stand against a mitigation of punishment under §§ 21, 49 para. 1 Criminal Code. However the findings made so far are not sufficient to answer this question especially in the light of events dragging on several hours; it remains unclear whether the defendant G., when he made the decision to maltreat the victim, was already substantially restricted in his capacity for control or not . . .

The findings of the court of fact on the sentence—and therefore also those on the prerequisites of § 21 Criminal Code—are quashed as a whole. The new judge of fact will (with the benefit of expert advice) have critically to analyses the findings about the defendants' inebriation, especially with regard to G.'s capacity to drive and the absence of information regarding M. If necessary it will at least have to be examined in relation to the defendant G. whether the prerequisites for sending him to a treatment center (§ 64 Criminal Code) are present and whether this measure should therefore be ordered in addition to the punishment.

German Criminal Code

§ 20 (Lack of Culpability Due to Mental Disorders)

Who at the time of the commission of the offense due to a pathological mental disorder, a profound consciousness disorder, debility or other serious mental abnormality, is incapable of understanding the wrongness of the act or incapable of acting in accordance with such understanding, acts without culpability.

§ 21 (Diminished Culpability)

If the capacity of the offender to understand the wrongness of his act or to act in accordance with such understanding is substantially diminished at the time of the commission of the offense due to one of the reasons indicated in § 20, the sentence can be mitigated according to § 49 para. 1.

§ 323a (Extreme Intoxication)

(1) Who intentionally or negligently puts himself into a state of intoxication with alcoholic beverages or other intoxicants will be punished with imprisonment of not more than five years or a fine if he commits an unlawful act in this state and may not be punished because he did not act culpably due to the intoxication or if this cannot be excluded.

(2) The punishment must not be more severe than the punishment provided for the offense committed in the intoxicated state.

(3) The offense may only be prosecuted upon complaint or authorization if the act committed in the drunken state may only be prosecuted upon complaint or authorization.

NOTES

1. *Cameron* sets out the standard common law position that "intoxication does not, in itself, constitute a mental disease" and that it may negative intention but does not count as an excuse if it is self-induced. In contrast, German criminal law considers intoxication under the rubric of "culpability" (or "blameworthiness," i.e., absence of excuse) rather than "*mens rea.*" Although the text of §§ 20, 21 Criminal Code does not explicitly mention intoxication, nobody expresses doubts (in case law or in the literature) that being under the influence of chemical substances which impair thinking (and thus the ability to understand that one is about to do wrong) or a person's capacity to control themselves, or both, counts as one of the pathological circumstances listed in § 20 Criminal Code. There is some disagreement whether intoxication is a "pathological mental disorder" or a "profound consciousness disorder" (note that the Federal Court of Justice in the decision from 1990 leaves this open). But the general question of whether intoxication of any kind, self-induced or not, can, under certain conditions, exculpate an offender (i.e., constitute an excuse) is uniformly answered in the affirmative.

Exculpation in German criminal law presupposes extreme circumstances, that is, a very high degree of intoxication. Medical experts must confirm the existence of "profound consciousness disorder" or "pathological mental disorder" at the time of the offense and, in addition, the judges must conclude that the defendant could not understand the wrongfulness of his or conduct or control himself or herself anymore. 0.2 percent of alcohol in the blood, mentioned in the German ruling from 1990, refers to a possible state of diminished culpability (§ 21 Criminal Code). For lack of culpability, the blood alcohol level usually must be considerably higher, as a rough rule of thumb above 0.3 percent.

2. Does it make a difference whether intoxication is taken into account as negating *mens rea* or as an excuse? How about negating the voluntariness component of the act requirement in Anglo-American criminal law? Why should intoxication not be taken into account whenever, and wherever, it might be relevant to the analysis of criminal liability? Does it not make sense to say that a person was so intoxicated that he or she lacked the requisite intent? Or lacked the requisite voluntariness to satisfy the act requirement? That he or she had the requisite intent but nonetheless escapes criminal liability because of the incapacity to differentiate right from wrong or to control his or her actions?

3. Does the availability of (self- and other-induced) intoxication as an excuse mean that offenders who were extremely drunk can always expect to leave a German courtroom without negative consequences? The answer is: no. First, there is always the possibility of a "measure of rehabilitation and incapacitation" rather than criminal "punishment" if the latter cannot be chosen due to the lack of culpability.* One of the measures consists in committing offenders who are addicted to drugs or alcohol to a treatment facility (§ 64 Criminal Code).

---

* On the German two-track system of measures and punishments, see Chapter 1.B.iii.

Second, German law has an offense that is tailored to intoxication (§ 323a Criminal Code). The wrong captured by this offence is simple: to intoxicate oneself intentionally or negligently. As the legislature was aware that intoxication is not a rare phenomenon and that it would cause social uproar if every instance of getting very drunk could be punished, § 323a Criminal Code contains in addition an objective condition: intoxication will only be punished if the offender in fact committed an offense that cannot be punished because of § 20 Criminal Code. This is an objective condition in a legal-technical sense: the offender's *mens rea* need not extend to the commission of the offense. Thus, even if the individual could not have foreseen how he or she would react to the substances intentionally or negligently consumed, this does not preclude punishment according to § 323a Criminal Code. Note that the maximum punishment is five years' imprisonment, which is not much if the offense consisted, for example, in an act of murder under § 211, punishable by life imprisonment. Then again, within the five-year limitation, the punishment can match that "provided for the offense committed in the intoxicated state."* In England, a similar proposal to codify a new "fall-back" offense of "dangerous intoxication," with a maximum sentence of one year for a first offenses, and three years for a subsequent one, was rejected.[†]

4. Consider § 323a German Criminal Code in light of the culpability principle. Does § 323a create a strict liability crime, by punishing someone for an offense committed without the otherwise requisite *mens rea*? Or does the "intentional or negligent" intoxication take the place of the *mens rea* requirement of the offense committed in the state of intoxication? How is this different from familiar, and long criticized and now disfavored, common law constructions of substituted, or "transferred," intent—where a person is held strictly liable for one offense "while committing" another (the predicate), on the theory that proof of the *mens rea* for the first—predicate—offense suffices to establish the *mens rea* for the second?[‡] Or does the culpability principle only require proof of some *mens rea* with respect to some prior act, rather than the specific *mens rea* required for the offense in question? If so, then how closely linked must the prior act (here, of self-intoxication) be to the subsequent one (the crime committed while intoxicated)?[§] Similarly, what must be the link between the *mens rea* requirement for the first crime and that for the second? Note that proof of negligent intoxication suffices even if the offense eventually committed under intoxication would require proof of intent (never mind more detailed inquiries, within the realm of intent, whether the type of intent—*Absicht*, knowledge, or merely *dolus eventualis*, matches the mental state requirement of the offense committed under intoxication).

Or is § 323a perhaps better understood as not concerned with guilt, but with the identification and treatment of exceptionally dangerous persons, who have manifested their dangerousness through a propensity to become intoxicated and, in a state of intoxication, to commit criminal offenses? In that case, would the appropriate sanction—under the German two-track system—not be a measure of rehabilitation and incapacitation, rather than punishment? After all, the sanction formally attaches to the act of intoxication, rather than to the act committed in a state of intoxication. (Note that the original version of the provision was introduced in 1933 as part of the major legislative reform that introduced the two-track system, Law Against Dangerous Recidivists and Regarding Measures of Incapacitation and Rehabilitation ("Gewohnheitsverbrechergesetz") of Nov. 24, 1933, RGBl. I 995, art. 3, no. 17.)[¶]

---

* Recall in this context that the fine is considered the default punishment in German criminal law, that prison sentences are rarely imposed, and if imposed rarely exceed a sentence of five years' imprisonment. See Chapter 1.A.iii.

[†] Butler Committee on Mentally Abnormal Offenders (1975), 235–7 ("while voluntarily intoxicated do an act (or make an omission) that would amount to a dangerous offence if it were done or made with the requisite state of mind for such offence").

[‡] See the discussion of "felony" or "constructive" murder in Chapter 15.A.ii.

[§] See the discussion of time framing, and concurrence, in Chapter 7.A.

[¶] The immediately following provision in the German Criminal Code, § 323b [originally § 330b], criminalizes "endangering of a detoxification treatment," by supplying alcohol or drugs to someone under treatment for substance abuse pursuant to a measure of incapacitation or rehabilitation.

If the argument is that the offender is punished not for the crime committed under intoxication, but for the intoxication itself, reducing the second offense to a sentencing consideration, do you find this argument convincing? Or does it strike you as an instance of the tail wagging the dog, an unsatisfyingly formalistic circumvention of a fundamental principle such as the (now constitutionally anchored) culpability requirement? Even so, would this interpretation not raise concerns about proportionality? Would a sentence of five years' imprisonment for the mere act of intoxication, even an intentional one, not be disproportionate (especially given the relatively lower sentences in German criminal law)? (In the original version of the provision, the maximum punishment was two years, § 330a Criminal Code [old version]).*)

Note also that § 323a criminalizes intoxication in general, whether public or private. What, then, is the wrong (never mind the culpability) captured by the offense? Public intoxication statutes are regarded, rightly or wrongly, as offenses against "public order." Some may also seek to justify them as offenses against public morality—assuming this is an interest properly subject to protection by the criminal law, or law generally speaking. But what harm is an act of private intoxication? What *Rechtsgut* is violated by, intentionally or negligently, "putting [oneself] into a drunken state," i.e., having a few (too many?) beers while watching TV at home (alone or with friends)? Under U.S. constitutional law, might the criminalization of private conduct implicate due process concerns?[†]

5. More fundamentally, is § 323a German Criminal Code best thought of as an aggravated intoxication prohibition (with penalties up to five years' imprisonment) or as an attempt to deal with the contentious issue of the relevance of intoxication to criminal liability, not for the intoxication itself, but for offenses committed in an intoxicated state? Treating it as the latter, does § 323a strike the right (*a* right) balance between competing considerations? What are these competing considerations? Adhering to a principle like the culpability principle as enunciated by the German Federal Court of Justice—or the unfortunately named "moral voluntariness" principle of fundamental justice being developed by the Canadian Supreme Court—while, at the same time, preventing impunity for offenses committed in a state of self-induced intoxication?

Compare the German approach to the question of intoxication under § 323a to the common law's approach:

Cameron makes reference to a long-standing distinction between general and specific intent crimes, with intoxication being permitted as a defense only to the latter. This distinction had two effects: First, since the vast majority of offenses were labeled "general intent" crimes, it drastically limited the scope of intoxication as a defense; second, even in specific intent crimes, intoxication only provided a partial defense, to the extent that a general intent crime was available as a fallback option (the classic case being the homicide pair of murder, a specific intent crime, and manslaughter, a general intent crime). Once the defendant had cleared the general/specific intent hurdle, having established the availability of intoxication as a defense, he or she faced the next requirement, of sufficient intoxication, where the sufficiency of the intoxication was difficult to specify, except by reference to unhelpful standards like "prostration of the faculties."[‡]

The distinction between general and specific intent crimes came under attack almost as soon as it was posited, largely because it proved almost impossible to draw with any clarity, and in the end appeared to amount to little more than a way of expressing a particular court's judgment about which offenses—and perhaps even which defendants—should receive the benefit of an intoxication defense, and which should not, taking into account general

---

* This limitation was removed in 1941, permitting the imposition of any prison sentence; the current five-year maximum was introduced in 1969.

† See, e.g., *Stanley v. Georgia*, 394 U.S. 557 (1969) (private possession of obscene materials); *Lawrence v. Texas*, 539 U.S. 558 (2003) (private sexual conduct).

‡ For a general discussion from a comparative perspective, see Brian Foley, "Same Problem, Same Solution?: The Treatment of the Voluntarily Intoxicated Offender in England and Germany," 4 *Trinity College Law Review* (2001), 119.

considerations of policy, notably the policy against recognizing intoxication as a defense in the first place. Interestingly, the judicial defenders of the general/specific intent distinction, in unusual moments of refreshing candor, acknowledged the incompatibility of denying an intoxication defense to defendants charged with a general intent crime, which may not require what the Model Penal Code might call "conscious object," but would at least require *awareness* of some sort—again, anachronistically using MPC terminology, knowledge (i.e., awareness of a fact or practical certainty) or recklessness (i.e., awareness of a substantial risk). Consider the following passage from Lord Edmund-Davies's opinion in the leading English case on intoxication, *D.P.P. v. Majewski*, [1976] 2 All E.R. 142:

> Illogical though the present law may be, it represents a compromise between the imposition of liability upon inebriates in complete disregard of their condition (on the alleged ground that it was brought on voluntarily), and the total exculpation required by the defendant's actual state of mind at the time he committed the harm in issue.

And, a few years later, in an opinion by Justice McIntyre in the Canadian case of *R. v. Bernard*, [1988] 2 S.C.R. 833:

> [W]hatever the logical weaknesses may be, an overwhelming justification for the exclusion [of the drunkenness defence in general intent cases] may rest on policy, policy so compelling that it possesses its own logic. Intoxication, whether by alcohol or drugs, lies at the root of many if not most violent assaults: intoxication is clearly a major cause of violent crime. What then is preferable, a recognition of this fact and the adoption of a policy aimed at curbing the problem, or the application of what is said to be logic by providing in law that he who voluntary partakes of that which is the cause of the crime should for that reason be excused from the consequences of his crime? If that is logic, I prefer policy.

The Model Penal Code rejected the general/specific intent distinction (along with the concept of intent itself), but shied away from addressing that distinction's most glaring "logical" weakness (if we leave aside the questionable utility of an apparently categorical, but in fact entirely instrumental, distinction), namely its effect of barring the use of intoxication to negate an offense element in every case involving an offense with at least one element to which is attached a mental state requiring awareness: The Model Penal Code simply declared that intoxication, despite appearances (and "logic") to the contrary, could not negate recklessness (§ 2.08(2)).

Apart from the considerations of policy, mentioned above, can this position be explained in terms of the Model Penal Code's treatmentist approach?

Combined with the exclusion of intoxication as an excuse analogous to insanity (§ 2.08(3) and (4)), can the Model Penal Code's position be squared with the culpability principle in German law, even if intoxication evidence remains relevant to negate purpose and knowledge and, presumably, to negate the voluntariness components of the act requirement?

The U.S. Supreme Court has rejected a (due process) constitutional challenge to a Montana statute (§ 45-2-203) that declared, simply, that "voluntary intoxication "may not be taken into consideration in determining the existence of a mental state which is an element of [a criminal] offense.'" *Montana v. Egelhoff*, 518 U.S. 37 (1996). Along the way, the Court, in an opinion by Justice Scalia, cited an 1820 opinion by Justice Story who challenged the very coherence of a "defense" of intoxication:

> This is the first time, that I ever remember it to have been contended, that the commission of one crime was an excuse for another. Drunkenness is a gross vice, and in the contemplation of some of our laws is a crime; and I learned in my earlier studies, that so far from its being in law an excuse for murder, it is rather an aggravation of its malignity.
>
> *United States v. Cornell*, 25 F. Cas. 650, 657–658 (No. 14,868) (C.C. R.I. 1820).

Having found no historical support for a claim of a "fundamental principle" requiring the consideration of intoxication evidence in the determination of *mens rea*, Scalia went on to list what he considered the "considerable justification" for the challenged Montana provision:

> A large number of crimes, especially violent crimes, are committed by intoxicated offenders; modern studies put the numbers as high as half of all homicides, for example. Disallowing consideration of voluntary intoxication has the effect of increasing the punishment for all

unlawful acts committed in that state, and thereby deters drunkenness or irresponsible behavior while drunk. The rule also serves as a specific deterrent, ensuring that those who prove incapable of controlling violent impulses while voluntarily intoxicated go to prison. And finally, the rule comports with and implements society's moral perception that one who has voluntarily impaired his own faculties should be responsible for the consequences.

There is, in modern times, even more justification for laws such as § 45-2-203 than there used to be. Some recent studies suggest that the connection between drunkenness and crime is as much cultural as pharmacological—that is, that drunks are violent not simply because alcohol makes them that way, but because they are behaving in accord with their learned belief that drunks are violent. This . . . adds additional support to the traditional view that an intoxicated criminal is not deserving of exoneration . . .

Returning to the comparison between the German and the common law approach (particularly, the version found in the Model Penal Code), do similar considerations motivate each approach? How do the approaches differ? Does one choose logic over policy, and the other policy over logic? Does one strike a better (more consistent, more principled, etc.) balance between logic and policy than the other? Or is the relevant balance not between logic and policy, but rather between principle and expediency? Or some other contrast of values, or conceptions of criminal law?

6. In German criminal law, even if an offender was in a state of profound consciousness disorder or pathological mental disorder at the time of the offense, under certain conditions he or she can still be punished for the offense as such (and not just under § 323a Criminal Code). In its 2004 opinion excerpted above, the Federal Court of Justice refers to a legal construction called *actio libera in causa*. This Latin expression describes the following situation: the offender has already formed the intention to commit a certain crime (for instance, to assault a specific victim) while he was sober or only slightly intoxicated. He then disinhibits himself with alcohol, or drinks to "calm his nerves," or for other motives—and finally commits the intended crime in a state of complete drunkenness falling under § 20 Criminal Code. Applying *actio libera in causa*, he could be punished for assault. (Note that *actio libera in causa* may also apply to crimes of negligence, insofar as the defendant should have foreseen the possibility that his drinking would lead to the commission of the relevant criminal act in an intoxicated state under § 20 Criminal Code.)

There is an extensive debate in the German literature about this construction. Because it is nowhere written in the German Criminal Code, some argue that it means applying an uncodified rule to the offender's disadvantage, which clashes with the legality principle, art. 103 para. 2 Basic Law ("An act can be punished only if its punishability was specified by a law before the act was committed."). But the majority opinion argues that it is merely a matter of interpreting the term "at the time of the commission of the offense" in § 20 Criminal Code. If the conditions of *actio libera in causa* are present, it is said, the offense begins earlier: with the planning stage, and at this point the offender was not severely intoxicated. Is this a satisfactory response to the concern that *actio libera in causa* violates the principle of legality in the form of the prohibitions of vagueness and of analogy, or—in U.S. constitutional terms—the rule of lenity (or strict construction)?

The Federal Court of Justice has no principled objections to this construction but makes an exception if the crime is not a result offense (i.e., one composed of both act and harmful result, e.g., killing, causing bodily harm), but a conduct offense (i.e., one that consists only in the *act as such*, e.g., drunk driving). Here, the crime can only begin when the vehicle moves, not before that, and thus *actio libera in causa* is not available for this kind of offense (see Judgment of August 22, 1996, 4 StR 217/96, BGHSt 42, 235).

Would this construction not violate the concurrence requirement in German criminal law (under §§ 16, 8 Criminal Code, associated with the vagueness prohibition in art. 103 para. 2 Basic Law) and in Anglo-American criminal law (requiring coincidence of *actus reus* and *mens rea*)?* Wouldn't the objections to criminal liability under § 323a apply yet more clearly

---

* See Chapter 7.A.

to liability under *actio libera in causa*, which abandons the fiction that regards § 323a as imposing liability on the intoxication itself, rather than subsequent criminal act? What about the culpability principle? Does it require proof of *mens rea* at *some point*, or more narrowly during the commission of the proscribed act and the infliction of the proscribed result? Does it place any limits on how far the relevant "act" can be extended looking backward from the commission of the offense? Does the planning of a future offense constitute commission of the offense itself? Does that not amount to punishment for thoughts, without acts? Or is this an instance of transference of *mens rea* from one act to another, a controversial construction in light of the concurrence requirement and the *mens rea* requirement (or the culpability principle in German law, as applied to *mens rea*)?

More generally, is *actio libera in causa* needed if one has § 323a? Isn't one of the contributions of § 323a, perhaps its most significant contribution, to criminal law doctrine that it makes constructions such *actio libera in causa* unnecessary? Or does the difference between a crime that was planned in a sober state and crimes that "just happened" because the offender was drunk justify two different approaches (and two different punishment ranges)?

7. The two German decisions above refer not to § 20 Criminal Code, but to its "little brother," § 21 Criminal Code. For court practice, this is the more important provision. While intoxication calling for § 20 Criminal Code is rare (most persons would not be able to move once they reached the required degree of drunkenness), offenders' severe drunkenness often requires judgments about the applicability of § 21 Criminal Code. (Given the rarity of sufficient intoxication, in German and in U.S. law ("prostration of the faculties"), is the doctrinal excitement about the intoxication defense much ado about nothing? Or is this an issue that carries symbolic significance beyond its practical impact?)

Until a few years ago, the courts often mitigated punishment according to § 21 Criminal Code. This approach is reflected in the decision from 1990, which emphasizes the straightforward significance of blood alcohol levels. But the newer decision from 2004 reflects a growing uneasiness about rewarding persons after substance abuse with mitigated punishments. The Federal Court of Justice in this newer decision makes use of the fact that § 21 Criminal Code does not demand mitigation of punishment in all cases but merely provides that the punishment "*can* be mitigated" (this is a crucial difference in comparison with § 20 which does not allow for discretion). The Senate points out that, if there is something reprehensible about the offender's prior conduct, this can outweigh the fact of intoxication at the precise moment of an attack. What is the basis for the Senate's decision? That the sentencing judge was under the false impression that mitigation was mandatory in the face of addiction, and therefore did not consider the appropriateness of mitigating the sentence? Or that the sentencing judge incorrectly weighed the relevant factors? Either way, what guidelines, if any, does the Senate set out for use in this case, or by other judges in future cases?

8. What is the significance of expert testimony in German intoxication cases? Is there a danger of overreliance on experts, whose opinion on threshold blood-alcohol content (BAC) could take the place of an independent legal judgment regarding the criminal liability, or at least the sanction, appropriate in a particular case? If BAC levels drive the application of §§ 20 and 21, does the principle of legality require their publication in a legislative norm, with the attendant publicness, accessibility, and uniformity, along with opportunities for the consultation of expert evidence at legislative hearings (as, for instance, in the case of the offense of *per se* driving while intoxicated*)?

---

* See, e.g., N.Y. Vehicle & Traffic Law §§ 1192.2, 1192.2-a.

CAUSATION

Causation is among the topics that will either reveal significant differences between Anglo-American and German criminal law or not, depending on your point of view and the granularity of your inquiry. It is also an instance in which contemporary German criminal law may appear to bear a closer resemblance to (at least some strands) of the traditional common law approach to a doctrinal issue than to the contemporary American—and in particular the Model Penal Code-based—one. (Other examples include the analysis of accessorial liability, of attempt, and of certain aspects of the law of homicide.*) From afar, or from a functional perspective, little distinguishes the Anglo-American and the German analysis of causation: both agree that *sine qua non*/but-for/physical causation is necessary, but not sufficient, for criminal liability and that something else is needed.

Just what that "something else" is, and how it fits into the analysis of criminal liability is another matter, and one that the Model Penal Code and German criminal law address in different ways. In the case of the Model Penal Code, that elusive *je ne sais quoi* is conceptualized as part of the inquiry into causation: legal, or proximate, cause, to be assessed under a complex (if not Byzantine) scheme of causation requirements tailored to the mental state requirement attached to the result element of the offense in question (recall that the definition of the mental state requirements themselves depends on the type of offense element they accompany[†]), and culminating in a loose, if not vague, standard framed as an inquiry into whether the result was "too remote or accidental in its occurrence to have a [just] bearing on the actor's liability or on the gravity of his offense." German criminal law, by contrast, deals with the "something else" question under a different heading, of "objective imputation" (*objektive Zurechnung*), which is distinguished from the inquiry into causation (it is a matter of objective *imputation*), on the one hand, and from that into *mens rea* (it is a matter of *objective* imputation), on the other.

People v. Kibbe
Court of Appeals of New York
35 N.Y.2d 407, 321 N.E.2d 773 (1974)

Gabrielli, Judge.

The factual setting of the bizarre events of a cold winter night of December 30, 1970, as developed by the testimony, including the voluntary statements of the defendants, reveal the following: During the early evening the defendants were drinking in a Rochester tavern along with the victim, George Stafford. The bartender testified that Stafford was displaying and "flashing" one hundred dollar bills, was thoroughly intoxicated and was finally "shut off" because of his inebriated condition. At some time between 8:15 and 8:30 p.m., Stafford inquired if someone would give him a ride to Canandaigua, New York, and the defendants, who, according to their statements, had already decided to steal Stafford's money, agreed to drive him there in Kibbe's automobile. The three men left the bar and proceeded to another bar where Stafford was denied service due to his condition. The defendants and Stafford then walked across the street to a third bar where they were served, and each had another drink or two.

---

* See Chapters 10, 12.A, and 15.A.
† See Chapter 8.A.

After they left the third bar, the three men entered Kibbe's automobile and began the trip toward Canandaigua. Krall drove the car while Kibbe demanded that Stafford turn over any money he had. In the course of an exchange, Kibbe slapped Stafford several times, took his money, then compelled him to lower his trousers and to take off his shoes to be certain that Stafford had given up all his money; and when they were satisfied that Stafford had no more money on his person, the defendants forced Stafford to exit the Kibbe vehicle.

As he was thrust from the car, Stafford fell onto the shoulder of the rural two-lane highway on which they had been traveling. His trousers were still down around his ankles, his shirt was rolled up towards his chest, he was shoeless and he had also been stripped of any outer clothing. Before the defendants pulled away, Kibbe placed Stafford's shoes and jacket on the shoulder of the highway. Although Stafford's eyeglasses were in the Kibbe vehicle, the defendants, either through inadvertence or perhaps by specific design, did not give them to Stafford before they drove away. It was some time between 9:30 and 9:40 p.m. when Kibbe and Krall abandoned Stafford on the side of the road. The temperature was near zero, and, although it was not snowing at the time, visibility was occasionally obscured by heavy winds which intermittently blew previously fallen snow into the air and across the highway; and there was snow on both sides of the road as a result of previous plowing operations. The structure nearest the point where Stafford was forced from the defendants' car was a gasoline service station situated nearly one half of a mile away on the other side of the highway. There was no artificial illumination on this segment of the rural highway.

At approximately 10:00 p.m. Michael W. Blake, a college student, was operating his pickup truck in the northbound lane of the highway in question. Two cars, which were approaching from the opposite direction, flashed their headlights at Blake's vehicle. Immediately after he had passed the second car, Blake saw Stafford sitting in the road in the middle of the northbound lane with his hands up in the air. Blake stated that he was operating his truck at a speed of approximately 50 miles per hour, and that he "didn't have time to react" before his vehicle struck Stafford. After he brought his truck to a stop and returned to try to be of assistance to Stafford, Blake observed that the man's trousers were down around his ankles and his shirt was pulled up around his chest. A deputy sheriff called to the accident scene also confirmed the fact that the victim's trousers were around his ankles, and that Stafford was wearing no shoes or jacket.

At the trial, the Medical Examiner of Monroe County testified that death had occurred fairly rapidly from massive head injuries. In addition, he found proof of a high degree of intoxication with a .25%, by weight, of alcohol concentration in the blood.

For their acts, the defendants were convicted of murder, robbery in the second degree and grand larceny in the third degree. However, the defendants basically challenge only their convictions of murder, claiming that the People failed to establish beyond a reasonable doubt that their acts "caused the death of another', as required by the statute (Penal Law, § 125.25, subd. 2)* . . . In answering this question, we are required to determine whether the defendants may be convicted of murder for the occurrences which have been described. They contend that the actions of Blake, the driver of the pickup truck, constituted both an intervening and superseding cause which relieves them of criminal responsibility for Stafford's death. There is . . . no statutory provision regarding the effect of an intervening cause of injury as it relates to the criminal responsibility of one who sets in motion the machinery which ultimately results in the victim's death; and there is surprisingly little case law dealing with the subject. Moreover, analogies to causation in civil cases are neither controlling nor dispositive, since, as this court has previously stated: "A long distance separates the negligence which renders one criminally liable from that which establishes civil liability" (People v. Rosenheimer, 209 N.Y. 115, 123, 102 N.E. 530, 533); and this is due in large measure to the fact that the standard or measure of persuasion by which the prosecution must convince the trier of all the essential elements of the crime charged, is beyond a reasonable doubt (In re Winship, 397 U.S. 358, 361, 90 S.Ct. 1068, 25 L.Ed.2d 368). Thus, actions which may serve as a predicate for civil liability may not be sufficient to constitute a basis for the imposition of criminal sanctions because of the different purposes of these two branches of law . . . However, to be a sufficiently direct cause of death so as to warrant the imposition of a criminal penalty therefor, it is not necessary that the ultimate harm be intended by the actor. It will suffice if it can be said beyond a reasonable doubt, as indeed it can be here said, that the ultimate harm is something which should have been foreseen as being reasonably related to the acts of the accused . . .

We subscribe to the requirement that the defendants' actions must be a sufficiently direct cause of the ensuing death before there can be any imposition of criminal liability, and recognize, of course,

---

* [N.Y. Penal Law § 125.25(2) ("A person is guilty of murder in the second degree when . . . [u]nder circumstances evincing a depraved indifference to human life, he recklessly engages in conduct which creates a grave risk of death to another person, and thereby causes the death of another person.").—Eds.]

that this standard is greater than that required to serve as a basis for tort liability. Applying these criteria to the defendants' actions, we conclude that their activities on the evening of December 30, 1970 were a sufficiently direct cause of the death of George Stafford so as to warrant the imposition of criminal sanctions. In engaging in what may properly be described as a despicable course of action, Kibbe and Krall left a helplessly intoxicated man without his eyeglasses in a position from which, because of these attending circumstances, he could not extricate himself and whose condition was such that he could not even protect himself from the elements. The defendants do not dispute the fact that their conduct evinced a depraved indifference to human life which created a grave risk of death, but rather they argue that it was just as likely that Stafford would be miraculously rescued by a good [S]amaritan. We cannot accept such an argument. There can be little doubt but that Stafford would have frozen to death in his state of undress had he remained on the shoulder of the road. The only alternative left to him was the highway, which in his condition, for one reason or another, clearly foreboded the probability of his resulting death.

Under the conditions surrounding Blake's operation of his truck (i.e., the fact that he had his low beams on as the two cars approached; that there was no artificial lighting on the highway; and that there was insufficient time in which to react to Stafford's presence in his lane), we do not think it may be said that any supervening wrongful act occurred to relieve the defendants from the directly foreseeable consequences of their actions. In short, we will not disturb the jury's determination that the prosecution proved beyond a reasonable doubt that their actions came clearly within the statute and "cause(d) the death of another person."

Model Penal Code

§ 2.03. Causal Relationship Between Conduct and Result; Divergence Between Result Designed or Contemplated and Actual Result or Between Probable and Actual Result.

(1) Conduct is the cause of a result when:

(a) it is an antecedent but for which the result in question would not have occurred; and
(b) the relationship between the conduct and result satisfies any additional causal requirements imposed by the Code or by the law defining the offense.

(2) When purposely or knowingly causing a particular result is an element of an offense, the element is not established if the actual result is not within the purpose or the contemplation of the actor unless:

(a) the actual result differs from that designed or contemplated, as the case may be, only in the respect that a different person or different property is injured or affected or that the injury or harm designed or contemplated would have been more serious or more extensive than that caused; or
(b) the actual result involves the same kind of injury or harm as that designed or contemplated and is not too remote or accidental in its occurrence to have a [just] bearing on the actor's liability or on the gravity of his offense.

(3) When recklessly or negligently causing a particular result is an element of an offense, the element is not established if the actual result is not within the risk of which the actor is aware or, in the case of negligence, of which he should be aware unless:

(a) the actual result differs from the probable result only in the respect that a different person or different property is injured or affected or that the probable injury or harm would have been more serious or more extensive than that caused; or
(b) the actual result involves the same kind of injury or harm as the probable result and is not too remote or accidental in its occurrence to have a [just] bearing on the actor's liability or on the gravity of his offense.

(4) When causing a particular result is a material element of an offense for which absolute liability is imposed by law, the element is not established unless the actual result is a probable consequence of the actor's conduct.

German Federal Court of Justice
2 StR 549/89, BGHSt 37, 106 (July 6, 1990)
Leather Spray Case

Facts

The firm W-GmbH deals amongst other things with the manufacture of shoe and leather care articles. This includes leather sprays, which—contained in aerosol cans—are meant for spraying and are used for the care, waterproofing or coloring of in particular shoes and other items of clothing. These products are sold amongst other things by the subsidiary firms E-GmbH and S-GmbH. Whilst the first named firm sells articles of the brand "E" via grocery shops, supermarkets and chemists, the last named firm supplies shoe and leather specialist shops with articles of the brand "S." From late autumn 1980, reports of harm were received by the group of firms, in which it was stated that people had suffered health impairment after the use of leather sprays of the brands described. These impairments mostly expressed themselves in breathing difficulties, coughing, nausea, shivering fits and fever. Affected persons had to obtain medical help, often needed hospital treatment as in-patients and in not infrequent cases came first to intensive care units because of their life-threatening condition. The findings mostly revealed collections of fluid in the lungs (lung edema). In most cases, the condition soon improved—especially after administering cortisone preparations—and led to complete recovery.

The first reports of harm caused internal investigations within the firms. These related to spray cans which were returned. There were no manufacturing faults in these. It was only established that the active ingredient of silicone oil in one spray had been increased since the middle of 1980. This change of formula was reversed at the beginning of 1981. Nevertheless further reports of harm followed. Technical discussions with toxicologists of two chemical firms and an advisory doctor brought no enlightenment. The silicone oil ingredient was taken out of production. As it emerged that in 1980 the supplier of fluoro-carbon resins used in production had changed, these materials were obtained from March 1981 onwards from the previous suppliers once more. The reports of harm continued however; they now concerned not only leather sprays—as at the beginning—of brand "S" but also those of brand "E." In the middle of April 1981 there was therefore a short term cessation of production and sale for certain "E" sprays; this was however cancelled again after a few days when investigations in the firm's own chemical department were unproductive.

On May 12, 1981, there was a special meeting of the directorship. The only agenda item was the cases of harm which had become known. The participants included all the directors of the firm W-GmbH namely the defendants S. and Dr Sch., the co-defendant R. (who died in the meantime) and the earlier co-defendant O. (the proceedings against him were handled separately). The defendant Dr. B. who was the head of the central laboratory was called in as "chief chemist." He presented the facts. In so doing he referred in particular to the fact that according to the investigations so far no toxic properties were found in the sprays and therefore no cause existed for a recall of these products. He proposed commissioning an external institution with further investigations and the placing of warnings on all spray cans, and improvement, if necessary, of warnings already present. The directorship endorsed this proposal. They were united in considering the cessation of sales, recall or even warning action only if the further investigations should reveal a "genuine product defect" or a "provable consumer risk." Following this meeting the defendants W. and D. were comprehensively informed. W. was at that time a director in the firm S-GmbH and D. occupied the same position in the firm E-GmbH. Both adopted the decision made at the meeting for their respective areas of responsibility.

In the ensuing period there were further cases of harm to health after the use of leather sprays of the brands mentioned. Even after further investigations there was no success in identifying a definite substance as causing harm. In the course of time the warnings on the spray cans were amplified and improved. On the September 20, 1983, after interventions by the Federal Health Office and the Federal Ministry for Youth, Family and Health the firm W-GmbH began to implement a cessation of sales and a recall operation, but without admittedly abandoning completely the further use of the formulae used in the recalled products. The regional court convicted the defendants S., Dr Sch., W. and D. of having inflicted bodily harm on numerous users of the sprays partly through failing to make a timely recall of the products from the dealers, and partly through continuing production and sale of these products. It assumes negligent infliction of bodily harm for four cases of harm which occurred after the case of harm F. became known on February 14, 1981. A further 38 cases of harm, which occurred after the meeting of the directorship of May 12, 1981, are the court's basis for conviction for infliction of dangerous bodily harm. The regional court has accordingly sentenced the defendants as follows: S. and Dr. Sch. each for negligent infliction of bodily harm in four cases to fines and for infliction of dangerous bodily harm to sentences of imprisonment of one year and six months; W. for negligent infliction of bodily harm in three cases to a fine and for infliction of dangerous bodily harm to a sentence of imprisonment of one year; D. for negligent infliction of bodily harm and for infliction of dangerous bodily harm to an overall fine. In so far as sentences of imprisonment have been passed, the court has suspended their execution on probation.

Reasons

. . .

III.

The conviction of the defendants S., Dr. Sch., W. and D. withstands legal examination . . .

1. The defendants have, to the extent established by the criminal chamber, committed (1) negligent infliction of bodily harm and (2) infliction of dangerous bodily harm in the form of treatment endangering life (§§ 230, 223a Criminal Code*).

a) It has been established without legal error that, in all cases of harm which are the basis of the convictions, the impairments of the health of the users affected have been caused by the leather sprays used in each case (in particular "S-3-fach" (S-3-fold) and "E-Nässeschutz" (E-damp protection), but also other sprays with the same formula). The criminal chamber has—contrary to the doubts expressed by the complainants—not left open whether the cause of harm was in the composition of the sprays. Apart from the fact that this follows from the context of the reasons in the judgment, it has expressly established within the description of the facts that the cause could "only lie in possible toxicological effects of the individual raw materials alone or at least in combination with other raw materials." This finding which binds the court hearing the appeal in law suffices to affirm the causal relationship. None of this is changed by the fact that it has not been possible—as the chamber admits—to identify with scientific exactness the substance or combination of substances which give the products their specific aptitude to cause damage to health. It was not necessary in the present case to discover the content responsible for this, to know its chemical composition and to describe its toxic effects. If it has been established in a manner free from legal error that the composition of the product—even if it could not be more precisely explained—was the cause of the harm, then it is not necessary for proof of the causal connection to establish why this composition could cause harm, i.e., what according to scientific analysis and discovery was the reason for it in the end (thus also Kuhlen, Fragen einer strafrechtlichen Produkthaftung (Questions of a product liability in criminal law), 1989, p. 69 f. (72)). Certainly where causality cannot be explained in this way, all other possible causes of harm must be excluded. But this is what the criminal chamber has done here. It has concerned itself in detail with the question of whether the cases of harm could be traced back to other causes which do not lie in the composition of the spray. With expert assistance it has reached the conclusion—after discussion of all the possibilities which need to be considered—that such other causes have to be ruled out. In this connection it has correctly explained—and this could certainly not eliminate the causal connection but only attribution of the harm to the defendants—that in none of the cases of harm was a misuse of the leather sprays recorded which was not in accordance with the instructions for use. Although the regional court has explained in detail that the harmful consequences were not influenced by a particular disposition or habit of the injured user (allergy sufferer or smoker), such explanations were not even needed. This is because a causal connection would not thoroby bo put in quoction, and tho attribution of harm to the defendants' responsibility would remain unaffected in the light of the not inconsiderable proportion of allergy sufferers and smokers in the population as a whole. The product in question must, unless such groups were expressly warned about its use, be so composed that it can be used by them as well in accordance with the instructions without impairment of health.

The suspicion expressed by the complainants that the criminal chamber had reached the conclusion of a causal connection between product use and occurrence of harm only on the basis that one occurred after the other finds no support in the assessment of the evidence by the court of fact. That court has instead correctly taken into account the fact that in the individual cases the course of illness and recovery showed significant similarities which gave an important indication of one and the same cause taking effect, which here was the use of the sprays. The deviations recorded were insubstantial. Besides this, animal experiments with the formulae of the leather sprays in question had also resulted in comparable lung damage. In the light of this evidential position, the formation of the belief of the court of fact cannot be objected to legally. In view of the number of similar cases of harm it needs no special explanation to show that it was not a question of merely accidental coincidence; this was a purely theoretical possibility. As the

---

* [Now §§ 229, 224 StGB: § 229 StGB (Causing Bodily Harm through Negligence): Who causes bodily harm to another person through negligence will be punished with imprisonment of not more than three years or with a fine.
§ 224 para. 1 Nr. 5 StGB (Causing Bodily Harm by Dangerous Means): Whosoever causes bodily harm . . . 5. by methods that pose a danger to life, shall be liable to imprisonment from six months to ten years, in less serious cases to imprisonment from three months to five years.—Eds.]

chamber has explained, the small number of cases in relation to the overall production of the leather sprays was also not inconsistent with affirmation of a causal connection. The same applies finally for the fact likewise discussed by the chamber that the same products had been manufactured and sold for a long time without this having led to corresponding consumer complaints.

b) Criminal liability of the defendants for the bodily harm which had occurred from the use of the leather sprays arises from their position as directors of the manufacturing firm W-GmbH as well as of the sales firms S-GmbH and E-GmbH, as these firms brought the articles causing harm into circulation. As the criminal chamber has correctly recognized, conduct by positive action should be assumed in so far as harm arose through the use of those sprays which had been produced or sold after the special meeting of directors on May 12, 1981 (10 cases of harm). This is because production and sale of products by a GmbH (limited company) are to be attributed to its directors as their own action..... It is different with the far more numerous cases in which the leather spray causing harm had already reached the market at the decisive point in time but had not yet reached the consumer. In these cases (28 cases from the overall complex of infliction of dangerous bodily harm and all four cases by negligent infliction of bodily harm) the directors are only responsible from the viewpoint of omission.

... A person who brings consumer articles which endanger health into circulation is obliged to avert harm and must, if he culpably fails to comply with this duty, assume criminal liability for the harmful consequences caused thereby. The criminal chamber derives this duty to avert harm from the duty to ensure safety in civil law, i.e., the duty of product surveillance, and bases this directly on the principles which have been developed by the case law of the highest courts for the area of civil law product liability (beginning with BGHZ 51, 91—fowl pest—up to BGHZ 104, 323—fizzy drink bottle) ... Whether and, if appropriate, how far the civil law duties on harm prevention are in agreement with those founding criminal liability (see on this Kuhlen, Fragen einer strafrechtlichen Produkthaftung (Questions of a product liability in criminal law), 1989, p. 148 ff. (171 ff.); ... does not need to be decided in general. In any case, the defendants had a guarantor status here obliging them to avert harm ... This guarantor status follows from prior dangerous conduct which is contrary to a duty.

... A person who, by bringing products into circulation, causes risk to their consumers in breach of duty must in principle take responsibility for ensuring that this risk is not realized in corresponding harm. This applies particularly for the production and sale of consumer goods which are made in such a way that their use in accordance with instructions creates the risk of harm to the health of consumers contrary to their justified expectations. In this respect it is not only the person who causes harm by positive action who is liable (see Landgericht Aachen, JZ 1971, 507 (514 ff.)—thalidomide; ...), but also the person who omits to avert threatened harm..... .

In the present case, the criminal chamber has established the prerequisites of such a guarantor status free from legal error. The prior conduct of the four defendants creating the risk consists in the fact that, as directors of the participating companies, they brought on to the market leather sprays which threatened to cause harm to the health of the users when used in accordance with instructions ...

The prior conduct of the defendants was also objectively in breach of duty. This follows from the simple fact that the legal order—not without exception, but in principle—forbids the creation of risks from which physical harm for third parties will subsequently develop if no one intervenes in the course of events ... The general protection given to the legal interest in physical integrity (see art. 2 para. 2 1 Basic Law) is sufficient to provide the legal basis for this ...

As the defendants were accordingly in a guarantor position, the objection raised by the complainant S. that it was only after the directors' meeting of May 12, 1981, at the earliest that the impression of danger had become so strong that further sale of these products and leaving them in the market could appear "careless" must fail. The objective breach of duty in the prior conduct does not assume that the person acting has already thereby violated his duties of care and thus behaved negligently (for another view Schünemann, ZStW 96 (1984) 287 (295, 308); also Jakobs, StrafR AT, 29/45, p. 670). The legal disapproval of the consequence of the endangering suffices. It is not a question of whether the behavior of the person who causes it is reprehensible in the sense of personal culpability ...

c) The guarantor status which is accordingly to be affirmed gave rise—as the criminal chamber correctly assumes—to the duty to recall the leather sprays which had already entered the market (on the duty to recall see BGH, NStE § 223 StGB no. 5—almond and sugar cake); ... The contrary view of Schünemann, who in general rejects a duty of recall having significance in criminal law in cases of this kind (Schünemann, Unternehmenskriminalität und StrafR (Corporate criminality and criminal law), 1979, pp. 99 ff.); ... cannot be followed ...

... The claim that the producer, when the goods have left his area of control, has no other status in relation to the threatened occurrence of harm than any unconnected third party, is also incorrect. This view completely loses sight of the possibility of and responsibility for action by those causing the danger. The producer and the sales organization have the most comprehensive overview, as the notifications of harm are collected by them. A recall issued by them has, in comparison to the intervention of a third party, a greater chance of being followed because traders and consumers ought to assume them to be most likely to have the technical knowledge which is necessary to assess the defectiveness of the product, to estimate the extent of the threatened danger, and to make the right choice about the necessary measures for its elimination. . . . Finally, the recall ought not to remain unissued simply because such an action is costly and possibly injurious to the reputation (the "image") of the firms involved, and would lead to a decrease in sales as well as a decline in profits. When balancing the interests in question, economic view-points must take second place, and the protection of consumers from harm to health deserves the priority here . . .

d) The duty to recall was owed by the directors of the three companies—in each case to be complied with jointly. It extended in the case of the defendants S. and Dr Sch. (as well as the other directors of the parent company) to all leather sprays, but was limited in the case of the defendant W. to products of the brand "S.," and in the case of the defendant D. accordingly to products of the brand "E."

These duties of each individual defendant were not limited by the fact that the companies had several directors, and in the firm W-GmbH each of them was allotted a particular business area: the defendant S. business area I (chemistry), the earlier co-defendant R. business area II (tech-nology, purchasing, stock and transport) the defendant Dr. Sch. business area III (administration), and the earlier co-defendant O. business area IV (sales). In principle, the dividing up of the business areas amongst several directors of a company does not influence the responsibility of each individual for the management of the company as a whole . . .

e) The requirement to act applying to the individual director was to be distinguished from the duty to recall which applied to all the directors jointly. The regional court has not made this distinction. The criminal chamber states that recall was possible and also reasonable for each of the defendants . . . There are doubts about this assessment. It leaves out of account the fact that within a company which has several directors there is in principle overall management. According to this the directors are only authorized to act jointly. None of them may proceed without the cooperation of the others . . .

If accordingly—contrary to the view held by the regional court—the individual director was not entitled to order the recall on his own authority, this does, however, not change his comprehen-sive guarantor position imposing a duty to avert harm. It is true that his concrete duties to act, proceeding from this guarantor position, were limited. Each of them was only under a duty to do what was possible and reasonable for him to bring into existence a decision of the board of directors about the ordering and implementation of the required recall. None of the defendants has satisfied this duty to act; they have all omitted to take the action demanded of them.

f) . . . Causality is present in the case of crimes by omission if, on undertaking the action which duty required, the resulting harm mentioned in the definition of the crime would not have occurred, and the harm would thus not have happened if the action were in an experiment of thought added (consistent case law, recently BGH, StrVert 1984, 247 f.; BGH, NStZ 1985, 26 f.; . . .) . . . According to these principles there is no objection here to finding a causal relationship. The question of causality poses itself in the present case at three different levels. At the first level it had to be decided whether the required recall would have come into existence at all, at the second whether it would have reached the intermediate dealers in time, and at the third whether these dealers would have taken action with regard to the recall . . .

aa) The criminal chamber has explained the (hypothetical) causal relationship of the second and third steps without legal error . . .

bb) The (hypothetical) causal connection of the first step can likewise be confirmed on the basis of the findings made. Admittedly it must be borne in mind that—as already explained—the duty to act on the part of each individual defendant was limited to doing everything possible and reasonable for him in order to bring into existence a decision by the board of directors as a whole. It is accordingly decisive whether the fulfillment of this duty to act would have led to such a decision having been made. If this question is asked separately for each of the defendants, the answer to it could be doubtful, because it cannot be excluded that each of the directors would have failed in the attempt to bring about the necessary decision because of the resistance of the remaining directors rejecting the recall. But this nevertheless permits criminal liability on his part.

cc) This applies to the charge of infliction of dangerous bodily harm simply because the four defendants were in this respect co-perpetrators, so that each of them must permit the contributions of all the others to the omission to be attributed to him. Co-perpetration is also possible for crimes by omission (RGSt 66, 71 (74); . . .). It is present for instance when several guarantors who can only fulfill together a duty make the collective decision not to do it (Jescheck, in: LK, 10th edit., § 13 marginal no. 58).

That is the situation here. At the special meeting of the board of directors on May 12, 1981, in which all the directors of the firm W-GmBH took part, the participants made the unanimous decision to refrain from a comprehensive recall. This was the collectively made decision not to fulfill the duty to avert harm which was imposed on them jointly. It is the basis for the joint nature of the omission and consequently for co-perpetratorship. The defendants W. and D. entered the circle of co-perpetrators, although they were not directors of the parent company and their presence at the special meeting was not established. This is because they were (in any case) comprehensively informed following this meeting about the decision made there, they approved it and they adopted it for each of their areas of responsibility . . .

dd) Even in the cases which the regional court judged as negligent infliction of bodily harm, each one of the defendants is liable for his failure to make the required recall. Nothing is changed by the fact that he merely made a partial contribution to this, consisting of not speaking in favor of the recall decision necessary for averting harm . . .

In the area of responsibility for action in criminal law, there is no doubt that where several participants independently of each other bring about the result contained in the definition of the crime only through the totality of their active contributions, each individual contribution is causatory in the sense of founding liability (see Lenckner, in: Schönke-Schröder, StGB, 23rd edit., preliminary note §§ 13 ff. marginal no. 83; Rudolphi, in: SKStGB, 5th edit., preliminary note § 1 marginal no. 51a; . . .) . . .

What applies to responsibility for action must likewise apply for omissions. If the measure required for averting harm—here the recall to be decided on by the board of directors—can only come into existence by the collaboration of several participants, each person who, in spite of his competence to collaborate, fails to make his contribution to it creates a cause for the required measure not taking place . . . He cannot exonerate himself here by arguing that his efforts to bring about the required collegial decision would have remained fruitless because the other participants would have outvoted him. He would only be freed from his joint criminal responsibility if he had done everything that was possible and reasonable for him to do in order to obtain the required decision (similarly, although in relation to responsibility for action: BGHSt 9, 203 (215 f.); see also Oberlandesgericht Stuttgart, NStZ 1981, 27 f.; . . .). But this did not apply to the defendants; none of them took any initiative at all to bring about the decision to recall, so the question of what steps would have been possible, reasonable and therefore required for the individual director needs not to be answered here.

Accordingly, each of the defendants must take responsibility in criminal law for the failure to recall and the harmful consequences caused by it . . .

NOTES

1. As set out in Model Penal Code § 2.03, Anglo-American criminal law distinguishes between two aspects of the causation analysis: factual cause and legal (or proximate) cause. Factual cause is "but-for cause": "conduct is the cause of a result when it is an antecedent *but for* which the result in question would not have occurred."* Factual cause is rarely in issue; almost all causation cases are about legal, or proximate, cause: "the relationship between the conduct and result satisfies any *additional causal requirements* imposed by the Code or by the law defining the offense."†

These "additional causal requirements" for legal cause are set out in the remainder of § 2.03. In the Model Penal Code version, the crucial question is whether "the actual result . . . is not too remote or accidental in its occurrence to have a [just] bearing on the actor's liability or on the gravity of his offense." This deliberately flexible—and arguably vague—standard replaces a plethora of tests the common law had developed over time, ranging from intervening and supervening causes to Hart & Honoré's *actus novus interveniens* (defined as a "voluntary" intervening act, one that is "free, deliberate, and informed") to the more recent foreseeability test applied in *Kibbe*, all supplemented by a range of fact scenarios based, more or less, on real cases (victim conduct and characteristics ("the thin-skulled man"), third

---

* § 2.03(1)(a) (emphasis added).
† § 2.03(1)(b) (emphasis added).

party conduct (often featuring medical professionals)), and all designed to determine whether some act, or event, "broke the chain of causation" between the defendant's conduct and the result.

The Model Penal Code drafters rejected these tests as obscuring the ultimately normative question of whether the actual result is fairly attributable to the defendant. The flexible test "not too remote . . . to have a [just] bearing on the actor's liability" was designed to delegate the assessment of fair attributability to the fact finder, and the jury in particular: to "put[] the issue squarely to the jury's sense of justice."* The Model Penal Code's proximate cause standard was (unsuccessfully) attacked on vagueness grounds:

> Our strong "sense of justice" requires us to consider the remoteness of . . . adventitious outcomes when determining criminal liability, but our inability to express what feature of unusual or extended causal chains affects our sense of justice makes developing a precise and definite standard that will accommodate our sense of justice difficult, and we have found none better than the "too remote to have a just bearing" standard. . . . The only practical standard is the jury's sense of justice. . . .
>
> Despite the vagueness of the "not too remote" standard, however, the authors of the Model Penal Code ultimately decided that it represented the best solution, concluding that what was really involved was a communal determination by a jury about how far criminal responsibility should go in cases of this kind: a community's sense of justice on whether a defendant, otherwise clearly responsible under the criminal law, should be relieved of punishment because the result appeared too distant from his act. . . .
>
> The question, then, is whether the law can constitutionally accommodate this conflict [between the desirability of limiting criminal liability for results otherwise falling within the law's prohibition but whose occurrence was so far from the ordinary or expectable as to leave doubt about the justice of imposing such liability, and the impossibility of fashioning language to define the extent of such limitation in a way to assure acceptably consistent application] in what the most learned of our colleagues have concluded is the best way, or whether, because of the indefiniteness involved, the law must abandon the search. If we choose the latter course, we face an intolerable predicament, for we would be forced either to extend criminal responsibility regardless of remoteness, or to confine it restrictively, severely limiting its scope and effectiveness simply to avoid the possibility of arbitrary application. Therefore, we choose the former—the law is constitutional—and we do so as a matter of our own sense of sound policy.
>
> In many, many other areas the law cannot be precise but must be practical. Even in the fashioning of rules of liability, this Court bluntly has acknowledged that its sense of sound policy and justice may be the ultimate touchstone. . . .
>
> This "sense of justice" is clearly involved in many criminal cases. Juries possess not only the unwritten power of nullification, but juries also have the almost absolute ability to determine life and death in sentencing proceedings under our capital punishment law. The acknowledged power of jurors, seemingly irrationally, certainly not explicitly rationally, to exercise lenity by not convicting of certain charges when the rest of their verdict may clearly indicate guilt is but another example. What other explanation exists for our accommodation of jurors' instincts but our faith in their "sense of justice"? . . .
>
> As we said about our acceptance of jury nullification, our trust in juries to understand and apply the "not too remote" element "is indicative of a belief that the jury in a criminal prosecution serves as the conscience of the community and the embodiment of the common sense and feelings reflective of society as a whole." "[A]nd law in the last analysis must reflect the general community sense of justice."

> *State v. Maldonado*, 137 N.J. 536, 645 A.2d 1165 (1994).

Is the New Jersey Supreme Court's opinion in this case to be commended for its honest embrace of inevitable discretion or condemned for its all-too-cavalier attitude toward the principle of legality? Is the "sense of justice" an inevitable component of considered judgments about justice in particular cases, or just another name for irrationality in legal decision-making? Should legal norms and institutions facilitate, and guide, the exercise of the sense of justice or should they seek to eliminate, or at least minimize, its influence? Even if

---

* Commentaries § 2.03, cmt. (The explicit reference to "justice" in the standard did not find sufficient support and therefore was placed in brackets.)

the sense of justice can play a useful role in criminal law, can a group of laypersons, however representative of some community (the defendant's, the victim's, both?), be entrusted with its exercise and application? Consider these questions from the perspective of both U.S. and German criminal law.*

2. The New York Court of Appeal in *Kibbe* adopts a (perhaps deceptively) simple foreseeability test for proximate causation, i.e., the inquiry into whether the defendants' conduct was a "sufficiently direct cause" of the actual result in the case. (Like most courts dealing with causation issues, which are rare enough to begin with, it wastes little time on addressing the factual cause ("but-for") issue: no one doubted that *but for* the defendants' conduct the victim would not have found himself half naked without his glasses at night in the middle of a snow blown road etc.) Although the New York Penal Law is based substantially on the Model Penal Code (with the MPC's main drafter, Herbert Wechsler, also serving on the New York criminal code revision commission), it did not follow the Model Penal Code in all respects. One of the provisions the New York code did not adopt is the MPC's section on causation. Left with no statutory guidance, the New York Court of Appeal is forced to announce a standard of its own: the foreseeability test is the result. This standard takes the Model Code's drive to simplify the inquiry into proximate cause to another level, or perhaps in another direction. It replaces the traditional palette of intervening and supervening causes with a single standard, without however essentially punting the issue to the fact finder and a vague reference to excessive "remoteness" and "just bearing" (as the New Jersey Criminal Code did).†

The foreseeability standard takes the place, in the Model Penal Code, not only of the "remoteness" inquiry, but also of that into the relationship between the actual result and the actor's mental state regarding the statutorily proscribed result. Here, the Model Code drafters can once again be accused of losing the forest for the trees. Note that the proximate cause test differs depending on what mental state requirement accompanies the result element of the offense in question: there are (at least) three proximate cause tests, depending on whether the result *mens rea* is purpose or knowledge (§ 2.03(2)), recklessness or negligence (§ 2.03(3)), or none at all (§ 2.03(4)). The New York Court of Appeals ignores this rather convoluted, if well intentioned, taxonomy and instead adopts a single one-size-fits-all foreseeability standard, which—in Model Penal Code terms—most closely approximates the proximate cause standard meant to be used "[w]hen . . . negligently causing a particular result is an element of an offense" ("actual result is . . . within the risk of which the actor . . . should be aware").

3. As the *Leather Spray Case* makes clear, the crucial question in determining causality in German criminal law involves a hypothetical test that closely resembles the common law "but-for" test for factual causation: if one were to eliminate the act in question from the course of the event, would the result have occurred nevertheless? If the answer is: yes, then the act was not the cause of the result, if the answer is: no, causality is established. If the conduct in question consists of an omission, the test question needs to be modified but follows the same structure: would the result not have occurred if one adds the act omitted in a hypothetical reconstruction?‡

Having determined that a causal connection exists under this but-for test, German criminal law next inquires whether the result should be attributed to the offender.§ Had consumers used the leather sprays disregarding explicit instructions printed on the containers, production and sale of the sprays would still be a cause of these imprudent consumers' health problems. But consequences of misuse would not be attributed to the producers of the sprays.

---

* See generally Markus D. Dubber, *The Sense of Justice: Empathy in Law and Punishment* (2006) (sense of justice as empathic role-taking).

† See *State v. Maldonado,* 137 N.J. 536, 645 A.2d 1165 (1994).

‡ See the *Leather Spray Case,* para III.1.f.

§ On the distinction between causality and attribution, see a short remark in the *Leather Spray Case* (at para. III.1.a), which addressed the question of possible misuse of the sprays.

Consider *Kibbe*: from a German perspective, what the court really examines is not the matter of causation (since, after all, the but-for test was clearly met), but the matter of attribution. The mere finding of a causal relationship cannot be a sufficient basis for punishment. Every event in this world has millions of antecedents that are causally connected to it. In *Kibbe*, for instance, if the owner of the tavern in Rochester where victim and offenders met would not have opened his establishment, or if Stafford's parents had chosen not to have children, the incident would not have occurred as it did. But causal antecedents of this kind hardly are sufficient to attribute criminal responsibility. It makes sense that the court demands a "sufficiently direct cause," but under German criminal law this is something different than causality. Besides the fact that the analysis does not spell out this distinction, in substance there are no fundamental objections to be raised from the perspective of German criminal law.

Under German criminal law doctrine, "objective attribution" (*objektive Zurechnung*) is established as an additional filter besides causality: the offender's conduct must have created a wrongful risk of this specific result, and the result must be the product of this very risk. Applying the "wrongful risk" formula, one arrives for *Kibbe* at the same legal outcome as the New York Court of Appeals did: the death of Stafford can be attributed to the defendants. The case would have been decided the same way under German law.

What is at stake in designating the inquiry beyond the application of the "but-for" causation test as one into legal, or proximate, cause (as in Anglo-American law) or into "objective attribution" (as in German law)? Regardless of the label, the inquiry produced the same result in *Kibbe*. Would it have produced the same result under the Model Penal Code test? Or is the New York Court of Appeals' foreseeability test for legal causation particularly close to the German "wrongful risk" test for "objective attribution"? Both, after all, are objective (the German one arguably being more objective than the New York one, since it requires only actual risk creation, not even putative awareness of the risk, i.e., foreseeability (not actual *foresight*)).

But consider the Model Penal Code approach, which—in the case of the offense at issue in *Kibbe* (depraved indifference murder)—would have required (at least) that "the actual result [be] within the risk of which the actor is aware" (since, at the time—before *People v. Payne* (Chapter 15.A.ii)—New York courts interpreted depraved indifference as aggravated recklessness) (§ 2.03(3)). In other words, the Model Penal Code would have required actual foresight, not merely foreseeability. Would the result still be the same as that under the German "wrongful risk" test? Is there something inappropriate about introducing a subjective component into the legal, or proximate, cause inquiry? Is it, in fact, desirable, given that the defendant's attitude toward, or perception, of the likelihood of a certain result occurring in a certain way might affect the decision whether that result can fairly be attributed to him or her? Would the German test be able to accommodate this subjective element? Or should all subjective issues be confined to the inquiry into *mens rea*?* Or would that inquiry only consider the *mens rea* with respect to the abstract result category identified in the offense definition (e.g., "death of another human being," in the case of homicide), as opposed to the actual result (e.g., death by getting run over by a car in the middle of the road, as in *Kibbe*) and its connection to the defendant's actual conduct (e.g., abandoning a highly intoxicated person by the side of a rural two-lane highway at night in the dead of winter, with blowing snow)?

4. The *Leather Spray Case* plays an important role in German criminal law because it discusses a number of contested legal issues. Two of them concern genuine questions of causation. The first causation problem emerged because it could never be determined which chemical substance in the leather sprays actually had the toxic qualities that could explain the health problems suffered by a small minority of consumers. It remained somewhat mysterious that the products had been on the market for a considerable time without reports about consumer injuries. But the German Federal Court of Justice did not see the chemists'

---

* See the discussion of *error in persona* and *aberratio ictus*, Chapter 8.C.

puzzlement as crucial. The main point was rather to establish *that* the leather sprays caused the health problems rather than to establish the precise scientific explanation.

For a similar U.S. case, see *People v. Warner-Lambert Co.*, 51 N.Y.2d 295 (1980). In this case, the New York Court of Appeals likewise assumes the acceptability of indeterminate alternative cause-in-fact cases such as in the *Leather Spray Case*, but then moves on to explore the analysis of legal, or proximate, cause in this type of case:

> [An explosion in a Warner-Lambert factory killed six workers. The corporation and various of its officers were charged with manslaughter in the second degree in violation of section 125.15 of the Penal Law and six counts of criminally negligent homicide in violation of section 125.10 of the Penal Law.*]
>
> There can be no doubt that there was competent evidence before the Grand Jury here which, if accepted as true, would have been sufficient to establish the existence of a broad, undifferentiated risk of explosion from ambient MS dust which had been brought to the attention of defendants. . . .
>
> [The prosecution presented three theories as to the actual cause of the explosion.] [T]he proof with respect to the actual cause of the explosion is speculative only, and as to at least one of the major hypotheses—that involving oxygen liquefaction—there was no evidence that that process was foreseeable or known to any of the defendants. In sum, there is no proof sufficient to support a finding that defendants foresaw or should have foreseen the physical cause of the explosion. This being so there was not legally sufficient evidence to establish the offenses charged. . . .
>
> It has been the position of the People that but-for causation is all that is required for the imposition of criminal liability. Thus, it is their submission, reduced to its simplest form, that there was evidence of a foreseeable and indeed foreseen risk of explosion of MS dust and that in consequence of defendants' failure to remove the dust a fatal explosion occurred. The chain of physical events by which the explosion was set off, i.e., its particular cause, is to them a matter of total indifference. On oral argument the People contended that liability could be imposed if the cause of the explosion were the lighting of a match by an uninvited intruder or the striking of a bolt of lightning. In effect they would hold defendants to the status of guarantors until the ambient dust was removed. It thus appears that the People would invoke an expanded application of proximate cause principles lifted from the civil law of torts.
>
> We have rejected the application of any such sweeping theory of culpability under our criminal law, however. . . . The critical issue in *People v. Kibbe* [excerpted above] was whether the defendants should be held criminally liable for murder when the particular cause of death was vehicular impact rather than freezing. Under the theory now advanced by the People it would have been irrelevant that death had been the consequence of one particular chain of causation rather than another; it would have been enough that the defendants exposed their victim to the risk of death and that he died. . . . To analogize the actual situation in the case now before us to that in *Kibbe* it might be hypothesized that the abandoned victim in *Kibbe* instead of being either frozen to death or killed when struck by a passing motor vehicle was killed when struck by an airplane making an emergency landing on the highway or when hit by a stray bullet from a hunter's rifle—occasions of death not reasonably to have been foreseen when the defendants abandoned their victim.

Does this opinion conflate proximate cause analysis with *mens rea* analysis, or does it rather clarify the distinction between the two, by illustrating the significance of the causation inquiry in cases where the presence of general *mens rea* does not imply the presence of proximate causation (i.e., under the New York test (under *Kibbe*): foreseeability of the "particular result")?

5. The second causation issue in the *Leather Spray Case* concerns collective decision-making in firms (it also applies to other collectives). The classical test to assess causality between act or omission and a harmful result consists of "imagining away" the act or, in the case of an omission, "hypothetical addition of the required act." This test shows its limits under the circumstances present here. Each of the directors could argue: even if I had demanded a recall of the dangerous products, my colleagues would have outvoted me. The Federal Court of

---

* Another issue in the case was the propriety of charging a corporation with an offense against the person. On the general question of corporate criminal liability, see Chapter 11.

Justice nevertheless argued that each of the directors had made a sufficient contribution to be criminally liable for the bodily harm. In upholding the convictions of intentional infliction of bodily harm after the directors' meeting on May 12, 1981, the Court invoked the concept of co-perpetration (at para. III.1.f.cc). The point of labeling offenders "co-perpetrators" is precisely to allow attribution of an act committed by one person to another. The prerequisite is that there was a common plan to the crime. For instance, if two offenders had agreed to shoot at the cashier in a bank robbery, the shots fired by one of them count also as acts of the other. According to this simple logic, the Court argues in the *Leather Spray Case* that the agreement formed on May 12, 1981, means that the co-perpetrators are responsible for one another's future omissions.

Independent of this, the Court also argues that, even before there was an explicit, agreed upon common strategy, each director was under a duty to do his best in installing a recall-strategy (para. III.1.f.dd); the court rejected as irrelevant the objection that any attempt to discharge that duty would have failed because he would have been outvoted. There was some debate about this argument in the literature—in the end, it is thought to imply a relaxation of the otherwise well-rooted causality principle in German criminal law.

The *Leather Spray Case* thus combines questions of causation with questions of complicity (or, more generally, "liability for conduct of another," Model Penal Code § 2.06) and, arguably, conspiracy (in particular the controversial liability for conduct of a co-conspirator in furtherance of the underlying agreement under *Pinkerton v. United States*, 328 U.S. 640 (1946)). For now, it is enough to point out that, at least in traditional Anglo-American criminal law, a different—and lesser—causation standard applies in cases of liability for another's conduct; from the perspective of causation, A will be held liable for harm caused by B's conduct as long as A *facilitated* B's conduct, where "facilitation" is understood, literally, to require some contribution short of but-for causality. The Model Penal Code attempts to sidestep this issue by not differentiating between successful and attempted facilitation: "A person is an accomplice of another person in the commission of an offense if . . . with the purpose of . . . facilitating the commission of the offense, he . . . aids . . . or *attempts to aid* such other person in . . . committing it" (§ 2.06(3)(a)(ii)). (In sharp contrast, attempting aiding—as opposed to attempted abetting—is not criminalized in German criminal law.) All of these issues are developed further in Chapter 10.

6. Besides the causation issues mentioned above, the *Leather Spray Case* also figures as an important case in the category of crimes by omission via guarantor duties based on prior dangerous conduct. There is universal agreement in German case law and the literature that prior conduct of a defendant that consisted of the wrongful violation of a duty can establish a guarantor duty.[*] But in this case, the Federal Court of Justice introduced a distinction that was, and still is, highly controversial. According to parts of the literature, a guarantor duty is limited to cases of negligent prior conduct, and negligence presupposes more than doing something objectively dangerous: it must also be subjectively negligent, that is, the individual concerned must at the time of the prior conduct have been able to foresee harm. This is why the defense lawyers in the *Leather Spray Case* argued that before the directors' meeting on May 12, 1981, there might have been objective dangers for consumers but not sufficient data to label the directors' conduct as subjectively negligent. But the Court maintains that the creation of an objective danger at a time when the risk was not yet known suffices to create a duty to recall the product once the knowledge is present—and if this duty is not fulfilled, to generate criminal liability for bodily injury through this omission.[†] How does the inquiry into "subjective negligence" differ from one into the foreseeability of the risk analyzed under a reasonable person standard (which would turn on the question whether a reasonable person in the actor's situation would have been aware of the existence, nature, and magnitude of the risk)?

---

[*] On omission liability and guarantor duties, see Chapter 7.D.
[†] On the notion of "subjective negligence" in German criminal law, see Chapter 8.A.

COMPLICITY

Courts, and commentators, have long noted the confused state of the common law of accessorial liability—so long, in fact, that it is surprising that none of them ever managed to remedy the situation, though not always for lack of trying. This confusion recently has been transferred from domestic to international criminal law, which—not surprisingly—confronts various forms of joint criminal activity. German criminal law often is held up as a promising alternative, not only as a more sophisticated, or at least systematic, general approach to the question of accessorial liability, but also, more specifically, as a means of extending criminal liability to dominating figures who may lie beyond the reach of traditional common law complicity doctrine (a problem not unlike that addressed in a different way by various domestic criminal law innovations, particularly in U.S. federal criminal law, see the discussion of RICO and money laundering in Chapter 17.C.).

Here, it is interesting that German criminal law bears a certain—at least formal—resemblance to traditional common criminal law, which likewise had developed an intricate taxonomy of accessories and principals, though one built on the concept of "presence" rather than "act dominion" (*Tatherrschaft*), the central notion in the contemporary German criminal law of accessorial liability. The Model Penal Code had discarded the traditional common law taxonomy as empty and obfuscatory, and replaced it with a distinction between accomplice and principal that carried no doctrinal significance, in an attempt to clear the way to what the drafters considered the central substantive question: assessing each actor's culpability, regardless of label. German criminal law differentiates not only between accessory and principal, but also between inciters (abettors) and aiders; in fact, this last distinction is arguably the most significant one, insofar as an inciter-accessory is punished at the level of the principal, while an aider-accessory receives a discount (which can be substantial, for instance, from life to a sentence range starting with three years in prison up to fifteen years, § 49 para. 1 nr. 1 Criminal Code).

State v. Tally
Supreme Court of Alabama
102 Ala. 25, 15 So. 722 (1894)

McClellan, J.

John B. Tally, as judge of the ninth judicial circuit, is charged with complicity in the murder of R.C. Ross by the hands of Robert, John, James, and Walter Skelton. Tally was a brother-in-law to . . . the Skeltons . . . , having married their sister . . . The grievance they had against Ross lay in the fact that the latter had seduced, or been criminally intimate with a sister of . . . them and of Mrs. Tally . . .

[On Sunday, February 4, 1894,] Ross left his house in Scottsboro surreptitiously under and because of an apprehension that his life was in imminent peril at the hands of the Skeltons, who soon gave chase] . . .

The flight of Ross and the pursuit of the Skeltons at once became generally known in the town of Scottsboro, and was well nigh the sole topic of conversation that Sunday morning. Everybody knew it. Everybody talked only about it. Everybody was impressed with the probability of a terrible tragedy to be enacted on the road to Stevenson, or at the latter point.

The respondent was soon abroad. He went to the depot, where the telegraph office was. He remained about there most of that morning. E. H. Ross, a kinsman of the Ross who had fled, . . . addressed [a telegram] to R. C. Ross, Stevenson, Ala. Its contents were: "Four men on horseback with guns following. Look out." Ross handed it to the operator to be sent. Tally either saw this message, or in some way accurately divined its contents. He called for paper, and immediately wrote a message himself, "Do not let the party warned get away," [addressed to William Huddleston, mayor of Stevenson and a lifelong friend of Tally's] . . . The respondent then handed this telegram to the operator, remarking to him, "This message has something to do with that one you just received," said he wanted it sent, and paid for it. He then started towards the door, but turned to the operator, and said: "Just add to that message, 'say nothing.' " Tally left the office. This message was sent just after that of E. H. Ross to R. C. Ross . . . Tally then, his watch to prevent the sending or delivery of a telegram to R. C. Ross being over, went home . . .

[We must address three issues] two of fact and one of law: First (a question of fact), did Judge Tally, on Sunday, February 4, 1894, knowing the intention of the Skeltons to take the life of Ross, and after they had gone in pursuit of him, do any act intended to further their design, and aid them in the taking of his life? If he did, then, second (a question of law), is it essential to his guilt that his act should have contributed to the effectuation of their design to the death of Ross? And, if so, third (another inquiry of fact), did his act contribute to the death of Ross?

There can be no reasonable doubt that Judge Tally knew, soon after the Skeltons had departed, that they had gone in pursuit of Ross, and that they intended to take his life. Within a few minutes, he was informed by his wife that Ross had fled, and that the four Skeltons were pursuing him. He had seen three of them mounted and heavily armed. He knew the fourth, even keener on the trail than these, had gone on before. He knew their grievance. The fact that they intended to wreak vengeance, in the way they did, upon overtaking Ross, was known to all men in Scottsboro, as soon as the flight and pursuit became known . . .

[As to the first inquiry,] we therefore find and hold that John B. Tally, with full knowledge that the Skeltons were in pursuit of Ross with the intent to take his life, committed acts, namely, kept watch at Scottsboro to prevent warning of danger being sent to Ross, and, with like purpose, sent the message to Huddleston, which were calculated to aid, and were committed by him with the intent to aid, the said Skeltons to take the life of Ross under the circumstances which rendered them guilty of murder.

[W]e are next to consider and determine the second inquiry . . . [To begin with,] Judge Tally did not command, direct, incite, counsel, or encourage the Skeltons to the murder of Ross . . . Judge Tally was therefore not, on the view we take of the evidence, an accessory before the fact to the killing of Ross. To be guilty of murder, therefore, not being a common-law principal, and not being an accessory before the fact,—to be concerned in the commission of the offense within the meaning of our statute,—he must be found to have aided or abetted the Skeltons in the commission of the offense in such sort as to constitute him at common law a principal in the second degree. A principal in this decree is one who is present at the commission of a felony by the hand of the principal in the first degree, and who, being thus present, aids or abets, or aids and abets, the latter therein. The presence which this definition requires need not be actual, physical juxtaposition in respect of the personal perpetrator of the crime. It is enough, so far as presence is concerned, for the principal in the second degree to be in a position to aid the commission of the crime by others. It is enough if he stands guard while the act is being perpetrated by others to prevent interference with them, or to warn them of the approach of danger; and it is immaterial how distant from the scene of the crime his vigil is maintained, provided it gives some promise of protection to those engaged in its active commission. At whatever distance he may be, he is present in legal contemplation if he is at the time performing any act in furtherance of the crime, or is in a position to give information to the principal which would be helpful to the end in view, or to prevent others from doing any act, by way of warning the intended victim or otherwise, which would be but an obstacle in the way of the consummation of the crime, or render its accomplishment more difficult. This is well illustrated by the case of State v. Hamilton, 13 Nev. 386, in which a plan was arranged between Laurie and others to rob the treasure of Wells, Fargo & Co. on the road between Eureka and some point in Nye county. Laurie was to ascertain when the treasure left Eureka, and signal his confederates by building a fire on the top of a mountain in Eureka county, which could be seen by them in Nye county, 30 or 40 miles distant. This signal was given by him, and his confederates, advised by it, met the stage, attacked and attempted to rob it, and in the attempt killed one of the guards. Laurie was indicted with the rest for murder. . . . He was constructively present though 30 or 40 miles away, and he was guilty as a principal in the second degree in that from and across this distance he aided and abetted his confederates by the beacon lights which he set upon a hill. It was as if he had been endowed with a voice to compass the intervening space, and to advise his accomplices of the approach of the treasure, or as if his words had been transmitted over a telephone or a telegraph line to the ears of his distant confederates. . . .

So far, therefore, as presence goes, Judge Tally, on guard at Scottsboro, to prevent warning being sent to Ross, or intercepting, or attempting to intercept, messages of warning which had started on their flight, was in legal contemplation present at Stevenson,—the scene of the homicide,—standing over Huddleston, to stay him in the performance of his duty of delivering warnings to Ross. He was constructively there, and hence, for all practical legal purposes, actually there. Being thus present, did he aid or abet the killing of Ross?

It is said ... that "the words 'aid' and 'abet' are pretty much the synonyms of each other;" and this has doubtless come to be true in the law, though originally a different meaning attached to each. The legal definition of "aid" is not different from its meaning in common parlance. It means "to assist," "to supplement the efforts of another." "Abet" is a French word, compounded of the two words "a" and "beter,"—"to bait or excite an animal;" ... "To abet is to incite or encourage a person to commit a crime. An abettor is a person who, being present or in the neighborhood, incites another to commit a crime, and thus becomes a principal in the offense." ... [T]o be an aider or abettor when no assistance is given or word uttered, the person so charged must have been present by preconcert, special or general, or at least to the knowledge of the principal, with the intent to aid him ...

... The assistance given ... need not contribute to the criminal result in the sense that but for it the result would not have ensued. It is quite sufficient if it facilitated a result that would have transpired without it. It is quite enough if the aid merely rendered it easier for the principal actor to accomplish the end intended by him and the aider and abettor, though in all human probability the end would have been attained without it. If the aid in homicide can be shown to have put the deceased at a disadvantage, to have deprived him of a single chance of life which but for it he would have had, he who furnishes such aid is guilty, though it cannot be known or shown that the dead man, in the absence thereof, would have availed himself of that chance ...

[A]nd so we are come to a consideration of the effect, if any, produced upon the situation at Stevenson by the message of Judge Tally to Huddleston. Its effect upon the situation could only have been through Huddleston, and upon his action in respect of the delivery to Ross of the message of warning sent by Ed Ross. This latter message reached Huddleston ..., we suppose, about five minutes certainly not more than ten minutes before Ross arrived at Stevenson. Immediately upon the heels of it, substantially at the same time, Tally's message to Huddleston was received by the latter. Ed Ross' message imported extreme urgency in its delivery, ... and it was the manifest duty of Huddleston to deliver it at the earliest practicable moment of time.

Huddleston appears to have appreciated the urgency of the case, and at first to have intended doing his duty. Upon receiving the two messages, he went at once without waiting, to copy them, to the Stevenson Hotel, which is located very near the telegraph office, in quest of Ross, upon the idea that he might have already arrived ... Not finding him there (for he had not yet reached Stevenson), Huddleston returned to the door of the depot, upstairs, in which was the telegraph office. By this time the command which Judge Tally had laid upon him had overmastered his sense of duty, and diverted him from his purpose to deliver Ed Ross' message to Robert. Standing there at the door, he saw a hack approaching from the direction of Scottsboro. He said then that he supposed Ross was in that hack ...

[I]t was Huddleston's duty to go out to the road along which the hack was being driven, at a point opposite his own position at the depot, and near to it, and there and then have delivered the message or made known its contents to Ross ... He did not warn Ross, because he did not want Ross to get away, and this because Judge Tally had asked him not to let Ross get away ...

It remains to be determined whether the unwarranted delay in the delivery of the message to Ross, or in advising him of its contents, thus caused by Judge Tally, with intent thereby to aid the Skeltons to kill Ross, did, in fact, aid them or contribute to the death of Ross ...

Can it be doubted that Ross' utter ignorance of John Skelton's presence with the others at Stevenson made it easier for John Skelton to take his life? Can it be doubted that his ignorance of the presence of all four Skeltons when the first gun was fired by Robert Skelton at Bloodwood, when, had he known it, he could have fled in the appreciable time between the time of the firing of the first and other shots—the next one being fired by the same man—made it easier for them to take his life? Can it be doubted in any case that murder by lying in wait is facilitated by the unconsciousness of the victim? Or in any case that the chances of the intended victim would be improved, and his death rendered more difficult of accomplishment, if the first unfruitful shot apprises him of the number and the identity of his assailants, and the full scope and measure of their motive and purposes? We cannot believe otherwise ...

[W]e are impelled to find that John B. Tally aided and abetted the murder of Robert C. Ross ... and to adjudge that he is ... guilty of murder ...; and judgment deposing him from office will be entered on the records of this court.

People v. Kaplan
Court of Appeals of New York
76 N.Y.2d 140, 556 N.E.2d 415 (1990)

Titone, J.

Defendant Murray Kaplan was convicted of first degree criminal sale of a controlled substance (Penal Law § 220.43) because of his involvement in a narcotics network which operated out of a garment business office located in the Empire State Building. His primary contention on appeal is that although the culpable state required for the commission of this crime is "knowledge," the trial court should have instructed the jury that defendant could not be held liable as an accomplice unless he acted with the specific intent to sell a controlled substance. We conclude that such an instruction is not required and that, accordingly, the conviction should be affirmed.

From May 1, 1986 to February 17, 1987, the police investigated a cocaine ring which apparently operated out of an office maintained by defendant's cousin, Mike Kaplan, in the Empire State Building. Detective Janis Grasso, posing as a drug courier for someone named "Ronnie" from Atlantic City, engaged in a series of transactions, primarily with Mike Kaplan. The charges against defendant were based on his actions on October 15, 1986, when, pursuant to a prior phone call, Grasso went to Kaplan's office to purchase 10 ounces of cocaine and found Kaplan, Kaplan's brother and defendant present. After introducing Grasso to the other two men, Mike Kaplan told defendant "to take care of the young lady." Defendant got off the couch, walked to a file cabinet in the room, removed a manila envelope from it, and placed it on the desk in front of Grasso. She in turn took out $ 15,000 in prerecorded buy money and placed it on the table. Defendant picked up the money, took it over to the table and began counting it. At the same time, Grasso opened the manila envelope, took out a zip-lock plastic bag, and placed the drugs into her purse remarking that "it looks nice."

Defendant was subsequently charged with, inter alia, criminal sale of a controlled substance.[1] Before the case was submitted to the jury, defense counsel asked the court to instruct the jurors that in order to convict defendant as an accomplice they must find that he had "specific intent" to sell a controlled substance, and that he had to "share the intent or purpose of the principal actors." The court denied defendant's request, noting that the mental culpability required for criminal sale was not "intent" but "knowledge" and, further, that the standard charge for accomplice liability requires proof that the defendant "intentionally aided" the other participants. Following the court's charge, which tracked the language of the applicable statutes, the jury found defendant guilty of criminal sale. The Appellate Division, First Department, affirmed defendant's conviction, without opinion, and leave to appeal was granted by a Judge of this court.

Penal Law § 20.00 provides that a person may be held criminally liable as an accomplice when he performs certain acts and does so "with the mental culpability required for the commission" of the substantive crime. Despite this language, defendant argues, based on case law predating the present Penal Law, that even though the substantive crime with which he was charged—criminal sale of a controlled substance—requires only knowledge,[3] the statute should be construed to require proof of a more exacting *mens rea*, namely specific intent to sell.

Under section 2 of the former Penal Law, a person could be convicted as a principal if he "aid[ed] and abett[ed] in [the] commission [of a crime]." The former Penal Law, however, did not specifically state what type of acts were required for conviction. Consequently, in order to prevent the imposition of criminal liability for the principal's crime on someone who may have been merely present, the courts required proof that the aider or abetter " 'share[d] the intent or purpose of the principal actor' " (People v. La Belle, 18 NY2d 405, 412; see, People v. Morhouse, 21 NY2d 66, 73–74 [accomplice had knowledge of and shared guilty purposes of principle]; People v. Fasano, 11 NY2d 436, 443 [accomplice must be "engaged in a common purpose or design"]).

Defendant's argument is that this "shared intent or purpose" test required proof, in his case, that he acted with the specific intent to sell cocaine. However, any lack of clarity that previously existed under section 2 of the former Penal Law was eliminated by the adoption of section 20.00 of the revised Penal Law, which specifies that an accomplice must have acted with the "mental culpability required for the commission" of the particular crime. Further, we have already construed section 20.00 as not requiring specific intent within the meaning of Penal Law § 15.05 (1) when the

---

[1] The additional charges were (1) a conspiracy count, which was severed; (2) sale and possession counts arising out of an alleged August 26, 1986 incident, which were dismissed before trial; (3) a possession count arising out of the October 15, 1986 incident, which was dismissed on the prosecutor's motion and (4) sale and possession counts involving an incident occurring on August 5, 1986, as to which the jurors in the present action were unable to agree.

[3] Penal Law § 220.43 provides, in pertinent part, that "[a] person is guilty of criminal sale of a controlled substance in the first degree when he *knowingly* and unlawfully sells" (emphasis supplied).

substantive crime does not involve such intent (see, People v. Flayhart, 72 NY2d 737, 741). Finally, the "shared intent or purpose" language from our earlier cases, which appears occasionally even in cases arising under the modern statute (see, e.g., People v. Allah, 71 NY2d 830, 831 ["community of purpose"]), cannot be read for the proposition, advanced by defendant, that a specific wish to commit the principal's substantive crime is required in all circumstances, including those involving substantive crimes with mental states other than that defined in Penal Law § 15.05(1). Indeed, the "shared intent or purpose" test set forth in the case law merely establishes that acts undertaken in relative innocence and without a conscious design to advance the principal's crime will not support a conviction for accomplice liability. The same conclusion, however, is implicit in the specific requirement in Penal Law § 20.00 that the accomplice "solicit[], request[], command[], importune[], or intentionally aid[]" the principal, since all of the delineated acts import goal-directed conduct.

The distinction made here is a subtle, but important, one. It is well illustrated by our holding in People v. Flayhart (supra), in which we concluded that the defendants could be guilty as accomplices to the crime of criminally negligent homicide under Penal Law § 125.10, even though neither defendant had the victim's death as a "conscious object" (see, Penal Law § 15.05 [1]). This result flowed naturally from the fact that both defendants could be found to have "fail[ed] to perceive a substantial and unjustifiable risk" of death—the "mental culpability required for the crime" (Penal Law § 20.00 ["acting with the mental culpability required for the commission thereof"])—and that both engaged in deliberate conduct to advance the common enterprise, i.e., the egregious neglect of the victim.

Similarly, in People v. Lipton (54 NY2d 340), this court upheld various counts of a physician's conviction arising out of a scheme in which the defendant wrote prescriptions for controlled substances that were subsequently either used by himself and his codefendants or sold to others by one of his codefendants. The court's statement in dictum that the physician could not have been liable as an accomplice to an illegal sale absent a "specific interest in having the actual drugs sold to some third party" or some other form of "specific intent," was an apparent reference to the "intentionally aiding" requirement of Penal Law § 20.00, as distinguished from the statutory *mens rea* requirement that the accomplice act with the level of mental culpability required for the principal's crime. . . .

In defendant's case there was sufficient evidence for the jury to find that, knowing the substance in question was cocaine, defendant intentionally aided Mike Kaplan by delivering it to Detective Grasso. The evidence established that after being asked by Mike Kaplan to "take care of" Detective Grasso, defendant immediately went to a file cabinet drawer, retrieved a package containing cocaine, and gave the package to Grasso in exchange for money which defendant immediately began to count. That defendant neither negotiated nor arranged the transactions does not affect his liability as an accomplice, and the court was not required to include specific intent to sell as an element in its charge on accessorial liability. The elements were adequately conveyed when the court told the jury that it must find both that defendant acted with the specific intent required for the substantive offense, i.e., knowledge that the substance was cocaine, and that he "intentionally aided" the sale.

Standefer v. United States
Supreme Court of the United States
447 U.S. 10 (1980)

At common law, the subject of principals and accessories was riddled with "intricate" distinctions. 2 J. Stephen, A History of the Criminal Law of England 231 (1883). In felony cases, parties to a crime were divided into four distinct categories: (1) principals in the first degree who actually perpetrated the offense; (2) principals in the second degree who were actually or constructively present at the scene of the crime and aided or abetted its commission; (3) accessories before the fact who aided or abetted the crime, but were not present at its commission; and (4) accessories after the fact who rendered assistance after the crime was complete. By contrast, misdemeanor cases "d[id] not admit of accessories either before or after the fact," United States v. Hartwell, 26 F.Cas. No. 15, 318, pp. 196, 199 (CC Mass. 1869); instead, all parties to a misdemeanor, whatever their roles, were principals.

Model Penal Code

§ 2.06. Liability for Conduct of Another; Complicity

(1) A person is guilty of an offense if it is committed by his own conduct or by the conduct of another person for which he is legally accountable, or both.

(2) A person is legally accountable for the conduct of another person when:

(a) acting with the kind of culpability that is sufficient for the commission of the offense, he causes an innocent or irresponsible person to engage in such conduct; or

(b) he is made accountable for the conduct of such other person by the Code or by the law defining the offense; or

(c) he is an accomplice of such other person in the commission of the offense.

(3) A person is an accomplice of another person in the commission of an offense if:

(a) with the purpose of promoting or facilitating the commission of the offense, he

　(i)　solicits such other person to commit it; or

　(ii)　aids or agrees or attempts to aid such other person in planning or committing it; or

　(iii)　having a legal duty to prevent the commission of the offense, fails to make proper effort so to do; or

(b) his conduct is expressly declared by law to establish his complicity.

(4) When causing a particular result is an element of an offense, an accomplice in the conduct causing such result is an accomplice in the commission of that offense, if he acts with the kind of culpability, if any, with respect to that result that is sufficient for the commission of the offense.

(5) A person who is legally incapable of committing a particular offense himself may be guilty thereof if it is committed by the conduct of another person for which he is legally accountable, unless such liability is inconsistent with the purpose of the provision establishing his incapacity.

(6) Unless otherwise provided by the Code or by the law defining the offense, a person is not an accomplice in an offense committed by another person if:

(a) he is a victim of that offense; or

(b) the offense is so defined that his conduct is inevitably incident to its commission; or

(c) he terminates his complicity prior to the commission of the offense and

　(i)　wholly deprives it of effectiveness in the commission of the offense; or

　(ii)　gives timely warning to the law enforcement authorities or otherwise makes proper effort to prevent the commission of the offense.

(7) An accomplice may be convicted on proof of the commission of the offense and of his complicity therein, though the person claimed to have committed the offense has not been prosecuted or convicted or has been convicted of a different offense or degree of offense or has an immunity to prosecution or conviction or has been acquitted.

German Federal Court of Justice
4 StR 613/57, BGHSt 11, 268, NJW 1958, 836 (January 23, 1958)

Facts

The defendant P., together with the co-defendants M. and T., attempted in the night of April 21, 1952, to force an entry into A.'s food shop in order to steal there. Each of them was armed with a loaded pistol for this purpose. When P. broke the windowpane of the bedroom of the married couple A., which he had taken to be an office, and M. had pushed the casements open into the room, A. went to the window, pushed the casements shut, and "gesticulating and bellowing like a bear" placed himself in front of the window. M. and T. then each fired a shot at the window as a result of which Mrs. A., who was just getting out of bed, was seriously wounded. After this T. and M. ran one after the other to the street. At the front corner of the house, M., looking backwards, noticed that a person was following him at a distance of not more than 2 to 3 m. This was P. M. however took him for a pursuer and was afraid of being captured by him. In order to escape the supposedly threatened arrest and the exposure of his perpetration of a crime, he shot at the person coming after him; he expected his shot to have fatal consequences and approved of this possibility. The bullet hit P. on the right upper arm but only passed through the lined sleeve of his jacket and was caught in his rolled-up shirtsleeve.

P. had already once fired at least five shots at police officers in 1950 when they disturbed him in the attempt to steal brandy from a distillery. The defendants had also repeatedly taken loaded firearms with them on their theft expeditions. They had discussed the use of firearms to the effect that people should be fired at if there was a risk of arrest of one of the participants. The shot fired at P. corresponded with that agreement by all three defendants. M. intended to hit him in order to eliminate him as the supposed pursuer; he aimed at him so as to hit him in any case, no matter on what part of the body; he did not mind if the bullet was fatal provided it hit its target and disposed of the victim as a pursuer.

The finding of the criminal chamber that the defendant M. is guilty of attempted murder because he attempted to kill a human being in order to conceal another crime, namely the burglary just attempted, is not open to objection in law . . .

Reasons

The complicity of the defendant P. in this criminal attempt has also been established in a manner which is free from objection . . .

P. must allow this attempted murder by M., directed against the supposed pursuer, to be considered as his own and be punished for it as a co-perpetrator. Such a punishment does not assume that he himself has fulfilled a feature of the statutory definition of the crime of attempted murder. It is sufficient according to consistent case law if there is mental collaboration, even a preparatory act in such a way that the co-perpetrator supports the other co-perpetrator by advice given before the crime or reinforces his intention to kill at any point in time (BGH, NJW 51, 410 no. 23). He must contribute to causing the entire result of the crime as his own at the time of this mental collaboration, i.e. in the present case intending by his contribution to adopt the possible shooting of a pursuer. The regional court has given sufficient reasons for this by finding an arrangement once for all to use weapons to prevent threatened arrest and to share risks together as a community . . . This agreement, as it were, "obliged" M. to shoot.

P. also participated in the dominion over the crime in the period in question. He could at any time have controlled the actions of his two accomplices when in their vicinity and asked them this time, contrary to the agreement, not to shoot at pursuers. The fact that he did not do this up to the time of the firing of the shot is the basis of his joint responsibility for the shot fired at him . . . This shot, as it was meant for a supposed pursuer, corresponded with the agreement of all the participants, and therefore did not go beyond the scope of what was encompassed by the defendant's intention. The shot must therefore be fully attributed to him (see RGSt 54, 177, 179 f.).

Contrary to the opinion of the appeal in law it is not within this framework a question of whether P. at the moment of the shot was himself in agreement with it. After he had "set the ball rolling" with an intention to act as a co-perpetrator by his earlier contribution to the crime, only a change of mind in accordance with the principles of withdrawal from an attempt could have freed him from criminal liability. A pre-requisite for this would however have been that he either had induced his co-perpetrators to give up their intention to kill or he had in some other way removed from his own contribution to the crime its causal effect for the further criminal actions of others (RGSt 54, 177; 59, 412; JW 34, 692; BGH, NJW 51, 410, 23). The clear findings of the regional court showed that this did not happen here, and that the defendant held to their original agreement in constant collaboration with the two others right to the end and at the time of the firing of the shot.

German Federal Court of Justice
9 StE 4/62, BGHSt 18, 87, NJW 1963, 355 (October 19, 1962)
Staschynskij Case

Facts

The defendant who is now almost 31 years old comes from a village in West Ukraine near Lemberg. In the late summer of 1950 the defendant was apprehended on the railway without a ticket and sent to the transport police in Lemberg. The transport police department is part of the Soviet Russian state security service (at that time the MGB—Ministry of State Security; from 1954 the KGB—Committee for State Security with the Council of Ministers of the USSR). An MGB leader interrogated him without mentioning the travel without payment. He mentioned that he knew in detail about the anti-Soviet attitude of the St. family. St. would be able to do valuable state policy work for the MGB and thereby protect his family from serious consequences. Shortly after that St. submitted a written commitment to the MGB service with an unconditional requirement of silence. He received the codename "Oleg." . . .

In September 1957 St. had to report to S. in the restricted area of Karlshorst [a quarter in East Berlin —Eds.]. On his arrival all S. said to him to start with was: "The time has now come, a man from Moscow has arrived." At this moment St. realized, as he said, "with suddenness and shock," that the prior observation of R. was in preparation for his assassination. Inwardly disturbed, he saw the Moscow KGB man produce a weapon as to which S. claimed that it had already been used several times and always with success. It was a metal tube at least as thick as a finger and about 18 cm long, made of three parts screwed together. In the lower part there was a firing pin which, under tension, is released by pressure on a securable spring which then lights a powder charge (a percussion cap). By this a metal piston in the middle part is moved which crushes a glass ampoule in the muzzle. This glass ampoule of about 5ccm contained, according to the presenter, a transparent poison, which on destruction of the ampoule escaped forwards as a gas. A human being who had this gas shot into his face from a distance of about 50 cm would breathe it in and die immediately. No traces could be discovered, so it would not possible to establish a violent death. The poison gas was harmless for the assassin if he swallowed a certain antidote tablet beforehand and after the assassination immediately crushed an ampoule sewn into gauze and breathed in the escaping gas . . .

Shortly after this S. gave the defendant instructions for the assassination of R. On October 8, 1957, S. gave orders that St. was to travel to Munich immediately, and to carry out the assassination. He gave him the crime weapon, the anti-poison remedy, i.e., 10 preventative tablets—St. had to return at any event on the 10th day at the latest—, an ampoule sewn into gauze and two identity cards, one a forged identity card of the Federal Republic of Germany made out for "S. D." and one a travel pass by the Soviet Zone made out to "J." The defendant flew to Munich and lay in wait for R. On October 12, 1957, a little after 10 a.m. he discovered R. getting out of the tram and then approaching the building KPlatz 8. From now on the defendant acted "almost automatically," which he, as he immediately adds, does not intend to be understood as a ground of excuse. "Something like an electric shock went through me, my heart was in my mouth; without of course being unconscious I went into the house as if I was half dreaming and went up to the first upper floor." When he then heard R. coming in, he took the wrapped up weapon from his coat pocket, unscrewed the safety screw and went to meet R. He saw that R. suspected nothing. When they met on the upper third of the lower stairs, he going down on the left hand side and R. directly to the right in front of him, he lifted his right hand, directed the weapon at R.'s face and pulled the trigger. He only noticed that R. reeled forwards, and then he ran rapidly down the stairs. While still in the hallway, the defendant crushed the anti-poison ampoule and sniffed it.

In January 1959 St. was sent by S. to Munich in order to investigate there the residence and habits of the Ukrainian emigrant leader Stefan B., the head of the OUN (Organization of Ukrainian Nationalists). In April 1959 he was summoned to Moscow. Here a higher KGB officer G. took precise details about the result of his investigations in Munich. He then revealed to St. that according to a decision made "at the highest level" he now had to eliminate B. in the same way as R. St. flew as ordered to Munich on May 10, 1959. S. had given him the weapon again unpacked on the previous evening, an identity card in the name of "H. B.," the antidote and a key for the front door to KrStraße 7. On the second or third day of his presence in Munich, an opportunity for the crime unexpectedly presented itself to St., who had only intended to observe the house KrStraße 7 in the afternoon as instructed. He did not however use this opportunity. In August 1959 St. spent a holiday with his parents as he did every year. At the beginning of October 1959 after he had already secretly been hoping that the KGB would not expect any further assassinations of him, S. revealed to him the instructions had just come from "the highest level in Moscow" that St. must now eliminate B. After equipping him with a double-barreled weapon, the antidotes, an appropriate duplicate key for the house KrStraße 7 and an identity card in the name of "B," St. flew to Munich again on October 14, 1959. On the following morning, St. took the protective tablet and observed the house ZStraße 67, where B. had his office. Shortly before 1 p.m. he saw B arriving unaccompanied in a car and driving into the yard. From now on, as he says, "a form of focused automatic process" started inside him. Hope gave way to "compulsion" ("Now I must do it"). He released the safety catch of the weapon, which was rolled up in a newspaper, opened the front door, and entered the house. As he was about to climb the stairs, he heard a woman above him saying "goodbye" and coming downstairs. In order not to be seen by her, he turned to the lift door on the ground floor, and pressed the lift button. Whether the lift came, and whether he opened its door, he no longer knows in spite of his otherwise excellent memory. In any case he let the woman leave the house without her having been able to see his face. In the meantime his agitation had become tremendous. He can no longer remember whether he reached the upper floor by the lift or via the stairs. There he soon heard the front door opening. He then went down and saw that B., who had just come in with a basket with tomatoes—in any case "something red"—on his right arm, was trying with his left hand to pull out the door key which had apparently become stuck. In order to cover up this delay, St. bent down and made as if he was fumbling with his shoe lace, even though he was wearing shoes without laces. Immediately after this he went up to B. at the front door, and said as he went past something like "Isn't it working?" He grasped the outer door knob with his left hand, with his right hand directed the weapon covered with the newspaper at the head of the unsuspecting B., pressed both triggers at the same time, which was possible without any difficulty, and rapidly pulled the front door shut from the outside. He then crushed the antidote ampoule, breathed in the contents and ran in the direction of the "Hofgarten" [a park–Eds.]. B was found on the day of the crime at 1.05 p.m. dying on the half landing of the first floor. He died shortly afterwards. In November 1959 St. was presented by S. in the Karlshorster Soviet restricted area to a Soviet general, whom he presumed to be the KGB leader of East Berlin. Standing and with a glass of brandy in his hand, the general declared that St. had been awarded the military

Order of the "Red Banner," which the KGB chief Sch. in Moscow would hand over to him, for carrying out an "important government task."

Reasons

I.

R. and B. were insidiously killed and thus murdered (§ 211 Criminal Code) . . .

II.

1. *Perpetratorship.* The defendant was ordered to carry out both assassinations, according to the reliable outcome of the trial, by the "highest level" of the Soviet Union, at least by the government, with the participation of Sch., the chairman at that time of the Committee for State Security with the Council of Ministers of the USSR. This is proved by the established circumstances, especially the way in which the command was given, the conferment of the order of the "Red Banner" and the document about this. The expert v. Bu. has convincingly explained as follows in relation to the period since Stalin's death in 1953: Before this point in time, orders to kill and other arbitrary measures against Soviet citizens and other persons by the leader of the KGB (formerly MGB, NKVD and GPU) were frequent. Since about 1956 (20th Party Conference of the Communist Party) such measures, according to reliable information from the leader's office, had been permitted to be decided only by a committee consisting of several government members, and no longer by the KGB. This knowledge accorded with the detailed, uncontradictory and completely unembellished information from the defendant about the issue of orders. This information is emphasized by the fact that St. received the military Order of the Red Banner for carrying out "an important government task" (according to the Soviet general in Karlshorst and S. in Moscow) or, as the "official assessment" of the KGB of December 28, 1960 says, for the "treatment of an important problem." St.'s superiors had, when ordering both assassinations, laid down beforehand the essential features (victims, weapon, antidote, manner of use, times of crimes, places of crimes and journeys). They acted intentionally. The poisoned pistols prepared at their command "already used several times and always with success," the detailed orders and instructions for the crimes prove that they had in mind killings with the conscious exploitation of the victim's absence of suspicion or means of defending himself, that is, murders. As originators of the crimes, wire pullers in the truest sense, they had the intention of principal perpetrators. It is not necessary in a legal sense to establish which individual persons had this perpetrator's intention. These real originators of the crimes are therefore principal perpetrators, in fact indirect perpetrators.

2. Aiding. Contrary to the view of the Federal Prosecutors Office, which sees the defendant as the perpetrator (although it has not given more precise reasons for this) St. should in both cases only be convicted as a facilitator to murder (§ 49 Criminal Code) [old version, today § 27 Criminal Code—Eds.].

An aider in relation to murder, as in relation to all other crimes, is a person who does not commit the crime as his own, but only co-operates as a tool or assistant in the crime of another. The decisive factor here is the inward attitude to the crime. The German Imperial Court had in this way already distinguished principal perpetrators and aiders from each other in consistent case law (RGSt 31, 82; 44, 71; 57, 274; 66, 240; 74, 84 with further information). According to this case law a person who has a crime carried out entirely by others also falls to be considered as a principal perpetrator and on the other hand a person who fulfills all the features of the definition of a crime personally also falls to be considered as a mere aider. This so-called subjective participation doctrine has been endorsed in principle by the Federal Court of Justice in its case law from the outset (BGHSt 2, 150, 156; BGHSt 2, 169, 170; BGHSt 4, 20, 21; BGHSt 6, 226, 228; BGHSt 6, 248, 249; BGHSt 8, 70, 73). According to decisions of the Federal Court of Justice in particular a person who himself fulfills all the elements of the definition of the crime can be a mere aider (BGH, NJW 51, 120; NJW 54, 1374, 1375; . . .) even if such a participant in the crime should in most cases be convicted as principal perpetrator (see BGHSt 8, 70, 73) . . .

There is no reason to move away from this case law of the Federal Court of Justice which is described in the literature, not quite correctly, as the "subjective theory with incorporation of objective elements" (Schönke-Schröder, StGB, 10th edit., preliminary note. VIII 2 before § 47). The objective theory advocated in the literature (which is not at all uniform in this respect) offers no convincing alternative. It rejects any distinction between perpetration and participation (aiding) based on the feature of the perpetrator's will. The objective theory considers as crucial the actual happening, the "real division of power between the various people co-operating" (Maurach, Deutsches Strafrecht, Allgem. Teil, 2nd edit., 1958, pp. 515, 516), in which connection the decisive feature should be the perpetrator's dominion over the crime and the absence of any control of it by the aider.

According to this approach, it is not a question of the mere will to control the crime, rather, a person who fulfills an element of the crime himself is always a co-perpetrator, even if he has no interest in its success.

It may be left undecided whether the distinguishing feature of dominion over the crime declared to be decisive by this opinion is understood in much too narrow a way (excluding any psychological facts and emotional pressure or compulsion of the participants). It might provide an easy distinction between principal perpetration and aiding, but at the same time it is of questionable crudeness and poses the danger of no longer assessing each participant in the crime in the most just way. But above all this theory is questionable because, primarily in relation to homicide crimes but certainly not only with these, it excludes consideration of special backgrounds of crimes which are admittedly extremely powerful but alien to general criminology. The extraordinary power of special circumstances of this kind has been unanimously emphasized in the outcome in the present proceedings not only by the prosecution and defence but above all also by the two accessory prosecutors whose husbands were the victims of the crimes and their lawyers. The objective theory would perhaps be more convincing if judgment were only to be passed on participants in the crime who have followed crime motives known to criminology, and against the background of essentially uniform moral views of the general public and fairly stable conditions in state politics. It leaves out of account that this obviously only applies to part of current criminality. Political murders have of course always occurred in the world, as in Germany. Recently however certain modern states, under the influence of radical political opinions, in Germany under National Socialism, have moved to planning political murders or mass murder and to commanding the execution of such bloody deeds. The mere recipients of such commands are not subject to criminologically researched criminal impulses or to similar personal ones when committing these kinds of officially commanded crimes. Instead they find themselves in the morally confusing, sometimes hopeless situation of being ordered to commit the most reprehensible crimes by their own state which appears to many people as an unquestionable authority through skillful mass propaganda. They comply with such instructions under the influence of political propaganda or the authority to command or similar influences of their own state from which they are in contrast entitled to expect the preservation of law and order. These dangerous impulses to commit crimes proceed not from the recipients of the commands but from the holders of state power in flagrant misuse of this power. Commands of this kind to commit crimes are not even limited to the realm of the state concerned. The trial has shown that they also occur in the international realm.

These special circumstances of state-commanded crime do not in any way exempt the participants from culpability in criminal law. Every state community may and must require that everyone unconditionally refrains from crime, even crime demanded by misuse of state authority. Otherwise all order would be dissolved and the door opened to political crime. The internal ground for the accusation of culpability lies in the fact that the human being is destined for free, responsible and moral self-determination, and is therefore enabled to decide for the right and against the wrong, to order his conduct according to the norms of the legally required and to avoid what is legally prohibited as soon as he has attained moral maturity and as long as his aptitude for free moral self-determination has not been temporarily paralyzed or permanently destroyed by the pathological events mentioned in § 51 [old version, now § 20 German Criminal Code (Chapters 8.D and 14.C)—Eds.] (BGHSt 2, 194, 200). This should also be adhered to for the realm of regimes which commit crimes. In special circumstances, state commands to commit crimes may admittedly create grounds for reduction of punishment. However, a person who (1) willingly gives in to a political murder campaign, silences his conscience and makes the criminal goals of others the basis of his own conviction and his own actions, or who (2) in his area of responsibility or influence ensures that such commands are carried out unreservedly, or who (3) in doing so shows consensual zeal or exploits murderous state terrorism for his own purposes cannot appeal to the fact that he was only an assistant to his superiors. His thoughts and actions coincide with those of the real originator of the crime. He is as a rule a principal perpetrator.

It can however be different in a legal sense with those who disapprove of such commands to commit crimes and struggle against them, but nevertheless carry them out because of human weakness, as they are not a match for the superior strength of state authorities, and give in to them because they cannot summon up the courage for resistance or the intelligence for effective excuse, even if this means to placate their consciences temporarily by political slogans and to provide themselves with self-justification. There is no sufficient legal ground to equate such people from the outset, without exception and inevitably, with the originator of the crime, the unscrupulous perpetrator acting out of conviction and the convinced and willing recipient of the command, especially as the statute threatens even the aider with the full punishment for a perpetrator and only provides for a discretionary reduction of the punishment.

The objective theory is too schematically narrow on all these grounds. It needs further examination of its consequences. On this ground the case law so far, rightly understood, deserves preference (see also Kohlrausch-Lange, StGB, 42nd edit., preliminary note before § 47: influence "of overpowering factors").

The application of these legal principles to the proven inward attitude of the defendant in both assassinations reveals, on consideration of all the circumstances, that he did not intend these crimes as his own, that he had no interest of his own in them and no criminal intention of his own, that he gave in only reluctantly to the criminal intention of others, that in the end he submitted to the authority of his political leadership at that time against his conscience, and that he did not himself determine the mode of execution in any significant points. No material or political interests of his own existed as an indication of his intention as perpetrator. No payment for the crime was promised for him as for a hired henchman, and he also received none. The awarding of the decoration surprised and repelled him. He could not escape it. Regarding R. and B. as "enemies of the Soviet Union to be eliminated" did not spring from his own political inspiration. He had been indoctrinated in such ideas from his youth upwards without real success, and without them having become firm maxims for him and so as to numb his conscience. Admittedly St. committed both crimes outside the area of authority of his superiors. However this does not make him a perpetrator either. To say that he would only have needed to reveal himself to Western authorities fails to recognize the true factual situation. The defendant must be believed when he says that someone who has spent 11 years without interruption as an impressionable young man in the heart of the realm of Soviet authority, and has been continually indoctrinated there, has great difficulties in understanding Western ways of life and thought, coming to terms with them, leaving home, relations and his familiar language area for ever, and instead embracing unknown circumstances, dangers and influences, even if he already has a personal attachment here. He has also not so far learnt a vocation which can provide him with a living. Because of the "important government task" given to him he must also be believed when he says that he feared both the KGB in the careless "West," and after a change of allegiance he would, as a "traitor," be the subject of his superiors' revenge. The overall picture of all the circumstances of the crime therefore argues that the defendant was not a principal perpetrator. He is therefore to be convicted as an aider (§ 49 Criminal Code) [old version, now § 27 Criminal Code—Eds.].

[St. was sentenced to eight years' imprisonment.]

German Federal Court of Justice,
5 StR 98/94, BGHSt 40, 218 (July 26, 1994)

Facts

The object of the present proceedings is the killing of seven men who between 1971 and 1989 intended to flee from East Germany over the internal German border. The regional court held the defendants, as members of the National Defence Council, to be (jointly) responsible for the deaths of these fugitives. The regional court found the following facts: Since the beginning of 1949 until the middle of 1961 about 2.5 million Germans fled from East Germany into the West. When, in 1961, as a consequence of the world political situation, the stream of fugitives significantly increased, the Council of Ministers of the German Democratic Republic (GDR) decided on the August 12, 1961, after conversations with those responsible in the Soviet Union and in other states which were members of the Warsaw Pact, to close completely the border between East Germany and the Federal Republic of Germany. In the morning hours of August 13, 1961, the sectors border within Berlin were sealed off with barbed wire and barricades and later "secured" by a wall. On the remaining border between East Germany and West Germany, security installations were strengthened or built. Except on the Berlin borders, mines were laid and automatic firing devices set up. Numerous attempts at flight over the thus "secured" border of East Germany ended fatally for the fugitives because they trod on mines, were caught by automatic firing devices or were shot by members of the border troops to prevent their flight. According to Art. 48 Constitution of the GDR, the People's Chamber was the organ of superior state power in the GDR which was simultaneously entitled to make laws and execute them. Between the sittings of the People's Chamber, the Council of State exercised the powers of the People's Chamber under art. 66 GDR Constitution. Under art. 73 GDR Constitution the Council of State organized the defence of the country with the assistance of the National Defence Council. The National Defence Council was the central state organ which was responsible for the integrated direction of defence and security measures in the GDR (Staatsrecht der DDR, Lehrb., Berlin 1978, p. 350). The number of members of the National Defence Council fluctuated slightly; it amounted in 1971 to 14. Whilst the chairman of the National Defence Council was chosen by the People's Chamber (art. 50 GDR Constitution), the members were appointed by the Council of State (art. 73 GDR Constitution). The chairman of the National Defence Council from 1971 onwards was Erich Honecker, the Chairman of the Council of State and the Secretary General of the Central Committee of the SED [United Socialist Party of Germany: the East German communist party]. Apart from him, the members included, amongst others, the Chairman of the Council of Ministers, the Minister for National Defence, the Chiefs of the General Staff of the National People's Army and of the Political Head Office of the National People's Army, a department of the Ministry for National Defence at the same time subject to the Central Committee of the SED, as well as the first secretaries of the SED's district organizations from certain border areas. The leading role laid down in art. 1 GDR Constitution of the SED as the Marxist-Leninist party led to the politics of the GDR being in fact determined by the SED and its committees, in particular the Central Committee, the Politburo and the Secretariat, through a strong personal interconnection between organs of the party and state organs. The First Secretary of the Central Committee of the SED was in charge of the Politburo and the Secretariat. This was Honecker since 1971. The National People's Army and the "border troops of the GDR," hived off from the National People's Army at the beginning of the 1970s, were subordinate to the Ministry for National Defence. All the actions of the border troops, including the setting up of automatic firing devices at the border, the mining of the border and the deployment of firearms against fugitives were based on commands which went back to the "annual commands" of the Minister for National Defence. The necessary prerequisite for these annual commands was that they should be based on previous decisions of the National Defence Council.

The defendant K. was born in 1920 and became a member of the party executive after the founding of the SED, and then of the Central Committee, in 1957 the Chief of the Air Force of the National People's Army and Deputy Minister of National Defence. From 1967 to 1978 the defendant was Chief of the General Staff for the National People's Army and since 1967 member of the National Defence Council to which he belonged until 1989. The defendant S. was born in 1926 and was appointed in 1964 a Major General and called to the Ministry for National Defence as Deputy Chief of the General Staff for operational questions. When Honecker became Chairman of the National Defence Council in 1971, S., as member of the National Defence Council, took over his earlier tasks as secretary of this committee. He occupied this post until 1989. The defendant A. was born in 1919. He was a member of the Central Committee of the SED from 1963 and became a first secretary of the SED district organization in Suhl in 1968. In 1971, he became a deputy in the People's Chamber and in 1972, in his capacity as first secretary of the SED district organization in Suhl, a member of the National Defence Council to which he belonged until 1989.

The general command situation at the border of East Germany with West Germany for which the defendants as members of the National Defence Council took responsibility was to the effect that "border violations" by fugitives from East Germany were to be prevented in every case and by the employment of any means. In this context the death of the fugitive was accepted when a "border violation" could not otherwise be prevented. The border installations, the technical arrangement of which was laid out in such a way that they primarily prevented flight from East Germany, were guarded by border troops which were specially trained for this task. The members of the border troops were informed that a successful "border violation" would have "consequences" for the soldiers concerned. As in many cases a fugitive could not be stopped without the deployment of aimed firearms, fatal consequences could not be excluded with the use of the firearm, especially as the sub-machine gun "Kalashnikov Model 47" used at the border had a low capacity for accuracy particularly on continuous fire from a standing position. The commands deliberately gave the soldiers the impression that the "inviolability of the border" had priority over human life. In order to avoid the public taking notice, rescue measures had to take place in such a way that they were not observed by third parties. That led to substantial delays in the provision of medical assistance. Hospital doctors were not informed about the cause of the injuries. Doctors carrying out autopsies received no, or only vague, information about the more detailed circumstances of the deaths, and the death certificate contained no information about the cause of death. Even after the Border Act came into effect in 1982 (see on this BGHSt 39, 1, 9 ff.), soldiers were again ordered to employ firearms to the extent of the earlier order. Border soldiers who had prevented an attempted flight were commended, even if the fugitive had been killed. This general command situation at the border was based on the decisions of the National Defence Council, in which the defendants had been involved . . .

As a result of the measures at the border of East Germany with West Germany, large numbers of fugitives were killed. The following occurrences are the subject of the proceedings:

(1) On April 8, 1971, the 18-year-old E., in attempting to cross the minefield in the neighborhood of Schwickerthausen, trod on a land mine. This tore off his left foot but in spite of this he managed to reach the territory of West Germany. Here E. died, after several operations, on May 4, 1971, as a consequence of his injuries.

(2) On January 16,1973, the 29-year-old F. set off a fragmentation mine SM-70 installed in the neighborhood of Blütlingen in the district of Lüchow-Dannenberg and was severely injured by

numerous splinters. In spite of this he succeeded in reaching the territory of West Germany. F. died on January 17, 1973, in hospital as a result of his injuries.

(3) On July 14, 1974, the 25-year-old V set off three fragmentation mines SM-70 in the neighborhood of Hohegeiß and was severely injured by numerous splinters. 20 minutes later he was dragged by the feet by GDR border soldiers into the back area and loaded into a lorry which still waited for about a further 20 minutes. He was admitted to the Wernigerode Hospital almost two hours after the event, where he died on July 15, 1974, from the consequences of his injuries.

(4) On April 7,1980, the 28-year-old B. set off a fragmentation mine SM-70 at Veltheim in the district of Halberstadt and was severely injured by numerous splinters. After a series of operations in the hospital at Halberstadt, B. died on May 11, 1980, from the consequences of his injuries.

(5) On March 22, 1984, the 20-year-old M. set off a fragmentation mine SM-70 in the neighborhood of Wendehausen in the district of Mühlhausen and was severely injured by numerous splinters. He was rescued by border soldiers. A doctor who was summoned confirmed his death.

(6) On December 1, 1984, at 3.15 a.m. in Berlin two border soldiers fired at the 20-year-old C. with continuous fire when he was attempting to get over the wall with a ladder, and hit him in the upper region of the back. Medical assistance was refused to the victim. He was not delivered to the hospital of the People's Police until around 5.15 a.m. At this point, he had bled to death. If medical assistance had come sooner, C. would probably have survived. The marksmen were praised, and objection was only made to the overuse of ammunition. Criminal proceedings against the marksmen were the subject of a judgment of the Senate (BGHSt 39, 1), *Border Guard Case*, Chapter 2.A).—Eds.].

(7) In the night of February 5 to February 6, 1989, the 22-year-old G. and A. of the same age attempted to climb over the wall to West Berlin. G. was fatally hit in the chest by a shot fired by a border soldier. A was injured by a shot. The marksmen were formally praised; a dinner was held in their honor. The criminal proceedings against the marksmen were the subject of a judgment of the Senate (BGHSt 39, 168).

The regional court attributes to the individual defendants only the crimes which were committed after the commencement of their membership of the National Defence Council . . . The regional court found the defendants K. and S. guilty of incitement to homicide and the defendant A. of aiding with homicide. It therefore sentenced the defendant K. to a term of imprisonment of seven years and six months, the defendant S. to a term of five years and six months and the defendant A. to a term of three years and six months.

The appeals lodged by the public prosecutor's office against the defendants led to an alteration in the verdict for the defendants and besides this in the case of defendant A. to a higher sentence. Otherwise they were unsuccessful. The defendants' appeals were unsuccessful.

Reasons

The public prosecutor's office puts forward the view that the defendants were co-perpetrators with the border soldiers . . . The examination by the Senate results in the following:

1. The defendants are guilty of homicide as indirect perpetrators (§§ 212, 25 Criminal Code) . . .

a) . . .

b) According to the Criminal Code, the defendants are indirect perpetrators of homicide. The question of whether the border soldiers have acted culpably in each case can be left undecided because indirect perpetration falls to be considered even where there is an intermediary who was himself acting with unlimited culpability and as a principal perpetrator. The Senate has already decided that in cases of the present kind the border soldiers could be perpetrators and not only aiders (BGHSt 39, 1, 31 f.)

aa) The question of whether the background man to a perpetrator acting with unlimited culpability can be an indirect perpetrator is disputed.

The legislature has deliberately left the question open and confined itself to the formulation that a person who "commits" a crime "through another" can also be the perpetrator (§ 25 para. 1 Criminal Code) . . . The literature does not convey a uniform picture. "There is scarcely anything that is beyond question except the general principle that the indirect perpetrator must also in his person fulfill all the prerequisites of the perpetration" (Stratenwerth, StrafR AT I, 3rd edit., p. 224; . . .). A widely held view claims that indirect perpetration has to be ruled out if the intermediary fulfills the definition of the crime himself intentionally, wrongfully and culpably even if it was on the basis of an error of motive caused by the background man. The criminal responsibility of the person acting directly excludes for statutory reasons regarding him at same time as being the tool of another (Jescheck, Lehrb. des StrafR AT, 4th edit.,

p. 601; Jakobs, StrafR, 2nd edit., p. 532; . . . .) Others (Maurach/Gössel/Zipf, StrafR, part vol. 2, 7th edit., p. 260 (277); . . .)) hold indirect perpetration, even with a tool acting in a fully criminal way, as generally possible when the background man has the course of the event "under control," and therefore "a power reserve" remains for him "which enables him to employ someone acting directly as a mere tool" . . .

Extensive unanimity exists in the literature in the assessment of perpetrators who have acted within the framework of an organizational power apparatus. Some argue that the background man and everyone who within the framework of the hierarchy passes on the instruction for the crime with independent power to command (Roxin, in: LK, § 25 marginal no. 133) should be an indirect perpetrator, because the exchangeability of the intermediary gives control of the crime to the mastermind (Stratenwerth, p. 226; Roxin, in: LK, § 25 marginal no. 25, 128; . . .). In this connection, reference is also made to structures like the Mafia (Stratenwerth, p. 224) . . .

The Federal Court of Justice has explained in various decisions that the indirect perpetrator carries out the crime through another who is not himself a perpetrator (BGHSt 2, 169, 170; BGHSt 30, 363, 364). This description of the concept "indirect perpetrator" is however not fundamental in the decisions mentioned (BGHSt 35, 347, 351). In a line of further decisions, the Federal Court of Justice found indirect perpetration by the background man, with an intermediary acting with unlimited responsibility, without further reasoning. Thus BGHSt 3, 110 has assumed that a denunciation which had led to a wrongful (but not executed) sentence of the death penalty, constituted intentional illegal killing by the person making the denunciation as indirect perpetrator. The Court emphasized that wrongfulness had to be assessed in the same way for all participants, including the judge who passed the sentence of the death penalty, which meant that the judge as an intermediary acted wrongfully and culpably. BGHSt 32, 165, 178 (west runway) emphasizes that participation in acts of violence in the sense of § 125 Criminal Code [public rioting] could also occur through the absent mastermind as indirect perpetrator, because he "controlled the event by virtue of his superior will, and had brought about the result" (see on this BVerfGE 32, 236, 269; . . .). In the decision BGHSt 37, 106 [*Leather Spray Case*, Chapter 9.—Eds.] the Federal Court of Justice finds without further discussion perpetration by omission committed by directors of a company, without examining whether the persons involved with the later distribution of the product down to the retailer knew of the danger and therefore themselves acted with unlimited culpability . . .

bb) The Senate endorses the following:

(1) If someone acts without error and with undiminished culpability, his background man is as a rule not an indirect perpetrator. This applies in particular to cases in which the perpetrator who acts directly comprehensively controls and intends to control the event not only legally but above all factually. Then the background man has as a rule no dominion in the crime.

(2) There are however groups of cases in which, in spite of an intermediary who acts with full responsibility, the contribution of the background man leads almost automatically to the crime which this background man seeks to achieve. This can be the case if the background man takes advantage of the framework provided by organizational structures and his contribution to the crime causes processes corresponding to strict rules within them. Framework conditions of this kind need to be considered in particular for state and entrepreneurial (and similar) organizational structures and for command hierarchies. If in such a case the background man acts in the knowledge of these circumstances and if he also takes advantage in particular of the unconditional preparedness of the direct actor to commit the crime, and if the background man wants the result as the outcome of his own action, he is a perpetrator in the form of indirect perpetration.

He has dominion over the crime. He actually controls the event much more than is necessary with other groups of cases in which indirect perpetration is accepted without hesitation, for instance those involving the use of a "human tool" who acts fully responsible but who cannot be a perpetrator merely because he lacks a special personal duty or a special intention required by the definition of the crime. Even when tools are used who are mistaken or cannot act culpably, the indirect perpetrator may have far less control over the occurrence of the result than in cases of the kind described.

The background man in cases of the kind to be decided here has the comprehensive intention of dominion over the crime if he knows that the decision to break the law, which is yet to be made by the intermediary but which is predetermined by the framework conditions, represents no hindrance to the realization of the results desired by him. Not to treat the background man in such cases as the perpetrator would not do justice to the objective importance of his contribution to the crime, especially as responsibility frequently does not decrease but increases with increasing distance from the place of the crime (F.-C. Schroeder, Der Täter hinter dem Täter (The perpetrator behind the perpetrator), 1965, p. 166). Indirect perpetration understood in this way will fall to be considered not only in the face of misuse of state authority but also in cases of crimes organized by bodies like the Mafia, in which the spatial, temporal and hierarchical distance between the management of the organization responsible for the commands and the person acting directly argues against co-perpetration based on a division of labor. The problem of responsibility in business enterprises can also be resolved in this way. In addition to this, indirect perpetration understood in this way also falls to be considered in cases in which, as in the facts underlying the decision BGHSt 3, 110, the perpetrator for the pursuit of his own goals deliberately makes use of a state apparatus which acts illegitimately. With this solution it is not a question of the good or bad faith of the person acting directly which might be difficult to answer in the individual case.

cc) According to these principles it cannot be doubted that all three defendants, even A., have killed intentionally by indirect perpetration (§§ 212 I, 25 para. 1 Criminal Code)...

3. ... The change of the verdict does not affect the sentence for the defendants K. and S. For these defendants, who had been convicted by the regional court of incitement to homicide, the statutory punishment range remains unaffected.... This does not apply to the defendant A. The regional court has sentenced him to imprisonment for three years and six months for aiding the commission of homicide, but the statutory minimum sentence for homicide-as-a-perpetrator amounts to five years. The Senate, in order to avoid a further delay in proceedings, has sentenced the defendant A. for homicide, in accordance with § 354 para. 1 Code of Criminal Procedure, on the subsidiary application of the Chief Federal Prosecutor, to the lowest sentence of imprisonment permitted by statute, which is five years ...

German Criminal Code

§ 25 (Prinicipalship) [Perpetration]

(1) Who commits the offense himself or through another person, will be punished as a principal [perpetrator].

(2) If several persons commit the offense jointly, each will be punished as a principal (co-principals). [perpetrator (co-perpetrators)]

§ 26 (Incitement)

Who intentionally prompts another person to intentionally commit an unlawful act (inciter) will be punished as if he were a principal. [perpetrator]

§ 27 (Aiding)

(1) Who intentionally aids another in the intentional commission of an unlawful act will be punished as an aider.

(2) The sentence for the aider is to be based on the punishment range for the principal. [perpetrator] It must be mitigated according to § 49 para. 1.

Markus D. Dubber, "Criminalizing Complicity: A Comparative Analysis," 5 *Journal of International Criminal Justice* (2007), 977

The distinction between civil law and common law approaches [to complicity] can serve as no more than a rough analytic guidepost. Austrian law, for instance, is generally classified as a civil law system but deals with complicity in a quite uncivil—even common—way. In fact, modern Austrian complicity doctrine consciously distances itself from German complicity doctrine.

Even comparing German and American law on complicity isn't as straightforward a task as it might appear at first. Distilling American criminal law's approach to complicity already requires a preliminary exercise in *domestic* comparative criminal law. What is commonly referred to as "American criminal law" encompasses the criminal law of fifty states and federal criminal law, not to mention the District of Columbia, as well as the American Law Institute's influential Model Penal Code of 1962.

Our focus will be on American criminal law, not on Anglo-American law, which is often used synonymously with common law. The "Anglo-American" approach to complicity—or any other issue, for that matter—thus isn't any easier, or more worthwhile, to assemble than is the "common law" approach. Capturing the American law on complicity will prove tricky enough, without taking account of English (or perhaps British?) law as well.

[N]o domestic criminal law system can be said to have worked out an entirely satisfactory doctrine of complicity. German complicity doctrine often threatens to get bogged down in a web of differentiation, while at bottom resting the most significant distinction of them all (that between perpetrator and accomplice) on a nebulous concept found nowhere in the criminal code (*Tatherrschaft*). Modern American criminal law suffers from the opposite problem. The Model Penal Code approach to complicity lacks differentiation, having radically streamlined the common law's traditional complicity doctrine, which rivaled the German law of complicity in the number of distinctions, if not in systematic ambition.

Rather than choosing one domestic "model" over another, international criminal law ought to strike a better balance between differentiation and simplification. When all is said and done, and the forest is seen for the trees, the similarities between the two domestic systems outweigh the differences. Both systems reject "guilt by association," or by "mere presence." Both distinguish between perpetrators and accomplices, even if that distinction is less significant in the American system than in the German one. Most important, both systems are committed to complying with the general principle that criminal liability requires that each defendant—perpetrator and accomplice alike—satisfy each element of the offense as statutorily defined.

Here is the common core of accomplice liability in German and American criminal law: Complicity doctrine is simply one way of satisfying the conduct element of the offense, without affecting the question of whether the accomplice also satisfies any other elements of the offense (most notably, the result element). The perpetrator satisfies the conduct element directly. The accomplice satisfies it indirectly, through the perpetrator's act. The accomplice's liability is derivative only in this, limited, sense. In the end, the accomplice's liability must stand on its own, rather than deriving entirely from the principal's. The principal's act is imputed to the accomplice as his own.

Zooming in from this overview, it's easy to see that the details differ. Let's begin with the categories of perpetrators and accomplices. The German criminal code recognizes five of them, three types of perpetrator (covered in one section) and two types of accomplice (covered in two others):

(1) (direct) perpetrator (*[unmittelbarer] Täter*)—personally engages in the proscribed conduct,[4]
(2) indirect perpetrator (*mittelbarer Täter*)—uses another as an unwitting or unwilling tool to engage in the proscribed conduct,[5]
(3) co-perpetrator (*Mittäter*)—personally engages in the proscribed conduct jointly with another,[6]
(4) solicitor (*Anstifter*)—incites another to engage in the proscribed conduct,[7]
(5) facilitator (*Gehilfe*)—aids another in engaging in the proscribed conduct.[8]

Facilitators after the fact, i.e., after the offense has been committed, are treated in a separate chapter in the special part of the criminal code, dealing with obstruction of justice.[9] The offenses in this chapter include not only facilitation after the fact[10] and receiving stolen property,[11] but also obstruction of punishment[12] and—most notably—money laundering.[13]

The offense of obstruction of punishment is broadly defined to include preventing the imposition or infliction of a penal sanction for an unlawful criminal act and applies to official and private actors alike, with the former facing a stiffer punishment. In the case of criminal justice officials, including police officers, prosecutors, and judges, this provision puts teeth—at least on paper—into the principle of compulsory prosecution (*Legalitätsprinzip*), which requires the prosecution of all provable criminal acts.[14]

Unlike obstruction of punishment, the offense of money laundering of course is familiar to common law systems . . . Compare the German scheme with the traditional common law scheme, which distinguished between principals in the first degree, principals in the second degree, and

---

[4] StGB § 25(1).
[5] StGB § 25(1).
[6] StGB § 25(2).
[7] StGB § 26.
[8] StGB § 27. Commentators (and courts) recognize a sixth category, that of parallel perpetrator (*Nebentäter*), which we can safely ignore for our purposes since it's covered comfortably by category (1).
[9] StGB ch. 21.
[10] StGB § 257.
[11] StGB §§ 259–260a.
[12] StGB §§ 258–258a.
[13] StGB § 261.
[14] On the principle of compulsory prosecution, [see Chapter 5.C].

accessories before the fact. It went without saying that principals in the first degree included those who use another person to commit the offense. Accessories before the fact came in two varieties—solicitors and facilitators. The complete common law scheme thus looks like this, with, once again, three modes of perpetration and two of complicity:

(A) principal in the first degree: (direct) perpetrator—personally engages in the proscribed conduct,
(B) principal in the first degree: (indirect) perpetrator—uses another as an unwitting or unwilling tool to engage in the proscribed conduct,
(C) principal in the second degree—aids another in engaging in the proscribed conduct in his presence,
(D) accessory before the fact: solicitor—incites another to engage in the proscribed conduct,
(E) accessory before the fact: facilitator—aids another in engaging in the proscribed conduct not in his presence.

As in the German system, facilitation after the fact eventually was treated as a separate offense. The "accessory after the fact" disappeared along with the "accessory at the fact," who as early as the fourteenth century became the principal in the second degree.[17]

In the common law as in German law, ex post facilitators would face liability for obstructing justice or receiving stolen property, or some local variant, such as misprision of felony in U.S. federal criminal law.[18] ...

The Model Penal Code, and hence modern American criminal law, has replaced the traditional common law taxonomy with a more streamlined version, as it has done throughout the doctrine of criminal law. From the outside, the Model Penal Code scheme looks less like the German system than does the common law scheme; a look inside the doctrine, however, reveals closer substantive similarities between the Model Penal Code and the German system, if only because the Model Code presented the first comprehensive treatment of the question of accessorial liability in American law. Until the Code, legislators, judges, and commentators were content to simply state and restate the historically developed scheme, without aiming for systematic coherence.

The Model Penal Code does not distinguish between different degrees of principals; it also abandons the concept of accessory altogether and along with it any remnants of the historical distinction between accessories before, at, and after the fact. Instead, it speaks only in terms of principals and accomplices. In fact, the term "principal" appears nowhere in the Model Code. The term "perpetrator" or "actor" might be preferable, to further signal the Code's break with common law tradition on the issue of complicity. We'll continue to use "principal" here; it is used in the ALI's official commentaries on the Code and continues to be the term of choice in contemporary American discussions of the issue.

A closer look at the Model Penal Code provision on complicity reveals subsidiary distinctions familiar from the German and common law schemes.

(A) principal: (direct) perpetrator—personally engages in the proscribed conduct,[30]
(B) principal: (indirect) perpetrator—uses another as an unwitting or unwilling tool to engage in the proscribed conduct,[31]
(C) accomplice: solicitor—incites another to engage in the proscribed conduct,[32]
(D) accomplice: facilitator—aids another in engaging in the proscribed conduct.[33]

The basic structural distinction in the Model Penal Code scheme is not that between principal and accomplice, but between someone who commits an offense "by his own conduct" and someone whose criminal liability—if any—derives from "the conduct of another person for which he is legally accountable."[34] Within this scheme, the *principal* satisfies the objective conduct element of an offense through "his own conduct," or through the conduct of an "innocent or irresponsible person" for whose conduct he is therefore legally accountable by "caus[ing]" him to commit it. The *accomplice* satisfies the objective offense element of an offense through the principal's conduct for which he is "legally accountable" by soliciting or facilitating it ...

---

[17] The recognition of an accessory "at the fact," and its transformation into a principal, hints at the characteristic that ended up policing the line between principal and accessory, presence.

[18] 18 U.S.C. § 4 ("whoever, having knowledge of the actual commission of a felony cognizable ... conceals and does not as soon as possible make known the same to some judge or other [official]" guilty of misprision of felony).

[30] MPC § 2.06(1).

[31] MPC § 2.06(2)(a).

[32] MPC § 2.06(2)(c) & (3)(a)(i).

[33] MPC § 2.06(2)(c) & (3)(a)(ii).

[34] MPC § 2.06(1).

The Model Penal Code drafters' approach to the question of complicity—and to traditional doctrinal distinctions in this field—reflects their view of criminal law in general. As they saw it, the common law had become entangled in a web of underrationalized doctrinal rules that did more harm than good. They obscured the substantive questions that drove the ascription of criminal liability and therefore failed to constrain—and to guide—the discretion of those charged with applying, interpreting an—depending on one's view of the inevitability, and perhaps even the desirability, of judicial criminal lawmaking—defining and shaping them. While they tried to fix what they could, the Model Penal Code drafters repeatedly simply discarded familiar but hopeless doctrinal rules. The rejection of the common law scheme of principals and accessories in general, and of presence as the distinguishing characteristic among them in particular, is but one example of this attempt to make a fresh start. Others include the law of causation (where the drafters abandoned the baroque doctrine of proximate cause) and, most important, the law of culpable mental states (where the drafters created a novel streamlined taxonomy of subjective offense elements in place of the convoluted scheme of mens rea, intent, scienter, malice, willfulness, etc.).

The drafters' guiding principle was that each person's criminal liability should reflect his individual culpability. In their view, this principle could be used to inspect and to elucidate traditional doctrinal rules. In many cases, common law rules could be adjusted to better reflect the underlying principle. In others, the traditional rules had to be abandoned because they had developed in such a way that they made implementation of the principle impossible. The law of complicity fell somewhere in the middle of this spectrum from usefulness to uselessness. Its basic taxonomy was abandoned as unhelpful; many of the specifics were reshaped and retained . . .

No matter which strategy they deemed appropriate in particular cases—revision or reform—the Model Penal Code drafters were guided by a particular conception of individual culpability. While it is possible to interpret the Model Penal Code in light of a different conception, it is impossible to understand it otherwise. To simplify, the Model Penal Code drafters measured individual culpability in terms of dangerousness. To punish a person according to his individual culpability did not mean to mete out punishment proportionate to desert. Punishment was not an act of retribution, but of peno-correctional treatment. According to the then-orthodox treatmentist view of criminal law espoused by the Model Penal Code drafters, the concept of punishment itself was a taboo, which should be avoided and replaced with treatment according to the individual peno-correctional of each offender.

From the treatmentist perspective, [t]he accomplice is legally accountable for the principal's conduct insofar as, and only insofar as, his solicitation or facilitation of that conduct indicates that abnormal dangerousness which requires intervention in the form of peno-correctional treatment. Did the putative accomplice, through his soliciting or facilitating, reveal himself as the sort of person who requires penal intervention, for his own good as well as for the good of society at large? . . .

The Model Penal Code's wholehearted commitment to a once orthodox, but long since disfavored, treatmentist ideology focused on the identification and elimination of human dangers is troubling and anachronistic. The German complicity scheme is similarly hampered by its ultimate grounding in similarly outdated, and significantly more obscure ontological enthusiasms about the being of actness. The vague and underjustified concept of act dominion (*Tatherrschaft*) provides no greater doctrinal guidance than the infamously nebulous notion of presence, which the Model Penal Code was right to abandon. At the same time, the Model Penal Code provides little guidance of its own, leaving the differentiation of peno-correctional treatment to the post-conviction stage, at sentencing and, most important, during the correctional process itself. Here one might think that sentencing guidelines could prove useful; the U.S. Sentencing Guidelines' treatment of the distinction among various levels of participation in crime, however, is disappointingly perfunctory.[70]

NOTES

1. The Model Penal Code significantly revised the traditional common law approach to so-called accessorial liability, an area that had long been mired in technical distinctions among accessories and principals of various types and degrees that, much like other once-fundamental distinctions like that between felonies and misdemeanors, carried at least as much procedural as substantive significance. The excerpt from *Standefer* gives a quick overview of the traditional scheme; *Tally* shows it in operation (and along the way comments on the—often-ignored—distinction between "aiding" and "abetting," which had become so entrenched that the Model Penal Code retains it despite its origins in the muddled common law doctrine the drafters sought to leave behind). Today, the old distinctions remain

---

[70] U.S.S.G. §§ 3B.1.1 ("aggravating role") & 3B1.2 ("mitigating role").

significant for two, perhaps three, reasons: they may help in appreciating the Model Code's effort at reconceptualization, they may suggest parallels to the similarly fine grained German taxonomy, and—relatedly—they may suggest shortcomings in the Model Penal Code approach: Did the Model Penal Code go too far in flattening the traditional common law scheme? As in the case of *mens rea*, where the Code abandoned the traditional distinction between intent and other types of *mens rea*, it is worth considering whether the Code's complicity scheme fails to reflect significant distinctions, say, between principal and accessory, based on the concept of presence (or perhaps some other, more relevant, consideration, such as *Tatherrschaft*, or act dominion), or between aider and abettor (a distinction that makes no difference in American criminal law, and a big difference in German criminal law).

2. The *Kaplan* case from New York illustrates the Model Penal Code scheme in operation. Unlike in the case of causation (see Chapter 9), the New York criminal code revisers decided to adopt, or rather to adapt, the Model Penal Code's approach to complicity, and to forms of participation in criminal conduct more generally. In *Kaplan*, the New York Court of Appeals distinguishes the new (MPC-based) view of accomplice liability from the traditional conception, which turned on what the Model Code drafters considered unhelpfully vague notions such as "shared intent." Instead, the Model Code focuses on the individual liability (or, in treatmentist terms criminal dangerousness) of each *dramatis persona*: the accomplice's liability does not derive from the principal's. Instead, the distinction between accomplice and principal is misleading insofar as it detracts from the need to analyze each person's liability independently of the other—at issue is liability for an offense, whether directly as principal or indirectly, through attribution, as accomplice. The only thing that is attributed from the principal to the accomplice is the principal's behavior that satisfies the conduct element of the offense. The accomplice is treated as if the principal's conduct were his or her own; this completes the contribution of conduct attribution (under § 2.06: "Liability for Conduct of Another") to the analysis of the accomplice's criminal liability. The question whether the accomplice satisfies any or all of the remaining objective and subjective elements of the offense (attendant circumstance(s) and result, with their accompanying mental state requirements, if any) remains open.

Under the Model Penal Code's approach, there is no requirement of "shared intent." This means, among other things, that each participant in the offense (however labeled) may have a different mental state with respect to a given objective offense element (say, result in the case of homicide, to pick a popular example), generating liability for different offenses, or grades of offense (as, for instance, in the *Flayhart* case discussed in *Kaplan*). The accomplice is not "the principal's" accomplice (aider or abettor); the accomplice, like the principal, is criminally liable for that offense the objective and subjective elements of which he or she satisfies.

3. "Intent"—in the now familiar sense of purpose, or "conscious object," MPC § 2.02(2)(a)— does continue to play a central role in the Model Penal Code approach to participation in crime: the Code retained the traditional requirement of purpose (or "specific intent") for accomplice liability. The principal's conduct will be attributed to the accomplice only if it was the accomplice's purpose, i.e., conscious object, to aid or abet the principal. Knowledge is not enough. This question had been debated vigorously in the years preceding the Model Penal Code project, with distinguished judges chiming in on both sides of the issue.* Herbert Wechsler, Chief Reporter of the Model Penal Code project, unsuccessfully proposed the following provision, which would have required only knowledge:

(3) A person is an accomplice of another person in commission of a crime if: . . .
   (b) acting with knowledge that such other person was committing or had the purpose of committing the crime, he knowingly, substantially facilitated its commission; . . .

---

* Contrast *United States v. Peoni*, 100 F.2d 401 (2d Cir. 1938) (Hand, J.) with *Backun v. United States*, 112 F.2d 635 (4th Cir. 1940) (Parker, J.).

Other common law jurisdictions extend accomplice liability to knowing facilitation, even going so far as to suggest that requiring purpose would lead to "perverse consequences" and "absurd result[s]":

> If a man is approached by a friend who tells him that he is going to rob a bank and would like to use his car as the getaway vehicle for which he will pay him $100, . . . can he say "My purpose was not to aid the robbery but to make $100?" His argument would be that while he knew that he was helping the robbery, his desire was to obtain $100 and he did not care one way or the other whether the robbery was successful or not.
>
> $\qquad$ *R. v. Hibbert*, [1995] 2 S.C.R. 973 (Can.) (quoting A. W. Mewett and
> $\qquad$ M. Manning, Criminal Law (2nd ed. 1985), at p. 112).

Some jurisdictions, including New York, retained the purpose (as conscious object) requirement for complicity, but introduced a (separate) fallback offense of facilitation.*

4. One model of attributing criminal liability for unlawful events treats all the persons who have made a contribution to them alike. It labels the persons uniformly as perpetrators without attempting more fine-grained judgments. This model can be found in German law with respect to administrative penalties and with respect to negligent offenses. In these areas, the law does not distinguish between different types of perpetrator and other participants. When assessing intentional crimes, however, German law sorts those who intentionally participated in the crime into one of three categories: principal perpetrators, inciters, and aiders (§§ 25, 26, 27 Criminal Code).

Note that under current German law the distinction between perpetrators and *inciters* (as opposed to aiders) only has limited significance for the outcome in terms of available punishment ranges. In § 26, the German Criminal Code provides that inciters and principal perpetrators are to receive the same punishment. But courts would still not, if in doubt, leave open the question of whether someone is a perpetrator or merely an inciter. There seems to be an intuition that this needs to be decided as a matter of fair labelling, and also, *within* the punishment range the Code assigns to the offense, it is likely that in practice an inciter would receive a somewhat lighter sentence than the principal perpetrator. (Why?)

The potential sentence difference between perpetrators and *aiders* is more pronounced. The mitigation of the legal punishment range for aiders (which is now mandatory[†]) is of considerable significance, especially in the case of serious crimes. To apply § 49 para. 1 Criminal Code means, for instance, that in the case of murder the minimum penalty for aiding is three years' imprisonment (rather than mandatory life imprisonment for a perpetrator) and in the case of homicide [*Totschlag*] two years (compared to five years). For instance, had the defendant in *Staschynskij* been sentenced as a perpetrator, he would have received a life sentence, rather than eight years' imprisonment. (Why punish perpetrators and inciters the same? But not perpetrators and aiders? Put another way, why distinguish not between perpetrators and inciters, but between inciters and aiders? Is the distinction between the person who in fact engages in the proscribed conduct and others less significant than that among types of accomplices? What accounts for these distinctions? Consider the various rationales for punishment.)

The distinction between inciting and aiding in German criminal law also manifests itself in another way: Only attempted inciting is criminalized (as an attempt to commit the principal offense, § 30 para. 1 Criminal Code); attempted aiding is not punishable. By contrast, the Model Penal Code treats aiders and abetters alike; both are liable as participants since aiding and abetting are simply two forms of accomplice liability. Insofar as the principal's conduct is attributed to them, they are treated as though they had themselves engaged in the proscribed conduct, and are punished—or rather treated—accordingly. Moreover, under the Model

---

* See, e.g., N.Y. Penal Law § 115.00 ("A person is guilty of criminal facilitation . . . when, *believing it probable* that he is rendering aid . . . to a person who intends to commit a crime, he engages in conduct which provides such person with means or opportunity for the commission thereof and which in fact aids such person to commit a felony" (emphasis added)).

† See Criminal Code § 27 para. 2.

Penal Code attempted aiding is punishable. In fact, the Code treats attempted aiding as equivalent to aiding. 2.06(3)(ii) "(aids or agrees or *attempts to aid* such other person in planning or committing it"; emphasis added).*

5. The German Criminal Code does not give instructions on *how* to distinguish perpetratorship from aiding and inciting. Therefore, this question had to be dealt with by the literature and the courts. The judgment of the Federal Court of Justice in the *Staschynskij Case* from 1962 reflected a traditional approach in German case law: an approach which emphasizes subjective elements. The Court inquired whether the defendant had the will to be a principal perpetrator, if he *willed* the crime *as his own*. There are several possible explanations why German courts in the past favored this subjective approach. Like the focus on the "vicious will" still cited in common law opinions,[†] it reflects the influence of traditional moral assessments in criminal law. If the actor's motives and attitudes are the most important factors when assessing wrongful conduct, it makes sense to base also the perpetrator-participant distinction on a subjective basis.

Other reasons for favoring a subjective approach are more outcome-oriented: it allows more flexibility for judges with an eye to sentencing. For a famous older case from 1940 (the *Bathtub Case* (Imperial Court Judgment of February 19, 1940, g. R. 3 D 69/40, RGSt 74, 84)), one of the judges later explained that compassion with the female defendant prompted the court to opt for the subjective solution. (Note that classifying her as an inciter would not have had the desired effect.) The defendant, a young woman, wanted to help her sister who had secretly given birth to a baby out of wedlock. A major scandal was to be expected. Upon the urgent pleadings of the mother, the sister drowned the newborn immediately after birth in the bathtub; the mother had been too weak to do this herself. Convicting this young woman as "perpetrator of murder" would have meant to have her hanged in 1940, and only by "downgrading" her role to that of a "mere aider" could the Court spare her life. (See Fritz Hartung, "Der 'Badewannenfall': Eine Reminiszenz," *JuristenZeitung* [1954], 430. According to Judge Hartung's post-1945 recollection, he spontaneously suggested the extension of the subjective theory of perpetration in this case to spare the life of the young girl. Even assuming its reliability, what is the relevance of this revelation for purposes of criminal law doctrine?) Compassion with the defendant's situation also is a likely explanation for the outcome in the *Staschynskij Case*.

Couldn't discretion cut the other way, as well, to classify someone as perpetrator because he had the requisite will, even though his involvement was more minimal—and certainly more minimal than in the 1940 case, where the person engaged in precisely the conduct that proscribed in the offense definition? If the point is to tailor punishment to the culpability of each participant, wouldn't it make more sense to abandon the categorical distinction between perpetrator and aider in the first place? If this is not an option for a court interpreting the German Criminal Code, does the Imperial Court's adoption of a subjective theory of perpetration amount to judicial reform *sub rosa*?

More generally, did the decisions in the *Bathtub Case* and the *Staschynskij Case* amount to an exercise of "the court's" sense of justice? Does one need fine-grained and (apparently) categorical doctrinal distinctions to justify these exercises of judicial compassion, or would it be preferable to formulate a flexible standard that allows judges—or other factfinders—to consult their sense of justice?

6. Two things must be added: first, the introduction of objective criteria could also be observed in older German case law which was not *exclusively* oriented towards internal attitudes of the offender. In the ruling of 1958 reprinted above, the Federal Court of Justice had justified P.'s conviction as co-perpetrator of the attempted killing of his own person with his "dominion over the crime"—this meant to apply an objective standard. Secondly, today a merely subjective theory no longer is regarded as compatible with German law. In 1975, the

---

* See the discussion of causation and complicity in Chapter 9, Note 5.
† See Chapter 8.B.

German legislature introduced § 25 Criminal Code in its present wording, and the formulation in § 25 para. 1 (defining as perpetrator anyone "who commits the crime himself") means that the person who fulfilled the elements of the crime through her own acts *must* be classified as perpetrator. Neither the young woman in the *Bathtub Case* nor the defendant in the *Staschynskij Case* could be treated as aiders to murder under this formulation. (Is that a positive development?)

In general, modern case law of the German courts still sometimes refers to the offender's will, but only as one among several elements to decide between perpetratorship and mere participation in cases which are more complex than the straightforward "killing-with-one's-own-hand" type. Under such circumstances, the courts now have taken up the objective approach.

The objective approach asks who had dominion over the crime (*Tatherrschaft*) by looking at the events from the outside and by determining who moved them along. Dubber in his article expresses skepticism about the concept of "act dominion." But its functions are to prevent an exclusive focus on the subjective aspect of the inquiry and to convey a general idea of what it means to be a perpetrator (bearing in mind that the notion of "dominion" must be specified in more detail for each of the three variations of direct perpetrator, indirect perpetrator and co-perpetrator).

Given its specific function within the context of the development of German criminal law doctrine—on the heels of another doctrine that was also, apparently, adopted to serve a specific function, namely to prevent the execution of a particular defendant in a particular case—does "act dominion" have limited relevance outside of that context? What general idea of perpetration does it convey, apart from its function in the history of German criminal law doctrine? And to whom? Potential offenders?

7. At its most straightforward, perpetration includes the concept of direct perpetration (where someone in his own person carries out the relevant act that directly leads to the result described in the offense description, for instance, the death of another person). Carrying out the act in person is the most uncomplicated form of "dominion."

The two other variations (co-perpetrators and indirect perpetrators) often need more explanation. There are, of course, also uncomplicated cases of co-perpetratorship. But it is not uncommon that one can debate whether one of several persons involved in a crime scheme reached the threshold of being a perpetrator or merely aided the others. The relevant questions are: was there a common plan and was this common plan also jointly executed, typically with a division of labor? There is some debate whether someone who is not present at the scene of crime could ever be a co-perpetrator. (Recalling the traditional common law distinction between principal and accessory. See *Tally* (excerpted above).) The majority opinion in German criminal law doctrine accepts this possibility in rare cases if lack of participation at the stage of committing the crime is compensated by superior dominion in the planning stage (if the "mastermind" had sketched every detail of the offense and others acted in execution of his precise plan). (Again, recalling the notion of "constructive" presence in the traditional common law of principal and accessory. See *Tally*.)

Co-perpetratorship was the issue in the ruling from 1958. It might at first glance seem odd that P., the victim of attempted murder, could be convicted and punished as a co-perpetrator of this very crime, committed against himself. Nonetheless, his classification as co-perpetrator under the "act dominion" approach makes sense, since he had agreed with his co-defendants M. and T. that firearms should be used against pursuers during the course of their joint burglaries, and was present at the scene of the crime. (Does the fact that the act dominion theory generates, or at least justifies, this (at least initially) counterintuitive result give you pause?)

Even more complicated is the concept of indirect perpetratorship. Crucial is the indirect perpetrator's dominion in terms of knowledge or will power that he or she exercises over a "human tool." Uncontroversial examples include the intentional exploitation of another person's lack of knowledge or lack of culpability, for instance, making someone pull the trigger of a weapon after leading the person to believe that he was participating in a game or that the weapon was unloaded, or instructing a small child to take away goods in a shop. Under such circumstances, the person in the background will be sentenced as an indirect perpetrator. (Does one need a theory of act dominion to reach this result? Compare Model Penal Code § 2.06(2)(a) ("acting with the kind of culpability that is sufficient for the commission of the offense, he causes an innocent or irresponsible person to engage in such conduct").)

More controversial are cases like the one against the defendants Heinz Keßler, Fritz Streletz, and Hans Albrecht, former members of the GDR National Defense Council. Here, the direct perpetrators who fired shots at the inner German border or placed mines acted fully culpably. They could not be considered "human tools" in the narrow sense of this term as it is commonly used in the context of indirect perpetratorship. After all, the Federal Court of Justice had already decided in the *Border Guard Case* from 1992* that the members of the border troops had acted unlawfully and culpably. The defendants in the *National Defence Council Case* nevertheless were convicted as indirect perpetrators. This had a precedent in the *Staschynskij Case* where the Court had argued that those high up in the Soviet chain of command in Moscow were indirect perpetrators. (Was this decision any more, or less, convincing in the *Staschynskij Case*?)

However, the legislature's introduction of the new § 25 into the German Criminal Code— defining "perpetrator" as anyone "who commits the crime himself or through another person"—was generally interpreted to preclude labelling such "background men" [*Hintermänner*] as perpetrators, since they neither satisfied the elements of the crime themselves ("commits the crime himself") nor used another person as a mere tool ("through another person"). But this is precisely what the Federal Court of Justice did, setting the courts' course not only for crimes committed under the regime of a state which is dictatorial and violates human rights, but also for cases of organized crime, organized in the sense of stable organizational structures that last beyond their human members.

Note that the sentences for the former members of the National Defense Council are more severe than those for the members of the border troops, but that they are nevertheless mild sentences for intentional killing. (The defendants were not sentenced for murder but only for manslaughter [*Totschlag*]; in contrast to Staschynskij's crimes, the killings were not held to have been committed in an insidious manner, and therefore not to have constituted murder.†)

Are the (post-)GDR and Soviet cases better analyzed as criminal law cases applying standard categories of criminal law doctrine or, rather, as *sui generis* political cases in which the criminal law is employed in a pragmatic and flexible way to capture an assessment of a particular case, or types of case, within the context of a more general (negative) judgment about a political system, while *at the same time* exemplifying the commitment of (West) German criminal law to the rule of law, even in cases of those who commit atrocities in the name of another, fundamentally unjust, system? (Does the Cold War-era *Staschynskij Case* differ from the post-1989 GDR decisions in this respect?) Do these cases have implications for ordinary criminal law, or do they make "bad law"? Do they perhaps even draw into question the distinction between "regular" criminal law and "exceptional" criminal law, insofar as this distinction assumes that (all? most?) criminal law cases resolve themselves through the application of doctrinal categories?

8. *A note on some details in the* Staschynskij *Case.* From a contemporary perspective, it seems odd that the Federal Court of Justice refers several times to "motives not known to criminology"; this is a somewhat awkward way of referring to political crimes committed under the extreme pressures of dictatorships. And a procedural detail might need explanation: the Court mentions the wives of the two murder victims as "accessory prosecutors." Under the German Code of Criminal Procedure this position may be assumed by victims in cases involving certain serious crimes against the person.‡

---

* See Chapter 8.C.ii.
† For the concept of murder in German criminal law, see Chapter 15.A.ii.
‡ See Chapter 1.A.ii.

9. *State v. Tally* was a case about aiding. A decisive principle expressed there is mirrored in German case law. The Alabama Court states: "The assistance given need not contribute to the criminal result in the sense that but for it the result would not have ensued." In other words, a causal connection in the ordinary ("but for" or *sine qua non*) sense is not a necessary requirement. It suffices that the aider facilitates the perpetrator's act even if the latter might or would have succeeded without this help being given. This is how modern German courts see it, too. Under German law, one would also scrutinize whether the aider acted with the necessary intent (*Vorsatz*): he must have foreseen and approved of the crime as it was committed by the perpetrator.* The Anglo-American approach to the purpose requirement in complicity is discussed in Note 3.

On the question of causation, note that, in contrast to the common law rule set out in *Tally*, the Model Penal Code does not distinguish between aiding and attempting (or agreeing) to aid, thus eliminating the requirement of any causal link between the accomplice's act and the commission of the offense (§ 2.06(3)(a)(ii)). In other words, attempted complicity is complicity, if the offense was committed. (If the offense is not committed or attempted, conduct that would otherwise amount to complicity is treated as an attempt (§ 5.01(3)). The same applies if the offense is not committed, but is attempted by the principal, i.e., in a case of complicity in an attempt.)

10. *Sentencing.* When all is said and done, and all the doctrinal distinctions are viewed from a comfortable distance, why not radically simplify the doctrine of accessorial liability, adopt a unitary model of perpetration (direct or indirect), and then shift the task of differentiation to sentencing? Consider, for instance, the following provisions of the U.S. Sentencing Guidelines, on "Aiding and Abetting" and "Role in the Offense":

§ 2X2.1. Aiding and Abetting

The offense level is the same level as that for the underlying offense.

§ 3B1.1. Aggravating Role

Based on the defendant's role in the offense, increase the offense level as follows:
(a) If the defendant was an organizer or leader of a criminal activity that involved five or more participants or was otherwise extensive, increase by 4 levels.
(b) If the defendant was a manager or supervisor (but not an organizer or leader) and the criminal activity involved five or more participants or was otherwise extensive, increase by 3 levels.
(c) If the defendant was an organizer, leader, manager, or supervisor in any criminal activity other than described in (a) or (b), increase by 2 levels.

§ 3B1.2. Mitigating Role

Based on the defendant's role in the offense, decrease the offense level as follows:
(a) If the defendant was a minimal participant in any criminal activity, decrease by 4 levels.
(b) If the defendant was a minor participant in any criminal activity, decrease by 2 levels.
In cases falling between (a) and (b), decrease by 3 levels.

§ 3B1.3. Abuse of Position of Trust or Use of Special Skill

If the defendant abused a position of public or private trust, or used a special skill, in a manner that significantly facilitated the commission or concealment of the offense, increase by 2 levels. This adjustment may not be employed if an abuse of trust or skill is included in the base offense level or specific offense characteristic . . .

---

* For a discussion of the German law on intent, see Chapter 8.

§ 3B1.4. Using a Minor To Commit a Crime

If the defendant used or attempted to use a person less than eighteen years of age to commit the offense or assist in avoiding detection of, or apprehension for, the offense, increase by 2 levels.

11. *Renunciation or withdrawal.* The defense of renunciation in the U.S. and German law of complicity is discussed with the inchoate offences to which it also applies in Chapter 12.

CORPORATE CRIMINAL LIABILITY

Corporate criminal liability, at first glance, appears as a clear instance of a categorical difference between Anglo-American and German criminal law: one has it, the other does not. Even at second glance, the distinction does not quite disappear, but might instead begin to look less categorical, or at least more interesting, when it is seen in a wider historical and doctrinal context. A historical approach reveals that English criminal law categorically rejected the very possibility of corporate criminal liability as late as the turn of the nineteenth century, while German criminal law had long recognized corporate criminal liability, with both systems switching sides at roughly the same time. Moreover, support for corporate criminal liability in Germany continued throughout the nineteenth and early twentieth centuries, including from central figures in the German law of corporations (Otto von Gierke) and criminal law (Franz von Liszt). And, in the second half of the twentieth century, corporations were subjected to potentially substantial "administrative *fines*" (*Geldbußen*) for the commission of offenses on their behalf, which some observers on either side of the debate about corporate criminal liability have found difficult to distinguish in effect, if not in label, from "administrative *penalties*" (*Geldstrafen*). Still, no doubt remains that contemporary Anglo-American criminal law—including most commentators—does not raise principled objections to corporate criminal liability, whereas German criminal law—including most commentators—does.

N.Y. Central & Hudson River Railroad Co. v. United States
Supreme Court of the United States
212 U.S. 481 (1909)

Mr. Justice Day delivered the opinion of the Court.

[The railroad company and its assistant traffic manager were convicted of paying rebates to sugar companies, by charging them less than the published rate in order to prevent them from shipping sugar from New York City to Detroit by water rather than by train, in violation of the Elkins Act.]

The principal attack in this court is upon the constitutional validity of certain features of the Elkins act. 32 Stat. 847. That act, among other things, provides:

(1) That anything done or omitted to be done by a corporation common carrier subject to the act to regulate commerce, and the acts amendatory thereof, which, if done or omitted to be done by any director or officer thereof, or any receiver, trustee, lessee, agent or person acting for or employed by such corporation, would constitute a misdemeanor under said acts, or under this act, shall also be held to be a misdemeanor committed by such corporation, and upon conviction thereof it shall be subject to like penalties as are prescribed in said acts, or by this act, with reference to such persons, except as such penalties are herein changed. . . .

In construing and enforcing the provisions of this section, the act, omission or failure of any officer, agent or other person acting for or employed by any common carrier, acting within the scope of his employment, shall in every case be also deemed to be the act, omission or failure of such carrier, as well as of that person.

It is contended that these provisions of the law are unconstitutional because Congress has no authority to impute to a corporation the commission of criminal offenses, or to subject a corporation to a criminal prosecution by reason of the things charged. The argument is that to thus punish the corporation is in reality to punish the innocent stockholders, and to deprive them of their property without opportunity to be heard, consequently without due process of law...It is urged that... owing to the nature and character of its organization and the extent of its power and authority, a corporation cannot commit a crime of the nature charged in this case.

Some of the earlier writers on common law held the law to be that a corporation could not commit a crime. It is said to have been held by Lord Chief Justice Holt that "corporation is not indictable, although the particular members of it are." In Blackstone's Commentaries, chapter 18, § 12, we find it stated: "A corporation cannot commit treason, or felony, or other crime in its corporate capacity, though its members may in their distinct individual capacities." The modern authority, universally, so far as we know, is the other way. In considering the subject, Bishop's New Criminal Law, § 417, devotes a chapter to the capacity of corporations to commit crime, and states the law to be: "Since a corporation acts by its officers and agents their purposes, motives, and intent are just as much those of the corporation as are the things done. If, for example, the invisible, intangible essence of air, which we term a corporation, can level mountains, fill up valleys, lay down iron tracks, and run railroad cars on them, it can intend to do it, and can act therein as well viciously as virtuously." [In] Telegram Newspaper Company v. Commonwealth, 172 Massachusetts, 294...Mr. Chief Justice Field said: "We think that a corporation may be liable criminally for certain offenses of which a specific intent may be a necessary element. There is no more difficulty in imputing to a corporation a specific intent in criminal proceedings than in civil. A corporation cannot be arrested and imprisoned in either civil or criminal proceedings, but its property may be taken either as compensation for a private wrong or as punishment for a public wrong." It is held in England that corporations may be criminally prosecuted for acts of misfeasance as well as nonfeasance.

It is now well established that in actions for tort the corporation may be held responsible for damages for the acts of its agent within the scope of his employment....

In this case we are to consider the criminal responsibility of a corporation for an act done while an authorized agent of the company is exercising the authority conferred upon him...Applying the principle governing civil liability, we go only a step farther in holding that the act of the agent, while exercising the authority delegated to him to make rates for transportation, may be controlled, in the interest of public policy, by imputing his act to his employer and imposing penalties upon the corporation for which he is acting in the premises.

It is true that there are some crimes, which in their nature cannot be committed by corporations. But there is a large class of offenses...wherein the crime consists in purposely doing the things prohibited by statute. In that class of crimes we see no good reason why corporations may not be held responsible for and charged with the knowledge and purposes of their agents, acting within the authority conferred upon them. If it were not so, many offenses might go unpunished and acts be committed in violation of law, where, as in the present case, the statute requires all persons, corporate or private, to refrain from certain practices forbidden in the interest of public policy...

While the law should have regard to the rights of all, and to those of corporations no less than to those of individuals, it cannot shut its eyes to the fact that the great majority of business transactions in modern times are conducted through these bodies, and particularly that interstate commerce is almost entirely in their hands, and to give them immunity from all punishment because of the old and exploded doctrine that a corporation cannot commit a crime would virtually take away the only means of effectually controlling the subject matter and correcting the abuses aimed at.

State of Louisiana v. Chapman Dodge Center, Inc. & Swindle
Louisiana Supreme Court
428 So.2d 413 (La. 1983)

Defendants, Chapman Dodge Center, Inc., and John Swindle were charged by bill of information with 20 counts of theft, in violation of La. Stat. Ann.-R.S. § 14:67. On July 13–16, 1981, defendants were tried before a six person jury which found them guilty of the lesser included offense of unauthorized use of a movable in violation of LSA-R.S. § 14:68. Thereafter, the trial court sentenced Chapman Dodge Center, Inc., to pay $100 on each of the 20 counts and actual court costs pursuant to LSA-C.Cr.P. Art. 887; in addition to the $100 fines and court costs, defendant John Swindle was sentenced to serve six months in parish prison on each of the 20 counts, the sentences to run consecutively....

The question of the criminal liability of the corporate defendant in this cause is a...difficult proposition involving fundamental issues of the nature of criminal responsibility. These issues have not been generally considered with respect to corporations in this jurisdiction. Certainly our law contemplates corporate criminal defendants. Louisiana law delineates a number of acts the commission or omission of which creates corporate criminal responsibility.[3]

The problem of what criminal liability a corporation should bear for the unauthorized acts of its officers and managers is indeed a grave and troubling one. Recent allegations of corporate responsibility for large train derailments and massive pollution of water sources underscore the importance of this troubling topic. Certainly there is civil responsibility under such circumstances. The question is whether a corporation should be criminally responsible in the absence of a specific statute which defines and describes the corporate act, prohibits that act, and establishes a specific punishment therefor.

.... Our Civil Code in Article 427 defines a corporation as:

> ...an intellectual body, created by law, composed of individuals united under a common name, the members of which succeed each other, so that the body continues always the same, notwithstanding the change of the individuals which compose it, and which, for certain purposes, is considered as a natural person. (emphasis added).

The corporation as a fictitious person is capable of entering into contracts, owning property and making and receiving donations. In short, it is capable of doing virtually anything that a natural person is capable of doing.

A corporation by the very nature of its operation is dependent upon people to carry out its business. Some of these people may rightfully be regarded as the "mind" of the corporation. This group, known as the board of directors, is responsible for the direction that the corporation takes in its business activity. Plans for the corporation, developed by the board of directors, are transmitted to the officers of the corporation and through them to the employees. This latter group may be regarded as the "hands" of the corporation. But here our analogy to the human form must end. For unlike ordinary human hands, corporate "hands" have minds of their own and are capable of self direction.

When a corporation is accused of committing a crime which requires intent, it must be determined who within the corporate structure had the intent to commit the crime. If the crime was the product of a board of directors' resolution authorizing its employees to commit specific criminal acts, then intent on the part of the corporation is manifest. However, a more difficult question arises if the crime is actually committed by an employee of the corporation not authorized to perform such an act. Holding a corporation criminally responsible for the acts of an employee may be inconsistent with basic notions of criminal intent, since such a posture would render a corporate entity responsible for actions which it theoretically had no intent to commit.

Common law jurisdictions hold corporations criminally liable for the acts of low-ranking employees. In such jurisdictions, corporate criminal liability is based on an extension of the tort doctrine of vicarious liability. The theme of vicarious criminal liability, however, is varied. Some jurisdictions impose criminal liability where there has been an act or an authorization to act by a managerial officer, some where there has been an act committed within the scope of the actor's employment, and still others where there has been an act done which benefits the corporation. These varied applications notwithstanding, common law jurisdictions have found corporations liable for forms of homicide, theft, extortion —in short, virtually every crime other than rape and carnal knowledge.

Although this merger of tort and criminal law doctrine has found wide acceptance, it has also generated significant theoretical problems. Admittedly, tort law and criminal law are cousins, causing concern as to whether their relationship is within the prohibited degree such that a union of the two might produce unwanted offspring. It should be remembered that the main function of the law of torts is compensation and to a much lesser degree, deterrence.

Tort law attempts to distribute the loss of a harmful occurrence. Causation is the important ingredient therein. Holding a corporation vicariously liable for the torts of its employees dovetails with the idea of compensating the victim. The corporation is in a more likely position to compensate.

On the other hand, as mentioned earlier, the primary function of criminal law is to deter future criminal liability. To impose such liability on another party who had no part in the act and, as in the case of most corporate crimes, no intent to commit such an act, seems at first glance to be contrary to the purpose of our criminal legal system.

It is important to point out that while corporate criminal liability is recognized and applied in common law jurisdictions, the maxim that societas delinguere non potest (a corporation cannot do wrong) is still firmly recognized in the civil law.[9] Only the natural person acting for the corporation can incur criminal guilt...

---

[3] LSA-R.S. 12:172 (Failure to Keep Records); LSA-R.S. 37:850 (Violation of Embalming Laws); LSA-R.S. 14:106 (Obscenity); LSA-R.S. 47:1953 (Tax Assessment of Corporations); LSA-R.S. 51:125, 126 (Transactions Lessening Competition); LSA-R.S. 30:217 (Unauthorized Prospecting); LSA-R.S. 30:1096 (Pollution).

[9] [U]ntil 1942, La. Rev. Civil Code of 1870, Article 443 expressly stated that a corporation could not be convicted of any crime.

One of the most interesting aspects of the concept that a corporation may be guilty of an offense without specific statutory authority is the question of how one punishes a corporation. It cannot be imprisoned. Obviously it may not be sentenced to death in the sense that an individual may be. Of course, the charter may be revoked but obviously in that circumstance there would have to be a statute which authorizes this sanction.

The only method of punishing a corporation that is guilty of an offense . . . is by the imposition of a fine. Certainly it may be argued that a fine in such instances punishes those not guilty of the offense, for funds lost from the corporate treasury can be recouped either by withholding dividends from shareholders or increasing the price of the product to the consumer. On the other hand, serious fines levied against corporations can modify the behavior of corporate officers who want to keep their jobs, and the behavior of voting shareholders who will vote to elect officers that will avoid such costly fines. But obviously there are certain theoretical inconsistencies between a fine to a corporation for an offense . . . and the concept that the purpose of criminal statutes is to punish and deter.

But the most interesting theoretical problem arising from the idea that a corporation may be fined where it commits an offense such as theft or unauthorized use is presented by contemplation of the converse. What punishment should be exacted where the authorized penalty is only a jail term? This dilemma would arise if one of the managers or upper level employees of a company authorized the burglary of the home of a senior officer of a competitor in order to obtain vital information.[13] It would then not be possible to effectively punish the corporation as the burglary of an inhabited dwelling requires a minimum jail sentence which cannot be suspended . . .

The instant defendant is a closely held holding corporation which is accused of a basic "Ten Commandment Crime"—theft—and convicted of a lesser included offense. Thus the finder of fact in effect determined that the defendant corporation kept the money in question with fraudulent intent, but with the intent to eventually return the funds. The evidence further indicates that "retention" of the funds was not specifically authorized by the board of directors or by the president or any other officer of the corporation. The record does not indicate, moreover, that any of these entities had any real knowledge of that action. Of course the corporation, its board of directors, its parent corporations and its president are for all practical purposes the same entity—the individual defendant Swindle. Furthermore, as discussed earlier, the evidence preponderates that it was a party other than Swindle who determined to "retain the funds."

Thus, the facts of this case can be narrowed to a fine point. In so doing, however, broad questions of a complex nature are visited upon us. While recognizing the potential disservice to the jurisprudence we are nevertheless unable, within the confines of this appeal, to resolve these extremely complex issues. We simply determine that under the circumstances of this case, criminal intent has not been adequately established. . . . We hold that since this record reveals no evidence of complicity by the officers or the board of directors, explicit or tacit, that the actions of these managers and/or employees were insufficient to cause this corporate entity to be guilty of the offense of an unauthorized use of a movable.

We thus reverse as to both defendants and order their discharge.

Lemmon, Justice, dissenting in part.

The evidence supports a conclusion that a high managerial agent, in whom the corporation had vested the authority to manage its day-to-day business operations, knowingly committed a criminal offense on behalf of the corporation and for its benefit while acting in the scope of his employment. The corporation should therefore be held criminally liable. See Model Penal Code § 2.07(1)(c) . . .

People v. Congregational Khal Chaisidei Skwere, Inc.
Supreme Court of New York, Appellate Division, Third Department
232 A.D.2d 919, 649 N.Y.S.2d 499 (1996)

Yesawich, J.

On August 6, 1990, Chaim Kolodny, working as a driver for defendant, a corporation which owns and operates a children's summer camp, drove approximately 18 other employees of defendant to another camp for a basketball game. En route, the 15-person van broke down and most of the passengers reached their destination by other means. In the early morning hours of August 7, 1990, Kolodny, using defendant's recently acquired 1983 Chevrolet Suburban, drove to the other camp to retrieve the employees. The Suburban contained a front and back seat as well as a cargo area and was suited for six passengers. Kolodny and 16 others occupied the vehicle when they set off, in the

---

[13] Watergate revisited.

rain, for their own campground. On the way, the Suburban hydroplaned, left the road and ultimately struck a tree; two of the passengers died and seven others were injured.

In September 1990, defendant was indicted on two counts of criminally negligent homicide, seven counts of reckless endangerment in the second degree, one count of unsafe tires and one count of invalid inspection. Following a nonjury trial, which commenced in February 1995, defendant was found guilty on all charges. On each of the counts of criminally negligent homicide, defendant was sentenced to pay a $ 10,000 fine, and for each of the counts of reckless endangerment, a fine of $ 5,000 was imposed. Pursuant to Penal Law § 80.15, the fines merged into a maximum fine of $ 10,000. Defendant was also sentenced to an unconditional discharge with respect to its convictions for unsafe tires and invalid inspection. On this appeal, defendant challenges the sufficiency of the evidence underlying the convictions for criminally negligent homicide and reckless endangerment in the second degree . . .

The evidence, viewed most favorably to the People, is legally sufficient to sustain the convictions. Specifically, the trial testimony revealed that Philip Gross, defendant's executive director, purchased the Suburban on behalf of the corporation in late July 1990, shortly before its State inspection certificate was to expire, placed it in operation with a temporary certificate and failed to have it inspected within the 10 days allowed for that purpose. As a consequence, on the date of the accident the vehicle was being operated without a valid State inspection sticker, conduct that is proscribed both by the Vehicle and Traffic Law (*see*, Vehicle and Traffic Law § 306 [b]) and by the State Sanitary Code governing children's camps (*see*, 10 NYCRR 7-2.10 [c]). More importantly, the evidence credited by County Court at trial demonstrated that Gross had not taken any steps to evaluate the vehicle's safety before turning the keys over to Kolodny, but had, at most, delegated that task to the youthful driver without making any effort to ascertain the latter's ability to carry it out.[4] In addition, Kolodny had not been furnished the required safety training (*see*, 10 NYCRR 7-2.5 [k]).

Even without taking into consideration the fact that defendant was also in violation of its own rules as to transportation operators, Gross' conduct in allowing Kolodny to operate this lately purchased, uninspected, used vehicle to transport staffers and, on occasion, campers created a substantial and unjustifiable risk of injury or death. Gross' disregard of that risk was a "gross deviation from the standard of conduct that a reasonable person would observe in the situation" (Penal Law § 15.05 [3]; *see*, Penal Law § 15.05 [4]), sufficient to justify findings of criminally negligent homicide and reckless endangerment in the second degree (*see*, Penal Law §§ 120.20, 125.10). As Gross was undeniably a high managerial agent of defendant, his wrongdoing in this respect may form the basis for a finding of criminal liability on the part of the corporation (*see*, Penal Law § 20.20 [2] [b]).

Moreover, there is no question that defendant's failure to remedy the unsafe conditions that would have been uncovered by a timely inspection, prior to placing the vehicle in service, was a direct cause of the accident. The uncontroverted testimony of the People's expert established that the vehicle, which was traveling at a speed in excess of 60 miles per hour, hydroplaned as a result of the inadequacy of the tread depth of the two front tires, and that at least one of those tires would not have passed inspection. That an accident might occur in this fashion, as a result of Gross' dereliction, was foreseeable under the circumstances . . .

Ordered that the judgment is affirmed.

Thomas Weigend, "*Societas delinquere non potest?* A German Perspective," 6 *Journal of International Criminal Justice* (2008), 927

A. History, and a Compromise Solution

While the majority of European states have moved toward recognizing corporate criminal responsibility, Germany, along with a few allies, has so far held out in a position of at least partial denial. Germany recognizes an indirect form of corporate liability for wrongdoing of officers and managers of legal persons, but has so far refrained from making corporations subject to 'genuine' criminal sanctions. Germany's reluctance in that regard can be traced back to certain tenets of nineteenth-century idealistic philosophy. All the way until the end of the eighteenth century, criminal liability of collective entities had been a well-recognized and frequently practised phenomenon under the law applicable on the territory that today is Germany. For example, communities were fined for violations of the laws imposed by imperial or regional sovereigns. The ancient rule that corporations cannot be

---

[4] Unfortunately, Kolodny—who was 19 years old at the time—possessed very little automotive knowledge. He did not know the meaning of the term "tread" nor what a "bald tire" was; it is apparent that he did not comprehend the danger posed thereby. Indeed, when asked to "check out" the vehicle, he had reported only that one window was broken and that it did not have a radio.

held criminally responsible (*societas delinquere non potest*) had been abandoned in favour of a practical approach that made it possible for emerging regional powers to subdue recalcitrant local entities. It was only in the wake of Immanuel Kant's individualistic understanding of responsibility that the notion of the criminal guilt of a corporation lost credit. At the same time, the great German jurist Carl Friedrich von Savigny developed the 'fiction theory' of corporations, maintaining that the recognition of legal persons was rooted in the fiction that the individual will of each of their representatives was regarded as the will of the legal person. Such fiction, Savigny concluded, could lead to civil liability but never to criminal liability of the corporation. Although Savigny's theory was later challenged by Otto von Gierke, who postulated the existence of a 'real corporate person-ality' of legal persons, the Penal Code for the new German empire, written in 1870, adhered to Savigny's concept and limited criminal liability to natural persons...

[In 1968,] a legislative compromise had resolved the conflict between doctrinal opposition to corporate criminal responsibility and the practical demand for confiscating the profits of criminal activities from corporations. [Since then,] the Code on Administrative Infractions (*Gesetz über Ordnungswidrigkeiten*) permits the imposition of an administrative fine against a legal person if an organ, a representative or a person with control functions of the legal person committed a criminal offence or an administrative infraction by which an obligation of the legal person was violated or the legal person was enriched. In order to impose an administrative fine, it is not necessary to identify an individual officer or representative who did wrong; it only has to be shown that someone acting for the legal person in a capacity designated by the statute committed an offence. The offence can also consist in a culpable lack of supervision over lower-rank employees. The appropriate state agency can thus impose an administrative fine on a legal person when all that is known is the fact that one of its employees committed a criminal or administrative offence on behalf of the legal person and that a responsible officer of the legal person failed to prevent or discourage the commission of that offence through proper supervision of the subordinate. The maximum amount of an administrative fine against the legal person is one million Euro. If the legal person obtained an illicit profit from the offence, the fine can exceed one million Euro and is limited only by the amount of the legal person's gain. The Penal Code also provides for the possibility of confiscating the proceeds of a crime from a legal person when a natural person has committed a criminal offence on its behalf.

This legal arrangement... fulfils the main functions of corporate criminal responsibility. It permits the state to hold the corporation financially responsible for offences committed by its agents on its behalf, and even for offences of mere employees if they were not sufficiently supervised, and to deprive the corporation of any illicit profit it may have drawn from violations committed on its behalf. It can therefore be argued that the Federal Republic of Germany lives up to its commitment under various international conventions to provide for proportional and deterrent sanctions against legal persons.

...

D. "Fundamental" Objections

Given the deficiencies of the two "models" of corporate criminal responsibility, it is not surprising that a strong group of German theorists oppose the introduction of full-scale corporate liability. These authors argue that corporate criminal responsibility conflicts with basic tenets of German criminal law. They see three fatal deficiencies: corporations cannot act, corporations cannot be blamed, and corporations cannot be subject to criminal punishment.

To understand this argument remember that, according to traditional German doctrine, criminal law is a profoundly moral business. Criminal sanctions, as opposed to civil liability for damages or administrative sanctions, are said to have an inherent element of moral blame, a negative socio-ethical value judgment addressed to the offender and relating to the offence. This negative value judgment can be justified only when the person has acted (or omitted to act) according to his voluntary decision and could have avoided the act of wrongdoing. Attribution of blame, under these high standards, is not a pragmatic tool employed to bring about desired behaviour on the part of citizens, but the outcome of a dialogue between the state and the citizen, a dialogue with strong ethical overtones.

Seen from this perspective, the problems of corporate criminal responsibility become easily apparent. The criminal law presupposes the existence of and is addressed to a moral agent. His fault is the reason for the law's moral condemnation of his criminal act. A legal person, even though it can be subject to legal obligations, lacks all ingredients of a moral agent in the true sense: it has no moral conscience, it cannot recognize moral or legal norms, and it cannot stop itself from violating such norms. This significant difference suggests prima facie that criminal liability cannot be imposed on corporations, at least not in the same way as they are imposed on natural persons. If one wishes to make corporations criminally liable it would, in any event, be necessary to adapt and transform basic concepts of criminal law so that they 'fit' the special characteristics of a legal person. Whether or not such transformation is possible and, if so, desirable is the issue on which the debate in Germany has centred.

Let us now take a closer look at the requirements for individual criminal responsibility.

1. Corporations Do Not Act

The primary pre-condition for criminal liability is an act done by the offender. On the basis of an extensive debate among criminal law theorists in the 1950s and 1960s, there has emerged a consensus that an act is a volitional movement, typically geared toward an effect determined by the will of the actor. Corporations, it has been argued, cannot act in that sense, because they neither have a will nor can they make movements. This somewhat naturalistic argument against corporate criminal liability has been countered on several levels. Simply referring to positive law, some authors maintain that since the law confers obligations upon legal persons, the law must assume that legal persons can act to fulfil these obligations. Others refer not to positive law but to the views of society: since corporations are recognized in social life as actors with an identity distinct from their individual members, they claim, whatever is an expression of the "sense" of the corporation can be regarded as its act for the purposes of criminal law. A more sophisticated argument describes legal persons as self-referential, autopoietic systems which, just like natural persons, possess recursivity and self-reflexivity. What these authors have in common is a perspective of legal persons as anthropomorphous entities that act like humans do. That parallel is, however, more metaphoric than precise; and it may overlook a critical difference between natural and legal persons, namely that a legal person's identity exists on paper only—the natural persons acting on behalf of the corporation change over time so that there is no "real" identity and self-consciousness that links the corporation's present to its past or future. This difference may well give the corporation's "acts" a different quality from those of a natural person whose volition is linked to and part of a coherent personal history.

An alternative approach is to attribute the acts of the corporation's organs to the corporation itself. According to this view, legal persons can and do act, but only through their organs. It has correctly been pointed out, however, that there is no persuasive reason for attributing the corporate officers' acts to the corporation since the corporation as such lacks control over what its officers do.

None of the attempts to define "acts" of legal persons in parallel to those of natural persons thus comes across as truly convincing, at least as long we adhere to a naturalistic view of human acts. In order to make corporations "actors" under criminal law, we have to adapt the concept of an "act." Something like "organizational dominance" of certain processes would have to be regarded as an equivalent of a human act. If a persuasive reason for the necessity of this adaptation could be given—and needs of criminal policy might be cited in that context—it would further be necessary to precisely describe what it is that creates "organizational dominance." The fact that processes leading to harmful results have been controlled by the legal person's officers might be a relevant criterion in that respect. But, regardless of the fact that many jurisdictions have introduced corporate criminal responsibility, we still move in unchartered waters when we strive to find appropriate requirements for ascribing human acts to legal persons. The task of spelling out such requirements, at least in civil law systems, certainly belongs to the legislature, which is to give guidance to citizens and courts alike beyond merely stating that corporations can be held liable for acts of their officers, as the French Penal Code does.

2. Corporations Cannot be Morally Guilty

Matters become even more complicated when we consider the issue of a corporation's blameworthiness. Schuld—which I will interchangeably translate as "guilt" or "blameworthiness"—has been another hot topic of debate in German criminal law theory, especially after the Second World War. As early as in 1952, the Federal Court of Appeals declared in a landmark ruling that a person cannot be found guilty of a crime if he was unable to recognize the fact that his conduct was prohibited. In that judgment, the Court, referring to principles of natural law, declared that "man is directed toward free, responsible moral self-determination" and that only for that reason moral and legal blame can be imposed on him when he commits a crime. The Federal Constitutional Court has since then repeatedly declared that the rule *nulla poena sine culpa*, although not specifically mentioned in the German Basic Law of 1949, is an important constitutional principle. According to the Court, this principle is rooted in the protection of human dignity and the right to develop one's personality and is also supported by the fact that the Federal Republic of Germany is a state based on the rule of law.

It is easy to see that "moral self-determination" is not something that can easily be attributed to legal persons. For that reason, the German legislature did not provide for criminal punishment of corporations, but relegated their liability to the law of administrative infractions. In that part of the law, so the theory goes, sanctions, although they can amount to millions of Euro, do not imply moral blame and therefore can be applied to legal persons.

In recent years, however, several theorists have challenged the idea that criminal guilt presupposes moral self-determination and can therefore not be attributed to legal persons. The main lines of argument are similar to those used with respect to a corporation's ability to act. Some authors propose a concept of "corporate guilt," supposed to reflect popular thinking about the responsibility of corporations for harm caused under their name. Others maintain that the legislature, by providing for administrative sanctions against corporations, has indicated its belief that corporations can act culpably. Beyond that positivistic argument, many authors would be willing to re-define the concept of guilt to fit the conditions of decision-making of a corporation. They argue that although a legal person cannot be said to have a free will in the same way as is postulated for natural persons, a legal person does have a choice to act legally or in violation of the law, a choice that is eventually determined by its organs. One author even suggests that a corporation as such can act intentionally and negligently, depending on the kind of fault its organs or employees commit in defectively organising the corporation. Other writers would transfer the guilt of officers to the corporation, thereby sidestepping the question of whether a corporation itself can act culpably.

Yet others have gone so far as to abandon strict adherence to the guilt requirement and would regard the necessity to prove an actor's blameworthiness as only one factor in assessing the legitimacy of a criminal statute. If the evil to be repressed is serious enough and the sanction can generally be termed proportionate, then guilt in any traditional sense need not be a prerequisite for conviction.

The proposals to lower the traditional guilt standard have nevertheless met with serious opposition. For example, Günther Jakobs, one of Germany's leading criminal law theorists, has insisted that blameworthiness presupposes a capacity to comprehend the meaning of a moral norm and to take a position with respect to that norm; even an organ of a legal person, Jakobs maintains, cannot transfer that capacity to the legal person itself.

Jakobs' statement, I think, draws a correct conclusion from a "personal" concept of guilt. But it remains an open question whether the traditional concept of blameworthiness, which would indeed preclude introduction of corporate criminal responsibility, can be altered when activities of legal persons are concerned. Tatjana Hörnle has recently shown that the proclaimed connection between the guilt principle and the dignity of man is not so strict and close as had been assumed.[77] The guilt principle, Hörnle says, is necessary to protect the citizen against unwarranted reprobation, which would interfere with his right to freely develop his personality. The protection of the guilt principle is thus needed only to the extent moral reprobation is pronounced by formally convicting a person of a crime. Only when the reprobation inherent in criminal punishment is personal, Hörnle concludes, personal guilt is required. If that is correct, the very fact that legal persons do not partake of the autonomy and free will that forms the basis of human dignity means that the "guilt principle" in its traditional form need not be applied to them. To the extent that sanctions against corporations do not imply moral blame, corporations do not need protection against unwarranted blaming. In other words, sanctions against corporations may neither presume nor express the notion that the corporation has committed a moral wrong in the same sense in which a natural person could have culpably violated a norm. The guilt principle does thus not stand in the way of introducing sanctions that do not impose moral blame.

3. Criminal Sanctions do not Apply to Corporations

But there still is the third, somewhat related issue: Is a corporation a proper subject of criminal punishment? Leaving aside the facetious argument that you cannot put a company into prison, the main objection to punishing corporations is that a legal person cannot realize that it is being sanctioned and cannot make a conscious effort to avoid punishment in the future. Since a legal person has no conscience, criminal sanctions can neither make it realize its fault nor turn it into a better legal person.

This is a serious objection, and bland assertions that the preventive purposes of criminal punishment can still be reached miss the point. If sanctioning a corporation leads to law-abiding "behaviour" on the part of the corporation, this is not because the corporation has been impressed by the sanction and has decided to mend its ways, but because the consequences of punishing the corporation have had a collateral effect on natural persons, namely managers, shareholders, or customers, who then took measures to curb the violations. Corporations can be influenced through criminal sanctions only in a twice mediated way: the punishment of the legal person affects natural persons, and these natural persons change the corporation's leadership or organization. It is a legitimate question to ask

---

[77] T. Hörnle, 'Die verfassungsrechtliche Begründung des Schuldprinzips', in U. Sieber et al. (eds), Strafrecht und Wirtschaftsstrafrecht: Dogmatik, Rechtsvergleich, Rechtstatsachen (Köln: Heymanns, 2008), 325.

whether this detour is worth taking. Might it not be better to address criminal sanctions directly at those responsible for the wrongdoing ascribed to the corporation?

Assuming there exists a need, based on criminal policy concerns, to impose sanctions directly on the corporation, several authors have suggested that these sanctions should be distinguished from criminal penalties imposed on natural persons in order to avoid confusion between punishment connoting moral reproach and corporate punishment imposed without conferring reprobation. Nice linguistic distinctions have been made between criminal fines and corporate fines. Some authors have suggested a more radical approach. They would introduce prevention-oriented sanctions not conferring blame, such as German law recognizes, for example, for insane offenders. Such sanctions would resolve the problem of (the lack of) corporate guilt. It has been objected, however, that the whole idea of mobilizing the criminal law for sanctioning legal persons would be undercut if in the end one only imposed morally neutral sanctions (as already happens under the law of administrative infractions). Moreover, devising measures to reduce the dangerousness of enterprises is being seen as a typical function of administrative agencies, not of criminal courts.

The issue of naming and shaping sanctions for legal persons may indeed be heavily contingent not only on each jurisdiction's semantic possibilities, but more importantly, on the way a jurisdiction distinguishes among civil, administrative and criminal consequences of misconduct or impending risk. From the perspective of the offender, a fine is a fine, regardless of whether the imposed payment is deemed to have moral overtones, and whether it is mainly a reaction to past behaviour or an incentive for future conduct. Which sanction is regarded as "criminal" also varies from one jurisdiction to the other—some regard even illegal parking as a "criminal" offence (because there is no alternative system for minor violations), some entertain special—typically gray—areas between administrative and criminal law, and some make only a civil versus criminal distinction. Thus, to say that a sanction for legal persons is "criminal" (rather than civil or administrative or administrative-penal) may have a quite different meaning depending on the legal environment in which that sanction exists. Given these ambiguities, it may not be worthwhile to change a functioning system of corporate responsibility just in order to attach the label "criminal" to whatever sanctions are already in use, especially given the problems of distinguishing such "criminal" corporate sanctions from "truly criminal" sanctions against individuals.

NOTES

1. The issue of corporate criminal liability marks a fundamental point of difference between Anglo-American and German criminal law. Or so it seems. Weigend sets out, clearly and comprehensively, the objections to corporate criminal liability found in the German criminal law literature for decades. He also points out, however, that these objections are not universal and appear to be fading. In fact, a closer look at German legal history reveals that differences between the German position and the Anglo-American one may not be as radical, and as deeply entrenched, as might appear at first glance.* From a comparative standpoint, the standard histories of corporate criminal liability in Anglo-American and in Germany criss-crossed one another like ships in the dark right around the turn of the nineteenth century: According to stock histories, before 1800, English criminal law categorically rejected cor-porate criminal liability (because corporations couldn't be culpable), but then with breath-taking speed adopted corporate criminal liability (because the industrial revolution produced corporations, and in particular railways, that were both powerful and dangerous). Across the Channel, before 1800, corporate criminal liability was widely accepted in German law, but then the Enlightenment arrived (through Kant and Savigny) raising categorical objections to the very idea of corporate criminal liability (because corporations couldn't be culpable).

Viewed side-by-side, these stories are surprising and ultimately unconvincing. In fact, corporate criminal liability was widely accepted in English and German law before 1800. In fact, the rejection of corporate criminal liability in Germany was neither as categorical, nor as sudden as the standard account suggests. Gierke, in his monumental and still much-admired study *Das deutsche Genossenschaftsrecht* (published in four volumes between 1868 and 1913), argued forcefully for the long-standing existence of a specifically German conception of the

---

* See generally Markus D. Dubber, "The Comparative History and Theory of Corporate Criminal Liability," 16 *New Criminal Law Review* (2013), 203.

corporation as a person (in contrast to the Roman conception of the corporation as a fictional entity propagated by Savigny), evidenced by among other things the recognition of corporate criminal liability since the Middle Ages. Although the German Criminal Code of 1871 adopted the Romanist position, rejecting corporate criminal (but not civil!) liability as a logical impossibility, corporate criminal liability continued to attract distinguished supporters, including the leading German criminal law scholar of the late nineteenth and early twentieth century, Franz von Liszt.

Particularly vociferous objections to corporate criminal liability were raised after World War II, when German criminal law scholars rejected it as an alien notion radically at odds with the essence of German criminal law, the culpability (or guilt) principle (enunciated at this very time in the much-cited 1952 judgment of the Federal Court of Justice). (The alienness of the concept was figurative and literal: corporate criminal liability was, after all, widely accepted in the law of English and American occupiers, who nonetheless refrained from employing it.) German criminal law, as Weigend points out, "is a profoundly moral business." Or, in the language of the time, criminal liability presupposes "free responsible ethical self-determination," i.e., "personal-ethical guilt." The corporation being but a legal fiction, however, it was plain for all to see that it was incapable of "free responsible ethical self-determination," never mind—since it was not a "person" to begin with, of "personal-ethical guilt."

Now, at the same time as corporate criminal liability was rejected as beyond the pale (so far beyond the pale, in fact, that its invocation by occupation courts was treated as analogous to the use of capital punishment despite its disavowal in the German Basic Law*), explicitly non-punitive, administrative, sanctions for corporate misconduct were developed and first introduced in 1949 (see § 23 Economic Crimes Act (WiStG) (1949)). (In fact, the construction of non-punitive sanctions for corporate misconduct became the model for the general Administrative Offenses Act (*Ordnungswidrigkeitengesetz*) of 1968, mentioned by Weigend.) Since administrative fines, so the argument went, do not imply moral condemnation based on "personal-ethical guilt," triggered by an act of "free responsibly ethical self-determination," they do not implicate the culpability principle at the heart of German criminal law. Administrative sanctions did not punish retrospectively; instead, they were prospective "sharpened administrative orders" (*verschärfte Verwaltungsbefehle*).

2. Problem solved. Or was it? Even German commentators at the time sensed a sleight of hand, complaining that administrative fines for corporate misconduct were simply criminal punishments by another name. These voices, however, gained no more traction than did similar cries of "fraudulent labeling" (*Etikettenschwindel*) raised at the time of the introduction of the two-track system in the 1930s, which turns on the distinction between "punishments" and "measures." As Weigend points out, a fine is a fine (is a fine), at least to the person (or fictional entity!) paying it. Whether this means that administrative sanctions are as effective as criminal ones, or that the distinction between one type of sanction and the other (particularly given the prevalence of fines in German criminal law†), is another question perhaps worth considering. Does German criminal law, by both rejecting corporate criminal liability on principle and putting in place administrative sanctions with stiff fines as "sharpened administrative orders" try to have its cake and eat it too?‡

Compare this strategy to that of differentiating "measures" from "punishments," discussed in Chapter 1.B.iii. Are there any limits on the state's discretion to label one of its acts in one way or rather than another? To what extent does the rejection of corporate criminal liability depend on an outdated conception of crime and punishment?

---

* See Chapter 1.B.i.
† See Chapter 1.A.iii.
‡ See *Öztürk v. Germany*, 6 EHRR 409 (Eur. Ct. Hum. Rts. 1984) (relevance of classification as criminal offense (*Straftat*) or administrative offense (*Ordnungswidrigkeit*)); see generally Thomas Weigend, "The Legal and Practical Problems Posed by the Difference between Criminal Law and Administrative Penal Law," 59 *Revue internationale de droit pénal* (1988), 67.

What's the difference between conceiving of criminal law as "a profoundly moral business" based on notions like "moral self-determination" and "moral reprobation" (never mind "free responsible ethical self-determination" or "personal-ethical guilt") and one grounded in such things as a "vicious will"? Both have been invoked categorically to reject corporate criminal liability, one in Germany today, the other in England before the nineteenth century. Does it help instead to argue that corporations cannot perform an act, defined as the "expression or manifestation of one's personality": "Since they lack psychic-spiritual substance, they cannot express or manifest themselves."[*]

3. On the other side of the Atlantic, *N.Y. Central & Hudson River Railroad Co.* is generally taken to have settled the issue of corporate criminal liability in American criminal law. This is perhaps a lazy reading of the case, but does indicate the general lack of serious interest in the issue of corporate criminal liability; no court since then has expressed doubts about its constitutionality and, of course, *N.Y. Central* itself made it seem as though the issue had long before been settled. In fact, the Court's opinion amounts to little more than making this very point: we (and the English) have been holding corporations criminally liable for quite some time, therefore it cannot be unconstitutional to continue doing so. This is not a particularly convincing argument as a matter of constitutional law; it is also dubious in many other respects. As a matter of history, it is hardly compelling. If we disregard the fact that—as has already been pointed out—corporate criminal liability in fact was commonplace throughout English legal history since the Middle Ages, and instead follow the Court—and pretty much everyone else—in taking Blackstone's pronouncement (that a "corporation cannot commit treason, or felony, or other crime, in its corporate capacity: though its members may, in their distinct individual capacities"[†]) at face value, the gradual recognition of first civil and then criminal liability for corporations, first for some offenses then for others, over the course of the nineteenth century, first in England, then in the United States, does not establish the consistency of corporate criminal liability with the very principles of criminal liability that led Blackstone to declare its ineligibility for criminal liability. (What has changed? The concept of a corporation, the principles of criminal liability, or perhaps the Court's commitment to their enforcement?) Instead of turning attention to these questions, the Court is content to record recent judicial and legislative practice; corporate criminal liability has been accepted, often implicitly, therefore it is acceptable. (What do you make of the jump from civil liability to criminal liability? This is a common move among supporters of corporate criminal liability:[‡] if the corporation can commit a tort (or break a contract, never mind enter into one), it can commit a crime. Are you convinced?)

Apart from this description, however questionable, of current and recent law, the Court emphasizes the need for, or at least the advantages of, the recognition of corporate criminal liability. Corporations are powerful; they do dangerous things; therefore they must be punished, or rather legislatures must have the option of punishing them without fear of constitutional constraint. Public welfare demands no less. Is this a convincing argument? Is benefit to public welfare always (ever?) a knock-down argument? Are the dangers posed by modern corporations so great that the state has no option but to punish corporations? Consider the question from the perspective of the various theories of punishment (including the Model Penal Code's treatmentism—how does one assess the criminal dangerousness of a corporation)?

The Louisiana Supreme Court, in the *Chapman Dodge Case*, tries much harder than the U.S. Supreme Court to come to grips with the nature of corporate criminal liability. This is not surprising, perhaps, since Louisiana, as the only civil law jurisdiction in the United States, had rejected corporate criminal liability until 1942.[§] The corporation's "mind" and "hands" mentioned in the opinion refer to the so-called "identification" (or "alter ego") doctrine developed by English courts, adopted in other common law countries, which derives

---

[*] Claus Roxin, *Strafrecht: Allgemeiner Teil* (3rd edn. 1997), vol. 1, § 8 III.
[†] William Blackstone, *Commentaries on the Laws of England* (1765), vol. 1, 464.
[‡] See also Franz von Liszt, *Lehrbuch des deutschen Strafrechts* (10th ed. 1900), § 27 n.1.
[§] See n. 9 in the court's opinion.

corporate criminal liability from the criminal conduct of senior employees, the "directing mind" of the corporation. According to a recent summary by the Canadian Supreme Court,

> [i]n order to trigger [the identification doctrine's] operation and through it corporate criminal liability for the actions of the employee (who must generally be liable himself), the actor-employee who physically committed the offence must be the "ego," the "center" of the corporate personality, the "vital organ" of the body corporate, the "alter ego" of the corporation or its "directing mind."
>
> *Canadian Dredge and Dock Co. v. The Queen*, [1985] 1 S.C.R. 662 (Can.)

This approach is generally contrasted with the broad—*respondeat superior*—approach associated with U.S. federal criminal law and the criminal law of some states, which may extend corporate liability vicariously to the criminal acts of any employee committed within the scope of employment, regardless of his or her position in the corporation, provided the conduct was undertaken, at least in part, to benefit the corporation. The latter approach is often criticized as too broad, however breadth is measured in this case. Assuming that's a problem, is the cure of the "identification" doctrine with its bizarre combination of crude pseudo-physical anthropomorphism of hands and minds (though no feet, brains, or other internal organs) and pop psychology of egos and alter egos worse than the disease? Or is this post hoc rationalizations through various doctrinal "constructions" no different than other criminal law fictions (such as constructive possession, constructive territorial jurisdiction, constructive presence, and any number of other "deeming" provisions)?

4. *Congregational Khal Chaisidei*, a New York case, illustrates the Model Penal Code's approach to corporate criminal liability in everyday action, along with the matter-of-fact application of corporate criminal liability to an offense against the person (including criminally negligent homicide), not to mention "one count of unsafe tires and one count of invalid inspection" (two minor offenses under the New York Vehicle & Traffic Law). The corporate defendant's criminal liability is based on the finding that Gross, a "high managerial agent" of the corporation, engaged in "conduct constituting [an] offense ... within the scope of his employment and in behalf of the corporation." N.Y. Penal Law § 20.20(2) (b). The New York Penal Law provision is based on Model Penal Code § 2.07 (Liability of Corporations, Unincorporated Associations and Persons Acting, or Under a Duty to Act, in Their Behalf):

(1) A corporation may be convicted of the commission of an offense if:
   (a) the offense is a violation or the offense is defined by a statute other than the Code in which a legislative purpose to impose liability on corporations plainly appears and the conduct is performed by an agent of the corporation acting in behalf of the corporation within the scope of his office or employment, except that if the law defining the offense designates the agents for whose conduct the corporation is accountable or the circumstances under which it is accountable, such provisions shall apply; or
   (b) the offense consists of an omission to discharge a specific duty of affirmative performance imposed on corporations by law; or
   (c) the commission of the offense was authorized, requested, commanded, performed or recklessly tolerated by the board of directors or by a high managerial agent acting in behalf of the corporation within the scope of his office or employment.
(2) When absolute liability is imposed for the commission of an offense, a legislative purpose to impose liability on a corporation shall be assumed, unless the contrary plainly appears. ...
(4) As used in this Section:
   (a) "corporation" does not include an entity organized as or by a governmental agency for the execution of a governmental program;
   (b) "agent" means any director, officer, servant, employee or other person authorized to act in behalf of the corporation or association and, in the case of an unincorporated association, a member of such association;
   (c) "high managerial agent" means an officer of a corporation or an unincorporated association, or, in the case of a partnership, a partner, or any other agent of a corporation or association having duties of such responsibility that his conduct may fairly be assumed to represent the policy of the corporation or association.

(5) In any prosecution of a corporation or an unincorporated association for the commission of an offense included within the terms of Subsection (1)(a) . . . , other than an offense for which absolute liability has been imposed, it shall be a defense if the defendant proves by a preponderance of evidence that the high managerial agent having supervisory responsibility over the subject matter of the offense employed due diligence to prevent its commission. This paragraph shall not apply if it is plainly inconsistent with the legislative purpose in defining the particular offense . . .

Note the dissent in *Chapman Dodge*. Is the disagreement in the case about which standard to apply, or how to apply the standard to the facts of the case?

INCHOATE OFFENSES

A comparative analysis of the treatment of so-called inchoate liability in Anglo-American and German criminal law presents a diffuse picture, a mixture of similarities and differences, criss-crossing lines among specific doctrines and historical periods. Starting with attempt, the Model Penal Code's "substantial step" approach to locating the famed *locus poenitentiae* separating preparation from attempt, and its unabashed enthusiasm for attempt liability (and inchoate liability in general), are among the clearest manifestations of its commitment to treatmentism, i.e., the conception of criminal law as a rough guide to the identification and diagnosis of abnormally dangerous individuals to be subjected to peno-correctional treatment. They also mark one of the most prominent points of departure from traditional common law doctrine, which—incidentally—resembles the position of German criminal law on these issues, drawing the line between preparation and attempt far more closely to the consummation of the offense and mitigating punishment for attempt vis-à-vis the completed offense.

On the issue of conspiracy, the Model Penal Code again deviated substantially from the traditional common law position, by limiting conspiracy liability to agreements to commit acts criminal in themselves, as opposed to the old—and controversial—doctrine, which criminalized conspiracies to commit "corrupt, dishonest, fraudulent, or immoral, and in that sense illegal" acts. Here, as generally on the issue of solicitation, German criminal law is aligned with the Model Penal Code: while German criminal law also criminalizes agreements—as an attempt to participate, § 30 Criminal Code—there is no question that the object of the agreement must be a crime itself (otherwise, it would be impossible to attempt to participate in its commission).

A. Attempt

People v. Lehnert
Supreme Court of Colorado
163 P.3d 1111 (2007)

The defendant, Charity Lehnert, was charged with attempted first degree murder, possession of explosive or incendiary parts, committing a crime of violence, and two less serious offenses of drug possession. She was convicted of all but the drug charges, and she was sentenced to terms of thirty years for attempted murder and six years for possession of explosive devices, to be served concurrently.

Evidence at her trial indicated that in July 2001, the owner of a gun shop contacted the Denver Police Department and reported that a suspicious woman had attempted to buy gunpowder from him but refused to say why she wanted it. He declined to sell the gunpowder to her and instead notified the police. Through the license plate number he gave them, the police were able to identify the defendant.

Days later a friend of the defendant contacted the police, reporting that the defendant told her she was planning to kill two "pigs," using two pipe bombs. One of the officers was a male correctional officer at the Denver Women's Correctional Facility, where the defendant had been an inmate, and the other was a female officer named "Shelly." The friend testified that the defendant had borrowed a drill and made holes in the end caps of the bomb, and had asked for wooden clothespins to serve as a switch and a soldering iron to connect two small wires, saying that she only needed a few more parts to complete the bomb. The friend also testified that the defendant told her that she had learned how to construct bombs while in prison and had written instructions at her home. In addition, she testified that Lehnert had not only found out extensive family information and the home address of the correctional officer, but also had driven past his house numerous times.

The defendant's friend became concerned that the defendant was actually going to carry out the killings, and she called the police. In addition to telling the police about the defendant's statements and actions, she also told them that she had found in her home a business card for a second gun shop. By inquiring at the second gun shop, the police learned that the defendant had managed to purchase two boxes of shotgun shells.

A search warrant was issued for the defendant's apartment, where police discovered doorbell wire, electrical tape, a nine-volt battery, two metal pipes (which had been scored, weakening them and increasing their destructive potential), two metal end caps (with drilled out center holes), latex gloves, screwdrivers, wire cutters, safety glasses, magnets, two boxes of shotgun shells full of gunpowder, flashlight bulbs (sometimes used as an ignition device for a pipe bomb), and directions to the victim's house. In addition, the police found materials for making false identification cards, the defendant's driver's license, falsified birth certificates, an application for a new social security card, and a falsified high school transcript.

A police detective testified that the materials recovered from the defendant's apartment were explosive parts, capable of being assembled to make a bomb. The detective further testified that the defendant possessed everything required for a pipe bomb except a completed switch and that a switch could probably be made from the wire found at the scene or from a clothespin, which the defendant had tried to acquire from her friend.

At the close of the People's evidence, defense counsel moved for a judgment of acquittal on all counts, arguing that the evidence was insufficient to sustain the attempted first degree murder count because it did not include any evidence from which a reasonable jury could find that the defendant had yet taken a "substantial step" toward committing the murder, as required by the statute. The trial court disagreed and denied the motion. The court of appeals reversed the defendant's conviction for attempted murder, concluding that the evidence was insufficient. Largely because the pipe bombs were not fully assembled and placed in close proximity to the intended victim, the appellate court found that the defendant's conduct did not progress beyond "mere preparation." The People petitioned this court for a writ of certiorari.

A person commits criminal attempt in this jurisdiction if, acting with the kind of culpability otherwise required for commission of a particular crime, he engages in conduct constituting a substantial step toward the commission of that crime. See § 18-2-101(1), C.R.S. (2006).[1] . . .

Until 1963, Colorado had not codified the law of attempt in a general statute. In that year, the General Assembly enacted with few modifications the Model Penal Code's proposed codification, including its enumeration of specific kinds of conduct, which would, under certain circumstances, be considered sufficient, as a matter of law, to overcome a motion for judgment of acquittal. In 1971, with the adoption of the Colorado Criminal Code, the unadulterated Model Penal Code approach was abandoned in favor of the approach of the proposed Federal Criminal Code [which itself was fashioned after the Model Penal Code]. See ch. 121, sec. 1, § 40-2-101(1), 1971 Colo. Sess. Laws 414, 414–15; People v. Frysig, 628 P.2d 1004 (Colo. 1981) ("The original formulation of criminal attempt in the Colorado Criminal Code was patterned after proposed federal legislation."); The Nat'l Comm'n on Reform of Fed. Criminal Laws, Study Draft of a New Federal Criminal Code § 1001, at 61–62 (1970).

Prior to the enactment of a general criminal attempt statute, the sporadic treatment of attempt by this court focused largely on the dangerousness of the actor's conduct in terms of its proximity to, or the likelihood that it would result in, a completed crime. Emphasizing that neither preparation alone nor a "mere intention" to commit a crime could constitute criminal attempt, we described an attempt as "any overt act done with the intent to commit the crime, and which, except for the interference of some cause preventing the carrying out of the intent, would have resulted in the commission of the crime." Lewis v. People, 124 Colo. 62, 67, 235 P.2d 348, 350 (1951). By also making clear, however, that the overt act required for an attempt need not be the last proximate act necessary to consummate the crime, we implicitly acknowledged that acts in preparation for the last

---

[1] Section 18-2-101(1), reads in part:
A person commits a criminal attempt, if, acting with the kind of culpability otherwise required for commission of an offense, he engages in conduct constituting a substantial step toward the commission of the offense. A substantial step is any conduct, whether act, omission, or possession, which is strongly corroborative of the firmness of the actor's purpose to complete the commission of the offense.

proximate act, at some point attain to criminality themselves. The question of an overt act's proximity to, or remoteness from, completion of the crime therefore remained, without detailed guidance, a matter for individual determination under the facts of each case.

By contrast, the statutory requirement of a "substantial step" signaled a clear shift of focus from the act itself to "the dangerousness of the actor, as a person manifesting a firm disposition to commit a crime." See Model Penal Code § 5.01 cmt. 1 (1985); cf. People v. Thomas, 729 P.2d 972, 976 (Colo. 1986) ("[T]he probability of future dangerousness that has given rise to the justified legislative judgment that criminal attempt liability should be imposed . . . "). While some conduct, in the form of an act, omission, or possession, see § 18-2-101(1), is still necessary to avoid criminalizing bad intentions alone; and the notion of "mere preparation"[4] continues to be a useful way of describing conduct falling short of a "substantial step"; the ultimate inquiry under the statutory definition concerns the extent to which the actor's conduct is strongly corroborative of the firmness of his criminal purpose, rather than the proximity of his conduct to consummation of the crime. Even more directly than the Model Penal Code formulation, which makes strong corroboration of criminal purpose a necessary but not sufficient condition of a substantial step, see Model Penal Code § 5.01 (2)(1985) (not a substantial step "unless" strongly corroborative), the statute adopted by this jurisdiction in 1971 actually equates a substantial step with "any conduct that is strongly corroborative of the firmness of his purpose to complete the commission of the offense." § 18-2-101(1). The question whether particular conduct constitutes a substantial step, of course, remains a matter of degree and can no more be resolved by a mechanical rule, or litmus test, than could the question whether the actor's conduct was too remote or failed to progress beyond mere preparation. The requirement that the defendant's conduct amount to a "substantial step," statutorily defined as it now is, however, provides the fact-finder with a much more specific and predictable basis for determining criminality. Rather than leaving to the fact-finder (as well as the court evaluating the sufficiency of evidence) the task of resolving the policy choices inherent in deciding when acts of preparation have become criminal, the statutory requirement of a substantial step simply calls for a determination whether the actor's conduct strongly corroborates a sufficiently firm intent on his part to commit the specific crime he is charged with attempting.

By actually defining a "substantial step" as "any conduct . . . which is strongly corroborative of the firmness of the actor's purpose," the Colorado statute has no need to further enumerate particular circumstances in which strongly corroborative conduct may constitute a substantial step. Conduct strongly corroborative of the firmness of the actor's criminal purpose is sufficient in itself. Drawn as they are largely from decisional law, however, the acts enumerated in the former statute and Model Penal Code, such as searching out a contemplated victim, reconnoitering the place contemplated for commission of a crime, and possessing materials specially designed for unlawful use and without lawful purpose, remain useful examples of conduct considered capable of strongly corroborating criminal purpose, and in those instances where they do, of being sufficient to establish criminal attempt. See United States v. Rahman, 189 F.3d 88, 128–29 (2d Cir. 1999) (finding the factors listed in the Model Penal Code relevant to the existence of sufficient evidence of a "substantial step" in attempted bombing prosecution).

A motion for judgment of acquittal may be granted only if the relevant evidence, both direct and circumstantial, when viewed as a whole in the light most favorable to the prosecution, is not substantial and sufficient to support a conclusion by a reasonable mind that the defendant is guilty of the charge beyond a reasonable doubt.

According to this standard, there was evidence at the defendant's trial from which the jury could find that she repeatedly articulated her intent to kill two law enforcement officers with pipe bombs. Unlike many prosecutions for attempt, it was therefore unnecessary for the jury to be able to infer the defendant's criminal intent or purpose from her conduct. The jury need only have been able to find that the defendant committed acts that were strongly corroborative of the firmness of that purpose.

There was also evidence from which the jury could reasonably find that the defendant was determined to make the pipe bombs she needed to implement her plan and that she made substantial efforts and overcame hurdles to do so. Over many days she not only managed to acquire almost all of the materials required to create a bomb but also feloniously altered them to suit her criminal purpose, conduct for which she was separately convicted of possessing explosive or incendiary parts. When rebuffed in her attempt to acquire gunpowder directly from one gun shop, for example, she found a way to do so indirectly from another gun shop. There was testimony from

---

[4] Interestingly, although the term "overt act" appears in the statutory definition of "Conspiracy," see § 18-1-201, C. R.S. (2006), and conduct beyond "mere preparation" has at times been referred to as a requirement of attempt, see People v. Washington, 865 P.2d 145, 148 (Colo. 1994), neither has ever actually appeared in the criminal attempt statute of this jurisdiction.

which the jury could believe that she had eventually succeeded in acquiring all but a few necessary materials and that she had already acquired the drawings and written instructions necessary for final assembly.

Beyond the tenacity exhibited by the defendant in actually fabricating the bombs, her friend testified that she also had gathered significant personal information about one of her intended victims, including his address and information about his children and the car his family drove. There was evidence that she had reconnoitered his house and neighborhood more than once, reportedly being forced to leave on one occasion after being noticed. Finally there was evidence from which the jury could believe that she was simultaneously producing forged documents, which would permit her to assume false identities for purposes including the purchase of additional weapons.

The complexity of some criminal schemes, and the extent and uniqueness of the preparatory acts required to implement them without detection, lend themselves, by their very nature, to corroborating the actor's firmness of purpose. Regardless of the fact that the defendant was arrested before producing operational bombs or placing them within striking range of her victims in this case, there was in fact an abundance of evidence of her determined and sustained efforts to implement her plan, which could be found by reasonable jurors to be strongly corroborative of the firmness of her purpose to commit murder. Nothing more was required.

People v. Dlugash
Court of Appeals of New York
41 N.Y.2d 725, 363 N.E.2d 1155 (1977)

Jasen, Judge.

The criminal law is of ancient origin, but criminal liability for attempt to commit a crime is comparatively recent. At the root of the concept of attempt liability are the very aims and purposes of penal law. The ultimate issue is whether an individual's intentions and actions, though failing to achieve a manifest and malevolent criminal purpose, constitute a danger to organized society of sufficient magnitude to warrant the imposition of criminal sanctions....

On December 22, 1973, Michael Geller, 25 years old, was found shot to death in the bedroom of his Brooklyn apartment.... Defendant stated that, on the night of December 21, 1973, he, [Joe] Bush and Geller had been out drinking. Bush had been staying at Geller's apartment.... When Geller ... pressed his demand for rent money, Bush drew his .38 caliber pistol, aimed it at Geller and fired three times. Geller fell to the floor. After the passage of a few minutes, perhaps two, perhaps as much as five, defendant walked over to the fallen Geller, drew his .25 caliber pistol, and fired approximately five shots in the victim's head and face. Defendant contended that, by the time he fired the shots, "it looked like Mike Geller was already dead." ...

.... [T]he evidence did not establish, beyond a reasonable doubt, that Geller was alive at the time defendant fired into his body. To sustain a homicide conviction, it must be established, beyond a reasonable doubt, that the defendant caused the death of another person. The People were required to establish that the shots fired by defendant Dlugash were a sufficiently direct cause of Geller's death. While the defendant admitted firing five shots at the victim approximately two to five minutes after Bush had fired three times, all three medical expert witnesses testified that they could not, with any degree of medical certainty, state whether the victim had been alive at the time the latter shots were fired by the defendant.... Whatever else it may be, it is not murder to shoot a dead body.

The concept that there could be criminal liability for an attempt, even if ultimately unsuccessful, to commit a crime is comparatively recent. The modern concept of attempt has been said to date from Rex v. Scofield (Cald 397), decided in 1784. In that case, Lord Mansfield stated that "(t)he intent may make an act, innocent in itself, criminal; nor is the completion of an act, criminal in itself, necessary to constitute criminality. Is it no offence to set fire to a train of gunpowder with intent to burn a house, because by accident, or the interposition of another, the mischief is prevented?" ....

The most intriguing attempt cases are those where the attempt to commit a crime was unsuccessful due to mistakes of fact or law on the part of the would-be criminal. A general rule developed in most American jurisdictions that legal impossibility is a good defense but factual impossibility is not. Thus, for example, it was held that defendants who shot at a stuffed deer did not attempt to take a deer out of season, even though they believed the dummy to be a live animal. The court stated that there was no criminal attempt because it was no crime to "take" a stuffed deer, and it is no crime to attempt to do that which is legal. (State v. Guffey, 262 S.W.2d 152 (Mo.App.); see, also, State v. Taylor, 345 Mo. 325, 133 S.W.2d 336 (no liability for attempt to bribe a juror where person bribed was not, in fact, a juror).) These cases are illustrative of legal impossibility. A further example is Francis Wharton's classic hypothetical involving Lady Eldon and her French lace. Lady Eldon, traveling in Europe, purchased a quantity of French lace at a high price, intending to smuggle it into England without payment of the duty. When discovered in a customs search, the lace turned out to be of English origin, of little value and not subject to duty. The traditional view is that Lady Eldon is not liable for an attempt to smuggle. (1 Wharton, Criminal Law (12th ed.), s 225, p. 304, n.9)

On the other hand, factual impossibility was no defense. For example, a man was held liable for attempted murder when he shot into the room in which his target usually slept and, fortuitously, the target was sleeping elsewhere in the house that night. (State v. Mitchell, 170 Mo. 633, 71 S.W. 175.) Although one bullet struck the target's customary pillow, attainment of the criminal objective was factually impossible....

The New York cases can be parsed out along similar lines. One of the leading cases on legal impossibility is People v. Jaffe, 185 N.Y. 497, 78 N.E. 169, in which we held that there was no liability for the attempted receipt of stolen property when the property received by the defendant in the belief that it was stolen was, in fact under the control of the true owner. Similarly, in People v. Teal, 196 N.Y. 372, 89 N.E. 1086, a conviction for attempted subornation of perjury was overturned on the theory that the testimony attempted to be suborned was irrelevant to the merits of the case. Since it was not subornation of perjury to solicit false, but irrelevant, testimony, "the person through whose procuration the testimony is given cannot be guilty of subornation of perjury and, by the same rule, an unsuccessful attempt to that which is not a crime when effectuated, cannot be held to be an attempt to commit the crime specified." (196 N.Y., at p. 377, 89 N.E. at p. 1088.) Factual impossibility, however, was no defense. Thus, a man could be held for attempted grand larceny when he picked an empty pocket.

As can be seen from even this abbreviated discussion, the distinction between "factual" and "legal" impossibility was a nice one indeed and the courts tended to place a greater value on legal form than on any substantive danger the defendant's actions posed for society. The approach of the draftsmen of the Model Penal Code was to eliminate the defense of impossibility in virtually all situations. Under the code provision, to constitute an attempt, it is still necessary that the result intended or desired by the actor constitute a crime. However, the code suggested a fundamental change to shift the locus of analysis to the actor's mental frame of reference and away from undue dependence upon external considerations. The basic premise of the code provision is that what was in the actor's own mind should be the standard for determining his dangerousness to society and, hence, his liability for attempted criminal conduct.

In the belief that neither of the two branches of the traditional impossibility arguments detracts from the offender's moral culpability, the Legislature substantially carried the code's treatment of impossibility into the 1967 revision of the Penal Law. Thus, a person is guilty of an attempt when, with intent to commit a crime, he engages in conduct which tends to effect the commission of such crime. (Penal Law, s 110.00.) It is no defense that, under the attendant circumstances, the crime was factually or legally impossible of commission, "if such crime could have been committed had the attendant circumstances been as such person believed them to be." (Penal Law, s 110.10.) Thus, if defendant believed the victim to be alive at the time of the shooting, it is no defense to the charge of attempted murder that the victim may have been dead.

Turning to the facts of the case before us, we believe that there is sufficient evidence in the record from which the jury could conclude that the defendant believed Geller to be alive at the time defendant fired shots into Geller's head. Defendant admitted firing five shots at a most vital part of the victim's anatomy from virtually point blank range. Although defendant contended that the victim had already been grievously wounded by another, from the defendant's admitted actions, the jury could conclude that the defendant's purpose and intention was to administer the coup de grace.

Model Penal Code

§ 5.01 Criminal Attempt

(1) *Definition of Attempt.* A person is guilty of an attempt to commit a crime if, acting with the kind of culpability otherwise required for commission of the crime, he:

(a) purposely engages in conduct which would constitute the crime if the attendant circumstances were as he believes them to be; or

(b) when causing a particular result is an element of the crime, does or omits to do anything with the purpose of causing or with the belief that it will cause such result without further conduct on his part; or

(c) purposely does or omits to do anything which, under the circumstances as he believes them to be, is an act or omission constituting a substantial step in a course of conduct planned to culminate in his commission of the crime.

(2) *Conduct Which May Be Held Substantial Step Under Subsection (1)(c).* Conduct shall not be held to constitute a substantial step under Subsection (1)(c) of this Section unless it is strongly

corroborative of the actor's criminal purpose. Without negativing the sufficiency of other conduct, the following, if strongly corroborative of the actor's criminal purpose, shall not be held insufficient as a matter of law:

(a) lying in wait, searching for or following the contemplated victim of the crime;
(b) enticing or seeking to entice the contemplated victim of the crime to go to the place contemplated for its commission;
(c) reconnoitering the place contemplated for the commission of the crime;
(d) unlawful entry of a structure, vehicle or enclosure in which it is contemplated that the crime will be committed;
(e) possession of materials to be employed in the commission of the crime, which are specially designed for such unlawful use or which can serve no lawful purpose of the actor under the circumstances;
(f) possession, collection or fabrication of materials to be employed in the commission of the crime, at or near the place contemplated for its commission, where such possession, collection or fabrication serves no lawful purpose of the actor under the circumstances;
(g) soliciting an innocent agent to engage in conduct constituting an element of the crime.

(3) *Conduct Designed to Aid Another in Commission of a Crime.* A person who engages in conduct designed to aid another to commit a crime which would establish his complicity under Section 2.06 if the crime were committed by such other person, is guilty of an attempt to commit the crime, although the crime is not committed or attempted by such other person.

(4) *Renunciation of Criminal Purpose.* When the actor's conduct would otherwise constitute an attempt under Subsection (1)(b) or (1)(c) of this Section, it is an affirmative defense that he abandoned his effort to commit the crime or otherwise prevented its commission, under circumstances manifesting a complete and voluntary renunciation of his criminal purpose. The establishment of such defense does not, however, affect the liability of an accomplice who did not join in such abandonment or prevention.

Within the meaning of this Article, renunciation of criminal purpose is not voluntary if it is motivated, in whole or in part, by circumstances, not present or apparent at the inception of the actor's course of conduct, which increase the probability of detection or apprehension or which make more difficult the accomplishment of the criminal purpose. Renunciation is not complete if it is motivated by a decision to postpone the criminal conduct until a more advantageous time or to transfer the criminal effort to another but similar objective or victim.

German Federal Court of Justice
1 StR 234/97, BGHSt 43, 177, NJW 1997, 3453 (August 12, 1997)
Bärwurz Case

Facts

At the beginning of March 1994, unknown persons forced entry to the defendant's house, prepared warm food for themselves in the kitchen situated on the ground floor, and also drank the contents of bottles there containing various drinks. Besides this, pieces of home electrical equipment were taken up to the attic of the house. The police, who were notified by the defendant on March 6, 1994, therefore assumed that the perpetrators might return once more in the ensuing days in order to collect and take away the goods which had been placed ready for removal. In the night of March 8 to March 9, four police officers therefore stayed in the house, in order to be able capture possible burglars there. At the same time the defendant, a chemist, had decided on the afternoon of March 8, out of annoyance at the break-in, to place in the entrance hall on the ground floor a standard earthenware bottle with the inscription "Pure Hiekes Bavarian Forest Schnaps (Bayerwaldbärwurz)." He filled this with 178 ml. of a highly poisonous substance and 66 ml. of water, and corked it again. Knowing that consumption of the smallest quantities of this mixture could quickly lead to death, the defendant accepted that, by the placing of this bottle, burglars who might possibly appear in the house again might drink from the bottle, and could be fatally poisoned. The defendant later had reservations, as he had not informed the police officers carrying out surveillance, and he now recognized that they also were at risk from the bottle of poison. He pointed out its poisonous contents to the officers, who had not touched it. On the following morning, an officer from the Criminal Investigation Department asked him by telephone to remove the bottle. He refused to do this at first, but finally, following persuasion by the official, gave his agreement to the official securing the bottle.

The regional court sentenced the defendant to a fine of 90 daily amounts of 180 DM each for intentionally bringing harmful substances into circulation as foodstuffs (punishable according to § 51 para. 1 no. 1 LMBG (Food and Objects of Use Act)). The appeal in law lodged against the defendant by the public prosecutor's office objected to him not having been convicted of the crime of attempted homicide. The appeal was unsuccessful.

Reasons

I.

According to the opinion of the regional court, the defendant had not yet crossed the threshold to attempting the crime of homicide. Although according to his concept of the crime he had done everything to bring about the result sought after, he had not yet taken a step which would immediately lead to the completion of the crime as the occurrence of the result had still been too improbable according to his expectations. There is no objection to this in law.

1. A person attempts a crime by taking steps which will immediately lead to the completion of the crime as envisaged by him (§ 22 Criminal Code). For this, the perpetrator must undertake actions which according to his concept of the crime will lead directly to fulfillment of its definition if there is undisturbed progress without interludes. The commission of acts as described in the statutory definition is admittedly not necessary. It suffices if the perpetrator's action is a direct precursor to the fulfillment of an element in the definition of the crime or is in direct spatial and temporal connection with the fulfillment of the definition (BGHSt 40, 257, 268; see also BGHSt 26, 201, 202f.; BGHSt 28, 162, 163; 30, 363, 364ff.; BGHSt 37, 294, 296).

These principles serving to differentiate attempt from preparatory action have been developed by the case law for incomplete attempts: in the case of an incomplete attempt, the perpetrator has not yet done everything necessary according to his concept of the crime for the fulfillment of the definition of the crime. But they also apply to completed attempts, when the perpetrator has already completely committed the characteristic actions which are necessary according to his plan for the crime. The Federal Court of Justice points out that even completed actions by the perpetrator do not always have to lead directly to the fulfillment of the definition of a crime. Therefore, completion of perpetrator's actions must not necessarily mean that the perpetrator reached the stage of attempt (BGHSt 40, 257, 268; thus also Vogler, in: LK, 10th edit., § 22 marginal nos. 73ff.; . . . for another view Roxin JuS 1979, 1, 9ff.; . . . following him, Papageorgiou-Gonatas, Wo liegt die Grenze zwischen Vorbereitungshandlungen und Versuch? (Where does the boundary lie between preparatory actions and attempt) Diss. 1988, pp. 245ff.).

Cases have been decided in which the perpetrator's plan included necessary contributions of an intermediary. Here an attempt is assumed if the perpetrator has completed influencing the intermediary; it is thus not necessary that the intermediary should take an immediate step towards the crime by his own actions. A direct immediate step is present in any case when the indirect perpetrator lets the intermediary go with the idea that the intermediary will now undertake the criminal act in close connection with the conclusion of the exercise of the perpetrator's influence (BGHSt 4, 270 273; BGHSt 30, 363, 365f.; BGHSt 40, 257, 268f.). An attempt will be denied, however, if the influence on the intermediary will only be effective after a lengthy period, or if it remains uncertain whether or when it will take effect at all. Under such circumstances, the attempt begins only when the intermediary, whose conduct is attributed to the perpetrator via § 25 para. 1 Criminal Code [see Chapter 10], directly takes an immediate step himself towards the crime. The decisive factor for the differentiation between preparation and attempt is therefore whether, according to the plan for the crime, the individual actions of the perpetrator in their totality already contain an attack on the protected legal interest of such a kind that it is already endangered and the harm can follow directly (BGHSt 4, 270, 273; BGHSt 40, 257 (268); thus also Vogler, in: LK, § 22 marginal no. 76; Otto, NJW 1976, 578 (579) . . .) or whether the creation of such a danger is left to later actions of the intermediary which are still uncertain.

2. The principles developed for cases of indirect perpetration also apply when—as here—a trap is set for the victim in which he would only be caught through his own contribution. These cases also are characterized by the fact that the perpetrator, by virtue of his control of the event, makes the behavior of another useful for his success. They therefore demonstrate a structure similar to indirect perpetration, and the victim thereby becomes an "intermediary against himself" (see on this also Gössel, JR 1976, 248, 250; Papageorgiou-Gonatas, p. 249). Here also an attempt is only present, if, according to the plan for the crime, a concrete, direct endangering of the protected legal interest occurs.

It is true that the perpetrator takes an immediate step towards the crime if he sets his trap, and yet this attack only has a direct effect on the protected legal interest if the victim comes within the effective area of the prepared means for the crime. Whether that is the case depends on the plan for the crime. If it is certain for the perpetrator that the victim will appear and effect the behavior included in the plans for the success of the crime, a direct endangering (according to the plan for the crime) is present simply with the conclusion of the criminal action (for instance when the perpetrator puts a time bomb in a busy place; see on this also RGSt 66, 141 where it could be expected with certainty within that within a foreseeable period of time a light switch would be used and thus arson caused thereby). If on the other hand the perpetrator—as here—considers the appearance of the victim within the effective area of the means for the crime as merely possible, but still uncertain, or even not very probable (for instance when throwing away a brandy bottle filled with poison in a forest), then a direct endangering of a legal interest according to the plan for the crime only occurs if the victim actually appears and makes preparations to carry out the expected action which will cause him harm, and the danger for him therefore intensifies (BGH, NJW 1954, 567; . . . ; thus in the end result also Lackner, § 22 marginal no. 9; Otto, NJW 1976, 578 (579); Gössel, JR 1976, 251). This stage had not yet been reached in the present case . . .

3. On the application of the standards mentioned, the threshold between preparation and attempt has not yet been crossed in the present case. It is true that the defendant has done everything from his own point of view which he had to do himself to poison a possible burglar, yet harm to possible victims was not yet directly imminent according to his concept of the crime. In fact no burglars appeared again in the defendant's house before the securing of the bottle of poison. As the defendant knew, this was from the outset not very probable because of the risk of discovery associated with it. The suspicion that this could nevertheless occur was only based on the stolen goods placed ready for removal in the attic. It was scarcely to be expected that the perpetrators who, for the first crime, had reached the house via the second floor would consume anything on the ground floor in a repeat case, in view of the four police officers hidden in the house. This was also known to the defendant. He could at most still expect the burglars to appear later and to take the bottle of poison when there was no further police surveillance. Therefore even from his point of view a sufficiently concrete—i.e., direct—endangering of a possible victim in the sense of the above observations was not yet present. It was true that a concrete endangering existed for the observing police officers, but the defendant had not at first thought about this and therefore had also not included it in his intention. Therefore the assumption that attempted homicide by the defendant had already begun cannot be based on the endangering of the police officers.

German Criminal Code

§ 22 (Definition of Attempt)

A person attempts a crime by taking steps which will immediately lead to the completion of the crime as envisaged by him.

§ 23 (Criminal Liability for Attempt)

(1) An attempt to commit a felony will be punished; attempted misdemeanors only if the law explicitly states that attempts are to be punished.

(2) An attempt can be punished more leniently than the completed crime (§ 49 para. 1).

(3) If the offender did due to a gross lack of common sense not realize that the attempt could never have led to the completion of the crime, due to the nature of its object or the means by which it was to be committed, the court may dispense of punishment or mitigate the sentence (§ 49 para. 2).

NOTES

1. The Model Penal Code's treatment of attempt, and of inchoate offenses in general, illustrates its treatmentist approach particularly clearly. In the drafters' view, "the primary purpose of punishing attempts" was "to neutralize dangerous individuals."* As the New York Court of Appeals put it, in *People v. Dlugash*, 41 N.Y.2d 725 (1977):

> The criminal law is of ancient origin, but criminal liability for attempt to commit a crime is comparatively recent. At the root of the concept of attempt liability are the very aims and purposes of penal law. The ultimate issue is whether an individual's intentions and actions,

* Commentaries § 5.01, at 323.

though failing to achieve a manifest and malevolent criminal purpose, constitute a danger to organized society of sufficient magnitude to warrant the imposition of criminal sanctions...

The attempt has diagnostic significance, as an "indication that the actor is disposed toward [criminal] activity, not alone on this occasion but on others."[*] From a treatmentist perspective, which regards the apparatus of criminal law as a (rough, preliminary, if not amateurish) tool for the diagnosis of criminal dangerousness, there is no point in punishing attempts for the purpose of deterrence. After all, the consummated offense is also proscribed, and threatened with punishment. If a person ignored the threat of punishment for a successful attempt, it makes no sense to expect him or her to heed the threat of punishment for an unsuccessful one; the threat of punishment for an attempt, given that it requires the intent to consummate the offense, adds nothing to the threat of punishment for the offense itself.

Perhaps the punishment of attempts can be justified in another, less consequentialist (or treatmentist), way. One might, for instance, focus on the (psychic) harm caused by the attempt itself. A person who escaped serious physical harm, perhaps even death, by the skin of her teeth surely would have experienced considerable distress, provided she was aware of the attempt, perhaps even only after the fact. In this light, attempts (or at least certain attempts) would amount to attacks, i.e., to (consummated) assaults.[†] Criminal liability for attempt, however, does not require that the victim have been aware of the impending harm.[‡] Then again, criminal liability in general does not (always) require the infliction of harm; creating a risk of harm can be enough, regardless of whether the "victim" was aware of the risk facing him or her, so why should this be a problem for attempts? (Of course, the legitimacy of risk creating crimes is somewhat controversial itself, so they may not make for a particularly promising starting point for an attempt to justify attempts.[§]) But perhaps the focus on individual victims is misplaced; after all, criminal law, unlike tort law, is often said to concern itself with public, not private, harm. Even attempts, after all, can disturb the public peace, a significant point for those who regard the protection of the public (or the Queen's or King's) peace as the (or certainly one) function of criminal law.[¶]

Or is the burden on those who insist on distinguishing between attempted and consummated crimes in the first place? Are they simply holding on to an outmoded conception of criminal law that places criminal liability at the whim of moral luck? There may have been a time before general attempt liability, but perhaps this is a time best left behind. Isn't the medieval rule "where there is no harm done, no crime is committed; an attempt to commit a crime is no crime," just that: medieval?[**]

Consider Stephen Schulhofer's well-known critique of the relevance of harm in criminal law:

> The criminal law attributes major significance to the harm actually caused by a defendant's conduct, as distinguished from the harm intended or risked. If, for example, a person attacks his wife and tries to kill her, he will be guilty of assault and attempted murder even if she escapes unharmed. He will also commit a battery if she is injured, mayhem if the injury is of certain especially serious types, and murder if she dies. The applicable penalties generally increase accordingly. Yet both the defendant's state of mind and his actions may have been identical in all four of the cases supposed. The precise location of a knife or gunshot wound, the speed of intervention by neighbors or the police, these and many other factors wholly outside the knowledge or control of the defendant may determine the ultimate result. Accordingly, the differences in legal treatment would seem at first blush inconsistent with such purposes of the criminal law as deterrence, rehabilitation, isolation of the dangerous, and even retribution— in the sense of punishment in accordance with moral blame...

---

[*] Commentaries art. 5, at 294 (intro.).

[†] See, e.g., R.A. Duff, *Criminal Attempts* (1996) (attempts as "attacks" on rights or legally protected interests).

[‡] Contrast Restatement (Second) of Torts § 22 ("An attempt to inflict a harmful or offensive contact or to cause an apprehension of such contact does not make the actor liable for an assault if the other does not become aware of the attempt before it is terminated.").

[§] See Chapter 15.B.

[¶] See, e.g., *Commonwealth v. Slaney*, 345 Mass. 135, 185 N.E.2d 919 (Mass. 1962).

[**] Frederick Pollock & Frederic William Maitland, *The History of English Law Before the Time of Edward I* (2nd edn. 1898), vol. 2, 475 (citing Heinrich Brunner, *Deutsche Rechtsgeschichte* (1892), vol. 2, 558–64).

Emphasis on the harm caused can, of course, be understood as a vestige of the criminal law's early role as instrument of official vengeance. Actual damage was once prerequisite to the existence of a crime, and the doctrine that an attempt to commit a crime was in itself criminal developed slowly...

Stephen J. Schulhofer, "Harm and Punishment: A Critique
of Emphasis on the Results of Conduct in the Criminal Law,"
122 *University of Pennsylvania Law Review* (1974), 1497, 1498–1500.

According to the standard historical account, attempts did not enter English criminal law until the sixteenth century, in the (infamous) Court of Star Chamber (ordinarily not an auspicious beginning for a criminal law doctrine), and then were only punished in cases of felony.* To this day, German criminal law limits attempt liability to felonies (*Verbrechen*); attempts to commit a misdemeanor (*Vergehen*) are only punishable if the statute explicitly provides for it (§ 23 para. 1 Criminal Code) (however, in fact, most prohibitions of misdemeanors do contain a clause stating that attempts are to be punished).

Assuming that attempts are a legitimate basis for criminal liability, why would one punish some attempts, but not others (from the perspective of various rationales of punishment)? Why would one draw the line between more serious offenses, and less serious ones? Should it (instead?) matter what right (or legal interest: individual or public), or what type of offense (against the person, property, public order, health, etc.) is at stake?

2. Justifying punishing attempts is one question. Determining how to punish them is yet another. Here, again, the Model Penal Code's treatmentist colors shine especially bright. Breaking from common law tradition, the Code generally (except for the most serious offense category) punishes the attempt as it would the consummated offense. (The same applies to the other inchoate offenses in the Code as well, conspiracy and solicitation, for the same reason.) After all, the attempt is a symptom of "the antisocial disposition of the actor," regardless of whether the attempt succeeds, or fails. (Technically speaking, even the Model Code permits the imposition of a lower sentence, provided it remains within the range of sentences for offenses of the same grade and degree—e.g., second-degree felonies, punishable by between one and ten years' imprisonment, and a maximum $10,000 fine, in the Model Penal Code scheme, §§ 6.03(1); 6.06(2).)

Model Penal Code § 5.05. Grading of Criminal Attempt.

Except as otherwise provided... attempt [is a crime] of the same grade and degree as the most serious offense that is attempted.... An attempt... to commit a [capital crime or a] felony of the first degree is a felony of the second degree.

Model Penal Code Commentaries § 5.05, at 489–90.

The theory of the grading system may be stated simply. To the extent that sentencing depends upon the antisocial disposition of the actor and the demonstrated need for a corrective sanction, there is likely to be little difference in the gravity of the required measures depending on the consummation or the failure of the plan. It is only when and insofar as the severity of sentence is designed for general deterrent purposes that a distinction on the ground is likely to have reasonable force. It is doubtful... that the threat of punishment for the inchoate crime can add significantly to the net deterrent efficacy of the sanction threatened for the substantive offense that is the actor's object which he, by hypothesis, ignores.

The traditional rule, and that still in place in most U.S. jurisdictions, mitigates the punishment for attempt, often by half, compared to the sentencing prescribed for the consummated offense.

---

* Jerome Hall, "Criminal Attempt: A Study of Foundations of Criminal Liability," 49 *Yale Law Journal* (1940), 789, 796–7.

Cal. Penal Code § 664. Attempts; punishment.

Every person who attempts to commit any crime, but fails, or is prevented or intercepted in its perpetration, shall be punished where no provision is made by law for the punishment of those attempts, as follows:

(a) If the crime attempted is punishable by imprisonment in the state prison, the person guilty of the attempt shall be punished by imprisonment in the state prison for one-half the term of imprisonment prescribed upon a conviction of the offense attempted. However, if the crime attempted is willful, deliberate, and premeditated murder, ... the person guilty of that attempt shall be punished by imprisonment in the state prison for life with the possibility of parole ...

The U.S. Sentencing Guidelines, § 2X1.1(b)(1), prescribe a reduction in the applicable sentencing range for some, but not all, cases of attempt (and other inchoate offenses: conspiracy and solicitation):

(1) If an attempt, decrease by 3 levels, unless the defendant completed all the acts the defendant believed necessary for successful completion of the substantive offense or the circumstances demonstrate that the defendant was about to complete all such acts but for apprehension or interruption by some similar event beyond the defendant's control.

The German Criminal Code, too, provides for discretionary mitigation of punishment in cases of attempt: § 23 para. 2, for both completed attempts (the defendant completed all the acts he believed necessary for completion) and incomplete attempts.

But what justifies the traditional grading scheme? Why should attempts be punished less harshly than consummated offenses?

[E]ven from the point of view of the general deterrent, the sceptical argument which suggested that there is no case for punishing an attempt is ... mistaken. It is perfectly true that those who commit crimes intend to succeed, but this does not show that punishing a man for an unsuccessful attempt will not increase the efficacy of the law's threats. ... [F]irst, there must be many who are not completely confident that they will succeed in their criminal objective, but will be prepared to run the risk of punishment if they can be assured that they have to pay nothing for attempts which fail. ... [There must also] be many cases where men might with good or bad reason believe that if they succeed in committing some crime they will escape, but if they fail they may be caught. Treason is only the most obvious of such cases ...

A more difficult question concerns the almost universal practice of legal systems of fixing a more severe punishment for the completed crime than for the mere attempt ... [A] retributive theory in which severity of punishment is proportional to the allegedly evil intentions of the criminal is in grave difficulty; for there seems to be no difference in wickedness, though there may be in skill, between the successful and the unsuccessful attempt in this respect ... [From a deterrent perspective, there are crimes] whose consummation occupies a considerable space of time so that the criminal may have time between the attempt and its consummation to think again ... He might desist, but if he is already involved in the full penalty by virtue of merely having attempted to commit the crime, he may have no motive for desisting. Similar reasoning is presented when it is pointed out that if a man shoots and misses there is no reason why he should not shoot again if he is already liable to the full penalty for his unsuccessful attempt.

H.L.A. Hart, *Punishment and Responsibility:*
Essays in the Philosophy of Law (1968), 129–31.

[T]he most plausible explanation for more lenient treatment of attempts is that the community's resentment and demand for punishment are not aroused to the same degree when serious harm has been averted.

This explanation, however, raises further questions ... To what extent should the structure of penalties serve to express intuitive societal judgments that cannot be rationalized in terms of such instrumental goals as deterrence, isolation, rehabilitation, and even retribution—that is, condemnation reflecting the moral culpability of the act?

Stephen J. Schulhofer, "Attempt," in *Encyclopedia of Crime*
and Justice (1st edn. 1983), vol. 1, 91, 97.

Is at least one explanation—if not justification—for the practice (in Germany, the explicitly discretionary practice) a general sense of uneasiness about extending criminal liability to attempts in the first, so that mitigation of punishment can serve as a (partial) safety valve in particular cases, while also limiting the potential unfairness of the practice of punishing attempts as a whole?

3. Perhaps not surprisingly, the Model Penal Code's treatmentism also affected its approach to the age-old question of the distinction between preparation and attempt. While few people agreed on what test should be used for drawing the line between (non-punishable) "preparation" and (punishable) "attempt," never mind on how to apply a given test in a particular case, almost everyone agreed that the line was difficult to draw in the abstract and required a fact-intensive case-by-case analysis. Nonetheless, here are two of the tests that have been proposed—and often found wanting—over the years:

- *res ipsa loquitur* (the thing, or rather the act, speaks for itself; charitably interpreted, this test looks for acts by the defendant that taken by themselves—i.e., "objectively," "unambiguously," "unequivocally," or at least without additional evidence, for instance, in the form of a confession—"are sufficient in themselves to declare and proclaim the guilty purpose with which they are done," *King v. Barker*, [1924] N.Z.L.R. 865 (New Zealand).)
- last proximate act ("acts which would end in the consummation of the particular offense, but for the intervention of circumstances independent of the will of the party," *People v. Murray*, 14 Cal. 159 (1859)).

Eventually, courts became impatient with the available tests (others required "an appreciable fragment of the crime itself" or "the commencement of the consummation of the crime") and began to acknowledge their limited usefulness in particular cases. For instance, while still on the Massachusetts Supreme Judicial Court, Oliver Wendell Holmes in an influential opinion took into account not only the proximity of the act to the consummation of the offense but also the seriousness of the crime in question, suggesting that the line between preparation and attempt is crossed sooner in more serious crimes than in less serious ones.*

The Model Penal Code took these developments one step further and, rather than adjusting them, abandoned the existing tests as hopelessly confused and distracting altogether, replacing them with a broad standard: the "substantial step" test. The substantial step test was superior, in the eyes of the Model Code drafters, because it was explicitly flexible—it was a standard, rather than a rule—and therefore forced courts—and fact-finders in general—to make discretionary judgments in the light of the facts of each case, without the crutch of a formal, and only apparently determinative, "test." The drafters, then, guided this discretion in two ways—and, arguably, tried to have it both ways—by, first, defining the standard in broad functional terms and then listing a great many, and detailed, illustrative factual scenarios, § 5.01(2):

(a) lying in wait, searching for or following the contemplated victim of the crime;
(b) enticing or seeking to entice the contemplated victim of the crime to go to the place contemplated for its commission;
(c) reconnoitering the place contemplated for the commission of the crime;
(d) unlawful entry of a structure, vehicle or enclosure in which it is contemplated that the crime will be committed;
(e) possession of materials to be employed in the commission of the crime, which are specially designed for such unlawful use or which can serve no lawful purpose of the actor under the circumstances;
(f) possession, collection or fabrication of materials to be employed in the commission of the crime, at or near the place contemplated for its commission, where such possession, collection or fabrication serves no lawful purpose of the actor under the circumstances;
(g) soliciting an innocent agent to engage in conduct constituting an element of the crime.

The function of the inquiry into the line between preparation and attempt (i.e., the inquiry into the so-called *actus reus* of attempt), according to the Model Code, is to determine the

---

* *Commonwealth v. Kennedy*, 170 Mass. 18, 22 (1897).

seriousness of the actor's "criminal purpose" (understood in the MPC sense of "conscious object"). The *actus reus* inquiry, in other words, is in the end of evidentiary significance: the act of attempt (measured very roughly in terms of the preparation/attempt distinction) provides "corroboration" of the actor's purpose. Or in treatmentist terms, the act is relevant insofar as it affects the court's (or the jury's) diagnosis of the actor's dangerousness, which is based primarily on evidence of the actor's purpose to commit the offense.

Doesn't this fly in the face of the act requirement? Doesn't this amount to punishing someone for his or her intent, or thoughts, alone?

Now, as *Lehnert* makes clear, the Model Penal Code "substantial step" standard not only made explicit the flexibility of the inquiry into the *actus reus* of attempt, and its emphasis on *mens rea*, at the expense of *actus reus*; it also appeared to expand the scope of criminal liability for attempt by pushing back the line between preparation and attempt, farther away from the consummation of the offense. In other words, acts now qualified as an attempt that, under the old tests, would have amounted to preparation only, by—in the court's words—focusing on the steps that had been taken, rather than on the ones that remained. Of course, just how broad, or narrow, a flexible standard like the "substantial step" requirement turns out to be will depend on its application to particular fact scenarios. Could you argue that Lehnert did *not* take "substantial steps" toward the consummation of the offense? For purposes of drawing the line between preparation and attempt should it matter which offense one focuses on (in Lehnert's case, the choices included first degree murder, possession of explosive devices, and drug possession)?

4. With all the attention lavished on the supposed Rubicon separating preparation and attempt, it is important not to forget that criminal liability is regularly extended beyond this magical line. Take, for instance, the entire panoply of "possession" offenses, which criminalize no act at all, and certainly no act that could possibly be construed as one that crosses the line between preparation and attempt.* If the line between preparation and attempt marks that between non-punishability and punishability, why should pre-preparatory non-acts be punishable?

5. Note also that the preparation/attempt line also does not arise in every attempt case. The beginning of the Model Penal Code attempt section, § 5.01, can be used to illustrate different types of attempt scenarios.

> (1) *Definition of Attempt.* A person is guilty of an attempt to commit a crime if, acting with the kind of culpability otherwise required for commission of the crime, he:
> (a) purposely engages in conduct which would constitute the crime if the attendant circumstances were as he believes them to be; or
> (b) when causing a particular result is an element of the crime, does or omits to do anything with the purpose of causing or with the belief that it will cause such result without further conduct on his part; or
> (c) purposely does or omits to do anything which, under the circumstances as he believes them to be, is an act or omission constituting a substantial step in a course of conduct planned to culminate in his commission of the crime.

The question of the distinction between preparation and attempt under the Code arises only under (1)(c).[†] Subsections (1)(a) and (1)(b) cover cases of complete, rather the incomplete, attempt, i.e., cases where the actor had done everything necessary for the consummation of offense, and still failed.

6. Convicting a defendant under circumstances like those in *Lehnert* for *attempted murder* would be unthinkable under German criminal law; as in traditional common law, preparation to commit a criminal offense is not punishable as an attempt in German criminal law even if the potential offender's mind was firmly set on it, and Lehnert's conduct would not

---

* See Chapter 7.C.
[†] See § 5.01(2) ("Conduct Which May Be Held Substantial Step *Under Subsection (1)(c)*" (emphasis added).

have crossed the line between preparation and attempt, as that line is presently drawn in German law. That said, that there are a few norms in the German Criminal Code (and in other laws) that explicitly penalize acts which are in substance clearly preparation for a criminal act to follow. For instance, it is an offense to make or to store paper, printing devices etc. in preparation of counterfeiting money (§ 149 Criminal Code). The same holds for explosive materials made or stored with the intention to create an explosion endangering other persons or objects of considerable worth (§ 310 Criminal Code)—but the punishment range for conduct like Lehnert's under German law is only six months to five years' imprisonment. (How can the line between preparation and attempt, then, be said to mark the *locus poenitentiae* if, outside the specific doctrinal context of the law of attempt, some preparatory acts are punished?)

The task of delineating the boundary between mere preparatory acts and an attempted crime can be difficult. German law requires that the completion of the crime must have been imminent (§ 22 Criminal Code): The offender must have taken steps that will *immediately* lead to the completion of the crime as envisaged by him. In a case like *Lehnert*—that is, a case of incomplete attempt (where the defendant has not yet engaged in behavior she believes to be sufficient to consummate the offense—a conviction for attempted murder would only be possible if the perpetrator was a few minutes away from doing the final act. Imagine that the bombs had been completely assembled and stored in the trunk of Lehnert's car, but she still would need to drive to the victims' houses (or wherever she planned the detonations): even this would not count as attempted murder under § 22 Criminal Code.

The actual proximity of the completed crime is not just corroborative of the firmness of criminal purpose, as the court in *Lehnert* (following the Model Penal Code) would have it, but essential as such if the offender is to be punished *for the act* rather than for her intentions. Only if the ignition of the bombs was to occur within the next few minutes and without important intermediary steps, the threshold between preparation and attempt would have been crossed according to German law (if, for instance, she had arrived at the scene of crime, placed the bombs and was fumbling in her pockets for the lighter to set off the bombs). The Federal Court of Justice has ruled, for instance, that ringing the doorbell of a house suffices for attempted robbery, but only if according to the plan the victim is to be attacked immediately after the door is opened (Judgment of June 2, 1993, 2 StR 158/93, BGHSt 39, 236).

German law, in other words, uses an approach to the distinction between preparation and attempt that is familiar from the practice of common law courts before the Model Penal Code and, in several jurisdictions that did not follow the Code on this issue, even today, and would face the same objections.* What does it mean to require that steps leading "immediately" to the "completion of the crime"? What makes an intermediate step more important than another? Clearly the German standard is generally interpreted as communicating an intent to draw the preparation/attempt line fairly closely to the consummation of the offense, but what considerations drive the interpretation of what counts as "immediate" or "proximity" in this context? Physical, temporal, objective, or subjective? How does the decision in the *Bärwurz Case* address these questions? What determines which considerations matter in general, in a particular case?

Perhaps it would help to get a clearer sense of the rationale for punishing attempts in German criminal law in the first place. Several theories have been developed:[†]

- objective theory (no longer in favor): attempt is punishable insofar as it endangers the legal interest protected by the criminal statute in question (also known as dangerousness theory);

---

* See, e.g., New York Penal Law § 110.00 ("A person is guilty of an attempt to commit a crime when, with intent to commit a crime, he engages in conduct which tends to effect the commission of such crime."); *People v. Rizzo*, 246 N.Y. 334 (1927) ("The act or acts must come or advance very near to the accomplishment of the intended crime.").

[†] For a summary, see, e.g., Hans Joachim Hirsch, "Untauglicher Versuch und Tatstrafrecht," in Bernd Schünemann et al. (eds.), *Festschrift für Claus Roxin zum 70. Geburtstag am 15. Mai 2001* (2001), 711.

- subjective theory (arguably, still favored by courts): attempt is punishable insofar as it constitutes a "disobedience of the legal order that is unbearable for the legal community" (a variation: the "danger" posed by this disobedience) or, in another popular formulation, manifests a "will hostile to law" (*rechtsfeindlicher Wille*);*
- mixed theories (currently favored by criminal law professors): combining objective and subjective elements, with varying emphasis on one other the other, so that, in the popular so-called "impression theory" (*Eindruckstheorie*), an attempt is punishable insofar as it produces, or is capable of producing, an impression of disturbing the law (*rechtserschütternder Eindruck*) among others (or, in other formulations, of disturbing of the public's trust in the validity of the legal order (*Geltung der Rechtsordnung*), its legal consciousness (*Rechtsbewußtsein*), or legal peace (*Rechtsfrieden*)).

Do these theories justify punishing attempts? Do they provide guidance to courts in particular cases, for the differentiation between preparation and attempt (in the *Bärwurz Case*, for instance)? Do they draw the line too close (not close enough, at the appropriate level of proximity) to the consummation of the offense? Do they satisfy the principle of legality (prohibition of vagueness, analogy)?

7. In contrast to *Lehnert*, the attempted murder the public prosecutor's office pursued in the *Bärwurz Case* would have been a completed attempt: by placing the poisoned Schnaps, the defendant had already done everything required by his plans to kill the intruder (note that this was a case of conditional intent, *dolus eventualis*). Usually, cases of completed attempts are the ones where drawing the boundary between preparation and attempt is less difficult. Think about an offender aiming and firing his gun at the victim but missing his target—this is clearly a case of attempt even under the restrictive provision in § 22 Criminal Code. Here, however, the Court had to deal with an unusual situation: Can one find an attempted crime where the offender has completed setting a trap and thus has done everything deemed necessary but where completion would still largely be a matter of coincidence? After all, consummating murder in the *Bärwurz Case* would have required that the burglars turn up again, and turn up again despite the police presence in the house (they did not in fact), discover the bottle in the entrance hall, and feel thirst for alcohol again. This was all rather unlikely, and both courts, the regional court and the Federal Court of Justice, held that the danger was too remote to satisfy the requirements of an attempt. But if the offender could expect with greater certainty that in the near future the victim of the crime will come close to the trap set for it, the Court explains, this would suffice for an attempt (if, for instance, the chemist had intended to poison his wife and thus poisoned bottles of beer in the house, knowing that she drinks beer from the household supplies every evening).

   Do you agree with the result in this case? How would the Model Penal Code have dealt with the preparation/attempt question in the *Bärwurz Case*? And what rationale for the punishment of attempts in German criminal law is most consistent with the decision in the case? Was this attempt inept enough, i.e., unlikely enough to succeed, to remove it from the scope of attempt liability, despite the fact that the defendant had the requisite intent and had done everything he considered necessary to consummate the offense? Or is this a case not about attempt, but about intent? Because success was so unlikely? But does (should) the likelihood of success matter in cases of attempt (except in extreme cases of ineptitude)?

8. Note that the *Bärwurz Case* applies attempt liability to a case of conditional intent (*dolus eventualis*). Regardless of the interpretation of conditional intent,† the notion of an attempt to commit a non-purpose offense (in the sense of an offense that requires proof of a mental state short of "purpose" with respect to its result element) is controversial in Anglo-American criminal law. Many jurisdictions require proof of purpose—in the sense of specific intent, or conscious object, as opposed to knowledge or recklessness—for attempt liability. In the case of homicide, for instance, attempt liability would require proof of purpose to kill, so that the

---

* See, e.g., BGHSt 11, 324, 327 (1958).
† See Chapter 8.A.

only type of attempted homicide would, in effect, be attempted (purpose) murder.* The defendant in the *Bärwurz Case* therefore would have been acquitted of attempted murder for lack of the requisite *mens rea* (he did not have the specific intent to kill) even if he had been found to have committed the requisite *actus reus* (i.e., crossed the line between preparation and attempt).

The Model Penal Code occupies a middle position. For attempt liability it requires "purpose" with respect to the result element of the object offense (defined as "conscious object," i.e., *Absicht* § 2.02(2)(a)) or, at least, "the belief that [the conduct] will cause such result" (§ 5.01(1)(b)). Even under the Model Code, therefore, the *Bärwurz* defendant would have lacked the requisite *mens rea* for attempt (insofar as a belief that a result will occur is closer to a belief in the virtual certainly of its occurrence, i.e., to *Wissentlichkeit*, than it is to a belief in its possibility, i.e., to *dolus eventualis*).

Does it make sense to see the *actus reus* and *mens rea* of attempt as related, so that an expansion of one could be compensated by a contraction of the other? In other words, does the discrepancy between German criminal law and the Model Penal Code diminish if one thinks of one as combining a narrow *actus reus* test with a broad *mens rea* test (Germany), and vice versa? (Of course, the Model Penal Code drafters presumably would not have seen matters in this way as their treatmentist agenda sought to diagnose dangerousness, not to balance doctrinal categories.)

9. U.S. criminal law (under the Model Penal Code) and German criminal law both reject the impossibility defense. Moreover, they reject it in the same way, indirectly, by statutory definition. The Model Penal Code, in § 5.01(1)(a), provides that a person commits an attempt if he "purposely engages in conduct which would constitute the crime *if the attendant circumstances were as he believes them to be*" (emphasis added), with the high-lighted clause serving to eliminate the impossibility defense in all cases. Previously—and still in several American jurisdictions—legal, though not factual, impossibility provided a defense against a charge of attempt.

Similarly, the revision of the German Criminal Code in 1975 introduced a definition of attempt that, among other things, put to rest disputes about the punishability of impossible attempts, in much the same terms as the Model Code had done a decade earlier. An attempt now required steps toward the "completion of the crime *as envisaged by [the actor].*"† The predecessor provision (§ 43 Criminal Code (old version)) had made no mention of the actor's belief, leaving open the possibility of an impossibility defense in the event that belief turned out to be mistaken:

(1) Whoever manifested the decision to commit a felony or misdemeanor through acts that contain the commencement of the commission of that felony or misdemeanor, is punishable for attempt, if the intended felony or misdemeanor did not reach completion.

Note the arguably broader scope of attempt liability in comparison to current German law, which—in § 25 Criminal Code (current version)—requires "taking steps which will immediately lead to the completion of the crime," rather than merely "contain the commencement" of its commission. Furthermore, the standard in § 43 Criminal Code (old version) closely resembles one of the tests found in common law cases prior to the Model Penal Code.‡

From a treatmentist perspective, rejecting the impossibility defense outright makes sense: the impossibility of success does not reflect on the "anti-social character" of the person trying to succeed. What is the justification for eliminating the defense from the perspective of other

---

* See, e.g., *R. v. Ancio*, [1984] 1 S.C.R. 225 (Can.).
† Criminal Code § 22 (emphasis added); see also § 23 para. 3.
‡ See Note 3. See further *Regina v. Cheeseman*, 1 Leigh & C.C.C. 140 (1862) ("commencement of the consummation of the crime"); see generally "Criminal Law—Attempt to Commit Murder—The Line Between Preparation and Attempt," 36 *Columbia Law Review* (1936), 676 ("conduct should be made criminal as soon as the anti-social character of the actor has been manifested in such a way that a significant probability of harm to society is indicated," citing Ferri's Italian Penal Code art. 56 (1930)).

rationales of punishment? From the perspective of the various rationales for the punishment of attempt under German criminal law?*

The similarities between the Model Penal Code and German criminal law extend to the exceptions from the rule of the punishability of impossible attempts. Both allow for mitigation of punishment in the case of inept attempts: MPC § 5.05(2) (if attempt "so inherently unlikely to result or culminate in the commission of a crime that neither such conduct nor the actor presents a public danger warranting the grading [of the attempt at the level of "the most serious offense which is attempted"] the Court shall exercise its power...to enter judgment and impose sentence for a crime of lower grade or degree or, in extreme cases, may dismiss the prosecution") and § 23 para. 3 Criminal Code (court may dispense with punishment or mitigate the sentence if "the offender, due to a gross lack of common sense, did not realize that the attempt could never have led to the completion of the crime, due to the nature of its object or the means by which it was to be committed"). Note also that both in German criminal law and the MPC merely imaginary crimes, or cases of "true legal impossibility" (*Wahndelikte*) are not to be punished: if the actor engages in conduct he or she believes mistakenly to be a crime (for instance, if an actor were to mistakenly believe that adultery is still a crime in Germany, even though the criminal prohibition was abolished in 1969).

What could justify these exceptions, all of which cover types of impossible attempt committed by persons with the requisite intent to engage in criminal conduct (and, at least in the case of inept attempts, possibly to inflict serious harm, as for instance in unsuccessful murder attempts through witchcraft)? Or are they simply efforts to provide a *de minimis* safety valve for cases that would push the rejection of impossibility too far (measured how)?[†]

B. Conspiracy

Like corporate criminal liability, conspiracy often serves as a convenient point of distinction between Anglo-American and German criminal law, and the common law and the civil law of crimes more generally: one has it, the other does not. The distinction even figured in Allied discussions leading up to the Nuremberg War Crimes Tribunal:

> During much of the discussion, the Russians and French seemed unable to grasp all the implications of the concept; when they finally did grasp it, they were genuinely shocked. The French viewed it entirely as a barbarous legal mechanism unworthy of modern law, while the Soviets seem to have shaken their head in wonderment—a reaction, some cynics may believe, prompted by envy. But the main point of the Soviet attack on conspiracy was that it was too vague and so unfamiliar to the French and themselves, as well as to the Germans, that it would lead to endless confusion.
>
> Bradley F. Smith, *Reaching Judgment at Nuremberg* (1977), 51.

Even more so than in the case of corporate criminal liability, however, this is a distinction that becomes less tangible when seen in historical and doctrinal context. For one, a particularly troubling feature of the traditional common law concept of conspiracy was its extension to agreements to commit acts not criminal in themselves. (This was a relevant point at Nuremberg since, as none other than Herbert Wechsler—later the chief drafter of the Model Penal Code—pointed out at the time, "some of the elements of the conspiracy charged, (notably violation of treaties, atrocities committed upon German nationals on racial, religious and political grounds and atrocities committed prior to the state of war) [were] not embraced within the ordinary concept of crimes punishable as violations of the laws of war."[‡] This feature of conspiracy, however, was rejected by the Model Penal Code drafters. The

---

* See Note 6.
† Compare MPC § 2.12 ("De Minimis Infractions").
‡ Herbert Wechsler, "Memorandum for the Attorney General, Dec. 29, 1944 (Doc. 27)," in Bradley F. Smith (ed.), *The American Road to Nuremberg: The Documentary Record 1944–1945* (1982), 84, 86.

Model Penal Code also dismissed another controversial feature of the law of conspiracy, particularly in federal criminal law, which generally extended liability for offenses committed by co-conspirators without the need to satisfy the ordinary prerequisites for accessorial liability (the *Pinkerton* rule). And even though the German Criminal Code does not contain a provision bearing the label "conspiracy," it does criminalize agreements to commit an offense as a form of attempted participation.

Pinkerton v. United States
Supreme Court of the United States
328 U.S. 640 (1946)

Mr. Justice Douglas delivered the opinion of the Court.

A conspiracy is a partnership in crime. It has ingredients, as well as implications, distinct from the completion of the unlawful project. As stated in United States v. Rabinowich, 238 U.S. 78, 88, 35 S.Ct. 682, 684, 685:

> For two or more to confederate and combine together to commit or cause to be committed a breach of the criminal laws is an offense of the gravest character, sometimes quite outweighing, in injury to the public, the mere commission of the contemplated crime. It involves deliberate plotting to subvert the laws, educating and preparing the conspirators for further and habitual criminal practices. And it is characterized by secrecy, rendering it difficult of detection, requiring more time for its discovery, and adding to the importance of punishing it when discovered.

Moreover, it is not material that overt acts charged in the conspiracy counts were also charged and proved as substantive offenses. "If the overt act be the offense which was the object of the conspiracy, and is also punished, there is not a double punishment of it." The agreement to do an unlawful act is even then distinct from the doing of the act.

Walter and Daniel Pinkerton are brothers who live a short distance from each other on Daniel's farm. They were indicted for violations of the Internal Revenue Code. The indictment contained ten substantive counts and one conspiracy count. The jury found Walter guilty on nine of the substantive counts and on the conspiracy count. It found Daniel guilty on six of the substantive counts and on the conspiracy count . . .

There is . . . no evidence to show that Daniel [who was in prison at the time] participated directly in the commission of the substantive offenses on which his conviction has been sustained, although there was evidence to show that these substantive offenses were in fact committed by Walter in furtherance of the unlawful agreement or conspiracy existing between the brothers. The question was submitted to the jury on the theory that each petitioner could be found guilty of the substantive offenses, if it was found at the time those offenses were committed petitioners were parties to an unlawful conspiracy and the substantive offenses charged were in fact committed in furtherance of it.

. . . We have here a continuous conspiracy. There is here no evidence of the affirmative action on the part of Daniel which is necessary to establish his withdrawal from it . . . [S]o long as the partnership in crime continues, the partners act for each other in carrying it forward. It is settled that "an overt act of one partner may be the act of all without any new agreement specifically directed to that act." Motive or intent may be proved by the acts or declarations of some of the conspirators in furtherance of the common objective.

. . . The criminal intent to do the act is established by the formation of the conspiracy. Each conspirator instigated the commission of the crime. The unlawful agreement contemplated precisely what was done. It was formed for the purpose. The act done was in execution of the enterprise. The rule which holds responsible one who counsels, procures, or commands another to commit a crime is founded on the same principle. That principle is recognized in the law of conspiracy when the overt act of one partner in crime is attributable to all. An overt act is an essential ingredient of the crime of conspiracy . . . If that can be supplied by the act of one conspirator, we fail to see why the same or other acts in furtherance of the conspiracy are likewise not attributable to the others for the purpose of holding them responsible for the substantive offense.

A different case would arise if the substantive offense committed by one of the conspirators was not in fact done in furtherance of the conspiracy, did not fall within the scope of the unlawful project, or was merely a part of the ramifications of the plan which could not be reasonably foreseen as a necessary or natural consequence of the unlawful agreement. But as we read this record, that is not this case.

Affirmed.

People v. McGee
Court of Appeals of New York
49 N.Y.2d 48, 399 N.E.2d 1177 (1979)

Cooke, Chief Judge.

Two trials are considered here. Out of one evolve appeals by defendants McGee, Edwards and Tolliver, who were convicted, after a jury trial, of one count of conspiracy in the third degree and 28 counts of bribery in the second degree. From the other, arise appeals by defendants Quamina and Waters, who were convicted, upon a jury verdict, of one count of conspiracy in the third degree and 10 counts of bribery in the second degree.

[T]he People's theory was that the defendants proposed an arrangement whereby Rochester Police Officers Gerald Luciano and Gustave J. D'Aprile, members of the Vice Squad, would be paid to prevent the arrest of defendants' gambling associates while enforcing the law against competitors....The officers were offered monetary and other benefits in exchange for their assistance...

[In late 1973 and early 1974, Quamina and Waters met with the officers on several occasions.] Defendants McGee, Edwards and Tolliver were later brought into the operation....On November 13, [1974] there was a meeting with Edwards and McGee at which the group discussed the scope of police activity, as well as weekly payments to the police. No payments were made at that meeting....At various intervals during the ensuing months, Edwards made payments to the officers...

McGee argues that the Trial Judge erred in charging the jury that he could be found guilty of the substantive offense of bribery by virtue of his status as a conspirator. After determining that there was sufficient evidence of an agreement among the defendants to go to the jury on the conspiracy count, the court charged that each conspirator could be convicted of bribery on the basis of acts of any one of the coconspirators committed in furtherance of the conspiracy (see Pinkerton v. United States, 328 U.S. 640, 66 S.Ct. 1180, 90 L.Ed. 1489). The court also charged that McGee alone could be convicted of the bribery if he solicited, requested, commanded, importuned or intentionally aided another to engage in that offense (see Penal Law, § 20.00). McGee is correct in his contention that the portion of the charge concerning conspirator liability was erroneous. It is held that liability for the substantive offense may not be independently predicated upon defendant's participation in an underlying conspiracy. As there was no evidence of McGee's complicity in the bribery counts submitted to the jury,[1] and thus no basis for accomplice liability, there must be a reversal of the conviction of bribery and a dismissal of the indictment as to those counts.

In rejecting the notion that one's status as a conspirator standing alone is sufficient to support a conviction for a substantive offense committed by a coconspirator, it is noted that the Legislature has defined the conduct that will render a person criminally responsible for the act of another. Conspicuously absent from section 20.00 of the Penal Law is reference to one who conspires to commit an offense. That omission cannot be supplied by construction. Conduct that will support a conviction for conspiracy will not perforce give rise to accessorial liability. True, a conspirator's conduct in many instances will suffice to establish liability as an accomplice, but the concepts are, in reality, analytically distinct. To permit mere guilt of conspiracy to establish the defendant's guilt of the substantive crime without any evidence of further action on the part of the defendant, would be to expand the basis of accomplice liability beyond the legislative design.

The crime of conspiracy is an offense separate from the crime that is the object of the conspiracy. Once an illicit agreement is shown, the overt act of any conspirator may be attributed to other conspirators to establish the offense of conspiracy and that act may be the object crime. But the overt act itself is not the crime in a conspiracy prosecution; it is merely an element of the crime that has as its basis the agreement. It is not offensive to permit a conviction of conspiracy to stand on the overt act committed by another, for the act merely provides corroboration of the existence of the agreement and indicates that the agreement has reached a point where it poses a sufficient threat to society to impose sanctions. But it is repugnant to our system of jurisprudence, where guilt is generally personal to the defendant, to impose punishment, not for the socially harmful agreement to which the defendant is a party, but for substantive offenses in which he did not participate.

We refuse to sanction such a result and thus decline to follow the rule adopted for Federal prosecutions in Pinkerton v. United States, 328 U.S. 640, 66 S.Ct. 1180, 90 L.Ed. 1489. Accessorial conduct may not be equated with mere membership in a conspiracy and the State may not rely solely on the latter to prove guilt of the substantive offense.

---

[1] The trial court dismissed two bribery counts on the ground that there was no agreement on November 13 to pay the specific amount of $50 to each officer as charged in the indictment. The court determined, however, that there was sufficient evidence of an agreement among defendants and the remaining counts were submitted to the jury.

People v. Washington
Court of Appeals of New York
8 N.Y.3d 565, 869 N.E.2d 641 (2007)

Cipatrick, J.

The question presented by this appeal is whether a conditional agreement to murder a person in the future can be subject to prosecution under our conspiracy law...

Defendant, while incarcerated at Rikers Island on child endangerment and promotion of prostitution charges, confided in fellow inmate, Martin Mitchell, who, unbeknownst to defendant, was a government informant, that he was willing to pay $ 5,000 to have the 14-year-old complaining witness in his child endangerment case killed. Mitchell, who was nearing release from Rikers Island, informed a New York City Police Department (NYPD) detective of his conversation with defendant. At the detective's request, Mitchell again met with defendant and told defendant that he knew of a hitman who would kill the intended victim. During this conversation defendant gave Mitchell a telephone number so that he could make contact with defendant's associates once he was released in order to arrange for the contract killing.

On August 23, 2002, Mitchell, who was now released from incarceration, visited defendant at Rikers Island. Their conversation was recorded as Mitchell was wired with a tape recorder at the request of the NYPD. During this meeting, defendant changed the intended victim of the contract killing from the complaining witness to a rival named "Seven," who had months earlier allegedly shot defendant in the head. Defendant also stated that he would now pay $ 4,000 to have Seven killed and expressed optimism that he would soon be getting out of jail...

Defendant argues that the evidence against him was legally insufficient to support a finding that he entered into an agreement to kill Seven since he conditioned any action on his release from jail, ... and that there was no agreement since he and the undercover officer [who posed as a hitman] never discussed price.

Section 105.15 of the Penal Law provides that "[a] person is guilty of conspiracy in the second degree when, with intent that conduct constituting a class A felony be performed, he agrees with one or more persons to engage in or cause the performance of such conduct." Furthermore, it is well settled that "[a] conspiracy consists of an agreement to commit an underlying substantive crime..., coupled with an overt act committed by one of the conspirators in furtherance of the conspiracy" (*People v Caban*, 5 NY3d 143, 149, 833 N.E.2d 213, 800 N.Y.S.2d 70 [2005]).

We are here presented with the question whether conditions placed on an agreement can negate the existence of a conspiracy. The federal circuit courts provide some guidance in this regard since they have considered whether a purported agreement that is conditioned by a defendant can be considered an agreement to commit an unlawful act under conspiracy law. The First and Eighth Circuits have adopted the approach that an agreement with a condition will be effective only if the defendant subjectively believes the condition is likely to be fulfilled (*United States v Anello*, 765 F.2d 253, 262 [1st Cir 1985]; *United States v Brown*, 946 F.2d 58, 61 [8th Cir 1991]). The Appellate Division here relied upon the First Circuit's holding in *United States v Palmer* (203 F.3d 55, 64 [1st Cir 2000]), which followed *Anello*, where the federal court held that "[l]iability should attach if the defendant reasonably believed that the conditions would obtain." In *Anello*, the defendant had conditioned his purchase of marijuana on its quality. The defendant, however, proceeded with obtaining the funds to purchase the drugs in anticipation that his quality concerns would be met. The court found "that the 'quality' condition was unlikely to prove a serious impediment" (*Anello*, 765 F.2d at 263) to the formation of the agreement to purchase the marijuana, since the defendant subjectively believed that the condition would be fulfilled and, as such, proceeded to fulfill his obligations under the agreement.

Three other circuits take a different approach, holding that conditions to an agreement are legally irrelevant (*see United States v Grassi*, 616 F.2d 1295, 1302 [5th Cir 1980]; *United States v Prince*, 883 F.2d 953, 958 [11th Cir 1989]), unless the conditions are so unlikely to be met that the agreement is illusory (*United States v Podolsky*, 798 F.2d 177, 179 [7th Cir 1986]). We need not go as far as this to resolve this case; even under the *Anello*, *Palmer* and *Brown* test, defendant's conviction would be upheld. Defendant reasonably believed the condition to the execution of the planned murder—his release from prison—would occur...

Here, neither party imposed a condition on entry into the agreement that was unacceptable to the other. Similarly, ... an "agreement" to murder a victim is effectuated when the co-conspirators accept the defendant's invitation to kill the victim.... Thus, the determinative factor is whether there was an agreement—not whether agreed-upon conditions made the performance of the agreement contingent upon the happening of an event.

Here, the conditions that defendant imposed on the performance of the agreement—to commit a murder—were that nothing was to happen to Seven until defendant was released from jail and was able to secure money to pay for the hit. These requirements were not "conditions" negating the existence of an agreement to kill Seven—they were terms of the agreement. In other words, defendant's wish to delay the killing and payment until he was released from prison was not a demand in negotiations that prevented the parties from reaching the agreement to kill Seven, but a temporal component of the agreement accepted by both parties.

A conspiratorial agreement will be found where there is a "concrete and unambiguous... expression of [defendant's] intent to violate the law" (*People v Schwimmer*, 66 A.D.2d 91, 95–96, 411 N.Y.S.2d 922 [2d Dept 1978]). Both Mitchell's and the undercover's testimony reveal that defendant entered into an agreement to commit the underlying substantive crime of murder in the first degree, and that there were overt acts committed in furtherance of that goal...

Model Penal Code

§ 5.03 Criminal Conspiracy

(1) Definition of Conspiracy. A person is guilty of conspiracy with another person or persons to commit a crime if with the purpose of promoting or facilitating its commission he:

(a) agrees with such other person or persons that they or one or more of them will engage in conduct which constitutes such crime or an attempt or solicitation to commit such crime; or
(b) agrees to aid such other person or persons in the planning or commission of such crime or of an attempt or solicitation to commit such crime.

(2) Scope of Conspiratorial Relationship. If a person guilty of conspiracy, as defined by Subsection (1) of this Section, knows that a person with whom he conspires to commit a crime has conspired with another person or persons to commit the same crime, he is guilty of conspiring with such other person or persons, whether or not he knows their identity, to commit such crime.

(3) Conspiracy With Multiple Criminal Objectives. If a person conspires to commit a number of crimes, he is guilty of only one conspiracy so long as such multiple crimes are the object of the same agreement or continuous conspiratorial relationship.

. . .

(5) Overt Act. No person may be convicted of conspiracy to commit a crime, other than a felony of the first or second degree, unless an overt act in pursuance of such conspiracy is alleged and proved to have been done by him or by a person with whom he conspired.

(6) Renunciation of Criminal Purpose. It is an affirmative defense that the actor, after conspiring to commit a crime, thwarted the success of the conspiracy, under circumstances manifesting a complete and voluntary renunciation of his criminal purpose.

. . .

German Federal Court of Justice
2 StR 500/58, BGHSt 12, 306, NJW 1959, 777 (December 12, 1958)

Reasons

The defendant, whilst on detention awaiting trial for suspicion of arson, agreed with his cell companions H. and S. to break out of the institution. They discussed together various options for breaking out, and then made a plan to strike the guard on the head with a mug during change of shifts. The defendant was then to tie him up, so that H. and S. could take possession in the meantime of the service pistols which were kept in a cupboard; they would then force the breakout with the pistols. They also discussed the possibility of removing the window grill to their cell with a spanner, which they would steal from a Volkswagen which visited the institution regularly, and then escape through the window. While they then observed the guards on their rounds during the following nights, they considered further how they could obtain money after a successful breakout, and go underground; they decided to break into a certain bar, give the landlady a blow on the head and take away her money.

The criminal chamber finds this to be—as the seriousness of the plan is expressly established—a conspiracy for aggravated prison riot under § 122 para. 3 Criminal Code [old version, see now

§ 121 para. 3—Eds.]* and a robbery under § 249 Criminal Code. The application of § 49a para. 2 Criminal Code [old version, now § 30 para. 2 Criminal Code—Eds.]† to this conspiracy does not in itself meet with any reservation. First of all, so far as the conspiracy concerned an act according to § 122 para. 3 Criminal Code, the judgment must be understood to the effect that the rioters had agreed *jointly and personally* to commit acts of violence against the officials of the institution. . . . The planned act was a felony so far as the defendant personally was concerned, simply because the tying up of the prison guard, which was to be carried out by him, would have been an act of violence in the sense of the statute even if the official was unconscious (see BGH in NJW 53, 350). If a conspiracy in a narrow sense under § 49a para. 2 Criminal Code [now § 30 para. 2; that is: an agreement to jointly commit a felony—Eds.] were to be denied, on the basis that *only* the defendant was to commit acts of violence, the defendant would still have declared to others his willingness to commit a felony which is also covered by § 49a para. 2 Criminal Code [now § 30 para. 2—Eds.].

Insofar as the defendant and his cell companions also considered the possibility of escaping by removing the cell grid with a spanner, the conspiracy is not a criminal offence. This is because this type of breakout is only a misdemeanor under § 122 para. 2 Criminal Code[old version].‡ But the three cell companions were certainly not undecided on whether they wanted to break out and the way in which they intended to break out. They were instead equally ready for both forms of break out, and wanted to carry it out in the manner which first became available to them.

It is true that § 49a para. 2 Criminal Code [now § 30 para. 2—Eds.] assumes that the conspirators must have been in agreement about the felony which is to be committed. Uncertainty about the type of felony to which the conspiracy relates excludes its application. But an uncertainty in this sense is not present if the participants contemplate several possibilities of legal interest violation in the conspiracy, and include each of them in their intention; nor is this so when out of two simultaneously planned possibilities of commission, one is a felony and the other is only a misdemeanor and a conspiracy in this respect not criminal.

The three prisoners finally abandoned the break-out plan. In so far as the plan related to the commission of a felony under § 122 para. 3 Criminal Code, they abandoned it because the plan of striking a guard down seemed to them "on more detailed consideration to be too dangerous." The criminal chamber considers that this did not take place voluntarily, and the defendant was therefore not absolved from punishment under § 49a para. 3 Criminal Code [now § 31 para. 1].§ It is not possible to agree with this view. It is admittedly not explained in the judgment in what way the plan seemed to them to be too dangerous. However as matters stood only the following fears fall to be considered: that either the guard could be severely or fatally injured, or the attempt could fail and they would then have to expect severe punishment. If they no longer intended to undertake these risks, their decision to refrain from the implementation of the intended felony was voluntary and not based on external compulsion. The judgment in particular offers no grounds for saying that they had come to the conviction that the execution of their plan was impossible, and that they therefore, i.e., in the certain foresight that it would fail, had given up the plan (see in particular RGSt 47, 74, 78). Thus in so far as the defendant has conspired with H. and S. to commit an aggravated riot under § 122 para. 3 Criminal Code, he remains immune from punishment according to § 49a para. 3 no. 2 Criminal Code [now § 31 para. 1 no. 3—Eds.].

Now the three detainees conspired further to commit a robbery. In this respect the prerequisites of § 49a para. 2 Criminal Code are also present. It is part of the concept of conspiracy that the participants seriously intended to commit the crime, i.e., that they decided to carry it out and thus have a *definite* intention to fulfill the definition of the crime. Mere consideration or preliminary discussions, with the reservation of a later final decision about whether the crime is to be committed, do not suffice. The defendant and his cell companions had the serious and definite intention to rob the landlady. The implementation of the crime admittedly had the success of the intended break-out as a necessary prerequisite. But this circumstance does not remove the necessary definiteness from their intention to commit the felony. It was merely uncertain whether they would succeed in the break-out. This uncertainty is not inconsistent with the assumption of a conspiracy to rob, because it did not concern the decision of the rioters but the possibility of its fulfillment.

---

* [German Criminal Code (old version) § 122 para. 3
Those rioters who commit acts of violence against prison officials or other persons who have to guard them, will be punished with imprisonment from one year to ten years imprisonment.—Eds.]
   † [StGB § 30 is reproduced below—Eds.].
   ‡ [German Criminal Code (old version) § 122 para. 2
The same punishment range [as in para. 1, imprisonment from six months to five years] applies if prisoners band together and with joint forces and violently attempt to escape.—Eds.]
   § [The text of this provision can be found in Chapter 12.D (on renunciation).—Eds.]

The Imperial Court had stated in an earlier decision (RGSt 16, 133) that the decision to fulfill the definition of the crime, which is inherent in an attempt, is also present if the perpetrator intends to complete the crime only under certain factual conditions, the future occurrence of which is still uncertain when the decision is made. However, in the decisions RGSt 68, 341; 70, 203 and 71, 53, the Imperial Court has stated that the intention to carry out the action in accordance with the definition of the crime is insignificant if it is still dependent upon a "condition." The "conditional" intention in RGSt 68, 341 and 70, 203 is evidently equated with the "uncertain" intention and thus with the case in which the perpetrator has still reserved the final decision on whether he intends to carry out the crime at all. However then there is still no decision to commit the crime.

Mere consciousness on the part of the perpetrator that the realization of his plan is dependent on an external condition, whether this is a particular factual situation or the occurrence or non-occurrence of an event, does not make his intention either a conditional or an indeterminate intention. This is because in such a state of affairs, no new ("final") decision is necessary for the implementation of the crime, but only the occurrence or non-occurrence of the event or the presence of a certain factual situation. In the overwhelming majority of cases the implementation of a criminal plan is dependent on such prerequisites of a factual kind, which are outside the perpetrator's will. It would however be inappropriate to negate in principle the final intention to carry out the crime solely because of this dependency. In the individual case the idea of substantial hindrances or of great uncertainty about the occurrence of a certain event may cause the perpetrator still not to make a final decision; that is however a question of fact.

Here the defendant and his two companions have not conspired to commit a robbery in case they should decide to break out of the detention institution. They had firmly decided to do both things. They wanted to carry out the robbery if the break-out should succeed. In this respect also a conspiracy in the sense of § 49a para. 2 Criminal Code [now § 30 para. 2—Eds.] is present.

The rioters, by abandoning the planned break-out, have at the same time given up the robbery which was the subject of the conspiracy. As this was only possible if the break-out succeeded, they have, if the retreat from the riot was voluntary, also voluntarily given up the carrying out of the robbery. As has already been explained, they have withdrawn voluntarily from the plan to strike the guard down and to force their way out with the stolen pistols. The possibility which they had in mind at the same time of removing the grid of the cell window and escaping through the window, did not present itself to them because they could not get themselves an appropriate spanner. It is not necessary to examine whether it would be inconsistent with the finding of a voluntary withdrawal from robbery if they had abandoned the plan to strike down the guard but had adhered for the time being to their plan to escape through the window. That is not how the matter lies. They had instead, according to the findings in the judgment, entirely given up the plan for the break-out on the basis of a unified decision, i.e., abandoned at the same time the use of both the ways they had considered. . . .

Accordingly the defendant and his companions have also voluntarily given up the conspiracy to commit robbery. . . . He is therefore to be acquitted (§ 354 para. 1 German Code of Criminal Procedure).

German Federal Court of Justice
3 StR 233/04, BGH NJW 2005, 1668 (March 10, 2005)
Landser Case

Facts

The Kammergericht [the Higher Regional Court of Berlin]* has sentenced the defendant R. to three years and four months imprisonment for formation of a criminal organization as ringleader [§ 129 paras. 1, 4 Criminal Code, reproduced below] in combination with dissemination of propaganda material of organizations hostile to the Constitution [§ 86] and incitement of hatred [§ 130] in two cases as well as with public incitement to commit crimes [§ 111], approval of crimes [§ 140], defamation of the state and its symbols [§ 90a]and defamations of religions [§ 166]. A corresponding verdict was given against the co-defendants M. and W. (who have not lodged appeals in law), except that they were not convicted as ringleaders in the sense of § 129 para. 4 Criminal Code.

According to the findings, the defendant R. was from 1992 a member and from 1993 the head of the music group "Landser" which had formed from members of the extreme right scene in Berlin and played so-called Punk or Oi!-Skin music. After he had taken over leadership of the group, the

---

* [The Higher Regional Court in Berlin is called "Kammergericht," a unique title in the German court system. It kept the historical name (which meant literally "Chamber Court" and goes back to the German Royal Court being seated in the capital Berlin) but serves the same functions as any other Higher Regional Court in Germany.—Eds.]

defendant R. pursued the goal of influencing the youth of Germany by radical right wing propaganda texts, which were criminal and therefore had a particular emboldening effect in the scene, in order to stir up hatred and emotions, and thus make the group an instrument of political struggle. These efforts were shared by the other members of the group. They therefore refrained in future from public appearances and generally accessible rehearsals. These were held secretly instead at changing locations. Between the end of 1992 and the middle of 2001 the group, the composition of which changed in the course of time, with the exception of the defendant R., and which in 1997 consisted in its final form of the three defendants, brought a music cassette and several CDs onto the market, in collaboration with various persons from within and outside Germany. The CDs were primarily recorded and produced abroad. They were marketed within Germany in conspiratorial ways in the right-wing radical scene, sold there with great rapidity and founded the reputation of "Landser" as the cult group of the young people's extreme right spectrum.

The conviction of the defendant R. under § 129 para. 1 and 4 Criminal Code is based on his membership of the group in the period from 1997 in its final form. The verdict in relation to the remaining crimes committed concomitantly is based on the texts of several songs with a radical right-wing, racist or anti-foreigner content, which are contained in the CDs "Ran an den Feind" ["Rush the Enemy"] and "Best of Landser" published in 2000 and 2001. The defendant's appeal in law objects to violation of procedural and substantive law.

Reasons

. . .

II.

1. The verdict against the defendant R. for founding a criminal association as ringleader (§ 129 para. 1, 4 Criminal Code) is not open to objection.

a) The Kammergericht Berlin is of the opinion that the three members of the music group "Landser" formed a criminal association in the sense of § 129 para. 1 Criminal Code after the entry of the co-defendant W. in 1997 within a very short time. It bases this assessment mainly on the following considerations:

The group had shown the required organizational structure and developed the necessary binding general will for a (criminal) association, and considered itself to be a unified unit. It had therefore distinguished itself from a gang [*Bande*] in the criminal law sense, which need not show organizational structures nor a general will superimposed over the will of the individual members of the gang. The activity of a gang need not go beyond its members working together, each out of his own interest, in a safe and effective carrying out of crimes, and obtaining spoils and gain. A gang need not to pursue any goals endangering society which go beyond the immediate criminal activities.

The organizational structure of the music group "Landser" was indicated by the fact that they had a special name and had since the beginning of 1996 a logo which creates an identity. Besides this, within the group it was not only the musical tasks which had been allocated to the individual members. The defendant R. had, as singer and guitarist, been the creative head of the group on the basis of his superior capabilities. He had determined its National Socialist orientation and he had composed the texts of its songs without which the success of the band would not have been conceivable. The co-defendant W. was entrusted with the external tasks of the organization. Thus he had been responsible for three rehearsal venues, and had contributed considerably by his connections in the radical right-wing scene to the production and marketing of the CD "Ran an den Feind." The co-defendant M. had on the other hand only been able to deal with a few other tasks besides musical ones because of his working activities. He had sometimes transported R. and W. to the rehearsal venues and collected R.'s mail from his mother.

This minimum of internal structure had been amplified by the external structures of their supporters in the right wing radical environment, which had been used systematically by the group for the production of the CDs. The group had relied on this "network" in the accomplishment of their criminal aims, and should have felt itself protected by it.

This alone did not however suffice to classify them as a criminal association in the sense of § 129 para. 1 Criminal Code because organizational structures of this kind could easily be found with music groups which disseminate criminal texts. The protective purpose of § 129 para. 1 Criminal Code required that only groups which posed a danger for public security should be covered. This was only the case if the group had "an important position in the relevant market." Such a high market significance had in fact been achieved by the group "Landser" with the release of the CD "Republik der Strolche" [Republic of Rascals] recorded by another composition of the group in 1995. This position had not been lost by the change in the group's composition and the pause in its activities of several months before the entry of the co-defendant W.

Within the group a binding communal will had also been present. Admittedly R. had not led the group in an authoritarian fashion and no hierarchical structure existed. Instead, all the members had made the decisions jointly, even though frequently on the basis of their shared interests and, in recognition of the competence of the defendant R., unanimously by nodding.

As the commission of crimes, i.e., the dissemination of messages inviting acts of violence, stirring up hatred, denigrating the Constitution of the Federal Republic and resurrecting National Socialism, had been in the foreground of the group's activities, and public security had been significantly endangered thereby, the group had fulfilled all the prerequisites of a criminal organization in the sense of § 129 para. 1 Criminal Code.

b) The findings of the Kammergericht do not reveal legal errors in the end result. A criminal organization is a voluntary organizational union intended to last for a certain duration, consisting of at least three persons, who, subordinating the will of the individual to the will of the whole, pursue joint (criminal) purposes, and who are in such a relationship to each other that they feel themselves to be an integrated unit (see BGHSt 28, 147; BGHSt 31, 202, (204f.); BGHSt 31, 239; BGHSt 45, 26 (35).

aa) These prerequisites were fulfilled here according to the reasoning in the judgment.

Within the music group "Landser" there was an organizational structure for the collaboration of the three members of the group, in order to realize the jointly pursued goals. This is sufficiently proved by the findings about the composition of new songs by the defendant R., the rehearsing of new pieces, the general course of the rehearsal operations, the recording or production of CDs, and the largely conspiratorial implementation of all these activities. The Kammergericht has correctly concluded from the group's name, and the emblem used for the group, that the members of the group felt themselves to be an integrated unit.

The individual members of the group had subordinated themselves to the group will. It is true that the Kammergericht has not established that the defendants gave themselves binding rules by which all the decisions within the group were to be made. This was however not necessary here. This is because it simply follows from the successful collaboration over several years in which three CDs were brought on the market that every individual member of the group must have been subordinated to the goal supported by the joint will of the group. Otherwise the criminal intentions of the participants could not have been implemented in the manner present here.

bb) The further circumstances on which the Kammergericht bases its view of the law are, however, not constitutive for the presence of a criminal organization, and not appropriate to differentiate it from other interactions of several people for the attainment of criminal goals. In this respect the following applies:

If the observations of the Kammergericht are to be understood as meaning that only its embedding into or use of external structures of the radical right wing scene (the "network") had provided the "Landser" group with the degree of organization required for an association in the sense of § 129 para. 1 Criminal Code, this cannot be followed. Such a unilateral or reciprocal amplification of organizational structures could only produce consequences in relation to the crime definition if both "organizations" could give rise to criminal liability, at least in their collaboration. This was not the case here, because there is no indication that the parts of the radical right-wing scene with which the defendants collaborated formed jointly with them a more extensive criminal organization including the organization "Landser." Besides this, the statutory distinction between the organization and its supporters would be eliminated through this construction by the Kammergericht.

That the Kammergericht refers, over and above this, to the organization's pursuit of goals that endanger society beyond direct criminal activities as a fundamental feature to distinguish an organization in the sense of § 129 para. 1 Criminal Code from other forms of collaboration of several people in the pursuit of criminal purposes, in particular of a gang, finds no support in the statute. It can admittedly be deduced from the statutory materials that the legislature considered political or politically motivated groupings in particular as criminal organizations (Hohmann, wistra 1992, 85 with further references). The conclusion cannot however be drawn from this, nor from the nature of the crime, the systematic position of § 129 within the Criminal Code or the legal interest of public security protected by it, that the provision is only applicable to organizations of this kind (for another view Hohmann, wistra 1992, 85; Walischewski, StV 2000, 583,585). Such a limitation of the area of application cannot be deduced from the wording of the provision nor is it suggested by the provisions of art. 9 para. 2 GG,* which is the basis of the norm in its origin (see only v. Bubnoff, in: LK-StGB, 11th edit., § 129 marginal no. 5; Lenckner, in: Schönke/Schröder, StGB, 26th edit., § 129 marginal no. 1).

Nor does the assessment of the music group "Landser" as a criminal association depend on the fact that it had attained "a significant position in the relevant market." This is an unsuitable criterion for demarcation. § 129 para. 1 Criminal Code does not require that the association concretely plans or prepares even only one of the crimes towards which it is orientated (BGH, NJW 2005, 80 [81 with further references]). Criminal liability under this provision cannot accordingly require that these crimes are committed and the association obtains by this a high degree of esteem with like-minded persons. It suffices that it was oriented towards the commission of crimes like stirring up hatred, denigration of the state, dissemination of propaganda material for organizations opposed to the Constitution etc.

German Criminal Code

§ 30 (Attempted Participation)

(1) Who attempts to prompt another to commit a felony or to incite another to commit a felony, will be punished according to the provisions about the attempt of a felony. The sentence is to be mitigated according to § 49 para. 1. § 23 para. 3 will apply.

(2) In the same way will be punished who declares his willingness or who accepts the offer of another or who agrees with another to commit or to incite the commission of a felony.

§ 129 (Forming Criminal Organizations)

(1) Who founds an organization the aims or activities of which are directed at the commission of crimes or who participates in such an organization as a member, recruits members or supporters for it or supports it, will be punished with imprisonment of not more than five years or a fine.

(2) Para. 1 will not be applied
1. if the organization is a political party which the Federal Constitutional Court has not declared to be unconstitutional,
2. if the commission of crimes is of merely minor significance for the aims or activities, or
3. if the aims or activities concern crimes according to §§ 84 to 87.

(3) The attempt to found an organization described in para. 1 will be punished.

(4) If the offender is one of the ringleaders or hintermen or the case is otherwise especially serious, the penalty is imprisonment from six months to five years; . . .

§ 129a (Forming Terrorist Organizations)

(1) Who founds an organization the aims or activities of which are directed at the commission of
1. murder (§ 211), homicide (§ 212) or genocide (§ 6 Code of International Criminal Law) or a crime against humanity (§ 7 Code of International Criminal Law) or a war crime (§§ 8, 9, 10, 11 or § 12 Code of International Criminal Law) or
2. crimes against personal liberty in cases of § 239a or § 239b [abduction for blackmail; taking of hostages], or who participates in such a group as a member will be punished with imprisonment from one to ten years.

(2) In the same way will be punished who founds an organization the aims or activities of which are directed at
1. causing serious physical or mental harm to another person, namely of the kind described in § 226 [grievous bodily harm],
2. crimes under §§ 303b, 305, 305a [computer sabotage, destruction of buildings, destruction of important means of production] or crimes endangering the general public under §§ 306 to 306c [arson], §§ 307 para. 1 to 3, 308 para. 1 to 4, 309 para. 1 to 5 [explosions, abuse of ionizing radiation], §§ 313, 314 [flooding, common danger by poisoning], or § 315 para. 1, 3 or 4 [dangerous interruption of rail, ship or air traffic], § 316b para. 1 or 3 [disruption of public services] or § 316c para. 1 to 3 [attacks on air and sea traffic] or § 317 para. 1 [disruption of telecommunication services],

---

* [Associations whose aims or activities contravene the criminal laws, or that are directed against the constitutional order or the concept of international understanding, are prohibited.—Eds.]

3. committing crimes against the environment under § 330a para. 1 to 3 [severe endangerment through release of poison],
4. committing crimes under the following provisions of the Weapons of War Control Act ... ; or
5. committing offences under § 51 para. 1 to 3 of the Weapons Act;
    or who participates in such a group as a member, if one of the crimes is intended to seriously intimidate the population, to coerce public authority or an international organization through the use of force or the threat of the use of force, or to significantly impair or destroy the basic political, constitutional, economic or social structures of a state or an international organization, and which, regarding the mode of acting or the consequences, can seriously harm a state or an international organization.

(3) If the aims or activities of the organization are directed at threatening the commission of one of the crimes listed in para. 1 or 2, the punishment will be imprisonment from six months to five years.

(4) If the offender is one of the ringleaders or hintermen, he will be punished with imprisonment of not less than three years in cases under para. 1 and 2, and imprisonment from one to ten years in cases under para. 3.

(5) Who supports an organization as described in para. 1, 2 or 3 will be punished with imprisonment from six months to ten years in cases under para. 1 and 2, and imprisonment of not more than five years or a fine in cases under para. 3. Who recruits members or supporters for an organization as described in para. 1 or para. 2, will be punished with imprisonment from six months to five years.

NOTES

1. What does it mean that persons have founded "a partnership in crime" as the U.S. Supreme Court describes conspiracy in *Pinkerton v. United States*? The American category of "conspiracy" as developed in this older leading case is broad and the legal consequences sketched there deserve critical discussion from a comparative perspective.

While the German Criminal Code does not have a section explicitly devoted to "conspiracy," it contains several provisions dealing with pre-crime communication and criminal organizations in its general and special part (e.g., § 30 para. 2 and §§ 129, 129a Criminal Code). Both legal systems therefore have provisions to address situations in which two or more persons reached an agreement to commit crimes in the future but never reached the stage of actually attempting them. Having such legal instruments allows prosecution even if the "partners in crime" did not come close to committing the crime. This is especially useful in legal systems like Germany's with a high threshold for what actions qualify as attempt (requiring "steps which will immediately lead to completion"*). But, legal systems with a wider reach of provisions concerning attempts are also confronted with situations in which the persons involved did not proceed beyond the mere verbalization of an agreement long before actually taking action. The Model Penal Code, for instance, combines a broad definition of attempt with a broad definition of conspiracy, and of inchoate offenses generally speaking. From a treatmentist perspective, there is no reason not to interfere as soon as a sufficiently reliable diagnosis of dangerousness has been made.

Now, federal criminal law has not adopted the Model Penal Code approach to conspiracy.[†] There is no general law of attempt in federal criminal law; the attempt to a commit a federal offense is punishable only if explicitly provided by statute. That said, in the absence of a federal criminal code worthy of that title (as opposed to a—more or less—alphabetical listing of offense definitions, preceded by a fragmentary general part), federal courts are free to consult the Model Penal Code in crafting federal criminal law doctrine.[‡] At any rate, *Pinkerton* was decided before the Model Penal Code was drafted (and then rejected by the Code drafters).

---

* See Criminal Code § 22 (in Chapter 12.A).
† For more discussion on this point, see Note 6.
‡ See, e.g., *United States v. Ivic*, 700 F.2d 51, 66 (2d Cir. 1983) (adopting Model Penal Code approach to attempt).

2. As a matter of critical analysis of the positive law, the question arises: what is the rationale behind the crime of conspiracy? If there are general reasons not to punish persons for their plans, communications and mere preparations, why should one make exceptions for conspiracies? The U.S. Supreme Court in *Pinkerton* seems to assume that "plotting to subvert the law" is reprehensible. This could be interpreted as saying that conspirators attack the legal order through the mere demonstration of their subversive attitudes. Perhaps a more convincing answer would point to a greater degree of dangerousness due to the pressures that (even small) groups tend to exercise on individuals, an especially important point if one looks at criminal organizations (which receive extensive attention in German criminal law, which focuses less on conspiracies in the sense of "agreements" than in the sense of "groups of persons"). Another argument could be that the likelihood of having a firm intention (rather than a more volatile state of mind) is higher when one expresses one's intention to other persons and comes to an agreement with them. What do you make of the U.S. Supreme Court's argument that conspiracy ought to be punished because it requires "more time for its discovery"?

The crime of conspiracy has long been a controversial feature of Anglo-American criminal law. Although current U.S. criminal law retains conspiracy as a crime—and in fact makes frequent use of it in all manner of criminal prosecutions—conspiracy today is often favorably contrasted with conspiracy yesterday, without however addressing the more fundamental objections to the very notion of conspiracy liability in the first place. Conspiracy today differs from conspiracy yesterday mainly in that it limits permissible objects of a criminal conspiracy to criminal conduct. Traditionally, a conspiracy was a crime even if its object was merely an objectionable act of some sort, crime or no crime:

> In order that a combination may be punishable it must be formed to do either an unlawful act or a lawful act by criminal or unlawful means. . . . It is not essential, however, to criminal liability that the acts contemplated should constitute a criminal offense for which, without the elements of conspiracy, one alone could be indicted. It is an offense independent of the crime or unlawful act which is its purpose; and it will be enough if the acts contemplated are corrupt, dishonest, fraudulent, or immoral, and in that sense illegal. A conspiracy will be indictable, if the end proposed or the means to be employed are, by reason of the combination, particularly dangerous to the public interests, or particularly injurious to some individual, although not criminal.

State v. Kemp, 126 Conn. 60, 77–78 (1939).

This broadly defined conspiracy turned out to be a usefully flexible tool in many different contexts, including nineteenth century labor disputes, where union members found themselves labeled, and punished, as conspirators, even though the object of their conspiracy, higher wages, was not illegal if pursued by each individually.[*]

Even with the limitation to criminal objects, and cases like *Pinkerton* notwithstanding, conspiracy has continued to draw concern among commentators and judges (including on the U.S. Supreme Court[†]). Not so among the Model Penal Code drafters. They embraced conspiracy enthusiastically, as they did all inchoate offenses. Conspiracy, to them, was but another indicator of criminal dangerousness. The result was a broad and flexible definition of conspiracy, tailored to perform its diagnostic function, which differed from the traditional common law one in several important respects. The Model Penal Code drafters rejected the application of criminal conspiracy liability to non-criminal conspiracies (i.e., agreements with non-criminal objects). They retained the "overt act" requirement, but limited it to lesser offenses (§ 5.03(5)) (requirement of overt act in pursuance of conspiracy does not apply to first- and second-degree felonies). Perhaps most important, they recognized the doctrine of so-called "unilateral" conspiracy (§ 5.04 ("Incapacity, Irresponsibility or Immunity of Party to Solicitation or Conspiracy")):

---

[*] See R.S. Wright, *The Law of Criminal Conspiracies and Agreements* (1887).
[†] See *Krulewitsch v. United States*, 336 U.S. 440, 445 (1949) (Jackson, J., concurring).

(1) [I]t is immaterial to the liability of a person who . . . conspires with another to commit a crime that:
  (a) he or the person . . . . . . with whom he conspires does not occupy a particular position or have a particular characteristic which is an element of such crime, if he believes that one of them does; or
  (b) the person . . . . . . with whom he conspires is irresponsible or has an immunity to prosecution or conviction for the commission of the crime.

In other words, as long as the defendant thought that her "partner in crime" was indeed a partner—rather than someone who pretended to be (say, because she is in fact an undercover police officer) or could not have been (because of something other than lack of intent to go through with the agreement)—conspiracy liability attached. Finally, as with attempt (and solicitation), conspiracies were generally punished at the level of the object offenses (§ 5.05(1) ("crimes of the same grade and degree as the most serious offense which . . . . . . is an object of the conspiracy," again except for conspiracies to commit first-degree felonies, which were downgraded to second-degree status).

Unlike federal law (at issue in *Pinkerton*), the Model Penal Code does not permit conviction of, and punishment for, both the conspiracy and the object offense, if the object offense was committed. (Then again, federal law does not recognize unilateral conspiracies.) Moreover, the Model Penal Code rejected the *Pinkerton* rule itself, which allowed prosecutors to piggyback liability (under an accomplice theory) for any offense committed "in furtherance of the conspiracy," provided the commission of that offense was reasonably foreseeable, without further proof of the ordinary prerequisites for accomplice liability. In treatmentist terms, the automatic extension of criminal liability may lead to a false dangerousness diagnosis. (See Note 6.)

3. One scenario that could possibly be called "conspiracy" concerns persons who might not have yet planned specific crimes in a more detailed way (i.e., with view to locations, objects, victims, points in time) but who have formed a *general agreement* to commit crimes. Under German law, it is a criminal offense to found an organization the aims or activities of which are directed at the commission of crimes, or to be a member of such an organization or to support it, § 129 Criminal Code. Due to a wave of a terrorist attacks by some (self-defined) left-wing extremists calling themselves the "Red Army Fraction," which began in the 1970s, § 129a (Forming Terrorist Organizations) was introduced into the German Criminal Code in 1976. Note that § 129a Criminal Code does not attempt to define "terrorism" in general; terrorist organizations are distinguished from other criminal organizations in the kinds of object crime (very serious crimes) and higher punishment in § 129a para. 1; § 129a para. 2 also requires that the offenders aim at some effects on the population, the government or international organizations.

One has to keep in mind that the term "organization" [*Vereinigung*] in §§ 129, 129a Criminal Code must be taken seriously. The two brothers in *Pinkerton v. United States* would not qualify as an organization in this sense. The *Landser Case* points out what the requirements for a criminal organization in general are, and especially where the difference to a gang [*Bande*] lies. Note that the organization must have at least three members and that it must not only have a certain stability, but also a degree of dominion over individual members. The agreement of three or more people to commit, for instance, a bank robbery as a group would not suffice to make them a "criminal organization." For "mere" gangs, criminal liability can be based on § 30 para. 2 Criminal Code but not on § 129 Criminal Code.

The closer analogy to the "organization" in §§ 129, 129a Criminal Code in U.S. criminal law is the "enterprise" in the federal RICO statute,* which provides, in 18 U.S.C. § 1962(c) that "[i]t shall be unlawful for any person employed by or associated with any enterprise engaged in, or the activities of which affect, interstate or foreign commerce, to conduct or participate, directly or indirectly, in the conduct of such enterprise's affairs through a pattern of racketeering activity or collection of unlawful debt." The term "enterprise," in turn, is

---

* Discussed in greater detail in Chapter 17.C.

defined as "any individual, partnership, corporation, association, or other legal entity, and any union or group of individuals associated in fact although not a legal entity" (18 U.S.C. § 1961(4)), while "pattern of racketeering activity" requires at least two acts of "racketeering activity" committed within ten years of each other (18 U.S.C. § 1961(5)).

Some states also have begun to recognize the "gang" as a term of art in criminal law. Take, for instance, the California Street Terrorism Enforcement and Prevention Act, enacted in 1988 "to seek the eradication of criminal activity by street gangs by focusing upon patterns of criminal gang activity and upon the organized nature of street gangs," which includes the following provision:

> § 186.22. (a) Any person who actively participates in any criminal street gang with knowledge that its members engage in or have engaged in a pattern of criminal gang activity, and who willfully promotes, furthers, or assists in any felonious criminal conduct by members of that gang, shall be punished by imprisonment in a county jail for a period not to exceed one year, or by imprisonment in the state prison for 16 months, or two or three years.

"Criminal street gang" is defined in subsection (f) as "any ongoing organization, association, or group of three or more persons, whether formal or informal, having as one of its primary activities the commission of one or more of the criminal acts enumerated in..., having a common name or common identifying sign or symbol, and whose members individually or collectively engage in or have engaged in a pattern of criminal gang activity."

Other American jurisdictions, however, have shied away from (explicitly) criminalizing membership in an organization:

> [N.Y.] Penal Law § 120.07 states: "A person is guilty of gang assault in the first degree when, with intent to cause serious physical injury to another person and when aided by two or more other persons actually present, he causes serious physical injury to such person or to a third person."
>
> When analyzing the legislative intent in this case, it is particularly significant to consider not only the language that was used in drafting the statute, but what was omitted. The word "gang" does not appear in the statutory description of the crime. Contrary to defendants' contention that a prosecution under the statute requires evidence of gang affiliation, there is no element requiring that any of the participants in the offense be affiliated with an organization or even with each other prior to the commission of the assault. In contrast to the California Street Terrorism Enforcement and Prevention Act..., New York's Penal Law defining "gang assault" does not require evidence of an association with an organized group of any kind.... In contrast, the only requirement under New York's Penal Law §§ 120.06 and 120.07, other than the intentional infliction of injury, is that there be at least three persons actually present to assist in the commission of the assault. It is apparent that the New York State Legislature rejected the elements of "gang membership" as outlined in the California statute.
>
> People v. Fatal, 187 Misc. 2d 334, 723 N.Y.S.2d 609 (2001)

One of the concerns raised about the criminalization of conspiracy, and in particular the joint trial of defendants charged with conspiracy, is that it permits attribution of "guilt by association," a danger vividly captured by Justice Jackson's concurrence in *Krulewitch v. United States*, 336 U.S. 440 (1949) (Jackson, J., concurring):

> A co-defendant in a conspiracy trial occupies an uneasy seat. There generally will be evidence of wrongdoing by somebody. It is difficult for the individual to make his own case stand on its own merits in the minds of jurors who are ready to believe that birds of a feather are flocked together. If he is silent, he is taken to admit it and if, as often happens, co-defendants can be prodded into accusing or contradicting each other, they convict each other.

A conspiracy may, technically, refer to an agreement in American criminal law, but it is all too easily treated as a group ("the conspiracy"), with each member—the conspirators—punished for their membership. No matter how true this description might ring, American criminal law nonetheless has insisted on defining conspiracy not as a group, no matter how organized or disorganized, but as an agreement (and as a result facilitating conviction by removing an element, as illustrated by the *Fatal* case quoted above).

4. Do you find the arguments made by the Federal Court of Justice in the *Landser Case* convincing? Does it, for instance, really follow from the fact that a music group has managed to bring three CD's on the market over several years that the "individual members have been subordinated to the joint will"?

What about requiring "subordinating the will of the individual to the will of the whole" in the first place? What sort of conception of a collective is at play here? At what point does this conception become difficult to distinguish from the very sort of "personality" that Gierke considered as the quintessentially German view of the corporation (*Genossenschaft*)? Is there a connection between the construction of something like "the will of the whole" and the construction of corporate intent?* The fine distinctions drawn in German criminal law between different types of collectivities, and between "organizations" and "gangs" in particular, and between individual wills and the will of the whole, are strikingly different than the descriptions of, say, enterprise in federal RICO cases, which tend to focus on commercial relationships (also owing to the necessary foundation of the RICO statute itself in the federal power to regulate interstate commerce).†

5. At the core of what is meant by "conspiracy" are cases in which two or more persons have agreed *to commit a specific crime. People v. Washington* and the similar case from 1958 decided by the German Federal Court of Justice deal with such circumstances: two persons agreeing to commit a crime in the future. Under German law, § 30 para. 2 Criminal Code requires agreement about a *Verbrechen* (a felony with minimum punishment of one year's imprisonment, for instance, murder, intentional homicide, robbery, but not burglary or bodily injury with dangerous means‡). Both rulings address the question of conditional agreement; in both cases, the necessary condition was the defendant's release from prison. And both come to a comparable general line of argument: if the intention to commit the crime has been formed, the fact that it is made dependent on an external condition does not necessarily mean that there is no serious (and thus punishable) agreement. But note the slightly different standards expressed in the courts' opinions (whether the offender must "reasonably believe that the condition would obtain" or whether it is sufficient that there is "no great uncertainty about the occurrence"). Do they, in the end, amount to the same thing?

6. Another set of question arises if a crime is actually committed *and* the perpetrator had a prior agreement with another person about this very crime. *Pinkerton* reflects the rule in U.S. federal criminal law that offenders can be punished for *both* the agreement to commit a specific crime and the actual commission of this crime. Under German law, there would only be a conviction for the actual crime. Punishment for the agreement under § 30 para. 2 Criminal Code serves an ancillary function. Although one can, of course, distinguish at the descriptive level the act of communicating from the act of committing the crime, it would be seen as unjust to punish both the creation of a danger and the manifestation of that very danger (namely the occurrence of the object crime). Can the federal rule be defended on normative grounds? Perhaps by drawing a normative distinction between the subversive act of expressing criminal attitudes through conspiring and the act of causing tangible harm through the crime? Could this distinction account for the Supreme Court's position that the agreement to commit a crime might cause greater "injury to the public" than the commission of the crime itself? Recall in this context the rationales for the punishment of another inchoate offense, attempt, developed in German criminal law, discussed in Chapter 12.A (e.g., manifesting a "will hostile to law").

Note that the Federal Court of Justice had in the *Landser Case* no objections to punishing the defendant for both membership in the criminal organization *and* crimes committed with the help of the lyrics used by the group "Landser" (incitement to hatred, etc.§). This seems defensible. The idea of a criminal organization is that it is aimed not at one specific crime but

---

* See Chapter 11.
† See Chapter 17.C.
‡ See Chapter 5.D.
§ See Chapter 17.A.

at an indeterminate number of not-yet-specified criminal activities. Therefore, founding such an organization and being a member in it does not amount to a wrongdoing identical to the commission of specific crimes in the course of the organization's existence.*

Or does it? While the wrongdoing may not be identical, wouldn't it be enough if there were some (substantial?) overlap between the danger and its manifestation? Is this a case where an organization is founded for one purpose, and then its members commit crimes unrelated to that purpose? More generally, what justifies criminalizing membership in a "criminal organization" in and of itself, if not the increased danger of the commission of criminal offenses resulting from the existence of that organization? Otherwise, when would constitutional concerns arise about the (criminal) prohibition of membership in an organization, under the freedom of association? (The free-speech implications of the criminalization of the specific conduct in question will be discussed in Chapter 17.C.)

The Model Penal Code likewise rejects the dual liability rule (for conspiracy and object) of federal criminal law mentioned in *Pinkerton*, but on different grounds. From a treatmentist perspective, the indicated rehabilitative or incapacitative peno-correctional treatment reflects a diagnosis of criminal dangerousness; the commission of an offense simply manifests the very dangerousness that had been diagnosed on the basis of inchoate conduct of one form or another (attempt, conspiracy, solicitation). To punish someone twice for the manifestation of the same danger would be to overprescribe peno-correctional treatment. Punishing someone for both the consummated version and the inchoate version of a given offense makes no more sense in cases of conspiracy than in cases of attempt (which even federal criminal law "merges" into its object offense). In the end, does the disagreement between the Model Penal Code drafters and the U.S. Supreme Court come down simply to a disagreement about the proper diagnosis of criminal dangerousness associated with criminal conspiracies?[†] Does the Model Penal Code approach to criminal law provide the resources to resolve disagreements of this nature? How is one to choose among different proposed peno-correctional diagnoses, at the level of general rules (as here) or in particular cases?

7. Still another question—besides the issue of cumulative punishment—arises if on the basis of a prior conspiracy the crime is actually committed. Does the fact of having being involved in a conspiracy make each of the conspirators a perpetrator of the crime, even if they were not involved physically in the specific offense? While *Pinkerton v. United States* answered this affirmatively, *People v. McGee* rejects this position. This corresponds to German law. Even if two or more persons had agreed about committing a specific crime (§ 30 para. 1 Criminal Code), when it comes to the actual criminal act, the normal rules of perpetratorship and participation apply. A person can only be a co-perpetrator if he has sufficient dominion (*Tatherrschaft*) over the act that fulfils the definition of the crime. This usually means that he has to be present at the scene of the crime; only if he has taken a very dominant role in the planning stage is an exception to this rule conceivable. (Again, note the parallels between the German criminal law's approach to the analysis of participation in crime and the pre-Model Penal Code common law approach, both of which distinguish sharply between principals/ perpetrators, who are present, and accessories/aiders, who are not.)

The parallels between *McGee* and German criminal law extend beyond the result, to the rationale. In a striking passage, the New York Court of Appeals rejects *Pinkerton* because "it is repugnant to our system of jurisprudence, where guilt is generally personal to the defendant." Does this rather cryptic reference to the "personalness" of "guilt" hint at an unenunciated principle of personal guilt similar to that developed in German criminal law (and, in a different formulation, Canadian criminal law)? (On the culpability principle, see Chapter 1.) Or could this be read as consistent with the Model Penal Code's own version of the personalness of guilt, namely an ascription of criminal liability that reflects the

---

* Again, a comparison with the concept of "enterprises" under RICO might be instructive. See Chapter 17.C.
† See *Callanan v. United States*, 364 U.S. 587 (1961) (dismissing the traditional merger rule in conspiracy as a "common-law procedural nicet[y]" and concluding that "the danger which a conspiracy generates is not confined to the substantive offense which is the immediate aim of the enterprise").

dangerousness of each offender as accurately as possible, given the crude tools of (preliminary) diagnosis and classification provided by the criminal law? After all, the New York Penal Law was revised in light of the Model Penal Code, and the Code had rejected *Pinkerton* long before *McGee* was decided. (See Note 6.) Note that the New York Penal Law also followed the Model Penal Code's recognition of so-called "unilateral" conspiracies, perhaps the most drastic manifestation of the Code's treatmentist (and "personal") approach to conspiracy. (See Note 2.)

8. The *actus reus* of conspiracy is the agreement. Any other requirement (say, in the form of an act in furtherance of the agreement) is considered to be of evidentiary significance, which presumably explains why the Model Penal Code drafters felt free to do away with the "overt act" requirement altogether in serious cases (first and second degree felonies), where—from their perspective—the very seriousness of the object crime provides sufficient indication of dangerousness. § 5.03(5). The overt act requirement in conspiracy is often contrasted with the act requirement in the law of attempt, which—at least in the traditional common law approach—is supposed to be more demanding because, in the absence of an agreement, it is the *actus reus* of attempt. Of course, that contrast diminishes if one dilutes the act requirement in the law of attempt. Recall that the Model Penal Code's approach to attempt liability makes do with a "substantial step," assessed in light of the evidentiary question of whether it is "strongly corroborative of the actor's criminal purpose."* The "overt act" requirement in conspiracy, in other words, appears to perform the same evidentiary function as does the act requirement in attempt. At the end of the day, what is left of the act requirement in the law of conspiracy?

C. Solicitation

The inclusion of the new offense of solicitation in the Model Penal Code is in keeping with the Code's treatmentist approach to criminal law in general, and to inchoate liability in particular. The provision has been criticized as both too broad and, at the same time, as duplicative, given the availability of other modes of inchoate liability, including the combination of attempt and accessorial liability (notably inciting, or abetting), as illustrated by § 30 para. 1 StGB.

Benson v. People
Supreme Court of California
57 Cal.2d 240 (1962)

Traynor, J.

Petitioner seeks a writ of prohibition to restrain the Superior Court of Los Angeles County from taking further proceedings against him under a count of an indictment charging him with soliciting perjured testimony in violation of Penal Code section 653f.[†]

The Department of Social Welfare had been conducting an investigation of adoption practices in Los Angeles County. Mrs. Evelyn Scheingold, an investigator, visited petitioner, an attorney, and told him that she was pregnant, that she wished to have the child adopted, and that the child's father was unknown, since she had been living with her husband and another man. The husband's consent would normally be necessary for an adoption, for a legitimate child "cannot be adopted without the consent of its parents..." (Civ. Code, §§ 224, 226.) To make the husband's consent unnecessary, the wife must show that she is not cohabiting with him and must rebut the statutory presumptions favoring the child's legitimacy. In a custody proceeding the wife may present testimony establishing

---

* See Chapter 12.A.

† [Penal Code § 653f.
Every person who solicits another... to commit or join in the commission of... perjury... is punishable by imprisonment in the county jail not longer than one year or in the state prison not longer than five years, or by a fine of not more than five thousand dollars. Such offense must be proved by the testimony of two witnesses, or of one witness and corroborating circumstances.—Eds.]

that she has lived apart from her husband for a sufficient length of time to rebut the presumptions that the husband is the child's father.

Mrs. Scheingold testified before the grand jury that in contemplation of a custody proceeding petitioner said to her: "'There are ways of getting around the law, and I'm the only lawyer in town who knows how to do it.' He said, 'I will help you get a witness to establish that your husband could not have been the father. I know how to get around these Courts.' "She testified further: "I said, 'Mr. Benson, my big problem is how I am going to get a witness to testify that I have not been with my husband for a period of time.'

"He said, 'You have a girl friend here, haven't you?'"

"I said, 'Yes, but I am afraid she may say the wrong things. She's pretty nervous.'"

"Mr. Benson said, 'Don't worry. I'll talk to her. She will say the right things.'"

Subsequently, Mrs. Scheingold introduced Miss Terri Pallato, a fellow investigator, to petitioner as a friend. Mrs. Scheingold testified that Miss Pallato, "told Mr. Benson that she had never seen my husband, that she did not know him, that she did not know whether or not this was his baby, but she was willing to swear in the affirmative to both of these points . . .

"Mr. Benson assured her that there was nothing to it. He said that Terri and I would go into the Judge's chambers and he would ask whether or not she knew my husband and whether or not this could be his baby, and she would answer that this could not be his baby."

"Mr. Benson said that Terri should say that she knew my husband, but that I had been living out here in Los Angeles for over 11 months and this could not be his child."

Miss Pallato testified: "He said, 'All we do is we three, you, her and me, will walk into the Judge's chambers and he will ask you those two questions.'"

"Now, he didn't repeat the questions, but he meant, 'Do you know Evelyn's husband' and 'Do you know that this is not his baby?'"

"And he said, 'All you do is answer yes to both those questions.'"

"So I said, 'Well, I'm terribly nervous about it, Mr. Benson.' I said, 'I don't do this every day of my life . . .'"

"He said, 'Look, there's absolutely nothing to it.' . . ."

Petitioner contends, however, that he could not have committed the crime of solicitation since the perjury would not have occurred because the fact that Mrs. Scheingold was an investigator who was not even pregnant would have precluded a custody proceeding. Petitioner's alleged acts nevertheless fall clearly within Penal Code section 653f.

That section is designed not only to prevent solicitations from resulting in the commission of the crimes solicited, but to protect "inhabitants of this state from being exposed to inducement to commit or join in the commission of the crimes specified . . ." "Purposeful solicitation presents dangers calling for preventive intervention and is sufficiently indicative of a disposition towards criminal activity to call for liability. Moreover, the fortuity that the person solicited does not agree to commit the incited crime plainly should not relieve the solicitor of liability . . ." (Model Penal Code, § 5.02, comment [Tent. Draft No. 10, 1960] 82.)

The act solicited must, of course, be criminal. If the solicitor believes that the act can be committed "it is immaterial that the crime urged is not possible of fulfilment at the time when the words are spoken" or becomes impossible at a later time. This rule was clearly enunciated as early as 1864 in Commonwealth v. Jacobs, 91 Mass. (9 Allen) 274, 275. In that case a statute made criminal the solicitation of another to leave the state to offer himself as a draft substitute for the solicitor. The court rejected defendant's contention that since the person solicited, without the solicitor's knowledge, had been rejected as physically unfit by the army before the solicitation, the impossibility of completing the act barred a conviction.

Solicitation itself is the evil prohibited by the Legislature, and prosecution therefor is particularly appropriate for the very case in which the crime solicited does not take place.

Model Penal Code

§ 5.02 Criminal Solicitation

(1) *Definition of Solicitation.* A person is guilty of solicitation to commit a crime if with the purpose of promoting or facilitating its commission he commands, encourages or requests another person to engage in specific conduct which would constitute such crime or an attempt to commit such crime or which would establish his complicity in its commission or attempted commission.

(2) *Uncommunicated Solicitation.* It is immaterial under Subsection (1) of this Section that the actor fails to communicate with the person he solicits to commit a crime if his conduct was designed to effect such communication.

NOTES

1. German law, like the Model Penal Code and California law, contains a prohibition against solicitation, § 30 para. 1 Criminal Code.* Section 30 para. 1 Criminal Code supplements the provision on incitement (§ 26 Criminal Code), which only applies if the principal perpetrator actually commits the crime or at least reaches the stage of a punishable act. If there is no such unlawful act by the person whom the inciter had hoped would become a perpetrator, he or she cannot be punished for incitement. Like the provision about agreements in § 30 para. 2 Criminal Code, § 30 para. 1 is limited to cases in which the object offense is a felony (a *Verbrechen* in the sense of the German Criminal Code, that is, punished with a mandatory minimum of one year's imprisonment†).

But note that there is an exemption in the German Criminal Code which in effect parallels California law: although false testimony is (unless sworn with a false oath) not a felony in the sense of § 30, § 159 Criminal Code makes solicitation for any case of false testimony a criminal offense. It seems that in both legal systems the legislature (probably correctly) assumed that the inclination to influence witnesses is widespread and that for this specific offense deterrence is particularly important to counteract the temptation to solicit such conduct. The Model Penal Code also explicitly criminalizes soliciting witness tampering (§ 241.6).‡ Is there something about these offenses that makes the explicit criminalization of their solicitation more appropriate than for other offenses?

2. Section 30 para. 1 Criminal Code does not, in so many words, criminalize "solicitation" as a separate offense. Instead it criminalizes "attempted participation," or more precisely, attempted inciting (but not attempted aiding). Section 30 para. 1 treats attempted inciting as an attempt, rather than as a separate offense of solicitation. But if attempt law can handle attempted inciting, what's the point of a separate solicitation offense? In fact, the Model Penal Code Commentaries acknowledge that solicitation "may, indeed, be thought of as an attempt to conspire." Commentaries § 5.02, at 365–66. So who needs solicitation as a separate offense if attempt and conspiracy are already criminalized? According to the Model Penal Code Commentaries, "[p]urposeful solicitation presents dangers calling for preventive intervention and is sufficiently indicative of a disposition towards criminal activity to call for liability." If solicitation is designed to capture cases not already covered by the broad definition of attempt and conspiracy under the Model Code, does it cross the line of the acceptable extension of criminal liability in the pursuit of the identification of the criminally dangerous? In other words, isn't solicitation either redundant and therefore unnecessary or unjustified? For an expression of judicial skepticism about the (then-)new offense of solicitation, see *People v. Lubow*, 29 N.Y.2d 58 (1971). Does calling a doubly inchoate offense like attempted conspiracy by another name ("solicitation") do more than obscure a troubling expansion of the criminal law? On the illegitimacy of multiply inchoate offenses, see, e.g., *R. v. Déry*, [2006] 2 S.C.R. 669 (attempt to conspire to possess).

3. The Supreme Court of California, in *Benson*, argued that it does not matter if the crime solicited could have been undertaken. This view is shared in German law doctrine. Even in the case of an attempt, punishment is not excluded if completion of the crime would have been impossible—for example, if an abortive substance was administered to a woman who was in fact not pregnant.§

In other words, the impossibility defense is rejected for all inchoate offenses, attempt and solicitation, and conspiracy as well. This comes as no surprise under the Model Penal Code treatmentist scheme (see the discussion of impossibility: Chapter 12.A, Note 9). For a justification from another perspective, in terms of the significance of "the subjective point

---

* See Chapter 12.B.
† See Chapter 5.D.
‡ For other offenses defined in terms of solicitation, see Model Penal Code §§ 210.5 (assisted suicide) (see Chapter 15.A.v), 224.8 (commercial bribery), 224.9 (contract rigging), 240.1, 240.3, 240.5, 240.7 (bribery and related offenses), and 251.2, 251.3 (prostitution).
§ See Criminal Code § 23 para. 3, in Chapter 12.A.

of view" rather than criminal dangerousness, see the opinion of the Canadian Supreme Court in *United States v. Dynar*, [1997] 2 S.C.R. 462 (which, incidentally, also rejects the Model Penal Code's notion of a unilateral conspiracy):

> [S]ince the offence of conspiracy only requires an intention to commit the substantive offence, and not the commission of the offence itself, it does not matter that, from an objective point of view, commission of the offence may be impossible. It is the subjective point of view that is important, and from a subjective perspective, conspirators who intend to commit an indictable offence intend to do everything necessary to satisfy the conditions of the offence. The fact that they cannot do so because an objective circumstance is not as they believe it to be does not in any way affect this intention. The intention of the conspirators remains the same, regardless of the absence of the circumstance that would make the realization of that intention possible. It is only in retrospect that the impossibility of accomplishing the common design becomes apparent.

4. If one considers the rationale of a prohibition against solicitation, from a German perspective, the most obvious answer is that the crime to be committed would cause harm, violate a right or a legal good. The prohibition of solicitation serves to prevent the danger of this happening in a similar way as the criminalization of the other inchoate offenses, attempt and conspiracy, as well as the recognition of incitement as a mode of liability for the consummated offense.

The Supreme Court of California argues that citizens ought to be protected against being exposed to inducements. But if those approached reject such proposals, the mere fact that they might feel offended about being proposed this way is hardly a convincing a reason for criminal punishment. If one looks at the punishment, under German law solicitation is punished like the agreement between persons to commit the crime. One can question this choice of the legislature: after all, when two persons conspire, the probability of the crime being carried out seems higher than in the case of mere solicitation. Therefore, one could argue that conspiracy is more dangerous and deserves more serious punishment than mere solicitation. After all, insofar as solicitation is an attempted conspiracy, punishing both equally would deviate from the general principle of punishing the attempt less severely than the consummation.

Again, from the Model Penal Code's perspective, solicitation and conspiracy, as all other inchoate offenses (and modes of participation) are but indicators of criminal dangerousness that allow courts to hazard a preliminary diagnosis and impose a general peno-correctional treatment regime, to be fine-tuned by expert penologists (parole and probation officers, correctional officials). In this light, even the unmailed letter, the "telephone message initiated but never delivered," can serve as a sufficient indicator of criminal dangerousness: "It is immaterial that the actor fails to communicate with the person he solicits to commit a crime if his conduct was designed to effect such communication."* Under the German approach to attempt liability, does this behavior amount to "disobedience of the legal order that is unbearable for the legal community," or has the person engaging in it manifested a "will hostile to law" that deserves, permits, or perhaps even requires punishment to prevent danger to the "public's trust in the validity of the legal order"? (See Chapter 12.A.)

D. Renunciation

Both the Model Penal Code and German criminal law recognize a doctrine of renunciation, or withdrawal, but take different approaches to this issue both at the level of conceptualization and of application. (Some common law jurisdictions deny the relevance of renunciation, perhaps reflecting a narrower conception of attempt than that found in the Model Penal Code, see Chapter 12.A.) Interestingly, both systems have some difficulty integrating the

---

* Model Penal Code § 5.02(2), Tent. Draft No. 10.

question into their analysis of criminal liability. Under the Model Penal Code renunciation can perhaps be seen as a rebuttal of the (apparently, and exceptionally, rebuttable) presumption of abnormal dangerousness attached to a finding of the requisite purpose for attempt liability. German criminal law instead categorizes withdrawal as neither an element-negating "defense," nor a justification or an excuse, but as an unusual "personal exemption from *punishment*" rather than from criminal liability.*

People v. Sisselman
Supreme Court of New York, Appellate Division
147 A.D.2d 261, 542 N.Y.S.2d 801 (1989)

Yesawich, J.

Defendant was convicted of conspiracy in the fourth degree and solicitation in the fourth degree for paying Dennis Patterson $ 250 to break the limbs of Louis Marrero, who defendant suspected was dating his extramarital girlfriend, giving her drugs or both. Patterson, acting as a police agent, recorded two telephone conversations during which defendant solicited Patterson to perform the assault, which in fact was never accomplished. . . .

At trial, defendant, through his own testimony and that of his longtime friend, Marty Biederman, asserted that he had renounced the assault scheme prior to finding out that Patterson was a police informant by directing him not to carry out the assault. County Court excluded, as inadmissible hearsay, testimony proffered by Biederman that defendant said he had told Patterson not to commit the crime . . .

County Court gave the jury a renunciation charge suggested by the Committee on Criminal Jury Instructions of the State of New York (*see,* 1 CJI[NY] 40.10 [4a], at 959–960; [4b], at 964–965), which defined the two elements of the affirmative defense as (1) voluntary and complete renunciation of the criminal enterprise, and (2) a substantial and successful effort to prevent the object crime. The jury was further instructed that for the effort to be deemed successful, the "effort must have been the sole and motivating inducement for Dennis Patterson to have abandoned any further effort and intention to commit such a crime." Convicted, defendant now appeals.

Defendant argues that the quoted charge language deprived him of the renunciation defense because he simply could not be the "sole and motivating" factor in preventing the object crime since Patterson, as a police agent, never intended to commit the assault. . . .

"Renunciation does not negate the commission of the inchoate crime" (*People v. Johnston*, 87 AD2d 703, 704), but rather offers those guilty of such crimes an incentive to take steps to prevent the object or substantive crime, in exchange for which the defendant is excused from liability. Unlike charges based upon accessorial conduct or criminal facilitation where only substantial efforts to prevent the object crime are required to invoke the renunciation defense (Penal Law § 40.10 [1], [2]), charges of conspiracy and solicitation give way to the renunciation defense only where "the defendant prevented the commission of such crime" (Penal Law § 40.10 [4]). The statute does not go so far as to say that defendant's efforts must be the "sole" reason that the object crime was not committed; indeed, such a reading would thwart the purpose of the provision where, for instance, two co-conspirators acted in concert to prevent the consummation of the object crime, and to that extent the pattern instruction is an overstatement of the law.

The real problem here is that defendant was in no position to prevent the object crime since Patterson never intended to carry out the solicited assault. Despite this inability on defendant's part to literally comply with the statute, it would be unfair to deny him the renunciation defense merely because his coconspirator lacked criminal intent, for, in addition to encouraging prevention of the substantive crime, the renunciation defense is predicated upon the premise that complete and voluntary "renunciation manifests a lack of the firmness of purpose that evidences individual dangerousness." (ALI Model Penal Code and Commentaries § 5.03 [6], Comment 6, at 457–458; *see also,* ALI Model Penal Code and Commentaries § 5.01 [4], Comment 8, at 359; § 5.02 [3], Comment 3 [d], at 382). Consequently, although defendant was incapable of preventing the object crime, he should be given the opportunity to rebut the prima facie indication of firmness of purpose which follows from the People's proof of solicitation and the overt act in furtherance of the conspiracy (*see,* ALI Model Penal Code and Commentaries § 5.01 [4], Comment 8, at 359). County Court should have charged that defendant's efforts to prevent the object crime would be deemed

---

* Entrapment shares this neither-nor status. See Chapter 14.B.

successful if they would have prevented the crime in the event that Patterson had intended to carry out the object crime.

Model Penal Code

§ 5.01 Criminal Attempt

. . . .

(4) *Renunciation of Criminal Purpose.* When the actor's conduct would otherwise constitute an attempt under Subsection (1)(b) or (1)(c) of this Section, it is an affirmative defense that he abandoned his effort to commit the crime or otherwise prevented its commission, under circumstances manifesting a complete and voluntary renunciation of his criminal purpose. The establishment of such defense does not, however, affect the liability of an accomplice who did not join in such abandonment or prevention.

Within the meaning of this Article, renunciation of criminal purpose is not voluntary if it is motivated, in whole or in part, by circumstances, not present or apparent at the inception of the actor's course of conduct, which increase the probability of detection or apprehension or which make more difficult the accomplishment of the criminal purpose. Renunciation is not complete if it is motivated by a decision to postpone the criminal conduct until a more advantageous time or to transfer the criminal effort to another but similar objective or victim.

§5.02. Criminal Solicitation.

. . . .

(3) *Renunciation of Criminal Purpose.* It is an affirmative defense that the actor, after soliciting another person to commit a crime, persuaded him not to do so or otherwise prevented the commission of the crime, under circumstances manifesting a complete and voluntary renunciation of his criminal purpose.

§ 5.03. Criminal Conspiracy.

. . . .

(6) *Renunciation of Criminal Purpose.* It is an affirmative defense that the actor, after conspiring to commit a crime, thwarted the success of the conspiracy, under circumstances manifesting a complete and voluntary renunciation of his criminal purpose.

§ 2.06. Liability for Conduct of Another; Complicity.

. . . .

(6) Unless otherwise provided by the Code or by the law defining the offense, a person is not an accomplice in an offense committed by another person if:

. . .

(c) he terminates his complicity prior to the commission of the offense and
　(i) wholly deprives it of effectiveness in the commission of the offense; or
　(ii) gives timely warning to the law enforcement authorities or otherwise makes proper effort to prevent the commission of the offense.

German Federal Court of Justice
StR 665/87, BGHSt 35, 184 (January 13, 1998)

Facts

The defendant had informed M., the new partner of the defendant's divorced wife B., that he would shoot him if he did not leave his wife alone, but that he would be ready to tolerate contacts between them if both of them would pay him 100,000 DM to cover his debts. As this threat had no effect, in rage about the refusal of the payment of money he made the decision to kill them both at the next opportunity.

On the evening of December 16, 1986, in the expectation of at least being able to kill his former wife, he drove to a parking lot of the business in which she was employed. He carried a butcher knife as well as a kitchen knife with him. Whilst he waited in his car for the appearance of his ex-wife, M. also arrived in his vehicle. He had agreed with her to meet her at the parking place—as he had already done on previous days—and accompany her home. M. parked his car about 10 m away from her car. When getting out of the car, he noticed the defendant. With the intention of speaking to the defendant again about the demands for money, M. went to his car, opened the car door and greeted the defendant. The defendant, in anger about the non-payment of the desired sum, and with the intention to kill—which was completely unexpected by M.—stabbed him powerfully with the butcher knife in the abdomen. In doing so he injured the witness's small intestine, stomach and large intestine. M. fled but the defendant caught up with him and tried to stab him again. The witness, desperately defending himself, succeeded in snatching the knife from the defendant and throwing it over a fence. Then he ran to another parking lot of the firm, about 50 m away. The defendant ran back to his car and pursued the witness in the vehicle with the object of killing him by running him down. M. evaded him, jumped through a 5 m wide hedge strip and crouched down behind it. He felt himself beginning to faint, and realized he was unable to continue his flight. The defendant drove into the hedge in order to break through it and to run the witness down. His car penetrated the hedge almost completely, but then remained stuck there. Consequently the defendant climbed out of the vehicle and "left M. alone and hurriedly ran—either because he thought that M. would not survive the serious wound inflicted on him anyway, or because he feared that he would 'miss' his ex-wife as a result of the lapse in time which had occurred—taking the kitchen knife with him" to her vehicle. "Having arrived there, he gave B., who had arrived at her car . . . in rage about the refused money payment, and with the unconditional intention of killing her, a total of about 17 stab wounds by means of the kitchen knife to the upper part of her body and the abdomen by which, amongst other things, her heart, her aorta, and her pulmonary artery . . . were severed." B. bled to death. After he had stabbed his ex-wife, the defendant returned to the other parking lot and stood next to the witness M. who was crouching wounded on the ground. The regional court sentenced the defendant to life imprisonment for murder (base motives) and to a further sentence of imprisonment of twelve years for attempted murder.

The defendant objected to a violation of substantive law.

Reasons

. . . 2. The reasoning with which the regional court has denied a withdrawal from attempted murder (§ 24 para. 1 Criminal Code), which it considered to be possible according to one version of the facts, does not stand up to legal examination. The Court argues that if the defendant left M. alone because he was afraid that he would "miss" his ex-wife, the attempt was admittedly incomplete, but the withdrawal had not occurred voluntarily. . . .

b) The view taken by the judge of fact in his finding that voluntariness was absent is not justified. He has taken into account that the defendant, when he left the witness M. alone, might have done so because he considered the killing of his ex-wife to be of greater priority than that of the witness. Such reasoning of a defendant does not justify the denial of voluntariness. According to consistent case law, when deciding about the presence of this feature the decisive factor is whether the defendant still "remained the master of his decisions and considered the implementation of his plan for the crime still to be possible . . . , and thus was not prevented by an external predicament nor rendered incapable by psychological pressure from completing the crime" (BGHSt 7, 296, 299; further, amongst others, BGHSt 21, 216 "emotional compulsion makes the perpetrator incapable"). It depends on whether the circumstance in question appears to be a "compelling hindrance" for the perpetrator (BGH, in: Holtz, MDR 1982, 969; 1986, 271). The reason why the defendant refrained from further pursuit of M. was not however of this kind. Instead, the abandoning of his course of action was the result of sober consideration.

c) Voluntariness, according to consistent case law (amongst others, BGHSt 7, 296, 299; BGHSt 9, 48 ff.; BGHSt 33, 142, 145 f.; BGH, NJW 1980, 602), is also not excluded by the fact that the defendant did not refrain from further attacks on the witness from a motive deserving moral approval.

d) Further, it is not inconsistent with affirmation of the prerequisites for withdrawal that the defendant did not abandon the implementation of his plan as a whole but only refrained from pursuing the witness, now turning against his ex-wife whose killing he regarded as having greater priority. Admittedly a person can only withdraw from a crime so as to free himself from punishment if he gives up the implementation of his criminal intention fully and finally. That however only applies in relation to the individual crime in the substantive law sense (BGHSt 33, 142 (144 f.) = NJW 1985, 1788).

e) The Senate does not fail to recognize that the opinion held by the case law does not always lead to satisfactory results. That also explains why a substantial part of the literature has turned against the "psychologizing" way that the case law has of looking at the issue, and regards a normative assessment of the motive for withdrawal as required. It is not necessary here to deal with the special features of the various theories developed under this aspect, and the reservations existing against the details of these. The Senate confines itself in this respect to indicating that the concept of voluntariness used in § 24 Criminal Code requires demarcation according to psychologizing criteria. This element does not permit a purely normative interpretation (appropriately, Lackner, StGB, 17th edit., § 24 note 3 b, bb). Those theories admittedly take account of the rationale behind the withdrawal regime more than the view held by the case law. However they are not reconcilable with the wording of the statute. A remedy, as Lackner (loc. cit.) correctly concludes, is possible only by way of an amendment of the law.

3. The conviction of the defendant for attempted murder must be quashed on the grounds explained . . .

German Criminal Code

§ 24 (Withdrawal)

(1) Who voluntarily gives up the further execution of the crime or prevents its completion will not be punished for the attempt. If the crime remains uncompleted independent of further actions by the offender who abandoned his plan, he will not be punished if he has made voluntary and earnest efforts to prevent completion of the crime.

(2) If two or more persons participated in the commission of the crime, the person who voluntarily prevents its completion will not be punished for the attempt. However, his voluntary and earnest efforts to prevent the completion of the crime suffice for exemption from punishment if the crime remains uncompleted independent of his further actions or if it is completed independent of his prior contributions.

§ 31 (Withdrawal from Attempted Participation)

(1) A person will not be punished under § 30 if he voluntarily
1. gives up the attempt to prompt another to commit a felony and averts any existing danger that the other may commit the felony,
2. after having declared his willingness to commit a felony, gives up his plan or
3. after having agreed to commit a felony or having accepted the offer of another to commit a felony, prevents the commission of the offence.

(2) If the crime remains uncompleted independent of further actions by the offender who abandoned the plan or if it is completed independent of his prior contributions, his voluntary and earnest efforts to prevent the completion of the crime suffice for exemption from punishment.

NOTES

1. German law (§§ 24, 31 Criminal Code) leaves offenders extensive opportunities for withdrawal in the case of attempts, or rather inchoate offenses more generally, assuming one reads § 30 Criminal Code as recognizing, in effect, solicitation (para. 1) and conspiracy (para. 2). According to current German criminal law doctrine, withdrawal does not negate an offense element, nor does it justify or excuse the criminal act because it occurs after it. Instead it is considered to be a personal exemption from punishment (*persönlicher Strafaufhebungsgrund*), i.e., it is limited to the specific person who satisfies the conditions for withdrawal and exempts that person from punishment (as opposed to the ascription of criminal liability): even though the offender satisfies all three levels in the analysis of criminal liability (criminality, unlawfulness, guilt), he or she nonetheless escapes punishment.*

From the viewpoint of defense lawyers, establishing withdrawal often is the most important issue in a case of inchoate crime, especially in cases involving serious attacks on a person. Being punished only for assault and not for attempted murder means a significant lowering of the punishment range.

---

* On the analysis of criminal liability, see Chapter 6.

If one compares German statutory and case law with § 5.01(4) and § 5.02(3) Model Penal Code, there are some similarities, not only concerning the existence of withdrawal as a legal option but also with regard to some details. For instance, the exclusion of voluntariness in a withdrawal if the defendant was motivated by circumstances "which increase the probability of detection or apprehension" (§ 5.01(4)) is also part of German case law.

But there appear to be differences concerning the rationale behind the concept of withdrawal, as perhaps reflected in the difference between the expressions "renunciation" on the one hand, "withdrawal" on the other. The Model Penal Code's approach is based on the notion expressed in § 5.01(4), that a "complete and voluntary renunciation of [the actor's] criminal purpose" be manifested. The legal relevance of renunciation is thus based on the offender's subjective state of mind. In keeping with the Model Penal Code's treatmentist approach, renunciation can be seen as a rebuttal of the presumption of dangerousness ordinarily attached to the commission of acts that satisfy the criteria for an inchoate offense (attempt, solicitation, conspiracy, and—in jurisdictions like New York—facilitation) or for participatory liability (complicity).* A subjective approach to renunciation is also consistent with a character-based approach to criminal liability that would regard renunciation as evidence of the absence of the requisite malice (or "vicious will").

The leading German approach is different. Using the expression "withdrawal" (*Rücktritt*) emphasizes the *act* of giving up as such rather than what this might tell us about the offender as a person (or her mental state). This approach points to victims' interests: the law offers a personal exemption from punishment as an incentive to prevent or abstain from further harm.

Over the years, the rationale of the German Criminal Code's recognition of withdrawal from an attempt has been much debated in German criminal law, resulting in a spectrum of theories, including:

- "rationale of punishment" theory: withdrawal renders punishment unnecessary for specific or general deterrence purposes :

  > The actor who freely abandons an attempt indicates that his criminal will was not as strong as would have been required for commission of the offense. His dangerousness, which initially manifests itself in the attempt, in retrospect reveals itself as significantly lesser. For this reason the law abstains from punishing "the attempt as such." For a punishment appears unnecessary to prevent the actor from criminal acts in the future, to deter others, or to reinstate the disturbed legal order.
  >
  > German Federal Court of Justice, BGHSt 9, 48, 52 (1956).

- golden bridge theory (since v. Liszt): punishment exemption gives offender an incentive to abandon the attempt by "building him a golden bridge," thus allowing him to "return to legality";
- element-negating and justification theories: withdrawal negates liability by negating the requisite intent (v. Hippel) or functioning as a justification (Binding); largely abandoned, because it would extend to accomplices and because "an attempt remains an attempt" and cannot be undone.

In the U.S., the renunciation (abandonment, withdrawal) defense itself, rather than merely its rationale, remains controversial. Some jurisdictions (including California) reject the defense altogether:

> [T]he character of the abandonment..., whether it be voluntary (prompted by pangs of conscience or a change of heart) or nonvoluntary (established by inference in the instant case), is not controlling. The relevant factor is the determination of whether the acts of the perpetrator have reached such a stage of advancement that they can be classified as an attempt. Once that attempt is found there can be no exculpatory abandonment. "One of the purposes of the criminal law is to protect society from those who intend to injure it. When it is established that the defendant intended to commit a specific crime and that in carrying out this intention he

---

* See Model Penal Code Commentaries § 5.01, at 359.

committed an act that caused harm or sufficient danger of harm, it is immaterial that for some collateral reason he could not complete the intended crime.

People v. Staples, 6 Cal. App. 3d 61 (1970).

Other jurisdictions recognize it in the criminal code (e.g., N.Y. Penal Law § 40.10) or in case law (e.g., *People v. Kimball*, 109 Mich. App. 273 (1981)).

Why would we recognize a defense of renunciation? Attempt is defined as an offense; if someone has engaged in conduct that matches the definition of this offense, he or she has committed the offense. Unless a justification or excuse is available, criminal liability has been established. Why should attempt (or any other inchoate offense) get special treatment? Can other offenses be undone? Can I escape criminal liability for theft if I return the goods I stole (assuming, of course, I had the requisite intent to keep them permanently)? If I, a trustee, return the money I borrowed from a trust fund fully intending to put it back in full, and perhaps even with interest, once I had put it to work for a purpose not authorized by the conditions of the trust? If I pay for the best treatment available anywhere in the world to straighten the nose I broke, perhaps even making it look better than before?

In jurisdictions that, like Germany, already mitigate the punishment for an attempt compared to the consummated offense, don't attempters already have an incentive not to consummate the offense? Why is the additional incentive necessary, or useful, given that the original incentive was ineffective (since renunciation doesn't come into play unless the offender has crossed the line between preparation and attempt)?

While the recognition of renunciation as a defense to liability is controversial, its relevance at sentencing is widely acknowledged (see, e.g., the following excerpts from the U.S. Sentencing Guidelines):*

§ 3E1.1. Acceptance of Responsibility

(a) If the defendant clearly demonstrates acceptance of responsibility for his offense, decrease the offense level by 2 levels . . .

[Official] Commentary:

1. In determining whether a defendant qualifies under subsection (a), appropriate considerations include, but are not limited to, the following:
   (a) truthfully admitting the conduct comprising the offense(s) of conviction . . . [A] defendant who falsely denies, or frivolously contests, relevant conduct that the court determines to be true has acted in a manner inconsistent with acceptance of responsibility;
   (b) voluntary termination or withdrawal from criminal conduct or associations;
   (c) voluntary payment of restitution prior to adjudication of guilt;
   (d) voluntary surrender to authorities promptly after commission of the offense;
   (e) voluntary assistance to authorities in the recovery of the fruits and instrumentalities of the offense;
   (f) voluntary resignation from the office or position held during the commission of the offense;
   (g) post offense rehabilitative efforts (e.g., counseling or drug treatment); and
   (h) the timeliness of the defendant's conduct in manifesting the acceptance of responsibility.

§ 5K2.16. Voluntary Disclosure of Offense (Policy Statement)

If the defendant voluntarily discloses to authorities the existence of, and accepts responsibility for, the offense prior to the discovery of such offense, and if such offense was unlikely to have been discovered otherwise, a departure below the applicable guideline range for that offense may be warranted. For example, a downward departure under this section might be considered where a defendant, motivated by remorse, discloses an offense that otherwise would have remained undiscovered. This provision does not apply where the motivating factor is the defendant's knowledge that discovery of the offense is likely or imminent, or where the defendant's disclosure occurs in connection with the investigation or prosecution of the defendant for related conduct.

---

* On the Guidelines, see Chapter 1.A.iii.

Under the rationales underlying renunciation as a *complete* defense or exemption from punishment, why would it not suffice to take it into account at the sentencing stage? Would its consideration at sentencing—rather than an all-or-nothing approach—allow for a more nuanced appreciation of the specific circumstances of the act and the offender?

2. Section 24 Criminal Code (as well as the text of § 5.01(4) Model Criminal Code) covers different circumstances of voluntary withdrawal. The main provision for single perpetrators in § 24 para. 1 sentence 1 Criminal Code describes two different scenarios; it applies to incomplete attempts (variation 1) and to complete attempts (variation 2). An attempt is complete if the offender believes (after the act which counts as an attempt) that he has already done everything necessary for the result to occur. If he believes that further action would be required, the attempt is incomplete (the standards are subjective—it does not matter whether the victim was in fact already fatally wounded but whether the offender thought this to be the case, see for the case law on this point for instance Federal Court of Justice, Judgment of November 12, 1987, 4 StR 541/87, BGHSt 35, 90).

In variation 2 (completed attempt), the offender must prevent the completion of the crime. This means that he has to do something *actively* which helps (in the case of attempted killing) the victim to survive. If he does so, for instance by calling an ambulance, he will be spared punishment for attempted killing. But variation 1 (applicable to incomplete attempts only) offers the reward of "no punishment" to offenders while requiring less from them: all they have to do is to remain *passive*. In such cases, no demonstration of "practical remorse," no act of helping the victim is necessary. It suffices that the offender chose voluntarily not to shoot again, stab again etc. although he could have done so.

The German case from 1988 shows how far this goes. The issue was whether the defendant withdrew from the attempted murder of M. when he left him alone lying wounded behind the hedge and returned to his ex-wife's car. The regional court had, when establishing the facts, left it open whether the defendant did this because "he thought that M. would not survive the serious wound inflicted on him anyway, or because he feared that he would 'miss' his ex-wife as a result of the lapse in time which had occurred." The decision of the German Federal Court of Justice to quash the conviction meant in effect that another chamber at the regional court had to reexamine the facts. If the defendant had thought that M. was already mortally wounded, the situation would have been one of completed attempt, and remaining passive after the first attacks could not spare him criminal punishment. However, the regional court believed it could leave open what the defendant actually thought—because the judges assumed that even if this had been an incomplete attempt, the withdrawal would not have been voluntary, leading to the same result: no exemption from punishment. (Does this case suggest that the formal distinction between withdrawal in complete and incomplete attempts can obscure the substantive inquiry into the issue of withdrawal?)

On this, the Federal Court of Justice disagreed. In its opinion, if the defendant *really* had thought that M. was not mortally wounded, and under this belief did not try to stab him again or otherwise "to finish him off," his withdrawal would qualify as voluntary. This means that a murderer who must for merely practical reasons (because he cannot be at two places at the same time) make a choice between either "finishing off" the first victim or killing the second victim, will be rewarded with "withdrawal from attempted murder" if he opts for killing the second victim. This outcome is morally objectionable if one assumes that norms like § 24 Criminal Code should be connected to some sign of goodwill on the offender's part. The cold-blooded, vicious preference for killing victim 2 does not seem to deserve a reward. But the controversial decision of the German Federal Court of Justice rejects such moral objections with the short reference to its "consistent case law" on the matter. At the end of the decision, it refers briefly to commentators that have called for an application of some "normative" standards to the inquiry into the voluntariness of a withdrawal. The Court argues that the wording of the statute requires a strictly "psychological" approach to the question of whether an actor's withdrawal from an attempt can be classified as "voluntary" or not.

Again, § 24 provides:

> Who voluntarily gives up the further execution of the crime or prevents its completion will not be punished for the attempt. If the crime remains uncompleted independent of further actions by the offender who abandoned his plan, he will not be punished if he has made voluntary and earnest efforts to prevent completion of the crime.

Do you agree that this wording demands a purely "psychological" rather than a "normative" inquiry into the question of voluntariness? Is it possible to cleanse the inquiry into voluntariness from all "normative" elements? Is it desirable? Are courts equipped to produce diagnoses of the precise "psychological" motivation underlying an apparent withdrawal, or are they better suited to make "normative" judgments? Or is this the sort of fine grained diagnosis courts engage in all the time, or at least any time they inquire into a defendant's mental state, or *mens rea*? Or is there a difference between diagnosing motive and intent?* Are "normative" and "moral" or "ethical" standards the same? In other words, is a "normative" approach to this issue inappropriate because it imports irrelevant "moral" or "ethical" considerations into a "legal" analysis? But isn't the question of withdrawal one that explicitly engages considerations of "mercy" or "reward" that otherwise are difficult to accommodate in an analysis of legal liability (as opposed to the imposition of punishment)? Consider the Court's approach—and the resolution of the particular issue—from the perspective of the various rationales proposed for the withdrawal defense in attempt in German criminal law and under the Model Penal Code. Does it make sense under any, all, none of them?

The Court acknowledges that withdrawal applies only when the actor "gives up the implementation of his criminal intention fully and finally." See also Model Penal Code § 5.01(4) (no withdrawal if "motivated by a decision to postpone the criminal conduct until a more advantageous time or to transfer the criminal effort to another but similar objective or victim"). The Court, however, limits the scope of this restriction to "the individual crime in the substantive law sense," meaning that it applies only to the postponement of a specific crime perpetrated against a specific victim. If the crime scenario involves two victims, as in the present case, the decision the offender can "withdraw" from the attempt against one victim in order to focus on the other victim instead. Again, consider this argument from the perspective of the various proposed rationales for the withdrawal doctrine in German and U.S. criminal law.

---

* On motive and *mens rea*, see Chapter 8.A.

13

JUSTIFICATIONS

A Note on Defenses. Before delving into a comparative analysis of the doctrinal niceties of various justifications and excuses, it is worth taking a quick look at the structural conceptualization of these defense types in American and German criminal law. We have already raised the much-pondered question of the substantive distinction between justification and excuse, assuming one should—or could—be drawn in the first place, not to mention whether there is even a need to carve out any space for a separate inquiry into defenses, given that the common law seemed to do just fine for centuries with just *actus reus* and *mens rea*.

For present purposes, let us assume that there is, or could be, a distinction between *actus reus* and *mens rea*, on one hand, and defenses, let's call them justifications and excuses, on the other, and that this distinction might actually do some analytic work, ever so often, at least if used carefully and as a means to an end, rather than an end in itself. In this light, the distinction between justification and excuse resembles that among different offense element types (conduct, attendant circumstance, result), which plays an important role in the Model Penal Code—most notably in the key provision on *mens rea*, which defines various mental states differently depending on which offense element type they accompany. Or as the Code drafters put it, "[w]hile these terms are not airtight categories, they have served as a helpful analytical device in the development of the Code."*

The first thing to note about defenses of justification and excuse is that they are, well, *defenses*. This conceptualization is not obvious; in fact, it can be seen as distinctive of a common law, procedure-centric, approach. As defenses, justifications, and excuses fit into a view of criminal law as moving from offense to defense, from prosecution to defense, from case-in-chief to defense. This view of the substantive criminal law is shaped by the criminal process, more specifically the adversarial criminal process, a constant give-and-take and back-and-forth between the parties under the (more or less) watchful eye of the judge, and in at least a few (if supposedly paradigmatic) cases, also of the jury.

Associated with this procedural view of substantive criminal law are important procedural questions that often drive the substantive debate.† For instance, the classification of an issue as offense- or defense-related, in the mind of a common lawyer, in the end raises questions about the assignment, and even the level, of the burden of proof. For the common lawyer, the operative distinction among defenses is that between an ordinary defense and an affirmative defense, not between a justification and an excuse. An ordinary defense, in particular an (offense) element-negating defense, in this sense is not a proper defense, and as a result is often cited in scare quotes, like so: "defense." An element-negating defense is not a defense properly speaking because it does not shift the burden of proof onto the defense. It is instead an offense element upside down, regarded from the perspective of the defense rather than of

---

* Commentaries § 5.01, at 301 n.9.
† This phenomenon is not limited to the law of defenses. Consider also the interplay between evidentiary and substantive approaches to *mens rea* and causation, see, e.g., Chapters 8 and 9 (negligence vs. recklessness, implied malice vs. malice, willful ignorance vs. knowledge, intending the consequences of one's action vs. intent or cause, rebuttable vs. irrebuttable presumptions).

the prosecution; it is simply an obstacle in the prosecution's path to carrying its burden of proving the elements of the offense (beyond a reasonable doubt).

Affirmative defenses are defenses properly speaking because in American law (not in German law) they shift all, or part, of the burden of proof onto the defense. They come in different varieties, some more burdensome for the defendant than others. Under the Model Penal Code, for instance, an affirmative defense only shifts the burden of production onto the defendant, i.e., the burden of producing some evidence supporting a defense if that evidence has not already entered the record as part of the prosecution's case-in-chief. Once this modicum of evidence has been introduced, the burden shifts back onto the prosecution to disprove the affirmative defense. Under the New York Penal Law, by contrast, affirmative defenses are affirmative all the way down: they place the burden of persuasion, not just the burden of production (evidentiary burden), on the defendant. Under the New York Penal Law, that burden is proof by a preponderance of the evidence; other codes have imposed higher burdens, including proof beyond a reasonable doubt.*

Where an issue is placed along the divide between offense and defense may even have constitutional significance. In *Patterson v. New York*, 432 U.S. 197 (1977), the U.S. Supreme Court limited the constitutional requirement of proof beyond a reasonable doubt to *offense* elements. At the same time, the legislature was free to shift the burden onto the defendant on any issue relating to a *defense*. (*Patterson* concerned the then-new defense of extreme emotional disturbance, which substantively broadened the traditional provocation defense in murder, but at the same time transformed it into an affirmative defense, thus adding a procedural hurdle.)

In Germany, by contrast, where the judge overseeing the "inquisitorial" process is charged with determining the truth and with collecting all the evidence necessary to that end, process takes a back seat to substance. The order of inquiry is not shaped by a procedural order, but by the analysis of the substantive issue at stake: who is criminally liable for what? There are prerequisites of criminal liability, and the process is designed to help the court determine whether they have been met. One prerequisite is criminality: does the defendant's behavior match the definition of an offense? Another is unlawfulness: was that formally criminal behavior also unlawful, generally speaking? And the remaining prerequisite is responsibility: is the defendant blameworthy for the formally criminal and unlawful behavior? Justification is not a defense; it is simply the absence of unlawfulness. Excuse is not a defense; it is the absence of responsibility (or culpability, guilt).

There are different ways of structuring these, procedure- and substance-driven, approaches to the analysis of criminal liability. The most obvious, and basic, structural distinction in the common law approach is that between offense and defense. There are occasionally hints of another line, based on the assignment of the burden of proof, which would fall between offense elements and justification, on one side, and excuse, on the other, insofar as often (though certainly not consistently) justifications are "ordinary" defenses and excuses "affirmative" ones. In the substance-based (German) approach, the basic distinction is less obviously that between offense elements, on one hand, and justifications and excuses, on the other. At least as likely a candidate is the distinction between offense and justification, on one side, and excuse, on the other. Offense and justification, one might suggest, are concerned with the analysis of acts, whereas excuse focuses on the actor. More specifically, offense and justification could both be seen as investigating the unlawfulness of the act, with the offense analysis establishing a strong presumption of unlawfulness rebuttable only in exceptional cases, namely those where a justification is available (establishing that the conduct is not unlawful after all, generally speaking). There are even those who regard justifications as silent negative offense elements—so that every offense definition includes, implicitly, the absence of justifications.

Now, before we turn to the various justifications and excuses in action, we should point out that we will encounter some doctrines that look and feel like defenses, but do not fit easily

---

* See, e.g., *Leland v. Oregon*, 343 U.S. 790 (1952) (insanity).

into the dichotomy of justification and excuse. People disagree about whether a given defense counts as a justification or as an excuse, whether this is because they have different conceptions of the defense in question or, more fundamentally, of the distinction between justification and excuse. Then there are those doctrines that seem to fit into neither category—they are *hors catégorie*, neither fish nor fowl. Technically speaking, they do not concern the assessment of criminal liability; they do not interfere with the conclusion that a criminal unlawful culpable act has been committed. Rather than with liability, they deal with punishability, with exceptional cases in which liability does not imply punishability.

Not surprisingly, given that German criminal law is considerably more concerned about the proper categorization of defenses as justification or excuse, it has also devoted more effort to identifying those doctrines that resist categorization.* They include so-called "personal exemptions" or "exceptions" from punishability (*persönliche Strafausschließungs-* or *Strafaufhebungsgründe*). It turns out, for instance, that a key doctrine like withdrawal from an attempt (§§ 24, 31 Criminal Code) falls in this category for "policy reasons"; so does, in the special part, obstruction of justice to benefit a relative (§ 258 para. 6), in this case to take account of conflicts that resemble—but don't quite rise to the level of—a necessity situation; or, retrospectively, "active repentance," as, for instance, through extinguishing a fire in cases of arson (§ 306e Criminal Code; see also §§ 314a, 320, 330b).

Finally, there are exceptional circumstances in which the court may refrain from imposing punishment altogether, or in part. For instance, we will encounter one case (the *Daschner Case* in Chapter 13.A) in which the court issues a warning with a suspended sentence (under § 59 Criminal Code); the court can also refrain from punishment in cases where the offender has already suffered enough as a result of the offense (§ 60 Criminal Code). The farther we travel down the road from liability, to punishability, to punishment, the more we shift from the law of crime (criminal law) to the law of punishment (sentencing law). In the United States, at least in federal law, similar sentencing considerations are addressed in the U.S. Sentencing Guidelines, excerpts from which are sprinkled throughout this book.

Justifications. It is one of the puzzles of modern criminal law theory, and—given its penchant for taxonomic sophistication and accuracy—of modern German criminal law theory in particular, that no widely accepted systematic account of justification defenses has emerged. There is a general sense of what distinguishes a justification from an excuse, that, as the Model Penal Code drafters put it, "[t]o say that someone's conduct is 'justified' ordinarily connotes that the conduct is thought to be right, or at least not undesirable," while "to say that someone's conduct is 'excused' ordinarily connotes that the conduct is thought to be undesirable but that for some reason the actor is not to be blamed for it."[†]

Within the category of justifications, however, there is little sense of how one justification relates to another. Instead, commentators often stress the great, and ever changing, variety of reasons for "thinking" facially criminally conduct "to be right," as many reasons as there are norms, so many, in fact, that the search for a comprehensive account of justifications is futile: "The considerations that can result in precluding the material unlawfulness of an act that fulfills the definition of an offense are so multifarious, and the number of justifications arising from all parts of the legal order is so great and—notably in the case of state interventions—dependent on so many changing needs, that uniform principles, which also have substantive significance, can always only have limited validity."[‡] Examples are said to include changes in "the criminal and civil legal order" and "police laws," even changes in "views regarding the right to discipline, compulsory vaccination, the private sphere or the right to demonstrate." (Note that, under this conception, justificatory norms are not limited to those set out in the criminal code; recall, in this context, the question of the recognition of non-statutory, "common law," duties in omission liability, and of the distinction between criminal and civil negligence, discussed in Chapters 7 and 8, respectively.)

---

* For a comprehensive analysis of defenses in American criminal law, see Paul H. Robinson, *Criminal Law Defenses: A Systematic Analysis* (1982).
† Model Penal Code Commentaries art. 3, introduction, at 2–3.
‡ Claus Roxin, *Strafrecht: Allgemeiner Teil* (4th edn. 2006), vol. 1, 615.

Undeterred by the prospect of futility, the German criminal law literature nonetheless has produced some candidates for a general principle of justification. Chief among these are what one might call "balance theories," according to which conduct justified insofar as its benefit in a particular case outweighs its detriment—where the relevant balance is measured in any number of ways, including, for instance, social interests, institutions, or relationships, legal interests or goods, or values. These accounts are likely to assign pride of place to the necessity defense, which is explicitly framed as a balance of conflicting "interests" (in § 34 Criminal Code) or "harms or evils" (in Model Penal Code § 3.02).* In fact, the Model Penal Code drafters considered the defense of necessity the justification *par excellence*, defining it at the beginning of the Code's article on general principles of justification under the heading "Justification Generally: Choice of Evils."

Balance theories of justification, however, are often said to face the difficulty of integrating the justification of *consent*. Some theorists, then, have proposed supplementing the balance principle with another principle, according to which some acts—namely consented-to ones—are justified because they do not involve the violation of an interest in the first place. These theories have the disadvantage of not in fact producing one principle of justifications, but two. (Why cannot cases of consent simply be treated as specific—extremely lopsided—instances of interest balancing?)

Of course, one might also take the opposite tack, and regard *consent* as the paradigmatic justification, and necessity as the outlier. A consent-based account presumably would rely on the often-cited fundamental importance of autonomy in the criminal law, if not in the legal order of a state under the rule of law as a whole. A consent-centered account might even invoke the fact that necessity is a newcomer on the justification scene, having been recognized as a justification (as opposed to as an excuse) in the German Criminal Code only in 1975 (in the Model Penal Code in 1962), not to mention that some continue to reject the very notion of necessity as a justification.† It would be odd if the system of justifications were to rest on an only recently and incompletely acknowledged defense.

Does the order of appearance of justifications in a Code's general part imply a hierarchy? Does firstness imply firstness, as it may in the special part of criminal law,‡ and as it does in American constitutional law, where the "firstness of the First Amendment" has been a common refrain?§ Here it is interesting to note that, while the Model Penal Code treats necessity first, explicitly assigning it paradigmatic status, followed by Execution of Public Duty, and then self-defense (followed by Law Enforcement and a grab bag of defenses under the tellingly diffuse heading "Use of Force by Persons with Special Responsibility for Care, Discipline or Safety of Others") the German Criminal Code treats self-defense before necessity (and no other justifications). In fact, recall that the German Criminal Code did not contain a provision on justifying necessity for the first century of its existence (1871–1975),¶ nor did the Prussian Criminal Code of 1851, upon which it is based, contain any provision we would now recognize as a justification other than self-defense.** Historically speaking, then, the justification of self-defense in German criminal law clearly can claim priority over the justification of necessity. One would therefore think that a comprehensive account of justifications, at least in German criminal law, might build on self-defense (rather than necessity, or consent). This has not been the case, however. It turns out, in fact, that the conception of self-defense in German criminal law is itself contested, or at least complex, with different accounts competing for attention, reflecting the broad characterization of the defense as, literally, emergency defense (*Notwehr*) rather than self-defense, which leaves room for an account of the defense that posits law, or right, as the object of protection, rather than the person.

---

* See Chapter 13.B.
† See *R. v. Perka*, Chapter 13.B.
‡ See Part III.
§ See Edmond Cahn, "The Firstness of the First Amendment," 65 *Yale Law Journal* (1956), 464.
¶ See RStGB §§ 53–54.
** See PrStGB § 41.

A. Self-Defense and Defense of Another (*Notwehr*)

We begin our discussion of justifications with self-defense because self-defense is the first justification to appear in the German Criminal Code, and is treated first in German criminal law textbooks; this was also the practice of American textbooks and casebooks, at least until the Model Penal Code first codified necessity, placing it at the beginning of its article on "general principles of justification." (The subject of the relationship between self-defense and necessity will arise in both this section, and the following one, on necessity.)

Self-defense is a popular, and a rewarding, topic for comparative analysis, at various levels of detail. The broad German conception of self-defense, or rather of *Notwehr* (emergency defense), as at least partly, if not primarily, a defense of the legal order differs from the standard Anglo-American conception of the defense in individual terms, as a defense of self. This difference at the level of conceptualization—reflected in the oft-repeated German legal maxim that "right need not make way for wrong"—also has noteworthy implications at the doctrinal level, for instance, in the traditional, though now somewhat less categorical, rejection of a duty to retreat in German criminal law, along with a general requirement of proportionality. Then there is of course "putative self-defense," an old chestnut of comparative criminal law, that will allow us to take a comparative glance at the Anglo-American and German treatment of mistakes regarding the presence of the prerequisites for self-defense, and mistakes regarding defense elements in general (including another comparative look at the concept of reasonableness*). Another important, though somewhat less heavily canvassed, subject that first arises in the present section is the doctrinal significance of battered-woman's syndrome in cases where a victim of domestic abuse is charged with the homicide of the abuser. (We will return to this question later on, in Chapters 13.B (necessity) and 15.A.iii (provocation).)

Last, but not least, the section on self-defense includes some of the more controversial, and notorious, cases in the recent history of Anglo-American and German criminal law: *People v. Goetz* and *Daschner*.

People v. Goetz
Court of Appeals of New York
68 N.Y.2d 96, 497 N.E.2d 41 (1986)

Chief Judge Wachtler

A Grand Jury has indicted defendant on attempted murder, assault, and other charges for having shot and wounded four youths on a New York City subway train after one or two of the youths approached him and asked for $5. The lower courts, concluding that the prosecutor's charge to the Grand Jury on the defense of justification was erroneous, have dismissed the attempted murder, assault and weapons possession charges. We now reverse and reinstate all counts of the indictment.

The precise circumstances of the incident giving rise to the charges against defendant are disputed, and ultimately it will be for a trial jury to determine what occurred. We feel it necessary, however, to provide some factual background to properly frame the legal issues before us. Accordingly, we have summarized the facts as they appear from the evidence before the Grand Jury. We stress, however, that we do not purport to reach any conclusions or holding as to exactly what transpired or whether defendant is blameworthy. The credibility of witnesses and the reasonableness of defendant's conduct are to be resolved by the trial jury.

On Saturday afternoon, December 22, 1984, Troy Canty, Darryl Cabey, James Ramseur, and Barry Allen boarded an IRT express subway train in The Bronx and headed south toward lower Manhattan. The four youths rode together in the rear portion of the seventh car of the train. Two of the four, Ramseur and Cabey, had screwdrivers inside their coats, which they said were to be used to break into the coin boxes of video machines.

---

* See also Chapter 8.C.

Defendant Bernhard Goetz boarded this subway train at 14th Street in Manhattan and sat down on a bench towards the rear section of the same car occupied by the four youths. Goetz was carrying an unlicensed .38 caliber pistol loaded with five rounds of ammunition in a waistband holster....

It appears from the evidence before the Grand Jury that Canty approached Goetz, possibly with Allen beside him, and stated "give me five dollars." Neither Canty nor any of the other youths displayed a weapon. Goetz responded by standing up, pulling out his handgun and firing four shots in rapid succession. The first shot hit Canty in the chest; the second struck Allen in the back; the third went through Ramseur's arm and into his left side; the fourth was fired at Cabey, who apparently was then standing in the corner of the car, but missed, deflecting instead off of a wall of the conductor's cab. After Goetz briefly surveyed the scene around him, he fired another shot at Cabey, who then was sitting on the end bench of the car. The bullet entered the rear of Cabey's side and severed his spinal cord...

On December 31, 1984, Goetz surrendered to police in Concord, New Hampshire, identifying himself as the gunman being sought for the subway shootings in New York nine days earlier. Later that day, after receiving Miranda warnings, he made two lengthy statements, both of which were tape recorded with his permission. In the statements, which are substantially similar, Goetz admitted that he had been illegally carrying a handgun in New York City for three years. He stated that he had first purchased a gun in 1981 after he had been injured in a mugging. Goetz also revealed that twice between 1981 and 1984 he had successfully warded off assailants simply by displaying the pistol.

According to Goetz's statement, the first contact he had with the four youths came when Canty, sitting or lying on the bench across from him, asked "how are you," to which he replied "fine." Shortly thereafter, Canty, followed by one of the other youths, walked over to the defendant and stood to his left, while the other two youths remained to his right, in the corner of the subway car. Canty then said "give me five dollars." Goetz stated that he knew from the smile on Canty's face that they wanted to "play with me." Although he was certain that none of the youths had a gun, he had a fear, based on prior experiences, of being "maimed."

Goetz then established "a pattern of fire," deciding specifically to fire from left to right. His stated intention at that point was to "murder [the four youths], to hurt them, to make them suffer as much as possible." When Canty again requested money, Goetz stood up, drew his weapon, and began firing, aiming for the center of the body of each of the four. Goetz recalled that the first two he shot "tried to run through the crowd [but] they had nowhere to run." Goetz then turned to his right to "go after the other two." One of these two "tried to run through the wall of the train, but...he had nowhere to go." The other youth (Cabey) "tried pretending that he wasn't with [the others]" by standing still, holding on to one of the subway hand straps, and not looking at Goetz. Goetz nonetheless fired his fourth shot at him. He then ran back to the first two youths to make sure they had been "taken care of." Seeing that they had both been shot, he spun back to check on the latter two. Goetz noticed that the youth who had been standing still was now sitting on a bench and seemed unhurt. As Goetz told the police, "I said '[y]ou seem to be all right, here's another,'" and he then fired the shot which severed Cabey's spinal cord. Goetz added that "if I was a little more under self-control...I would have put the barrel against his forehead and fired." He also admitted that "if I had had more [bullets], I would have shot them again, and again, and again."

After waiving extradition, Goetz was brought back to New York and arraigned on a felony complaint charging him with attempted murder and criminal possession of a weapon. The matter was presented to a Grand Jury in January 1985, with the prosecutor seeking an indictment for attempted murder, assault, reckless endangerment, and criminal possession of a weapon...On January 25, 1985, the Grand Jury indicted defendant on one count of criminal possession of a weapon in the third degree (Penal Law § 265.02), for possessing the gun used in the subway shootings, and two counts of criminal possession of a weapon in the fourth degree (Penal Law § 265.01), for possessing two other guns in his apartment building. It dismissed, however, the attempted murder and other charges stemming from the shootings themselves.

Several weeks after the Grand Jury's action, the People, asserting that they had newly available evidence, moved for an order authorizing them to resubmit the dismissed charges to a second Grand Jury. Supreme Court, Criminal Term, after conducting an in camera inquiry, granted the motion. Presentation of the case to the second Grand Jury began on March 14, 1985...

On March 27, 1985, the second Grand Jury filed a 10-count indictment, containing four charges of attempted murder (Penal Law §§ 110.00, 125.25 [1]), four charges of assault in the first degree (Penal Law § 120.10[1]), one charge of reckless endangerment in the first degree (Penal Law § 120.25), and one charge of criminal possession of a weapon in the second degree (Penal Law § 265.03 [possession of loaded firearm with intent to use it unlawfully against another]). Goetz was arraigned on this indictment on March 28, 1985, and it was consolidated with the earlier three-count indictment.

On October 14, 1985, Goetz moved to dismiss the charges contained in the second indictment alleging . . . that the prosecutor's instructions to that Grand Jury on the defense of justification were erroneous and prejudicial to the defendant so as to render its proceedings defective . . .

In an order dated January 21, 1986, Criminal Term granted Goetz's motion to the extent that it dismissed all counts of the second indictment, other than the reckless endangerment charge . . . The court . . . held . . . that the prosecutor, in a supplemental charge elaborating upon the justification defense, had erroneously introduced an objective element into this defense by instructing the grand jurors to consider whether Goetz's conduct was that of a "reasonable man in [Goetz's] situation." The court . . . concluded that the statutory test for whether the use of deadly force is justified to protect a person should be wholly subjective, focusing entirely on the defendant's state of mind when he used such force.[2] . . .

Penal Law article 35 recognizes the defense of justification, which "permits the use of force under certain circumstances." One such set of circumstances pertains to the use of force in defense of a person, encompassing both self-defense and defense of a third person (Penal Law § 35.15). Penal Law § 35.15(1) sets forth the general principles governing all such uses of force: "[a] person may . . . use physical force upon another person when and to the extent he reasonably believes such to be necessary to defend himself or a third person from what he *reasonably believes* to be the use or imminent use of unlawful physical force by such other person" (emphasis added).

Section 35.15(2) sets forth further limitations on these general principles with respect to the use of "deadly physical force": "A person may not use deadly physical force upon another person under circumstances specified in subdivision one unless (a) He *reasonably believes* that such other person is using or about to use deadly physical force . . . or (b) He *reasonably believes* that such other person is committing or attempting to commit a kidnapping, forcible rape, forcible sodomy or robbery" (emphasis added).

Thus, consistent with most justification provisions, Penal Law § 35.15 permits the use of deadly physical force only where requirements as to triggering conditions and the necessity of a particular response are met. As to the triggering conditions, the statute requires that the actor "reasonably believes" that another person either is using or about to use deadly physical force or is committing or attempting to commit one of certain enumerated felonies, including robbery. As to the need for the use of deadly physical force as a response, the statute requires that the actor "reasonably believes" that such force is necessary to avert the perceived threat.

Because the evidence before the second Grand Jury included statements by Goetz that he acted to protect himself from being maimed or to avert a robbery, the prosecutor correctly chose to charge the justification defense in section 35.15 to the Grand Jury. . . . When the prosecutor had completed his charge, one of the grand jurors asked for clarification of the term "reasonably believes." The prosecutor responded by instructing the grand jurors that they were to consider the circumstances of the incident and determine "whether the defendant's conduct was that of a reasonable man in the defendant's situation." It is this response by the prosecutor—and specifically his use of "a reasonable man"—which is the basis for the dismissal of the charges by the lower courts.

As expressed repeatedly in the Appellate Division's plurality opinion, because section 35.15 uses the term "he reasonably believes," the appropriate test, according to that court, is whether a defendant's beliefs and reactions were "reasonable to him." Under that reading of the statute, a jury which believed a defendant's testimony that he felt that his own actions were warranted and were reasonable would have to acquit him, regardless of what anyone else in defendant's situation might have concluded. Such an interpretation defies the ordinary meaning and significance of the term "reasonably" in a statute, and misconstrues the clear intent of the Legislature, in enacting section 35.15, to retain an objective element as part of any provision authorizing the use of deadly physical force.

Penal statutes in New York have long codified the right recognized at common law to use deadly physical force, under appropriate circumstances, in self-defense. These provisions have never required that an actor's belief as to the intention of another person to inflict serious injury be correct in order for the use of deadly force to be justified, but they have uniformly required that the belief comport with an objective notion of reasonableness . . .

In 1961 the Legislature established a Commission to undertake a complete revision of the Penal Law and the Criminal Code. The impetus for the decision to update the Penal Law came in part from the drafting of the Model Penal Code by the American Law Institute, as well as from the fact that the

---

[2] The court did not dismiss the reckless endangerment charge because, relying on the Appellate Division decision in *People v. McManus*, 108 A.D.2d 474, 489 N.Y.S.2d 561, it held that justification was not a defense to a crime containing, as an element, "depraved indifference to human life." As our reversal of the Appellate Division in *McManus* holds, justification is a defense to such a crime. Accordingly, had the prosecutor's instructions on justification actually rendered the Grand Jury proceedings defective, dismissal of the reckless endangerment count would have been required as well.

existing law was poorly organized and in many aspects antiquated. Following the submission by the Commission of several reports and proposals, the Legislature approved the present Penal Law in 1965 and it became effective on September 1, 1967. The drafting of the general provisions of the new Penal Law, including the article on justification, was particularly influenced by the Model Penal Code. While using the Model Penal Code provisions on justification as general guidelines, however, the drafters of the new Penal Law did not simply adopt them verbatim.

The provisions of the Model Penal Code with respect to the use of deadly force in self-defense reflect the position of its drafters that any culpability which arises from a mistaken belief in the need to use such force should be no greater than the culpability such a mistake would give rise to if it were made with respect to an element of a crime. Accordingly, under Model Penal Code § 3.04(2)(b), a defendant charged with murder (or attempted murder) need only show that he "*believe[d]* that [the use of deadly force] was necessary to protect himself against death, serious bodily injury, kidnapping or [forcible] sexual intercourse" to prevail on a self-defense claim (emphasis added). If the defendant's belief was wrong, and was recklessly, or negligently formed, however, he may be convicted of the type of homicide charge requiring only a reckless or negligent, as the case may be, criminal intent (see, Model Penal Code § 3.09[2]).

The drafters of the Model Penal Code recognized that the wholly subjective test set forth in section 3.04 differed from the existing law in most States by its omission of any requirement of reasonableness. The drafters were also keenly aware that requiring that the actor have a "reasonable belief" rather than just a "belief" would alter the wholly subjective test ...

New York did not follow the Model Penal Code's equation of a mistake as to the need to use deadly force with a mistake negating an element of a crime, choosing instead to use a single statutory section which would provide either a complete defense or no defense at all to a defendant charged with any crime involving the use of deadly force. The drafters of the new Penal Law adopted in large part the structure and content of Model Penal Code § 3.04, but, crucially, inserted the word "reasonably" before "believes" ...

We cannot lightly impute to the Legislature an intent to fundamentally alter the principles of justification to allow the perpetrator of a serious crime to go free simply because that person believed his actions were reasonable and necessary to prevent some perceived harm. To completely exonerate such an individual, no matter how aberrational or bizarre his thought patterns, would allow citizens to set their own standards for the permissible use of force. It would also allow a legally competent defendant suffering from delusions to kill or perform acts of violence with impunity, contrary to fundamental principles of justice and criminal law.

We can only conclude that the Legislature retained a reasonableness requirement to avoid giving a license for such actions ... [T]he drafters of section 35.15 were proposing a single section which, for the first time, would govern both the use of ordinary force and deadly force in self-defense or defense of another. Under the 1909 Penal Law and its predecessors, the use of ordinary force was governed by separate sections which, at least by their literal terms, required that the defendant was in fact responding to an unlawful assault, and not just that he had a reasonable ground for believing that such an assault was occurring. Following the example of the Model Penal Code, the drafters of section 35.15 eliminated this sharp dichotomy between the use of ordinary force and deadly force in defense of a person. Not surprisingly then, the integrated section reflects the wording of Model Penal Code § 3.04, with the addition of "reasonably" to incorporate the long-standing requirement of "reasonable ground" for the use of deadly force and apply it to the use of ordinary force as well ...

Statutes or rules of law requiring a person to act "reasonably" or to have a "reasonable belief" uniformly prescribe conduct meeting an objective standard measured with reference to how "a reasonable person" could have acted ...

Goetz ... argues that the introduction of an objective element will preclude a jury from considering factors such as the prior experiences of a given actor and thus, require it to make a determination of "reasonableness" without regard to the actual circumstances of a particular incident. This argument, however, falsely presupposes that an objective standard means that the background and other relevant characteristics of a particular actor must be ignored. To the contrary, we have frequently noted that a determination of reasonableness must be based on the "circumstances" facing a defendant or his "situation." Such terms encompass more than the physical movements of the potential assailant. [T]hese terms include any relevant knowledge the defendant had about that person. They also necessarily bring in the physical attributes of all persons involved, including the defendant. Furthermore, the defendant's circumstances encompass any prior experiences he had which could provide a reasonable basis for a belief that another person's intentions were to injure or rob him or that the use of deadly force was necessary under the circumstances.

Accordingly, a jury should be instructed to consider this type of evidence in weighing the defendant's actions. The jury must first determine whether the defendant had the requisite beliefs under section 35.15, that is, whether he believed deadly force was necessary to avert the imminent use of deadly force or the commission of one of the felonies enumerated therein. If the People do not prove beyond a reasonable doubt that he did not have such beliefs, then the jury must also consider whether these beliefs were reasonable. The jury would have to determine, in light of all the "circumstances," as explicated above, if a reasonable person could have had these beliefs . . .

Order reversed.

State v. Kelly
Supreme Court of New Jersey
97 N.J. 178, 478 A.2d 364 (1984)

Wilentz, C.J.

On May 24, 1980, defendant, Gladys Kelly, stabbed her husband, Ernest, with a pair of scissors. He died shortly thereafter at a nearby hospital. The couple had been married for seven years, during which time Ernest had periodically attacked Gladys. According to Ms. Kelly, he assaulted her that afternoon, and she stabbed him in self-defense, fearing that he would kill her if she did not act.

Ms. Kelly was indicted for murder. At trial, she did not deny stabbing her husband, but asserted that her action was in self-defense. To establish the requisite state of mind for her self-defense claim, Ms. Kelly called Dr. Lois Veronen as an expert witness to testify about the battered-woman's syndrome. After hearing a lengthy voir dire examination of Dr. Veronen, the trial court ruled that expert testimony concerning the syndrome was inadmissible on the self-defense issue . . .

Ms. Kelly was convicted of reckless manslaughter. . . . [T]he Appellate Division affirmed the conviction. We granted certification, 91 N.J. 539, 453 A.2d 859 (1983), and now reverse.

Defendant raises [several] issues on appeal[, including] that the trial court erred in excluding expert testimony on the battered-woman's syndrome . . .

The Kellys had a stormy marriage. Some of the details of their relationship, especially the stabbing, are disputed. The following is Ms. Kelly's version of what happened . . .

The day after the marriage, Mr. Kelly got drunk and knocked Ms. Kelly down. Although a period of calm followed the initial attack, the next seven years were accompanied by periodic and frequent beatings, sometimes as often as once a week. During the attacks, which generally occurred when Mr. Kelly was drunk, he threatened to kill Ms. Kelly and to cut off parts of her body if she tried to leave him. Mr. Kelly often moved out of the house after an attack, later returning with a promise that he would change his ways . . .

[The day of the stabbing, Ms. Kelly went to a friend's house] with her daughter, Annette, to ask Ernest for money to buy food. He told her to wait until they got home, and shortly thereafter the Kellys left. After walking past several houses, Mr. Kelly, who was drunk, angrily asked "What the hell did you come around here for?" He then grabbed the collar of her dress, and the two fell to the ground. He choked her by pushing his fingers against her throat, punched or hit her face, and bit her leg.

A crowd gathered on the street. Two men from the crowd separated them, just as Gladys felt that she was "passing out" from being choked. Fearing that Annette had been pushed around in the crowd, Gladys then left to look for her. Upon finding Annette, defendant noticed that Annette had defendant's pocketbook. Gladys had dropped it during the fight. Annette had retrieved it and gave her mother the pocketbook.

After finding her daughter, Ms. Kelly then observed Mr. Kelly running toward her with his hands raised. Within seconds he was right next to her. Unsure of whether he had armed himself while she was looking for their daughter, and thinking that he had come back to kill her, she grabbed a pair of scissors from her pocketbook. She tried to scare him away, but instead stabbed him . . .

In the past decade social scientists and the legal community began to examine the forces that generate and perpetuate wife beating and violence in the family. What has been revealed is that the problem affects many more people than had been thought and that the victims of the violence are not only the battered family members (almost always either the wife or the children). There are also many other strangers to the family who feel the devastating impact, often in the form of violence, of the psychological damage suffered by the victims.

Due to the high incidence of unreported abuse (the FBI and other law enforcement experts believe that wife abuse is the most unreported crime in the United States), estimates vary of the number of American women who are beaten regularly by their husband, boyfriend, or the dominant male figure in their lives. One recent estimate puts the number of women beaten yearly at over one million. See California Advisory Comm'n on Family Law, Domestic Violence app. F at 119 (1st report 1978). The state police statistics show more than 18,000 reported cases of domestic violence in New Jersey during the first nine months of 1983, in 83% of which the victim was female. It is clear that the American home, once assumed to be the cornerstone of our society, is often a violent place.

While common law notions that assigned an inferior status to women, and to wives in particular, no longer represent the state of the law as reflected in statutes and cases, many commentators assert that a bias against battered women still exists, institutionalized in the attitudes of law enforcement agencies unwilling to pursue or uninterested in pursuing wife beating cases.

Another problem is the currency enjoyed by stereotypes and myths concerning the characteristics of battered women and their reasons for staying in battering relationships. Some popular misconceptions about battered women include the beliefs that they are masochistic and actually enjoy their beatings, that they purposely provoke their husbands into violent behavior, and, most critically, as we shall soon see, that women who remain in battering relationships are free to leave their abusers at any time.

As these cases so tragically suggest, not only do many women suffer physical abuse at the hands of their mates, but a significant number of women kill (or are killed by) their husbands. In 1978, murders between husband and wife or girlfriend and boyfriend constituted 13% of all murders committed in the United States. Undoubtedly some of these arose from battering incidents. Federal Bureau of Investigation, Crime in the United States 1978 (1978). Men were the victims in 48% of these killings. Id.

As the problem of battered women has begun to receive more attention, sociologists and psychologists have begun to focus on the effects a sustained pattern of physical and psychological abuse can have on a woman. The effects of such abuse are what some scientific observers have termed "the battered-woman's syndrome," a series of common characteristics that appear in women who are abused physically and psychologically over an extended period of time by the dominant male figure in their lives. Dr. Lenore Walker, a prominent writer on the battered-woman's syndrome, defines the battered woman as one who is repeatedly subjected to any forceful physical or psychological behavior by a man in order to coerce her to do something he wants her to do without concern for her rights. Battered women include wives or women in any form of intimate relationships with men. Furthermore, in order to be classified as a battered woman, the couple must go through the battering cycle at least twice. Any woman may find herself in an abusive relationship with a man once. If it occurs a second time, and she remains in the situation, she is defined as a battered woman.

According to Dr. Walker, relationships characterized by physical abuse tend to develop battering cycles. Violent behavior directed at the woman occurs in three distinct and repetitive stages that vary both in duration and intensity depending on the individuals involved.

Phase one of the battering cycle is referred to as the "tension-building stage," during which the battering male engages in minor battering incidents and verbal abuse while the woman, beset by fear and tension, attempts to be as placating and passive as possible in order to stave off more serious violence.

Phase two of the battering cycle is the "acute battering incident." At some point during phase one, the tension between the battered woman and the batterer becomes intolerable and more serious violence inevitable. The triggering event that initiates phase two is most often an internal or external event in the life of the battering male, but provocation for more severe violence is sometimes provided by the woman who can no longer tolerate or control her phase-one anger and anxiety.

Phase three of the battering cycle is characterized by extreme contrition and loving behavior on the part of the battering male. During this period the man will often mix his pleas for forgiveness and protestations of devotion with promises to seek professional help, to stop drinking, and to refrain from further violence. For some couples, this period of relative calm may last as long as several months, but in a battering relationship the affection and contrition of the man will eventually fade and phase one of the cycle will start anew.

The cyclical nature of battering behavior helps explain why more women simply do not leave their abusers. The loving behavior demonstrated by the batterer during phase three reinforces whatever hopes these women might have for their mate's reform and keeps them bound to the relationship.

Some women may even perceive the battering cycle as normal, especially if they grew up in a violent household. Or they may simply not wish to acknowledge the reality of their situation. T. Davidson, Conjugal Crime, at 50 (1978) ("The middle-class battered wife's response to her situation tends to be withdrawal, silence and denial . . . ").

Other women, however, become so demoralized and degraded by the fact that they cannot predict or control the violence that they sink into a state of psychological paralysis and become unable to take any action at all to improve or alter the situation. There is a tendency in battered women to believe in the omnipotence or strength of their battering husbands and thus to feel that any attempt to resist them is hopeless.

In addition to these psychological impacts, external social and economic factors often make it difficult for some women to extricate themselves from battering relationships. A woman without independent financial resources who wishes to leave her husband often finds it difficult to do so because of a lack of material and social resources.

Even with the progress of the last decade, women typically make less money and hold less prestigious jobs than men, and are more responsible for child care. Thus, in a violent confrontation where the first reaction might be to flee, women realize soon that there may be no place to go. Moreover, the stigma that attaches to a woman who leaves the family unit without her children undoubtedly acts as a further deterrent to moving out.

In addition, battered women, when they want to leave the relationship, are typically unwilling to reach out and confide in their friends, family, or the police, either out of shame and humiliation, fear of reprisal by their husband, or the feeling they will not be believed.

Dr. Walker and other commentators have identified several common personality traits of the battered woman: low self-esteem, traditional beliefs about the home, the family, and the female sex role, tremendous feelings of guilt that their marriages are failing, and the tendency to accept responsibility for the batterer's actions.

Finally, battered women are often hesitant to leave a battering relationship because, in addition to their hope of reform on the part of their spouse, they harbor a deep concern about the possible response leaving might provoke in their mates. They literally become trapped by their own fear. Case histories are replete with instances in which a battered wife left her husband only to have him pursue her and subject her to an even more brutal attack.

The combination of all these symptoms—resulting from sustained psychological and physical trauma compounded by aggravating social and economic factors—constitutes the battered-woman's syndrome. Only by understanding these unique pressures that force battered women to remain with their mates, despite their long-standing and reasonable fear of severe bodily harm and the isolation that being a battered woman creates, can a battered woman's state of mind be accurately and fairly understood.

The voir dire testimony of Dr. Veronen, sought to be introduced by defendant Gladys Kelly, conformed essentially to this outline of the battered-woman's syndrome . . .

Dr. Veronen described the various psychological tests and examinations she had performed in connection with her independent research. These tests and their methodology, including their interpretation, are, according to Dr. Veronen, widely accepted by clinical psychologists. Applying this methodology to defendant (who was subjected to all of the tests, including a five-hour interview), Dr. Veronen concluded that defendant was a battered woman and subject to the battered-woman's syndrome.

In addition, Dr. Veronen was prepared to testify as to how, as a battered woman, Gladys Kelly perceived her situation at the time of the stabbing, and why, in her opinion, defendant did not leave her husband despite the constant beatings she endured.

Whether expert testimony on the battered-woman's syndrome should be admitted in this case depends on whether it is relevant to defendant's claim of self- defense, and, in any event, on whether the proffer meets the standards for admission of expert testimony in this state. We examine first the law of self- defense and consider whether the expert testimony is relevant.

. . . The use of force against another in self-defense is justifiable "when the actor reasonably believes that such force is immediately necessary for the purpose of protecting himself against the use of unlawful force by such other person on the present occasion." N.J. Stat. Ann. § 2C:3-4(a). Further limitations exist when deadly force is used in self-defense. The use of such deadly force is not justifiable unless the actor reasonably believes that such force is necessary to protect himself against death or serious bodily harm . . . [N.J. Stat. Ann. § 2C:3–4(b)(2)].

Self-defense exonerates a person who kills in the reasonable belief that such action was necessary to prevent his or her death or serious injury, even though this belief was later proven mistaken. "Detached reflection cannot be demanded in the presence of an uplifted knife," Justice Holmes aptly said, *Brown v. United States*, 256 U.S. 335, 343, 41 S.Ct. 501, 502, 65 L.Ed. 961, 963 (1921); and the law accordingly requires only a reasonable, not necessarily a correct, judgment.

While it is not imperative that actual necessity exist, a valid plea of self-defense will not lie absent an actual (that is, honest) belief on the part of the defendant in the necessity of using force. While no case in New Jersey has addressed the point directly, the privilege of self-defense does not exist where the defendant's action is not prompted by a belief in its necessity: "He has no defense when he intentionally kills his enemy in complete ignorance of the fact that his enemy, when killed, was about to launch a deadly attack upon him." W. LaFave & A. Scott, Criminal Law § 53, at 394 (1972).[7] . . .

Honesty alone, however, does not suffice. A defendant claiming the privilege of self-defense must also establish that her belief in the necessity to use force was reasonable. As originally proposed, the

---

[7] See also Restatement of Torts 2d § 63 (1965) at 101. Under principles of self-defense as a justification for the torts of assault and battery—which closely parallel criminal self-defense principles—no privilege of self-defense exists for one acting in ignorance of another's intent to inflict harm on him.

new Code of Criminal Justice would have eliminated the reasonableness requirement, allowing self-defense whenever the defendant honestly believed in the imminent need to act. This proposed change in the law was not accepted by the Legislature. N.J. Stat. Ann. § 2C:3–4 as finally enacted retains the requirement that the defendant's belief be reasonable.[8]

Gladys Kelly claims that she stabbed her husband in self-defense, believing he was about to kill her. The gist of the State's case was that Gladys Kelly was the aggressor, that she consciously intended to kill her husband, and that she certainly was not acting in self-defense.

The credibility of Gladys Kelly is a critical issue in this case. If the jury does not believe Gladys Kelly's account, it cannot find she acted in self-defense. The expert testimony offered was directly relevant to one of the critical elements of that account, namely, what Gladys Kelly believed at the time of the stabbing, and was thus material to establish the honesty of her stated belief that she was in imminent danger of death.[10] . . .

. . . Dr. Veronen would have bolstered Gladys Kelly's credibility. Specifically, by showing that her experience, although concededly difficult to comprehend, was common to that of other women who had been in similarly abusive relationships, Dr. Veronen would have helped the jury understand that Gladys Kelly could have honestly feared that she would suffer serious bodily harm from her husband's attacks, yet still remain with him. This, in turn, would support Ms. Kelly's testimony about her state of mind (that is, that she honestly feared serious bodily harm) at the time of the stabbing.

On the facts in this case, we find that the expert testimony was relevant to Gladys Kelly's state of mind, namely, it was admissible to show she honestly believed she was in imminent danger of death . . .

We also find the expert testimony relevant to the reasonableness of defendant's belief that she was in imminent danger of death or serious injury. [T]he expert's testimony, if accepted by the jury, would have aided it in determining whether, under the circumstances, a reasonable person would have believed there was imminent danger to her life.

At the heart of the claim of self-defense was defendant's story that she had been repeatedly subjected to "beatings" over the course of her marriage. While defendant's testimony was somewhat lacking in detail, a juror could infer from the use of the word "beatings," as well as the detail given concerning some of these events (the choking, the biting, the use of fists), that these physical assaults posed a risk of serious injury or death. When that regular pattern of serious physical abuse is combined with defendant's claim that the decedent sometimes threatened to kill her, defendant's statement that on this occasion she thought she might be killed when she saw Mr. Kelly running toward her could be found to reflect a reasonable fear; that is, it could so be found if the jury believed Gladys Kelly's story of the prior beatings, if it believed her story of the prior threats, and, of course, if it believed her story of the events of that particular day.

The crucial issue of fact on which this expert's testimony would bear is why, given such allegedly severe and constant beatings, combined with threats to kill, defendant had not long ago left decedent . . . . The expert could clear up [this issue], by explaining that one of the common characteristics of a battered wife is her inability to leave despite such constant beatings; her "learned helplessness"; her lack of anywhere to go; her feeling that if she tried to leave, she would be subjected to even more merciless treatment; her belief in the omnipotence of her battering husband; and sometimes her hope that her husband will change his ways.

R. v. Williams (Gladstone)
Court of Appeal, Criminal Division
[1987] 3 All ER 411

Lord Lane CJ

The facts were somewhat unusual and were as follows. On the day in question the alleged victim, a man called Mason, saw a black youth seizing the handbag belonging to a woman who was shopping. He caught up with the youth and held him, he said with a view to taking him to a nearby police station, but the youth broke free from his grip.

---

[8] The rejected form of § 2C:3–4 was patterned after § 3.04 of the Model Penal Code. The purpose of the proposed Code and M.P.C. provisions was to prevent one who killed in the honest but mistaken and unreasonable belief in the necessity of the action from being convicted of a crime like murder, which is premised on an act motivated by unlawful purpose.

[10] The factual contentions of the parties eliminated any issue concerning the duty to retreat. If the State's version is accepted, defendant is the aggressor; if defendant's version is accepted, the possibility of retreat is excluded by virtue of the nature of the attack that defendant claims took place. We do not understand that the State claims defendant breached that duty under any version of the facts. If, however, the duty becomes an issue on retrial, the trial court will have to determine the relevancy of the battered-woman's syndrome to that issue.

Mason caught the youth again and knocked him to the ground, and he then twisted one of the youth's arms behind his back in order to immobilise him and to enable him, Mason, so he said, once again to take the youth to a police station. The youth was struggling and calling for help at this time, and no one disputed that fact.

Upon the scene then came the appellant who had only seen the latter stages of this incident. According to Mason he told the appellant first of all that he was arresting the youth for mugging the lady and secondly, that he, Mason, was a police officer. That was not true. He was asked for his warrant card, which obviously was not forthcoming, and thereupon something of a struggle ensued between Mason on the one hand and the appellant and others on the other hand. In the course of these events Mason sustained injuries to his face, loosened teeth and bleeding gums.

The appellant put forward the following version of events. He said he was returning from work by bus, when he saw Mason dragging the youth along and striking him again and again. He was so concerned about the matter that he rapidly got off the bus and made his way to the scene and asked Mason what on earth he was doing. In short he said that he punched Mason because he thought if he did so he would save the youth from further beating and what he described as torture.

There was no doubt that none of these dramatis personae was known to each other beforehand . . .

One starts off with the meaning of the word "assault." "Assault" in the context of this case, that is to say using the word as a convenient abbreviation for assault and battery, is an act by which the defendant, intentionally or recklessly, applies unlawful force to the complainant. There are circumstances in which force may be applied to another lawfully. Taking a few examples: first, where the victim consents, as in lawful sports, the application of force to another will, generally speaking, not be unlawful. Secondly, where the defendant is acting in self-defence: the exercise of any necessary and reasonable force to protect himself from unlawful violence is not unlawful. Thirdly, by virtue of section 3 of the Criminal Law Act 1967, a person may use such force as is reasonable in the circumstances in the prevention of crime or in effecting or assisting in the lawful arrest of an offender or suspected offender or persons unlawfully at large. In each of those cases the defendant will be guilty if the jury are sure that first of all he applied force to the person of another, and secondly that he had the necessary mental element to constitute guilt.

The mental element necessary to constitute guilt is the intent to apply unlawful force to the victim. We do not believe that the mental element can be substantiated by simply showing an intent to apply force and no more.

What then is the situation if the defendant is labouring under a mistake of fact as to the circumstances? What if he believes, but believes mistakenly, that the victim is consenting, or that it is necessary to defend himself, or that a crime is being committed which he intends to prevent? He must then be judged against the mistaken facts as he believes them to be. If judged against those facts or circumstances the prosecution fail to establish his guilt, then he is entitled to be acquitted.

The next question is, does it make any difference if the mistake of the defendant was one which, viewed objectively by a reasonable onlooker, was an unreasonable mistake? In other words should the jury be directed as follows: "Even if the defendant may have genuinely believed that what he was doing to the victim was either with the victim's consent or in reasonable self-defence or to prevent the commission of crime, as the case may be, nevertheless if you, the jury, come to the conclusion that the mistaken belief was unreasonable, that is to say that the defendant as a reasonable man should have realised his mistake, then you should convict him."

. . . The reasonableness or unreasonableness of the defendant's belief is material to the question of whether the belief was held by the defendant at all. If the belief was in fact held, its unreasonableness, so far as guilt or innocence is concerned, is neither here nor there. It is irrelevant. Were it otherwise, the defendant would be convicted because he was negligent in failing to recognise that the victim was not consenting or that a crime was not being committed and so on. In other words the jury should be directed first of all that the prosecution have the burden or duty of proving the unlawfulness of the defendant's actions; secondly, if the defendant may have been labouring under a mistake as to the facts, he must be judged according to his mistaken view of the facts; thirdly, that is so whether the mistake was, on an objective view, a reasonable mistake or not.

In a case of self-defence, where self-defence or the prevention of crime is concerned, if the jury came to the conclusion that the defendant believed, or may have believed, that he was being attacked or that a crime was being committed, and that force was necessary to protect himself or to prevent the crime, then the prosecution have not proved their case. If however the defendant's alleged belief was mistaken and if the mistake was an unreasonable one, that may be a powerful reason for coming to the conclusion that the belief was not honestly held and should be rejected.

Even if the jury come to the conclusion that the mistake was an unreasonable one, if the defendant may genuinely have been labouring under it, he is entitled to rely upon it.

Model Penal Code

§ 3.04. Use of Force in Self-Protection

(1) Use of Force Justifiable for Protection of the Person. Subject to the provisions of this Section and of Section 3.09 [dealing with mistakes], the use of force upon or toward another person is justifiable when the actor believes that such force is immediately necessary for the purpose of protecting himself against the use of unlawful force by such other person on the present occasion.

(2) Limitations on Justifying Necessity for Use of Force.
(a) The use of force is not justifiable under this Section:
    (i) to resist an arrest which the actor knows is being made by a peace officer, although the arrest is unlawful; ...
(b) The use of deadly force is not justifiable under this Section unless the actor believes that such force is necessary to protect himself against death, serious bodily harm, kidnapping or sexual intercourse compelled by force or threat; nor is it justifiable if:
    (i) the actor, with the purpose of causing death or serious bodily harm, provoked the use of force against himself in the same encounter; or
    (ii) the actor knows that he can avoid the necessity of using such force with complete safety by retreating or by surrendering possession of a thing to a person asserting a claim of right thereto or by complying with a demand that he abstain from any action which he has no duty to take, except that:
        (1) the actor is not obliged to retreat from his dwelling or place of work, unless he was the initial aggressor or is assailed in his place of work by another person whose place of work the actor knows it to be; ...

§ 3.05. Use of Force for the Protection of Other Persons

(1) Subject to the provisions of this Section and of Section 3.09, the use of force upon or toward the person of another is justifiable to protect a third person when:
(a) the actor would be justified under Section 3.04 in using such force to protect himself against the injury he believes to be threatened to the person whom he seeks to protect; and
(b) under the circumstances as the actor believes them to be, the person whom he seeks to protect would be justified in using such protective force; and
(c) the actor believes that his intervention is necessary for the protection of such other person.

German Federal Court of Justice
4 StR 505/86, BGH NStZ 1987, 172 (October 30, 1986)

Facts

According to the findings the defendant made his way in the night of July 31, 1985,—shortly after midnight—with his loaded small bore rifle to his company premises, where he suspected that there was a thief. There he apprehended H. who had been previously convicted on several occasions for theft, and who immediately fled when he saw the defendant. Despite the defendant calling "Stop or I shoot" H. continued his flight and ran on to a rising concrete ramp. When he had reached the upper end of this, the defendant fired from a distance of about 7 m. The shot hit H. on the right side of the back of his head, and he fell to the ground fatally wounded. The police later found a vehicle jack underneath the dead man; the iron lever which belonged to this object was close to his side.

The defendant made a statement to the effect that the fugitive had turned round with a raised arm holding in his hand an object like a pipe when he had closed in on him to a distance of 7 m. Thinking that H. would throw this at him from above or rain blows on him, he lifted his gun, pressed it into his right hip, held it up in the direction of the attacker and fired. He had intended "to defend himself and to arrest the other man."

The regional court sentenced the defendant for homicide to a prison sentence of one year and six months. It suspended the implementation of the sentence on probation. The defendant's appeal in law led to the quashing of the judgment.

Reasons

bb) The criminal chamber excludes the application of § 32 Criminal Code on the ground that the defendant had "exceeded the boundaries to the exercise of self-defense . . . set by § 32 Criminal Code." It denied the necessity of the means of defense chosen by him. Its observations on this are however not free from doubt.

The scope of necessary defense is determined by the overall circumstances under which the attack and the defense took place, and in particular by the strength of and danger posed by the attacker, and by the defense options open to the person attacked (BGH, NStZ 1981, 138). In principle the person attacked may choose the means of defense within his reach (including a firearm and even one which he carries without permission: BGH, NStZ 1986, 357), which may be expected to result in an immediate and final removal of the danger (BGHSt 25, 229.230; BGH, NJW 1980, 2263; NStZ 1982, 285; NJW 1984, 986). But boundaries are set to the use of firearms in such a way as to endanger life. It is certainly not forbidden from the outset (see BGH, Judgment of April 15, 1980, 1 StR 130/80). It can however only be the final means of defense (BGHSt 26, 143,146). As a rule the defender is first required to threaten its use (see BGH, Judgment of March 13, 1980, 4 StR 24/80). If this does not suffice, the defender must if possible attempt a less dangerous use of the weapon before the fatal shot (see BGHSt 26, 143,146). This could involve unaimed warning shots (BGH, in Holtz, MDR 1979, 985) or, if these do not suffice, shots in the legs in order to make the attacker unable to fight (see BGHSt 25, 229. 230), i.e. such defensive measures which on the one hand will without doubt be effective as defense and which on the other hand do not unnecessarily exceed the intensity and danger of the attack (BGH, NStZ 1981, 138; 1982, 285; 1983, 117).

The regional court has made no observations on whether the defendant regarded the attack to be so threatening that he believed he would only be able to meet it with a fatal shot in the head. This does not seem obvious, as the attacker was still 7 m away. The regional court has however observed that the defendant had believed that he was permitted to shoot as he did. It considers this mistake an avoidable mistake of law because he could "recognize that it was not necessary for him to defend himself at the price of the attacker's life." These observations are ambiguous. They would not be open to objection in law if the defendant had believed that he was permitted to kill an attacker by an aimed shot at the head even if less dangerous defensive measures were available to him. But they do not stand up to the examination in law, if—which according to the observations of the regional court cannot be excluded—objectively less dangerous defensive measures were admittedly available to the defendant but he believed that an aimed shot at the head of the victim was necessary to defend himself from an attack which threatened his life. In this case the defendant's mistake about the necessity of his action would be a mistake about facts and not a mistake of law (BGH, NJW 1968, 1885; BGHSt 26, 256,257; BGH, in Holtz, MDR 1980, 453). If the defendant was thus mistaken—which cannot be excluded from the outset, according to the observations of the regional court—about the necessity of his defensive action, he could not be convicted in accordance with § 16 para. 1 sentence 1 Criminal Code of homicide; but the possibility of negligent homicide would have to be examined.

<hr>

German Federal Court of Justice
3 StR 503/01, BGH NStZ-RR 2002, 203; BGH NStZ 2001, 590 (April 18, 2002)
Family Tyrant Case

Facts

The regional court established the following:

The defendant had been married to Detlef M., the subsequent victim, since February 1997 by a second marriage. During the marriage, M. often—primarily under the influence of alcohol—struck the defendant for trivial reasons with his fists all over the body and in the face, causing her numerous bruises. The defendant did not dare to oppose Detlef M., as he would not put up with any contradiction, but took it as a cause to ill-treat the defendant in a more violent physical manner. In February 1998 she made her first attempt to separate from her husband. She went with her children, including their son A. who was born in March 1997, to a battered wives refuge. However, she re-established telephone contact with Detlef M. of her own accord after a week and returned to him after he had promised to change his behavior. But in spite of this promise he struck the defendant again—mainly under the influence of alcohol—and in the summer of 1998, for the first time, her daughter Kathrin, who was born in 1984, when she wanted to assist her mother who was being throttled by M. In October or November 1998 the defendant moved with the children into an apartment of her own. After about four weeks however she sought contact with Detlef M. again who in the ensuing period succeeded in exciting her sympathy. Frequent meetings began again in which Detlef M. returned to his old habits. As Detlef M. under the influence of alcohol also became involved in quarrels with the defendant's neighbors, she received notice to quit her apartment. In late autumn 1999, the defendant found a new home. However in the following period she spent time during the day in M.'s apartment with the children, and mostly only returned in the late evening to her own apartment. Acts of violence also occurred in M.'s apartment. Since the end of 1999 Detlef M. also began to abuse his step-daughter Kathrin sexually by making her have sexual intercourse and oral intercourse with him on a number of occasions. The defendant discovered this from M. as well as from her daughter Kathrin, who also confided in her teacher who facilitated contact with a lawyer. On May 15, 2000, the defendant and Kathrin had a conversation with this lawyer in which they were informed that, according to information from the police, the arrest of M. could not be assumed with 100% certainty. Because of these uncertainties, the defendant and her daughter Kathrin were not prepared to report M. to the police, because they feared that their lives would be in danger if he was not arrested despite the report.

The defendant spent the evening of May 17, 2000, with the children as usual in M.'s apartment. During dinner there had already been conflicts, at first verbal, which were then continued by M. (who had drunk alcohol throughout the day) mainly with the stepdaughter Kathrin in the living room. M. was sitting on a sofa, with Kathrin sitting on another sofa diagonally to him, and a coffee table standing between them. The longer the quarrel continued, "the more it became clear" to the defendant "that it would come to blows again this evening. She feared that she and possibly also Kathrin would be beaten up again by M." The defendant did not see any possibility of being able to leave M.'s apartment with the children unmolested, according to the findings of the judgment under challenge, nor a possibility of calling others to help. On the other hand she was no longer prepared to put up with everything from M. The defendant therefore went into the kitchen, took a 25 cm long kitchen knife tapering to a point, and returned to the living room. At first she remained standing in the doorway. She hoped that M. would come to his senses on seeing the knife, but she was prepared to use the knife against M. in case he attacked Kathrin. She also accepted that she could possibly inflict fatal injuries on him.

When M. saw the defendant armed with a knife, he rose, turned "bellowing" in Kathrin's direction, and went up to her. The defendant knew from experience that M. would now rain blows on Kathrin so she went up to M., who stopped when he noticed the defendant, took a step backwards, stumbled and fell back on the sofa. The defendant feared that when M. got up again, he would go for her, and she stabbed him in the left side of the chest three times in rapid sequence with the knife. One of these stab wounds pierced his heart. This wound was fatal, but did not lead to M. immediately losing the power of movement. He cried out with pain, rose from the sofa and went in Kathrin's direction. The defendant did not recognize that he was already fatally injured, and stabbed M. four times in the back as he moved away from her. He took a few more steps into the entrance hall where he collapsed, dead. There the defendant stabbed him another 44 times as he was lying on the ground, until he moved no longer. The defendant and Kathrin first took M.'s corpse to the bath and then removed the most flagrant traces of the crime. They both conferred, and decided not to report what had happened to the police. In the ensuing days they wrapped M.'s corpse up and brought it in the defendant's car to a forest where they buried it. The crime and the corpse remained undiscovered until the beginning of January 2001.

The regional court acquitted the defendant of the charge of homicide because it was of the view that, at the point in time of the stabbing, an attack by M. against the defendant or her daughter had been imminent, and the defense used by the defendant was suitable, required and appropriate, in order to avert M.'s attack on her or Kathrin's health or life.

The public prosecutor's office lodged an appeal in law against this judgment. The appeal was successful.

Reasons

a) The regional court has taken an objective self-defense situation as a basis for its legal assessment of the first three stab wounds in M.'s chest which led to his death. It has however made no findings that at this point in time there was objectively an attack on the part of the victim. The circumstances of the crime also do not simply suggest such a factual (still) existing or imminent new attack, as M. on seeing the defendant armed with a knife and coming towards him had paused in his movements, taken a step backwards and as a result of stumbling was now lying more or less helpless on the sofa. The district court has only established in this connection that the defendant feared an attack by M. Such a mere subjective fear that an attack was imminent does not create on its own a self-defense situation (see Lenckner/Perron, in: Schönke/Schröder, StGB, 25th edit., § 32 marginal no. 27). If the defendant drew the erroneous conclusion from M.'s conduct that a new attack was imminent, then at most the legal principles of putative self-defense fell to be considered (Lenckner/Perron, § 32 marginal no. 28, 65) . . . The assumption of the regional court that the first three fatal stabbings of M. by the defendant were justified by an objective self-defense situation lack a factual foundation.

b) Additionally the judgment contains contradictory findings about the defendant's mental concept regarding the further course of events at the point in time when she fetched the knife from the kitchen. In the findings the regional court explains that the defendant hoped that M. would come to his senses on seeing the knife and leave her in peace. Within the assessment of the evidence, however, it explains as the basis of its conviction that the defendant had already fetched the knife with the intention of killing and that she knew from experience that M. had never so far given in. Although it was admittedly within the realms of possibility that the threat with a knife would have had an intimidating effect, it was however primarily to be expected "that the knife could actually intensify his rage, and the defendant would then have to use it to prevent anything further happening." If these observations are to be understood as meaning that the defendant knew that the sight of the knife would, in the sense so to speak of an automatic mechanism, increase M.'s rage so that she would be compelled to use the knife, the regional court should then have discussed whether the defendant was not obliged to escape from the anticipated self-defense situation, and leave the apartment with the children

Whether she should already have left the apartment on the basis of the existing marriage with M. can be left undecided. Earlier decisions of the Federal Court of Justice have admittedly required of spouses under certain circumstances that they should refrain from a method of defense which would be reliable but fatal, even if the application of a less severe method might be less effective in removing the danger (BGH, GA 1969, 117; BGH, NJW 1969, 802; . . .). Whether this case law still should be adhered to (restrictively, BGH, NJW 1984, 986 with discussion by Spendel, JZ 1984, 507; critically also Tröndle/Fischer, StGB, 50th edit., § 32 marginal no. 19), does not need to be decided by the Senate. Under the circumstances existing here, the defendant was already obliged to show restraint, as in the past, even when separations from M. had already been effected successfully, she had always come back to him on her own initiative without compulsion or necessity, in spite of her negative experiences, and had thereby herself contributed to M. being able to ill-treat her and her daughter Kathrin physically. Even on the day of the crime she had, in spite of ill-treatment experienced previously again and again, gone into a situation with her eyes open which held the danger of an escalation. It was at least to be expected of her that she would leave M.'s apartment with the children on the first sign of a possibly escalating quarrel. It has not been established that she could not have done this at an earlier point in time, perhaps during supper. Although the regional court has observed that the defendant had—later—seen no possibility of being able to leave M. unmolested, this finding is not substantiated with facts . . .

3. For the new trial the Senate draws attention to the need for the judge of fact, if he should again come to the conclusion that the defendant had acted in self-defense with the first three fatal knife stabbings, to examine the subsequent happenings more carefully than before. It is not evident why the defendant should have the benefit of putative self-defense for the stabbings in M's back and the further stabbings when he was already lying on the ground (inflicted with the intention of killing). The regional court has not referred to objective circumstances for its opinion that this was not at least attempted homicide. The course of events points against a continuous and constant subjective assessment of the occurrences by the defendant. The occurrences established show objectively at least two distinctive turning points, i.e., one when M. turned away from the defendant and went into the hall, and the other when he finally collapsed there.

Regional Court (*Landgericht*, LG) Frankfurt am Main
5/27 KLs 7570 Js 203814/03 (4/04), NJW 2005, 692
Daschner Case

Facts

G, who took part in the present proceedings as a witness, overpowered and killed an 11-year-old boy in order to extort ransom money from the family of the—already dead—child. After G had been observed three days after the abduction when collecting the money and—he had in the meantime bought a Mercedes car—had been later arrested, the police investigations concentrated first on establishing the whereabouts of the victim: it was provisionally assumed that the child was still alive and was held in a hiding place. During the period when G was being questioned, the police found a substantial part of the ransom money in his residence and a piece of paper on which details of the preparation for the crime were written down. These discoveries revealed a strong suspicion that G was a sole or co-perpetrator of the abduction. As G had deliberately misdirected the official investigations on several occasions by the statements he gave, the defendant Wolfgang Daschner (D) instructed the defendant E to threaten G with the use of physical force when he was further questioned in order to make G reveal the hiding place. D was at that time acting head of the authority in place of the otherwise competent Chief Constable who was absent on leave. E as "incumbent leader K12" led the subsection taking part in the investigations, "General Investigations." The defendants knew that the situation about evidence was not certain and in particular it had not yet been resolved whether there were co-perpetrators besides G who also had a say about the fate of the child. Further it was not possible to be certain at this point in time from the results of the investigation that G had again lied in his statements about an alleged hiding place. The defendants also knew that a phased plan with various measures worked out by the leaders of the section involved—including, amongst other things, a confrontation of G by members of the victim's family—was not necessarily doomed to fail. D prepared a written note about his order and the further events which stated, amongst other things:

> On September 30, 2002, at around 10.45 p.m. DI E told me that the suspect Magnus G had still given no information as to the whereabouts of the missing child. In case of further refusal, I have ordered the application of direct force. It can be assumed from the facts that Jakob M, provided he is still alive, faces acute danger to his life (from withdrawal of food and fluids and external temperature).
>
> On Oct. 10, 2002, at 6.15 a.m. DI E and DI Mü told me that G had now voluntarily made a statement. In accordance with the information he gave, further suspects had been arrested, and residences searched without result. Jakob M was allegedly held in a hut at the Langener Waldsee (according to the description it could also be the Walddorfer Badesee). Several hundred people are being brought together there at the moment. Because of the extensive terrain, and the absence of possibilities for limiting it, a long search operation is to be expected.
>
> The officer interrogating G was of the opinion that he had told the truth. In contrast, the police psychologist S held the view that it was a tissue of lies.
>
> To save the life of the abducted child, I have ordered that G

following prior threat
under medical surveillance
by the infliction of pain (with no injuries)

> is questioned once more. The establishment of the whereabouts of the abducted child admits of no delay and in this respect the police have a duty within the framework of proportionality to take all measures to save the life of the child. In parallel to this the police chief Mü was charged to investigate whether a truth drug can be obtained.
>
> The questioning of G is not to solve the crime but exclusively to save the abducted child's life.
>
> The moral reservations raised by DI W were set aside in a further discussion with AD R, DI W and DI Mü (8 a.m.). DCS E was directed to prepare the accused G for the imminent proceedings.
>
> At 8.25 a.m. Mr. E stated that G had admitted as a "might be" that Jacob M was dead. Later he supplemented this statement by identifying a hut in the area of the Langener Waldsee and the location of the body at Birstein. Because of the giving of the confession, the measure was unnecessary.

The 22nd criminal chamber of the regional court of Frankfurt a. M. established in the criminal proceedings against G that the threat of the defendant E was illegal for violation of arts. 1 and 104 para. 1 sentence 2 GG and art. 3 ECHR, and that therefore four interrogations of G, three police notes and an unofficial copy should not be used for evidence purposes (LG Frankfurt a. M., StV 2003, 325). G was finally sentenced to life imprisonment as an overall sentence for murder concomitantly with extortionate robbery resulting in death and for false accusation concomitantly with deprivation of freedom in two cases.

In the present criminal case, the regional court found the defendant E guilty of coercion in office and the defendant D of inducing a subordinate to commit coercion in office and gave both defendants a conditional discharge.

Reasons

The defendant E is guilty of coercion in the sense of § 240 para. 1 Criminal Code. By threatening G on the morning of October 1, 2002, that under medical supervision pain would be inflicted on him, but without injuries, in order to force him to reveal the whereabouts of the abducted child, he has held out the prospect of a severe evil, making it clear that he would not be the implementer, but that he spoke on behalf of and representing the management of the authority and therefore had influence over the realization of the threat.

The defendant D is guilty of inducing a subordinate to commit this crime under § 357 para. 1 Criminal Code in combination with § 240 para. 1 Criminal Code. As Deputy Chief Constable, D was the superior of E and gave a binding direction to him to commit the crime which E also carried out.

According to the defendants' idea and the choice of words used, the infliction of pain which was in prospect was to be substantial and so strong that it would leave no room for G to have the will to resist. By directing that a particular officer should be brought in, it was suggested that a quite specific and particularly effective infliction of harm was intended. The preventative presence of a doctor signalized physical impairments to health which needed medical surveillance. The threat had the desired effect. It caused G to give up his resistance and to reveal where the child was. This follows from the fact that G had not previously been prepared to make a statement in this respect to the witness M nor in the confrontation with his mother on the morning of Oct. 1, 2002, nor to the witnesses Pr and Pe. The appeal by E to G's conscience and the attempt to awaken sympathy with the child's fate could have no effect, as G knew that the child was already dead. In view of the very short time when E was alone in the room with G, it could only have been the exclusive effect of the threat of application of violence that caused G to give up his resistance.

Both defendants knew what they were doing and intended the consequence which occurred. No grounds of justification were present, and the threat of the evil was to be regarded as reprehensible in relation to the purpose sought (§ 240 para. 2 Criminal Code)...

Even if one were to follow the legal opinion which applies the criminal law grounds of justification effective for private persons to sovereign action as well, the actions of both defendants are [not] justified by defence of self or another (§ 32 Criminal Code)...

§ 32 Criminal Code requires that an emergency defence situation is objectively present at the time of the crime (Tröndle/Fischer, StGB, 52nd edit. [2004], § 32 marginal no. 3). This was not so, as the child was already dead. Yet both defendants thought rescue of the child was possible. The defendants were not however making the kind of mistake that would exclude intention about the factual prerequisites of a ground of justification: the defence is necessary in the sense of § 32 Criminal Code if on the one hand it is appropriate for defence and on the other hand represents the least severe remedy (Lenckner/Perron, in: Schönke/Schröder, StGB, 26th edit. [2001], § 32 marginal no. 34). The threat of the infliction of pain was however not, in the light of its nature and extent, the least severe remedy as under the graduated approach other measures were available...

Besides this, the action was neither required in the sense of § 32 Criminal Code... because it violated art. 1 para. 1 sentence 1 GG.

This fundamental principle of the Constitution is found again in art. 104 para. 1 sentence 2 GG, according to which detained persons may not be psychologically or physically mistreated. Under art. 1 para. 1 sentence 1 GG, human dignity is inviolable. No-one may be turned by state power into an object, an epitome of anxiety in the face of pain.

This legal concept has also found expression in international treaties and conventions, as for example in art. 3 ECHR, which has statutory force in Germany.

Respect for human dignity is the foundation of this constitutional state. The author of the Constitution has put it quite deliberately at the beginning of the Constitution. The right to life and freedom from bodily harm is on the other hand only stipulated in art. 2 para. 2 GG. This has its basis in the history of this state. The documents from the period of the origin of the Federal Republic of Germany make it quite clear that the atrocities of the National Socialist regime were still very vividly in the minds of the members of the Parliamentary Council. Its fundamental concern was never to let such things happen again, and to put a stop by the composition of this Basic Law to any such attempt. It should not be possible for human beings to be treated for a second time as repositories of knowledge which the state wants to wring out of them, even if this is in the interests of justice. Thus it must be declared that art. 1 para. 1 sentence 1 GG is unalterable. The author of the Constitution has given expression in art. 79 para. 3 GG to the idea of "nipping it in the bud," and excluded amendment of this constitutional principle even if an appropriate majority for an amendment of the Basic Law was present. For this reason art. 79 para. 3 GG is described as an "eternity clause." The strict prohibition of even just threatening an accused with force is already the result of a balancing of all the interests to be considered. This was undertaken when the Basic Law was established. It is quite essentially a question of the protection and of the viability of the administration of criminal justice. The judgments of the criminal courts are based on correct police work in proceedings conforming to the concept of the constitutional state. The constitutional state would be given up for lost if it did not follow this strict requirement...

An exception from the unambiguous statutory position would mean that the constitutional law protection of human dignity in its absoluteness would be breached and opened up to a balancing exercise which would be tantamount to the breach of a taboo.

Such exceptions have been discussed within the framework of scenarios involving terrorist attacks. They would relate to borderline cases in which the protection of the human dignity of the perpetrator would be set against the possible death and therefore the protection of the lives of thousands of human beings (the "ticking bomb" cases). In the context of this discussion, one of the views propounded is that the human dignity of the victims requires the state to undertake everything, if necessary even applying emotional or physical pressure, in order to save the lives of threatened human beings. In a balancing exercise, the human dignity of the perpetrator would have to take second place.

According to the view of Brugger (JZ 2000, 164) relativization of the prohibition of torture only comes into consideration in, for instance, a type of case in which several features are exhibited, which qualify the occurrence as a unique and extreme exceptional situation. The troublemaker must be the only certainly identified person who has caused the danger and can also remove it. The application of force must be the only measure promising results.

Herdegen (in: Maunz/Dürig/Herzog, GG, 42nd edit [2003], art. 1 marginal nos. 45ff.) seeks to make a "differentiation of the core of dignity and the further protected area." "Fringe zones of the protected area open to the balancing exercise" are to be created. He further states that the required balancing exercise should not be carried out on the "internormative plane (conflict) of art 1 para. 1 sentence 1 GG and art 2 para. 2 sentence 1GG." Herdegen aims instead at a balancing exercise already "inherent in the norm" in the "concretization of the claim to dignity," according to which in the individual case the threat or infliction of physical evil should not violate the claim to dignity.

According to another view (Roxin in: Festschrift for Eser, 2005) the perpetrator's attack on the victim's human dignity does not legitimate the state in itself then attacking the perpetrator's human dignity. The fact that it does not put itself on the same level with the criminal expresses its moral superiority . . .

Hilgendorf (JZ 2004, 331) warns that abuse could never be excluded. There would no longer be any legal boundaries with "formalized" torture, and the supposed perpetrator would be exposed to the limitless use of arbitrary power.

Hecker (KJ 2003, 210) points out, correctly according to the chamber's opinion, that in the light of the level of present day professional standards for police interrogation and examination techniques, the threat or infliction of pain would be a return to the techniques of the Middle Ages.

In summary it can be established that even the supporters of a relativization of human dignity formulate the pre-requisites for such an extreme exceptional situation very carefully and restrictively. The fundamental doubts remain and it is common to the abstract cases that measures of force are considered only as a last resort if they can be employed against a perpetrator who is ascertained with certainty and they promise results . . .

It is not the task of this chamber to intervene in the abstract discussion of constitutional law principles as this is not necessary for the assessment of the present individual case. The legal situation is unambiguous. The exceptional cases discussed are theoretical borderline cases which possibly in terms of their assessment move into a legal grey area and reach the boundaries of legal science. But the present case does not represent an extreme exceptional situation of this kind; it is within a context in which application of measures of force could not come into consideration, for the simple reason that the incriminating factors had not yet been ascertained with sufficient certainty and the permissible investigation measures had not yet by any means been exhausted . . .

The prerequisites for an especially serious case in the sense of § 240 para. 4 nr. 3 Criminal Code, in the category of a perpetrator abusing his powers or his position as the holder of an office, are certainly fulfilled, as the defendant E in his capacity as a detective in a responsible position . . .

In spite of the presence of this category, the court however sees massive extenuating circumstances in this case which are inconsistent with the increased level of punishment of six months to five years imprisonment and make it appear unreasonable. There is a very strong argument for a less severe assessment in the fact that both defendants were trying, exclusively and urgently, to save the child's life. In addition to this, the defendant D felt that he had special responsibility as, in deputizing for the Chief Constable, he was acting for the head of the authority. He was thereby charged with a burden of responsibility to which he was unaccustomed, and therefore felt he was under a special duty. He had thought long and hard in the night about the situation and the right way to proceed, and saw a conflict which he had not yet encountered in his forty years of service. Besides this, he was under strong pressure to produce results from his superior authority and the public.

A further extenuating circumstance to be considered for both defendants is that G's provoking and unscrupulous behavior in the statements he made strained the nerves of the investigating officers to the utmost extent. He was legally trained and he knew how to formulate and present his false statements in such a way that they constantly generated uncertainties, hopes, and disappointments and offered no certitudes. He gave the impression that he was deliberately playing with the child's life, and directing the police deployment and rescue strategy in a false direction in order to gain time and possibly bring about the boy's death.

Besides this, exceptionally hectic conditions prevailed. The police officers had been on duty for an unusually long time, and were exhausted and weary. The defendant E had worked through the night and the defendant D had only slept for a few hours. The defendants' tense state substantially diminishes the accusation of guilt as it lowered the threshold for commission of the crime. They both found themselves at the edge of their resilience. Moreover their lives had been heretofore blameless.

The defendant D had demonstrated an honorable and responsible frame of mind by recording the facts in his written note on Oct. 1, 2002, and making this public. He should be respected for this in an age in which shifting responsibility and blame to others are more likely to be the order of the day.

The consequences of the crimes should also be considered so as to mitigate punishment. The involvement of the media both before and during the criminal proceedings was immense. This created a great burden for the defendants and their families, and in part led to a "pillorying" effect—whether intended or not. Besides this, both of them became associated with dreadful torture scenes from crisis areas.

The long duration of the proceedings should be considered in mitigation. The trial stretching over several weeks and likewise the long duration of the investigatory proceedings was an enormous burden for the defendants; and the confrontation with witness G, a convicted murderer, who was in almost complete denial about his crime, put himself in the spotlight as a victim, and still lied, must in particular be emphasized here.

Both defendants have experienced setbacks in their careers: the defendant D was transferred to the Hessian Ministry for the Interior in Wiesbaden and the defendant E was not able to carry out relevant measures relating to criminal procedure. Finally, allowance must be made in both cases for the fact that this was the first case when such a conflict situation—even though it was not insoluble—was dealt with by the courts . . .

In view of the special circumstances adduced, the chamber refrains from subjecting the defendants to punishment. Instead it reserves the power to impose a fine under § 59 Criminal Code [and instead issues a warning]. The strict prerequisites of this provision are fulfilled. There are no doubts about a favorable social prognosis for both defendants. The overall assessment of this crime and of the personality of both defendants indicates special circumstances which make it advisable here to refrain from imposing punishment. The crime has admittedly not arisen from an unavoidable conflict situation, as numerous alternative courses of action were still available. The defendants were however faced from a subjective point of view with a situation which had a certain proximity to grounds of justification and excuse. Besides this, reference is made to the grounds for determination of punishment discussed at the start in which the motive of saving the child's life is pervasive.

§ 59 Criminal Code furthermore requires that the defense of the legal order not require imposition of a punishment. The mere warning is not expected to seriously diminish the population's sense of justice or loyalty to law . . . .

The wide public resonance gives rise to the hope that the dangers of deviating from the absoluteness of art. 1 para. 1 sentence 1 GG will have become apparent.

German Criminal Code

§ 32 (Self-defense)

(1) Who commits a crime in a situation when this was appropriate as an act of self-defense does not act unlawfully.

(2) Self-defense means defensive action that is necessary to avert an imminent unlawful attack on oneself or another.

§ 33 (Excessive Self-defense)

An offender who exceeds the limits of self-defense out of confusion, fear or terror will not be punished.

NOTES

1. Comparing the law on self-defense and defense of another across the legal systems reveals similarities, but also significant differences. To start with a similarity: § 32 Criminal Code, § 35.15 New York Penal Law and English law (see *R. v. Williams (Gladstone)* (above)) do not differentiate between self-defense and defending another. In the following sections, referrals to "self-defense" are used as a matter of abbreviation; this includes the defense of another

person. (The Model Penal Code treats defense of another in a separate section, § 3.05 (above), but in fact defines it as constructive self-defense.) Note that the German term *Notwehr* ("emergency defense"), which is translated as "self-defense," does not distinguish between self and other to begin with.

Compare the scope of self-defense to the scope of other defenses, notably necessity and duress. Under the German Criminal Code, necessity as a justification (*Notstand* or "emergency situation"), § 34 Criminal Code, likewise extends to "another," whereas necessity as an excuse extends only to "a relative or person close to" the actor, § 35 Criminal Code. Under the Model Penal Code, both necessity as a justification (§ 3.01) and duress (§ 2.09) extend to "another." Does this difference in scope reflect a difference in rationale?

Looking at the question of which circumstances may trigger lawful self-defense, note that the German approach is rather broad. Section 32 para. 2 Criminal Code requires "an imminent unlawful act" and "defensive action that is necessary to avert" the attack. There are no limitations concerning the kind of attack. A justification of self-defense is not restricted to cases of physical force applied against the attacked person, but extends, for instance, to attacks on property (including incidents like trespassing or taking goods of minor value), attacks on honor and any other individual legal good (*Rechtsgut*).

Necessity as a justification likewise does not restrict the class of legal goods to which it applies, § 34 Criminal Code ("life, limb, freedom, honor, property or another legal interest"); necessity as an excuse, by contrast, only applies to life, limb, and freedom, § 35 Criminal Code.

The restriction to *individual* legal goods is significant. Self-defense is not available in the case of threats to *public* legal goods (public order, public safety, etc.); their protection is entrusted exclusively to the state itself, to preserve its monopoly on violence. But how is self-defense regarding individual legal goods compatible with the state's monopoly on violence? Or does the monopoly on violence require that justified use of force be limited to use of force in compliance with a state order?* Should self-defense perhaps be considered an excuse instead? See William Blackstone, *Commentaries on the Laws of England* (1769), vol. 4, 178–82:

> In . . . instances of justifiable homicide, it may be observed that the slayer is in no kind of fault whatsoever, not even in the minutest degree; and is therefore to be totally acquitted and discharged, with commendation rather than blame. But that is not quite the case in excusable homicide, the very name whereof imports some fault, some error or omission; so trivial, however, that the law excuses it from the guilt of felony, though in strictness it judges it deserving of some little degree of punishment. . . .
>
> Homicide in self-defence or *se defendendo*, upon a sudden affray, is . . . excusable, rather than justifiable, by the English law. . . . They cannot therefore legally exercise this right of preventive defence but in sudden and violent cases, when certain and immediate suffering would be the consequence of waiting for the assistance of the law. Wherefore, to excuse homicide by the plea of self-defence, it must appear that the slayer had no other possible (or at least probable) means of escaping from his assailant.

2. Section 32 StGB does not include a general proportionality test that would require weighing the harm done through the defensive action against the harm prevented. Defendants can be justified if they cause serious physical injury to fend off attacks on property. This absence of a proportionality requirement reflects the foundation of self-defense in German criminal law on the so-called "principle of law-protection" (*Rechtsbewährungsprinzip*): "right need not make way for wrong" ("*Das Recht braucht dem Unrecht nicht zu weichen*"). This (supraindividual) principle of law protection is contrasted with the (individual) "principle of self-protection" (*Selbstschutzprinzip*). The prevailing view combines both principles, with different emphases placed on one or the other. Generally speaking, the greater weight rests on the principle of law-protection, the less room is thought to remain for considerations of proportionality.

Why does this stand-your-ground principle amount to a justification for the recognition of self-defense as a defense? What is the role of the state in this account of self-defense? How

---

* See, e.g., Model Penal Code §§ 3.03 (Execution of Public Duty), 3.07 (Use of Force in Law Enforcement).

does this principle (also occasionally captured in the Latin maxim "*vim vi repellere licet,*" or force may be met with force) relate to the state's monopoly on violence?

Significantly, the stand-your-ground principle is taken to imply the absence of a proportionality requirement (which is seen as introducing an improper balancing of right against wrong) as well as the absence of a general, or specific, duty to retreat. What role does this conception assign to the attacker in a self-defense case? Does the unlawful aggressor forfeit her right to protection under the law, since it is the aim of law protection that justifies the use of force against? Is this primacy of the protection of law compatible with the constitutional right to life, and the incommensurability of life reflected in other doctrines of German criminal law (for instance, the inapplicability of necessity as justification in cases of homicide*)?

3. A key term which is common to the different self-defense provisions is "necessary." The meaning of this term is somewhat ambiguous. It could be read as providing some normative boundaries, such as a proportionality test. But it is worth emphasizing that this is not the way it is interpreted in German law. In the Federal Court of Justice ruling from 1986 (concerning the deadly shot at a burglar), the Court explains the established case law: an act of defense is necessary if it is the only means available to end the attack immediately and finally. If it is the last resort to avert an attack on property, fatally wounding a burglar who runs away with stolen goods can be justified under § 32 Criminal Code. However, the Court reminds us that careful examination is required to determine whether there were less dangerous defensive measures available to the defendant, which might have been equally effective. Especially if firearms are involved, the courts demand that other conceivable defensive acts such as showing the weapon to the attacker or firing warning shots need to be considered. If (but only if) they would have been equally effective, i.e., if they would have stopped the attack immediately and finally, then a more violent way of defense was not necessary. If, however, the attack could not be stopped with less intrusive means, defense with deadly force will be regarded as necessary.

The general rule in German law which rejects a proportionality principle is open to some exceptions, in the form of "social" or "social ethical" limitations. It has been argued that these limitations can be read into the requirement in § 32 German Criminal Code that the act of self-defense be not only necessary, but "appropriate" (*geboten*). (Courts also have invoked the "appropriateness" to generate other limitations on the right to self-defense, notably a duty to retreat (see below).) Does this vague standard raise concerns in light of the principle of legality?[†] Does it provide courts with sufficient guidance? Is it compatible with the principle of law-protection? Or with the principle of self-protection, for that matter? Does the consideration of "social" or "social ethical" factors compromise the legal nature of the inquiry into criminal liability? Should such judgments be left to a jury, which is often said to function as a representative, or at least an indicator, of the applicable "social ethical" norms?

At any rate, these "social ethical" limitations (whether or not based on the legal concept of "appropriateness") are conceptualized as external constraints designed to filter out exceptional cases when allowing this defense would be considered extremely unfair towards the attacking person. So while there is no general principle of proportionality, "extreme disproportionality" might nonetheless exceed the bounds of self-defense. The classic case that illustrates both the categorical rejection of any proportionality requirement in the German law of self-defense and the possible consideration of proportionality on social ethical grounds in extreme cases is the *Fruit Thief Case* (RGSt 55, 82 (1920)), in which the Imperial Court of Justice upheld the acquittal on the basis of self-defense (or rather defense of property) of a man who had shot and seriously wounded another as he was making off with fruits from the defendant's tree. Today, the case would be judged differently due to the mentioned consideration of social ethical concerns, grounded in the requirement of "appropriateness" (though not of necessity) of the use of deadly force. But note that the label "not appropriate" (*nicht*

---

* See Chapter 6.C.
† See Chapter 2.

geboten) will even today be reserved to the use of deadly force when defending property of really trivial economic value (perhaps a few euros). Beyond such a threshold, the filter of "appropriateness" does not preclude the use of deadly force in defense of property.

The Model Penal Code drafters were clear on this issue, though they encountered considerable resistance at the American Law Institute's discussion of their draft: while the use of physical force in defense of property was permissible in general, the use of *deadly* force was never justified. (Under the Model Penal Code's, "deadly force" is defined broadly, as "force which the actor uses with the purpose of causing or which he knows to create a substantial risk of causing death or serious bodily harm" (§ 3.11(2)). In particular, "purposely firing a firearm in the direction of another person or at a vehicle in which another person is believed to be constitutes deadly force," § 3.11(2).)

The Model Penal Code position may have been controversial; it was not new, however. See *Ayers v. State*, 60 Miss. 709 (1883) ("No man is required by law to yield possession of his property to the unlawful claim of another. He may defend his possession; and while he may not kill to prevent the trespass, he may kill to protect his own person against a deadly assault made by the trespasser on him."); N.Y. Penal Law § 35.25.

Burglary, traditionally defined as trespass with the intent to commit a crime (most often larceny), presents a more controversial case. To the extent that it is categorized as a property offense, the use of *deadly* force to prevent its commission should not be justified under the general rule. This is the position of the Model Penal Code (§ 3.06(3)(d)—deadly force justified to avert burglary only in case of actual danger to persons, and not only to property). Many jurisdictions, including New York, however, take the opposite view. N.Y. Penal Law (§ 35.20(3)—deadly force justified to avert burglary). In New York, then, I would be justified in killing a burglar even if neither I nor anyone else was in fact in danger of physical—never mind deadly—harm. Not so under the Model Penal Code. According to the Code drafters, their position reflected "[t]he basic judgment that 'the preservation of life has such moral and ethical standing in our culture and society, that the deliberate sacrifice of life merely for the protection of property ought not to be sanctioned by law.'"*

Is this position—and this rationale—consistent with the Model Penal Code's treatmentist orientation? Does the German position, which insists on the justifiability of the use of deadly force to protect any individual legal interest (including life, physical integrity, property, honor), reflect a different "moral and ethical standing" of "the preservation of life" in German "culture and society"? (Or is it the other way around, with the absence of legal limitations on the use of self-defensive force indicating a—social ethical?—commitment to "the preservation of life" so strong and so widely shared as to make legal constraints unnecessary?) German criminal law categorically rejects the necessity defense in cases of homicide because of an appreciation of life's immeasurable and incommensurable value?[†] Is this position in the law of necessity inconsistent with the position on the use of deadly force in the law of self-defense? Or is the relevant distinction one between an innocent victim (in the case of necessity) and a guilty one (in the case of self-defense), or at least one who acts unlawfully (if not necessarily with guilt, in the sense of an absence of an excuse)?

Does it even make sense to compare German and U.S. (Model Penal Law) law on self-defense, given the radical difference in the availability of firearms in both "cultures and societies"? How does the likelihood that the person pleading self-defense used a firearm affect the norms of self-defense? In the American legal and social-political context, a "stand-your-ground" provision that does away with the traditional retreat requirement in cases involving the use of deadly force in self-defense appears as an affirmation of the constitutional right to bear (and use) arms, and is supported by the National Rifle Association, an influential gun rights organization.

---

* Model Penal Code Commentaries § 3.06, at 72.
† See the discussion of *Dudley & Stephens* in Chapter 6.C.

Florida Statutes Chapter 776. Justifiable Use of Force

§ 776.012 Use of force in defense of person

A person is justified in using force, except deadly force, against another when and to the extent that the person reasonably believes that such conduct is necessary to defend himself or herself or another against the other's imminent use of unlawful force. However, a person is justified in the use of deadly force and does not have a duty to retreat if:

(1) He or she reasonably believes that such force is necessary to prevent imminent death or great bodily harm to himself or herself or another or to prevent the imminent commission of a forcible felony; or

(2) Under those circumstances permitted pursuant to s. 776.013.

§ 776.013 Home protection; use of deadly force; presumption of fear of death or great bodily harm

. . .

(3) A person who is not engaged in an unlawful activity and who is attacked in any other place where he or she has a right to be has no duty to retreat and has the right to stand his or her ground and meet force with force, including deadly force if he or she reasonably believes it is necessary to do so to prevent death or great bodily harm to himself or herself or another or to prevent the commission of a forcible felony.

Note that even this heavily criticized provision only eliminates the duty to retreat, but leaves the general limitation of the use of deadly force to defend against similar physical force in place. The underlying norm is that force may be met with force, rather than more generally that right may stand its ground against wrong.

Despite the association between the stand-your-ground principle and the principle of law-protection in German criminal law, the rejection of a duty to retreat in American law was traditionally associated with a particular set of social norms that assigned the protection of "honor" pride of place, and saw retreat in the face of a challenge as an act of cowardice. From this "hip-pocket ethics of the Southwest," enlightened American criminal law was said to distinguish itself by insisting on a duty to retreat, for a "really honorable man, a man of truly refined and elevated feeling, would perhaps always regret the apparent cowardice of a retreat, but he would regret ten times more after the excitement of the contest was past, the thought that he had the blood of a fellow-being on his hands."[*] Beale, writing at the dawn of the twentieth century, contrasts this "refined" rule with the "brutal doctrine" that dismisses a duty to retreat, based as it is "in the ethics of the duelist, the German officer [!], and the buccaneer," as exemplified, in his view, by the following passage from a 1902 opinion of the Missouri Supreme Court:

The right to go where one will, without let or hindrance, despite of threats made, necessarily implies the right to stay where one will, without let or hindrance. These remarks are controlled by the thought of a lawful right to be in the particular locality to which he goes or in which he stays. It is true, human life is sacred, but so is human liberty. One is as dear in the eye of the law as the other, and neither is to give way and surrender its legal status in order that the other may exclusively exist, supposing for a moment such an anomaly to be possible. In other words, the wrongful and violent act of one man shall not abolish or even temporarily suspend the lawful and constitutional right of his neighbor. And this idea of the non-necessity of retreating from any locality where one has the right to be is growing in favor, as all doctrines upon sound reason inevitably will . . .

State v. Bartlett, 71 S.W. 148 (Mo. 1902).

In fact, Beale draws precisely that connection between necessity and the duty to retreat which German criminal law denies:

No killing can be justified, upon any ground, which was not necessary to secure the desired and permitted result; and it is not necessary to kill in self-defense when the assailed can defend himself by the peaceful though often distasteful method of withdrawing to a place of safety.

---

[*] Joseph H. Beale, Jr., "Retreat from a Murderous Assault," 16 *Harvard Law Review* (1903), 567, 581.

Are you convinced? Does necessity imply a duty to retreat? In all cases? Only in cases of the use of deadly force? (Massachusetts, for instance, imposes a general duty of retreat, not only in deadly force cases.*) If necessity implies a duty to retreat, and necessity is an element of self-defense, no matter what force is used, then why wouldn't the duty to retreat apply across the board, to all cases of self-defense?

4. Note in this context the recognition of "honor" among the legal goods subject to protection under the right of self-defense—along with any other (individual) legal good—and, explicitly, under justifying (though not excusing) necessity (§§ 34, 35 Criminal Code), as well as the extensive chapter in the German Criminal Code devoted to libel and defamation provisions (ch. 14 Criminal Code), which is generally regarded as protecting the legal good of honor:[†]

> The target of insult [§ 185 Criminal Code] is the inner honor, which every human has as the carrier of spiritual and ethical values, as well as his significance as such, his good reputation in the society of fellow humans. The essential basis of this inner honor and therefore the core of every human's honorability is the inalienable personal dignity he possesses from birth, which the Basic Law affirms as inviolable in art. 1 Basic Law and explicitly obliges all state power to respect and protect.
>
> German Federal Court of Justice, BGH NJW 1958, 228.

In the United States, the criminal (and, for that matter, civil) legal protection of "honor" is complicated by the so-called firstness of the First Amendment, which subjects state action that might "chill" the exercise of the right to free speech to particular scrutiny (even to the point where courts have found a constitutional *mens rea* requirement in cases implicating First Amendment rights[‡]). In contrast, the article setting out the right to free expression in the German Basic Law, art. 5, explicitly recognizes "the right to personal honor" as a limit on that right. Interestingly, while criminal libel laws remain on the books of many American states, they are treated as dead letter. The case most closely associated with limits on even *civil* liability for libel was argued by none other than the Chief Reporter of the Model Penal Code, Herbert Wechsler, who two years after the completion of the Model Penal Code convinced the U.S. Supreme Court, in *New York Times v. Sullivan*, 376 U.S. 254 (1964), to require public officials to establish "actual malice"—not surprisingly (given the Model Code's approach to *mens rea*) interpreted to mean knowledge of, or at least recklessness regarding, the falsity of the claim in question.

For a rare more recent attempt to bring a criminal libel prosecution, see *Mink v. Knox*, 613 F.3d 995 (10th Cir. 2010). The criminal prosecution in this case, based on a Colorado college student's allegedly libelous online depiction of a professor, was not only dismissed, but resulted in a civil rights suit brought by the student against the prosecutor, and contributed to the repeal of Colorado's criminal libel statute shortly thereafter.

In the United States, and common law countries more generally, the protection of honor in criminal law is generally associated with the (controversial) traditional rationale of the (partial) defense of "provocation," or—in the modern, Model Penal Code based, parlance—"extreme (mental or) emotional disturbance" in cases of intentional homicide. The protection of honor is also occasionally invoked in cases of so-called "honor killings," in which the defendant raises a "cultural defense," arguing that American criminal law should respect the norms of culture in which the protection of personal honor is valued more highly, and therefore considered more deserving of protection even through violent acts, including homicide.[§] In contrast, honor

---

* *Commonwealth v. Niemic*, 427 Mass. 718, 722, 696 N.E.2d 117 (1998).

† For a brief overview of the (contested) significance of honor in German criminal law, see Thomas Winter, "Deutschland," in Silvia Tellenbach (ed.), *Die Rolle der Ehre im Strafrecht* (2007), 95.

‡ See, e.g., *United States v. X-Citement Video, Inc.*, 513 U.S. 64 (1994).

§ See, e.g., Pascale Fournier, Pascal McDougall, and Anna R. Dekker, "Dishonour, Provocation and Culture: Through the Beholder's Eye?," 16 *Canadian Criminal Law Review* (2012), 161 (exploring "the (Western) 'provocation defence,' an institution which is historically rooted in male honour and whose concrete operation in Canada has sometimes been to uphold homicidal schemes that are no stranger to notions of bruised honour"). (See the discussion of homicide in Chapter 15.A.iii.)

killings in German criminal law are often classified as driven by "base motives," which identify the actor as a "murderer," subject to mandatory life imprisonment.*

5. Another element of self-defense is that the attack (or, more precisely the force against which the defendant is said to have defended himself) be "unlawful." This question has attracted considerable attention in German criminal law, much less so in American criminal law. Consider the almost comically ill-drafted Model Penal Code's definition of unlawful force, in § 3.11(1), which appears to have been dropped in from another time and place, replete with references to notoriously ill-defined concepts borrowed from the law of torts ("privilege") and similarly ill-defined traditional criminal law concepts studiously avoided elsewhere in the Code ("intent"):

> "unlawful force" means force, including confinement, which is employed without the consent of the person against whom it is directed and the employment of which constitutes an offense or actionable tort or would constitute such offense or tort except for a defense (such as the absence of intent, negligence, or mental capacity; duress; youth; or diplomatic status) not amounting to a privilege to use the force. Assent constitutes consent, within the meaning of this Section, whether or not it otherwise is legally effective, except assent to the infliction of death or serious bodily harm.

In German criminal law, the classic illustration of the prerequisite of the unlawfulness of the attack is the case of the dueling self-defense claims: A's (purported) self-defense against B's act of self-defense, which is taken to illustrate the "impossibility" of self-defense against a lawful attack. A's defense cannot be lawful if B's (prior) act is already lawful; right can only be on one side. In that case, A could not qualify for self-defense as a justification—though he or she may invoke a mistake regarding a justification (specifically "putative self-defense").†

Is the supposed "logical" impossibility of self-defense as a justification against an attack that is itself lawful more than a matter of definition? Does the answer to this question depend (in part) on whether you favor one account of self-defense over another ("law-protection" vs. "self-protection")?

6. *Unlawful force.* The definition of self-defense in terms of protection against unlawful "force"—as opposed to an unlawful attack—may require separate treatment of the defense of property. (Recall that German criminal law speaks in terms of *Notwehr*, emergency defense, generally, rather than self-defense.) As noted previously, the Model Penal Code draws a sharp distinction between defense of property and defense of person (self and other), rejecting the use of deadly force (defined broadly to include "force which the actor uses with the purpose of causing or which he knows to create a substantial risk of causing death or serious bodily harm," § 3.11(2)) to protect property interests. At the same time, the conception of self-defense as the "use of force upon or toward another" has caused difficulties for courts in cases dealing with attempts to justify, in terms of self-defense, offenses against property, rather than against the person. In *Boget v. State*, 74 S.W.3d 23 (Ct. Crim. App. Tex. 2002), the Texas Court of Criminal Appeals allowed the defense against a charge of criminal mischief because "a rule that allows a charge on self-defense where a person kills another, but prohibits the defense when a person merely damages the other's property" is "illogical" and inconsistent with the statutory purpose of "encouraging the use of restraint in defensive situations," under the following facts:

> Boget said that when he approached the vehicle, the truck "took off" toward him and hit him. The impact caused Boget to hit the front windshield, flip over the top of the truck, and land in the truck bed. According to Boget, he then began hitting the back windshield and rear windows with his flashlight.

Do you agree?

7. *Subjective vs. objective.* It is now widely accepted, in American and German criminal law, that defenses—more specifically justifications—have a subjective aspect, just as offenses do.

---

* See, e.g., BGH, 5 StR 538/01 (2002).
† See Note 8.

Defenses are occasionally said to "mirror" offenses, although it is not always clear just how close—or fruitful—the connection between offense and defense analysis really is. It is generally agreed that a defendant is not entitled to a justification simply because its elements are objectively satisfied (the mirror image of a strict, or absolute, liability offense), no matter what attitude or awareness, if any, she may have had toward them. So I cannot claim the justification of self-defense even though the person I pushed down the stairs was, unbeknownst to me, about to stab me with a stiletto.* But doesn't this distinction turn on a difference in motive? And aren't motives supposed to be irrelevant for purposes of criminal liability, at least in Anglo-American criminal law?†

At the same time, a defendant may be entitled to some defense (whether it's called self-defense or something else—like "putative self-defense," discussed in Chapter 13.A, Note 8) even if the elements have not objectively satisfied, as long as she *believed* they have been. The latter cases are far more common, though perhaps less interesting, than the former.

8. *Mistaken self-defense.* Very often in cases of self-defense or defense of another, the legal discussion centers on defendants' errors. As the remark by Justice Holmes quoted in *State v. Kelly* ("detached reflection cannot be demanded in the presence of an uplifted knife") points out, in the stressful situation created by an attack, mistaken perceptions and judgments are frequent. In a similar way, the psychological stress created by the erroneous belief of being under attack can lead persons to misread the situation. Also, after criminal investigations have begun, it can be expected that defendants claim to have seen things in a more benign way than they really did. This leads to the problem of reconstructing the defendant's actual state of mind at the time of the offense. But in terms of substantive criminal law, as opposed to the law of evidence, the interesting question is how legal systems respond to actual (or "honest") though mistaken beliefs.

One possible solution is to apply merely subjective standards in the examination of self-defense and to assess both the presence of an attack and necessity of a defense based on the defendant's actual beliefs. This purely subjective approach can be found in the English case of *Williams (Gladstone)* (and in the Model Penal Code—at least according to the (questionable) reading by the New York Court of Appeals in *Goetz* (more on this point in Note 10)). A second approach applies an objective filter to subjective beliefs. In this mode, New York law uses the term "reasonably believes" twice, referring to the presence of unlawful physical force by another and to the necessity of the defense. Section 32 Criminal Code does not, in contrast to the New York Penal Law, refer to a "reasonable belief." Here, we find the third approach: the prerequisites in § 32 Criminal Code must be present objectively. There must *in fact* have been an imminent unlawful act, and it must have been objectively necessary to fend it off in the way the actor did. German criminal law doctrine does not treat cases in which defendants merely believed themselves to be attacked (but were not) as cases of "self-defense," strictly speaking. This might sound as if German law was stricter than American law—it is not, it only treats such cases under a different label and with a differently structured analysis.

The label is "putative self-defense" (*Putativnotwehr*) or, more generally, "error about the existence of justifying circumstances" (*Erlaubnistatbestandsirrtum*). There has been a big debate in the German criminal law literature about how to deal with imagined attacks and other comparable errors of fact. The German Criminal Code does not explicitly mention errors about the existence of justifying circumstances. Case law and the majority opinion in the literature today opt for applying § 16 Criminal Code to errors concerning the presence of justifying circumstances. The wording of § 16 Criminal Code covers errors about facts that constitute the elements of the crime‡ but the idea is that erring about a fact concerning an element in a justification is comparable.

---

* For an airing of these issues in American criminal law, see Paul H. Robinson, "A Theory of Justification: Societal Harm as a Prerequisite for Criminal. Responsibility," 23 *UCLA Law Review* (1975), 266; George P. Fletcher, "The Right Deed for the Wrong Reason: A Reply to Mr. Robinson," 23 *UCLA Law Review* (1975), 293.

† See Chapter 8.A.

‡ See Chapter 8.C.

It may be worth pausing to see how the majority opinion in German criminal law lands on this position. Since the German Criminal Code doesn't address the issue, one basic question is whether mistakes regarding defense elements should be treated under § 16 or § 17 Criminal Code. Under § 17, mistakes regarding defense elements would at best make out an excuse, and as in the case of mistakes of law regarding the existence of *offense*, would be relevant only if they were avoidable.*

Today, there is a general consensus that treatment under § 16 Criminal Code is preferable, for various reasons, including (1) that a mistake regarding the presence of a defense element more closely resembles a mistake regarding the presence of an offense element than it does a mistake regarding the existence of an offense (in other words, that it is more like a "mistake of fact" than a "mistake of law") and (2) that the requirement of unavoidability would violate the constitutional "culpability principle" insofar as it would treat negligent (but avoidable) conduct as intentional conduct. (Recall here the related distinction between (a) the New York position, which—as set out in *Goetz*—disregards unreasonable mistakes altogether and convicts of an intent crime even if the mistake was negligent and (b) the Model Penal Code position, which tailors criminal liability to the type of mistake, limiting liability to a negligence offense in the event of a negligently unreasonable mistake, on the other.)†

9. Note that the outcome in English law resembles the outcome in German law: in *R. v. Williams (Gladstone)*, the Court of Appeal argues that the jury had to decide whether the defendant in fact believed in the existence of an unlawful attack. The belief need not have been reasonable, though reasonableness of the belief may be taken as evidence of its actuality: all other things being equal, the fact finder is more likely to find that the defendant in fact held a certain belief if holding that belief would have been reasonable under the circumstances (i.e., if a reasonable person would have held it). But this is a matter of proof. On the substantive question, the English Court comes to a similar conclusion as German case law: if honestly held, even an unreasonable error about the existence of an attack suffices for the justification of defense of another. (This subjective approach can also be found in the English law of mistake of fact, most notoriously in the case of *DPP v. Morgan*, in which the House of Lords held that an actual ("honest"), though mistaken, belief regarding consent in a rape case precluded criminal liability, without drawing a distinction between mistakes regarding an offense element or a defense element, i.e., between (non-)consent as an element of rape or as a justification.‡)

Under this approach, even if the defendant's misperception is based on silliness or prejudices, he will not be punished for intentional killing or otherwise harming the supposed attacker (but he can be convicted of a negligent crime under German law, § 16 para. 1 sentence 2 Criminal Code). German law and English law can lead to results that might appear unfair from the victim's perspective. Imagine for instance that the actor injured another because he believed he was about to be attacked—but the ostensible attacker had done nothing whatsoever to create such a misconception; the error was based solely on the actor's paranoia and racist views. If the law does not demand screening for reasonableness, even the most offensive beliefs stand in the way of a conviction for intentional bodily injury (provided that this "defense" would have satisfied the "necessity" requirement in the case of a real attack§).

The Model Penal Code addresses mistakes regarding defense elements in a separate provision:

Section 3.09. Mistake of Law as to Unlawfulness of Force or Legality of Arrest; Reckless or Negligent Use of Otherwise Justifiable Force...

(1) The justification afforded by Sections 3.04 to 3.07, inclusive, is unavailable when:

(a) the actor's belief in the unlawfulness of the force or conduct against which he employs protective force or his belief in the lawfulness of an arrest which he endeavors to effect by force is erroneous; and

---

* See Chapter 8.C.ii.
† On the culpability principle, see Chapter 3.A.
‡ *Morgan v. DPP* [1975] 2 WLR 913, [1976] AC 182; but see now Sexual Offences Act 2003, §§ 74–77.
§ See Note 10.

(b) his error is due to ignorance or mistake as to the provisions of the Code, any other provision of the criminal law or the law governing the legality of an arrest or search.

(2) When the actor believes that the use of force upon or toward the person of another is necessary for any of the purposes for which such belief would establish a justification under Sections 3.03 to 3.08 but the actor is reckless or negligent in having such belief or in acquiring or failing to acquire any knowledge or belief which is material to the justifiability of his use of force, the justification afforded by those Sections is unavailable in a prosecution for an offense for which recklessness or negligence, as the case may be, suffices to establish culpability....

Subsection (1) restates the Model Code's general rejection of mistake of law as a defense, applying it to defenses, rather than offenses.* A mistake of law regarding a defense (justification) element (or the existence of a defense) is no more of an excuse than is a mistake of law regarding an offense element (or the existence of an offense). Similarly, subsection (2) applies the Model Code's general approach to mistakes of fact to defenses, rather than offenses: a mistake of fact is relevant insofar, and only insofar, as it negates an offense element—in particular a required mental state, *mens rea*. So, in the context of a defense like self-defense, a mistaken belief regarding the conditions (or elements) of self-defense is relevant insofar, and only insofar, as it negates an element of the offense in question: for instance, the effect of a defendant's mistaken belief that she must defend herself against an imminent attack will depend on the nature of her belief and on the definition of the offense with which she is charged. If she is reckless in holding the mistaken belief (i.e., under the Model Penal Code definition of reckless, she consciously disregards a substantial and unjustifiable risk that she may be mistaken), then she will be acquitted if (1) the offense with which she is charged requires a mental state "higher" than recklessness: knowledge, purpose and (2) no other, lesser included, offense (requiring recklessness or negligence) exists. The same applies *mutatis mutandis* in cases of a negligent mistake (so that she will only escape liability for offenses that require a mental state "higher" than negligence: recklessness, knowledge, purpose).

In other words, the New York Court of Appeals in *Goetz* misinterprets the Model Penal Code as adopting a purely subjective approach to mistakes regarding defense elements. The fact that the Model Code section on self-defense does not refer to reasonableness reflects the drafters' general discomfort with this vague term, not their rejection of an objective aspect of the analysis of mistakes. In fact, they elsewhere clarify that "'reasonably believes' or 'reasonable belief' designates a belief which the actor is not reckless or negligent in holding" (§ 1.13 (16)). Reckless and negligent mistakes, thus, are simply two forms of unreasonable belief.

The New York Court of Appeals reads the relevant provision of the New York Penal Law as retaining an all-or-nothing approach to the law of self-defense: reasonable belief exculpates, unreasonable belief does not. The murder defendant who makes a reasonable mistake is acquitted, the one who makes an unreasonable mistake is convicted of murder. The Model Penal Code instead differentiates between two types of unreasonable mistake (without referring to "reasonableness"): if the mistake was reckless—and an applicable recklessness offense exists—then the defendant holding this belief is acquitted of an offense requiring a higher mental state (murder), but guilty of a recklessness offense (manslaughter); if the mistake is negligent—and an applicable negligence offense exists—then she is guilty of a negligence offense (negligent homicide).

10. If one were to analyze *Goetz* according to German law, it might appear as if Goetz would have been acquitted in Germany even if his belief that the four young men were about to victimize him was unreasonable.† However, this conclusion would be premature. Even if the offender in fact did believe that he was about to be attacked, his defense must still have been necessary. The crucial test concerns the hypothetical scenario: if there really had been an attack, would this kind of defense have been necessary?

Here it might be helpful to distinguish between two questions: what are the facts the offender believed, and what is the correct assessment of necessity based on these facts? The

---

* See the discussion in Chapter 8.C.ii.
† See George P. Fletcher and Steve Sheppard, *American Law in a Global Context* (2005), 563–4.

person who (perhaps erroneously) believed he was about to be attacked can also err about additional facts, for instance, by believing that one of the attackers held a knife or another weapon in his hand (which allows more intense measures of defense), or by not realizing that other, less harmful, means for effective defense were at hand. Again, such errors about facts will be treated under German law according to § 16 para. 1 Criminal Code (see the Federal Court of Justice ruling from 1986).

But in cases like *Goetz*, the decisive question is: how far may citizens go in self-defense? This is a normative question, a question of law, which must not be left to the subjective assessment of the offender but decided for all acts of self-defense. It is inconsistent if a legal system dismisses as irrelevant mistakes of law based on defendants' idiosyncratic views about the law (which both the German the American system do*) but leaves the scope of self-defense in particular cases to individuals' personal predilections. There ought to be a normative filter, and therefore there are good reasons for a solution like that in New York law, i.e., to demand "reasonable belief" concerning the necessity of the defensive action.

Under German law, the assessment "was this necessary?"[†] follows objective standards. If Goetz would have pursued his vigilant activities in a German city, he might have under certain circumstances gotten away with using firearms against presumed attackers—but not under the circumstances as described in the ruling by the New York Court of Appeals. Even if Goetz believed that the four young men were about to assault him or to rob him: firing without prior warning and aiming for the center of the body of each of the young men indicates that even the first shot (and certainly not the last shot on Cabey) was not necessary to ward off an attack. Goetz's conduct therefore would be labeled "unlawful" under German law.[‡]

11. In considering *Goetz*, it may be useful to recall the procedural posture of the case when it reached the New York Court of Appeals. The case was before the court on an appeal by the prosecution from the trial court's dismissal of an indictment based on what the trial court had found to have been an erroneous instruction by the prosecutor to the grand jury on the law of self-defense, specifically the standard applicable to beliefs regarding the presence of the elements of the defense. (The prosecutor, rather than the judge, instructs the grand jury because no official charge has been filed. The grand jury decides whether or not to bring charges, an indictment. The petit jury then decides at trial whether the charges have been proved. The judge instructs the petit jury.) The question was not whether Goetz was entitled to an acquittal on self-defense grounds, but whether the prosecution had misinstructed the grand jury on what it would take for him to be acquitted on self-defense grounds. In other words, the case was not about whether Goetz succeeded in raising the defense, but whether he was deprived of the opportunity to raise it in the first place. No trial had taken place at the time. The question was whether the grand jury's indictment (i.e., the formal charge) was flawed, not how the case should be resolved on the facts, and on the merits, or even whether there was sufficient evidence in the record at the time to support a finding that, even based on a correct statement of the law of self-defense, Goetz would be entitled to raise the defense, never mind to successfully raise it, resulting in an acquittal. In fact, after the New York Court of Appeals reinstated the indictment, Goetz was tried before a (different) jury and was acquitted of assault and attempted murder. He was, however, convicted of possession of an illegal weapon for which he served eight and a half months in prison.

12. But what about the aforementioned remark by Justice Holmes ("detached reflection cannot be demanded in the presence of an uplifted knife"), which draws attention to psychological limits in life-threatening situations? Should we not have some degree of understanding for overreactions under certain circumstances? From a German perspective, this is an occasion to point out the usefulness of distinguishing excuses from justifications.

---

* See Chapter 8.C.

[†] See German Criminal Code § 32.

[‡] For similar concerns about the need to cabin defenses through the use of objective tests in the law of *necessity*, see Chapter 13.B; see also Model Penal Code § 3.02 ("harm or evil sought to be avoided...*is* greater than that sought to be prevented by the law defining the offense charged").

Section 33 Criminal Code excuses an offender whose defensive action was not objectively necessary if he acted out of confusion, fear or terror. If more aggressive emotions like anger, resentment, hatred, or a desire for retaliation motivated the offender, however, the excuse does not apply. (How can we tell the difference?) The circumstances of the *Goetz* case indicate that he acted for the latter kind of motives—accordingly, he would not even be excused under German law.

13. Note, in § 33 Criminal Code, the explicit recognition of the doctrinal significance of motive: only the person who exceeds the limits of self-defense "out of confusion, fear or terror" will "not be punished" (as opposed to acts that remain within the limits of self-defense, which are "not unlawful," § 32 Criminal Code); on the other end of the spectrum, compare the consideration—as an aggravating element—of "base motives" as the distinctive characteristic of a "murderer" in the German law of homicide, § 211 para. 2(2) Criminal Code (e.g., pleasure, sexual gratification, greed).[*]

14. In a case like *State v. Kelly*, on the other hand, the defendant would have had good chances of acquittal under German law. To come to this result, a German court would not need to engage in an extensive discussion of the situation of battered wives in general or the particular history of the marriage in the particular case.[†] The facts as they are stated for the day of the crime show a very violent attitude of the husband towards the defendant at this very moment in time: he choked, punched and bit her. Even if these two persons were not spouses in a "stormy marriage," if they were acquaintances or strangers before the violent first attack of the man, one could assess the defendant's stabbing as necessary defense. Before coming to a conclusion, a German court would ask the following questions according to the established analysis of "errors about justifying circumstances": Suppose this was in fact a second attack as Ms. Kelly believed it to be, did the defendant have other means to effectively defend herself? Might she have stopped the attack by fighting without a weapon? Obviously not, as the first attack showed. Or could she have saved herself by simply showing her scissors and thus deterring the attacker? Again, the effectiveness of doing this would have been highly questionable—the attacker, in his agitated state, might have simply snatched away the scissors and used them against her. Therefore, even without applying the excuse in § 33 Criminal Code, the defendant probably would be spared punishment under German law.

Again, it may help to keep in mind the procedural posture of the *Kelly* case. In this opinion, the New Jersey Supreme Court considers an appeal from a manslaughter conviction, which argued—among other things—that the trial court had improperly excluded testimony on battered woman syndrome. As in *Goetz*, the court thus is not addressing the case on its merits, i.e., it is not undertaking an analysis of criminal liability; it is addressing the specific issue before it: should the trial court have permitted expert testimony on the question of battered woman syndrome? Whether Ms. Kelly might have had available to her other arguments, or whether the case required a consideration of battered woman syndrome, is thus beside the point; she had raised the issue and had requested expert testimony to bolster her claim; this request was denied; she was convicted by a jury (of manslaughter, though not of murder); she appealed.

The *Kelly* case is significant because it is one of the earliest cases discussing the possible relevance of battered woman syndrome evidence in general, and to the issue of self-defense in particular. Consider the various ways in which battered woman syndrome evidence might be relevant? Voluntariness? *Mens rea*? Provocation? Self-defense (reasonableness of belief? honesty of belief?)? Diminished capacity? Insanity?

Does it matter just how battered woman syndrome evidence fits into the analysis of criminal liability? Does the defense, or its consideration in the context of a reasonable woman standard, institutionalize negative stereotypes of women?[‡]

---

[*] On the contested role of motives in substantive criminal law, see Chapter 8.A.
[†] Compare the discussion of the broad conception of self-defense in German criminal law, in Note 3.
[‡] See Anne Coughlin, "Excusing Women," 82 *California Law Review* (1994), 1.

Both *Kelly* and *Goetz* are often seen as fitting into a general trend to subjectivize the once (purportedly) objective "reasonable man" standard.* Can we draw a principled distinction between battered woman syndrome evidence and evidence of racist beliefs? Is one characteristic more reasonable than the other? More relevant?

15. In the German *Family Tyrant Case* from 2002, the Federal Court of Justice considers whether the defendant had a duty to retreat, i.e., to leave the apartment rather than defending herself against her husband's attack. Note that this normally will be expected neither in cases of self-defense nor in the case of an erroneously assumed attack (putative self-defense): attacked persons are in general entitled to defend themselves actively rather than to flee.

But some restrictions have been developed in the German case law. Section 32 para. 1 Criminal Code states that the defense must also be "appropriate." Referring to this notion of "appropriateness," under certain circumstances courts will not classify actions of defense as justified despite the fact that within the category "active defense" a less harmful alternative had not been available and thus the act was "necessary." If battered women after years of ill treatment finally defend themselves with a weapon and with fatal consequences, they typically choose such drastic measures because they are physically weaker and attempts to ward off an attack without recourse to a weapon would therefore not be effective.

What could be reasons why courts demand flight, if flight is feasible, and consider active resistance as not being "appropriate"? One example would be if the attacker was a child or mentally impaired. (Why should that matter?) Another set of cases is based on the notion of provocation (see also Model Penal Code § 3.04(2)(b)(i) ("the actor, with the purpose of causing death or serious bodily harm, provoked the use of force against himself in the same encounter")). In the 2002 case, if the defendant displayed the knife although she knew that this would increase her husband's rage, this might be considered provocation. If the person who is later attacked has knowingly contributed to an increase in tension, he or she may be obliged to flee if an attack is imminent—but only if this is possible, otherwise even the person who added provocative elements to a tense situation may defend herself. The demand that provocation obliges the provoker to flee, if possible, is not restricted to battered women cases—the courts apply it to different kinds of reprehensible conduct on the part of the person who is later attacked.

A second and more controversial restriction on active resistance has been developed in older cases, which the Federal Court of Justice cites in its 2002 decision. The notion here is that within marriages and within families the person attacked must be more considerate towards the attacker than they need to be if he was a stranger. They have to leave the scene of the attack, if possible, rather than choose active defense if the latter would seriously injure the attacker. This approach required also accepting minor injuries if these minor injuries could only be avoided by defending oneself in a way which will kill or seriously injure the attacking family member (contrast Model Penal Code § 3.04(2)(b)(ii)(1) ("the actor is not obliged to retreat from his dwelling": so-called castle doctrine)).

It might be somewhat easier to understand this notion of "appropriateness" if considering a child who physically attacks a parent—under such circumstances, the parent ought not to grab a knife but rather leave the room or endure a minor injury. But this case law met criticism as it implies that wives and partners must accept, for instance, another slap in the face if the only way to avert this would be to use a knife, a gun or other weapon against the violent partner. The Federal Court of Justice leaves this open in the 2002 case—but still demands that the defendant should have left the apartment before the violence spiked up. (Does this mark a change in "social ethical" norms? How, by whom, would this be measured?)

It is obvious that the German Federal Court of Justice did not hear expert witnesses on the situation of battered women. If the judges had done so, they might not have so easily embraced the idea that "just go" might be an easy option for women in problematic and violent marriages. The description of the marital history in the German case sounds familiar if one has read about the typical cycles of violence and contrition described by the expert witness in *Kelly*. More sensitivity to battered women's situation would be advisable for

---

* Compare the related discussion in the context of *mens rea*, and negligence in particular, in Chapter 8.A.

German courts—but there is no broad discussion about this in the forensic literature or appellate court decisions. In general one can say that feminists' work has not been very influential in German criminal law doctrine and practice. The role of battered woman syndrome in criminal law is, however, not uncontroversial from a feminist perspective.* At any rate, is there something about the German doctrine of self-defense that complicates the consideration of evidence of battered woman syndrome evidence? Does evidence of battered woman syndrome affect the "social ethical" norms governing the interpretation of the "appropriateness" of the use of force in self-defense?

16. Note how the German Federal Court of Justice's 2002 opinion in the battered woman case draws attention to the fact that each action undertaken by a defendant must be examined separately, even if these actions occur rapidly one after the other. The numerous stabbings undertaken by the female defendant in the German case had a different meaning if judged according to the criminal law, much like the shots which Goetz fired individually at his four victims. After the first victim was hit with the first bullet, it was hardly plausible that Goetz could have believed he was still in danger or being robbed, and it is dubious that belief in the necessity of self-defense could possibly be assumed for the very last shot at Cabey.

17. The question of whether defense of another can be "appropriate" also played a central role in the famous *Daschner Case*. Daschner, the vice president of the Frankfurt police force, was tried for inducing a subordinate police officer to commit a crime (§ 357 Criminal Code): coercing another person to an act (here: a statement about the whereabouts of the boy) through the threat of violence (§ 240 para. 1 Criminal Code). The question here was whether Daschner's order was justified. Had the young boy whom Gäfgen had kidnapped to extort money still been alive, Gäfgen would have attacked the boy's liberty, health and life. As the victim of the kidnapping was already dead, however, this was not a case of defense of another—but the police officers did not know this. The regional court therefore considered an error about a justifying circumstances (putative defense of another); according to German case law, this would be a case for § 16 para 1 Criminal Code.†

For an assumed attack as well as for a real attack, the first question is whether the defensive measure was *necessary*.‡ Somewhat mysteriously, the regional court held that "other measures were available." This referred to the fact that the police officers had discussed other ways of getting Gäfgen to speak. One of the ideas was to confront Gäfgen with the kidnapped boy's juvenile sister whom he knew. The court held that threatening violence would not have been necessary because a less intrusive measure was still available. But this is highly questionable—several persons had already tried in vain to get Gäfgen to reveal where he had hidden the boy, among them Gäfgen's own mother. It was not very likely that further appeals to his conscience would have been an effective strategy to save the boy's life.

As an additional argument, the court states that the threat was not *appropriate* in the sense of § 32 para. 1 Criminal Code. Here lies the center of the legal debate. The court expresses the widespread opinion that police officers may never, even if this is the only means to save a kidnapping victim's life, threaten or use violence to induce a statement by the kidnapper. The argument relies on the notion of human dignity, a central right in the German Basic Law (art. 1 para. 1 Basic Law), which is, again according to the majority opinion, not open to a weighing of interests. Some writers have criticized this because it means sacrificing the victim of the kidnapping for our shared interest in the absoluteness of a prohibition against torture. Of course, this interest is of high importance and plays a central role in international conventions—but at the price of a human life? Also, some commentators pointed to the fact that Gäfgen was not tortured—violence was not applied but only threatened. Should the threat of violence be treated differently than the actual infliction of violence?

---

* See Anne Coughlin, "Excusing Women," 82 *California Law Review* (1994), 1.
† See Note 8.
‡ See Note 3.

Note that the regional court in the end reached a kind of compromise: the defendants were convicted but received one of the mildest reactions available in the German Criminal Code, even milder than a fine: a mere warning (§ 59 Criminal Code).*

18. The *Daschner Case* judgment also considers—and rejects—the defense of necessity, both as justification (§ 34) and as excuse (§ 35 Criminal Code).[†]

B. Necessity

Although self-defense tends to attract the bulk of comparative attention, necessity is worth a closer look (and not only because of its relationship to self-defense!). For instance, it is interesting to discover that the justification of necessity, until recently, spent its doctrinal career in both Anglo-American and German criminal law as a judge-made defense, in the shadowed crevices of criminal codes. This is surely less surprising, and noteworthy, in Anglo-American criminal law, given its long aversion to codification in general, than it is in German criminal law. Until the revision of the German Criminal Code in 1975, self-defense was the only justification set out in the German Criminal Code. There was a necessity provision in the original 1871 Code, but it set out an excuse, rather than a justification based on a balancing of interests (or legal goods, or "harms or evils," in the Model Penal Code formulation).[‡] Justifying necessity in German criminal law, by contrast, was not recognized until 1927, in a decision by the German Supreme Court, as a "supra-statutory" defense. And so it came about that the justification of necessity was first codified in a common law jurisdiction, the American Model Penal Code, in 1962, while it persisted as a judge-made doctrine in codified German criminal law for another decade or so.

Necessity is a schizophrenic defense—it is generally thought to come in two versions, as a justification and as an excuse (*pace* the Canadian Supreme Court's decision in *R. v. Perka* (below))—with the inevitably attendant doctrinal anxieties about the relationship between the two sides of its personality. Among the distinctions we will encounter is that based on the source of the necessity: another person or circumstances. Some insist that circumstantial necessity can only function as a justification (Model Penal Code), others that circumstantial necessity can only function as an excuse (*Perka*). Personal necessity is generally recognized as a defense (an excuse), though not necessarily under the name of necessity, but of "duress" (Model Penal Code and *Perka*). Under German criminal law, personal and circumstantial necessity both can amount to either justifying or excusing necessity, depending on the case.

People v. Craig
Court of Appeals of New York
78 N.Y.2d 616, 585 N.E.2d 783 (1991)

Hancock, Judge.

Defendants were arrested on May 7, 1985 and charged with the violation of trespass (Penal Law § 140.05[§]) when they refused to leave the office of a United States Representative after conducting a peaceful demonstration in which they voiced their opposition to the policy of the United States in imposing an embargo of Nicaragua. In a nonjury trial, Rochester City Court rejected the defense of justification under Penal Law § 35.05(2), which, under certain circumstances, provides that conduct that would otherwise be illegal may be justified as necessary to avoid a greater evil. County Court affirmed and defendants have appealed to this Court by leave . . .

---

* Compare the *Border Guard Case* and *Dudley & Stephens*, in Chapters 8.C.ii and 6.C, respectively.
[†] See Note 13.
[‡] For more on this provision, and on excusing necessity in general, see Chapter 14.A.

[§] [N.Y. Penal Law § 140.05 ("A person is guilty of trespass when he knowingly enters or remains unlawfully in or upon premises. Trespass is a violation.").—Eds.]

City Court... precluded defendants from offering testimony of expert witnesses to substantiate their contentions concerning the imminence and seriousness of the injuries allegedly resulting from the Government's policies. The court reasoned that Penal Law § 35.05(2) called for a subjective, state-of-mind standard of proof and that the only relevant question was whether a defendant's "intent or state of mind was such that it raises itself to the defense of justification." It, therefore, excluded expert opinions of third parties as irrelevant.

In a written decision, City Court found that the prosecution had disproved the defense of justification beyond a reasonable doubt[1] and had established defendants' guilt of trespass under Penal Law § 140.05....On appeal, defendants' primary argument is that City Court erred in its interpretation of Penal Law § 35.05(2) as establishing a subjective rather than an objective standard and in its exclusion of defendants' proffered expert testimony...

The general notion that conduct which would otherwise be criminal may be justified as necessary to avoid a greater harm, now codified in New York in Penal Law § 35.05(2), may be traced to cases in the early English common law. In the older English cases, it was a defense to a criminal charge that a defendant committed an act to save a life or to put out a fire. And prisoners might escape from a burning jail without violating the law. In the United States, early Federal cases also recognized the defense of necessity (see, e.g., United States v. Ashton, 24 Fed. Cas. No. 14,470 [C.C.D.Mass.1834] [sailors charged with mutiny justified their refusal to obey captain's orders on ground that ship was not seaworthy]). Where the defense was permitted in the common law, the cases generally required the existence of an "impending danger, present, imminent and not to be averted" (Note, Necessity as a Defense, 21 Colum. L. Rev. 71, 72–73).

The view that necessity for avoiding a greater evil might afford a justification for prohibited conduct was adopted in 1962 by the American Law Institute in Model Penal Code § 3.02. Section 3.02 reflects the judgment that a "choice of evils" defense "like the general requirements of culpability, is essential to the rationality and justice of the criminal law, and is appropriately addressed in a penal code." The essential concept of the Model Code provision is that conduct which "the actor believes to be necessary to avoid a harm or evil to himself or to another" is justifiable, provided that "the harm or evil sought to be avoided" is greater than that "sought to be prevented by the law" being broken (§ 3.02[a]). The provision is not, by its terms, limited to cases involving imminent danger. Nevertheless, the examples given in the commentaries to section 3.02 are of emergency situations involving immediate threat of harm reminiscent of the older common-law cases—e.g., destroying property to prevent spread of a fire, entering a vacant cabin as refuge in a mountain blizzard and using provisions, jettisoning cargo or violating an embargo to save a vessel.

New York's first recognition of the defense of necessity came in 1965 with the adoption of Penal Law § 35.05(2) as part of the revised Penal Law....Although derived from Model Code § 3.02, section 35.05(2) is more limited than the Model Code provision and contains restrictive language not found in section 3.02 (e.g., in the requirements that conduct to be justified must be "necessary as an *emergency measure* to avoid an *imminent* public or private injury which *is about to occur*" and that "the desirability and *urgency* of avoiding such injury clearly outweigh the desirability of avoiding" the prohibited conduct [emphasis added]). The Staff Notes of the Temporary State Commission on Revision of the Penal Law and Criminal Code indicate that section 35.05(2) was envisioned as providing a defense of justification "in rare and highly unusual circumstances." As illustrative of conduct which would be justifiable under the section, the Staff Notes cite, inter alia, the "burning of real property of another in order to prevent a raging forest fire from spreading into a densely populated community."

Section 35.05(2) differs from the Model Code provision in another significant particular. Unlike the Model Code which contains a standard for justifiability that is partially subjective (i.e., "[c]onduct that the actor *believes to be necessary* to avoid a harm or evil to himself or to another" [§ 3.02(1)] [emphasis added]), the New York statutory standard is, by its terms, objective. There is no reference in section 35.05(2) to what the actor intends, or believes to be necessary. In this respect, the section is also unlike Penal Law § 35.15 which bases justification for the use of physical force on the actor's reasonable belief that such force is necessary to defend himself or a third person (§ 35.15) and for the use of deadly force on the actor's reasonable belief that the other person is using or about to use deadly physical force (§ 35.15[a]).

In *People v. Goetz*, 68 N.Y.2d 96, 506 N.Y.S.2d 18, 497 N.E.2d 41, we emphasized that the words "reasonably believes" in Penal Law § 35.15 embody in the justification standard for self-defense elements which are subjective (i.e., what the actor believes) as well as objective (i.e., whether a reasonable person could have had these beliefs). From the plain wording of section 35.05(2) and the

---

[1] Justification is a defense, not an affirmative defense. If a defendant's conduct is justified on the ground of necessity or choice of evils under Penal Law § 35.05(2), it is not unlawful. When the defense is raised, the People must prove beyond a reasonable doubt that defendant's conduct was not justified.

omission of any language suggesting that justification was intended to depend on any belief held by the actor, we agree with defendants' contention that the statute sets forth a standard that is, by its terms, objective only.[3]

Section 35.05(2) specifies that whenever "evidence relating to the defense of justification under this subdivision is offered by the defendant, the court shall rule as a matter of law whether the claimed facts and circumstances would, if established, constitute a defense." Thus, the court must decide, as a threshold legal question, whether the defense will lie. We turn to whether under the objective standard in section 35.05(2), the avoidance of the harm resulting from the Government's actions in Nicaragua, as postulated by the defendants, could be the basis for a justification defense under the statute. Put another way, the question is: does the harm which defendants sought to avoid by conducting a protest in an effort to change governmental policy constitute an "imminent public or private injury" (§ 35.05) which, as intended by the Legislature, could justify their conduct as a "necessary [preventative]...emergency measure"?

To ascertain the type of situation envisioned by the Legislature in enacting section 35.05(2), we, of course, look first to the statute, giving the words their natural and obvious meaning. It is apparent that the language of the statute bears both on the nature of the conduct to be justified and the harm to be avoided. The conduct must be "necessary as an emergency measure to avoid an imminent public or private injury which is about to occur" (§ 35.05). The requirement that the conduct be "necessary as an emergency measure" to avoid the injury contemplates conduct which is not only warranted by the circumstances as an emergency response but is also reasonably calculated to have an actual effect in preventing the harm. It rules out conduct that is tentative or only advisable or preferable or conduct for which there is a reasonable, legal alternative course of action. And the requirement that the impending injury must be "imminent" and "about to occur" denotes an impending harm which constitutes a present, immediate threat—i.e., a danger that is actual and at hand, not one that is speculative, abstract or remote.

From the foregoing analysis, we conclude that the harm resulting from governmental actions in Nicaragua, as described by defendants, lacks the immediacy required by the statute. Moreover, the actions of defendants in committing a trespass in Congressman Eckert's office cannot be viewed as an emergency measure reasonably calculated to avoid the harm or as a necessary choice over alternative, legal courses of action designed to effect a change in the policy of the Administration. We conclude that the claimed facts and circumstances offered by defendants would not, if established, constitute a defense under section 35.05(2)...

We note that courts in other jurisdictions in cases arising out of protest demonstrations have reached similar conclusions, applying the common law or analogous statutes (see, e.g., *Andrews v. People*, 800 P.2d 607, 609–610 [Colo.1990] [rejecting "choice of evils defense" where defendants blocked road leading to nuclear weapons plant, under statute virtually identical to New York's, because conduct was not effective to achieve the purpose or necessary in the face of available legal alternatives and the threatened harm was long-term and speculative, not definite and imminent]; *People v. Stiso*, 93 Ill.App.3d 101, 48 Ill.Dec. 687, 416 N.E.2d 1209 [1981] [no defense of necessity under statute similar to Model Penal Code for obstructing clinic performing abortions]).

Inasmuch as the claimed facts and circumstances pertaining to the situation in Nicaragua would not, if established, constitute a justification defense, we do not reach defendants' contention that the court erred in excluding their proffered expert testimony....

R. v. Perka
Supreme Court of Canada
[1984] 2 S.C.R. 232

Dickson J.

[The appellants were on their way from Colombia to Alaska when, some two hundred miles off the Canadian coastline, their ship developed mechanical problems. They decided to seek refuge on the shoreline to make temporary repairs. The ship ran aground near Vancouver Island and the captain, to prevent the ship's capsizing, offloaded the cargo, 33.49 tons of marijuana worth $6,000,000 or $7,000,000. Charged with importing cannabis into Canada and with possession for the purpose of trafficking, the appellants produced expert witnesses on marine matters who testified that the

---

[3] Although the operative standard is objective, it would seem virtually inevitable that a defendant who acted under circumstances which made the defense applicable would have done so with the subjective intention of avoiding the greater evil of the imminent injury. We need not address the hypothetical situation where actual necessity existed but the actor did not have the intention of avoiding the greater evil. Here, unquestionably, defendants believed that their conduct would in some way avoid the greater evil in Nicaragua. Nor need we address the situation where—under an objective/reasonable person standard—the action was necessary but necessity-in-fact did not exist.

decision to come ashore was, in the opinion of one witness, expedient and prudent and in the opinion of another essential. The appellants appealed to the Canadian Supreme Court from the reversal by the intermediate appellate court of their acquittal at trial.—Eds.]

II. The necessity defence

(a) History and background

From earliest times it has been maintained that in some situations the force of circumstances makes it unrealistic and unjust to attach criminal liability to actions which, on their face, violate the law. Aristotle, *Ethics* (Book III, 1110 a), discusses the jettisoning of cargo from a ship in distress and remarks that "any sensible man does so" to secure the safety of himself and his crew. Pollard, Sergeant at Law, arguing for the defendant in the case of *Reniger v. Fogossa* (1551), 1 Plowden 1 at p. 18, 75 E. R. 1, maintained:

in every law there are some things which when they happen a man may break the words of the law, and yet not break the law itself; and such things are exempted out of the penalty of the law, and the law privileges them although they are done against the letter of it, for breaking the words of the law is not breaking the law, so as the intent of the law is not broken. And therefore the words of the law of nature, of the law of this realm, and of other realms, and of the law of God also will yield and give way to some acts and things done against the words of the same laws, and that is, where the words of them are broken to avoid greater inconveniences, or through necessity, or by compulsion . . .

In *Leviathan* (Pelican ed., 1968), p. 157, Hobbes writes:

If a man by the terrour of present death, be compelled to doe a fact against the law, he is totally excused; because no law can oblige a man to abandon his own preservation. And supposing such a law were obligatory: yet a man would reason thus, if I doe it not, I die presently: if I doe it I die afterwards: therefore by doing it there is time of life gamed: nature therefore compells him to the fact.

To much the same purpose Kant, in *The Metaphysical Elements of Justice* (translator Ladd, 1965), discussing the actions of a person who, to save his own life sacrifices that of another, says at p. 41:

A penal law applying to such a situation could never have the effect intended for the threat of an evil that is still uncertain (being condemned to death by a judge) cannot outweigh the fear of an evil that is certain (being drowned). Hence, we must judge that, although an act of self-preservation through violence is not inculpable, it still is unpunishable.

In those jurisdictions in which such a general principle has been recognized or codified it is most often referred to by the term "necessity." Classic and harrowing instances which have been cited to illustrate the arguments both for and against the principle include the mother who steals food for her starving child, the shipwrecked mariners who resort to cannibalism (*R. v. Dudley and Stephens* (1884), 14 Q.B.D. 273), or throw passengers overboard to lighten a sinking lifeboat (*United States v. Holmes* (1842), 26 Fed. Cas. 360), and the more mundane case of the motorist who exceeds the speed-limit taking an injured person to the hospital.

In the United States a general defence of necessity has been recognized in the statutory law of a number of states and has found its way into the Model Penal Code of the American Law Institute. Attempts have been made, with mixed success, in American jurisdictions to apply the defence to multifarious types of conduct, including cases involving prison escapes, *United States v. Bailey* (1980), 444 U.S. 394; social protests and civil disobedience, *United States v. Moylan* (1969), 417 F. 2d 1002 (4th Cir.); *certiorari* denied 397 U.S. 910; *United States v. Cullen* (1971), 454 F. 2d 386 (7th Cir.), and unorthodox medical treatments, *United States v. Randall*, 104 Daily Wash. L. Rep. 2249; *United States v. Richardson* (1978), 588 F. 2d 1235.

In England, opinion as to the existence of a general defence of necessity has varied. Blackstone, in his *Commentaries on the Laws of England* (1941) (abridged edition of William Hardcastle Browne, edited by Bernard C. Gavit), mentioned two principles capable of being read as underlying such a defence. In Book IV, c.2, p. 761, he says: "As punishments are only inflicted for the abuse of that free will, which God has given to man, it is just that a man should be excused for those acts, which are done through unavoidable force and compulsion." Then under the rubric "Choice Between Two Evils" he writes:

Choice Between Two Evils. This species of necessity is the result of reason and reflection and obliges a man to do an act, which, without such obligation, would be criminal. This occurs, when a man has his choice of two evils set before him, and chooses the less pernicious one. He rejects the greater evil and chooses the less. As where a man is bound to arrest another for a capital offence, and being resisted, kills the offender, rather than permit him to escape.

Stephen, *A History of the Criminal Law of England* (1883), vol. II, p. 108, refers to compulsion by necessity as one of the curiosities of the law, "a subject on which the law of England is so vague that, if cases raising the question should ever occur the judges would practically be able to lay down any rule which they considered expedient." At pp. 109–10 he concedes it just possible to imagine cases in which the expedience of breaking the law would be so overwhelmingly great that people might be justified in doing so but says that "these cases cannot be defined beforehand, and must be adjudicated upon by a jury afterwards."

Later English commentators have had even more doubts on the matter. *Halsbury's Laws of England*, 4th ed., vol. 11, para. 26, has this to say on the subject:

Necessity. Although there are cases in which it is not criminal for a person to cause harm to the person or property of another, there is no general rule giving rise to a defence of necessity, and it seems that, outside the specific cases mentioned, it is no defence to a crime to show that its commission was necessary in order to avoid a greater evil to the defendant or to others.

While Glanville Williams (6 C.L.P. 216 (1953)) has been able to assert "with some assurance" that the defence of necessity is recognized by English law, the authors of Smith & Hogan, *Criminal Law*, 4th ed. (1978), at pp. 193–4, state that: "The better view appears to be that a general defence of necessity is not recognized by the English courts at the present time."

A Working Party of the English Law Commission proposed to resolve this uncertainty by recognizing a general defence of necessity, but one that was carefully circumscribed to prevent its being invoked in extravagant and inappropriate cases. The English Law Commission, however, rejected the working party proposal and instead made two counter-proposals (Law Com. No. 83, Part IV) which recognized the possibility of the existence of a defence of necessity at common law but clearly disapproved of its principles. The commission proposed: "First, that no attempt should be made to establish the defence by legislation. Secondly, that the proposed Act should expressly abolish any such defence as may exist at common law." . . .

(b) The conceptual foundation of the defence

[T]he "defence" of necessity . . . is capable of embracing two different and distinct notions. As Mr. Justice Macdonald observed succinctly but accurately in [*R. v. Salvador, Wannamaker, Campbell and Nunes* (1981), 59 C. C. C. (2d) 521, 21 C. R. (3d) 1, 45 N.S.R. (2d) 192 (N.S.S.C.A.D.)], at p. 542: "Generally speaking, the defence of necessity covers all cases where non-compliance with law is excused by an emergency or justified by the pursuit of some greater good."

Working Paper 29 of the Law Reform Commission of Canada Criminal Law The General Part: Liability and Defences (1982), p. 93, makes this same point in somewhat more detail:

The rationale of necessity, however, is clear. Essentially it involves two factors. One is the avoidance of greater harm or the pursuit of some greater good, the other is the difficulty of compliance with law in emergencies. From these two factors emerge two different but related principles. The first is a utilitarian principle to the effect that, within certain limits, it is justifiable in an emergency to break the letter of the law if breaking the law will avoid a greater harm than obeying it. The second is a humanitarian principle to the effect that, again within limits, it is excusable in an emergency to break the law if compliance would impose an intolerable burden on the accused.

Despite any superficial similarities, these two principles are in fact quite distinct and many of the confusions and the difficulties in the cases (and, with respect, in academic discussions) arise from a failure to distinguish between them.

Criminal theory recognizes a distinction between "justifications" and "excuses." A "justification" challenges the wrongfulness of an action which technically constitutes a crime. The police officer who shoots the hostage-taker, the innocent object of an assault who uses force to defend himself against his assailant, the good Samaritan who commandeers a car and breaks the speed laws to rush an accident victim to the hospital, these are all actors whose actions we consider *rightful*, not wrongful. For such actions people are often praised, as motivated by some great or noble object. The concept of punishment often seems incompatible with the social approval bestowed on the doer.

In contrast, an "excuse" concedes the wrongfulness of the action but asserts that the circumstances under which it was done are such that it ought not to be attributed to the actor. The perpetrator who is incapable, owing to a disease of the mind, of appreciating the nature and consequences of his acts, the person who labours under a mistake of fact, the drunkard, the sleepwalker: these are all actors of whose "criminal" actions we disapprove intensely, but whom, in appropriate circumstances, our law will not punish.

Packer, *The Limits of the Criminal Sanction* (1968), expresses the distinction thus at p. 113:

> ... conduct that we choose not to treat as criminal is "justifiable" if our reason for treating it as noncriminal is predominantly that it is conduct that we applaud, or at least do not actively seek to discourage: conduct is "excusable." If we deplore it but for some extrinsic reason conclude that it is not politic to punish it.

It will be seen that the two different approaches to the "defence" of necessity from Blackstone forward correspond, the one to a justification, the other to an excuse. As the examples cited above illustrate, the criminal law recognizes and our *Criminal Code* codifies a number of specific categories of justification and of excuse. The remainder, those instances that conform to the general principle but do not fall within any specific category such as self-defence on the one hand or insanity on the other, purportedly fall within the "residual defence" of necessity.

As a "justification" this residual defence can be related to Blackstone's concept of a "choice of evils." It would exculpate actors whose conduct could reasonably have been viewed as "necessary" in order to prevent a greater evil than that resulting from the violation of the law. As articulated, especially in some of the American cases, it involves a utilitarian balancing of the benefits of obeying the law as opposed to disobeying it, and when the balance is clearly in favour of disobeying, exculpates an actor who contravenes a criminal statute. This is the "greater good" formulation of the necessity defence: in some circumstances, it is alleged, the values of society, indeed of the criminal law itself, are better promoted by disobeying a given statute than by observing it.

With regard to this conceptualization of a residual defence of necessity, I retain the scepticism I expressed in [*Morgentaler v. The Queen* (1975), 20 C.C.C. (2d) 449, 53 D.L.R. (3d) 161, [1976] 1 S.C.R. 616]. It is still my opinion that, "[n]o system of positive law can recognize any principle which would entitle a person to violate the law because on his view the law conflicted with some higher social value." The *Criminal Code* has specified a number of identifiable situations in which an actor is justified in committing what would otherwise be a criminal offence. To go beyond that and hold that ostensibly illegal acts can be validated on the basis of their expediency, would import an undue subjectivity into the criminal law. It would invite the courts to second-guess the Legislature and to assess the relative merits of social policies underlying criminal prohibitions. Neither is a role which fits well with the judicial function. Such a doctrine could well become the last resort of scoundrels and, in the words of Edmund Davies L.J. in *Southwark London Borough Council v. Williams et al.*, [1971] Ch. 734 [at p. 746], it could "very easily become simply a mask for anarchy."

Conceptualized as an "excuse," however, the residual defence of necessity is, in my view, much less open to criticism. It rests on a realistic assessment of human weakness, recognizing that a liberal and humane criminal law cannot hold people to the strict obedience of laws in emergency situations where normal human instincts, whether of self-preservation or of altruism, overwhelmingly impel disobedience. The objectivity of the criminal law is preserved; such acts are still wrongful, but in the circumstances they are excusable. Praise is indeed not bestowed, but pardon is, when one does a wrongful act under pressure which, in the words of Aristotle in *The Nicomachean Ethics* (translator Rees, p. 49), "overstrains human nature and which no one could withstand."

George Fletcher, *Rethinking Criminal Law*, describes this view of necessity as "compulsion of circumstance" which description points to the conceptual link between necessity as an excuse and the familiar criminal law requirement that in order to engage criminal liability, the actions constituting the *actus reus* of an offence must be voluntary. Literally, this voluntariness requirement simply refers to the need that the prohibited physical acts must have been under the conscious control of the actor. Without such control, there is, for purposes of the criminal law, no act. The excuse of necessity does not go to voluntariness in this sense. The lost Alpinist who, on the point of freezing to death, breaks open an isolated mountain cabin is not literally behaving in an involuntary fashion. He has control over his actions to the extent of being physically capable of abstaining from the act. Realistically, however, his act is not a "voluntary" one. His "choice" to break the law is no true choice at all; it is remorselessly compelled by normal human instincts. This sort of involuntariness is often described as "moral or normative involuntariness." Its place in criminal theory is described by Fletcher at pp. 804–5 as follows:

> The notion of voluntariness adds a valuable dimension to the theory of excuses. That conduct is involuntary—even in the normative sense—explains why it cannot fairly be punished. Indeed, H. L. A. Hart builds his theory of excuses on the principle that the distribution of punishment should be reserved for those who voluntarily break the law. Of the arguments he advances for this principle of justice, the most explicit is that it is preferable to live in a society where we have the maximum opportunity to choose whether we shall become the subject of criminal liability. In

addition Hart intimates that it is ideologically desirable for the government to treat its citizens as self-actuating, choosing agents. This principle of respect for individual autonomy is implicitly confirmed whenever those who lack an adequate choice are excused for their offenses.

I agree with this formulation of the *rationale* for excuses in the criminal law. In my view, this *rationale* extends beyond specific codified excuses and embraces the residual excuse known as the defence of necessity. At the heart of this defence is the perceived injustice of punishing violations of the law in circumstances in which the person had no other viable or reasonable choice available; the act was wrong but it is excused because it was realistically unavoidable.

Punishment of such acts, as Fletcher notes at p. 813, can be seen as purposeless as well as unjust:

... involuntary conduct cannot be deterred and therefore it is pointless and wasteful to punish involuntary actors. This theory... of pointless punishment, carries considerable weight in current Anglo-American legal thought.

Relating necessity to the principle that the law ought not to punish involuntary acts leads to a conceptualization of the defence that integrates it into the normal rules for criminal liability rather than constituting it as a sui generis exception and threatening to engulf large portions of the criminal law. Such a conceptualization accords with our traditional legal, moral and philosophic views as to what sorts of acts and what sorts of actors ought to be punished. In this formulation it is a defence which I do not hesitate to acknowledge and would not hesitate to apply to relevant facts capable of satisfying its necessary prerequisites.

(c) Limitations on the defence

If the defence of necessity is to form a valid and consistent part of our criminal law it must, as has been universally recognized, be strictly controlled and scrupulously limited to situations that correspond to its underlying rationale. That rationale as I have indicated, is the recognition that it is inappropriate to punish actions which are normatively "involuntary." The appropriate controls and limitations on the defence of necessity are, therefore, addressed to ensuring that the acts for which the benefit of the excuse of necessity is sought are truly "involuntary" in the requisite sense.

In *Morgentaler v. The Queen* (1975), 20 C.C.C. (2d) 449 at p. 497, 53 D.L.R. (3d) 161 at p. 209, [1976] 1 S.C.R. 616 at p. 678, I was of the view that any defence of necessity was restricted to instances of non-compliance "in urgent situations of clear and imminent peril when compliance with the law is demonstrably impossible." In my opinion, this restriction focuses directly on the "involuntariness" of the purportedly necessitous behaviour by providing a number of tests for determining whether the wrongful act was truly the only realistic reaction open to the actor or whether he was in fact making what in fairness could be called a choice. If he was making a choice, then the wrongful act cannot have been involuntary in the relevant sense.

The requirement that the situation be urgent and the peril be imminent, tests whether it was indeed unavoidable for the actor to act at all. In Lafave and Scott, *Handbook on Criminal Law* (1972), p. 338, one reads:

It is sometimes said that the defense of necessity does not apply except in an emergency—when the threatened harm is immediate, the threatened disaster imminent. Perhaps this is but a way of saying that, until the time comes when the threatened harm is immediate, there are generally options open to the defendant to avoid the harm, other than the option of disobeying the literal terms of the law—the rescue ship may appear, the storm may pass, and so the defendant must wait until that hope of survival disappears.

At a minimum the situation must be so emergent and the peril must be so pressing that normal human instincts cry out for action and make a counsel of patience unreasonable.

The requirement that compliance with the law be "demonstrably impossible" takes this assessment one step further. Given that the accused had to act, could he nevertheless realistically have acted to avoid the peril or prevent the harm, without breaking the law? Was there a legal way out? I think this is what Bracton means when he lists "necessity" as a defence, providing the wrongful act was not "avoidable." The question to be asked is whether the agent had any real choice: could he have done otherwise? If there is a reasonable legal alternative to disobeying the law, then the decision to disobey becomes a voluntary one, impelled by some consideration beyond the dictates of "necessity" and human instincts.

The importance of this requirement that there be no reasonable legal alternative cannot be overstressed.

Even if the requirements for urgency and "no legal way out" are met, there is clearly a further consideration. There must be some way of assuring proportionality. No rational criminal justice system, no matter how humane or liberal, could excuse the infliction of a greater harm to allow the actor to avert a lesser evil. In such circumstances we expect the individual to bear the harm and refrain from acting illegally. If he cannot control himself we will not excuse him. According to Fletcher, this requirement is also related to the notion of voluntariness [at p. 804]:

> ...if the gap between the harm done and the benefit accrued becomes too great, the act is more likely to appear voluntary and therefore inexcusable. For example, if the actor has to blow up a whole city in order to avoid the breaking of his finger, we might appropriately expect him to endure the harm to himself. His surrendering to the threat in this case violates our expectations of appropriate and normal resistance to pressure. Yet as we lower the degree of harm to others and increase the threatened harm to the person under duress we will reach a threshold at which, in the language of the Model Penal Code, "a person of reasonable firmness" would be "unable to resist." Determining this threshold is patently a matter of moral judgment about what we expect people to be able to resist in trying situations. A valuable aid in making that judgment is comparing the competing interests at stake and assessing the degree to which the actor inflicts harm beyond the benefit that accrues from his action.

I would therefore add to the preceding requirements a stipulation of proportionality expressible, as it was in *Morgentaler*, by the proviso that the harm inflicted must be less than the harm sought to be avoided.

(d) Illegality or contributory fault

The Crown submits that there is an additional limitation on the availability of the defence of necessity. Citing *R. v. Salvador, Wannamaker, Campbell and Nunes* (1981), 59 C. C. C. (2d) 521, 21 C. R. (3d) 1, 45 N.S.R. (2d) 192 (N.S.S.C.A.D.), it argues that because the appellants were committing a crime when their necessitous circumstances arose, they should be denied the defence of necessity as a matter of law....

...I have considerable doubt as to the cogency of such a limitation. If the conduct in which an accused was engaging at the time the peril arose was illegal, then it should clearly be punished, but I fail to see the relevance of its illegal character to the question of whether the accused's subsequent conduct in dealing with this emergent peril ought to be excused on the basis of necessity. At most the illegality—or . . . the immorality—of the preceding conduct will colour the subsequent conduct in response to the emergency as also wrongful. But that wrongfulness is never in any doubt. Necessity goes to excuse conduct, not to justify it. Where it is found to apply it carries with it no implicit vindication of the deed to which it attaches. That cannot be over-emphasized. Were the defence of necessity to succeed in the present case, it would not in any way amount to a vindication of importing controlled substances nor to a critique of the law prohibiting such importation. It would also have nothing to say about the comparative social utility of breaking the law against importing as compared to obeying the law. The question, as I have said, is never whether what the accused has done is wrongful. It is always and by definition, wrongful. The question is whether what he has done is voluntary. Except in the limited sense I intend to discuss below, I do not see the relevance of the legality or even the morality of what the accused was doing at the time the emergency arose to this question of the voluntariness of the subsequent conduct.

In *Salvador*, Jones J.A., cited sources in support of his view that illegal conduct should act as a bar to the necessity defence. These sources do not support that view but do support a closely related notion—that if the accused's own "fault" (including negligence or recklessness) is responsible for the events giving rise to the necessity, he may not rely on the necessity defence.

This limitation has found expression in several American state statutes codifying the necessity defence, such as those of New York and Illinois and has been adopted by the United States National Commission on Reform of Federal Criminal Laws which recommended that the defence apply only "where the situation developed through no fault of the actor." A parallel is sometimes drawn between such a limitation and the restrictions placed on the availability of the largely analogous defence of duress: see, e.g., Ashworth, "Reason, Logic and Criminal Liability," 91 L.Q.R. 102 at p. 106 (1975). In my view, the accused's fault in bringing about the situation later invoked to excuse his conduct *can* be relevant to the availability of the defence of necessity, but not in the sweeping way suggested by some of the commentators and in some of the statutory formulations. In so far as the accused's "fault" reflects on the moral quality of the action taken to meet the emergency, it is irrelevant to the issue of the availability of the defence on the same basis as the illegality or immorality of the actions preceding the emergency are irrelevant. If this fault is capable of attracting criminal or civil liability in its own right, the culprit should be appropriately sanctioned. I see no basis, however, for "transferring" such liability to the actions taken in response to the emergency, especially where to do so would result in attaching criminal consequences on the basis of negligence to actions which would otherwise be excused.

In my view, the better approach to the relationship of fault to the availability of necessity as a defence is based once again on the question of whether the actions sought to be excused were truly "involuntary." If the necessitous situation was clearly foreseeable to a reasonable observer, if the actor contemplated or ought to have contemplated that his actions would likely give rise to an emergency requiring the breaking of the law, then I doubt whether what confronted the accused was in the relevant sense an emergency. His response was in that sense not "involuntary." "Contributory fault" of this nature, but only of this nature, is a relevant consideration to the availability of the defence.

It is on this point that the analogy to duress is especially enlightening. Section 17 of the *Criminal Code* provides:

> 17. A person who commits an offence under compulsion by threats of immediate death or bodily harm from a person who is present when the offence is committed is excused for committing the offence if he believes that the threats will be carried out and if he is not a party to a conspiracy or association whereby he is subject to compulsion . . .

The rationale for the proviso making the defence unavailable to a member of a criminal conspiracy or association, is the same as that articulated with regard to the common law defence of duress by Lord Morris of Borth-y-Gest in *Director of Public Prosecutions for Northern Ireland v. Lynch* [1975] A.C. 653 at p. 670:

> In posing the case where someone is "really" threatened I use the word "really" in order to emphasise that duress must never be allowed to be the easy answer of those . . . who readily could have avoided the dominance of threats nor of those who allow themselves to be at the disposal and under the sway of some gangster-tyrant.

If s. 17 and the comments of Lord Morris of Borth-y-Gest embody a notion of "contributory fault" it is not per se on account of the accused's participation in criminal or immoral activity at the time he became subject to threats, nor on account of any simple negligence on his part, but rather on account of the clear foreseeability of his becoming subject to such threats and domination and the consequent conclusion that he was not "really" threatened.

In my view, the same test is applicable to necessity. If the accused's "fault" consists of actions whose clear consequences were in the situation that actually ensued, then he was not "really" confronted with an emergency which compelled him to commit the unlawful act he now seeks to have excused. In such situations the defence is unavailable. Mere negligence, however, or the simple fact that he was engaged in illegal or immoral conduct when the emergency arose will not disentitle an individual to rely on the defence of necessity.

(e) Onus of proof

Although necessity is spoken of as a defence, in the sense that it is raised by the accused, the Crown always bears the burden of proving a voluntary act. The prosecution must prove every element of the crime charged. One such element is the voluntariness of the act. Normally, voluntariness can be presumed, but if the accused places before the court, through his own witnesses or through cross-examination of Crown witnesses, evidence sufficient to raise an issue that the situation created by external forces was so emergent that failure to act could endanger life or health and upon any reasonable view of the facts, compliance with the law was impossible, then the Crown must be prepared to meet that issue. There is no onus of proof on the accused. . . .

(f) Preliminary conclusions as to the defence of necessity

It is now possible to summarize a number of conclusions as to the defence of necessity in terms of its nature, basis and limitations:

(1) the defence of necessity could be conceptualized as either a justification or an excuse;
(2) it should be recognised in Canada as an excuse, operating by virtue of s. 7(3) of the Criminal Code;
(3) necessity as an excuse implies no vindication of the deeds of the actor;
(4) the criterion is the moral involuntariness of the wrongful action;
(5) this involuntariness is measured on the basis of society's expectation of appropriate and normal resistance to pressure;
(6) negligence or involvement in criminal or immoral activity does not disentitle the actor to the excuse of necessity;
(7) actions or circumstances which indicate that the wrongful deed was not truly involuntary do disentitle;

(8) the existence of a reasonable legal alternative similarly disentitles; to be involuntary the act must be inevitable, unavoidable and afford no reasonable opportunity for an alternative course of action that does not involve a breach of the law;

(9) the defence only applies in circumstances of imminent risk where the action was taken to avoid a direct and immediate peril;

(10) where the accused places before the court sufficient evidence to raise the issue, the onus is on the Crown to meet it beyond a reasonable doubt.

(g) The judge's charge

. . .

In my view, the trial judge was correct in concluding that on the evidence before him he should instruct the jury with regard to necessity. [But he did not properly put the question of the existence of a reasonable legal alternative, i.e., of a "legal way out," before the jury.] In my view, this was a serious error and omission going to the heart of the defence of necessity. The error justifies a new trial.

V. Conclusion

On the basis of all the above, it is my conclusion that the Court of Appeal was correct in the result in ordering a new trial . . . .

I would dismiss the appeals.

German Federal Court of Justice
1 StR 483/02, BGHSt 48, 255, NJW 2003, 2464 (March 25, 2003)

Facts

The regional court found the defendant guilty of the insidiously committed murder of her husband but in view of the presence of exceptional circumstances imposed a sentence of imprisonment of nine years instead of life imprisonment. The defendant's appeal in law led, in response to the substantive complaint, to the quashing of the verdict and sentence; the findings of facts remain unaffected.

A.

I.

According to the findings of the regional court, the defendant shot her sleeping husband F. with his own revolver on September 21, 2001, at around midday. He had continually seriously injured and humiliated her over many years by increasingly aggressive acts of violence and insults. When she committed the crime she could no longer see any route of escape to protect herself and their two daughters from further acts of violence.

The defendant met F. in 1983 and became friendly with him. He was already at that time a member of a motorcycle gang. He soon became violent towards the defendant and hit her in the face. Nevertheless the defendant married him in 1986. Later, after the birth of the first daughter J., he struck her with his fists in the face, or in the region of the stomach, and kicked her, if anything in daily life did not meet his wishes, or the defendant did not comply with his "commands" with the expected rapidity. Besides this, he began increasingly to demand the defendant's help in every daily task. She also had to clear away anything which he left lying around. When the defendant became pregnant with her second daughter T., he showed her no consideration in this respect, and gave her kicks and punches in the abdominal region. The defendant traced the fact that T. was born with a cleft palate and lip back to this. The acts of violence finally assumed such proportions that the defendant made the decision in May 1988 to separate from her husband. She went to a battered wives refuge. Her parents were not prepared to take her in, because they feared pursuit by F. However after he had promised improvement, the defendant returned to him after four weeks. In 1993 there was a further attack, in which he beat her until she remained prostrate on the ground. He then kicked her as she lay there with his army boots several times; from this she suffered bruising of the kidneys. In the clinic however the defendant pretended that she had had a fall in order to cover this up. On another occasion, F. pushed the defendant's head against the wall of a room several times with such violence that it became extensively smeared with blood, and the defendant fell unconscious to the ground. He himself assumed that he had killed her. Since the middle of the 1990s, he struck her whenever he thought that she had done anything wrong. In one case he struck her in the face with his fist in the middle of the night during her sleep, because in his view she had given him cause for jealous dreams; her split lip had to be treated surgically.

After the couple had finally bought a house plot, and F. himself lent a hand in the garden, he expected the defendant to provide the necessary tools or assistance at a nod from him; at the same time he regularly called her a "slut," a "whore" or a "cunt," and gave her boxes on the ears or kicks. If he noticed that this treatment could be observed by neighbors, he sent the defendant into the house, followed her, and then gave her further punches and kicks there. In the new environment his acts of violence became yet more intensive and frequent. He would strike his wife with a baseball bat or other objects which happened to be within reach. Finally he ill-treated and humiliated her even before his friends in his motorcycle club: at Christmas in 2000, he struck her in the presence of the assembled members of the club, and forced her to kneel in front of him and to repeat after him that she was a "slut" and the "lowest of the low."

The defendant accepted the constant insults and physical injuries without protest or even resistance; she thought that her husband would otherwise become angrier and retaliate more forcefully. After F. had made himself independent in April 2001 as landlord of a bar, his acts of violence increased further. He did not only strike the defendant. The daughters J. and T. also received blows "in the neck," when, in his opinion, they behaved in a rebellious or disrespectful way. The defendant, who had to remain available for F. in every free minute for lending a hand with all the everyday tasks, and had to wait on him, was scarcely able to sleep after the opening of the bar. She reached the limits of her psychological and physical ability to withstand stress through the continued insults and acts of violence. She became continually thinner. In the summer of 2001 she became pregnant by F. for a third time but suffered a miscarriage in August, i.e., about a month before the crime. In the last two days before the crime F. had extraordinarily violent fits of rage. He became worked up because he feared that he would not get to his bar to open it punctually. He blamed the defendant for this because she had not awoken him earlier. When he became agitated about a door rattling in the wind, and the defendant tried to pacify him, he hit her powerfully several times; this threw her to the ground. Then he kicked her with his bare foot. A short time later he suddenly gave her such a powerful punch in the stomach that she doubled up in pain. Then he boxed her ears violently. He was now furious because the defendant had bumped against a door; he reproached her over the fact that the door could have been damaged. Then, wearing army boots, he kicked the defendant, who was now finally lying on the ground, at least ten times, knelt on her, and struck her with his fists in the face. He pulled her towards him with her hair and bit her in the cheek. As a result of her injuries the defendant could not go to their bar that day, and had also to cancel a visit to the dentist. When F. at about 3.30 a.m. on the day of the crime came home from his bar, he quarreled again with the defendant. He abused her for half an hour, spat at her and struck in the face so that she bled from her mouth. Finally he went to bed, whilst the defendant remained awake, because she had to get the children ready for school at six o'clock. Later, at about nine o'clock, when tidying up in the house she came upon F.'s illegally acquired eight-shooter revolver "double action," Aminius brand, 22 calibre Magnum, together with ammunition. Her husband normally kept this at the bar, in order to protect himself against acts of revenge by enemy motorcycle gangs and robberies.

The defendant considered her situation to be completely hopeless, since she had noticed some weeks before that her general condition, because of the double burden of the household and the bar, as well as because of her husband's abuse and acts of violence, had significantly worsened. She therefore believed that she would soon "no longer be able to withstand" the growing acts of violence, and feared that the violence could also assume worse proportions against the daughters, and she herself, because of her poor general state of health, would be continually less able to do anything about it. After three failed suicide attempts by means of tablets in the past, she came to realize that suicide was no solution, as her daughters would then be exposed without protection to her husband's acts of violence. From the summer of 2001 at the latest she had therefore to an increased extent given attention to the idea of bringing an end to her husband's life. She saw no other way out in her situation in order to escape violence by F., and to guarantee freedom from harm for herself and her daughters. She thought she would not be able to manage a separation from F. even with the help of state or charitable institutions. For such a situation he had repeatedly threatened her—after she had returned from the battered wives refuge—that he would do something to the daughters. He would also be able to find her at any time. Even if he went into prison, she would not be safe from him. He would finally "come out again" some time or other. Besides this, he could also order his friends from the motorcycle gang even from prison to do something to her. The defendant took these threats seriously. F. and the motorcycle gang to which he belonged were in fact known to the courts as extremely violent. The defendant, on finding the revolver, struggled with herself for a long time as to whether this was the opportunity to commit the act which she had already considered for some time. She decided she would dare to take the step and to kill her husband. She saw this as the "only possible solution" for ending the relationship with her husband which was so ruinous for her. She went into the bedroom, and from a distance of about 60 cm she fired the contents of the whole of the revolving breech of the eight shooter revolver in a matter of seconds at her sleeping husband. Two shots hit their target and led immediately to his death.

II.

The regional court considered the defendant's testimony in relation to the prior history of the crime to be credible. It was confirmed by further forms of evidence. In so far as the defendant had claimed a situation of self-defense, however, the criminal chamber regarded her account as refuted. On this basis the chamber convicted the defendant of murder which was not justified by self-defense. The presence of other statutory grounds of justification or excuse was not examined by the chamber. In place of the sentence of life imprisonment the criminal chamber, according to the principles developed by the Federal Court of Justice in BGHSt 30, 105 opted for mitigated punishment in accordance with § 49 para. 1 no. 1 Criminal Code, because of the extraordinary circumstances under which the defendant committed the crime.

Reasons

B.

The defendant's appeal in law is essentially well-founded. The verdict does not stand up to examination in substantive law . . . . The criminal chamber should have examined whether the prerequisites of an excusing necessity were present, and—if this was not the case—whether the defendant was mistaken about this, avoidably or unavoidably (§ 35 Criminal Code).

II.

. . .

2. The assessment that the defendant had deliberately and with hostile intent taken advantage of the fact that her husband was unsuspecting and defenseless in order to kill him is supported by the findings. F. had so to speak "taken" his absence of suspicion "with him into his sleep" (see BGHSt 23, 119, 121). The defendant had in the past allowed humiliations and mistreatment by her husband to wash over her without resistance. He could not therefore be considered to have expected a severe physical attack by the defendant at the time he fell asleep. The defendant deliberately shot her husband in his sleep because she did not dare to face him with open hostility. Her capacities for understanding and control were not restricted in any substantial way. She had concerned herself over a long period with the idea of killing F., and had also struggled with herself about this for a long time directly before carrying out the crime.

3. The regional court was likewise correct in affirming the unlawfulness of the defendant's act in the end result. It excluded self-defense, although it admittedly did not discuss the question of a justifying necessity (§ 34 Criminal Code). However, on the basis of the findings made, the prerequisites for this were obviously not present. Acceptance of a justifying necessity assumes a balancing of interests. This must have as its outcome that the protected interest substantially outweighs the one which has been harmed (§ 34 sentence 1 Criminal Code). It is obvious that the legal interests which were to be protected here, the physical safety of the defendant and their daughters, did not outweigh the interest harmed by the crime, i.e., the life of F. as the legal interest which was destroyed. The result of this balancing exercise would not turn out in the defendant's favor even if an intensified situation with acute danger to the life of a member of F's family were to be assumed (see on the so-called balancing of "life against life": Lenckner/Perron, in: Schönke/Schröder, StGB, 26th edit., § 34 marginal nos. 30, 31; Rengier, NStZ 1984, 21 [22]; see further on the question of a justification for killing the so-called "house or family tyrant" in situations of intensified danger: Roxin, StrafR AT, 3rd edit., § 16 marginal no. 76; Hillenkamp, in: Festschr. f. Koichi Miyazawa, 1995, p. 141, 146; . . .).

4. On the basis of the findings made, the criminal chamber should however have examined the question of whether the defendant acted in an excusing necessity or had perhaps made a mistake—avoidable or unavoidable—about its prerequisites (§ 35 Criminal Code). In the case of such a necessity or of an unavoidable mistake about the presence of excusing circumstances, an acquittal would have to be considered. In a case of an avoidable mistake, the punishment would have to be mitigated under § 49 para. 1 Criminal Code . . .

a) When a present danger for the life or limb of the perpetrator, a relative, or another person close to him exists, an unlawful act is excused and will not be punished if the danger could not have been averted otherwise than by the act (§ 35 para. 1 sentence 1 Criminal Code). The findings made so far by the chamber suggest that a present danger of this kind existed for the defendant and her children, and an excuse for the act does not therefore appear to be excluded from the outset. The criminal chamber should therefore also have considered whether such a danger could be averted otherwise than by the act. It should have made further findings on this subject which were necessary for this assessment.

aa) According to consistent case law, a danger in the sense of § 35 para. 1 Criminal Code is a state of affairs in which on the basis of factual circumstances there is a probability of a harmful event occurring (see only BGHSt 18, 271). This also includes a situation in which danger is continually threatened over a long period and this persistent risk can at any time change into actual harm (BGH, NJW 1979, 2053, 2054). In this respect the starting point for excusing necessity, present danger, differs from that for self-defense which assumes a present attack. In the present case, the assumption is unavoidable that the defendant and her children found themselves in a situation of long-term danger, resulting from F., for their physical safety and possibly also for their lives. The husband's acts of violence against the defendant had gone on for about 15 years. They had continually increased in the months and days before the crime, and had already led to serious injuries to the defendant. They were by now also directed against their daughters. According to the chamber's findings it therefore appeared that there was a probability bordering on certainty of the infliction of future injuries as well.

A danger is a present one where the probability of the occurrence of harm according to an objective judgment from an ex ante point of view has intensified to such an extent that measures necessary for the protection of the threatened legal interest must be introduced immediately in order to prevent harm. With a long-term danger, such an intensification of the danger is to be assumed if the harm can occur at any time, even if the possibility remains open that the harm may not happen for a while (BGH, NJW 1979, 2053 [2054]; see also BGHSt 5, 371, 373). On the basis of this standard, a "present danger" in the sense of § 35 para. 1 Criminal Code existed here. It could be realized at any time even if F. was sleeping at the time of the act; he had already ill-treated the defendant in the past when awakening from sleep and without any concrete cause. Besides this, his awakening and the immediate resumption of a quarrel with physical abuse could be expected. Immediate action was therefore in principle required to avoid the occurrence of further harm.

bb) A finding of an excusing necessity was not excluded here simply because the defendant had perhaps "herself caused" the danger resulting from F., or because it would have been reasonable for her on the basis of the marriage to have accepted the danger which went with it (§ 35 para. 1 sentence 2 Criminal Code). A "causing of the danger" in this sense does not fall to be considered just because the defendant had remained with her husband for many years in spite of the ill-treatment and insults. The marriage to him as such was, in the light of the seriousness of the long-term repeated ill-treatment, not a legal relationship on the basis of which the defendant could have been expected to accept the danger of further violent physical attacks.

cc) The question of an excuse for the defendant can therefore depend on whether the danger could otherwise—than by the crime—have been averted for her. The chamber has not assessed the facts from this point of view and has made no findings about it. That will have to be redressed. The following will apply:

The danger could not have been averted otherwise than through the emergency act if this would have been the only suitable means to counter the emergency situation effectively (BGH, NJW 1966, 1823,1824f.; NStZ 1992, 487). The other options of averting the danger which obviously fell to be considered here were seeking help of the authorities or of charitable institutions, in particular the defendant and the daughters moving out of the family house into, for instance, a battered wives refuge, but also the seeking of refuge with the police with a request for help. The latter would obviously be linked with bringing a criminal charge. The defendant did not however attempt to liberate herself in this way from her desperate situation. In these circumstances, the danger could only be assessed as not capable of being otherwise averted if, on the basis of concrete grounds in the individual case, it would have been doubtful from the outset whether the alternative courses of action would have been sufficiently effective. If long-term danger exists, averting it must not be limited merely to postponing the danger (BGHSt 5, 371,375; BGH, NJW 1979, 2053, 2054). One could argue that the alternatives for averting the danger would not have been effective if, for instance, the authorities had not intervened effectively in the past, in spite of a request for help and knowledge of the situation, so that it had to remain uncertain whether they would take decisive action with lasting effects in the actual emergency situation (BGH, NJW 1966, 1823, 1824f.; NJW 1979, 2053, 2054), or if help from the police would not have removed the emergency situation effectively (on this, BGH, GA 1967, 113). According to the findings so far, it cannot be reliably assessed whether the defendant was without promising and effective alternative courses of action for the aversion of the danger threatening her and the children, although this seems to be rather unlikely. Even if pursuit by F. was to be feared in the case of a move and the claiming of assistance, it remains to be assessed how seriously the threats he made were actually to be taken. Finally it should be assumed in principle on complete knowledge of the objective facts that family members who had got into difficulties in this way are accorded effective help by state authorities and charitable institutions.

... The requirements to be placed on the finding of other means of averting long-term danger should, not least on normative grounds and especially when the destruction of the legal interest of life is in question, not be too high. This corresponds with the duty of state authorities (the police, but also, e.g., youth offices) to intervene effectively. Therefore the long-term danger which arises from a "family tyrant's continually repeated substantial acts of violence for the other family members, can as a rule, in the sense of § 35 para. 1 Criminal Code, be averted otherwise than through the killing of the "tyrant" by claiming the help of third persons, in particular state authorities.

b) The defendant could however not be punished for her crime even if the danger could have been averted, if she had, on the commission of the crime, erroneously assumed circumstances which would excuse her, and if she could not have avoided this mistake (§ 35 para. 2 Criminal Code). According to the findings of the chamber so far—which it admittedly made without regard to § 35 Criminal Code—the defendant was animated by the idea that her situation was hopeless and that she could only protect herself and her children from further attacks by killing F. She saw this as "the only possible solution." On such a view of things by the defendant, the chamber ought to have assessed whether this understanding of the situation could have been avoided by her (see BGH, GA 1967, 113, 114)...

III.

For the new trial and decision, the Senate refers to the following:

1. If the new trial should reveal that the danger resulting from F. could have been otherwise averted, but that the defendant did not recognize this, the question of avoidability of such a mistake (§ 35 para. 2 Criminal Code) depends on whether the defendant conscientiously examined possible ways out. The requirements for this duty of examination are to be determined according to the concrete circumstances (BGH, NStZ 1992, 487). In particular the seriousness of the crime and the circumstances under which the examination took place are of importance, and especially the period which was available to her and whether calm reflection was a possibility for the perpetrator; if appropriate it will depend upon why her insight into the factual situation was distorted . With the killing of a human being, one of the most serious crimes and an attack on the highest individual legal interest was at issue. Therefore strict requirements will need to be placed on the defendant's duty of examination. It would argue for the avoidability of a corresponding mistake if it were to emerge in the new trial that the defendant had a long period for consideration before the crime, in which she could have made inquiries about the other possibilities for averting the danger and sought advice. It is rather unlikely that her physical and psychological constitution after the lengthy ill-treatment and humiliations by F. would have hindered her in assessing her options realistically (in any case if it were to be shown once again that her capacity neither for control nor for insight was substantially reduced).

2. If the new judge of fact comes to the conclusion that the mistake of the defendant was avoidable, the punishment will be reduced under §§ 35 para. 2, 49 para. 1 no. 1 Criminal Code...

German Federal Court of Justice
4 StR 352/88, BGHSt 35, 347 (September 15, 1988)
King of the Cats (*Katzenkönig*) Case

Facts

According to the findings, the defendants lived together in a "neurotic tangled relationship" characterized by "mysticism, false knowledge and misconception." The defendant H. succeeded, in deliberate cooperation with P., in at first successfully leading the easily influenceable defendant R. to believe that they were threatened by pimps and gangsters, and then in forcing him into the role of protector. Later, by means of theatrical tricks, pretense of hypnotic and clairvoyant powers, and the carrying out of mystical cult activities they brought him to believe in the existence of the "king of the cats" who had embodied evil for thousands of years, and threatened the world. R.—who had a limited critical capability and who was also trying hard, because of his love for Barbara H., to believe them—imagined himself in the end to be chosen, together with the other two, to take up the battle against the "king of the cats." At their command he had to undertake tests of courage, be baptized as a Catholic, and swear eternal faithfulness to Barbara H. In this mode, he was first used by her and P. as a tool for their own fun. When the defendant H. in the middle of 1986 heard of the marriage of her earlier friend Udo N., she decided, out of hate and jealousy, to have his wife (Annemarie N.) killed by R., by exploiting his superstition. With the tacit agreement of P., who—as she knew—wanted to get rid of his rival, the defendant H. deluded R. into believing that because of the many faults committed by him the "king of the cats" demanded a human sacrifice in the form of Mrs. N.; if he did not carry out the act within a short period of time, he would have to leave her, and humanity or millions of human beings would be destroyed by the "king of the cats." R., who knew that it would be murder, tried in vain to find a way out by referring to the Fifth Commandment. H. and P. continually pointed out that the prohibition on killing did not apply to them as it was a divine assignment, and they had to save humanity. After he had had to swear to Barbara H. "by appeal to Jesus" to kill a human being, and she had indicated to him that, on breach of his oath, his "immortal soul" would be "cursed for eternity," he finally decided to carry out the act. He was plagued by pangs of conscience but he balanced against this the danger for millions of human beings, whom he could save by the sacrifice of Mrs. N.

Late on the evening of July 30, 1986, R. visited Mrs. N. in her flower shop under the pretext of wanting to buy roses. In accordance with the advice given to him by P.—in agreement with Barbara H.—R. stabbed the unsuspecting and defenseless Mrs. N. from behind in the neck, face and body with a sheath knife which P. had let him have for this purpose, in order to kill her. As other people rushed to help Mrs. N., who was now desperately defending herself, R. desisted from further implementation of the crime in order to be able to escape unrecognized in accordance with his "assignment"; he was reckoning on the death of his victim, which did not occur.

The regional court sentenced the defendants H. and P. to life imprisonment for attempted murder, and the defendant R. to a nine-year imprisonment and to confinement in a psychiatric hospital. By their appeals in law the defendants R. and P. have objected to violation of substantive law.

Reasons

The regional court has correctly convicted all the defendants as perpetrators of attempted murder.

1. The defendant R.

The criminal chamber has without legal error determined the presence in relation to this defendant of the prerequisites for attempted insidious murder. R. "stabbed Mrs. N. personally with the intention of killing her in order to fulfill his assignment"; in doing so he deliberately exploited her absence of suspicion and defenselessness. The murder attempt was completed as the defendant believed after the conclusion of the last implementing act that the consequence would occur (BGHSt 35, 90, 92 with further references). He did not withdraw from this attempt in such a way as to release himself from punishment, because he made no effort to avert the result (§ 24 para. 1 sentence 1 Criminal Code).

The regional court has correctly assumed that the defendant was responsible for his actions. The criminal chamber, on expert advice, was convinced that the defendant does not suffer from debility or a pathological mental disorder. Certainly he has a "highly abnormal personality," which is "neurotically profoundly disturbed and distorted." This condition ... and the "successful work by the defendants H. and P. in convincing" R. led to him living in "delusional certainties" at the time of the crime. The regional court has not classified this personality type expressly under one of the characteristics of § 20 Criminal Code. It can however be deduced with sufficient clarity from its observations that it should be characterized as another serious mental abnormality in the sense of that provision. This did not impair the defendant's capacity for understanding, because he knew that the killing of a human being was prohibited, and he knew all the factual circumstances. Besides this, his ability to control was not removed, as the defendant could have withdrawn from the assignment. The fact that, according to the observations of the criminal chamber, the delusions and the "pathological feelings resulting from this" led the defendant substantially astray was considered by it through the application of § 21 Criminal Code.

The defendant R. cannot rely on self-defense or defense of others (§ 32 Criminal Code), as neither he nor others, as he knew, were exposed to a present unlawful attack by the victim. Justifying necessity under § 34 Criminal Code is not present simply because an actual present danger was lacking. Admittedly the defendant believed in such a danger. This mistake about the factual prerequisites for § 34 Criminal Code does not however benefit the defendant as a mistake about the crime definition, because § 34 Criminal Code additionally presupposes predomination of the weight of the interest to be protected over that to be sacrificed and does not allow a balancing of "life against life" (OGHSt 1, 321, 334; 2, 117, 121; Dreher/Tröndle, 44th edit., § 34 marginal no. 10). The fact that the defendant has balanced this conflict of interest defectively does not, as an error in assessment, lead to the exclusion of intention, but to a mistake of law—avoidable, according to the findings—in accordance with § 17 Criminal Code (see S/S-Lenckner, 23rd edit., § 34 marginal no. 51; Dreher/Tröndle, loc.cit., 18). Accordingly he would, as a police officer, taking into consideration his individual capabilities and also his delusions, have been able to recognize the impermissibility in law of a quantitative estimation of human life as the absolute highest value by an appropriate exercise of his conscience and a consultation, which he could have been expected to make, with a person in a position of trust, e.g., a priest.

The criminal chamber has also correctly denied an exclusion of guilt under § 35 Criminal Code simply because the perpetrator did not have the intention to avert the supposed danger from himself, a relative or another person close to him (see LK-Hirsch, 10th edit., § 35 marginal no. 38 with further references) He did not fear his own death because H. and P. had led him to believe that he had already lived several times, and his soul would certainly return again; he was not thinking of relatives or persons close to him. The regional court has not examined whether the defendant has the benefit of an extra-statutory excusing necessity going beyond the area of application of § 35 Criminal Code (see Lackner, 17th edit., before § 32 note III 3 with further references). That does not however lead to the quashing of the verdict. Such a ground of excuse or for excluding punishment (see Lackner, loc. cit.) can, if it exists at all, at the most be allowed to the perpetrator under the prerequisite that a conscientious examination of the presence of a necessity situation has taken place (see the case law before § 35 Criminal Code, new version, came into effect . . .) . . . This was lacking with the defendant, as the observations of the regional court on the avoidability of an error of law in relation to § 34 Criminal Code prove.

2. The defendant P.

The regional court has also correctly convicted the defendant P. as perpetrator. He has jointly with the defendant H. committed the crime "through another" in the sense of § 25 para. 1 Criminal Code. They acted from base motives. Both of them are not merely inciters just because the co-defendant R. was also to be classified as a perpetrator . . . The question of whether the background man of a perpetrator acting culpably can be an indirect perpetrator has not yet been decided by the highest courts . . .

In the literature, the question of the demarcation between incitement and indirect perpetration is disputed . . .

The demarcation depends in the individual case on the type and consequences of the mistake and the intensity of the influence of the background man (see BGHSt 32, 38, 42). An indirect perpetrator of a homicide or attempted homicide crime is in any case the person who, with the help of the mistake deliberately provoked by him, intentionally causes and controls the event, so that the mistaken person, on an evaluating consideration, is to be regarded as a—even though (still) acting culpably—tool.

c) This, according to the findings, is the situation here. On the one hand the defendants H. and P. have caused defendant R. to have delusions and have later deliberately exploited these in order to exclude his legal reservations as well as his pangs of conscience, and to cause him to carry out the crime intended by them according to their plans and ideas. In this psychological manner they controlled the planning of the crime. In addition to this they determined substantial parts of the implementation of the crime. P. handed over the crime weapon to the defendant R. and explained, in response to his question as to how he should carry out the crime, that he should stab from behind as the "Japanese and leathernecks" had done "in the Second World War," as the victim would then immediately be dead; no witnesses should be present. R. adhered to these and other instructions. On the other hand R. was mistaken in relation to the crime not only as to the fact that his actions were forbidden; in addition to this he was substantially restricted in his capacity to control. He found himself in a narrow network of relationships and influence which the defendants H. and P. exploited for the purpose of controlling him, using it in such a way that he could only free himself with difficulty from their determining influence.

The defendants H. and P. have thereby induced him to commit the crime, and controlled the implementation of the crime by virtue of their influence and their superior knowledge . . .

German Federal Constitutional Court
BVerfGE 115, 118 (February 15, 2006)
Aviation Security Act Case

Facts

The constitutional complaint challenges the armed forces' authorization by the Aviation Security Act to shoot down, by the direct use of armed force, aircraft that are intended to be used as weapons in crimes against human lives.

On September 11, 2001, four passenger planes of US American airlines were hijacked in the United States of America by an international terrorist organization and caused to crash . . . On January 5, 2003, an armed man captured a sports plane, circled above the banking district of Frankfurt/Main and threatened to crash the plane into the high-rise of the European Central Bank if he was not granted the possibility of making a phone call to the United States of America . . . The police ordered major alert, the city center of Frankfurt was cleared, high-rises were evacuated. Slightly more than half an hour after the capture, it was evident that the hijacker was a mentally confused person acting on his own . . .

Both incidents caused a large number of measures aimed at preventing unlawful interference with civil aviation, at improving the security of civil aviation as a whole and at protecting it, in doing so, also from dangers that are imminent where aircraft are taken command of by people who want to abuse them for objectives that are unrelated to air traffic . . .

In the Federal Republic of Germany, factual as well as legal measures have been taken whose intended objectives are to increase the security of air traffic and to protect it from attacks.

Since October 1, 2003, a "National Air Security Center" (Nationales Lage- und Führungszentrum "Sicherheit im Luftraum"), which has been established in Kalkar on the Lower Rhine, has been operational . . . The main function of the center is to avert dangers that emanate from so-called renegade planes, which are civil aircraft that have been taken command of by people who want to abuse them as weapons for a targeted crash. Once an aircraft has been classified as a renegade—be it by NATO, be it by the National Air Security Center itself—the responsibility for the measures required for averting such danger in the German air space rests with the competent authorities of the Federal Republic of Germany.

The legal basis for these measures is laid down in the Act on the New Regulation of Aviation Security Functions (Gesetz zur Neuregelung von Luftsicherheitsaufgaben) of January 11, 2005 (Federal Law Gazette I p. 78).

Pursuant to its § 1, the Aviation Security Act serves to provide protection from attacks on the security of air traffic, in particular from hijackings, acts of sabotage and terrorist attacks . . . The operations that are permissible in accordance with the Aviation Security Act and the principles that apply as regards their choice are specified in §§ 14 and 15 of the Aviation Security Act. Pursuant to § 15 para. 1 Aviation Security Act, operations intended to prevent the occurrence of an especially grave accident within the meaning of § 14 para. 1 and 14 para. 3 Aviation Security Act may be taken only if the aircraft from which the danger of such accident emanates has previously been checked by the armed forces in the air space and if it has then been unsuccessfully tried to warn and to divert it. If this prerequisite has been met, the armed forces may, pursuant to § 14 para. 1 Aviation Security Act, force the aircraft off its course in the air space, force it to land, threaten to use armed force, or fire warning shots. Pursuant to § 14 para. 3 Aviation Security Act, the direct use of armed force against the aircraft is permissible only if the occurrence of an especially grave accident cannot be prevented even by such measures. This, however, only applies where it must be assumed under the circumstances that the aircraft is intended to be used as a weapon against human lives, and where the direct use of armed force is the only means to avert this imminent danger . . .

Reasons

The armed forces' authorization pursuant to § 14 para. 3 Aviation Security Act (Luftsicherheitsgesetz—LuftSiG) to shoot down by the direct use of armed force an aircraft that is intended to be used against human lives is incompatible with the right to life under art. 2 para. 2 sentence 1 Basic Law in conjunction with the guarantee of human dignity under art. 1 para. 1 Basic Law to the extent that it affects persons on board the aircraft who are not participants in the crime.

. . .

The fundamental right to life guaranteed by art. 2 para. 2 sentence 1 Basic Law is subject to restrictions if these are part of a statute pursuant to art. 2 para. 2 sentence 3 Basic Law . . . The Act, however, that restricts the fundamental right must in its turn be regarded in the light of the fundamental right and of the guarantee of human dignity under art. 1 para. 1 Basic Law, which is closely linked with it. Human life is the vital basis of human dignity as the essential constitutive principle, and as the supreme value, of the constitution (see BVerfGE 39, 1, 42; 72, 105, 115; 109, 279, 311). All human beings possess this dignity as persons, irrespective of their qualities, their physical or mental state, their achievements and their social status (see BVerfGE 87, 209, 228; 96, 375, 399). It cannot be taken away from any human being. What can be violated, however, is the claim to respect which results from it (see BVerfGE 87, 209, 228). This applies irrespective, inter alia, of the probable duration of the individual human life (see BVerfGE 30, 173, 194, on the human being's claim to respect of his or her dignity even after death).

In view of this relation between the right to life and human dignity, the state is prohibited, on the one hand, from encroaching upon the fundamental right to life by measures of its own, thereby violating the ban on the disregard of human dignity. On the other hand, the state is also obliged to protect every human life. This duty of protection demands of the state and its bodies to shield and to promote the life of every individual, which means above all to also protect it from unlawful attacks, and interference, by third parties (see BVerfGE 39, 1, 42; 46, 160, 164; 56, 54, 73). Also this duty of protection has its foundations in art. 1 para. 1 sentence 2 of the Basic Law, which explicitly obliges the state to respect and protect human dignity (see BVerfGE 46, 160, 164; 49, 89, 142; 88, 203, 251).

What this obligation means in concrete terms for state action cannot be definitely determined once and for all (see BVerfGE 45, 187, 229; 96, 375, 399–400). Art. 1 para. 1 Basic Law protects the individual human being not only against humiliation, branding, persecution, outlawing and similar actions by third parties or by the state itself (see BVerfGE 1, 97, 104; 107, 275, 284; 109, 279, 312). Taking as a starting point the idea of the constitution-creating legislature that it is part of the nature of human beings to exercise self-determination in freedom and to freely develop themselves, and that the individual can claim, in principle, to be recognized in society as a member with equal rights and with a value of his or her own (see BVerfGE 45, 187, 227–228), the obligation to respect and protect human dignity generally precludes making a human being a mere object of the state (see BVerfGE 27, 1, 6; 45, 187, 228; 96, 375, 399). What is thus absolutely prohibited is any treatment of a human being by public authority which fundamentally calls into question his or her quality of a subject, his or her status as a legal entity (see BVerfGE 30, 1, 26; 87, 209, 228; 96, 375, 399) by its lack of the respect of the value which is due to every human being for his or her own sake, by virtue of his or her being a person (see BVerfGE 30, 1, 26; 109, 279, 312–313). When it is that such a treatment occurs must be stated in concrete terms in the individual case in view of the specific situation in which a conflict can arise (see BVerfGE 30, 1, 25; 109, 279, 311).

In the situation in which these persons are at the moment in which the order to use direct armed force against the aircraft involved in the aerial incident pursuant to § 14 para. 4 sentence 1 Aviation Security Act is made, it must be possible, pursuant to § 14 para. 3 Aviation Security Act, to assume with certainty that the aircraft is intended to be used against human lives. As has been stated in the reasoning for the Act, the aircraft must have been converted into an assault weapon by those who have brought it under their command (see Bundestag document 15/2361, p. 20); the aircraft itself must be used by the perpetrators in a targeted manner as a weapon for the crime, not merely as an auxiliary means for committing the crime, against the lives of people who stay in the area in which the aircraft is intended to crash (see Bundestag document 15/2361, p. 21). In such an extreme situation, which is, moreover, characterized by the cramped conditions of an aircraft in flight, the passengers and the crew are typically in a desperate situation. They can no longer influence the circumstances of their lives independently from others in a self-determined manner.

Also the findings that are supposed to be gained from reconnaissance measures and checks pursuant to § 15 para. 1 Aviation Security Act are, in the opinion of the Cockpit Association, vague at best, even with ideal weather conditions…Under these circumstances, the assessment of the motivation and the objectives of the hijackers of an aircraft that is made on the basis of the facts ascertained were said to probably remain, as a general rule, speculative to the very end…

Even if in the area of police power, insecurities concerning forecasts often cannot be completely avoided, it is absolutely inconceivable under the applicability of art. 1 para. 1 Basic Law to intentionally kill persons such as the crew and the passengers of a hijacked plane, who are in a situation that is hopeless for them, on the basis of a statutory authorization which even accepts such imponderabilities if necessary. It need not be decided here how a shooting down that is performed all the same, and an order relating to it, would have to be assessed under criminal law (on this, and on cases with comparable combinations of circumstances see, for instance, Decisions of the Supreme Court of Justice for the British Zone in Criminal Matters (Entscheidungen des Obersten Gerichtshofs für die Britische Zone in Strafsachen—OGHSt) 1, 321, 331 et seq., 335 et seq.; 2, 117, 120 et seq.; Roxin, Strafrecht, Allgemeiner Teil, vol. I, 3rd ed. 1997, pp. 888–889; Erb, in: Münchener Kommentar zum Strafgesetzbuch, vol. 1, 2003, § 34, marginal nos. 117 et seq.;…). What is solely decisive for the constitutional appraisal is that the legislature may not, by establishing a statutory authorization for intervention, give authority to perform operations of the nature regulated in § 14 para. 3 Aviation Security Act vis-à-vis people who are not participants in the crime and may not in this manner qualify such operations as legal and thus permit them. As missions of the armed forces of a non-warlike nature, they are incompatible with the right to life and the obligation of the state to respect and protect human dignity.

In complying with duties of protection, the state and its bodies have a broad margin of assessment, valuation and organization (see BVerfGE 77, 170, 214; 79, 174, 202; 92, 26, 46). Unlike the fundamental rights in their function as subjective rights of defence [against the state], the state's duties to protect which result from the objective contents of the fundamental rights are, in principle, not defined (see BVerfGE 96, 56, 64). How the state bodies comply with such duties of protection is to be decided, as a matter of principle, by themselves on their own responsibility (see BVerfGE 46, 160, 164; 96, 56, 64). This also applies to their duty to protect human life. It is true that especially as regards this protected interest, in cases with a particular combination of circumstances, if effective protection of life cannot be achieved otherwise, the possibilities of choosing the means of complying with the duty of protection can be restricted to the choice of one particular means (see BVerfGE 46, 160, 164–165). The choice, however, can only be between means the use of which is in harmony with the constitution...

... The authorization to use direct armed force against an aircraft on board of which there are only people who want to abuse it within the meaning of § 14 para. 3 of the Aviation Security Act is proportional in the narrower sense. According to the result of the overall weighing between the seriousness of the encroachment upon fundamental rights that it involves and the weight of the legal interests that are to be protected (see on this BVerfGE 90, 145, 173; 104, 337, 349; 110, 141, 165), the shooting down of such an aircraft is an appropriate measure of averting danger which is reasonable for the persons affected if there is certainty about the elements of the offence... Under the combination of circumstances that is assumed here, it is these people themselves who, as offenders, have brought about the necessity of state intervention, and they can avert such intervention at any time by refraining from realizing their criminal plan. It is the people who have the aircraft under their command who determine the course of events on board, but also on the ground in a decisive manner. Their killing can only take place if it can be established with certainty that they will use the aircraft that is under their control to kill people, and if they keep to their plan even though they are aware of the danger to their lives that this involves for them. This reduces the gravity of the encroachment upon their fundamental rights... On the other hand, those in the target area of the intended plane crash whose lives are intended to be protected by the measure of intervention under § 14 para. 3 of the Aviation Security Act by which the state complies with its duty of protection, as a general rule do not have the possibility of averting the attack that is planned against them and in particular, of escaping it.

What must also be kept in mind, however, is that the application of § 14 para. 3 Aviation Security Act will possibly affect not only extremely dangerous installations on the ground but will possibly also kill people who are staying in areas in which, in all probability, the wreckage of the aircraft that is shot down by the use of armed force will come down. The state is constitutionally obliged to protect also the lives—and the health—of these people... This aspect, however, does not concern the continued existence in law of the regulation under § 14 para. 3 of the Aviation Security Act, but its application in the individual case. Pursuant to the opinions submitted in the proceedings, the application is intended to be refrained from anyway if it must be assumed with certainty that people on the ground would suffer damage or even lose their lives by plane wreckage falling down on densely populated areas. Concerning the question whether the provision meets also the proportionality requirements of constitutional law, it is sufficient to establish that combinations of circumstances are conceivable in which the direct use of armed force against an aircraft which only has attackers on air traffic on board can avert the danger to the lives of those against whom the aircraft is intended to be used as the weapon for the crime without the shooting down of the aircraft encroaching at the same time upon the lives of others... This makes § 14 para. 3 Aviation Security Act also proportional in the narrower sense to the extent that it permits the direct use of armed force against a pilotless aircraft or against an aircraft which only has attackers on board...

Tatjana Hörnle, "Hijacked Airplanes: May They Be Shot Down?," 10 *New Criminal Law Review* (2007), 582

In the aftermath of September 11, 2001, and an incident in 2003, when a mentally disturbed man in a small airplane flew over the city of Frankfurt threatening to crash himself into a skyscraper, the German parliament (in addition to other provisions) passed a law to tighten security measures with respect to air traffic. This law, which became effective on January 15, 2005, was called Luftsicherheitsgesetz. Among other measures, it contained a highly controversial provision, allowing "the use of weapons against an airplane, if under the given circumstances one could presume that this airplane was going to be used against the lives of other human beings, and if the use of weapons was the only means against this present danger." The president of the republic, Horst Köhler, had, when signing the law, expressed doubts whether it was compatible with the German constitution, and soon it was brought before the Federal Constitutional Court. On February 15, 2006, the court declared section 14 III to be unconstitutional.

The ruling contains two different chains of reasoning. The first concerns the relationship between the state governments and the federal government in Germany. The states are responsible for averting dangers to public security and, so argued the court, it is not permissible to use the federal air force for this purpose....

The second chain of arguments is probably more noteworthy for observers outside Germany: the Federal Constitutional Court stated that human rights provisions prohibit shooting down an airplane if it is carrying passengers and crew members. The judges had no objections against deadly action if terrorists were to get hold of a plane and fly it without crew or passengers. However, if persons other than the offenders are aboard, the court tells us that their right to life and their human dignity would be violated if missiles were fired at the plane. . . .

Resorting to a result-oriented assessment, the drafters of the American Model Penal Code held that the justification labeled "choice of evils" should be applied if the goal is to safe a greater number of lives. In stark contrast to this position, German contributions express disdain for such calculations if they lead to the killing of a human being. German criminal courts also have refuted such thoughts if they considered them (which they hardly do). Obviously, it would be unfair to label the American tradition as straightforwardly consequentialist as there are many American contributions in the field of moral philosophy exploring and defending limits to this way of thinking. However, even in view of the wide-ranging positions to be found in the American discussion, one can still conclude that there is a difference between the legal cultures . . .

Those who do not acknowledge a justification keep searching for ways to spare the pilot criminal punishment. The way to achieve this would be to excuse him. There is a provision about "excusing necessity" in § 35 of the German Penal Code that exempts offenders from punishment who act to avert a present danger to life. This provision does not require a weighing of conflicting interests. However, the excuse is limited to situations when the offender himself (or someone with whom he has a close relationship, such as a family member) is in danger. The wording is unequivocal: it does not cover circumstances when the offender acts on behalf of persons whom he does not know . . .

German Criminal Code

§ 34 (Justifying Necessity)

Who commits an offense in imminent danger to life, limb, freedom, honor, property or another legal good which cannot be averted otherwise to avert the danger from himself or another person, does not act unlawfully, if, upon weighing the conflicting interests, in particular the affected legal goods and the degree of danger, the protected interest substantially outweighs the one interfered with. This only applies if the act committed is an appropriate way to avert the danger.

§ 35 (Excusing Necessity)

(1) Who commits an unlawful act in imminent danger to life, limb or freedom which cannot be averted otherwise to avert the danger from himself, a relative or a person close to him, acts without guilt. This does not apply if the offender could be expected under the circumstances to accept the danger, in particular, because he himself had caused the danger or because he was under a special legal obligation; however, the sentence may be mitigated according to § 49 para. 1 unless the offender was required to accept the danger because of a special legal obligation.

(2) If at the time of the commission of the act the offender mistakenly assumes that circumstances exist which would excuse him under para. 1, he will only be punished if the mistake was avoidable. The sentence will be mitigated according to § 49 para. 1.

NOTES

1. Can an offender be justified if he acted with the aim of averting danger? What could be the reason to forego criminal punishment in such cases? If the imminent danger stems from the unlawful attack of another person, the justification of self-defense, or defense of another applies—and under such circumstances, it is not difficult to explain why the attacker must accept being harmed: he brought this situation upon himself. (What is the significance of bringing the situation giving rise to self-defense upon oneself? Does the attacker consent to the use of defensive force against him? Or is it a causal claim, in the sense that the attacker caused another's defense against himself? Or does the attacker forfeit something by attacking unlawfully? If so, what? The right to protection of the law, of the *criminal* law, of the state? How far does this forfeiture go? Does the attacker, through his unlawful attack, remove himself from the realm of law altogether? Does he become an outlaw, strictly speaking? A person who is not entitled, by law, to protection, but at best by mercy?*)

---

* Compare, in this respect, the discussion of causing the conditions of one's defense, Note 7.

The point of necessity cases often is that the victims of the danger-averting act are innocent third parties who were neither endangered themselves (and thus did not profit themselves from the act in question) nor responsible for creating the danger. (What is the definition, and significance, of "innocence" in this context?) Consider the examples mentioned in *People v. Craig*: the offender breaks into a cabin to escape a blizzard or destroys property to prevent the spread of the fire. How can it be justified to the owner of the property and to the owner of the cabin that this is lawful? Granting a justification to the offender implies that the law demands acceptance of harm from the owners although they could argue that they are not responsible for fires and blizzards. (Consider the doctrinal significance of this notion of "acceptance." Does the owner of the cabin have the right to defend himself, or his property, against the freezing mountaineer? Why, or why not? Does it matter whether he has a duty to aid (see, e.g., § 323c Criminal Code)? And where does this expectation of "acceptance" come from? What conception of law and community does it reflect? How does it relate to the idea of a reasonable person?)

In *R. v. Perka*, Justice Dickson explores possible modes of thinking about necessity in criminal law theory. One could explain necessity with a utilitarian calculus: if in the end more is saved than harmed, the overall advantage might be seen as sufficient for justification. However, there are arguments against this explanation: a utilitarian calculus neglects individuals' rights and individuals' duties. (In what sense does a utilitarian calculus neglect rights? Duties? What is the relationship between these rights and duties? Is the idea that one cannot have one without the other?) For this reason, German criminal law doctrine favors another explanation, which points to duties of solidarity. In the examples mentioned above, the property owners owe some degree of solidarity to their fellow human beings and for this reason have to make sacrifices. (What is the (legal) source of this duty of solidarity to our fellow human beings? Can one not have a conception of necessity as balancing interests, or rights, or legal goods that does not seek to maximize utility, and in that sense does not involve a utilitarian calculus? Would this conception also require the assumption of a broad duty of interhuman solidarity?)

The defense of necessity (as a justification) did not appear in the German Criminal Code until 1975. Originally, the German Criminal Code contained the following provision, which frames necessity as an excuse:

§ 54. A punishable act is not present when the act, except in a case of self-defense (*Notwehr*), was committed in an emergency (*Notstand*), for which the actor is not responsible (*unverschuldet*), to save the actor or a relative of the actor from a present danger to body or life.

Compare this provision with the current version of §§ 34 and 35 (justifying and excusing necessity, respectively). Before the introduction of the current provisions, justifying necessity was recognized only as a judicially created defense in German criminal law: in the 1927 case of a doctor who had performed an abortion (a crime) to save the life of the suicidal mother, the Imperial Court developed the defense of "supra-statutory justificatory necessity." The Court balanced the competing legal goods at stake, the life of the mother and the "existence of the fetus," concluding that the former outweighed the latter in light of the fact that the sentencing range for homicide exceeded that for abortion. The 1975 reform is generally thought to have replaced this "casuistic" construction with a codified formulation of the defense.

Is there something about necessity as a justification that complicates its integration into a system of criminal law? Is there something incoherent—or at least internally inconsistent, or counterproductive—about a criminal law system that that authorizes, rather than merely tolerates (as in cases of excuse), the intentional violation of its norms? Does the answer depend on one's general conception of criminal law (or even of law, generally speaking)?

Note that the Model Penal Code, completed in 1962, featured a justifying necessity provision before the German Criminal Code did. Can the defense be squared with the Model Penal Code's treatmentist orientation? Is a person who inflicts criminal harm less dangerous if she does so in order to prevent greater criminal harm? Consider this passage from the Model Penal Code Commentaries (partially quoted in *Craig*):

[A] principle of necessity, properly conceived, affords a general justification for conduct that would otherwise constitute an offense. It reflects the judgment that such a qualification on criminal liability, like the general requirements of culpability, is essential to the rationality and justice of the criminal law, and is appropriately addressed in a penal code. Under this section, property may be destroyed to prevent the spread of a fire. A speed limit may be violated in pursuing a suspected criminal. An ambulance may pass a traffic light. Mountain climbers lost in a storm may take refuge in a house or may appropriate provisions. Cargo may be jettisoned or an embargo violated to preserve the vessel. An alien may violate a curfew in order to reach air raid shelter. A druggist may dispense a drug without the requisite prescription to alleviate grave distress in an emergency.

Commentaries § 3.02, at 9–10.

What does it mean to say that "rationality and justice" require the recognition of a necessity (balance-of-evils) defense? If "the rationality and justice of the criminal law" demand a necessity defense, how could German criminal law have done without it for so long? Is the problem the recognition of a balance-of-harms defense, or the recognition of a balance-of-harms *justification* defense?

The Model Penal Code is resolutely utilitarian, and more specifically treatmentist, in outlook. Does this account for its unproblematic recognition of necessity? (Then again, what is treatmentist about the reference to "rationality and justice" in the above passage? Does the Model Code's approach to justification—and excuse?—reflect the treatmentist focus on a diagnosis of dangerousness, or is it perhaps even meant to function as a corrective on treatmentism in light of "rationality and justice"?) Do (some) legal systems struggle to accommodate necessity as a justification because they reject utilitarianism (in this particular case, in a particular version, in general)? In other words, is necessity problematic *insofar as* it is based on a utilitarian (or, more generally, consequentialist) rationale? If so, how can legal systems that do not categorically reject utilitarian considerations—including, for instance, Canadian criminal law—dismiss necessity as a justification? Why is utilitarianism acceptable, for instance, in the general rationale of punishment (deterrence, incapacitation, rehabilitation), but not in the case of the defense of necessity?

What would a non-utilitarian account of necessity as justification look like? Is one reason why German criminal law has resisted recognizing necessity as justification that this defense does not fit easily with an account of criminal law that assigns pride of place to the maintenance of law—or right—for its own sake?

Compare the rationale of self-defense in German criminal law: self-defense is justified because "right" need not cede to "wrong." This rationale of law protection may have difficulty accounting for limitations on the right to self-defense. Does it apply at all to the defense of justifying necessity? What is the "wrong" in the defense of necessity against which "right" is protected (recall the example of the much-invoked "innocent" owner of the mountain cabin)? Under this account, just why does the cabin owner have to "accept" becoming the victim of a property offense, given that she was doing nothing wrong? The answer appears to be a general norm of solidarity (which presumably also underlies the general duty-to-aid provision, § 323c Criminal Code). Is this the sort of extraneous "social ethical" factor that is also now said to generate limitations on the right of self-defense*? Does this mean that a legal system that does not recognize a (criminally enforceable) general duty to aid—like American criminal law—could not justify a necessity justification, at least on no-utilitarian grounds?

Does the reference to a general norm of solidarity imply that the cabin-owner would be in the wrong after all (legally? or just socially, ethically?) if she used force to prevent the hiker from climbing through her window to seek shelter from the storm? Or would this still amount to a confrontation of right and right? If so, at what point could the hiker be expected to just remain outside and "accept" his chances in the snow storm?

Aside from the question of why the victim of an offense committed under justifying necessity should accept her plight (i.e., her bad luck, rather than the hiker's), what about the prior question of what puts the hiker in the right to begin with? (Likewise, does saying that an

---

* See Chapter 13.A.

attacker must accept the consequences of actions in self-defense also explain why the target of the attack, as opposed to the state—which holds the monopoly on violence—is justified in using self-defensive force in the first place?) Necessity as an *excuse* rests on the actors' dire straits, but what makes the act under justifying necessity lawful if not the balancing of interests? And what is the balancing of interests if not a utilitarian weighing of costs and benefits? How else is a conflict of right and right to be resolved?*

2. A comparison of New York law, see *People v. Craig*, and German law shows that both legal systems incorporate norms providing a justification in situations of necessity: § 35.02 New York Penal law and § 34 Criminal Code. Another question is how to handle cases where the offender was convinced that the danger really existed while in reality it did not, or at least not as an imminent danger. In *People v. Craig*, the New York Court argues for objective standards. The offender's subjective conviction does not suffice to make his conduct lawful.

Here the New York Court of Appeals, as it did in *Goetz* on the issue of self-defense, distances itself from the Model Penal Code, emphasizing what it regards as significant distinctions between the New York Penal Law and the Model Penal Code. In both cases, the New York court casts the New York version of the defense in question as narrower than the Model Penal Code's: *Goetz* insists that the New York version of self-defense is narrower than the Model Penal Code insofar as it is not purely subjective, but installs an objective filter of "reasonableness" (even though the court then turns around and develops an exceedingly flexible, "subjectivized," account of reasonableness that takes into account the characteristics of the defendant and the circumstances in which he found himself). In *Craig*, the court appears to go a step further: it reads the New York necessity provision as doing away with any subjective inquiry whatsoever; necessity, according to *Craig*, is "objective only." It is unclear whether the court actually means what it says; in a footnote, the court leaves open how it would deal with a case where (a) "actual necessity existed but the actor did not have the intention of avoiding the greater evil" or where, conversely, (b) the necessity conditions are met "under an objective/reasonable person standard," but not in fact. (On the first scenario, objective justifications without a subjective aspect, see Chapter 13.A.)

The Model Penal Code, on closer inspection, is significantly less subjective on the issue of necessity than the New Court of Appeals recognizes. Recall that in the case of self-defense, the Model Penal Code—contrary to the opinion in *Goetz*—does not endorse a purely subjective standard; although it does not refer to reasonable beliefs in the definition of self-defense, it provides for the punishability of defendants acting under reckless or negligent beliefs according to the nature of their mistake (recklessness offenses for recklessly unreasonable mistakes, negligence offences for negligently unreasonable ones). In the case of necessity, the Model Penal Code does refer to reasonableness, but similarly provides for (fall-back) liability for unreasonable mistakes in the same way: "(2) When the actor was reckless or negligent . . . in appraising the necessity for his conduct, the justification afforded by this Section is unavailable in a prosecution for any offense for which recklessness or negligence, as the case may be, suffices to establish culpability" (§ 3.02(2)).

In fact, there is one element of necessity that is purely objective in the Model Penal Code. Mistakes regarding the *necessity* of the conduct do not bar the defense (if they are reasonable, they support a full defense, and if they are not, they support a partial defense, from an intention offense to a recklessness or negligence one, depending on the nature of the mistake); mistakes regarding the *balancing* of the "the harm or evil sought to be avoided" against "that sought to be prevented by the law defining the offense charged," however, do. According to the Model Penal Code Commentaries, the point of this requirement was to prevent the application of the necessity defense to someone who "genuinely believes that the life of another is less valuable than his own financial security." Does this different treatment of the necessity element and the balancing element of the necessity defense make sense? Or is

---

* For recent attempts—both drawing on Hegel—to generate non-utilitarian (and non-communitarian) accounts of justifying necessity, see Alan Brudner, "A Theory of Necessity," 7 *Oxford Journal of Legal Studies* (1987), 339; Michael Pawlik, *Der rechtfertigende Notstand* (2002).

it an arbitrary attempt to limit the scope of a defense (perhaps to make it more palatable to legislatures)? The Model Code Commentaries attempt to frame the distinction in terms of that between mistakes of law and mistakes of fact:

> What is involved [in balancing mistakes] may be described as an interpretation of the law of the offense, in light of the submission that the special situation calls for an exception to the criminal prohibition that the legislature could not reasonably have intended to exclude given the competing values to be weighed.
>
> Commentaries § 3.02, at 12.

Even if this distinction applied (even in cases involving the balancing not of different qualities, but quantities, of harm), does it end the inquiry if one does not accept, unlike the Model Penal Code, that mistake of law is not an excuse—absent reliance on a prior misstatement of law?*

On its face, as *Craig* points out, the New York Penal Law version of the defense is "objective only" regarding both the necessity and the balancing element. The New York legislature, however, indeed went out of its way to stress the limits of the defense of necessity: acts must be "necessary as an *emergency measure* to avoid an *imminent* public or private injury which *is about to occur*" and that "the desirability and *urgency* of avoiding such injury clearly outweigh the desirability of avoiding" the prohibited conduct (emphases in *Craig*). What function do the italicized terms serve other than to signal the legislature's anxiety about the potential scope of the necessity defense, or perhaps even about the desirability of the defense of necessity as justification in the first place? At what point does the defense become so narrow as to have been rendered pointless?

3. A more bizarre version of mistaken beliefs is described in the *King of the Cats Case*. The defendant R., who attempted to murder Mrs. N., thought this to be necessary to save millions of human beings who would otherwise be killed by the vicious "king of the cats." The Federal Court of Justice did not apply § 34 Criminal Code due to the lack of an imminent danger. Nevertheless, in a rather condensed passage, the Court talks about the weighing of interests at the heart of § 34. This might seem odd at first glance: why consider the weighing-of-interest question if there was no danger at all? The answer points to a feature of German criminal law that we mentioned above: the doctrine of errors about justifying circumstances, based on an analogous application of the provision regarding errors about offense elements in the German Criminal Code, § 16 Criminal Code (Chapter 8.C). With this doctrine of errors about justifying circumstances, German law considers offenders' subjective beliefs, which might lead to the result that they will not be punished. The test under such circumstances is a hypothetical scenario: if the offender's belief regarding an imminent danger had been true, would the weighing of interests have led to a justification? The judges thus had to consider: what if the "king of cats" really existed and demanded a human sacrifice? Would it then be permissible to kill one person to save millions? The Court does not dwell on this strange scenario but states briefly that a balance of "life against life" is not permissible. We will come back to this limit on justifying necessity in Note 6.† At this point, suffice it to note that under German law, unlike under New York law, it is conceivable that, as in the case of putative self-defense discussed in Chapter 13.A, an actor can be acquitted in a case of putative necessity even if the danger was only in his or her imagination.

Does this mean that German criminal law would reach a different result in a case like *Craig*? No, because it would not have been enough for the political activists to have honestly believed that the harm of committing a minor crime such as trespass might be outweighed by the long-term benefits of preventing future harm; they must have believed in the existence of an imminent danger, rather than merely in the possibility of future harm. The doctrine of mistake about justifying circumstances only exempts from punishment if *all* the conditions of the justification were fulfilled, where the imagined attack, danger etc. were in fact present.

---

* See Chapter 8.C.ii.
† See also the discussion of *Dudley & Stephens* in Chapter 6.C.

Within the "justifying necessity" provision in § 34 Criminal Code, the crucial passage requires that "upon weighing the conflicting interests, in particular the affected legal goods and the degree of danger, the protected interest substantially outweighs the one interfered with." This has been interpreted to mean that killing another person will not be justified under § 34 Criminal Code, even if this is the only way of averting a very serious danger to another person's health or life, on the ground that life is the supreme legal good, i.e., the legal good that outweighs all others. Internal balancing of life—i.e., of one life against another, or of fewer lives against more—is held to be similarly impermissible, as a categorical matter.* As a result, then, in German law, justifying necessity is not available as a defense in cases of homicide. (Recall that this was also the position of the court in *Dudley & Stephens*, in Chapter 6.C.) There is no similar limitation in the Model Penal Code, though the exclusion of homicide from the purview of certain defenses, notably the (excuse) defense of duress, has a long tradition in common law countries.[†]

This leads to legal outcomes such as in the battered woman case decided by the German Federal Court of Justice in 2003. Compare this case to *State v. Kelly* (Chapter 13.A): in both cases a woman killed her husband after years of serious abuse. However, there is one crucial difference: in the German case, the husband was asleep while the wife shot him. The legal consequence was that the defendant was not acting in self-defense because § 32 Criminal Code presupposes an imminent attack. This is the reason why the German case appears in the section on necessity, rather than in that on self-defense. For the German battered woman case, the question was: did she act in a state of necessity, under § 34 (justifying necessity) or § 35 (excusing necessity) Criminal Code?[‡]

Note that the Federal Court of Justice in the German battered woman case did not reject the justification defense because the danger was not imminent. The requirements for a present attack (self-defense, § 32 Criminal Code) and imminent danger (§ 34 Criminal Code) are not identical: in the case of self-defense, the attack must occur within minutes; in the case of necessity it suffices that harm would occur at some point in the not-too-distant future, even many hours later. Does this distinction make sense, apart from differences in the precise current formulation of the relevant sections of the German Criminal Code (§§ 32 and 34 Criminal Code)? What, at bottom, is the difference between the *Not* (necessity, emergency) in *Notwehr* and the *Not* in *Notstand*? What would account for differentiating between the imminence of harm in the form of an attack and the imminence of harm in some other form, other than an attempt to differentiate between the scope of self-defense and necessity? And what would be the rationale for drawing the distinction between self-defense and necessity, and for drawing it on this ground, in this way? Is the lapse of time between the act purportedly justified under self-defense or necessity and the harm it is meant to avert a promising candidate for drawing a serviceably clear line between self-defense and necessity? (Recall here that the imminence requirement in justifying necessity, while less stringent than the "presence" requirement in self-defense, nonetheless is not flexible enough to cover the conduct of the defendants in *Craig*.)

It is worth pointing out here that, in American criminal law, the fact that the victim was asleep would not automatically remove a case from the realm of self-defense, despite the presence of an imminence requirement in the law of self-defense. The question would remain whether the defendant (reasonably) believed that the elements of self-defense were satisfied, though presumably a fact finder, everything else being equal, would be less likely to find that the defendant held the requisite belief (actually and reasonably) if the victim was asleep,

---

* See Note 6.
  † See, e.g., William Blackstone, *Commentaries on the Law of England* (1769), vol. 4, 30 ("he ought rather to die himself than escape by the murder of an innocent"); see also, illustrating the compromise position of permitting a partial defense (from murder to manslaughter), the New Jersey Code of Criminal Justice, N.J. Stat. § 2C:2–9(b) ("In a prosecution for murder, the defense is only available to reduce the degree of the crime to manslaughter."). For more on duress, see Chapter 14.A.
  ‡ Excusing necessity is discussed in Note 8; for a discussion of "insidiously committed murder," the crime of conviction in the German case (intentional murder under aggravating circumstances, § 211 Criminal Code), see Chapter 15.A.

rather than awake, at the time of the purportedly self-defensive action. Consider, for instance, the well-known case of *State v. Leidholm*, 334 N.W.2d 811 (N.D. 1983), which featured expert evidence on battered-woman's syndrome:

> Janice Leidholm was charged with murder for the stabbing death of her husband, Chester Leidholm, in the early morning hours of August 7, 1981, at their farm home near Washburn. She was found guilty by a McLean County jury of manslaughter and was sentenced to five years' imprisonment in the State Penitentiary with three years of the sentence suspended. Leidholm appealed from the judgment of conviction . . .
>
> According to the testimony, the Leidholm marriage relationship in the end was an unhappy one, filled with a mixture of alcohol abuse, moments of kindness toward one another, and moments of violence. The alcohol abuse and violence was exhibited by both parties on the night of Chester's death.
>
> Early in the evening of August 6, 1981, Chester and Janice attended a gun club party in the city of Washburn where they both consumed a large amount of alcohol. On the return trip to the farm, an argument developed between Janice and Chester which continued after their arrival home just after midnight. Once inside the home, the arguing did not stop; Chester was shouting, and Janice was crying.
>
> At one point in the fighting, Janice tried to telephone Dave Vollan, a deputy sheriff of McLean County, but Chester prevented her from using the phone by shoving her away and pushing her down. At another point, the argument moved outside the house, and Chester once again was pushing Janice to the ground. Each time Janice attempted to get up, Chester would push her back again.
>
> A short time later, Janice and Chester re-entered their home and went to bed. When Chester fell asleep, Janice got out of bed, went to the kitchen, and got a butcher knife. She then went back into the bedroom and stabbed Chester. In a matter of minutes Chester died from shock and loss of blood.

On these facts, the North Dakota Supreme Court overturned the conviction on the ground that the following jury instruction on self-defense was incorrect:

> The circumstances under which she acted must have been such as to produce in the mind of reasonably prudent persons, regardless of their sex, similarly situated, the reasonable belief that the other person was then about to kill her or do serious bodily harm to her.

Instead, the court held that, in a self-defense case,

> an accused's actions are to be viewed from the standpoint of a person whose mental and physical characteristics are like the accused's and who sees what the accused sees and knows what the accused knows. For example, if the accused is a timid, diminutive male, the factfinder must consider these characteristics in assessing the reasonableness of his belief. If, on the other hand, the accused is a strong, courageous, and capable female, the factfinder must consider these characteristics in judging the reasonableness of her belief.

More specifically, the court made clear that this (confusingly named) "subjective standard of reasonableness" (also familiar from *Kelly* and *Goetz*), required the fact finder (i.e., the jury or, in a bench trial, the court) "to consider expert testimony, once received in evidence, describing battered woman syndrome and the psychological effects it produces in the battered spouse when deciding the issue of the existence and reasonableness of the accused's belief that force was necessary to protect herself from imminent harm."

It is useful, once again, to keep in mind the procedural posture of the *Leidholm* case before the North Dakota Supreme Court. The court did not hold that Ms. Leidholm in fact satisfied the elements of self-defense; the court held instead that the trial court had misinstructed the jury on the law of self-defense in a way that may have prejudiced Ms. Leidholm by precluding the jury from properly considering the evidence of battered woman syndrome offered in her case. Even with a correct instruction, the jury would have been free to reject the claim of self-defense on any of the elements of self-defense, most notably her (actual and reasonable) belief in the necessity to use deadly force "to prevent imminent and unlawful harm."

At any rate, as noted previously, the decisive issue in the German battered woman case from 2003 was not the imminence element of the necessity defense, but the balancing requirement. The Court held that "the physical safety of the defendant and their daughters did not outweigh the interest harmed by the crime, i.e., the life of [the husband] F. as the legal interest which was destroyed." Although the Court does not devote much space to the decisive weighing question, it is worth taking a closer look. In the German literature, it is common to point to a difference between "defensive necessity" (*Defensivnotstand*) and other cases of justifying necessity ("aggressive necessity," *Aggressivnotstand*). We have mentioned that danger-averting acts often harm those who had nothing to do with the danger, such as the owner of the cabin into which the offender broke to escape the blizzard, discussed in Note 1 above. Note the difference in the German battered woman case: the source of the danger was the same person as the victim of the defensive act (the husband). Under such circumstances, the situation is closer to the situation of self-defense and therefore is called "defensive necessity." For this reason, one could argue that the weighing of interests that § 34 Criminal Code demands must take such "closeness to self-defense" into account. But the Federal Court of Justice did not seriously consider justifying the defendant's act and shows reluctance to extend the rationale underlying self-defense to cases of non-"present" attacks (i.e., future harm that satisfies the "present attack" element of self-defense under § 34 Criminal Code).

Does it make sense to distinguish between self-defense (*Notwehr*) and "defensive necessity" (*defensiver Notstand*)? If A, who engages in a "present attack" against D, has to "accept" the consequences of D's defensive action, why wouldn't B, who threatens D with the threat of "imminent" harm? Isn't "defensive necessity" closer to self-defense than to "aggressive necessity"—and in fact to necessity in general—insofar as the expectation of "solidarity" that is cited as a rationale for necessity in general, and aggressive necessity in particular, doesn't apply? What does the classification of an act of necessity as "defensive" or "aggressive" have to do with the balancing of interests? Is the idea that the person who triggers an act of defensive necessity forfeits (part of) the "protection of the law" or that his or her interests are weighted less than those of the "innocent" cabin owner?

4. The distinction between so-called *defensive* necessity and self-defense raises the more general question of the relationship between necessity and self-defense. In the present materials, and in the German Criminal Code, self-defense is treated before necessity. But why? Couldn't one think of necessity as the more general justification defense and of self-defense as the more specific? Is there some reason other than numerical priority in the German Criminal Code or, for that matter, historical priority in German criminal law (recall that the defense of justifying necessity was not recognized in Germany until the 1920s and did not appear in the German Criminal Code until 1975), why self-defense should be treated as somehow prior to, or more fundamental than, necessity? The Model Penal Code (and other American criminal codes based on it, including the New York Penal Law), deal with necessity first, and then move on to other, more specific, defenses.

Compare the structure of justification defenses as reflected in the Model Penal Code with that in the German Criminal Code:

Model Penal Code

Article 3. General Principles of Justification

...

§ 3.02. Justification Generally: Choice of Evils.
§ 3.03. Execution of Public Duty.
§ 3.04. Use of Force in Self-Protection.
§ 3.05. Use of Force for the Protection of Other Persons.
§ 3.06. Use of Force for the Protection of Property.
§ 3.07. Use of Force in Law Enforcement.
§ 3.08. Use of Force by Persons with Special Responsibility for Care, Discipline or Safety of Others.

German Criminal Code

Fourth Title. Self-Defense, Necessity and Duress

§ 32. (Justifying) Self-Defense
§ 33. Excessive (Excusing) Self-Defense
§ 34. Justifying Necessity
§ 35. Excusing Necessity

Does the priority of self-defense over necessity reflect one conception of criminal law, and the priority of necessity over self-defense, another? If so, what's the difference between the two? Is the former categorical, deontological, right-based, and the latter conditional, utilitarian, interest-based? If necessity is the fundamental, fallback, justification that may apply when other, more specific, ones do not, and if, more specifically, self-defense is merely an instance of necessity, could we simply do away with a separate defense of self-defense? If, for instance, both necessity and self-defense turn on the balancing of competing interests (or legal goods, or "harms"—let's leave aside the unfortunately named "evils"), why couldn't the "general justification" of necessity deal with cases of self-defense? Similarly, if "acceptability" is the principle that drives both self-defense and necessity (in the first case because the attacker brought the harm upon himself, and in the second because an innocent victim of an action justified by necessity is bound by a duty of solidarity), then could one replace the provisions on self-defense and necessity with a general provision recognizing a defense in cases where the victim can be expected to "accept" the harm?

5. *A note on other justifications.* As the above excerpts make clear, many of the justifications set out in the Model Penal Code do not appear in the German Criminal Code. (In the pursuit of broad criminal law reform, the Model Penal Code was not addressed only at legislators, but also at judges, lawyers, and law teachers. More than a model piece of criminal legislation, it was a treatise and textbook of criminal law.*) This is not to say that these defenses are not recognized in German criminal law; instead many are addressed elsewhere.

For instance, "execution of public duty" (MPC § 3.03) and "use of force in law enforcement" (MPC § 3.07) is addressed in § 127 StPO [German Criminal Procedure Code] and the police laws of the various *Länder.*[†] "Use of Force by Persons with Special Responsibility for Care, Discipline or Safety of Others" (MPC § 3.08) is covered in the Mariners Law (§ 106 *Seemannsgesetz* (captain's authority)) and the Air Safety Law (§ 12 *Luftsicherheitsgesetz* (pilot's authority)). The use of force by prison authorities is governed by the Prison Act [StVollzG].[‡]

Parental discipline (MPC § 3.08) used to be recognized in the German Civil Code (§ 1631 BGB), but this is no longer the case. In fact, § 1631 para. 2 Civil Code (BGB) now explicitly provides that: "Children have a right to an upbringing without violence. Physical punishments, psychological injuries and other degrading measures are prohibited." This contemporary approach in the Civil Code's provisions on family law is seen to preclude references to necessity (§ 34 Criminal Code) as a justification for parental discipline that otherwise would satisfy the elements of assault (§ 223 Criminal Code: "physically mistreats or harms the health of another person").[§]

Consent as a justification (MPC § 2.11) is also not defined as a general defense in the German Criminal Code, though it is recognized as a defense in cases of assault (§ 228 Criminal Code).[¶]

Does the legality principle require exhaustive and specific definitions of justifications? In the criminal code? In any statute? Even a non-criminal statute (e.g., the civil code)? Does the answer to the last question depend on the relationship between civil and criminal liability? More specifically, does it depend on whether a successful justification defense categorically precludes both criminal and civil liability or not?

* See Herbert Wechsler, "The Challenge of a Model Penal Code," 65 *Harvard Law Review* (1952), 1097.
† See, e.g., pt. IV ("coercion") PolG NRW [Police Law of the Land North Rhine-Westfalia].
‡ See, e.g., StVollzG titles 12 ("direct coercion") and 13 ("disciplinary measures"). For further discussion, see Chapter 13.D.
§ See generally Manfred Heinrich, "Elterliche Züchtigung und Strafrecht," 6 *ZIS-Strafrecht* (2011), 431, <http://www.zis-online.com/dat/artikel/2011_5_577.pdf>. For a discussion of the constitutionality of a parental discipline defense along similar lines by the Canadian Supreme Court, see *Canadian Foundation for Children, Youth and the Law v. Canada (Attorney General)*, [2004] 1 S.C.R. 76 (upholding constitutionality of defense, narrowly construed to apply to "minor corrective force of a transitory and trifling nature" used "by way of correction," excluding "corporal punishment of children under two or teenagers" and "degrading, inhuman or harmful conduct," such as "discipline by the use of objects," "blows or slaps to the head," or "outbursts of violence against a child motivated by anger or animated by frustration").
¶ For further discussion of consent (as element-negating "defense" and general justification), see Chapter 13.C.

6. What about the weighing of interests if the question is not "one life against another life" but "one life against hundreds, thousands, millions of others" (i.e., quantitative, rather than qualitative, balancing)? If one reads the wording of § 34 Criminal Code, one could come to the conclusion that under such circumstances one person's interest in not being sacrificed is outweighed by the interest of the many others who could be saved. But this is not how § 34 Criminal Code is interpreted by German courts and the vast majority in the German literature.* Why is that? What is more respectful of the value of life: to sacrifice one life to save a thousand, or *not* to sacrifice one life to save a thousand? Should it matter whether the lives saved include one's own? Why should a person be expected, in a situation of necessity, to "accept" violations of any legal good, but never of the legal good of life, no matter how many lives of other persons are at stake? Why does the duty of solidarity, said to undergird the defense of necessity, stop at life?

The short passage in the *King of the Cats Case* mentions that § 34 Criminal Code does not "allow a balancing of life against life." This is meant to exclude justification. It is worth to note which precedents are cited there: "OGHSt" refers to criminal law decisions of the Supreme Court of Justice for the British Zone on German territory after the Second World War (*Oberster Gerichtshof für die Britische Zone in Strafsachen*). The two opinions cited in the *King of the Cats Case* dealt with cases involving defendants who as doctors had worked in mental hospitals and had produced lists with patients to be killed in the so-called "euthanasia"—program, mainly in the years 1940 and 1941. When indicted as aiders to murder after 1945, the defendants had argued that, had they refused cooperation, other doctors with stronger commitment to National Socialist (NS) ideology would have haven taken their place and handed in much longer lists. The court did not object to this factual assertion and pointed out that some mental hospitals had indeed been emptied out entirely by NS doctors. Nevertheless, the judges insisted that the assembly of the lists was not justified, contrary to the conclusion of the trial court. However, they acknowledged a "personal exemption from punishment" (*persönlicher Strafausschließungsgrund)* if the motive was solely to rescue patients. This could not be established clearly for the individual defendants, thus the case went back to the trial court.† Compare this fact-specific (compromise?) resolution to that adopted in other cases, including *Dudley & Stephens* and the *Border Guard Case*.‡

The court's approach was controversial at the time, with several German criminal law scholars arguing that, based on the court's findings, the defendants were entitled to an excuse, i.e., a finding of no criminal *liability*, rather than merely to an exemption from *punishment*. The court, however, stressed the "uniqueness" of the situation facing the defendants, which in its view required a *sui generis* disposition on the facts of the case by means of a *personal* exemption rather than the application of a general rule (be it in the form of an excuse or a justification). According to the court, "state sponsored mass criminality" represented a "unique criminal scenario incapable of generalization" (OGHSt 1, 338). Interestingly, however, the court did not reject the legal relevance of an ethical norm out of hand, conceding instead that "the community indeed is not justified in ascribing guilt to someone who does what ethical law (*das Sittengesetz*) unambiguously demands, even if it results in the violation of a norm." The cases before it, however, did not rise to the level of such a conflict between ethical and legal norms (OGHSt 2, 123).

Personal exemptions from punishment, which are said to "lie beyond unlawfulness and guilt," occupy a somewhat uneasy place in German criminal law doctrine. Frequently cited examples include: withdrawal from an attempt or conspiracy (§§ 24, 31 Criminal Code), underage incest participants (§ 173 para. 3), abortion during the first twenty-two weeks of the pregnancy (§ 218a para. 4), obstruction of justice to avoid punishment (§ 258 para. 4), reporting money laundering (§ 261 para. 9), or "active regret" through extinguishing an

---

* Compare *Dudley & Stephens*, Chapter 6.C, where this categorical position would require resort to necessity as an excuse.

† Supreme Court of Justice for the British Zone, Judgment of March 5, 1949, against Dr. P. et al., 19/49, OGHSt 1, 321; also Judgment of July 23, 1949, against C. et al., 161/49, OGHSt 2, 117.

‡ See Chapters 6.C and 8.C.ii, respectively.

arsonous fire (§ 306e). These personal punishment exemptions, of course, are legislatively defined, unlike the exemption enunciated in the OGH cases. Does this make a difference? Do they have anything in common? What is gained, or lost, by not classifying them as either an excuse or a justification? Or are they perhaps best thought of as (mandatory) sentencing guidelines that preclude the imposition of any punishment?

Consider the possible relevance of citing, in this context, a case involving Nazi atrocities, and more specifically of Nazi eugenics, in this case the destruction of mental patients' "lives not worth living." Might the categorical rejection of any balancing involving human life, be it of one life against another (more or less valuable, or "worth living") or of one life against many (not to mention of life against some other, lesser, legal good) also reflect an attempt to categorically condemn these frequent, and systematic, practices under the Nazi regime? In other words, is the sanctity of life not only a fundamental principle of constitutional priority, but also a taboo? Is the German criminal law on necessity, and on the justifiability of homicide in particular, therefore at least in part of symbolic significance that emerges only against the historical backdrop?

The notion of "sacrificing some to save the lives of a greater number" drew a lot of attention in the *Aviation Security Act Case* from 2006. In the *Aviation Security Act Case*, the German Federal Constitutional Court had to decide whether it would, from the constitutional point of view, be appropriate to label the shooting down of a hi-jacked airplane a lawful act. The Court held that it is constitutionally permissible to shoot down a hi-jacked airplane if the only persons on board are the hi-jackers (from the perspective of criminal law, this would be a straightforward case of others-defense and thus justified). Much more difficult are judgments if uninvolved passengers or crew members were killed (under such circumstances, it is not possible to point to self-defense/defense of others—this justification only applies if the victim of the defensive act is the attacker). The German Federal Constitutional Court points to human dignity, art. 1 para. 1 Basic Law: the innocent passengers would be treated as "mere objects."

Do you think this is convincing? What about protective duties of state organs towards citizens (after all, in the case of hi-jacked airplanes, only the state has the means to end the attack)? And, again, from a criminal law perspective, what about the duty of solidarity said to underlie the defense of justifying necessity? Are there no circumstances, is there no proportion between lives sacrificed and lives saved, that would impose a duty upon even an innocent person to accept interference with the legal good of life, as in the case of other legal goods? Is the "innocent" person who must "accept" violations of other legal goods—the paradigmatic mountain cabin owner, for instance—treated as any less of a "mere object" than the similarly innocent passengers on that hi-jacked plane? In this context, does it matter whether "the state" inflicts the harm (though, of course, from the perspective of criminal law, as opposed to constitutional law, it is not the state that faces criminal liability, but the person, or persons, accountable for the commission of the offense—the killing of the plane passengers), or a "private person" (as in the case of the defendant who burned down one house on the outskirts to save the entire town from an oncoming firestorm)?

7. The Canadian Supreme Court in *Perka* spends a good deal of time on the question of what it calls "illegality or contributory fault." This reference to illegality should not be confused with the requirement of unlawfulness in the law of self-defense. There, the defense is available only if the attack is "unlawful." Here, the defense is *not* available if the *defendant's* act is "illegal." In the first case, unlawfulness allows the defense, in the second, it precludes it, or so the argument goes. *Perka* rejects this position—after all, what good would a defense be that does not cover conduct that is, at least *prima facie* (in the sense of satisfying the elements of a criminal offense), "illegal"? The question of the relevance of "contributory fault" is perhaps less easily dismissed. The Model Penal Code deals with this issue in some detail:

§ 3.02. Justification Generally: Choice of Evils

. . .

(2) When the actor was reckless or negligent in bringing about the situation requiring a choice of harms or evils or in appraising the necessity for his conduct, the justification afforded by this

Section is unavailable in a prosecution for any offense for which recklessness or negligence, as the case may be, suffices to establish culpability.

In other words, the Model Penal Code treats the issue of "contributory fault" as it does a mistake regarding the element of "necessity" (though, again, not a mistake regarding the element of balancing, which is objective in the Model Penal Code's conception of the defense*). The defendant's liability reflects the type of fault, or mistake: recklessness or negligence will not preclude liability for offenses requiring proof of recklessness or negligence, respectively, if any. Compare also the Model Penal Code's similar treatment of mistakes regarding the elements of other defenses, including self-defense.[†] Also contrast the analogous—but less generous—provision in the Code's definition of duress (§ 2.09):[‡] Recklessly exposing oneself to duress bars the defense altogether; negligent exposure, as in the case of necessity, will either amount to a complete defense or, at worst, support criminal liability for an applicable negligence offense, if any.

German criminal law doctrine closely tracks this approach. Negligence (*Fahrlässigkeit*) in bringing about the justifying necessity (under § 34 Criminal Code) does not necessarily bar the defense, but exposes the defendant to liability for a negligence offense, should one exist that covers the conduct in question. If an offender intentionally created the necessity situation, this will be considered in the process of interest weighing required by § 34 German Criminal Code, but it is conceivable that it does not render the defense inapplicable. With view to duress—i.e., excusing necessity under § 35 Criminal Code—the text of § 35 Criminal Code precludes the defense if the defendant had to accept the danger, namely because he "himself caused the danger." A standard explanation of treating duress (excusing necessity, § 35 Criminal Code) somewhat less generously than (justifying) necessity (§ 34 Criminal Code) is that the defendant acting under duress "did something unlawful, i.e., socially disapproved, that does not deserve exculpation if he is also responsible for his situation," whereas someone acting under justifying necessity acted "to preserve interests that do not lose their otherwise significant predominance on account of his responsibility for the necessity situation."[§] The Model Penal Code Commentaries acknowledge that rejecting duress in cases where the defendant recklessly caused the necessity situation represents a "deliberate departure" from the general rule that liability match individual culpability (in the sense of a mode of culpability, here: recklessness), pointing to "the exceptional nature of the defense."[¶] Do you find the proposed explanations for the differential treatment of necessity and duress convincing? Aren't defenses, and excuse defenses in particular, "exceptional" by definition? What's exceptionally exceptional about duress?

Consider this question also in the broader context of the question of defense bootstrapping, or "causing the conditions of one's own defense."** Beyond the realm of necessity (and duress), consider, for instance, the treatment of "provocation" (or "initial aggressors") in the law of self-defense. Here, both the Model Penal Code and some interpretations of German criminal law (the German Criminal Code does not explicitly address this question, the discussion centers around the word "appropriate" (*geboten*) in § 32 Criminal Code) are considerably more generous than they are in the case of necessity (never mind duress). One might think, for instance, that—as in the case of necessity (and duress)—self-defense would not be available in the event of an intentional provocation (*Absichtsprovokation*), i.e., provoking another with the specific intent (purpose, conscious object, *Absicht*) to cause him or her to engage in conduct that satisfies the conditions for an exercise of one's right to self-defense. Indeed, this assumption is frequently made by those who interpret the German self-defense provision in § 32 Criminal Code. Yet, the American Model Penal Code refers to

---

* See Note 2.

[†] See Chapter 13.A.

[‡] See Chapter 14.A.

[§] Claus Roxin, *Strafrecht: Allgemeiner Teil* (4th edn. 2006), vol. 1, 751.

[¶] Commentaries § 2.09, at 379 and n.48.

** See generally Paul H. Robinson, "Causing the Conditions of One's Own Defense: A Study in the Limits of Theory in Criminal Law Doctrine," 71 *Virginia Law Review* (1985), 1.

the ostensible self-defender who "with the purpose of causing death or serious bodily harm, provoked the use of force against himself in the same encounter" only in the cases involving the use of *deadly* self-defensive force. § 3.04(2)(b)(i) (where deadly force is defined fairly broadly as "force which the actor uses with the purpose of causing or which he knows to create a substantial risk of causing death or serious bodily harm," § 3.11(2)).

Some German commentators likewise insist that even intentional provocation does not preclude self-defense as long as the provocative conduct is itself not unlawful, as for instance a police officer's lawful exercise of his duties, "even if he hopes to provoke the affected person through his duty compliant intervention so that he can take a swipe at him in self-defense." Why? Because "it is only demanded that people behave lawfully," and "the law cares not about the motivating disposition," so that "the right to self-defense cannot be affected by this either."* Recall that self-defense (*Notwehr*) in German criminal law, as a justification, is grounded traditionally in the objective conception of maintenance, or protection, of law (which also accounts for the principle that right need not cede to wrong, and the rejection of a general legal duty to retreat). Here, the provocateur's motivation is beside the point because, insofar as he is "in the right," he protects law nonetheless.

Do you agree with the treatment of the self-defensive provocateur under the Model Penal Code or in German criminal law? Does the degree, or nature, of the provocation matter, or the provoked's ability to resist it, apart from the provoker's intent, or from the lawfulness of his conduct?

8. *Excusing necessity and duress.* If the act in question is not justified, the possibility of excusing necessity remains, at least in the German legal system. In the extensive analysis of necessity that Justice Dickson provides in *R. v. Perka*, he also points out the difference between justification and excuse—this distinction is a familiar and central feature in German criminal law doctrine.† With respect to necessity, Justice Dickson assumes that this must be *either* justification *or* excuse (and he expresses his preference for an excuse). German law, however, provides for another solution: not "either-or," but both; the German Criminal Code contains two provisions about necessity, justifying necessity (§ 34) and excusing necessity (§ 35). (The German Criminal Code initially recognized only excusing necessity; justifying necessity was added in 1975. See Note 1.)

Excusing necessity, under § 35 Criminal Code, does not affect the unlawfulness of the act, but operates on the third level of the analysis of criminal liability: guilt (responsibility, blameworthiness). If § 35 applies, the offender "acts without guilt." Unlike § 34, this defense is framed not in terms of a balancing of interests, or legal goods; the emphasis instead lies on the necessity itself. Even if the balancing of legal goods does not come out (decisively) in the defendant's favor, he or she may nonetheless escape punishment if the straits were so dire that it would be unfair to cast blame.

American criminal law, and the Model Penal Code in particular, also recognizes both a justificatory and an excusing version of necessity, broadly understood. It should be pointed out here that *Perka*, in insisting that there can only be necessity as an *excuse*, is not the norm in the common law, not only because both justificatory and excusing varieties of necessity have been recognized, but also because, if only one type of necessity is accepted, it tends to be necessity as a justification, rather than as an excuse. Recall that *Dudley & Stephens* is generally read as (and often criticized for) recognizing necessity only as a justification; if only it had recognized necessity as an excuse, it would have reached the correct result, or so the story goes.‡ Note also that even in *Perka* itself, the dissent—by Justice Wilson—chided the majority for concluding that "the appropriate jurisprudential basis on which to premise the defence of necessity is exclusively that of excuse." Justice Wilson had no difficulty conceiving of, and making room for, necessity as a justification, suggesting unremarkably that "an act is

---

* Roxin, *Strafrecht*, vol. 1, 688.
† See Chapter 6.A.
‡ See Chapter 6.C.

justified on grounds of necessity if the court can say that not only was the act a necessary one but it was rightful rather than wrongful."

Perka is unusual in another—and more important—respect, namely in its wide-ranging exploration of the "history and background" of the necessity defense, and the nature of justification and excuse, from which Justice Dickson attempts to derive a coherent doctrine of necessity. Whether this attempt is successful is another question, as is whether the resulting account of necessity has less to do with the distinction between justification and excuse than with the concept of "moral involuntariness" and, ultimately, an obscure but apparently deeply felt anxiety about the abuse of the defense by "scoundrels": whereas necessity as a justification "could 'very easily become simply a mask for anarchy,'" necessity as an excuse is supposedly "much less open to criticism." Do you find this convincing? Wouldn't you expect just the opposite?

Notwithstanding *Perka* and Canadian criminal law, then, American criminal law recognizes necessity both as a justification (balance of evils, choice of evils) and as an excuse. Unlike German criminal law (and *Perka*), however, the Model Penal Code limits necessity as an excuse to cases where the exigency giving rise to the commission of the offense originates from another person, rather than circumstances. In other words, excusing necessity comes in the form of personal, but not of circumstantial, duress. This narrow conception of the defense of necessity as an excuse, rather than the absence of excusing necessity altogether, accounts for the unavailability of excusing necessity in *Dudley & Stephens*, at the time the case was decided as well as under the Model Penal Code. For more on duress, and the limitations on the defense, which reflect the same anxiety about its abuse that figure so prominently in *Perka*, see Chapter 14.A.

9. *Necessity and domestic violence.* Note that the court in the German battered woman case from 2003 analyzed the defendant's criminal liability under the doctrine of necessity, rather than self-defense (as American courts would have done), and more specifically necessity as an excuse, not as a justification.* One question was: Could the danger have been averted otherwise? The Federal Court of Justice does not answer this conclusively but refers the case back to the trial court for examining the relevant facts. But the judges at the Federal Court of Justice give some hints: they say that it is "rather unlikely" that the defendant had no other alternatives. This implies that § 35 para. 1 Criminal Code—requiring that the "imminent danger . . . cannot be averted otherwise"—could not be satisfied. (In that case, necessity as a justification, under § 34, would also be unavailable, since § 34 contains the exact same requirement: without necessity, neither justifying nor excusing necessity applies.) In the next step, the Federal Court of Justice draws the trial court's attention to the question of an error about *excusing* circumstances (*Entschuldigungstatbestandsirrtum*) and the avoidability of such an error (§ 35 para. 2 Criminal Code).

(Note here the contrast to errors about justifying circumstances, which need not be unavoidable to preclude liability.† In other words, mistakes about a justification element are treated like mistakes regarding an offense element, under § 16 Criminal Code (which do not need to be unavoidable), and mistakes about an excuse element are handled like mistakes of law, under § 35 para. 2 Criminal Code (which do). Unlike mistakes about the presence of a justification element, however, mistakes about the presence of an excuse element are treated explicitly in the German Criminal Code, in § 35 para. 2, making the analogous application of the mistake of law provision, § 17 Criminal Code, unnecessary.)

When the ruling describes the desperation the defendant had reached after fifteen years of horrible abuse by her violent and dominating husband, the conclusion is not far-fetched that she thought, in fact, that it was impossible to free herself and her daughters other than through eliminating the source of their suffering. Thus, the decisive question appears to be: was such an error avoidable? If not, § 35 para. 2 Criminal Code declares that the defendant

---

* On the inapplicability of self-defense in these cases, under German law, see Chapter 13.A.
† See Chapter 8.C.

will not be punished. Unfortunately, in the last section of the judgment, the Federal Court of Justice demands "strict requirements" regarding unavoidability.* In contrast to *State v. Kelly*, nowhere in the judgment does the court attempt to illuminate the specific psychological situation of battered women. Had the judges done this like the New Jersey Supreme Court in *State v. Kelly*, they might have developed an understanding that "strict requirements" concerning the defendants' assessment of their situation might be inappropriate. If the Court assumed that the defendant acted under an avoidable error about a present danger that could not be averted by other means, the legal consequence according to § 35 para. 2 in connection with § 211 Criminal Code† would be a mitigation of punishment according to § 49 para. 1 Criminal Code, rather than a complete excuse.‡ This would result in imprisonment between three years and fifteen years; note that a prison sentence of more than two years may not be suspended (§ 56 Criminal Code).

What, if anything, is at stake in the classification of a defense as a justification or as an excuse, in the context of prolonged domestic violence? Is the only thing that matters the outcome, regardless of the message of societal disapproval that accompanies it? Recall here the discussion of battered woman syndrome evidence, and attendant efforts to characterize abuse victims' actions against their abusers as justified, rather than as merely excused.

10. The provision about excusing necessity in the German Criminal Code, § 35 para. 1, narrows the scope of application by demanding that the danger must exist for the defendant or a relative or a person close to him or her. If the offender acts for altruistic reasons, with the goal to avert dangers to persons not close to him personally, § 35 Criminal Code does not apply. (Traditionally, this limitation also applied to the common-law defense of duress; the Model Penal Code, however, removed it, instead resting the defense exclusively on an inquiry into the reasonableness of the assessment of the necessity situation, regardless of the prior relationship between the defendant and the third party threatened. § 2.09 ("against his person or the person of another").)

In cases like the *Aviation Security Act Case*, therefore, neither § 34 nor § 35 Criminal Code could exempt from punishment. This does not seem a satisfying outcome if the defendant sincerely believed that he or she is doing the right thing by intentionally killing a human being as the only way to save a great number of lives. This has prompted discussions about an extra-legal excuse (*übergesetzlicher entschuldigender Notstand*). Constitutional doctrine permits the application of non-statutory principles *in favor* of the offender (as consistent with the principle of legality§). Since this subject is hotly debated, however, a legislative decision would be preferable, to close the gap in the criminal law if an offender acted in an altruistic way, saving others from a serious danger, while these others were not his kin (see § 35 Criminal Code), and where he acted under considerable time pressure.

There are two reasons supporting an argument that the legislator should close this gap by acknowledging an excuse: first, it is not a matter of personal fault that reliable information is not available. It is easier to excuse conduct if a decision had to be made very quickly and thus was not based on reliable information. Second, the atypical, altruistic background mitigates the offender's culpability. To arrive at this judgment, one has to take a close look at the quality of the offender's motives. Previous invocations of an extra-legal excuse, by doctors who were prosecuted after World War II for assembling partial lists of mental patients for National Socialist euthanasia programs, were met with skepticism; it was unclear whether all the defendants, who claimed that they had sacrificed a few to save the many, were totally

---

* On the general question of avoidability in the doctrine of mistake, also in relation to the common-law concept of reasonableness, see Chapter 8.C.

† See Chapter 15.A.

‡ German Criminal Code (Special Reasons for Mitigations in the Criminal Code) § 49
(1) If a mitigation of punishment according to this provision is required or allowed, the following applies for this mitigation . . . 1. life long imprisonment is substituted by imprisonment of not less than three years . . . .".

§ See Chapter 2.

immune to considering their career prospects and did not in fact support the euthanasia policies they later claimed to have opposed.*

But it would be unfair to compare a pilot's personal situation with these arguably dubious cases. The pilot would be aware that with the decision to kill he would run into personal difficulties, and one could hardly suspect that, unlike in the case of the doctors, some kind of ideological prejudice against *the victims* might have tainted purportedly his or her altruistic motive. However, one could argue that retaining criminal punishment could have the side effect of deterring actions in borderline cases, that is, if the information at hand might not be entirely reliable. Refusing an extra-legal excuse and connecting the rule "do not shoot" (or more specifically: do not shoot unless you are convinced of the reliability of your information) with criminal punishment may well have this deterrent effect. However, the question of justice remains: it seems unfair, even contradictory, to impose murder liability on someone who acted out of an altruistic motive and under time pressure, while extending a full excuse to someone who acted for the purpose of self-preservation (or the preservation of his or her relatives).†

We have discussed the legality principle in Chapter 2 (*nulla poena sine lege*, no punishment without law)—but note that the requirement of a legislative decision even under German law (art. 103 para. 2 Basic Law) only applies to changes to the criminal law that are detrimental to defendants. Do you think that an excuse could be the best approach for altruistic interventions in order to save many lives at the cost of one or a few lives? Note that the German Federal Constitutional Court explicitly leaves open how the criminal law should address the case. This could be understood as hinting in favor of an excuse. From the constitutional point of view, it is only the wrongful/not wrongful dichotomy that matters; accepting an excuse, as opposed to a justification, might be compatible with the human dignity argument. Why?

11. *Some additional notes on the* King of the Cats Case. The defendant R. who had stabbed Ms. N. was sentenced to nine years imprisonment, a lesser punishment than the persons in the background, R. and Ms. H., received for attempted murder. The reason for this was that the Court had mitigated the criminal punishment according to § 21 and § 17 Criminal Code (avoidable mistake of law).‡ In addition to the criminal punishment, a measure of prevention was ordered, i.e., confinement in a psychiatric hospital. (§ 63 Criminal Code allows this measure in the case of insanity or diminished responsibility.)

In German criminal law textbooks, the *King of the Cats* case is mostly cited under the heading "indirect perpetratorship." While there is general agreement that persons who act without culpability, such as children, can be labeled "human tools" if a person in the background acts as indirect perpetrator,§ this is somewhat less evident if the direct perpetrator acts under an avoidable mistake of law (and thus culpably, in the sense of without excuse!). But the Federal Court of Justice established that it is possible to punish *both* the person at the scene of the crime *and* the background person, *as perpetrators*. This was later confirmed with respect to the shootings at the German Border: criminal punishment for the border guards and the members of the GDR's National Defense Council.¶ (Compare the doctrine of "constructive presence" in the traditional common law of accessorial liability above.**)

12. Recall the *Daschner Case*, which we first encountered in Chapter 13.A, on self-defense. Now reconsider it in light of the necessity defense, as a justification (§ 34 Criminal Code) and as an excuse (§ 35 Criminal Code). The court rejects necessity as a justification because

---

* See the discussion in Note 6.
† See generally Tatjana Hörnle, "Shooting Down a Hijacked Plane: The German Discussion and Beyond," 3 *Criminal Law and Philosophy* (2009), 111; Tatjana Hörnle, "Hijacked Airplanes: May They Be Shot Down?," 10 *New Criminal Law Review* (2007), 582; see also Michael Bohlander, "In Extremis: Hijacked Airplanes, 'Collateral Damage' and the Limits of Criminal Law," *Criminal Law Review* [2006], 579.
‡ See Chapter 8.C.ii.
§ See Chapter 10.
¶ See Chapter 2.
** See Chapter 10.

Daschner's acts were no more necessary or appropriate (*angemessen*) under § 34 Criminal Code than they were necessary or appropriate (*geboten*) under § 32 Criminal Code (self-defense). Necessity as an excuse (§ 35 Criminal Code) likewise was not available:

> The responsibility for the abducted child arose from the police duty to avert danger. A close relationship as required by § 35 Criminal Code was not present. According to this provision only relatives and persons who are close to the victim are excused, because of the personal relationship and the conflict situation, and not police officers.

At the same time, the court rejected the argument that an exculpating, if not justifying, "extra-statutory necessity" might apply, for several reasons, some specific to the case, others of more general significance:

> There was no insoluble conflict of duties that would exclude guilt. As already stated, the action undertaken was not the only irrefutably necessary measure for assistance. The abduction case was not essentially different from the known instances in case law in which the perpetrators killed their victims at the start, and yet sought to extort money by the deception that they were still alive. It was not a unique individual case, but sadly not untypical in its category. Besides this it has to be considered that an application of extra-statutory necessity to state organs' powers to intervene can lead to a breakdown of the law regarding the state organization and competence (see Böckenförde, NJW 1978, 1881). When applying it in constitutional law the danger exists that the extra-statutory necessity "leads" to an "extra-constitutional necessity and an open general authority for overcoming necessities and emergencies" would arise. Every constitutional or statutory limit on [state] powers would thereby become only a provisional one.

Recall, however, that in the end, despite the rejection of any and all defenses, justifications and excuses, the defendant was found guilty but received a "warning" rather than a "punishment," under a rarely used provision of the German Criminal Code, § 59 StGB. (Compare the resolution in *Dudley & Stephens*, combining a guilty verdict and an executive pardon.*)

13. *Torture, self-defense, and necessity.* Compare the judgments in the *Daschner Case* (2005) and the *Aviation Security Act Case* (2006) with this excerpt from the infamous "torture memo" prepared by John Yoo for the U.S. Department of Justice's Office of Legal Counsel in 2002:

> You have asked for our Office's views regarding the standards of conduct under the Convention Against Torture and Other Cruel, Inhuman and Degrading Treatment or Punishment, as implemented by Sections 2340–2340A of title 18 of the United States Code. . . . We conclude . . . that Section 2340A[†] proscribes acts inflicting, and that are specifically intended to inflict, severe pain or suffering, whether mental or physical. Those acts must be of an extreme nature to rise to the level of torture within the meaning of Section 2340A and the Convention . . .
>
> Even if an interrogation method . . . might arguably cross the line drawn in Section 2340 . . . , we believe that under the current circumstances certain justification defenses might be available that would potentially eliminate criminal liability.
>
> Standard criminal law defenses of necessity and self-defense could justify interrogation methods needed to elicit information to prevent a direct and imminent threat to the United States and its citizens.
>
> **A. Necessity**
>
> . . . It appears to us that under the current circumstances the necessity defense could be successfully maintained in response to an allegation of a Section 2340A violation. On September 11, 2001, al Qaeda launched a surprise covert attack on civilian targets in the United States that led to the deaths of thousands and losses in the billions of dollars. According to public and governmental reports, al Qaeda has other sleeper cells within the United States that may be planning similar attacks. Indeed, al Qaeda plans apparently include efforts to develop and deploy chemical, biological and nuclear weapons of mass destruction. Under these circumstances, a detainee may possess information that could enable the United States to prevent

---

* See Chapter 6.C.

† [18 U.S.C. § 2340A

Whoever outside the United States commits or attempts to commit torture shall be fined under this title or imprisoned not more than 20 years, or both, and if death results to any person from conduct prohibited by this subsection, shall be punished by death or imprisoned for any term of years or for life.—Eds.]

attacks that potentially could equal or surpass the September 11 attacks in their magnitude. Clearly, any harm that might occur during an interrogation would pale to insignificance compared to the harm avoided by preventing such an attack, which could take hundreds or thousands of lives.

Under this calculus, two factors will help indicate when the necessity defense could appropriately be invoked. First, the more certain that government officials are that a particular individual has information needed to prevent an attack, the more necessary interrogation will be. Second, the more likely it appears to be that a terrorist attack is likely to occur, and the greater the amount of damage expected from such an attack, the more that an interrogation to get information would become necessary. Of course, the strength of the necessity defense depends on the circumstances that prevail, and the knowledge of the government actors involved, when the interrogation is conducted . . .

B. Self-Defense

Even if a court were to find that a violation of Section 2340A was not justified by necessity, a defendant could still appropriately raise a claim of self-defense . . . .

The threat of an impending terrorist attack threatens the lives of hundreds if not thousands of American citizens. Whether such a defense will be upheld depends on the specific context within which the interrogation decision is made. If an attack appears increasingly likely, but our intelligence services and armed forces cannot prevent it without the information from the interrogation of a specific individual, then the more likely it will appear that the conduct in question will be seen as necessary. If intelligence and other information support the conclusion that an attack is increasingly certain, then the necessity for the interrogation will be reasonable. The increasing certainty of an attack will also satisfy the imminence requirement. Finally, the fact that previous al Qaeda attacks have had as their aim the deaths of American citizens, and that evidence of other plots have had a similar goal in mind, would justify proportionality of interrogation methods designed to elicit information to prevent such deaths.

To be sure, this situation is different from the usual self-defense justification, and, indeed, it overlaps with elements of the necessity defense. Self-defense as usually discussed involves using force against an individual who is about to conduct the attack. In the current circumstances, however, an enemy combatant in detention does not himself present a threat of harm. He is not actually carrying out the attack; rather, he has participated in the planning and preparation for the attack, or merely has knowledge of the attack through his membership in the terrorist organization. Nonetheless, leading scholarly commentators believe that interrogation of such individuals using methods that might violate Section 2340A would be justified under the doctrine of self-defense, because the combatant by aiding and promoting the terrorist plot "has culpably caused the situation where someone might get hurt. If hurting him is the only means to prevent the death or injury of others put at risk by his actions, such torture should be permissible, and on the same basis that self-defense is permissible." Michael S. Moore, "Torture and the Balance of Evils," 23 Israel L. Rev. 280, 323 (1989) (symposium on Israel's Landau Commission Report).

Thus, some commentators believe that by helping to create the threat of loss of life, terrorists become culpable for the threat even though they do not actually carry out the attack itself. They may be hurt in an interrogation because they are part of the mechanism that has set the attack in motion, *id.* at 323, just as is someone who feeds ammunition or targeting information to an attacker. Under the present circumstances, therefore, even though a detained enemy combatant may not be the exact attacker—he is not planting the bomb, or piloting a hijacked plane to kill civilians—he still may be harmed in self-defense if he has knowledge of future attacks because he has assisted in their planning and execution . . .

This memo was widely criticized and eventually withdrawn. The criticism, however, generally focused on another part of the memo, which defends a narrow definition of "torture," making invocation of the defenses discussed in the above excerpt unnecessary. Note that, at this point, no interrogators have been prosecuted for torture. In 2009, U.S. Attorney General Holder announced that the Department of Justice "would not prosecute anyone who acted in good faith and within the scope of the legal guidance given by the Office of Legal Counsel regarding the interrogation of detainees." In 2012, an investigation into the question "whether any unauthorized interrogation techniques were used by CIA interrogators, and if so, whether such techniques could constitute violations of the torture statute or any other applicable statute" was closed on the ground that "the admissible evidence would not be sufficient to obtain and sustain a conviction beyond a reasonable doubt."

14. *Sentencing.* Justification or excuse, or both, should the consideration of necessity be left to sentencing? (Justice Wilson, in her dissent in *Perka*, argues that justifying necessity should function as a defense that precludes liability, whereas excusing necessity merely mitigates punishment.) In all cases, or at least in cases that support, but do not quite make out, a necessity defense? Or is necessity an all-or-nothing affair? Consider the U.S. Sentencing Guidelines' policy statement on a downward departure for "lesser harms"*:

§ 5K2.11. Lesser Harms (Policy Statement)

Sometimes, a defendant may commit a crime in order to avoid a perceived greater harm. In such instances, a reduced sentence may be appropriate, provided that the circumstances significantly diminish society's interest in punishing the conduct, for example, in the case of a mercy killing. Where the interest in punishment or deterrence is not reduced, a reduction in sentence is not warranted. For example, providing defense secrets to a hostile power should receive no lesser punishment simply because the defendant believed that the government's policies were misdirected.

In other instances, conduct may not cause or threaten the harm or evil sought to be prevented by the law proscribing the offense at issue. For example, where a war veteran possessed a machine gun or grenade as a trophy, or a school teacher possessed controlled substances for display in a drug education program, a reduced sentence might be warranted.

C. Consent

Consent is a fascinating issue in criminal law that often gets lost in the justification shuffle, assuming it is even recognized as a possible justification to begin with. Consent is a justification defense of potentially enormous scope, which may help to explain, but hardly to justify, why it has received so little attention. The Model Penal Code nicely captures consent's ambivalent position in criminal law, as either obviously relevant or possibly relevant, or both: consent is obviously relevant insofar as it negates an element of non-consent in the definition of an offense (i.e., as an element-negating "defense" or *Tatbestandsausschließungsgrund*), yet it is also possibly relevant as a justification (*Rechtferti-gungsgrund*) that, as a general principle of criminal liability, would apply to all offenses, including—and in particular—to those that are not defined in terms of the absence of consent. However, it is conceived, considerations of consent as a defense quickly give rise to urgent concerns about limiting its scope, which ordinarily trigger unusually frank references to "social norms" and "good morals" that are supposed to draw a sufficiently clear line between, say, a "boxing match" (to cite a classic example) and a "fist fight" (or a "bar brawl").

State v. George
Court of Appeals of Missouri
937 S.W.2d 251 (1996)

Reinhard, Judge.

Defendant appeals after he was convicted by a jury of one count of second degree assault, § 565.060, Rev. Stat. Mo. 1994, and one count of third degree assault, § 565.070, Rev. Stat. Mo. 1994...

The evidence reveals that on December 2, 1993, defendant was a patient at the psychiatric intensive care unit at St. Anthony's Hospital in South St. Louis County. About mid day defendant became angry, agitated, and upset... Hospital security was notified. When Dusty Barnes and Mary Ann Erger, security personnel within the hospital, responded to the call, defendant was moving up and down the hallway saying that "somebody was going to get hurt."... When he screamed that he wanted a light for his cigarette, Barnes approached defendant and offered him a light. As defendant leaned forward, Barnes dropped his lighter and brought defendant to the floor.

Defendant punched Barnes in the eye... While Erger was helping to control and hold down defendant, he bit her leg through her trousers... The bite later became infected, and she had to

---

* On the Guidelines, see Chapter 1.A.i.

have an incision to remove a hematoma. Erger was able to work only part time for approximately two months...

Section 565.080, Rev. Stat. Mo. 1986, provides:

1. When conduct is charged to constitute an offense because it causes or threatens physical injury, consent to that conduct or to the infliction of the injury is a defense only if:

(1) The physical injury consented to or threatened by the conduct is not serious physical injury; or

(2) The conduct and the harm are reasonably foreseeable hazards of

    (a) The victim's occupation or profession; or

    (b) Joint participation in a lawful athletic contest or competitive sport; or

(3) The consent establishes a justification for the conduct...

2. The defendant shall have the burden of injecting the issue of consent....

Defendant urges that because of the nature of the guards' job, they consented to assaultive behavior. The state, however, argues that the security officers did not consent to defendant's conduct, and although they may have consented to "minor physical injuries which arise out of ordinary interactions" by virtue of their occupation, defendant exceeded the scope of any such consent.

When the Missouri legislature adopted a version of the Model Penal Code, it included a provision that was not in the model code. Our research reveals that few states, which adopted statutes similar to the Model Penal Code, have included a provision setting forth consent as a defense by nature of one's occupation. See e.g., Me.Rev.Stat.Ann. Tit. 17-A, § 109 (West 1995); N.D.Cent.Code § 12.1-17-08 (1995); Tex. Penal Code Ann. § 22.06 (West 1996)...

The trial court in this case also relied upon § 10.13 of the new Missouri Criminal Code: A Manual for Court Related Personnel (n.d.). This manual discusses § 565.080 and provides "if the injury is a reasonably foreseeable hazard of the victim's employment he may be deemed to consent to the risk of injury by accepting the employment. An example would be military or police training exercises."

In *Tanksley v. State*, 656 S.W.2d 194, 195 (Tex.Ct.App.1983), an imprisoned defendant called a jailer to the holding cell window. The defendant, while holding a sharpened toothbrush handle, stated that he would stab the jailer in the eye when the holding cell door was opened. The defendant was convicted of aggravated assault. At trial, the jailer admitted that "inmates are sometimes belligerent, that while he was rarely threatened, he had been insulted 'verbally' and abused a few times while working in the jail." Id.

On appeal, the defendant argued that "by the nature of the jailer's employment he consented... to any assault as a risk of his occupation, within the meaning of Tex.Pen.Code Ann. § 22.06(2)(A) (1974)." The court found that the provisions of the Texas Code "do not define effective consent to mean engaging in an occupation having a risk of assault." Although a "victim's express or apparent assent to an accused's conduct is effective as a defense if the victim knew that such conduct was a risk of his occupation," the court found the jailer did not assent to the defendant's conduct.

In the case at hand, defendant relies upon the literal reading of § 565.080 to support his contention that he was entitled to the consent defense. Defendant... relies upon... cases... involving the issue of assumption of risk. We do not find either case to be persuasive. Assumption of risk cases are civil matters involving money damages, an award of which will benefit the victim. These matters differ from criminal cases, which involve not only the defendant and the victim, but also the public.

For example, in *State v. Fransua*, 85 N.M. 173, 510 P.2d 106 (App.1973), defendant and victim were in a bar drinking heavily. After an argument, defendant stated that if he had a gun, he would shoot victim. The victim then brought defendant a gun and told him "if he wanted to shoot me to go ahead." Defendant shot victim, and at trial, defendant argued that victim consented to the shooting. The court disagreed...:

It is generally conceded that a state enacts criminal statutes making certain violent acts crimes for at least two reasons: One reason is to protect the persons of its citizens; the second, however, is to prevent a breach of the public peace. While we entertain little sympathy for either the victim's absurd actions or the defendant's equally unjustified act of pulling the trigger, we will not permit the defense of consent to be raised in such cases... [T]he public has a stronger and overriding interest in preventing and prohibiting acts such as these.

An intentional assault which occurs while working as a hospital guard differs from participating in military or police training exercises. In the latter example, an individual has consented to reasonably foreseeable injuries that may occur. In this case, however, there was no evidence that the security officers consented to the assault. Defendant said he was glad he had punched Barnes in the face, and then he bit Erger. This was an intentional assault.

By enacting the consent statute, the legislature did not intend to legalize intentional criminal assaults on persons engaged in the security profession. Rather, the legislature intended to "accommodate the assault law to reality, in that many acts which our society considers to be quite acceptable, and even desirable, are technically assaults by whatever rational definition that term may be given." *State v. Floyd*, 466 N.W.2d 919, 922 (Iowa Ct.App.1990).

For instance, in *State v. Floyd*, supra, a fight erupted during an aggressive basketball game. The court discussed the issue of consent to an assault occurring during a sporting event and found that the legislature "contemplated a person who commits acts during the course of play, and the exception seeks to protect those whose acts otherwise subject to prosecution are committed in furtherance of the object of the sport." The court found at the time of the altercation, defendant and his victims were not "voluntary participants in a sport." The court added, however, that even if the defendant and his victims were sport participants, "[i]t strains the imagination and contorts the concept of foreseeability beyond recognition to assert that the brutal assaults carried out by defendant . . . could have been 'reasonably foreseeable incident[s].' "

In the present case, it would be illogical to condone defendant's intentional assault of two guards simply because of the victims' profession. The consent statute was intended to protect acceptable acts committed during employment that would otherwise be subject to prosecution but which are committed in furtherance of one's employment. Authorizing a person to assault a worker who attempts to calm a person's abusive or disruptive behavior would not further the statute's intention. Rather, allowing the consent statute to legalize intentional assaults would thwart the purpose of Missouri's statutes criminalizing assaultive behavior . . .

Furthermore, . . . [c]ommon sense suggests that while the statute's terms insinuate consent is a defense to foreseeable and intentional assaults occurring within the victim's occupation, the statute cannot reasonably be construed to provide a defense to such conduct. We can infer that a security guard at a hospital or other business who is aware of previous assaults against his or her co-workers does not consent to future assaults against him or her. Without such an inference, it is foreseeable that convenience store workers, service station attendants, or bank tellers, who are working where previous assaults have occurred, would be assaulted, and the assailant would go unpunished for such behavior. We do not think the legislature intended the consent defense to encompass such situations.

We conclude that the trial court did not err. . . .

Judgment affirmed.

Model Penal Code

§ 2.11. Consent

(1) In General. The consent of the victim to conduct charged to constitute an offense or to the result thereof is a defense if such consent negatives an element of the offense or precludes the infliction of the harm or evil sought to be prevented by the law defining the offense.

(2) Consent to Bodily Injury. When conduct is charged to constitute an offense because it causes or threatens bodily injury, consent to such conduct or to the infliction of such injury is a defense if:
a) the bodily injury consented to or threatened by the conduct consented to is not serious; or
b) the conduct and the injury are reasonably foreseeable hazards of joint participation in a lawful athletic contest or competitive sport or other concerted activity not forbidden by law; or
c) the consent establishes a justification for the conduct under Article 3 of the Code.

(3) Ineffective Consent. Unless otherwise provided by the Code or by the law defining the offense, assent does not constitute consent if:
a) it is given by a person who is legally incompetent to authorize the conduct charged to constitute the offense; or
b) it is given by a person who by reason of youth, mental disease or defect or intoxication is manifestly unable or known by the actor to be unable to make a reasonable judgment as to the nature or harmfulness of the conduct charged to constitute the offense; or
c) it is given by a person whose improvident consent is sought to be prevented by the law defining the offense; or
d) it is induced by force, duress or deception of a kind sought to be prevented by the law defining the offense.

R. v. Jobidon
Supreme Court of Canada
[1991] 2 S.C.R. 714

Gonthier J.

At issue in the present appeal is the role of consent in the criminal offence of assault. More particularly, the issue is whether the absence of consent is an essential element of this offence when it relates to a fist fight where bodily harm is intentionally caused...

The appellant, Jules Jobidon, was charged with manslaughter for the unlawful act of killing Rodney Haggart—through the offence of assault (alternatively, through an act of criminal negligence). The incident leading to the charge was a fist fight between the two men, in a parking lot outside a hotel near Sudbury, Ontario, on September 19, 1986. At the date of the killing, Rodney Haggart was 25 years old. He had consumed some beer. His blood alcohol level, measured a few hours after the incident, was 160 milligrams of alcohol per 100 millilitres of blood, but the trial judge found that Haggart appeared "perfectly fine" and "perfectly normal." Jobidon, a young, fit and powerful man, had also been drinking beer prior to the fight, but in the opinion of the trial judge was not inebriated...

While Haggart and Jobidon stood facing each other, Jobidon struck Haggart with his fist, hitting him with great force on the head and face. Haggart was knocked backward onto the hood of a car. The trial judge determined that Haggart was rendered unconscious by this initial punch and that he appeared to be "out cold." He was not moving and offered no resistance to the appellant.

Immediately after throwing that first punch, Jobidon continued forward. In a brief flurry lasting no more than a few seconds he struck the unconscious victim a further four to six times on the head. The trial judge found that there was no interval between Haggart's fall and the continued punching. The punches were part of "one single continuing transaction...one fluid event, punctuated by specific blows." The judge noted that the most reliable witness testified that it all happened so quickly he thought Haggart would bounce off the hood and resume the fight....

The trial judge found that Jobidon did not intend to kill Haggart, nor did he intend to cause the deceased serious bodily harm. However, the possibility of injury more serious than a bruise or bloody nose, such as a broken nose, was contemplated. Jobidon intentionally hit Haggart as hard as he could, but believed he was fighting fair. He did not depart intentionally from the kind of fight that Haggart had consented to. Jobidon believed that Haggart had consented to a fair fight, the object of which was to hit the other man as hard as physically possible until that person gave up or retreated. The trial judge also found that, although mistaken, and not supported by objective facts, Jobidon honestly believed that after Haggart had been struck onto the hood of the car he was merely stunned, but still capable of fighting back, and still trying to fight.

Jobidon was tried before a judge of the Supreme Court of Ontario, and was found not guilty of manslaughter. The judge held that Haggart's consent negated assault, and held further that Jobidon had not been criminally negligent. The respondent appealed the judge's holding of assault to the Ontario Court of Appeal, which allowed the appeal, set aside the acquittal, and substituted a guilty verdict on the charge of manslaughter....

The [assault section in the Canadian Criminal Code] now reads:

265. (1) A person commits an assault when
(a) without the consent of another person, he applies force intentionally to that other person, directly or indirectly;...
(2) This section applies to all forms of assault, including sexual assault, sexual assault with a weapon, threats to a third party or causing bodily harm and aggravated sexual assault.
(3) For the purposes of this section, no consent is obtained where the complainant submits or does not resist by reason of
  (a) the application of force to the complainant or to a person other than the complainant;
  (b) threats or fear of the application of force to the complainant or to a person other than the complainant;
  (c) fraud; or
  (d) the exercise of authority.
(4) Where an accused alleges that he believed that the complainant consented to the conduct that is the subject matter of the charge, a judge, if satisfied that there is sufficient evidence and that, if believed by the jury, the evidence would constitute a defence, shall instruct the jury, when reviewing all the evidence relating to the determination of the honesty of the accused's belief, to consider the presence or absence of reasonable grounds for that belief.

3. The Role and Scope of Consent in Assault

... Provincial courts of appeal have grappled with the issue on numerous occasions in recent years, sometimes arriving at divergent conclusions. Legal academics have experienced similar consternation. One has noted that the present state of the law in Canada is "confusing and conflicting." Another text states "this area of the law is so nebulous that it is difficult to be very precise" (Mewett and Manning, *Criminal Law* (2nd ed. 1985), at p. 566). In 1984, the Law Reform Commission of Canada phrased the problem in more detailed terms:

> As regards the present law, it is clear that sometimes, as in the case of mere touching, consent is a defence, and that in general, where the contact is intended to cause death or serious harm, consent is no defence. It is also clear that even in circumstances going beyond mere touching (for example, in surgical operations and in lawful sports) consent can prevent the force from being unlawful. *What is unclear is the extent to which the same rule applies or does not apply in Canada outside the operating theatre and the sports arena, for example, in sado-masochistic circumstances.* [Emphasis added.]

> (Working Paper 38: *Assault*, at p. 24.)

It is the purpose of the remaining analysis to clarify the role of consent in relation to a fist fight or brawl.

(a) The General Influence of the Common Law on the Code's Definition of Assault

Just as the common law has built up a rich jurisprudence around the concepts of agreement in contract law, and volenti non fit injuria in the law of negligence, it has also generated a body of law to illuminate the meaning of consent and to place certain limitations on its legal effectiveness in the criminal law. It has done this in respect of assault. In the same way that the common law established principles of public policy negating the legal effectiveness of certain types of contracts—contracts in restraint of trade for example—it has also set limits on the types of harmful actions to which one can validly consent, and shelter an assailant from the sanctions of our criminal law.

... That common law is rich and extensive, with roots reaching back well into the decades preceding Canada's adoption of the *Code* of 1892. For instance it provided that, as a general rule, consent would only be valid or legally effective if it was given freely by a rational and sober person. (See Russell on Crime, op. cit., at p. 678.)

Thus in *R. v. March* (1844), 1 Car. & K. 496, 174 E.R. 909, the English criminal court, speaking through Lord Tindal C.J., held that a fraudulently obtained consent to common assault was no consent at all (p. 911). The parallel in our Code is in s. 265(3)(c). In *R. v. Lock* (1872), L.R. 2 C.C.R. 10, an English criminal court held that eight-year-old boys were too young to understand the nature of a sexual act with a grown man to be able to consent to it. Submission by a young child to an older, stronger person, an authority figure, would not be considered consensual. The consent would in all probability have been obtained under a coerced and ill-informed will ...

As for consent in the context of fist fights, the English common law displayed a similar penchant for limiting its role as an exculpatory defence. However it is vital to note that the basis of the concern was different than in the case of fraud, threats, or forced "consents." The early cases often did not explicitly acknowledge that different basis, but hints of it may be identified. It was a concern that the offence of assault—more particularly the element of consent—be informed by considerations of public policy. Such considerations were thought sufficiently important to justify nullifying the legal validity of consent as a defence to a charge of assault.

For instance, in *Wright's Case* (1603), Co. Litt. f. 127 a–b, the English criminal court held that, not only would a man be punished at law for procuring another to sever his hand—to assist his career as a mendicant—but the person effecting the task would also be liable to criminal sanction, irrespective of the other's consent. In *Matthew v. Ollerton* (1693), Comb. 218, 90 E.R. 438, it was held that a man may not license another to beat him as that act amounted to a breach of the peace. This principle was repeated in *Boulter v. Clarke* (1747), Bull. N.P. 16, where it was determined that it is no defence to a charge of assault that the two persons fought by mutual consent. Coleridge J. reaffirmed the doctrine in *R. v. Lewis* (1844), 1 Car. & K. 419, 174 E.R. 874, a case involving a fight between two men outside a dance hall, which had resulted in the death of a man from blows sustained to his head. Coleridge J. stated, at p. 875: "it ought to be known, that, whenever two persons go out to strike each other, and do so, each is guilty of an assault."

It will be seen that this nullification of the defence of consent in fist fight cases in England has continued forward uninterruptedly to the present day. In Canada the same principle was applied for many decades before the appropriateness of such invalidation was ever brought into question. Indeed it was for reasons of public policy that the Court of Appeal nullified Haggart's consent ...

Whether consent is formally categorized as part of the *actus reus* of the offence, or as a defence, its essential function remains unaltered—if consent is proved, or if absence of consent is not proved, an individual accused of assault will *generally* be able to rely on the consent of the complainant to bar a conviction. He will be able to lean on the consent as a defence to liability. This basic reality has been widely recognized. English and Canadian courts widely refer to consent as being in the nature of a defence. Leading treatises on criminal law conceive it this way. See Watt, op. cit., at p. 216; Clarkson and Keating, op. cit., at pp. 283–92; G. Williams, *Textbook of Criminal Law* (2nd ed. 1983), at pp. 549 and 576–8; and Law Reform Commission of Canada, Working Paper 38, *Assault*, op. cit., at p. 24. We have also observed, in the general interpretative section above, that the law confers on s. 8(3) an open and developmental view of the common law's role. Section 8(3) strongly suggests preservation of the common law approach to consent in assault.

Assault has been given a very encompassing definition in s. 265. It arises whenever a person intentionally applies force to a person "directly or indirectly," without the other's consent. The definition says nothing about the degree of harm which must be sustained. Nor does it refer to the motives for the touching. If taken at face value, this formulation would mean that the most trivial intended touching would constitute assault. As just one of many possible examples, a father would assault his daughter if he attempted to place a scarf around her neck to protect her from the cold but she did not consent to that touching, thinking the scarf ugly or undesirable. (Even an argument for implied consent would not seem to apply in a case like this.) That absurd consequence could not have been intended by Parliament. Rather its intention must have been for the courts to explain the content of the offence, incrementally and over the course of time.

... Policy-based limits are almost always the product of a balancing of individual autonomy (the freedom to choose to have force intentionally applied to oneself) and some larger societal interest. That balancing may be better performed in the light of actual situations, rather than in the abstract, as Parliament would be compelled to do.

With the offence of assault, that kind of balancing is a function the courts are well-suited to perform. They will continue to be faced with real situations in which complicated actions and motivations interact, as they have in the past.... The common law is the register of the balancing function of the courts—a register Parliament has authorized the courts to administer in respect of policy-based limits on the role and scope of consent in s. 265 of the Code.

...

Section 14 [of the Criminal Code] nullifies consent to the infliction of death in a broad and open-textured fashion. It provides:

14. No person is entitled to consent to have death inflicted on him, and such consent does not affect the criminal responsibility of any person by whom death may be inflicted on the person by whom consent is given.

[T]he appellant [argues] that by enacting s. 14 of the Code, Parliament reflected its intention to negate consent solely in situations where death was intended to be caused. With other situations, and with forms of conduct like the fist fight between Jobidon and Haggart where that consequence was not intended, consent should be given full legal effect. In other words, the appellant suggested a version of the interpretative principle expressed by the maxim expressio unius est exclusio alterius. But this argument also fails.

Section 14 is an absolute exclusion of consent to death in all circumstances. It follows neither from logic nor from the structure of the Code that absent death, consent to any or all forms of bodily injury is permissible, regardless of the circumstances. The section speaks only of consent to the infliction of death. It does not comment on consent to other consequences, any more than it comments on sexual offences or any other form of assault. It stands on its own.

...

(d) Summary of the Common Law

(i) The English Position

Attorney General's Reference makes it clear that a conviction of assault will not be barred if "bodily harm is intended *and/or* caused." Since this test is framed in the alternative, consent could be nullified even in situations where the assailant did not intend to cause the injured person bodily harm but did so inadvertently. In Canada, however, this very broad formulation cannot strictly apply, since the definition of assault in s. 265 is explicitly restricted to *intentional* application of force. Any test in our law which incorporated the English perspective would of necessity have to confine itself to bodily harm intended and caused.

(ii) The Canadian Position

The preceding analysis reveals division in the Canadian jurisprudence. Decisions by courts of appeal in Manitoba, Ontario, Nova Scotia and (lately) Saskatchewan would nullify consent to intentionally inflicted bodily harm arising from a fist fight. Their approach is contained, respectively, in *Buchanan* (1898), *Cullen* (1948), *Squire* (1975), *Jobidon* (1988), *Gur* (1986), *McIntosh* (1991), and *Cey* (1989) . . . .

On the other side are decisions of appellate courts in New Brunswick (*MacTavish* (1972)), Quebec (*Abraham* (1974)), Saskatchewan (*Setrum* (1976)), and Alberta (*Bergner* (1987) and *Loonskin* (1990)).

Although there is certainly no crystal-clear position in the modern Canadian common law, still, when one takes into account the combined English and Canadian jurisprudence, when one keeps sight of the common law's centuries-old persistence to limit the legal effectiveness of consent to a fist fight, and when one understands that s. 265 has always incorporated that persistence, the scale tips rather heavily against the validity of a person's consent to the infliction of bodily injury in a fight.

The thrust of the English common law is particularly important in this regard because it has been consistent for many decades, indeed, centuries. It became an integral component of the Canadian common law and has remained so to this day. Many of the seemingly pivotal pro-consent decisions made by courts in the 1970s were either obiter or were pronounced upon insufficient consideration of the important role of the traditional common law. Moreover they were decided prior to the decision in *Attorney General's Reference* (1981), which offered a very authoritative pronouncement of the common law position. . . . In light of these many considerations, I am of the view that the Canadian position is not as opaque or bifurcated as one might initially think.

Notwithstanding this conclusion, given the residual indeterminacy which admittedly lingers in the recent Canadian cases, it is useful to canvass policy considerations which exert a strong influence in this appeal, for they rather decisively support the respondent, bringing down the scales even more surely in support of the decision in the court below.

(e) Policy Considerations

Foremost among the policy considerations supporting the Crown is the social uselessness of fist fights. As the English Court of Appeal noted in the *Attorney General's Reference*, it is not in the public interest that adults should willingly cause harm to one another without a good reason. There is precious little utility in fist fights or street brawls. These events are motivated by unchecked passion. They so often result in serious injury to the participants. Here it resulted in a tragic death to a young man on his wedding day.

There was a time when pugilism was sheltered by the notion of "chivalry." Duelling was an activity not only condoned, but required by honour. Those days are fortunately long past. Our social norms no longer correlate strength of character with prowess at fisticuffs. Indeed when we pride ourselves for making positive ethical and social strides, it tends to be on the basis of our developing reason. This is particularly true of the law, where reason is cast in a privileged light. Erasing longstanding limits on consent to assault would be a regressive step, one which would retard the advance of civilised norms of conduct.

Quite apart from the valueless nature of fist fights from the combatants' perspective, it should also be recognized that consensual fights may sometimes lead to larger brawls and to serious breaches of the public peace. In the instant case, this tendency was openly observable. At the prospect of a fight between Jobidon and the deceased, in a truly macabre fashion many patrons of the hotel deliberately moved to the parking lot to witness the gruesome event. That scene easily could have erupted in more widespread aggression between allies of the respective combatants. Indeed it happened that the brothers of Jobidon and Haggart also took to each other with their fists.

Given the spontaneous, often drunken nature of many fist fights, I would not wish to push a deterrence rationale too far. Nonetheless, it seems reasonable to think that, in some cases, common law limitations on consent might serve some degree of deterrence to these sorts of activities.

Related to a deterrence rationale is the possibility that, by permitting a person to consent to force inflicted by the hand of another, in rare cases the latter may find he derives some form of pleasure from the activity, especially if he is doing so on a regular basis. It is perhaps not inconceivable that this kind of perversion could arise in a domestic or marital setting where one or more of the family members are of frail or unstable mental health. As one criminal law theorist has written:

> . . . the self-destructive individual who induces another person to kill or to mutilate him implicates the latter in the violation of a significant social taboo. The person carrying out the killing or the mutilation crosses the threshold into a realm of conduct that, the second time, might be more easily carried out. And the second time, it might not be particularly significant whether the victim consents or not. Similarly, if someone is encouraged to inflict a sado-masochistic beating on a consenting victim, the experience of inflicting the beating might loosen the actor's inhibitions against sadism in general.

> (G. Fletcher, *Rethinking Criminal Law* (1978), at pp. 770–71.)

Of course this appeal does not concern sadism or intentional killing. But it comes close to mutilation. In any event, the weight of the argument could hold true for fights. If aggressive individuals are legally permitted to get into consensual fist fights, and they take advantage of that license from time to time, it may come to pass that they eventually lose all understanding that that activity *is* the subject of a powerful social taboo. They may too readily find their fists raised against a person whose consent they forgot to ascertain with full certitude. It is preferable that these sorts of omissions be strongly discouraged.

Wholly apart from deterrence, it is most unseemly from a moral point of view that the law would countenance, much less provide a backhanded sanction to the sort of interaction displayed by the facts of this appeal. The sanctity of the human body should militate against the validity of consent to bodily harm inflicted in a fight.

Some would say the offence of assault should not be concerned with these considerations. They might argue that in respect of street fights, deterrence and express disapprobation of the law is already contained in other provisions of the Criminal Code. For instance, Parliament has seen fit to prohibit "prize-fighting," on penalty of criminal sanction, in s. 83.

However, while it is true that s. 83 prohibits prize-fighting, it is unlikely that section would apply to the situation giving rise to this appeal, nor to the wide range of cases which arise in like fashion. The definition of prize-fighting is:

> **83**(2) . . . an encounter or fight with fists or hands between two persons *who have met for that purpose by previous arrangement* made by or for them, but a boxing contest between amateur sportsmen . . . shall be deemed not to be a prize fight. [Emphasis added.]

Since it is a condition of this offence that the fight be arranged previously, it is questionable whether the facts of this case would warrant a conviction on that basis. Although the trial judge found that the parties agreed to continue their fight outside the hotel, nonetheless it was essentially a spontaneous, *ad hoc* event. (In any event, this issue has not been raised in this appeal.)

The policy preference that people not be able to consent to intentionally inflicted harms is heard not only in the register of our common law. The Criminal Code also contains many examples of this propensity. As noted above, s. 14 of the Code vitiates the legal effectiveness of a person's consent to have death inflicted on him under any circumstances. The same policy appears to underlie ss. 150.1, 159 and 286 in respect of younger people, in the contexts of sexual offences, anal intercourse, and abduction, respectively. All this is to say that the notion of policy-based limits on the effectiveness of consent to some level of inflicted harms is not foreign. Parliament as well as the courts have been mindful of the need for such limits. Autonomy is not the only value which our law seeks to protect.

Some may see limiting the freedom of an adult to consent to applications of force in a fist fight as unduly paternalistic; a violation of individual self-rule. Yet while that view may commend itself to some, those persons cannot reasonably claim that the law does not know such limitations. All criminal law is "paternalistic" to some degree—top-down guidance is inherent in any prohibitive rule. That the common law has developed a strong resistance to recognizing the validity of consent to intentional applications of force in fist fights and brawls is merely one instance of the criminal law's concern that Canadian citizens treat each other humanely and with respect.

Finally, it must not be thought that by giving the green light to the common law, and a red light to consent to fights, this Court is thereby negating the role of consent in all situations or activities in which people willingly expose themselves to intentionally applied force. No such sweeping conclusion is entailed. The determination being made is much narrower in scope.

(f) Conclusion

How, and to what extent is consent limited?

The law's willingness to vitiate consent on policy grounds is significantly limited. Common law cases restrict the extent to which consent may be nullified; as do the relevant policy considerations. The unique situation under examination in this case, a weaponless fist fight between two adults, provides another important boundary.

The limitation demanded by s. 265 as it applies to the circumstances of this appeal is one which *vitiates consent between adults intentionally to apply force causing serious hurt or non-trivial bodily harm to each other in the course of a fist fight or brawl*. (This test entails that a minor's apparent consent to an adult's intentional application of force in a fight would also be negated.) This is the extent of the limit which the common law requires in the factual circumstances of this appeal. It may be that further limitations will be found to apply in other circumstances. But such limits, if any, are better developed on a case by case basis, so that the unique features of the situation may exert a rational influence on the extent of the limit and on the justification for it.

Stated in this way, the policy of the common law will not affect the validity or effectiveness of freely given consent to participate in rough sporting activities, so long as the intentional applications of force to which one consents are within the customary norms and rules of the game. Unlike fist fights, sporting activities and games usually have a significant social value; they are worthwhile. In this regard the holding of the Saskatchewan Court of Appeal in *R. v. Cey* (1989), 48 C.C.C. (3d) 480, is apposite.

The court's majority determined that some forms of intentionally applied force will clearly fall within the scope of the rules of the game, and will therefore readily ground a finding of implied consent, to which effect should be given. On the other hand, very violent forms of force which clearly extend beyond the ordinary norms of conduct will not be recognized as legitimate conduct to which one can validly consent.

There is also nothing in the preceding formulation which would prevent a person from consenting to medical treatment or appropriate surgical interventions. Nor, for example, would it necessarily nullify consent between stuntmen who agree in advance to perform risky sparring or daredevil activities in the creation of a socially valuable cultural product. A charge of assault would be barred if the Crown failed to prove absence of consent in these situations, in so far as the activities have a positive social value and the intent of the actors is to produce a social benefit for the good of the people involved, and often for a wider group of people as well. This is a far cry from the situation presented in this appeal, where Jobidon's sole objective was to strike the deceased as hard as he physically could, until his opponent either gave up or retreated. Fist fights are worlds apart from these other forms of conduct.

Finally, the preceding formulation avoids nullification of consent to intentional applications of force which cause only minor hurt or trivial bodily harm. The bodily harm contemplated by the test is essentially equivalent to that contemplated by the definition found in s. 267(2) of the Code, dealing with the offence of assault causing bodily harm. The section defines bodily harm as "any hurt or injury to the complainant that interferes with the health or comfort of the complainant and that is more than merely transient or trifling in nature."

On this definition, combined with the fact that the test is restricted to cases involving adults, the phenomenon of the "ordinary" schoolyard scuffle, where boys or girls immaturely seek to resolve differences with their hands, will not come within the scope of the limitation. That has never been the policy of the law and I do not intend to disrupt the status quo. However, I would leave open the question as to whether boys or girls under the age of 18 who truly intend to harm one another, and ultimately cause more than trivial bodily harm, would be afforded the protection of a defence of consent . . .

Appeal dismissed.

German Federal Court of Justice
2 StR 505/03, BGHSt 49, 166 (May 26, 2004)

Facts

The regional court has sentenced the defendant to imprisonment for one year and ten months for negligent homicide and suspended the sentence on probation. According to the findings, the defendant's partner, R., showed great interest in the carrying out of unusual sexual practices, primarily so-called "bondage games." This included amongst other things that the defendant (who had no interest in these "games" and himself remained dressed during them) had to exert pressure with an object on her throat in order to cause the temporary lack of oxygen that she wanted which had the effect of arousing her. In the past, cords or ropes were used for this strangulation session. After bondage games of this kind had no longer taken place for a while, because the defendant had expressed doubts about safety, Mrs R., on May 18, 2002, the day of the crime, asked him to carry out a bondage game again and herself prepared the necessary equipment for this (cords, a piece of wood and a metal tube). The defendant resisted at first but then complied with her wish. However, because of the corpulence of Mrs. R., who had clearly increased in girth over the recent period, he expressed doubts as he feared, by attaching her legs over her abdomen to her head, that she would no longer be able to breathe. But she dispelled his doubts and asked him this time to use the metal tube instead of the cord used so far. The defendant also expressed reservations about this at first, but allowed himself to be persuaded, and tied up his partner as she wanted. At first for the strangulation session he used the piece of wood which had been laid out, but then at the request of his partner he went over to using the metal tube to throttle her. In doing so he recognized that the use of an object which did not fit the contours of the neck was dangerous, and he also explained this to her. However he then let himself be persuaded by his partner to use it, and at her request even strengthened its effect.

He regarded a fatal outcome as possible as a result of his violent pressure on the neck of the victim, but trusted that this would not happen. His personal capabilities put him in a position to recognise the dangerous nature of his act, and to fulfill the care requirements arising from it. He pressed the metal tube against Mrs. R.'s neck repeatedly, with intervals. These actions lasted at least three minutes. He thereby achieved the desired compression of the vessels in the neck, and in particular the arterial and venous blood supply to the brain, but also a massive injury to the bones in the neck which he did not intend, caused by the metal tube. These injuries were however not fatal; in fact Mrs. R. died from the consequences of the massive compression of the vessels in her neck, and the cessation of the oxygen supply to the brain caused by this, with ensuing cardiac arrest. When Mrs. R. was no longer articulating audibly, the defendant untied her in the belief that she had fallen asleep, as was usual after such activities in the past. In the afternoon he began to have doubts because of the passage of time, and discovered that Mrs. R. was no longer alive. He abandoned an initial plan to commit suicide and reported to the police where he handed in a farewell letter composed by him, and explained that he had killed Mrs. R.

The regional court found that a (conditional) intention to kill on the part of the defendant had not been proved. He had admittedly recognized the dangerous nature of his violent act but had sincerely trusted that death would not occur. The court also denied infliction of bodily harm resulting in death. The defendant's act had not been contrary to good morals (§ 228 Criminal Code), he had carried out the actions causing physical injury (compression of the vessels in the neck by means of the tube) with the effective consent of the victim. The defendant's conduct was therefore only to be assessed as negligent homicide. The defendant and the public prosecutor's office contested this decision by their appeals in law . . .

Reasons

II.

Appeal in law by the public prosecutor's office. In so far as the appeal contests the denial of an intentional crime of homicide, it is unfounded. The regional court found without legal error within the required overall survey of all the objective and subjective circumstances of the crime (see BGHSt 36, 1 [9f.] . . .), that the defendant had sincerely trusted that Mrs. R.'s death, recognized by him as possible, would not occur. The judgment cannot however be affirmed, because the court denied a crime of infliction of bodily harm causing death.

1. The defendant caused the victim to have a cardiac arrest, and therefore to die, by the massive compression of the vessels in the neck, and the consequential cessation of supply of oxygen to the brain; the specific danger inherent in the assault on the victim's neck was therefore realized in the fatal outcome. The defendant can be accused of negligence in relation to the causing of the death, as the regional court has correctly established, so that the elements in the definition of § 227 Criminal Code* (see BGHSt 31, 96 [98]; BGH, NJW 1992, 1708; . . .) are present.

The defendant is a perpetrator as he had the decisive control over the event leading to the death. The fact that R. jointly controlled the event, as she gave him instructions, and on several occasions dispelled his reservations in relation to the dangerous nature of his actions, is not inconsistent with this . . .

2. The defendant's action is, however, contrary to the view of the regional court, not justified by the victim's consent.

a) According to § 228 Criminal Code bodily harm inflicted with the consent of the injured person is unlawful if the act violates good morals in spite of the consent. The concept of "good morals" is not concerned with extra-legal ethical and moral categories. In order to satisfy the requirement that state punishment must be predictable, the concept of good morals must be limited to its legal core. Violation of values of individual social groups or of the criminal court dealing with the crime does not suffice. If the inconsistency with good morals cannot be established with certainty according to legal standards, a conviction is ruled out (see BGH, NJW 2004, 1054 = NStZ 2004, 204 with further references).

There is dispute as to the detailed criteria to be invoked as a basis for assessment of the inconsistency of the act with good morals. First of all it is disputed whether the act is to be considered according to the type and scope of the attack on the legal interest alone, or whether (or

---

* [German Criminal Code (Bodily Harm with Deadly Consequences) § 227
(1) If the offender causes the injured person's death through the infliction of bodily harm (§§ 223 to 226), the punishment will be imprisonment of not less than three years. (2) In less serious cases, the punishment will be one to ten years imprisonment.—Eds.]

to what extent) the purpose pursued by the act or the circumstances which underlie it are of importance for the judgment as to violation of good morals. According to case law which goes back to the Imperial Court and part of the literature, the purpose as well the aims and motives of the participants underlying the act are to be included as the decisive factor in the assessment, especially when it is a question of morally reprehensible purposes (BGHSt 4, 24 [31] = NJW 1953, 473; RGSt 74, 91 [94]; see also Oberlandesgericht Düsseldorf, NStZ-RR 1997, 325 [327]; Landgericht Mönchengladbach, NStZ-RR 1997, 169 [170]; BayObLG, NJW 1999, 372 [373]...; Stree, in: Schönke/Schröder, § 228 marginal no. 8; Lackner/Kühl, StGB, 24th edit., § 228 marginal no. 10; Berz, GA 1969, 145).

The primary argument against this approach which only or as a priority takes account of the purpose of the action is that it frequently leads to unclear differentiations and distances itself too much from protection of legal goods interest (see Tröndle/Fischer, StGB, 51st edit., § 228 marginal no. 9; Hardtung, in: MünchKomm-StGB, § 228 marginal no. 25). To focus on the actor's purpose would no longer take exclusive account, as prescribed by statute, of the crime as the point of reference for violation of good morals because it includes aspects which would only concern the inconsistency of the consent itself with good morals (see Hirsch, in: LK-StGB, 11th edit., § 228 marginal no. 9, and the same in: 50 Jahre BGH, Festgabe d. Wissensch. IV, p. 199, 218; Otto, in: Festschr. f. Tröndle, 1989, p. 157, 168).

According to more recent case law and the view overwhelmingly advocated in the literature, the decisive issue is whether the offender's conduct is unacceptable for the legal order because of the special importance of the legal good, having regard to the scope of the physical injury and the degree of danger for the life and limb of the victim, in spite of the consent of the holder of the legal interest. Account must accordingly be taken of the type of assault, the results of the physical injury and the degree of possible danger to life when making a judgment as to inconsistency with good morals in the sense of § 228 Criminal Code. General preventive welfare interventions by the State into autonomous decisions made by the holder of a legal interest can only be legitimate in the area of serious injuries ... The goal pursued by the act is, according to this view, only exceptionally of importance for assessing inconsistency with good morals under § 228 Criminal Code, namely when the physical injury would be regarded as contrary to good morals if it was considered on its own, but such a negative assessment is compensated for by a positive—or at any rate understandable—purpose. Even with serious impact on bodily integrity, the scope for autonomous decisions by the holder of the legal interest is accordingly not exceeded if a positive purpose exists, for instance in the case of medical interventions which endanger life but are carried out for the purpose of preserving life (see Hirsch, in: LK, § 228 marginal no. 9; Tröndle/Fischer, § 228 marginal no. 10) ...

b) The Senate, in agreement with the judgment of the 3rd Criminal Senate of December 11, 2003 (NJW 2004, 1054, administering of narcotics with fatal consequences) and the prevailing doctrine, holds that, for the assessment of whether the act is contrary to good morals according to § 228 StGB, the weight of the attack on the legal good—and therefore an objective criterion—is crucial. Here, primarily the scope of the physical ill-treatment or harm to health accepted by the victim and the degree of danger to life and limb associated with it are decisive.

c) This legal approach has not been considered by the regional court.

    aa) The defendant's actions cannot accordingly be regarded as violating good morals merely because of the specific sexual motivation.

        The view of the Imperial Court, according to which in the case of sadomasochistic practices the physical injuries occurred "for indecent purposes" and therefore are a violation of good morals in spite of a possible consent (see RG, JW 1928, 2229, with critical comment Bohne, JW 1929, 1015; HRR 1931, 1611) has to be given up, not least because of changed moral opinions (see on this the overwhelming tendency of the recent literature according to which sadomasochistic activities are not simply to be classified as contrary to good morals because of an "abnormal" sexual purpose: Hirsch, in: LK, § 228 marginal no. 9; Stree, in: Schönke-Schröder, § 228 marginal no. 7; Tröndle/Fischer, § 228 marginal no. 10; Paeffgen, in: NK-StGB, § 228 marginal no. 37; Roxin, StrafR AT I, 13th edit., § 13 marginal no. 38...; Maurach/Schroeder/Maiwald, StrafR BT I, 8th edit., § 8 marginal no. 14; Frisch, in: Festschr.f. Hirsch, pp. 485, 502; May, Die Anwendbarkeit des § 226a StGB bei einverständlichen sadistischen und masochistischen Körperverletzungen (The applicability of § 226a StGB to sadistic and masochistic physical injuries inflicted with agreement), 1996, p. 97f.; Niedermair, Körperverletzung mit Einwilligung und die guten Sitten (Physical injury with consent and good morals), 1999, p. 192; Sitzmann, GA 1991, 71 [79]).

        Sadomasochism is an "existing and practiced form of sexual life" which occurs in heterosexual, homosexual, pedophiliac variations, or restricted to auto-eroticism. Sadomasochistic occurrences appear to be lacking in uniformity and are practiced by married couples and singles, and in monogamous and promiscuous relationships . . . . It is hardly possible to find an unambiguous general opinion in the population that sadomasochistic practices were inconsistent with good morals. Besides this an argument against an evaluation of inconsistency with good morals is that this would contradict assessments of the 4th Statute for the Reform of Criminal Law of November 23, 1973 (BGBl I, 1725). This Statute replaced the earlier description of the crimes in the 13th Chapter of the Special Part of the German Criminal Code as "Moral crimes" by that of "Crimes against sexual self-determination" and has thereby moved another legal interest into the foreground (see Roxin, § 13 marginal no. 38; Niedermair, p. 188).

bb) As explained, the Senate considers the extent or the significance of the threatened violation of the legal interest as decisive, with the result that when a certain degree of physical impairment or a possible danger to life is reached, consent does not have a justifying effect. Whether this boundary has been exceeded has to be decided on the basis of an assessment carried out "ex ante." The Senate can leave open here which intensity of injury invited the assessment of inconsistency with good morals and whether—or under what prerequisites— further purposes or other circumstances are to be included in the assessment. In any case, the act is inconsistent with good morals if, on objective consideration of all the crucial circumstances, the consenting person is brought into concrete danger of death by the action causing physical injury. The purpose of § 228 Criminal Code as well as the legislative assessment to be derived from § 216 Criminal Code* argue in favor of this limitation. They limit the power of individual agreements to justify homicide or severe physical injury. The law pursues a social interest in the maintenance of these legal interests, even against the will of the person affected. Interference by the holder of the legal interest himself (in the form of suicide or self-injury) is admittedly not punishable; however in the general public interest, the possibility of making existential dispositions about one's own body or life is limited. The protection of the legal interests "freedom from bodily harm" and "life" against interferences by third parties is accordingly not simply placed at the disposal of the individual, but only within a framework which is tolerable for the legal order.

cc) Measured by this, the boundaries within which the defendant's actions can be accepted by the general public have been exceeded in the present case. The strangulation of the victim for a period of at least three minutes carried out with intervals and thus with alternating strengthening and reduction of the pressure, with the help of a rigid metal tube not fitting the contours of the neck brought the victim, in a way which the defendant could recognize, not only into an abstract danger to life but into a concrete danger. This is because . . . the risk of directly causing the death of his partner by his action was neither calculable not controllable for the defendant. . . . This leads to the quashing of the judgment on the appeal in law of the public prosecutor's office . . . .

German Criminal Code

§ 228 (Consent)

Who causes bodily harm with the consent of the injured person only acts unlawful if the act is inconsistent with good morals despite the consent.

NOTES

1. *Types of consent.* In the German criminal law literature, there is fundamental agreement that consent bears on the question of criminal liability, given the high status German criminal law assigns to persons' autonomy. Those who are injured through a crime as a rule are entitled to declare their lack of interest in the protection of the legal good (*Rechtsgut*).[†] (But see Note 4 for exceptions to this rule.) The Model Penal Code, as well as Canadian criminal law, likewise acknowledges the potential relevance of consent in the analysis of criminal liability.

---

* [See Chapter 15.A.—Eds.]

[†] On the concept of legal good, also in relation to the harm principle, see Chapter 3.B.

If the significance of consent is widely recognized, the precise nature of that significance, i.e., the role of consent in the analysis of criminal liability remains somewhat less clear. The Model Penal Code sets out two possibilities (§ 2.11(1)), consent as element-negation and consent as justification (German criminal law refers to these two types of consent as *Einverständnis* and *Einwilligung*, respectively):

> The consent of the victim to conduct charged to constitute an offense or to the result thereof is a defense if such consent negatives an element of the offense or precludes the infliction of the harm or evil sought to be prevented by the law defining the offense.

It goes without saying that consent is relevant insofar as its presence negates an offense element requiring its absence. For instance, the definition of assault in the Canadian Criminal Code, at issue in *Jobidon*, conveniently defines assault as "without the consent of another person, [applying] force intentionally to that other person, directly or indirectly" (§ 265(1)). Obviously, if a person consented to the application of force, that application did not occur "without the consent" of that person.

More interesting questions arise in the case of offenses that are not defined in terms of the absence of consent. Does consent apply to them as well? Here, there are again two possibilities. One is to continue to treat consent as merely an offense element-negating "defense" (*Einverständnis*) by reading a non-consent element into the definition of an offense. For example, it is generally acknowledged in German criminal law that theft requires *nonconsensual* interference with another's possession, even though the definition of theft in the German Criminal Code (§ 242 Criminal Code) makes no explicit reference to lack of consent (defining theft as taking property away from another with the intention of unlawfully appropriating it, however, "taking away" is interpreted uniformly as requiring lack of consent. The other option is to recognize consent as a broad justification (*Einwilligung*) that operates at the second level of the analysis of criminal liability (unlawfulness), rather than the first (definition of the offense). As a freestanding justification, then, consent would apply across the board, even to offenses that do not include a non-consent element. (In fact, it would make little sense to apply it to offenses that do.)*

Consent as justification (*Einwilligung*) is framed by the Model Penal Code as consent that "precludes the infliction of the harm or evil sought to be prevented by the law defining the offense." Note, however, that the Model Penal Code does not label this defense as a justification; in fact, the consent provision in the Code, § 2.11, appears in article 2 (General Principles of Liability), rather than article 3 (General Principles of Justification). Placement in article 2, where the Code also addresses *actus reus* and *mens rea* (in §§ 2.01 and 2.02, respectively), reflects consent's status as an element-negating "defense" (*Einverständnis*). Article 2 contains a grab bag of other defenses that can be seen as straddling the lines between different levels in the analysis of criminal liability, e.g., § 2.08: intoxication (level 1 (definition)/level 3 (excuse)); § 2.09: duress (*mens rea*/excuse); § 2.10: military orders (justification/excuse), or between substantive and procedural criminal law, e.g., § 2.12: de minimis; § 2.13: entrapment.

This ambiguity in classification of consent, it is worth nothing, is not confined to the Model Penal Code. In German criminal law, too, there is disagreement about whether consent should be considered as an element-negating "defense" or a justification. One argument that has been advanced in favor of the former classification invokes a liberal, individualistic, concept of legal good (*Rechtsgut*), which is thought to require that consent "already" negate the criminality of the conduct (at the first level of the analysis of criminal liability) rather than "only" its unlawfulness (at the second level).† Assuming, for argument's sake, that consent has the same effect, regardless of its classification, does this distinction make a (symbolic?) difference?

---

* See generally Vera Bergelson, *Victims' Rights and Victims' Wrongs: Comparative Liability in Criminal Law* (2009); Vera Bergelson, "The Right to Be Hurt: Testing the Boundaries of Consent," 75 *George Washington Law Review* (2007), 165.
† See Claus Roxin, *Strafrecht: Allgemeiner Teil* (4th edn. 2006), vol. 1, 545.

2. *The scope of consent.* In the German Criminal Code, § 228 StGB, unlike Model Penal Code § 2.11, does not tell us what the pre-conditions for valid consent are (it only mentions inconsistency with good morals as a negative condition). Nevertheless, German case law and criminal law doctrine affirm some essential conditions for the validity of consent in a similar way as the Canadian Criminal Code and the Model Penal Code. The victim's choice can only be autonomous if external pressure (such as force or threats) is absent and if the victim is mature (not a child) and psychologically able (not suffering from a mental disease) to understand the nature and degree of harmfulness of the conduct in question. Legal competence also means, of course, that the legal good in question is at the victim's disposition—which is not the case if it is a public good (such as the environment or the functioning of the courts in the case of perjury), or if there was a co-owner in the case of a property offense.

There is a debate about how much deception can invalidate consent if victims were aware of the extent to which they might be harmed but erred in the area of motives (if, for instance, the person giving consent for donation of blood expected a higher financial compensation). Errors merely concerning motives are considered irrelevant by the majority in the German literature: the consent remains valid. (Note that here motives are, once more, considered irrelevant for purposes of criminal liability.*) This doctrine parallels the—contested—common law distinction between fraud in the factum and fraud in the inducement, with only the former vitiating consent, which has been captured in various ways, including, for instance:

> [I]f deception causes a misunderstanding as to the fact itself (fraud in the factum) there is no legally recognized consent because what happened is not that for which consent was given, whereas consent induced by fraud is as effective as any other consent, so far as direct and immediate legal consequences are concerned, if the deception relates not to the thing done but merely to some collateral matter (fraud in the inducement).
>
> *Boro v. People*, 163 Cal. App. 3d 1224, 210 Cal.Rptr. 122 (1985) (defendant passed off sexual intercourse as medical treatment: fraud in the inducement).

> The distinction involved in this case is between fraud in the inducement and fraud in the factum. The former applies to situations where consent is obtained by misrepresentations ("No, I'm not married."); the latter applies to misrepresentations about the nature of the act itself.
>
> *United States v. Hughes*, 48 M.J. 214 (C.M.A. 1998) (defendant passed himself off as another man, the victim's boyfriend: fraud in the factum).

The Model Penal Code rejects this distinction as unhelpful and ill-grounded (why should pretending to be the victim's husband be fraud in the factum, rather than in the inducement? why should it matter whether it is classified as one or the other?), and instead precludes consent as "ineffective" that is "induced by . . . deception of a kind sought to be prevented by the law defining the offense." Whether this approach does anything to clarify the inquiry, as opposed to reclassifying it as a question of statutory interpretation, is another question. Might one instead differentiate between misrepresentations affecting the victim's consent to each element in the definition of an offense and those affecting her reasons for giving the consent?[†]

3. Note that the issue of consent appears in different forms. In one variation, the victim explicitly or implicitly declares *consent to the harm* as such. In the German case, Mrs. R. had declared that she wanted her partner to mistreat her physically and to hurt her health by throttling her and thus causing a lack of oxygen (a pathological physical condition). However, the American and Canadian cases concern a second variation of consent: the victims did not consent to be bitten in the leg or to receive blows to particularly sensitive body parts—they

---

* See Chapter 8.A.

† For a detailed exploration of the analysis of fraudulently obtained consent in the context of a Canadian case involving a defendant who had not informed his sex partners of his HIV infection, see *R. v. Cuerrier*, [1998] 2 S.C.R. 371 (besides fraud in the factum, fraud vitiates consent in sexual assault cases where the defendant's objectively dishonest behavior creates a significant risk of serious bodily harm).

only agreed to participate in a risky activity such as a fist fight or guarding mentally ill persons. In German criminal law doctrine, these are called "*risk consent*"-cases.

And there is a third, conceptually different category: cases in which the injured person declared nothing at all, neither explicitly nor implicitly, but in which one can legitimately assume consent: for instance, if after a traffic accident, an unconscious person needs surgery but cannot declare consent to surgery. According to German case law, surgeons and other doctors taking invasive measures need consent—lacking consent, these actions are labeled "bodily harm." This serves to protect not only bodily integrity against unwanted surgeries etc., but also, of course, patients' autonomy. But if it is evident that immediate medical measures are necessary to avert serious risks, German courts acknowledge a justification of "assumed consent."*

Under the Model Penal Code, cases of assumed, or constructive, consent to medical treatment are addressed in § 3.08, entitled "Use of Force by Persons with Special Responsibility for Care, Discipline or Safety of Others," which also covers discipline by persons in parental or quasi-parental situations of power and responsibility, including, well, parents and guardians, but also prison wardens, pilots, captains, and their subordinates, along with anyone "authorized or required by law to maintain order or decorum in a vehicle, train or other carrier or in a place where others are assembled." Although a doctor (or "other therapist or a person assisting him at his direction") is lumped in with this group, it turns out that the justification requires not only status, but also a remedial purpose ("promoting the physical or mental health of the patient") and, most relevant for present purposes, the patient's actual or, in the absence of the capacity to consent, constructive consent, either through another person (e.g., a parent) or a "reasonable person" in the patient's position.

Consider two threads that could be seen to hold these provisions together: hierarchy and consent. From one perspective, § 3.08 conceptualizes the situations within its scope in relational terms: the "justification" arises from the status relationship between the "offender" and the "victim." The former is responsible for the other's well-being (as "parent," "teacher," "prison warden," "pilot," "captain," or "doctor") and therefore is entitled (justified?) to "punish" or to "treat" the latter (as "child," "student," "prison inmate," "passenger," or "patient"), even by engaging in conduct that on its face violates a criminal prohibition (involving the "use of force"), within the scope of his or her responsibility, and attendant authority. From the other perspective, the "offender" is justified in using force against the "victim" because the latter has "consented" to it (actually, or constructively); here, the relationship between the two is conceptualized as egalitarian, one person consenting to another person's conduct.

Is one conceptualization preferable to the other? Are some relations more appropriately conceptualized as hierarchical than others? Where does the doctor-patient relationship fit on the hierarchy-equality divide, or is it a spectrum? Do they reflect more general underlying conceptions not only of the various roles at issue, but also of the nature of criminal law, of punishment, or at least of justification? Consider also how the conceptualization of these relationships might shift over time, and how these shifts might affect criminal law doctrine. Consider, in particular, the recognition of "children's rights" or "patients' rights."

Of course, as soon as one expands the concept of consent to include "constructive," "implied," or "assumed," consent, it becomes possible to redefine (some?) status relationships in terms of consent: by entering into the hierarchical status relationship, I "consent" (implicitly, or through small-print boiler-plate provisions even explicitly) to subjecting myself to the authority of whoever occupies the superior position (by getting on a plane, I "subject" myself to the pilot's authority, by getting myself convicted of a crime (by committing it in the first place?), I in some sense consent to the prison warden's authority over me, and so on. This works better for some relationships than for others (how does the child consent, even constructively, to the parent's authority?).

With respect to risk consent, German courts would be expected to decide the same way the Court of Appeals of Missouri did in *State v. George*. To work in a profession that typically

---

* See, e.g., Federal Court of Justice, Judgment of March 25, 1988, BGHSt 35, 246.

involves rough interactions means to declare implicit consent to this risk (the same applies to contact sports). If the issue was minor injuries inflicted negligently, one can thus assume valid consent even if the particular victim claims not to have considered such injuries. However, if the bodily harm goes beyond scratches, small bruises and the like, and if the injury was inflicted intentionally, the offender cannot point to victims' consent as being implicitly declared by participating in risky activities. To achieve this legal outcome, it is not even necessary to consider limitations of consent such as the "good morals" in § 228 Criminal Code. From the perspective of German criminal law, it is simply a matter of interpreting the content of victims' implicit consent. (Why is that? In *George*, why would the victims' job-related consent to harm be limited to its non-intentional infliction?)

Wouldn't the scope of even this implicit consent depend on the nature of the activity, even within an employment context? Returning to the sports analogy, compare the victims in *George* with the (professional?) boxer, mixed martial artist, American football player, ice hockey player, or practitioner of any number of violent contact sports involving the intentional infliction of often serious physical harm. More radically, can the police officer working a dangerous beat be said to have consented to the risk of even the intentional infliction of physical harm, and even death? What if a particular police officer joined the police force, or perhaps even sought out a particularly dangerous assignment, precisely because of the high risk associated with it? Does it make a difference whether the risk-creating conduct is criminal? But if it isn't criminal, then why would the question of a defense (here, of consent) even arise? In fact, of course, the infliction of physical harm, and certainly of death, on a police officer, rather than being treated as subject to a consent defense, implicit or explicit, is instead treated as a particularly serious crime. But why is that? And does this fact tell us anything about the consent defense?

4. Legal disputes about consent often concern the question of boundaries. Should individual autonomy prevail in every situation, should individuals be allowed to justify any interference with their legal goods (however serious) through their consent? This is a debated question in the area of legal philosophy and criminal law theory. Those who advocate a strong conception of autonomy might answer that it is not the state's business (and thus not the task of the criminal law) to be paternalistic and protect people's life and health if they do not wish to be protected this way. Justice Gonthier argues in *R. v. Jobidon* that "all criminal law is 'paternalistic' to some degree—top-down guidance is inherent in any prohibitive rule." Criminal law theorists, however, tend to have something else in mind when they call a prohibition "paternalistic": Paternalistic norms are paternalistic from the perspective of the victim. They rely on the argument "it is for you own good if we ignore your wishes." In contrast, in ordinary cases of robberies, sexual assault etc. victims do not consent and thus the criminal law protects their rights against unwanted interference by others.

Justice Gonthier's remark points to a general conception of criminal law that finds it difficult to accommodate a consent defense. A criminal law that is concerned with the protection of the public peace, or the King's peace in the case of the common law, or that is regarded as an exercise of the state's (or the King's) police power (defined, for instance, by Blackstone as the power to establish "the due regulation and domestic order of the kingdom, whereby the individuals of the state, like the members of a well-governed family, are bound to conform their general behavior to the rules of propriety, good neighborhood, and good manners, and to be decent, industrious, and inoffensive") is inherently hierarchical, and more specifically, paternalistic (since the state, or the King, function as *parens patriae*).* Whether this conception of criminal law captures the design and operation of a particular criminal law regime is another question, of course. Moreover, it is not obvious that every unequal power relationship, or the notion of sovereignty, is "inherently" paternalistic in this sense; the connection between positivism in the sense of a command theory of law (as associated with John Austin) and paternalism may appear closer to some than to others.

---

* On the police power, see Chapter 3; see generally Markus D. Dubber, *The Police Power: Patriarchy and the Foundations of American Government* (2005).

The German Criminal Code contains two provisions that might be labeled "paternalistic boundaries to consent." Section 216 Criminal Code prohibits intentional killing even if the deceased had "expressly and earnestly" (autonomously) requested it, and § 228 Criminal Code declares consent irrelevant if the act is inconsistent with "good morals."

With respect to § 216 Criminal Code, there is a debate whether this is a truly paternalistic norm. One could argue, for instance, that it is beyond human imagination to grasp what death means and that for this reason no one can decide about his or her own death in a truly autonomous way. However, this is not a very plausible assumption, at least if the "victim" of a crime according to § 216 Criminal Code is a mature, rational person suffering from a highly painful, hopeless disease. The more plausible explanation points to the protection of a public taboo against intentional killing (in order to avoid slippery-slope-scenarios leading to the killing of the merely "too expensive" chronically ill).

Similar provisions also appear in criminal codes in common law countries, including § 14 of the Canadian Criminal Code (cited in *Jobidon*). *Jobidon* does not explore the legitimacy of this provision, merely considering its significance for the interpretation of the assault statute, and its non-consent element in particular. The various constitutional arguments—weighing (justified) "paternalism" against "autonomy" in the context of criminal prohibitions of assisted suicide—were considered at length by the United States Supreme Court in *Washington v. Glucksberg*, 521 U.S. 702 (1997); *Vacco v. Quill*, 521 U.S. 793 (1997) (upholding the prohibition in both cases).

With respect to § 228 Criminal Code, it seems even more dubious why the legislature deems consent and thus autonomous decisions irrelevant. And the matter is not just one of criminal policy. Section 228 Criminal Code also poses problems for judges who merely interpret the law as it stands. The problem of legal interpretation is: what are "good morals"? This question was easily answered by the older case law of the Imperial Court cited by the Federal Court of Justice. One who defines the task for criminal law in general as "protecting moral values or moral convictions held by the public" has no problem with a norm such as § 228 Criminal Code. However, this is not the view taken by the contemporary German legislature or the German courts. The Federal Court of Justice mentions the 4th Statute for the Reform of the Criminal Code from 1973, which, among other changes, relabeled the relevant chapter in the German Criminal Code by deliberately abolishing the old expression "moral crimes." Also, the courts today are hesitant to simply invoke moral standards and moral conviction. For instance, the German Federal Court of Justice has refrained from labeling sadomasochistic sexual practices immoral. The Court's solution is to emphasize dangerousness instead: if the consensual causation of bodily harm encompasses dangers for life, § 228 Criminal Code will be applied and consent is deemed irrelevant. (But what is the connection between dangerousness and good (or bad) morals? Doesn't § 228 Criminal Code explicitly require an inquiry into "good morals"?)

Regarding fist fights, the Bavarian Higher Regional Court has arrived at a similar result as the Canadian Supreme Court, pointing out that such fights endanger life and are generally inacceptable due to the very severe bodily harm that might occur (Judgment of September 7, 1998, NJW 1999, 372). But German courts in general are more reluctant to focus on "policy considerations," social utility and specifically deterrence as arguments.

5. *Consent and sexual assault.* Note that the Canadian Criminal Code, as interpreted in *Jobidon*, contains only a single assault provision (§ 265); there is no separate definition of sexual assault, or rape, for that matter. In Canadian criminal law, as elsewhere, consent issues frequently arise in sexual assault cases, many of which turn on a claim of mistaken belief regarding the presence of consent. The Canadian Criminal Code addresses this issue in the following, detailed, provisions:

273.1 (1) Subject to subsection (2) and subsection 265(3), "consent" means, for the purposes of sections 271, 272 and 273 [sexual assault], the voluntary agreement of the complainant to engage in the sexual activity in question.

(2) No consent is obtained, for the purposes of sections 271, 272 and 273, where

(a) the agreement is expressed by the words or conduct of a person other than the complainant;

(b) the complainant is incapable of consenting to the activity;

(c) the accused induces the complainant to engage in the activity by abusing a position of trust, power or authority;

(d) the complainant expresses, by words or conduct, a lack of agreement to engage in the activity; or

(e) the complainant, having consented to engage in sexual activity, expresses, by words or conduct, a lack of agreement to continue to engage in the activity.

(3) Nothing in subsection (2) shall be construed as limiting the circumstances in which no consent is obtained.

273.2 It is not a defence to a charge under section 271, 272 or 273 that the accused believed that the complainant consented to the activity that forms the subject-matter of the charge, where

(a) the accused's belief arose from the accused's

(i) self-induced intoxication, or

(ii) recklessness or wilful blindness; or

(b) the accused did not take reasonable steps, in the circumstances known to the accused at the time, to ascertain that the complainant was consenting.

Note that under German law, there is no similar solution. Even the most stupid, reckless or willfully blind error about the other person's consent will free a defendant from criminal liability.*

In a recent Canadian case, *R. v. J.A.*, [2011] 2 S.C.R. 440, the Court applied this framework to determine "whether a person can perform sexual acts on an unconscious person if the person consented to those acts in advance of being rendered unconscious": K.D. had consented to J.A.'s choking her, understanding that she might black out, then lost consciousness for "less than three minutes," while J.A. engaged in sexual intercourse with her. The Court affirmed J.A.'s sexual assault conviction on the ground that:

the Criminal Code makes it clear that an individual must be conscious throughout the sexual activity in order to provide the requisite consent. Parliament requires ongoing, conscious consent to ensure that women and men are not the victims of sexual exploitation, and to ensure that individuals engaging in sexual activity are capable of asking their partners to stop at any point.

In dissent, Fish, J., argued that the "mission" of the Code's consent provisions

is not to "protect" women against themselves by limiting their freedom to determine autonomously when and with whom they will engage in the sexual relations of their choice. Put differently, they aim to safeguard and enhance the sexual autonomy of women, and not to make choices for them.

Paternalism or autonomy? Both? Neither?

D. Law Enforcement

Like the defense of consent, the defense of "law enforcement" does not appear in the German Criminal Code; German law instead addresses the topic in other statutes, notably state administrative "police law" statutes (*Polizeigesetze*). The Model Penal Code section on law enforcement also sits on the margins of American substantive criminal law, insofar as it covers a subject that in American law generally is considered a matter of procedural criminal law, and of *constitutional* criminal procedure in particular. Constitutional criminal procedure, however, tends to focus on the legality of the arrest, rather than the legality of the use of force incident to the arrest, and even the legality of the arrest is only relevant indirectly,

---

* For a critique, see Tatjana Hörnle, "Der Irrtum über das Einverständnis des Opfers bei einer sexuellen Nötigung," 112 *Zeitschrift für die gesamte Strafrechtswissenschaft* (2000), 356.

insofar as it affects the legality of the evidence gathered during, or as a result of, the arrest. Even in *Tennessee v. Garner*, the U.S. Supreme Court case excerpted in this section, the constitutionality of the use of deadly force is analyzed in terms of the Fourth Amendment's protection against "unreasonable searches and seizures." Note that *Garner* is not a criminal case; it is a civil case brought by Garner's father against the City of Memphis, its mayor, the Memphis Police Department, its director, and the individual police officer under the Civil Rights Act of 1871, 42 U.S.C. § 1983, a federal post-Civil War statute which provides, in part:

> Every person who, under color of any statute, ordinance, regulation, custom, or usage, of any State . . . , subjects, or causes to be subjected, any citizen of the United States or other person within the jurisdiction thereof to the deprivation of any rights, privileges, or immunities secured by the Constitution and laws, shall be liable to the party injured in an action at law . . . .

Garner straddles not only the line between substantive and procedural criminal law, but also that between substantive criminal law and constitutional law: the Model Penal Code provision on the justification of law enforcement—drafted as a defense in criminal prosecutions against those who use deadly force—is adopted as a rule governing the constitutional analysis under the Fourth Amendment.

Tennessee v. Garner
Supreme Court of the United States
471 U.S. 1 (1985)

Justice White delivered the opinion of the Court.

At about 10:45 p.m. on October 3, 1974, Memphis Police Officers Elton Hymon and Leslie Wright were dispatched to answer a "prowler inside call." Upon arriving at the scene . . . Hymon . . . saw someone run across the backyard. The fleeing suspect, . . . Edward Garner, stopped at a 6-feet-high chain link fence at the edge of the yard. With the aid of a flashlight, Hymon was able to see Garner's face and hands. He saw no sign of a weapon, and, though not certain, was "reasonably sure" and "figured" that Garner was unarmed. He thought Garner was 17 or 18 years old and about 5'5" or 5'7" tall.[2] While Garner was crouched at the base of the fence, Hymon called out "police, halt" and took a few steps toward him. Garner then began to climb over the fence. Convinced that if Garner made it over the fence he would elude capture, Hymon shot him. The bullet hit Garner in the back of the head. Garner was taken by ambulance to a hospital, where he died on the operating table. Ten dollars and a purse taken from the house were found on his body.

In using deadly force to prevent the escape, Hymon was acting under the authority of a Tennessee statute and pursuant to Police Department policy. The statute provides that "[i]f, after notice of the intention to arrest the defendant, he either flee or forcibly resist, the officer may use all the necessary means to effect the arrest." Tenn. Code Ann. § 40-7-108 (1982). The Department policy was slightly more restrictive than the statute, but still allowed the use of deadly force in cases of burglary. The incident was reviewed by the Memphis Police Firearm's Review Board and presented to a grand jury. Neither took any action.

Garner's father then brought this action in the Federal District Court for the Western District of Tennessee, seeking damages under 42 U.S.C. § 1983 for asserted violations of Garner's constitutional right . . . After a 3-day bench trial, the District Court entered judgment for all defendants. It dismissed the claims against the Mayor and the Director for lack of evidence . . . The Court of Appeals reversed and remanded. It reasoned that the killing of a fleeing suspect is a "seizure" under the Fourth Amendment,[6] and is therefore constitutional only if "reasonable." . . . Officers cannot resort to deadly force unless they "have probable cause . . . to believe that the suspect [has committed a felony and] poses a threat to the safety of the officers or a danger to the community if left at large."[7] . . . .

A police officer may arrest a person if he has probable cause to believe that person committed a crime . . . To determine the constitutionality of a seizure "[w]e must balance the nature and quality of the intrusion on the individual's Fourth Amendment interests against the importance of the governmental interests alleged to justify the intrusion." . . .

---

[2] In fact, Garner, an eighth-grader, was 15. He was 5'4" tall and weighed somewhere around 100 or 110 pounds.

[6] "The right of the people to be secure in their persons . . . against unreasonable searches and seizures, shall not be violated . . . " U.S. Const., Amdt. 4.

[7] The Court of Appeals concluded that the rule set out in [§ 3.07 of] the Model Penal Code "accurately states Fourth Amendment limitations on the use of deadly force against fleeing felons."

The intrusiveness of a seizure by means of deadly force is unmatched. The suspect's fundamental interest in his own life need not be elaborated upon. The use of deadly force also frustrates the interest of the individual, and of society, in judicial determination of guilt and punishment. Against these interests are ranged governmental interests in effective law enforcement. It is argued that overall violence will be reduced by encouraging the peaceful submission of suspects who know that they may be shot if they flee . . .

Without in any way disparaging the importance of these goals, we are not convinced that the use of deadly force is a sufficiently productive means of accomplishing them to justify the killing of nonviolent suspects. The use of deadly force is a self-defeating way of apprehending a suspect and so setting the criminal justice mechanism in motion. If successful, it guarantees that that mechanism will not be set in motion. And while the meaningful threat of deadly force might be thought to lead to the arrest of more live suspects by discouraging escape attempts,[9] the presently available evidence does not support this thesis. The fact is that a majority of police departments in this country have forbidden the use of deadly force against nonviolent suspects . . .

. . . Where the suspect poses no immediate threat to the officer and no threat to others, the harm resulting from failing to apprehend him does not justify the use of deadly force to do so. It is no doubt unfortunate when a suspect who is in sight escapes, but the fact that the police arrive a little late or are a little slower afoot does not always justify killing the suspect . . .

[By contrast,] where the officer has probable cause to believe that the suspect poses a threat of serious physical harm, either to the officer or to others, it is not constitutionally unreasonable to prevent escape by using deadly force. Thus, if the suspect threatens the officer with a weapon or there is probable cause to believe that he has committed a crime involving the infliction or threatened infliction of serious physical harm, deadly force may be used if necessary to prevent escape, and if, where feasible, some warning has been given . . .

It is insisted that the Fourth Amendment must be construed in light of the common-law rule, which allowed the use of whatever force was necessary to effect the arrest of a fleeing felon, though not a misdemeanant . . . Most American jurisdictions also imposed a flat prohibition against the use of deadly force to stop a fleeing misdemeanant, coupled with a general privilege to use such force to stop a fleeing felon . . .

It has been pointed out many times that the common-law rule is best understood in light of the fact that it arose at a time when virtually all felonies were punishable by death.[11] "Though effected without the protections and formalities of an orderly trial and conviction, the killing of a resisting or fleeing felon resulted in no greater consequences than those authorized for punishment of the felony of which the individual was charged or suspected." American Law Institute, Model Penal Code § 3.07, Comment 3, p. 56 (Tentative Draft No. 8, 1958) (hereinafter Model Penal Code Comment). Courts have also justified the common-law rule by emphasizing the relative dangerousness of felons.

Neither of these justifications makes sense today. Almost all crimes formerly punishable by death no longer are or can be. And while in earlier times "the gulf between the felonies and the minor offences was broad and deep," 2 Pollock & Maitland 467, n. 3, today the distinction is minor and often arbitrary. Many crimes classified as misdemeanors, or nonexistent, at common law are now felonies. These changes have undermined the concept, which was questionable to begin with, that use of deadly force against a fleeing felon is merely a speedier execution of someone who has already forfeited his life. They have also made the assumption that a "felon" is more dangerous than

---

[9] We note that the usual manner of deterring illegal conduct—through punishment—has been largely ignored in connection with flight from arrest. Arkansas, for example, specifically excepts flight from arrest from the offense of "obstruction of governmental operations." The commentary notes that this "reflects the basic policy judgment that, absent the use of force or violence, a mere attempt to avoid apprehension by a law enforcement officer does not give rise to an independent offense." Ark.Stat.Ann. § 41-2802(3)(a) (1977) and commentary. In the few States that do outlaw flight from an arresting officer, the crime is only a misdemeanor. See, e.g., Ind.Code § 35-44-3-3 (1982). Even forceful resistance, though generally a separate offense, is classified as a misdemeanor. E.g., Ill.Rev.Stat., ch. 38, 31–1 (1984); Mont.Code Ann. § 45-7-301 (1984); N.H.Rev.Stat.Ann. § 642:2 (Supp.1983); Ore.Rev.Stat. § 162.315 (1983).

This lenient approach does avoid the anomaly of automatically transforming every fleeing misdemeanant into a fleeing felon —subject, under the common- law rule, to apprehension by deadly force —solely by virtue of his flight. However, it is in real tension with the harsh consequences of flight in cases where deadly force is employed. For example, Tennessee does not outlaw fleeing from arrest. The Memphis City Code does, § 22-34.1 (Supp.17, 1971), subjecting the offender to a maximum fine of $50, § 1-8 (1967). Thus, Garner's attempted escape subjected him to (a) a $50 fine, and (b) being shot.

[11] The roots of the concept of a "felony" lie not in capital punishment but in forfeiture. 2 F. Pollock & F. Maitland, The History of English Law 465 (2d ed. 1909) (hereinafter Pollock & Maitland). Not all felonies were always punishable by death. Nonetheless, the link was profound. Blackstone was able to write: "The idea of felony is indeed so generally connected with that of capital punishment, that we find it hard to separate them; and to this usage the interpretations of the law do now conform. And therefore if a statute makes any new offence felony, the law implies that is shall be punished with death, viz. by hanging, as well as with forfeiture . . ." 4 W. Blackstone, Commentaries * 98.

a misdemeanant untenable. Indeed, numerous misdemeanors involve conduct more dangerous than many felonies.[12]

There is an additional reason why the common-law rule cannot be directly translated to the present day. The common-law rule developed at a time when weapons were rudimentary. Deadly force could be inflicted almost solely in a hand-to-hand struggle during which, necessarily, the safety of the arresting officer was at risk. Handguns were not carried by police officers until the latter half of the last century. Only then did it become possible to use deadly force from a distance as a means of apprehension. As a practical matter, the use of deadly force under the standard articulation of the common-law rule has an altogether different meaning—and harsher consequences—now than in past centuries . . .

The District Court concluded that Hymon was justified in shooting Garner because state law allows, and the Federal Constitution does not forbid, the use of deadly force to prevent the escape of a fleeing felony suspect if no alternative means of apprehension is available. This conclusion made a determination of Garner's apparent dangerousness unnecessary. The court did find, however, that Garner appeared to be unarmed, though Hymon could not be certain that was the case. Restated in Fourth Amendment terms, this means Hymon had no articulable basis to think Garner was armed.

. . . [T]he fact that Garner was a suspected burglar could not, without regard to the other circumstances, automatically justify the use of deadly force. Hymon did not have probable cause to believe that Garner, whom he correctly believed to be unarmed, posed any physical danger to himself or others.

. . . While we agree that burglary is a serious crime, we cannot agree that it is so dangerous as automatically to justify the use of deadly force. The FBI classifies burglary as a "property" rather than a "violent" crime. Although the armed burglar would present a different situation, the fact that an unarmed suspect has broken into a dwelling at night does not automatically mean he is physically dangerous. This case demonstrates as much. In fact, the available statistics demonstrate that burglaries only rarely involve physical violence. During the 10-year period from 1973 [to] 1982, only 3.8% of all burglaries involved violent crime . . .

German Federal Court of Justice
2 StR 82/04, NStZ 2005, 31 (June 30, 2004)

Facts

According to the findings B., who was later killed, spent the evening of July 27, 2002, in a clubhouse in N. During the course of the evening he took alcohol and cocaine, but his alcohol consumption was virtually unnoticeable in its external effects. B. left the clubhouse in the early morning of July 28, 2002, together with M. At the corner of T-Straße/A. they put money into a cigarette machine, but it produced no cigarettes. Both of them were angry and they each rained blows on the machine with a loose paving slab which was lying around. Because of the noise caused by this, two witnesses called the police independently of each other at 4.27 a.m. and informed them that people were there breaking into a vending machine.

The defendant, a police sergeant with the police authority at N., and Sergeant L. were then sent with their patrol car to the place of the crime. B. and M. tried to hide behind a beer cart. The defendant and Sergeant L. approached the beer cart from the other side, Sergeant L. shouting loudly "Stop, stay where you are—police!." Whilst M. was arrested by Sergeant L. behind the beer cart, B. freed himself from the defendant's grasp and struck at him at head height. The defendant backed away from the blows and called on B. to lie down. He however ran away across a terrace between tables and chairs in the direction of T-Straße, pulling as he did so at one of the chained chairs. The defendant believed that B. wanted to attack him with the chair, and pulled his pepper spray out of his belt. B. asked "Do you want to shoot me?." Because of the distance, and the fact that they were both moving, the pepper spray had no real effect.

At the end of the terrace, a palate of cobblestones was kept, and to the left of it lay a disorderly heap of these cobblestones with a weight of about 3 kg each. B. took at least one of these stones, and threw it in the direction of the defendant's head. The defendant was standing at a distance of 3 to 4 m from him. Because of this, the defendant drew his gun and waved it in the air in order to give a warning shot. B. at this moment hurled a second stone with great force at the defendant. It only just missed his head. B. turned back again in order to pick up a third stone. The defendant realised that he was in considerable danger from the stones, and lowered his weapon in order to shoot B. in the legs. He pressed the trigger of the weapon. The shot hit B., who was just bending down, 81 cm above the ground in the back. It completely opened up his aorta, so that he bled to death within a short period.

---

[12] White-collar crime, for example, poses a less significant physical threat than, say, drunken driving.

The regional court acquitted the defendant of the charge of negligence homicide. The appeals in law of the accessory prosecutors and of the public prosecutor's office were unsuccessful.

Reasons

...

2. Examination of the disputed judgment in respect of the substantive objections raised by all the appellants in law has revealed no legal error.

There is also no objection to the assessment of the judge of fact that the defendant, at the moment of the unlawful attack, had available no less severe method, which nevertheless promised success, of defending himself from the danger. In the light of the threat to life from the throwing of the stones the defendant did not need to rely on a warning shot or simple physical restraint. He was instead permitted to defend himself in such a way that the danger was averted immediately and finally, and also to use a firearm for this purpose, although only in such a way as not to exceed unnecessarily the intensity and danger of the attack (see BGHSt 27, 336, 337; BGH NJW 1980, 2263; NStZ 1981, 138; . . .). According to general principles of self-defense law, the person attacked is entitled to choose the method of defence which guarantees an immediate and final removal of the danger. Amongst several possibilities for defense, he only has to take the one which is less drastic for the attacker if he has the time available to choose as well as to estimate the danger, and if the defense which is less dangerous for the attacker is appropriate to dispel the danger without doubt, immediately and finally (consistent case law; see BGH NStZ 1982, 285; 1983, 117; 1994, 581, 582; 2001, 591, 592; 2002, 140; . . .). The regional court has denied the presence of these prerequisites here with reasoning which is free from error. Although the public prosecutor's office in its appeal in law criticizes the judge of fact for having only relied on presumptions, the office also points out no facts which substantiate that a warning shot and a retreat of several steps by the defendant would have ended the attack.

The defendant could also not be expected to retreat from B.'s attack. The legal provisions for self-defense only requires a person who is unlawfully attacked to take flight or to evade the attack in another way if special circumstances limit his right of self-defense (see BGH NJW 1980, 2263), for example when he himself has carelessly or intentionally provoked the attack. The position is also no different for police officers (see BayObLandesgericht MDR 1991, 367). The relevant provisions here of the Thuringian Police Functions Act do not limit the individual right of self-defense (§ 58 para. 2 PAG*). In the case of a present unlawful attack on life and limb of a police officer the question of how far he can defend himself does not in particular depend on which legal interest has previously been harmed by the attacker. The permissible extent of the necessary defense in the sense of § 32 para. 2 Criminal Code is also determined here by the concrete circumstances of the attack, in particular by the strength of and danger posed by the attacker and by the means of defence which are available to the person attacked. Special circumstances restricting the right of self-defense were not present here. The defendant was therefore permitted to direct a shot at the legs of the attacker, who was bending to pick up another cobble stone, in order to render him incapable of fighting. The deviation of the shot caused by the swerving of the weapon, which was in itself trivial, from the intended target, which led through a movement by the victim to a fatal injury, falls into the range of typical risks associated with self-defense and is therefore covered by the justification.

NOTES

1. Law enforcement situations in which police officers have to apply force (with guns or by other means, including the use of force incident to an arrest), and therefore engage in conduct that on its face satisfies the elements of an offense (assault, homicide, coercion, unlawful imprisonment, etc.) are not rare. (Compare doctors, and in particular surgeons, whose very job consists of conduct that matches the definition of assault, if not homicide, in the event of botched operation.) Every legal system has to arrive at a compromise between effective police work and citizens' individual rights to freedom and bodily integrity. If one analyzes typical situations, there are two standard types: first, the arrest of a suspect who flees the scene of a presumptive crime without attacking the arresting police officers; second, subjects attacking police officers or other persons in a way that requires defense.

---

* [PAG Thüringen § 58 para. 2
The consequences in civil law and criminal law of the provisions concerning self-defense and necessity remain unaffected.— Eds.]

Typical arrest cases (mere flight, no resistance) are somewhat complicated to assess under German law. The federal law, that is, the German Code of Criminal Procedure, does not answer all questions. There is a provision, in the Criminal Procedure Code, not the Criminal Code, authorizing police officers and public prosecutors to arrest suspects if the facts create an urgent suspicion that the arrested person has committed a criminal offense (§ 127 para. 2 Code of Criminal Procedure). However, this norm says nothing about the means used to affect an arrest. Boundaries between permissible and impermissible reliance on force and specifically the use of guns are drawn in the state's police laws (codified in state police statutes, *Polizeigesetze*). Federal law governing police work deals only with the conduct of criminal investigations. All other aspects of police work are covered by state law, that is, the police statutes in the sixteen German states. This is why the German Federal Court of Justice cites the Police Functions Act (*Polizeiaufgabengesetz*) of Thuringia. Policies and customs of local police departments in conflict with the state's police statute would be legally irrelevant.

The framework provided by these police laws resembles that set out in *Tennessee v. Garner*. For instance, the Police Functions Act of Thuringia (§ 65 para. 1) provides that guns may be used against persons "to stop a person trying to escape an arrest or the verification of identity, if there is a high degree of suspicion that this person has committed a) a felony or b) a misdemeanor if facts support the conclusion that the person carries guns or explosives." Police laws in other German states contain the same rule. Most medium severity offenses in the German Criminal Code are not felonies in the technical sense, which are defined in § 12 para. 1 Criminal Code as offenses with a minimum statutory punishment of at least one year's imprisonment (as opposed to a *maximum* statutory punishment of at least one year's imprisonment as in American law*). Robbery, rape and homicide are felonies under German law, but burglary and assault are not. Therefore, the use of guns to arrest the unarmed offender of a misdemeanor is not authorized by the German police laws.

There are a few felonies in the German Criminal Code that do not fall into the category of violent crime, e.g., currency counterfeiting (§ 146), organized fraud (§ 263 para. 5), judicial bribery (§ 332 para. 2), and perversion of justice (§ 339). Since under the Thuringia police statute (and other German police statutes), the use of a firearm is permitted on suspicion of commission of a felony, with no additional requirement of dangerousness (either based on the violent nature of the felony or other indicia of dangerousness), using a firearm in the execution of an arrest for these offenses would be covered. This might raise the additional question of constitutional limits, under German law, on the state's authorization of the use of force for the purpose of law enforcement. The issue in *Garner*, of course, was whether the general common law rule, which permitted the use of deadly force (which, under the Model Penal Code, includes "purposely firing a firearm in the direction of another person or at a vehicle in which another person is believed to be," with no distinction between the shooter's specific aim at one part of the body or another) in all felony cases, and only in felony cases, passed constitutional muster. Citing, among other things, the existence of nonviolent felonies, the Court rejected this blanket rule in favor of one that turns on an analysis of the offender's dangerousness.

2. Another question is what police officers are entitled to do if an offender resists arrest and attacks the officer or other persons. The point of § 58 para. 2 Police Functions Act of Thuringia, cited by the Federal Court of Justice, is to clarify that a police officer who injures or kills under such circumstances is entitled to claim the justification of self-defense. If shooting at the attacker is the only way to end the attack, as the German Federal Court of Justice says "without doubt, immediately and finally," a police officer acts with justification. There is no fundamental conflict between the criminal law justification of self-defense (or other-defense), § 32 Criminal Code, and the states' police laws. Use of guns is typically allowed according to the police laws if there is present danger for life or limb.† (Why would the police officer need a separate authorization in situations that are covered by the general

---

* See Chapter 5.D.

† See, e.g., Thuringian Police Functions Act § 65 para. 1 nr. 1.

justification of self-defense? Might one expect police officer to use more restraint in the face of an attack on their person than ordinary citizens? If so, why? Because police officers are better trained or because the relationship between the state and state officials, on the one hand, and citizens, on the other, might influence the evaluation?)

3. There are cases where police officers could, from the point of view of German criminal law, claim the justification of other-defense while the police laws do not permit the use of weapons. Imagine an offender who, after a residential burglary, runs away not only to escape arrest but also to keep stolen property, for instance, a jewelry case. Under such circumstances, there still is a present attack: an attack on property. If there are no other means available, such an attack may be stopped according to § 32 Criminal Code with deadly force.* But police officers who use a gun in such a situation typically do not act in accordance with the police laws as the police laws typically do not permit the use of guns merely for the protection of property. In other words, the police laws are stricter than the general criminal law justifications.

There is a dispute in Germany how to deal with this contradiction in the law. The Federal Court of Justice in our case stresses that it is to be taken seriously if the applicable police law explicitly states that the self-defense provisions remain unaffected. According to this view, in a case such as *Tennessee v. Garner*, the crucial question is: did the police officer act to defend the home owner's property (of a non-trivial value)? In *Tennessee v. Garner*, the value involved might have been too trivial, and it seems likely that the police officer did not know about the stolen items Garner was carrying with him. But under other circumstances, gun use against a burglar is justified under German law. Within the literature, there are however voices criticizing this result. They argue that the states' police laws are more detailed and more specific about officers' gun use and therefore should not be circumvented by pointing to § 32 Criminal Code. What could be the point of the more specific provision, if not to supersede the more general one, according to a familiar maxim of statutory interpretation? (Again, in light of *Garner*'s constitutional analysis, do constitutional constraints come into play here, to favor—or perhaps require—one resolution of this question of statutory interpretation rather than another? At what point does the suspect's constitutionally protected inviolable right to dignity, for instance, place limits on the use of deadly force? By a state official, as opposed to by a private citizen? What about the immeasurable value of life, which is seriously threatened by the use of deadly force in general, and of a firearm in particular? Or does the constitutional argument cut the other way, by suggesting that the *officer's* constitutional rights would be infringed by denying him or her the full benefit of the general self-defense provisions of the German Criminal Code? On what basis? Equality? Or on the constitutional basis of the self-defense provisions themselves, regardless of their application to particular groups?)

4. The Court's decision in *Garner* constitutionalizes the Model Penal Code's treatment of the criminal law justification of use of force in law enforcement, i.e., it holds that the Model Penal Code's provision captures the limits on police use of force for the purpose of law enforcement emanating from the Fourth Amendment's prohibition of unreasonable searches and seizures. But, of course, the Model Penal Code provision also operates as a criminal law norm (whether constitutionalized or not).

Section 3.07. Use of Force in Law Enforcement.

(1) Use of Force Justifiable to Effect an Arrest. [T]he use of force upon or toward the person of another is justifiable when the actor is making or assisting in making an arrest and the actor believes that such force is immediately necessary to effect a lawful arrest.

(2) Limitations on the Use of Force.

(a) The use of force is not justifiable under this Section unless:

    (i) the actor makes known the purpose of the arrest or believes that it is otherwise known by or cannot reasonably be made known to the person to be arrested; and

    (ii) when the arrest is made under a warrant, the warrant is valid or believed by the actor to be valid.

---

* See the *Fruit Thief Case* discussed in Chapter 13.B.

(b) The use of deadly force is not justifiable under this Section unless:
   (i) the arrest is for a felony; and
   (ii) the person effecting the arrest is authorized to act as a peace officer or is assisting a person whom he believes to be authorized to act as a peace officer; and
   (iii) the actor believes that the force employed creates no substantial risk of injury to innocent persons; and
   (iv) the actor believes that:
      (1) the crime for which the arrest is made involved conduct including the use or threatened use of deadly force; or
      (2) there is a substantial risk that the person to be arrested will cause death or serious bodily harm if his apprehension is delayed.

5. *Public duty and legal authority.* The Model Penal Code distinguishes the justification of use of force in law enforcement from a general justification of execution of public duty, which is designed to cover the exercise of state power in general, not limited to a specific conduct (use of force) or specific purpose (e.g., law enforcement or crime prevention).

Section 3.03. Execution of Public Duty.

(1) Except as provided in Subsection (2) of this Section, conduct is justifiable when it is required or authorized by:
(a) the law defining the duties or functions of a public officer or the assistance to be rendered to such officer in the performance of his duties; or
(b) the law governing the execution of legal process; or
(c) the judgment or order of a competent court or tribunal; or
(d) the law governing the armed services or the lawful conduct of war; or
(e) any other provision of law imposing a public duty.
   . . .

Compare this provision with § 25 of the Canadian Criminal Code:

Protection of Persons Administering and Enforcing the Law

25. (1) Every one who is required or authorized by law to do anything in the administration or enforcement of the law
(a) as a private person,
(b) as a peace officer or public officer,
(c) in aid of a peace officer or public officer, or
(d) by virtue of his office,
is, if he acts on reasonable grounds, justified in doing what he is required or authorized to do and in using as much force as is necessary for that purpose . . .
   . . .

Note the reference to "private persons" in § 25 Canadian Criminal Code; note also that Model Penal Code § 3.07 makes no reference to the official status of the person claiming the law enforcement justification except in § 3.07(2)(b), dealing with the use of *deadly* force. This raises the question whether the law enforcement justification—and more generally the public duty justification—turn on conduct or status? Or do they differ in this respect, with one (perhaps the law enforcement justification?) more conduct-based than the other? Does it matter whether one conceives of the law enforcement justification, say, as conduct-based, so that it is in principle available to anyone, regardless of status (perhaps with allowances made based on the special obligations, experience, and training of state officials), or as conduct-based, so that it is conceived primarily as a justification available to state officials in the exercise of their official duties?[*]

In this context, does it make a difference whether the justification is set out in the criminal code, which is presumably addressed to the broader public, rather than state officials, or in an administrative law code, dealing with—say—police law, dedicated to defining the roles of state officials?[†]

---

[*] For a case exploring the different norms governing the use of force, and of deadly force in particular, by police officers and others, see *People v. Peña*, 169 Misc.2d 75, 641 N.Y.S.2d 794 (N.Y. Sup. Ct. 1996); see also *R. v. Brennan*, [1989] O.J. No. 2054 (historical and statutory context of § 25 Canadian Criminal Code).
[†] See Note 1.

14

EXCUSES

There are at least as many conceptions of "excuse" as there are of "justification," probably more. Unlike in the case of justification, however, the search for a common denominator has been pursued with considerable effort, and with greater success. There is now a wide range of comprehensive conceptions of excuse, or rather of that prerequisite for criminal liability the absence of which is classified as an excuse, including, in rough order of significance: guilt, culpability, responsibility, blameworthiness, reproachability, accountability, and avoidability (where the first two or three are more likely to be treated as formal doctrinal categories, with the remaining terms serving as synonyms or, more ambitiously, expositions—and in the case of the last listed, a rationale—of the first two or three). The basic idea is that even an *act* that satisfies the elements of an offense—notably, the mental state requirements (also known as "modes of culpability") or subjective offense elements—and is unlawful generally speaking, should not result in criminal liability for the *actor* unless he or she can also be blamed (held responsible or accountable, or reproached, etc.) for it.

The Model Penal Code's treatmentist approach can accommodate the concept of justification insofar as the actor who engages in behavior that, in an exceptional case, on balance protects rather than "inflicts or threatens harm to individual or public interests,"* even though it matches the definition of an offense. In this way, the actor can be said to have shown him- or herself not to possess the requisite abnormal dangerousness that would trigger the state's interference to prescribe, and administer, the indicated peno-correctional treatment; in other words, justifications serve to rebut the ordinary presumption of criminal dangerousness arising from the commission of an act that matches the definition of an offense.†

A similar treatmentist account may account for some excuses—excusing necessity (whether triggered by circumstances or another person (duress)) or, perhaps, entrapment come to mind—as they, too, can be said to rebut the ordinary diagnosis of criminal dangerousness upon commission of a criminal offense insofar as the actor faced an extraordinary situation of coercion that he or she could not have been expected to withstand. The person who drives a stranger to a bank robbery at gunpoint is neither abnormally heroic nor abnormally dangerous. A treatmentist account of what one might call incapacity, rather than inability, offenses is more difficult to generate. It can hardly be said that persons who suffer from a mental disease or defect that renders them incapable of telling right from wrong, or of exercising sufficient self-control to keep themselves from committing acts they recognize as wrong, are less criminally dangerous than those who do not; in fact, they are more likely to be considered *more* dangerous. (Of course, radical treatmentists, including at least some of the psychiatrists who contributed to the Model Penal Code project, would merely take this observation as another illustration of the misguidedness of distinguishing between punishment and treatment in the first place, and therefore of the very project of defining an "insanity" defense for a sliver of the offender population, rather than recognizing "mental disease or defect" as characteristic of all criminal behavior.) At any rate, the Model Penal Code drafters appeared content to invoke the notion of "blame" when it came to the

---

* Model Penal Code § 1.02(1)(a).
† For a similar account of renunciation in the law of inchoate offenses, see Chapter 12.D.

conception of an excuse, perhaps regarding—at least certain—excuses as a limit on the treatmentist regime, rather than as an aspect of it.*

In this respect, the Model Penal Code is significantly less ambitious than the so-called "functional" theory of guilt (*funktionale Schuldtheorie*) developed in German criminal law in the late twentieth century, which was explicitly designed to take on the traditional "normative" approach (*normative Schuldtheorie*) outlined above. According to the functional account,[†] which has had a greater impact on the scholarly literature than on the courts, guilt (*Schuld*) is "a deficit in the actor's legal motivation" or "in loyalty to law (*Rechtstreue*)" and calls for an exercise of the state's penal power only if accepting this deficit interferes with the ultimate aim of punishment: stabilizing the validity of existing norms and affirming society's loyalty to law, i.e., positive general prevention (Chapter 1.A.i).

A. Duress

The defense of duress has faced its fair share of definitional and taxonomical challenges. Does "duress" encompass only emergency situations caused by threats made by one person against another? Or does it also include extremely dire straits not attributable to a person? For that matter, is it a separate defense at all, or is it just a variety of necessity, a synonym for necessity as an excuse? No matter what it is called, how far does it reach? Does it extend to all offenses, or are there some—in particular murder—that are so serious, inflict such grave harm on another (innocent) person, or violate a *Rechtsgut* so (uniquely?) important, that we can expect everyone, even the non-heroic, to resist any compulsion, no matter how great, personal or circumstantial, to commit it? Likewise, does it reach threats only to the offender him- or herself, or also to others? If so, to whom: relatives, friends, members of his or her political (social?) community, or any person whatsoever? (What's the connection between this question and the question of whom I am duty-bound to protect, under the law of omission liability?[‡] Do the answers to this question reflect different conceptions of criminal law?) Do we even need a defense of duress, or can it be handled under necessity *as a justification*, which after all also requires an emergency ("necessity") situation? Or even as an element-negating defense that negates the requisite *mens rea* (perhaps assuming that the *mens rea* requires proof of a certain motive, in the sense of a reason for acting)?

Duress, however classified, forces the criminal law directly to face its underlying conception of the person, and its commitment to a focus on acts, rather than actors. Duress, particularly in its Anglo-American version, makes explicit the silent assumption that the person in criminal law is the "reasonable" person, and as a result raises clearly the question of just who this reasonable person is, and just how far we are willing to go in tailoring the conception of the reasonable person to the particularities of the offender and "the situation."

Dixon v. United States
Supreme Court of the United States
548 U.S. 1 (2006)

Justice Steven delivered the opinion of the Court.

In January 2003, petitioner Keshia Dixon purchased multiple firearms at two gun shows, during the course of which she provided an incorrect address and falsely stated that she was not under indictment for a felony. As a result of these illegal acts, petitioner was indicted and convicted on one count of receiving a firearm while under indictment in violation of 18 U.S.C. § 922(n) and eight counts of making false statements in connection with the acquisition of a firearm in violation of § 922 (a)(6). At trial, petitioner admitted that she knew she was under indictment when she made the

---

* See Model Penal Code Commentaries art. 3, introduction, at 2–3 (conduct "thought to be undesirable but . . . for some reason the actor is not to be blamed for it").

[†] See, e.g., Günther Jakobs, *Das Schuldprinzip* (1993).

[‡] See Chapter 7.D.

purchases and that she knew doing so was a crime; her defense was that she acted under duress because her boyfriend threatened to kill her or hurt her daughters if she did not buy the guns for him.

Petitioner contends that the trial judge's instructions to the jury erroneously required her to prove duress by a preponderance of the evidence instead of requiring the Government to prove beyond a reasonable doubt that she did not act under duress . . .

There is no federal statute defining the elements of the duress defense. We have not specified the elements of the defense and need not do so today. Instead, we presume the accuracy of the District Court's description of these elements: (1) The defendant was under an unlawful and imminent threat of such a nature as to induce a well-grounded apprehension of death or serious bodily injury; (2) the defendant had not recklessly or negligently placed herself in a situation in which it was probable that she would be forced to perform the criminal conduct; (3) the defendant had no reasonable, legal alternative to violating the law, that is, a chance both to refuse to perform the criminal act and also to avoid the threatened harm; and (4) that a direct causal relationship may be reasonably anticipated between the criminal act and the avoidance of the threatened harm.

Petitioner argues here, as she did in the District Court and the Court of Appeals, that federal law requires the Government to bear the burden of disproving her defense beyond a reasonable doubt and that the trial court's erroneous instruction on this point entitles her to a new trial. There are two aspects to petitioner's argument in support of her proposed instruction that merit separate discussion. First, petitioner contends that her defense "controverted the mens rea required for conviction" and therefore that the Due Process Clause requires the Government to retain the burden of persuasion on that element. Second, petitioner argues that the Fifth Circuit's rule is "contrary to modern common law."

The crimes for which petitioner was convicted require that she have acted "knowingly," § 922(a) (6), or "willfully," § 924(a)(1)(D).[3] . . . Although the Government may have proved these elements in other ways, it clearly met its burden when petitioner testified that she knowingly committed certain acts—she put a false address on the forms she completed to purchase the firearms, falsely claimed that she was the actual buyer of the firearms, and falsely stated that she was not under indictment at the time of the purchase—and when she testified that she knew she was breaking the law when, as an individual under indictment at the time, she purchased a firearm.

Petitioner contends, however, that she cannot have formed the necessary mens rea for these crimes because she did not freely choose to commit the acts in question. But even if we assume that petitioner's will was overborne by the threats made against her and her daughters, she still knew that she was making false statements and knew that she was breaking the law by buying a firearm. The duress defense . . . may excuse conduct that would otherwise be punishable, but the existence of duress normally does not controvert any of the elements of the offense itself.[4] . . . Like the defense of necessity, the defense of duress does not negate a defendant's criminal state of mind when the applicable offense requires a defendant to have acted knowingly or willfully; instead, it allows the defendant to "avoid liability . . . because coercive conditions or necessity negates a conclusion of guilt even though the necessary mens rea was present." United States v. Bailey, 444 U.S. 394, 402, 100 S. Ct. 624 (1980).[5] . . . The fact that petitioner's crimes are statutory offenses that have no counterpart in the common law also supports our conclusion that her duress defense in no way disproves an element of those crimes . . . Here, consistent with the movement away from the traditional dichotomy of general versus specific intent and toward a more specifically defined hierarchy of culpable mental states, Congress defined the crimes at issue to punish defendants who act "knowingly," § 922(a)(6), or "willfully," § 924(a)(1)(D). It is these specific mental states, rather than some vague "evil mind," Brief for Petitioner 42, or " 'criminal' intent," Martin v. Ohio, 480 U.S. 228, 235, 107 S. Ct. 1098 (1987), that the Government is required to prove beyond a reasonable doubt. The jury instructions in this case were consistent with this requirement and, as such, did not run afoul of the Due Process Clause

---

[3] Although § 922(n) does not contain a mens rea requirement, the relevant sentencing provision, § 924(a)(1)(D), requires that a violation be committed willfully.

[4] [T]here may be crimes where the nature of the mens rea would require the Government to disprove the existence of duress beyond a reasonable doubt. See 1 W. LaFave, Substantive Criminal Law § 5.1, p 333 (2d ed. 2003) (hereinafter LaFave) (explaining that some common-law crimes require that the crime be done "maliciously"); Black's Law Dictionary 968 (7th ed. 1999) (defining malice as "[t]he intent, without justification or excuse, to commit a wrongful act").

[5] Professor LaFave has explained the duress defense as follows: "The rationale of the defense is not that the defendant, faced with the unnerving threat of harm unless he does an act which violates the literal language of the criminal law, somehow loses his mental capacity to commit the crime in question. Nor is it that the defendant has not engaged in a voluntary act. Rather it is that, even though he has done the act the crime requires and has the mental state which the crime requires, his conduct which violates the literal language of the criminal law is excused . . . ." 2 LaFave § 9.7(a), at 72.

when they placed the burden on petitioner to establish the existence of duress by a preponderance of the evidence.

Having found no constitutional basis for placing upon the Government the burden of disproving petitioner's duress defense beyond a reasonable doubt, we next address petitioner's argument that the modern common law requires the Government to bear that burden. In making this argument, petitioner recognizes that, until the end of the 19th century, common-law courts generally adhered to the rule that "the proponent of an issue bears the burden of persuasion on the factual premises for applying the rule." Fletcher, Two Kinds of Legal Rules: A Comparative Study of Burden-of-Persuasion Practices in Criminal Cases, 77 Yale L. J. 880, 898 (1967–1968). In petitioner's view, however, [the publication of the Model Penal Code in 1962] established a contrary common-law rule that now prevails in federal courts . . .

As petitioner notes, the [Model Penal] Code would place the burden on the government to disprove the existence of duress beyond a reasonable doubt. See Model Penal Code § 1.12 (stating that each element of an offense must be proved beyond a reasonable doubt); § 1.13(9)(c), at 91 (defining as an element anything that negatives an excuse for the conduct at issue); § 2.09, at 131–132 (establishing affirmative defense of duress). Petitioner argues that the Code reflects "well established" federal law as it existed at the time. But . . . no such consensus existed when Congress passed the Safe Streets Act in 1968. And even if we assume Congress' familiarity with the Code and the rule it would establish, there is no evidence that Congress endorsed the Code's views or incorporated them into the Safe Streets Act.

In fact, the Act itself provides evidence to the contrary. Despite the Code's careful delineation of mental states, see Model Penal Code § 2.02, at 94–95, the Safe Streets Act attached no explicit mens rea requirement to the crime of receiving a firearm while under indictment, § 924(a), 82 Stat. 233 ("Whoever violates any provision of this chapter . . . shall be fined not more than $5,000 or imprisoned not more than five years, or both"). And when Congress amended the Act to impose a mens rea requirement, it punished people who "willfully" violate the statute, a mental state that has not been embraced by the Code, see Model Penal Code § 2.02(2), at 94–95 (defining "purposely," "knowingly," "recklessly," and "negligently"); Explanatory Note, p 97 ("Though the term 'wilfully' is not used in the definitions of crimes contained in the Code, its currency and its existence in offenses outside the criminal code suggest the desirability of clarification"). Had Congress intended to adopt the Code's structure when it enacted or amended the Safe Streets Act, one would expect the Act's form and language to adhere much more closely to that used by the Code. It does not, and, for that reason, we cannot rely on the Model Penal Code to provide evidence as to how Congress would have wanted us to effectuate the duress defense in this context.

Congress can, if it chooses, enact a duress defense that places the burden on the Government to disprove duress beyond a reasonable doubt. In light of Congress' silence on the issue, however, it is up to the federal courts to effectuate the affirmative defense of duress as Congress "may have contemplated" it in an offense-specific context. Oakland Cannabis Buyers' Cooperative, 532 U.S., at 491, n. 3, 121 S. Ct. 1711. In the context of the firearms offenses at issue—as will usually be the case, given the long-established common-law rule—we presume that Congress intended the petitioner to bear the burden of proving the defense of duress by a preponderance of the evidence. Accordingly, the judgment of the Court of Appeals is affirmed.

It is so ordered.

Justice Breyer, with whom Justice Souter joins, dissenting.

Courts have long recognized that "duress" constitutes a defense to a criminal charge. Historically, that defense "excuse[d] criminal conduct" if (1) a "threat of imminent death or serious bodily injury" led the defendant to commit the crime, (2) the defendant had no reasonable, legal alternative to breaking the law, and (3) the defendant was not responsible for creating the threat. United States v. Bailey, 444 U.S. 394, 409–410, 100 S. Ct. 624 (1980); see also 2 W. LaFave, Substantive Criminal Law § 9.7(b), pp 74–82 (2003) (hereinafter LaFave). The Court decides today in respect to federal crimes that the defense must bear the burden of both producing evidence of duress and persuading the jury. I agree with the majority that the burden of production lies on the defendant, that here the burden of persuasion issue is not constitutional, and that Congress may allocate that burden as it sees fit. But I also believe that, in the absence of any indication of a different congressional intent, the burden of persuading the jury beyond a reasonable doubt should lie where such burdens normally lie in criminal cases, upon the prosecution.

My disagreement with the majority in part reflects my different view about how we should determine the relevant congressional intent. Where Congress speaks about burdens of proof, we must, of course, follow what it says. But suppose, as is normally the case, that the relevant federal statute is silent? The majority proceeds on the assumption that Congress wished courts to fill the gap by examining judicial practice at the time that Congress enacted the particular criminal statute in question...

I would assume instead that Congress' silence typically means that Congress expected the courts to develop burden rules governing affirmative defenses as they have done in the past, by beginning with the common law and taking full account of the subsequent need for that law to evolve through judicial practice informed by reason and experience. That approach would produce uniform federal practice across different affirmative defenses, as well as across statutes passed at different points in time.

My approach leads me to conclude that in federal criminal cases, the prosecution should bear the duress defense burden of persuasion. The issue is a close one. In Blackstone's time the accused bore the burden of proof for all affirmative defenses. See 4 W. Blackstone, Commentaries * 201; Patterson v. New York, 432 U.S. 197, 201–202, 97 S. Ct. 2319 (1977). And 20th-century experts have taken different positions on the matter. The Model Penal Code, for example, recommends placing the burden of persuasion on the prosecution. ALI, Model Penal Code § 1.12, p 16, § 1.13(9)(c), p 18, § 2.09, pp 37–38 (1985). The Brown Commission recommends placing it upon the defendant. National Commission on Reform of Federal Criminal Laws, 1 Working Papers 278 (1970). And the proposed revision of the federal criminal code, agnostically, would have turned the matter over to the courts for decision. S. 1722, 96th Cong., 1st Sess., § 501 (1979). Moreover, there is a practical argument that favors the Government's position here, namely that defendants should bear the burden of persuasion because defendants often have superior access to the relevant proof.

Nonetheless, several factors favor placing the burden on the prosecution. For one thing, in certain respects the question of duress resembles that of mens rea, an issue that is always for the prosecution to prove beyond a reasonable doubt. See In re Winship, 397 U.S. 358, 364, 90 S. Ct. 1068 (1970); Martin v. Ohio, 480 U.S. 228, 234, 107 S. Ct. 1098 (1987). The questions are not the same. The defendant's criminal activity here was voluntary; no external principle, such as the wind, propelled her when she acted. The Nicomachean Ethics of Aristotle, p 54 (R. W. Browne transl. 1865). Moreover, her actions were intentional. Whether she wanted to buy the guns or not, and whether she wanted to lie while doing so or not, she decided to do these things and knew that she was doing them. Indeed, her action was willful in the sense that she knew that to do them was to break the law. See Ratzlaf v. United States, 510 U.S. 135, 136–137, 114 S. Ct. 655 (1994).

Nonetheless, where a defendant acts under duress, she lacks any semblance of a meaningful choice. In that sense her choice is not free. As Blackstone wrote, the criminal law punishes "abuse[s] of th[e] free will"; hence "it is highly just and equitable that a man should be excused for those acts, which are done through unavoidable force and compulsion." 4 William Blackstone, Commentaries on the Laws of England 27 (1769).

And it is in this "force and compulsion," acting upon the will, that the resemblance to lack of mens rea lies. See also Austin, Ifs and Cans, in Proceedings of the British Academy 123–124 (1956) (noting difference between choosing to do something where one has the opportunity and ability to do otherwise and choosing to do something where one lacks any such opportunity or ability). Davis v. United States, 160 U. S. 469 (1895), allocated the federal insanity defense burden to the Government partly for these reasons. That case, read in light of Leland v. Oregon, 343 U.S. 790, 797, 72 S. Ct. 1002 (1952), suggests that, even if insanity does not always show the absence of mens rea, it does show the absence of a "*vicious* will." Davis, supra, at 484, 16 S. Ct. 353 (citing Blackstone; emphasis added).

For another thing, federal courts (as a matter of statutory construction or supervisory power) have imposed the federal-crime burden of persuasion upon the prosecution in respect to self-defense, insanity, and entrapment, which resemble the duress defense in certain relevant ways. In respect to both duress and self-defense, for example, the defendant's illegal act is voluntary, indeed, intentional; but the circumstances deprive the defendant of any meaningful ability or opportunity to act otherwise, depriving the defendant of a choice that is free. Insanity, as I said, may involve circumstances that resemble, but are not identical to, a lack of mens rea. And entrapment requires the prosecution to prove that the defendant was "predisposed" to commit the crime—a matter sometimes best known to the defendant...

[F]our Circuits now place the burden of persuasion on the prosecution across the board; one places the burden on the prosecution if the statute requires mens rea but not otherwise; and four have held or suggested that the burden should be on the prosecution if the statute requires an intentional or willful state of mind, but not if the statute requires only knowledge. While the Circuits are divided, apparently only one (the Fifth) agrees with the position taken by the Court today.

Further, while I concede the logic of the Government's practical argument—that defendants have superior access to the evidence—I remain uncertain of the argument's strength. After all, "[i]n every criminal case the defendant has at least an equal familiarity with the facts and in most a greater familiarity with them than the prosecution." Tot v. United States, 319 U.S. 463, 469, 63 S. Ct. 1241 (1943). And the strict contours of the duress defense, as well as the defendant's burden of production, already substantially narrow the circumstances under which the defense may be used.

A defendant may find it difficult, for example, to show duress where the relevant conduct took place too long before the criminal act. That is because the defendant must show that he had no alternative to breaking the law. And that will be the more difficult to show the more remote the threat. See also LaFave, § 9.7, p 77–79 (duress generally requires an "immediate" or "imminent" threat, that the defendant "take advantage of a reasonable opportunity to escape," and that the defendant "terminate his conduct 'as soon as the claimed duress . . . had lost its coercive force' "). More important, the need to prove mens rea can easily present precisely the same practical difficulties of proof for the prosecutor. Suppose for example the defendant claims that an old lady told him that the white powder he transported across the border was medicine for her dying son. Cf. United States v. Mares, 441 F.3d 1152 (CA10 2006).

It is particularly difficult to see a practical distinction between this affirmative defense and, say, self-defense. The Government says that the prosecution may "be unable to call the witness most likely to have information bearing on the point," namely, the defendant. But what is the difference in this respect between the defendant here, who says her boyfriend threatened to kill her, and a battered woman who says that she killed her husband in self-defense, where the husband's evidence is certainly unavailable? See also Jacobson, 503 U.S. 540, 112 S. Ct. 1535 (entrapment; need to prove "propensity"). Regardless, unless the defendant testifies, it could prove difficult to satisfy the defendant's burden of production; and, of course, once the defendant testifies, cross-examination is possible . . .

Finally, there is a virtue in uniformity, in treating the federal statutory burden of persuasion similarly in respect to actus reus, mens rea, mistake, self-defense, entrapment, and duress. The Second Circuit, when imposing the burden of persuasion for duress on the prosecution, wrote that differences in this respect create "a grave possibility of juror confusion." United States v. Mitchell, 725 F.2d 832, 836 (1983). They risk unfairness as well.

Model Penal Code

§ 2.09. Duress

(1) It is an affirmative defense that the actor engaged in the conduct charged to constitute an offense because he was coerced to do so by the use of, or a threat to use, unlawful force against his person or the person of another, which a person of reasonable firmness in his situation would have been unable to resist.

(2) The defense provided by this Section is unavailable if the actor recklessly placed himself in a situation in which it was probable that he would be subjected to duress. The defense is also unavailable if he was negligent in placing himself in such a situation, whenever negligence suffices to establish culpability for the offense charged.

German Federal Court of Justice
1 StR 230/53, BGHSt 5, 371 (March 5, 1954)

The defendant was examined before the court as a witness in two sets of criminal proceedings against F., at first under oath, then twice unsworn, and finally under oath again. On each occasion she deliberately gave false testimony in favor of F. F. had induced her to do so by the threat that he would kill her if she did not give untrue evidence. The regional court sentenced the defendant to an overall sentence of nine months' imprisonment for repeated perjury and for repeated false unsworn testimony. Her appeal in law succeeds.

Reasons

The offenses of perjury (§ 154 Criminal Code)* and deliberately giving false unsworn testimony (§ 153 Criminal Code)† were explained in the judgment without legal error. The appeal in law does not dispute this. It claims however that the regional court incorrectly denied the presence of the

---

* [German Criminal Code (Perjury) § 154

(1) Who falsely takes an oath before a court or another authority competent to demand oaths will be punished with imprisonment of not less than one year.

(2) In less serious cases the punishment is imprisonment from six months to five years.—Eds.]

† [German Criminal Code (False Unsworn Testimony) § 153

Who gives false unsworn testimony as a witness or expert before a court or other authority competent to examine witnesses and experts under oath will be punished with imprisonment from three months to five years.—Eds.]

prerequisites for coercion necessity which frees from guilt (§ 52 Criminal Code)[*] [now no longer part of the Criminal Code—Eds.]; it had also not sufficiently examined whether the defendant had at least erroneously assumed the presence of this ground for excluding guilt. The objections are well founded.

The regional court accepts that the defendant had been threatened by F. with danger to life and limb if she did not give the false testimony demanded by him. It also considers it to have been proved that the defendant testified and swore falsely out of fear from these threats . . . The judge of fact nevertheless denied the defendant the protection of § 52 Criminal Code on the basis of the following reasoning: When the defendant was examined on April 5, 1951, under oath and unsworn on April 20 and June 6, 1951, F. was in custody pending trial and would thereby have been prevented from fulfilling his threats; the defendant was therefore not at the time of these examinations in the present danger which § 52 assumes. At the time of the examination of the defendant under oath on July 31, 1952, F. was at large; the defendant could however have averted the danger by informing the court of the threat. Moreover she had also been in a position to do this at the time of the earlier examinations. These explanations do not fully explore the legal situation.

a) Present nature of the danger: the threats of F. had not suddenly put the defendant in a danger which she could only answer by an immediate defense. The danger lasted for a longer period. Such a long-term danger can be present and form the basis of necessity under § 52 Criminal Code . . . This is the case when the long-term danger is so compelling that it can turn into harm at any time, and thus also immediately, even though the possibility remains that the occurrence of the harm may be deferred for a while, as can for instance be the case with the danger of a ruinous house collapsing (RGSt 59, 69; see further RGSt 60, 318; OGHSt 1, 369). Besides this, the present nature of a long-term danger has been accepted in the case law if the harm which was to be feared according to the course of things was admittedly not imminent but could only be averted by immediate present action. This view becomes especially apparent in some decisions of the Imperial Court about the necessity situation in the case of perjury—RGSt 66, 98, 22, 397— . . . Whether this opinion should in principle be followed (see, against this, H. Mayer, JW 32, 2291 ff. and 3068 f.) can be left undecided here. The detention of F. in custody pending trial at the time of the examinations of the defendant on April 5, April 20 and June 8, 1951, excluded the present nature of the danger if it was established that the detention would last beyond the hearings in which the defendant had to give her testimony; it suffices that this is probable for the retrospective observer to an extent bordering on certainty. If on the other hand an immediate release of F. after the hearing was to be expected, the fulfillment of his threats could become imminent in such a way that the danger would assume a present nature. It follows from the judgment that the judge of fact was persuaded that, if the defendant had testified truthfully, F. would not have been at large after any of the three examinations; moreover this did not occur in spite of the untrue testimonies of the defendant favoring F. although admittedly in the case of the last examination only because F. was taken into custody in relation to another case immediately after his acquittal. The view of the regional court that there was no present danger for the defendant at the time of the three examinations mentioned cannot be objected to in law . . .

It cannot however be deduced from the judgment that the defendant recognized all this and did not erroneously regard the danger as present. The regional court is admittedly of the view that the defendant could have recognized that F. would be further detained if she had given true testimonies. However this does not say anything about the beliefs which she actually formed. If she could only have recognized but did not actually know that F. would be kept in custody, then she can at most be accused of having considered coercion necessity through negligence. It would not suffice for punishment for the two unsworn false statements, because such a crime is only threatened with punishment when committed intentionally. The oath violation committed on April 5, 1951, could admittedly be punishable as a negligent false oath under § 163 Criminal Code,[†] if the defendant through negligence considered the prerequisites of coercion necessity, which were not in truth fulfilled, to be present (RGSt 66, 222, 227); however the observations of the regional court so far do not suffice for the finding of negligence . . .

b) Whether the danger could be averted: If a danger forms the basis of a true necessity situation under § 52 Criminal Code . . . , then all measures necessary to avert this danger completely are

---

[*] [German Criminal Code (old version, until 1975) § 52
(1) The act will not be punished if the offender was coerced to act by irresistible force or by a threat posing a present danger for life or limb for himself or a relative.—Eds.]
[†] [Today, this is German Criminal Code § 161
If a person commits one of the offenses in §§ 154 to 156 negligently, the punishment will be imprisonment of not more than one year or a fine.—Eds.]

excused. If it is a question of a present long-term danger, the defense need not be limited to preventing the immediate occurrence of the harm and thus postponing the danger . . . The regional court is evidently of the view that the defendant could have averted the danger in all four cases, in particular also in her examination under oath of July 31, 1952, by appealing for the protection of the courts. The judgment does not however reveal whether the judge of fact had regard here to what has just been explained; he also expressed no view on the measures the courts could take and would have taken for the protection of the defendant. As a result, the reasons given by the regional court do not support its decision. Additionally the judgment does not deal with the question of whether the defendant was aware of that legitimate way out of the danger, if it existed at all. If she was not, then if the danger was present, or if it was considered by her to be present, she could not be punished for an intentional crime . . .

The fact that the defendant could not avert the danger simply by refusing to testify (see RGSt 66, 222, 226 f.) has been correctly recognized by the criminal chamber, as F. had not demanded that she should not make incriminating statements but that she should make a particular false statement in his favor.

Following all this, the case needs further elucidation by the judge of fact.

NOTES

1. The U.S. Supreme Court, in *Dixon*, comes to the same conclusion as the majority opinion in German law, that duress can be an excuse but does not negate *mens rea*. While it is commonly accepted in common law systems that duress is an excuse, rather than an element-negating "defense," this was not always so. For a particularly exhaustive exploration of the struggle to categorize duress,* where the Canadian Supreme Court undertakes to "examine the theoretical nature of the common law defence of duress, and determine its relationship to basic mens rea principles," and in the process traces, among other things, its own recent jurisprudence on the subject, reversing its decision in *R. v. Paquette*, [1977] 2 S.C.R. 189, in which it had held that duress can negate *mens rea* (as well as serve as a separate excuse).

> The defence of "duress per minas" ("duress by threat") has a long history at common law. References to the defence can be found in the writings of such venerable commentators as Hale and Blackstone (see J. Ll. J. Edwards, "Compulsion, Coercion and Criminal Responsibility" (1951), 14 Mod. L. Rev. 297, at pp. 298–99; and P. Rosenthal, "Duress in the Criminal Law" (1989–90), 32 Crim. L.Q. 199, at pp. 200ff.). In spite of the defence's antiquity, however, many important aspects of its nature and its details have remained unresolved, or have been shrouded with uncertainty. As Professor Edwards, supra, observed in 1951 (at p. 297):
>
> "Judged by the absence of any satisfactory modern authority, it must be very rare for the accused to set up as a defence that he committed the alleged crime under the compulsion of another person. Indeed the whole field of learning on this defence to criminal liability is both meagre and unsatisfactory."

In *Hibbert*, the Court, at long last, concludes that duress can serve as an excuse, but that it cannot negate the *mens rea* for party liability under Canadian law (purpose, intention in common). It leaves open, however, the possibility that duress *may* negate where "the mental state specified by Parliament in its definition of the offence is such that the presence of coercion can, as a matter of logic, have a bearing on the existence of mens rea." In other words, if the legislature makes it clear that "threats of death or bodily harm" *can* negate the mental state requirement in a given statute then there is no reason why they *cannot* serve this function. The Court doesn't provide an example, but its discussion of *Paquette* suggests that mental states requiring, or precluding, a certain motive might qualify. Why? But is motive not supposed to be irrelevant to criminal liability? See the discussion of motive in Chapter 8.A.

2. *Dixon* cites the Model Penal Code, and the Code's duress section certainly does recognize duress as a separate "affirmative defense," rather than an element-negating one:

---

* See *R. v. Hibbert*, [1995] 2 S.C.R. 973.

Section 2.09. Duress.

(1) It is an affirmative defense that the actor engaged in the conduct charged to constitute an offense because he was coerced to do so by the use of, or a threat to use, unlawful force against his person or the person of another, which a person of reasonable firmness in his situation would have been unable to resist.

But note that the duress provision appears in article 2, on general principles of liability, rather than in article 4, on responsibility (or article 3, on general principles of justification). In a sense, then, the Model Penal Code's treatment, at least structurally, if not substantively, reflects the traditional ambiguity surrounding the categorization of duress. (Although it should be pointed out that article 4 includes no excuses other than insanity and diminished capacity. Other defenses that might be labeled "excuses"—inability excuses, that is, as opposed to incapacity excuses, like insanity—also appear in article 3 (e.g., mistake of law, § 2.04(3); pathological and other-induced intoxication, § 2.08(4); military orders, § 2.10; entrapment, § 2.13).) The second half of article 2 is also home to a number of (other?) wobbler defenses, that—at least on some accounts—straddle the line between various levels in the analysis of criminal liability (e.g., mistake: level one (criminality) and level three (excuse); intoxication: same; military orders: excuse or justification; and—at least traditionally—duress: criminality and excuse; consent: criminality and justification; entrapment: criminality and excuse).

This placement reflects the Model Penal Code's drafters' non-doctrinaire approach to the question of classification. As with other formal distinctions—notably between types of offense element: conduct, attendant circumstance, result (see Chapter 7)—they believed that a distinction was only as important as its usefulness. The ultimate question, then, is, what difference does the distinction make?

This question has an answer in the case of duress (and in the case of other defenses), as *Dixon* and *Hibbert* illustrate: the burden of proof is more likely to rest on the defendant on an excuse than on an element-negating "defense." In fact, in the United States, saddling the defendant with the burden of proof on an offense element (or rather on its "negation") is unconstitutional;* at the same time, there are essentially no constitutional constraints on placing the burden of proof on the defendant with respect to an excuse.[†] Note, then, that the Model Penal Code, in § 2.09, does not identify duress as an "excuse," but as an "affirmative defense," which means that the defendant bears the burden of proof on this issue (or, more precisely, the burden of production, not of persuasion, under the Model Penal Code's definition of an affirmative defense, § 1.12: if there is no evidence to support the defense already on the record, based on the prosecution's case-in-chief, the defendant bears the burden of producing sufficient evidence to raise the issue, at which point the burden of persuasion, i.e., the burden of proof strictly speaking, shifts to the prosecution).

None of this, of course, makes any sense from the German perspective. The common law idea that the defendant has to prove a defense by a preponderance of evidence is alien to German procedural law. If the state convicts a person, the state has to prove beyond a reasonable doubt not only all objective and subjective elements of the crime, but also the non-existence of justifying or excusing circumstances. The defendant might be in a better position to alert the court to the possibility of such circumstances, but the burden of proof always lies with the state. If the German legislature were to consider the shifting the burden of proof, it seems likely that the German Federal Constitutional Court would declare such a law to be unconstitutional. The constitutional culpability principle (see Chapter 3) could be invoked along with the presumption of innocence, which under German constitutional law can be interpreted as requiring the state to bear the burden of proof.

In his dissenting opinion, Justice Breyer mentions that the question of burden of proof is decided differently in the Federal Circuits. From the German perspective, again, this would

---

* *In re Winship*, 397 U.S. 358 (1970).
[†] *Patterson v. New York*, 432 U.S. 197 (1977).

provoke sharp criticism because it can hardly be justified to defendants that such coincidental developments produce just outcomes. (Of course, the absence of a provision on duress, or for that matter, a comprehensive and systematic federal criminal code, is also not conducive to consistency in federal criminal law.*)

So-called circuit splits are not uncommon, even in criminal law, given that the U.S. Supreme Court, considering the scope of federal law and the Court's limited docket, does not, and cannot, take up every case in which a circuit split exists, though the existence of a circuit split certainly is among the reasons advocates raise in support of their application for a writ of certiorari, or "cert" for short, the granting of which signals the Court's decision to consider a case. At the same time, of course, adherence to the principle of *stare decisis*, or precedent, also is designed to assure consistency within a given body of law, and a given jurisdiction, so that once the U.S. Supreme Court resolves a circuit split, all federal courts are bound to follow the Supreme Court's decision, just as all lower federal courts within a given federal circuit are bound to follow the decisions of the federal circuit court that sits atop the federal judicial hierarchy in that circuit. (The same applies, analogously, to state courts.) From the perspective of a common law system accustomed to the principle of *stare decisis*, then, a system that does not follow this principle may invite similar questions about the possibility of inconsistent judicial decisions.

3. The German Criminal Code contained until 1975 a provision tailored to duress, § 52 Criminal Code old version (excerpted in a footnote to the 1954 decision of the German Federal Court of Justice excerpted above). In its 1954 decision, the Federal Court of Justice calls duress "coercion necessity" (*Nötigungsnotstand*)—reflecting the classification in German criminal law of duress as a subgroup of the larger group of necessity cases. When the German legislature revised the General Part of the Criminal Code in 1975 and introduced two general provisions about necessity (§§ 34, 35, see Chapter 13.B), the idea was that a more specific rule for coercion necessity was no longer needed. Therefore, the German Criminal Code now does not contain a norm referring explicitly to coercion necessity or duress.

The view that duress and necessity are closely related, as two sides of the same coin, is widespread in common law jurisdictions as well. To once again quote from *Hibbert*, the leading Canadian case on duress, comparing and contrasting duress, necessity, and self-defense:

> The defences of self-defence, necessity and duress all arise under circumstances where a person is subjected to an external danger, and commits an act that would otherwise be criminal as a way of avoiding the harm the danger presents. In the case of self-defence and duress, it is the intentional threats of another person that are the source of the danger, while in the case of necessity the danger is due to other causes, such as forces of nature, human conduct other than intentional threats of bodily harm, etc. Although this distinction may have important practical consequences, it is hard to see how it could act as the source of significant juristic differences between the three defences.

In Germany, the abolition of § 52 Criminal Code in 1975 opened a debate whether such cases now fall under § 34 (justifying necessity) or § 35 (excusing necessity) Criminal Code. Some argue that it does not make a difference if present danger stems from natural sources or a threat by a human being, and that the weighing of interests required in § 34 Criminal Code can lead to the result that the offender who commits a crime under coercion is justified. (There is a recent argument in favor of categorizing duress a justification, rather than an excuse, in the context of Anglo-American criminal law.† If one follows this opinion, in a case such as *Dixon v. United States* the defendants could point to a justification because the wrongdoing was of a minor nature while the threat was considerable.

In the common law literature, the distinction between personal and circumstantial duress also has been challenged, on the ground that the actor's blameworthiness does not depend on the

---

* On (the failure of) federal criminal code reform, see Ronald L. Gainer, "Federal Criminal Code Reform: Past and Future," 2 *Buffalo Criminal Law Review* (1998), 45.

† See Peter Westen and James Mangiafico, "The Criminal Defense of Duress: A Justification, Not an Excuse—And Why It Matters," 6 *Buffalo Criminal Law Review* (2003), 833, 937–9.

source of the threat, but on whether he or she reasonably could be expected to resist it. That distinction, however, is commonly drawn, also in the Model Penal Code, which apparently intended to preclude claims of circumstantial (or situational) duress indirectly by requiring "the use of, or a threat to use, *unlawful force*," which (in article 3) is defined, not as unjustified force, but as "force...employed without the consent of the person against whom it is directed and the employment of which constitutes an offense or actionable tort or would constitute such offense or tort except for a defense (such as the absence of intent, negligence, or mental capacity; duress; youth; or diplomatic status) not amounting to a privilege to use the force" (§ 3.11(1)). The Code drafters, it appears, were concerned about impunity: personal duress merely shifts liability from the coerced to the coercer, whereas situational duress eliminates it altogether. Is this a convincing rationale? Why else would it matter whether the coercing force is "unlawful"? If the force were lawful, would it be any less coercive?

According to the majority in the German literature, a criminal offense under duress can only be excused (§ 35 Criminal Code). The proponents of this view can point to the decision made in the former § 52 Criminal Code, which did not provide a justification but only an excuse. Moreover, if the criminal offense committed under the coercive influence is of a kind that might trigger self-defense of the victim (the offender was under a threat for his life and thus coerced to assault the victim, for instance), this victim should be entitled to self-defense. Under German law, self-defense presupposes an unlawful attack (see Chapter 7), and if the offender under duress were justified, this would imply that the victim was confronted with a lawful act. However, if the coerced offender is only excused, this cannot block the victim's right to self-defense (self-defense test, *Notwehrprobe*).

Apart from the context of the German doctrinal debate, which turns on details of German legislative history (and the frequently invoked self-defense test, which does not generate a rationale for a classification, but serves as a test whether the classification is sound, in the sense of not leading to absurd, or otherwise objectionable, results). What is at stake in this debate? Would it not be the case that, if the balance of interests favors the defendant, "duress" would qualify as a justification, since it satisfies, by hypothesis, the requirements of justifying necessity under § 34 Criminal Code? Isn't the point of duress precisely to provide a defense, if "only" an excuse rather than a justification, even in cases where the interest balancing does not favor the defendant?

4. In cases of coercion often a decisive question is: was there really a present danger, and could the offender have averted the danger in a different way? For perjury and other false testimony, the German regional court held that there is no danger if the threatening person is in custody while the threatened witness has to testify. Do you find this convincing? The German Federal Court of Justice accepted this assessment of danger but found a way out by pointing to the defendant's erroneous belief that there was a present danger. The next question would be whether the danger could be averted otherwise, or whether, as the U.S. Supreme Court puts it, there was a reasonable, legal alternative to violating the law.

It is not surprising that the test for duress resembles that for necessity, or balance of evils, on this point: after all, they both presuppose a situation of necessity. Now recall that the Model Penal Code drew a distinction between necessity and duress when it comes to the actor's responsibility for the necessity situation in the first place. Recklessly or negligently bringing about the necessity situation does not bar the necessity defense altogether; it limits criminal liability to any applicable offenses that require recklessness or negligence (§ 3.02(2)). In the case of duress, recklessness in this respect does preclude the defense; only negligence has the effect of limiting liability to a negligence offense, if any (§ 2.09(2)). See Chapter 13.B (causing the conditions of one's defense).

5. While the Model Penal Code limits the defense of duress in certain respects (e.g., personal duress only, requiring unlawful force, precluding recklessly caused necessity situation), it lacks other popular limitations. Unlike the German provision on excusing necessity, and other common law provisions, the Model Penal Code section on duress covers threats made to any person, not only relatives and those close to the defendant. Similarly, unlike duress provisions in several common law jurisdictions, the Model Penal Code's duress provision does not exclude any offenses from the scope of the defense; most notably, the Code does not bar the defense in cases of homicide, instead generally relying on the inquiry into the question whether the person under threat could reasonably have been expected to refrain from committing the offense.

The Model Penal Code's reasonableness test is discussed in the following excerpt from the New Jersey Supreme Court's opinion in *State v. Toscano*, 74 N.J. 421 (1977):

> Commentators have expressed dissatisfaction with the common law standard of duress. Stephen viewed the defense as a threat to the deterrent function of the criminal law, and argued that "it is at the moment when temptation is strongest that the law should speak most clearly and emphatically to the contrary." Stephen, 2 History of the Criminal Law in England 107 (1883). A modern refinement of this position is that the defense should be designed to encourage persons to act against their self-interest if a substantial percentage of persons in such a situation would do so. Hall, General Principles of Criminal Law (2d ed. 1960), 446–47. This standard would limit its applicability to relatively minor crimes and exclude virtually all serious crimes unless committed under threat of imminent death.
>
> Others have been more skeptical about the deterrent effects of a strict rule. As the Alabama Supreme Court observed in an early case:
>
> "That persons have exposed themselves to imminent peril and death for their fellow man, and that there are instances where innocent persons have submitted to murderous assaults, and suffered death, rather than take life, is well established; but such self sacrifice emanated from other motives than the fear of legal punishment." (97 Ala. 5, 12, 12 So. 301, 303 (1893))
>
> Building on this premise, some commentators have advocated a flexible rule which would allow a jury to consider whether the accused actually lost his capacity to act in accordance with "his own desire, or motivation, or will" under the pressure of real or imagined forces. The inquiry here would focus on the weaknesses and strengths of a particular defendant, and his subjective reaction to unlawful demands. Thus, the "standard of heroism" of the common law would give way, not to a "reasonable person" standard, but to a set of expectations based on the defendant's character and situation.
>
> The drafters of the Model Penal Code and the New Jersey Penal Code sought to steer a middle course between these two positions by focusing on whether the standard imposed upon the accused was one with which "normal members of the community will be able to comply..." They stated:
>
> "[L]aw is ineffective in the deepest sense, indeed it is hypocritical, if it imposes on the actor who has the misfortune to confront a dilemmatic choice, a standard that his judges are not prepared to affirm that they should and could comply with if their turn to face the problem should arise. Condemnation in such case is bound to be an ineffective threat; what is, however, more significant is that it is divorced from any moral base and is injust. Where it would be both 'personally and socially debilitating' to accept the actor's cowardice as a defense, it would be equally debilitating to demand that heroism be the standard of legality." (Model Penal Code s 2.09, Comment at 7 (Tent.Draft No. 10, 1960), quoting Hart, "The Aims of the Criminal Law," 23 Law & Contemp.Prob. 401, 414 and n. 31 (1958); New Jersey Model Penal Code s 2C:2B9, Commentary at 71 (1971).)
>
> Thus, they proposed that a court limit its consideration of an accused's "situation" to "stark, tangible factors which differentiate the actor from another, like his size or strength or age or health," excluding matters of temperament.

Why require "stark, tangible" factors? (What is a "stark, tangible" factor anyway?) Is it to prevent defendants from claiming characteristics that are difficult to confirm because they do not manifest themselves externally? (Often, courts and commentators express anxiety about abuse of the duress defense. Is this concern unique to duress, or more serious than in the case of other defenses?) Or is it also meant to retain an element of objectivity in the duress reasonableness test? Does it, or should it, differ from other reasonableness tests (reasonable beliefs in the presence of defense elements, or the absence of offense elements, say)?

6. Note the American and German cases excerpted above both feature women defendants. (So does a recent leading Canadian case on duress, *R. v. Ruzic*, [2001] 1 S.C.R. 687.) While there are also many duress cases with male defendants (including *Hibbert*, [1995] 2 S.C.R. 973, *Paquette*, [1977] 2 S.C.R. 189, and *Toscano*, 74 N.J. 421 (1977), cited above), if female defendants are overrepresented in duress cases, this may reflect persistent expectations and stereotypes about women's susceptibility to male influence, as captured most clearly in the traditional defense of *feme covert*, or coverture. Until the early 1970s, some American jurisdictions continued to recognize this defense, which established a presumption of coercion if a married woman committed an offense in the presence of her husband.* The practice was still widespread enough in 1962, the year of the Model Penal Code's publication, for the Code to expressly disavow it in its duress provision, § 2.09:

> (3) It is not a defense that a woman acted on the command of her husband, unless she acted under such coercion as would establish a defense under this Section. [The presumption that a woman, acting in the presence of her husband, is coerced is abolished.]

In England, a "marital coercion" defense, introduced in 1925 to replace the marital coercion *presumption*, persists to this day: "on a charge against a wife for any offence other than treason or murder it shall be a good defence to prove that the offence was committed in the presence of, and under the coercion of, the husband." Criminal Justice Act 1925, § 47. (For a recent invocation of the defense, see John F. Burns, "Official's Speeding Fine Builds to Lurid Scandal," *N.Y. Times*, February 16, 2013, at A16.)

7. *Sentencing.* If a duress defense is unsuccessful at trial, it may nonetheless affect the sentence imposed. The U.S. Sentencing Guidelines list "coercion and duress" among possible grounds for a downward departure from the prescribed guideline range in exceptional cases. (On the Guidelines, see Chapter 1.)

§ 5K2.12. Coercion and Duress (Policy Statement)

> If the defendant committed the offense because of serious coercion, blackmail or duress, under circumstances not amounting to a complete defense, the court may depart downward. The extent of the decrease ordinarily should depend on the reasonableness of the defendant's actions, on the proportionality of the defendant's actions to the seriousness of coercion, blackmail, or duress involved, and on the extent to which the conduct would have been less harmful under the circumstances as the defendant believed them to be. Ordinarily coercion will be sufficiently serious to warrant departure only when it involves a threat of physical injury, substantial damage to property or similar injury resulting from the unlawful action of a third party or from a natural emergency. Notwithstanding this policy statement, personal financial difficulties and economic pressures upon a trade or business do not warrant a downward departure.

B. Entrapment

The defense of entrapment is an odd fit for an analysis of criminal liability; it is an even odder fit than the defense of duress, which we discussed above, and with which it is often paired, as carrot and stick. (Despite these efforts at portraying entrapment and duress as two sides of the same compulsion coin, the distinction between enticement and threat so far has attracted far less attention than that, say, between commission and omission.) It is treated as a procedural doctrine in uncomfortable substantive garb. It comes in two varieties: objective and subjective, the objective variety being the more obviously procedural, and thus also more oddly fitting, of the two. Traditionally, entrapment—in Anglo-American criminal law at least—turned on an inquiry into the defendant's "predisposition" to commit the offense in question. If, and once, predisposition was present, state officials (or those acting on their behalf) could entrap the eventual defendant to their hearts' delight, without any effect on the defendant's criminal liability. (Unlike in German criminal law, the question of the entrapper's, rather than the entrappee's, criminal liability under ordinary norms of accessorial liability—see Chapter 10—generally did not attract much attention.) This had the practical effect of rendering the defense of entrapment essentially unavailable to anyone with a criminal record, as well as turning the consideration of the issue of entrapment into an

---

* See generally David Rosenberg, "Coverture in Criminal Law: Ancient 'Defender' of Married Women," 6 *U.C. Davis Law Review* (1973), 101.

inquiry into the defendant's "criminal" character in general. Instead, the Model Penal Code (and other jurisdictions) preferred to frame entrapment as an objective inquiry, in the sense of not focusing on the defendant's predisposition (which could be mistaken for a *sui generis* mental state requirement or a reflection of criminal character) but instead on the appropriateness of the behavior of state officials (and their surrogates) in the lead-up to the eventual commission of the offense. This addressed one problem, but created another: it now was unclear just what the question of entrapment had to do with the defendant's criminal liability, in other words why an inquiry into the procedural aspect of the case should affect the substantive question of liability. Different legal systems have found different ways to address this question, ranging from outright acquittal to a dismissal to consideration at sentencing.

People v. Calvano
Court of Appeals of New York
30 N.Y.2d 199, 282 N.E.2d 322 (1972)

Gibson, Judge.

The alleged commission by the defendant on November 15, 1968 of criminal acts unrelated to those for which he was on trial was proven by the People, who seek to justify the production of this ordinarily irrelevant evidence (1) as probative of disposition refuting the defense of entrapment, interposed to a charge of crime committed prior thereto, on November 11, 1968; and (2) as countering the defense of duress, interposed to a charge of crime committed thereafter, on November 19, 1968 . . .

Through the efforts of undercover police officers, aided by an informer, the defendant was indicted, and subsequently arrested and tried, upon charges of criminal possession of . . . and criminally selling a dangerous drug . . . , each committed on November 11, 1968, and with like possession and sale . . . , each committed on November 19, 1968. Defendant was, by verdict of a jury, acquitted of the . . . November 11 [charges] and convicted of the . . . November 19 [charges].

As to the November 11 transaction, involving a sale of heroin to the undercover officers, after they had been introduced to defendant by their informer, defendant . . . assert[ed] that he had been framed by the informer, . . . interpos[ing] the defense of entrapment.

As to the November 19 transaction, another sale to the same undercover officers was involved. Defendant, having interposed the defense of duress, testified that, following threats and physical compulsion by the officers, he gave to his friend, subsequently identified as an informer, $28 which the officers had given him and accompanied the informer to an unfamiliar area where the latter entered a house and returned with an envelope which defendant later gave to the officers.

On cross-examination bearing upon both the November 11 and November 19 transactions, defendant was asked whether, on November 15, 1968, he had possessed and had sold to these same officers a substance which he represented to be heroin, and this he categorically denied. Thereafter, the People recalled one of the detectives, who testified that on November 15 defendant sold to him and to the other detective envelopes containing a white powder, [which turned out not to be heroin] . . . There was and is no suggestion that any conviction followed and ordinarily, of course, the People would be bound by defendant's denials on cross-examination and would not be permitted to produce proof in contradiction. The People . . . contend that it "was properly admitted to establish the defendant's intent relative to the sales of heroin charged, after the element of intent was placed squarely in issue by the defenses of entrapment and duress."

. . . Section 40.05 of the Penal Law provides for [the defense of entrapment], as follows: "In any prosecution for an offense, it is an affirmative defense that the defendant engaged in the proscribed conduct because he was induced or encouraged to do so by a public servant, or by a person acting in cooperation with a public servant, seeking to obtain evidence against him for the purpose of criminal prosecution, and when the methods used to obtain such evidence were such as to create a substantial risk that the offense would be committed by a person not otherwise disposed to commit it. Inducement or encouragement to commit an offense means active inducement or encouragement. Conduct merely affording a person an opportunity to commit an offense does not constitute entrapment."

Duress is also constituted a defense, and section 40.00 of the Penal Law, defining it, provides, so far as here pertinent: "In any prosecution for an offense, it is an affirmative defense that the defendant engaged in the proscribed conduct because he was coerced to do so by the use or threatened imminent use of unlawful physical force upon him or a third person, which force or threatened force a person of reasonable firmness in his situation would have been unable to resist."

It is provided by section 25.00 (subd. 2) of the Penal Law that when an affirmative defense is raised, "the defendant has the burden of establishing such defense by a preponderance of the evidence" and we have recently found unwarranted the "(c)oncern (that) has been expressed whether constitutional due process limitations are invaded by placing the burden of persuasion on a defendant with respect to the defense of entrapment."

Thus, the defendant was under the burden of proving entrapment by showing that he was "a person not... disposed to commit" the drug crimes charged, and of proving duress by satisfying the jury that he was coerced to commit them by the use or threat of force overcoming his will; and the People... were, therefore, entitled to refute his proof by evidence of his intent or disposition to commit criminal acts of that nature...

The People contend that proof of another crime is proper to rebut the defense of duress for the same reason that renders it competent to refute the claim of entrapment, that is, to rebut the denial, implicit in each defense, of any criminal intent. Concluding, as we have, that proof of other sales would be competent to rebut the entrapment defense interposed in a narcotics prosecution, it is rather clear that parity of reasoning compels the same conclusion with respect to the duress defense. Under each defense there is asserted, and a defendant may prima facie prove, absence of the criminal intent ordinarily inferable from the admitted acts of commission; under one he asserts that he was persuaded, under the other that he was coerced, i.e., "induced or encouraged" in one case (entrapment) or "coerced" in the other (duress). Indeed, the terms "induced" and "coerced" differ only in respect of the pressures exerted; so that, if prior criminal acts of the same nature may properly be proved to rebut the defense that defendant was "coerced" into the transgression, like proof may properly be received in refutation of a claim that he was "induced or encouraged" to transgress. In one case, as in the other, his intent— meaning his will and volition—is overcome by force or by persuasion, as the case may be, exerted by another. And thus, because—and only because—defendant tenders the issue of innocent intent which has admitted acts would otherwise belie, the People should be permitted, in respect of each defense, to prove a disposition inconsistent with an intent or disposition free of criminality...

Appellant contends, however, that insofar as the proof of his acts of November 15 was tendered to refute his defense of entrapment asserted against the charges of crime committed November 11, the evidence was not relevant—that "predisposition" may not be shown by proof of subsequent acts. Ordinarily, of course, the statutory test of whether a defendant was not "disposed to commit" a drug offense would look to prior acts; but that is not to say that acts subsequently occurring or physical conditions existing as of a later time may not in some cases reflect a disposition or condition antedating the criminal act charged; and certainly they may have that effect when shown as part of a continuing transaction or a chain of events initiated before and continuing after the offense in issue. In other cases, a subsequent incident alone may sometimes be of such a nature and so related to disposition as to render proof of the incident relevant.... In this case, clearly, proof of defendant's alleged criminal acts intermediate the November 11 and November 19 incidents was, under the circumstances, relevant to the jury's consideration of defendant's disposition and volition...

Model Penal Code

§ 2.13. Entrapment

(1) A public law enforcement official or a person acting in cooperation with such an official perpetrates an entrapment if for the purpose of obtaining evidence of the commission of an offense, he induces or encourages another person to engage in conduct constituting such offense by either:

(a) making knowingly false representations designed to induce the belief that such conduct is not prohibited; or

(b) employing methods of persuasion or inducement which create a substantial risk that such an offense will be committed by persons other than those who are ready to commit it.

(2) Except as provided in Subsection (3) of this Section, a person prosecuted for an offense shall be acquitted if he proves by a preponderance of evidence that his conduct occurred in response to an entrapment. The issue of entrapment shall be tried by the Court in the absence of the jury.

(3) The defense afforded by this Section is unavailable when causing or threatening bodily injury is an element of the offense charged and the prosecution is based on conduct causing or threatening such injury to a person other than the person perpetrating the entrapment.

German Federal Court of Justice
1 StR 221/99, BGHSt 45, 321 (November 18, 1999)

Facts

In July 1997 a police informer (PI) spoke to the defendant, an Italian citizen, about an insurance matter. In the course of the conversation, the PI—a fellow countrymen of the defendant—asked if he knew someone who could get a kg of cocaine. The defendant stated that he did not carry out any such transactions, and he also had no appropriate contacts. In the following weeks, the PI made two further inquiries. He held out to the defendant the prospect of a profit in the sum of about 5000 DM. The defendant again refused each time. Only after a fourth inquiry—about a month after the first—the defendant promised that he would ask around. The defendant spoke to "E.," known by him to be a drug consumer, who referred him to a mutual acquaintance, the co-defendant I. I. thought it possible that a further fellow countryman, the co-defendant C., from whom he regularly obtained cocaine for his own consumption, had a sufficient supply at his disposal. I. was introduced to the PI by the defendant. The PI explained that there was a financially powerful purchaser behind him who was ready to pay more than 100,000 DM for 1 kg of cocaine. I. promised to try to obtain a supplier. The defendant remained part of the operation as intermediary to the PI. The co-defendant I. turned to the co-defendant C., who asked his supplier. The supplier was ready to sell a kg of cocaine for 60,000 DM. With the prospect of a purchase price of 100,000 DM, the defendant and the two co-defendants expected a profit in the sum of 40,000 DM, which they intended to share with the PI. The participants reached an agreement that the transaction should be conducted in October 1997. Between the defendant I. and the PI there were several conversations regarding the place for handing over the drug and the method of payment, in which I. acted as a spokesperson and the defendant assisted.

At the handover of about 1 kg of cocaine to the police fake purchaser introduced by the PI, and after receipt of the purchase price, the three defendants were arrested. The PI's manager, an official of the Bavarian Criminal Police Office, had given the PI in summer or early summer 1997 a promise of confidentiality, and instructed the PI "not to incite anyone." He was informed by the PI about the events from July 1997: "To start with, no names had been mentioned, and everything had been fairly vague." The regional court found that the initiative for the drug transaction came only from the PI, and the defendant was only ready after the fourth attempt to take part in it. The criminal chamber has accepted that there was not the slightest ground for saying that the defendant had had other opportunities to obtain the drug than "the gradual and relatively time-consuming establishment of contacts to suppliers" of drugs via the co-defendants. The criminal chamber regarded the crime definition of impermissible dealing with narcotics in other than a trivial quantity [§ 29a para. 1 nr. 2 Narcotics Act*—Eds.] as fulfilled. In assessing the punishment, it declined, on the basis of an overall assessment, a less serious case, but has considered, in the defendant's favor, his confession and his prior life which was essentially free of convictions. "The persistent provocation to commit the crime by an agent provocateur, which was not in any way fostered by the defendant in the initial phase was also" of "considerable importance".

The regional court sentenced the defendant to imprisonment for three years and nine months for impermissible trading in narcotics of an amount that was not trivial. The defendant's appeal in law objected that the regional court had not sufficiently considered the use of the agent provocateur. The appeal in law was partially successful and led to the quashing of the order as to legal consequences; in other respects it was unfounded.

Reasons

B.

I.

The Senate has examined whether the regional court had sufficiently taken into account the fact that the defendant had been induced to carry out the crime by a PI. This did not amount to a procedural obstacle. The verdict is free of legal error. On the other hand the sentencing decision cannot stand. According to the findings, the defendant had been induced to carry out the crime which was the subject of the judgment by an impermissible provocation which was attributable to the state, which represents a violation of the principle of a fair trial under art. 6 para. 1 sentence 1 of the ECHR. This

---

* [§ 29a Narcotics Act

(1) With not less than one year imprisonment will be punished who
    1. as a person over the age of 21 years gives drugs to a person under 18 years, . . .
    2. deals with narcotics in other than a trivial quantity, produces or possesses them.

(2) In less serious cases the punishment will be imprisonment between three months and five years.—Eds.]

violation should have been expressed by the regional court in the reasons for the judgment and appropriately compensated for in the sentence . . .

II.

The Federal Court of Justice has already given attention to the question of provocation to commit crimes on several occasions:

1. The employment of informers (PIs) and undercover investigating police officers (UIPs) is in principle permissible for combating especially dangerous crimes which are difficult to resolve, and this includes in particular dealing in drugs. This also applies if these persons act as agents provocateurs (see BGHSt 32, 115, 121f.; BGHSt 32, 345, 346; BGHSt 40, 211, 215; BGHSt 41, 42, 43; BVerfGE 57, 250, 284; BVerfG [3rd chamber of the Second Senate], NJW 1987, 1874, 1875 . . .; finally BGH, NJW 1998, 767, besides this BVerfG, Judgment of April 29, 1998, 2 BvR 174/98 . . .).

2. Previously the views of the Criminal Senates [of the German Federal Court of Justice—Eds.] about the legal consequences of exceeding the boundaries of the permissible use of agents provocateurs were not uniform. The 2nd Criminal Senate had originally held the view that exceeding the boundaries led to forfeiture of the state's criminal claim and created an obstacle to proceedings . . . In the meantime, the 1st Criminal Senate had decided in its seminal judgment of May 23, 1984 that such an influence did not cause an obstacle to proceedings, but had to be considered within the framework of sentencing (BGHSt 32, 345, 345). In this decision, the Senate emphasized that conduct by the PI provoking the crime could only be accepted within boundaries set by the constitutional rule of law principle. The boundaries of permissible provocation to commit crimes would be exceeded if an overall assessment showed that the conduct of the police agent provocateur had gained such importance that the perpetrator's own contribution took second place in comparison to it. In the case to be decided at that time the Senate had, on factual grounds alone, not established that these boundaries were exceeded. It had regarded it as decisive that the influence on the defendant there was limited to repeated enticing offers. The defendant had reacted from the start not by declining them but by showing a continually growing interest and meeting on several occasions with the agent provocateur outside his homeland . . .

The Senate has stated that even exceeding the boundaries of permissible employment of an agent provocateur did not lead to an procedural obstacle "because of forfeiture of the state's claim to criminal punishment due to contradictory conduct (BGHSt 32, 345) and also not to the exclusion of evidence (BGHSt 32, 345, 355). It has instead regarded any influence of the agent provocateur on the perpetrator as an important ground for reduction in punishment (sentencing solution). The area of discretion available to the judge of fact extended—depending on the lasting nature of the influence— from declining to find an especially serious case, in spite of the presence of one or more situations where punishment could be increased, to the acceptance of a less serious case and even to the discontinuance of proceedings under §§ 153, 153a German Criminal Code of Procedure* in the case of a misdemeanor . . .

This case law favoring the sentencing solution has been followed by the 2nd, 4th and 5th Criminal Senates of the Federal Court of Justice (BGH, NJW 1985, 1764; NStZ 1995, 506; NStZ 1999, 501 . . .

3. In the literature, the sentencing solution has overwhelmingly met with approval . . .

III.

In cases of employment of an agent provocateur in breach of the Convention, the Senate regards the sentencing solution as appropriate to create the compensation necessary in the individual case for violation of the Convention.

1. The ECtHR in its judgment of June 9, 1998, in *Teixeira de Castro v. Portugal* saw a violation of the right to a fair trial protected by art. 6 ECHR in a drug transaction provoked by a police officer and in sentencing the complainant to imprisonment for six years for drug dealing . . . The ECtHR came to the conclusion "that the activities of both police officers went beyond those of an undercover investigator, because they incited the commission of a crime, and because there are no indications that this would have been committed without their intervention. This intervention as well as its utilization in the disputed criminal proceedings meant that the complainant did not have a fair trial ab initio and in the end result. Therefore a violation of art. 6 para. 1 ECHR is present" . . .

The decision of the ECtHR was based on the following facts: two plain clothes officers of the Portuguese police, posing as drug purchasers, approached a person who was suspected of dealing in drugs in small quantities. In spite of persistent questioning, the person could not name any dealers in hashish. The officers then stated that they were now interested in buying heroin. The person approached replied that the complainant, whose address he did not know, was someone who

* [See Chapter 5.C—Eds.]

could find that kind of thing. After ascertaining the address, they then called together on the complainant. The officers explained that they wanted it to buy 20 g of heroin for the equivalent of just under 2000 DM. The complainant agreed. He drove to an intermediary, who bought 20 g of heroin mixture from a supplier, which the complainant handed over to the police officers. The complainant was arrested and sentenced to six years imprisonment for the drug transaction on the basis of, amongst other things, the statements of the two police officers.

In order to examine the question of whether the activities of the two police officers went beyond the permissible boundaries, the ECtHR has taken the following circumstances as a basis: It remained unclear whether suspicion had existed against the complainant, who had no previous convictions, before the provocation. In any case there was no proof that the defendant had been ready to commit crimes.... Investigatory proceedings had also not been instituted previously against the complainant. The crime had therefore been committed because of the exertion of influence by the police, who had not merely "passively investigated," and the conviction had essentially been based on the statements of the two police officers who had been investigating undercover.

2. This interpretation of the Convention on Human Rights by the ECtHR must be taken into account.
...The ECtHR emphasizes that the admissibility of evidence is primarily regulated by the provisions of national law, and it is in principle a matter for the national courts to assess the evidence collected by them. The task of the Court consists in establishing whether the proceedings in their totality, including the presentation of evidence, were fair...

b) The Human Rights Convention which, according to art. II Ratification Act of August 7, 1952, has become part of German law and therefore ranks as an (ordinary) federal statute (BVerfGE 74, 358, 370), must be considered as an aid to interpretation in the application of national law. According to the case law of the Federal Constitutional Court, when statutes are applied in criminal proceedings, the court must always examine whether the application and interpretation are in harmony with the international law obligations of the Federal Republic of Germany "because it must not be assumed that the legislature, in so far as it has not clearly said so, intends to deviate from international law obligations of the Federal Republic of Germany or to facilitate the violation of such obligations" (BVerfGE 74, 358, 370).

c) Notwithstanding some special features of the facts assessed by the ECtHR, the observations of the Court are relevant in cases of the present kind as well.

aa) In the facts assessed by the ECtHR, the police officials had received an indication from a third party that the complainant was someone "who could find such stuff"...It was unclear whether "the competent authorities had rational grounds for the assumption that the complainant was a drug dealer"; he had "on the contrary no previous convictions," and no investigatory proceedings had previously been instituted against him. In the present proceedings there was, according to the findings, no indication that the defendant had dealt in drugs before the provocation to commit the crime. Investigatory proceedings had also not yet been instituted against him. He gave an express refusal to the first question by the PI and only agreed a month later, after the fourth contact, "to ask around"...

bb) There is no difference which is significant for the purpose of the decision between the Portuguese police officers (investigating undercover) whose provocation to commit a crime has been assessed by the ECtHR, and the PI used in the case of the defendant...In a factual respect, the activity of the PI which is to be attributed to the state corresponds to the effects produced by the UIP in Portugal as assessed by the ECtHR...

3. The decision of the ECtHR of June 6, 1998, that the complainant had not had a fair trial, and that therefore he had to be compensated for the deprivation of freedom suffered, does not mean that criminal proceedings after a provocation to commit a crime by a police agent provocateur must not be initiated because of an obstacle to proceedings.

a) The finding by the ECtHR that the activities of both police officers as well as the use of the statements in the criminal proceedings which were the subject of the dispute had caused the complainant to have had "no fair trial ab initio" (no 39 of the reasons) could admittedly indicate that the Court assumed that criminal proceedings ought not to have been implemented against the complainant...In the judgment of the ECtHR of June 9, 1998, it is in the end left open whether provocation to commit a crime constitutes a violation of the principle of a fair trial on its own, or whether such provocation is only a breach of the Convention in combination with the later criminal proceedings (in particular the "fairly severe punishment").

b) Recognition of a procedural obstacle would only fall to be considered in German law if the judge of fact could not take provocation to commit a crime into account in the sentencing decision, by refraining from punishment, or otherwise by application and interpretation of criminal law and criminal procedural law in an appropriate manner (thus also BGHSt 35, 137, 140, on the violation of the requirement for expedition under art. 6 ECHR).

... The following considerations argue against seeing a procedural obstacle in German procedural law in an impermissible provocation to commit a crime: the uniform treatment of all cases of provocation does not do justice to the great differences, in particular in relation to the extent of the subsequent culpable behavior of a person provoked. If, for example, a so far unsuspected drug dealer is by chance asked by a PI whether he could obtain any drugs, and the person approached then independently develops extensive activities which lead to the import of large quantities of especially dangerous narcotics, it would be unreasonable on grounds of justice to accept a procedural obstacle. Likewise having regard to the intensity of any initial suspicion, to the persistence in the provocation to commit a crime, and the degree of attributability of the actions of private individuals to the state, there can be borderline cases, and cases which in relation to the guilt of the person provoked are far apart from each other ... Recognition of a procedural obstacle would amount to the principle "all or nothing" rather than assessing the different circumstances ...

5. If a person who is unsuspected, and at first not inclined to commit a crime, is induced to do so by a PI managed by an officeholder in a manner which is attributable to the state, and if this leads to criminal proceedings, this is not compatible with the right to a fair trial under art. 6 para. 1 sentence 1 of the ECHR ... Admittedly not all provocation to commit crimes by a PI is impermissible:

The deployment of a PI is based on the objectives recognized by the case law of uncovering criminal structures, crushing latent criminality or preventing the continuance of long-term crimes (BGHSt 32, 115, 122). In so far as the activity of a PI relates to purely obtaining information without concrete suspicion of crime, the deployment has a preventive purpose of averting danger. The activity of the PI can however extend to co-operation in crimes, and even to their initiation. In this case the PI becomes an agent provocateur. Affirmation of the permissibility of such provocation by a PI can point to the danger posed by the persons to be enticed and the need to stop them from committing future crimes.

Provocation to commit a crime is however only permissible if the PI is deployed against a person who is suspected ... of having participated in a crime already committed or being ready to commit a future crime; adequate factual grounds must be present for this. This applies independently of whether the deployment of the PI originally (up to the time of the provocation) served the preventive aversion of danger or from the outset the purpose of investigating crimes already committed. The legality of the deployment of an agent provocateur must, even in the case of "mixed purposes" be assessed in a uniform way by the rules in the Criminal Procedure Code (Rieß, in: Löwe/Rosenberg, StPO, 24th edit., § 163 marginal no. 64) ...

According to this standard, there is no provocation to commit a crime if a PI, without exerting any other influence, merely asks a third party whether he could obtain narcotics. Likewise there is no provocation if the PI only exploits obviously recognizable preparedness to commit or to continue the commission of crimes. On the other hand, the PI will be active as an agent provocateur provoking the crime if, over and above merely "joining in," he influences and stimulates the perpetrator in the direction of awakening preparedness to commit the crime or intensification the planning of the crime to a significant degree (see Rieß, in: Löwe/Rosenberg, § 163 marginal no. 66) ...

IV.

The sentencing in the judgment under challenge does not do justice to the requirements of a fair trial when assessing an impermissible state provocation to commit a crime ...

The findings do not permit the rejection of a less serious case in accordance with § 29a para. 2 Narcotics Act by the regional court and the imposition of a sentence of imprisonment of three years and nine months. In the light of the above observations, a sanction in the region of the minimum punishment is suggested, and detailed explanations would have been needed as to why the criminal chamber deviated so far from the minimum punishment in spite of the defendant's not very important contribution to the crime and the instrumentalization of someone not previously suspected by impermissible state provocation to commit the crime.

Jacqueline E. Ross,
"Tradeoffs in Undercover Investigations: A Comparative Perspective,"
69 *University of Chicago Law Review* (2002), 1501

In the United States, but almost nowhere else, entrapment is a defense wholly relieving the defendant from liability. Most Western European legal systems instead treat entrapment as a mode of complicity that fails to excuse the target but implicates the investigator in the crime. Defining entrapment subjectively rather than objectively, the American test largely focuses on the offender's predisposition. Even powerful inducements will fall short of entrapment if the offender is predisposed to commit the crime. By contrast, the offender's predispositions are less important to

European legal systems that focus on the undercover agent's complicity. Suppose an agent offered a suspect too tempting an opportunity to commit a crime—securing, for instance, essential resources such as hard-to-get ingredients for a bomb or criminal contacts that the offender would not have been likely to locate on his own. If so, the agent may be complicit in the attempted crime, despite the target's subjective willingness to commit it. Even if the investigator has not entrapped the target, he may himself have engaged in illegal conduct by handling contraband, transferring funds, or using false documents. European legal systems treat such conduct as criminal unless a law expressly exempts the investigator from liability for specified acts . . . .

Agents incur a risk of criminal liability not only by participating in crimes undercover, but also by postponing the arrest of targets until the conclusion of the covert investigation . . . . If a country lacks prosecutorial discretion and requires prosecution of all apparent offenses committed by police officials and civilians alike, undercover operatives may face a very real danger of punishment unless they confine their activities within legislatively defined bounds.

NOTES

1. Under the heading "entrapment" (in Germany, the expression "provocation"—as in *agent provocateur*—is common) we have listed cases that deal with consequences of clandestine police activities, conduct by plainclothes officers (police officers not in uniform), undercover agents (police officers who assume a different identity), or police informers (who are not part of the police force but work under the supervision of a managing police officer).

One question that appears in this context (see the excerpt by Jacqueline Ross) is whether police officers or police informers can themselves become criminal defendants if they have overstepped the scope of permissible conduct. The legal situation in Germany corresponds to Ross's account: if an officer or informant fulfills the definition of a crime (by purchasing narcotics, receiving child pornography via internet etc.), he or she is punishable—unless a justification is provided either by the Criminal Code or the Code of Criminal Procedure (which regulates the investigation of past crimes), or the German states' police laws (which concern the prevention of future events). (German law distinguishes between backward-looking (investigative) and forward-looking (preventive) functions of the police; the former is governed by the federal Codes of Criminal Law and Criminal Procedure, the latter by state police statutes. See Chapter 5.) Often, undercover agents and police informers act for "mixed purposes" (investigation of both past and future crimes). In these cases, the German Federal Court of Justice in the decision excerpted above states that the conduct must be justified according to the Code of Criminal Procedure.

While the legal situation is simple (no justification means punishability), it would be naïve to expect that this will always be executed. We have described the rule of compulsory prosecution (*Legalitätsprinzip*) as one of the cornerstones of German criminal procedural law (see Chapter 5.C), but in real life, obviously, one has to expect imperfection, especially if those instigating criminal investigations would be pursuing them against colleagues.

The same discrepancy between norm and fact characterizes the application of criminal law to state officials, and police officers, in general; using the American criminal process as the backdrop, possibly criminal conduct needs to be reported (by a concerned bystander, if there is one, by a suspect, who may have little interest in pursuing the matter, or a fellow police officer), reported cases need to be internally investigated, investigated cases need to be brought to the attention of a prosecutor, the prosecutor needs to decide to pursue the matter, a grand jury needs to be willing to indict, a trial jury (or judge) needs to be willing to convict, and a judge needs to be willing to impose a meaningful sentence. Consider, as one notorious example, the struggle to prosecute the police officers who were videotaped brutally beating Rodney King in Los Angeles, in 1991. After they were acquitted in state court, they were prosecuted in federal court. Even after their conviction there, the trial judge dramatically reduced their sentence on the basis of a host of mitigating factors, including their special vulnerability as prison inmates.*

---

* See *United States v. Koon*, 833 F. Supp. 769 (C.D. Cal. 1993), aff'd in part & rev'd in part, 518 U.S. 81 (1996) (discussed in Chapter 1.A.i).

Entrapment is different, however, because it amounts to the criminalization of police work itself, rather than the use of criminal law to deal with police violence or other forms of abuse of power. Entrapment paradoxically provides an opportunity for criminal conduct, for the purpose of law enforcement, to ferret out crime. It is not criminal conduct by itself, but indirectly, through imputation of the "offender's" conduct to the entrapper/instigator-facilitator, under the application of ordinary rules of accessorial liability (see Chapter 10). (Of course, the entrapper may, along the way, also commit criminal offenses as a principal, perhaps to insinuate himself into the "target's" favor.)

It is this obvious question that has received little attention in American criminal law, in theory and in practice: when is the entrapper criminally liable for the entrappee's criminal conduct? (Instead, entrapment is considered almost exclusively in light of its possible relevance to the criminal liability of the *entrapped*, as discussed below in Note 2.)

If the entrapper intentionally facilitated, or solicited, the commission of an offense by the entrapped, why is the latter's criminal conduct not imputed to the latter, and, if so, why is the entrapper not subject to criminal liability (assuming the other offense elements are satisfied)? If, for instance, the entrapper facilitated (never mind solicited!) the commission of a homicide, why is he or she not liable for at least negligent homicide, if not manslaughter (i.e., reckless homicide), assuming absence of intention (in the sense of knowledge or purpose) with respect to the result element of death? (Presumably *not* because he or she lacked the requisite accessorial intent, which no more requires a "criminal" motive than does intent in any other criminal doctrinal context; see Chapter 8.A.) Would the entrapper have to rely on a defense of abandonment (renunciation)?* Or a justification? (Surely not an excuse.) Which one? Necessity? Law enforcement? Public duty? Under what legal authority? Set out where?

2. The second set of problems concerns the impact of entrapment or provocation on the legal outcome in the proceedings against the person who was entrapped or provoked. One first question is which conduct of police agents and informers, and at what time, prior to the commission of a crime influences its legal assessment.[†] Another question concerns the nature of the legal consequences: a substantive defense, a procedural device, or merely a reason to mitigate punishment? While the Model Penal Code and the statutes following it address these questions, there is nothing to be found in the German Criminal Code. The notion of provocation and its impact is developed in case law. Here again, we have an example why it would be erroneous to expect that in Germany, commonly labeled a "civil law system" in contrast to "common law systems," every detail of criminal law is codified. Strict requirements for codification derived from *nulla poena sine lege* (no punishment without law, art. 103 para. 2 Basic Law, see Chapter 2) only apply to the offense definitions in the special part of the Criminal Code. There are considerable gaps in the general part of the German Criminal Code with respect to general principles, definitions of concepts, justifications, and excuses. These gaps must be filled by case law.

Why would the principle of legality not apply to matters other than offense definitions? (Does it matter which theory of punishment one adopts?) Consider the various aspects of the principle: specificity, legislativity, prospectivity, publicity (see Chapter 2). What if the legislature eliminated the entire general part? Transferred the general part into a separate code? Transformed it into a set of regulations or instructions, say, for judges, or prosecutors, or police officers? Defense attorneys? Witnesses? Defendants? Suspects? Researchers? What if these guidelines were not published? Is the idea that there are different types of criminal law norms (conduct rules and decision rules, say), and different parts of a code, are addressed to different audiences (the public, state officials)?[‡] That it would be "functional" to codify each

---

* See Model Penal Code § 2.06(6)(c) ("he terminates his complicity prior to the commission of the offense and (i) wholly deprives it of effectiveness in the commission of the offense; or (ii) gives timely warning to the law enforcement authorities or otherwise makes proper effort to prevent the commission of the offense").

† See, e.g., *Jacobson v. United States*, 503 U.S. 540 (1992).

‡ See Meir Dan-Cohen, "Decision Rules and Conduct Rules: On Acoustic Separation in Criminal Law," 97 *Harvard Law Review* (1984), 625.

set of rules separately (in a code of conduct, and a code of adjudication, say)?* Would it be constitutional? Consistent with the principle of legality? Are there any constitutional constraints on the legislature's decision about what to include in the general part? Is there a constitutional minimum general part of a criminal code?

3. Which conduct should count as impermissible entrapment or provocation, to be taken into account in favor of the entrapped or provoked defendant? Ross highlights differences between American and European law. However, if one compares the two decisions, by the Court of Appeals of New York and the German Federal Court of Justice, similarities also appear. Both courts presuppose that entrapment or provocation requires conduct by a public servant or a person acting in cooperation with a public servant. This feature obviously does not relate to the defendant's perception as the defendant is unaware of cooperating with someone representing the state. If one were to describe the psychological situation, it would not make sense to assume that undercover agents and police informers exert stronger psychological influence than a private person, for instance, a defendant's close friend or partner.

That said, the focus on the defendant's predisposition to commit the offense, prior to state inducement, reflects the subjective aspect of the entrapment defense (in its subjective version). Note, however, that the Model Penal Code rejected the subjective version of entrapment for an objective one. Subjective entrapment focuses on the defendant, and on the defendant's "predisposition" to commit the offense in particular; in the presence of predisposition, state inducement is immaterial.

The inquiry into "predisposition" has proved difficult to distinguish from a wide ranging exploration of the defendant's criminal character or lifestyle, while at the same time limiting the scope of the defense. Consider the following entrapment instruction in a New York case: "In general the purpose of the defense of entrapment is to prevent a conviction of persons who *although not criminals or predisposed to become criminals*, nevertheless commit a crime because induced or encouraged to do so by pressure exerted by the police or people acting in cooperation with them" (emphasis added). This instruction was rejected on appeal, *People v. Missrie*, 300 A.D.2d 35, 751 N.Y.S.2d 16 (2002), on the ground that the "although not criminals" phrase left the jury with the "erroneous impression that the defense is available to 'non-criminals' only and thus strips a defendant with a criminal record of the benefit of the defense as a matter of law." Instead, the court argued, "[a] defendant's criminal record is only one factor to be considered by the jury in assessing his predisposition; an instruction that renders the entrapment defense unavailable to a defendant with a criminal record precludes the jury from considering any other factor." Can this "erroneous impression" be prevented through a more carefully phrased instruction, or is it inevitable in a predisposition-centered account of entrapment?[†]

Objective entrapment, by contrast, focuses on the state; it is concerned with state misconduct, not the predisposition of offenders. Under the Model Penal Code, the doctrine of entrapment serves not to safeguard the "innocence of the defendant" but "to deter wrongful conduct on the part of the government." Model Penal Code Commentaries § 2.13, at 406–7. Under an objective view of entrapment, in other words, the "innocence" of the defendant is beside the point:

> Permissible police activity does not vary according to the particular defendant concerned; surely if two suspects have been solicited at the same time in the same manner, one should not go to jail simply because he has been convicted before and is said to have a criminal disposition.
>
> *Sherman v. United States*, 356 U.S. 369, 383
> (1958) (Frankfurter, J., concurring)
> (quoted in Model Penal Code Commentaries § 2.13, at 412).

---

* Paul H. Robinson, Peter D. Greene, and Natasha R. Goldstein, "Making Criminal Codes Functional: A Code of Conduct and a Code of Adjudication," 86 *Journal of Criminal Law and Criminology* (1996), 304.

† See also *United States v. Mendoza-Prado*, 314 F.3d 1099 (9th Cir. 2002) ("[t]he character of the defendant is one of the elements—indeed, it is an essential element—to be considered in determining predisposition").

Now, many jurisdictions that follow the traditional, subjective, approach to entrapment, including New York and federal law, supplement this *criminal law* defense with a *constitutional* defense of objective entrapment: "outrageous government (mis)conduct." This defense, however, may be so narrow as to be illusory. It originates from *United States v. Russell*, 411 U.S. 423 (1973), where the U.S. Supreme Court, in dictum, remarked that "we may some day be presented with a situation in which the conduct of law enforcement agents is so outrageous that due process principles would absolutely bar the government from invoking judicial processes to obtain a conviction." Since then, federal courts have been generally hostile to the defense, declaring it "moribund," *United States v. Santana*, 6 F.3d 1 (1st Cir. 1993), and even "stillborn," *United States v. Boyd*, 55 F.3d 239 (7th Cir. 1995). State courts have been somewhat more sympathetic.* In a leading case, *People v. Isaacson*, 44 N.Y.2d 511 (1978), the New York Court of Appeals listed "illustrative" factors to test an outrageous conduct defense:

(1) whether the police manufactured a crime which otherwise would not likely have occurred, or merely involved themselves in an ongoing criminal activity;
(2) whether the police themselves engaged in criminal or improper conduct repugnant to a sense of justice;
(3) whether the defendant's reluctance to commit the crime is overcome by appeals to humanitarian instincts such as sympathy or past friendship, by temptation of exorbitant gain, or by persistent solicitation in the face of unwillingness; and
(4) whether the record reveals simply a desire to obtain a conviction with no reading that the police motive is to prevent further crime or protect the populace.

In the view of the German Federal Court of Justice, the crucial point in the discussion about entrapment and provocation is that the state forfeits (or is estopped from exercising) its right to criminal punishment if state officials have induced the commission of crime. Inducing the crime with one hand, while punishing it with the other is contradictory conduct. (Compare the defense of ignorance of law as executive estoppel, based on good-faith reliance on an official misstatement of law, see, e.g., MPC § 2.04(3); *People v. Studifin*, 132 Misc. 2d 326 (N.Y. Sup. Ct. 1986); see also *United States v. Nichols*, 21 F.3d 1016, 1018 (10th Cir. 1994) (constitutional, due process, defense of "entrapment by estoppel" implicated where "an agent of the government affirmatively misleads a party as to the state of the law and that party proceeds to act on the misrepresentation so that criminal prosecution of the actor implicates due process concerns"; defendant's reliance must be "reasonable in light of the identity of the agent, the point of law misrepresented, and the substance of the misrepresentation").)

While the first requirement for entrapment (public servant or person acting in cooperation with a public servant) is not overly problematic, the more difficult question is: what kind of conduct remains within the range of undercover agents' and informers' acceptable communication and interactions with potential offenders, and what kind of conduct constitutes legally relevant entrapment or provocation? Again, the approaches are comparable. The framework provided by the German Federal Court of Justice corresponds to § 2.13(1)(b) Model Penal Code. According to German case law, it is permissible to ask, to join in, and to exploit an "obviously recognizable preparedness," but not to influence and motivate the perpetrator in the direction of beginning to develop preparedness to commit the crime. (Think again about the supposed irrelevance of motive to criminal liability, Chapter 8.A.)

4. But comparative analysis reveals a difference in the area of legal consequences. Under American law, entrapment leads to acquittal. From the perspective of German criminal law doctrine, a question towards the proponents of this approach would be: why? Entrapment or provocation cannot justify the crime; it does not make it lawful. Therefore, from a German perspective, possible alternatives could be: excuse or a public-policy-exemption from

---

* See, e.g., *State v. Vallejos*, 123 N.M. 739, 945 P.2d 957 (1997) (objective entrapment present if "police conduct created a substantial risk that an ordinary person would have been caused to commit the crime" and "police conduct exceeded the standards of proper investigation"); see *State v. Lively*, 130 Wash.2d 1, 921 P.2d 1035 (1996) (successful invocation of outrageous government conduct defense).

punishment beyond wrongdoing and guilt (*persönlicher Strafaufhebungsgrund*) (see, e.g., withdrawal from attempt, § 24 Criminal Code, Chapter 12.D). Add to these, in American and Canadian criminal law, an element-negating "defense" and a procedural device (judicial stay of proceedings after assessment of guilt).

American criminal law has struggled to answer this question. No one argues that entrapment qualifies as a justification. Element-negation and excuse are more promising candidates. Both rely on an analogy between entrapment and duress, another defense that has straddled the line between element-negation and excuse. To recall the New York Court of Appeals's discussion in *Calvano*:

> Under each defense there is asserted, and a defendant may prima facie prove, absence of the criminal intent ordinarily inferable from the admitted acts of commission; under one he asserts that he was persuaded, under the other that he was coerced, i.e., "induced or encouraged" in one case (entrapment) or "coerced" in the other (duress). Indeed, the terms "induced" and "coerced" differ only in respect of the pressures exerted; so that, if prior criminal acts of the same nature may properly be proved to rebut the defense that defendant was "coerced" into the transgression, like proof may properly be received in refutation of a claim that he was "induced or encouraged" to transgress. In one case, as in the other, his intent—meaning his will and volition—is overcome by force or by persuasion, as the case may be, exerted by another.

To the extent that this passage relies on an analogy between entrapment and duress, it provides little support for the view that entrapment negatives an offense element, in particular any required mental state, given that the traditional view of duress as relevant to *mens rea* has been widely discredited. What's at stake in entrapment, it would seem, is not the intent (or some mental state) with respect to any or all of the elements of the offense, but at best the decision to commit the offense in the first place. The question, then, is one of the motive, or cause, for forming the requisite intent. (Under this view, a defendant is predisposed if the state inducement is not the but-for-cause of his or her criminal conduct.)

If the analogy to duress, then, is to support classifying entrapment as an excuse, it is not particularly helpful for a different reason: not because duress is not considered an excuse (*pace* occasional contrary arguments that ought to be classified as a justification, see Chapter 14.A), but because the reason why duress is considered an excuse does not apply to entrapment. The difference between "induced" and "coerced" is significant. Duress is an excuse insofar as the coercion is sufficient to overcome the resistance of non-heroic mere mortals; there is no similar requirement of the futility of reasonable resistance in the case of entrapment.

Canadian criminal law—which also follows an objective theory of entrapment, see *R. v. Mack*, [1988] 2 S.C.R. 903—has developed a different approach. Rather than treat entrapment as a substantive defense, the Canadian Supreme Court frames it "as an aspect of the abuse of process doctrine which enable[s] a court to enter a stay of proceedings in circumstances where allowing the accused to stand trial would offend the courts' sense of justice."

The German Federal Court of Justice takes yet another approach: the so-called sentencing solution. Do you think that the Court's arguments in support of the sentencing solution against the alternative of "acquittal" are convincing? In practice, this means that at least a suspended prison sentence will be the outcome, if not a fine. Even if the defendant was provoked to commit a felony with a high minimum statutory punishment of two years' imprisonment or more (there are not many in German criminal law; examples are homicide, aggravated robbery, or importing narcotics in other than a trivial quantity, §§ 212, 250 Criminal Code, § 30 Narcotics Act), a mild punishment usually will be possible. This is because most of these offense definitions provide for a considerably lower punishment in unspecified "less serious cases," in the range that allows for suspension (under § 56 Criminal Code, prison sentences of up to two years can be suspended).

5. The decision of the German Federal Court of Justice also is of interest as it demonstrates the increasing influence of the European Court of Human Rights on German case law. Because of the fair trial provisions in Article 6 of the European Convention on Human Rights, German courts integrate the European Court's judgments to develop procedural principles. Technically, the victory of the Portuguese claimant meant personal affirmation and the right

to compensation from the Portuguese state. But the influence of decisions goes beyond individual cases. The original idea behind the European Convention of Human Rights was that there ought to be some minimal common human rights standards across Europe. Today, the judges at the European Court of Human Rights show greater ambition to design criminal justice policies as a part of this broad project.

C. Insanity

The insanity defense, in Anglo-American criminal law, is of almost exclusively symbolic significance, because it is also most never raised and, if it is raised, rarely succeeds. Which is not to say, of course, that it is insignificant; quite to the contrary, its practical insignificance only highlights its symbolic significance as a *liminal* question: like duress, insanity brings criminal law face to face with its own limits, not in terms of the type of conduct its special part may cover, but in terms of its subjects. As excuses, duress and insanity, explore the threshold not of criminal acts, but of criminal actors. Unlike duress (or excusing necessity), however, insanity is not concerned with the actor's response to an external stimulus, in the form of compulsion originating from another person or "circumstances"; instead, insanity directly investigates the characteristics of the person him- or herself. (In this sense, insanity—and infancy—is an *incapacity* excuse, whereas duress—as well as military orders and subjective entrapment—is an *inability* excuse; unlike the insane person, the person who acts under duress does not lack normal internal capacities, but is unable to exercise them under certain external circumstances.)

Interestingly, while the insanity tests in German and (modern, Model Penal Code-based) Anglo-American law are very similar—both framed as the lack of capacity to distinguish right from wrong (cognitive incapacity) or to keep oneself from doing wrong (volitional incapacity)—they differ radically in scope. Most importantly, the German insanity provision is regularly, and frequently, applied to cases of intoxication, which are categorically excluded from the scope of the Anglo-American conception of the insanity defense (except in the very rare case of involuntary intoxication, or what the Model Penal Code calls intoxication that is "not self-induced" or "pathological"). (On intoxication, see Chapter 8.D.) As a result, the insanity defense in German criminal law functions as a broad defense that matches its title of "lack of culpability capacity due to mental disorders" (§ 20 Criminal Code) and has considerable practical significance, rather than as a defense that, despite its superficially similar title of "mental disease or defect excluding responsibility" (Model Penal Code § 4.01) in fact arises in so few cases as to only have symbolic significance.

United States v. Ewing
U.S. Court of Appeals for the Seventh Circuit
494 F.3d 607 (7th Cir. 2007)

Sykes, Circuit Judge.

John Ewing, Jr., is a paranoid schizophrenic plagued by delusions that society is engaged in a conspiracy to read his thoughts. After becoming convinced a state court judge was part of that conspiracy, Ewing attacked the judge with a Molotov cocktail. For this he was indicted on two federal charges and at trial raised a defense under the federal insanity statute . . .

Ewing asked the regional court to instruct the jury that "wrongfulness" for purposes of the insanity defense means "moral as well as criminal wrongfulness," and further that "moral wrongfulness" is determined according to the defendant's subjective beliefs about morality or moral justification. The regional court denied this request and instead adopted the government's alternative instruction that defined wrongfulness as "contrary to public morality, as well as contrary to law." The jury rejected Ewing's insanity defense and found him guilty. Ewing now appeals . . .

Ewing's insanity defense was premised on the theory that Ewing believed his actions were justified based on his delusion that Judge Miller was part of a mind-reading conspiracy. Dr. Robert Chapman, Ewing's expert, testified that to Ewing, the delusions of mind reading were akin to mental slavery from which he had to escape by whatever means necessary. Dr. Chapman reported that Ewing made the following statements during one of his examinations: "I didn't consider what I was going to do as illegal or criminal because I was in the right, and what [Judge Miller] was doing was illegal, reading my mind and conspiring with others to steal my ideas for commercial purposes—commercial profit. I never considered arrest." . . .

Under the Insanity Defense Reform Act of 1984 ("IDRA"), it is an affirmative defense to a prosecution for a federal crime if "at the time of the commission of the acts constituting the offense, the defendant, as a result of a severe mental disease or defect, was unable to appreciate the nature and quality or the wrongfulness of his acts." 18 U.S.C. § 17(a). The defendant has the burden of proving insanity by clear and convincing evidence. Id. § 17(b).

The statute does not define "wrongfulness." In the context of the insanity defense, courts and scholars have generally proposed three alternative definitions for the term: (1) legal wrongfulness, as in "contrary to law"; (2) moral wrongfulness, as in "contrary to public morality," determined objectively by reference to society's condemnation of the act as morally wrong; or (3) moral wrongfulness, as in "contrary to personal morality," determined subjectively by reference to the defendant's belief that his action was morally justified (even if he appreciated that it was illegal or contrary to public morality) . . .

Although various formulations of the insanity defense were proposed throughout the twentieth century, the language of the IDRA closely resembles the common-law *M'Naghten* standard. Compare 18 U.S.C. § 17 with Model Penal Code § 4.01 (adopting a combination of the *M'Naghten* test and an "irresistible impulse" test), and Durham v. United States, 94 U.S. App. D.C. 228, 214 F.2d 862 (D.C. Cir. 1954) (establishing the so-called "Durham test" focusing on whether defendant's conduct was "the product of a mental disease or defect"), overruled by United States v. Brawner, 153 U.S. App. D.C. 1, 471 F.2d 969 (D.C. Cir. 1972) (adopting Model Penal Code § 4.01). The precise language of the *M'Naghten* test has been altered at common law and by state statute, but its essential elements are codified in the IDRA: to establish the affirmative defense of insanity, the defendant has the burden of proving that at the time of the offense, as a result of a severe mental disease or defect, he was unable to appreciate the nature and quality or wrongfulness of his acts.

The IDRA, as we have noted, does not define "wrongfulness"; the term is admittedly susceptible of the multiple definitions discussed above. Because the statute adopts the elements of the *M'Naghten* test, however, we may infer that wrongfulness carries the same meaning as in *M'Naghten's Case* and the common law that developed around it.

M'Naghten's Case, 8 Eng. Rep. 718 (1843), concerned a British common-law trial with facts not unlike those at issue in this appeal. In 1843, acting under a delusion that the Tory political party was persecuting him, Daniel M'Naghten shot and killed Edward Drummond, private secretary to Prime Minister Sir Robert Peel.[5] M'Naghten presented an insanity defense based on the theory that a defendant could not be found guilty of any act committed while he was laboring under a delusion, regardless of whether the act was a direct product of that delusion. The jury found M'Naghten not guilty by reason of insanity. In response to public and royal outrage following the verdict, the House of Lords asked the judges of the Queen's Bench to answer five questions regarding the proper formulation of the insanity defense. Their responses served as the basis for the development of American law on the insanity defense over the next 150 years.

Although the language of the *M'Naghten* insanity test comes from a particular passage of the case, it is helpful to review each of the judges' relevant responses to understand the meaning of that language. The first question from the House of Lords posited circumstances quite similar to Ewing's defense here, in which "the accused knew he was acting contrary to law, but did the act complained of with a view, under the influence of insane delusion, of redressing or revenging some supposed grievance or injury, or of producing some supposed public benefit." 8 Eng. Rep. at 720. The judges responded that such a defendant "is nevertheless punishable according to the nature of the crime committed, if he knew at the time of committing such crime that he was acting contrary to law; by which expression we understand your Lordships to mean the law of the land." Id. at 722.

In response to the next two questions regarding the proper inquiry to be submitted to a jury in an insanity defense case, the judges provided the test used in most American courts over the next century:

[T]o establish a defense on the ground of insanity, it must be clearly proved that, at the time of committing the act, the party accused was labouring under such a defect of reason, from

---

[5] M'Naghten apparently shot Drummond under the mistaken belief that he was Prime Minister Peel. See generally Richard Moran, Knowing Right From Wrong 7 (1981).

disease of the mind, as not to know the nature and quality of the act he was doing, or, if he did know it, that he did not know he was doing what was wrong.

Id. The judges explained that they used the term "wrong" instead of "illegal" to prevent "confound [ing] the jury, by inducing them to believe that an actual knowledge of the law of the land was essential in order to lead to a conviction." Id. at 723. Rather, the proper inquiry was "[i]f the accused was conscious that the act was one that he ought not to do, and if that act was at the same time contrary to, the law of the land." Id.

The final response bearing on wrongfulness came from the fourth question posed, which is again of particular relevance to Ewing's defense: "If a person under an insane delusion as to existing facts, commits an offence in consequence thereof, is he thereby excused?" Id. at 720. The judges answered:

[W]e think he must be considered in the same situation as to responsibility as if the facts with respect to which the delusion exists were real. For example, if under the influence of his delusion he supposes another man to be in the act of attempting to take away his life, and he kills that man, as he supposes, in self-defence, he would be exempt from punishment. If his delusion was that the deceased had inflicted a serious injury to his character and fortune, and he killed him in revenge for such supposed injury, he would be liable to punishment.

Id. at 723.

These responses shed light on two aspects of the original *M'Naghten* test critical to the meaning of wrongfulness. First, they demonstrate that the relevant inquiry, according to the Queen's Bench, was not a defendant's actual knowledge of the criminal law under which he was accused, but rather whether the defendant understood the difference between right and wrong.[6] The second point, illustrated by the judges' fourth response, is that the right-versus-wrong test asked not whether the defendant believed he was justified based on his delusional view of reality, but whether society would judge his actions an appropriate response to his delusions. Thus, as applied to M'Naghten, the judges' responses illustrate that his conduct was not properly excused because his deluded belief in a governmental conspiracy against him—even if true—did not justify his knowingly wrongful act of murder.[7]

Accordingly, "criminality" or "contrary to law" is too narrow a definition of wrongfulness, and "subjective personal morality" is too broad. The second of the alternative definitions of wrongfulness—contrary to objective societal or public morality—best comports with the rules established in *M'Naghten's Case*. This conclusion is consistent with the holdings of American courts that analyzed the issue prior to 1984, when Congress adopted the IDRA. Although case law relevant to our specific inquiry is sparse, a brief canvas of those cases that are on point supports our conclusion that the *M'Naghten* wrongfulness inquiry is to be judged according to objective societal standards of morality.

We begin with People v. Schmidt, 216 N.Y. 324, 110 N.E. 945, 34 N.Y. Cr. 51 (N.Y. 1915), which Ewing cites to support his assertion that American courts have traditionally read *M'Naghten* to espouse the subjective definition of wrongfulness. In particular, Ewing relies on language from *Schmidt* in which then-Judge Cardozo explained how a New York statute adopting the *M'Naghten* test might provide a defense for someone who because of mental illness believed himself directed by God to commit a crime—the so-called "deific decree" defense. See id. at 949 ("If, however, there is an insane delusion that God has appeared to the defendant and ordained the commission of a crime, we think it cannot be said of the offender that he knows the act to be wrong."). Ewing argues that Cardozo's approving reference to the deific decree defense demonstrates that the *M'Naghten*

---

[6] *M'Naghten's Case* thus refutes Ewing's contention that the second of the possible definitions of wrongfulness (societal or public morality) is not meaningfully distinct from the first (criminality). See Brief of Defendant-Appellant at 34 ("[A]lmost all cases giving rise to an insanity plea involve serious crimes where there is likely to be no difference between publicly accepted moral standards and the law. A public morality standard frustrates legislative intent by rendering Congress's choice of the word 'wrongfulness' in lieu of criminality meaningless." (citation omitted)). *M'Naghten's Case* demonstrates that "wrongfulness" is substituted for "criminality" not to create two (or more) distinct moral codes by which a defendant's conduct could be judged, but rather to ensure that the inquiry remains focused on a defendant's ability to understand wrongfulness, rather than his actual knowledge of the law. Compare State v. Hamann, 285 N.W.2d 180, 183 (Iowa 1979) ("[Rejecting the subjective definition] is not to say, as has sometimes been suggested, that sanity would thereby be measured by legal knowledge.... The determination is to be made on the basis of a person's ability to understand it when something is prohibited by law.").

[7] Like Ewing, M'Naghten argued not that he thought Drummond was directly attacking him, but rather that he believed his act an appropriate response to the looming conspiracy against him. Presumably, the bench's answers would lead to a different result had M'Naghten argued that he believed his life to be in imminent danger from Drummond at the moment he committed the murder.

wrongfulness inquiry focuses on the defendant's personal beliefs about morality or moral justification.

Ewing's reliance on this aspect of *Schmidt* is misplaced. Cardozo's opinion for the Court of Appeals of New York carefully distinguished between the deific decree defense and the sort of insanity defense brought in *M'Naghten's Case* and asserted by Ewing here. Relying on the response provided to the first *M'Naghten* inquiry, Cardozo concluded that a defense based on a defendant's personal definition of wrongfulness would not suffice to prove insanity under *M'Naghten*. Cardozo explained the difference between the two defenses:

> A delusion that some supposed grievance or injury will be redressed, or some public benefit attained, has no such effect in obscuring moral distinctions as a delusion that God himself has issued a command. The one delusion is consistent with knowledge that the act is a moral wrong, the other is not.

Id. at 948. *Schmidt* does not support Ewing's proposed subjective definition of wrongfulness. To the contrary, the case supports our conclusion that moral wrongfulness is determined by reference to societal or public standards of morality.

People v. Rittger, 54 Cal. 2d 720, 7 Cal. Rptr. 901, 355 P.2d 645 (Cal. 1960), also supports an objective rather than subjective definition of wrongfulness. California had judicially adopted the *M'Naghten* rule in the absence of a state statute on the insanity defense. In *Rittger*, a jury had rejected an insanity defense premised on the defendant's disturbed belief that he had to murder his victim for his own future protection. In affirming the conviction, the California Supreme Court held:

> The fact that a defendant claims and believes that his acts are justifiable according to his own distorted standards does not compel a finding of legal insanity . . . This is necessarily so if organized society is to formulate standards of conduct and responsibility deemed essential to its preservation or welfare, and to require compliance, within tolerances, with those standards.

355 P.2d at 653 (citation omitted) . . .

There is nothing in the IDRA to suggest that wrongfulness should be interpreted more broadly than or contrary to the traditional understanding of the *M'Naghten* test. We conclude that wrongfulness for purposes of the federal insanity defense statute is defined by reference to objective societal or public standards of moral wrongfulness, not the defendant's subjective personal standards of moral wrongfulness . . .

Model Penal Code

§ 4.01. Mental Disease or Defect Excluding Responsibility

(1) A person is not responsible for criminal conduct if at the time of such conduct as a result of mental disease or defect he lacks substantial capacity either to appreciate the criminality [wrongfulness] of his conduct or to conform his conduct to the requirements of law.

(2) As used in this Article, the terms "mental disease or defect" do not include an abnormality manifested only by repeated criminal or otherwise anti-social conduct.

§ 4.02. Evidence of Mental Disease or Defect Admissible When Relevant to Element of the Offense . . .

(1) Evidence that the defendant suffered from a mental disease or defect is admissible whenever it is relevant to prove that the defendant did or did not have a state of mind which is an element of the offense.

. . .

§ 4.03. Mental Disease or Defect Excluding Responsibility Is Affirmative Defense; Requirement of Notice . . .

(1) Mental disease or defect excluding responsibility is an affirmative defense.
(2) Evidence of mental disease or defect excluding responsibility is not admissible unless the defendant, at the time of entering his plea of not guilty or within ten days thereafter or at such later time as the Court may for good cause permit, files a written notice of his purpose to rely on such defense.

. . .

German Federal Court of Justice
2 StR 707/94, StV 1995, 405 (March 24, 1995)

Reasons

The regional court sentenced the defendant to imprisonment for four years and six months for sexual coercion.* The defendant bases his appeal in law against this on a substantive objection ... The appeal was essentially successful in its substantive complaint.

Denial of the presence of the prerequisites of §§ 20, 21 Criminal Code[†] does not stand up to legal examination. The considerations on which, following the observations of the expert, the regional court has based its finding that the defendant was capable at the time of commission of the crime, to appreciate the unlawfulness of his actions are incomplete. Although the findings require this, the regional court did not discuss the possibility that the defendant was in an acute phase of his illness at the point in time of the crime.

According to the findings, the defendant suffered a schizophrenic psychosis while serving sentences of imprisonment arising from earlier convictions and was treated in the psychiatric department of the prison. According to the observations of the expert who had spoken to the defendant several times from 1989 to 1993 in custody, treatment with specifically antipsychotic medicines led to a substantial improvement of the "symptoms which were at times acute."

The overall development indicates that originally a psychosis of the schizophrenic order was present which was not completely cured. According to the expert's diagnosis, the defendant now suffered from a "residual syndrome of a schizophrenia which was formerly of the paranoid hallucinatory nature, but at present was no longer acute." The regional court is of the same view as the expert, that the defendant's capacity for understanding, which remained in spite of impairment by the residual syndrome, allowed the defendant to recognize the fact that his act was forbidden. However, it did not include in its assessment the defendant's conduct during the conversation in the accessory prosecutor's [the victim's—Eds.] residence which preceded the crime and which lasted several hours. The regional court established the following, amongst other things, about this:

> The defendant continued to talk insistently to the accessory prosecutor, and when doing so he frequently and abruptly changed the subject so that it was difficult for her to recognize a connection. He spoke about a number of things, for instance about Helmut Kohl,[‡] the injustices in this world, or about his relationship with his parents which he regarded as bad.... The defendant also made accusations against the accessory prosecutor that she only pretended to have an ecological mindset; it was time for her who had been so favored in life to get to know about life in a different way. Once he threw spent matches at the ceiling saying: "That's evil, you won't get rid of it!"

The regional court ought to have concerned itself with these clear symptoms of a new acute phase of his illness. During acute phases of schizophrenia, the person affected is in general prevented to motivate herself in accordance with norms (see Jähnke in LK 11. A. § 20 marginal no. 40). As absence of criminal capacity in the sense of § 20 Criminal Code can accordingly not be excluded, the absence of discussion necessitates the quashing of the verdict.

German Criminal Code

§ 20 (Lack of Culpability Capacity Due to Mental Disorders)

Who at the time of the commission of the offense due to a pathological mental disorder, a profound consciousness disorder, debility or other serious mental abnormality, is incapable of understanding the wrongness of the act or incapable of acting in accordance with such understanding, acts without culpability.

§ 21 (Diminished Culpability Capacity)

If the capacity of the offender to understand the wrongness of his act or to act in accordance with such understanding is substantially diminished at the time of the commission of the offense due to one of the reasons indicated in § 20, the sentence can be mitigated according to § 49 para. 1.

---

* [Coercing the victim to sexual acts other than intercourse through violence or force, § 178 (old version) at the time of the offense, now § 177 para. 1 StGB.—Eds.]

† [Reproduced immediately below.—Eds.]

‡ [The German chancellor at the time of the offense.—Eds.]

NOTES

1. In Germany, the question of "diminished culpability" (§ 21 Criminal Code, mitigation of punishment) or "lack of culpability" (§ 20 Criminal Code, excuse) often plays a role in criminal trials. These norms get invoked not only if offenders suffer from insanity but also, importantly in practice, because intoxication might lead to such an excuse or mitigation of punishment (see Chapter 8.D). But pathological mental conditions of a more permanent nature, such as a psychosis, also can excuse offenders.

As we noted in the discussion of intoxication, American criminal law—and common law jurisdictions in general—draws a sharp distinction between insanity and intoxication. Intoxication, if it is relevant at all, serves to negate *mens rea*, or rather only certain varieties of *mens rea* (notably "specific intent," which may include purpose and knowledge, but not "general intent," which may encompass recklessness and negligence). The defense of intoxication is controversial to begin with, and its boundaries jealously guarded. Not surprisingly, then, the line separating intoxication from insanity is also heavily policed. The Model Penal Code, for instance, makes explicit, in its intoxication provision, that "[i]ntoxication does not, in itself, constitute mental disease within the meaning of Section 4.01 [the Code's insanity provision]" (§ 2.08(3)). Intoxication can function as an excuse only if it is "pathological" or "not self-induced," where pathological intoxication is defined as "intoxication grossly excessive in degree, given the amount of the intoxicant, to which the actor does not know he is susceptible" (§ 2.09(4)). Needless to say, this provision is all but irrelevant for practical purposes, since intoxication in criminal cases (and presumably general speaking) tends to be self-induced. (Of course, any comparative analysis of intoxication in criminal law should keep in mind the existence of the extreme intoxication provision in the German Criminal Code, § 323a StGB, which serves as a broad, if incomplete, fallback provision in cases where an intoxication defense succeeds. See Chapter 8.D.)

2. On the procedural background: as we have mentioned already for other excuses, under German law defendants do not carry a burden of proof (see Chapter 14.A)—if there is the suspicion of a mental disorder, the state has to prove full culpability, and the court has to make sure that evidence is available. (Technically speaking, at least under the Model Penal Code, defendants also do not carry the burden of *proof* on affirmative defenses. They carry the burden of production, i.e., of introducing enough evidence to raise the issue, assuming no such evidence has entered the record as part of the prosecution's case-in-chief. In other words, the prosecution bears the burden of (dis)proof on the defense, beyond a reasonable doubt, only if there is some evidence in the record that supports it.) In the German inquisitorial criminal trial, introduction of evidence is organized in a different way than in adversarial trials. It is the responsibility of the court to introduce witnesses, experts and other evidence if there are hints that this might elucidate what has happened. This is called the principle of state investigation (*Amtsermittlungsgrundsatz*), one of the main principles of the trial, see § 244 para. 2 German Code of Criminal Procedure: "In order to establish the truth, the court must, *ex officio*, extend the taking of evidence to all facts and means of proof relevant to the decision." The presiding judge therefore will order an expert to examine the defendant if he or she suspects that there might be a mental disorder. Obviously, if this happens against the defendant's explicit wishes and the defendant refuses to cooperate, the expert's report might be of limited significance. However, under the rules of evidence in the German Code of Criminal Procedure, it is not up to the defendant to choose whether insanity will be a topic in the proceedings or not.

In common law jurisdictions, whether the prosecution may raise evidence of insanity over the defendant's objective is a controversial question. The arguments were recently canvassed by the Canadian Supreme Court in *R. v. Swain*, [1991] 1 S.C.R. 933. Given Canada's extensive preventive detention regime for defendants found "not criminally responsible on account of a mental disorder" (NCR), a defendant may prefer to take his or her chances with the jury and forego the insanity defense (Canadian Criminal Code pt. XX.1). The Court acknowledged the significance of the right to conduct one's own defense, but concluded that the prosecution may raise the issue of insanity against the defendant's express wishes in limited circumstances, notably after the defense itself has "put the accused's capacity for criminal intent in issue":

> The appellant argues that it is a principle of fundamental justice that an accused person be able to participate in a meaningful way in his or her defence and to make fundamental decisions about the conduct of his or her defence—such as waiving the defence of insanity . . . It is argued that the functioning of the adversarial system is premised on the autonomy of an accused to make fundamental decisions about his or her defence which require certain consequences and risks to be weighed. The appellant's argument is reflected in the words of Stewart J. in Faretta v. California, 422 U.S. 806 at p. 834 (1975):
>
> > "The right to defend is personal. The defendant, and not his lawyer or the State, will bear the personal consequences of a conviction. It is the defendant therefore, who must be free personally to decide whether in his particular case counsel is to his advantage. And although he may conduct his own defence ultimately to his own detriment, his choice must be honored out of 'that respect for the individual which is the lifeblood of the law.' "
>
> This court has, on numerous occasions, acknowledged that the basic principles underlying our legal system are built on respect for the autonomy and intrinsic value of all individuals . . . .
>
> This court has also recognized the constructs of the adversarial system as a fundamental part of our legal system. In Borowski v. Canada (Attorney-General) (1989), 47 C.C.C. (3d) 1 at p. 13, 57 D.L.R. (4th) 231, [1989] 1 S.C.R. 342, Sopinka J., . . . stated:
>
> > "[A] court's competence to resolve legal disputes is rooted in the adversary system. The requirement of an adversarial context is a fundamental tenet of our legal system and helps guarantee that issues are well and fully argued by parties who have a stake in the outcome . . . ."
>
> Given that the principles of fundamental justice contemplate an accusatorial and adversarial system of criminal justice which is founded on respect for the autonomy and dignity of human beings, it seems clear to me that the principles of fundamental justice must also require that an accused person have the right to control his or her own defence.

3. In German insanity cases, the central issue typically is the experts' diagnosis, the psychiatric and psychological evaluation. Without psychiatric training, the legal terms in § 20 Criminal Code "pathological mental disorder" and "other serious mental abnormality" are not easy to understand. (Is that a problem for the principle of legality?) The element of "other serious mental abnormality" was added in the reform of the German Criminal Code's General Part in 1969. The purpose was to extend full and partial excuses beyond the "traditional" mental diseases (covered by the expression "pathological mental disorder") familiar to the drafters of the original 1871 Code, given that scientific knowledge in this area has progressed since 1871. (For that reason, it is surprising to a German reader that the common law of insanity heavily relies on views developed in the 19th century in the *M'Naghten Case*. Psychiatrists often express similar astonishment —but one might perhaps argue about the significance of psychiatric expertise here.) Note that both psychiatrists' state of knowledge and its consequences for the criminal law are not always uncontroversial. A dispute preceded the legislature's decision to add "other serious mental abnormality." With regard to some more recent extensions in diagnostic manuals and classification schemes (for instance, sexual identity disorders such as pedophilia), one can in principle challenge the view that such conditions should ever excuse offenders in criminal proceedings.

But note that German law does not allow the court to simply conclude from a psychiatrist's diagnosis of a mental disorder that the offender was excused. Section 20 Criminal Code requires examination in two separate steps: first, diagnosis of pathological mental disorder, profound consciousness disorder (for instance, hypnosis, sleep inertia, epilepsy, severe exhaustion, fatigue, confusion, or intoxication) or debility, or another serious mental abnormality; second, the court must find that the offender was incapable of appreciating the wrongfulness of his action or of acting in accordance with such appreciation. With this second step of assessment (which is seen as the courts' prerogative, not the psychiatrists'), courts have an instrument to deny an excuse and also deny a mitigation of punishment (§ 21 Criminal Code) even if defendants have been diagnosed as being seriously mentally abnormal.

Do you think that such a clear cut division between psychiatric and legal evaluation is convincing? Why should the courts', or more generally fact-finders', role be limited to the second step? Conversely, why should psychiatric expert testimony be limited to the issue of mental disorder? Rather than assigning different steps in the analysis of insanity to different experts or at least institutional actors (psychiatric or legal), why not instead recognize that each step in the analysis may be informed by psychiatric evidence, while at the same acknowledging that the judgment in the end, as a whole, is a legal one?

Experts also play a key role in insanity cases in common law jurisdictions. Frequently, courts are skeptical of expert testimony on the issue of insanity and generally insist on characterizing the issue of insanity as legal, rather than medical. Experts are free to provide a diagnosis of some medical condition or other, but whether this condition amounts to, say, a "mental disease or defect" within the meaning of the Model Penal Code's insanity provision is framed as no less of a legal question than is the ultimate question whether this condition caused the requisite incapacity (to tell right from wrong, or to control one's actions). For a fairly typical discussion of the relevance of expert testimony in this context, consider this passage from the Canadian case of *R. v. Stone*, [1999] 2 S.C.R. 290 (Binnie, J., concurring and dissenting):

> [C]ourts have insisted that the definition of "disease of the mind" must be a matter of law, and is not to be dictated by medical experts. Medical input, of course, is nevertheless an essential component. As La Forest J. stated in R. v. Parks, [1992] 2 S.C.R. 871, at p. 898, quoting Martin, J.A. in R. v. Rabey (1978) 37 C.C.C. (2d) 461:
>
>> "Disease of the mind" is a legal term, not a medical term of art; although a legal concept, it contains a substantial medical component as well as a legal or policy component.
>
> Martin J.A. described the "policy function" in *Rabey* as relating to:
>
>> ... (a) the scope of the exemption from criminal responsibility to be afforded by mental disorder or disturbance, and (b) the protection of the public by the control and treatment of persons who have caused serious harms while in a mentally disordered or disturbed state.

More generally, it may be useful to consider the significance of experts in the context of the "adversarial" common law process as a whole; here, it is worth noting that trials often present a battle of experts, each with often radically opposing, but similarly scientifically objective, findings, which tend to bolster the case of one side, rather than other. In particular, a criminal defendant may produce his or her own psychiatric expert, whose testimony may well paint a picture of his or her mental condition that supports a finding of insanity, assuming of course that the defense is pursuing that trial strategy.* Finally, it should be kept in mind that the defendant has the right to have his or her case tried before a jury. In that event, the jury will make the final determination of whether the insanity defense succeeds or not. Whether a jury, or a judge without a jury, is more or less deferential to expert testimony is difficult to say, if only because the jury is—and may—not be required to provide an account of its decision-making process, or reveal the basis for its decision.†

4. That *M'Naghten* continues to shape insanity law in much of the common law world is surprising not only because it was decided in 1843, but also because the Law Lords in *M'Naghten* went out of their way to stress that no precedential significance should be attached to their opinions whatsoever, for the simple reason that they were, literally, merely advisory, since there was no live case or controversy before the court.

In the United States, the *M'Naghten* (cognitive) right/wrong test was very soon supplemented by a (volitional) "irresistible impulse" test. See, e.g., the instruction given one year after *M'Naghten*, in Commonwealth v. Rogers, 7 Met. (Mass.) 500 (1844):

> The term "insanity," as used in this defense, means such a perverted and deranged condition of the mental and moral faculties as to render a person incapable of distinguishing between right and wrong, or unconscious at the time of the nature of the act he is committing, or where, though conscious of the nature of the act, and able to distinguish between right and wrong, and know that the act is wrong, yet his will—by which I mean the governing power of his mind—has

---

* See, e.g., *People v. Kohl*, 72 N.Y.2d 191 (1988) (four experts: two (presented by defense) finding mental disease or defect, two (presented by prosecution) finding none).

† See generally *R. v. Connor*, [2004] UKHL 2 (jury secrecy).

been, otherwise than voluntarily, so completely destroyed that his actions are not subject to it, but are beyond his control.

For an earlier English case, see *R. v. Oxford*, 9 Car. & P. 525, 546, 173 Eng. Rep. 941, 950 (1840) ("If some controlling disease was, in truth, the acting power within [the defendant] which he could not resist, then he will not be responsible").

An alternative approach, under New Hampshire law, applied the defense broadly to any act that was "the offspring or product of mental disease in the defendant."* That approach was plucked from obscurity in a famous opinion by Judge Bazelon in *Durham v. United States*, 214 F.2d 862, 874–5 (D.C. Cir. 1954), who installed it as the federal insanity test in the federal D.C. Circuit: "The rule . . . is simply that an accused is not criminally responsible if his unlawful act was the product of mental disease or mental defect."

The Model Penal Code, published in 1962, also took on the challenge of reforming, and modernizing, *M'Naghten,* but instead of replacing it with a different test altogether, it integrated and updated *M'Naghten's* cognitive test and the volitional "irresistible impulse" test into a two-pronged standard, combining the structure of the *Rogers* test with the flexibility of the *Pike/Durham* test. The D.C. Circuit Court of Appeals, in *United States v. Brawner*, 471 F.2d 969 (1972), eventually discarded the *Durham* rule in favor of the Model Penal Code approach, which by then had been adopted by most federal circuits, and in many states.

The Model Penal Code was seen as an advance over *M'Naghten* not only because it recognized volitional incapacity as a ground of exculpation, but also because it revised the cognitive test, by broadening and making it more flexible, thereby making room for the incorporation of developments in general and forensic psychiatry and other sciences of the mind, as well as in criminal law and policy. Whereas the traditional *M'Naghten* standard required total impairment of the relevant cognitive capacity, the Model Penal Code used "the more realistic standard of lack of substantial capacity."† Likewise, under the Code's formulation of the cognitive prong, the relevant capacity is no longer the capacity to *know* that the act was wrong, but to *appreciate* that it was. This change was meant to bring within the scope of the defense defendants who may have a "largely detached or abstract awareness" of their acts' wrongfulness, without that awareness "penetrat[ing] to the affective level." What's at stake here, put another way, is a "broader sense of understanding than simple cognition" (MPC Commentaries § 4.01, at 166.) According to a 1963 report by the New York criminal code revision commission:

> There is, first, the difficulty that inheres in the ordinary meaning of the word "know," as applied to persons suffering from serious mental disease. The fact that the defendant is able to verbalize the right answer to a question, to respond, for example, that murder or stealing is wrong, or the fact that he exhibited a sense of guilt as by concealment or by flight, is often taken as conclusive evidence that he knew the nature and the wrongfulness of his behavior. Yet one of the most striking facts about the abnormality of many psychotics is that their way of knowing is entirely different from that of the ordinary person. In psychiatric terms, their knowledge is usually divorced from all affect, which is to say that it is like the knowledge children have of propositions they can state but cannot understand; it has no depth and is divorced from comprehension. The present statute [modeled on *M'Naghten*] makes it very difficult to put this point before the jury, though it often is the crucial point involved. . . . The knowledge that should be deemed material in testing responsibility is more than merely surface intellection; it is the appreciation sane men have of what it is that they are doing and of its legal and its moral quality.
>
> 1963 Second Interim Report of the Temporary Commission
> on the Revision of the Penal Law and Criminal Code
> (NY Legis Doc, 1963, No. 8, pp. 18–19)

The distinction between "knowledge" and "appreciation" also plays a role in other—and much older—reformulations of the *M'Naghten* cognitive test, though with slight variations.

---

* See, e.g., *State v. Pike*, 49 N.H. 399, 402 (1869–70).
† *People v. Westergard*, 113 A.D.2d 640, 497 N.Y.S.2d 65 (1985).

Consider, for instance, the definition of insanity in the Canadian Criminal Code (unchanged in the relevant portions since 1892):

16. (1) No person shall be convicted of an offence in respect of an act or omission on his part while he was insane.
(2) For the purposes of this section a person is insane when he is in a state of natural imbecility or has disease of the mind to an extent that renders him incapable of appreciating the nature and quality of an act or omission or of knowing that an act or omission is wrong.

Here, too, the capacity to appreciate rather than (merely) to know is required, but not with respect to the wrongfulness of the conduct in question; there, knowledge is enough. Canadian courts have drawn the line between appreciation and knowledge in a similar way:

In contrast to the position in England under the *M'Naghten* Rules, where the words used are "knows the nature and quality of his act," s. 16 of the Code uses the phrase "appreciating the nature and quality of an act or omission." The two are not synonymous. The draftsman of the Code, as originally enacted, made a deliberate change in language from the common law rule in order to broaden the legal and medical considerations bearing upon the mental state of the accused and to make it clear that cognition was not to be the sole criterion. Emotional as well as intellectual awareness of the significance of the conduct is in issue.

Just how significant is the move from knowledge to appreciation? Or from total incapacity to lack of "substantial capacity"? For that matter, what does it mean to say that someone lacked "the substantial capacity" as opposed to lacking "the capacity"? Is lacking "the substantial capacity" the same as having a "substantially diminished" capacity, § 21 StGB? In that case, is § 20 StGB significantly narrower, in this respect, than Model Penal Code § 4.01, or any of the other common law insanity definitions that require not a lack of capacity, but of substantial capacity? If this difference is significant, would a defendant suffering from a lack of *substantial* cognitive capacity, rather than a lack of cognitive capacity, period, qualify for a complete insanity defense under these common law tests, but only for a finding of diminished responsibility, and therefore a sentence reduction, under the German Criminal Code (§ 21)? (For more on diminished responsibility, and sentencing, see Note 10.)

Or do these changes—from knowledge to appreciation, and from incapacity to substantial incapacity—do little more than signal a more expansive view of the insanity defense? And how expansive should the realm for an insanity defense become? Should, for instance, psychopaths—who may lack empathy, but may have highly developed cognitive capacities—escape criminal responsibility? Could not many (most, all?) of those who engage in criminal conduct (and quite possibly many others besides) be said to lack the "substantial" capacity for empathy? How far can we push the requirement of affective, or emotional, knowledge, without drawing the entire project of blame and punishment into question? Would that be a problem? Many psychiatrists at the time of the drafting of the Model Penal Code did not think so. They called for abandoning the insanity defense precisely because it manifested, in criminal law doctrine, the fiction of a non-pathological concept of crime and its attendant atavist notion of deserved punishment, instead of the modern scientific concept of peno-correctional treatment. (On treatmentism and the Model Penal Code, see Chapter 1.A.i.)

5. If the comparative perspective were limited to analyzing the insanity defense within the Model Penal Code and in the German Criminal Code, it would appear that there are strong parallels. This is, however, not the case if one compares the realities of contemporary criminal practice in the U.S. jurisdictions with German criminal law. Since *Brawner*, the Model Penal Code test has lost influence, as jurisdictions across the U.S. have scaled back the insanity defense in various ways. Some abandoned insanity as a separate defense, limiting evidence of insanity to *mens rea*. See, e.g., Kan. Stat. Ann. § 22-3220 ("It is a defense to a prosecution under any statute that the defendant, as a result of mental disease or defect, lacked the mental state required as an element of the offense charged. Mental disease or defect is not otherwise a defense.").

Others turned the clock back to *M'Naghten*, and eliminated the volitional prong; this was the U.S. Congress's response to John Hinckley's acquittal on volitional incapacity grounds of charges arising from his attempt to assassinate President Reagan.*

Some jurisdictions limited the scope of the cognitive prong. For instance, Arizona eliminated the reference, in the cognitive prong, to awareness of the nature and quality of one's acts; at the same time, the Arizona Supreme Court held that evidence of mental disease or defect could only go to the issue of insanity as a separate defense, not to *mens rea*. Ariz. Rev. Stat. § 13-502(A) ("a mental disease or defect of such severity that the person did not know the criminal act was wrong"). The U.S. Supreme Court upheld the (federal) constitutionality of this statute, on the ground that "the insanity rule, like the conceptualization of criminal offenses, is substantially open to state choice" (*Clark v. Arizona*, 548 U.S. 735 (2006); see also id. at 749–52 (overview of the panoply of insanity doctrines found throughout American criminal law)).

More modestly, other jurisdictions retained their insanity test in substance, but shifted the burden of proving insanity onto the defendant.[†]

6. The question discussed in *United States v. Ewing* would be answered in a similar way by German courts and in the German criminal law literature. In both legal systems, the description of the insanity excuse contains a cognitive element: if the offender was, due to the mental disorder, not capable of appreciating the wrongfulness of the conduct, he will be excused. In the English translation of § 20 Criminal Code, the German term *Unrecht* sometimes is translated with "unlawfulness," sometimes with "wrongfulness." The expression *Unrecht* is somewhat ambiguous because it refers, outside of legal contexts, also to moral judgments. Therefore, the interpretation of the legal term *could*, in a parallel way to *United States v. Ewing*, be disputed in a German context. However, it is generally agreed that *Unrecht* does not refer to the offender's idiosyncratic moral ideas but must be interpreted in an objective way. (Consider this question in light of the German culpability principle. See Chapter 3.A.)

In a decision concerning mistake of law (§ 17 Criminal Code, this norm contains the same cognitive requirement as § 20 Criminal Code: the offender must understand the wrongfulness of his act), the German Federal Court of Justice had to decide about the meaning of "wrongfulness": Judgment of May 19, 1999, 2 StR 86/99, BGHSt 45, 97. The two defendants, a married couple from Switzerland, helped their business partner, a German citizen, Dr. Schneider, to escape arrest by fleeing to Florida. In Germany, Schneider had committed economic crimes causing many millions of dollars in damage (because he was notorious, the identity of "Dr. S." as he is called in the judgment is known—as the reader must have noticed by now, German courts do not use full names). The Swiss friends of Dr. Schneider were accused of obstruction of punishment (§ 258 Criminal Code, see Chapter 5.C). It remained unclear whether they had been informed about § 258 Criminal Code. Their attorney in Geneva told them that they had not committed an offense under Swiss law, and they claimed to have acted under a mistake of law, § 17 Criminal Code.

But the German Federal Court of Justice held, parallel to the federal appellate court in *Ewing*, that "appreciating wrongfulness" does not mean knowing the precise content of a statute. It is hardly imaginable that a court would decide differently: otherwise, except for a few specialists in criminal law, almost everybody would act under mistake of law. (Is this a reason to adopt this interpretation of "appreciating wrongfulness" or—as a matter of policy rather than of statutory interpretation—to abandon, or at least reformulate, the mistake of law defense, perhaps along the lines of a reliance on official misstatement of the law? (See Chapter 8.C.ii.) Common sense recommends the middle approach as taken by the German Federal Court of Justice as well as the American court: neither is it necessary to know the statute's text nor does subjective moral assessment suffice to deny awareness of wrongfulness.

---

* See Insanity Defense Reform Act of 1984 (IDRA); see generally Peter W. Low, John C. Jeffries, Jr., and Richard J. Bonnie, *The Trial of John W. Hinckley, Jr.: A Case Study in the Insanity Defense* (1986).

[†] See, e.g., *People v. Kohl*, 72 N.Y.2d 191 (1988) (1984 reform of N.Y. Penal Law).

While the general approach is similar, there remains a difference with regard to one detail. The court in *Ewing* makes reference to "societal or public standards of moral wrongfulness." A German court would avoid the word "moral" and rather talk about incompatibility with the "legal order," to denote awareness of the difference between the legal and the moral. In the Judgment of May 19, 1999, the Federal Court of Justice accordingly avoids claims about moral wrongfulness but refers to the legal good of a "functioning criminal justice system" and the defendants' awareness of having interfered with this legal good. (Does this reflect a difference in form, or in substance? Is one formulation more problematic than the other, or in a different way?)

7. While the interpretation of the term "wrongfulness" follows a similar approach, with respect to the *scope* of the insanity defense, comparative analysis reveals a noticeable difference. Traditional Anglo-American law (and some contemporary re-formulations of statutes, see Note 5), following the *M'Naghten* test, focuses on the cognitive side: the impact of mental disorders on the appreciation of wrongfulness. German law—and the Model Penal Code—is based on the assumption that mental disorders can affect the offender in two different ways, not just on the cognitive level, but also on the level of control. Section 20 Criminal Code describes two possible consequences of mental disorders: the offender can be "incapable of appreciating the wrongfulness of the offense" *or* "incapable of acting in accordance with any such appreciation." In other words, the condition can affect understanding *or* affect control; it can manifest itself as either cognitive or volitional incapacity.

This way of phrasing the insanity defense expands its potential scope. Cases are rare in which an offender is delusional to such a degree that he is truly unaware of society's or the legal order's judgments about this kind of conduct. If it comes to serious crimes, usually even a person who is schizophrenic or in other ways undisputedly mentally ill knows that society or the legal order condemns this. The focal point in the German case from 1995 reprinted above, when it was heard again by a trial court, would not be an exploration of whether the offender knew that it was wrong to sexually attack women. It can be expected that he was aware of that. However, like in many other cases of impulsive violence, sexual misconduct etc., a possible mental disorder requires attention because it might have eliminated his (volitional) capacity to control himself. An excuse drafted as narrowly as the *M'Naghten* test is deficient from the German point of view.

Consider whether the elimination of the volitional prong violates the constitutional culpability principle in German law. Clearly, it would pass constitutional muster in the United States today. As mentioned previously, many American jurisdictions never followed the Model Penal Code's adoption of a volitional prong, others dropped it, and yet others eliminated the insanity defense—as a separate excuse—altogether (see Note 5). Even Canadian criminal law, which has undergone an extensive reconsideration in light of constitutional principles,* has retained the *M'Naghten* test virtually unchanged since the adoption of the Canadian Criminal Code in 1892. Can you reconcile a commitment to autonomy with the rejection of volitional insanity as an excuse? Or might respect for the autonomy of accused persons cut the other way entirely, and preclude rather than support the recognition of a broad insanity defense (and perhaps any insanity defense), and most particularly of an insanity defense that turns on a finding that the accused lacked the requisite capacity for autonomy? (In this context, consider the concerns raised about the recognition of battered-woman's syndrome in domestic violence cases, see Chapter 13.A.)

8. If a mental disorder made the defendant believe she acted in a justified way, under German law the question would arise: does one need § 20 Criminal Code at all or should the offender go unpunished because of an error about justifying circumstances (see for this Chapter 13.A)? The test for "errors about justifying circumstances" is: if the facts were as the defendant erroneously believed them to be, would he then be justified? This requires accepting the defendant's deranged view of the world. At first glance, this might seem odd,

---

* See, e.g., *R. v. Wholesale Travel Group Inc.*, [1991] 3 S.C.R. 154. ("Criminal law is rooted in the concepts of individual autonomy and free will...").

if one takes *United States v. Ewing* or the *King of the Cats Case* (Chapter 13.B) as examples. (Note that in the *King of the Cats Case* the defendant R. was diagnosed—only—with mental abnormality that did not amount to a full excuse. For the sake of explanation, imagine someone more similar to Ewing suffering from a fully developed "classical" mental disease such as paranoid schizophrenia.) However, the German approach, which examines "errors about justifying circumstances" even if the offender obviously suffered from a mental disease, does not lead to unreasonable outcomes. The more serious the crime, the less likely it becomes that even from the perspective of the defendants' bizarre visions they could claim a justification: *even if* Judge Miller *had been* part of a conspiracy to read Ewing's thoughts, there was neither a present attack that would allow self-defense nor a balance-of-interests justification for throwing a Molotov cocktail; and the same holds for attempted murder (neither self-defense nor justifying necessity) *even if* the monstrous king of cats existed.

9. *Hypnosis, mental disturbances, and mental disorders.* Section 20 of the German Criminal Code is far broader than the defense of insanity in common law jurisdictions. Even if one compares apples and apples, rather than the German test to *M'Naghten*, and uses an insanity test that includes both a cognitive and a volitional prong, § 20 Criminal Code covers more ground than, say, § 4.01 of the Model Penal Code. For instance, several of the classic examples of "insanity" in German criminal law—hypnosis, sleep inertia—would be handled under the voluntariness aspect of the act requirement (discussed in Chapter 7.A). Recall Model Penal Code § 2.01:

Section 2.01. Requirement of Voluntary Act; Omission as Basis of Liability; Possession as an Act

(1) A person is not guilty of an offense unless his liability is based on conduct which includes a voluntary act or the omission to perform an act of which he is physically capable.
(2) The following are not voluntary acts within the meaning of this Section:
   (a) a reflex or convulsion;
   (b) a bodily movement during unconsciousness or sleep;
   (c) conduct during hypnosis or resulting from hypnotic suggestion;
   (d) a bodily movement that otherwise is not a product of the effort or determination of the actor, either conscious or habitual.

Other cases that would fall under § 20 Criminal Code—severe forms of exhaustion, fatigue, or confusion—similarly might fall under the rubric of involuntariness, insofar as they result in bodily movements that cannot be classified as "a product of the effort or determination of the actor, either conscious or habitual" (§ 2.01(2)(d)), though a person in this condition also may well not have formed the requisite *mens rea*.

Intoxication is the exception, and an important one, given the frequency with which § 20 Criminal Code is applied to cases of intoxication. Apart from the traditional anxiety surrounding intoxication as a defense, the common law conception of insanity would not be an easy fit for cases of intoxication for another reason, which would also apply to the above-mentioned cases of hypnosis etc.: the extension of § 20 beyond mental diseases and disorders to *disorders* that lack permanence and depth compared to the term disease. One might describe alcoholism as a disease, but severe intoxication as a mere disorder or mere disturbance. In fact, those who suffer from the disease of alcoholism, i.e., "alcoholics," may well disqualify themselves from the benefit of § 20 because their consumption of a given quantity of alcohol may not lead to the same pathological effects as it does with the occasional social drinker who goes on an atypical drinking binge.

10. *Diminished responsibility, diminished capacity.* The concept of diminished responsibility, or diminished capacity, has for some time occupied an uneasy place in American criminal law.* Some jurisdictions recognized it as a partial defense in murder cases, resulting in

---

* See generally Stephen J. Morse, "Undiminished Confusion in Diminished Capacity," 75 *Journal of Criminal Law and Criminology* (1984), 1.

manslaughter liability despite an intent to kill (much like provocation, see Chapter 15.A.iii). See, e.g., *People v. Henderson*, 60 Cal.2d 482 (1963) ("Under the ... rule of diminished responsibility even though a defendant be legally sane according to the *M'Naghten* test, if he was suffering from a mental illness that prevented his acting with a malice aforethought or with premeditation and deliberation, he cannot be convicted of murder of the first degree."). In this version, the defense was regarded as a(nother) way to soften the rigid *M'Naghten* rule.* The Model Penal Code, already having expanded the insanity defense beyond *M'Naghten*, included a general provision to point out that—much like intoxication, and mistake—evidence of mental disease or defect may nonetheless be relevant on the issue of *mens rea*, even if it does not amount to a separate insanity defense.† The Code also retains a version of the traditional diminished responsibility-manslaughter rule insofar as "extreme mental disturbance"—and not merely extreme emotional disturbance, which tends to get all the attention—can make out a case of voluntary manslaughter (MPC § 210.3(1)(b)).

Even if diminished responsibility does not amount to a full, or partial, defense, in a particular case, or in general, it may be taken into account in sentencing, as in § 21 Criminal Code and, for instance, under the U.S. Sentencing Guidelines:

§ 5K2.13. Diminished Capacity (Policy Statement)

A downward departure may be warranted if (1) the defendant committed the offense while suffering from a significantly reduced mental capacity; and (2) the significantly reduced mental capacity contributed substantially to the commission of the offense. Similarly, if a departure is warranted under this policy statement, the extent of the departure should reflect the extent to which the reduced mental capacity contributed to the commission of the offense.

However, the court may not depart below the applicable guideline range if (1) the significantly reduced mental capacity was caused by the voluntary use of drugs or other intoxicants; (2) the facts and circumstances of the defendant's offense indicate a need to protect the public because the offense involved actual violence or a serious threat of violence; (3) the defendant's criminal history indicates a need to incarcerate the defendant to protect the public; or (4) the defendant has been convicted of an offense under chapter 71 [obscenity], 109A [sexual abuse], 110 [sexual exploitation], or 117 [transportation for illegal sexual activity], of title 18, United States Code.

Commentary
Application Note:
1. For purposes of this policy statement—
"Significantly reduced mental capacity" means the defendant, although convicted, has a significantly impaired ability to (A) understand the wrongfulness of the behavior comprising the offense or to exercise the power of reason; or (B) control behavior that the defendant knows is wrongful.

Note here the reference to "significantly impaired ability," which tracks § 21 Criminal Code, as does the recognition of volitional incapacity (despite the absence of a volitional prong in the federal insanity provision, discussed in *Ewing*), yet the persistent rejection of intoxication-based incapacity, even for purposes of sentencing.

---

* Compare *People v. Westergard*, 113 A.D.2d 640, 497 N.Y.S.2d 65 (N.Y. App. Div. 1985) (rejecting the defense in New York because revised New York Penal Law already "ameliorate[d]" *M'Naghten* rule by defining insanity in terms of substantial, rather than complete, incapacity).

† See, e.g., Model Penal Code § 4.02(1); *State v. Breakiron*, 108 N.J. 591, 532 A.2d 199 (1987).

PART III

THE SPECIAL PART

The general part has attracted the lion's share of interest in comparative criminal law, and in criminal law as a whole. For some time, criminal law scholarship has tended to wrestle with general principles of criminal liability, raising (and raising again, and again), fundamental questions such as the nature of criminal liability, culpability, responsibility, of harm and/or wrong, the concepts of justification and of excuse, the core of self-defense, of necessity, and the significance of insanity, duress, intoxication, and mistake, and, of course, last but not least, the question of just what justifies state punishment in the first place. This was not always so. Until fairly recently, in American law schools, criminal law was taught one crime at a time, and criminal law exams consisted of "issue spotters," hypotheticals that sent students on a truffle hunt for offenses that the protagonists might have committed. And, recently, the study of the special part, at least in the common law world, has begun to attract more scholarly attention, perhaps a sign of general-part fatigue on the part of criminal law scholars who have leapt into the bramble bush of general principles once too often.

Focusing on the general part in comparative criminal law makes sense; it is easier to engage in a conversation across systems about fundamental principles, about bedrock assumptions, than it is about the details of the definition of a specific offense. Herbert Wechsler, who, as Chief Reporter of the American Law Institute's Model Penal Code project, oversaw an ambitious preparatory comparative analysis of domestic American criminal law, regarded the special part as a reflection of "variations in social conditions and public attitudes from state to state."* This means that comparative analysis of the special part is hard; but it also means that it is worth doing, and for the same reason. It is here, in the conception of the rights and interests with which the criminal law is to concern itself, the crafting of types, groups, and classes of offenses, and even the drafting of specific offenses that comparative analysis finds interesting similarities and differences, which may or may not track the results of the comparative analysis of the general part.

In our discussion of the special part, we will continue to draw on the Model Penal Code as the common denominator of American criminal law. Given the diversity of offense definitions throughout the fifty-plus jurisdictions that make up "American criminal law," we will pay particular attention to one jurisdiction in particular, New York. New York criminal law makes for a useful point of comparison for several reasons. Its criminal code, though based on the Model Penal Code, also retains significant elements of traditional common law doctrine, it is among the most influential American jurisdictions in general, and in the area of criminal law in particular, and its courts, led by the New York Court of Appeals, have had an opportunity to develop an extensive body of criminal jurisprudence since the revision of the New York Penal Law in 1967.

---

* Herbert Wechsler, "The Challenge of a Model Penal Code," 65 *Harvard Law Review* (1952), 1097, 1132.

A. Protected Rights and Interests: The Structure of the Special Part

Before we turn to specific offenses, we begin with a note on the abstract. The structure of the special part is a reflection of the rights and interests the protection of which ostensibly is the function of criminal law. Just what are the "individual" and "public interests" at the heart of "the provisions governing the definition of offenses," and what role do they play in the special part of Anglo-American and German criminal law?

Consider the following tables of contents, of the special parts of the Model Penal Code, the New York Penal Law, and the German Criminal Code:

Model Penal Code (1962)

Part II. Definition of Specific Crimes

[Offenses Against Existence or Stability of the State]	Offenses Involving Danger to the Person
Offenses Against Property	Offenses Against the Family
Offenses Against Public Administration	Offenses Against Public Order and Decency
[Additional Articles]	

New York Penal Law (1967)

Part Three—Specific Offenses

Title G   Anticipatory Offenses
Title H   Offenses Against the Person Involving Physical Injury, Sexual Conduct, Restraint and Intimidation
Title I   Offenses Involving Damage to and Intrusion upon Property
Title J   Offenses Involving Theft
Title K   Offenses Involving Fraud
Title L   Offenses Against Public Administration
Title M   Offenses Against Public Health and Morals
Title N   Offenses Against Public Order, Public Sensibilities and the Right to Privacy
Title O   Offenses Against Marriage, the Family, and the Welfare of Children and Incompetents
Title P   Offenses Against Public Safety

German Criminal Code (*Strafgesetzbuch*, StGB) (1975)

Special Part

1: Offenses Against Peace, High Treason and Endangering the Democratic Rule of Law
2: Treason and Endangering External Security
3: Offenses Against Foreign States
4: Offenses Against Constitutional Organs as well as During Elections and Ballots
5: Offenses Against the National Defense
6: Resistance to State Authority
7: Offenses Against Public Order
8: Counterfeiting of Money and Stamps
9: False Unsworn Testimony and Perjury
10: Casting False Suspicion
11: Offenses Which Relate to Religion and Philosophy of Life
12: Offenses Against Personal Status, Marriage and the Family
13: Offenses Against Sexual Self-determination
14: Insult
15: Violation of the Realm of Personal Privacy and Confidentiality
16: Offenses Against Life
17: Offenses Against Bodily Integrity
18: Offenses Against Personal Freedom
19: Theft and Misappropriation
20: Robbery and Extortion
21: Accessory After the Fact and Receiving Stolen Property
22: Fraud and Breach of Trust
23: Falsification of Documents

24: Offenses of Insolvency
25: Punishable Greed
26: Offenses Against Competition
27: Damaging Property
28: Offenses Dangerous to the Public
29: Offenses Against the Environment
30: Offenses in Public Office

Comparative analysis of the special parts of criminal codes, even at the abstract level of tables of contents, can reveal significant structural similarities and differences, for instance:

- the placement of certain provisions within the general or the special part,
  - ♦ So, for instance, inchoate offenses appear in the general part of the Model Penal Code [MPC], and the German Criminal Code [Strafgesetzbuch, StGB] but in the special part of the New York Penal Law [NYPL]. See MPC art. 5; StGB ti. 2; NYPL arts. 100–115.
- the choice of interests thought to require penal protection,
  - ♦ For instance, one will not find an analogue to StGB's extensive chapter on libel and slander, designed to protect the legal good of honor, in the MPC or the NYPL. See StGB ch. 14 (§§ 185–200). Conversely, there is no equivalent to the NYPL article on gambling offenses in the StGB. See NYPL art. 225.
- the definition of these interests,
  - ♦ Here, as elsewhere, the details, of course, require further analysis, but a comparison of the offenses grouped under, say, offenses "against the family" in various codes produces interesting results. The MPC, for instance, lists bigamy, polygamy, incest, abortion, endangering welfare of children, and persistent non-support (of children), MPC art. 230; the StGB, in its chapter on "offenses against personal status, marriage, and the family," includes the above (minus abortion), but adds, at the very beginning, the crime of "falsification of personal status," which criminalized misrepresenting a child status to "a public authority responsible for the maintenance of personal status registers." StGB § 169. Compare also MPC ("Offenses Involving Danger to the Person") with NYPL ti. H ("Offenses Against the Person Involving Physical Injury, Sexual Conduct, Restraint and Intimidation"), or MPC art. 213 ("Sexual Offenses") with StGB ch. 13 ("Offenses Against Sexual Self-Determination").
- the ordering of these interests in the special part,
  - ♦ Whereas the special part of the French Penal Code [Code Pénal] and the NYPL begins with crimes against the person, the special part of the StGB and the MPC first define crimes against the state. See Code Pénal bk. 2; NYPL ti. H; StGB §§ 80–163; MPC art. 200. (Strictly speaking, the drafters of the MPC did not produce model offenses against the state because they "are peculiarly the concern of the federal government" and "inevitably affected by special political considerations.")
  - ♦ Even within a set of provisions dedicated to the protection of a particular interest, different penal codes have adopted different ordering principles. So, many American penal codes and the Code Pénal order crimes against the person in descending order of seriousness, while the NYPL moves from the less serious to the more serious. See MPC art. 210; Code Pénal art. 211-1; NYPL arts. arts. 120, 125
  - ♦ Yet more specifically, within a given a set of offenses built around one aspect of a more general interest, such as offenses against life within the category of offenses against the person, codes adopt different ordering guidelines. The NYPL, for instance, within the article on homicide, moves from negligent homicide to murder; the MPC and the StGB instead descend in order of seriousness, from murder to negligent homicide. NYPL art. 125; MPC art. 210; StGB ch. 16.
- the classification of particular offenses within the framework of protected interests,
  - ♦ For example, the NYPL and the StGB classify abortion as a crime against the person whereas the MPC categorizes it as an offense against the family. See NYPL § 125.40–125.60; StGB §§ 218–219b; MPC § 220-3. Bestiality, in the NYPL, is a form of "sexual misconduct" (besides nonconsensual sexual intercourse, and sexual conduct with a

dead human body), § 130.20(3); in Germany, after having been removed from the criminal code in 1969, it recently was added to the Animal Protection Act (*Tierschutzgesetz*) as an administrative offense subject to a maximum €25000 fine.
- or outside that framework altogether,
  - ◆ Legislators have struggled to fit computer crimes into their codes. See, e.g., Connecticut General Statutes §§ 53a-250 to 53a-261 ("computer-related offenses"); NYPL §§ 156.00–156.50 ("offenses involving computers").
  - ◆ RICO also has become a code within a code. See, e.g., 18 U.S.C. §§ 1961–1968 ("racketeer influenced and corrupt organizations," better known as RICO); NYPL §§ 460.00–460.80, 470.00–470.20 ("The Organized Crime Control Act").
  - ◆ As has terrorism. See, e.g., Canadian Criminal Code pt II.1 ("terrorism").
  - ◆ Sometimes, legislators have just thrown in the towel. See, e.g., Conn. Gen. Stat. §§ 53a-211 to 53a-222 ("miscellaneous offenses").
- the decision whether or not to include in the criminal code
  - ◆ a particular offense,
    - ■ For instance, there is no general duty-to-aid statute, like StGB § 323c, in the MPC or the NYPL, or any other American criminal code, with a few, limited, exceptions (see, e.g., 12 Vermont Statutes § 519; Wisconsin Statutes § 940.34). Conversely, the StGB does not include an offense of prostitution, unlike both the MPC, § 251.2, and the NYPL, art 230.
  - ◆ a group of offenses,
    - ■ Perhaps most important, offenses of drug possession and distribution occupy two entire articles of the NYPL, but appear nowhere in the StGB, which addresses narcotics (other than alcohol) only in prohibitions against intoxication in general and against intoxication while operating "any vehicle engaged in rail, suspension rail, water or air traffic." See NYPL §§ 220.00–220.65, 221.00–221.55; StGB §§ 315a, 323a. Offenses of drug possession and distribution in Germany are instead defined in a separate code. See German Narcotics Act of 1981; see also Canadian Controlled Drugs and Substances Act of 1996.
  - ◆ or a type, or class, of offense
    - ■ Most American penal codes include some, but not all, minor offenses. Infractions, violations, and the like instead are defined in a variety of other state codes, state regulations, and the laws promulgated by lower-level governmental entities, including counties, cities, towns, and villages. German criminal law, by contrast, deals with these offenses in a separate code, the Administrative Offenses Act (*Gesetz über Ordnungswidrigkeiten,* OWiG).

In the chapters that follow we move on to a comparative analysis of specific offense clusters. Giving an overview of the enormous scope and variety of the special part of any given contemporary criminal system, never mind of two (or more), is a hopeless endeavor. We have selected some offenses that, we hope, will allow for some interesting comparative reflection, without trying to add up to even an illustrative sample of the teeming and constantly evolving—and more often than not, expanding—bodies of norms, offenses, rules, regulations, and orders that make up the special parts of the systems under consideration.

Offenses against the person come first (even though they do not necessarily lead off the special part of criminal codes, as we just saw). Along with old standbys like the various forms of homicide, we will also touch on assisted suicide and stalking (*Nachstellung*). Next we turn to sexual offenses, which we address in a section entitled "offenses against sexual autonomy," thereby privileging a particular—recent—conceptualization of these offenses, as a violation of an aspect of the victim's autonomy as a person, rather than, say, as an offense against morals, or against the victim's female, or virginal, honor, or against her father's, or husband's honor, or property interest. We close by touching on some crimes of particular comparative interest: the Holocaust denial and *Rechtsbeugung* (literally "law bending") provisions in the German Criminal Code (§§ 130, 339), and the RICO and money laundering provisions of (primarily) U.S. federal criminal law.

OFFENSES AGAINST THE PERSON

Offenses against the person have played a central role in the history of criminal law, or at least in the development of criminal law doctrine. In English criminal law, the law of homicide had a general part *avant la lettre*; there was a doctrine of homicide *se defendendo* before there was a general doctrine of self-defense and when Blackstone turned his mind to what we now would consider matters of justification and excuse, his mind was on homicide in particular, not crime in general:

> [H]omicide, or the killing of any human creature, is of three kinds: justifiable, excusable, and felonious. The first has no share of guilt at all; the second very little; but the third is the highest crime against the law of nature, that man is capable of committing....
>
> In...instances of justifiable homicide,...the slayer is in no kind of fault whatsoever, not even in the minutest degree....But that is not quite the case in excusable homicide, the very name whereof imports some fault, some error, some omission; so trivial however, that the law excuses it from the guilt of felony....
>
> Excusable homicide is of two sorts; either *per infortunium*, by misadventure [where a man..., without any intention of hurt, unfortunately kills another]; or *se defendendo*, upon a principle of self-preservation....Homicide in *self-defence*, or *se defendendo*, upon a sudden affray, is excusable rather than justifiable....This species of self-defence must be distinguished from that [which is] calculated to hinder the perpetration of a capital crime; which is not only a matter of excuse but of justification. But the self-defence, which we are now speaking of, is that whereby a man may protect himself from an assault, or the like, in the course of a sudden brawl or quarrel, by killing him who assaults him...This right of natural defence does not imply a right of attacking: for, instead of attacking one another for injuries past or impending, men need only have recourse to the proper tribunals of justice. They cannot therefore legally exercise this right of preventive defence, but in sudden and violent cases; when certain and immediate suffering would be the consequence of waiting for the assistance of the law.
>
> William Blackstone, *Commentaries on the Laws of England* (1769), vol. 4, 182.*

Whether Blackstone, or his contemporaries, regarded homicide as an "offense against the person" is another matter. Recall that the dominant conception of crime was as a violation of the king's peace; if homicide was an offense against the person, it therefore would have been against the person of the king, rather than against the person of the individual human being whose life has come to a premature end. Or put another way, homicide became an *offense* against the person, and therefore a crime, only insofar as it affected the king and his peace, even if it could in some sense be construed as an offense *against the person* of that unlucky royal subject. For that reason, homicide *se defendendo* was treated as merely pardonable, and in that sense excused, rather than as justified; *se defendendo* or not *se defendendo*, any homicide deprived the king of one of his subjects, an offense that was punishable absent a royal dispensation, an act of sovereign mercy. Only as an exercise of royal authority—by enforcing or executing his law, or preventing its violation—could homicide be justified. (On the structure of justifications, see Chapter 13.)

---

* See also William Blackstone, *Commentaries on the Laws of England* (1768), vol. 3, at 120–1 (discussing, in the law of private wrong (tort), rather than of public wrong (crime), instances of "justifiable or lawful" battery, defined as "*unlawful* beating of another" (original emphasis)).

A. Homicide

Homicide is often treated as the most serious offense and, for that reason, tends to get pride of place in discussions of criminal offenses. This treatment is thought to reflect a commitment to the centrality of the individual person in contemporary law in general, and criminal law in particular: the individual person is the central figure in a state under the rule of law, a *Rechtsstaat*, and the right to life is the most fundamental right of the person, therefore homicide, as the violation of the right to life, is the most serious offense. Perhaps this is so. One reason why this view is rarely questioned, however, may be that the seriousness of homicide is compared to that of other offenses against the person. The question, however, is not whether homicide is the most serious offense against the person, but whether it is the most serious offense, period. Is it more serious than the most serious offense against the state? Than, say, high treason? If so, why do both the German Criminal Code and the Model Penal Code open their respective special parts with the most serious offenses against the state, not homicide? Even within the realm of offenses against the person, is homicide simply an assault with a different result element (death rather than harm short of death)? Or is homicide qualitatively different? Is it unique? Is "the murderer" qualitatively different than other offenders (including the "manslaughterer")? If so, does the murderer deserve a qualitatively different punishment to match?

i. Overview

To frame comparative analysis, it makes sense to set out statutory definitions of the various forms of homicide before taking a look at the particular cases, and the interpretive and doctrinal issues they raise. Besides giving an overview of the law of homicide in Anglo-American and German law, these excerpts highlight different approaches to the task of criminal legislation, in form and substance.

Model Penal Code

Part II. Definition of Specific Crimes
Offenses Involving Danger to the Person
Article 210. Criminal Homicide

§ 210.0. Definitions

In Articles 210–213, unless a different meaning plainly is required:
(1) "human being" means a person who has been born and is alive;
(2) "bodily injury" means physical pain, illness or any impairment of physical condition;
(3) "serious bodily injury" means bodily injury which creates a substantial risk of death or which causes serious, permanent disfigurement, or protracted loss or impairment of the function of any bodily member or organ;
(4) "deadly weapon" means any firearm, or other weapon, device, instrument, material or substance, whether animate or inanimate, which in the manner it is used or is intended to be used is known to be capable of producing death or serious bodily injury.

§ 210.1. Criminal Homicide

(1) A person is guilty of criminal homicide if he purposely, knowingly, recklessly or negligently causes the death of another human being.
(2) Criminal homicide is murder, manslaughter or negligent homicide.

§ 210.2. Murder.

(1) Except as provided in Section 210.3(1)(b), criminal homicide constitutes murder when:
    (a) it is committed purposely or knowingly; or
    (b) it is committed recklessly under circumstances manifesting extreme indifference to the value of human life. Such recklessness and indifference are presumed if the actor is engaged or is an accomplice in the commission of, or an attempt to commit, or flight after committing or attempting to commit robbery, rape or deviate sexual intercourse by force or threat of force, arson, burglary, kidnapping or felonious escape.

(2) Murder is a felony of the first degree [but a person convicted of murder may be sentenced to death, as provided in § 210.6*].

§ 210.3. Manslaughter.

(1) Criminal homicide constitutes manslaughter when:
    (a) it is committed recklessly; or
    (b) a homicide which would otherwise be murder is committed under the influence of extreme mental or emotional disturbance for which there is reasonable explanation or excuse. The reasonableness of such explanation or excuse shall be determined from the viewpoint of a person in the actor's situation under the circumstances as he believes them to be.
(2) Manslaughter is a felony of the second degree.

§ 210.4. Negligent Homicide.

(1) Criminal homicide constitutes negligent homicide when it is committed negligently.
(2) Negligent homicide is a felony of the third degree.

New York Penal Law

Part Three—Specific Offenses
Title H—Offenses Against the Person Involving Physical Injury, Sexual Conduct, Restraint and Intimidation
Article 125. Homicide, Abortion and Related Offenses

§ 125.00 Homicide defined.

Homicide means conduct which causes the death of a person or an unborn child with which a female has been pregnant for more than twenty-four weeks under circumstances constituting murder, manslaughter in the first degree, manslaughter in the second degree, criminally negligent homicide, abortion in the first degree or self-abortion in the first degree.

§ 125.05 Homicide, abortion and related offenses; definitions of terms.

[omitted]

§ 125.10 Criminally negligent homicide.

A person is guilty of criminally negligent homicide when, with criminal negligence, he causes the death of another person.
    Criminally negligent homicide is a class E felony.

§ 125.11 Aggravated criminally negligent homicide.

§ 125.12 Vehicular manslaughter in the second degree.

§ 125.13 Vehicular manslaughter in the first degree.

§ 125.14 Aggravated vehicular homicide.

[omitted]

§ 125.15 Manslaughter in the second degree.

A person is guilty of manslaughter in the second degree when:
1. He recklessly causes the death of another person; or
2. ...
3. He intentionally causes or aids another person to commit suicide.
Manslaughter in the second degree is a class C felony.

§ 125.20 Manslaughter in the first degree.

A person is guilty of manslaughter in the first degree when:
1. With intent to cause serious physical injury to another person, he causes the death of such person or of a third person; or

---

* [In 2009, the American Law Institute withdrew § 210.6 "in light of the current intractable institutional and structural obstacles to ensuring a minimally adequate system for administering capital punishment."—Eds.]

2. With intent to cause the death of another person, he causes the death of such person or of a third person under circumstances which do not constitute murder because he acts under the influence of extreme emotional disturbance, as defined in paragraph (a) of subdivision one of section 125.25. The fact that homicide was committed under the influence of extreme emotional disturbance constitutes a mitigating circumstance reducing murder to manslaughter in the first degree and need not be proved in any prosecution initiated under this subdivision; or

3. ...

4. Being eighteen years old or more and with intent to cause physical injury to a person less than eleven years old, the defendant recklessly engages in conduct which creates a grave risk of serious physical injury to such person and thereby causes the death of such person.

Manslaughter in the first degree is a class B felony.

§ 125.21 Aggravated manslaughter in the second degree.

§ 125.22 Aggravated manslaughter in the first degree.

[omitted]

§ 125.25 Murder in the second degree.

A person is guilty of murder in the second degree when:

1. With intent to cause the death of another person, he causes the death of such person or of a third person; except that in any prosecution under this subdivision, it is an affirmative defense that:

   (a) The defendant acted under the influence of extreme emotional disturbance for which there was a reasonable explanation or excuse, the reasonableness of which is to be determined from the viewpoint of a person in the defendant's situation under the circumstances as the defendant believed them to be. Nothing contained in this paragraph shall constitute a defense to a prosecution for, or preclude a conviction of, manslaughter in the first degree or any other crime; or

   (b) The defendant's conduct consisted of causing or aiding, without the use of duress or deception, another person to commit suicide.

   Nothing contained in this paragraph shall constitute a defense to a prosecution for, or preclude a conviction of, manslaughter in the second degree or any other crime; or

2. Under circumstances evincing a depraved indifference to human life, he recklessly engages in conduct which creates a grave risk of death to another person, and thereby causes the death of another person; or

3. Acting either alone or with one or more other persons, he commits or attempts to commit robbery, burglary, kidnapping, arson, rape in the first degree, criminal sexual act in the first degree, sexual abuse in the first degree, aggravated sexual abuse, escape in the first degree, or escape in the second degree, and, in the course of and in furtherance of such crime or of immediate flight therefrom, he, or another participant, if there be any, causes the death of a person other than one of the participants; except that in any prosecution under this subdivision, in which the defendant was not the only participant in the underlying crime, it is an affirmative defense that the defendant:

   (a) Did not commit the homicidal act or in any way solicit, request, command, importune, cause or aid the commission thereof; and

   (b) Was not armed with a deadly weapon, or any instrument, article or substance readily capable of causing death or serious physical injury and of a sort not ordinarily carried in public places by law-abiding persons; and

   (c) Had no reasonable ground to believe that any other participant was armed with such a weapon, instrument, article or substance; and

   (d) Had no reasonable ground to believe that any other participant intended to engage in conduct likely to result in death or serious physical injury; or

4. Under circumstances evincing a depraved indifference to human life, and being eighteen years old or more the defendant recklessly engages in conduct which creates a grave risk of serious physical injury or death to another person less than eleven years old and thereby causes the death of such person; or

5. Being eighteen years old or more, while in the course of committing rape in the first, second or third degree, criminal sexual act in the first, second or third degree, sexual abuse in the first degree, aggravated sexual abuse in the first, second, third or fourth degree, or incest in the first, second or third degree, against a person less than fourteen years old, he or she intentionally causes the death of such person.

Murder in the second degree is a class A-I felony.

§ 125.26 Aggravated murder.

[omitted]

§ 125.27 Murder in the first degree.

A person is guilty of murder in the first degree when:

1. With intent to cause the death of another person, he causes the death of such person or of a third person; and
   (a) Either:
   (i) the intended victim was a police officer . . . who was at the time of the killing engaged in the course of performing his official duties, and the defendant knew or reasonably should have known that the intended victim was a police officer; or
   (ii) the intended victim was a peace officer . . . who was at the time of the killing engaged in the course of performing his official duties, and the defendant knew or reasonably should have known that the intended victim was such a uniformed court officer, parole officer, probation officer, or employee of the division for youth; or
   (iii) the intended victim was an employee of a state correctional institution or was an employee of a local correctional facility . . ., who was at the time of the killing engaged in the course of performing his official duties, and the defendant knew or reasonably should have known that the intended victim was an employee of a state correctional institution or a local correctional facility; or
   (iv) at the time of the commission of the killing, the defendant was confined in a state correctional institution or was otherwise in custody upon a sentence for the term of his natural life, or upon a sentence commuted to one of natural life, or upon a sentence for an indeterminate term the minimum of which was at least fifteen years and the maximum of which was natural life, or at the time of the commission of the killing, the defendant had escaped from such confinement or custody while serving such a sentence and had not yet been returned to such confinement or custody; or
   (v) the intended victim was a witness to a crime committed on a prior occasion and the death was caused for the purpose of preventing the intended victim's testimony in any criminal action or proceeding whether or not such action or proceeding had been commenced, or the intended victim had previously testified in a criminal action or proceeding and the killing was committed for the purpose of exacting retribution for such prior testimony, or the intended victim was an immediate family member of a witness to a crime committed on a prior occasion and the killing was committed for the purpose of preventing or influencing the testimony of such witness, or the intended victim was an immediate family member of a witness who had previously testified in a criminal action or proceeding and the killing was committed for the purpose of exacting retribution upon such witness for such prior testimony. As used in this subparagraph "immediate family member" means a husband, wife, father, mother, daughter, son, brother, sister, stepparent, grandparent, stepchild or grandchild; or
   (vi) the defendant committed the killing or procured commission of the killing pursuant to an agreement with a person other than the intended victim to commit the same for the receipt, or in expectation of the receipt, of anything of pecuniary value from a party to the agreement or from a person other than the intended victim acting at the direction of a party to such agreement; or
   (vii) the victim was killed while the defendant was in the course of committing or attempting to commit and in furtherance of robbery, burglary in the first degree or second degree, kidnapping in the first degree, arson in the first degree or second degree, rape in the first degree, criminal sexual act in the first degree, sexual abuse in the first degree, aggravated sexual abuse in the first degree or escape in the first degree, or in the course of and furtherance of immediate flight after committing or attempting to commit any such crime or in the course of and furtherance of immediate flight after attempting to commit the crime of murder in the second degree; provided however, the victim is not a participant in one of the aforementioned crimes and, provided further that, unless the defendant's criminal liability under this subparagraph is based upon the defendant having commanded another person to cause the death of the victim or intended victim pursuant to section 20.00 of this chapter, this subparagraph shall not apply where the defendant's criminal liability is based upon the conduct of another pursuant to section 20.00 of this chapter; or
   (viii) as part of the same criminal transaction, the defendant, with intent to cause serious physical injury to or the death of an additional person or persons, causes the death of an

additional person or persons; provided, however, the victim is not a participant in the criminal transaction; or

(ix) prior to committing the killing, the defendant had been convicted of murder as defined in this section or section 125.25 of this article, or had been convicted in another jurisdiction of an offense which, if committed in this state, would constitute a violation of either of such sections; or

(x) the defendant acted in an especially cruel and wanton manner pursuant to a course of conduct intended to inflict and inflicting torture upon the victim prior to the victim's death. As used in this subparagraph, "torture" means the intentional and depraved infliction of extreme physical pain; "depraved" means the defendant relished the infliction of extreme physical pain upon the victim evidencing debasement or perversion or that the defendant evidenced a sense of pleasure in the infliction of extreme physical pain; or

(xi) the defendant intentionally caused the death of two or more additional persons within the state in separate criminal transactions within a period of twenty-four months when committed in a similar fashion or pursuant to a common scheme or plan; or

(xii) the intended victim was a judge . . . and the defendant killed such victim because such victim was, at the time of the killing, a judge; or

(xiii) the victim was killed in furtherance of an act of terrorism . . . ; and

(b) The defendant was more than eighteen years old at the time of the commission of the crime.

2. In any prosecution under subdivision one, it is an affirmative defense that:

(a) The defendant acted under the influence of extreme emotional disturbance for which there was a reasonable explanation or excuse, the reasonableness of which is to be determined from the viewpoint of a person in the defendant's situation under the circumstances as the defendant believed them to be. Nothing contained in this paragraph shall constitute a defense to a prosecution for, or preclude a conviction of, manslaughter in the first degree or any other crime except murder in the second degree; or

(b) The defendant's conduct consisted of causing or aiding, without the use of duress or deception, another person to commit suicide. Nothing contained in this paragraph shall constitute a defense to a prosecution for, or preclude a conviction of, manslaughter in the second degree or any other crime except murder in the second degree.

Murder in the first degree is a class A-I felony.

German Criminal Code

Special Part
Chapter Sixteen
Offenses Against Life

§ 211 (Murder)

(1) Murderers will be punished with life imprisonment.

(2) A murderer is who for pleasure of killing, for sexual gratification, out of greed or otherwise base motives, insidiously or cruelly or by means that pose a danger to the public, or in order to facilitate or to cover up another offense, kills a human being.

§ 212 (Manslaughter)

(1) Who kills a human being without being a murderer will be punished as a manslaughterer with imprisonment of not less than five years.

(2) In especially serious cases the punishment will be life imprisonment.

§ 213 (Less Serious Cases of Manslaughter)*

If the manslaughterer, without his own fault, was provoked to rage by the killed person through maltreatment or serious insult inflicted on him or a relative, and thereby was carried away immediately to commit the offense, or in another less serious case, the punishment will be imprisonment from one to ten years.

---

* [§§ 214 & 215 were repealed in 1941: § 214 contained an offense description similar to the one now in § 211 StGB regarding killing in order to facilitate or to cover up another offense, and § 215 increased punishment for simple homicide if the victim was the offender's parent or a grandparent.—Eds.]

§ 216 (Killing on Request)*

(1) If a person was incited to kill another person by the victim's explicit and earnest request, the punishment will be imprisonment from six months to five years.

(2) The attempt is punishable.

§ 221 (Abandonment)

(1) Who

1. brings a human being into a helpless situation; or
2. abandons a human being in a helpless situation although he is obliged to care for him or otherwise is obliged to give assistance,
   and thereby exposes him to a danger of death or serious injury of health, will be punished with imprisonment from three months to five years.

(2) The punishment will be imprisonment from one to ten years if the offender commits the offense against his child or a person entrusted to him for education or care; or through the offense causes serious injury to the victim's health.

(3) If the offender causes the death of the victim the punishment will be imprisonment of not less than three years.

(4) In less serious cases under para. 2 the punishment will be imprisonment from six months to five years, in less serious cases under para. 3 imprisonment from one to ten years.

§ 222 (Negligent Homicide)

Who causes the death of a human being through negligence will be punished with imprisonment of not more than five years or a fine.

NOTES

1. The categories of offenses against life in Anglo-American criminal law differ from those in German law. This complicates comparisons. Both systems distinguish between three types of homicide: murder-manslaughter-negligent homicide and *Mord-Totschlag-fahrlässige Tötung*. At the bottom end, negligent homicide and *fahrlässige Tötung* are roughly comparable (apart from the question of the general relationship between the mental states of negligence and *Fahrlässigkeit*, explored in Chapter 8.A).

The top and intermediate types of homicide, however, do no match up quite so nicely. In the Anglo-American scheme, murder and manslaughter differ primarily in the mental state requirement attached to the result element, death: murder requires intent (knowledge, purpose), manslaughter requires recklessness. (Leaving aside so-called "voluntary manslaughter" for the moment.) In the German scheme, *Mord* differs from *Totschlag* not in the requisite mental state (intent, or *Vorsatz*, in both cases), but in certain aggravating circumstances, which mark the offender as a murderer (*Mörder*). Note, here, that the murder provision in fact defines a murderer, rather than murder, that is the actor, rather than the act. (For further discussion of this instance of *Täterstrafrecht*, or actor criminal law, as distinct from *Tatstrafrecht*, or act criminal law, see Chapter 15.A.ii.)

The use of aggravating circumstances is familiar from the American law of homicide, though here it is used to distinguish between different degrees of murder: first degree murder is second degree murder, plus one or more aggravating circumstances. New York Penal Law § 125.27(1)(a) provides a fairly common list of aggravating circumstances, which turn on a range of factors, including characteristics of the victim [(i), (ii), (iii), (v), (xii)], the offender [(iv), (ix), (x)], or the act [(vi), (vii), (viii), (xi), (xiii)]. The distinction between first and second degree murder was significant in American criminal law because it traditionally marked the line between (at least potentially) capital and non-capital murder.

---

* [§ 217 was repealed in 1998; it provided for mitigation of punishment if a mother killed a child born out of wedlock while or immediately after giving birth; §§ 218–219b concern abortion; § 220, which criminalized abortion advertisements, was repealed in 1974; § 220a, on genocide, was repealed in 2002 when it became part of the new International Criminal Law Code.—Eds.]

So-called voluntary manslaughter differs from murder not in the requisite mental state regarding the resulting death. It is murder (i.e., intentional homicide), plus *provocation* (in traditional common law terms) or *extreme emotional or mental disturbance* (in Model Penal Code lingo, § 210.3(1)(b)) or *extreme emotional disturbance* (under the New York Penal Law, § 125.20(2), and many other Model Penal Code-based American criminal codes). Voluntary manslaughter is called, misleadingly, "voluntary," to distinguish it from "involuntary" manslaughter, which requires only recklessness, not intention. ("Misleadingly" because voluntariness is generally treated as a matter of *actus reus*, not *mens rea*; voluntary manslaughter is not voluntary, but intentional. On voluntariness, see Chapter 7.A.)

German criminal law also recognizes provocation as a mitigating factor, but only within the realm of *Totschlag*, not within the realm of homicide in general. Provocation reduces what otherwise would be a case of *Totschlag* to a case of *minder schwerer Totschlag*, i.e., manslaughter to a less serious case of manslaughter.

2. But if one moves beyond the obstacles of translation, the basic structure, especially of the section on homicide in the Model Penal Code, is not unfamiliar to a German reader.

(Here it is worth noting that the New York Penal Law homicide scheme, in its basic structure, follows that of the Model Penal Code—though as we'll see, it supplemented, and obscured, that structure with a great many details. The traditional common law scheme did not distinguish between manslaughter and negligent homicide. Instead, it differentiated between murder (and, within murder, often between first and second degree murder) and manslaughter, with what we now would call negligent homicide treated as an instance of homicide without "malice," the distinguishing feature of murder. The Model Penal Code discarded the term "malice"—which comes in "express" and "implied" varieties—as hopelessly vague; nonetheless, it survives in the law of murder in jurisdictions that do not follow the Model Penal Code in general, or on this point in particular.)

While it would be conceivable that a legal system would work with one or two offense descriptions to capture all cases of punishable killing, using a variety of offense definitions, and their attendant sanctions, serves to better capture the objective features of killing another human being and the nuances of offenders' *mens rea* and culpability. Whether a legal system opts for four to six categories (German Criminal Code: murder, manslaughter, less serious cases of manslaughter, negligent homicide) or three basic categories (Model Penal Code: murder, manslaughter, negligent homicide) is a matter of detail.

That said, perplexing from the perspective of a German reader is the intricacy of the New York Penal Law homicide provisions. To multiply the categories of negligent homicide, manslaughter and negligent homicide with variations such as "aggravated," "first and second degree," plus special descriptions for vehicular homicide results in a multitude of offense descriptions. The complexity of this system certainly overburdens lay people's ability to understand, and, from the perspective of legal comparison, invites the question: why these complicated distinctions and this (in comparison to the conciseness and neatness of the Model Penal Code scheme) vastly increased number of offenses?

No one would mistake the New York Penal Law's homicide scheme for a model of statutory drafting, in form or in substance. (Unlike the Model Penal Code, the New York code was not a model piece of legislation, nor was it drafted by a group of distinguished academics, lawyers, and judges; it was, and has remained, a political document, for better, and for worse.) While the New York Penal Law in general is modeled on the Model Penal Code (Herbert Wechsler was a member of the New York code revision commission), the Model Code had a greater influence on the Penal Law's general part than on its special part. In some cases the Penal Law drafters simplified the Model Code's overly complex approach to a doctrinal issue, in others they overcomplicated the Model Code's straightforward solution. The homicide provisions combine elements of the Model Penal Code approach with remnants of traditional common law doctrine, such as "depraved indifference" murder (see the next section). Over the years, the legislature added provisions that further complicated the original scheme, presumably in response to some felt need for political action (which, in the field of criminal law, tends to result in addition, rather than in subtraction, of provisions).

There is, however, also the more general, and more interesting, matter of common law statutory drafting, which traditionally has been fond of detail, preferring a list of specific provisions, accompanied by a list of definitions, to a statement of general norms. From the perspective of this tradition, the German Criminal Code looks surprisingly indefinite, and incomplete, leaving much to the interpretation, and even creation, of others. Those "others," in the common law world, of course, would be the judges. In Germany, however, the assumption traditionally has been that professors, i.e., legal scientists, will fill the gaps left (intentionally) by the drafters, with judges then choosing between rival scientific theories, although this division of labor appears to have shifted in recent decades, as judges have taken a more active role.* The Model Penal Code tried to find a middle ground, by often resorting to general provisions, and having acknowledged, and in fact embraced, the inevitability of residual judicial discretion in even the most detailed and comprehensive code, then adding a set of general interpretive norms to guide the exercise of that discretion. See, e.g., §§ 1.02 ("principles of construction"), 2.02(3)–(10) (interpretation of mental state requirements).

Leaving the New York Penal Law's homicide provisions aside, one function of a multiplicity of offense definitions, and offense types and degrees, could be the indirect development of a differentiated law of sentencing without the use of separate sentencing guidelines, assuming, of course, a systematic arrangement of offense definitions, and attendant specific sentence prescriptions. Of course, this may not be seen as particularly desirable in a system that delegates sentencing largely to judicial discretion, such as the Model Penal Code and German criminal law.† Alternatively, one might leave matters of sentencing to sentencing guidelines, which can draw the same distinctions, explicitly and directly:

U.S. Sentencing Guidelines § 2A1.4. Involuntary Manslaughter

(a) Base Offense Level:
   (1) 12, if the offense involved criminally negligent conduct; or
   (2) (Apply the greater):
      (A) 18, if the offense involved reckless conduct; or
      (B) 22, if the offense involved the reckless operation of a means of transportation.

ii. Murder

Murder/*Mord* sits atop the hierarchy of homicides in both systems. Also in both systems, the question arises whether murder is more than merely the most serious type of homicide, *primus inter pares*, or whether something more separates it from the other types of homicide, and perhaps even from all other offenses. The distinction between murder, on one side, and manslaughter and negligent homicide, on the other, in the Model Penal Code appears to be much less pronounced than in the German Criminal Code, or perhaps in the common law generally speaking. Note, for instance, that the Model Penal Code begins with an overall definition of "homicide," and only then defines the various types of homicide, starting with murder and then descending through its line-up of mental states (purpose, knowledge, recklessness, negligence). In contrast, the German Criminal Code launches directly into a definition of murder(er), followed by manslaughter, then a host of other provisions (including abortion), and returning to negligent homicide only at the end of the chapter on offenses against life. The German Criminal Code also tries to capture something unique about murder, or more precisely, about those who commit it, in terms that recall similar attempts in the traditional common law jurisprudence of murder, which turned on the concept of malice, and malice aforethought in particular. (Interestingly, the drafters of the Prussian

---

* For an interesting exploration of some of these issues, see Henry M. Hart, Jr. and Albert M. Sacks, *The Legal Process: Basic Problems in the Making and Application of Law* (William N. Eskridge and Philip P. Frickey eds., 1994) [1958], 749–73.

† See Gerard E. Lynch, "Towards a Model Penal Code, Second (Federal): The Challenge of the Special Part," 2 *Buffalo Criminal Law Review* (1998), 297.

Criminal Code of 1851, on which the German Criminal Code is based, rejected as too vague a proposed general definition of homicide (*Tötung*) as "an unlawful act or omission causing the death of a human being.")* The New York Penal Law, we'll see, occupies an uncomfortable middle position between the Model Penal Code and the German Criminal Code, which has created considerable confusion among New York courts, as the next case illustrates.

Intentional and depraved indifference murder

The New York Penal Law distinguishes between two types of (second-degree) murder: intentional and depraved indifference murder. The former is based on the Model Penal Code homicide scheme, based on distinctions among mental state requirements regarding the result element of homicide: death; the former reflects the traditional common law approach to murder, driven by the inquiry into malice. Are these approaches compatible? And how do they match up against the German Criminal Code's consideration of "base motives"?

People v. Payne
Court of Appeals of New York
3 N.Y.3d 266, 819 N.E.2d 634 (2004)

Rosenblatt, J.

We once again address the crime of depraved indifference murder and where it fits within the Penal Law's statutory framework. In the appeal before us, defendant, armed with a twelve-gauge shotgun, went to the deceased's home and shot him at point-blank range. After acquitting defendant of intentional murder—the first count in a two-count indictment—the jury was improperly allowed to consider depraved indifference murder and found defendant guilty.

The Appellate Division affirmed, and a Judge of this Court granted leave to appeal. We reverse. Defendant did not commit depraved indifference murder.

Defendant and the deceased, Curtis Cook, had been friends for nearly twenty years, but their relationship began to sour in 1998. In March of that year, Cook was arrested and accused of sexually abusing an eight-year-old girl, a playmate of defendant's daughter . . .

On April 27, 1998, defendant drank large amounts of alcohol at a local bar, while Cook drank at home. When defendant's girlfriend arrived at the tavern to take him home, she told defendant that Cook telephoned her to complain about defendant's dog. This infuriated defendant, because Cook had been belligerent toward the girlfriend and defendant had warned him never to communicate with her.

Following a telephone conversation with Cook, defendant went to his closet and took out a twelve-gauge shotgun. He referred to the weapon as an "elephant gun." With the loaded weapon in hand, defendant walked next door to confront Cook. After the two exchanged words, defendant shot Cook at point-blank range, killing him. The wound was below the heart and just above the navel. Defendant admitted the shooting and presented a justification defense, which by its verdict the jury rejected.[1]

Pursuant to Penal Law § 125.25 (2), a person is guilty of depraved indifference murder when "under circumstances evincing a depraved indifference to human life, he recklessly engages in conduct which creates a grave risk of death to another person, and thereby causes the death of another person." In People v. Gonzalez (1 NY3d 464, 807 N.E.2d 273, 775 N.Y.S.2d 224 [2004]), the Court reversed a depraved indifference murder conviction for legal insufficiency. There, the defendant kicked in the door of a barber shop, pulled a gun from his waistband and, at close range, shot the victim several times. We held that because it evinced an intent to kill, a homicide of that type could not constitute depraved indifference murder. Indifference to the victim's life, we explained, contrasts with the intent to take it. Here, as in Gonzalez, the evidence established defendant's intent to kill.

The prosecution seeks to distinguish Gonzalez, asserting that here defendant's conduct was not "overtly intentional" in that he did not plan or contrive the shooting, and that the jury could have concluded that the homicide was merely instinctive—the result of a reckless act in arming himself before confronting Cook. This theory is flawed and reveals a fundamental misunderstanding of the concepts underlying depraved indifference murder.

To begin with, intentional murder does not require planning or contrivance. The premeditation element was eliminated in the 1967 Penal Law. Secondly, by the prosecution's theory, homicides

---

* Georg Beseler, *Kommentar über das Strafgesetzbuch für die Preußischen Staaten* (1851), 342–3 (discussing § 222 of the 1830 draft).

---

[1] Neither side asked that the jury consider lesser included charges.

could be routinely categorized and sustained as depraved indifference murder whenever the defendant brought a weapon to a contentious confrontation. Inasmuch as it is "reckless" to arm oneself under those circumstances or to wield a weapon carelessly (the argument goes) any homicide that results could qualify as depraved indifference murder. That is not the law. If it were, every homicide, particularly intentional ones, would be converted into depraved indifference murder.

Moreover, the prosecutor's position is based on the erroneous notion that the wanton disregard for human life inherent in every intentional homicide amounts to depraved indifference murder. In Gonzalez, this Court rejected that contention, holding that the reckless conduct must be "so wanton, so deficient in a moral sense of concern, so devoid of regard for the life or lives of others, and so blameworthy as to warrant the same criminal liability as that which the law imposes upon a person who intentionally causes the death of another" (1 NY3d at 469).

The use of a weapon can never result in depraved indifference murder when, as here, there is a manifest intent to kill . . .

This Court differentiated cases like the one before us (and Gonzalez) from homicides in which a defendant lacking the intent to kill (but oblivious to the consequences and with depraved indifference to human life) shoots into a crowd or otherwise endangers innocent bystanders. People v. Jernatowski (238 NY 188, 144 N.E. 497, 41 N.Y. Cr. 325 [1924]) is a prominent example of this genre. There, the defendant fired shots into a house, killing the wife of a man with whom he had a confrontation. Similarly, in People v. Fenner (61 N.Y.2d 971, 463 N.E.2d 617, 475 N.Y.S.2d 276 [1984]), defendant fired into a fleeing crowd. In People v. Russell (91 N.Y.2d 280, 693 N.E.2d 193, 670 N.Y.S.2d 166 [1998]), defendant shot and killed an innocent bystander during a gun battle and in People v. Gomez (65 N.Y.2d 9, 478 N.E.2d 759, 489 N.Y.S.2d 156 [1985]), defendant struck a child with a car, accelerated, and killed another child while speeding on crowded sidewalks. The case before us involves a crime directed at a single individual—and, moreover, an intentional killing—as opposed to the generalized depraved indifference exemplified in the above cases.

We have recognized another species of depraved indifference murder in which the acts of the defendant are directed against a particular victim but are marked by uncommon brutality—coupled not with an intent to kill, as in Gonzalez and the case before us, but with depraved indifference to the victim's plight. Instances include where, without the intent to kill, the defendant inflicted continuous beating on a three-year-old child (see People v. Poplis, 30 N.Y.2d 85, 281 N.E.2d 167, 330 N.Y.S.2d 365 [1972]), fractured the skull of a seven-week-old baby (see People v. Bryce, 88 N.Y.2d 124, 666 N.E.2d 221, 643 N.Y.S.2d 516 [1996]), repeatedly beat a nine-year-old (see People v. Best, 85 N.Y.2d 826, 648 N.E.2d 782, 624 N.Y.S.2d 363 [1995]) or robbed an intoxicated victim and forced him out of a car on the side of a dark, remote, snowy road partially dressed and without shoes in subfreezing temperatures (see People v. Kibbe, 35 N.Y.2d 407, 321 N.E.2d 773, 362 N.Y.S.2d 848 [1974]; see also People v. Mills, 1 NY3d 269, 804 N.E.2d 392, 772 N.Y.S.2d 22 [2003]).

As the drafters of the Penal Law put it, "depraved indifference murder is 'extremely dangerous and fatal conduct performed without specific homicidal intent but with a depraved kind of wantonness: for example, shooting into a crowd, placing a time bomb in a public place, or opening the door of the lion's cage in the zoo' " (Denzer and McQuillan, Practice Commentary, McKinney's Cons Laws of NY, Book 39, Penal Law § 125.25, at 235 [1967]).

Thus, if a defendant fatally shoots the intended victim once, it could be murder, manslaughter in the first or second degree or criminal negligence (or self-defense), but not depraved indifference murder. Moreover, it should be obvious that the more the defendant shoots (or stabs or bludgeons) the victim, the more clearly intentional is the homicide. Firing more rounds or inflicting more wounds does not make the act more depravedly indifferent, but more intentional. Absent the type of circumstances in, for example, Sanchez (where others were endangered), a one-on-one shooting or knifing (or similar killing) can almost never qualify as depraved indifference murder . . .

Defendant did not commit depraved indifference murder within the meaning of the statute. Therefore, the order of the Appellate Division should be reversed and the indictment dismissed.

German Federal Court of Justice
1 StR 49/93, BGH NJW 1993, 1664 (February 18, 1993)

Facts

The defendant had come to know two young foreign women, who were related to each other, in a bar, and had immediately begun a relationship with one of them. He took them both into his residence and placed them, for the purpose of carrying out prostitution, at another bar, which was run by the later victim A. The defendant agreed with A. that A. would let the defendant have a quarter of the earnings which each of the two witnesses obtained by carrying out prostitution in the bar. This agreement was observed for about two weeks. Then the witnesses left the defendant's residence after it had become evident that he had another girl friend, and went into accommodation provided by A. After relationships between the witnesses and the defendant had ceased, and A. himself had to pay for the accommodation of the witnesses, he stopped making the payments to the defendant. Demands by the defendant to the witnesses to pay him directly were as ineffective as his attempt to induce the witnesses to transfer their activity to another bar. The defendant did not intend to resign himself to loss of his source of income, and made continual but fruitless efforts to cause A. to make further payments. This resulted in repeated (verbal) disputes between the defendant and A., which—in this respect nothing precise can be deduced from the reasons in the judgment—evidently extended over some days or even weeks. After repeatedly announcing his intention, the defendant shot A. with a pistol on January 15, 1992, during such a dispute. The regional court sentenced the defendant to life imprisonment for murder committed out of greed.

His appeal in law succeeded with its substantive objection, as the findings of the regional court do not support the finding of greed.

Reasons

2. [T]he criminal chamber sees the element of greed in the definition of murder fulfilled because the defendant's "decisive motive" was "...his unrestrained striving for a continuous source of income from the earnings of the girls" and he "did not intend to resign himself" to a refusal of payments by A.

3. These considerations do not stand up to legal examination.

a) Greed means a striving for material goods or advantages which in its lack of restraint and consideration far exceeds the extent that is tolerable and which as a rule is driven by uninhibited compulsive selfishness (BGHSt 29, 317).

It is a prerequisite for this that the perpetrator's wealth—objectively or at least according to his own ideas—increases directly as a result of the victim's death, or that in any case a prospect, which is otherwise not present, of a direct increase in his wealth arises from the crime. That is the case, for instance, if the perpetrator intends by the victim's death to give himself the opportunity of taking away a valuable object belonging to the victim (see BGHSt 29, 317 (318)), if he will become the victim's heir as a result of his death (Jähnke, in: LK, 10th edit., § 211 marginal no. 8), if he is the beneficiary of a life insurance policy taken out on the victim's life (see BGHSt 32, 38 (40, 43)), or if the perpetrator kills the victim in order to obtain a reward (Jähnke, in: LK, § 211 marginal no. 8). Even the intention of freeing oneself from a burdensome debt or a duty of maintenance by the killing satisfies the greed element according to the case law (see OGHSt 1, 81; BGHSt 10, 399).

b) An association of this kind, or one comparable with it, between the victim's death and an enrichment of the perpetrator is not evident here. The death of A. excluded any future payments by him to the defendant. The reasons for the judgment do not contain any findings that as a result of A's death parts of the witnesses' incomes obtained by prostitution would go to the defendant in some other way, or that he at least believed that this would happen. The reasons for the judgment only reveal that the defendant killed A. out of rage and irritation that the increase in his income which he hoped to obtain failed to materialize; but his crime did not bring him any nearer to this goal either objectively or in his mind. This does not justify the finding of greed.

4. On the basis of its contrary view, the criminal chamber has differentiated between killing out of greed on the one hand and the motives additionally present of "rage and irritation," and has seen in this "no independent base motive" in the sense of § 211 Criminal Code. The criminal chamber called on to make the new decision will if necessary have to take the following into account in the examination of this element of murder: A killing occurs out of a base motive if the motive for the crime is at the lowest level according to general moral evaluation, and is therefore especially contemptible. Whether this is the case will be assessed on the basis of an overall evaluation which includes the circumstances of the crime, the perpetrator's background, and his personality (see BGHSt 35, 116 (127)...). This overall evaluation can if necessary also include whether the defendant—also—killed A. in order to make it clear "that he...was to be taken seriously now and in the future."

German Federal Court of Justice
3 StR 90/69, BGHSt 23, 119 (October 8, 1969)

Reasons

The regional court gave the defendant two life sentences for murder in two cases. The defendant killed Mrs. M. and their son, with whom he had been living until then, with an axe while they were both sleeping.

The defendant's appeal in law, which is based on the violation of procedural and substantive law, is directed against this judgment. The appeal is unsuccessful.

1. The finding of the regional court that the defendant killed Mrs. M. and the boy insidiously meets with no legal reservations.

In the decision BGH, NJW 66, 1823, the Federal Supreme Court has admittedly observed that the killing of an unconscious person cannot be insidious because that person cannot resist the attack (BGH, loc. cit. p. 1824), i.e., in the light of his condition it could not be insidious even if the attack would have been recognizable in time. Dreher equates the sleeping person to the unconscious person (Schwarz-Dreher, StGB, 30th edit., § 211 note 1 B b). That cannot however be acceded to; the sleeping person is a different type of case.

A person kills insidiously if he deliberately exploits his victim's absence of suspicion and defenselessness in order to kill him (BGHSt [GSSt] 11, 139, 143). A person is unsuspecting if he—at least at this time—is not expecting an attack by the perpetrator on his life (BGHSt 7, 218). The sleeping person is as a rule unsuspecting when he falls asleep. He abandons himself to sleep in the confidence that nothing will happen to him; in this confidence he resigns himself to defenselessness. From this point of view BGH, LM no. 5 on § 211 StGB approves conviction for murder (see further BGHSt 8, 216, 218; BGH, Judgment of May 15, 1956, 5 StR 112/56 in Pfeiffer-Maul-Schulte, StGB, p. 531 below). On the other hand the unconscious person is overcome by his condition without being able to prevent it; he cannot be deceived in an expectation that nobody will harm him.

Admittedly the intention to kill must be present while the victim is still unsuspecting (see BGHSt 19, 321). He is, however, unsuspecting not only *before* he falls asleep. A person who lies down to sleep takes his unsuspecting state with him into sleep. It accompanies him, even if he is no longer aware of it. The especially dangerous and "treacherous" features of the killing which expose the perpetrator to life imprisonment lie in the fact that he surprises his victim in a helpless situation, and thereby prevents him from resisting the attack on his life or at least making it more difficult. The statute is less concerned with the perpetrator here than with the victim (BGHSt [GSSt] 11, 139, 143, 144). In this sense the killing of a sleeping person is the almost classic example of insidiousness. Whether an exception to this must apply if someone has been overcome by sleep against his will (see BGH, Judgment of June 21, 1967, 4 StR 199/67) can remain open here.

The disputed judgment does justice to these principles. According to the findings neither Mrs. M. nor her son was expecting an attack when they laid themselves down to sleep. They took no measures of any kind for their safety, and did not lock the bedroom door "in full confidence that they were under no threat of danger from the defendant." This absence of suspicion and defenselessness was deliberately exploited by the defendant. The offense element of insidious action is thereby fulfilled (see also BGH, NJW 67, 1140, 1141, last paragraph). The fact that the son possibly awoke directly before the attack on him, and was therefore no longer unsuspecting, does not exclude the finding of insidiousness in this respect (see BGHSt 22, 77, 79).

The circumstances decisive for this legal assessment were apparent to the defendant—despite his drunkenness—"at a glance" (see BGHSt 6, 120, 121).

2. The finding of base motives is also not open to objection in the end result.

A motive for killing is base if, according to general moral evaluation, it is at the lowest level, induced by unrestrained, compulsive selfishness, and therefore especially reprehensible, even contemptible (BGHSt 3, 132). The regional court sees in the defendant's "feelings of revenge for unjust treatment and humiliations suffered, and jealousy" the impulses which governed him in relation to the crime; it regards these as base.

The lust for revenge can be a base motive (BGH, NJW 58, 189) but it need not be (BGH, Judgment of October 31, 1967, 5 StR 399/67; Judgment of August 27, 1968, 5 StR 180/68). According to the findings in the judgment, the defendant felt the conduct of Mrs. M., who had expelled him from the new home which had been partly furnished by him, to be especially ungrateful and selfish. She had deprived him, at any rate as he saw it, of the fruits of labor and care over the years; he, who had cared well for her and her children over fifteen years, felt himself humiliated and disowned. When it is taken further into consideration that Mrs. M. was partly to blame for the rift between her and the defendant because of her expensive purchases, and that he saw her action from his point of view as completely unjustified, doubts could—from this limited perspective—arise as to whether the crime appears to be reprehensible to such a high degree that it must arouse a definite feeling of contempt.

A single motive cannot however be evaluated on its own when deciding the question of whether a killing deserves this judgment. The evaluation must extend to the motives for the killing as a whole; it depends on the overall circumstances (BGH, NJW 54, 365, Judgment of September 2, 1960, 4 StR 275/60). The defendant's further "predominating" consideration, that if he could not keep what he had made for himself then others, his life companion and his son, should not have it, is of decisive significance here. The regional court correctly characterizes the decision to extinguish both lives with this objective as detestable and contemptible. Finally there is also the defendant's jealousy. He had no really convincing reason for this and he let it become so overpowering that it not only gave part of the stimulus to kill, but also found its expression in incision injuries which the defendant additionally inflicted on the dead woman in the genital area. According to his own words, he had not given Mrs. M. to anyone else, and he had the feeling that he must cut "that" out. Such excessive jealousy is not humanly comprehensible and stands at the lowest level (see on this BGHSt 3, 180, 182,183).

The overall picture of the beliefs and considerations inducing the defendant to commit the crime is accordingly characterized by ruthless egoism which the defendant, setting aside all natural inhibitions and ties, expressed in such a manner as to disavow the least degree of that moral responsibility which applies to everyone. The impulse behind his crime deserves no understanding of any kind, but only contempt (see BGHSt 3, 132, 133).

NOTES

1. In the original version of the German Criminal Code, the *Reichsstrafgesetzbuch* [RStGB] of 1871, the definition of murder in § 211, taken almost verbatim from the Prussian Criminal Code of 1851, read as follows:

> Who intentionally and with deliberation (*mit Überlegung*) kills a human being is punished by death for murder.

In 1941, however, § 211 was revised, and has remained unchanged to this day. This revision reflected a particular conception of penality, *Täterstrafrecht*, which sought to classify offenders according to types (*Tätertypen*) and was championed by several German criminal law theorists at the time, most notably Georg Dahm:

> Under this conception, the act was significant only as a symptom of the actor's characteristics . . . As with many other reforms implemented between 1933 and 1945, one can think of this conception of penality as a National Socialist innovation or as having deeper roots, particularly in the Progressive school of criminal law and criminology associated in Germany with Franz v. Liszt [1851–1919], depending on whether one emphasizes its specific racist, nationalistic, and communitarian aspects or its general shift of focus onto the offender's personality and the diagnosis of penal abnormality.
>
> In contemporary German criminal law, *Täterstrafrecht* is generally invoked as the contrast to *Tatstrafrecht*, the generally accepted conception of criminal law; at the same time, it is acknowledged that *Täterstrafrecht* is alive and well in juvenile criminal law, which turns on the diagnosis of "harmful tendencies." It is even said to help *limit* the scope of criminal law by insisting that criminal liability requires not only commission of the proscribed conduct but also possession of the requisite characteristics in general (as, for instance, . . . insufficient loyalty to law) and in particular (as envisaged in the conception of the offense).
>
> Markus D. Dubber, "Criminal Jurisdiction and Conceptions of Penality in Comparative Perspective," 63 University of Toronto Law Journal (2013), 247, 272.*

The revision of § 211 was the perhaps most significant, but not the only, reform based on *Täterstrafrecht*. A year earlier, in 1940, the primary basis of criminal jurisdiction had been changed from territoriality—based on the *locus criminis*—to active personality—based on the offender's citizenship, or rather membership in the German *Volk*. If crime was, in the final analysis, an act of disloyalty to the German people, or the *Führer*, it made sense that criminal jurisdiction attach to the actor, and more specifically to the actor who owed a duty of loyalty in the first place, as a member of the German *Volk*.[†] Unlike in the case of the definition of murder in § 211, Germany since has reverted to territoriality as the primary jurisdictional basis.[‡]

---

* See generally Richard Wetzell, *Inventing the Criminal: A History of German Criminology from 1880–1945* (2000).

† See Georg Dahm, "Verrat und Verbrechen" ["Treason and Felony"], 95 *Zeitschrift für die gesamte Strafrechtswissenschaft* (1935), 283; Friedrich Schaffstein, "Das Verbrechen als Pflichtverletzung," in Karl Larenz (ed.), *Grundfragen der neuen Rechtswissenschaft* ["Felony as Violation of Duty"] (1935), 108.

‡ See Albin Eser, "Die Entwicklung des Internationales Strafrechts im Lichte des Werkes von Hans-Heinrich Jescheck," in Theo Vogler (ed.), *Festschrift für Hans-Heinrich Jescheck zum 70. Geburtstag* (1985), vol. 2, 1353–77.

2. Apart from the shift of focus from act to actor, the 1941 reform also made another significant change: it eliminated the requirement of premeditation, or deliberation (*Überlegung*). This is particularly interesting from a comparative perspective, because the pre-1941 murder definition in the German Criminal Code closely resembled the traditional common law definition of murder, which likewise required premeditation. That requirement, however, was heavily criticized as vague and pointless and was abandoned by the Model Penal Code.

Consider this fascinating discussion of the revised German murder provision in a 1949 decision by the U.S. Military Court of Appeals in the American Occupation Zone, some thirteen years *before* the completion of the Model Penal Code in 1962, but over a decade after the publication of a critique of the premeditation requirement, by Herbert Wechsler, in "A Rationale of the Law of Homicide," a groundbreaking article on American criminal law, published in 1937—four years before the reform of § 211 Criminal Code—which lays out Wechsler's treatmentist approach to criminal law, and eventually to the American Law Institute's Model Penal Code project, which he went on to lead after the war:

> The draftsmen of the Military Government laws were not content to leave amended Sec. 211 untouched. If they had thought that the section expressed some Nazi ideology they could have used the powers granted them under Control Council Law No. 11 and abrogated it. . . . [A]lthough the section was amended by the Nazis, it represented a penological thinking long under consideration by many persons other than Nazis. . . .
>
> [T]he purpose and background of the 1941 Amendment to Sec. 211 of the German Criminal Code . . . was most certainly to meet the objections that many students of the criminal law had been making to both the penological theory and the practical application of the premeditation concept. The commentators seem in thorough accord. So we find them saying:
>
> "Assuming that other factors indicate of his character [sic], such as knowledge, intent and motive are the same, of what additional importance is it that his act was the product of or was preceded by more or less deliberation? It may be argued that the more carefully considered and the less impulsive the act is, the more it indicates basic perversion of the actor's conceptions of good and evil. But it is surely not self-evident that the man who acts on wrong principles is a more dangerous man than one who acts without considering what is good. There are, moreover, other objections to this view of the significance of deliberation. In the first place, it ignores that passion may influence deliberation as well as lead to action without deliberation, so that deliberate as well as impulsive action may be contrary to the actor's real notions of good and evil. In the second place, it does not embrace either deliberation about means rather than ends or acts which are preceded by but are not in accord with the results of deliberation. And yet it is extremely difficult in most cases to discover in what terms the actor deliberated or what was the relationship between deliberation and act. These objections are not avoided by stating the significance of deliberation in another way. Thus it may be said that reflection prior to action indicates that the actor lacks the sort of desires that will prevent such an act, since reflection is the opportunity to bring such desires into play, an opportunity which, by hypothesis, is not afforded by impulsive action; whereas, action without reflection does not permit of that inference because if the actor had deliberated he might not have acted as he did. But in order to draw from these premises the conclusion that the man who acts deliberately is more dangerous than the man who acts impulsively, it must be asserted that the probability that the former's deliberations will result in wrong judgments is greater than the probability that the latter will not reflect before acting. This proposition also requires proof."[30]
>
> . . .
>
> The practical objection to the insistence upon premeditation lies in the complexities of its application. So again we have adverse comment:
>
> "The most striking phase of the development of the English law was the reduction of 'malice aforethought' to a term of art signifying neither 'malice' nor 'forethought' in the popular sense. Strikingly analogous in the judicial development of the American law of homicide is the narrow interpretation of 'deliberation' and 'premeditation' to exclude the two elements which the words normally signify: a determination to kill reached (1) calmly and (2) some appreciable

[30] [Jerome Michael & Herbert Wechsler,] A Rationale of the Law of Homicide II, 37 *Columbia Law Review*, 1283, 1284.

time prior to the homicide. The elimination of these elements leaves, as Judge Cardozo pointed out, nothing precise as the crucial state of mind but intention to kill."[34]

U.S. Mil. Gov't v. Rockenhaeuser, Court of Appeals, U.S. Mil. Gov't Courts,
U.S. Area of Control in Germany (Case No. 88, Opinion No. 70, September 20 1949),
3 Court of Appeals Reports Opinions Nos. 1–1083, at 82, 88–89, 90–91 (1949).

The original definition of murder, in the German Criminal Code of 1871 and the Prussian Criminal Code of 1851, closely resembled the definition of murder (or first degree murder) in American criminal law. The Model Penal Code eliminated the central element of premeditation; the criminal codes that were revised on the basis of the Code, including the New York Penal Law, generally followed suit:

> [The new murder provision] defines the basic crime as intentional killing, making no mention of premeditation and deliberation, which were, of course, elements of the former first degree offense and the factors which differentiated it from second degree murder. If those words denoted planning or preparation to kill formulated over a considerable period of time, there might be validity to the distinction drawn between intentional homicides of a premeditated and of an unpremeditated character. The inherent difficulty of precise definition, however, has produced a judicial construction of "premeditation" so broad that it includes a determination to kill formed a fleeting second before the homicidal act. Under that formulation—almost inevitable because of the impossibility of a definition based upon length of time—the determination of whether premeditation has occurred in a particular instance frequently amounted to no more than an exercise in semantics, and a jury's decision . . . turned upon an issue which not even experienced attorneys truly understand.

Proposed New York Penal Law, Commission Staff Notes § 130.25 (1964).

Other jurisdictions continue to struggle to make sense of this elusive concept. See, e.g., *State v. Thompson*, 204 Ariz. 471, 65 P.3d 420 (2003) ("if the only difference between first and second degree murder is the mere passage of time, and that length of time can be 'as instantaneous as successive thoughts of the mind,' then there is no meaningful distinction between first and second degree murder").

But, even assuming that courts in fact made a hash of the concept of premeditation, whose fault is that? Premeditation's? Or the courts'? Is it impossible to define premeditation, or deliberation? Is it any harder to define premeditation than any number of other concepts, like intention, or baseness, or indifference, or depravity, or conscious object(ive), or insiduousness?

3. Section 211 Criminal Code lists two types of circumstance that upgrade a killing from manslaughter *(Totschlag)* to murder *(Mord)*: *objective* conditions accompanying the killing (insidiously or cruelly or by means that pose a danger to the public) and *subjective* elements, that is, motives (the main term is: base motives—*niedere Beweggründe*—with examples of base motives listed: pleasure of killing, sexual gratification, greed, and the motive to facilitate or to cover up another offense). This way of differentiating murder from other, lesser, forms of homicide, in terms of the offender's motives that reflect a baseness, or meanness, of character, or disposition (*Gesinnung*) has roots that precede the arrival of National Socialist criminal law, and extend back to medieval law (a common feature of Nazi "reform" proposals, in fact, which tended to call for a return to a pre-liberal, truly German, state of legal affairs). Consider, for instance, Georg Beseler's 1851 comments on the then-freshly minted murder provision, § 175, in the new Prussian Criminal Code, upon which the original, pre-1941, version of § 211 in the German Criminal Code was based:

> The basic contours of this doctrine [of murder], as they have been worked out in common German criminal law and Prussian legislation, can already be found as an expression of old German legal ideas in the [Constitutional Criminalis] Carolina [of 1532], even if the actor's deliberation had been emphasized instead of the stealth, which the old law associated with the concept of murder. In this sense, the Prussian General Land Law, pt II, ti. 20, § 826, provided:
>
> > "Whoever, with the premeditated intent to kill in fact commits homicide, shall receive the punishment of the wheel from above as a murderer."

---

[34] A Rationale of the Law of Homicide, 37 *Columbia Law Review* 707, 708.

The [French] *Code pénal* shares this view, by labelling that which German criminal law calls murder, *assassinat* and requiring premeditation in its definition. The lying in wait (*guet-apens*), which is also listed, is only added as a particular manner of acting that reveals premeditation and therefore could have been omitted from the code.

Georg Beseler, *Kommentar über das Strafgesetzbuch für die Preußischen Staaten* (1851), 343–4.

4. At first glance, the definitions of murder in German law on the one hand, and the Model Penal Code (and also in New York Penal Law), on the other, might appear similar: in both systems a mixture of subjective and objective circumstances are used to develop the concept of murder. However, on second view, the picture is more complicated.

Some parallels can be found with respect to what is called "depraved indifference murder" in New York law. In *People v. Payne*, the New York Court of Appeals lists examples for depraved indifference that are similar to objective elements in § 211 Criminal Code. Most notably, both New York and German criminal law regard killing another person by shooting into a crowd, driving onto a crowded sidewalk and similar examples of killing "by means that pose a danger to the public" (§ 211 Criminal Code) as murder. Also, there is overlap between the element "cruelly" in § 211 Criminal Code and the second type of depraved indifference murder mentioned in *Payne* (reflecting "uncommon brutality" in the sense of "depraved indifference to the victim's plight"). According to German case law, cruelty requires the infliction of additional pain, physical or psychological, that is, severe pain beyond the level that is unavoidable in killing a human being (see, e.g., Federal Court of Justice, Judgment of September 30, 1952, 1 StR 243/52, BGHSt 3, 180; Judgment of June 17, 2004, 5 StR 115/03, BGHSt 49, 189). "Cruel" overlaps with, but is not identical to "brutal" (thus there arguably remains a difference to *Payne*, which does not differentiate between "uncommon brutality" and cruelty). The German Federal Court of Justice pointed out in the Judgment from 1952 that it is not decisive whether an observer would describe the mode of acting (in this case: numerous stabs with a knife) as cruel. What matters is if the individual victim suffered severe pain, which is not the case if they lost consciousness at the beginning. Therefore, acts of extreme violence may be brutal without necessarily also being "cruel" in the sense of § 211 Criminal Code.

Note that "cruel" (*grausam*) is treated as an objective offense element—an attendant circumstance in Model Penal Code lingo. Does that make sense? Is the offender's perception irrelevant given that the ultimate question is whether he or she qualifies as a "murderer"? Would the act be any less "cruel" if the offender did not know that the victim was unconscious?

Interestingly, the New York Court of Appeals struggled for many years with a similar question: how to classify "depraved indifference," or more specifically how to fit "depraved indifference," this holdover from the traditional common law lexicon, into the Model Penal Code scheme of mental state (which, ironically, was designed in large part to eliminate precisely these concepts, which the Code drafters considered moralistic, vague, and—at best—obfuscatory, out of step with the treatmentism they favored, which required a diagnosis of abnormal dangerousness, not of moral abnormality). Like German courts, the Court of Appeals decided not to characterize it as a mental state requirement (i.e., a subjective offense element). Instead, it referred to "objective circumstances," a *sui generis* element beyond *actus reus* and *mens rea*:

The Penal Law does not expressly define the term "element." However, it does set forth what the "elements" of an offense are and identifies them, as does the common law, as a culpable mental state (mens rea) and a voluntary act (actus reus) (Penal Law, § 15.10). Both are required in all but the strict liability offenses (id.). Consistent with that provision, the statutory definition of depraved mind murder includes both a mental element ("recklessly") and a voluntary act ("engaging in conduct which creates a grave risk of death to another person") (see Penal Law, § 125.25, subd. 2; §§ 15.05, 15.10). Recklessness refers to defendant's conscious disregard of a substantial risk (Penal Law, § 15.05, subd. 3) and the act proscribed, the risk creating conduct, is defined by the degree of danger presented. Depraved mind murder resembles manslaughter in the second degree (a reckless killing which includes the requirement that defendant disregard a substantial risk [Penal Law § 125.15, subd. 1; § 15.05, subd. 3]), but the depraved mind murder statute requires in addition not only that the conduct which results in death present a grave risk of death but that it also occur "[u]nder circumstances evincing a depraved indifference to human life." This additional requirement refers to neither the mens rea nor the actus reus. If it states an element of the crime at all, it is not an element in the traditional sense but rather a definition of the factual setting in which the risk creating conduct must occur— objective circumstances which are not subject to being negatived by evidence of defendant's intoxication.

People v. Register, 60 N.Y.2d 270 (1983).

Can German and New York court be seen as facing the same difficulty (and, incidentally, addressing it in oddly similar ways)? Is the challenge in both cases how to make room in a system of criminal law doctrine for an alien, and antiquated, norm? The same alien and antiquated norm that stems from a conception of crime as an expression of meanness, or baseness, and its punishment as a public reflection of that status?

Shifting our comparative analysis from the New York Penal Law to the Model Penal Code, is there an analogue to the inquiry into "base motives" in the Model Penal Code? Consider the reference to "circumstances manifesting extreme indifference to the value of human life." What is the significance of adding "depravity" into the mix? Is there a difference between "extreme indifference" and "depraved indifference"? The Model Penal Code drafters certainly thought there is, but perhaps they are wrong; perhaps any inquiry into extreme indifference, particularly in cases of homicide sufficiently serious, and exceptional even for the already serious offense of homicide, inevitably slips into the sort of moralistic search for meanness, malice, and wickedness, they hoped to leave behind and, if so, perhaps it is better to bring this search out into the open, rather than to force it underground, under the cover of an inquiry into a sort of heightened, or "extreme," form of recklessness:

As the commentary to the Model Penal Code explains, the culpability for non-intentional murder is extreme recklessness—i.e., the disregard of such a high degree of risk created by the actor's conduct that it "cannot fairly be distinguished in grading terms from homicides committed purposely or knowingly" (Model Penal Code § 210.2, Comment 4, at 21). That is because "purposeful or knowing homicide demonstrates precisely such indifference to the value of human life. Whether recklessness is so extreme that it demonstrates similar indifference is not a question, it is submitted, that can be further clarified. It must be left directly to the trier of fact under instructions which make it clear that recklessness that can fairly be assimilated to purpose or knowledge should be treated as murder and that less extreme recklessness should be punished as manslaughter" (id. at 22).

People v. Sanchez, 98 N.Y.2d 373 (2002)

Then again, perhaps the Model Penal Code drafters were wrong in a normative sense: is the inquiry into baseness not only inevitable, but desirable? Is the post-1941 version of § 211 German Criminal Code with its emphasis on "base motives" preferable to the pre-1941 one?

5. Leaving aside the issue of depravity and baseness, let us take a closer comparative look at the subjective aspect of the law of murder. Here, it is useful to recall our previous comparative analysis of the hierarchy of mental states, and to pay particular attention to the definition of the various modes of culpability in the New York Penal Law and the Model Penal Code, on one side, and German criminal law (though not the German Criminal Code, which does not address this issue), on the other. So, when the New York Penal Law defines murder as "with intent" causing the death of another person, note that "intentionally" is defined in the New York Penal Law "with respect to a result"—in this case, "death of another person"—as having the "conscious objective . . . to cause such result." In other words, "with intent" is the New York Penal Law equivalent of "purposely" in the Model Penal Code, which is there defined— again, with respect to a result element—as having the "conscious object . . . to cause such a result." Comparatively speaking, then, the mental state of "with intent" in the New York Penal Law, or its Model Penal Code analogue of "purposely," is not to be confused with the German mental state of *Vorsatz*, often translated as "intention." The better translation is *Absicht*, which is only one form of *Vorsatz*, which also encompasses knowledge and conditional intention. (For detailed discussion, see Chapter 8.A.)

Also note a distinction between the New York Penal Law and the Model Penal Code on this point. Where the New York Penal Law recognizes only "intentional"—in the sense of purposeful—murder (apart from depraved indifference murder), the Model Penal Code definition of murder encompasses both purposeful and knowing homicide: only under the Model Penal Code, then, would a defendant who was merely aware of a "practical certainty" of the result of death have the requisite *mens rea* for murder. In sum, the New York Penal Law recognizes two forms of murder: with purpose ("with intent") and with depraved indifference. The Model Penal recognizes three: with purpose, with knowledge, and with extreme indifference. Manslaughter, by contrast, requires recklessness with respect to the result element, and negligent homicide requires, well, negligence (disregarding voluntary manslaughter, or homicide that would be murder but for provocation, or extreme (mental or) emotional disturbance).

According to German law, the dividing line between murder (*Mord*) and simple homicide (*Totschlag*) is *not* drawn along the difference between purposefully killing another person on the one hand and conditional intention or knowledge on the other hand, nor—for that matter—at the line between knowledge and conditional intention: all types of intention (*Vorsatz*) are treated as equivalent. Even if the victim's death was the conscious object of the offender, the crime still will be labeled *Totschlag* (§ 212) rather than *Mord* (§ 211) if neither the objective conditions of insidiousness, cruelty or means posing a danger to the public, nor base motives were present. Motives count, according to § 211 Criminal Code, but not a difference between types of *Vorsatz*. (This also implies, of course, that it is at least theoretically possible to be convicted of murder based on proof of conditional intention only, provided one acted with the requisite base motives.)

6. Note that the German Federal Court of Justice aims to make trial courts assess "baseness of motives" without lapsing into general assessments of the offender's character. In the case decided in 1993, the facts supported the general moral judgment that the defendant was a greedy person. He financially exploited the two young women as a pimp and started the disputes with the later victim A. in order to continue this exploitation. (A footnote to the case: in Germany, prostitution is not a crime; it is a legal activity governed by statute, Law to Regulate the Legal Relations of Prostitutes from December 20, 2001, Federal Gazette—BGBl I p. 3983; penalized, however, are human trafficking, pimping, and exploitation of prostitutes (§§ 180a, 181a, 232 Criminal Code).) However, the obvious general greediness of the defendant did not translate into his murder liability. The Court analyzes the motive for the particular act of killing, not the broader motivational background. Killing A. did not increase the defendant's chances of again participating in the women's earnings; it had the opposite effect, as the women had made their money in A.'s bar. Rage and frustration about a source running dry are not the same as greed, the Court argues. (This may be so. But why should this make a difference for purposes of liability under criminal law, apart from the statutory language? Is acting out of greed worse than acting out of rage? More easily deterred? And once the court gets into the business of hazarding a detailed diagnosis of the defendant's greed, how should it define the context? Where did the defendant's greed end and his rage begin? How does the court differentiate between motives, and rank them according to their relative significance at a particular moment in time? Does the irrationality of behavior necessarily indicate the weakness of a given motive at a given moment, as opposed to its overpowering, blinding, strength?)

7. Among the objective conditions that upgrade manslaughter (*Totschlag*) to murder (*Mord*) according to § 211 Criminal Code, the element "insidiously" (*heimtückisch*) is the most complicated and controversial. The main principles are laid out in the German Federal Court of Justice decision from 1969. It is established case law that the first prerequisite is the victim's lack of suspicion, and the second, that the victim, due to his or her not suspecting a serious attack, was defenseless. A classic example is shooting at a victim who is unaware of the attacker from behind. The case law furthermore presupposes that the particular victim at the time of the crime was generally capable of harboring suspicion. This presupposition leads to the restrictive view that very young children can only be killed insidiously if an adult

guardian's absence of suspicion is exploited (see for such cases Federal Court of Justice, Judgment of November 4, 1952, 2 StR 261/52, BGHSt 4, 13), and also that someone who became unexpectedly unconscious, for instance, fainted, cannot be killed insidiously. However, as the Court argues in the Judgment from 1969, this does not apply to sleeping persons as they have taken absence of suspicion with them in the state of sleep. (What does this mean? What sort of theory of—the psychology, physiology, phenomenology of—sleep does this assume? Is this a scientific observation, or a normative assessment? If the former, how would we test this? Does it make sense to base the distinction between murder and manslaughter, between mandatory life imprisonment (§ 211 Criminal Code) and a minimum five year prison sentence (§ 212), on this sort of speculative analysis?)

From the perspective of criminal law theory, one can criticize the offense element "insidiously" in its interpretation by the German Federal Court of Justice. This case law is based on rather old-fashioned, male assumptions about "fair fights." The underlying logic assumes offender and victim as two persons of roughly equal strength and fighting capacity, and thus a fair chance for the victim of effective self-defense if the offender had proceeded openly. Under such circumstances, one might deem it reprehensible if the chances to defend oneself are undermined by the offender's insidious—i.e., cowardly—attack. (Compare this conception with that reflected in the German doctrine of self-defense, which does not countenance a duty to retreat. See Chapter 13.A.)

This model, however, does not fit other situations. Think about victims who are not of equal strength and who could not have fought back effectively in an open fight. If the offender attacks such a victim after a verbal argument that gave clear indications of his will to attack physically, he will only be liable for manslaughter despite the fact that suspicion had not improved the victim's chances of survival and that under such conditions intimidating the victim before the attack has nothing to do with fairness. Furthermore, the interpretation chosen by the German Federal Court of Justice leads to problematic results in cases of battered-women-as-offenders/family-tyrants-as-victims—if women, after years of abuse, kill their husband or partner. Typically, they do this when their husband/partner either sleeps (as in BGHSt 48, 255, in Chapter 13.B) or is distracted in other ways. One could hardly blame battered women for not having sought a "fair open fight" with their male partners. Nevertheless, if they kill their sleeping or distracted mate, they will be charged with murder, not just manslaughter, because this falls under "insidious killing." With respect to the German battered women case reprinted here, we have seen that the German courts neither apply the justifying or excusing necessity defense nor do they acknowledge the special situations of battered women with another defense. This problem is enlarged because the charge will be one for murder rather than for manslaughter.

That said, the same issue would arise in a criminal law system that does not require proof of insidiousness, or other base motives. More specifically, the battered woman who kills her sleeping abuser also would have satisfied the elements of murder, defined as intentional homicide (New York Penal Law) or as purposeful or knowing homicide (Model Penal Code), with no need to investigate the depravity, or extremeness, of her indifference toward the value of human life as indicated by her act—since these are merely alternative, or supplemental, routes to satisfying the elements of murder (see Note 5). Instead, the defendant would have to rely on a defense (most commonly self-defense) to prevent murder liability (see Chapter 13). Interestingly, however, the question of holding a defendant to an inapposite standard of conduct would present itself, as it does in German criminal law, but in a different context, namely as part of the interpretation and application of the standard of reasonableness. The traditional one-size-fits all, though in fact male-centered, "reasonable man" standard, has given way to a more contextualized ("subjective") conception of reasonableness. Recall, for instance, the battered-woman's syndrome case of State v. Leidholm, 334 N. W.2d 811 (N.D. 1983), in which the North Dakota Supreme Court held that instead of contemplating a standard of "reasonably prudent persons, regardless of their sex, similarly situated," the reasonableness inquiry should consider "the standpoint of a person whose mental and physical characteristics are like the accused's and who sees what the accused sees and knows what the accused knows."

8. *Motives.* It is an old saw of (at least Anglo-American) criminal law that motives are supposed to be irrelevant to criminal liability (see Chapter 8.A). Is the German murder provision, in fact, a sentencing provision, that requires the imposition of a qualitatively different sentence on a qualitatively different crime (or criminal)? If so, could—or perhaps should—the consideration of motives be left entirely, and explicitly, to sentencing? See, e.g., U.S.S.G. § 2A1.2, comment. (n.1) ("If the defendant's conduct was exceptionally heinous, cruel, brutal, or degrading to the victim, an upward departure may be warranted."); see generally U.S.S.G. § 5K2.8 ("Examples of extreme conduct include torture of a victim, gratuitous infliction of injury, or prolonging of pain or humiliation."). Is the consideration of motives any less troubling under the heading of "assessment of criminal liability" than under that of "assessment of punishment"?

Felony murder

The felony (or constructive) murder rule is among the most controversial doctrines in Anglo-American criminal law. Almost universally condemned by commentators for decades,* frequently criticized by (dissenting) judges, declared unconstitutional in Canada, rejected by the Model Penal Code, and abolished in England, the rule nonetheless is alive and well in the vast majority of American jurisdictions, including New York. There are about as many versions of the rule as there are formulations of it, but the basic idea is to impose *murder* liability on deaths caused during the commission of a *felony*, without the need to establish intent, or some other mental state, with respect to the death. So, for instance, if I commit a robbery—i.e., if I engage in conduct that matches every objective and subjective element of the definition, or if you prefer, the *actus reus* and the *mens rea*, of robbery—and accidentally kill my victim during the robbery, I will be liable not only for the robbery (the so-called "predicate felony") but also for murder. Variations on this theme include, for instance,

(1) the nature of the predicate felony (which may or may not be limited to certain, perhaps violent, felonies, or to felonies on a statutory list),
(2) the relationship between the predicate felony and the homicide (if the relationship is too close, as for instance between a lesser included offense—like assault—and homicide, the "merger rule" may preclude application of the felony murder rule),
(3) the identity of the perpetrator of the homicide (does it extend to deaths caused by non-perpetrators of the predicate felony (victims, police officers, bystanders) or by other participants in the predicate felony (accomplices, co-conspirators)?),
(4) the identity of the homicide victim (does it extend to deaths of non-victims of the predicate felony (police officers, bystanders, fellow participants in the predicate felony)?), and
(5) the relationship between the predicate felony and death (does it extend to deaths that occur after the completion of the predicate felony (e.g., during flight from the predicate felony)).

People v. Burroughs
Supreme Court of California
35 Cal. 3d 824 (1984)

Defendant Burroughs, a 77-year-old self-styled "healer," appeals from a judgment convicting him of unlawfully selling drugs, compounds, or devices for alleviation or cure of cancer (Health & Saf. Code, § 1707.1); felony practicing medicine without a license (Bus. & Prof. Code, § 2141.5, now § 2053); and second degree felony murder (Pen. Code, § 187) in the treatment and death of Lee Swatsenbarg.

Burroughs challenges his second degree murder conviction by contending the felonious unlicensed practice of medicine is not an "inherently dangerous" felony, as that term has been used in our previous decisions to describe and limit the kinds of offenses which will support application of the

---

* For two recent exceptions, see Guyora Binder, *Felony Murder* (2012); David Crump, "Reconsidering the Felony Murder Rule in Light of Modern Criticisms: Doesn't the Conclusion Depend upon the Particular Rule at Issue?," 32 *Harvard Journal of Law and Public Policy* (2009), 1155.

felony-murder rule. We conclude that while the felonious unlicensed practice of medicine can, in many circumstances, pose a threat to the health of the individual being treated, commission of that crime as defined by statute does not inevitably pose danger to human life. Under well-established principles it cannot, therefore, be made the predicate for a finding of murder, absent proof of malice. As a consequence, we must reverse defendant's second degree felony-murder conviction . . .

Lee Swatsenbarg had been diagnosed by the family physician as suffering from terminal leukemia. Unable to accept impending death, the 24-year-old Swatsenbarg unsuccessfully sought treatment from a variety of traditional medical sources. He and his wife then began to participate in Bible study, hoping that through faith Lee might be cured. Finally, on the advice of a mutual acquaintance who had heard of defendant's ostensible successes in healing others, Lee turned to defendant for treatment.

During the first meeting between Lee and defendant, the latter described his method of curing cancer. This method included consumption of a unique "lemonade," exposure to colored lights, and a brand of vigorous massage administered by defendant. Defendant remarked that he had successfully treated "thousands" of people, including a number of physicians. He suggested the Swatsenbargs purchase a copy of his book, *Healing for the Age of Enlightenment*. If after reading the book Lee wished to begin defendant's unorthodox treatment, defendant would commence caring for Lee immediately. During the 30 days designated for the treatment, Lee would have to avoid contact with his physician.

Lee read the book, submitted to the conditions delineated by defendant, and placed himself under defendant's care. Defendant instructed Lee to drink the lemonade, salt water, and herb tea, but consume nothing more for the ensuing 30 days. At defendant's behest, the Swatsenbargs bought a lamp equipped with some colored plastic sheets, to bathe Lee in various tints of light. Defendant also agreed to massage Lee from time to time, for an additional fee per session.

Rather than improve, within two weeks Lee's condition began rapidly to deteriorate. He developed a fever, and was growing progressively weaker. Defendant counseled Lee that all was proceeding according to plan, and convinced the young man to postpone a bone marrow test urged by his doctor.

During the next week Lee became increasingly ill. He was experiencing severe pain in several areas, including his abdomen, and vomiting frequently. Defendant administered "deep" abdominal massages on two successive days, each time telling Lee he would soon recuperate.

Lee did not recover as defendant expected, however, and the patient began to suffer from convulsions and excruciating pain. He vomited with increasing frequency. Despite defendant's constant attempts at reassurance, the Swatsenbargs began to panic when Lee convulsed for a third time after the latest abdominal massage. Three and a half weeks into the treatment, the couple spent the night at defendant's house, where Lee died of a massive hemorrhage of the mesentary in the abdomen. The evidence presented at trial strongly suggested the hemorrhage was the direct result of the massages performed by defendant.

Defendant's conviction of second degree felony murder arose out of the jury's determination that Lee Swatsenbarg's death was a homicide committed by defendant while he was engaged in the felonious unlicensed practice of medicine. The trial court ruled that an underlying felony of unlicensed practice of medicine could support a felony-murder conviction because such practice was a felony "inherently dangerous to human life."[1] Consequently, the trial judge instructed the jury that if the homicide resulted directly from the commission of this felony, the homicide was felony murder of the second degree.[2] This instruction was erroneous as a matter of law.

When an individual causes the death of another in furtherance of the perpetration of a felony, the resulting offense may be felony murder. This court has long held the felony-murder rule in disfavor. "We have repeatedly stated that felony murder is a 'highly artificial concept' which 'deserves no

---

[1] Felony practicing medicine without a license violates section 2053 of the Business and Professions Code (formerly § 2141.5) which states: "Any person who willfully, under circumstances or conditions which cause or create a risk of great bodily harm, serious physical or mental illness, or death, practices or attempts to practice, or advertises or holds himself or herself out as practicing, any system or mode of treating the sick or afflicted in this state, or diagnoses, treats, operates for, or prescribes for any ailment, blemish, deformity, disease, disfigurement, disorder, injury, or other physical or mental condition of any person, without having at the time of so doing a valid, unrevoked or suspended certificate as provided in this chapter, or without being authorized to perform such act pursuant to a certificate obtained in accordance with some other provision of law, is punishable by imprisonment in the county jail for not exceeding one year or in the state prison."

[2] Second degree felony murder was defined for the jury as, "The unlawful killing of a human being, whether intentional, unintentional or accidental, which occurs as a direct causal result of the commission of or attempt to commit a felony inherently dangerous to human life, namely, the crime of practicing medicine without a license under circumstances or conditions which cause or create risk of great bodily harm, serious mental or physical illness, or death, and where there was in the mind of the perpetrator the specific intent to commit such crime, is murder of the second degree. The specific intent to commit such felony, i.e., practicing medicine without a license under circumstances or conditions which cause or create risk of great bodily harm, serious mental or physical illness, or death, and the commission of or attempt to commit such crime must be proved beyond any doubt." (CALJIC No. 8.32.)

extension beyond its required application.' " (*People* v. *Dillon* (1983) 34 Cal.3d 441, 462–463 [194 Cal. Rptr. 390, 668 P.2d 697]) For the reasons stated below, we hold that to apply the felony-murder rule to the facts of the instant case would be an unwarranted extension of this highly "anachronistic"[3] notion.

At the outset we must determine whether the underlying felony is "inherently dangerous to human life." We formulated this standard because "[if] the felony is not inherently dangerous, it is highly improbable that the potential felon will be deterred; he will not anticipate that any injury or death might arise solely from the fact that he will commit the felony."

In assessing whether the felony is inherently dangerous to human life, "we look to the elements of the felony in the abstract, not the particular 'facts' of the case." This form of analysis is compelled because there is a killing in every case where the rule might potentially be applied. If in such circumstances a court were to examine the particular facts of the case prior to establishing whether the underlying felony is inherently dangerous, the court might well be led to conclude the rule applicable despite any unfairness which might redound to the defendant by so broad an application: the existence of the dead victim might appear to lead inexorably to the conclusion that the underlying felony is exceptionally hazardous. We continue to resist such unjustifiable bootstrapping.

In our application of the second degree felony-murder analysis we are guided by the bipartite standard articulated by this court in *People* v. *Henderson*, 19 Cal.3d 86. In *Henderson*, we stated a reviewing court should look first to the primary element of the offense at issue, then to the "factors elevating the offense to a felony," to determine whether the felony, taken in the abstract, is inherently dangerous to human life, or whether it possibly could be committed without creating such peril. In this examination we are required to view the statutory definition of the offense as a whole, taking into account even nonhazardous ways of violating the provisions of the law which do not necessarily pose a threat to human life.

The primary element of the offense in question here is the practice of medicine without a license. The statute defines such practice as "treating the sick or afflicted." One can certainly conceive of treatment of the sick or afflicted which has quite innocuous results —the affliction at stake could be a common cold, or a sprained finger, and the form of treatment an admonition to rest in bed and drink fluids or the application of ice to mild swelling. Thus, we do not find inherent dangerousness at this stage of our investigation.

The next level of analysis takes us to consideration of the factors which elevate the unlicensed practice of medicine to a felony: "circumstances or conditions which cause or create a risk of great bodily harm, serious mental or physical illness, *or death*." That the Legislature referred to "death" as a separate risk, and in the disjunctive, strongly suggests the Legislature perceived that one may violate the proscription against the felonious practice of medicine without a license and yet not necessarily endanger human life . . .

The statute at issue can also be violated by administering to an individual in a manner which threatens risk of serious mental or physical illness. Whether risk of serious physical illness is inherently dangerous to life is a question we do not reach; however, we believe the existence of the category of risk of serious mental illness also renders a breach of the statute's prohibitions potentially less than inherently dangerous to life. . . .

While conceding . . . the possibility that mental illness may be inherently dangerous, we note . . . there are occasions when this need not be the case. It is not difficult, for example, to envision one who suffers from delusions of grandeur, believing himself to be the President of the United States. An individual who purports without the proper license to be able to treat such a person need not be placing the patient's life in jeopardy, though such treatment, if conducted, for example, without expertise, may lead to the need for more serious psychiatric attention.

Consequently, we are disinclined to rule today that the risks set forth in section 2053 are so critical as to render commission of this felony of necessity inherently dangerous to human life. Indeed, were we to interpret either the risk of great bodily harm or serious mental illness as being synonymous with the risk of death for purposes of the felony-murder rule, we would be according those terms a more restrictive meaning than that which the Legislature obviously meant them to have in the definition of the felony itself. Such a reading would require that an unlicensed practitioner of medicine actually perform treatment under circumstances or conditions which necessarily place the very life of the patient in jeopardy before such a practitioner could be susceptible to a conviction for *felonious* unlicensed practice. We possess grave doubts that the Legislature intended such a result.

---

[3] . . . In *People* v. *Dillon*, 34 Cal.3d 441, 462–472, we reaffirmed the first degree felony-murder rule despite serious reservations as to its rationality and moral vitality, because we regarded ourselves bound by the explicit statutory provision (Pen. Code, § 189) from which that rule derived. The second degree felony-murder rule, by contrast, is a creature of judicial invention, and as the Chief Justice's concurring opinion suggests the time may be ripe to reconsider its continued vitality. We decline to do so here, however, since that issue has not been raised, briefed, or argued.

Moreover, our analysis of precedent in this area reveals that the few times we have found an underlying felony inherently dangerous (so that it would support a conviction of felony murder), the offense has been tinged with malevolence totally absent from the facts of this case. In *People* v. *Mattison* (1971) 4 Cal.3d 177 [93 Cal.Rptr. 185, 481 P.2d 193], we held that poisoning food, drink, or medicine with intent to injure was inherently dangerous. The wilful and malicious burning of an automobile (located in a garage beneath an occupied home) was ruled inherently dangerous in *People* v. *Nichols* (1970) 3 Cal.3d 150, 162–163 [89 Cal.Rptr. 721, 474 P.2d 673]. Finally, we held kidnaping to be such an offense in *People* v. *Ford*, 60 Cal.2d 772, 795.

To hold, as we do today, that a violation of section 2053 is not inherently so dangerous that by its very nature, it cannot be committed without creating a substantial risk that someone will be killed, is consistent with our previous decisions in which the underlying felony has been held not inherently hazardous. We have so held where the underlying felony was felony false imprisonment, possession of a concealable firearm by an ex-felon, escape from a city or county penal facility, and in other, less potentially threatening circumstances.

Finally, the underlying purpose of the felony-murder rule, to encourage felons to commit their offenses without perpetrating unnecessary violence which might result in a homicide, would not be served by applying the rule to the facts of this case. Defendant was or should have been aware he was committing a crime by treating Swatsenbarg in the first place.[5] Yet, it is unlikely he would have been deterred from administering to Lee in the manner in which he did for fear of a prosecution for murder, given his published beliefs on the efficacy of massage in the curing of cancer. Indeed, nowhere is it claimed that defendant attempted to perform any action with respect to Swatsenbarg other than to heal him—and earn a fee for doing so.

This clearly is a case in which conviction of felony murder is contrary to our settled law, as well as inappropriate as a matter of sound judicial policy. The instruction regarding felony murder was erroneous. Accordingly, defendant's second degree murder conviction is reversed.

In addition to asserting the felonious unlicensed practice of medicine will not provide the predicate for a felony-murder conviction because felonious unlicensed medical practice is not inherently dangerous to human life, Burroughs claims the trial court erroneously refused to give an instruction, requested by defendant, on the purportedly lesser included offense of involuntary manslaughter. [W]hile there was no evidence to suggest Swatsenbarg's demise was the intended consequence of Burroughs' treatment of the decedent, there was substantial evidence that this treatment, the administering of "deep abdominal massages" in particular, was performed "without due caution and circumspection," and was the proximate cause of Lee Swatsenbarg's death. Thus, on the evidence presented, Burroughs was susceptible to a possible conviction of involuntary manslaughter, and the jury should have been so instructed . . .

Bird, C. J., Concurring.

The majority reverse appellant's second degree felony-murder conviction on the ground that practicing medicine without a license is not an inherently dangerous felony. I agree with that conclusion, as well as with the directions that on retrial appellant may be prosecuted for involuntary manslaughter. However, I would rest the reversal on a broader ground. The time has come for this court to discard the artificial and court-created offense of second degree felony murder.

. . . Felony murder has been described as "a highly artificial concept that deserves no extension beyond its required application." "[The] rule is much censured 'because it anachronistically resurrects from a bygone age a "barbaric" concept that has been discarded in the place of its origin' . . . and because 'in almost all cases in which it is applied it is unnecessary' and 'it erodes the relation between criminal liability and moral culpability' . . . "

. . . The second degree felony-murder rule is, "as it has been since 1872, a judge-made doctrine without any express basis in the Penal Code." Therefore, the power to do away "with . . . the 'barbaric' anachronism which we are responsible for creating" lies with this court . . .

Accordingly, this court should take the long-overdue step and eliminate the second degree felony-murder rule.[2] . . .

The history of the felony-murder rule is in reality a history of limitation. [After a series of cases limiting the doctrine beginning in the nineteenth century, it was abandoned in England] by the Homicide Act of 1957. Section 1 of the act provided in relevant part: "Where a person kills another in the course or furtherance of some other offence, the killing shall not amount to murder unless

---

[5] He had been convicted of practicing medicine without a license in 1960.

[2] This court would not be the first to take such a step. In *People* v. *Aaron* (1980) 409 Mich. 672 [299 N.W.2d 304], the Michigan Supreme Court . . . reviewed the common law doctrine of felony murder and concluded that "it violates the basic premise of individual moral culpability upon which our criminal law is based." As a result, the court abolished the felony-murder rule in Michigan. . . .

done with the same malice aforethought (express or implied) as is required for a killing to amount to murder when not done in the course or furtherance of another offense."[16]

In the United States, the rule has followed a somewhat similar path. Since the state of English common law in 1776 served as the basis for the development of American jurisprudence, Blackstone's version of the felony-murder rule[17] became an integral part of the common law of the first 13 states. Not surprisingly, the Atlantic separation did nothing to reduce the amount of criticism to which the doctrine has been subjected. As early as 1854, this criticism appears to have resulted in the statutory abolition of the felony-murder rule in Ohio.

Oliver Wendell Holmes questioned the rule's deterrent effect in 1881. "[If] a man does an act with intent to commit a felony, and thereby accidentally kills another, ... [the] fact that the shooting is felonious does not make it any more likely to kill people. If the object of the rule is to prevent such accidents, it should make accidental killing with firearms murder, not accidental killing in the effort to steal; while, if its object is to prevent stealing, it would do better to hang one thief in every thousand by lot." (Holmes, The Common Law (1881) pp. 57–58.)

Two states, Hawaii and Kentucky, have followed Ohio in abolishing the felony-murder rule by statute. The comment to the Hawaii statute is instructive.

"Even in its limited formulation the felony-murder rule is still objectionable. It is not sound principle to convert an accidental, negligent, or reckless homicide into a murder simply because, without more, the killing was in furtherance of a criminal objective of some defined class. Engaging in certain penally-prohibited behavior may, of course, evidence a recklessness sufficient to establish manslaughter, or a practical certainty or intent, with respect to causing death, sufficient to establish murder, but such a finding is an independent determination which must rest on the facts of each case ...

"In recognition of the trend toward, and the substantial body of criticism supporting, the abolition of the felony-murder rule, and because of the extremely questionable results which the rule has worked in other jurisdictions, the Code has eliminated from our law the felony-murder rule."

The drafters of the Model Penal Code concluded that the felony-murder rule should be abandoned. (Model Pen. Code, § 201.2, com. 4 (Tent. Draft No. 9, 1959) p. 33) However, concern over possible political opposition to the idea led them to insert a provision in section 201.2(b)'s definition of reckless murder, to the effect that "recklessness and [extreme] indifference [to the value of human life] are [rebuttably] presumed if the actor is engaged or is an accomplice in the commission of, or an attempt to commit or flight after committing or attempting to commit [one of seven enumerated felonies]." (see Model Pen. Code, § 210.2, subd. (1)(b))

While New Hampshire is the only state to have adopted the Model Penal Code formulation, several other states require that the accused exhibit a mens rea above and beyond the mere intent to commit a felony. Arkansas requires that the defendant cause death "under circumstances manifesting extreme indifference to the value of human life." (Ark. Stat. Ann., § 41.1502.) The Texas Penal Code provides that the act causing death must be "clearly dangerous to human life." (Tex. Pen. Code Ann., § 19.02(a)(3).) The Delaware first degree murder statute mandates that the accused at least have acted with criminal negligence in the course of committing certain enumerated felonies or recklessly in the course of committing nonenumerated felonies. (Del. Code, tit. 11, § 636(a)(2), (6) (1979)) ...

Perhaps the most objectionable and often criticized feature of the felony-murder rule involves its vicarious application to accomplices who did not participate in the acts which caused the victim's death. Accordingly, legislatures in 10 states have adopted statutes which provide an affirmative defense for such persons in certain limited circumstances.[22]

... In 1959 the drafters of the Model Penal Code listed seven major limitations which had been imposed by various state courts.[24] The intervening 25 years have done little to reduce the need for or

---

[16] Criticism of the felony-murder rule and the concept of presumed or constructive malice appears in virtually every country whose legal system, based on the tradition of English common law, is "blessed" with this relic of our medieval heritage. India abolished the felony-murder rule by statute in 1951. None of the nations of continental Europe has a concept of criminal law analogous to the felony-murder rule.

[17] "[When] an involuntary killing happens in consequence of an unlawful act, it will be either murder or manslaughter according to the nature of the act which occasioned it. If it be in prosecution of a felonious intent, or in it's [sic] consequences naturally tended to bloodshed, it will be murder; but if no more was intended than a mere civil trespass, it will only amount to manslaughter."

[22] The New York statute (N.Y. Pen. L., § 125.25(3)) is typical.

[24] (1) The felonious act must be dangerous to life. (2) The homicide must be a natural and probable consequence of the felonious act. (3) Death must be "proximately" caused. (4) The felony must be *malum in se*. (5) The act must be a common law felony. (6) The period during which the felony is in the process of commission must be narrowly construed. (7) The underlying felony must be 'independent' of the homicide. Model Penal Code § 201.2, comment 4 (Tent. Draft No. 9, 1959) at 37.

number of limitations on the rule. The most important of these include requirements that the underlying felony be inherently dangerous, that the killing be committed by one of the felons, that the duration of the felony be strictly construed, and that the purpose of the underlying felony be independent of the killing.

California's approach to the rule mirrors these developments ... The reasons for limiting the rule were well summarized over a decade ago in *People* v. *Satchell*, 6 Cal.3d 28. This court observed that the felony-murder rule is "usually unnecessary for conviction ... " In almost all cases in which the rule is applied, conviction "can be predicated on the normal rules as to murder and as to accomplice liability ... "

The second degree felony-murder rule erodes the important relationship between criminal liability and an accused's mental state. That relationship has been described as "the most basic principle of the criminal law." ...

The second degree felony-murder rule, as a strict liability concept, violates this most important principle. Not only does it obliterate the distinction between intended and unintended homicides, but it seeks to apply the same ponderous sanction to any participant in the criminal conspiracy or enterprise from which a death results. Thus, the doctrine has been applied where a co-defendant served only in a getaway driver capacity, where the co-defendant was present at the scene of the killing but did not fire the fatal shot, and where the victim died from a heart attack precipitated by the fright induced by commission of the felony.

Legal commentators have been virtually unanimous in their condemnation of the felony-murder rule because it ignores the significance of the actor's mental state in determining his criminal liability. As the drafters of the Model Penal Code concluded in 1959, "principled argument in ... defense [of the felony-murder rule] is hard to find." (Model Pen. Code, § 201.2, com. 4.)

As noted earlier, the rule is perhaps the last vestige of an archaic and indiscriminate philosophy still present in our modern system of criminal law. "The rationale of the doctrine is that one who commits a felony is a bad person with a bad state of mind, and he has caused a bad result, so that we should not worry too much about the fact that the fatal result he accomplished was quite different and a good deal worse than the bad result he intended. Yet it is a general principle of criminal law that one is not ordinarily criminally liable for bad results which differ greatly from intended results." (LaFave & Scott, Criminal Law (1972) p. 560.)

... [T]he harshness of the rule, which leads some juries to disregard the law and others to follow it only with great reluctance, results in haphazard application of the criminal sanction. As the Ohio Supreme Court concluded more than a century ago in deciding to abandon the felony-murder rule, "crime is more effectually prevented by the *certainty* than by any unreasonable *severity* of punishment disproportionate to the turpitude and danger of the offense." In my view, it is far preferable to do away with an irrational doctrine than to permit it to be applied in an irrational manner ...

As Holmes so eloquently stated, "It is revolting to have no better reason for a rule of law than that so it was laid down in the time of Henry IV. It is still more revolting if the grounds upon which it was laid down have vanished long since, and the rule simply persists from blind imitation of the past." (Holmes, Collected Legal Papers (1920) p. 187.) It is time this court laid this ill-conceived rule to rest.

Richardson, J.

I respectfully dissent. In my view, the unauthorized practice of medicine "under circumstances or conditions which cause or create a risk of great bodily harm, serious physical or mental illness, or death" (Bus. & Prof. Code, § 2053) fully supports application of the second degree felony-murder rule.

Relying on hypertechnical and irrelevant distinctions between great bodily harm, serious physical and mental injury, and the risk of death, the majority ignores the "rational function that [the felony-murder rule] is designed to serve." As we have frequently reiterated, that purpose "is to deter those engaged in felonies from killing negligently or accidentally." ... [In] *People* v. *Taylor* (1970) 11 Cal. App.3d 57 [89 Cal.Rptr. 697], ... the Court of Appeal upheld a second degree murder conviction under the felony-murder rule when the underlying felony was furnishing of heroin to the victim. "In other words the felony was not done with the intent to commit injury which would cause death. Giving a felony-murder instruction in such a situation serves rather than subverts the purpose of the rule. 'While the felony-murder rule can hardly be much of a deterrent to a defendant who has decided to assault his victim with a deadly weapon, it seems obvious that in the situation presented in the case at bar, it does serve a rational purpose: knowledge that the death of a person to whom heroin is furnished may result in a conviction for murder should have some effect on the defendant's readiness to do the furnishing.'" Similarly, here, knowledge that the death of a "sick or afflicted" person whom the unauthorized practitioner treats, "willfully, under circumstances or conditions which cause or create a risk of great bodily harm, serious physical or mental illness, or death," may have an effect on such person's willingness to so practice.

The majority's fine distinctions become even more dubious when one considers the holding in *People* v. *Nichols* (1970) 3 Cal.3d 150 [89 Cal.Rptr. 721, 474 P.2d 673], approving a second degree murder conviction premised on the burning of an automobile ... How can the underlying felony at issue here be less "inherently dangerous to human life" than the burning of an automobile?

In enacting Business and Professions Code section 2053, the Legislature clearly sought to impose a greater penalty in those cases where the unauthorized practice of medicine causes significant risks that may lead to death. The use of the felony-murder rule in this context clearly furthers the goal of deterring such conduct. The underlying conduct proscribed by section 2053 is manifestly "inherently dangerous to life." Viewed in the abstract, improper treatment of the "sick and afflicted" under the dangerous circumstances and conditions specified in that section is almost synonymous with inherently dangerous conduct.

R. v. Martineau
Supreme Court of Canada
[1990] 2 S.C.R. 633

Lamer C.J.C.:

The facts of this case are not central to the disposition of this appeal, and, therefore, may be briefly summarized as follows. On February 7, 1985, the bodies of James McLean and Ann McLean were found in the bathroom of their home, a trailer, in Valleyview, Alberta. A police investigation led to Martineau and one Patrick Tremblay. Martineau, who was 15 at the time, was charged with both murders and was transferred to adult court.

Martineau was tried by a judge and jury starting on September 12, 1985. Thirty witnesses gave evidence including the accused. The evidence revealed that Martineau and his friend, Tremblay, had set out one evening armed with a pellet pistol and rifle respectively. Martineau testified that he knew that they were going to commit a crime, but that he thought it would only be a "b and e" [breaking and entering]. After robbing the trailer and its occupants, Martineau's friend Tremblay shot and killed the McLeans.

As they left the trailer, Martineau asked Tremblay why he killed them and Tremblay answered, "they saw our faces." Martineau responded, "But they couldn't see mine 'cause I had a mask on." They drove James McLean's car to Grande Prairie where they abandoned it. The respondent was convicted of second degree murder ...

... Section 213(a) of the *Code* defines culpable homicide as a murder where a person causes the death of a human being while committing or attempting to commit a range of listed offences, whether or not the person means to cause death or whether or not he or she knows that death is likely to ensue if that person means to cause bodily harm for the purpose of facilitating the commission of the offence or flight after committing or attempting to commit the offence. The introductory paragraph of the section, therefore, expressly removes from the Crown the burden of proving beyond a reasonable doubt that the accused had subjective foresight of death. This section stands as an anomaly as regards the other murder provisions, especially in light of the common law presumption against convicting a person of a true crime without proof of intent or recklessness: *R. v. Sault Ste. Marie (City)* (1978), 40 C.C.C. (2d) 353 at pp. 362–3, 85 D.L.R. (3d) 161, [1978] 2 S.C.R. 1299, per Dickson J., as he then was.

A conviction for murder carries with it the most severe stigma and punishment of any crime in our society. The principles of fundamental justice require, because of the special nature of the stigma attached to a conviction for murder, and the available penalties, a *mens rea* reflecting the particular nature of that crime. The effect of s. 213 is to violate the principle that punishment must be proportionate to the moral blameworthiness of the offender, or as Professor Hart puts it in *Punishment and Responsibility* (1968), at p. 162, the fundamental principle of a morally based system of law that those causing harm intentionally be punished more severely than those causing harm unintentionally. The rationale underlying the principle that subjective foresight of death is required before a person is labelled and punished as a murderer, is linked to the more general principle that criminal liability for a particular result is not justified except where the actor possesses a culpable mental state in respect of that result. In my view, in a free and democratic society that values the autonomy and free will of the individual, the stigma and punishment attaching to the most serious of crimes, murder, should be reserved for those who choose to intentionally cause death or who choose to inflict bodily harm that they know is likely to cause death. The essential role of requiring subjective foresight of death in the context of murder is to maintain a proportionality between the stigma and punishment attached to a murder conviction and the moral blameworthiness of the offender. Murder has long been recognized as the "worst" and most heinous of peace-time crimes. It is, therefore, essential that to satisfy the principles of fundamental justice, the stigma and punishment attaching to a murder conviction must be reserved for those who either intend to cause death or who intend to cause bodily harm that they know will likely cause death. In this regard, I refer to the following works as support for my position . . . : Cross, "The Mental Element in Crime," 83 L.Q.R. 215 (1967); Ashworth, "The Elasticity of *Mens rea*" in *Crime, Proof and Punishment* (1981); Williams, *The Mental Element in Crime* (1965), and Williams, "Convictions and Fair Labelling," [1983] C.L.J. 85.

In sum then, I am of the view that a special mental element with respect to death is necessary before a culpable homicide can be treated as murder. That special mental element gives rise to the moral blameworthiness that justifies the stigma and punishment attaching to a murder conviction. For all the foregoing reasons . . . I concluded that it is a principle of fundamental justice that a conviction for murder cannot rest on anything less than proof beyond a reasonable doubt of subjective foresight of death. Therefore, since s. 213 of the *Code* expressly eliminates the require-ment for proof of subjective foresight, it infringes ss. 7 and 11(d) of the Charter.*

As regards s. 1 of the Charter,[†] there is no doubt that the objective of deterring the infliction of bodily harm during the commission of certain offences because of the increased risk of death is of sufficient importance to warrant overriding a Charter right. Further, indiscriminately punishing for murder all those who cause death irrespective of whether they intended to cause death might well be thought to discourage the infliction of bodily harm during the commission of certain offences because of the increased risk of death. But it is not necessary in order to achieve this objective to convict of murder persons who do not intend or foresee the death. In this regard the section unduly impairs the Charter rights. If Parliament wishes to deter persons from causing bodily harm during certain offences, then it should punish persons for causing the bodily harm. Indeed, the conviction for manslaughter that would result instead of a conviction for murder is punishable by, from a day in jail, to confinement for life. Very stiff sentences for the infliction of bodily harm leading to death in appropriate cases would sufficiently meet any deterrence objective that Parliament might have in mind. The more flexible sentencing scheme under a conviction for manslaughter is in accord with the principle that punishment be meted out with regard to the level of moral blameworthiness of the offender. To label and punish a person as a murderer who did not intend or foresee death unneces-sarily stigmatizes and punishes those whose moral blameworthiness is not that of a murderer, and thereby unnecessarily impairs the rights guaranteed by ss. 7 and 11(d) of the Charter. In my view then, s. 213(a), indeed all of s. 213, cannot be saved by s. 1 of the Charter.

German Federal Court of Justice
3 StR 535/91, BGHSt 38, 295 (May 15, 1992)

Facts

The Higher Regional Court Koblenz sentenced the defendant to youth detention of six years and six months for attempted murder of three human beings concomitantly with intentionally causing an explosion, a further attempted murder of two human beings, two further attempted murders each of one human being, assistance to attempted murder of seventeen human beings, and attempted murder of four human beings each concomitantly with intentionally causing an explosion, and all crimes concomitantly with membership of a terrorist organization and a violation of the Weapons Act.

The appeal in law of the Chief Federal Prosecutor is limited to the verdict on the Zürich crimes. The appeal challenges the defendant's acquittal of attempted murder in relation to the killing of the passer-by K. and of robbery resulting in death under § 251 Criminal Code.

On the crimes committed in Zürich, the Higher Regional Court has essentially established the following facts: The defendant joined the RAF [Red Army Faction, a left-wing terrorist group active in Germany during that time—Eds.] at the end of October 1978 at the age of 20 and belonged to it until the end of July/beginning of August 1981. In this period, besides other terrorist acts of violence which are the subject of the conviction, he committed a robbery with C., W., and B. with loaded weapons at the Schweizerische Volksbank (Swiss People's Bank) in Zürich at which they carried off more than 548,000 Swiss francs. On the ensuing flight they were pursued by bank employees, others to whom the employees had given the alarm, and police officers. The perpetrators fired several shots at the

---

* [Can. Charter of Rights and Freedoms § 7
Everyone has the right to life, liberty and security of the person and the right not to be deprived thereof except in accordance with the principles of fundamental justice."); 11(d) ("Any person charged with an offence has the right (d) to be presumed innocent until proven guilty according to law in a fair and public hearing by an independent and impartial tribunal.—Eds.]
† [Can. Charter of Rights and Freedoms § 1
The Canadian Charter of Rights and Freedoms guarantees the rights and freedoms set out in it subject only to such reasonable limits prescribed by law as can be demonstrably justified in a free and democratic society.—Eds.]

pursuers which were at least partly aimed. After the group of perpetrators had fled into the shopping center located underneath the square in front of the railway station, an exchange of fire began between them and a police officer P. who was pursuing them. A shot aimed by one of the perpetrators at the police officer missed him and fatally wounded the passer-by K.

The Higher Regional Court has refused to convict for murder of the passer-by K. because it was not able to establish an intention . . . The appeal in law of the Chief Public Prosecutor led to an alteration of the verdict, but the sentence was not affected by this.

Reasons

1.

a) The Higher Regional Court has without legal error denied an intentional killing of the passer-by K. There is no objection to the fact that the court of fact did not find conditional intent, because it was not able to establish that the person who fired the fatal shot which missed its mark had recognized that besides the police officer P., Mrs. K. and possibly the witness F. were in the field of fire. The fact that he ought to have seen these persons does not suffice for knowledge about the concrete danger of the shot fired for passers-by who were not participating which justifies a conclusion that their killing was accepted, any more than the general knowledge of the presence of persons in the shopping mall, as long as the person firing the shot thinks that at least his field of fire was free.

b) The Higher Regional Court should however have convicted the defendant in relation to the death of the passer-by K. for robbery resulting in death under § 251 Criminal Code, because he caused the death of this woman in a grossly negligent way with his co-perpetrators by the robbery. This qualified offense description definition has not been included by the court of fact in its examination.

According to the findings Mrs. K. was hit by a shot (which was aimed at the police officer P. but missed him) by one of the perpetrators, and fatally injured. The fact that this exchange of shots only occurred after completion during the escape in the context of defense against pursuers is not inconsistent with the assessment that this amounted to robbery resulting in death. This is because the danger which is specially characteristic of a robbery was thereby realized, which justifies acceptance of a connection between robbery and the resulting death in the sense of § 251 Criminal Code.

It is admittedly disputed in the literature whether an action which no longer serves the taking away of a good in the end phase of a robbery still falls under § 251 Criminal Code (see, on the state of the dispute, with further references, Herdegen, in: LK, 10th edit., § 251 marginal nos. 4 ff.) . . . The overwhelming view however applies § 251 Criminal Code to the phase between completion of the taking away and the final conclusion of the robbery event (Lackner, StGB, 19th edit., § 251 marginal no. 1; Eser, in: Schönke-Schröder, StGB, 24th edit., § 251 marginal no. 4; Dreher-Tröndle, StGB, 45th edit., § 251 marginal no. 2; Geilen, Jura 1979, 502, 557). This opinion must be agreed with . . .

In the case of crimes of robbery, in particular the armed bank robbery present here, there is a danger specific to the crime not only at the time of taking away, which is usually realized when the perpetrator is surprised, but no less during the following phase of flight and securing of the stolen material. This is because frequently the victims of robberies themselves or with the help of the police and other third parties will attempt to follow the escaping perpetrators and recover the stolen goods. The risk that an armed perpetrator will use his weapon not only for the theft, but also as defense against pursuers and to secure the stolen material, should not be assessed as smaller. The view that it is the specific danger peculiar to the basic definition of the crime which needs to be realized (Geilen, in: Festschr. f. Welzel, p. 681) therefore argues to a considerable extent against any limitation to only those coercive acts required within the statutory offense description of robbery which precede the taking away of goods. No sufficient reason can be identified for placing the perpetrator who shoots his way out in a better position than the one who uses his firearm for the taking away.

It is therefore irreconcilable with the protective purpose of § 251 Criminal Code to except the perpetrator of robbery from punishment if he uses violence after the taking away, in order to secure the stolen material or his flight, and thereby causes the death of another . . .

No further reasoning is necessary to demonstrate that the use of firearms in a shopping mall containing people is negligent to a flagrant degree . . .

German Criminal Code

§ 251. (Robbery Causing Death)

If through the robbery (§§ 249 and 250) the offender causes the death of another person at least by gross negligence, the punishment will be life imprisonment or imprisonment of not less than ten years.

NOTES

1. In a footnote in her concurrence in the California case of *People v. Burroughs*, one of the most extensive judicial critiques of the felony murder in American jurisprudence, Chief Justice Bird remarks that "none of the nations of Continental Europe has a concept of criminal law analogous to the felony-murder rule." The validity of this comparative conclusion depends on how close the analogy would need to be. It is true that within the section about homicide in the German Criminal Code nothing is to be found that resembles the felony murder rule. The offender in the German case decided by the Federal Court of Justice in 1992 could not, after the case went back to the trial court and § 251 Criminal Code (Robbery Causing Death) was applied, be convicted of murder. Therefore, if the decisive element is seen in the stigma attached to the expression "murder," as Chief Justice Lamer argues in the Canadian case of *R. v. Martineau*, it makes sense to conclude that there is nothing analogous to the felony murder rule in German law.

However, the more pragmatically minded will have noted that § 251 Criminal Code allows for the highest sanction possible, that is, life imprisonment—a punishment not available in German law for simple manslaughter (*Totschlag*)—i.e., homicide short of murder (*Mord*)—though it is available for especially serious cases of *Totschlag*. Besides § 251, there are a few other similarly constructed provisions in the German Criminal Code that define an offense as causing death by the commission of some other offense and prescribe a discretionary maximum punishment of life imprisonment: sexual child abuse causing death (§ 176b), sexual assault causing death (§ 178), abduction causing death (§ 239a para. 3), arson causing death (§ 306c). Pointing to these norms, one could argue that despite the lack of a felony murder rule in the strict sense a similar solution (a functional equivalent) can be found in German criminal law if one emphasizes the sentencing perspective.

However, the scope of possible functional equivalents to the felony murder rule in German law is much narrower. It would be inconceivable to arrive at a sentence in the range of murder cases if the initial crime was only illegally practicing medicine. This is just a very minor misdemeanor in German law.* (Of course, if this offense had been classified as a misdemeanor under California law, the *felony* murder rule would not have been implicated.) Under German law, a conviction for negligent homicide would have been the most that Burroughs could have expected. (Note that felony murder also would not have been an option under the New York Penal Law, which limits eligible predicate felonies to those enumerated in the criminal code, see N.Y. Penal Law § 125.25(3) (robbery, burglary, kidnapping, arson, rape, and escape).)

More generally, an assessment of felony murder rules and functionally similar provisions depends on the construction of such rules. The strong words by Chief Justice Bird in *Burroughs* about a "barbaric anachronism" and the criticism by Chief Justice Lamer in *Martineau* are appropriate if the law ties harsh sanctions to the mere causation of death. This is obvious within the German legal system with its characteristic commitment to the culpability principle in the Basic Law (see, e.g., Chapter 1.A). But the heading of § 251 Criminal Code (and the similar provisions in this Code mentioned above) should not mislead readers to assume that the causal connection between execution of a felony and

---

* Law about the Professional Exercise of the Art of Healing without Certification (*Heilpraktikergesetz*) § 5

Who practices the art of healing without the required permit to work as a physician and without a certification according to § 1, will be punished with imprisonment of not more than one year or a fine.

death is the decisive factor that justifies the high punishment. Rather, these norms require that the offender acts with gross negligence (*leichtfertig*). Coincidental and accidental developments that could not have been foreseen would not suffice to apply § 251 Criminal Code.

But note again the difference between recklessness and negligence (*Fahrlässigkeit*), or rather gross negligence (*Leichtfertigkeit*), in this case. The American concept of recklessness requires that the offender consciously disregards a substantial risk (see for the definition in the Model Penal Code, Chapter 8.A), and Chief Justice Lamer in *Martineau* also argues that the *mens rea* requirement needs to be subjective foresight. Such subjective foresight of the possible deadly consequences is not required for the application of § 251 Criminal Code. According to German law, objective foreseeability of a substantial and obvious risk suffices. The degree of the risk is determinative, regardless of whether the individual offender had recognized it.*

Consider whether you think that life imprisonment is only justifiable in the case of subjective foresight (see *Martineau*). An argument in support of the German solution is that not even giving a single thought to the destructive impact of one's conduct on others' lives can be more blameworthy compared to the offender who shows minimum responsibility by at least thinking about possible consequences (if the degree of risk in the first case was considerably higher than in the second case). What effect would this argument have on the law of *mens rea* generally speaking? Would this imply that in general negligence (objective foreseeability) offenses might in particular cases be punished more harshly than recklessness (subjective foresight) offenses? (Also note that negligence does not require proof that the defendant, in a particular, had *not* considered the risk his or her conduct would pose to others; it requires proof that a reasonable person would have recognized the risk, regardless of whether the defendant did or did not.) Or is this argument limited to conduct that causes death? If so, would this require a consideration not only of the risk of harm, but also the degree of harm, so that what would amount to negligence in a homicide case might be different from what would amount to negligence in an assault case?

2. If an offender acts together with other perpetrators, according to German law they all must have been grossly negligent with respect to the resulting death. The outcomes therefore are fairly similar to what New York penal law tries to achieve with a (rather complicated) system of defenses for participants, § 125.25(3)(b)–(d). If it was unforeseeable for one perpetrator or participant that the others were likely to engage in dangerous conduct during the course of a felony (if he could not have known that someone had a weapon hidden in his coat), he or she would fall neither under § 251 Criminal Code nor under the New York norm on murder in the second degree. In a case like the one decided by the German Federal Court of Justice in 1992, however, if all the members of a group engaging in armed robberies were aware of the presence of weapons, those who did not shoot have to expect life imprisonment under § 251 Criminal Code (if they had actually formed an agreement to shoot, they would be co-perpetrators of murder if all act for financial gain and thus with greed, see § 211 Criminal Code; on co-perpetration, see Chapter 10). Therefore, the German court did not need to establish who of the group of terrorists fired the shot that killed Mrs. K.

The New York provision on accomplice felony murder cases, § 125.25(3)(b)–(d), attempts to address what Chief Justice Bird, in *Burroughs*, called "[p]erhaps the most objectionable and often criticized feature of the felony-murder rule . . . its vicarious application to accomplices who did not participate in the acts which caused the victim's death." It is one thing to punish the principal in the predicate felony for murder under the felony murder doctrine; it is quite another to extend murder liability to accomplices.

Note, however, that the New York Penal Law provision sets up an affirmative defense, which means, under the New York Penal Law definition of an affirmative defense, which differs from the Model Penal Code on this point, MPC § 1.12, that the defendant bears the burden of establishing the defense, by a preponderance of the evidence, § 25.00(2). The

---

* See generally Gunther Arzt, "Leichtfertigkeit und recklessness," in Walter Stree et al. (eds.), *Gedächtnisschrift für Horst Schröder* (1978), 119; see also the discussion of *mens rea* in Chapter 8.A.

provision gives "a defendant an opportunity to fight his way out of a felony murder charge by persuading a jury, by way of affirmative defense, that he not only had nothing to do with the killing itself but was unarmed and had no idea that any of his confederates were armed or intended to engage in any conduct dangerous to life." It "is based upon the theory that the felony murder doctrine, in its rigid automatic envelopment of all participants in the underlying felony, may be unduly harsh in particular instances; and that some cases do arise, rare though they may be, where it would be just and desirable to allow a nonkiller defendant of relatively minor culpability a chance of extricating himself from liability for murder—though not, of course, from liability for the underlying felony."*

Similarly, the U.S. Supreme Court has placed constitutional limits on the imposition of capital punishment in accomplice felony murder cases. *Enmund v. Florida*, 458 U.S. 782 (1982) (under Eighth Amendment "cruel and unusual punishments" clause, overturning death sentence imposed on robbery getaway driver in felony murder case, without proof that he "killed or attempted to kill" or "intended or contemplated that life would be taken"); but see *Tison v. Arizona*, 481 U.S. 137 (1987) (proof of intent to kill not constitutionally required, since "reckless indifference to the value of human life may be every bit as shocking to the moral sense as an 'intent to kill'"). In capital cases, then, causing death during a predicate felony may function as an aggravating circumstance on the basis of proof of some mental state regarding the resulting death, rather than as a separate theory of murder liability. See also N.Y. Penal Law § 125.27(1)(a)(vii) (first degree murder as intentional homicide during commission of predicate felony).

3. *Sentence mitigation.* In the end, it may make more sense to regard the sections in the German Criminal Code that most resemble the felony murder rule not as rules of liability, but as sentencing provisions, albeit sentencing provisions that also require proof of gross negligence with respect to the aggravating factor (death). The U.S. Sentencing Guidelines provide for downward departure from the prescribed sentencing range in felony murder cases where the defendant lacked the requisite *mens rea* for murder with respect to the result element of death:

> If the defendant did not cause the death intentionally or knowingly, a downward departure may be warranted. For example, a downward departure may be warranted if in robbing a bank, the defendant merely passed a note to the teller, as a result of which the teller had a heart attack and died. The extent of the departure should be based upon the defendant's state of mind (e.g., recklessness or negligence), the degree of risk inherent in the conduct, and the nature of the underlying offense conduct.
>
> U.S.S.G. § 2A1.1, comment (n.2(B)).

Does this provision limit the potential unfairness of the felony murder rule, or does it undercut its rationale, or both?

5. In the face of such widespread criticism of the felony murder in Anglo-American law, combined with its puzzling persistence, it may be worth taking a step back and looking at little more closely at both the criticism, and its object. Take the Model Penal Code's abandonment of the felony murder. While it is true that the Code does not recognize a separate category entitled "felony murder," it transformed felony murder from a rule of substantive criminal law into an evidentiary one:

§ 210.2. Murder.

(1) [C]riminal homicide constitutes murder when: . . .
(b) it is committed recklessly under circumstances manifesting extreme indifference to the value of human life. Such recklessness and indifference are presumed if the actor is engaged or is an accomplice in the commission of, or an attempt to commit, or flight after committing or attempting to commit robbery, rape or deviate sexual intercourse by force or threat of force, arson, burglary, kidnapping or felonious escape.

---

* Richard G. Denzer and Peter McQuillan, *Practice Commentary, McKinney's Consolidated Laws of New York* (1967), Book 39, Penal Law § 125.25, 237.

Under the Model Penal Code, then the felony murder rule survives as a rebuttable presumption of the recklessness and indifference sufficient for murder liability (or, if you prefer, it has been converted from an irrebuttable presumption into a rebuttable one). How likely is it that a defendant would be able to rebut this presumption given the nature of the offenses that give rise to it?

Consider also the following excerpt, which attempts to refocus the discussion on the felony murder rule as it actually exists, rather than as it tends to be criticized:

> [T]he felony murder rule is not a strict liability rule, at least not in the form in which it is found in almost every American jurisdiction. [M]ost American jurisdictions condition felony murder either on a short list of inherently dangerous predicate offenses, or simply on the dangerousness of the underlying felony or the means by which it was perpetrated. [M]ost of the remaining jurisdictions condition it on some level of culpability with respect to the risk of death, or on proximate cause standards that condition liability on the foreseeability of death. When felony murder is conditioned on dangerous predicate offenses, it is not a strict liability crime, but a crime of negligence, as [Kenneth] Simons explains:
>
>> "On first impression, any grading differential for which no formal culpability is required seems inconsistent with retributivism. Consider felony-murder as an example. We punish the felony at a certain level. We do not otherwise punish nonculpable homicide. Thus, adding a penalty to the felony because it resulted in death seems no more justifiable than punishing someone for an accidental, non-negligent homicide today simply because he committed a felony last year. But this analysis is incorrect. Often, culpably doing X, which happens to cause Y, amounts to negligence (or to a higher culpability, such as recklessness) as to Y. Consider a more specific felony murder example. If armed robbery is the predicate felony, then it is not difficult to conclude that an armed robber should foresee, and often does foresee, a significant risk that robbery will result in a death. Thus, the robber is ordinarily negligent and often reckless as to the risk of death."
>
> This analysis suggests that formal strict liability as to death (i.e. the lack of any explicit culpability requirement) can nevertheless be consistent with substantive culpability.
>
> Guyora Binder, "Meaning and Motive in the Law of Homicide,"
> 3 *Buffalo Criminal Law Review* (2000), 755 (quoting Kenneth W. Simons,
> "When is Strict Liability Just?," 87 *Journal of Criminal
> Law and Criminology* (1997), 1075, 1121–2).

iii. Manslaughter

Descending the hierarchy of types of homicide, we move from murder (*Mord*) to manslaughter (*Totschlag*), which—in the common law world—comes in two varieties: voluntary and involuntary manslaughter. One thing both varieties of manslaughters have in common is that they are both misnomers, or rather one misnomer twice over. "Voluntary" here should be read as "intentional," and "involuntary" as "non-intentional." Voluntary manslaughter is, in fact, intentional homicide that is not murder. And involuntary manslaughter is, in fact, non-intentional homicide that—at least in modern American criminal law—is not negligent homicide, i.e., reckless homicide.

We will deal with voluntary manslaughter first, then with its involuntary cousin. Since voluntary manslaughter is murder plus provocation—or provocation's modern version, "extreme emotional disturbance"—the law of voluntary manslaughter is less about homicide than about this partial defense, or ground of mitigation, depending on your point of view.

Voluntary manslaughter (murder with provocation/ extreme emotional disturbance)

The Model Penal Code substantially revised the traditional doctrine of provocation, which was framed in colorful terms such as "sudden quarrel" and "heat of passion," along with "cooling off" periods. The first case comes to us from New York, which revised its provocation provision in light of the Model Penal Code. But before we turn our attention to matters of extreme emotional disturbance, it is useful to get a quick sense of what came before, with a short excerpt from a Washington case that gives a brief overview of the provocation doctrine, *State v. Gounagias*, 88 Wash. 304 (1915):

The doctrine of mitigation is briefly this: That if the act of killing, though intentional, be committed under the influence of sudden, intense anger, or heat of blood, obscuring the reason, produced by an adequate or reasonable provocation, and before sufficient time has elapsed for the blood to cool and reason to reassert itself, so that the killing is the result of temporary excitement rather than wickedness of heart or innate recklessness of disposition, then the law, recognizing the standard of human conduct as that of the ordinary or average man, regards the offense so committed as of less heinous character than premeditated or deliberate murder. Measured as it must be by the conduct of the average man, what constitutes adequate cause is incapable of strict definition.

People v. Roche
Court of Appeals of New York
98 N.Y.2d 70, 772 N.E.2d 1133 (2002)

Graffeo, J.

In this prosecution stemming from the brutal stabbing by defendant of his common-law wife, the Appellate Division reversed defendant's conviction of murder in the second degree based on the trial court's failure to charge the jury concerning the affirmative defense of extreme emotional disturbance. Because the evidence at trial was insufficient to support the defense of extreme emotional disturbance, we reverse . . . and reinstate defendant's conviction . . .

[T]he People offered proof that the victim was stabbed 12 to 14 times in the face, back and chest . . . A trail of blood on the furniture, walls and floors throughout the living room, hallway and kitchen suggested a violent struggle. Forensic evidence indicated the two deep, and ultimately fatal, stab wounds to the victim's chest had been inflicted last, after she had collapsed on the kitchen floor. The murder weapon was never found.

Gilberto Franco and Norma Ruiz, tenants in the apartment building who were acquainted with defendant and the victim, testified at trial that they had seen the couple arguing in the building lobby earlier that day. Franco recounted that in a conversation he had with defendant two weeks before the stabbing, defendant confided that his wife was crazy and hooked on drugs, that he was tired and wanted to leave but that he couldn't live at his sister's house. At around 4:00 P.M. on the day of the crime . . . Franco heard defendant and the victim engaged in a loud argument . . .

About 40 or 50 minutes later, Franco and Ruiz heard defendant yelling in the hallway outside their apartment. They opened their door and saw defendant running down the stairs, exclaiming that his wife had killed herself and that someone should call the police . . . After Franco contacted the police from a nearby store, he and a friend went to defendant's apartment . . . Franco saw defendant emerge carrying a duffle bag. When asked where he was going, defendant replied, "I have to take everything out of here because the police is going to check it out." . . .

Defendant went to his sister's apartment where he was greeted by Pedro Malave, her son-in-law. Defendant told Malave that his wife was dead and that she had tried to kill herself two days before. Defendant changed his socks after requesting a clean pair and threw the pair he had been wearing in the garbage. When defendant's sister arrived, he had a private conversation with her in which he revealed that, in the course of an argument, he had hit his wife and believed that she was dead. She advised him to go to the police.

Thereafter, defendant appeared at the police station and announced: "My wife killed herself. I want to find out who did this. That's why I'm here." . . . Defendant told the police that his wife had been out the night before and had not come home until 5:00 A.M. She had slept most of the morning but then sent him on a series of errands that afternoon, first requesting that he retrieve some items she had thrown out of the window, then asking him to purchase pain reliever, and later sending him to buy cigarettes . . . [He further told the police that he found her dead when he returned.]

The thrust of [defendant's] defense was that the police had the "wrong man" and had rushed to judgment in charging defendant with the crime without searching for the true killer. The defense emphasized the absence of physical evidence linking defendant to the stabbing, his lack of a motive to kill his wife, and the failure of the police to conduct various tests which the defense contended might have revealed the identity of the actual perpetrator.

At a charge conference . . . defendant requested that the lesser included offense of extreme emotional disturbance manslaughter be submitted to the jury . . .

The affirmative defense of extreme emotional disturbance . . . "allows a defendant charged with the commission of acts which would otherwise constitute murder to demonstrate the existence of mitigating factors which indicate that, although not free from responsibility for [the] crime, [defendant] ought to be punished less severely." . . . A defendant cannot establish an extreme emotional disturbance defense without evidence that he or she suffered from a mental infirmity not rising to the level of insanity at the time of the homicide, typically manifested by a loss of self-control. And not all mental infirmities merit a manslaughter charge based on extreme emotional disturbance . . . To prove such an affirmative defense, a defendant must demonstrate, first, that he or she acted under the influence of an extreme emotional disturbance, and second, that there was a reasonable explanation or excuse for that disturbance. The first, subjective element is met if there is evidence that defendant's conduct at the time of the incident was actually influenced by an extreme emotional disturbance. The second is an objective element and requires proof that defendant's emotional disturbance was supported by a reasonable explanation or excuse. This is "determined by viewing the . . . external circumstances as the defendant perceived them to be . . . , however inaccurate that perception may have been, and assessing from that standpoint whether the explanation or excuse . . . was reasonable."

A defendant who pursues an inconsistent defense at trial, such as outright denial of involvement in the crime, may nevertheless be entitled to a manslaughter charge based on extreme emotional disturbance . . . And it is possible for a defendant to establish the presence of such a disturbance without psychiatric testimony . . . These circumstances do, however, impact whether sufficient evidence to support the defense has been presented . . . In the absence of requisite proof, an extreme emotional disturbance charge should not be given because it would invite the jury to engage in impermissible speculation concerning defendant's state of mind at the time of the homicide . . .

Applying these principles to the case, we conclude . . . the proof was insufficient to support either element of the defense. Beginning with the subjective element, the record is devoid of evidence that he actually suffered from a mental infirmity at the time of the stabbing. Defendant cannot rely on his statements to the police since he asserted he had not harmed his wife in any respect. Evidence of mental infirmity is not discernible from defendant's remarks to . . . his sister because he neither claimed that he suffered a loss of self-control nor used any other language suggesting that he killed the victim while under the influence of a mental disability. Similarly, defendant's behavior prior to and immediately after the crime was not indicative of extreme emotional disturbance. Soon after the killing, defendant contrived a false explanation for the victim's wounds . . . Moments later, defendant had the presence of mind to gather items in a duffle bag and remove them from the apartment so they would not be discovered by the police—conduct inconsistent with the loss of self-control associated with the defense . . .

Defendant contends that the brutal nature of the stabbing constituted evidence that he acted under the influence of a mental infirmity. While proof concerning the nature of the wounds defendant inflicted is relevant, we have never held that a jury may infer the presence of an extreme emotional disturbance based solely on proof that the crime was especially violent or brutal . . .

Even if sufficient evidence of the subjective element of extreme emotional disturbance were present in this case, proof of the objective element is lacking. Defendant points to the fact that he and the victim had been arguing and that the victim apparently sent him on a number of errands on the afternoon of the murder, causing him to climb the stairs to the fifth-floor apartment numerous times. This falls far short of the type of tumultuous relationship that might meet the objective component when coupled with other provocation . . . In the absence of proof that defendant's history or mental status rendered him unusually sensitive to these verbal exchanges and demands, no reasonable jury could have concluded that a resulting loss of self-control or similar disability constituted "an understandable human response deserving of mercy" under these circumstances . . .

German Federal Court of Justice
4 StR 48/04, NStZ 2004, 500 (April 22, 2004)

Facts

The regional court has sentenced the defendant to imprisonment of nine years and six months for homicide. The defendant's appeal in law leads, on the substantive objection, to quashing of the sentence.

Reasons

1. The reasoning by which the lay assessors court has rejected a less serious case of homicide in the sense of the first alternative of § 213 Criminal Code meets with decisive legal objections.

According to the regional court's findings, violent verbal and physical clashes had arisen over some years between the defendant and his partner C. who was 17 years younger. On the day of the crime another dispute arose, in the course of which the defendant killed his partner by inflicting twenty knife wounds after she had asked him to leave their joint home immediately, and in this context had said: "When I see you here, it hurts my eyes. You disturb me here. You're not a man any more, you're too old. I have found another man who is better than you in bed and more handsome than you, he is coming now!"

Within the framework of sentencing, the regional court determined that the statement by the defendant's partner uttered immediately before the crime represented a severe insult, in particular in relation to the defendant's capability for sexual performance. This insult had however not "directly driven" the defendant "to commit the crime, as primarily other motives" had been causatory "for it— namely narcissistic injury to feelings in the light of the announcement that a new partner had already been lined up, together with rage and disappointment in view of the demand now made, contrary to the original promise, to leave the home immediately."

The regional court admittedly correctly found that a motivation situation in which other circum- stances causing the crime relegated the anger resulting from a serious insult to a subordinate role is not covered by the first alternative of § 213 Criminal Code (see BGHR StGB § 213 alternative 2 Opferverhalten 3; BGH StV 1983, 60, 61). Such a motivation situation is however not substantiated by the regional court's findings. According to these it was rather the statements of his partner in their totality which "immediately caused the defendant, who felt himself to be profoundly humiliated and devalued by them, to feel considerable rage resulting from injury to his feelings." The regional court has further established that the defendant "in this rage" made the decision "immediately to kill" his partner. The different evaluation of the motives causing the crime which the regional court used as a basis for sentencing is not reconcilable with these findings. Nor do the observations of the experts reveal anything different. They have seen the affective initial situation for the crime on the one hand in the demand to leave immediately, but on the other hand, and equally importantly, in the fact that the defendant could not compensate for the further statements by his partner, in particular bearing in mind his character and personality structure; they had represented an extreme humiliation and devaluation for him. It is not comprehensible why the hurtful statements by his partner should have been on the one hand one of the causes for a considerable affective excitement of the defendant, and on the other hand should merely have played a subordinate role in causing the crime . . .

NOTES

1. Behind differences in terminology, one can find similar notions with regard to the evaluation of offenses. In the German Criminal Code, the provision labeled "less serious cases of manslaughter" (§ 213) aims to address similar cases to those falling under the norms about voluntary manslaughter in the Model Penal Code (§ 210.3(1)(b)) and in the New York Penal Law (§ 125.20(2)). Both systems set out to define circumstances in homicide cases that warrant less blame and less punishment, with a mixture of subjective and objective factors.

Under the New York Penal Law (and the Model Penal Code), the subjective prong of the extreme emotional disturbance defense, or EED for short, ("extreme mental or emotional disturbance," under the Model Penal Code) requires that the defendant *in fact* have been extremely emotionally disturbed when he or she committed the homicide. Just what amounts to EED is left unclear, though the New York Court of Appeals explains that the defendant cannot make out an extreme emotional disturbance defense unless there is evidence that "he or she suffered from a mental infirmity not rising to the level of insanity at the time of the homicide, typically manifested by a loss of self-control."

In German law the offender must be driven by rage, and the requirement that the offense must have been committed immediately after the maltreatment or insult (§ 213 Criminal Code) is also meant to ensure a close connection between the offender's emotional state and the homicide.

The Model Penal Code's (and therefore also the New York Penal Law's) approach instead has moved from a set of strict rules defining the scope of the defense, as illustrated in the excerpt from *Gounagias*, to a general standard framed in terms of reasonableness that leaves considerable discretion to the fact-finder. The following excerpt from *People v. Patterson*, 39 N.Y.2d 288 (1976), explains why:

An action influenced by an extreme emotional disturbance is not one that is necessarily so spontaneously undertaken. Rather, it may be that a significant mental trauma has affected a defendant's mind for a substantial period of time, simmering in the unknowing subconscious and then inexplicably coming to the fore. The differences between the present New York statute and its predecessor [from 1881] . . . can be explained by the tremendous advances made in psychology since 1881 and a willingness on the part of the courts, legislators, and the public to reduce the level of responsibility imposed on those whose capacity has been diminished by mental trauma.

The sort of "simmering" long-term build-up of "mental trauma" that would not have been covered by the traditional rule-based doctrine of provocation but that should not be disqualified from consideration as a mitigating factor is illustrated by the California case of *People v. Berry*, 18 Cal. 3d 509 (1976), decided the same year as *Patterson*. In that case, the defendant had killed his wife Rachel after a ten-day period during which she taunted him with the fact that she was sexually attracted to, and having relations with, another man. On the day of the homicide, the defendant had waited for twenty hours for Rachel to return home. When she returned, she said, "I suppose you have come here to kill me." His response was ambiguous; she started to scream at him. The defendant grabbed her by the shoulder and tried to stop her screaming, and eventually strangled her to death with a telephone cord. The defense psychiatrist testified that as a result of the cumulative series of provocations, "defendant at the time he fatally strangled Rachel was in a state of uncontrollable rage, completely under the sway of passion." The California Supreme Court reversed Berry's conviction:

> The Attorney General contends that the killing could not have been done in the heat of passion because there was a cooling off period, defendant having waited in the apartment for 20 hours. However, the long course of provocatory conduct, which had resulted in intermittent outbreaks of rage under specific provocation in the past, reached its final culmination in the apartment when Rachel began screaming...

A more recent, English, case, *R. v. Ahluwalia*, [1992] 4 All E.R. 889, illustrates the difficulty of applying the traditional provocation rule to a domestic violence case in which the woman kills her abuser:

> On 9th May 1989 the appellant, after enduring many years of violence and humiliation from her husband, threw petrol in his bedroom and set it alight. Her husband sustained terrible burns from which, after lingering painfully for six days, he died on 15th May.
> The appellant was indicted for murder. [S]he was convicted of murder... The learned judge then imposed upon her the mandatory sentence of life imprisonment...
> The appellant had suffered violence and abuse from the deceased from the outset of the marriage. He was a big man; she is slight. Her complaints of violence were supported by entries in her doctor's notes. Thus, in October 1981, there is a record of her being hit three or four times on the head with a telephone and thrown to the ground. In September 1983, a note states she was 'pushed' by her husband whilst pregnant and sustained a bruised hand. The next month she had a broken finger due to another argument. She made attempts at suicide in 1983 and again in 1986. The Croydon Crown Court granted her an injunction to restrain the deceased from hitting her in 1983. In 1986 the deceased abused the appellant and tried to run her down at a family wedding. She obtained her second injunction from the court after the deceased had held her throat and threatened her with a knife. He threatened to kill her and threw a mug of hot tea over her. Despite the court order, the deceased continued his violence which intensified after January 1989...
> The classic definition of provocation in law is that given by Devlin J. (as he then was) and which was approved by this court in R. v. Duffy [1949] 1 All E.R. 932. He said:
> "Provocation is some act, or series of acts done (or words spoken)... which would cause in any reasonable person and actually causes in the accused, a sudden and temporary loss of self-control, rendering the accused so subject to passion as to make him or her for the moment not master of his or her mind."...
> In the present case the learned judge followed that direction faithfully. He repeated it almost verbatim when he first directed the jury on provocation... His final direction read:
> "Sudden loss of self-control. That is what you have to consider and consider in the context of the facts as described by the defendant herself."...
> We consider that the learned judge's direction was in accordance with the well established law and cannot be faulted.

Of course, to set up a standard that would not dismiss this type of case under the subjective prong of the extreme emotional disturbance test is not to say that it will not fail under its objective, reasonableness, prong.

Both legal systems demand an objective assessment of subjective emotions. The American norms ask for a "reasonable explanation or excuse" for the emotional disturbance. Under-lying § 213 Criminal Code is a similar notion, which is phrased, however, in a less abstract and general mode. The provision instead defines a "less serious case" of manslaughter (*Totschlag*), which sets out prerequisites that typically cause emotional turbulence: "maltreatment or serious insult inflicted on him or a relative."

Furthermore, the state of "rage" (*Zorn*) must have occurred "without his own fault," which leads to similar outcomes as the requirement that an outside observer set the standard for reasonableness. In both legal systems, an offender's individual proneness to rage leading to overreactions that are hard to understand for a reasonable person would preclude mitigation. (Why does the psychological characteristic of proneness to rage affect the attribution of fault, unless the defendant is to be faulted for having this characteristic in the first place, or the characteristic is insufficiently ingrained, or acute, to determine behavior? Consider the German culpability principle in this context. And does the requirement of absence of fault, or rather guilt (*Schuld*), not more naturally refer to behavior by the defendant that gave rise to the emotional stimulus, either by placing him- or herself in the situation or by engaging in specific conduct in that situation?) On causing the conditions of one's defense, see Chapter 13.B.

2. *On the formulation of offense descriptions in criminal statutes.* From the German point of view, it is a virtue that criminal codes be relatively short (and thus accessible) and well-organized. This ideally means describing the relevant elements not too specifically, without too much detail, but in a way that is abstract enough to cover a multitude of possible cases in one offense description. Against this background, generalizing descriptions are preferable to, for instance, listing specific groups of victims such as police officers, peace officers, employees of correctional institutions etc. (see § 125.26 New York Penal Law). In general, the German Criminal Code uses more abstract, but also shorter and fewer offense description.

However, comparing the provisions about voluntary manslaughter to § 213 Criminal Code, we can see an exception: here, the German statute is more casuistic, describing specific situations rather than trying to express the principles of evaluation in a more abstract way. The American provisions are more convincing if the task is to formulate general conditions. The German, more specific, requirements might be too narrow: while "maltreatment" and "serious insult" certainly grasp important examples for understandable agitation, it is conceivable that there might be other reasons for emotional disturbance that can be reasonably explained or excused. (Compare the discussion of psychiatric experts in the context of the insanity defense, in Chapter 14.C.) But note that § 213 Criminal Code also contains a very generally phrased, open formulation: "in another less serious case." This leaves courts ample discretion to rely on the lower punishment range should they find the minimum sanction for manslaughter (*Totschlag*) in § 212 Criminal Code too severe. (But, in that case, what standard would guide the exercise of that discretion? How would we tell a more serious case from a less serious one?)

It may be worth noting in this context that the current German provocation provision, in § 213 Criminal Code, is almost identical—except for the reference to "another less serious case"—to the provocation provision in the Prussian Criminal Code of 1851, upon which the original German Criminal Code of 1871 was based:

Prussian Criminal Code of 1851
§ 177 (Manslaughter in the heat of passion
[*Totschlag im Affekt*])

If the manslaughterer, without his own fault, was provoked to rage by the killed person through maltreatment or serious insult inflicted on him or his relatives, and thereby was carried away immediately to commit the offense, lifelong hard imprisonment [*Zuchthausstrafe*] is precluded, and a sentence of not under two years' imprisonment [*Gefängniß*] is to be imposed.

3. What is the rationale behind milder punishment for cases of so-called voluntary manslaughter? Consider again the possible rationales behind the insanity defense (see Chapter 14.C). The general question of what it means to act culpably might not only be relevant for deciding about a defense (no punishment), but also for explaining why some offenses deserve less punishment than others. According to the *M'Naghten* rule and its traces in the American law, for instance in the New York Penal Law, the cognitive element matters: the appreciation of wrongfulness (which can be distorted due to a mental disorder). German law and the Model Penal Code assume that mental disorders can also affect the offender's self-control (see § 20 Criminal Code and Model Penal Code § 4.01) and thus eliminate or diminish culpability. This second explanation, which points to diminished capacity for the exercise of self-control, could also be used to justify the lesser punishment for offenders acting in a state of emotional turbulence.

Obviously, however, a breakdown of self-control cannot as such explain the legal situation in Germany or New York. Severe emotional disturbance also diminishes self-control if the reasons for getting into this emotional state fail under a standard of reasonableness. This shows that across legal cultures the question "how culpable was this act?" is not judged solely with view to the individual offender's psychological state at the time of the offense. Rather, the answers to questions such as "can society develop some degree of understanding for mitigating circumstances?" or "has the victim contributed to the emotional escalation in a blameworthy way?" seem to be crucial. (Who is best situated to reflect societal empathy here? A judge or a jury? And under which conditions might it be defensible to attribute a share of responsibility to the victim?)

More generally, once a rationale for mitigating on the basis of provocation, or extreme emotional disturbance, has been found, the question arises why it should not extend to other offenses besides murder. Attempted murder? If attempted murder, assault (if the provoked person inflicts physical harm that happens to fall short of death, without the intent to kill)? Offenses against property (if the provoked defendant destroys the provoker's property, intentionally or not, or for that matter, someone else's property)? If one takes a historical view, at least in the Anglo-American context, provocation never made the transition from a doctrine within the law of homicide to a general principle, from the special part to the general part. It is a general defense that remains limited to a specific offense.

4. Apart from its awkward position, with one foot in the special part and the other in the general part, the doctrine of provocation, or of extreme emotional disturbance, has attracted considerable criticism. Much like the doctrines of "insidious" murder and the conception of "no retreat" self-defense in German criminal law can be seen as reflecting a paradigm of men engaged in fair and honorable fistfights among equals, so the doctrine of provocation has been criticized for its patriarchal roots in a world of good men who reasonably lose their temper when their honor has been sullied. The classic provocation scenario, in Anglo-American criminal law at least, is the cuckolded husband who happens upon his wife in the arms of another man and, then, in a righteous fury kills one or the other, or just as likely, both, before coming to his senses.*

Calls for abolition of the defense of provocation have been made throughout the common law world, on the grounds that, among other things, it legitimizes violence against women and gay men, shifts responsibility to the victim, and discriminates against women who seek to invoke the defense. It was abolished outright in New Zealand in 2009 (Crimes (Provocation Repeal) Amendment Act 2009, § 5). In England, the defense was revised, and instead framed as a "loss of control" defense:

Coroners and Justice Act 2009
§ 54 Partial defence to murder: loss of control

(1) Where a person ("D") kills or is a party to the killing of another ("V"), D is not to be convicted of murder if—
(a) D's acts and omissions in doing or being a party to the killing resulted from D's loss of self-control,
(b) the loss of self-control had a qualifying trigger, and
(c) a person of D's sex and age, with a normal degree of tolerance and self-restraint and in the circumstances of D, might have reacted in the same or in a similar way to D.

---

* See, e.g., Donna A. Coker, "Heat of Passion and Wife Killing: Men Who Batter/Men Who Kill," 2 *Southern California Review of Law and Women's Studies* (1992), 71.

(2) For the purposes of subsection (1)(a), it does not matter whether or not the loss of control was sudden.

(3) In subsection (1)(c) the reference to "the circumstances of D" is a reference to all of D's circumstances other than those whose only relevance to D's conduct is that they bear on D's general capacity for tolerance or self-restraint.

(4) Subsection (1) does not apply if, in doing or being a party to the killing, D acted in a considered desire for revenge.

(5) On a charge of murder, if sufficient evidence is adduced to raise an issue with respect to the defence under subsection (1), the jury must assume that the defence is satisfied unless the prosecution proves beyond reasonable doubt that it is not.

(6) For the purposes of subsection (5), sufficient evidence is adduced to raise an issue with respect to the defence if evidence is adduced on which, in the opinion of the trial judge, a jury, properly directed, could reasonably conclude that the defence might apply.

(7) A person who, but for this section, would be liable to be convicted of murder is liable instead to be convicted of manslaughter.

(8) The fact that one party to a killing is by virtue of this section not liable to be convicted of murder does not affect the question whether the killing amounted to murder in the case of any other party to it.

§ 55 Meaning of "qualifying trigger"

(1) This section applies for the purposes of section 54.

(2) A loss of self-control had a qualifying trigger if subsection (3), (4) or (5) applies.

(3) This subsection applies if D's loss of self-control was attributable to D's fear of serious violence from V against D or another identified person.

(4) This subsection applies if D's loss of self-control was attributable to a thing or things done or said (or both) which—
(a) constituted circumstances of an extremely grave character, and
(b) caused D to have a justifiable sense of being seriously wronged.

(5) This subsection applies if D's loss of self-control was attributable to a combination of the matters mentioned in subsections (3) and (4).

(6) In determining whether a loss of self-control had a qualifying trigger—
(a) D's fear of serious violence is to be disregarded to the extent that it was caused by a thing which D incited to be done or said for the purpose of providing an excuse to use violence;
(b) a sense of being seriously wronged by a thing done or said is not justifiable if D incited the thing to be done or said for the purpose of providing an excuse to use violence;
(c) the fact that a thing done or said constituted sexual infidelity is to be disregarded.

(7) In this section references to "D" and "V" are to be construed in accordance with section 54.

Note how this revision removed the traditional requirement of "sudden" loss of control immediately following the triggering event, to expand the relevant time frame in light of cases like *Ahluwalia*, in Note 1. At the same time, the revision narrowed the scope of what may count as a "qualifying trigger" by providing that "the fact that a thing done or said [?] constituted sexual infidelity is to be disregarded," thus removing a—if not *the*—classic paradigm of the defense from its purview altogether.

5. Note that in the New York Penal Law, though not in the Model Penal Code, extreme emotional disturbance is classified as an affirmative defense (which, according to N.Y. Penal Law § 25.00(2), places the burden of establishing the defense on the defendant by a preponderance of the evidence). This classification was challenged on constitutional (due process) grounds and produced a significant opinion by the U.S. Supreme Court:

After a brief and unstable marriage, the appellant, Gordon Patterson, Jr., became estranged from his wife, Roberta. Roberta resumed an association with John Northrup, a neighbor to whom she had been engaged prior to her marriage to appellant. On December 27, 1970, Patterson borrowed a rifle from an acquaintance and went to the residence of his father-in-law. There, he observed his wife through a window in a state of semiundress in the presence of John Northrup. He entered the house and killed Northrup by shooting him twice in the head.

[Patterson was convicted of second-degree murder, which in New York has two elements: (1) "intent to cause the death of another person"; and (2) "caus(ing) the death of such person or of a third person." N.Y. Penal Law § 125.25 (McKinney 1975). A person accused of murder may raise an affirmative defense that he "acted under the influence of extreme emotional disturbance for which there was a reasonable explanation or excuse." If successful, this defense reduces the defendant's liability to manslaughter.]

We cannot conclude that Patterson's conviction under the New York law deprived him of due process of law . . . [The affirmative defense of] extreme emotional disturbance . . . , which the [New York] Court of Appeals described as permitting "the defendant to show that his actions were caused by a mental infirmity not arising to the level of insanity, and that he is less culpable for having committed them," does not serve to negative any facts of the crime which the State is to prove in order to convict of murder. It constitutes a separate issue on which the defendant is required to carry the burden of persuasion . . .

Patterson v. New York, 432 U.S. 197 (1977)

The upshot of *Patterson* was that the federal constitution, and the due process clause in particular, requires the state to bear the burden of proof (beyond a reasonable doubt) on all offense elements, but not on any issue the legislature had categorized as a defense element, rather than an offense element. Acknowledging that this holding "may seem to permit state legislatures to reallocate burdens of proof by labeling as affirmative defenses at least some elements of the crimes now defined in their statutes," the Court noted that "there are obviously constitutional limits beyond which the States may not go in this regard," without, however, specifying what these limits might be.

Patterson had argued that evidence of extreme emotional disturbance served to negate *mens rea*—specifically, the mental state requirement attached to the result element of murder, in this case intent—so that even under the Court's dualistic approach set out in *Patterson*, the state was constitutionally required to bear the burden of proof on the issue. The Court, however, categorized—or rather found that the New York legislature had categorized—extreme emotional disturbance as a "separate issue" instead, which "does not serve to negative any facts of the crime which the State is to prove in order to convict of murder." Of course, as in the case of evidence of a mental disease or defect, see Model Penal Code § 4.02, there is no reason why evidence of extreme emotional disturbance might not be relevant both to the issue of *mens rea* and to a separate defense (presumably an excuse) that would be available even if *mens rea* has been proved. One difficulty in *Patterson* was that shifting the burden on the defense may lead the jury as fact-finder to shift it on the offense element of *mens rea* as well, thus relieving the state of its constitutional obligation to establish all offense elements (beyond a reasonable doubt).

6. Insofar as the doctrines of provocation (traditional common law), extreme emotional disturbance (N.Y. Penal Law and Model Penal Code), manslaughter in heat of passion (Prussian Criminal Code), and less serious case of manslaughter (German Criminal Code) all serve to reduce the otherwise applicable sentence for murder, it is worth considering whether they might be transformed into, or supplemented with, an explicit, and more broadly framed, sentencing provision:

U.S. Sentencing Guidelines
§ 5K2.10. Victim's Conduct (Policy Statement)

If the victim's wrongful conduct contributed significantly to provoking the offense behavior, the court may reduce the sentence below the guideline range to reflect the nature and circumstances of the offense. In deciding whether a sentence reduction is warranted, and the extent of such reduction, the court should consider the following:

(1) The size and strength of the victim, or other relevant physical characteristics, in comparison with those of the defendant.

(2) The persistence of the victim's conduct and any efforts by the defendant to prevent confrontation.

(3) The danger reasonably perceived by the defendant, including the victim's reputation for violence.

(4) The danger actually presented to the defendant by the victim.

(5) Any other relevant conduct by the victim that substantially contributed to the danger presented.

(6) The proportionality and reasonableness of the defendant's response to the victim's provocation. Victim misconduct ordinarily would not be sufficient to warrant application of this provision in the context of offenses under Chapter Two, Part A, Subpart 3 (Criminal Sexual Abuse). In addition, this provision usually would not be relevant in the context of non-violent offenses. There may, however, be unusual circumstances in which substantial victim misconduct would warrant a reduced penalty in the case of a non-violent offense. For example, an extended course of provocation and harassment might lead a defendant to steal or destroy property in retaliation.

Involuntary manslaughter (reckless homicide)

If voluntary manslaughter is all about provocation, or extreme emotional disturbance, then involuntary manslaughter is all about *mens rea*, and in particular about recklessness. At this point, then, a comparative analysis of the law of homicide will come to resemble a comparative analysis of the *applied* law of *mens rea* (see Chapter 8): in contemporary American criminal law, just as voluntary manslaughter is about recklessness, so negligent homicide is, not surprisingly, about negligence. Still, *mens rea* certainly is a subject of sufficient importance to deserve a closer look, in action, so to speak, in the context of a particular set of related offenses, the various types of homicide, which themselves occupy a central role in the special part of criminal law. Of course, as we have mentioned before, at least in Anglo-American criminal law the law of homicide was, for the longest time, a general part *avant la lettre*, as doctrines of the general part tended to first see the light of day as doctrines of the law of homicide.

It is useful to get a sense of the traditional common law before the arrival of the Model Penal Code, not only to see what came before, but also because common law doctrines continue to play a significant role in many American jurisdictions. So we begin with a pre-Model Penal Code case from Pennsylvania that nicely sets out the classic homicide scheme against the backdrop of an interesting set of facts, before moving on to a decidedly more contemporary German case, which deals with the potential criminal liability for exposing unwitting sex partners to HIV.

Commonwealth v. Malone
Supreme Court of Pennsylvania
354 Pa. 180 (1946)

Opinion by Mr. Chief Justice Maxey

This is an appeal from the judgment and sentence under a conviction of murder in the second degree. William H. Long, age 13 years, was killed by a shot from a 32-caliber revolver held against his right side by the defendant, then aged 17 years. These youths were on friendly terms at the time of the homicide . . .

On the evening of February 26, 1945, when the defendant went to a moving picture theater, he carried in the pocket of his raincoat a revolver which he had obtained at the home of his uncle on the preceding day. In the afternoon preceding the shooting, the decedent procured a cartridge from his father's room and he and the defendant placed it in the revolver.

After leaving the theater, the defendant went to a dairy store and there met the decedent. Both youths sat in the rear of the store ten minutes, during which period the defendant took the gun out of his pocket and loaded the chamber to the right of the firing pin and then closed the gun. A few minutes later, both youths sat on stools in front of the lunch counter and ate some food. The defendant suggested to the decedent that they play "Russian Poker."[1] Long replied: "I don't care; go ahead." The defendant then placed the revolver against the right side of Long and pulled the trigger three times. The third pull resulted in a fatal wound to Long. The latter jumped off the stool and cried: "Oh! Oh! Oh!" and Malone said: "Did I hit you, Billy? Gee, Kid, I'm sorry." Long died from the wounds two days later.

The defendant testified that the gun chamber he loaded was the first one to the right of the firing chamber and that when he pulled the trigger he did not "expect to have the gun go off." He declared he had no intention of harming Long, who was his friend and companion. The defendant was indicted for murder, tried and found guilty of murder in the second degree and sentenced to a term in the penitentiary for a period not less than five years and not exceeding ten years . . .

---

[1] It has been explained that "Russian poker" is a game in which the participants, in turn, place a single cartridge in one of the five chambers of a revolver cylinder, give the latter a quick twirl, place the muzzle of the gun against the temple and pull the trigger, leaving it to chance whether or not death results to the trigger puller.

Appellant alleges certain errors in the charge of the court and also contends that the facts did not justify a conviction for any form of homicide except involuntary manslaughter. This contention we overrule. A specific intent to take life is, under our law, an essential ingredient of murder in the first degree. At common law, the "grand criterion" which "distinguished murder from other killing" was malice on the part of the killer and this malice was not necessarily "malevolent to the deceased particularly" but "any evil design in general; the dictate of a wicked, depraved and malignant heart": 4 Blackstone 199. Among the examples that Blackstone cites of murder is "coolly discharging a gun among a multitude of people," causing the death of someone of the multitude.

In Pennsylvania, the common law crime of murder is divided into two degrees, and murder of the second degree includes every element which enters into first degree murder except the intention to kill. When an individual commits an act of gross recklessness for which he must reasonably anticipate that death to another is likely to result, he exhibits that "wickedness of disposition; hardness of heart; cruelty; recklessness of consequences and a mind regardless of social duty" which proved that there was at that time in him "that state or frame of mind termed malice" . . .

The trial judge . . . erred in charging that "A person on trial for murder cannot be convicted of any offense if the testimony shows that the death was accidental." Death may be accidental though it resulted from a malicious act intentionally committed. In such a case the means were not accidental; the result was.[3] In the instant case if the defendant had by some negligent, unintentional act, caused Long to fall off the stool at which he was sitting in the store and if, as a result of that fall, Long had sustained a fatal injury, both the initial act and the death might be correctly characterized as accidental. But when the defendant knowing that a revolver had at least one loaded cartridge in it, pressed the muzzle of that revolver to the side of Long and pulled the trigger three times, his act cannot be characterized as accidental, even if his statement that he had no intention to kill Long is accepted (as the jury accepted it). The way the trial judge used the word "accidental" throughout the charge must have been confusing to the jury and might easily have misled it into acquitting the accused on the theory that since the death of Long was accidental, "the defendant cannot be convicted of any offense," (as the trial judge said). The latter should have made it clear to the jury that even though Long's death might have been unintended and, therefore, accidental, the evidence showed that the act which caused the victim's death was not accidental. This was the view the jury took of the case despite the court's instructions . . . Of such and similar errors, the appellant cannot complain; they were prejudicial only to the Commonwealth . . .

The killing of William H. Long by this defendant resulted from an act intentionally done by the latter, in reckless and wanton disregard of the consequences which were at least sixty per cent certain from his thrice attempted discharge of a gun known to contain one bullet and aimed at a vital part of Long's body. This killing was, therefore, murder, for malice in the sense of a wicked disposition is evidenced by the intentional doing of an uncalled-for act in callous disregard of its likely harmful effects on others. The fact that there was no motive for this homicide does not exculpate the accused. In a trial for murder proof of motive is always relevant but never necessary.

German Federal Court of Justice
1 StR 262/88, BGHSt 36, 1 (November 4, 1988)
AIDS Case

Facts

The defendant, an American citizen living in the Federal Republic, voluntarily underwent an AIDS test in February 1986 when being treated for an acute sexual disease in the US hospital in Nuremberg. This revealed that he was infected with the so-called human immune deficiency virus (HIV). When telling this to the defendant at the beginning of June 1986, the responsible doctor, Dr S., informed him in a detailed discussion about the nature and effects of the AIDS disease (acquired immune deficiency syndrome). He gave special emphasis to an explanation of the necessary protective measures in connection with sexual intercourse—including homosexual intercourse. Dr S. pointed out forcefully and in detail to the defendant, who had already been treated sixteen times since 1965 by the military medical services for sexual diseases, that he was "infectious for the rest of his life" and therefore would have to use "condoms as a matter of principle" for sexual intercourse for the protection of his partners. As the AIDS pathogen, although especially concentrated in the semen and blood, was present in every other bodily fluid, he ought not to engage in oral, vaginal or anal

---

[3] If A maliciously beats B intending to do him enormous bodily harm without killing him and B dies as result of the beating, A can be found guilty of murder in the second degree, though death was "accidental" in the sense that it was not intended by A.

intercourse without a condom. By unprotected intercourse of these kinds he could pass on the pathogen to his partners and cause them to have "a fatal disease." It made no difference here whether sexual intercourse resulted in ejaculation or not. In the context of further medical examinations, in which no symptoms appeared indicating that AIDS had already broken out, Dr S. advised the defendant again in the middle of July 1986 about the possibility of infecting others with the virus.

Regardless of this the defendant had unprotected sexual relations—by anal intercourse—twice in August 1986 in a homosexual club with an Italian whose identity remains unknown, without pointing out his HIV infection to his partner. In both cases he carried out anal intercourse without a condom at first and then interrupted it and continued it with a condom to ejaculation. "The defendant knew at least on the second occasion that his actions were apt to transmit the AIDS virus to his partner. He accepted and condoned the fact that his partner could become ill and run the risk of dying" (case 1 of the conviction). Whether this resulted in the Italian being infected could not be established. When the defendant at the end of August 1986 was treated again for a fresh outbreak of gonorrhea, Dr S. reprimanded him severely because he had obviously not observed the advice given to him for the protection of his intimate partners, and advised him again forcefully about the consequences of unprotected sexual intercourse. Besides this the psychiatrist at the US hospital brought home to the defendant once again the consequences of his behavior. However, the defendant had unprotected sexual contacts at least twice in the following period, in December 1986 and in January 1987, at a homosexual meeting place with a German, the witness D., without informing him about his HIV infection. In this case the defendant, who had had homosexual relations several times already with D., engaged in the first of the two contacts by first having oral sex practiced on him without a condom, breaking off shortly before ejaculation, then using a condom—brought by D.—and finally completing anal intercourse with ejaculation. In the later contact the defendant proceeded first in the same manner, and then attempted after oral intercourse to introduce his unprotected member into D.'s anus. As this caused him pain, the defendant abandoned the attempt and then carried out anal intercourse with a condom—brought by D.—to the stage of ejaculation. "The defendant knew on each occasion that unprotected oral sex was apt to transmit the AIDS virus to D. However in order to satisfy his sexual urge he accepted and condoned the fact that D. could become ill and run the risk of death" (cases 2 and 3 of the conviction). An investigation undertaken later gave no proof of D. having been infected. The regional court convicted the defendant of attempted infliction of dangerous bodily harm in three cases and sentenced him to a total term of imprisonment of two years, but acquitted him of other charges (NJW 1988, 2311).

The defendant's appeal in law by which he objected to the violation of procedural and substantive law was not well founded insofar as it applied to the guilty verdict.

Reasons

I.

The regional court did not err in law in considering the objective features of an attempt to inflict dangerous bodily harm by way of "treatment endangering life" (§ 223 para. 1, § 223a para. 1, 2 [now: § 224—Eds.], §§ 22, 23 Criminal Code) to be present in each case.

1. The criminal chamber correctly assumes that the infection of another with the immunodeficiency virus (HIV) causing the acquired immune deficiency syndrome AIDS fulfills the objective definition of bodily harm.* Any causing or exacerbation of a condition which deviates disadvantageously from the normal condition of the victim's physical functions is to be regarded as harm to health in the sense of §§ 223 ff. Criminal Code, regardless of the way in which the impairment occurs; it does not need to be associated with a feeling of pain (BGH, in: Dallinger, MDR 1975, 723; Hirsch, in: LK, 10th edit., § 223 marginal no. 11 with further references). It is recognized in the case law and the literature that even infecting another with a disease which is not entirely trivial—also, and in particular, with a sexually transmitted disease—represents a worsening of health. Because a person infected with HIV himself becomes infectious with the entry of the virus into his organism, and this remains for the total length of his ensuing life (see on this and on other medical aspects Pschyrembel, Klinisches Wörterbuch, 255th edit. (1986), keyword Aids; . . .), this principle must apply likewise, and especially for infection with the immune deficiency syndrome AIDS—so far incurable and as a rule fatal when it occurs . . . Harm to health here, and therefore bodily harm, occurs—as with other dangerous infections—with the mere infection as such, as this—objectively—changes the victim's normal

---

* [German Criminal Code (Inflicting Bodily Injury) § 223

(1) Who physically maltreats another person or damages another person's health, will be punished with imprisonment of not more than five years or with a fine. (2) The attempt is punishable.—Eds.]

physical condition profoundly. Besides this many people infected with HIV have a short flu-like episode some weeks after the infection.

2. The regional court's assumption that the defendant's behavior had in each case been apt to bring about an infection of his partner and therefore harm the latter's health in the sense of § 223 para. 1 Criminal Code is likewise not open to objection on legal grounds.

The criminal chamber—expertly advised by two scientists, Prof. Dr. F. and Prof. Dr. K., who had been active for years in medical research into AIDS—relies on the following factual considerations: AIDS is transmitted by viruses which appeared in all bodily fluids, but were especially concentrated in the blood and semen. The further the disease progressed, the stronger was the incidence of the virus (virus load). The infection, for which a so-called gateway was necessary into the person affected, occurred primarily by sexual contacts. In general any sexual intercourse—and even only on one occasion—was apt to infect the partner. The infection risk, which depended in other respects on the composition of the organisms of both partners, was especially great with homosexual contacts, and in particular with unprotected anal intercourse—because of small injuries to the mucus membrane (microlesions) which were as a rule unavoidable. In the light of possible transmission via the mucus membrane in the mouth or through injuries in the mouth region, unprotected oral intercourse also represented an infection risk. Even if less dangerous, these practices were also apt to cause infection without ejaculation, as even in this way—as occurs with the possibility of a pregnancy following coitus interruptus—seminal fluid, even though in small amounts, and other secretions could be transferred.

This judgment of the criminal chamber is based on careful and critical assessment of the two expert opinions and in particular does not contradict the available findings according to the current state of medical research . . .

3. In all the cases the regional court correctly assumes that the defendant's behavior corresponding to the definition is to be assessed as "treatment endangering life" in the sense of § 223a para. 1 Criminal Code.*

According to the established case law of the Federal Court of Justice such treatment does not need actually to bring the victim's life in the individual case into danger in an outwardly recognizable way. It is sufficient if it is apt to cause this—even though considering the actual circumstances of the individual case—because of its general danger (BGHSt 2, 160 (163); see also Oberlandesgericht Köln, NJW 1983, 2274). According to the current medical findings about the course of AIDS, the infection leads—in the main after a latent phase of several years without distinctive clinical features—in the case of the overwhelming number of carriers of the virus via various stages finally to the complete picture of the disease; here the disease, which has not so far been accessible to any effective therapy, as a rule takes a fatal course (Laufs-Laufs, NJW 1987, 2259; Buchborn, MedR 1987, 261 f.). In the light therefore of the considerable probability of a lethal outcome to the infection, the behavior of an HIV infected person—at any rate so long as no secure cure option exists—who has sexual intercourse without the protection of a condom, and therefore in a manner generally apt to cause infection, is in principle also in general apt to bring his partner's life into danger. It therefore represents, as the literature and case law already quoted does not doubt, "treatment endangering life" in the sense of the criminal statute.

II.

Contrary to the view of the appeal in law, the regional court has also assumed without legal error that the defendant had in each case acted with—conditional—intention to harm.

1. According to the consistent case law of the Federal Court of Justice on the demarcation between conditional intention and conscious negligence, the perpetrator acts intentionally when he recognizes the occurrence of the result in the definition of the crime as possible and not entirely unlikely, and therefore agrees with it in such a way that he accepts and condones the realization of the definition, or at least comes to terms with it for the sake of the objective which he seeks, even if the occurrence of the result is in itself not desired by him; conscious negligence occurs however if the perpetrator is not in agreement with the realization (recognized as possible) of the definition, and earnestly—and not merely vaguely—trusts in the result not occurring (BGHSt 7, 363 (368 f.); BGH, NStZ 1982, 506; 1983, 407; 1984, 19; 1988, 175). As both these forms of culpable mind are close to each other in the border area, for conditional intention to be present, both elements of the internal side of the crime, i.e. the knowledge element as well as the volitional element, must be examined in each individual case and be proved by factual findings. In particular the assessment of the voluntative intention

* [German Criminal Code § 224 (dangerous bodily harm, formerly § 223a)

(1) Who causes bodily harm . . . 5. by a treatment that endangers life, will be punished with imprisonment from six months to ten years, in less serious cases with imprisonment from three months to five years.—Eds.]

element must concern itself with the findings in the judgment about the perpetrator's personality and also take into consideration the significant circumstances at the time of occurrence of the crime (BGH, in: Holtz, MDR 1977, 105 and in: Holtz, MDR 1977, 458; BGH, NStZ 1987, 424; 1988, 175). An overall view is therefore required of all the objective and subjective circumstances of the crime. Various aspects of evaluation can take prime place here according to the special nature of the case. Indications as to the perpetrator's attitude to the protected legal interests can emerge from his past life as well as from his statements before, during or after the crime. In particular "the objective size and closeness of the danger as known to the perpetrator" can be taken up to prove conditional intention (Jescheck, Lehrb. des StrafR AT, 4th edit, § 29 III 3a).

The Senate—considering criticism expressed on this subject in the literature (recently in particular Herzberg, JuS 1986, 249; . . .) sees no cause to abandon these principles of demarcation developed in consistent case law either generally or specially for the assessment of criminal law liability in connection with AIDS. They also apply when a person infected with HIV has sexual intercourse without protective measures in the knowledge of his infection. In this area also intentional action requires the knowledge and intention of the realization of the definition of the crime and the approval of the result thus forms the essential distinguishing feature. Bearing in mind the knowledge which has been widely disseminated in the meantime about the risk of infection on unprotected sexual contacts, it is likely that, in a case of the present kind, the perpetrator recognizes the possibility of infection of his partner, and if in spite of this he adheres to his course of conduct, he accepts and condones the danger associated with this or, in order to be able to pursue his sexual urge, comes to terms with its occurrence. However there is no room here for stereotyped findings. A comprehensive examination of the voluntative intention element—for differentiation from consciously negligent action—always remains indispensable . . .

It is admittedly not permissible simply to conclude from the perpetrator's knowledge of his HIV infection and the fact that unprotected sexual intercourse is in general apt to transmit the virus, that he has accepted and condoned an infection of his partner. However the state of the perpetrator's knowledge, in so far as it permits conclusions about his intention, can be referred to within the overall assessment of the actual facts which has to be undertaken by the judge of fact. It must also be borne in mind that in cases like the present, in which the perpetrator, after creating the cause, can himself no longer influence the course of events and control it, the question of how far he has made the danger "unshielded," and then let it take its course, can acquire special significance. The perpetrator's assertion that he had believed or hoped that nothing would happen is not inconsistent with the assumption of an approval if it is left to chance as to whether the danger which he knows about is realized. On the other hand the perpetrator having had reason for the opinion that the risk of infection was only minor in the circumstances of the actual case can argue against this assumption. It can however also be of consequence, as a circumstance in favor of the assumption of conditional intention, that, even in the case of a statistically small risk of infection, any unprotected sexual contact can be the one out of many which transmits the virus, and that therefore every individual instance on its own carries with it in reality the full risk of infection.

2. The regional court has not violated these legal principles.

a) The criminal chamber reached the conclusion, on the basis of an assessment of the evidence which was free of legal errors, that the defendant knew in each case about the possibility of infection of the partner as a result of the sexual contact. The chamber concerned itself here with the possibility that the defendant could have assumed that no, or at any rate only a quite unlikely, risk of infection existed, either generally with sexual intercourse without ejaculation, or in particular by the practices chosen by him in each case. It bases its finding of the presence of the intellectual intention elements, however, in all three cases, crucially on the fact that the defendant had been comprehensively and forcefully advised before the commission of the crimes about the danger resulting from his HIV infection, and that Dr S. had in particular indicated to him expressly and unmistakably on the first—detailed—consultation that in the future he should only have any sexual intercourse, whether of the vaginal, oral or anal kind, with the use of condoms for the protection of his partner, and that it made no difference here whether ejaculation occurred as a result of the intercourse or not. Certainly the criminal chamber takes into consideration in cases 2 and 3 in the defendant's favor that this explanation—after commission of the first crime—was subject to a certain relativization, in that the defendant had informed himself by an English language brochure about "Safer Sex." After assessment of the type, content and orientation of the brochure (according to which oral sexual intercourse without ejaculation merely carries a diminished risk) the chamber however reached the conviction "that it was clear even to the defendant that the detailed explanation by a doctor here, which related to his individual case, had priority over general suggestions for behavior." The conclusion reached by the regional court that the claimant had not seriously trusted that "an infection was excluded or that the degree of probability was so small that it could be considered to be completely insignificant" is not open to objection on legal grounds.

b) The considerations which led the regional court to find the volitional intention element in each case likewise withstand examination.

   aa) The criminal chamber in case 1 first stresses in relation to the grounds for finding the intention element that "simply on the basis of the defendant's high level of knowledge" because of the instructions given to him it could be assumed that he had accepted and condoned the possible infection and possible danger to life of his partner, or had come to terms with such consequences. This assessment of the evidence meets with no prevailing doubts. As already explained, substantial circumstantial evidence of the presence of the volitional intention element can be deduced from the quality and intensity of the knowledge which the perpetrator has about the danger of his course of conduct in the individual case. In this respect the regional court correctly considers the extremely intensive form of the explanation by a doctor and the fact that when describing the risk of infection from unprotected anal intercourse he had made no distinction between that with and that without ejaculation.

   Besides this the criminal chamber derived its conclusion as to the presence of the intention element "from the overall circumstances of the crime," and based it on further grounds discussed in detail. Contrary to the view of the appeal in law the regional court could draw the conclusion from the statements of the witnesses heard about earlier statements by the defendant—the detective I., the examining magistrate W. and the doctor Dr S.—that he had first had unprotected anal intercourse on the day in question with the same partner on two occasions. The consideration which is employed in this context as a piece of circumstantial evidence for the defendant's preparedness to endanger, that it was clear to him "as experienced sexually" that "traces of semen could still be present" on his member "which came from the first act of sexual intercourse on this day," has a sufficient factual basis . . .

   On the basis of this evidence, the conclusion drawn by the criminal chamber that the defendant had accepted and condoned the infection of his partner which he had recognized as possible cannot be objected to on legal grounds. The conclusions which the judge of fact draws from the established facts do not need to be absolutely conclusive. It suffices that they are possible and comprehensible (BGHSt 10, 208 (210); BGHSt 26, 56 (63); BGHSt 29, 18 (19 f.)). That is the case here.

   bb) In cases 2 and 3 the regional court, proceeding from the defendant's state of knowledge as described, considered that he "had no condoms with him at the time of both sexual contacts with D., although he would have been especially required to do so." Further, the criminal chamber in the context of its assessment of the evidence stresses the fact that the defendant had attempted in the second act of sexual intercourse to introduce his member into D's anus without a condom. The criminal chamber could consider both circumstances to be apt to characterize the defendant's inward attitude to the infection—recognized by him as possible—of his partner and his preparedness to endanger. These circumstances, in the overall review of the evidential indications discussed, permit the conclusion "that D's fate was a matter of complete indifference to the defendant," and that he thereby accepted and condoned the infecting of D.

3. . . .

4. The finding that the defendant had in each case committed an attempt to inflict dangerous bodily harm with conditional intention is not put in question by the fact that the regional court, in spite of the *fatal* danger associated with an infection, has not established a conditional intention to kill. The judgment under challenge remains within the framework of established case law which has continually indicated that a much higher threshold exists for the intention to kill than for the intention to endanger or to injure (see BGH, StrVert 1984, 187; 1986, 421; BGH, NStZ 1983, 407; 1984, 19; 1988, 175). The criminal chamber could not establish that this threshold was crossed here. In particular it derives doubts about the condoning of a fatal outcome from the fact that a variable incubation period is expected with AIDS, which in some circumstances is very long, and that the defendant possibly shared the hope of many people infected with HIV that in this period a cure for AIDS would be found, and that the disease in relation to himself and also his partners, if he had indeed infected them, would only break out after discovery of such a cure. Contrary to the criticism expressed in the literature in this respect (Herzberg, NJW 1987, 1465; Geppert, Jura 1987, 672; Prittwitz, JA 1988, 501 f.), the decision of the regional court contains no methodological contradiction. This is shown simply by the distinction in the statute between—conditionally—intentional killing and intentional infliction of bodily harm "by means of treatment endangering life" (§ 223a Criminal Code). It is quite possible that the perpetrator knows all the circumstances which make his actions a treatment endangering life, without—as a result of whatever facts there may be in the actual situation—accepting and condoning that his action would lead to the victim's death (BGH, Judgment of June 11, 1985, 1 StR 200/85).

III.

The regional court correctly assumed that the defendant could not escape liability either from the viewpoint of so-called permitted risk or with regard to the argument that the partner in question intentionally endangered himself on his own responsibility.

1. A case of permitted risk—whether because of an exclusion from the definition of the crime or a ground of justification—is not in any case present if a person infected by HIV has sexual intercourse without protective measures (general opinion, see Eberbach, Rechtsprobleme der HTLV-III-Infektion—Aids—(Legal problems of the HTLV-III-Infection—AIDS) 1986, p. 10; Herzberg, JuS 1987, 778; Arloth, MedR 1987, 291; . . . see also Regional Court München I, AIFO 1987, 648 (649)). There is a contrast here with commonplace and widely spread infections like for instance the common cold, which are almost ubiquitous, from which it is therefore scarcely possible to be shielded in human communal life and which additionally as a rule cause no substantial danger to the health of others. The defendant's conduct was not socially permissible because every HIV transmission represents a lifelong invasion into the life interests of the person infected which is highly probable to have a fatal outcome, and because in the case of sexual intercourse, as the most important method of transmission for AIDS, the danger of infection can be, if not completely excluded, at least screened out in a reasonable way by the use of condoms, and thereby substantially reduced. Over against this, the degree of probability that an infection will occur is of no consequence (thus also Prittwitz, JA 1988, 440).

2. The defendant's actions also do not have to remain unpunished from the viewpoint of action at one's own risk or of a risk consciously entered into by the partners. It is true that the new case law of the Federal Court of Justice laid down by the Senate means that a person who merely causes, facilitates or promotes another to endangering himself intentionally on his own responsibility is not as a rule punishable because of an—attempted or completed—infliction of bodily harm or homicide crime, even if the risk consciously entered into by this person is realized (BGHSt 32, 262; see further BGH, NStZ 1984, 452; 1985, 25; 1986, 266; 1987, 406; BGH, NJW 1985, 690). Whether these legal principles—developed in particular in the context of cases of death following communal use of drugs—are applicable at all to sexual relations with people infected with HIV (denied by Helgerth, NStZ 1988, 262) does not need any decision here. In any case the criminal liability of the perpetrator, as is explained in the case law quoted, begins where because of superior specialist knowledge he understands the risk better than the person endangering himself. This is the situation when someone who knows that he is infected with HIV has sexual relations with another person whom he has not informed about his infectiousness and the danger to life associated with his infection (likewise the main view; see Eberbach, ZRP 1987, 396 f.; Geppert, Jura 1987, 671; Herzberg, NJW 1987, 2284; . . . ; for another view Bruns, MDR 1987, 356 and NJW 1987, 2282 as well as Herzog/Nestler-Tremel, StrVert 1987, 370 . . .).

No different considerations apply if the person affected who did not recognize the concrete risk of HIV transmission is prepared for the fact that he is having sexual intercourse with a person who belongs to one of the so-called risk groups. Even in such cases he has a claim to the protection of criminal law, because there is no question of transferring responsibility for the avoidance of such a serious danger from the person from whom the danger proceeds, and who knows it, to the person endangered, even if he also behaved carelessly. In particular, so far as homosexuals and prostitutes are concerned, there are indications that for the members of these risk groups "by now a very high and broad sensitivity (readiness to receive the prevention message) for AIDS" can be assumed (Rosenbrock, AIFO 1988, 166). On this ground also the partner can as a rule trust that no one will have unprotected sexual intercourse with him knowing but remaining silent about his own infection . . .

NOTES

1. If one were to evaluate a case like *Commonwealth v. Malone* according to the standards expressed in the Model Penal Code and state law following this approach, it would be analyzed as a potential case of involuntary manslaughter, i.e., reckless homicide. *Malone*, however, applies the traditional common law homicide scheme, which revolved around the concept of malice. Murder required proof of malice, manslaughter did not. Malice came in two (evidentiary) varieties: express and implied. Express malice required proof of intent to kill. Implied malice instead required proof of "gross recklessness" regarding death, which was tantamount to homicidal intent, and therefore malice. A contemporary version of this scheme appears in the California Penal Code, originally drafted in 1872:

Cal. Penal Code

§ 187

(a) Murder is the unlawful killing of a human being . . . with malice aforethought . . .

§ 188

Such malice may be express or implied. It is express when there is manifested a deliberate intention unlawfully to take away the life of a fellow creature. It is implied, when no considerable provocation appears, or when the circumstances attending the killing show an abandoned and malignant heart . . .

The Model Penal Code abandoned this talk of abandoned and malignant hearts, malice implied, express, and aforethought, and replaced it with the familiar taxonomy of mental states (purpose, knowledge, recklessness, negligence), designed to diagnose criminal dangerousness, rather than degrees of malignancy.

Given the absence of purpose (conscious object, § 2.02(2)(a)(i)), and assuming the absence of knowledge (practical certainty, § 2.02(2)(b)(ii)), regarding the result element of homicide (death of another human being, § 210.1), the question under the Model Penal Code would be whether Malone acted with (i) extreme recklessness regarding the result element ("recklessly under circumstances manifesting extreme indifference to the value of human life"), in which case he would be liable for murder, § 210.2(1)(b), (ii) with ordinary recklessness, in which case he would be liable for manslaughter, § 210.3(1)(a), or (iii) with negligence, in which case he would be liable for negligent homicide, § 210.4. The definitions of recklessness and negligence would not be specific to the law of homicide, but would be taken from the general provision on "kinds of culpability," § 2.02(2):

(c) Recklessly.

A person acts recklessly with respect to a material element of an offense when he consciously disregards a substantial and unjustifiable risk that the material element exists or will result from his conduct. The risk must be of such a nature and degree that, considering the nature and purpose of the actor's conduct and the circumstances known to him, its disregard involves a gross deviation from the standard of conduct that a law-abiding person would observe in the actor's situation.

(d) Negligently.

A person acts negligently with respect to a material element of an offense when he should be aware of a substantial and unjustifiable risk that the material element exists or will result from his conduct. The risk must be of such a nature and degree that the actor's failure to perceive it, considering the nature and purpose of his conduct and the circumstances known to him, involves a gross deviation from the standard of care that a reasonable person would observe in the actor's situation.

For more detailed discussion of these definitions, and the Model Penal Code *mens rea* scheme in general, see Chapter 8.A.

The New York Penal Law would follow the same general approach, though it would inquire not into Malone's "extreme indifference to the value of human life," but into his "depraved indifference to human life," under N.Y. Penal Law § 125.25(2). To what extent the reference to "depravity" supplements, or undermines, the Model Penal Code reform of the traditional analysis of the *mens rea* of homicide is explored in Chapter 15.A.ii.

2. Under German law, playing Russian Roulette with deadly consequences could lead to a conviction for manslaughter (*Totschlag*), § 212 Criminal Code, or negligent homicide, § 222. Under the circumstances described in *Commonwealth v. Malone*, there are no "base motives," thus no reason to apply § 211 Criminal Code, murder (boredom, seeking a thrill or whatever the defendant's motives were would not count as base motives). A conviction for manslaughter, § 212 Criminal Code, would require proof of conditional intention. The category of recklessness does not exist in German law, thus the category of "reckless homicide" does not exist. Simple manslaughter, § 212 Criminal Code, requires *Vorsatz*, i.e., at least conditional intention (or purpose or knowledge which, however, are not typical states of minds with respect to Russian Roulette). As discussed in detail in Chapter 8.A, conditional intention shares some features with recklessness, and circumstances that are

assessed as recklessness in American law often will be assessed as conditional intention in German law. But the concepts are not identical. Conditional intention is similar to the cognitive element that § 2.02(2)(c) Model Penal Code defines with the words "consciously disregards a substantial and unjustifiable risk." Risk awareness is part of the German concept of conditional intent as well, but the concept requires more: a volitional element that the German Federal Court of Justice defines as condoning or accepting the harmful outcome or at least coming to terms with it (see Chapter 8.A). This volitional element needs to be proved in addition to risk awareness.

It is hard to predict with certainty whether a German trial would find that Malone honestly and seriously hoped for a harmless outcome (in which case he would have lacked conditional intention, and would only have acted negligently) rather than having accepted the other's death as part of the thrill seeking game (which would make out conditional intention). The statistical likelihood of a deadly shot if the trigger was pulled not once but thrice certainly would be a strong indicator for conditional intention. Therefore, a German court probably would convict for manslaughter (*Totschlag*) and not just for negligent homicide.

But, again, it would be premature to conclude that cases of involuntary manslaughter (i.e., reckless homicide) under American law necessarily will be treated as manslaughter (§ 212) under the German Criminal Code. The court, after all, could find that the defendant had in fact trusted that a bullet would not be fired, despite this being a somewhat irrational expectation under circumstances. Trust in a positive outcome in spite of a substantial risk can be present even if this seems entirely irrational to a detached, reasonable observer. And particularly if the defendant was not an adult and the action typical of juvenile risk seeking, the court might find that he held an irrational, but psychologically real, trust that the risk will not materialize.

3. The *AIDS Case* required the German Federal Court of Justice to evaluate the trial court's assessment of conditional intention, both with respect to the attempted infliction of bodily harm by way of "treatment endangering life" (now § 224 para. 1 no. 5 Criminal Code, until 1998 § 223a) and also with respect to attempted homicide or murder. (On the *mens rea* requirement in cases of attempt under German law, which can be satisfied by any type of intention (*Vorsatz*): purpose, knowledge, or conditional intention, see Chapter 8.A.) As the defendant's sexual partners either could not be identified or showed no infection with HIV, the court examined the question of attempt. One of the main points of the judgment was to resolve the question of conditional intent with respect to two different accusations: first, the accusation of having attempted to inflict bodily harm by way of a treatment endangering life (§ 224 para. 1 no. 4 Criminal Code; this crime of endangerment appears in the German Criminal Code's section on bodily injury, not in the section on homicide); and, second, the accusation of attempted homicide. If the court had found conditional intention for attempted homicide, another question would have been if this also fulfilled the elements of murder (*Mord*), § 211 Criminal Code ("base motive" of sexual gratification)—however, this proved to be unnecessary because it was held to not even amount to manslaughter (*Totschlag*).

The German Federal Court of Justice did not object to the trial court's finding of conditional intention with respect to "treatment endangering life," now § 224 para. 1 no. 5 Criminal Code. In these passages of the judgment, the Court reaffirms the features of conditional intention and its distinction from what is called "conscious negligence" (or advertent negligence, conscious *culpa*), that is, risk awareness coupled with the sincere hope for a harmless outcome. (See Chapter 8.A.) But note that in its more recent case law the Federal Court of Justice urges trial judges to be careful with ascriptions of the *volitional* element with respect to manslaughter (*Totschlag*) or murder (*Mord*). This is the point of the "threshold" requirement mentioned in the *AIDS Case* (Chapter 15.A.iii). The Federal Court of Justice assumes that human beings in general are more inhibited in killing another human being than they are in merely injuring another or merely endangering the lives of others. Only for this reason, with view to the threshold requirement specific to homicide and murder, could the Court accept it as consistent to find, on the one hand, conditional intent for "treatment endangering life," yet not to find such intent concerning the sexual partners' possible death after an infection with HIV, on the other. At first glance, this might seem puzzling. But it makes sense, from a psychological perspective, to distinguish between acceptance of risk of death, and acceptance of death, if one realizes that thoughts and hopes of human beings can be irrational. (What is the evidence for this "threshold"?

4. In the last sections of the *AIDS Case*, the Federal Court of Justice leaves the issue of "subjective offense elements" and returns to the objective side. The question addressed here is whether it would be sufficient that a defendant's conduct causes a result described in the offense definition, or whether other "filters" should be applied, which would allow attributing outcomes not to the offender but to the victim (see the discussion of causation, Chapter 9). The Court mentions drug crimes. A person selling drugs to a customer will not be convicted of negligent homicide if the customer takes or injects the drug him- or herself and dies of an accidental overdose. Although the sale of the drug is causally connected to this death, the Federal Court of Justice has held that responsibility lies with the drug user who knowingly and voluntarily endangers him- or herself (see Federal Court of Justice, Judgment of February 14, 1984, 1 StR 808/83, BGHSt 32, 262).

In the case of sexual contacts, one could argue in a similar manner that having intercourse with persons from high-risk groups (such as drug users or persons with a highly promiscuous life style) amounts to knowing and voluntary self-endangerment. However, the Court precludes the attribution of outcomes to the victim through self-endangerment where the defendant had a higher degree of knowledge vis-à-vis the victim. Thus, only if the defendant had informed his partners about the HIV-infection would he have been spared criminal liability if they nevertheless opted for unprotected sexual intercourse. (What's the connection between this approach and an analysis in terms of consent? Why would the defendant's behavior not qualify as sexual assault, or some form of nonconsensual sexual conduct? See, e.g., *R. v. Cuerrier*, [1998] 2 S.C.R. 371 (fraudulently obtaining consent through non-disclosure of HIV infection).)

iv. Negligent homicide

Negligent homicide, or as the New York Penal Law calls it redundantly, "criminally" negligent homicide, is a relative newcomer to the Anglo-American law of homicide. (By contrast, the Prussian Criminal Code of 1851 already contained a provision on negligent homicide. § 184 PStGB *(fahrlässige Tötung)*.) Its existence presupposes a concerted effort to differentiate between recklessness and negligence in general, a project that did not make serious headway until the Model Penal Code drafters took it on. In the traditional homicide scheme, homicide came in two kinds, murder and manslaughter, each with two subcategories, first and second degree, on one side of the divide, and voluntary and involuntary manslaughter, on the other. More generally, though, manslaughter functioned as a catch-all category for homicide that was not murder, for one reason or another—including not only voluntary manslaughter (intentional, but provoked, homicide) and involuntary manslaughter (non-malicious homicide), but also imperfect self-defense (i.e., unreasonable mistakes regarding the elements of self-defense) and diminished responsibility (mental disturbance not rising to the level of insanity).

People v. Beiter
Supreme Court of New York, Appellate Division
77 A.D.2d 214, 432 N.Y.S.2d 947 (1980)

Simons, Justice.

The issue on this appeal is the sufficiency of the People's evidence to sustain the jury's finding that defendant was guilty of criminal negligence in causing the death of David A. Schifano in a motor vehicle accident (Penal Law, § 125.10).

The accident happened at about 2:00 a.m. on December 4, 1977. Defendant had been working the previous evening as a waitress in the Country House Restaurant in East Rochester. At about 11:00 p.m., after completing work, she went to a discotheque on the floor below the restaurant and there she visited with friends until she left between 1:30 a.m. and 2:00 a.m. to drive home alone in her 1968 Chevrolet sedan. While at the discotheque, she had two or three "Singapore Slings."

The accident occurred on Plank Road in Penfield, New York, near the Landmark Inn. Plank Road is a two-lane paved highway, straight and level for a considerable distance from the scene of the accident in both directions. On the night of the accident, the weather was clear and the road was dry. Defendant had entered Plank Road by turning right from an intersecting highway about .2 of a mile west of the scene and she was proceeding east when the accident occurred. There was no street lighting in the area at the time but there was some illumination of the road from a neon beverage sign in the window of the Inn and lights in the parking lot behind it. Three or four vehicles were parked on the shoulder of the road near the Inn.

Immediately before the accident, decedent and his companion, Leonard Colantoni, left the Landmark Inn to go home. They started across Plank Road walking north to south to enter Colantoni's van which was parked on the south side of the road.

When Colantoni was in the road, about 10 feet ahead of decedent, he observed the headlights of defendant's car to the west. He watched the car as it approached them and then yelled to decedent to hurry because the car was traveling fast. After reaching the side of the road, Colantoni heard a loud noise, saw broken glass and saw something fly and hit the road as the car continued on without stopping. Colantoni estimated defendant's speed at 60 miles per hour, "maybe more."

After the accident, Colantoni found articles of decedent's clothing in the road, his body in a ditch approximately 141 feet from the point of impact and decedent's severed leg about 20 feet from the body. Decedent apparently was killed instantly by the impact. The pathologist testified that there were several major injuries and that decedent's blood alcohol level was .11 per cent by weight.

The only other witness to the accident was defendant. She testified that she was proceeding easterly on Plank Road at 40 miles per hour, that there was no other traffic on the highway and that just after passing the Inn she saw two men about 40 feet in front of her, one off the road to her right, and the other just behind him. As she approached, she drove her car slightly to the left to avoid them. She did not realize that she had hit anyone but she slowed down after noticing that her radio went off and her windshield was cracked. Nevertheless, she drove on home and it was there, after examining the damage to her car, that she realized that she had hit someone and called the police. Colantoni had testified that defendant did not apply her brakes and that he did not hear a horn at any time. Defendant admitted that she did not apply her brakes and she could not recall sounding her horn. Defendant took a breathalyzer test at 4:50 a. m. and it resulted in a reading of .07 per cent.

Defendant was indicted on three counts: Criminal Negligence; Leaving the Scene of an Incident; and Operating a Motor Vehicle under the Influence of Alcohol or Drugs. The criminal negligence count charged defendant with causing decedent's death "by operating a motor vehicle while under the influence of alcohol at an excessive rate of speed on a straight level road and thereby failing to observe" decedent, although there was no obstruction to her vision. The jury convicted defendant of criminal negligence and leaving the scene but acquitted her of driving while under the influence of alcohol.

Section 125.10 of the Penal Law provides that "(a) person is guilty of criminally negligent homicide when, with criminal negligence, he causes the death of another person." A person acts with criminal negligence with respect to a result or circumstance "when he fails to perceive a substantial and unjustifiable risk that such result will occur or that such circumstance exists. The risk must be of such nature and degree that the failure to perceive it constitutes a gross deviation from the standard of care that a reasonable person would observe in the situation."

Considering the evidence in the light most favorable to the People, as we must, the proof established that defendant was operating her automobile at night on a straight and level rural road, partially illuminated by the lights of a nearby tavern, at a speed of 60 miles per hour in a 40 mile-per-hour zone, at a time when there were three or four other cars parked in the vicinity on the shoulder of the highway; that she saw two men when they were approximately 40 feet in front of her, swerved slightly to the left to avoid hitting them but struck one man, damaging the right headlight, right front fender and right side of the windshield of the car. We do not think that this evidence establishes a "gross deviation" from the standard of care of a reasonable person under the circumstances.

The People place considerable emphasis on defendant's failure to sound her horn or apply her brakes after she observed the pedestrians. Defendant was confronted suddenly by an unanticipated situation, however, and even if her spontaneous reaction to the emergency was wrong, it did not constitute a gross deviation from the standard of reasonable care. Under familiar rules, if an emergency is the result of defendant's own inattention it may not serve as an excuse for her negligent conduct. But the existence of the emergency situation does provide a different standard of reasonableness for judging her actions after the emergency was created. "It is . . . not the conduct after the emergency has arisen which is *not* excused, but the prior negligence" (Prosser, Torts (4th ed.), § 33, p. 170 (emphasis added)). Thus, although defendant may have failed to exercise the required care before she observed the pedestrians, her failure to sound her horn or brake after being confronted with the emergency cannot serve to magnify her criminal culpability and it is at least arguable that her swerve to the left to avoid striking Schifano was the most reasonable course of action under the conditions.

The issue, then, is whether defendant's illegal speed and her failure to perceive the danger, considering the traffic, road conditions and lighting conditions existing that night constituted criminal negligence.

In People v. Haney, 30 N.Y.2d 328, 333 N.Y.S.2d 403, 284 N.E.2d 564, the Court of Appeals, recognizing the difficulty of clarifying the elements necessary to establish criminal negligence, observed that "two main considerations should be emphasized. Firstly, criminal liability cannot be predicated upon every careless act merely because its carelessness results in another's death; and, secondly, the elements of the crime 'preclude the proper condemnation of inadvertent risk creation unless "the significance of the circumstances of fact would be apparent to one who shares the community's general sense of right and wrong"' (Model Penal Code, Tent. Draft No. 9, at p. 53). The court noted that the quantum of proof required for criminal negligence is " 'appreciably greater than that required for ordinary civil negligence by virtue of the "substantial and unjustifiable" character of the risk involved and the factor of "gross deviation" from the ordinary standard of care' (Commission Staff Notes, Gilbert Criminal Code and Penal Law (1971), p. 2-248; cf. Prosser, Law of Torts (4th ed.), § 31; Restatement, Torts, § 282)."

In *Haney* the Court of Appeals tested the legal sufficiency of an indictment, not the evidence after trial. Defendant Haney was accused of striking and killing a pedestrian in mid-intersection while driving an automobile through a red light on a city street at a speed of 52 miles per hour during daylight hours. The court held the indictment sufficient and stated that it was for the trier of the facts to evaluate defendant's conduct and his failure of perception and to determine whether defendant's conduct constituted a gross deviation from the standard of reasonable care.

By contrast, this defendant was driving down a straight and level highway in a sparsely populated area with her lights on. The area was dark and the road free of other traffic, circumstances in which she could reasonably expect that anyone crossing the road would see her headlights and conduct themselves accordingly. Seeing the victim from 40 feet away, she swerved, albeit not enough, to avoid striking him. Such conduct does not constitute a gross deviation from the ordinary standard of care held by those who share "the community's general sense of right and wrong."

The judgment should be modified by reversing the conviction for criminal negligence, dismissing the first count of the indictment charging that crime and vacating the sentence and as so modified the judgment should be affirmed.

Hancock, Justice (dissenting)

In my opinion, there is in this record ample evidence from which a jury could have concluded that defendant, after consuming alcoholic beverages, drove her automobile at night at a dangerously high rate of speed and without keeping a careful lookout past a lighted restaurant the glare from which impaired her vision and where there was a likelihood of pedestrian traffic, and that by doing so she created a substantial and unjustifiable risk; that defendant failed to perceive that risk; and that the failure to perceive it constituted a gross deviation from the standard of care that a reasonable person would have observed in the situation.

To support a finding of excessive speed by the defendant, the jury had before it not only the testimony of the eye witness that defendant's car was "hauling ass" and going "60 miles an hour, maybe more" but the physical evidence of high speed from the substantial damage to the automobile and the multiple fractures and massive injuries to the deceased resulting from an impact of such force as to sever the aorta in three places, wrench the right leg completely away from the pelvis and propel deceased's body a distance of 141 feet from the point of impact, as well as defendant's admissions on cross-examination and in her statement to the police that she was in a hurry and that she did not know how fast she was traveling. Based on defendant's own statements, the jury could have inferred that from her frequent trips past the restaurant she was either aware or should have been aware of the facts that the glare from the restaurant would reduce her ability to see and that there was a likelihood that there would be parked cars and pedestrian traffic on the highway in front of the restaurant. Further, defendant's testimony that she did not see the cars which were parked on the highway, did not observe the two pedestrians until she was 40 feet away, heard no noise from the impact, saw nothing hit the windshield despite the extensive damage it sustained, and that she was not immediately aware that she had hit someone would, taken together, support a conclusion by a trier of the facts either that defendant's senses and powers of observation were impaired or that she was not paying attention and keeping a careful lookout.

The jury could have inferred solely from defendant's conduct under the circumstances that she must have been oblivious to the substantial risks she was creating by driving her automobile in the manner described. There is, moreover, direct evidence that defendant failed to perceive these risks; i.e., her testimony that she saw no "problem at all in getting by" the pedestrians when she saw them for the first time in front of her car at a distance of 40 feet and that she did not sound her horn or apply her brakes but "just swerved over a little bit" to the left. I cannot agree with the majority that, as a matter of law, defendant's failure to perceive the risks did not constitute a gross deviation from the ordinary standard of care held by one who shares the community's general sense of right and wrong. In my opinion, it was for the jury to "evaluate the actor's failure of perception and determine whether, under all the circumstances, it was serious enough to be condemned." (Model Penal Code, Tent. Draft No. 4, (April 25, 1955), p. 126).

Finally, I must disagree with the majority's reliance on the emergency rule. First, the emergency doctrine was not charged; nor was there any request for such charge. Second, the emergency, if there was one, was in large measure the product of defendant's own conduct in driving too fast under the prevailing conditions without keeping a sufficiently careful lookout. Under such circumstances, the rule is inapplicable. Third, the gravamen of the charge against defendant does not lie in her negligent actions or omissions after she recognized the emergency but rather in her failure to perceive the risks in operating her automobile under the prevailing circumstances in a manner which contributed to the emergency. The emergency rule, even if applied, could not exonerate her from criminal liability for her pre-emergency failures and omissions.

German Federal Court of Justice
4 StR 26/70, BGHSt 24, 31 (November 26, 1970)

Reasons

1. The defendant was driving his car on the evening of October 15, 1968 at around 7:45 p.m. after a considerable consumption of alcohol, on Federal Route 27, improved to motorway standard, from S. to E.F. at a speed of 100 to 120 km per hour. His blood alcohol content amounted to at least .19%. He was approximately in the middle of the two-lane carriageway and had dipped his headlights because of oncoming traffic. When he switched to full beam again, he noticed a motor cyclist travelling in the same direction about 30 to 50 m in front of him and moving from the left edge of the overtaking lane to the right towards the middle of the carriageway. In spite of sharp braking by the defendant, his car hit the motorcycle and pushed it a further 40 to 50 m in front of the car before it came to a standstill. The rider of the motorcycle was fatally injured.

The local court and the criminal chamber [of the appellate court—Eds.] convicted the defendant of negligent homicide concomitantly with negligent endangering of road traffic. The criminal chamber found that it could not establish that the accident would have been avoidable for a sober driver at the same—possibly permissible—speed. It based the defendant's conviction on the fact that he had not driven at a lower speed of 30 to 40 km per hour at the most, which would have been suited to the alcohol induced impairment of his capacity for perception and reaction, and which would have resulted in him being able to avoid the accident.

The Higher Regional Court Stuttgart which was called upon to decide the defendant's appeal in law intends to quash the judgment ... According to the opinion of the Higher Regional Court Stuttgart, the conviction of the defendant would have required a finding that he could have avoided the accident if he had been driving at the same speed in a sober condition. But it regarded itself as prevented from recognizing this by the judgment of the Higher Regional Court Celle of August 1, 1968 (VRS 36, 276). According to the view of this court, when considering the question of whether the traffic accident of a driver who is unfit to drive was avoidable, account should not be taken of whether a sober driver could have avoided the accident when driving at the actual speed in question. It is necessary instead to examine the speed which the driver, having regard to the influence of alcohol on him and the traffic situation, ought—regardless of the fact that because he was unfit to drive he should not have driven at all—not to have exceeded, and whether the accident would have been avoidable at this speed ... Because the Higher Regional Court Stuttgart wished to deviate from the decision of the Higher Regional Court Celle—it has referred the following legal question for decision:

When examining whether an accident caused by a driver who was unfit to drive because of alcohol was avoidable, should account be taken of whether the same driver driving at the same speed in a sober condition could have prevented the accident, or must investigation first be made as to the (lower) speed this driver ought not to have exceeded, taking into consideration the influence of alcohol on him and the traffic conditions, and is this speed then to be referred to when examining avoidability?

II.

The reference is permissible. . . .

III.

In this case the Senate cannot endorse the view of the referring Higher Regional Court Stuttgart...

A causal connection between conduct by the defendant contrary to traffic rules and the killing of the motorcyclist with whom he collided would not exist if the same result would also have occurred following conduct complying with traffic rules, or if the judge of fact was not persuaded that this could be excluded on the basis of significant facts (BGHSt 11, 1, 7). The examination of the causality of conduct contrary to traffic rules must regard the critical traffic situation which led directly to the harmful result (BGH, VRS 20, 129, 131; 23, 369, 370; 24, 124, 126; 25, 262). When considering the question of what conduct by the perpetrator complying with traffic rules would be, it is necessary to proceed on the basis of the actual facts rather than hypothetical scenarios (BGHSt 10, 369, 370). The question of what conduct would have complied with traffic rules must accordingly be answered having regard to the breach of the rules which falls to be considered as the direct cause of the accident. According to these principles, when considering the question of whether the defendant's behavior caused the death of the motorcyclist, account cannot be taken of whether he would still have collided with the motorcyclist if he had himself been sober when driving at a speed of 100 to 120 km per hour (an unobjectionable speed in the case of a sober driver). It is necessary instead to proceed on the basis of the rule of § 9 para. 1 sentence 1 Road Traffic Ordinance, according to which the driver of the vehicle must adapt his speed in such a way that he is always in a position to satisfy his obligations in traffic, and that if necessary he can stop the vehicle in good time. Accordingly the driver, even on roads facilitating fast traffic (federal routes, motorways) ought to drive only so fast that he can always stop within the section of road which he can see (for instance BGH, VRS 21, 241 and especially BGHSt 16, 145). In deciding the speed which the defendant ought not to have exceeded directly before catching sight of the motorcyclist killed in the collision, a significant role is played by the fact that his blood alcohol content was at least .19%. With this blood alcohol content, which substantially reduced his capacity for perception and reaction, he ought not to have driven at a speed which would have been reasonable for him in a sober condition. He was admittedly unconditionally unfit to drive and was acting contrary to the provisions of § 316 Criminal Code* when taking part in traffic at all. If he did this, however, he ought not to have further increased the abstract dangers already arising from his incapacity to drive by driving excessively fast. He ought instead to have exercised the increased care necessitated by his condition and ought to have driven only so fast that he could still comply with his obligations in traffic, even taking into account that his capacity for perception and reaction were reduced by a substantial consumption of alcohol.

The fact that the defendant was unconditionally incapable of driving with a blood alcohol content of .19% and therefore ought not to have taken part in public road traffic at all (§ 316 Criminal Code) must be left out of consideration when deciding whether his actual driving behavior caused the motorcyclist's death. Participation in traffic which is impermissible because of personal defects cannot be assessed differently from impermissible participation in it with a vehicle which is unroadworthy because of defective brakes or worn tires... If a person who is not permitted to participate in public road traffic because of something relating to his person (incapacity to drive caused by alcohol) or his vehicle (defective brakes or tires) nevertheless takes part in it, he is subject to a duty of special care which is increased because of this personal or material defect. If a traffic accident occurs, he is not responsible for it simply because of his impermissible participation in road traffic, but only if and in so far as he does not take into account his personal defects or the defects in his vehicle in the way he drives and thereby causes an accident. Driving in a condition which is unfit for it, or with a vehicle which is unroadworthy thus cannot be the sole cause of an accident. The cause of an accident can only be driving which does not correspond with the driver's condition or with that of his vehicle. It is therefore incorrect for the referring Higher Regional Court to see the defendant's breach of duty as being solely his participation in road traffic in a condition in which he was unfit to drive, and to compare this with driving in a sober condition at the same speed.

The reason given by the Bavarian Higher Regional court in an unpublished decision of May 12, 1965, quoted by Mühlhaus (DAR 70, 125, 127) that it was not possible "without arbitrariness to establish a speed as being still allowed which could be compared with the actual speed" is unpersuasive. The degree to which the capacity for perception and reaction of the driver who was under the influence of alcohol is reduced, and the—reduced—speed which corresponds to this reduced capacity for perception and reaction can—if necessary with the help of an expert—be

---

* [§ 316 German Criminal Code

(1) Who drives a vehicle in traffic (§§ 315 to 315d) although due to consumption of alcoholic beverages or other intoxicants he is not in a condition to drive the vehicle safely will be punished with imprisonment not exceeding one year or a fine unless the offence is punishable under § 315a or § 315c.

(2) According to para. 1 will also be punished who commits the offense negligently.—Eds.]

determined. This does not establish a "permitted" speed, but only a speed which actually corresponds to the reduced capacity for perception and reaction . . .

The referring Higher Regional Court alludes to the fact that a driver who is under the influence of alcohol and therefore deliberately drives more slowly than he should in a sober condition but nevertheless causes an accident because of his reduced capacity for reaction could not be heard with the argument that, after all, he had driven more slowly because of his drunkenness. This consideration is admittedly correct, but has no consequences for the case which has to be decided. If a drunken driver causes an accident even at a slower speed because of his impaired capacity for reaction induced by alcohol, it only follows from this that he still drove too fast in his condition . . .

NOTES

1. If one compares the provisions on negligent homicide in the German Criminal Code and in New York Penal Law, one might expect that the outcome of cases would be similar because the wording in the statutes is similar. In both legal systems, causing the death of a person through negligence is a criminal offense. Also, in both legal systems the starting points are "ordinary standards of care," which can (such as in the case of participation in traffic) be found in statutes and regulations, but also in written and unwritten codes of conduct below the world of formal legal norms. But beyond such similarities, the case law shows remarkable differences. For a German reader, the notion expressed by the court in *Beiter* that there is a considerably higher threshold for criminal negligence than for civil negligence is alien. German law does not demand a *gross* deviation from the ordinary standards of care for a conviction according to § 222 Criminal Code.

As mentioned previously, in our general discussion of *mens rea*, see Chapter 8.A, the distinction between criminal and civil negligence is central to American criminal law, and not merely to the American law of homicide. This is not surprising, since it marks the line between criminal and civil liability, by definition. However much American courts might struggle to define criminal negligence, they would all agree that, whatever criminal negligence is, it must be different than, and more demanding than, civil negligence. The Model Penal Code, and the New York Penal Law pursuant to it, makes this point by insisting on a "gross" deviation from the standard of care and by requiring the failure to perceive a "substantial and justifiable" risk.

As a perceived newcomer, criminal liability for negligence is often met with suspicion, and juries can be reluctant to apply it, particularly to traffic accidents resulting in death, and—as *Beiter* illustrates—appellate courts can be even more reluctant to affirm those convictions a jury does hand down. It does not help matters that criminal liability for negligence is limited to very serious offenses, most notably homicide.

2. Even if one follows the standard of "gross deviation from ordinary standards of care," however, the result in *Beiter* is surprising, given that the driver was under the influence of alcohol (the .07% of blood alcohol level was established about three hours after the accident, it must have been higher at the time of driving) and drove approximately 60 miles per hour rather than the speed limit of 40 miles per hour. In fact, note that the appellate court in this case overturned a jury conviction for insufficiency of evidence, i.e., on a factual, rather than a legal, ground. Reversals on this basis are very rare, as the fact-finder (in this case a jury) is given great deference; to overturn a jury verdict for insufficiency of evidence, the appellate court must find, viewing the evidence in the light most favorable to the people, that there is no "valid line of reasoning and permissible inferences which could lead a rational person to the conclusion reached by the jury on the basis of the evidence at trial and as a matter of law satisfy the proof and burden requirements for every element of the crime charge." *People v. Bleakley*, 69 N.Y.2d 490, 515 N.Y.S.2d 761 (1981).

By contrast, a German court surely would have, with such excessive speeding, followed the arguments of the dissenting Judge Hancock and affirmed the conviction of negligent homicide (which does not necessarily mean imprisonment—note that among the 649 persons convicted in Germany in 2010 for negligent homicide in street traffic, 428 were sentenced only to a fine). (Under the New York Penal Law, negligent homicide is punishable by up to four years in prison, probation, or fine. N.Y. Penal Law §§ 60.01, 70.00.)

If the defendant in *Beiter* had not exceeded the posted speed limit, the case would have been comparable to the German case in which there was no speed limit at the place of the accident, meaning that ordinarily a driver would have been allowed to drive 100 km/h (app. 60 mph) under prevailing road conditions. Nonetheless, the German Federal Court of Justice has developed an approach that would support convicting drunk drivers of negligent homicide even in this case. The starting point is that there must be a connection between the fact that the driver was intoxicated and the occurrence of the accident. The German court does not argue that the mere fact of being drunk is a sufficient basis for a finding of negligent homicide. It is one thing to punish the act of drunk driving (the endangerment connected with this), another, to punish for the death of a person; in the latter case, the deadly result must be attributable to the defendant's deviation from the required standard of conduct. It is conceivable that an accident is entirely unrelated to the driver's condition (imagine, for example, that a person commits suicide by jumping from a bridge onto a highway in front of a car—under such circumstances, an accident is unavoidable for sober and for drunk drivers alike). However, the German Federal Court of Justice emphasizes that drivers have a duty to be able to brake in time and that alcohol impairs perception as well as the time for reaction, and for this reason postulates a duty to drive more slowly to cope with the typical dangers in street traffic. From this point of view, the defendant in *Beiter* would have been convicted even if she had obeyed the speed limit. Do you think that this is a convincing solution—despite the fact that a drunk driver blocking traffic by driving at 10 miles per hour on a German motorway would hardly escape sanctions with the argument that he fulfilled his duties with this "compromise"?

3. According to established case law of the German Federal Court of Justice concerning negligent crimes, persons are entitled to have confidence that others they encounter will obey the required standard of conduct (*Vertrauensgrundsatz*, principle of trust). Thus, for instance, a sober driver need not take into account that drunk pedestrians might step onto the road. However, and this seems to be a rule of fairness, it is also established German case law that this principle of trust only applies if the person invoking it complied with the required standard of conduct, so that the principle would not apply to Beiter vis-à-vis the eventual victim. To make sense of—if not to justify—the decision in *Beiter*, it is helpful to keep in mind not only the widespread reluctance to impose criminal liability for negligent homicide in traffic cases, but also to consider the sympathetic nature of the defendant, along with the victim's risky behavior immediately preceding the accident. Would the court have reached the same conclusion if the roles of offender and victim had been reversed in this case? Does the court's decision in *Beiter* reflect not only the reluctance to apply negligent homicide to fatal traffic accidents (many of which presumably could support a negligent homicide conviction, and not only in cases of drunk driving), and thereby to dramatically expand the scope of criminal law, but also the inherent flexibility of the concept of ("gross") negligence (involving "substantial" risks) itself?

The New York Court of Appeals has since placed more formal limits on the scope of negligent homicide in traffic cases. In *People v. Boutin*, 75 N.Y.2d 692 (1990), the court overturned a negligent homicide conviction on the following facts:

> On the night of November 26, 1985, defendant was driving a truck southbound in the right-hand lane of Interstate 87, commonly known as the Adirondack Northway. The night was overcast and dark, the weather was rainy with fog, and the pavement was slushy and wet. One hundred and fifty miles from the Canadian border, a marked police car, with emergency lights flashing, was stopped with all four tires in the right-hand lane behind a disabled tractor trailer, which also extended onto the roadway approximately six feet. Defendant's truck hit the police car. Both the State trooper and the driver of the disabled vehicle who was seated with him inside the police vehicle were killed. At the scene, defendant told police he had not seen the flashing lights. The passenger in defendant's truck said the same thing at trial.

These facts did not support a conviction of negligent homicide because:

> unless a defendant has engaged in some blameworthy conduct creating or contributing to a substantial and unjustifiable risk of death, he has not committed the crime of criminally negligent homicide; his "nonperception" of a risk, even if death results, is not enough...
>
> In the present case, there is no question that defendant's failure to see the vehicle stopped in the lane ahead of him resulted in the fatal accident. That failure may well constitute civil negligence. But the proof does not establish *criminal* negligence. [T]he evidence does not show that defendant was engaged in any criminally culpable risk-creating conduct—e.g., dangerous speeding, racing, failure to obey traffic signals, or any other misconduct that created or contributed to a "substantial and unjustifiable" risk of death. Rather, it establishes only that defendant inexplicably failed to see the vehicle until he was so close that he could not prevent the collision. Though it resulted in two tragic deaths, that unexplained failure, without more, does not constitute criminally negligent homicide.

4. A procedural note on the German case, and *stare decisis*: German courts are not in general obliged to follow precedents by other courts. If there is a dispute about the interpretation of the German Criminal Code, appeals in law often end with the Higher Regional Courts (*Oberlandesgerichte*), which hear appeals from local courts, where the vast majority of cases are initially tried. The Federal Court of Justice only hears appeals in law for serious crimes, which are initially tried at a Regional Court (*Landgericht*). For this reason, most cases never make it to the Federal Court of Justice—and this could mean that the German Criminal Code (although federal law) is interpreted differently in different regions. To promote uniformity, the Judiciary Act (*Gerichtsverfassungsgesetz*) demands that a Higher Regional Court, if they want to deviate from established case law of another Higher Regional Court or from the Federal Court of Justice's case law, must refer the question to the Federal Court of Justice (§ 121 para. 2 GVG).

v. Assisted suicide

The issue of the criminalization of assisted suicide explores the outer limits of the law of homicide, and of the law of crimes against life in general. It also implicates the law of consent, and its interaction with the state's interest in protecting the interest in, right to, or legal good of, life, even as it comes into conflict with personal autonomy and dignity, not to mention the distinction between omission and commission, and various conceptions of accessorial liability.

People v. Duffy
Court of Appeals of New York
79 N.Y.2d 611, 594 N.E.2d 814 (1992)

Titone, Judge.

According to the evidence adduced below, Jason Schuhle—a 17-year-old youth—met defendant on a street in the Village of McGraw, New York, during the early morning hours of August 6, 1988. Schuhle—who, at the time, was extremely distraught over having recently broken-up with his girlfriend—immediately imparted to defendant his desire to kill himself. At defendant's invitation, Schuhle then accompanied him back to defendant's apartment. There, for approximately the next half hour or so, Schuhle—who had been drinking heavily—continued to express suicidal thoughts and repeatedly importuned defendant to shoot him. In response to these entreaties, defendant provided Schuhle with some more alcohol and challenged him several times to jump headfirst off the porch of his second-story apartment. Finally, defendant—who later explained to the police that he was "tired" of hearing Schuhle complain about wanting to die—told Schuhle that he had a gun which he could use to kill himself. Defendant then retrieved a British .303 caliber Enfield rifle from his gun cabinet, and handed it to Schuhle, along with a number of bullets. He then urged Schuhle to "put the gun in his mouth and blow his head off." Moments later, Schuhle loaded the rifle, pointed the barrel at himself and pulled the trigger. He later died as a result of the massive injuries he suffered.

Defendant was thereafter indicted for two counts of manslaughter in the second degree. The first count alleged that he had intentionally caused or aided Schuhle in committing suicide (see, Penal Law § 125.15[3]), and the second alleged that he had recklessly caused Schuhle's death (see, Penal Law § 125.15[1]). After a jury trial, defendant was acquitted of the first count but convicted of the second.

On appeal, however, the Appellate Division reversed and dismissed the indictment. The court—with one Justice concurring in result only—concluded that defendant's conviction for reckless manslaughter (see, Penal Law § 125.15[1]) could not be sustained because, in its view, Penal Law § 125.15, when read as a whole, clearly evinced a legislative intent "that a person be found guilty of manslaughter in the second degree for causing or aiding a suicide only when he or she acts intentionally."

At the outset, we note that the conduct with which defendant was charged clearly fell within the scope of section 125.15(1)'s proscription against recklessly causing the death of another person. As the People aptly observe, a person who, knowing that another is contemplating immediate suicide, deliberately prods that person to go forward and furnishes the means of bringing about death may certainly be said to have "consciously disregard[ed] a substantial and unjustifiable risk" that his actions would result in the death of that person (see, Penal Law § 15.05[3]; § 125.15[1]). Accordingly, unless the Appellate Division correctly concluded that, despite the apparent applicability of section 125.15(1), it was nevertheless specifically contemplated by the Legislature that second degree manslaughter prosecutions involving suicide-related homicides would be maintainable solely pursuant to section 125.15(3), defendant's prosecution for reckless manslaughter cannot be said to have been improper.

As a general rule, a statutory prohibition against a particular type of conduct will not be deemed to constitute the exclusive vehicle for prosecuting that conduct unless the Legislature clearly intended such a result. Defendant argues that the Legislature evinced just such an intention here when it specifically proscribed only "intentionally caus[ing] or aid[ing] another person to commit suicide" in section 125.15(3). We disagree.

Nothing in the language or the legislative history of section 125.15(3) suggests that the Legislature intended to foreclose second degree manslaughter prosecutions for recklessly causing a suicide. Rather, by all indications, section 125.15(3) was simply meant to serve as a means of prosecuting those who, while having intentionally caused or aided another person to kill him- or herself, were not, in the Legislature's judgment, as culpable as intentional murderers.

Nor can we discern any reason why the Legislature would have wanted to limit criminal liability for causing a suicide to those instances where the accused acted intentionally. An individual who—like defendant—consciously disregards a substantial and unjustifiable risk that his actions will lead to another person's killing him- or herself and thereby causes that person's death may be just as culpable as one who intentionally causes or aids another to commit suicide (see, Staff Notes, op. cit., at 339 [noting that section 125.15(3)'s proscription against intentionally causing or aiding a suicide applies even where the defendant is motivated by "sympathetic" concerns, such as the desire to relieve a terminally ill person from the agony of a painful disease]). In the absence of a clear indication to the contrary, we are simply unwilling to ascribe to the Legislature an intent to criminalize the latter conduct while at the same time subjecting the former to no penal sanction at all.

Having concluded that a person may be convicted of second degree manslaughter for having engaged in reckless conduct which results in another person's committing suicide (see, Penal Law § 125.15[1]), we now turn to the question whether defendant's conduct here was a "sufficiently direct cause" of Schuhle's death to subject him to criminal liability. Defendant, stressing the fact that it was Schuhle—not he—who loaded the rifle and pulled the trigger, urges us to answer this question in the negative. We find defendant's argument to be unpersuasive.

Generally speaking, a person will not be held criminally accountable for engaging in conduct which results in another person's death unless it can be demonstrated that his actions were "an actual contributory cause of death, in the sense that they 'forged a link in the chain of causes which actually brought about the death' " (Matter of Anthony M., 63 N.Y.2d 270, 280, quoting People v. Stewart, 40 N.Y.2d 692, 697). The proof adduced below, when viewed in a light most favorable to the People, indicates that defendant gave Schuhle a rifle and a number of rounds of ammunition knowing full well that Schuhle had been drinking heavily and was in an extremely depressed and suicidal state, and that he then began taunting Schuhle to "put the gun in his mouth and blow his head off." In light of this evidence, we must disagree with defendant that Schuhle's act of loading the rifle and using it to kill himself constituted an intervening cause which—as a matter of law—relieved defendant of criminal responsibility. The jury could rationally have concluded that the risk of Schuhle's taking these actions was something which defendant should have, under the circumstances, plainly foreseen. There is therefore no basis, on this Court's review, to disturb the jury's verdict.

Accordingly, the order of the Appellate Division should be reversed and the case remitted to that court for consideration of the facts.

German Federal Court of Justice
1 StR 168/83, BGHSt 32, 28 (July 5, 1983)
Sirius Case

Facts

In 1973 or 1974 the defendant came to know the witness H. in a discotheque. She had been born in 1951 and was "at the time still a dependent young woman, burdened with complexes." She developed an intensive friendship with the defendant, who was four years older, in which sexual contacts remained insignificant. The subject matter of the relationship was principally discussions about psychology and philosophy, which occurred in meetings some months apart, and in telephone conversations which were more frequent and sometimes lasted several hours. In the course of time the defendant became a teacher and adviser to the witness in all questions of life. He was always there for her. She trusted and believed him blindly. In the course of their numerous philosophical discussions, the defendant told the witness that he was an inhabitant of the star Sirius. The Sirians were a race who were philosophically at a much higher level than human beings. He had been sent to earth with the mission of ensuring that certain worthy human beings, including the witness, could carry on living with their souls on another planet or on Sirius after the complete disintegration of their bodies. In order that she could attain this goal, the witness needed further spiritual and philosophical development. When the defendant recognized that the witness placed complete faith in him, he decided to enrich himself by exploitation of this trust at her expense. He explained to the witness that she could attain the capability of living on after her death on another celestial body if the monk Uliko, who was known to him, undertook a period of total meditation. This would make it possible for her body to pass through several planes during her sleep, and thereby undergo a spiritual development. The monastery in which the monk lived would have to be paid 30,000 DM for this. The witness believed the defendant. As she did not possess sufficient money, she obtained the necessary sum by a bank loan. The defendant spent the money on himself. Whenever the witness inquired about Uliko's efforts in the ensuing months, the defendant put her off. Later he explained to her that the monk had fallen into great danger in his attempts, but he had nevertheless obtained no result because her consciousness had built up a strong barrier against further spiritual development. The reason for this was in the witness's body; the block could only be removed by the destruction of the old body, and the obtaining of a new one. When the defendant noticed that the witness was still completely convinced of the correctness of his explanations, he devised a plan of obtaining further financial benefit from her confidence. The defendant deluded her into believing that a new body was ready for her in a red room by Lake Geneva, in which she would discover herself again as an artist when she separated herself from her old body. However, even in her new life, she needed money. This could be obtained by her taking out a life insurance for 250,000 DM (500,000 DM in the case of death by accident) and designating him irrevocably as the person entitled to receive payment, and leaving her "present life" by a fake accident. After payment he would deliver the insurance sum to her. The witness took out an insurance policy in accordance with the defendant's proposals. Insurance protection began on the 1. 12. 1979. The monthly insurance premium amounted to 587.50 DM. The witness handed over 4000 DM to the defendant in cash, because, as he told her, she needed the money, which he would bring to her immediately, as "starting capital" after her awakening at Lake Geneva. The payment of the insured sum could be delayed. The witness was to end her "present life" according to the defendant's first plan by a simulated motor accident, and, according to a later plan, by getting into a bath and letting a hairdryer, which would be switched on, fall into the bath water.

At the request of and in accordance with the instructions of the defendant, the witness attempted to carry out this plan on January 1, 1980, in her home in W., after she had previously, following a suggestion by the defendant, done some things which were to indicate that she had been unintentionally snatched from life. However, the fatal electric shock did not materialize. For "technical reasons" the witness only felt tingling in her body when she immersed the hairdryer. The defendant, who was staying in B., was surprised when the witness answered the telephone call he made to check on the situation. For about three hours in approximately 10 telephone conversations he gave her instructions for continuing the attempt to quit her life. Then he abandoned any further efforts because he regarded them as hopeless. The witness acted in complete confidence on the defendant's statements. She let the hairdryer fall into the water in the hope that she would immediately awaken in a new body. The idea of a "suicide" in the real sense, by which "her life would be ended forever," did not occur to her. She disapproved of suicide. Human beings had no right to do it. The defendant was aware that the conduct of the witness, who was dependent on him, was entirely determined by his pretenses and instructions.

The regional court sentenced the defendant to an overall term of imprisonment of seven years for attempted murder, fraud,* and infliction of bodily injury.†

The appeal in law was unsuccessful.

Reasons

. . .

II.

The appeal in law claims that the defendant was incorrectly convicted of attempted murder by indirect perpetration; only non-criminal participation in attempted suicide could be considered. There is however no objection to the verdict.

1. The question of the distinction between "criminal perpetration of homicide and non-criminal participation in suicide" (Roxin, in: Festschr. f. Dreher, p. 332) cannot be answered in the abstract in cases in which the person who takes his own life under the influence or with the involvement of another person does not show one of the psychological conditions which are listed in § 20 Criminal Code nor finds himself in a necessity situation in the sense of § 35 Criminal Code, but is induced by deceit to undertake the action causing death. The distinction depends in the individual case on the type and consequences of the error. If the error conceals from the person whose life is at stake the fact that he is setting up a cause for their own death, the person who has caused the error and with the help of the error has consciously and intentionally triggered the event which is to lead or leads to the death of the person deceived is a perpetrator of an (attempted or completed) crime of homicide by virtue of his superior knowledge by which he directs the mistaken person and makes him a tool against himself (Bottke, GA 1983, 31; Jähnke, in: LK, preliminary note § 211 marginal nos. 25 and 26; Lackner, StGB, 15th edit., preliminary note § 211 note 3b; Roxin, in: LK, § 25 marginal no. 83; Samson, in: SKStGB, § 25 marginal no. 30).

2. That is the situation here. According to the findings of the court of fact, the defendant did not delude the victim into believing that she would enter a transcendental existence through the gate of death, but induced her mistakenly to believe that she would—although apparently lying as a corpse in the bath— continue her earthly life as a human being, although physically and spiritually so changed that higher development to an astral being was guaranteed. Mrs. H.'s conviction that her physical and psychological identity and individuality would merely undergo modifications not only arose from the idea that she, as the defendant told her, would remain on this planet and needed money to cover her living expenses, but also from the fact that he deceived her into thinking that she would find tranquillizers in the red room by Lake Geneva and the necessary papers in the neighboring room. What Mrs. H. did not suspect or intend was what the defendant was seeking to attain: the electric shock—which was expected by both of them as certain –was to put an end to her life as the victim of the fraud, and provide the defendant with the insurance money which his victim assumed would be the financial basis of the new phase of her life. The defendant who also decisively controlled the actual event by instructions lasting for hours, committed as a consequence a crime of attempted indirect killing of another. This legal finding is not called in question by the fact that Mrs. H succumbed to completely incredible suggestions, even though she exhibited no mental disorders. The defendant had opened up the psyche of his victim to these suggestions. The astonishing aspect of this occurrence does not exonerate him.

. . .

4. The view of the court of fact that the defendant intended to cause the death of a human being out of greed, and therefore should be convicted of attempted murder, and the determination of the sentence, are not open to objection.

NOTES

1. According to German law, causing or aiding another person to commit suicide will not necessarily lead to criminal punishment. The German Criminal Code does not contain in its

---

* [German Criminal Code (Fraud) § 263

(1) Who with the intent of obtaining an unlawful financial benefit for himself or for a third person diminishes the assets of another by pretending false facts or by distorting or suppressing true facts and thus causing or maintaining an error will be punished with imprisonment of not more than five years or a fine. (2) The attempt is punishable.—Eds.]

† [German Criminal Code (Inflicting Bodily Injury) § 223

(1) Who physically maltreats another person or damages another person's health, will be punished with imprisonment of not more than five years or with a fine. (2) The attempt is punishable.—Eds.]

section on homicide in the special part a norm similar to § 125.15(3) New York Penal Law, and the provisions in the general part concerning inciting and aiding (§§ 26, 27 Criminal Code) require that a main perpetrator has committed a criminal offense. Because suicide is not a criminal offense (those who survive cannot be charged with attempting to kill themselves), punishment of participants cannot be based on §§ 26, 27 Criminal Code. The consequence of this is that it is not against the law to cause or to aid another person to commit suicide—provided it is a "genuine" suicide. This is the case under two conditions: the deceased him- or herself carried out the act leading to death and did so without cognitive or volitional deficits.

The doctrinal background in American criminal law is similar. As in German criminal law, aiding or abetting suicide cannot generate accomplice liability since neither suicide nor attempted suicide, is a crime. Unlike in German criminal law, however, American legislatures have stepped in and explicitly criminalized the offense of assisted suicide. The Model Penal Code created a new offense of "aiding or soliciting suicide": "A person who purposely aids or solicits another to commit suicide is guilty of a felony of the second degree if his conduct causes such suicide or an attempted suicide, and otherwise of a misdemeanor." § 210.5. The New York Penal Law instead classified "intentionally caus[ing] or aid[ing] another person to commit suicide" as a form of second degree manslaughter. § 125.15(3).

2. Lack of punishment under German law is important in practice for what is called medically assisted suicides: suicides by persons who are terminally ill or experience great pain, or both, and are capable of deciding autonomously about ending their life, but need assistance in the stage of preparation. There have been discussions if, with regard to such cases, a norm ought to be added to the German Criminal Code that would apply to members of suicide organizations or persons who take fees; but the German legislature so far has refrained from taking action. This is not to say that medical practitioners (and others willing to help) may not face legal risks when they assist patients in the preparation of a suicide. First, the framework of regulations for the medical profession (ärztliches Standesrecht) condemns this practice; second, the Narcotics Act and the criminal norms therein have to be taken into account if a patient asks for drugs to end her life; and third, the Federal Court of Justice has in older rulings affirmed convictions of medical practitioners for omission offenses if the doctor was present and did not resuscitate after the patient lost consciousness.*

In the United States, this behavior would clearly fall under the criminal prohibition of aiding suicide, not only under the Model Penal Code and the New York Penal Law, but also in many other American jurisdictions. At the same time, however, "[i]t is established under New York law that a competent person may refuse medical treatment, even if the withdrawal of such treatment will result in death." *Quill v. Koppell*, 870 F. Supp. 78, 84 (S.D.N.Y. 1994). This distinction, between the criminalization of assisted suicide, on one hand, the permissibility of refusing life-sustaining treatment, has been challenged on constitutional equal protection grounds insofar as it impermissibly differentiates among "competent persons who are in the final stages of fatal illness and wish to hasten their deaths" and are "similarly situated, except for the previous attachment of life-sustaining equipment." *Quill v. Vacco*, 80 F.3d 716, 727 (2d Cir. 1996). The U.S. Supreme Court, however, rejected this challenge on the ground that the distinction between withdrawal of life-support systems and assisted suicide, or as the Court put it, between "between letting a patient die and making that patient die," is rational, and therefore constitutionally sufficient, even if difficult to draw:

> Granted, in some cases, the line between the two may not be clear, but certainty is not required, even were it possible. Logic and contemporary practice support New York's judgment that the two acts are different, and New York may therefore, consistent with the Constitution, treat them differently. By permitting everyone to refuse unwanted medical treatment while prohibiting anyone from assisting a suicide, New York law follows a longstanding and rational distinction.
>
> *Vacco v. Quill*, 521 U.S. 793 (1997).

* Judgment of July 4, 1984, 3 StR 96/84, BGHSt 32, 367; see also Judgment of February 7, 2001, 5 StR 474/00, BGHSt 46, 279.

In the end, the Supreme Court's opinion turns on the distinction between omission and commission. Even if the distinction is "longstanding and rational," does it make sense? Cannot every omission be reframed as a commission? More specifically, cannot failing to continue to provide life-sustaining treatment be recharacterized as discontinuing or withdrawing it, or for that matter of acting according to the patient's wishes? And if so, why is withdrawing treatment any less of a commission than providing medication?

3. We now turn to cases that are not considered "true" suicides according to German law. The criminal prohibition in § 216 Criminal Code with the title "Killing on Request" refers to situations in which the person who wants to die does not commit the act of killing herself but asks another person to perform this act (for instance, a quadriplegic asks a relative or doctor to administer a deadly drug, or a person who is unfamiliar with weapons asks another to shoot her). Under such circumstances, although the offender only acted because of the "victim's" explicit and earnest request, he will nevertheless be punished under German law (but with lower punishment compared to manslaughter (*Totschlag*), § 212 Criminal Code). The decisive line of criminalization under German law does not depend solely on an assessment of autonomy but also on the external circumstance of who performed the deadly act. (Of course, there is also the question of what precisely counts as the "deadly act"— activating a mechanism that administers a drug, pulls a trigger, releases a gas, etc., by flipping a switch by hand, batting an eye lid, exhaling, etc., or swallowing a pill, drinking a liquid, etc. Is the distinction between "the deadly act" and "the very last act just before the deadly act" easier to draw, or more relevant, than that between commission and omission?).

Consider the reasons for punishing killing on request (such as: protection of taboos; doubts about autonomy if the suicidal candidate does not want to do the final step himself; slippery-slope-arguments). These arguments were explored in detail in the other recent U.S. Supreme Court case considering, and rejecting, a constitutional attack on a criminal law assisted suicide prohibition, in *Washington v. Glucksberg*, 521 U.S. 702 (1997). Unlike the challenge in *Quill* (in Note 2), that in *Glucksberg* was framed not in terms of equal protection, but in terms of substantive due process. (Note that both cases focused on the constitutional rights of the patient, not on those of the person whose conduct would be subject to criminal punishment. The criminal provision is only indirectly relevant, insofar as its existence affects the constitutional rights of the person who stands to benefit from the criminalized conduct. The criminal nature of the prohibition, by itself, is not considered constitutionally significant.) The Supreme Court was no more impressed with the constitutional arguments in *Glucksberg* than it was with those raised in *Quill*, its companion case, finding that the challenged provision was justifiable on any number of grounds:

> Washington's assisted-suicide ban implicates a number of state interests . . .
>
> First, Washington has an "unqualified interest in the preservation of human life." The State's prohibition on assisted suicide, like all homicide laws, both reflects and advances its commitment to this interest. Model Penal Code § 210.5, Comment 5, at 100 ("[T]he interests in the sanctity of life that are represented by the criminal homicide laws are threatened by one who expresses a willingness to participate in taking the life of another"). This interest is symbolic and aspirational as well as practical:
>
> > "While suicide is no longer prohibited or penalized, the ban against assisted suicide and euthanasia shores up the notion of limits in human relationships. It reflects the gravity with which we view the decision to take one's own life or the life of another, and our reluctance to encourage or promote these decisions." New York State Task Force on Life and the Law, When Death is Sought: Assisted Suicide and Euthanasia in the Medical Context 131–132 (May 1994).
>
> . . .
>
> Relatedly, all admit that suicide is a serious public-health problem, especially among persons in otherwise vulnerable groups. The State has an interest in preventing suicide, and in studying, identifying, and treating its causes.
>
> Those who attempt suicide—terminally ill or not—often suffer from depression or other mental disorders. Research indicates, however, that many people who request physician-assisted suicide withdraw that request if their depression and pain are treated. The New York Task Force, however, expressed its concern that, because depression is difficult to diagnose, physicians and medical

professionals often fail to respond adequately to seriously ill patients' needs. Thus, legal physician-assisted suicide could make it more difficult for the State to protect depressed or mentally ill persons, or those who are suffering from untreated pain, from suicidal impulses.

The State also has an interest in protecting the integrity and ethics of the medical profession. [T]he American Medical Association, like many other medical and physicians' groups, has concluded that "[p]hysician-assisted suicide is fundamentally incompatible with the physician's role as healer." And physician-assisted suicide could, it is argued, undermine the trust that is essential to the doctor-patient relationship by blurring the time-honored line between healing and harming.

Next, the State has an interest in protecting vulnerable groups—including the poor, the elderly, and disabled persons—from abuse, neglect, and mistakes. The Court of Appeals dismissed the State's concern that disadvantaged persons might be pressured into physician-assisted suicide as "ludicrous on its face." We have recognized, however, the real risk of subtle coercion and undue influence in end-of-life situations. If physician-assisted suicide were permitted, many might resort to it to spare their families the substantial financial burden of end-of-life health-care costs.

The State's interest here goes beyond protecting the vulnerable from coercion; it extends to protecting disabled and terminally ill people from prejudice, negative and inaccurate stereotypes, and "societal indifference." The State's assisted-suicide ban reflects and reinforces its policy that the lives of terminally ill, disabled, and elderly people must be no less valued than the lives of the young and healthy, and that a seriously disabled person's suicidal impulses should be interpreted and treated the same way as anyone else's.

Finally, the State may fear that permitting assisted suicide will start it down the path to voluntary and perhaps even involuntary euthanasia. The Court of Appeals struck down Washington's assisted-suicide ban only "as applied to competent, terminally ill adults who wish to hasten their deaths by obtaining medication prescribed by their doctors." Washington insists, however, that the impact of the court's decision will not and cannot be so limited. If suicide is protected as a matter of constitutional right, it is argued, "every man and woman in the United States must enjoy it." [W]hat is couched as a limited right to "physician-assisted suicide" is likely, in effect, a much broader license, which could prove extremely difficult to police and contain. Washington's ban on assisting suicide prevents such erosion.

Leaving their constitutional significance aside, do you find these arguments convincing? How do they match up against the protection of the patient's autonomy, assuming, of course, that the patient is in fact autonomous in the relevant sense, at the relevant time? Is the German position on assisted suicide consistent with the categorical rejection of the propriety of balancing the value of one human life against another in the German law of justifying necessity (see Chapter 13.B), or with the criminalization of consensual homicide, § 216 (see Chapter 15.A.i)?

4. The two cases reprinted above belong to yet another category: incidents that are not free and autonomous suicides because of deficiencies in the suicidal person's knowledge, faculty of judgment, and autonomy in the sense of not being under the influence of others etc. According to German law, if a person consciously exploits such a deficiency and promotes the victim's suicide, this person will be punished as the indirect perpetrator of homicide or murder. An uncontroversial example would be giving a syringe containing poison to a self-injecting diabetes patient with the lie that it contained insulin. This was the line of thinking in the *Sirius Case* and therefore the defendant was convicted for attempted murder by indirect perpetration. (The figure of the indirect perpetrator is indicated in § 25 para. 1 Criminal Code, and the details are developed in case law. See Chapter 10.)

If a German court had to decide *People v. Duffy*, it would probably have convicted the defendant of manslaughter (*Totschlag*, § 212 Criminal Code)—despite the fact that German law, other than New York law, includes neither the notion of manslaughter as "reckless homicide" (see Chapter 15.A.i) nor a prohibition of intentionally aiding another to commit suicide. But a German court could rely on the notion of indirect perpetratorship here as well. The defendant was the indirect perpetrator of homicide because he dominated the events in the interaction with Schuhle. Schuhle was a minor, and he was severely drunk. This lack of autonomy makes his act not a genuine suicide. That the defendant provided even more alcohol and urged Schuhle to kill himself with the gun suffices to establish a degree of dominion over the act (*Tatherrschaft*, see for this concept Chapter 10) that makes him the indirect perpetrator of the killing.

B. Reckless Endangerment

We now leave the world of homicide behind, a world steeped in doctrinal history reaching back hundreds of years, which recalls the Constitutio Criminalis Carolina of 1532 and a time in English criminal law when there was little criminal law doctrine beyond the realm of the law of murder and manslaughter (and suicide, *felonia de se*, that "double offence; one spiritual, in invading the prerogative of the Almighty and rushing into his immediate presence uncalled for; the other temporal, against the king, who hath an interest in the preservation of all his subjects"*).

The offense of reckless endangerment is of considerably more recent vintage. It was introduced into American criminal law by the drafters of the Model Penal Code, as a general and explicit criminalization of risk, rather than harm. It was designed as a comprehensive and flexible backdrop offense that could be used to cover criminalization gaps foreseen and unforeseen; more important, it was a reflection of the Model Penal Code's treatmentist approach that sought to identify abnormally dangerous persons who posed a threat to identified individual and public interests, i.e., to prevent harm, rather than to punish those who inflicted it. In this sense, reckless endangerment is the quintessential Model Penal Code offense. (On treatmentism and the Model Penal Code, see Chapter 1.A.i.)

The implicit, and offense-specific, criminalization of endangerment is commonly seen as a central feature of contemporary criminal law, and German criminal law in particular. The discussion of reckless endangerment therefore also provides a doctrinal framework for the exploration of the various types of endangerment offenses in modern criminal law.

People v. Rodriguez
Supreme Court of New York
110 Misc. 2d 828, 442 N.Y.S.2d 948 (1981)

Defendants have been indicted for the offenses of arson in the third degree [and] reckless endangerment in the first degree . . . [D]efendants contend that setting fire to an unoccupied store to which New York City fire fighters responded and entered cannot be the predicate upon which the crime of reckless endangerment may properly be charged . . .

Section 120.25 of the Penal Law provides: "A person is guilty of reckless endangerment in the first degree when, under circumstances evincing a depraved indifference to human life, he recklessly engages in conduct which creates a grave risk of death to another person." . . . It is alleged that the defendants arranged several fires in various neighborhood supermarkets, ostensibly in order to eliminate competition with their own supermarkets. It is further alleged that large quantities of gasoline were used to start these fires; thus requiring the response of certain firemen who had to enter the structures to extinguish the fires . . .

A trial jury could find that by setting fires with large quantities of gasoline, the defendants thereby created a grave risk of death to certain named firemen who quite foreseeably responded, and that at the time the defendants so acted they were aware of this substantial and unjustifiable risk. Fires are inherently dangerous—particularly to those charged with the awesome responsibility to extinguish them. Every year firemen die in the course of fire fighting, and any conflagration creates imminent peril for the fire fighters. In the summer of 1978, six firemen perished while fighting a single blaze in an unoccupied supermarket in Brooklyn. At least some of the fires allegedly set by the defendants herein could be found to have been of so serious and perilous a nature that fighting them posed a grave risk of death to the firemen who did so. The response of New York City firemen to such a serious fire(s) was not only foreseeable—it was inevitable. It would be spurious to suppose that firemen would not respond. Unquestionably, the defendants' conscious disregard of the risk would be a gross deviation from the standard of conduct that a reasonable person would observe. Finally, the circumstances alleged could be found to have been so calloused and extremely dangerous as to evince a depraved indifference to human life.

The contention that reckless endangerment requires a criminal act directed at someone who is present at the time the act is committed is without merit. There is nothing in the statutory definition of reckless endangerment or the term "recklessly," which so narrowly restricts its application

---

* William Blackstone, *Commentaries on the Laws of England* (1769), vol. 4, 189.

(see Penal Law, §§ 120.25, 15.05, subd 3; see, also, *People v. Graham*, 41 AD2d 226). "All that is necessary is the creation of a certain degree of risk to 'another person'." *(People v. Graham*, supra, p 227.) The proximity of another person is relevant only insofar as it bears on the degree of risk to which such other person may be exposed, and as it relates to the alleged recklessness of the defendant, e.g., the foreseeability of the harm to another. A trial jury could properly find that the firemen who responded were sufficiently near in time and space to be within the zone of danger and to have been exposed to a grave risk of death after they arrived. Considering the proximity of the firemen and the certainty of their response, a jury could further find that the defendants' actions were criminally reckless.

The contention that the basis for this charge of reckless endangerment is the mere allegation that firemen *may* respond is fallacious. Here, firemen actually did respond as in virtual certitude they would be expected to. The prospectiveness of their response reflects on the recklessness of the defendants. While the alleged acts of arson may not have been specifically directed at firemen, the defendants must have known that firemen would respond and should have known that those responding would be endangered. It would indeed be disingenuous to argue that fire fighting is not extremely hazardous...

Reckless endangerment is not simply a "catch-all" crime for arsonists. It is a crime for anyone who recklessly creates a grave risk of death to another person, whether he creates that risk by driving a car, shooting a gun, or starting a fire. The relatively modern offense of reckless endangerment was designed to fill a gap in the law of assault (2 Wharton's Criminal Law, § 203 [14th edn. Torcia]). Now the pattern is complete. "If a defendant acts recklessly and kills another, he is guilty of manslaughter; if he injures another, he is guilty of [assault]; if he endangers another, he is guilty of reckless endangerment." (Id., p 335.)

A person who starts a fire under circumstances evincing a depraved indifference to human life and recklessly causes the death of another person may properly be charged with both arson and homicide (Penal Law, § 125.15, subd 1 or § 125.25, subds 2, 3). If the other person is not killed but is seriously injured, the perpetrator may then be properly charged with both arson and assault (Penal Law, § 120.00, subd 2; § 120.05, subd 4 or 6; § 120.10, subd 3). It follows that if the other person is neither killed nor seriously injured, but is recklessly exposed to a grave risk of death, then the perpetrator may be properly charged with both arson and reckless endangerment....

Accordingly, the motions to dismiss the indictments are denied.

German Federal Court of Justice
3 StR 341/93, BGHSt 39, 322 (September 8, 1993)

Facts

In the night September 19 to September 20, 1992, a celebration was taking place in the house of the H. family in which all the guests taking part (approximately thirty, including the defendant and the later victims) drank considerable quantities of alcohol during the course of the evening, and the defendant observed this. Carrying out an idea which he had already considered before midnight, the defendant lit a piece of clothing at about 1:30 a.m. in one of the bedrooms in the upper storey of the house, the layout of which was known to him. His purpose was to set the building on fire. Whilst he then mingled with the guests on the ground floor, the 12-year-old son of the married couple H. was still in the parental bedroom in the upper storey at the time of the arson. A guest, M., was sleeping in a room near him. The fire spread quickly and thick smoke developed. The child succeeded after the outbreak of the fire in climbing over the canopy of the house to get to safety. M. on the other hand suffered from carbon monoxide poisoning which led a little later to his death. At the time of the arson the defendant—who was therefore significantly limited in his capacity for control—had a maximum blood alcohol concentration of .21% and M. of .238%.

When the 22-year-old son of the house owner, N., who had been outside the house at the time the fire broke out, noticed the fire, he decided immediately to try to reach the upper storey. He intended either "to bring some things in the upper storey out of the fire to safety" or to attempt "to rescue people," perhaps his 12-year-old brother or other persons. N., who at this point in time had a blood alcohol concentration of .217%, reached the corridor in the upper storey before the arrival of the fire brigade, where he collapsed unconscious. He died a little later, likewise from the consequences of carbon monoxide poisoning. The regional court sentenced the defendant to juvenile detention of four years for especially aggravated arson* concomitantly with negligent homicide...

---

* [The arson offenses were reformed in 1998. The judgment is based on the old law. At that time, the norm about especially aggravated arson was § 307 Criminal Code, and § 307 para. 1 Nr. 1 upgraded aggravated arson to especially aggravated arson if the offender caused the death of a person who was present in the rooms set on fire at the

The defendant by his appeal in law objects to the violation of substantive law. The appeal was unsuccessful.

Reasons

2. The conviction of the defendant for especially aggravated arson in accordance with § 307 no. 1 Criminal Code does not reveal legal error. Contrary to the view of the complainant, there is no objection in the law to the verdict in relation to negligent homicide committed concomitantly (to the detriment of N.) either. In this respect the definition in § 307 no. 1 Criminal Code is not fulfilled, as the victim had not been in the building set on fire at the time of the crime.

a) The regional court has correctly proceeded on the basis that the arson caused the occurrence of N.'s death and this consequence was foreseeable for the defendant. His death is also attributable to the defendant.

It is true that N. himself, by his decision to go into the burning upper storey of the house to take rescue measures, created an additional cause for the later occurrence of his death, in addition to arson by the defendant. The causal connection between the intentional arson and the later death is not however interrupted by the "voluntariness" of his rescue action. N. would not have exposed himself to the dangerous situation without the arson. It is recognized that a cause does not lose its significance in the legal sense if other causes additionally contribute to the bringing about of the result. A causal connection should only be denied if a later event removes the continuing effect of the original condition, and for its part brought about the result on its own by opening up a new chain of causes (RGSt 5, 202, 203; BGHSt 4, 360,361 f.; BGHSt 7, 112, 114...) That is not the case here.

It also follows from the disputed judgment that the defendant was in a position by his knowledge and capabilities to recognize that his behavior could lead to the death of a rescuer. It is not necessary here that he could foresee the consequences of his act in detail; it suffices that they were essentially foreseeable in their importance (BGHSt 37, 179,180; BGH, NStZ 1981, 350). This was possible for the defendant, according to the findings of the disputed judgment, in spite of his inebriation. He was in a position to evaluate the direct effects of the fire and to consider that members of the family affected could enter the burning house on the basis of an "autonomous decision to rescue" and endanger their lives in order to rescue material assets or family members.

b) The regional court has correctly assumed that the attribution of the death complies with the principles developed in the case law and in the literature on so-called conscious self-endangerment (see BGHSt 32, 262 ff.; BGHSt 36, 1,17, 18; BGHSt 37, 179, 180 ff.; BGH, NStZ 1984, 452; ... Schroeder, in: LK, 10th edit., § 16 marginal nos. 181 ff.; Rudolphi, in: SKStGB, preliminary note § 1 marginal nos. 79 ff.; Cramer, in: Schönke/Schröder, 24th edit., § 15 StGB marginal no. 157—each with further references). According to this view, in the area of physical injury and homicide crimes, an injury and in particular the death of a human being should not be attributed to a third party who has generated a cause for it, if the result is the consequence of a conscious self-endangerment which is autonomously intended and carried out, and the involvement of the third party has not gone beyond the mere causing or furthering of the act of self-endangerment. The case law developed in a case like BGHSt 32, 262 ff. (the victim died from an overdose of injected heroin after communal and consensual consumption of narcotics) can however not be mechanically transferred to cases in which a third party has been induced to take self-endangering action by criminal conduct of a perpetrator. The case law does not for instance apply if it follows from the protective purpose of the norm that the causer of the danger must take responsibility for the self-endangerment of others resulting from this (see BGHSt 37, 179, 180 ff.).

There is a need to limit the principle of criminal immunity where the victim consciously endangers himself, in particular when the perpetrator without involvement or agreement by the victim creates the obvious possibility of a conscious self-endangerment by establishing a substantial danger to a legal interest of the victim or persons close to him, and thereby creates an understandable motive for dangerous attempts to rescue (see Rudolphi, JuS 1969, 549,557); Frisch, Tatbestandsmäßiges Verhalten und Zurechnung des Erfolges (Conduct complying with the crime definition and attribution of the result), 1988, pp. 481 ff. . . .). It is correct to include these persons who endanger themselves in such situations within the protective area of criminal law provisions. In the same way as the perpetrator benefits from the averting of the result if the rescue succeeds, he has to take responsibility for it in the case of failure. Different considerations may apply if a rescue attempt is senseless from the outset or associated with obviously

---

time of the offense. The legislature realized that the condition "present in the rooms" was not sensible in light of the particularly serious dangers facing firefighters. Therefore, present law defines an act of arson as especially aggravated arson if the offender puts another human being in danger of death, § 306b para. 2 no. 1.—Eds.]

disproportionate risks (see also BGH, NJW 1964, 1363). It is obvious that such a case is not present here. What was in the end the trigger for the action of the later victim, the idea of saving human life or the idea of preserving material assets or a particular object from his parents' house from destruction, is insignificant here. The crucial point is that in any case N. went into the burning upper storey of the house with the intention of rescue, and that at the established point in time his behavior was to be expected and help was objectively necessary. This is because all the family's material assets were in the upper storey of the house and M. was still sleeping there. The rescue operation was not manifestly foolish. Further witnesses had also attempted, after the intervention by N., to get into the upper storey in time to save M.

NOTES

1. With respect to crimes of endangerment, a comparative analysis of statutes and case law reveals differences as well as some similarities. The German Criminal Code does not contain a *general* prohibition of endangerment comparable to § 120.25 New York Penal Law. However, scattered across the special part of the German Criminal Code, there are a number of endangerment offenses with more specific definitions of dangerous conduct. If one compares the two approaches (general norm such as § 120.25 New York Penal Law or a number of descriptions relating to specific situational contexts such as in the German Criminal Code), one could argue that the American approach has its advantages in terms of conciseness, while the German solution is less systematic, more casuistic and historically contingent.

Of course, these approaches are not mutually exclusive. The Model Penal Code also features a host of specific offense definitions that explicitly criminalize threats to various protected interests. In fact, the special part of the Code begins with a section on "offenses *involving danger* to the person," rather than offenses against the person. And note that the definition of crime at the outset of the Code, in § 1.02(1)(a), already refers to "conduct that unjustifiably and inexcusably inflicts *or threatens* substantial harm to individual or public interests" (emphases added).

2. The concept of endangerment figures in German criminal law less as an explicit offense element, or offense, than as an analytic tool that captures a type of offense, and draws further distinctions within that type. It is common in German criminal law doctrine to distinguish two species of endangerment offenses that can be found in the German Criminal Code: *concrete endangerment* and *abstract endangerment* offenses.

Abstract endangerment offenses consist in acts that are typically dangerous; for conviction of an abstract endangerment offense, however, it is not necessary to name an individual, or group of individuals, who was actually endangered (never mind harmed), and the offender cannot escape conviction by arguing that in the specific situation he or she in fact endangered no one. Consider a defendant accused of drunk driving who points out that on this lonely stretch of road at 4:00 a.m. his car did not come near any other human being. Assuming she is in fact intoxicated, of course, the driver will nevertheless, under German law, be held liable for drunk driving under § 316 Criminal Code because this is an abstract endangerment offense. Another abstract endangerment offense is aggravated arson: setting residential buildings or churches on fire (§ 306a para. 1 Criminal Code). It does not matter whether at the particular point in time the buildings were occupied or not.

In contrast, concrete endangerment offenses require that the offender's conduct created a risk for one (or more) person or persons. For instance, in the section on homicide, one finds an offense entitled "abandonment," § 221 Criminal Code (see Chapter 15.A). For conviction of this offense, it will not suffice to argue that this kind of behavior is typically dangerous. Rather, it must be proved that the individual victim in fact faced a risk of serious damage to health or death. Similarly, it is a traffic offense with a somewhat higher punishment if the drunk driver does in fact almost collide with another traffic participant (§ 315c Criminal Code, endangering road traffic). Among arson offenses, German law also recognizes several concrete endangerment offenses in the form of especially aggravated arson that apply if individuals were in fact present in the burning building or were exposed to risks to health or life (§§ 306a para. 2, 306b Criminal Code).

For further discussion of the taxonomy of endangerment offenses in German criminal law, including intermediate categories such as "abstract-concrete" and "potential" endangerment offenses, see the *Töben Case* judgment below in Chapter 17.A.

Is this a mere classification exercise that may serve an analytic function by focusing the interpretation and application of a given offense definition? How do we know whether an offense falls into one category or the other (or perhaps in between, see the *Töben Case* judgment)? Or does the classification do any normative work? For instance, does the classification of an offense as an abstract endangerment offense help to legitimate it by connecting it, however remotely, to a legal good—an individual or public interest—that it serves to protect? As opposed to classifying it simply as a *malum prohibitum* offense? Are concrete endangerment offenses more legitimate than abstract endangerment ones? Or is the general trend toward endangerment offenses in general, and abstract endangerment offenses in particular, if there is one, a troubling development that *undermines* the legitimacy of criminal law? Because it extends the scope of criminal law into the preventive sphere, and thereby not only expands state penal power, but also further dilutes the legitimatory significance of the legal good principle (*Rechtsgutsprinzip*), as the *locus poenitentiae* is removed farther and farther from an actual violation of a legal good?

3. The German court in the ruling from 1993 had to deal not with mere endangerment but with the actual causing of death (negligent homicide, § 222 Criminal Code). But the problem it discusses would have arisen even if the relevant offense description had referred to endangerment. The question was: does it matter that the person who is endangered or hurt—for instance, a fire fighter or other person arriving for the purpose of rescue—entered the zone of danger by his own voluntary act? At this point, one sees similarities in the results. Both courts, the New York court as well as the German court, argue that the arsonist is responsible for such dangers and the ensuing death. The German Federal Court of Justice is more specific about the relevant doctrinal concepts. It points out that the rescuer's choice to enter the burning building neither interrupts causality nor qualifies as the kind of self-endangerment that prevents the attribution of the result to the arsonist.

In contrast to the New York court, the German Federal Court of Justice also hints that circumstances are conceivable under which danger or harm would *not* be attributed to the offender. There are cases of self-endangerment which preclude attribution to the offender, namely if attempts of rescue "are senseless from the outset or associated with obviously disproportionate risks."

As in previous cases, and in the discussion of causation, here too it should be pointed out that American criminal law would address this question of "objective attribution" as part of the inquiry into causation, which consists of both a factual, or physical, cause prong and a proximate, or legal, cause one. Victim self-endangerment—or, for that matter, victim self-harm, as in the *Duffy* case (in Chapter 15.A.v)—is among the factors that may preclude offender's conduct from being labeled the proximate, or legal, cause of the proscribed result.

At any rate, why would this not be a case of professional consent, as in *State v. George*, discussed in Chapter 13.C? Isn't danger to life and limb part of a fire fighter's job description? In fact isn't this the reason why fire fighters—and, say, police officers—earn the respect of their fellow citizens?

4. Consider the potential scope of the reckless endangerment offense as illustrated by *Rodriguez*. Why could reckless endangerment not function as an automatic add-on to any arson charge? To any charge involving an offense that is likely to attract the attention of "first responders," who may endanger themselves as they rush to the scene? Given the definition of the offense, would they even have to leave the station house, or receive the call? The *Rodriguez* court notes the large quantity of gasoline used, the proximity of the firemen, and the certainty of their response. Are any of these facts required for the imposition of liability for reckless endangerment in this case? In German doctrinal terms, is this a crime of abstract endangerment, or of concrete endangerment?

C. Stalking

Continuing on our trajectory from classic to modern offenses against the person, we have reached "stalking." This offense, unlike the previous ones, is so new it does not even appear in the Model Penal Code (which was completed in 1962). Stalking offenses sprang up across the landscape of American criminal law in the 1990s, with California leading the way (Cal. Penal Code § 646.9). Criminal stalking laws have since appeared in other countries, including Germany. Recently, cyber stalking has attracted particular attention, as a form of criminal stalking through the Internet or by other electronic means.

People v. Stuart
Court of Appeals of New York
100 N.Y.2d 412, 797 N.E.2d 28 (2003)

In 1999, the Legislature criminalized "stalking." The crime contemplates an intentional course of conduct with no legitimate purpose in which the offender targets a particular person. The conduct must be likely to place the victim in reasonable fear of material harm, or cause the victim mental or emotional harm (see Penal Law § 120.45). In seeking reversal of his conviction, defendant contends that the anti-stalking statute is unconstitutionally vague both on its face and as applied to him. We disagree and therefore affirm the order of the Appellate Term upholding the conviction.

I. Facts

Although defendant had not previously known his victim, a 22-year-old student, he approached her outside a card store and presented her with a bouquet of flowers on Valentine's Day 2000. Complainant refused the gift, but defendant insisted she take it, introduced himself as "Paul," and shook her hand. Ultimately she took the flowers and walked away.

Later that month, defendant stood "shoulder-to-shoulder" next to complainant at a local coffee shop. He asked her to sit down and have a cup of coffee with him. After she declined, defendant asked her to dinner. She refused, telling him that her boyfriend would not appreciate his advances. Undeterred, defendant presented her with a heart-shaped box of chocolates and a portrait of her that he had drawn. On the portrait defendant had inscribed complainant's first name. Disquieted by this unwanted attention, complainant "made it clear" to defendant that she did not want any further contact with him. After he insisted that complainant accept the gifts, she took them and left the coffee shop to go to a library. Defendant followed her, twice ducking behind trees when complainant looked over her shoulder. When she got to the library, she described defendant to a security guard. A friend then accompanied complainant to the police precinct, where she turned in a written report of the incident. Worried, she spent the night at the friend's house.

A few days later, complainant went to an athletic club on the second floor of a building near her home. From the street below, passersby could see the club's patrons. Defendant positioned himself where he could see complainant and stare at her while she was working out. Increasingly frightened, she called a friend to meet her at the club and accompany her as she left. Once on the street, they saw defendant handing out flyers. Complainant and her friend then went to a bank to withdraw money. Defendant followed and watched them wait in line at the ATM.

The next day, defendant trailed complainant twice. During a break in her classes, he followed her to a delicatessen where she bought lunch. That evening, he followed her home. Rather than go to her dormitory room, complainant took refuge in a delicatessen on the ground floor of her building, where she telephoned her father and stayed for 40 minutes, afraid to leave. During that entire time, defendant paced outside, staring at her through the windows. When complainant left the deli, defendant was still in the area and began walking toward her.

The following day, defendant watched complainant and her friend have lunch and tracked the pair while they shopped, coming within five feet of them. Whenever they looked back at him, defendant would try to hide behind walls or trees. The two friends then walked to the police precinct. Defendant suspended his pursuit only when the two women approached the station house, where complainant filed another report.

For almost every day over the ensuing five weeks, defendant followed complainant to various locations, including her dormitory, school and gymnasium, and to stores and restaurants in the neighborhood. When she caught sight of him, defendant would often duck behind a corner and peek out to leer at her. She was frequently accompanied by her friend, who saw defendant following complainant two to three times a week.

Fearful and distraught, complainant again contacted the police and altered her daily patterns, trying to shake defendant off. His intrusive behavior only intensified, and on April 5, 2000, for the first time, he trailed her outside her neighborhood. On that day, complainant went shopping in uptown Manhattan. When taking the subway home, she saw defendant enter her subway car. Defendant did not approach her, but stood several feet away, staring and smirking. Afraid to go home, complainant again spent the night at her friend's house. The following day, she went to the police and filed another report.

The day after that, she saw defendant tracking her once more. For a fifth time, complainant went to the police station, where she broke down in tears. Police arrested defendant the next day and charged him with one count of third-degree stalking (Penal Law § 120.50[3]), two counts of fourth-degree stalking (Penal Law § 120.45[1], [2]) and one count of first-degree harassment (Penal Law § 240.25).

Before trial, defendant moved to dismiss the fourth-degree stalking charges, claiming that Penal Law § 120.45 is unconstitutionally vague both on its face and as applied to him. He argued that the statute fails to provide adequate notice of what conduct it prohibits and does not give sufficient guidance to those charged with enforcing it. The trial court rejected defendant's arguments, concluding that, as applied to him, the statute satisfied the requirements of due process. Defendant waived his right to a jury trial and the court found him guilty of both counts of fourth-degree stalking.[2]

II. New York's Anti-Stalking Statute

In 1992, the Legislature amended the menacing and harassment statutes in its first effort to penalize stalking-type behavior. Concluding that these amendments were not up to the task and that "stalking behavior...had become more prevalent...in recent years," the Legislature in 1999 enacted the "Clinic Access and Anti-Stalking Act," creating a new, separate crime known as stalking. The lawmakers were moved by the "unfortunate reality [] that stalking victims have been intolerably forced to live in fear of their stalkers" and that "stalkers who repeatedly follow, phone, write, confront, threaten or otherwise unacceptably intrude upon their victims, often inflict immeasurable emotional and physical harm upon them" (id.). Accordingly, like the other 49 states and the District of Columbia before it, New York enacted an anti-stalking law to give greater protections to stalking victims and "provide clear recognition of the dangerousness of stalking."

The Act, codified at Penal Law § 120.45, provides in relevant part:

"A person is guilty of stalking in the fourth degree when he or she intentionally, and for no legitimate purpose, engages in a course of conduct directed at a specific person, and knows or reasonably should know that such conduct:

(1) is likely to cause reasonable fear of material harm to the physical health, safety or property of such person, a member of such person's immediate family or a third party with whom such person is acquainted; or

(2) causes material harm to the mental or emotional health of such person, where such conduct consists of following, telephoning or initiating communication or contact with such person, a member of such person's immediate family or a third party with whom such person is acquainted, and the actor was previously clearly informed to cease that conduct[.]"

On this appeal, defendant contends that Penal Law § 120.45 is unconstitutionally vague both on its face and as applied to him. As he did in the courts below, he argues that the statute neither gives people adequate notice of what conduct it proscribes nor provides adequate guidance to those charged with enforcing it.

III. The Vagueness Doctrine

. . .

IV. The Constitutionality of New York's Anti-Stalking Law

The statute contains a preamble followed by three subsections. The preamble provides that a person is guilty of stalking in the fourth degree if he or she (1) intentionally and for no legitimate purpose (2) engages in a course of conduct directed at a specific person (3) when he knows or reasonably should know that his conduct will have either of two consequences: first, that it is likely to cause reasonable fear of material harm to the victim's (or other specified third-party's) physical health, safety or property (see subsection [1]); or second, that the conduct causes material harm to the victim's

---

[2] The prosecution dropped the harassment charge and defendant was acquitted of the third-degree stalking charge.

mental or emotional health and consists of following, telephoning or initiating communication with the victim (or other specified third-party) after being clearly told to stop (see subsection [2]).

Defendant's principal attack is on the words "no legitimate purpose." He argues that the Legislature's failure to define the term renders the statute unconstitutionally vague. He contends that an ordinary person would not know what the phrase means, and that this uncertainty will result in arbitrary enforcement. Defendant asserts that the vagueness problem is exacerbated because the law does not contain a specific intent requirement.

We note at the outset that the statute does contain a mens rea requirement of intent, in that a person cannot be guilty of stalking by accident, inadvertence or chance encounter. To be convicted, the person must have intended to engage in a course of conduct targeted at a specific individual. Defendant argues that this intent requirement is not enough; he claims that the statute must contain a requirement that the offender intend a specific result, such as fear or harm. We disagree. In People v. Nelson (69 N.Y.2d 302, 514 N.Y.S.2d 197, 506 N.E.2d 907), this Court upheld a jostling statute as against a vagueness challenge even though the statute did not specifically require larcenous intent. Like the statute before us today, it prohibited "a certain intentional course of conduct regardless of the wrongdoer's underlying purpose or motive." We observed that the jostling statute "clearly delineates specific conduct easily avoided by the innocent-minded" and thus "should present no difficulty for a citizen to comprehend that he must refrain from acting with the intent to bring his hand into the proximity of a stranger's pocket or handbag unnecessarily" (id. at 307). Similarly, defendant could not reasonably have failed to realize that his intentional course of conduct directed at the complainant for over a month was unlawful under the anti-stalking statute.

The Legislature's decision to require intent as to a particular course of conduct—as opposed to a specific result—was purposeful. In following the lead taken by the drafters of the Model Anti-Stalking Code, the Legislature enacted Penal Law § 120.45 recognizing that many stalkers are mentally or emotionally disturbed and that trying to discern their specific motivations would prove difficult, if not impossible. The statute thus focuses on what the offenders do, not what they mean by it or what they intend as their ultimate goal. In this manner, the law could properly reach those "delusional stalkers who believe either that their victims are in love with them or that they can win their victims' love by pursuing them" (Note, Anti-Stalking Laws: Do they Adequately Protect Stalking Victims?, 21 Harv. Women's L J 229, 254 [1998]). If the Legislature had required that the stalker intend to frighten or harm the victim, the statute would be debilitated and a great many victims endangered. Stalkers would be free to continue as long as they harbored the notion that they stood to win, rather than harm, their prey. We cannot tell how many stalkers intend no harm. The Legislature did not want to give them license.

In considering defendant's conduct, we cannot conclude that the phrases "course of conduct" or "directed at a specific person" are in any way vague. From February 14 to April 8 he unflaggingly trailed complainant, from the sidewalk where he first presented her with a bouquet of flowers, to the subway car 30 city blocks away where he simply "smirked" at her. This deliberate and intentional conduct, repeated day after day, was aimed at one victim. Thus, defendant cannot reasonably contend that this was not a willful "course of conduct" "directed at a specific person" or that this description is in any way vague as to him.

The anti-stalking statute also requires that the offender know or reasonably should know that his conduct is likely to cause reasonable fear of material harm to the victim's physical health, safety or property (see Penal Law § 120.45[1]). And, in the case of subsection (2), the statute specifies that the offender must follow, telephone or initiate communication with the victim after being told to stop. These provisions are important because they eliminate the concern that a particular course of conduct will be deemed criminal based merely on the subjective fear or sensibilities of the alleged victim. The fear must be reasonable and not idiosyncratic; the harm (or likely harm) must be material. These are objective terms easily understood. Like with the jostling statute in Nelson, the anti-stalking law is "easily followed by most citizens of this State, provides objective criteria... [and] is not dependent upon the subjective conclusions of a complainant or an arresting officer" ...

[W]e are satisfied that an ordinary understanding of the phrase "no legitimate purpose" means the absence of a reason or justification to engage someone, other than to hound, frighten, intimidate or threaten. The common understanding of that phrase and the various other provisions of the anti-stalking statute, when read as a whole, furnished defendant with adequate notice that his unrelenting pursuit of complainant was unlawful, particularly after she told him that she wanted no contact with him.

Besides the "no legitimate purpose" element, the statute contains lucid provisos clearly applicable to defendant's conduct: The course of conduct must be intentional; it must be aimed at a specific person; and the offender must know (or have reason to know) that his conduct will (or likely will) instill reasonable fear of material harm in the victim. In the case of subsection (2), the offender must have been told to cease his conduct after having followed, telephoned or initiated communication with the victim. Defendant has offered no explanation for having inflicted himself on complainant, nor has he attempted to show that his intrusive behavior involved some valid purpose other than hounding her to the point of harm. This is not legitimate, and defendant has given us no reason to conclude that it could have been anything but illegitimate. Lastly, he has not argued to this Court that complainant was never in fear, reasonable or otherwise, or that she suffered no harm, whether it be material or not.

We therefore conclude that sections 120.45(1) and (2) of the Penal Law, as applied to defendant's conduct, are not unconstitutionally vague. It follows that, because there exists at least one constitutional application of the statute, it is not invalid on its face.

German Federal Court of Justice
3 StR 244/09, BGHSt 54, 189 (November 19, 2009)

Facts

The accused became acquainted with the witness L in April 2006 and carried on a relationship with her until the end of 2007. After the separation there were repeated arguments as the accused did not want to accept it . . .

On the March 29, 2008, he rang at the door of the house which included the witness's flat. The witness opened the bathroom window and asked the accused to go away. But he announced that he would wait until the following morning to see who came out of the house; besides this he threatened the witness with death and called her a "tart" and a "whore."

At midday on April 24, 2008, the accused called the witness several times and stated that he would not leave her in peace. On the afternoon of the same day he intercepted her on the way back from her work, and during the following period observed her flat with a binocular and threatened the witness by telephone and by shouting loudly that he would stick a knife in her neck, cut her throat and kill her; he also described her as a slut.

On May 13, 2008, the accused called the witness again several times, rang at her front door and called out that he wanted to know what was happening in the flat. After the witness had asked him to go, he threatened her that he could break down the door of the flat and cut her throat faster than the police could arrive.

On May 20, 2008, the accused called the witness and said he would break down the door of her flat that day and kill her; if he saw her on the street he would hit her hard in the face.

On July 3, 2008, at around 4 am the witness received a call from the accused in which he told her that the date of the court hearing, 16 July, 2008, would not be a nice day for her; everybody knew that he would knock her out and kill her.

The witness took the threats of the accused seriously and was anxious for her life. She gave up substantial parts of her leisure activities because of his behavior. Because of her anxiety about him she, for instance, did not if possible leave her flat or open the door in the evening any more. She no longer switched on lights in the flat in the evening, in order to make the accused believe that she was not at home. During the day she only left her flat and her place of work after taking special safety precautions, and took care not to linger on the street alone. Because of her anxiety and the limitations associated with it she lost weight significantly.

Reasons

. . .

a) § 238 Criminal Code was inserted into the Criminal Code by the 40th Criminal Law Amendment Act of March 22, 2007 (BGBl I 354). According to the intention of the legislature, persistent advances which radically interfere with the victim's life (and are discussed under the English concept of "stalking") over and above the already existing definitions of crimes which would fall to be considered—as for example coercion (§ 240 Criminal Code), threat (§ 241 Criminal Code), insult (§ 185 Criminal Code) or infringement of an order under the Protection from Violence Act (§ 4 GewSchG)—were by this norm to be capable of being prosecuted under a further crime definition, so as to attain a better protection of the victim and to close gaps in criminality (BTDrucks, 16/575 p. 1; Büttner ZRP 2008, 124; on the previous legal situation see Valerius JuS 2007, 319, 320; see also Kinzig ZRP 2006, 255, 256 with observations on the regimes in the USA, the Netherlands and Austria). The new crime thereby serves to protect people's own lifestyles from deliberate, persistent and serious molestations to their way of life (Mosbacher NStZ 2007, 665).
b) The act constituting the offence under § 238 para. 1 no. 1 Criminal Code is the unauthorized pursuit through persistent direct and indirect approaches of the victim, and more precisely determined threats in the sense of § 238 para. 1 nos. 1 to 5 Criminal Code.

aa) The concept of pursuit . . . covers stalking, creeping up to, waylaying, visiting, tracking, luring, setting a trap for and having her hounded by third parties (Kinzig/Zander JA 2007, 481, 483; Valerius p. 321). In the context of § 238 Criminal Code the concept thus in principle describes all actions which are directed towards intrusion into the sphere of the victim's personal life by direct or indirect approaches to her, and thereby impairing her freedom of action and decision (BTDrucks. 16/575 p. 7; Wolters in SK-StGB § 238 marginal no. 7). However, all the forms of action to which penalization extends are exhaustively described in § 238 para. 1 nos. 1 to 5 Criminal Code. Whilst § 238 para. 1 Criminal Code describes variants in nos. 1 to 4 which are concretized more precisely, § 238 para. 1 no. 5 Criminal Code admittedly widely opens the spectrum of possible criminal acts by including in the criminality, without more precise restrictions, every activity which is "comparable" to the actions covered by § 238 para. 1 nos. 1 to 4 Criminal Code. Whether this could give rise to concerns with regard to the certainty requirement in constitutional law does not however need any more detailed consideration here.

§ 238 para. 1 no. 1 Criminal Code is to cover physical approaches to the victim like waylaying, tracking, standing in the front of the house and other forms of frequent presence in the neighborhood of the victim's residence or workplace. What is necessary is deliberate visits in spatial proximity to the victim (BTDrucks. 16/575 p. 7; Lackner/Kühl, StGB 26th edit. § 238 marginal no. 4; Wolters loc. cit. marginal no. 10; Mitsch NJW 2007, 1237, 1238; Valerius loc. cit. p. 321). § 238 para. 1 no. 2 Criminal Code covers advances through undesired calls, emails, SMSs, letters, written messages on the windscreen or similar, and indirect contact approaches via third parties (BTDrucks. 16/575 p. 7; Wolters loc. cit. marginal no. 11; Mitsch loc. cit. p. 1239).

The actions of the accused accordingly fulfil the prerequisites of pursuit in the variants of § 238 para. 1 nos. 1 and 2 Criminal Code. In the incident on March 29, 2008, the accused made a visit in the victim's spatial proximity by ringing at her flat and communicating with the witness through an open window; therefore the prerequisites of § 238 para. 1 no. 1 Criminal Code were present. The actions of the accused on April 24 and May 13, 2008, in each case fulfil the prerequisites of § 238 para. 1 nos. 1 and 2 Criminal Code as the accused made a visit in the physical proximity of the witness as well as establishing contact with her by telephone. § 238 para. 1 no. 2 Criminal Code covers the successful establishment of communication between the perpetrator and the victim besides the mere attempt, in spite of its equivocal wording in this respect (Fischer, StGB 56th edit. § 238 marginal no. 14). Finally the prerequisites of § 238 para. 1 no. 2 Criminal Code are likewise satisfied by the actions of the accused on May 20 and July 3, 2008.

bb) Persistent action on the part of the perpetrator as required by the definition is also present here.

The concept of "persistent" is also used in another place in the Criminal Code . . . and it is there interpreted as a rule as being repeated action or continual behavior which reveals disregard of a prohibition, or indifference on the part of the perpetrator (Fischer loc. cit. § 184 e marginal no. 5; Valerius loc. cit. p. 322; see also BGHSt 23, 167, 172 f.). In § 238 para. 1 Criminal Code the characteristic serves on the one hand to limit the definition; on the other hand it is to express the "stalking" type of offence and to differentiate individual actions regarded in themselves by the legislature as socially acceptable (BTDrucks. 16/575 p. 7) from unwanted "stalking" (Kinzig/Zander loc. cit. p. 484; Mitsch, critical in this respect, loc. cit. p. 1240). Objective factors of time as well as subjective and normative elements of intransigence and hostility to law are inherent in the concept of persistence in the sense of § 238 Criminal Code (Fischer loc. cit. § 238 marginal no. 19; Wolters loc. cit. marginal no. 15); it is not simply fulfilled by mere repetition. This feature of the definition describes instead a particular obstinacy expressed in the commission of an act and an increased indifference on the part of the perpetrator to the statutory prohibition which at the same time indicates the danger of further commission of it. Accordingly, repeated commission is always a prerequisite, but does not suffice on its own (Lackner/Kühl loc. cit. marginal no. 3; Gazeas JR 2007, 497, 502). Instead it is necessary that action is taken in disregard of the contrary will of the victim or in indifference to her wishes with the intention to behave in this way again and again in the future. It is inherent in persistence that the perpetrator intransigently insists on his attitude and holds tenaciously to his decision although the victim's contrary interests are known to him. The necessary negative stance and the intensified indifference towards the statutory prohibition are manifested in the fact that the perpetrator deliberately ignores the contrary will stated expressly or conclusively by the victim (see Wolters loc. cit.). The persistence follows from an overall assessment of the various actions in which, in particular, the gap in time between the attacks and their intrinsic connection are of importance . . .

The overall assessment of the behavior of the accused which is accordingly necessary reveals that he acted persistently in the sense explained. The district court has established events on a total of five days in which on single days several separate advances by the accused occurred. It is true that in between individual approaches by the accused there were in part also larger gaps in time of up to about six weeks. However the accused molested the witness over a long period of more than three months altogether, and on many days with particular insistence. While doing so he was aware all the time that the witness, who amongst other things had obtained an interim injunction against him, did not want to have any more contact with him. His behavior was nonetheless characterized by continual obstinate endeavors to plague the witness. The intensity of the harm to the witness by the actions of the accused must also be regarded as substantial; the accused even harassed his victim, for instance, during the night and by the severe threats and insults uttered committed in each case at least one further crime . . .

c) The definition of the crime has been formulated by the legislature as a crime of result (see BTDrucks. 16/3641 p. 14; Wolters loc. cit. marginal no. 2; Mosbacher loc. cit. p. 667; Neubacher/Seher, JZ 2007, 1029, 1030); the action must lead to a serious encroachment on the victim's lifestyle. The concept of lifestyle encompasses in a quite general way the freedom of human decision and action (BTDrucks. 16/575 p. 7; Wolters loc. cit. marginal no. 4). It is encroached upon if the victim is induced by the perpetrator's action to adopt behavior which she would not have shown without the perpetrator being involved; what must therefore always be established is a forced change of circumstances of life (BTDrucks. 16/ 575 p.8; Wolters loc. cit. marginal no. 5). This wide feature of the definition is subjected, by the wording of the statute, to a limitation that the encroachment must be serious. It thereby covers in the actual context results which are of consequence, grave and to be taken seriously and which substantially, and in a manner which can be objectivized, go beyond modifications of lifestyle which are average, normally to be accepted and reasonably to be expected (BTDrucks. 16/3641 p. 14; OLG Hamm NStZ-RR 2009, 175; Wolters loc. cit. marginal no. 3; Mosbacher loc. cit.; Mitsch, critically, loc. cit. p. 1240). Less important measures of self-care like for example the use of a telephone-answering machine and the installation of a so-called call tracer for the purpose of securing evidence, are not therefore sufficient. Further security precautions by the victim as, for instance, leaving home only in the company of third parties, a change of workplace or home, and darkening the windows of one's home are on the other hand to be regarded as serious (BTDrucks. 16/575 p. 8; OLG Hamm loc. cit.; Lackner/Kühl loc. cit. marginal no. 2; Wolters loc. cit. marginal no. 6). Accordingly the definition of the crime protects neither the over-anxious, nor the especially hardened who do not allow themselves to be affected by the pursuit (see Wolters loc. cit. marginal no. 2; Mitsch loc. cit.; Mosbacher loc. cit.).

According to these standards the necessary consequence of the crime is present, having regard to the limitations, which have been established and are capable of being objectivized, to the lifestyle which the molestations of the accused caused the witness to lead. It cannot admittedly be deduced from the findings that this result was caused by individual actions by the accused; it was rather that the combination of all the advances led to the encroachments on the lifestyle of the witness.

d) Against this background the behavior of the accused is to be assessed as a unified pursuit . . .

German Criminal Code

§ 238 (Stalking)

(1) Who unlawfully stalks a person by persistently

1. seeking his proximity,
2. trying to establish contact with him by means of telecommunication or other means of communication or through third persons,
3. abusing his personal data for the purpose of ordering goods or services for him or causing third persons to make contact with him,
4. threatening him or a person close to him with injuries to life, bodily integrity, health or freedom, or
5. committing similar acts

and thereby seriously infringes his lifestyle will be punished with imprisonment of not more than three years or a fine.

(2) The punishment will be three months to five years if the offender places the victim, a relative of the victim or another person close to the victim in danger of death or serious injury of health.

(3) If the offender causes the death of the victim, a relative of the victim or another person close to the victim the punishment will be imprisonment from one to ten years.

(4) Cases under para. 1 may only be prosecuted upon complaint unless the prosecuting authority considers that due to a special public interest prosecution is required.

NOTES

1. The German case and the New York case exemplify conduct typical of what is described by the term "stalking": an offender harassing an unknown woman with intense, unwanted attention from initial presents to tracing her steps, and an ex-boyfriend who harasses his ex-girlfriend with continued acts of hostility after the separation. Had the events taken place in New York, the German case would fall under New York Penal Law § 120.45(1). If the facts in *People v. Stuart* were to be assessed according to German law, the defendant's acts would fall under the description of conduct in § 238 para. 1 Nr. 1 Criminal Code. In addition, under German law, however, it would need to be proved that the defendant's conduct had a certain objective consequence. At this juncture, the German legislature and the New York legislature took slightly different paths: while New York law focuses on victims' subjective states (either fear or harm to mental or emotional health), the German Criminal Code instead requires an objective element as a result of the defendant's conduct, i.e., an infringement of lifestyle. According to the German Federal Court of Justice, this must consist in a coerced change in the victim's course of life, a change that is more than an average modification such as use of a telephone answering machine. But the description of the victim's situation in *Stuart* (she repeatedly stayed at a friend's house and altered her daily patterns) would suffice to fulfill the objective element "infringement of lifestyle" in § 238 para. 1 Criminal Code. Although only New York law explicitly demands that "the actor was previously clearly informed to cease that conduct," the interpretation of the element "persistently" leads to similar results: The German Federal Court of Justice requires that the offender "disregard the contrary will of the victim."

2. Note that the German Federal Court of Justice expressed constitutional objections to § 238 para. 1 no. 5 Criminal Code ("committing similar acts"). This passage is an *obiter dictum* because § 238 para. 1 no. 5 was not at issue in the case before the court. The legislative idea behind § 238 para. 1 no. 5 Criminal Code was that human inventiveness to create new modes of harassment is not to be underestimated, and that it is therefore necessary to have an open catch-all description. (Is this not true of criminal inventiveness in general and, if so, would this not justify the proliferation of catch-all provisions in the criminal law?) But it is likely that if a case comes up which cannot be placed under § 238 para. 1 nos. 1–4 Criminal Code, the court will then submit it to the Federal Constitutional Court with the question whether no. 5 is compatible with the prohibition against vagueness in art. 103 para. 2 Basic Law. Such submissions from a local or regional court to the Federal Constitutional Court are permitted under art. 100 Basic Law if a court has doubts about the constitutionality of a norm; see, e.g., the *Life Imprisonment Case*, in Chapter 1.B.i (doubts about the constitutionality of life imprisonment).

Are there no other vagueness problems with the German stalking statute? What does "lifestyle" (*Lebensgestaltung*) mean, and how would I know whether I "seriously infringed" it, or for that matter that infringing someone's lifestyle would trigger criminal punishment? Does it matter whether other offenses protect the victim's lifestyle from infringement, serious or not? For instance, should I be expected to recognize that I would expose myself to criminal punishment if I were to persistently seek another person's proximity (no. 1), or send that person emails (no. 2), and thereby cause a serious infringement on that person's lifestyle (whether or not I am aware of this effect)? Does the court not place a great deal of weight on the element of "persistence," which it reads very narrowly? Does the word bear this interpretive weight on its face? Or even in light of the fact that it appears elsewhere in the German Criminal Code, and has been interpreted there? Does it matter that the other appearance of the term, in § 184e, occurs in a different and entirely unrelated part of the

Criminal Code, in a provision criminalizing the "persistent" violation of a legal order—to refrain from engaging in prostitution in certain locations or at certain times?

In the United States, several stalking laws have faced vagueness challenges, with mixed results. For instance, the Kansas Supreme Court struck down a provision that defined stalking as "an intentional and malicious following... directed at a specific person when such following or course of conduct seriously alarms, annoys or harasses the person, and which serves no legitimate purpose" on the ground that, "[i]n the absence of an objective standard, the terms 'annoys,' 'alarms' and 'harasses' subject the defendant to the particular sensibilities of the individual victim" (*State v. Bryan*, 259 Kan. 143, 910 P.2d 212 (1996)). In contrast, the South Dakota Supreme Court, in *State v. Asmussen*, 668 N.W.2d 725 (S.D. 2003), rejected a vagueness challenge against a provision that defined stalking as "willfully, maliciously, and repeatedly harass[ing] another person" and "harass" as "a knowing and willful course of conduct directed at a specific person which seriously alarms, annoys, or harasses the person, and which serves no legitimate purpose," without reference to an objective standard.

How, in terms of vagueness, does the New York stalking provision compare to the Kansas, South Dakota, and German ones?

3. Aside from the constitutional issue of vagueness, there is also the question of whether stalking statutes are necessary, given the existence of other statutes dealing with similar behavior. For instance, the New York Penal Law also criminalizes "harassment," which includes "stalking-like behavior." See *People v. Furey*, 2 Misc. 3d 1011A, 784 N.Y.S.2d 922 (N.Y. Crim. Ct. 2004) (rejecting double jeopardy claim by distinguishing between harassment as a public order offense and stalking as an offense that inflicts physical and emotional harm on individual victims, and by pointing out that the former requires an "intent to harass, annoy or alarm" on the part of the stalker, while the latter focuses on the victim's fear of harm).

OFFENSES AGAINST SEXUAL AUTONOMY: RAPE AND SEXUAL ASSAULT

After the law of homicide—which has changed remarkably little over the past decades, or the past centuries, depending on where you look, and whom you ask—and two non-homicidal offenses against the person that have only recently appeared in the special part of criminal law, we now turn to a group of traditional offenses that has significantly evolved in recent years, at least in name, and at least in the German Criminal Code. In 1975, the section known since 1871* as "offenses against morality" was rebranded "offenses against sexual autonomy," and purged of several offenses, including adultery and bestiality.[†]

State v. Rusk
Court of Appeals of Maryland
289 Md. 230, 424 A.2d 720 (1981)

Murphy, C.J.:

Edward Rusk was found guilty by a jury of second degree rape in violation of Maryland Code, Art. 27, sec. 463(a)(1), which provides in pertinent part:

> A person is guilty of rape in the second degree if the person engages in vaginal intercourse with another person:
> (1) By force or threat of force against the will and without the consent of the other person.

On appeal, the Court of Special Appeals, sitting en banc, reversed the conviction; it concluded . . . that in view of the prevailing law as set forth in *Hazel v. State*, 221 Md. 464, 157 A.2d 922 (1960), insufficient evidence of Rusk's guilt had been adduced at trial to permit the case to go the jury . . .

At the trial, the 21-year-old prosecuting witness, Pat, testified that on the evening of September 21, 1977, she attended a high school alumnae meeting where she met a girl friend, Terry. After the meeting, Terry and Pat agreed to drive in their respective cars to Fells Point to have a few drinks . . . Rusk approached them [at a bar] and said "hello" to Terry. Terry, who was then conversing with another individual, momentarily interrupted her conversation and said "Hi, Eddie." Rusk then began talking with Pat and during their conversation both of them acknowledged being separated from their respective spouses and having a child. Pat told Rusk that she had to go home early because it was a weeknight . . . Rusk asked Pat the direction in which she was driving and after she responded, Rusk requested a ride to his apartment. Although Pat did not know Rusk, she thought that Terry knew him. She thereafter agreed to give him a ride. Pat cautioned Rusk on the way to the car that "I'm just giving a ride home, you know, as a friend, not anything to be, you know, thought of other than a ride;" and he said, "Oh, okay." . . .

---

* In fact, since 1851. See Prussian Criminal Code ti. 12 ("felonies and misdemeanors against morality").

[†] Bestiality is once against prohibited, though not as a crime, but as an administrative offense, and not in the Criminal Code, but in the Animal Protection Act (see Part III introduction). Incest and bigamy remained in the Criminal Code, but were moved into the category of "offenses against personal status, marriage and the family." The criminal incest prohibition was recently upheld by the German Constitutional Court in a controversial decision (see Chapter 3.B).

After a twenty-minute drive, they arrived at Rusk's apartment. Pat testified she was totally unfamiliar with the neighborhood. She parked the car at the curb on the opposite side of the street from Rusk's apartment but left the engine running. Rusk asked Pat to come in, but she refused. He invited her again, and she again declined. She told Rusk that she could not go in even if she wanted to because she was separated from her husband and a detective could be observing her movements ... Notwithstanding her repeated refusals, Pat testified that Rusk reached over and turned off the ignition to her car and took her car keys. He got out of the car, walked over to her side, opened the door and said, "Now, will you come up?" Pat explained her subsequent actions:

> "At that point, because I was scared, because he had my car keys, I didn't know what to do. I was someplace I didn't even know where I was ... I didn't know whether to run. I really didn't think at that point, what to do. Now, I know that I should have blown the horn. I should have run. There were a million things I could have done. I was scared, at that point, and I didn't do any of them."

Pat testified that at this moment she feared that Rusk would rape her. She said, "[I]t was the way he looked at me, and said 'Come on up, come on up;' and when he took the keys, I knew that was wrong."

It was then about 1 a.m. Pat accompanied Rusk across the street into a totally dark house. She followed him up two flights of stairs. She neither saw nor heard anyone in the building ... Rusk unlocked the door to his one-room apartment, and turned on the light. According to Pat, he told her to sit down. She sat in a chair beside the bed. Rusk sat on the bed. After Rusk talked for a few minutes, he left the room for about one to five minutes. Pat remained seated on the chair. She made no noise and did not attempt to leave. She said that she did not notice a telephone in the room. When Rusk returned, he turned off the light, and sat down on the bed. Pat asked if she could leave; she told him that she wanted to go home and "didn't want to come up." She said, "Now [that] I came up, can I go?" Rusk, who was still in possession of her car keys, said he wanted her to stay.

Rusk then asked Pat to get on the bed with him. He pulled her by the arms to the bed and began to undress her, removing her blouse and bra. He unzipped her slacks and she took them off after he told her to do so. Pat removed the rest of her clothing, and then removed Rusk's pants because "he asked me to do it." After they were both undressed Rusk started kissing Pat as she was lying on her back. Pat explained what happened next:

> I was still begging him to please, you know, let me leave. I said, "you can get a lot of other girls, down there, for what you want," and he just kept saying, "no"; and then I was really scared, because I can't describe, you know what was said. It was more the look in his eyes, and I said, at that point—I didn't know what to say; and I said, "If I do what you want, will you let me go without killing me?" Because I didn't know, at that point, what he was going to do; and I started to cry; and when I did, he put his hands on my throat, and started lightly to choke me; and I said, "If I do what you want, will you let me go?" And he said, yes, and at that time, I proceeded to do what he wanted me to do.

Pat testified that Rusk made her perform oral sex and then vaginal intercourse.

Immediately after the intercourse, Pat asked if she could leave. She testified that Rusk said, "Yes," after which she got up and got dressed and Rusk returned her car keys. She said that Rusk then "walked me to my car, and asked if he could see me again; and said, 'Yes'; and he asked me for my telephone number; and I said, 'No, I'll see you down Fells Point sometime,' just so I could leave." ...

She reported the incident to the police at about 3:15 a.m. ... [Rusk's friend David Carroll testified on the defendant's behalf, saying that when Rusk had left the bar at which he had met Pat, he] saw Rusk walking down the street arm-in-arm with a woman. He said "[s]he was kind of like, you know, snuggling up to him like ... She was hanging all over him then." Carroll was fairly certain that Pat was the woman ...

According to Rusk, when they arrived in front of his apartment Pat parked the car and turned the engine off. They sat for several minutes "petting each other." Rusk denied switching off the ignition and removing the keys ... Rusk testified that Pat came willingly to his room and that at no time did he make threatening facial expressions ... Rusk explained that after the intercourse, Pat "got uptight."

> Well, she started to cry. She said that—she said, "You guys are all alike," she says, "just out for," you know, "one thing." ...

Rusk denied placing his hands on Pat's throat or attempting to strangle her. He also denied using force or threats of force to get Pat to have intercourse with him.

In reversing Rusk's second degree rape conviction, the Court of Special Appeals [noted that] *Hazel* ... recognized that force and lack of consent are distinct elements of the crime of rape. It said:

Force is an essential element of the crime and to justify a conviction, the evidence must warrant a conclusion either that the victim resisted and her resistance was overcome by force or that she was prevented from resisting by threats to her safety...If the acts and threats of the defendant were reasonably calculated to create in the mind of the victim—having regard to the circumstances in which she was placed—a real apprehension, due to fear, of imminent bodily harm, serious enough to impair or overcome her will to resist, then such acts or threats are the equivalent of force....

Hazel did not expressly determine whether the victim's fear must be "reasonable."...The vast majority of jurisdictions have required that the victim's fear be reasonably grounded in order to obviate the need for either proof of actual force on the part of the assailant or physical resistance on the part of the victim. We think that, generally, this is the correct standard...

We think the reversal of Rusk's conviction by the Court of Special Appeals was in error [for the reason that it] "trampled upon the first principle of appellate restraint...[because it] substituted [its] own view of the evidence...for that of the judge and jury..." In view of the evidence adduced at the trial, the reasonableness of Pat's apprehension and fear was plainly a question of fact for the jury to determine...

Just where persuasion ends and force begins in cases like the present is fundamentally a factual issue...Considering all the evidence in the case, with particular focus upon the actual force applied by Rusk to Pat's neck, we conclude that the jury could rationally find that the essential elements of second degree rape had been established...

Cole, J. dissenting:

I agree with the Court of Special Appeals that the evidence...was insufficient to convict...

While courts no longer require a female to resist to the utmost or to resist where resistance would be foolhardy, they do require her acquiescence in the act of intercourse to stem from fear generated by something of substance. She may not simply say, "I was really scared," and thereby transform consent or mere unwillingness into submission by force. These words do not transform a seducer into a rapist. She must follow the instinct of every proud female to resist, by more than mere words, the violation of her person by a stranger or an unwelcomed friend. She must make it plain that she regards such sexual acts as abhorrent and repugnant to her natural sense of pride. She must resist unless the defendant has objectively manifested his intent to use physical force to accomplish his purpose. The law regards rape as a crime of violence. The majority today attenuates this proposition. It declares the innocence of an at best distraught young woman. It does not demonstrate the defendant's guilt of the crime of rape...

I find it incredible for the majority to conclude that on these facts, without more, a woman was *forced* to commit oral sex upon the defendant and then to engage in vaginal intercourse. In the absence of any verbal threats to do her grievous bodily harm or the display of any weapon and threat to use it, I find it difficult to understand how a victim could participate in these activities and not be willing...

This was a married woman with children...He had not forced his way into her car; he had not taken advantage of a difference in years or a state of intoxication or mental or physical incapacity on her part. He did not grapple with her. She got out of the car, *walked with him* across the street and *followed* him up the stairs to his room. She certainly had to realize they were not going upstairs to play *Scrabble.*

Once in the room she waited while he went to the bathroom where he stayed for five minutes. In his absence, the room was lighted but she did not seek a means of escape...

Upon his return, he turned off the lights and pulled her on to the bed. There is no suggestion or inference to be drawn from her testimony that he yanked her on the bed or in any manner physically abused her by this conduct. As a matter of fact there is no suggestion by her that he bruised her or hurt her in any manner, or that the "choking" was intended to be disabling...

He did not rip her clothes off or use any greater force than was necessary to unfasten her garments...

In my judgment the State failed to prove the essential element of force beyond a reasonable doubt...

People v. Jovanovic
Supreme Court of New York, Appellate Division
263 A.D.2d 182, 700 N.Y.S.2d 156 (1999)

Saxe, J.

On this appeal of his conviction for...sexual abuse..., defendant Oliver Jovanovic asks us to examine certain issues regarding the application of the Rape Shield Law (Crim. Proc. L. § 60.42)...

The Evidence at Trial

The People's case against Jovanovic was primarily founded upon the testimony of the complainant. She told a detailed story of becoming acquainted with Jovanovic through communications over the Internet, both by e-mail and by so-called "instant messages," as well as in a number of lengthy telephone conversations.

Their first contact took place during the summer of 1996. The complainant, a Barnard undergraduate who was home for the summer in Salamanca, a small town in upstate New York, went on-line and logged onto a "chat room" called "Manhattan," hoping to find other Columbia students there. [Their online communications intensified in the fall of 1996.]

After more e-mails back and forth during the late night/early morning hours of November 21, 1996, at about 2:30 a.m., the complainant referred to things getting "kind of intimate," and then, at about 5:00 a.m., Jovanovic ended his message with "Should I call you, or you call me." That afternoon her e-mail message included her phone number, with the message that she would be home around 3:00 that night.

He called at about 3:00 a.m. on November 22nd, and they spoke for approximately four hours. According to the complainant's trial testimony, Jovanovic invited her to see a movie with him that night, and she gave him the address of her dormitory . . .

The Complainant's Narrative of the Events of November 22–23, 1996

Jovanovic arrived at 8:30 p.m. on November 22, and suggested that they get something to eat. When they finished dinner at around 10:15, he said it was too late for the movie they had agreed upon, and asked if she wanted to see a video at his apartment instead. She said "I don't know"—explaining in her testimony that although she did not want to, she has trouble being assertive. Finally she agreed. He drove to three video rental outlets, but did not find what he wanted. He said he had some videos at his apartment, which was located in Washington Heights, and they proceeded to drive there, arriving at about 11:30 p.m.

Jovanovic gave her some tea . . . and a book of photographs by Joel-Peter Witkin, depicting corpses placed in grotesque poses. They watched a video entitled "Meet the Feebles," in which Muppet-like characters engage in sexual or violent behavior . . .

When the movie was over, she said it was getting late and she should go, but they began a conversation that ranged from the subjects of East Timor, media control of the news, and religion, to the subject of people with multiple personalities. Jovanovic told her he had another personality called the "Wise Philosopher" whom he can turn into when he encounters pain. To demonstrate, he told her to twist his wrist, which she did; she testified that he appeared to be "in" a personality that did not feel pain.

When he introduced the subject of good and evil, the complainant told him that she did not believe that evil existed. He looked stern, and in a voice she also characterized as "stern," told her to take off her sweater. He then repeated this directive in a louder voice. The complainant testified that she did not know what to do, thought it was a joke, but nevertheless removed her sweater. Then he told her to take off her pants, and she complied. He instructed her to lie down, and he tied her legs and arms to the frame of the futon . . . ; she explained that she did not protest because she did not know what to think.

[According to complainant's testimony, Jovanovic then proceeded to hold her captive for 20 hours during which time, over her repeated objections, he tied her up, bit her, dropped hot wax on her skin and molested her with a baton.]

The complainant's next memory was of waking some time on Saturday, November 23, 1996 . . . . Jovanovic untied her for a time and attempted to give her some instruction in self-defense. When she tried to run, he tied her up again.

Then, that evening, . . . the complainant found that she was able to untie her legs, and stood up. The complainant testified that [Jovanovic] then looked frightened. At this point, although she said he still sought to restrain her, she continued to run and to fight him off, . . . unlocking the apartment door and finally escaping . . .

Subsequent Events

The complainant took the subway to her dormitory at about 10:00 p.m., fell asleep, woke up, showered, and after Luke called her at 1:00 a.m., she went to Luke's apartment . . . The next morning she returned to her dormitory.

On Sunday night, November 24, 1996, she logged on to the computer at her school library and retrieved an e-mail message sent by Jovanovic the night before at 10:35 p.m. In it, he said she had forgotten her gold chain when she left the apartment, and that he could mail it if she gave him her zip code, or he could drop it off. He also said, "I have a feeling the experience may not have done you as much good as I'd hoped, because you weren't acting much smarter at the end than you were at the beginning." He closed with the words, "I hope you managed to get back all right."

The complainant sent Jovanovic a long e-mail the following day, in which her remarks included assertions that she was "purged by emotions, and pain," and that she was "quite bruised mentally and physically, but never been so happy to be alive." She said "Burroughs best sums up my state . . . the taste is so overpoweringly delicious, and at the same time, quite nauseating."

They continued their on-line communications later that day.

The Redacted Statements

With the foregoing narrative by the complainant, the People were able to present to the jury a compelling story of a woman being drawn into a cyberspace intimacy that led her into the trap of a scheming man. [Jovanovic] was . . . precluded from inquiring into several highly relevant statements contained in the complainant's e-mails to him . . .

[First] Redacted E-Mail

[O]n November 19th, the complainant sent Jovanovic a long message relating how she became involved with "Luke." She told of "fingering" Luke to chat with, and how Luke's "x-intrest [sic]," Karen, was unhappy about the complainant's new friendship with Luke and sent the complainant an e-mail warning her to stay away from him. The court deleted from this e-mail the following paragraphs . . .

"the boy calls, tells lots and lots of a life led like burroughs: heroin addicted, bisexual atheist. My kinda comrad. so he seduced me. come to Ufm, I did[,] come to my appartment, I did[,] then he got me.

"Oh he sighed and pulled out an agonized tale of being young in Edinborough and on a field trip for highschool . . . there were 'very nice boys' (according to the chaperons) who worked at the hotel, so said chaperons let luke and his teen friends hang out with the big boys for a night on the town. Unfortunately for poor luke, one took a liking to him, (this is liking with twisted glint in the eye mind you). yes yes, so young man took young boy (luke) to empty hotel room [where he raped him].

"'oh wow' I perked up all the time thinking snuff film snuff film snuff film murder plot present, I presented offer of assistance. Luke said sure, then told me more, about his old boyfriend gillian, what he taught him. and about ginger and this one dominatrix who lives on the 10th floor."

[Second] Redacted E-Mail

Jovanovic answered, shortly thereafter on November 19th, "[t]hen he got you? How suspenseful," although the court precluded the first four words, "[t]hen he got you?" The complainant's response on November 20th, contained a further personal confession that the court also deleted from the evidence, in which the complainant had replied, "No duh, there's more, more interesting than sex, yes he did catch me, no sex, but he was a sadomasochist and now I'm his slave and its [sic] painful, but the fun of telling my friends 'hey I'm a sadomasochist' more than outweighs the torment."

[Third] Redacted E-Mail

Jovanovic's responsive e-mail on November 20th said, "You're submissive sometimes? Should have told me earlier." The complainant's next message in reply, also on November 20th included the following critical information, which was also redacted: "and yes, I'm what those happy pain fiends at the Vault call a 'pushy bottom'."[4]

While the vast majority of the electronic correspondence between Jovanovic and the complainant was introduced into evidence, the preclusion of the foregoing statements . . . had an enormous impact on the defense. Basically, it left the jury with a distorted view of the events. Moreover, in the absence of proof that Jovanovic had reason to believe, prior to their meeting, that they both had intended to participate in consensual, nonviolent sadomasochism that night, his ability to testify in a credible manner as to this defense was irreparably impaired. Indeed, the limitation imposed by the court served to insulate the complainant from being fully cross-examined even as to those statements which were admitted into evidence, which evinced or implied some degree of interest in sadomasochism.

---

[4] The defense explains that The Vault is a club catering to sadomasochists, and a "pushy bottom" is a submissive partner who pushes the dominant partner to inflict greater pain.

These messages were ruled inadmissible on the ground that they were covered by the protection of the Rape Shield Law (Crim. Proc. L. § 60.42), in that they constituted evidence of the complainant's prior sexual conduct, having the effect of demonstrating her "unchastity." In addition to the messages themselves, based upon the trial court's understanding of the Rape Shield Law, Jovanovic was precluded from questioning either the complainant or Luke as to whether the two had mutually engaged in consensual sadomasochism . . . For the following reasons, we conclude that the Rape Shield Law (Crim. Proc. L. § 60.42) does not support the ruling precluding Jovanovic from inquiring into the full complement of the complainant's statements to him.

The Statute

The Rape Shield Law represents a rejection of the centuries-old legal tradition holding that, as Professor Wigmore stated, "the character of a woman as to chastity is of considerable probative value in judging the likelihood of [her] consent" (1 Wigmore, A Treatise on the Anglo-American System of Evidence in Trials at Common Law § 62, at 464 [3d ed 1940]). No longer does our society generally accept the premise that a woman who is "unchaste," i.e., unmarried and sexually active, is more likely than a "chaste" woman to consent to the sexual advances of any man. It is because society now views such evidence as generally irrelevant that the Legislature enacted a law prohibiting the use of such evidence: the law "bar[s] harassment of victims and confusion of issues through raising matters relating to the victims' sexual conduct that have *no proper bearing* upon the defendant's guilt or innocence" (Preiser, Practice Commentaries, McKinneys Cons Laws of NY, Book 11A, Crim. Proc. L. § 60.42, at 9 [emphasis added]; *See also*, Berger, *Man's Trial, Woman's Tribulation: Rape Cases in the Courtroom*, 77 Colum L Rev. 1, 15-22). Thus, it is critical to the theory behind the Rape Shield Law that evidence of the victim's character for chastity is generally irrelevant to a rape prosecution.

In accordance with this premise, Crim. Proc. L. § 60.42 provides that, "Evidence of a victim's *sexual conduct* shall not be admissible in the prosecution for [a sex] offense or an attempt to commit [a sex] offense unless such evidence:

1. proves or tends to prove specific instances of the victim's prior sexual conduct with the accused; or
2. proves or tends to prove that the victim has been convicted of [prostitution] within three years prior to the sex offense which is the subject of the prosecution; or
3. rebuts evidence introduced by the people of the victim's failure to engage in sexual intercourse, [oral sexual conduct, anal sexual conduct] or sexual contact during a given period of time; or
4. rebuts evidence introduced by the people which proves or tends to prove that the accused is the cause of pregnancy or disease of the victim, or the source of semen found in the victim; or
5. is determined by the court after an offer of proof by the accused outside the hearing of the jury, or such hearing as the court may require, and a statement by the court of its findings of fact essential to its determination, to be relevant and admissible in the interests of justice" (emphasis added).

The importance of this statute is in no way diminished by the discussion and conclusions that follow. We fully recognize that a woman's character or reputation for chastity is irrelevant to a charge that she was sexually assaulted. Our holding is simply that the Rape Shield Law, by its terms, is inapplicable to the evidence the trial court held to be inadmissible . . .

Although the Rape Shield Law is grounded upon a recognition that evidence of a victim's character for chastity is generally irrelevant to a rape prosecution, even the drafters of Rape Shield legislation recognized that information about the victim's past sexual conduct is not *always* irrelevant. Indeed, the inclusion of exceptions within Crim. Proc. L. § 60.42 is due to our Legislature's recognition of the possibility that certain types of sexual history evidence will be relevant. The bill was specifically drafted "to strike a reasonable balance between protection of a victim's privacy and reputation while not infringing on the defendant's right to a fair trial based on the presumption of innocence." A blanket exclusion which covered clearly *relevant* sexual conduct evidence would unduly circumscribe a defendant's constitutional right to cross-examine witnesses and present a defense. Consequently, for instance, "the bill deems proof of the victim's past sexual conduct with the accused or acts of prostitution as relevant," and, accordingly, creates an exception for such evidence. By the same token, the "interests of justice" exception contained in subdivision (5) of the statute was included to ensure that relevant evidence not otherwise admissible could be introduced.

[T]he redacted communications from the complainant to Jovanovic . . . fall within several of the exceptions contained in the statute.

First, given the highly intimate nature of some of this information, the statements, as a practical matter, should be viewed as the equivalent of "prior sexual conduct with the accused" (subd [1]). These statements, made to Jovanovic in the context of a relationship being developed on-line, as part and parcel of the ongoing conversation that led up to their in-person encounter, are really part of the complainant's verbal repartee with him, in which each participant tells the other of their interests and preferences. Viewed with the purpose of her statements in mind, even if the Rape Shield Law were to apply to statements, the redacted statements should therefore have been held to be admissible as falling within the first exception to the Rape Shield Law (Crim. Proc. L. § 60.42 [1]).

The exception for past conduct with the accused is included in the statute because a "history of intimacies" would "tend to bolster a claim of consent" (Berger, *op. cit.*, at 58). The statements here, especially in view of their intimate nature, have the same sort of potential of shedding light on the motive, intent, and state of mind of these two people in their subsequent encounter...

[Second], given the relevance of the redacted statements to the issues presented to the jury, even if none of the statute's other exceptions covered the complainant's statements to Jovanovic, the "interests of justice" exception of Crim. Proc. L. § 60.42 (5) would be applicable. That exception was included in order to give courts discretion to admit what was otherwise excludable under the statute, where it is determined that the evidence is relevant.

Even if no other exception applied, the precluded communications from the complainant to Jovanovic were highly relevant. The defense did not seek to introduce them to demonstrate the complainant's "unchastity" and thereby impugn her character or her honesty. Instead, the fact that the complainant made these statements to Jovanovic is relevant to establish that she purposefully conveyed to Jovanovic an interest in engaging in consensual sadomasochism with him.

Because the jury could have inferred from the redacted e-mail messages that the complainant had shown an interest in participating in sadomasochism with Jovanovic, this evidence is clearly central to the question of whether she consented to the charged...sexual abuse. The People emphasize that it is not whether she initially consented that is relevant, but whether she withdrew her consent and whether defendant continued to act despite the withdrawal of consent. However, the strength of the evidence as to the extent to which the complainant initially indicated to Jovanovic an interest in participating in sadomasochism with him *is* relevant to a determination of whether that consent was withdrawn.

Furthermore, the e-mails Jovanovic received from the complainant, particularly her statements, "now I'm his slave and its [*sic*] painful, but the fun of telling my friends 'hey I'm a sadomasochist' more than outweighs the torment," and "yes, I'm what those happy pain fiends at the Vault call a 'pushy bottom,'" could illuminate Jovanovic's understanding and beliefs as to the complainant's willingness to participate in sadomasochism with him, and, as such, are also relevant to Jovanovic's state of mind...

We conclude that the trial court's rulings erroneously withheld from the jury a substantial amount of highly relevant, admissible evidence...

Accordingly, the judgment of the Supreme Court, New York County...convicting defendant, after a jury trial, of...sexual abuse in the first degree...should be reversed...and the matter remanded for a new trial.

Mazzarelli, J. P. (concurring in part and dissenting in part).

While I agree with the majority's conclusion that a new trial is required because the trial court misapplied the Rape Shield Law when it precluded material evidence which may have affected the conviction on the kidnapping and sex abuse counts, a different perspective informs my analysis...

With respect to the redacted e-mails, I would also find that the complainant's statements concerning her interest in sadomasochistic practices should have been admitted, because the Rape Shield Law, which is designed to preclude introduction of "[e]vidence of a victim's sexual conduct," is not meant to exclude statements of interest in sex...

However,...I would...find that the [second] redacted November 20th e-mail was properly redacted because it concerned a direct statement relating to the complainant's prior conduct, her sadomasochistic relationship with her boyfriend. This redaction was also appropriate because the transmission described behavior which would serve only to disparage the complaining witness's reputation...

Unlike the majority, I would not find the [second] redacted November 20th e-mail admissible under...the interest of justice exception to the Rape Shield Law. Since Crim. Proc. L. § 60.42 (5) is designed to allow the introduction of material which has been deemed presumptively inadmissible, the proffered evidence merits careful scrutiny. Given the complainant's right to sexual self-determination, I would find that the inflammatory nature of the evidence of her prior sexual conduct would, in the eyes of the jury, outweigh the probative value of this evidence. Presenting this information could mislead the jury to conclude that the complainant was more likely to consent to the charged sexual offenses because she had previously consented to similar, violent acts...

The Rape Shield Law was expressly drafted for the purpose of protecting those persons who are sexually active outside a legally sanctioned relationship. It serves the very important policy objective of removing certain impediments to the reporting of sex crimes. Specifically, the law was drafted to encourage victims of sex offenses to prosecute their attackers without fear that their own prior sexual activities, regardless of their nature, could be used against them at trial. In enacting the Rape Shield Law, the Legislature sought to prevent muddling the trial with matters relating to a victim's prior sexual conduct which have no proper bearing on the defendant's guilt or innocence, but only serve to impugn the character of the complainant and to prejudice the jury. To limit its applicability and protections as the majority holds would only serve to turn the clock back to the days when the main defense to any such charge was to malign the complainant. Here, where a victim's sexual preferences are widely disapproved, it is crucial that evidentiary determinations be made with heightened concern that a jury may act on the very prejudices that the statute seeks to exclude.

German Federal Court of Justice
1 StR 521/98, BGHSt 44, 228 (November 3, 1998)

Facts

The defendant and the victim were in a car on the night of October 21, 1997, on the return journey from a meeting when the defendant tried to make sexual advances towards the victim. In spite of repeated pleas by the victim to stop, and to let her get out, he drove to "the car park by the Waldsee." There he parked "in front of a small piece of woodland not 100 m from the nearest house in the residential area." The frightened victim, who had seen a light in a house, tried several times to reach the house. She was however held fast by the defendant and dragged back into the car. After the last attempt to escape "he grabbed her hand and carried her struggling back to the car." There he had unprotected sexual intercourse with the resisting victim against her will. The regional court sentenced the defendant, a Turkish national, to two years and eleven months imprisonment for rape.

The public prosecutor's office raised a substantive complaint by its appeal in law lodged against the defendant. The appeal pursued by the Chief Federal Prosecutor was successful in relation to the sentence.

Reasons

II.

The regional court has correctly convicted the defendant of rape under § 177 para. 1 no. 1 Criminal Code in the version of the 33rd Criminal Law Amendment Act (33. StrÄndG) of July 1, 1997 (BGBl I, 1607) applying at the time of the crime. It has however rejected the presence of the third alternative of § 177 para. 1 Criminal Code, because, in the case of application of force as the method of committing the crime, "no room" existed "for the alternative of exploitation of a defenseless situation which the legislature has introduced to close gaps in the law." Such a situation was "not present due to the nearness of houses and the victim's resistance which was merely insufficient." This view does not stand up to legal examination.

1. The regional court admittedly correctly assumed that the third alternative in § 177 para. 3 Criminal Code (exploitation of a situation in which the victim is defenseless and at the mercy of the perpetrator's influence) was inserted by the 33rd Statute for the Amendment of Criminal Law (33. StrÄndG) with the objective of closing gaps in the law. It was to cover cases in which no force is exercised, nor is there a threat of present danger to the life or limb the victim, but the victim allows the act to take its course out of fear of the perpetrator because she finds herself in a hopeless situation and resistance appears to her to be ineffectual (BT-Dr 13-7324, pp. 2, 6; see BGH, Judgment of September 8, 1998, 1 StR 439/98). It is not possible however to draw from this goal pursued by the legislature the conclusion propounded by the regional court that the third alternative only applies if neither of the first two alternatives is fulfilled.

... The wording itself of § 177 para. 1 Criminal Code which links each of the three alternatives through the word "or" and thereby treats them as being of equal status argues against the assumption of a definition which merely takes effect subsidiarily ... The classification of the third alternative as of equal status to the two other alternatives of § 177 para. 1 Criminal Code can additionally be based on the legislative materials. According to these, the exploitation of a situation in which the victim is defenseless and exposed to the perpetrator's influence should be expressly placed as the third alternative besides the methods of committing the crime of "force" and "threat of present danger to life or limb" ...

2. The regional court was accordingly not prevented on legal grounds from affirming the presence of the third alternative of § 177 para. 1 Criminal Code in addition to the first alternative ... It has however

additionally found that the victim was not defenseless and exposed to the defendant's influence. This does not stand up to examination.

. . . [A] hopeless situation is present when the victim's opportunities for protection and defense are diminished to such a degree that the victim is exposed to the unimpeded influence of the perpetrator (see BGHSt 22, 178f.; BGHSt 24, 90, 93) . . .

b) The victim accordingly finds herself as a rule in a hopeless situation when she sees herself alone confronted with the perpetrator, and cannot reckon upon another person's help. It is not necessary that every opportunity for defense should be completely eliminated. Therefore the view referred to by the regional court that the victim was capable of resistance "that was merely insufficient" was not appropriate to deny the existence of a hopeless situation in the sense of the third alternative . . .

c) According to the findings made, the victim found herself in a defenseless situation in the sense of the third alternative of § 177 para. 1 Criminal Code . . . She was in the car park by the Waldsee with the defendant alone and was carried by him back to the parked car in the end, in spite of her attempts to escape and her resistance. The nearest residential area was admittedly "not 100 m away," but still so far distant that the victim could not simply get there. Besides this it was night-time and a light was still burning in one house only. In view of these circumstances help from others was improbable. The defendant had obviously deliberately exploited this by heading for the car park by the Waldsee.

III.

The sentence cannot remain as a result of the changed legal assessment.

1. When a perpetrator by his action fulfils two crime definitions, it can have the effect of increasing the punishment . . .

2. As the sentence is accordingly to be quashed, it can remain open whether the further objection of the public prosecutor's office is justified that the regional court in determining the sentence incorrectly took account of the fact that the defendant was a foreigner. However, the Senate observes with regard to the new trial:

The fact that a defendant is a foreigner does not in any case justify on its own the finding of increased sensitivity as to punishment which must be taken into account so as to reduce the sentence. Whether the execution of a sentence of imprisonment has unusual effects on a perpetrator depends on his overall personal circumstances, which can also include problems of communication, different habits of life and impeded family contacts (see BGHSt 43, 233, 234: . . .).

The regional court has not found anything of this kind. It can instead be deduced from the judgment that the defendant has been living in Germany since 1972, is employed here as a factory worker, and has started a family. In these circumstances, it is unlikely that the defendant, who has obviously transferred the focus of his life to Germany, is particularly sensitive to punishment because his is of foreign nationality (see BGHR StGB § 46 para. 2 Lebensumstände 17).

Tatjana Hörnle, "Penal Law and Sexuality: Recent Reforms in German Criminal Law," 3 *Buffalo Criminal Law Review* (2000), 639

Sexual offenses . . . in the German Criminal Code [have been frequently revised] during the last thirty years . . . The first reform movement took place in the late 1960s and early 1970s . . . In this period, the basic assumptions about the reasons for penal norms governing sexual behavior changed. Since the enactment of the German Criminal Code (StGB) in the nineteenth century, the relevant section was labeled "Offenses against Morality" (Straftaten wider die Sittlichkeit). In 1973, this was changed to Offenses against Sexual Autonomy, in order to reflect the fact that these rules protect the rights of individuals, not morality. The general tendency of the early reform movement can be described coherently by the word "liberalization." Many provisions that reflected traditional morals were abolished because the offenses described were not harmful to a person. For example, consensual homosexual acts between male adults were punishable in Germany until 1969, paid homosexual contact until 1973 . . . The 1969 reform of the German Criminal Code also decriminalized adultery and bestiality. Laws governing pornography were also liberalized. The reform of 1973 legalized, in principle, the distribution of pornography among adults; however, the law contains numerous restrictions to prevent distribution to children and juveniles.

. . . Sexual offenses began to occupy the legislature again in the 1990s. The first topic addressed during this second wave of changes was the treatment of pornographic materials depicting sex with children. Provisions governing the sexual abuse of juveniles were reformed in 1994. One major project was the modification of sexual abuse and rape in 1997. [O]ne year later ... the definitions of a number of sexual offenses [were revised].

... The second wave of German reform projects is entirely different from the first. The legislative work in the 1960s and 1970s abolished or narrowed criminal provisions. The [recent] tendency reverses this trend: Each of the reform acts just mentioned extended the reach of the criminal law. The number of offenses is growing, offense descriptions have been expanded to include more forms of behavior, and sentence length ranges have been increased to provide for aggravated punishments. In addition, regulations concerning parole and preventive forms of confinement have been stiffened.

... The reform laws governing sexual abuse and rape probably cannot be explained without reference to the work of female writers who exposed the gender-based views of male legislators, lawyers, and judges. After several futile attempts, the feminist critique finally gained influence in parliament and paved the way for a new definition of the conduct constituting sexual abuse and rape. The more stringent laws passed in 1998 were influenced by a markedly increased public interest in, and awareness of, sex offenses, especially offenses with child victims ... Another strand of argument criticizes the entire corpus of laws in the 1990s for this intensification of the scope and severity of the criminal law. If the first wave can be characterized as liberalization, one could label the second as an "anti-liberal backlash." ...

1. Rape and Sexual Abuse

a) Force, Threat, and Defenselessness

As I have already mentioned, the official title of the sexual offenses-section of the German Criminal Code [since 1973 has been] "Offenses Against Sexual Autonomy." For the American reader, this might be misleading: The choice of words does not imply that the German legislature favors a comprehensive protection of sexual autonomy similar to those which Stephen Schulhofer advocates in his recent book, *Unwanted Sex: The Culture of Intimidation and the Failure of Law*. On the contrary, many acts that violate another person's right to sexual autonomy could not be punished until 1997, and some are still beyond the reach of the criminal law today. Until 1997, German law followed the traditional approach to defining prohibited behavior, which still is characteristic in most U.S. states: Sexual acts performed against the other person's will were punishable only if the offender applied *physical force* or *threatened to do so*. Criminal punishment was not possible, however, if the circumstances allowed the offender to compel non-consensual sex without resorting to physical violence or threats of violence.

In addition to the narrow legislative choice, German courts tended to limit the criminal law's reach even further. The highest German court, the Bundesgerichtshof, employs a restrictive interpretation of force ...

With respect to the force or threat requirement, there are remarkable parallels between the German and American discussion ... German commentators have justly criticized the Bundesgerichtshof because its narrow reading of the rape provision does not adequately protect the victims' interests. Paradoxically, the Court's ruling required the victims to fight, even in completely hopeless situations, at remote places, or in the face of an offender obviously much stronger, thereby forcing the victim to risk serious injury or death. The more "sensible victim" had to see the assailant acquitted in court.

The reformulation of Section 177 of the German Criminal Code in 1997 eased these problems considerably by extending the criminal law's protective reach. In addition to force and threat, a third variation of criminal behavior was introduced: Now sexual abuse or rape can also occur if the offender takes advantage of a situation in which the victim is defenseless in the offender's hands. The reasons given for the new law state that an offender deserves punishment when "the victim surrenders without resistance because she was in a powerless position, and resistance was pointless due to the superiority of the offender." The reasoning continues arguing that especially offenses in which the offender takes the victim to a deserted place and the victim is alone with the physically superior offender should no longer go unpunished.

Interpreting the crucial phrases "powerless position" and "superiority" expansively, one could include situations where the victim yielded to *social pressure*, for example, when an employer threatens an employee with discharge. The addition in the legislative reasoning concerning "deserted place" cases does not necessarily restrict the law's scope; as the use of the word "especially" leaves the application to other types of situations open. It is, however, very unlikely that such a broad reading will be adopted by the German courts. Most commentators reject the notion of social pressure as irrelevant and reduce the definition of "powerless position" to *physical circumstances* that limit the victim's ability to run away or to fight the offender. This is the case, for example, when the victim is alone in an apartment with the offender without being able to flee or when the victim's physical or mental capacities are impaired ... For instance, under the new German law grabbing a stranger in a remote place, carrying her into the woods, and having sex with her constitutes a sexual offense, even if the victim does not resist because she is terrified. The result would be the same if a man noticed a severely drunk woman in a bar, carried her to a booth, and had sex with her.

German authors do not uniformly approve of this extension of rape and sexual abuse to situations of physical helplessness. Some regard it as too wide. Others require that the offender not only makes use of the victim's powerless position, but also *creates* the powerless position. Accordingly, the man who meets a biking or jogging woman in a deserted place, or the man who encounters a drunk woman, could not be punished if the victim were smart enough not to endanger herself with futile resistance...[T]his distinction is irrelevant from a victim's perspective. The situation is no less threatening, and the incident no less harmful, when the victim is surprised in a powerless situation which the offender did not create.

With the amendment governing situations in which the victim is powerless, the new German Penal Law covers cases that clearly are worthy of punishment, though they once went unpunished. In addition to the examples of stranger rape just mentioned, the legal provisions also apply to some standard constellations of acquaintance or date rape. Particularly in such cases, lack of physical resistance on the woman's part, and thus, the fact that the man did not need to use force, traditionally excluded criminal sanctions (both in the US and Germany), even when the woman made it unmistakably clear that she did not want sex. When the perpetrator and his victim are in a locked room or apartment, or when persons on a date drive to a remote place before the situation escalates, the new wording in the German Criminal Code now allows for punishment. Obviously, the new language neither remedies the problem that the offender who is acquainted with his victim typically will claim that she consented (or at least that he mistakenly thought she did), nor the problem that acquaintance rape is less likely to be prosecuted vigorously in the criminal justice system... Situations not covered by the new wording remain.... The new German law still imposes duties upon the victims. Even though the victim is no longer required to resist a physically superior man, she still has a duty to run away or to seek help if possible. This raises the question of whether the protective reach of the criminal law should exclude those who, for personal reasons, are less capable of protecting their own interests. Interestingly, New York law employs a more comprehensive approach: Section 130.55 New York Penal Law (sexual abuse in the third degree) prohibits sexual acts with another person without the other's consent.

Despite the improved protection for victims provided by contemporary German criminal law, there still is reason to think critically about the general outline of rape law: Should the offenders' observable behavior matter, or should the issue of the victims' consent be emphasized? (Of course, an offense based on lack of consent would need to carry a shorter sentence than an offense based on the use of force and the exploitation of the victim's helplessness). With respect to these topics, the German discussion lags behind the American... The issue of consent is important in German criminal law, but only insofar as actual consent precludes punishment for any sexual offense (except in the cases of vulnerable victims...). The question of how far lack of consent as such, or clearly expressed verbal protests should matter beyond the narrow scope of positive law has been largely neglected. [U]nder German law, one can ignore verbal protests against one's sexual acts without necessarily committing an offense. German penal theorists argue that only the more severe forms of coercion deserve punishment.

This view is, however, hard to justify. It cannot be reconciled with a comparative evaluation of the harm caused by different offenses. From the victim's perspective, an unwanted intrusion into the most personal and intimate area of life is not a minor incident—provided the contact is more than a brief touching. Unwanted sexual contacts are humiliating and degrading. Compared to simple property offenses, the negative impact of sexual offenses on the quality of the victims' life is far more profound, especially in situations involving the most demeaning sexual impositions such as forced intercourse or other forms of penetration. It is thus the *unwanted sexual contact as such*—and not the accompanying force or threat—which is at the core of the harm done through sexual offenses.

...

d) Marital Status

The most hotly debated question in the recent German legislative reform concerns the issue of rape within marriage...The exemption for marital rape was abolished.... The struggle to end unfair benefits for rapists who are married to their victims developed in similar ways in both countries. Political resistance to the inclusion of rape or other forced, degrading sexual contact within marriage slowly weakened. Finally, in the 1990s, all German political parties agreed that the right to determine freely and independently the occurrence of sexual acts is not dependent upon marital status. Marriage does not permit the enforcement of sexual relations against one partner's will...

N.Y. Penal Law

§ 130.05 Sex offenses; lack of consent

1. Whether or not specifically stated, it is an element of every offense defined in this article that the sexual act was committed without consent of the victim.

2. Lack of consent results from:
(a) Forcible compulsion; or
(b) Incapacity to consent; or
(c) Where the offense charged is sexual abuse or forcible touching, any circumstances, in addition to forcible compulsion or incapacity to consent, in which the victim does not expressly or impliedly acquiesce in the actor's conduct; or
(d) Where the offense charged is rape in the third degree as defined in subdivision three of section 130.25 [nonconsensual sexual intercourse], or criminal sexual act in the third degree as defined in subdivision three of section 130.40 [nonconsensual oral or anal sexual conduct], in addition to forcible compulsion, circumstances under which, at the time of the act of intercourse, oral sexual conduct or anal sexual conduct, the victim clearly expressed that he or she did not consent to engage in such act, and a reasonable person in the actor's situation would have understood such person's words and acts as an expression of lack of consent to such act under all the circumstances.

3. A person is deemed incapable of consent when he or she is:
(a) less than seventeen years old; or
(b) mentally disabled; or
(c) mentally incapacitated; or
(d) physically helpless; or
(e) committed to the care and custody or supervision of the state department of corrections and community supervision or a hospital, as such term is defined in subdivision two of section four hundred of the correction law, and the actor is an employee who knows or reasonably should know that such person is committed to the care and custody or supervision of such department or hospital . . . ; or
(f) committed to the care and custody of a local correctional facility, as such term is defined in subdivision two of section forty of the correction law, and the actor is an employee, not married to such person, who knows or reasonably should know that such person is committed to the care and custody of such facility . . . ; or
(g) committed to or placed with the office of children and family services and in residential care, and the actor is an employee, not married to such person, who knows or reasonably should know that such person is committed to or placed with such office of children and family services and in residential care . . . ; or
(h) a client or patient and the actor is a health care provider or mental health care provider charged with rape in the third degree as defined in section 130.25 [nonconsensual sexual intercourse], criminal sexual act in the third degree as defined in section 130.40 [nonconsensual oral or anal sexual conduct], . . . , or sexual abuse in the third degree as defined in section 130.55 [nonconsensual sexual contact], and the act of sexual conduct occurs during a treatment session, consultation, interview, or examination.

Canadian Criminal Code

§ 265

Assault

265. (1) A person commits an assault when
(a) without the consent of another person, he applies force intentionally to that other person, directly or indirectly;
(b) he attempts or threatens, by an act or a gesture, to apply force to another person, if he has, or causes that other person to believe on reasonable grounds that he has, present ability to effect his purpose; or
(c) while openly wearing or carrying a weapon or an imitation thereof, he accosts or impedes another person or begs.

Application

(2) This section applies to all forms of assault, including sexual assault, sexual assault with a weapon, threats to a third party or causing bodily harm and aggravated sexual assault.

Consent

(3) For the purposes of this section, no consent is obtained where the complainant submits or does not resist by reason of
(a) the application of force to the complainant or to a person other than the complainant;
(b) threats or fear of the application of force to the complainant or to a person other than the complainant;
(c) fraud; or
(d) the exercise of authority.

Accused's belief as to consent

(4) Where an accused alleges that he believed that the complainant consented to the conduct that is the subject-matter of the charge, a judge, if satisfied that there is sufficient evidence and that, if believed by the jury, the evidence would constitute a defence, shall instruct the jury, when reviewing all the evidence relating to the determination of the honesty of the accused's belief, to consider the presence or absence of reasonable grounds for that belief.

§ 271

Sexual assault

271. Everyone who commits a sexual assault is guilty of
(a) an indictable offence and is liable to imprisonment for a term not exceeding 10 years and, if the complainant is under the age of 16 years, to a minimum punishment of imprisonment for a term of one year . . .

§ 272

Sexual assault with a weapon, threats to a third party or causing bodily harm

272.(1) Every person commits an offence who, in committing a sexual assault,
(a) carries, uses or threatens to use a weapon or an imitation of a weapon;
(b) threatens to cause bodily harm to a person other than the complainant;
(c) causes bodily harm to the complainant; or
(d) is a party to the offence with any other person.

Punishment

(2) Every person who commits an offence under subsection (1) is guilty of an indictable offence and liable
(b) . . . to imprisonment for a term not exceeding fourteen years . . .

§ 273

Aggravated sexual assault

273.1 (1) Every one commits an aggravated sexual assault who, in committing a sexual assault, wounds, maims, disfigures or endangers the life of the complainant.

(2) Every person who commits an aggravated sexual assault is guilty of an indictable offence and liable
(b) . . . to imprisonment for life.

§ 273.1

Meaning of "consent"

273.1 (1) Subject to subsection (2) and subsection 265(3), "consent" means, for the purposes of sections 271, 272 and 273, the voluntary agreement of the complainant to engage in the sexual activity in question.

Where no consent obtained

(2) No consent is obtained, for the purposes of sections 271, 272 and 273, where

(a) the agreement is expressed by the words or conduct of a person other than the complainant;
(b) the complainant is incapable of consenting to the activity;
(c) the accused induces the complainant to engage in the activity by abusing a position of trust, power or authority;
(d) the complainant expresses, by words or conduct, a lack of agreement to engage in the activity; or
(e) the complainant, having consented to engage in sexual activity, expresses, by words or conduct, a lack of agreement to continue to engage in the activity . . .

§ 273.2

Where belief in consent not a defence

273.2 It is not a defence to a charge under section 271, 272 or 273 that the accused believed that the complainant consented to the activity that forms the subject-matter of the charge, where
(a) the accused's belief arose from the accused's
  (i) self-induced intoxication, or
  (ii) recklessness or wilful blindness; or
(b) the accused did not take reasonable steps, in the circumstances known to the accused at the time, to ascertain that the complainant was consenting.

German Criminal Code

§ 177 (Sexual Coercion; Rape)

(1) Who coerces another person
1. by force;
2. by threat of imminent danger to life or limb; or
3. by exploiting a situation in which the victim is defenseless and at the mercy of the offender,
to endure sexual acts by the offender or a third person on their own person or to engage in sexual activity with the offender or a third person, will be punished with imprisonment of not less than one year.

(2) In especially serious cases the punishment will be imprisonment of not less than two years. An especially serious case typically is present if
1. the offender performs sexual vaginal intercourse with the victim or performs similar sexual acts with the victim, or allows them to be performed on himself by the victim, which are of a particularly degrading nature, especially if they involve penetration of the body (rape); or
2. the offense is committed jointly by more than one person.

(3) The punishment will be imprisonment of not less than three years if the offender
1. carries a weapon or another dangerous instrument with him;
2. carries another instrument or other means with him for the purpose of preventing or overcoming the resistance of another person through force or threat of force; or
3. by the offense places the victim in danger of serious injury to health.

(4) The punishment will be imprisonment of not less than five years if the offender
1. uses a weapon or another dangerous instrument during the commission of the offense;
2. or if the offender
  a) seriously physically abuses the victim during the offense; or
  b) by the offenses place the victim in danger of death.

(5) In less serious cases under para. 1, the punishment will be imprisonment from six months to five years, in less serious cases under para. 3 and 4 imprisonment from one to ten years.

NOTES

1. During the last decade, not much has changed in German substantive criminal law with respect to sexual offenses in the area described above: sexual coercion and rape. In 1998, the legislature differentiated between rape (penetration, not only vaginal, but also oral and anal) as a special case of sexual coercion (§ 177 para. 2 StGB) and all other cases of sexual touching, which fall under the general label of "sexual coercion."

Section 177 StGB has remained unchanged since 1998. Public interest—and the attention of parliament—has shifted to sexual offenses against children and child pornography: with regard to such crimes, offense descriptions were extended, new offenses created and punishments increased in the last ten years. However, with regard to adult victims, the law still requires, besides lack of consent, additional elements such as force, threat with imminent danger for life or limb, or a defenseless position. There are a few other offense definitions in the section titled "Offenses against Sexual Autonomy" (or, in another translation, "Offenses against Sexual Self-Determination") that define acts as sexual abuse even if the victim was an adult: if the offender abused a certain, casuistically defined position of power in relationship to the victim. Under such circumstances, the question of consent is irrelevant; such forms of sexual abuse can be committed against hospital patients, prisoners, arrestees, or patients in psychotherapy or other medical treatment if the offender was a therapist, corrections officer, police officer etc.*

But the German Criminal Code still does not provide protection against sexual touching without consent in form of a general offense definition that focuses on lack of consent as the crucial element of wrongdoing. As a result, German criminal law protects sexual autonomy only partially. (Compare N.Y. Penal Law §§ 130.20 ("A person is guilty of sexual misconduct when: 1. He or she engages in sexual intercourse with another person without such person's consent . . . Sexual misconduct is a class A misdemeanor.").)

2. *Sexual autonomy.* Consider the recognition in the German Criminal Code of a category of offenses against sexual autonomy, and the attendant conception of sex offenses as violations of the legal good (*Rechtsgut*) of sexual autonomy. (As Tatjana Hörnle points out, this conception of sex offenses also has been proposed by some American writers, e.g., Stephen Schulhofer, "Taking Sexual Autonomy Seriously: Rape Law and Beyond," 11 *Law and Philosophy* (1992), 35, and *Unwanted Sex: The Culture of Intimidation and the Failure of Law* (1998).) Insofar as it regards sex offenses as violations of autonomy, does this view capture the specific nature, and the specific wrong, of these offenses? How does sexual autonomy relate to autonomy generally speaking, to privacy as a legal good and to human dignity? To other aspects of personal autonomy, such as physical, or psychological autonomy? Does the conceptualization of sex offenses as violations of sexual autonomy presuppose a general conception of crime as a violation of autonomy? Reclassifying sex offenses from "offenses against morality" to "offenses against sexual autonomy" qualified as a "liberal" reform insofar as it not only removed the legal assessment of sexual conduct from the moral realm but also, and more generally and arguably more importantly, did away with the category of "offenses against morality" altogether, thus rejecting the criminalization of immoral conduct of any kind (a position reaffirmed, if not necessarily respected, in cases considering the constitutionality of other criminal prohibitions, see the German Constitutional Court's judgment in the *Incest Case*, discussed in Chapter 3.B.). But does this liberal reclassification of sex *offenses* deprive them of their nature as *sex* offenses? Does integrating sex offenses into a generic liberal conception of crime and criminal law drain them of their essentially, and uniquely, gendered aspect, their grounding in the facts of endemic and deeply ingrained societal notions of gendered power, facts that feminist scholars so powerfully captured, documented, and interpreted over the course of several decades? How does a project to protect women's sexual autonomy through criminal law connect with a world in which "women are socialized to passive receptivity; may have or perceive no alternative to acquiescence; may prefer it to the escalated risk of injury and the humiliation of a lost fight; submit to survive"?[†]

In 1985, Canada fundamentally reconceptualized sex offenses by integrating them into the law of assault. There is no separate definition of sexual assault; instead sexual assault is treated as a form of the general crime of assault (Can. Crim. Code § 265 (above)), with follow-up provisions specifying aggravated forms of sexual assault (§§ 272, 273) and, most

---

* See Criminal Code §§ 174a–174c. (Compare N.Y. Penal Law § 130.05(3)(e)–(h).)
† Catharine A. MacKinnon, *Toward a Feminist Theory of the State* (1989), 172.

recently and significantly, setting out the "meaning of 'consent'" and the scope of the mistake of fact defense when applied to the lack of consent element in sexual assault cases (§§ 273.1, 273.2).

This reform tends to be portrayed as recognizing sexual assault as a violation of sexual autonomy, an aspect of personal autonomy (integrity, or dignity), which in turn is placed at the historical heart of "the common law":

> Society is committed to protecting the personal integrity, both physical and psychological, of every individual. Having control over who touches one's body, and how, lies at the core of human dignity and autonomy. The inclusion of assault and sexual assault in the Code expresses society's determination to protect the security of the person from any non-consensual contact or threats of force. The common law has recognized for centuries that the individual's right to physical integrity is a fundamental principle, "every man's person being sacred, and no other having a right to meddle with it, in any the slightest manner": see Blackstone's Commentaries on the Laws of England (4th ed. 1770), Book III, at p. 120. It follows that any intentional but unwanted touching is criminal.
>
> R. v. Ewanchuk, [1999] 1 S.C.R. 330.

Leaving aside the rather Whiggish account of English criminal law driving this passage from a leading Canadian Supreme Court's on consent in sexual assault cases, does the Canadian reform expand the scope of the criminal law's protection of violations of sexual autonomy at the price of normalizing sexual assault by denying a qualitative distinction between sex offenses and other offenses? Does the later addition of specific provisions addressing the key issue of consent in sex cases reflect this tension, and, if so, do these provisions resolve it, or merely highlight it?

3. *Consent.* A criminal law system that frames sex offenses as violations of the victim's sexual autonomy and defines sexual assault in terms of the absence of consent, without reference to traditional requirements of the use of force, or "forcible compulsion," inevitably will place particular pressure on the concept of consent. (Not that consent does not play a significant role in systems that retain some version of a force requirement, as illustrated by the detailed, and increasingly complex, N.Y. Penal Law provision on consent, § 130.05.) Consider Can. Crim. Code §§ 273.1, 273.2, which supplement the subsections on consent in the general assault provision, § 265(3)–(4), and set out a more narrowly drawn consent definition in sexual assault cases (requiring a "voluntary agreement of the complainant to engage in the sexual activity in question"), followed by a requirement that the accused "take reasonable steps, in the circumstances known to the accused at the time, to ascertain that the complainant was consenting," or be precluded from raising the defense of mistake of fact regarding the presence of consent.

The effort to come to grips with the central concept of consent in Canada's sexual autonomy based law of sexual assault has not been limited to the legislature. The Canadian Supreme Court has produced a number of opinions on the subject, most recently in a case that raised the question of the relevance, or indeed the possibility, of advance consent to sexual conduct. *R. v. J.A.*, [2011] 2 SCR 440. (More specifically, the issue was, in the words of the court, "whether a person can perform sexual acts on an unconscious person if the person consented to those acts in advance of being rendered unconscious.") Along the way, Chief Justice McLachlin provided the following remarks on the subject of "The Concept of Consent in the Jurisprudence":

> The jurisprudence has consistently interpreted consent as requiring a conscious, operating mind, capable of granting, revoking or withholding consent to each and every sexual act...
>
> As held by Major J. in R. v. Ewanchuk, [1999] 1 S.C.R. 330, "[t]he absence of consent... is subjective and determined by reference to the complainant's subjective internal state of mind towards the touching, at the time it occurred." The trier of fact must determine what was going on in the mind of the complainant in response to the touching... Moreover,... the complainant is not required to express her lack of consent. Rather, the absence of consent is established if the complainant was not experiencing the state of mind of consent while the sexual activity was occurring...

> The jurisprudence of this Court also establishes that there is no substitute for the complainant's actual consent to the sexual activity at the time it occurred. It is not open to the defendant to argue that the complainant's consent was implied by the circumstances, or by the relationship between the accused and the complainant. There is no defence of implied consent to sexual assault.
>
> The cases on the mens rea defence of honest but mistaken belief in consent take the same view. At common law, this was a standard defence of mistake of fact: the accused was not guilty if he honestly believed a state of facts, which, if true, would have rendered his conduct lawful: Pappajohn v. The Queen, 1980 CanLII 13 (SCC), [1980] 2 S.C.R. 120, at pp. 134 and 139. In *Ewanchuk*, this Court held that it is not sufficient for the accused to have believed that the complainant was subjectively consenting in her mind: "In order to cloak the accused's actions in moral innocence, the evidence must show that he believed that the complainant communicated consent to engage in the sexual activity in question." It thus is not sufficient for the accused to have believed the complainant was consenting: he must also take reasonable steps to ascertain consent, and must believe that the complainant communicated her consent to engage in the sexual activity in question...

The court concluded that "the tenor of the jurisprudence undermines" the concept of advance consent:

> The definition of consent for sexual assault requires the complainant to provide actual active consent throughout every phase of the sexual activity. It is not possible for an unconscious person to satisfy this requirement, even if she expresses her consent in advance. Any sexual activity with an individual who is incapable of consciously evaluating whether she is consenting is therefore not consensual within the meaning of the Criminal Code.

At what point does a consent requirement in the definition of an offense designed to protect sexual autonomy—or, for that matter, any other form, or aspect, of personal autonomy—become counterproductive? What limits, if any, does the victim's right to autonomy place on the interpretation of offenses meant to protect that right? (Compare, in this context, the discussion of consent, in Chapter 13.C, and of assisted suicide, in Chapter 15.A.v.)

Consider also provisions setting out situations in which consent to sexual conduct is impossible, based on the permanent or temporary individual incapacity to consent or on the relationship between the participants in the sexual activity. Do these provisions enhance, or protect, autonomy, or diminish it? See §§ 174a–174c, 179 Criminal Code; N.Y. Penal Law § 130.05(3)(e)–(h); see also *State v. Olivio*, 123 N.J. 550, 589 A.2d 597 (1991) ("The difficulty in making that determination [of the incapacity to consent based on mental defect] inheres in its implications for both mentally-defective persons who are vulnerable and need the special protection of our laws from the sexual intrusions of others and persons whose mental deficiencies need not be an impediment to the enjoyment of a reasonably normal life, including consensual sexual relations.").

4. When interpreting the elements "defenseless" and "at the mercy of the offender" in § 177 para. 1 no. 3 Criminal Code, the decisions of the German Federal Court of Justice tend to narrow the scope of application of this norm. If a healthy person who could have attempted physical resistance remained passive (and the offender therefore did not need to apply force), the norm will not apply unless the victim remained passive because he or she was physically weaker and feared bodily injury or death (see, e.g., Judgment of April 4, 2007, 4 StR 345/06, BGHSt 51, 280) and there was no opportunity to seek help from others or to escape. If the victim could have obtained help or escaped (but was too timid or too stressed to do so), German courts would not acknowledge a "defenseless situation" and the defendant would not be convicted. Therefore, in a case like *State v. Rusk*, the fact that the victim was on her own for several minutes while the defendant was in the bathroom would suffice for a German court to deny application of § 177 para. 1 no. 3. The fact that he still had her car keys probably would not change this outcome.

However, if it was proven that the offender did in fact choke the victim, this should be a straightforward case for the offense element "force"; everything that happened after this application of force ought to be considered as sexual coercion or rape if the choking made the victim endure or perform sexual acts. It is thus hard to understand why Justice Cole pointed out in the dissenting vote the circumstances *before* the choking (which might shed a negative light on the victim's presence of mind but that is not the legal question at stake). To hold that choking does not satisfy the element of "force" is to narrowly interpret "force" as requiring "disabling force." In German criminal law doctrine, it is common to distinguish between *vis absoluta* (absolute force, that would be: disabling force, such as knocking the victim unconscious or handcuffing) and *vis compulsiva* (coercive force, which does not aim to disable but to influence the victim's decision-making). It is uncontroversial that *vis compulsiva* suffices for any offense description that requires force. If the offender, for example, slaps the victim in the face to make her hand over money, "consent" to sex etc., this is considered "force" although it (other than *vis absoluta*) does not eliminate the option to still say no.

5. The German Code on Criminal Procedure does not contain restrictions on evidence about a victim's prior sexual conduct comparable to American rape shield laws, despite several German legislative projects during the last decades to improve the procedural position of victims. Such laws (e.g., the Second Law for the Protection of Victims of July 29, 2009, BGBl I, 2280) have introduced a number of provisions concerning better information and better support for victims in the German Code on Criminal Procedure (see, for instance, the section on rights for injured persons in §§ 406d–406h or witnesses' right to assistance by a legal counsel, § 68b). Also, it appears that the victim's rights movement in Germany is gaining strength, insofar as considerable public attention focuses on the issue of sexual abuse of children. However, it would be premature to generalize this phenomenon. One has to keep in mind, that, despite some compromises achieved by victim's rights groups (which were traditionally, compared to the United States, less powerful in the public arena), measures that seriously limit effective defense will meet strong resistance (from, among others, criminal defense lawyers, who exert considerable public influence). Accordingly, strategies of "blaming the victim" and specifically questions concerning prior sexual behavior by defense counsels are not blocked in German procedural criminal law. Section 68a German Code on Criminal Procedure asks that witnesses may only be asked questions concerning their personal sphere of life it this is strictly necessary. In practice, this does not come close to the effects of rape shield laws because defense attorneys will, of course, insist that illuminating the victim's sexual past is strictly necessary.

That said, having rape shield laws on the books is one thing. Enforcing them is another. In *Jovanovic*, the dissenter accuses the majority of "turn[ing] the clock back to the days when the main defense to [a rape] charge was to malign the complainant." Do you agree?

More generally, persistent efforts by liberal advocates of women's rights to protect the rights of victims of rape, and of domestic violence, in the criminal process bear no obvious relationship to the powerful conservative victims' rights movement in the United States, which formed an important part of the comprehensive tough-on-crime agenda of the so-called "war on crime" that produced the crisis of American mass incarceration documented in Chapter 1.A.*

---

* See generally Markus D. Dubber, *Victims in the War on Crime: The Use and Abuse of Victims' Rights* (2002).

OTHER OFFENSES

In this, the final, chapter on the special part of criminal law, we turn our attention to a grab bag of miscellaneous offenses that have little in common besides—hopefully—a shared potential for interesting, perhaps even revealing, comparative analysis. We begin by taking a parallel look at so-called hate crimes, in U.S. criminal law, and the criminalization of Holocaust denials in the German Criminal Code. Next up is the treatment (or non-treatment) in criminal law of misconduct by various state officials, including police officers, prosecutors, and judges, with particular attention to the fascinating German crime of law bending (*Rechtsbeugung*), a felony that criminalizes judicial decision-making for the benefit, or to the detriment, of a party. We then move on to two innovations of American criminal law, and U.S. federal criminal law in particular, that have proved to be popular tools in the various wars on organized crime, drug crime, or simply crime unmodified: RICO and money laundering. Our discussion of money laundering will take us full circle, back to the case of the money laundering interior decorators at the beginning of this book.

A. "Hate Crimes" and Holocaust Denial (§ 130 German Criminal Code)

The ill-defined category of "hate crimes," ranging from offenses that criminalize the commission of acts motivated by animus against one group or another to sentencing enhancements for ordinary offenses committed with that animus, has attracted much attention in the United States. While some see hate crime as the paradigm of crime, others argue that hate crimes punish inner motives, and run afoul of freedom of speech, or at least of thought. The crime of publicly denying the genocide "committed under the rule of National Socialism" (§ 130 Criminal Code) in German criminal law has escaped similar critical attention, although there has been some debate about the status of the offense as an endangerment offense and, relatedly, the legal good (*Rechtsgut*) it is designed to protect.

State v. Wyant
Supreme Court of Ohio
64 Ohio St. 3d 566 (1992)

Herbert R. Brown, Justice.

. . . [Ohio] Rev. Code § 2927.12 reads:

(A) No person shall violate section 2903.21, 2903.22, 2909.06, or 2909.07, or division (A)(3), (4), or (5) of section 2917.21 of the Revised Code by reason of the race, color, religion, or national origin of another person or group of persons.

(B) Whoever violates this section is guilty of ethnic intimidation. Ethnic intimidation is an offense of the next higher degree than the offense the commission of which is a necessary element of ethnic intimidation.

The statute creates enhanced criminal penalties for some people who commit aggravated menacing (Rev. Code § 2903.21), menacing (Rev. Code § 2903.22), criminal damaging or endangering

(Rev. Code § 2909.06), criminal mischief (Rev. Code § 2909.07), or certain types of telephone harassment (Rev. Code § 2917.21[A][3], [4], or [5]).

The predicate offenses to ethnic intimidation are already punishable acts under other statutes. [T]he enhanced penalty results solely from the actor's reason for acting, or his motive. We must decide whether a person's motive for committing a crime can support either a separate, additional crime, or an enhanced penalty for an existing crime.

Motive, in criminal law, is not an element of the crime. In their textbook, 1 Substantive Criminal Law (1986) 318, Section 3.6, LaFave and Scott argue that if defined narrowly enough, motive is not relevant to substantive criminal law, although procedurally it may be evidence of guilt, or, in the case of good motive, may result in leniency. Other thought-related concepts such as intent and purpose are used in the criminal law as elements of crimes or penalty-enhancing criteria, but motive itself is not punished.

There is a significant difference between why a person commits a crime and whether a person has intentionally done the acts which are made criminal. Motive is the reasons and beliefs that lead a person to act or refrain from acting. The same crime can be committed for any of a number of different motives. Enhancing a penalty because of motive therefore punishes the person's thought, rather than the person's act or criminal intent . . .

Culpable mental state, or intent, is usually required to find one guilty of a crime. "Intent" refers to the actor's state of mind or volition at the time he acts. Did A intend to kill B when A's car hit B's, or was it an accident? This is not the same as A's motive, which is why A intentionally killed B. When A murders B in order to obtain B's money, A's intent is to kill and the motive is to get money. One can have motive without intent, or intent without motive. For instance, the wife of a wealthy but disabled man might have a motive to kill him, and yet never intend to do so. A psychopath, on the other hand, may intend to kill and yet have no motive.

Purpose to commit an additional criminal act is frequently seen in criminal statutes as a basis for enhanced penalty or as creating a separate, more serious crime. For example, burglary is a trespass "with purpose" to commit a theft offense or felony. Purpose in this context is not the same as motive. What is being punished is the act of trespass, plus the additional act of theft, or the intent to commit theft. Upon trespassing, A's intent is to commit theft, but the motive may be to pay debts, to buy drugs, or to annoy the owner of the property. The object of the purpose is itself a crime. Thus the penalty is not enhanced solely to punish the thought or motive.

Criminal penalties are often enhanced using the concept of an aggravating circumstance. These also are distinguishable from motive. For example, under Rev. Code § 2929.04, any of a number of aggravating circumstances can increase the penalty for aggravated murder to death. Among these is murder committed "for the purpose of" escaping another offense. The basis for enhancing the penalty in this case is once again an additional act or intent. Escaping another offense is in itself a crime. The enhanced penalty for murder does not stem from motive (i.e., preference of life on the street to life in prison), but from the additional act of escape, or the intent to escape.

Rev. Code § 2929.04(A)(2) declares murder for hire to be an aggravating circumstance. This is not properly seen as enhancing the penalty for a mercenary motive. Hiring is a transaction. The greater punishment is for the additional act of hiring or being hired to kill. The motive for the crime (such as jealousy, greed or vengeance) is not punished.

Some aggravating circumstances involve the identity of the victim, such as a peace officer or governmental official. Rev. Code § 2929.04(A)(1), (6). The legislature has decided, in these instances, that acts against certain individuals are more serious criminal acts. Imposing a higher penalty for killing the Governor than for killing an ordinary citizen is similar to imposing a higher penalty for stealing a painting worth $1,000 than for stealing one worth only $5.

Under the above analysis, the legislature could decide that blacks are more valuable than whites, and enhance the punishment when a black is the victim of a criminal act. Such a statute would pass First Amendment analysis because the motive or the thought which precipitated the attack would not be punished. However, Rev. Code § 2927.12 could not have been written that way because such a statute would not survive analysis under the Equal Protection Clause of the Fourteenth Amendment to the United States Constitution . . .

Based upon the foregoing authorities and our analysis of the statute, we find that the effect of Rev. Code § 2927.12 is to create a "thought crime." This violates Section 11, Article I of the Ohio Constitution, and the First and Fourteenth Amendments to the United States Constitution.

Conduct motivated by racial or religious bigotry can be constitutionally punished under the criminal code without resort to constructing a thought crime. In fact, the behavior which is alleged in each case before us can be punished under the criminal statutes identified in Rev. Code § 2927.12 . . .

German Federal Court of Justice
1 StR 184/00, BGHSt 46, 212, NStZ 2001, 305 (December 12, 2000)
Töben Case

Facts

The defendant [Fredrick Töben; the Court, as usual, does not mention the name but the incident was well-reported in the media—Eds.], who was born in Germany in 1944, is an Australian citizen. He emigrated in 1954 with his parents to Australia. After he had studied Philosophy, German and English there, he came to Germany in 1970/1971 where he worked as a teacher in a technical college. Then he studied in Germany. In 1977 he went to Africa and in 1980 he returned to Australia and worked there as a teacher. In 1996 the defendant joined some like-minded people in Australia to form the "Adelaide Institute," of which he is the director. Since 1992 he has occupied himself with the Holocaust. He composed circular letters and articles which he made available over the internet, in which he propounded "revisionist" theses. These, under the pretext of academic research, disputed the murder of Jews committed under National Socialist rule and represented it as an invention of "Jewish circles" who thereby intended to pursue financial claims and to defame Germans politically. Three publications by the defendant are the subject matter of the conviction:

Internet case 1: Between April 1997 and March 1999—the exact point in time has not been established—the defendant stored on an Australian server websites which could be retrieved from the homepage of the Adelaide Institute via its internet address. These pages contained three English language articles by the defendant with the headings "About the Adelaide Institute," "Impressions of Auschwitz" and "More impressions of Auschwitz." In these it is stated, amongst other things: In the meantime we have established that the original number of four million dead at Auschwitz . . . was reduced to 800,000 at the most. This alone is good news, because it means that about 3.2 million people did not die in Auschwitz—a ground for celebration." "We declare proudly that so far there is no evidence that millions of people were killed in human gas chambers." "None of these assertions have ever been substantiated by any facts or written documents, with the exception of questionable statements by witnesses which have frequently sprung from the feverish brains of those who were after a pension from the German state."

Internet case 2: In August 1998 a local court judge convicted Günter Deckert because he had insulted Max Mannheimer, a survivor of Auschwitz. The defendant then wrote an "open letter" to the judge from Australia, and sent this at the same time to numerous further addressees, in Germany as well, and to, amongst others, the Berlin newspaper "Sleipnir." He inserted the English language text of the letter into the homepage of the Adelaide Institute. In the letter he accused Mannheimer of telling lies about Auschwitz, and he wrote, amongst other things: "I visited Auschwitz in April 1997 and on the basis of my own researches I have now reached the conclusion that in the war years the camp never had human gas chambers in operation."

Internet case 3: At the end of December 1998 / beginning of January 1999 the defendant inserted a further website into the homepage of the Adelaide Institute. This page contained an English language article by the defendant with the heading. " . . . New Year Thoughts, 1999." It stated, amongst other things: "In this first month of the penultimate year before the turn of the century, we can look back on a five year work and establish with certainty: The Germans never destroyed European Jews in deadly gas chambers in the concentration camp at Auschwitz or elsewhere. Therefore all Germans and ethnic Germans can live without the guilt complex forced on them by which a malignant way of thinking has enslaved them for half a century." "Even though Germans can now breathe a sigh of relief, they must prepare themselves for being further defamed, as people like Jeremy Jones of the organized Australian Jews do not change fundamentally overnight. Their Auschwitz cudgel was a good instrument for them which they have brandished against all those who are not in agreement with their political convictions in order to 'make them functional,' as Jones expresses himself."

The regional court could, in relation to the internet cases, neither establish that the defendant had on his own initiative dialed holders of online connections in Germany or anywhere else in order to communicate the web pages mentioned to them (to "push"), nor that internet users in Germany—except the investigating police officer—had dialed the homepage of the Adelaide Institute.

The regional court imposed on the defendant an overall sentence of imprisonment of ten months for insult* concomitantly with denigration of the memory of the dead† in three cases, and in one case

---

* [German Criminal Code (Insult) § 185
An insult will be punished with imprisonment of not more than one year or a fine and, if the insult is committed by means of an assault, with imprisonment of not more than two years or a fine.—Eds.]
† [German Criminal Code (Denigration of the Memory of the Dead) § 189]

(case 2) additionally concomitantly with incitement to hatred. The appeal in law of the public prosecutors office was mainly successful with its substantive objection.

Reasons

D.

Appeal in law of the public prosecutors office: The appeal in law of the public prosecutors office is mainly successful with its substantive objection; German criminal law applies also for incitement to hatred committed concomitantly in the internet cases 1 and 3.

I.

The statements in the internet cases 1 and 3 have a content of incitement to hatred under § 130 para. 1 nos. 1 and 2 Criminal Code as well as under § 130 para. 3 Criminal Code.

1. In both internet cases the so-called qualified Auschwitz lie (BGH, NStZ 1994, 140; BGHSt 40, 97) is present, which fulfils the definition of § 130 para. 1 no. 2 Criminal Code (abuse alternative) and § 130 para. 1 no. 2 Criminal Code (incitement alternative).

a) By the use of obviously untrue factual assertions (BVerfGE 90, 241; BGH, NStZ 1994, 140; NStZ 1995, 340) not only is the fate of the Jews under National Socialist rule represented as false history, but this assertion is also associated with the motive of alleged gagging and exploitation of Germany in favor of the Jews. In case 1 the qualification is particularly clear with the formulation:" ... frequently sprung from the feverish brains of those who were after a pension from the German state ," and in case 3 in particular by the formulation "guilt complex," "enslaved" and "Auschwitz cudgel."

b) The regional court has therefore accepted without legal error that the statement element of the definition in § 130 I no. 2 Criminal Code, at least in the form of insulting (see v. Bubnoff, in: LK-StGB, 11th edit., § 130 marginal no. 22), has occurred. An especially injurious form of contempt is present, in case 1 in particular by the formulation "a ground for celebration" and in case 3 in particular by the formulation "by which a malignant way of thinking has enslaved them for half a century long." As the assertions had a tendency to awaken and to stir up hostile feelings against the Jews in general and against Jews living in Germany, an attack against human dignity is also present (BGH, NStZ 1981, 258; see also BGHSt 40, 97, 100; v. Bubnoff, in: LK-StGB, § 130 marginal nos. 12, 18; Lenckner, in: Schönke/Schröder, StGB, 25th edit., § 130 marginal no. 7).

c) According to the findings, incitement to hatred in the sense of § 130 para. 1 no. 1 Criminal Code is also present (see on this BGHSt 31, 226 [231]; BGHSt 40, 97, 100; ... The findings substantiate that the statements were calculated to generate an increased hostility, going beyond mere disapproval and contempt, against Jews living in Germany (see BGHSt 40, 97, 102).

2. At the same time—and this is likewise charged—an act of genocide committed under National Socialist rule is denied and played down (§ 130 para. 3 Criminal Code). The internet pages personally composed by the defendant were directly accessible by an indeterminate—as to number and individuality—circle of persons and therefore public ...

3. . . . . .

4. The prerequisites of the clause which exempts from punishment in § 130 para. 5 Criminal Code in association with § 86 para. 3 Criminal Code* (see on this BGHSt, 46, 36) are not present. The statements do not facilitate science, research or teaching (BVerfG, Judgment of November 30, 1988, 1 BvR 900/88; BVerwG, NVwZ 1988, 933); they are also not protected by the basic right to free expression of opinion[†] (BVerfGE 90, 241; BVerfG, NJW 2001, 61).

Who denigrates the memory of a dead person will be punished with imprisonment of not more than two years or a fine.—Eds.]

   * [Section 130 para. 6 (formerly, at the time of the decision, § 130 para. 5) StGB refers to the "exemption from punishment" clause in § 86 para. 3 StGB. Section 86 StGB is titled "Dissemination of propaganda materials for unconstitutional organizations" (practically important for propaganda materials that pursue the goals of former National Socialist organizations. § 86 para. 1 no. 4 StGB). According to § 86 para. 3 StGB, the prohibitions do not apply if the act serves "civil education, control of movements against the Constitution, art or science, research or teaching, reporting about current events or history, or similar purposes."—Eds.]

   † [See Basic Law art. 5

(1) Every person has the right freely to express and disseminate his opinions in speech, writing, and pictures and to inform himself without hindrance from generally accessible sources. Freedom of the press and freedom of reporting in broadcasting and films are guaranteed. There shall be no censorship. (2) These rights find their limits in the provisions of general laws, in provisions for the protection of persons or minor age, and in the right to personal honor. (3) Art and science, research, and teaching are free. The freedom of teaching does not release from allegiance to the constitution.—Eds.]

5. The tendency to disturb the peace is a common element in § 130 para. 1, 3 Criminal Code which must accompany the statement.

a) The requirement of a tendency to disturb the peace renders incitement to hatred under § 130 para. 1 and 3 Criminal Code an abstract–concrete crime of endangerment see BGHSt, 39, 371 . . . ; this form of crime is also described by some as a "potential crime of endangerment" (BGH, NJW 1994, 2161; see also Sieber, NJW 1999, 2065, 2067, with further references). The categorization of the crime is of secondary significance; in any case, such crimes of endangerment are a subgroup of abstract crimes of endangerment (Senate, NJW 1999, 2129).

b) Therefore the occurrence of a concrete danger is not necessary for the tendency to disturb the peace (thus however Rudolphi, in: SK-StGB, 6th edit., § 130 marginal no. 10; Roxin, StrafR AT, vol. 1, 3rd edit., § 11 marginal no. 28; . . .). The judge of fact however is required to examine whether the action in question has a tendency to cause danger in the general view (see BGH, NJW 1999, 2129). What is necessary is a conclusive tendency to disturb the peace; it cannot just exist in the abstract, and must—even though on the basis of a generalizing view of the matter—be concretely established (Oberlandesgericht Hamburg, MDR 1981, 71; Oberlandesgericht Koblenz, MDR 1977, 334; Oberlandesgericht Köln, NJW 1981, 1280; v. Bubnoff, in: LK-StGB, § 130 marginal no. 4; . . . Streng, in: Festschr.f. Lackner, p. 140). Therefore, it is possible to present evidence showing that the tendency to disturb the peace is absent in an individual case . . .

d) Accordingly it suffices for the tendency to disturb the peace that justified—and therefore concrete—grounds are present for the fear that the attack will shake confidence in reliable protection provided by law (BGHSt 29, 26; BGHSt .46, 36; BGH, NStZ 1981, 258).

6. The acts had a tendency to disturb the public peace.

a) . . . In regard to the information opportunities on the internet, i.e., on the ground of actual circumstances, it had to be expected—and, according to the findings so far, it also mattered to the defendant—that the publications would become known to a wider public in Germany.

b) The defendant pursued the goal of disseminating revisionist theses, and he also intended that everyone worldwide—and therefore also in Germany—could read the articles. He also intended thereby actively to intervene in the formation of opinions by disseminating the theses in German "revisionist" circles, as the "open letter" with its circle of distributors shows in case 2.

c) It is obvious that the defendant's publications were automatically available to every internet user in Germany. The publications could also be further disseminated by German users within the country. The fact that it was German internet users—notwithstanding the use of the English language—who belonged, and were intended to belong, to the circle of addressees of the publications also in particular arises from their content, which has almost exclusive reference to Germany (for instance: "we are investigating the assertion that Germans systematically killed 6 million Jews"; "The hunting season for Germans has opened"; "Therefore all Germans and ethnic Germans can live without the guilt complex forced on them"; "Germans can be proud again").

d) The regional court has therefore correctly found that the defendant created a source of danger which had a tendency severely to disturb the flourishing mutual cooperation between Jews and other groups in the population and to impair Jews in their feeling of security and in their trust in protection by the law.

II.

German criminal law applies for the abstract–concrete crime of endangerment of incitement to hatred under § 130 para. 1 and 3 German Criminal Code in the internet cases. Its applicability arises from § 3 in combination with § 9 Criminal Code. This is because a crime within the country (§ 3 Criminal Code) is present, as the result belonging to the definition has occurred within the Federal Republic (§ 9 para 1 alternative 3 Criminal Code).

1. Interpretation of the element "result belonging to the definition" must follow the ratio legis of § 9 Criminal Code. According to the basic concept of the provision, German criminal law—even for criminal actions undertaken abroad—is to apply in so far as harm to legal interests or endangerment occurs within the country, the avoidance of which is the purpose of the criminal provision in question (BGHSt 42, 235, 242; Gribbohm, in: LK-StGB, 11th edit., § 9 marginal no. 24) . . .

2. Extensions of punishability beyond actual harm can be achieved by the legislature through various formulations of an endangerment crime. The legislature can create concrete endangerment crimes

(like § 315c Criminal Code*), or abstract-concrete (like §§ 130 para. 1 and 3, Criminal Code and purely abstract endangerment definitions (like § 316 Criminal Code [see BGH, Judgment of November 26, 1970, Chapter 15.A.iv—Eds.])... The fact that concrete crimes of endangerment—as a subgroup of result crimes—have a spatial place of result where concrete danger has occurred is widely undisputed (see only Gribbohm, in: LK-StGB, § 9 marginal no. 20, and Hilgendorf, NJW 1997, 1873, 1875, with further references). Abstract-concrete crimes of endangerment are situated between concrete and purely abstract endangerment crimes. They are comparable with concrete crimes of endangerment from the legal viewpoint which is relevant here of the place of result...

3. With abstract-concrete crimes of endangerment a result in the sense of § 9 Criminal Code has occurred where the act in question unfolds its danger in regard to the protected legal interest. In relation to incitement to hatred under § 130 para. 1 and 3 Criminal Code, this is the concrete tendency to disturb the peace in the Federal Republic of Germany (Collardin, CR 1995, 618: specific to the Auschwitz lie, if the perpetrator intends to operate in Germany; Kuner, CR 1996, 453 [456], on statements on the internet; Beisel/Heinrich, JR 1996, 95; ...).

This also corresponds with the legislature's intention in the creation of the definition of incitement to hatred in 1960. This intention was to oppose dynamism in advance of direct violations of human dignity which had been proved historically to be dangerous, and to counteract such developments at their earliest stages (Streng, p. 508: "climate protection").

In 1994, when the denial element was inserted in the definition in § 130 para. 3 Criminal Code, the legislature again emphasized the intention "of preventing the poisoning of the political climate by the playing down of the violent and arbitrary rule of National Socialism" (Report of the Legal Committee of the Dt. BT, BT-Dr 12/8558, p. 8; ...). The legislature therefore intended to provide criminal law protection in early stages; even the "poisoning of the political climate" was to be stopped. The creation of such a crime was—as the taking into account of the "political climate" shows—also determined by the fact that concrete endangerment or even an individual violation of a legal interest can only very seldom be traced directly back to an individual statement....

... In so far as a view is held by many in the legal literature that, abstract crimes of endangerment could have no place of result in the sense of § 9 Criminal Code (KG, NJW 1999, 3500; Gribbohm, in: LK-StGB, § 9 marginal no. 20; Tröndle/Fischer, § 9 marginal no. 3; Eser, in: Schönke/Schröder, StGB, 25th edit., § 9 marginal no. 6, Lackner/Kühl, § 9 marginal no. 2; Jakobs, StrafR AT, 2nd edit., p. 117; Horn/Hoyer, JZ 1987, 965 [966]; Tiedemann/Kindhäuser, NStZ 1988, 337 [346]; Cornils, JZ 1999, 394), these writers do not always distinguish sufficiently between purely abstract and abstract-concrete crimes of endangerment. But even where the view is held that abstract-concrete or potential crimes of endangerment—as a sub-case of abstract crimes of endangerment—had no place of result (Hilgendorf, NJW 1997, 1873; Satzger, NStZ 1998, 112) that is not convincing.

... By inclusion of the element of a (concrete) tendency to disturb the peace in the definition of § 130 para. 1 and 3 Criminal Code, the legislature has described the close relationship of the occurrence of the result to the definition of the crime, and thereby determined the result belonging to the definition...

4. For the application of German criminal law to incitement to hatred under § 130 para. 1 and 3 Criminal Code in cases of the present kind, a starting point providing legitimacy in public international law is present. The crime concerns an important legal interest within the country, which also shows a special objective connection with the territory of the Federal Republic of Germany (see Jescheck/Weigend, p. 179; Hilgendorf, NJW 1997, 1873 [1876]; Derksen, NJW 1997, 1878 [1880]; Martin, ZRP 1992, 19 [22]). The violation of this legal interest is to be stopped by this criminal provision. The speech crime under § 130 para. 1 Criminal Code protects parts of the domestic population in advance from direct violations of human dignity, and intends—because of Germany's special history—to counteract the instigation of an inherent dynamism proved historically to be dangerous. The denial element of the definition in § 130 para. 3 Criminal Code has a special connection to the Federal Republic of Germany on the ground of the uniqueness of the crimes committed against the Jews under National Socialist rule (see v. Bubnoff, in: LK-StGB, § 130 marginal no. 45; Lackner/Kühl, § 130 marginal no. 8a; Common measure of the Council of the European Union concerning the combating of racism and hostility to foreigners of the 15. 7. 1996, ABIEG of July 24, 1996, no. L 185 p. 5).

---

* [German Criminal Code (Endangering Road Traffic) § 315c
(1) Who in road traffic
1. drives a vehicle, although (a) due to consumption of alcoholic beverages or other intoxicants; or (b) due to mental or physical defects, he is not in a condition to drive the vehicle safely ... and thereby endangers the life or limb of another person or property belonging to another of considerable value will be punished with imprisonment of not more than five years or a fine.—Eds.]

German Criminal Code

§ 130 (Incitement to Hatred)

(1) Who, in a manner capable of disturbing the public peace,

1. incites hatred against segments of the population or calls for violent or arbitrary measures against them; or
2. assaults the human dignity of others by insulting, maliciously maligning, or defaming segments of the population,

will be punished with imprisonment from three months to five years.

(2) With imprisonment of not more than three years or with a fine will be punished who

1. a) disseminates,
   b) publicly displays, posts, presents, or otherwise makes accessible,
   c) offers, gives or makes accessible to a person under eighteen years, or
   d) produces, obtains, supplies, stocks, offers, announces, advertises, undertakes to import or export in order to use them or copies obtained from them according to no. a to c or in order to facilitate such use by another person,

   written materials (§ 11 para. 3) which incite hatred against segments of the population or a national, racial or religious group, or a group characterized by ethnic customs, which call for violent or arbitrary measures against them, or which assault the human dignity of others by insulting, maliciously maligning or defaming segments of the population or a previously indicated group

2. disseminates a presentation of the content indicated in no. 1 through broadcasting or telecommunication services.

(3) Who approves of, denies or downplays an act committed under the rule of National Socialism of the kind indicated in § 6 para. 1 Code of International Criminal Law publicly or in a meeting, in a manner capable of disturbing the public peace, will be punished with imprisonment of not more than five years or a fine.

(4) Who publicly or in a meeting disturbs the public peace in a manner that violates the dignity of the victims by approving of, glorifying, or justifying the National Socialist regime of violence and arbitrariness will be punished with imprisonment of not more than three years or a fine.

(5) Para. 1 shall also apply to written materials (§ 11 para. 3) of the content indicated in para. 3 and 4.

Tatjana Hörnle, "Offensive Behavior and German Penal Law," 5 *Buffalo Criminal Law Review* (2001), 255

Several provisions of the German Penal Code deal with conduct perceived to be intolerable and offensive. Punished are public sexual acts, dissemination of certain obnoxious kinds of pornography (e.g., pornography with children), public display of pornography in general, and incest. Also offensive are abusive statements against minorities, denial of the Nazi genocide, insults against religious denominations, disturbance of religious ceremonies, mistreatments of dead bodies, and desecration of burial sites.

Attempts to justify the prohibition of such behavior within the framework of contemporary German penal theory have led to difficulties. Most of these acts do not result in tangible harm to a specific person. In the absence of obvious damages, it is difficult to reconcile these parts of the German Penal Code with general principles concerning the proper range of the criminal law. The most straightforward explanation would simply point to the fact that the actor violated a *moral rule*. It would be easy to make that claim for most of the listed acts; their prohibition, indeed, is compatible with prevailing moral standards. Such a moral justification, however, runs contrary to the premises of modern German penal theory.

Today almost everyone agrees that conduct must not be prohibited solely on moral grounds. Violating conventional moral standards is thus no longer considered a valid reason for criminal sanctions.

German courts and German scholars justify some of the prohibitions, namely those against pornography, on the grounds that these prohibitions protect minors from harmful influences. The majority of prohibitions against offensive conduct, however, do not aim specifically to protect minors. Thus, another explanation is needed: These prohibitions are said to protect a *collective good*, that is, *public peace*. It is, however, unclear what "public peace" means. According to a common definition, it is "the condition of general security as well as general trust in the further existence of safe conditions and the sense of security within the population." However, pointing to "general security" does not yield a satisfying explanation: Every crime, by definition, violates "general security." To define the protected good as "no crimes" is pointless. The amount of *public trust* in the general security could be a real phenomenon. In theory, the psychological condition "trust" could be measured with the instruments of social psychology. But such measurements are difficult and certainly not possible within the context of legal decisionmaking. Statements about "public trust" inevitably stem from a merely subjective point of view. Talking of "public trust" hides personal perceptions of the wrong done by offensive conduct behind a pseudo-objective label. It is thus not feasible to justify penal prohibitions with the popular notion of "public peace." . . .

NOTES

1. In a wider, colloquial, sense, one could call *all* offenses that are motivated by offenders' resentments against groups of "others" hate crimes. However, for the purpose of legal classification, the expression "hate crimes" mainly is used to describe acts that would be criminal offenses anyhow (physical assaults, property crimes, trespassing, menacing, etc.) but that might deserve increased punishment insofar as they were motivated by hate (see for this group the discussion in *State v. Wyant*). Another type of offense penalizes the expression of racist or otherwise extremist statements as such. Such offenses are speech—or rather statement—offenses that target the expression of opinions. The crime of Holocaust denial and other variations of "incitement to hatred" in § 130 Criminal Code are examples of this type of offense.

As an example of the first type of hate crime, as sentence enhancer, consider the New York Penal Law's Hate Crimes Act of 2000, which also includes a lengthy legislative preamble:

N.Y. Penal Law § 485.00 Legislative findings.

The legislature finds and determines as follows: criminal acts involving violence, intimidation and destruction of property based upon bias and prejudice have become more prevalent in New York state in recent years. The intolerable truth is that in these crimes, commonly and justly referred to as "hate crimes," victims are intentionally selected, in whole or in part, because of their race, color, national origin, ancestry, gender, religion, religious practice, age, disability or sexual orientation. Hate crimes do more than threaten the safety and welfare of all citizens. They inflict on victims incalculable physical and emotional damage and tear at the very fabric of free society. Crimes motivated by invidious hatred towards particular groups not only harm individual victims but send a powerful message of intolerance and discrimination to all members of the group to which the victim belongs. Hate crimes can and do intimidate and disrupt entire communities and vitiate the civility that is essential to healthy democratic processes. In a democratic society, citizens cannot be required to approve of the beliefs and practices of others, but most never commit criminal acts on account of them. Current law does not adequately recognize the harm to public order and individual safety that hate crimes cause. Therefore, our laws must be strengthened to provide clear recognition of the gravity of hate crimes and the compelling importance of preventing their recurrence. Accordingly, the legislature finds and declares that hate crimes should be prosecuted and punished with appropriate severity.

§485.05 Hate crimes.

1. A person commits a hate crime when he or she commits a specified offense* and either:
    (a) intentionally selects the person against whom the offense is committed or intended to be committed in whole or in substantial part because of a belief or perception regarding the race, color, national origin, ancestry, gender, religion, religious practice, age, disability or sexual orientation of a person, regardless of whether the belief or perception is correct, or
    (b) intentionally commits the act or acts constituting the offense in whole or in substantial part because of a belief of perception regarding the race, color, national origin, ancestry, gender, religion, religious practice, age, disability or sexual orientation of a person, regardless of whether the belief or perception is correct.

---

* [Specified offenses include, for instance, menacing, assault, homicide, stalking, sex offenses, robbery, burglary, trespass, arson, and criminal mischief. See § 485.05(3).—Eds.]

American prosecutors have used "hate crime" legislation such as this in perhaps unantici-pated ways. For instance, a Queens prosecutor used the above New York statute in prosecu-tions of defendant charged with "singling out elderly victims for nonviolent crimes like mortgage fraud because they believed older people would be easy to deceive and might have substantial savings or home equity."* This, even though, as a fellow prosecutor pointed out, "criminals that prey on the elderly, they love the elderly—this is their source of wealth." (Compare the sentencing enhancement for "Hate Crime Motivation or Vulnerable Victim" in the U.S. Sentencing Guidelines, in Note 5.)

In general, however, hate crime legislation appears to be sparingly used. For instance, in 2011, there were 122 convictions from a hate crime arrest in New York State, compared to 105,577 felony convictions alone.[†]

Cases in which hate crime legislation is used often attract considerable media attention. See, e.g., Eric Eckholm, "Amish Sect Leader and Followers Guilty of Hate Crimes," *N.Y. Times*, September 20, 2012, at A1 (federal prosecution of a group of Amish defendants who had cut the beards and hair of other Amish men and women to "suppress the victims' practice of religion"); Marc Santora, "Woman Accused of Hate-Crime Murder in Subway Push," *N.Y. Times*, December 29, 2012, at A1 (New York "hate-crime murder" prosecution of a woman accused of pushing a man under an oncoming subway train because "I hate Hindus and Muslims ever since 2001 when they put down the twin towers I've been beating them up"); Kate Zernike, "Jury Finds Spying in Rutgers Dorm Was a Hate Crime," *N.Y. Times*, March 17, 2012, at A1 (New Jersey prosecution of a college student who used a webcam to spy on his roommate having sex with another man).

In fact, among early criticisms of hate crime statutes was the claim that they amounted to (merely) symbolic criminal lawmaking. See, e.g., James B. Jacobs and Kimberly A. Potter, "Hate Crimes: A Critical Perspective," 22 *Crime and Justice* (1997), 1 (arguing that "[c]reation of a hate crime category fills political and symbolic functions but is unlikely to provide a useful indication of the state of various prejudices or to reduce crime generated by prejudice"); see also Frederick M. Lawrence, *Punishing Hate: Bias Crimes Under American Law* (1999).

Under German law, there is no "hate crime" provision that enhances punishment if the offender, for instance, assaults another person motivated by his resentments against the victim's race, national origin, religion, or for similar reasons. The reasons behind the absence of such a norm are different from those expressed in *State v. Wyant*. The reservations expressed in the opinion against "thought crimes" and motives-as-crucial-elements-in-sentencing are rarely shared in the German discussion. Although there are a few criminal law theorists who would agree with Justice Brown, he would not find much support among German legislators, judges and criminal law scholars. According to a widespread opinion, motives do matter for the assessment of a crime. The proponents of this view usually point to § 211 Criminal Code, the provision on murder, which draws the line between simple homicide and murder (among other criteria) by referring to the baseness of motives (see Chapter 15.A.ii).

Of course, to point out that motives do matter is not to say that they should. (For a detailed discussion of the distinction between murder (*Mord*), § 211 Criminal Code, and manslaugh-ter (*Totschlag*), § 212, including the role of motives in this context, see Chapter 15.A.ii and iii.) The claim that motives are irrelevant for criminal liability, never mind for sentencing, is contested in Anglo-American criminal law as well.[‡] In fact, *Wyant* was among the cases reversed by the U.S. Supreme Court's opinion in *Wisconsin v. Mitchell*, 508 U.S. 476 (1993), which emphasized that it had long been deemed permissible to account for motive in sentencing and that "hate crime" statutes, at core, served as sentence-aggravating schemes.

Without recounting the discussion of this point in Chapter 8.A, to say that "if defined narrowly enough, motive is not relevant to substantive criminal law" (see *Wyant* above,

---

* Anne Barnard, "A Novel Twist for Prosecution of Hate Crimes," *N.Y. Times*, June 22, 2010, at A1.

† Hate Crime in New York State, N.Y. Div. Crim. Just. Services (October 2012); 2007–2011 Dispositions of Adult Arrests, N.Y. Div. Crim. Just. Services (April 2012); see generally "Unprosecuted Hate Crimes," *N.Y. Times*, August 14, 2012, at A22.

‡ See generally Carissa Byrne Hessick, "Motive's Role in Criminal Punishment," 80 *Southern California Law Review* (2006), 89.

citing LaFave and Scott) simply begs the question. The question is not whether one can define motive "narrowly enough" to find little or no evidence of it in Anglo-American criminal law, but whether motive, properly defined, or ordinarily defined, or sensibly defined, does play a role in the analysis of criminal liability, and, even more clearly, in sentencing, including in capital sentencing. (Recall, for instance, the parallels between the distinguishing characteristics set out in the German murder provision, § 211 Criminal Code, and the aggravating factors listed in the definition of first degree murder in the New York Penal Law, § 125.27, see Chapter 15.A.) In fact, *Wyant* itself can be read as making this very point; the norms and doctrines the court cites are only examples of the irrelevance of motive, if motive is "defined narrowly enough" to exclude them. Define motive more broadly and they illustrate the relevance of motive instead. For a more sophisticated argument, see Heidi Hurd, "Why Liberals Should Hate 'Hate Crime' Legislation," 20 *Law and Philosophy* (2001), 215.

The main difference between German and Anglo-American criminal law on motive, in the end, may be that the motive-is-irrelevant maxim only appears in the latter. The maxim, though overstated, may well reflect an unease about the consideration of motive, at least for purposes of criminal liability, if not of sentencing, that appears to be considerably more prevalent in Anglo-American than in German criminal law. That is surprising insofar as this unease can be seen as stemming from a commitment to the liberal distinction—often attributed to Kant—between the realms of legality and morality, with motives relevant—in fact, decisive—only in the latter, while the former does not inquire into internal motives, either for obeying or disobeying its external norms.

Recently, after well-publicized incidents of right-wing extremists committing violent crimes in Germany, there have been several proposals to amend the German Criminal Code by explicitly mentioning racist motives etc. as aggravating factors. The reason why this has not happened yet is a simple, technical one: § 46 para. 2 Criminal Code lists factors that should be taken into account, and one factor there is "disposition" (*Gesinnung*). For this reason, according to present law, it is already possible to aggravate sentences in cases of hate crimes in comparison with the same act committed for other motives. Such increases must stay within the statutory punishment range for the crime; however, these ranges are usually much broader than the scope actually used in practice, leaving enough room to accommodate a stricter assessment of crimes committed with base motives. (Is a general provision granting courts the discretion to consider the defendant's "disposition" preferable to one like N.Y. Penal Law § 485.05 that sets out aggravating circumstances in detail?)

2. A German reader of *State v. Wyant* is likely to object to the idea that the identity of the victim might be an aggravating circumstance, exemplified in the opinion by drawing an analogy between "[i]mposing a higher penalty for killing the Governor than for killing an ordinary citizen" and "imposing a higher penalty for stealing a painting worth $1,000 than for stealing one worth only $5." A German judge who would use such a comparison would meet public outrage and would be accused of violating human dignity (this would be a safe method to damage one's career permanently). Kant's insistence that human beings stand out exactly because they do *not* have a price (developed in the Groundwork of the Metaphysics of Morals, 1785) is not only popular with German scholars and universally acknowledged in the legal domain when it comes to explaining that necessity can never justify killing a human being ("the ordinary citizen") to save the life of another, higher-ranking person (see Chapter 13.B); after the experiences under the National Socialist regime, it also violates a strong social taboo to imply that the identity of the victim and its personal characteristics might be relevant to the wrongdoing of killing.

In fairness to the court in *Wyant*, the opinion does not in fact differentiate between the worth of a governor's life and that of an ordinary citizen; it instead uses the mentioned analogy, however clumsily, to make the point that occasionally "aggravating circumstances involve the identity of the victim, such as a peace officer or governmental official," reflecting a legislative judgment "that acts against certain individuals are more serious criminal acts." To illustrate, the court cites Ohio Rev. Code § 2929.04(A)(1), which lists as an aggravating factor in a murder case if "[t]he offense was the assassination of the president of the United States...."

Leaving aside the decision in *Wyant*, concerns about the possibility of differentiating among the value of victims' lives underlie some of the criticism of the U.S. Supreme Court's affirmation, in *Payne v. Tennessee*, of the constitutionality of victim impact statements in capital sentencing hearings (discussed in Chapter 1.A.ii). Is the murder of a homeless person any less serious, does it have any less of an "impact," than the murder of a beloved mother whose surviving family members and friends can take the witness stand to testify about their loss? (Of course, homicide is unique in being both the most serious and the least harmful crime: it extinguishes the person it harms, its only direct victim, and in that sense has an "impact" only on others, on its indirect victims.)

But let's get back to the presidential assassination statute cited in *Wyant*. Aggravated punishments for offenses against public officials are a common feature of American criminal law, and the American law of capital (and, more generally, first degree) murder in particular. Recall the discussion, in Chapter 15.A, of New York's first degree murder provision, N.Y. Penal Law § 125.27(1)(a), which lists, among the aggravating circumstances that differentiate first degree from second degree murder:

(i) the intended victim was a police officer . . . who was at the time of the killing engaged in the course of performing his official duties, and the defendant knew or reasonably should have known that the intended victim was a police officer; or

(ii) the intended victim was a peace officer . . . who was at the time of the killing engaged in the course of performing his official duties, and the defendant knew or reasonably should have known that the intended victim was such a uniformed court officer, parole officer, probation officer, or employee of the division for youth; or

(iii) the intended victim was an employee of a state correctional institution or was an employee of a local correctional facility . . . , who was at the time of the killing engaged in the course of performing his official duties, and the defendant knew or reasonably should have known that the intended victim was an employee of a state correctional institution or a local correctional facility; or . . .

(v) the intended victim was a witness to a crime committed on a prior occasion and the death was caused for the purpose of preventing the intended victim's testimony in any criminal action or proceeding whether or not such action or proceeding had been commenced   ; or

(xii) the intended victim was a judge . . . and the defendant killed such victim because such victim was, at the time of the killing, a judge . . . .

Are these provisions justifiable (in light of what rationale(s) of punishment)? Is there a difference, in terms of the relevant legal good(s) or in some other sense, between assassinating a president and committing a murder, between a crime committed against a state official (or a witness) and one committed against a private citizen? Does it matter whether the public official was performing her public function at the time of the offense?

N.Y. Penal Law § 120.08 Assault on a peace officer, police officer, fireman or emergency medical services professional

A person is guilty of assault on a peace officer, police officer, fireman or emergency medical services professional when, with intent to prevent a peace officer, police officer, a fireman, including a fireman acting as a paramedic or emergency medical technician administering first aid in the course of performance of duty as such fireman, or an emergency medical service paramedic or emergency medical service technician, from performing a lawful duty, he causes serious physical injury to such peace officer, police officer, fireman, paramedic or technician.

N.Y. Penal Law § 120.11 Aggravated assault upon a police officer or a peace officer

A person is guilty of aggravated assault upon a police officer or a peace officer when, with intent to cause serious physical injury to a person whom he knows or reasonably should know to be a police officer or a peace officer engaged in the course of performing his official duties, he causes such injury by means of a deadly weapon or dangerous instrument.

Does it make a difference whether the differentiation among victims occurs at the level of the offense definition or at sentencing? Whether the offense is "motivated" by the victim's official status?

U.S. Sentencing Guidelines § 3A1.2. Official Victim

(a) If (1) the victim was (A) a government officer or employee; (B) a former government officer or employee; or (C) a member of the immediate family of a person described in subdivision (A) or (B); and (2) the offense of conviction was motivated by such status, increase by 3 levels.

(b) If subsection (a)(1) and (2) apply, and the applicable Chapter Two guideline is from Chapter Two, Part A (Offenses Against the Person), increase by 6 levels.

(c) If, in a manner creating a substantial risk of serious bodily injury, the defendant or a person for whose conduct the defendant is otherwise accountable—

   (1) knowing or having reasonable cause to believe that a person was a law enforcement officer, assaulted such officer during the course of the offense or immediate flight therefrom; or

   (2) knowing or having reasonable cause to believe that a person was a prison official, assaulted such official while the defendant (or a person for whose conduct the defendant is otherwise accountable) was in the custody or control of a prison or other correctional facility, increase by 6 levels.

3. The German Criminal Code contains a number of speech offenses aimed at prohibited media content (and, in most offense definitions, also at face-to-face-interactions if they are public). Besides incitement to hatred (§ 130 Criminal Code), other examples are the prohibitions against propaganda and symbols used by National Socialists (and other organizations hostile to the Constitution) (§§ 86, 86a Criminal Code); public approval of crimes (§ 140 Criminal Code); and defamation of religions (§ 166 Criminal Code). There are two sets of questions to be asked with respect to such prohibitions of speech. First, what is the rationale of the prohibition, what are the legal goods protected, and can this conduct actually harm or endanger them? Second, is the relevant conduct protected under the constitutional free speech guarantee?

The German Federal Court of Justice and the majority opinion in the German literature point to "public peace" as the protected legal good. While this is fairly plausible with regard to many acts described in § 130 para. 1 Criminal Code (straightforward incitements such as, for instance, a call to violence against Turks in a live speech delivered to an audience of German right-wing juveniles), it is less so for typical cases of Holocaust denial that fall under § 130 para. 3 Criminal Code. In contemporary societies, those who publish revisionist pseudo-historical opinions about the Holocaust in books or online tend to be social outcasts who hardly will become the focal points of powerful political movements. Such activities are, in other words, annoying and offensive but not dangerous. (How powerful would a political movement have to be to endanger the "public peace"? Could the denial of the Holocaust at a public demonstration threaten the public peace, without the presence of a political movement?) There are debates about the question whether historical events are correctly labeled genocide, which might under certain circumstances even escalate into actual violent fights (consider the dispute about the genocide against Armenians in 1915 and 1916). However, the genocides committed by the National Socialist regime are beyond serious dispute (other genocides are not covered by § 130 para. 3 and 4 Criminal Code). The Federal Court of Justice mentions in the *Töben Case* the "poisoning the political climate" that is to be prevented with § 130 para. 3 Criminal Code. Do you think that this is a convincing justification for a criminal norm? Is a healthy political climate a legal good (*Rechtsgut*) and, if so, one that could justify invoking criminal sanctions? How would one distinguish between a healthy political climate, and a poisoned one? And is the threat of criminal sanction for certain contributions to public debate a promising means to produce a healthy political climate, or might it have the opposite effect? (On the *Rechtsgut* principle, see Chapter 3.B.)

The issue of freedom of speech is not extensively discussed in the decision by the German Federal Court of Justice. Of course, the German Constitution protects the right to freedom of expression, art. 5 Basic Law (see the *Töben Case* above). However, the Basic Law itself (art. 5 para. 2) allows restricting freedom of expression with "general laws." Constitutional doctrine demands a balancing between the right in art. 5 para. 1 Basic Law (which is in general emphasized as an important human right) and the protective purpose of the restrictive law in question. However, if the speech involves Holocaust denial, the balancing tends to be a short affair. The German Federal Constitutional Court never has questioned that norms criminalizing Holocaust denial and other expressions of National Socialist ideology are "general laws" in the sense of art. 5 para. 2 Basic Law and that it is constitutionally permissible to restrict freedom of speech in these cases (see, e.g., Judgment of April 13, 1994, 1 BvR 13/94, BVerfGE 90, 241). According to contemporary German social and legal culture, the right to freedom of speech is of crucial importance but stops short of covering speech that clearly and obviously is incompatible with the founding narrative of the modern German state. At the center of this founding narrative is the rejection of the National Socialist worldview and abhorrence for the crimes committed through this regime. (Does this mean that the speech is offensive by itself, even without considering its possible effect on the public peace?)

Compare the U.S. Supreme Court's decision in *R.A.V. v. City of St. Paul*, 505 U.S. 377 (1992), which struck down the following city ordinance ("St. Paul Bias-Motivated Crime Ordinance"):

> Whoever places on public or private property, a symbol, object, appellation, characterization or graffiti, including, but not limited to, a burning cross or Nazi swastika, which one knows or has reasonable grounds to know arouses anger, alarm or resentment in others on the basis of race, color, creed, religion or gender commits disorderly conduct and shall be guilty of a misdemeanor.

Without getting into the niceties of First Amendment jurisprudence, suffice it to say that the Supreme Court, in a controversial decision, found that this ordinance was not saved by the so-called "fighting words" doctrine, first recognized in *Chaplinsky v. New Hampshire*, 315 U.S. 568 (1942). Chaplinsky had been convicted under a statute that prohibited addressing "any offensive, derisive or annoying word to anyone who is lawfully in any street or public place ... or to call him by an offensive or derisive name." According to the complaint, Chaplinsky had called the town marshall "a God-damned racketeer" and "a damned Fascist." The Court upheld the conviction, arguing that:

> There are certain well-defined and narrowly limited classes of speech, the prevention and punishment of which have never been thought to raise any constitutional problem. These include the lewd and obscene, the profane, the libelous, and the insulting or "fighting words"—those that by their very utterance inflict injury or tend to incite an immediate breach of the peace. It has been well observed that such utterances are no essential part of any exposition of ideas, and are of such slight social value as a step to truth that any benefit that may be derived from them is clearly outweighed by the social interest in order and morality.

Note that courts in other common law countries may strike a different balance between the protection of free speech rights and the criminalization of hate speech. See, e.g., *R. v. Keegstra*, [1990] 3 S.C.R. 697 (upholding public incitement to hatred provision in Canadian Criminal Code).* As the dissent in *Keegstra* makes clear, however, the issue is likely to be controversial.

4. The decision by the German Federal Court of Justice in the *Töben Case* is frequently cited in commentaries to the German Criminal Code and criminal law treatises, not because it contains spectacularly new points concerning § 130 Criminal Code but because of the decision on jurisdiction. There was a lively discussion whether German courts are entitled to apply German criminal law to acts committed in Australia by an Australian citizen. Did the German criminal proceedings represent an attempt to "police the Internet"? (On jurisdiction, see Chapter 4.)

The question of jurisdiction arose because none of the provisions extending German jurisdiction to acts committed abroad applied. There was neither an offender of German nationality nor a German victim (under the active or passive personality principle, see § 7 Criminal Code), and § 130 Criminal Code is included neither on the list of domestic legal goods that can be attacked from abroad (under the nationality principle, § 5) nor on the list of crimes that allow for universal jurisdiction (§ 6 Criminal Code). But the Court argued that Töben's offense was committed in Germany (under the territoriality principle, § 9). This might sound strange at first; the key, however, is § 9 Criminal Code and the way the place of

---

* See also L.W. Sumner, *The Hateful and the Obscene: Studies in the Limits of Free Expression* (2004).

crime commission is defined there. According to this norm, the place of the offense is not only defined by the place of the act (in Internet cases: where the offender worked at the keyboard or touchscreen of a computer), but also by the place where the result element of the crime occurred. Thus, the crucial question in the *Töben Case* was whether crimes of Holocaust denial require proof of a result, and if so, where that result manifested itself.

(The expansion of the territoriality principle to cover cases, in which at least one element of the offense definition has been satisfied within the territory of the state is also a familiar feature of the law of criminal jurisdiction in common law countries—and smaller governmental entities, such as American states. See, e.g., N.Y. Crim. Proc. L. § 20.00(1) (N.Y. criminal law applies to an offense if "[c]onduct occurred within this state sufficient to establish: (a) An element of such offense").)

The starting point is the categorization of § 130 Criminal Code as an offense of endangerment. The court mentions the categories of concrete and abstract endangerment, discussed in Chapter 15.B. Obviously, § 130 does not belong into the established category of concrete endangerment offenses because these require identifying a specific victim and a specific instance of danger (for an example concerning the traffic offense in § 315c Criminal Code, cited in the *Töben Case* above: "at 3:15 a.m., the drunk defendant's car at the speed of 70 miles per hour only narrowly missed the motorcycle of Mr. X"). In contrast to such concrete endangerment offenses, Holocaust denial does not almost harm, or even endanger, a specific victim. With regard to the established other category, abstract endangerment offenses, a majority in the literature had argued that offenses of abstract endangerment do not have a result element. However, the German Federal Court of Justice pointed to a third category, of "concrete-abstract endangerment offenses." It argues that the wording of § 130 Criminal Code explicitly demands that the act must be "capable of disturbing the public peace." In this, the Court sees proximity to concrete endangerment offenses. (Does it make sense to classify the capacity to disturb the peace as a result, rather than an attendant circumstance? On offense element types, see Chapter 7.)

The next step was to consider whether the possible effect "disturbance of public peace" was to be expected specifically in Germany (rather than in all states worldwide where citizens have access to the Internet, that is, basically everywhere). Here, the judges point to German history.

Note that the Court wished to avoid the conclusion that German public prosecutors now may try to enforce German standards for Internet content everywhere. The judgment emphasizes that prosecution by German authorities must be legitimate according to public international law, which requires a "special objective connection with the territory of the Federal Republic of Germany." Most Internet content which would be illegal if measured according to the German Criminal Code does not have such a special connection to Germany. The German Criminal Code is, for instance, more restrictive than some other countries with respect to free and unhindered distribution of pornography (§ 184 Criminal Code contains limitations in order to restrict access of juveniles, also applicable to Internet providers in Germany). If content providers in other countries do not act in accordance with German law, though in accordance with their own legal system, they need not fear getting arrested when traveling to Germany if the "special connection" of their Internet content to Germany is lacking.

Nevertheless, the judgment in the *Töben Case* has met with a lot of criticism in the literature. If the logic of the Federal Court of Justice is taken up in other jurisdictions, this might limit freedom of movement. Imagine a puritan, strictly religious state. A public prosecutor in such a country might well point to the German Federal Court of Justice when protecting his own "insulted" citizens by arresting those responsible for "lewd" or otherwise religiously objectionable Internet content if they enter this country.

5. *Sentencing.* The U.S. Sentencing Guidelines provide for a sentence enhancement on the basis of certain victim characteristics: (1) if the offender intentionally chose a victim "because of" any of a number of actual or perceived characteristics (race, gender, sexual orientation, etc.) or (2) if the offender knew or should have known that the victim had another characteristic, vulnerability. Does this amount to an objectionable differentiation among victims? An objectionable consideration of motive, in sentencing, rather than in the assessment of criminal liability?

§ 3A1.1. Hate Crime Motivation or Vulnerable Victim

(a) If the finder of fact at trial or, in the case of a plea of guilty or nolo contendere, the court at sentencing determines beyond a reasonable doubt that the defendant intentionally selected any victim or any property as the object of the offense of conviction because of the actual or perceived race, color, religion, national origin, ethnicity, gender, gender identity, disability, or sexual orientation of any person, increase by 3 levels.

(b) (1) If the defendant knew or should have known that a victim of the offense was a vulnerable victim, increase by 2 levels.

    (2) If (A) subdivision (1) applies; and (B) the offense involved a large number of vulnerable victims, increase the offense level determined under subdivision (1) by 2 additional levels . . .

Commentary

Application Notes:

2. For purposes of subsection (b), "vulnerable victim" means a person (A) who is a victim of the offense of conviction and any conduct for which the defendant is accountable under §1B1.3 (Relevant Conduct); and (B) who is unusually vulnerable due to age, physical or mental condition, or who is otherwise particularly susceptible to the criminal conduct.

Subsection (b) applies to offenses involving an unusually vulnerable victim in which the defendant knows or should have known of the victim's unusual vulnerability. The adjustment would apply, for example, in a fraud case in which the defendant marketed an ineffective cancer cure or in a robbery in which the defendant selected a handicapped victim. But it would not apply in a case in which the defendant sold fraudulent securities by mail to the general public and one of the victims happened to be senile. Similarly, for example, a bank teller is not an unusually vulnerable victim solely by virtue of the teller's position in a bank.

B. Bending the Law (*Rechtsbeugung*)

The offense of law bending (*Rechtsbeugung*) is one of the most intriguing features of the special part of German criminal law, especially from a comparative perspective. First, it defines as a felony, and threatens with serious punishment, judges—or any other state official in charge of a legal matter at a particular point—for conduct in their official capacity, i.e., supervising and deciding cases, including criminal cases. Second, and more interesting, it defines the criminal conduct in question, the nature of the official misconduct, as "bending the law" in favor of one party or the other. Third, comparatively speaking, there is nothing like it in American criminal law; to the contrary, American law generally goes out of its way to shield state officials, and especially judges, from liability for conduct in their official capacity.

Mireles v. Waco
Supreme Court of the United States
502 U.S. 9 (1991)

PER CURIAM.

A long line of this Court's precedents acknowledges that, generally, a judge is immune from a suit for money damages. [The Court, however, has recognized that a judge is not absolutely immune from criminal liability, *Ex parte Virginia*, 100 U.S. 339, 348–349, 25 L. Ed. 676 (1880) . . .] Although unfairness and injustice to a litigant may result on occasion, "it is a general principle of the highest importance to the proper administration of justice that a judicial officer, in exercising the authority vested in him, shall be free to act upon his own convictions, without apprehension of personal consequences to himself." *Bradley* v. *Fisher*, 80 U.S. 335, 13 Wall. 335, 347, 20 L. Ed. 646 (1872).

In this case, respondent Howard Waco, a Los Angeles County public defender, filed suit in the United States District Court for the Central District of California under Rev. Stat. § 1979, 42 U.S. C. § 1983, against petitioner, Raymond Mireles, a judge of the California Superior Court, and two police officers, for damages arising from an incident in November 1989 at the Superior Court building in Van Nuys, Cal. Waco alleged that after he failed to appear for the initial call of Judge Mireles' morning calendar, the judge, "angered by the absence of attorneys from his courtroom," ordered the police officer defendants "to forcibly and with excessive force seize and bring plaintiff into his courtroom." App. to Pet. for Cert. B-3, P7(a). The officers allegedly "by means of unreasonable force and violence seized plaintiff and removed him backwards" from another courtroom where he was waiting to appear, cursed him, and called him "vulgar and offensive names," then "without necessity slammed" him through the doors and swinging gates into Judge Mireles' courtroom. *Id.*, at B-4, P7 (c). Judge Mireles, it was alleged, "knowingly and deliberately approved and ratified each of the aforedescribed acts" of the police officers. *Ibid.* Waco demanded general and punitive damages. *Id.*, at B-5 and B-6.

Judge Mireles moved to dismiss the complaint as to him, pursuant to Federal Rules of Civil Procedure 12(b)(1) and (6), for failure to state a claim upon which relief could be granted. The District Court dismissed the claim against the judge and entered final judgment as to him, pursuant to Rule 54(b), on grounds of "complete judicial immunity." App. to Pet. for Cert. D-2. On Waco's appeal, the United States Court of Appeals for the Ninth Circuit reversed that judgment. *Waco* v. *Baltad*, 934 F.2d 214 (1991). The court determined that Judge Mireles was not immune from suit because his alleged actions were not taken in his judicial capacity. It opined that Judge Mireles would have been acting in his judicial capacity if he had "merely directed the officers to bring Waco to his courtroom without directing them to use excessive force." *Id.*, at 216. But "if Judge Mireles requested and authorized the use of excessive force, then he would not be acting in his judicial capacity." *Ibid.*

Taking the allegations of the complaint as true, as we do upon a motion to dismiss, we grant the petition for certiorari and summarily reverse.

Like other forms of official immunity, judicial immunity is an immunity from suit, not just from ultimate assessment of damages. Accordingly, judicial immunity is not overcome by allegations of bad faith or malice, the existence of which ordinarily cannot be resolved without engaging in discovery and eventual trial. *Pierson* v. *Ray*, 386 U.S. at 554 ("Immunity applies even when the judge is accused of acting maliciously and corruptly"). See also *Harlow* v. *Fitzgerald*, 457 U.S. 800, 815–819, 73 L. Ed. 2d 396, 102 S. Ct. 2727 (1982) (allegations of malice are insufficient to overcome qualified immunity).

Rather, our cases make clear that the immunity is overcome in only two sets of circumstances. First, a judge is not immune from liability for nonjudicial actions, *i.e.*, actions not taken in the judge's judicial capacity. Second, a judge is not immune for actions, though judicial in nature, taken in the complete absence of all jurisdiction.

We conclude that the Court of Appeals erred in ruling that Judge Mireles' alleged actions were not taken in his judicial capacity. This Court . . . made clear that "whether an act by a judge is a 'judicial' one relate[s] to the nature of the act itself, *i.e.*, whether it is a function normally performed by a judge, and to the expectations of the parties, *i.e.*, whether they dealt with the judge in his judicial capacity." A judge's direction to court officers to bring a person who is in the courthouse before him is a function normally performed by a judge. See generally Cal. Civ. Proc. Code Ann. §§ 128, 177, 187 (West 1982 and Supp. 1991) (setting forth broad powers of state judges in the conduct of proceedings). [California Civ. Proc. Code Ann. § 128 (West Supp. 1991) provides in pertinent part: "Every court shall have the power to do all of the following: . . . (5) To control in furtherance of justice, the conduct of its ministerial officers, and of all other persons in any manner connected with a judicial proceeding before it, in every matter pertaining thereto."] Waco, who was called into the courtroom for purposes of a pending case, was dealing with Judge Mireles in the judge's judicial capacity.

Of course, a judge's direction to police officers to carry out a judicial order with excessive force is not a "function normally performed by a judge." But if only the particular act in question were to be scrutinized, then any mistake of a judge in excess of his authority would become a "nonjudicial" act, because an improper or erroneous act cannot be said to be normally performed by a judge. If judicial immunity means anything, it means that a judge "will not be deprived of immunity because the action he took was in error . . . or was in excess of his authority." Accordingly, as the language in *Stump* indicates, the relevant inquiry is the "nature" and "function" of the act, not the "act itself." In other words, we look to the particular act's relation to a general function normally performed by a judge, in this case the function of directing police officers to bring counsel in a pending case before the court.

Nor does the fact that Judge Mireles' order was carried out by police officers somehow transform his action from "judicial" to "executive" in character. [I]t is "the nature of the function performed, not the identity of the actor who performed it, that inform[s] our immunity analysis." A judge's direction to an executive officer to bring counsel before the court is no more executive in character than a judge's issuance of a warrant for an executive officer to search a home.

Because the Court of Appeals concluded that Judge Mireles did not act in his judicial capacity, the court did not reach the second part of the immunity inquiry: whether Judge Mireles' actions were taken in the complete absence of all jurisdiction. We have little trouble concluding that they were not. If Judge Mireles authorized and ratified the police officers' use of excessive force, he acted in excess of his authority. But such an action—taken in the very aid of the judge's jurisdiction over a matter before him—cannot be said to have been taken in the absence of jurisdiction.

German Federal Court of Justice
1 StR 201/09, NStZ 2010, 92 (June 24, 2009)

The regional court had sentenced the defendant for bending the law (*Rechtsbeugung*) in forty-seven cases and attempted bending the law in seven cases to imprisonment of three years and six months. The defendant's appeal in law remained without success.

1. The findings, made without legal error, support the verdict of guilty for bending the law under § 339 Criminal Code. Bending of the law can also be committed by violation of procedural provisions (see BGHSt 42, 343, 344; BGHR StGB § 339 Bending of the law 6—in each case with further references). Certainly not every violation of the law is to be seen as "bending" the law; this element of the definition contains a normative element and should only cover infringements in the administration of justice in which the perpetrator departs from law and statute [*Recht und Gesetz*] deliberately [*bewußt*] and in a grave manner in favor of or to the disadvantage of a party (see BGHSt loc. cit., with further references). Such fundamental infringements of law are present here.

a) According to the findings, the defendant, as a judge acting in the local court in care issues in 54 cases in respect of people in nursing homes, has authorized measures restricting freedom under § 1906 para. 1 or 4 Civil Code—as for example fitting bed guards, confinement to a bed, armchair or wheelchair or use of a protective cover, and also extension of the confinement. In so doing, contrary to the statutory duty of which he was aware, he systematically refrained from hearing the persons concerned personally beforehand and obtaining a direct impression of them. The defendant intended in this way to enable himself to decide the proceedings more easily and quickly, to save himself work, and in particular to have more time for family, hobbies and other activities. The defendant drew up records of hearings on pre-prepared forms, and put them in the procedural files in order to give the impression that the hearings were properly carried out. In seven cases he recorded hearings with persons who at the alleged time of the hearing had already died. When in one case the office of the local court pointed out to him that at the date of the alleged hearing the person concerned had already died, the defendant altered the content of the procedural files retrospectively.

b) The defendant, by systematically violating the duty to give a hearing under § 70c FGG (Statute on Matters of Non-Contentious Jurisdiction) and at the same time pretending he was taking a proper course of action under procedural law by false records of hearings, has deliberately departed from law and statute in such a grave manner that it must be seen as a fundamental violation of the law.

   aa) The statutorily prescribed duty to give a hearing not only has the purpose of including the person affected in the decision-making process by giving him a legal hearing in the general sense (Jansen/Sonnenfeld FGG, 3rd edit., § 70c marginal no. 3); the provision is also to guarantee that the court in matters concerning confinement and care can better perform its control function towards witnesses and experts. The court ought not, in such important affairs which affect the basic freedom rights of the persons affected by the particular measures, to make any decisions only on the basis of evidence and without its own observations as a foundation (see BT-Dr 11/4528, p. 90; Jansen/Sonnenfeld loc. cit., marginal no. 1).

   bb) The defendant has, in the cases of which he is accused, decided about the applications under § 1906 Civil Code either alone according to the situation in the file or on the basis of information which he had obtained from short superficial conversations with the care staff about the condition of the persons affected. He did not give the persons affected a personal hearing in any of the cases nor did he obtain a direct impression of their condition in the nursing home. He has thereby neglected his judicial duty to give a hearing not only in the individual case, for example due to professional overwork, but has systematically dispensed with hearings on the basis of irrelevant considerations, namely "in order to optimize his free time." By proceeding in this way he has nullified the reinforcement which the duty to hold a hearing was intended to give to the legal position of persons in the proceedings who are in special need of protection because of their age or state of health (see BT-Dr 11/4528, p. 89). Furthermore, as he did not even obtain a personal impression of the persons affected, he lacked an important basis for the decision about the approval of the measures sought.

   cc) By systematically dispensing with the holding of judicial hearings the defendant has deliberately committed a violation of law [*Rechtsbruch*] to the disadvantage of the persons affected by authorizing measures restricting freedom under § 1906 para. 1 or 4 Civil Code. Not only has he exposed the persons affected to the concrete danger of a disadvantage through breach of his duty to give a hearing on the basis of irrelevant considerations, namely to have more free time (see BGHSt 42, 343); he has in fact directly violated their legal status by authorizing the measure in question in the case. This is because the decision was consequently not based on personal impressions or wishes or other possible statements which could have had an effect on the decision. The violation of procedure therefore led in each individual case to a decision which was defective in objective law. Contrary to the view of the appeal in law, the main focus of the reprehensibility therefore does not lie in omitting the hearing, but in the authorization of measures restricting freedom with an insufficient basis for the decision. The hypothetical question of whether the defendant would, if a hearing had been held, have proceeded to an authorization of the measures in question just the same is of no significance when considering whether the defendant has "committed bending of the law to the disadvantage of a party."

c) The findings also support an intention [*Vorsatz*] to commit the crime. The intention must be directed towards violation of law to the advantage or disadvantage of a party; a specific purpose [*besondere Absicht*] is not needed (see *Fischer* § 339 marginal no. 17). These prerequisites are fulfilled here. The local court's conclusion, based on the cover-up activities, that he was aware of the seriousness of the violations of procedure committed by him to the disadvantage of the persons affected meets with no legal doubts.

In order to give the appearance of a proper hearing, the defendant had developed a form containing boxes to be marked with a cross, which were to document the state of health of the person affected, like for example, "not responsive" or "responsive and in every respect / partially / not orientated." Besides this he had had the following sentence printed on the form: "The person affected stated on the reason for the hearing: nothing." In the cases with which he is charged, the defendant in each case filed a hearing form dated with the day of the resolution, although he had not held any hearing at all in accordance with § 70c FGG. He has thus introduced documents with an incorrect content into the procedural files in order to fake a procedure corresponding with the statutory provisions. Having regard to the large number of cases in which the defendant has methodically kept secret the serious violations of procedure committed by him, the local court's assumption that the defendant bent the law deliberately and for irrelevant motives, in particular to optimize his free time, is not open to objection on appeal. The mere fact of systematic action to increase his own free time is enough to suggest that his actions were not directed towards the welfare of the persons affected . . .

German Federal Court of Justice
5 StR 94/96, NStZ-RR 1997, 36 (June 20, 1996)

Facts

The defendant, who was born in 1915, assisted in 1950 as an associate judge at the Supreme Court (OG) of the German Democratic Republic (GDR) [East Germany, under Communist rule until the re-unification in 1990—Eds.] under presiding judge B. in a first instance judgment for crimes under art. 6 of the GDR Constitution against nine members of the "Jehovah's Witnesses." Sentences of life imprisonment were passed on two defendants and of between eight to 15 years on seven of them. The defendant had in each case agreed with shorter sentences—of between five and 15 years. In 1952 the defendant fled from the GDR. Investigatory proceedings which had been taken against him in respect of the charge in the Federal Republic of Germany before the Unification Treaty came into effect were finally abandoned by the state prosecutor in 1966.

The regional court Berlin abandoned the proceedings against the defendant (who was accused of bending of the law concomitantly with nine cases of deprivation of freedom) on limitation grounds. The appeal in law by the public prosecutor's office was unsuccessful. The senate acquitted the defendant on the basis of the disputed judgment on factual grounds.

Reasons

. . .

3. Conviction of the defendant for bending the law does not come into consideration. The differing legal assessment by the judge of fact, who assumes conditional intention on the part of the defendant and regards this as sufficient, misses the point that according to the less severe intermediate law—§ 244 DDR-StGB (Criminal Code of the GDR)—direct intention would be necessary (see Senate, NJW 1996, 857 (862)). On the basis of the findings made by the judge of fact the senate may safely exclude the possibility that the prerequisites for directly intentional bending of the law are present.

a) The application of the criminal norm of art. 6 of the East German Constitution* was obviously contrary to the principle of the constitutional state. This however does not in itself justify assuming

---

* [East German Constitution art. 6

Agitation for boycott against democratic institutions and organizations, agitation to murder democratic politicians, articulation of hate against religions, race and nations, militaristic propaganda and agitation for war, and all other activities which are aimed against equal rights, are felonies in the sense of the Criminal Code.—Eds.]

bending of the law, at any rate in so far as it depends on subjective circumstances (see BGH, NJW 1996, 857 (858)). No other consideration can apply for the application of the criminal norm to the findings which formed the basis for the judgment of the East German Supreme Court. In this connection the senate is not failing to appreciate that assuming the presence of "agitation for war and boycott," and in particular of spying, could not seriously withstand critical examination according to constitutional state criteria. It verges on over-extension of the definition of the crime, but it should not be the basis of an accusation of directly intentional bending of the law against a judge working in the GDR, having regard to the time of the crime, in the period of the Cold War and in the starting phase of the GDR (which was highly unsure of itself) (see also on this BGH NJW 1996, 857). The assessment of the judge of fact that in the judgment of the Supreme Court of the GDR the religious convictions of those sentenced by it had been left out of account is also shown, having regard to the observations in the judgment of the Supreme Court of the GDR on the irrelevance of religious motives, to be insufficiently reliable as evidence of directly intentional bending of the law. Admittedly the findings of the disputed judgment suggest that in the proceedings before the Supreme Court at this special point in particular, but also the proceedings in general, were conducted in a manner contrary to the principle of the constitutional state. For the defendant, especially having regard to his position as associate judge, this cannot sufficiently substantiate the accusation of directly intentional bending of the law.

b) Certainly conviction of the defendant for bending the law could in principle be suggested due to the completely unreasonably excessive sentences. Even the lower prison sentences, for which the defendant voted are in an intolerable disproportion to the conduct of which those sentenced were defendant, and this disproportion in any case in itself objectively justified the accusation of bending of the law (see on this only BGH, GA 1958, 241; BGH, NJW 1960, 974f.). Nevertheless the senate definitely rules out here, on the basis of the special features of the case, that even in this respect the necessary unconditional intention to bend the law [*unbedingter Rechtsbeugungsvorsatz*] can be proved. As he did what he could by his proved voting conduct to secure lower sentences, in contradiction to the presiding judge and the reporting judge, the assumption that he could nevertheless deliberately still have decided here for sentences which were so excessive as to bend the law is in the end so unlikely that proof of it can be ruled out.

German Criminal Code

§ 339 (Bending the Law [*Rechtsbeugung*])

A judge, another public official or an arbitrator who in conducting or deciding a legal case is guilty of bending the law for the benefit or to the detriment of a party will be punished with imprisonment from one to five years.

NOTES

1. How do legal systems deal with misconduct of judges, committed in the course of their judicial activities? There are two rather different categories of (possible) judicial misconduct: first, aberrations that are typically motivated by the individual judge's self-interest. (Note that this is a phenomenological description; the wording of § 339 German Criminal Code does not presuppose self-interested acts. It would apply even if the judge does not stand to benefit, or seek to benefit, from his or her behavior; the offense merely requires an act "for the benefit or to the detriment of a party.") The second group of cases that has occupied German courts consists of judicial decisions that are part of systemic injustice within a state regime of injustice.

The main problem when drafting and interpreting statutes that penalize judicial misconduct has to do with judicial independence, an organizational principle based on the idea that state power must be divided (separation of powers to achieve "checks and balances"). For instance, the German Constitution provides in art. 97 para. 1 Basic Law: "Judges are independent and subject only to the law." Consider the impact it would have on judges if every mistake and every minor departure from legal rules could be sanctioned.

Within the German system, it is not common to speak of "judicial immunity" such as the U.S. Supreme Court does in *Mireles v. Waco*. However, the basic underlying notion is similar:

there must be some leeway for judges to make mistakes. The crucial question is where to draw the line. Despite the U.S. Supreme Court's insistence on the principle of judicial immunity, the ruling itself points out that judges are not absolutely immune from criminal liability, and furthermore the newspaper report demonstrates that in severe cases corrupt judges are not immune against criminal charges.

With regard to cases of judicial injustice within a state regime of injustice, an additional question arises: whether these injustices may and should be rectified after a change of regimes has made this possible, rectified by punishing the judges who were active under the old regime.

2. If we turn to the first group, personal motives of self-interest, we find judges acting for financial gain (such as in the case reported by the *New York Times*) or in order to save time by circumventing tedious tasks (see the German case from 2009 excerpted above), and also situations in which emotional gratification is sought through abusive acts against other persons (see *Mireles v. Waco*). German law allows for criminal convictions under certain circumstances. Criminal convictions for "bending of the law" are rare: for instance, in 2010, nobody was convicted under § 339 Criminal Code.

The offense in § 339 Criminal Code tends to be translated as "perversion of justice." *Rechtsbeugung*, however, literally means "bending the law" (or, perhaps, "bending right"). Note that this wording indicates that more is needed than a simple aberration from the law. "Bending" implies a stronger degree of wrongdoing. The case law of the German Federal Court of Justice requires, as repeated in the decision from 2009 reprinted here, that the offender "departs from law and statute deliberately (*bewußt*) and in a grave manner." Section 339 does not criminalize departures from legal norms that are either, objectively, minor violations, or are, subjectively, made only negligently: intention (*Vorsatz*) is required; after a revision of § 339 in 1974, it is clear that conditional intention suffices. (On the use of the previous legal requirement of direct intention (*dolus directus*), i.e., knowledge or purpose, in post-1945 cases to preclude the application of *Rechtsbeugung* to judgments under National Socialism, see Note 3.) As German commentators have pointed out, it is not clear how the requirement of a "deliberate" (*bewußt*, or "conscious") departure from law and statute as part of the objective aspect of the offense definition is consistent with the recognition that, since 1974, conditional intention (as opposed to knowledge, or purpose) is enough to satisfy the subjective aspect of the offense definition. However this question is resolved, it is clear that the German Federal Court of Justice is eager to limit the scope of the offense definition, to prevent its application to mere errors of interpretation or application and in the name of protecting judicial independence.

In the 2009 case, the court found a deliberate and grave departure and convicted the defendant whose behavior was characterized by persistent circumvention of procedural requirements, which he tried to conceal. By German standards, a sentence of three years and six months is rather high, and it seems especially severe if one takes into account that the defendant's disregard for procedural requirements might have had limited effect on the outcome (whatever that may say about the significance of these requirements in actual practice). It is not unlikely that, had he actually heard the men and women in nursing homes, the judge would have allowed measures such as confinement to bed, so that the same results would have been achieved. (Consider how far considerations concerning the impact of procedural misconduct on the outcome of cases should matter. What is the legal good— *Rechtsgut*—at issue in this offense? According to German criminal law doctrine, it is the public legal good of administration of justice (*Rechtspflege*), and only indirectly the individual legal goods of the parties involved.) The sentencing decision in this case hints that, *if* judges do conclude that the standards of judicial conduct have been violated in a grave manner and deliberately, they will not show much empathy for a deviant colleague who has damaged the profession's reputation. (But does the protection of the reputation of the judiciary justify use of the criminal sanction, with a maximum punishment of up to five years in prison?)

If *Mireles v. Waco* were a German case, the judge who had to decide about the civil claim for damages (brought by Waco, the public defender) could invoke a provision in the German Civil Code: A judge who breaches his official duties will only be responsible for any resulting damage arising if the breach of duty consists in a criminal offence (§ 839 para. 2 sentence 1 German Civil Code)—this makes the civil claim dependent on the question of bending the law, § 339 Criminal Code. However, with regard to the specific facts in *Mireles v. Waco*, it is conceivable that Judge Mireles actually could be convicted under § 339 Criminal Code (and thus also successfully sued under the Civil Code for damages) if it could be proved that he ordered the police officers to seize a defense attorney with excessive force. The presence of "excessive force" probably would suffice to make out a grave and deliberate departure from procedural requirements, and thus "bending the law" in the sense of § 339 Criminal Code.

This is precisely what makes § 339 Criminal Code so interesting from a comparative perspective: It is a crime of official misconduct as such. It is one thing to deny judges absolute immunity from general crimes committed during their tenure; it is another to create a crime specifically directed at the exercise of their judicial function. Judges who violate § 339 are criminal judges, rather than criminals who happen to be judges; rather than not shield them from criminal liability, their judicial status makes it possible in the first place, and makes it possible not just for any behavior, but for their judicial behavior.

What's noteworthy about the crime of bending the law from a comparative perspective, however, is not only the notion of criminalizing judicial misconduct; it is the conceptualization of the crime as not merely an instance of bias, but as a very specific bias: bias by means of "bending the law." What could this possibly mean? Section 339 Criminal Code is based on § 314 of the Prussian Criminal Code of 1851, which interestingly labeled the offense not *Rechtsbeugung* but abuse of office (*Amtsmißbrauch*) and defined the offense not in terms of bending the law, but straightforwardly—and broadly—as committing an "injustice" (*Ungerechtigkeit*).

Beyond this institutional context, the question is whether the notion "bending the law" itself reflects a conception of the nature of law, and of the judicial function. Does the idea of bending the law reflect a positivistic conception of law? One that views law as a collection of essentially self-executing commands that reduce the judicial function to the application of legislative rules under a syllogism of juristic logic, with no room for interpretation, and certainly none for a conception of the judicial role that recognizes the jurisgenerative aspect of judging?

3. This last question figures prominently in the second type of *Rechtsbeugung* case, regarding judges within a system of injustice, which attracted considerable attention after the breakdowns of, first, the National Socialist regime and, then, the Communist regime in the former German Democratic Republic.

The first time around, after 1945, the prohibition against bending the law was not applied against former judges, thanks to the case law of the German Federal Court of Justice. In the first years of its existence the Court set a high threshold for the subjective state of mind of judges: it established the interpretation that bending the law (now § 339, until 1974 § 336 Criminal Code) required direct intention (*dolus directus*), that is, a knowing or purposeful departure from the law in force at the time of the decision (see, e.g., BGH, Judgment of December 7, 1956, 1 StR 56/56), a threshold for liability that proved impossibly high. This narrow interpretation and the ensuing lack of criminal convictions for bending of law after 1945 provoked criticism.* Requiring direct intention had the effect that former NS-judges were practically immune from later prosecution. Judges who had harbored doubts about the legality of statutory norms before 1945, but applied them nonetheless, could later not be convicted for bending the law—because they only had conditional intent concerning the unlawfulness of what they were doing. And those who were committed to NS-ideology also lacked the requisite intent—because they did not even suspect an inconsistency between the fundamental requirements of legality and the positive statutory law.

Of course, to even raise the question of whether positive law can nonetheless conflict with law, generally speaking, assumes that there is a distinction between the two, and that there is such a thing as law apart from statute. Or to put this point in several other ways: that there is

---

* See Ingo Müller, *Hitler's Justice: The Courts of the Third Reich* (1991).

Law besides law, right beyond (or beneath) law, or that there is such a thing as "natural law," and if there is, that it has any significance to the daily business of law, and more particularly, of judging, rather than being another—confusing—name for morality, which, everyone agreed, was to be kept out of the realm of law. In other words, the question was whether there was only one conception of law, and that conception was a thoroughgoing positivism that denied the existence of law beyond positive law and strictly limited judges to enforcing the positive law, regardless of its content. Under this conception, judges would have been beyond reproach for their official conduct during the Nazi era if they followed the statutory law (however, they still might have been prosecuted if they departed in a more creative way from positive law, for instance, by finding a way around statutes that had been drafted and enacted before the era of National Socialism).*

Do you think that criminal convictions after the breakdown of a state of injustice, and in particular criminal punishment for bending the law, are the appropriate means to amend these injustices in general? Or are there reasons that support the claim that a juxtaposition of natural law and positive law should be avoided?

4. After the German Democratic Republic ceased to exist in 1990, the question arose whether GDR judges could be punished for bending the law. The judgment of the German Federal Court of Justice from 1996 invokes the requirement of direct intention (i.e., knowledge or *Wissentlichkeit*), rather than conditional intention; in this case, the applicable law—as the "less severe intermediate law"—was the bending the law provision in the *East German Criminal Code*, § 244, which required direct intention. However, note that the acquittal in this case is not entirely representative. This judgment refers to the defendant's position as an associate judge, rather than as presiding judge, and to the special situation in the starting phase of the GDR (the defendant's high age and his early decision to leave the GDR in 1952 also might have played a role, although the ruling does not say so). In the early 1990s, there was a large wave of indictments for bending the law against former GDR judges, and of those at least 181 prosecutions led to convictions[†]—quite a difference to the treatment of judges in the National Socialist regime who were met with much more empathy by the West German judiciary in the 1950s.

C. "Organized Crime": RICO and Money Laundering

The two offenses featured in this section are prime examples of U.S. federal criminal lawmaking in the name of the war on organized crime. They reflect a paradigm of crime far removed from the familiar scenario featuring an interaction between two persons, one of whom appears as "the offender" and the other as "the victim," an appearance to be confirmed, or rejected, by the state with the help of a trial. In the world of RICO and money laundering, the state sees itself as pitted against a powerful and complex criminal organization—the Mafia in one case, drug cartels in the other—that can be vanquished only through ingenuity and persistence in substantive and procedural criminal law.

i. RICO

We begin with RICO (i.e., the Racketeer Influenced and Corrupt Organizations Act), the older, more complex, and more ambitious of the two.

---

* See Markus D. Dubber, "Judicial Positivism and Hitler's Injustice," 93 *Columbia Law Review* (1993), 1807.
[†] See Klaus Marxen, Gerhard Werle, and Petra Schäfter, *Die Strafverfolgung von DDR-Unrecht, Fakten und Zahlen* [Criminal Proceedings for Injustice Committed in the GDR, Facts and Numbers] (2007), 41 table 21.

People v. Capaldo
Supreme Court of New York, New York County
151 Misc. 2d 114, 572 N.Y.S.2d 989 (N.Y. Sup. Ct. 1991)

This case arises out of a well-publicized investigation into the activities of various union officials, painting contractors and alleged organized crime members of the Luchese crime family during the period December 1978 until June, 1990. In essence it is alleged that a criminal enterprise existed in New York City and Long Island to control and corrupt the affairs of District Council No. 9 of the International Brotherhood of Painters and Allied Trades ("Painters Union").

The indictment which resulted from the investigation accuses eight defendants and contains 153 counts. Seven of the eight defendants were officials of various District Councils of the Painters Union during the period in question. The eighth defendant, Daniel Rech, was employed by a painting contractor. All eight defendants are charged in the first count of the indictment with Enterprise Corruption, in violation of Penal Law Section 460.20...

Each of the defendants has moved to dismiss the Enterprise Corruption charge contained in Count One, claiming that the Penal Law Article upon which the charge is grounded is unconstitutionally vague...

Article 460 of the Penal Law, part of the New York "Organized Crime Control Act" ("OCCA"), is a progeny of the federal "Racketeer Influenced and Corrupt Organizations" Law ("RICO"). Like RICO, the article is designed to "thwart the activities of organized crime activity." Although OCCA is based upon RICO, it is clear from both the language of OCCA and the legislative history that the New York State Legislature intended to draft a narrower and more precise statute than RICO. The legislature was aware of and sought to avoid the wide scope and sweep of RICO.

That scope is extremely broad. 18 USC 1962(c) makes it unlawful "for any person employed by or associated with any enterprise engaged in or the activities of which affect, interstate or foreign commerce to conduct or participate, directly or indirectly, in the conduct of such enterprise's affairs through a pattern of racketeering activity..." There is no requirement that the "enterprise" be criminal in nature. As a result RICO has spawned substantial civil and criminal litigation having nothing to do with organized crime.

The drafters of OCCA were also concerned about what they regarded as vague language in RICO. For example, the term "enterprise" is not defined in RICO. "Pattern of racketeering activity" is defined merely as "requiring at least two acts of racketeering activity." Because of RICO's vagueness, there have been suggestions that the law may be vulnerable to constitutional attack.

The failure of the RICO statute to precisely define "enterprise" has not prevented courts from concluding that use of that term therein is constitutional. Indeed, the use of that undefined term has been defended as "necessary in view of the fluid nature of criminal associations." United States v. Swiderski, 593 F.2d 1246, 1249 (D.C. Cir. 1978), cert. denied, 441 U.S. 933 (1979).

The term "pattern of racketeering activity" has also found judicial approval. Racketeering activity means any offense from an extensive list of federal and state crimes listed in the statute. 18 U.S.C 1961. The limited definition of "pattern" contained in RICO has also survived challenges that it is too vague. See, United States v. Angiulo, 897 F.2d 1169, 1179 (1st Cir. 1990), in which the court declined to invalidate the statute as vague "simply because potential uncertainty exists regarding the precise reach of the statute in marginal fact situations..."

The United States Supreme Court has on occasion had difficulty discerning what Congress intended a RICO "pattern" to involve. In Sedima, S.P.R.L. v. Imrex Co., 473 U.S. 479 (1985), the Court expressed dismay that Congress had failed to properly define the term at all but had simply required that a "pattern" include at least two acts of racketeering activity. The court concluded that "pattern" involved something more than two acts, and after examining RICO's legislative history, settled on "continuity plus relationship" as the additional requirement.

Almost five years later, in H. J. Inc. v. The Northwestern Bell Tel. Co., 109 S. Ct. 2893 (1989), the Court conceded that "continuity plus relationship" meant different things to different circuits. Nevertheless, it held firm to the Sedima requirement that, in order to establish a RICO pattern, the government had to show "that the racketeering predicates are related, and that they amount to or pose a threat of continued criminal activity." H.J. Inc., supra at 2900.

Justice Scalia, in a concurring opinion in which three other justices joined, derided the "relationship" requirement as not "much more helpful [to the lower courts] than telling them to look for a pattern—which is what the statute already says." As for the continuity requirement, Justice Scalia wrote:

> Today's opinion has added nothing to improve our prior guidance, which has created a kaleidoscope of circuit positions, except to clarify that RICO may in addition be violated when there is a "threat of continuity." It seems to me this increases rather than removes the vagueness. There

is no reason to believe that the Courts of Appeals will be any more unified in the future, than they have in the past, regarding the content of this law.

Despite these criticisms, no challenge to RICO's constitutionality has ever succeeded in federal court.

Aware of the controversies and ambiguities surrounding RICO, the OCCA drafters sought to limit the statute's applicability and enact "more rigorous definitions." Legislative findings, § 460.00. For example, the OCCA statute, unlike RICO, requires that there be a "criminal enterprise." That phrase is defined in Penal Law Section 460.10(3):

> Criminal Enterprise" means a group of persons sharing a common purpose of engaging in criminal conduct, associated in an ascertainable structure distinct from a pattern of criminal activity, and with a continuity of existence, structure and criminal purpose beyond the scope of individual criminal incidents.

The limiting nature of this phase was described by Assemblyman Melvin H. Miller, one of the authors of OCCA, in a letter dated July 16, 1986 to the Governor's Counsel urging adoption of the legislation:

> The most fundamental difference between the measure approved by the Assembly and all prior versions is the requirement of each defendant's association with a criminal enterprise. Other proposals would have permitted, as does federal law, prosecution of individuals who engage in a pattern of criminal activity without further proof that the criminal activity was accomplished for the purpose of participating in or advancing the affairs of a criminal enterprise with a separate, distinct and ascertainable structure and a continuity of existence and purpose beyond the scope of the pattern itself.
>
> The members of the Codes Committees felt that the extraordinary sanctions allowed under the Act should be reserved for those who not only commit crimes but do so as part of an organized criminal enterprise. Present law is adequate to punish ordinary white-collar crime . . . For that reason, it was not the sponsors' intent to redefine or sanction a new conduct already punishable under current law. Similarly, mere corruption of a legitimate enterprise by a pattern of criminal activity is insufficient to justify prosecution under this Act. Since the pattern of criminal activity is separately prosecutable there is no need to further prosecute the same conduct merely because the defendant is associated with a legitimate enterprise. Rather, the bill now requires association with an ascertainably distinct criminal enterprise in addition to corruption of a legitimate enterprise by criminal activity. In this way we are assured that the Act will only be applied to those who knowingly and voluntarily seek to advance an organized criminal enterprise by their misconduct.

The OCCA drafters also crafted a very specific description of what constitutes a "pattern of criminal activity." Penal Law Section 460.10 reads:

> 4. "Pattern of criminal activity" means conduct engaged in by persons charged in an enterprise corruption count constituting three or more criminal acts that:
> (a) were committed within ten years of the commencement of the criminal action:
> (b) are neither isolated incidents, nor so closely related and connected in point of time or circumstance of commission as to constitute a criminal offense or criminal transaction, as those terms are defined in section 40.10 of the criminal procedure law; and
> (c) are either: (i) related to one another through a common scheme or plan or (ii) were committed, solicited, requested, importuned or intentionally aided by persons acting with the mental culpability required for the commission thereof and associated with or in the criminal enterprise.

The resultant statutory scheme is significantly clearer and more limited than RICO. The complaint of vagueness lacks merit with respect to OCCA. The definitional requirements for a criminal enterprise emphasize a group structure distinct from the criminal acts committed, and it is difficult to perceive how a member of such a criminal organization can profess ignorance that he was violating OCCA.

As noted, RICO has survived all constitutional attacks based on vagueness and over-broadness. The drafters of OCCA, who had the benefit of the federal experience, drafted a narrower and more precise statute . . . Therefore, the motion to dismiss Count One of the indictment on constitutional grounds is denied.

German Criminal Code

§ 129 (Forming Criminal Organizations)

(1) Who founds an organization the aims or activities of which are directed at the commission of crimes or who participates in such an organization as a member, recruits members or supporters for it or supports it, will be punished with imprisonment of not more than five years or a fine.

(2) Para. 1 will not be applied

1. if the organization is a political party which the Federal Constitutional Court has not declared to be unconstitutional,
2. if the commission of crimes is of merely minor significance for the aims or activities, or
3. if the aims or activities concern crimes according to §§ 84 to 87.

(3) The attempt to found an organization described in para. 1 will be punished.

(4) If the offender is one of the ringleaders or hintermen or the case is otherwise especially serious, the penalty is imprisonment from six months to five years; . . .

NOTES

1. German law does not contain a provision in substantive criminal law that closely resembles the offense definitions in RICO and OCCA, as described in *People v. Capaldo*. The introduction of the Racketeer Influenced and Corrupt Organizations Act in 1970 also has to be seen against the background of the divide between federal criminal law and state criminal law and the expansion of federal criminal law, in this case in the name of a comprehensive, national war on organized crime, and the Mafia in particular, the paradigmatic example of a far flung and multifaceted "criminal enterprise." While American criminal law has been mainly state law for centuries, here, federal criminal law is taking the lead in the American war on organized crime, and state criminal law is following suit, much later, and—in the case of New York's Organized Crime Control Act—more circumspectly.

This is not to say that anxieties about "organized crime" never reached the German legislature. In the 1990s, several amendments to statutes carried the name of "organized crime" in their title or the legislative materials explicitly referred to organized crime.* These acts contained a large number of amendments, both to the Code of Criminal Procedure, extending the scope of investigative measures in organized crime cases, and to the Criminal Code. The latter mainly addressed questions of how to seize the financial gains achieved by organized crime. For instance, in 1992, the legislature introduced a new sanction called "Vermögensstrafe" (*property punishment*, § 43a Criminal Code) which consisted of confiscating an offender's property as a whole or in part:

(1) [T]he court may, in addition to a sentence of life imprisonment or of more than two years' imprisonment, require the payment of a monetary amount that is limited by the value of the offender's property (property punishment). Property gains subject to forfeiture are disregarded in the property assessment. The value of the property may be estimated.

Section 43a was declared unconstitutionally vague by the German Federal Constitutional Court in 2002, Judgment of March 20, 2002, 2 BvR 794/95, BVerfGE 105, 135.

2. If one turns to the Special Part of the German Criminal Code, there is no general prohibition against unspecified "patterns" of criminal activity or "racketeering" activity. In the German legal system, the legislature (if the idea of such a general "pattern offense" were to come up) would be aware that the way it is formulated in RICO and OCCA might not survive constitutional scrutiny. Unlike the U.S. federal courts, the German Federal Constitutional Court probably would find a violation of the constitutional vagueness

---

* See, e.g., Gesetz zur Bekämpfung des illegalen Rauschgifthandels und anderer Erscheinungsformen der Organisierten Kriminalität (Act to Combat Illegal Drug Trade and other Forms of Organized Crime) of July 15, 1992, Federal Gazette I p. 1302; Gesetz zur Verbesserung der Bekämpfung der Organisierten Kriminalität (Act for the Improvement of Combating Organized Crime) of May 4, 1998, Federal Gazette I p. 845.

prohibition, art. 103 para. 2 Basic Law, presumably for the reasons suggested by the New York Court of Appeals in *Capaldo*, and which led the New York legislature to try to draft a "narrower and more precise" statute. (But is the problem with RICO its vagueness, or its overbreadth? On the specificity principle, see Chapter 2.)

However, there are of course traces of "combating organized crime" in the German Criminal Code's special part. Take, for instance, the norms in the German Criminal Code titled "Forming Criminal Organizations" and "Forming Terrorist Organizations" (§§ 129, 129a Criminal Code); note, however, that §§ 129 and 129a Criminal Code are older than the so-called war on organized crime. But there are differences: §§ 129, 129a Criminal Code penalize acts that influence the existence and the size of an *organization as such*: founding, recruiting, participating as a member etc. The purpose is to extend applicability of the criminal law by introducing criminal prohibitions against conspiracies (see the discussion in Chapter 12.B). In contrast, the norms in RICO and OCCA aim at the *criminal activities themselves*, described with the words "pattern of racketeering activity" and "pattern of criminal activity."

Another question is whether, instead of recognizing a new offense, punishment should be enhanced in the case of pattern offenses. In the German Criminal Code, a related notion is expressed in the definitions of some medium-severity crimes (which are, according to the German categorization, misdemeanors (*Vergehen*)). If offenders have committed burglary or receiving of stolen goods, the punishment range will be somewhat expanded if they acted as members of a gang devoted to these types of crime or if they acted for the purpose of making continuous profit (§§ 244a, 260a Criminal Code). For instance, the minimum sanction is no longer a fine but imprisonment of one year (§ 244a Criminal Code, aggravated gang theft), or six months (§ 260a Criminal Code, receiving as member of a gang or commercially). But this kind of increased punishment is reserved for a few specific offenses (see also money laundering, § 261 para. 4 sentence 2, and fraud, § 263 para. 5 Criminal Code) rather than being broadened to a general pattern offense. If members of a criminal organization regularly commit felonies such as bank robberies, for example, the punishment ranges already will be broad enough to accommodate the particulars of each case, e.g., among other things, the dangerousness of criminal organizations.

3. *From conspiracy to RICO.* A century ago, Judge Learned Hand dubbed conspiracy "the darling of the modern prosecutor's nursery."[*] RICO was developed as a more powerful alternative to conspiracy in the attempt to break up large criminal networks. In the hands of aggressive federal prosecutors, it soon became "the new darling of the prosecutor's nursery."[†] (It apparently competes for the affections of federal prosecutors with the federal mail fraud statute: "To federal prosecutors of white-collar crime, the mail fraud statute is our Stradivarius, our Colt .45, our Louisville Slugger, our Cuisinart—and our true love."[‡] Unlike in the case of RICO, however, the U.S. Supreme Court has since then intervened, twice, to limit the scope of mail fraud, most recently in *Skilling v. United States*, 561 U.S. ___ (2010), discussed in Chapter 2.B.)

Consider the following attempt to capture the ways in which RICO addresses perceived shortcomings of traditional conspiracy doctrine, from *United States v. Elliott*, 571 F.2d 880 (5th Cir. 1978):

> In this case we deal with the question of whether and, if so, how a free society can protect itself when groups of people, through division of labor, specialization, diversification, complexity of organization, and the accumulation of capital, turn crime into an ongoing business. Congress fired a telling shot at organized crime when it passed the Racketeer Influenced and Corrupt Organizations Act of 1970, popularly known as RICO. 18 U.S.C. §§ 1961 et seq. (1970). Since the enactment of RICO, the federal courts, guided by constitutional and legislative dictates, have been responsible for perfecting the weapons in society's arsenal against criminal confederacies . . .

---

[*] *Harrison v. United States*, 7 F.2d 259 (2d Cir. 1925). (See the discussion of conspiracy in Chapter 12.B.)
[†] Barry Tarlow, "RICO: The New Darling of the Prosecutor's Nursery," 49 *Fordham Law Review* (1980), 165.
[‡] Jed S. Rakoff, "The Federal Mail Fraud Statute (Part 1)," 18 *Duquesne Law Review* (1980), 771.

Predictably, the government and the defendants differ as to what this case is about. According to the defendants, what we are dealing with is a leg, a tail, a trunk, an ear—separate entities unaffected by RICO proscriptions. The government, on the other hand, asserts that we have come eyeball to eyeball with a single creature of behemoth proportions, securely within RICO's grasp...

Simply stated, this is a case involving a group of persons informally associated with the purpose of profiting from criminal activity. The facts giving rise to this generalization, however, are considerably more complex. Evidence presented during the 12 day trial implicated the six defendants and 37 unindicted co-conspirators in more than 20 different criminal endeavors...

...

B. RICO to the Rescue: The Enterprise Conspiracy

In enacting RICO, Congress found that "organized crime continues to grow" in part "because the sanctions and remedies available to the Government are unnecessarily limited in scope and impact." Thus, one of the express purposes of the Act was "to seek the eradication of organized crime...by establishing new penal prohibitions, and by providing enhanced sanctions and new remedies to deal with the unlawful activities of those engaged in organized crime." Pub.L. 91-452, § 1, 84 Stat. 922 (1970).

Against this background, we are convinced that, through RICO, Congress intended to authorize the single prosecution of a multi-faceted, diversified conspiracy by [creating] a new statutory concept: the enterprise.

"To achieve this result, Congress acted against the backdrop of hornbook conspiracy law. Under the general federal conspiracy statute, the precise nature and extent of the conspiracy must be determined by reference to the agreement which embraces and defines its objects. Whether the object of a single agreement is to commit one or many crimes, it is in either case that agreement which constitutes the conspiracy which the statute punishes."
Braverman v. United States, 317 U.S. 49, 53, 63 S.Ct. 99, 102 (1942).

In the context of organized crime, this principle inhibited mass prosecutions because a single agreement or "common objective" cannot be inferred from the commission of highly diverse crimes by apparently unrelated individuals. RICO helps to eliminate this problem by creating a substantive offense which ties together these diverse parties and crimes. Thus, the object of a RICO conspiracy is to violate a substantive RICO provision—here, to conduct or participate in the affairs of an enterprise through a pattern of racketeering activity—and not merely to commit each of the predicate crimes necessary to demonstrate a pattern of racketeering activity. The gravamen of the conspiracy charge in this case is not that each defendant agreed to commit arson, to steal goods from interstate commerce, to obstruct justice, and to sell narcotics; rather, it is that each agreed to participate, directly and indirectly, in the affairs of the enterprise by committing two or more predicate crimes. Under the statute, it is irrelevant that each defendant participated in the enterprise's affairs through different, even unrelated crimes, so long as we may reasonably infer that each crime was intended to further the enterprise's affairs. To find a single conspiracy, we still must look for agreement on an overall objective. What Congress did was to define that objective through the substantive provisions of the Act.

C. Constitutional Considerations

The "enterprise conspiracy" is a legislative innovation in the realm of individual liability for group crime. We need to consider whether this innovation comports with the fundamental demand of due process that guilt remain "individual and personal". See Kotteakos v. United States, 328 U.S. 750, 772 (1946).

The substantive proscriptions of the RICO statute apply to insiders and outsiders—those merely "associated with" an enterprise—who participate directly and indirectly in the enterprise's affairs through a pattern of racketeering activity. 18 U.S.C. § 1962(c). Thus, the RICO net is woven tightly to trap even the smallest fish, those peripherally involved with the enterprise. This effect is enhanced by principles of conspiracy law also developed to facilitate prosecution of conspirators at all levels. Direct evidence of agreement is unnecessary: "proof of such an agreement may rest upon inferences drawn from relevant and competent circumstantial evidence—ordinarily the acts and conduct of the alleged conspirators themselves." Additionally, once the conspiracy has been established, the government need show only "slight evidence" that a particular person was a member of the conspiracy. Of course, "a party to a conspiracy need not know the identity, or even the number, of his confederates."

Undeniably, then, under the RICO conspiracy provision, remote associates of an enterprise may be convicted as conspirators on the basis of purely circumstantial evidence. We cannot say, however, that this section of the statute demands inferences that cannot reasonably be drawn from circumstantial evidence or that it otherwise offends the rule that guilt be individual and personal. The Act does not authorize that individuals "be tried en masse for the conglomeration of distinct and separate offenses committed by others." Kotteakos, 328 U.S. 750. Nor does it punish mere association with conspirators or knowledge of illegal activity; its proscriptions are directed against conduct, not status. To be convicted as a member of an enterprise conspiracy, an individual, by his words or actions, must have objectively manifested an agreement to participate, directly or indirectly, in the affairs of an enterprise through the commission of two or more predicate crimes. One whose agreement with the members of an enterprise did not include this vital element cannot be convicted under the Act. Where, as here, the evidence establishes that each defendant, over a period of years, committed several acts of racketeering activity in furtherance of the enterprise's affairs, the inference of an agreement to do so is unmistakable.

It is well established that "the government is not required to prove that a conspirator had full knowledge of all the details of the conspiracy; knowledge of the essential nature of the plan is sufficient." United States v. Brasseaux, 509 F.2d 157, 160 n. 3 (5th Cir. 1975). The Supreme Court explained the policy behind this rule in Blumenthal v. United States, 332 U.S. 539, 556–57 (1947):

> "For it is most often true, especially in broad schemes calling for the aid of many persons, that after discovery of enough to show clearly the essence of the scheme and the identity of a number participating, the identity and the fact of participation of others remain undiscovered and undiscoverable. Secrecy and concealment are essential features of successful conspiracy. The more completely they are achieved, the more successful the crime. Hence the law rightly gives room for allowing the conviction of those discovered upon showing sufficiently the essential nature of the plan and their connections with it, without requiring evidence of knowledge of all its details or of the participation of others. Otherwise the difficulties, not only of discovery, but of certainty in proof and of correlating proof with pleading would become insuperable, and conspirators would go free by their very ingenuity."

. . .

Our society disdains mass prosecutions because we abhor the totalitarian doctrine of mass guilt. We nevertheless punish conspiracy as a distinct offense because we recognize that collective action toward an illegal end involves a greater risk to society than individual action toward the same end. That risk is greatly compounded when the conspirators contemplate not a single crime but a career of crime. "There are times when of necessity, because of the nature and scope of the particular federation, large numbers of persons taking part must be tried together or perhaps not at all . . . When many conspire, they invite mass trial by their conduct." Kotteakos, 328 U.S. at 773.

In the end, it is useful to think of RICO as creating not just one tool, but as assembling an entire tool kit for the federal war on organized crime. Its substantive provisions are defined to give federal prosecutors maximum flexibility in constructing a strategy for building a circumstantial case by casting a wide net to catch, first, the smallest fish they can credibly threaten with the massive and diverse penalties—including civil sanctions, criminal penalties, and property forfeiture—that RICO holds in store for those associated with a sprawling "criminal enterprise," which may be held together by nothing more than the common "purpose of profiting from criminal activity," and then start a chain that leads from one fish to a bigger one, then to another, until they have reached the "chairman of the board." Courts, as *Elliott* illustrates, often see themselves as contributing to this pursuit of organized crime, by "perfecting the weapons in society's arsenal against criminal confederacies." In this environment, it is not difficult to see why what *Elliott* calls "constitutional and legislative dictates" and "constitutional considerations" may provide guidance, but little constraint.*

---

* See generally Gerard E. Lynch, "RICO: The Crime of Being a Criminal," 87 *Columbia Law Review* (1987), 661.

ii. Money laundering

This is our second encounter with money laundering. Our very first case, *United States v. Blarek*, was a money laundering case, against two interior decorators who—in Judge Weinstein's telling—entered into a Faustian bargain with an "ill-famed and powerful criminal client," a Colombian drug lord by the name of José Santacruz Londoño: he fed their obsession to create art, and they cleaned his dirty drug money in return. *Blarek* was about *sentencing* interior decorators for money laundering. The following case is about how they, and others like them, become ensnared in the net of the criminal law of money laundering in the first place.

Unlike RICO, federal money laundering has a direct analogue in German criminal law. What is more, similar issues arise in both systems, including the possible application of money laundering statutes to criminal defense lawyers' fees.

United States v. Campbell
U.S. Court of Appeals for the Fourth Circuit
977 F.2d 854 (4th Cir. 1992)

Ervin, Chief Judge:

The United States appeals from the district court's grant of Ellen Campbell's motion for judgment of acquittal on charges of money laundering, 18 U.S.C. § 1956(a)(1)(B)(i), and engaging in a transaction in criminally derived property, 18 U.S.C. § 1957(a)...

In the summer of 1989, Ellen Campbell was a licensed real estate agent working at Lake Norman Realty in Mooresville, North Carolina. During the same period, Mark Lawing was a drug dealer in Kannapolis, North Carolina. Lawing decided to buy a house on Lake Norman...

Lawing represented himself to Campbell as the owner of a legitimate business, L & N Autocraft, which purportedly performed automobile customizing services. When meeting with Campbell, Lawing would travel in either a red Porsche he owned or a gold Porsche owned by a fellow drug dealer, Randy Sweatt, who would usually accompany Lawing. During the trips to look at houses, which occurred during normal business hours, Lawing would bring his cellular phone and would often consume food and beer with Sweatt. At one point, Lawing brought a briefcase containing $ 20,000 in cash, showing the money to Campbell to demonstrate his ability to purchase a house.

Lawing eventually settled upon a house listed for $ 191,000 and owned by Edward and Nancy Guy Fortier... After negotiations, Lawing and the Fortiers agreed on a price of $ 182,500, and entered into a written contract. Lawing was unable to secure a loan and decided to ask the Fortiers to accept $ 60,000 under the table in cash and to lower the contract price to $ 122,500.[1]... The Fortiers agreed...

Thereafter Lawing met the Fortiers... and Campbell in the Mooresville sales office with $ 60,000 in cash. The money was wrapped in small bundles and carried in a brown paper grocery bag. The money was counted, and a new contract was executed reflecting a sales price of $ 122,500. Lawing tipped... Campbell with "a couple of hundred dollars."...

The money laundering statute under which Campbell was charged applies to any person who:

> knowing that the property involved in a financial transaction represents the proceeds of some form of unlawful activity, conducts or attempts to conduct such a financial transaction which in fact involves the proceeds of specified unlawful activity...knowing that the transaction is designed in whole or in part...to conceal or disguise the nature, the location, the source, the ownership, or the control of the proceeds of specified unlawful activity...
>
> 18 U.S.C. § 1956(a)(1).

The district court found, and Campbell does not dispute, that there was adequate evidence for the jury to find that Campbell conducted a financial transaction which in fact involved the proceeds of Lawing's illegal drug activities. The central issue in contention is whether there was sufficient evidence for the jury to find that Campbell possessed the knowledge that: (1) Lawing's funds were the proceeds of illegal activity, and (2) the transaction was designed to disguise the nature of those proceeds.

---

[1] Lawing's explanation to Campbell of this unorthodox arrangement was that the lower purchase price would allow Lawing's parents to qualify for a mortgage. Lawing would then make the mortgage payments on his parent's behalf. Lawing justified the secrecy of the arrangement by explaining that his parents had to remain unaware of the $ 60,000 payment because the only way he could induce their involvement was to convince them he was getting an excellent bargain on the real estate.

In assessing Campbell's culpability, it must be noted that the statute requires actual subjective knowledge. Campbell cannot be convicted on what she objectively should have known. However, this requirement is softened somewhat by the doctrine of willful blindness. In this case, the jury was instructed that:

The element of knowledge may be satisfied by inferences drawn from proof that a defendant deliberately closed her eyes to what would otherwise have been obvious to her. A finding beyond a reasonable doubt of a conscious purpose to avoid enlightenment would permit an inference of knowledge. Stated another way, a defendant's knowledge of a fact may be inferred upon willful blindness to the existence of a fact.

It is entirely up to you as to whether you find any deliberate closing of the eyes and inferences to be drawn from any evidence. A showing of negligence is not sufficient to support a finding of willfulness or knowledge.

I caution you that the willful blindness charge does not authorize you to find that the defendant acted knowingly because she should have known what was occurring when the property at 763 Sundown Road was being sold, or that in the exercise of hindsight she should have known what was occurring or because she was negligent in failing to recognize what was occurring or even because she was reckless or foolish in failing to recognize what was occurring.

Instead, the Government must prove beyond a reasonable doubt that the defendant purposely and deliberately contrived to avoid learning all of the facts.

As outlined above, a money laundering conviction under section 1956(a)(1)(B)(i) requires proof of the defendant's knowledge of two separate facts: (1) that the funds involved in the transaction were the proceeds of illegal activity; and (2) that the transaction was designed to conceal the nature of the proceeds. In its opinion supporting the entry of the judgment of acquittal, the district court erred in interpreting the elements of the offense. After correctly reciting the elements of the statute, the court stated, "in a prosecution against a party other than the drug dealer," the Government must show "a purpose of concealment" and "knowledge of the drug dealer's activities." This assertion misstates the Government's burden. The Government need not prove that the defendant had the purpose of concealing the proceeds of illegal activity. Instead, as the plain language of the statute suggests, the Government must only show that the defendant possessed the knowledge that the transaction was designed to conceal illegal proceeds. This distinction is critical in cases such as the present one, in which the defendant is a person other than the individual who is the source of the tainted money. It is clear from the record that Campbell herself did not act with the purpose of concealing drug proceeds. Her motive, without question, was to close the real estate deal and collect the resulting commission, without regard to the source of the money or the effect of the transaction in concealing a portion of the purchase price. However, Campbell's motivations are irrelevant. Under the terms of the statute, the relevant question is not Campbell's purpose, but rather her knowledge of Lawing's purpose.[4]

The sufficiency of evidence regarding Campbell's knowledge of Lawing's purpose depends on whether Campbell was aware of Lawing's status as a drug dealer. Assuming for the moment that Campbell knew that Lawing's funds were derived from illegal activity, then the under the table transfer of $ 60,000 in cash would have been sufficient, by itself, to allow the jury to find that Campbell knew, or was willfully blind to the fact, that the transaction was designed for an illicit purpose. Only if Campbell was oblivious to the illicit nature of Lawing's funds could she credibly argue that she believed Lawing's explanation of the under the table transfer of cash and was unaware of the money laundering potential of the transaction. In short, the fraudulent nature of the transaction itself provides a sufficient basis from which a jury could infer Campbell's knowledge of the transaction's purpose, if, as assumed above, Campbell also knew of the illegal source of Lawing's money.[5] As a result, we find that, in this case, the knowledge components of the money

---

[4] We have no difficulty in finding that Lawing's purpose satisfied the statutory requirement that the transaction be "designed in whole or in part ... to conceal or disguise the nature, the location, the source, the ownership, or the control of the proceeds of specified unlawful activity ...." 18 U.S.C. § 1956(a)(1)(B). The omission of $ 60,000 from all documentation regarding the sales price of the property clearly satisfies this standard—concealing both the nature and the location of Lawing's illegally derived funds. See United States v. Lovett, 964 F.2d 1029, 1034 (10th Cir. 1992) (money laundering transaction need not necessarily conceal the identity of the participants in the transaction; concealment of the funds themselves is sufficient), petition for cert. filed, June 22, 1992. Accordingly, we need not address the Government's alternative argument that Lawing concealed ownership of the funds by placing title to the Lake Norman property in the name of his parents.

[5] In this respect the present case is completely distinguishable from the principal case relied upon by the district court, United States v. Sanders, 929 F.2d 1466 (10th Cir.), cert. denied, 116 L. Ed. 2d 109 (1991). In that case, the court overturned two money laundering convictions of a defendant who, with funds admittedly derived from an illegal source, had purchased two automobiles. Unlike the present case, there was nothing irregular about the transactions

laundering statute collapse into a single inquiry: Did Campbell know that Lawing's funds were derived from an illegal source?

The Government emphasizes that the district court misstated the Government's burden on this point as well, by holding that the Government must show Campbell's "knowledge of the drug dealer's activities." As the text of the statute indicates, the Government need only show knowledge that the funds represented "the proceeds of some form of unlawful activity." 18 U.S.C. § 1956(a)(1). Practically, this distinction makes little difference. All of the Government's evidence was designed to show that Campbell knew that Lawing was a drug dealer. There is no indication that the jury could have believed that Lawing was involved in some form of criminal activity other than drug dealing. As a result, the district court's misstatement on this point is of little consequence.

The evidence pointing to Campbell's knowledge of Lawing's illegal activities is not overwhelming. First, we find that the district court correctly excluded from consideration testimony by Sweatt that Lawing was a "known" drug dealer. Kannapolis, where Lawing's operations were located, is approximately fifteen miles from Mooresville, where Campbell lived and worked, and, as the district court pointed out, there was no indication that Lawing's reputation extended over such an extensive "community."

However, the district court also downplayed evidence that we find to be highly relevant. [T]he Government presented extensive evidence regarding Lawing's lifestyle. This evidence showed that Lawing and his companion both drove new Porsches, and that Lawing carried a cellular phone, flashed vast amounts of cash, and was able to be away from his purportedly legitimate business for long stretches of time during normal working hours. The district court conceded that this evidence "is not wholly [sic] irrelevant" to Campbell's knowledge of Lawing's true occupation, but noted that Lawing's lifestyle was not inconsistent with that of many of the other inhabitants of the affluent Lake Norman area who were not drug dealers. Again, we find that the district court has drawn inferences from the evidence which, while possibly well-founded, are not the only inferences that can be drawn. It should have been left to the jury to decide whether or not the Government's evidence of Lawing's lifestyle was sufficient to negate the credibility of Campbell's assertion that she believed Lawing to be a legitimate businessman.

The statute under which Campbell was charged in Count 2 provides:

Whoever ... knowingly engages or attempts to engage in a monetary transaction in criminally derived property that is of a value greater than $ 10,000 and is derived from specified unlawful activity, shall be punished as provided in subsection (b).

18 U.S.C. § 1957(a).

The parties do not dispute that Campbell engaged in a monetary transaction in property of a value in excess of $ 10,000 or that the property was derived from "specified unlawful activity" as defined by the statute. Once again, the dispositive question is whether Campbell knew that Lawing's funds were the proceeds of criminal activity. As such, the discussion above with regard to the money laundering charge is completely applicable here. Because a jury could reasonably find that Campbell knew of, or was willfully blind to, Lawing's true occupation, it was error for the district court to grant a judgment of acquittal on this count as well ...

Julie Kay, "Heat is on Attorneys in Drug Trafficking Cases: Florida Lawyer Is Accused of Taking 'Dirty Money,'" *Miami Daily Business Review*, May 25, 2001.

[C]riminal defense attorney Neil Taylor is now on trial in U.S. District Court in Miami on charges of money laundering, conspiracy to obstruct justice and filing false tax returns in connection with accepting legal fees to represent an accused drug dealer. Taylor is charged with taking more than $1 million in illicit fees from accused drug lords Willie Falcon and Sal Magluta, in violation of a restraining order that froze the two men's assets, then hiding the source of the money on his tax forms.

When accepting payments of more than $10,000, all businesses, including law firms, are required to file Internal Revenue Service forms detailing names and full identification of those paying. Taylor, say prosecutors, conspired with the accused drug traffickers to make up a phony name and driver license for Wilfredo Alvarez, who was a courier for Falcon and Magluta, and who allegedly paid

themselves. The court found the transactions to be devoid of any attempt "to conceal or disguise the source or nature of the proceeds" and found that application of the money laundering statute to "ordinary commercial transactions" would "turn the money laundering statute into a 'money spending statute,' " a result clearly not intended by Congress. The present case, by contrast, presents a highly irregular financial transaction which, by its very structure, was designed to mislead onlookers as to the amount of money involved in the transaction.

Taylor's fee. Taylor's attorney, Robert Josefsberg, a partner at Podhurst Orseck Josefsberg in Miami, denies the charges.

Prosecutors have accused Falcon and Magluta in court of operating a $2 billion drug trafficking business. They allegedly spent $25 million on attorneys' fees through the 1990s. They were acquitted in 1996, but a jury foreman was later charged with taking a bribe in that trial. Falcon and Magluta, who remain behind bars, are facing a new federal indictment alleging conspiracy to intimidate and bribe witnesses.

Taylor...is the fourth lawyer—out of nearly 40 who represented Falcon and Magluta—to be prosecuted by the U.S. Attorney's office in Miami. The other three–Don Ferguson, Leonard Mark Dachs and Richard Martinez–all were convicted. "This has had a chilling effect on criminal defense lawyers," says Richard Sharpstein, another criminal defense attorney who used to specialize in drug cases. "I and most lawyers will not go near cases where the fees are questionable, 'cause they're absolutely not worth it."

The U.S. Department of Justice started clamping down on lawyers who represent alleged drug dealers in the early 1980s by seizing their fees as forfeiture funds. The crackdown was prompted by fear among tough-on-drugs politicians and law enforcement officials that the government was losing the war on illegal narcotics because cocaine and marijuana kingpins were hiring high-priced lawyers and winning acquittals.

In the mid-1980s, Congress passed tough money laundering laws, ... which gave federal prosecutors powerful new weapons in the narcotics war. It enabled them to put anyone who took money originating from drug trafficking or other illegal activities in prison.

But some defense attorneys say these statutes were never intended to be used against attorneys representing defendants in these cases. They point to an amendment, passed by Congress in 1994 after heavy lobbying by criminal defense lawyers, that excludes funds used "for the right to representation as guaranteed by the Sixth Amendment" from consideration in money laundering cases....

A broader problem, according to the South Florida defense bar, is that the government also is scrutinizing legal fees paid by those charged with white-collar crimes such as health care fraud and securities fraud....

Reuben Cahn, chief assistant to the federal public defender in Miami, angrily argues that the U.S. Attorney's pre-conviction seizure of defendants' assets and its targeting of defense attorneys essentially is forcing wealthy defendants to turn to public defenders for representation. The problem, he says, is that the P.D.'s office is supposed to represent the indigent and already is stretched thin.

"It's galling," Cahn says. "The U.S. Attorney's office has 221 regular attorneys and 40 special attorneys. We have 49 lawyers. It's a struggle to provide good representation to everyone."

To make sure the feds won't object to their collecting legal fees from "hot" clients, several criminal defense attorneys say they routinely meet with the line prosecutor in the case before accepting the client. But that is no guarantee of safe passage. In his opening statement, prosecutor Rubino acknowledged that Neil Taylor had met beforehand with the prosecutor in the Falcon/Magluta case to discuss his fees before taking on representation of the two defendants. But Taylor still was prosecuted....

[Taylor's trial ended in a mistrial after accusations surfaced that the lone hold-out juror for acquittal had taken a bribe. Julie Kay, "Money Laundering Trial Jurors Accused Holdout of Taking Bribe," *Miami Daily Business Review*, June 22, 2001, at A1.—Eds.]

German Federal Constitutional Court
2 BvR 1520/01, 2 BvR 1521/01, BVerfGE 110, 226 (March 30, 2004)

Facts

The complainants are lawyers. They objected to their conviction in a criminal court for money laundering through acceptance of a defence lawyer's fee and for being accessories after the fact in combination with money laundering in connection with receiving released securities.

... The regional court sentenced the complainants by a judgment of May 4, 2000, in each case to nine months imprisonment (the implementation of which it suspended) for intentional money laundering. According to the findings in the judgment the complainants took on the defence of two clients who were leading members of the "German Kings Club" which was founded in 1991 and were amongst the persons mainly responsible in its successor organization, the "European Kings Club" founded in 1992 (hereafter called EKC). The public prosecutor's office had a suspicion that the EKC was carrying on so-called letter transactions within the framework of a fraudulent snowball system; the EKC was promising its investors, on the purchase of a "letter" at the price of 1400 DM, the repayment of a total sum of 2400 DM in twelve monthly installments. A yield of this kind could not be achieved by reputable investment businesses on the capital market and could only be financed from the deposits of new investors. According to the findings of the criminal chamber the complainants after the arrest of their clients received in December 1994 a sum of 200,000 DM in cash in each case as an advance of fees for representation in the arrest warrant proceedings, although they knew for certain that the money came from the fraudulent actions committed by their clients. The Federal Court of Justice dismissed the complainants appeal in law directed against this...(BGHSt 47, 68). By a judgment of January 15, 2003, the regional court sentenced the complainants to nine months imprisonment for being accessories after the fact in combination with money laundering...

By their constitutional complaints the complainants objected to all the judgments issued in the criminal proceedings. They claimed amongst other things that the interpretation of the definition of money laundering on which the decisions were based infringed their right to free exercise of their profession guaranteed by art. 12 para. 1 Basic Law, and at the same time endangered the institution of criminal defence...

The constitutional complaints were unsuccessful in the end result.

Reasons

...

The interpretation that the acceptance of a fee or an advance on fees by a defence lawyer can be criminal money laundering in the sense of § 261 para. 2 no. 1 Criminal Code does not meet with any fundamental doubts in constitutional law...

Since the introduction of the criminal offence of money laundering, the question of including defence lawyers in the area of application of § 261 para. 2 no. 1 Criminal Code has been the subject of controversy. The leading doctrine reaches the conclusion that a defence lawyer is capable of committing money laundering like any other participant in business life (see Altenhain, in: Nomos Commentary on the StGB [NK-StGB], 2001, § 261 marginal nos. 126 ff.; Hefendehl, in: Festschrift for Roxin, 2001, pp. 145, 168; Neuheuser, in: MünchKomm-StGB, 2003, § 261 marginal no. 74; Peglau, wistra (Journal for Business Criminal Law) 2001, p. 461; Stree, in Schönke/Schröder, StGB, 26th edit. [2001], § 261 marginal no. 17; Tröndle/Fischer, StGB, 51st edit. [2003], § 261 marginal no. 32).

Because of possible dangers for the freedom of the legal profession and for the effectiveness of criminal defence, parts of the criminal law literature propose to limit the applicability of the definition to actions by defence lawyers; the reasoning diverges widely... The proponents of the (objective) definition solution refer to the legal concepts of social or professional appropriateness (see Bauer, in: Fragmentarisches Strafrecht [Fragmentary Criminal Law], 2003, p. 127, 143), demand a teleological reduction of the criminal definition (see Barton StV 1993, 156; Hoyer, in: SK-StGB, 2003, § 261 marginal no. 21; Laufhütte/Kuschel, in: LK, 11th edit. [2001], § 261 marginal no. 8;...) or regard the substantive law norm of § 261 Criminal Code as being "substituted" by § 137 Code of Criminal Procedure which guarantees the right of the defendant to defence of his choice (see Lüderssen, in Festschrift for Waltos, 2000, p. 329f.; the same, in Löwe/Rosenberg, StPO, 25th edit. [2002] preliminary note § 137 marginal no. 117). The Hamburg Higher Regional Court favors a restrictive interpretation (in conformity with the Constitution) of the objective definition and a "fee privilege" for defence lawyers (NJW 2000, 673): on a balancing of the competing legal interests protected in constitutional law the right of the defence lawyer to free exercise of his profession and the right of the defendant to legal assistance with his defence outweighed the public interest in effective combating of money laundering... The so-called justification solution derives from the position of the defence lawyer in procedural law...a ground of justification of its own kind (see Bernsmann, StV 2000, 40, 43f.; Ambos, JZ 2002, 70 80).

On application of the traditional methods of interpretation the acceptance of a fee or an advance on fees by a defence lawyer can fulfill the definition of the crime in § 261 para. 2 no. 1 Criminal Code if the fee is paid out of funds which derive from one of the predicate offences listed in § 261 para. 1 sentence 2 Criminal Code...

The criminal norm formulated as a general crime according to its wording forbids anyone to obtain money which derives from a listed offence. Therefore the defence lawyer falls to be considered like any other person as a capable perpetrator of money laundering. The receipt of a fee can realize the criminal act of "obtaining"...

The history of the origin of § 261 Criminal Code does not conflict with including defence lawyers among the possible perpetrators. The legislature has refrained from providing for exceptions for special types of cases in order not to weaken the goal pursued by the crime of money laundering, which was the effective combating of organized crime by economic isolation of dangerous criminals; this also applies to defence lawyers . . .

§ 261 para. 2 no. 1 Criminal Code signifies for defence lawyers an intrusion into their basic right of free exercise of their profession (art. 12 para. 1 Basic Law).

Art. 12 para. 1 Basic Law guarantees to the individual the free exercise of his vocation as the basis of his personal and economic way of life. The norm concretizes the basic right to free development of the personality in the realm of individual vocational performance and obtaining a livelihood (see BVerfGE 54, 301, 313; BVerfGE 75, 284, 292; BVerfGE 101, 331, 364ff.) . . .

The exercise of the profession of a lawyer which is characterized by the principle of a free legal profession is under the regime of the Basic Law subject to the free and unregulated self-determination of the individual lawyer (see BVerfGE 15, 226, 234; BVerfGE 50, 16, 29; BVerfGE 63, 266, 284). Protecting the exercise of the lawyers' profession from state control and supervision not only lies in the individual interest of the single lawyer or the single person seeking legal services. The lawyer is an "organ for the administration of justice" (see BRAO [Federal Lawyers Order] §§ 1 and 3) and is called to represent the interests of his client (see BVerfGE 10, 185, 198). His professional activity lies in the interest of the general public in an effective administration of justice, arranged in accordance with constitutional state principles (see BVerfGE 15, 226, 234; BVerfGE 34, 293, 302; BVerfGE 37, 67, 77ff.; BVerfGE 72, 51, 63ff.) . . .

The protection of art. 12 para. 1 Basic Law also encompasses criminal defence which is one of the important professional tasks of a lawyer (see BVerfGE 15, 226, 231; BVerfGE 22, 114, 119f.; BVerfGE 34, 293, 299; BVerfGE 39, 238, 242; . . .). The institution of criminal defence is guaranteed by the constitutional state principle of the Basic Law. The criminal process applied to investigation of the facts of a case, with its task of achieving the state claim to punish in order to protect legal interests of individuals and for the sake of the general public, must be formulated fairly (see BVerfGE 57, 250, 275ff.; consistent case law); its implementation is associated with substantial burdens and possible far-reaching consequences for the person affected. The individual must be able to have an active and effective influence on the course of the proceedings taken against him and on their outcome. Proceedings which are fair and in accordance with the constitutional state principle require "equality of arms" between the prosecution authorities on the one hand and the defendant on the other . . . The collaboration of a defence lawyer who stands by the side of the defendant advising him and brings to attention on his behalf the circumstances exonerating him is, apart from situations which are simple in nature, indispensable for the establishment of "equality of arms" (see Rzepka, Zur Fairness im deutschen Strafverfahren [On fairness in the German criminal process], 2000, p. 397ff.). The defendant's right to be defended in criminal proceedings by a lawyer of his choice and in whom he has confidence is not only statutorily guaranteed by § 137 para. 1 Code of Criminal Procedure and art. 6 para. 3 letter c ECHR, but at the same time by art. 2 para. 1 Basic Law in combination with the principle of the constitutional state, guaranteed in constitutional law by the Basic Law (see BVerfGE 26, 66, 71; BVerfGE 34, 293, 302; BVerfGE 38, 105, 111; BVerfGE 39, 156, 163; BVerfGE 66, 313, 318f.). By anchoring the right to defence in the concept of a criminal process which accords with the principle of the constitutional state, the Federal Constitutional Court has always emphasized free choice and confidence as prerequisites of an effective criminal defence (see BVerfGE 66, 313, 318f.; consistent case law) . . .

§ 261 para. 2 no. 1 Criminal Code intrudes into the defence lawyer's freedom of exercise of profession.

The statutory prohibition, applying equally for all taking part in business transactions, on obtaining tainted investments deriving from certain predicate offences impairs the freedom of decision of the defence lawyer in a special way when taking on a client because of the particular nature of his professional activity.

The circle of clients of a defence lawyer who engages in advocacy typically includes persons who have come under suspicion of an offence listed in the definition of money laundering and against whom investigative proceedings are therefore taken. The defence lawyer has to defend the client against suspicion of this crime . . .

The exercise of this professional task and the fact that the defence lawyer obtains from the defence relationship information about the actual events which form the basis of the accusation of the crime as well as about the financial circumstances of his client can significantly raise the risk of the defence lawyer incurring initial suspicion of money laundering himself (see W. Schmidt, StraFo 2003, 2 [4]).

The uncertainties and risks associated with § 261 para. 2 no. 1 Criminal Code not only result from the conditions of acting in the client relationship, but also from the wide version of the subjective part of the definition. The legislature has refrained from qualifying subjective characteristics of the definition; conditional intention or even gross negligence (*Leichtfertigkeit*) suffice for the ascription of guilt (see § 261 para. 5 Criminal Code). If the defence lawyer considers it to be possible at the time of receipt of the fee that it comes from a listed offence, and he condones this, he can be convicted of intentional money laundering (see Tröndle/Fischer, § 261 marginal no. 41). The perception of the facts by the person acting—apart from rare cases of a credible confession—will as a rule only become available from outward indicators; the assessment of these can scarcely be predicted with certainty even if in the end result they support the accusation in such a way as to convince the court that the defence lawyer had considered the criminal origin of his fee to be possible and had therefore acted intentionally.

This specific situation of risk will frequently present the defence lawyer before taking on clients for offences in the list in relation to money laundering with the question of whether he wants to undertake a defence at all which is associated with a risk, which is not insignificant and only calculable with difficulty, of his own criminal liability, and which moreover possibly only leads to a duty defence. His freedom of decision for or against taking on a client is thereby severely affected...

If the public prosecutor's office affirms an initial suspicion of money laundering against the defence lawyer and institutes investigatory proceedings against him, the defence lawyer cannot continue with the brief. The defence lawyer, being himself a defendant in the same complex of facts, cannot fulfill the role assigned to him in the constitutional state criminal process as an independent organ in the administration of justice of equal status as the public prosecutor's office and the court. His own position as defendant can lead to him being inclined to block the path to finding the truth or setting aside the interests of his client in order to protect himself as far as possible from being punished (BVerfGE 34, 293, 300f.). The conflict of interests which becomes obvious with his own position as defendant prevents a defence lawyer of choice from appropriately exercising his function of assistance (see BGHSt 45, 235, 248)...

The substantive criminal norm and the apparatus of criminal process assigned to it are in this respect also likely to endanger the relationship of confidence between the lawyer and the client.

The basic duties of a lawyer which establish his status include the duty of silence (see BVerfGE 76, 171, 189f.)...

A reasonable client will ask himself whether he can seriously reckon on the silence of his defence lawyer if investigations are being made against him for suspicion of money laundering in the same crime complex in which the defence is to take place... But if a client has to reckon with the revelation of confidential information by his own defence lawyer, then in the interest of self-protection he will be inclined to refrain from open and free communication with his defence lawyer. Effective criminal defence is no longer guaranteed under these conditions....

If a defendant then had to reckon with his defence lawyer, in the interest of self-protection, giving up the brief which he had taken on if the lawyer considers it to be merely possible that his client has committed the listed offence with which he is charged, he could, if informed by his lawyer at the commencement of the brief about the possible occurrence of this situation, see himself as prevented from open, unreserved and confident communication with his lawyer about a central point in relation to suspicion of the crime so as not to lose the lawyer of his choice.

Investigatory measures by public prosecutor's office against defence lawyers can disturb the relationship of confidence between lawyer and client even more deeply. If the public prosecutor searches the lawyer's office and confiscates his files, for instance, he can examine the concept behind the defence...

It cannot be unreservedly expected of the defence lawyer to respond to a situation of risk created by the legislature in relation to criminal law by relinquishing a brief of choice and an assignment as duty defence lawyer.

The institution of defence by a duty lawyer is a state welfare measure for the impecunious defendant and ensures proper conduct of proceedings in the interests of an administration of justice which conforms to the constitutional state principle. Through defence by a duty lawyer the state delegates this task, which is also in the public interest, to the legal profession. Defence by a duty lawyer is therefore, as the Federal Constitutional Court has held, a special form of employing private individuals in the public interest (see BVerfGE 39, 238, 241ff.; BVerfGE 68, 237, 253ff.). The position of the duty defence lawyer is characterized by smaller remuneration, which is statutorily fixed, the duty to take on the client (§ 49 BRAO, Federal Lawyers Act) and the duty to provide professional services of a highly personal nature (see BVerfGE 68, 237, 253f.), the choice of the duty defence lawyer by the president of the court (see § 143 Code of Criminal Procedure) including the possibility of his release from the duty (see BVerfGE 39, 238, 242), combined with the loss of freedom to terminate the brief in his own discretion . . . The assignment of a duty defence lawyer is also not a neutral issue from the point of view of the defendant too who has not yet been convicted and who has at his disposal financial resources which are not unquestionably established to be tainted until the legally binding conclusion of criminal proceedings against him . . .

An intrusion into the freedom of exercise of a defence lawyer's profession effected by this wide interpretation of the criminal norm in § 261 para. 2 no. 1 Criminal Code would not be justified in its full extent in constitutional law . . .

The balancing of interests in the examination of proportionality in the narrower sense must first take into account that the criminally sanctioned prohibition on accepting tainted money is, in relation to addressees who are defence lawyers, only minimally appropriate for clearly promoting the goal sought by the legislature in introducing the criminal provision in relation to money laundering. Perpetrators of organized crime would seldom chose the route of briefing and paying a defence lawyer in order to launder the proceeds of their crimes. The lawyer is an independent organ in the administration of justice and is subject to a number of special professional duties which go far beyond that measure of compliance with the law which is expected from everyone. Obligations of loyalty, registration proceedings and surveillance by special lawyers' tribunals offer an increased guarantee for a lawyer developing a professional ethos and behaving in a law-abiding manner.

Over against this the intrusion facilitated by § 261 para. 2 no. 1 Criminal Code, on its unlimited application to defence lawyers, into the freedom of exercise of their profession is serious. Fulfillment of the definition even with conditionally intentional action would endanger a lawyer's claim to remuneration even in cases of suspicion. A defence lawyer's freedom of decision for or against taking on a case would be clearly impaired by the possible risk, which is hard to predict, of his own criminality . . . The institution of defence by a lawyer of choice, which is guaranteed in constitutional law, is also endangered. The guarantee of freedom in taking on a defence lawyer is not only in the individual interest of the lawyer but also in the interest of the general public. The unlimited inclusion of defence lawyers within the circle of potential money launderers would endanger the institution of defence by a lawyer of choice because it—as explained above—could hinder the formation of a relationship of confidence between the defence lawyer and the client, and make criminal defence ineffective. Finally the defendant's right to effective assistance from a defence lawyer would also be endangered.

In the required balancing between the risks (for freedom of exercise of their profession and for the institution of defence by a lawyer of choice) associated with an unlimited inclusion of defence lawyers within the circle of perpetrators of money laundering on the one hand and the advantages to be expected from their inclusion in combating organized crime on the other hand, the disadvantages prevail. An unlimited inclusion of defence lawyers of choice in the circle of capable perpetrators of money laundering would be disproportionate.

The principle of proportionality admittedly does not require complete release of the defence lawyer from the threat of criminality under § 261 para. 2 no. 1 Criminal Code. The Basic Law does not ask for a space free of the criminal law in which the defence lawyer can accept tainted assets as fees to an unlimited extent and may, perhaps in co-ordination with the perpetrator of a listed offence or by a fictitious fee, thereby evade the aims of the legislature in prohibiting money laundering. Neither the basic right of freedom of exercise of profession nor the guarantee of freedom of choice of a defence lawyer in fair criminal proceedings support the release of a defence lawyer from the prohibition on money laundering if he deliberately [bewusst] obtains tainted money and thereby abuses his role as a defence lawyer in order to launder money . . . .

The intrusion into defence lawyers' freedom of exercise of profession and into the institution of defence by a lawyer of choice associated with § 261 para. 2 no. 1 Criminal Code is justified in constitutional law if the defence lawyer at the time of receipt of the fee (or of the advance on fees) knows for certain that this comes from a listed offence. The deliberate transmission of tainted investments under the cover of a relationship of confidence protected in constitutional law is a misuse of the privileged position of a defence lawyer which deserves no protection from the Constitution. If a defence lawyer knows for certain at the time of acceptance of a defence fee that the funds received come from a listed offence, then he is stepping outside his role as an organ of the administration of justice...

§ 261 para. 2 no. 1 Criminal Code can be interpreted in a restrictive way and in this interpretation is in harmony with the Constitution...

It is true that the legislature has ... designed § 261 para. 2 no. 1 Criminal Code as a "catch-all" definition (see BR-Dr 507/92, p.23f.; ...) ... It has however not sufficiently considered the tension arising in constitutional law in the special situation of acceptance of a fee by a defence lawyer of choice. It can admittedly be deduced from the statutory materials that the Criminal Law Committee of the German Association of Lawyers referred to the consequences of the norm for the holders of professional secrets in general in its written opinion (see Minutes of the 31st Session of the Law Committee of the German Bundestag of January 22, App. p. 152) ... The constitutional law dimension associated with an unlimited inclusion of defence lawyers has not been sufficiently discussed in the legislative proceedings...

The constitutional complaints remain unsuccessful in the end result.

... The judgment of the regional court of May 4, 2000, is not open to objection on constitutional grounds...

The regional court has decisively based its belief in the fact that the complainants had demanded unreasonably high advances of fees immediately after the arrest of their clients and the imminent collapse of the snowball system without a preceding written fee agreement, and also received these advances a short time later in cash. This, and the further incriminating circumstantial evidence, carefully established and reasonably assessed by the regional court, support the conclusion that the complainants have acted knowingly [*wissentlich*]...

German Criminal Code

§ 261 (Money Laundering; Hiding Unlawfully Obtained Benefits)

(1) Who hides an object which is a proceed of an unlawful act listed in sentence 2, conceals its origin or obstructs or endangers the investigation of its origin, its being found, its confiscation, its deprivation or its being officially secured, will be punished with imprisonment from three months to five years. Unlawful acts within the meaning of sentence 1 are

1. felonies;
2. misdemeanors under
   (a) § 332 para. 1, also in conjunction with para. 3, and § 334;
   (b) § 29 para. 1 sentence 1 Narcotics Act ... ;
3. misdemeanors under § 373 and § 374 para. 2 of the Fiscal Code ... ;
4. misdemeanors
   (a) under § 152a, § 181a, § 232 para. 1 and 2, § 233 para. 1 and 2, § 233a, § 242, § 246, § 253, § 259, §§ 263 to 264, § 266, § 267, § 269, § 271, § 284, § 326 para. 1, 2 and 4, § 328 para. 1, 2 and 4, and § 348;
   (b) under § 96 of the Residence Act and § 84 of the Asylum Procedure Act and § 370 of the Fiscal Code,
   which were committed on a commercial basis or by a member of a gang whose purpose is the continued commission of such offenses; and
5. misdemeanors under § 89a and under § 129 and § 129a para. 3 and 5, all of which also in conjunction with § 129b para. 1, as well as misdemeanors committed by a member of a criminal or terrorist organization (§ 129 and § 129a, all of which also in conjunction with § 129b para. 1) ... .

(2) In the same way will be punished who
obtains an object indicated in para. 1 for himself or a third person; or
stores an object indicated in para. 1 or uses it for himself or a third person if he knew the origin of the object at the time of obtaining it.

(3) The attempt is punishable.

(4) In especially serious cases the punishment is imprisonment from six months to ten years. An especially serious case typically will need to be found if the offender acts commercially or as a member of a gang whose purpose is the continued commission of money laundering.

(5) Who, in cases under para. 1 or 2, through gross negligence is unaware of the fact that the object stems from an unlawful act named in para. 1, will be punished with imprisonment of not more than two years or a fine.

. . .

NOTES

1. Organized crime statutes like RICO target persons engaged in the "core" activities of organized crime, described with such expressions as "pattern of racketeering activity"; money laundering statutes, an invention of the late twentieth century, instead are aimed at persons who assist the operation of a criminal enterprise by making its profits usable. The basic idea is that the step of "washing" money is essential for the profitability of large-scale organized crime and that therefore organized crime can be weakened if state agencies can intervene. One could imagine a money laundering statute narrowly drafted to target only offenders who are integral parts of criminal organizations and who work to disguise the criminal origin of financial assets: think of the Mafia accountant who expertly disguises the flow of income; for an offense definition that emphasizes the deceptive elements, see § 261 para. 1 Criminal Code. (Of course, such a statute may not only be unobjectionable, but also unnecessary, given the availability of standard norms of accessorial liability as well as the organized crime statutes themselves: the narrower, and less objectionable the statute is, the more redundant it becomes.)

However, typical money laundering laws also cover the mere acceptance of objects with tainted origins within otherwise perfectly ordinary business transactions (see § 261 para. 2 Nr. 1 Criminal Code, which makes it a crime to simply obtain an object stemming from one of the criminal offenses listed). This means that persons can be charged with money laundering who are not connected to "organized crime" in a systematic way and who do not attempt to disguise the criminal source of the money but merely accept money as payment despite indications that this money has been "earned" illegally by its pre-possessor. As a consequence of such broader laws, the real estate agent in *United States v. Campbell* and other business people, not to mention interior decorators, who accept large sums of cash fall under "organized crime" laws.

It is possible, of course, that casting the money laundering net wide is integral to the function of money laundering statutes. (Otherwise, why not simply criminalize *spending* dirty money?) At least in the context of U.S. federal criminal law, much like RICO, money laundering statutes help prosecutors expand the class of possible defendants who, when faced with stiff penalties— and the association with a criminal enterprise—may provide prosecutors with information that could prove useful in building a case against the participants in the criminal enterprise. Money laundering, in this sense, may function as a steppingstone to, or an extension of, RICO. Of course, if this instrumental use of substantive criminal law against one person to generate evidence against another is objectionable in the case of RICO, it presumably would be still more objectionable in the case of money laundering, as a proxy to RICO.

Consider the following laundry list of rationales for the criminalization of money laundering:

1. Laundering Removes the Incentive to Commit Predicate Offenses
2. Laundering is a Form of Complicity in Predicate Offenses
3. Laundering "Gets the Real Criminals" (i.e., Upper-Level Offenders)
4. Laundering Corrupts Professionals (e.g., Lawyers, Bankers, Accountants)
5. Laundering Jeopardizes Confidence in the Banking System

Peter Alldridge, "The Moral Limits of the Crime of Money Laundering," 5 *Buffalo Criminal Law Review* (2001), 279.

Can the criminal prohibition of money laundering be justified? What legal good does it protect? Does it endanger, or even violate, a legal good itself? Or is the claim that laundering money endangers or harms, indirectly, whatever legal good is endangered or harmed by the conduct of those who accumulate the dirty money that it launders? Judge Weinstein seems to hint at this justification when, in *Blarek,* he mentions "the thousands of teens whose lives had been ruined by Cali cartel drugs sold for the cash used to pay for Santacruz's extravagant lifestyle," including the interior decorations provided by Blarek and his partner.*

Do you find any of the mentioned justifications convincing? Are there others? How about that the criminal prohibition of money laundering drains criminal activity of its "life blood" or that it "disrupts criminal finance"? Or is the "fight against money laundering" separate from the war on organized crime, or the war on drugs? Is the disruption of criminal finance part of the protection of *noncriminal* finance?[†]

2. *Attorneys' fees.* Yet another problem arises with respect to the situation of defense counsel. They often have even more reason than sales people to suspect that the source of the payments for their services may be dubious. Should they be punished for money laundering if they accept such payments nevertheless? This question has been discussed extensively in the German literature (a substantial percentage of criminal law professors is active as defense counsel—developments that impact the role of defense counsel therefore tend be covered at some length in academic writing). The German Federal Court of Justice in its judgment of July 4, 2001, 2 StR 513/00, BGHSt 47, 68, rejected claims that § 261 para. 2 Criminal Code should not be applied to defense counsel.

But consider the impact that the threat to defense counsel of being convicted for money laundering can have beyond the individual case. This threat might have long term effects on the criminal justice system, effects that are detrimental to the idea of the constitutional state under the rule of law; it has been argued, for instance, that the application of money laundering prohibitions to criminal defense attorneys infringes not only defendants' rights but also the attorneys' constitutional freedom of profession (art. 12 para. 1 Basic Law).

Note that there is no office of public defender in the German legal system. If defendants cannot afford to hire an attorney by private contract, and if they are accused of a non-trivial offense or if the criminal proceedings are characterized by difficulties with regard to evidence or the law to be applied (§ 140 German Code of Criminal Procedure), the trial court will appoint a defense counsel at state expense. But this defense counsel can be any attorney willing to work as defense counsel. The defendant can choose who should be appointed as his duty defense counsel (see § 142 para. 1 German Code of Criminal Procedure: "Prior to the appointment of a defense counsel the accused shall be given the opportunity to name a defense counsel of his choice within a time limit to be specified. The presiding judge appoints this defense counsel unless there is an important reason for not doing so.").

While the German Federal Court of Justice in its decision of July 4, 2001 (2 StR 513/00, BGHSt 47, 68) had not objected to applying § 261 para. 2 to defense counsel, three years later the German Federal Constitutional Court in its ruling concerning the same case proved to be more sympathetic to defense counsel (in the decision excerpted above). The Constitutional Court stressed the importance of effective defense for a fair criminal trial and the public interest in a criminal justice system that respects the rule of law. Note also that the Federal Constitutional Court expressed a high degree of trust in defense counsel's integrity, which is expressed in the formulation that they are "organs of the administration of justice" in § 1 BRAO, the Federal Statute on Attorneys. The Constitutional Court at important points reached different conclusions than had the Federal Court of Justice. First, the Constitutional Court showed more awareness of differences in the quality of services provided by a privately paid defense counsel of choice in comparison to a duty defense counsel. The background: the

---

* *United States v. Blarek,* 7 F.Supp.2d 192, 196 (E.D.N.Y.1998).
  [†] See generally Mariano-Florentino Cuéllar, "The Tenuous Relationship Between the Fight Against Money Laundering and the Disruption of Criminal Finance," 93 *Journal of Criminal Law and Criminology* (2003), 311.

defense counsel may be the same person, but in the role of a duty defense counsel, fees are regulated and limited while privately hired counsel can, and often does, negotiate a higher fee.

Second, the Federal Constitutional Court introduced an important restriction. From defense counsel's point of view, the most troubling subsection in § 261 Criminal Code is para. 5: it suffices to be unaware of the object's origins in a grossly negligent (*leichtfertig*) way (on *Leichtfertigkeit*, see Chapter 8.A). The innovation of the Federal Constitutional Court was to stipulate different, higher, *mens rea* requirements specifically for defense counsel. For defense counsel, the Court held, neither gross negligence nor conditional intent (that is, awareness of the possibility that the sources are tainted, see the discussion of conditional intent in Chapter 8.A) will ground criminal liability. Only if defense counsel *positively knew* (*Wissentlichkeit, dolus directus*) that the funds for their payment are proceeds of one of the listed offenses, can they be punished for money laundering. (Does this raise concerns about the unequal application, or in this case the unequal *interpretation*, of a criminal prohibition, depending on one's occupation, or official function?)

The Federal Constitutional Court thus introduced a restrictive interpretation to § 261 Criminal Code, in order to preserve the statute's constitutionality. This raises a fundamental question of competence: may a constitutional court amend acts of legislation? For a discussion of this issue in the context of U.S. constitutional law, see *Skilling v. United States*, Chapter 2.B, where the majority adopted a narrow interpretation of the federal honest services provision instead of striking it down on vagueness grounds.

To get a sense of the relationship between attorneys' fees and money laundering in the U.S., it is useful to get a quick overview of the (fairly complex, or at least detailed) federal money laundering scheme. There are two main federal money laundering statutes, 18 U.S.C. § 1956 and § 1957:

> The most prominent is 18 U.S.C. 1956. Section 1956 outlaws four kinds of money laundering—promotional, concealment, structuring, and tax evasion laundering of the proceeds generated by designated federal, state, and foreign underlying crimes (predicate offenses)—committed or attempted under one or more of three jurisdictional conditions (i.e., laundering involving certain financial transactions, laundering involving international transfers, and stings). Its companion, 18 U.S.C. 1957, prohibits depositing or spending more than $10,000 of the proceeds from a Section 1956 predicate offense. Violations of Section 1956 are punishable by imprisonment for not more than 20 years; Section 1957 carries a maximum penalty of imprisonment for 10 years. Property involved in either case is subject to confiscation.
>
> Charles Doyle, "Money Laundering: An Overview of 18 U.S.C. 1956 and Related Federal Criminal Law," Congressional Research Service (February 8, 2012).

18 U.S.C. § 1956 is the more serious of the two types of money laundering, as it requires proof of one of the following:

- *intent* to promote the carrying on of specified unlawful activity;
- *intent* to engage in tax evasion or tax fraud;
- *knowledge* that the transaction was designed to conceal or disguise the nature, location, source, ownership or control of proceeds of the specified unlawful activity; or
  knowledge that the transaction was designed to avoid a transaction reporting requirement.

Section 1957 does not require proof of *mens rea* in the above variations; instead it inserts a $10,000 threshold amount for each transaction and the requirement that a financial institution must be involved in the transaction. "Although the prosecutor need not prove any intent to promote, conceal or avoid the reporting requirements, it still must be shown that the defendant knew the property was derived from some criminal activity and that the funds were in fact derived from a specified unlawful activity."*

Most relevant for present purposes, section 1957 (though not § 1956) includes an attorneys' fees exemption, covering "any transaction necessary to preserve a person's right to

---

* U.S. Dep't of Justice, U.S. Attorneys Manual, Criminal Resource Manual § 2101.

representation as guaranteed by the sixth amendment to the Constitution." The interpretation, and continued validity, of the exception, however, has been hotly contested. The Eleventh Circuit Court of Appeals, in *United States v. Velez*, 586 F.3d 875 (11th Cir. 2009), declared the exemption alive and well, but at the same time clarified why its continued existence is cold comfort for defense attorneys; they may escape a criminal money laundering conviction, but that does not mean their fees will not be subject to civil forfeiture:

> The Government argues that the exemption in § 1957(f)(1) has been "nullified" or "vitiated" because, shortly after the provision was enacted, the Supreme Court held in Caplin & Drysdale, Chartered v. United States, 491 U.S. 617, 626, 109 S. Ct. 2646, 109 S. Ct. 2667, 105 L. Ed. 2d 528 (1989) that the Sixth Amendment right to counsel does not protect the right of a criminal defendant to use criminally derived proceeds for legal fees. However, *Caplin & Drysdale*, which addresses a different statute governing the civil forfeiture of criminally derived proceeds, has no bearing on § 1957(f)(1) and indeed supports the conclusion that such proceeds have been statutorily exempted from criminal penalties....
>
> In Caplin & Drysdale, the Court addressed the constitutionality of 21 U.S.C. § 853, a federal forfeiture provision requiring individuals to surrender criminally derived assets and setting out the forfeiture process. Unlike section 1957, § 853 contains no express exemption for funds paid for legal representation. It simply requires the forfeiture of all criminally derived proceeds, without exception.....
>
> [T]he Court held...that Congress may require the forfeiture of criminally derived proceeds, even if those proceeds are used for legal representation, without running afoul of the Sixth Amendment right to counsel....
>
> The United States Solicitor General explained the distinction between civil forfeiture and criminal penalties in his 1989 brief to the Supreme Court in United States v. Monsanto, 491 U.S. 600, 109 S. Ct. 2657, 105 L. Ed. 2d 512 (1989), a companion case to *Caplin & Drysdale*. The brief states explicitly that, although the criminal defense bar had urged Congress "to exclude from [civil] forfeiture those assets that the defendant wants to use to pay an attorney," Congress ha[d] declined to do so." United States v. Monsanto, Gov't Br., 1989 WL 1115135, at *33–34....
>
> As the Government concedes, accepting its interpretation of § 1957(f)(1) would read all meaning out of the exemption. Section 1957 criminalizes only transactions involving criminally derived proceeds. It would therefore make little sense—and would be entirely superfluous—to read § 1957(f)(1) as an exemption from criminal penalties for non-tainted proceeds spent on legal representation, as those funds can always be used for any legal purpose. We do not believe Congress intended such an absurd result, which nullifies the provision and divorces it from its statutory context, thereby violating basic canons of statutory construction....
>
> The...plain language of § 1957(f)(1) clearly exempts criminally derived proceeds used to secure legal representation to which an accused is entitled under the Sixth Amendment.

Incidentally, the U.S. Supreme Court in *Caplin & Drysdale* in 1989 was no more moved than the German Federal Court of Justice would be twelve years later by the argument that the right to counsel means the right to *private* counsel:

> The [Sixth] Amendment guarantees defendants in criminal cases the right to adequate representation, but those who do not have the means to hire their own lawyers have no cognizable complaint so long as they are adequately represented by attorneys appointed by the courts. [N]othing in § 853 prevents a defendant from hiring the attorney of his choice, or disqualifies any attorney from serving as a defendant's counsel....

And if forfeiture under RICO and similar legislation directed at criminal drug enterprises does saddle defendants with inferior legal representation, that would be neither unintentional nor objectionable:

> [A] major purpose motivating congressional adoption and continued refinement of the racketeer influenced and corrupt organizations (RICO) and [drug enterprise] forfeiture provisions has been the desire to lessen the economic power of organized crime and drug enterprises. This includes the use of such economic power to retain private counsel. As the Court of Appeals put it: "Congress has already underscored the compelling public interest in stripping criminals...of their undeserved economic power, and part of that undeserved power may be the ability to

command high-priced legal talent." The notion that the Government has a legitimate interest in depriving criminals of economic power, even insofar as that power is used to retain counsel of choice, may be somewhat unsettling. But when a defendant claims that he has suffered some substantial impairment of his Sixth Amendment rights by virtue of the seizure or forfeiture of assets in his possession, such a complaint is no more than the reflection of "the harsh reality that the quality of a criminal defendant's representation frequently may turn on his ability to retain the best counsel money can buy." Morris v. Slappy, 461 U.S. 1, 23 103 S.Ct. 1610, 1622, 75 L.Ed.2d 610 (1983) (BRENNAN, J., concurring in result). Again, the Court of Appeals put it aptly: "The modern day Jean Valjean must be satisfied with appointed counsel. Yet the drug merchant claims that his possession of huge sums of money . . . entitles him to something more. We reject this contention, and any notion of a constitutional right to use the proceeds of crime to finance an expensive defense."

The dissent in the 5:4 decision in *Caplin & Drysdale* took a different view of the matter, arguing that the very integrity of the adversarial system of criminal justice, even the future of the criminal defense bar, was at stake:

> [O]ur chosen system of criminal justice is built upon a truly equal and adversarial presentation of the case, and upon the trust that can exist only when counsel is independent of the Government. Without the right, reasonably exercised, to counsel of choice, the effectiveness of that system is imperiled.
>
> Had it been Congress' express aim to undermine the adversary system as we know it, it could hardly have found a better engine of destruction than attorney's-fee forfeiture. . . .
>
> The long-term effects of the fee-forfeiture practice will be to decimate the private criminal-defense bar. As the use of the forfeiture mechanism expands to new categories of federal crimes and spreads to the States, only one class of defendants will be free routinely to retain private counsel: the affluent defendant accused of a crime that generates no economic gain. As the number of private clients diminishes, only the most idealistic and the least skilled of young lawyers will be attracted to the field, while the remainder seek greener pastures elsewhere.
>
> In short, attorney's-fee forfeiture substantially undermines every interest served by the Sixth Amendment right to chosen counsel, on the individual and institutional levels, over the short term and the long haul.

Note how the arguments on either side of the issue are eerily similar in Germany and the United States, despite supposedly different conceptions of the criminal trial, and of defense attorneys' role in it.

5. *Beyond domestic criminal law: the soft law of international money laundering.* As one might expect, money laundering is no longer framed as just a national matter (in the U.S., making it the business of federal law rather than of state law, the traditional center of American criminal law), but as a global phenomenon. As a global phenomenon, involving global banks and even global criminal networks, it pushes the boundaries of criminal law, which remains anchored in domestic legal systems that rely on international agreements and transnational collaboration—with the exception of international crimes subject to the jurisdiction of international criminal tribunals. And so, as with other global phenomena, global money laundering also has moved beyond the realm of criminal law and entered the sphere of so-called global administrative law. In fact, global money laundering may have left the realm of law, period, insofar as one draws a distinction between law and regulation, sovereign government and self-government, instead of distinguishing within the realm of law between its "hard" and its "soft" variety. Be that as it may, global banking institutions obviously have an interest—as does all business possibly subject to corporate criminal sanctions, or for that matter any kind of government regulation—to forestall the development of a global criminal law of money laundering, whatever form that might take and however that might be achieved, through the establishment of a regime of self-regulation.

Here is an example, featuring frequent references to the familiar self-regulatory tool of "due diligence":

Global Anti-Money-Laundering Guidelines for Private Banking
Wolfsberg AML Principles
(1st revision, May 2002*)

The following major International Private Banks
ABN AMRO Bank N.V.
Bank of Tokyo-Mitsubishi Ltd.
Barclays Bank
Citigroup
Credit Suisse Group
Deutsche Bank AG
Goldman Sachs
HSBC
J.P. Morgan Private Bank
Santander Central Hispano
Société Générale
UBS AG

have agreed to the following principles as important global guidance for sound business conduct in international private banking.

Global Anti-Money-Laundering Guidelines for Private Banking
Wolfsberg AML Principles

Preamble

The following guidelines are understood to be appropriate for private banking relationships. Guidelines for other market segments may differ. It is recognized that the establishment of policies and procedures to adhere to these guidelines is the responsibility of management.

1 Client acceptance: general guidelines
  1.1 General
    Bank policy will be to prevent the use of its worldwide operations for criminal purposes. The bank will endeavor to accept only those clients whose source of wealth and funds can be reasonably established to be legitimate. The primary responsibility for this lies with the private banker who sponsors the client for acceptance. Mere fulfilment of internal review procedures does not relieve the private banker of this basic responsibility.
  1.2 Identification
    The bank will take reasonable measures to establish the identity of its clients and beneficial owners and will only accept clients when this process has been completed.
    ...
  1.3 Due diligence
    It is essential to collect and record information covering the following categories:
    • Purpose and reasons for opening the account
    • Anticipated account activity
    • Source of wealth (description of the economic activity which has generated the net worth)
    • Estimated net worth
    • Source of funds (description of the origin and the means of transfer for monies that are accepted for the account opening)
    • References or other sources to corroborate reputation information where available.
    Unless other measures reasonably suffice to do the due diligence on a client (e.g. favorable and reliable references), a client will be met prior to account opening.
...

2 Client acceptance: situations requiring additional diligence/attention
  2.1 General
    In its internal policies, the bank must define categories of persons whose circumstances warrant additional diligence. This will typically be the case where the circumstances are likely to pose a higher than average risk to a bank.

---

* [In May 2012, these "Anti-Money-Laundering-Guidelines" were revised and renamed "Anti-Money Laundering *Principles*" (emphasis added). See generally <http://www.wolfsberg-principles.com/>—Eds.]

2.2 Indicators

The circumstances of the following categories of persons are indicators for defining them as requiring additional diligence:

- Persons residing in and/or having funds sourced from countries identified by credible sources as having inadequate antimony laundering standards or representing high risk for crime and corruption.
- Persons engaged in types of business activities or sectors known to be susceptible to money laundering.
- "Politically Exposed Persons" (frequently abbreviated as "PEPs"), referring to individuals holding or having held positions of public trust, such as government officials, senior executives of government corporations, politicians, important political party officials, etc., as well as their families and close associates.

. . .

4 Practices when identifying unusual or suspicious activities

4.1 Definition of unusual or suspicious activities

The bank will have a written policy on the identification of and follow-up on unusual or suspicious activities. This policy will include a definition of what is considered to be suspicious or unusual and give examples thereof.

Unusual or suspicious activities may include:

- Account transactions or other activities which are not consistent with the due diligence file
- Cash transactions over a certain amount
- Pass-through/in-and-out-transactions.

4.2 Identification of unusual or suspicious activities

Unusual or suspicious activities can be identified through:

- Monitoring of transactions
- Client contacts (meetings, discussions, in-country visits etc.)
- Third party information (e.g. newspapers, Reuters, internet)
- Private banker's/internal knowledge of the client's environment (e.g. political situation in his/her country).

4.3 Follow-up on unusual or suspicious activities

The private banker, management and/or the control function will carry out an analysis of the background of any unusual or suspicious activity. If there is no plausible explanation a decision will be made involving the control function:

- To continue the business relationship with increased monitoring
- To cancel the business relationship
- To report the business relationship to the authorities.

  The report to the authorities is made by the control function and senior management may need to be notified (e.g. Senior Compliance Officer, CEO, Chief Auditor, General Counsel). As required by local laws and regulations the assets may be blocked and transactions may be subject to approval by the control function.

5 Monitoring

5.1 Monitoring Program

A sufficient monitoring program must be in place. The primary responsibility for monitoring account activities lies with the private banker. The private banker will be familiar with significant transactions and increased activity in the account and will be especially aware of unusual or suspicious activities (see 4.1). The bank will decide to what extent fulfillment of these responsibilities will need to be supported through the use of automated systems or other means.

5.2 Ongoing Monitoring

With respect to clients classified under any category of persons mentioned in 2, the bank's internal policies will indicate how the account activities will be subject to monitoring.

6 Control responsibilities

A written control policy will be in place establishing standard control procedures to be undertaken by the various "control layers" (private banker, independent operations unit, Compliance, Internal Audit). The control policy will cover issues of timing, degree of control, areas to be controlled, responsibilities and follow-up, etc.

An independent audit function (which may be internal to the bank) will test the programs contemplated by the control policy.

7 Reporting

There will be regular management reporting established on money laundering issues (e.g. number of reports to authorities, monitoring tools, changes in applicable laws and regulations, the number and scope of training sessions provided to employees).

8 Education, training and information

The bank will establish a training program on the identification and prevention of money laundering for employees who have client contact and for Compliance personnel. Regular training (e.g. annually) will also include how to identify and follow-up on unusual or suspicious activities. In addition, employees will be informed about any major changes in anti-money-laundering laws and regulations.

All new employees will be provided with guidelines on the anti-money-laundering procedures.

9 Record retention requirements

The bank will establish record retention requirements for all anti-money-laundering related documents. The documents must be kept for a minimum of five years.

10 Exceptions and deviations

The bank will establish an exception and deviation procedure that requires risk assessment and approval by an independent unit.

11 Anti-money-laundering organization

The bank will establish an adequately staffed and independent department responsible for the prevention of money laundering (e.g. Compliance, independent control unit, Legal).

To what extent the formulation of the Wolfsberg AML principles had the effect of preventing the invocation of criminal law norms (or for that matter, money laundering) is unclear. In December 2012, HSBC, one of the banks that "agreed to [the Wolfsberg AML] principles as important global guidance for sound business conduct in international private banking," agreed to pay US$1.92 billion to settle federal and New York state claims of money laundering, thereby avoiding a criminal money laundering prosecution. New York and U.S. federal criminal law applied, even though HSBC is headquartered in London, because the bank was accused of having "transferred billions of dollars for nations like Iran and enabled Mexican drug cartels to move money illegally through its American subsidiaries." The inquiry also resulted in settlements with at least two other global banks, ING ($619 million) and Standard Chartered ($327 million settlement).

Apparently, the decision to accept a settlement from HSBC in lieu of a filing a criminal indictment was driven, at least in part, by the concern that HSBC had grown so large globally connected that it was "too big to fail," or in this case, too big to indict, with possibly devastating consequences on the global economy. Then again, others argued that the criminal money laundering statutes would lose their deterrent sting if they were not employed even in the face of strong evidence of pervasive criminal conduct. See generally Ben Protess and Jessica Silver-Greenberg, "HSBC to Pay $1.92 Billion to Settle Charges of Money Laundering," *N.Y. Times*, December 11, 2012, at A1.

Does this decision not to indict raise questions about the legitimacy and function of money laundering statutes? More fundamentally, does it raise concerns about the underlying conception of criminal law, and in particular of so-called white collar criminal law? About the unequal application of criminal law? Would a principle of compulsory prosecution be the answer (see Chapter 5.C)?

How would you explain this decision to Ms. Campbell, the real estate agent, or, for that matter, to Messrs. Blarek and Pellecchia, the interior decorators, from the first case in this book?

INDEX